The Blackwell Encyclopedia of Sociology

Volume IX

SE–ST

Edited by

George Ritzer

Blackwell
Publishing

BLACKWELL PUBLISHING
350 Main Street, Malden, MA 02148-5020, USA
9600 Garsington Road, Oxford OX4 2DQ, UK
550 Swanston Street, Carlton, Victoria 3053, Australia

The right of George Ritzer to be identified as the Author of the Editorial Material in this Work has been asserted in accordance with the UK Copyright, Designs, and Patents Act 1988.

First published 2007 by Blackwell Publishing Ltd

1   2007

Library of Congress Cataloging-in-Publication Data

Blackwell encyclopedia of sociology, the / edited by George Ritzer.
  p. cm.
Includes bibliographical references and index.
ISBN 1-4051-2433-4 (hardback : alk. paper) 1. Sociology—Encyclopedias. I. Ritzer, George.

HM425.B53 2007
301.03—dc22

                                        2006004167

ISBN-13: 978-1-4051-2433-1 (hardback : alk. paper)

A catalogue record for this title is available from the British Library.

Set in 9.5/11pt Ehrhardt
by Spi Publisher Services, Pondicherry, India
Printed in Singapore
by COS Printers Pte Ltd

The publisher's policy is to use permanent paper from mills that operate a sustainable forestry policy, and which has been manufactured from pulp processed using acid-free and elementary chlorine-free practices. Furthermore, the publisher ensures that the text paper and cover board used have met acceptable environmental accreditation standards.

For further information on
Blackwell Publishing, visit our website:
www.blackwellpublishing.com

Contents

sexual harassment

Kathrin Zippel

Sexual harassment refers to unwelcome sexual advances, requests for sexual favors, or other forms of unwanted attention of a sexual nature, in a workplace or elsewhere. Legal definitions distinguish between quid pro quo sexual harassment, where putting up with these behaviors is a condition of work, and behaviors that create an intimidating, offensive, hostile environment for the victim. Its forms can be physical, verbal, gestural, visual, or graphic. Behaviors that can be perceived as sexual harassment include unwelcome (sexual) jokes, remarks with sexual connotations or about private lives, gossip, repeated requests to go out, and any form of unwanted touching or invasion of personal space, as well as sexual advances or assault.

The overwhelming majority of victims are women; adolescent and young workers especially report sexual harassment experiences. Perpetrators are most often individual men or groups of men. Men, in particular those who are financially vulnerable, can experience sexual harassment as well (Uggen & Blackstone 2004). Same-sex harassment has also received attention, in particular, gender and sexual harassment among men.

Besides consequences such as loss of a job or not being promoted, victims experience psychological effects. Reactions cover a range of emotional and physical responses, including confusion, discomfort, anxiety, anger, and stress. Cultural representations of sexual harassment, however, often suggest an innocent flirt gone wrong, or that victims "asked" for it by dress or behavior. These representations may depict victims as revengeful, tapping into cultural repertoires similar to those around sexual violence.

Empirical research on the prevalence of the phenomenon has faced several methodological difficulties, partly because of its conceptualization, since the experience of sexual harassment depends on contextual factors. It usually includes related behaviors and several events, and hence is a dynamic or process rather than an isolated occurrence. Surveys have been conducted using the Sexual Experiences Questionnaire (SEQ) developed by Louise Fitzgerald and her colleagues; however, these studies tend to rely on self-reports, which raises the problem of subjective versus objective measures, including underreporting.

In the 1970s, second-wave feminists in the US criticized the social, legal, and cultural norms of behaviors and organizational practices concerning men's sexual advances toward women and the unwanted eroticization and sexualization of relationships in the workplace and elsewhere. Feminists questioned the conditions under which women "consent" to these behaviors in the context of unequal power relations.

While US law has defined sexual harassment primarily as discrimination based on sex at work and in education, sexual harassment also occurs between people in other hierarchical positions, for example, in the unequal power relationships between doctor and patient, psychologist and client, landlord and tenant, or between colleagues/peers.

Feminist theories view sexual harassment primarily as rooted in unequal gender relations and the abuse of power of men over women. Sexual harassment is the product of a gender system that maintains a dominant, (hetero)normative form of masculinity. In this view, sexual harassment is a problem because of different "sex roles," or assumptions about male sexual aggression and female passivity, that spill over into the workplace.

Organizational theories view sexual harassment as a problem perpetuated through gendered organizational and institutional structures. For example, the occupational status of the victim and supervisory authority of the perpetrator influence the perceptions and interpretations of sexual harassment. Women's lower status at work, sex segregation, gender gaps in authority, and other organizational factors contribute to and are perpetuated by sexual harassment.

Sociolegal and political approaches explore the relationship between emerging sexual harassment laws and individual and societal perceptions, for example, by asking questions about legal consciousness, sensitivity to gender issues, and interpretations of sexual harassment.

The experiences, interpretations, and perceptions of sexual harassment vary not only by gender but also by age, social class, and race. Research has recently begun to examine cross-national differences in individual, organizational, social, political, and legal interpretations of sexual harassment. For example, in several European countries sexual harassment is considered in the context of bullying, mobbing, or moral harassment, as a violation of workers' dignity or a form of violence against women.

SEE ALSO: Femininities/Masculinities; Gendered Organizations/Institutions; Sex and Gender; Sex Panics; Sexual Politics; Sexual Violence and Rape; Sexuality and the Law

REFERENCES AND SUGGESTED READINGS

Cahill, M. (2001) *The Social Construction of Sexual Harassment Law*. Aldershot, Ashgate.

Mac Kinnon, C. A. (1979) *Sexual Harassment of Working Women: A Case of Sex Discrimination.* Yale University Press, New Haven.

Saguy, A. (2003) *What is Sexual Harassment? From Capitol Hill to the Sorbonne.* University of California Press, Berkeley.

Uggen, C. & Blackstone, A. (2004) Sexual Harassment as a Gendered Expression of Power. *American Sociological Review* 69(1): 64–83.

Welsh, S. (1999) Gender and Sexual Harassment. *Annual Review of Sociology* 25: 169–90.

Zippel, K. (2005) *The Politics of Sexual Harassment: A Comparative Study of the United States, the European Union, and Germany.* Cambridge University Press, Cambridge.

sexual health

Laura M. Carpenter

Sexual health is both a lay expression and a technical term defined in national and international legal and public policy documents. As employed by social scientists, sexual health generally refers to a state of physical and emotional well-being in which an individual enjoys freedom from sexually related disease, dysfunction, coercion, and shame, and thus the ability to enjoy and act on her or his sexual feelings.

The concept is widely used in the United States, Canada, Australia, Europe, and Latin America.

Although scholars and policymakers have treated sexuality as a public health issue since the mid-1800s, few sociologists explicitly used the expression "sexual health" to describe their work before the mid-1990s (many still do not). In fact, the formal definition of sexual health dates only to 1975, when the World Health Organization (WHO) convened an international panel of human sexuality experts for the purpose of addressing a perceived shortage of sexuality educators and research opportunities. At that time, the youth counterculture, second-wave feminist, gay rights, and women's health movements were helping to transform understandings of gender, sexuality, and health in the West. Previously, reproductive health and sexual health had been treated as a single issue, with the emphasis on reproduction; the advent of highly effective contraceptives, along with increasing secularization and social acceptance of nonmarital sexuality in many societies, made a sharper distinction possible.

The 1975 WHO panel delineated the basic elements of sexual health as the "right to sexual information and ... pleasure," the "capacity to ... control sexual and reproductive behaviour," "freedom from ... psychological factors inhibiting sexual response and ... relationship," and "freedom from organic disorders, diseases, and deficiencies that interfere with sexual and reproductive functions." This definition bears the imprint of the WHO's 1946 definition of health as "a state of complete physical, mental, and social well-being and not merely the absence of disease or infirmity." It represents a fundamentally social rather than strictly biomedical understanding of sexual health, going beyond a narrow focus on disease, physiology, and reproduction to consider the social contexts in which sexual feelings and activity occur.

Pleasure, agency, and freedom from physiological and psychological disorders have been central components of all subsequent major definitions of sexual health. These elements also appear in lay definitions, as when the (US) Boston Women's Health Collective's *New Our Bodies, Ourselves* (1984) glossed sexual health as "a physical and emotional state of well-being that allows us to enjoy and act on our sexual feelings."

Definitions of sexual health have since evolved in response to broad social trends. In 1987, during a period marked by intense debate over social diversity and cultural relativism, the WHO Regional Office for Europe released a report (*Concepts on Sexual Health: Report on a Working Group*) contending that the culturally and temporally contingent nature of sexual health precluded a universal definition. The authors' concern that a single definition could be used to label some individuals or behaviors as unhealthy has informed subsequent definitions, which have recognized the importance of factors such as religion, age, disabilities, socioeconomic status, and sexual identity.

In the early 1990s an international coalition of women's health and development NGOs emerged as a major force in a series of population and development conferences sponsored by the United Nations. Coalition members were concerned with a broad range of issues related to sexuality, health, and human rights, including preventing mass rape and female genital mutilation (FGM) and ensuring women's ability to control their fertility, choice of partners, and sexual identity. The coalition succeeded in placing sexual health, framed as an aspect of reproductive health, on the international policy agenda and incorporating it into such documents as the 1994 International Conference of Population and Development (ICPD) Program of Action. The 1990s also saw a concerted effort to frame health as a human right and the development of the concept of sexual rights. Efforts to incorporate sexual health and sexual rights into international law and policy have consistently met with vigorous opposition by a Vatican-led alliance of religious/moral conservative governments and organizations.

The exact relationship between sexual health, reproductive health, and sexual rights is contested. ICPD delegates found it politically expedient to categorize sexual health as an aspect of the less controversial reproductive health. Other influential reports, such as that produced by the 1995 (US) National Commission of Adolescent Sexual Health, treat reproductive health as a component of sexual health. Definitions of sexual rights typically include access to sexual and reproductive health care and sexuality education as well as sexual and reproductive autonomy, bodily integrity, and the pursuit of sexual pleasure. The link between sexual health and sexual rights was made explicit in a 2000 joint report by the Pan American Health Organization (PAHO) and WHO (*Promotion of Sexual Health: Recommendations for Action*), written largely by Latin American sexologists: "Since protection of health is a basic human right, it follows that sexual health involves sexual rights." These widely publicized conferences contributed to a dramatic increase in the number of sociologists and demographers framing their research in terms of "sexual health."

In 2002, the WHO issued a revised definition of sexual health as "a state of physical, emotional, mental, and social well-being related to sexuality ... Sexual health requires a positive and respectful approach to sexuality and sexual relationships, as well as the possibility of having pleasurable and safe sexual experiences, free of coercion, discrimination, and violence." The task force further declared that the attainment of sexual health depended on having the "sexual rights of all persons ... respected, protected, and fulfilled."

National governments have also sought to define and incorporate sexual health into public policy. In 1999 and 2001, respectively, the Canadian and US governments, prompted by a host of similar concerns – including population aging; increasing social diversity; health and social welfare system restructuring; new reproductive technologies; and "unacceptably high" levels of sexually transmitted infections (STIs), infertility, sexual violence, and teen pregnancy – issued reports addressing sexual health. Health Canada's *Report from Consultations on a Framework for Sexual and Reproductive Health* and the US Surgeon General David Satcher's *The Surgeon General's Call to Action to Promote Sexual Health and Responsible Sexual Behavior* both explicitly acknowledged the importance of sexual health to children and older adults (previous definitions imply reproductive-age adults) and stressed the need for sexual responsibility at the individual and community levels (the latter referring to ensuring community members' access to sexuality education and health services and freedom from discrimination and violence). By contrast, a 2001 report from the British Department of Health (*National Strategy for Sexual Health and HIV*), produced as part of a wider health system reform initiative, construed sexual health in relatively narrow terms, reiterating the basic tenets of previous definitions, but focusing chiefly on reproductive issues and the prevention of HIV/STIs and unintended pregnancy, and avoiding reference to responsibility and pleasure. That said, the British framework resembles its Canadian counterpart in treating sexual health as a fundamental human right, whereas the US guidelines tend to frame it as an individual choice – a difference consistent with broader cultural tendencies.

The social trends that have influenced definitions of sexual health have also shaped the nature of sociological research. Historically, due to prevailing codes of morality, beliefs about the purpose of sex, and understandings of social problems, most studies of sexual-health topics focused on married couples of reproductive age or heterosexual adolescents (whose sexuality is presumed to be problematic). Furthermore, although definitions of sexual health are nominally gender-neutral, in practice the bulk of research on sexual health has centered on women – largely due to the physiology of pregnancy, gendered assumptions about family responsibilities, and the sexual double standard. For much of the twentieth century, studies tended to focus either on white middle-class people – typically cast as paragons of health and normalcy – or on economically disadvantaged people and/or members of racial/ethnic minorities, frequently framed as deviant or unhealthy. Study populations have become increasingly socially diverse since the 1970s, with scholars paying more attention to the effects of intersecting identities from the 1990s onward.

Despite the broad range of issues encompassed by leading definitions of sexual health, in practice, the vast majority of academic research on the topic focuses on STIs (including HIV/AIDS) and reproductive health. In developed nations, male and female sexual dysfunction are also common subjects; in the developing world, FGM and sexual violence are frequently studied. Researchers' preoccupation with the negative aspects of sexual health may stem from worldwide cultural and political difficulties in agreeing on a common definition of positive sexual health. With the advent of globalization, sociologists interested in sexual health have

become increasingly aware of the need for a global approach to many sexual health issues, such as the relationship of global sex tourism to STI transmission.

Early sociological work on sexual-health topics was generally motivated by concern with family and population dynamics. Approaches to many issues changed markedly starting in the 1970s, as second-wave feminism gave rise to new understandings of sexuality and gender, inspired the increasingly global women's health movement, and influenced two generations of feminist sociologists to direct attention to gender, sexuality, and bodies. From the 1930s onward, sociologists studied "sexual adjustment" – encompassing compatibility in sexual desire, preferred activities, and frigidity/impotence – as an aspect of "marital adjustment" or emotional well-being in marriage. The term "sexual adjustment" has largely fallen out of favor, and studies now consider these issues among same-sex and cohabiting couples and attend more closely to power and gendered expectations. Sociology's rich tradition of research on reproductive health and politics likewise began to cover new territory in the 1970s, especially the critical policy issues of childbirth, episiotomy, abortion rights, and menopause. Feminists, along with gay rights activists, have also helped to direct scholarly attention to stranger, acquaintance, and marital rape and rape culture, as well as sexuality-related hate crimes.

As scholarly interest in masculinity expanded from the 1990s onward, researchers have increasingly recognized the importance of attending to men's sexual health, beyond sexual dysfunction, both in its own right and in terms of its effects on female and male partners. Major foci to date include men's role in reproduction and birth control, STI transmission, male infertility, and sexual violence.

Gay rights activism, the increasing visibility of lesbigay people, and an increasing number of openly lesbigay sociologists have also influenced sexual health research agendas. Prior to the 1974 removal of homosexuality from the American Psychiatric Association's *DSM-III*, sexual desire for and contact with same-sex partners was largely studied as a sign of mental illness. Research addressing the relationship of sexual health to sexual identity/orientation has burgeoned since. The emergence of HIV/AIDS in 1982 prompted extensive research on gay men's sexual health, albeit much of it narrowly focused on HIV/AIDS. Lesbians' sexual health has received less attention because lesbians have not been a major risk group for HIV; however, sociologists have recently begun to explore lesbian and bisexual women's use of sexual health services. Research on social factors affecting the transmission, prevention, and diagnosis of STIs other than HIV/AIDS has continued throughout this era, with several recent studies offering compelling analyses of the ways gender and race intersect to shape the experience of living with, and seeking treatment for, STIs.

The aging of western populations, along with the unprecedented growth and deregulation of the pharmaceutical industry that began in the 1990s, have prompted increasing attention to sexual health after the menopause/climacteric. Analyses of the social causes and effects of sexual dysfunction – an umbrella term including erectile dysfunction (formerly called impotence) and premature ejaculation in men and dispareunia (painful intercourse), sexual aversion, and lack of desire in men and women (formerly called frigidity, in women) – have proliferated since the 1970s, due to new understandings of sexuality as essential to human happiness. From the late 1990s onward, researchers have charted the increasing medicalization of male and female sexual dysfunction and the pharmaceutical industry's role in setting research and treatment agendas. Over the same period, increasing scholarly interest in the lives of people with chronic illnesses and physical and mental disabilities has prompted a small but growing body of research on the sexual health of women and men with disabilities and/or chronic medical conditions.

Other aspects of sexual health examined by sociologists include:

- Sexual pleasure and desire, other than as related to dysfunction. Such research is relatively rare, especially among youth and people past reproductive age, and is seldom framed in terms of sexual health.
- Formal and informal sexuality education and the politics surrounding it. Comparisons of European and US approaches to sexual health education are especially interesting.

- The medical treatment of people born intersexed, especially genital surgery, as well as lay and medical opposition to that treatment.

Sociological studies of sexual health employ both quantitative and qualitative methods, with the former being somewhat more common, especially for issues deemed relevant to public health. By and large, research on sexual health is subject to the same methodological difficulties as research on sexuality in general (e.g., study participants' desire for privacy). However, the social and political climate in which scholars work may pose additional challenges. For example, since the late 1980s, conservative governments and grassroots organizations in the US and Britain have sought to impede and censor sexuality research by reducing and restricting funding and interfering in already-funded projects. In fact, the increasing popularity of the term "sexual health" may reflect an attempt by researchers worldwide to circumvent conservative opposition, under the assumption that research on sexuality is more likely to be deemed justifiable if it concerns health. Sociopolitical factors may also affect the implementation of public policy grounded in social scientific research. In the US, for example, conservative presidential administrations have overseen the removal of accurate contraception information from official websites and the promotion of "only-abstinence-until-marriage" sexual health education programs, despite evidence of their ineffectiveness. Policies in one nation may have global effects, as in the case of legislation forbidding international population programs that receive US funds from mentioning abortion.

SEE ALSO: AIDS, Sociology of; Family Planning, Abortion, and Reproductive Health; Female Genital Mutilation; New Reproductive Technologies; Safer Sex; Sex Education; Sexual Practices; Transnational and Global Feminisms; Viagra; Women's Health

REFERENCES AND SUGGESTED READINGS

Edwards, W. M. & Coleman, E. (2004) Defining Sexual Health: A Descriptive Overview. *Archives of Sexual Behavior* 33(3): 189–95.

Giami, A. (2002) Sexual Health: The Emergence, Development, and Diversity of a Concept. *Annual Review of Sex Research* 13: 1–35.

Hyde, J. (Ed.) (2002) Promoting Sexual Health and Responsible Sexual Behavior. Special issue, *Journal of Sex Research* 39(1).

Petchesky, R. P. (2003) *Global Prescriptions: Gendering Health and Human Rights*. Zed Books, London.

Petchesky, R. P. (2000) Sexual Rights: Inventing a Concept, Mapping an International Practice. In: Parker, R. G., Barbosa, R. M., & Aggleton, P. (Eds.), *Framing the Sexual Subject: The Politics of Gender, Sexuality, and Power*. University of California Press, Berkeley, pp. 81–103.

Rogstad, K. E. (Ed.) (1996) Men's Sexual Health. Special issue, *Sexual and Marital Therapy* 11(3).

Wingood, G. M. & Di Clemente, R. J. (Eds.) (2002) *Handbook of Women's Sexual and Reproductive Health*. Kluwer/Plenum, New York.

World Health Organization (2002) Definition of Sexual Health. Online. www.who.int/reproductive-health/gender/sexual_health.html.

sexual identities

Ken Plummer

The term identity is derived from the Latin root *idem*, implying sameness and continuity, and helps to provide a sense of who we are and of who other people are. It serves as a crucial bridge in social life between human beings and wider cultures; it implies a sense of meaning and a sense of categorization and differentiation; and it marks out differences – between ourselves and others. The idea of identity speaks of locating a person within a personal and social category. It suggests answer to the question "who am I?" placing one's self and life within a framework of past (what kind of person I was and how I became it), of present (of who I am now), and future (guiding the sense of who one will be and how one is different from others). Sexual and gendered identities help to locate people within sexual and gender cultural frameworks.

In some (usually more traditional) societies, identities are often assumed (they may be ascribed) and there is little debate about the nature of identities. Gender and sexuality may be taken for granted as a given identity. In other societies (usually modern ones prone to individualism), just who one is becomes a greater problem, and there is much discussion on the nature, origins, and impact of different kinds of identities. Some suggest that identities are more or less fixed and given from within – they are essentialist. They serve as an inner core of who one is. Much of biological, psychological, and psychotherapeutic thought is of this kind. Others suggest that identities themselves are historically and socially contingent, and that they are hence socially constructed. In this latter sense, people have to invent who they are – there is no inner core. Much of Meadian interactionist thought is of this kind. The analysis of identities covers a wide range of concerns from gender and sexual identities to ethnic identities, from occupational to nationalistic identities. Very often there are "hierarchies of identity" with master identities becoming key and conflicts being developed between them.

In recent times, with the emergence of postmodern culture, identities have increasingly come to be seen as highly unstable and precarious. For theorists like Anthony Giddens, Ulrich Beck, and Zygmunt Bauman, identities are destabilized and have to be worked at. Giddens, in his *Modernity and Self-Identity* (1991), suggests that identity becomes part of a "politics of life style" which has emerged to ask "how should we live?" in a post-traditional order and against the backdrop of existential questions. Lifestyle choice is increasingly important in the constitution of identity and daily activity. "Reflexively organized life planning becomes a central feature of the structuring of self-identity" (Giddens 1991: 5); self-identity is "the self as reflexively understood by the person in terms of her or his biography" (p. 53). For Bauman, "if the *modern* 'problem of identity' was how to construct an identity and keep it solid and stable, the *postmodern* 'problem of identity' is primarily how to avoid fixation and keep the options open" (1996: 18). Kenneth Gergen (1991) depicts a journey which he describes as "from the Romantic (via the Modern) to the Postmodern." For him, the postmodern means "the very concept of personal essences is thrown in doubt." The source of this change is "the technologies of social saturation" (low-tech and hi-tech), leading to a "multi-phrenic condition" and new patterns of relationships ("fractional," "microwave," etc.). All of this could mean that lifestyle choices have to be made around gender (how to be a man, what kind of man, how to see oneself as a man), or as a sexual being (how to be gay, how to identify oneself, etc.).

LESBIAN AND GAY IDENTITY

Ever since its arrival in academia during the 1970s, lesbian and gay studies have been haunted by the identity problem (Plummer 1981). From early studies such as Carol Warren's *Identity and Community in the Gay World* (1974) and Barbara Ponse's *Identities in the Lesbian World* (1978), through Richard Troiden's *Gay and Lesbian Identity* (1988) and William H. DuBay's (neglected) *Gay Identity: The Self Under Ban* (1987), the themes of classification and identity have been extremely prominent. In the now voluminous and magisterial compendiums, textbooks, readers, and handbooks that have been reproduced for lesbian and gay studies, identity always plays a prominent part. And articles on the field continue to multiply, though nowadays usually with increasing complexity. Without doubt, it has consistently been one of the big themes for understanding "lesbian and gay lives" historically, comparatively, and contemporaneously.

Broadly, research on gay identity has highlighted six questions:

1 What is the nature of the lesbian and gay identity? – the essentialist/phenomenalist question.
2 How did the identity of lesbian and gay emerge? – the historical question.
3 How do people come to acquire the lesbian/gay identity? – the question of stages and processes.
4 How do people manage the lesbian and gay identity? – the coming out/outing/passing problem.
5 How is the identity changing?
6 What are the political uses of lesbian and gay identities? – which highlights the politics of identity and the issue of citizenship rights.

This concern with identities is all part of a wider zeal to classify and order our identities and sexualities. In all this earlier work, there was a clear tendency to locate a fairly clear gay identity and a fairly identifiable pattern of coming out through stages (the popular coming out models of the 1970s and 1980s). It was usually linked to a community – identities became the bridge between the gay or lesbian person and the gay or lesbian community. Over time, the notions of identity became more complex as stage models of identity were challenged, variations of ethnicity and sexualities were confronted, and a politics of identity was developed. In all of this, boundaries were clearly being drawn, but in complex ways.

During the 1970s, a social science literature emerged which suggested the processes in which a person came to build up different kinds of sexual identity. These writings often delineated stages. Plummer (1975) suggested the stages of sensitization, signification, subculturalization, and stabilization. Troiden (1988) extends this and suggests a similar model: sensitization, identity confusion, assumption of a gay identity for oneself, and commitment to homosexuality as a way of life. Vivienne Cass (1979) suggested five movements: identity confusion, identity comparison, identity tolerance, identity acceptance, and identity pride. Nowadays, such models are seen as perhaps having relevance for the 1960s and the 1970s when homosexuality was heavily stigmatized; however, these days younger people are experiencing much more flexible ways of relating to the category of homosexual.

From at least the 1960s the idea of "coming out" became more and more significant as an aspect of gay and lesbian identity construction. Coming out has multiple meanings. In the earlier twentieth century, Delaney suggests that it seems to have meant "having one's first major homosexual experience." Subsequently, it meant primarily self-identification as homosexual. But toward the end of the twentieth century it came increasingly to mean disclosing who one is to family, friends, and indeed the wider world. In 1970, Barry Dank suggested how central this process was. Likewise, the gay and lesbian movement of the 1970s saw "coming out" as a political act: the making of homosexuality into a public event became a major force for change.

Times have changed. Ritch C. Savin Williams suggests in the early twenty-first century there has been much greater complexity and variability in the complex process of gay identity formation. He suggests a much wider range of terms available within which to locate oneself, with many refusing, resisting, and modifying sexual identity labels.

THE POLITICS OF IDENTITY AND ITS CRITICS

Identity politics became increasingly prominent from the late 1960s onwards, and is particularly associated with ethnic and religious minorities as well as with feminist and lesbian and gay movements. There is a clear move here from a class-based politics to a broader set of alliances. Experiences such as those of black, gay, or women's oppression become highlighted as the focus for creating a separate group identity – as blacks, gays, or feminists. By the 1980s it became clear that many sexual and gender identities were coming to be political categories. With reminiscences of Marx's dictum of a class becoming a class-in-itself – of the rise of political identity – and the model of black consciousness and black identity becoming more and more an issue, increasingly both the women's movement and the gay and lesbian movement came to center around a pivotal (and usually essentialized) identity. Indeed, without such identities becoming extant, much of the politics of the new social movements would not be possible.

A telling article by Steven Epstein (1985) on ethnic identity and gay identity suggested the parallel between black identity as a political and personal tool, and the gay identity as working in similar ways. The gay community, and indeed contemporary gay politics, require a clear identity around which to mobilize. This has remained the case for the vast majority of gays and lesbians since that time: there is a clear and strong identity. The notion of gay identity of true lesbians not only brought clarity to (an often unclear) life, it also firmly focused on a politics and galvanized action.

What was happening, though it may not have been clearly seen initially, was the development of a politics of identity. Gay identity became a political tactic. It also allowed rights to be attached to the identity. The new social movements (NSMs) have consistently been seen as generating a politics of identity which claims recognition as one of its main goals – collective, public, and political identities.

But there have also been a number of countermovements to this. First, critics suggest that actual sexual or gender identities are themselves much more complex than such simple terms suggest. Whilst we used to have rather simple terms of "passive" or "active" gays and "butch" and "femme" lesbians, increasingly these have become fragmented into many kinds: lesbian boys and male lesbians (Zita 1998), MSM (men who have sex with men), "female masculinity" (Halberstam 1998), or the range of "intersex" and "trans" identities (Preves 2003) – as well as broader ones such as "LGBT" (lesbian, gay, bisexual, and transgender identities). In general, though, critics suggest that the categories have oversimplified – even stereotyped and essentialized – complex experiences. Sexual and gender identities, for example, lie at the intersections of many other axes: ethnicity, nationality, age, disablement. These can readily hyphenate identities into "Asian gay identity" or "working-class, Native American lesbian identity."

Second, critics suggest that postmodern times have brought very different and largely unstable identities, as we have seen above: there is no fixed way of being sexual or gendered. They critique identity, and suggest instead that it is much more fluid, often characterized by narratives (Holstein & Gubrium 2000), seriality, performativity (Salih & Butler 2004), and hybridity. Stuart Hall (1997) talks of the diasporic experience as defined not "by essence or purity, but by the recognition of a necessary heterogeneity and diversity; by a conception of identity which lives with and through, not despite, difference; by *hybridity*."

QUEERING IDENTITY

"Gay identity," then, like all other identities, can presume too much. It is indeed usually an essentialist idea and cannot begin to capture the full complexities of what we might provisionally sense as "same-sex experience," which may be youthful or old, black or white, disabled or non-disabled, to engage in just a few of the most simplistic variations. So our notions of identities from which we speak have to become more varied, pluralized, and open than this, whilst indeed having to acknowledge some kind of continuities and boundaries (except in the most extreme, transgressive, and postmodern cases). Fixed clear voices seem now to have become weakened, identities ebb and flow, and voices now speak from a multiplicity of shifting and unsettled positions, constructing diverse narratives (stories of the lives of our lives) (Holstein & Gubrium 2000). These voices are always in dialogic process, and people speaking from various identities and positions may well find that these have to shift in the very processes of argumentation. But they cannot speak at all if they do not recognize the categories, however humbling and inadequate they may be. We need what might be called a *thin essentialism*. We need our identities, even as we change and modify them on a daily basis, and they are surely part of the continuing politics of citizenship. (And at times there may even be a need to "risk essentialism" to sense a strong, shared "we.")

These more radical tendencies in identity theory have since the late 1980s (in North America, largely as a humanities/multicultural-based response to a more limited social psychological approach classically found in "lesbian and gay studies" as indicated above) been linked to "queer." "Queer" is most definitely meant to take us beyond the boundaries and borders of heteronormativity. The roots of queer theory (if not the term) are usually seen to lie in the work of Eve Kosofsky Sedgwick in *Epistemology of the Closet* (1990). She argues that the central classifying device of the nineteenth and twentieth centuries – the overarching borders of society – is composed of the hetero/homo binary divide: "many of the major nodes of thought and knowledge in twentieth-century Western culture as a whole are structured – indeed fractured – by a chronic, now endemic crisis of homo/heterosexual definition, indicatively male, dating from the end of the nineteenth century" (1990: 1).

Identity is thus seriously questioned. Likewise, Judith Butler's *Gender Trouble* (1979) is interested in deconstructing the sex/gender divide (and hence less concerned with the deconstruction of the homo/heterosexual binary). For Butler, there can be no claim to any essential gender: it is all "performative," slippery, unfixed. If there is a heart to queer theory, then, it must be seen as a *radical stance around sexuality and gender that denies any fixed categories and seeks to subvert any tendencies toward normality within its study.* Queer theory, then, is a stance in which sexual categories are seen to be open, fluid, and non-fixed: both the boundaries of heterosexual/homosexual identities and sex/gender identities are challenged. Indeed, categories such as gay, lesbian, and heterosexual identity become "deconstructed." There is a decentering of identity.

Whether we can live with deconstructed identities in the future remains to be seen.

SEE ALSO: Class Consciousness; Coming Out/Closets; Essentialism and Constructionism; Female Masculinity; Freud, Sigmund; Gay and Lesbian Movement; Heterosexuality; Homosexuality; Hybridity; Identity: The Management of Meaning; Identity Politics/Relational Politics; Intersexuality; Lesbianism; Mead, George Herbert; New Social Movement Theory; Plastic Sexuality; Postmodern Sexualities; Queer Theory; Sex and Gender; Transgender, Transvestism, and Transsexualism; Women's Movements

REFERENCES AND SUGGESTED READINGS

Bauman, Z. (1996) From Pilgrim to Tourist: A Short History of Identity. In: Hall, S. & Du Gay, P. (Eds.), *Questions of Cultural Identity*. Sage, London.

Cass, V. C. (1979) Homosexual Identity Formation: A Theoretical Model. *Journal of Homosexuality* 4, 3 (Spring).

Cohler, B. J. & Galatzer-Levy, R. M. (2000) *The Course of Gay and Lesbian Lives*. University of Chicago Press, Chicago.

Epstein, S. (1985) Gay Politics, Ethnic Identity: The Limits of Social Constructionism. *Socialist Review* 17: 9–54.

Gergen, K. (1991) *The Saturated Self: Dilemmas of Identity in Contemporary Life*. Basic Books, New York.

Giddens, A. (1991) *Modernity and Self-Identity*. Polity Press, Cambridge.

Halberstam, J. (1998) *Female Masculinity*. Duke University Press, Durham, NC.

Hall, S. (1997) Subjects in History: Making Diasporic Identities. In: Lubiano, W. (Ed.), *The House That Race Built*. Pantheon, New York, pp. 289–99.

Holstein, J. & Gubrium, J. F. (2000) *The Self We Live By: Narrative Identity in a Postmodern World*. Oxford University Press, Oxford.

Mead, G. H. (1934) *Mind, Self, and Society*. University of Chicago Press, Chicago.

Plummer, K. (1975) *Sexual Stigma: An Interactionist Account*. Routledge & Kegan Paul, London.

Plummer, K. (Ed.) (1981) *The Making of the Modern Homosexual*. Hutchinson, London.

Preves, S. E. (2003) *Intersex and Identity: The Contested Self*. Rutgers University Press, New Brunswick, NJ.

Salih, S. (with Butler, J.) (Ed.) (2004) *The Judith Butler Reader*. Blackwell, Oxford.

Sedgwick, E. K. (1990) *Epistemology of the Closet*. University of California Press, Berkeley.

Troiden, R. R. (1988) *Gay and Lesbian Identity: A Sociological Study*. General Hall, Dix Hills, NY.

Woodward, K. (Ed.) (1997) *Identity and Difference*. Sage, London.

Zita, J. (1998) Male Lesbians and the Postmodernist Body. In: *Body Talk*. Columbia University Press, New York.

sexual markets, commodification, and consumption

Ken Plummer

Modern sexualities have become constituted through massive markets. Consumption has become a key social characteristic of the late twentieth century (see Robert Bocock's *Consumption*, 1993), and in parts of the world we are "born to shop." Consumption has played a growing role in the lives of individuals around the (wealthier) world, and one aspect of this is the deep and pervasive ways in which human sexualities have come to be marketed, commodified, distributed, and consumed across the world. In contrast with what Foucault, in the first volume of *The History of Sexuality*, called *ars erotica* (and the presumed spontaneity of sex though influenced by religion), contemporary sexualities are structured increasingly in global

capitalist markets (Altman 2000). This is no minor observation, although it is a much neglected one.

In one sense there is little new about this. There are several long-term historical institutions which have regulated sex through economic mechanisms. Prostitution, for example, has – rightly or wrongly – been commonly called the "oldest profession" and involved the financial supply of and demand for sex, among much else. In the twentieth century, this wider "sex industry" involves many workers and could properly be seen as an aspect of the sociology of work. Thus there are

> business owners and investors, independent contractors and non-sexual employees (waiters, cashiers, guards, drivers, accountants, lawyers, doctors) and middlemen who facilitate business processes (some travel agents, guides, estate agents, matrimonial agents, newspaper and magazine editors, Internet entrepreneurs). Sites involved include bars, restaurants, cabarets, clubs, brothels, discotheques, saunas, massage parlors, sex shops with private booths, motels, flats, dungeons for bondage and domination, Internet sites, cinemas and anywhere that sex is offered for sale on an occasional basis such as stag (men only) and hen (women only) events, shipboard activities or modeling parties. Products and services included erotic phone lines, escort and matrimonial services, films and videos, souvenirs, toys, clothes, equipment and live and virtual spectacles via web cameras. (Agustin 2005)

Likewise, many marital arrangements – from the bride dowry to family inheritance – are not new and have involved the regulation of sexuality through monetary means. But these have not typically involved the turning of sex into commoditized markets, such as "mail order brides" (Constable 2003), as is found today.

The contemporary ecology of sexual markets suggests looking at the workings of five major interlocking markets through which sexuality is consumed. These are:

1 The sale of sexualized corporeal bodies, in many versions of real live sex acts (Chapkis 1997): "prostitution" and sex work, trafficking of bodies, stripping, table dancing/lap dancing (Frank 2002), sex tourism (Ryan & Hall 2001), and sex parties. "Real sex" is on sale. Much of this is global, and

in rich/first world countries large numbers of men are purchasers of sex.

2 The sale of sexualized representations, through images and texts – in erotica, pornography, and Internet messaging. Not only is there a huge industry of pornography for men (straight and gay), but there are also now substantial markets for women. The widespread nature of this has been called the "pornographication" of culture (McNair 2002).

3 The sale of sexualized objects: most prominent here are "sex toys," from S/M costumes, nitrate inhalants ("Poppers"), and whips/harnesses to dildos, vibrators, inflated blowup dolls, and lingerie, organized through shops like Ann Summers (Storr 2004). Parties are organized; the "circuit party" organizes sex parties (usually gay) on a national and international scale (e.g., Westhaver 2005).

4 The sale of sexualized technologies: much of sex is also marketed through medical aids, from Viagra to contraceptives and transgender surgery, as well as cosmetic surgery (Haiken 1997).

5 The sale of sexualized relationships, including marriage (such as mail order brides), and meeting places, such as gay bars (Chasin 2000; Sender 2005), singles bars, or indeed almost any bar which can facilitate sexual relationships. Likewise, relationships can become subject to expensive therapy and standardized self-help books which can sell, for example, the 12 steps needed for a perfect relationship. Increasingly, relationships can be found in the marketplaces of cyberspace.

Some of these markets involve the explicit and direct selling of sex; others are more covert and indirect. Thus, the most conspicuous consumption is through direct markets where sex itself is the direct commodity for sale. By contrast, covert or indirect markets are those which use sexualities to sell something else – the massive worlds of advertising, entertainment, and sport are often sold through their sexual iconography. Thus stars from singers (Elvis Presley, Madonna) to film stars (Valentino in the 1920s to Tom Cruise) and sports stars (George Best to David Beckham) command

large sums while extracting "desires" from their audiences. Many objects are also sold that depend on an erotic connection: perfumes, clothes, holidays, music, dance, and so on, are linked to sex.

There is a landscape of erotica as a background to everyday life through film, television, advertising, video, and pop music – and indeed, even the city becomes a sexualized space. Websites, too, can provide online sexual pleasures, all neatly coded and organized according to a catalogue that transcends Krafft-Ebing's wilder taxonomies where consumers may find just what they desire, order and pay for it online, and subsequently meet their desires. It often parallels the McDonaldization of society (Ritzer 2004) as the McDonaldization of sexuality, being rendered rational, calculable, efficient, and predictable.

Sexual markets also span across the whole life cycle. Children enter systems of consumption and sexuality, even if they are not clear about them. Adolescents become saturated with sexual consumption, in the process developing desires of all kinds. In later life, the daily routines of sexual markets are unmistakable.

Tim Edwards in *Contradictions of Consumption* (1996) has suggested five fundamental meanings of consumption to consumers. These ideas are indicative of what could be developed in relation to sexuality. The first sees the consumer as king: sexual consumption indicates a kind of victor over the producer and retailer. The second sees sexual consumers as victims – as cultural dopes who cannot help but be persuaded about the latest sexual fashions. Third is the sexual consumer as criminal: the purchasing of illegal goods, and the many markets that sell sex against the law. Fourth is the anti-sexual consumer: someone who ostensibly rejects the increased dehumanization and crass commercialism of the consumer world. This type of consumer may turn to alternative and more spontaneous versions of sexuality (although paradoxically, such sexualities are also often sold in therapeutic markets, for example). Finally, the sexual consumer may also be a voyeur or pleasure seeker: a *flâneur* engaging with the proliferating erotic environment of images.

Consumption usually plays a symbolic role and may help to establish group boundaries, such as between men and women, gay and straight. It is not surprising that much of sexual consumption is linked to matters of gender: what it is to be a sexy man, or a sexy woman. There is growing research that suggests that what the symbols and culture propose for the sexuality of women are different from those for male sexuality. Thus women's consumption of sexuality and their desires can be shaped by the media: television's *Sex and the City*, advertising, women's magazines, websites, pop music, and, of course, fashion. Some feminists have argued this plays a key role for women and men. Notably, this is bound up with bringing back sexuality for women – sometimes a domesticated version, sometimes as an overstated self-expression (women become "self-made," autoerotic, choosing sexual display, seeking breakthrough sexual pleasure), as being desired, being sexy, feeling empowered (Storr 2004). Others see it as a sad reflection of shopping. The body is increasingly objectified, sex acts are more and more open to being sold, allied goods like underwear become sexualized, and the entire body is reconstructed as thin and beautiful through expensive cosmetic surgeries.

The commodification of sexuality, then, is seen as a rapidly expanding (and expensive) global market. Sexual consumption suggests the widespread growth of sexual pleasure and its accessibility where sex becomes "liberated." By contrast, sexual consumption may also be seen as a mechanism of dehumanization and disenchantment, a multibillion dollar industry which provides huge profits for organized crime, medical empires, and commercial companies that trade in a wide array of "sex." Desires are turned into markets and shaped and reinforced by them.

SEE ALSO: Consumption and the Body; Consumption, Girls' Culture and; Consumption, Masculinities and; Female Sex Work as Deviance; Sex Tourism; Gender, Consumption and; Globalization, Sexuality and; Homosexuality; Pornography and Erotica; Sex Tourism; Sexualities and Consumption; Viagra

REFERENCES AND SUGGESTED READINGS

Agustin, L. M. (2005) The Cultural Study of Commercial Sex. *Sexualities* 8(5).

Altman, D. (2000) *Global Sex*. University of Chicago Press, Chicago.

Attwood, F. (2005) Fashion and Passion: Marketing Sex to Women. *Sexualities* 8(4): 393–407.

Chapkis, W. (1997) *Live Sex Acts*. Routledge, London.

Chasin, A. (2000) *Selling Out: The Gay and Lesbian Movement Goes to Market*. Palgrave, Basingstoke.

Constable, N. (2003) *Romance on a Global Stage: Pen Pals, Virtual Ethnography, and "Mail Order" Marriages*. University of California Press, Berkeley.

Enloe, C. (1989) *Bananas, Beaches, and Bases*. Pandora, New York.

Farrar, J. (2002) *Opening Up: Youth Culture and Market Reform in Shanghai*. University of Chicago Press, Chicago.

Flowers, A. (1998) *The Fantasy Factory: Insider's View of the Phone Sex Industry*. University of Pennsylvania Press, Philadelphia.

Frank, K. (2002) *G Strings and Sympathy: Strip Club Regulars and Male Desire*. Duke University Press, Durham, NC.

Haiken, E. (1997) *Venus Envy: A History of Cosmetic Surgery*. Johns Hopkins University Press, Baltimore.

McNair, B. (2002) *Striptease Culture: Sex, Media, and the Democratization of Desire*. Routledge, London.

Ritzer, G. (2004) *The McDonaldization of Society*. Pine Forge Press, Thousand Oaks, CA.

Ryan, C. & Hall, C. M. (2001) *Sex Tourism, Marginal People, and Liminality*. Routledge, London.

Sender, K. (2005) *Business, Not Politics: The Making of the Gay Market*. Columbia University Press, New York.

Sonnett, E. (1999) Erotic Fiction by Women for Women: The Pleasure of Post-Feminist Heterosexuality. *Sexualities* (2)2: 167–87.

Storr, M. (2004) *Latex and Lingerie: Shopping for Pleasure at Anne Summers Parties*. Berg, Oxford.

Weitzer, R. (Ed.) (2000) *Sex for Sale*. Routledge, New York.

Westhaver, R. (2005) "Coming Out of Your Skin": Circuit Parties, Pleasure, and the Subject. *Sexualities* 8(3): 347–74.

sexual politics

Matthew Waites

"Sexual politics" refers to the contestation of power relations with respect to sex, gender, and sexuality. The concept originates in the second-wave feminist movement which emerged in the late 1960s and 1970s in western societies. Its definitive textual origin is Kate Millett's *Sexual Politics*, first published in 1970, one of the founding works of the emerging women's liberation movement which provided a social and political analysis of "patriarchy" – the social system of rule by men. For Millett, "sexual politics" expressed the idea that "sex is a status category with political implications," and this implied challenging the distinction between public and private which reproduced inequality between men and women by consigning concerns about sex and sexuality to a non-political private realm. The concept is now widely used in academia and in popular culture to refer to a range of struggles over sex, gender, and sexuality, although the scope and implications of sexual politics remain highly contested.

The idea of sexual politics was revolutionary for sociology. Power relations between men and women which had previously been interpreted as the appropriate expression of biological differences (e.g., in the work of Talcott Parsons) were acknowledged as the products of society, history, and culture, and hence as politically accountable. Feminists sought to distinguish sex, understood as biological difference, from gender, understood as socially defined – as in Ann Oakley's *Sex, Gender, and Society* (1972). Gradually, knowledge generated in feminist social movements began to challenge sociological orthodoxy.

One of the central concerns of Millett's *Sexual Politics* was with power and domination in relation to sexual activity itself, and indeed Millett argued that "coitus" "may serve as a model of sexual politics on an individual or personal plane." However, "sexual politics" as a phrase used in mainstream politics and culture sometimes became associated first and foremost with a focus on power inequalities relating to biological sex and gender rather than sexuality. During the 1970s, the emerging sociology of "sexual divisions" sometimes continued to neglect sexuality in its focus on work and the family. Sexual politics tended to imply that the politics of gender could be equated with the politics of socially defined relationships between two biologically given sexes. This assumption has more recently been challenged, however, in the context of developing technologies of body modification and surgery, by radical

transgender theorists and poststructuralist feminist theorist Judith Butler (1990), whose contestation of conceptions of sex as presocial and immutable defines what she now describes as the "new gender politics" (2004). Sexual politics today, then, has become a concept used to describe a wide variety of forms of intellectual work, social movement activity, and cultural politics contesting sex, gender, and sexuality by women, men, and transgender people, lesbian, gay, and bisexual people, queer people and heterosexual people, sadomasochists, pedophiles, anti-pornography campaigners, and many others.

Sexual politics politicized sociology with respect to gender and sexuality. Yet sexual politics also challenged traditional conceptions of the scope of politics as a discipline, pushing its research beyond the institutions of government and the public sphere to interrogate power-structured relationships in "private" life. Sexual politics thus tended to suggest the necessity of interdisciplinary analysis, yet political sociology – preoccupied with sophology and the sociology of government institutions – was initially ill equipped to serve as a forum for the necessary cross-fertilization. Over time, however, the idea of sexual politics has fostered interdisciplinary scholarship, and recently has contributed to the reinvention of political sociology as a more open and innovative field (Nash 1999).

Feminism in the United States, and to a lesser extent in the West more generally, became divided by "sex wars" between radical feminists and self-defined "pro-sex" feminists during the late 1970s and 1980s. Pornography was a central issue, for example in the radical feminist analysis of patriarchal oppression produced by Catharine MacKinnon and Andrea Dworkin (cf. Dworkin 1981); but such analyses were rejected by other "pro-sex"/"anti-censorship" feminists such as Carole Vance, who organized the Barnard conference on female sexuality in 1982 in response, placing greater emphasis on possibilities for women's sexual pleasure within heterosexuality (Vance 1992). Feminists remain divided over issues such as pornography and prostitution.

If, as is widely agreed among sociologists, the emergence of gay liberation and women's liberation movements from the late 1960s marked an important new phase in sexual politics, then it can be argued that contemporary sexual politics has again entered a new phase during the 1990s and in the new millennium. In the developed world, feminism has achieved a fundamental shift from the assumed model of the heterosexual nuclear family with a male "breadwinner" and corresponding gender norms of femininity and masculinity, to a situation in which it is assumed to be legitimate for both male and female partners in heterosexual relationships to engage in paid employment, and where diverse heterosexual masculinities and femininities are more acceptable, though still policed. Gay and lesbian movements have achieved a shift from a world structured by "the closet," as suggested by Eve Sedgwick in *Epistemology of the Closet* (1990) – one of the founding texts of "queer theory" (see below) – to a world now moving *Beyond the Closet* – the title of a study published in 2004 by US sociologist Steven Seidman. Transgender people have also experienced a significant shift toward public visibility and toleration, accompanied in some states by crucial legal reforms granting recognition of a change of gender, such as the 2004 Gender Recognition Act in the United Kingdom, though the state continues to institutionalize problematic forms of medicalization (e.g., the Act makes provision for "gender recognition" to be granted to individuals only where they are determined by a "Gender Recognition Panel" to have experienced "gender dysphoria" according to a report from a registered medical practitioner or psychologist; and also to be "living in the other gender" with the intention to continue doing so until death. In certain respects, such laws thus legally entrench, rather than destabilize, biomedical and binary conceptions of sex and gender).

Overall there have been significant changes, but contemporary developments do not suggest the future direction of social and political change will necessarily continue to be defined by the advance of these movements. Contemporary sexual politics in western states is marked, for example, by the emergence of men's movements campaigning on issues such as fathers' rights, which have a relationship to feminism that is frequently hostile. The contemporary cultural politics of sexuality has shifted profoundly, particularly in youth culture.

The issue of children's relationship to sexuality has come increasingly to the fore. Pedophile organizations and movements were able to emerge in the 1970s liberal climate in many western states to argue for the legitimacy of consensual relationships between adults and children. But with child sexual abuse emerging as a major public issue since the 1980s, such organizations and movements have increasingly gone underground. Libertarian critics such as Judith Levine in *Harmful to Minors* (2002) now warn of "the perils of protecting children from sex," emphasizing instead the need for sex education and openness. In this context, "age of consent" laws regulating young people's sexual behavior are increasingly subject to international comparison and contestation (Waites 2005).

The early 1990s witnessed the emergence of "queer politics," and relatedly "queer theory," in western states. "Queer" is a profoundly contested label: for some, queer has simply served as a rhetorically assertive synonym for "gay" or "gay, lesbian, and bisexual," but for others "queer" is fundamentally associated with a project of destabilizing the prevailing heterosexual/homosexual dichotomy. Queer theory is characterized by the influence of the French poststructuralist Michel Foucault, and associated above all with a challenge to "heteronormativity." Such a politics is critical of what is perceived as the liberal assimilationist politics of prominent lesbian and gay organizations discerned in demands for "lesbian and gay marriage" and "gays in the military" (see Warner 1999).

Meanwhile, in the "developing" world sexual politics is equally dynamic and fraught with conflict. In India, for example, where conceptions of national identity are structured by gendered signifiers such as "Mother India," Chetan Bhatt has discussed how women nevertheless obtain forms of political agency within Hindu nationalist movements. In Zimbabwe, as Oliver Phillips has documented, homosexuality has become politicized and labeled as an un-African "white man's disease" by President Robert Mugabe in the context of postcolonial struggles over national identity; and research by Jacqui Alexander has discerned similar postcolonial dynamics in the Caribbean (for extracts from all these, see Weeks et al. 2003).

Probably more than any other factor, HIV/ AIDS has played a huge role in transforming global sexual politics, forcing governments to address the most intimate areas of people's lives, and challenging deeply embedded cultural and religious traditions. Responses to HIV/AIDS have been analyzed in the context of globalization, with attention to the political economy of the crisis (Altman 2001). Research such as that of Ros Petchesky and the International Reproductive Rights Research Action Group demonstrates that the battles of sexual politics remain to be fought in much of the world, particularly Africa, but also criticizes the imposition of prescribed western agendas and solutions (Petchesky & Judd 1998).

SEE ALSO: AIDS, Sociology of; Coming Out/Closets; Feminism; Feminism, First, Second, and Third Waves; Femininities/Masculinities; Foucault, Michel; Gay and Lesbian Movement; Gender Ideology and Gender Role Ideology; Globalization, Sexuality and; Heterosexuality; Inequality/Stratification, Gender; Patriarchy; Queer Theory; Sex and Gender; Sexual Citizenship; Sexualities and Culture Wars

REFERENCES AND SUGGESTED READINGS

Altman, D. (2001) *Global Sex*. University of Chicago Press, Chicago.
Butler, J. (1990) *Gender Trouble*. Routledge, London.
Butler, J. (2004) *Undoing Gender*. Routledge, London.
Duggan, L. & Hunter, N. D. (Eds.) (1995) *Sex Wars: Sexual Dissent and American Political Culture*. Routledge, New York.
Dworkin, A. (1981) *Pornography: Men Possessing Women*. Women's Press, London.
Millett, K. (1972) *Sexual Politics*. Abacus, London.
Nash, K. (1999) *Contemporary Political Sociology: Globalization, Politics, and Power*. Blackwell, Oxford.
Oakley, A. (1972) *Sex, Gender, and Society*. Temple Smith, London.
Petchesky, R. & Judd, K. (Eds.) (1998) *Negotiating Reproductive Rights: Women's Perspectives Across Countries and Cultures*. Zed Books, London.
Sedgwick, E. (1990) *Epistemology of the Closet*. Penguin, London.
Seidman, S. (2004) *Beyond the Closet: The Transformation of Gay and Lesbian Life*. Routledge, London.
Vance, C. (1992) *Pleasure and Danger: Exploring Female Sexuality*, 2nd edn. Pandora, New York.
Waites, M. (2005) *The Age of Consent: Young People, Sexuality, and Citizenship*. Palgrave Macmillan, Basingstoke.
Warner, M. (1999) *The Trouble with Normal: Sex, Politics, and the Ethics of Queer Life*. Free Press, New York.
Weeks, J., Holland, J., & Waites, M. (Eds.) (2003) *Sexualities and Society: A Reader*. Polity Press, Cambridge.

sexual practices

Stephen K. Sanderson

Sexual practices have varied widely across time and space. In the broadest terms, societies are either *sex-positive* or *sex-negative*, with the majority the former (Bullough 1976). The Trobriand Islanders of Melanesia were described by Malinowski as unusually sexually permissive. Sex life may begin for young boys as early as age 10 and for young girls as early as age 6. Polynesian societies were also renowned for their high levels of sexual permissiveness. For example, among the ancient Hawaiians, "a little girl's clitoris was stretched and lengthened through oral stimulation. The penis received similar treatment so as to enhance its beauty and prepare it for sexual enjoyment later in life" (de Waal 2005: 107).

Homosexual relationships have also been common in a number of preliterate (and in modern) societies. In some North American Indian societies, a man known as a *berdache* dressed as a woman, performed women's roles, and engaged in sexual relations with other men, all with social approval. Other societies (e.g., India, Polynesia, Oman) have had the local equivalent of a *berdache*. Among the Azande of the Sudan, man–boy homosexual relations were common, and institutionalized homosexuality has been widespread throughout Melanesia. For example, among the Etoro of New Guinea, men and young boys sleep together in men's houses, and man–boy homosexual relations are common.

In agrarian civilizations, outside of western civilization, with its sex-negative Judeo-Christian tradition, sexual permissiveness has usually far exceeded restrictiveness. The Greeks were a fairly permissive culture, and are famed for their institutionalized form of homosexuality between older men and young boys. India was perhaps the most sex-positive of all the historical agrarian civilizations. Hindus thought that women enjoyed sex at least as much as men, and a wide range of sexual practices was considered acceptable. The Chinese were also quite open about sex and had a form of man–boy homosexuality that resembled the Greek pattern (Bullough 1976), and the same was true in Japan (Leupp 1995).

Freud and the Freudians dominated the study of human sexuality for many years. For Freud, sex was an overpowering biological drive that was repressed by society in varying ways and degrees. The Freudian tradition was kept alive in altered form by such thinkers as Reich and Marcuse. Kinsey emerged onto the scene in the late 1940s, and Masters and Johnson in the 1960s. Their work had little theory and has been referred to as a kind of "radical empiricism" (Brake 1982).

The currently dominant approach to explaining sexual practices seems to be *social constructionism*, which downplays the biological nature of humans and emphasizes that sexual practices are socially and culturally created. Among the earliest sociologists to take this approach, specifically in the form of symbolic interactionism, were John Gagnon and William Simon, as well as Ken Plummer. Social constructionists oppose "essentialism," or the notion that sexuality is largely a matter of biologically pre-given drives. For the constructionists, sexual practices are less biologically given than determined by society through complex webs of social interaction and social definition. Gagnon and Simon emphasized the importance of "sexual scripts"; for them, sexual conduct "is acquired and assembled in human interaction, judged and performed in specific cultural and historical worlds" (Gagnon 1977: 2). And, as Plummer tells us, "Sexuality has no meaning other than that given to it in social situations. Thus the forms and the contents of sexual meanings are another cultural variable, and why certain meanings are learnt and not others is problematic" (1982: 233).

Outside the symbolic interactionist tradition, social constructionist views of sexuality start with Foucault (1978). Foucault not only challenged biological essentialism, but also linked sex with power. Foucault was particularly interested in the development of a new science of sexuality in the nineteenth century, which he saw as part of the rise of a "disciplinary society" in which the state was increasingly trying to bring its citizens under control. Knowledge of sexuality was central to this control (Seidman 2003). Social constructionists in the Foucauldian tradition include Jeffrey Weeks and Steven Seidman. In Seidman's words, "We are born with bodies, but it is society that determines which parts of the body and which pleasures and acts are sexual. Also, the classification of sex acts into good and bad or acceptable and illicit is today understood as a product of social power: the dominant sexual norms express the beliefs of the dominant social groups" (2003: 39).

The leading alternative to social constructionism today is the *Darwinian* approach of sociobiologists and evolutionary psychologists. Donald Symons (1979), for example, has sought to show how Darwinian sexual selection has acted on human sexual desires by looking in particular at universal or extremely widespread sexual attitudes and practices. He points to such things as the overwhelming tendency of males everywhere to be aroused by visual sexual stimuli; to the apparently universal desire of men to mate with younger females; to copulation as primarily a service provided by females to males; and to the universal desire of males for a wide variety of sexual partners. Such preferences, when acted upon, help males to achieve higher levels of reproductive success than would be possible by a preference for older, less fecund females, or by being indifferent to the sight of naked females. Research in the Darwinian evolutionary tradition has also emphasized the widespread existence of sexual jealousy in both males and females. For males, sexual jealousy is seen as a way to avoid having one's mate inseminated by another man, whereas for females it is a way of holding onto mates who otherwise might abandon them for other females (Buss

2000). The Darwinian approach has made little headway in sociology, but it has been highly influential in psychology and anthropology (cf. Sanderson 2001: 177–94).

Two other recent approaches to human sexuality are Collins's (2004) interaction ritual theory and Posner's (1992) rational choice theory. Collins argues that sexual practices can best be understood as Goffmanian interaction rituals. If humans are hard-wired for anything it is "for the kinds of pleasure in emotional entrainment and rhythmic synchronization that make humans pursuers of interaction rituals" (2004: 227). Posner's rational choice theory is based on the notion that "the balance of private costs and private benefits determines the relative frequency of different sexual practices" (1992: 116). For example, in societies in which there is a high ratio of men to available women, opportunistic homosexuality and prostitution will be more frequent than in societies with an approximately equal ratio of men to available women.

The study of sexual practices has become an especially vigorous subfield of sociology, but is also of great interest to psychologists, anthropologists, and even historians. Despite major theoretical disputes, there has been a great deal of progress in this subfield and continued progress is likely to be both substantial and rapid.

SEE ALSO: Compulsory Heterosexuality; Globalization, Sexuality and; Heterosexuality; Homosexuality; Lesbianism; Oral Sex; Pornography and Erotica; Sadomasochism; Safer Sex; Sexuality

REFERENCES AND SUGGESTED READINGS

Brake, M. (1982) Sexuality as Praxis: A Consideration of the Contribution of Sexual Theory to the Process of Sexual Being. In: Brake, M. (Ed.), *Human Sexual Relations*. Pantheon, New York.

Bullough, V. L. (1976) *Sexual Variance in Society and History*. University of Chicago Press, Chicago.

Buss, D. M. (2000) *The Dangerous Passion: Why Jealousy is as Necessary as Love and Sex*. Free Press, New York.

Collins, R. (2004) *Interaction Ritual Chains*. Princeton University Press, Princeton.

de Waal, F. (2005) *Our Inner Ape*. Riverhead Books, New York.

Foucault, M. (1978) *The History of Sexuality*. Vol. 1. Trans. R. Hurley. Vintage, New York.

Gagnon, J. (1977) *Human Sexualities*. Scott, Foresman, Glenview, IL.

Leupp, G. P. (1995) *Male Colors: The Construction of Homosexuality in Tokugawa Japan*. University of California Press, Berkeley.

Plummer, K. (1982) Symbolic Interactionism and Sexual Conduct: An Emergent Perspective. In: Brake, M. (Ed.), *Human Sexual Relations*. Pantheon, New York.

Posner, R. A. (1992) *Sex and Reason*. Harvard University Press, Cambridge, MA.

Sanderson, S. K. (2001) *The Evolution of Human Sociality: A Darwinian Conflict Perspective*. Rowman & Littlefield, Lanham, MD.

Seidman, S. (2003) *The Social Construction of Sexuality*. Norton, New York.

Symons, D. (1979) *The Evolution of Human Sexuality*. Oxford University Press, New York.

sexual violence and rape

Liz Kelly

Rape attracted limited attention across the social sciences and humanities until it emerged as a key issue for feminists in the early 1970s. Most scholarship on the subject dates from this time, with the highest concentration appearing during the 1970s and 1980s. The first sociological study – Menachim Amir's *Patterns in Forcible Rape* (1971) – addressed the victimology of rape. But it, along with most previous work, was subjected to intense feminist critique, including in Susan Brownmiller's prescient *Against Our Will* (1975), which, in "giving rape its history," explored rape two decades before it became widely recognized. Rape was relatively invisible in feminist, policy, and research agendas during the 1990s outside the context of war/conflict. As we enter the twenty-first century, shoots of renewed interest are evident with a series of books and major research reports addressing theory (Cahill 2001), reporting and belief (Jordan 2004), rape in diverse contexts (Barstow 2002), and prevalence and attrition (Kelly et al. 2005).

CONTESTED CONCEPTS

Defining sexual violence and rape continues to vex social scientists, legal scholars, and practitioners, as debates about the boundary between consent and non-consent remain unresolved. The undisputed criminal status of rape lends the definitional issue a strong legal component, made more complex by the presence internationally of at least three competing conceptual frames: rape as forcible intercourse; rape as intercourse without consent; rape as intercourse in coercive circumstances. Albeit somewhat minor differences, they have significant implications for "what counts" in prevalence research and the evidential requirements to prove a case in court: in both instances, the requirement of force constitutes the narrowest definition. Alongside these foundational matters have been additional questions, including: whether all forms of penetration should be included; whether men can be raped; and whether rape is possible in marriage. Reformed legal definitions have tended to expand to encompass men and other forms of penetration, with the most contested issue remaining marital rape. Whether and how far legal definitions are echoed in research, not to mention shared by those experiencing unwanted sex, are recurring themes in empirical studies and commentaries. A key challenge from research has been to expand the concept of "real rape" (Estrich 1987), and feminist theorists (see, e.g., MacKinnon 1989) have problematized the consent/non-consent binary, suggesting continuities or, in one formulation, a continuum (Kelly 1987) of non-consent, only part of which is criminalized.

The issue of language has also proved thorny, with some seeking to reframe the issue as a crime of violence, replacing the word rape with "sexual assault," narrower and wider meanings of the word rape, and some using "sexual violence" to frame all forms of violence against women (Kelly 1987), while others limit its reach to explicitly sexualized assaults. How to refer to those who have been raped is also contested, with the term "victim" widely criticized yet remaining a legal status where crimes are reported, and "survivor," whilst preferred, taking on an increasingly therapeutic meaning.

FROM UNUSUAL TO EVERYDAY MATTERS

The wellspring for the creation of a knowledge base on rape was (re)discovery within feminist praxis of how often women and girls had had sex against their will. The critically important concepts of "silencing" and "naming" emerged from the practices of consciousness-raising and public "speakouts," practices which have strong correlates in the emphasis in feminist epistemology on qualitative approaches, on enabling and recording personal accounts in sociology and criminology, and on "reclaiming" testimonies (and activism) from the past through historical research (see, e.g., Kumar 1993; Sommerville 2004).

Viewed in retrospect, many early feminist texts reproduced the "deviant" construction of rapists. However, as feminist discourse became more nuanced, connections between rape and the construction of heterosexuality, masculinity, and femininity were increasingly explored (MacKinnon 1989; Lees 1993), and the limited progress made in terms of young women's belief in their right and ability to say no to unwanted sex documented (Holland et al. 1997). This issue has taken on even more profound implications as new research from Africa, and especially South Africa, demonstrates how difficult it is for women to negotiate safe sex in cultural contexts where force and coercion are commonplace and HIV infection an ever-present risk (Jewkes & Abrahams 2000). Brutalization through conflict has been increasingly addressed as a context in which levels of sexual violence increase, even at times encouraged by combatants (Barstow 2002). These studies highlight the continuing barriers to achieving the feminist goals of sexual freedom/agency for many women. However, rape research and more optimistic postmodern feminism do connect through the theoretical and material importance given to concepts and practices of sexual autonomy and its most recent variant, sexual sovereignty. Increasingly, legal reform attempts to build sexual offense statutes around these foundations for adults (see, e.g., recent legislation in South Africa and England and Wales). Law professor Stephen Schulhofer (1998: 9, 132) points out that a premise of the

right to sexual autonomy problematizes behaviors currently outside the reach of criminal law.

> [The law] still refuses to outlaw coercion and
> abuses of trust which prevent a woman from
> deciding freely whether to choose or refuse a
> sexual relationship. And when she does refuse,
> the law still fails to ensure that her clearly
> expressed preferences will be honoured and
> enforced. ... Conduct that forces a person to
> choose between her sexual autonomy and any
> of her other legally protected entitlements –
> rights to property, to privacy, and to reputa-
> tion – is by definition improper; it deserves to
> be treated as a serious criminal offence.

A more specific theoretical and practical literature has emerged within sociolegal studies,
and especially feminist jurisprudence, exploring
the content, success, and, all too often, failures
of legal reform (Rowland 2004). The courtroom
has proved a rich resource for exploring the
social construction of rape, heterosexuality,
and gender (Matoesian 1993; Ehrlich 2001),
and rape law, with its unique evidential requirements, is a paradigmatic example of the "hidden
gender of law" (Graycar & Morgan 2002).
Within these detailed explorations are unresolved debates as to whether emphasizing the
sexual element in the name and construction of
rape is a form of essentialism, whether it is a
unique form of crime/assault, and most recently
through notions of embodiment, whether law
can ever recognize and address the sexualized
elements and harms involved (Cahill 2001).

PREVALENCE, CONTEXTS, AND RESPONSES

Empirical research on rape began documenting
its nature, contexts, and consequences, moving
on to assess incidence and responses, especially
by the criminal justice system. More recently,
evaluative research has focused on rape crisis
groups, Sexual Assault Referral Centers, and
innovations such as forensic nursing. The
knowledge base overall, and with respect to prevalence, is considerably weaker than that on
domestic violence or sexual abuse in childhood
(Hagerman White 2001). Women's heightened
fear of crime is in large part connected to fear
of sexual attack in the public sphere; this

"phenomenology of fear" (Cahill 2001) was
documented in the 1980s in many studies on
women's safety.

> Most women experience the fear of rape as a
> nagging, gnawing sense that something awful
> could happen, and angst that keeps them from
> doing things they want and need to do, or from
> doing them at the time or in the way they
> might otherwise do. Women's fear of rape is a
> sense that they must always be on guard, vigi-
> lant and alert, a feeling that causes a woman to
> tighten with anxiety if someone is walking too
> closely behind her, especially at night.
> (Gordon & Riger 1989: 2)

Similar constraints only pertain for men and
boys if they are located in contexts where sexual assault is rife, such as prison or living on
the street.

Methodological innovation has been primarily through the development of surveys of violence against women, and the recognition that
not using the term "rape" and providing more
than one route into more detailed questions on
assaults increased disclosure. US college students have high reporting rates for victimization and perpetration (Schwartz 1997). The
Canadian Violence Against Women Survey
(Johnson & Sacco 1995) heralded what has been
termed the "third generation" of prevalence
research (Walby & Myhill 2001), although
many who have drawn on it subsequently have
entirely excluded or limited the questions on
sexual assault, prioritizing the more popular/
acknowledged issue of domestic violence. Using
telephone interviews, a national random sample
of 12,300 women took part. The key findings
with respect to sexual assault were: over a third
had been sexually assaulted; for almost 60 percent this involved more than one assault; four
in five (81 percent) were committed by known
men; only 6 percent (1 in 19) were reported
to the police (in comparison, a quarter of
those who had experienced domestic violence
reported at least one incident). These data raise
critical issues about the perception of rape as a
single, discrete event. The only recent prevalence study to include male and female respondents took place in the US and reported
prevalence rates for rape of 17.6 percent for
women and 3 percent for men (Tjaden &
Thoennes 1998).

The extent of unwanted sex that prevalence research revealed, especially within samples of US college students, led to several widely reported challenges, disputing the methods and analysis and referring to the findings as "advocacy numbers" (Gilbert 1991). An unfortunate legacy has been the inaccurate, but preferred, media concept of "date rape." Interestingly, surveys on male rape, using the same methodological tools, are seldom berated for "biased" findings and are more likely to meet comments as to the extent of underreporting.

The conventional orthodoxy about differential rates – both over time and across societies – of reported and recorded rapes has been that they reflect levels of (dis)trust in agencies and the state, rather than differences in levels of rape across societies. Some emerging data suggest more complex processes may be at play: for example, the very different societies of Australia, South Africa, and Sweden having high reporting rates per head of population. The Swedish data are especially intriguing since Sweden invariably heads global indexes on gender equality, suggesting that sexual (and domestic) violence does not decrease automatically as women's employment and political representation increase. Two recent studies (see Regan & Kelly 2003) revealed variable reporting patterns over time across Europe. The latter revealed at least three patterns: year-on-year increases for two decades across the UK and Scandinavia; flatter levels across the German-speaking countries; and sharp declines for many Central and Eastern European countries during the 1990s. Whilst some observations can be confidently made – such as the obvious impact of decreased capacity of, and trust in, state infrastructures in Central and Eastern Europe in the 1990s – more complex methodologies and theorization are needed to explain the variations in Western Europe.

Few contemporary studies explore questions central in early studies – the experiential realities of rape and/or its short- and long-term consequences (Kelly 1987) – and interest in the possibility of avoiding rape (Bart & O'Brien 1985) has also waned. In their place is a more therapeutic, "self-help" literature drawing heavily on psychological work on trauma and the practices initially developed in women's groups. Of particular interest, and in contrast to the above, is philosophy professor Susan Brison's (2002) reflection on her own experience of rape and how it changed not just her own sense of self, but her philosophical understanding of the self. In a rewarding combination of testimony and intellectual engagement, she echoes Judith Herman in noting the critical importance of the simultaneous disconnections from one's body, place in world, and relationships to others. For her, reconnecting to others and the embodied practice of women's self-defense (Seith & Kelly 2003) were critical in her remaking of her self.

TAKING STOCK, MOVING ON

From a marginal issue, the topic of rape has had an uneven intellectual trajectory over the last three decades. A number of substantive studies have established that it is much more common than previously thought, happens primarily in the context of routine interactions, and is more mundane than the media preoccupations and representations imply. In the research literature there are now detailed studies of rape in varying contexts, such as marriage, confinement in prison, mental hospital, or other residential setting, and coercive/deceptive sexual encounters with a range of professionals/authority figures, including therapists and religious leaders (Schwartz 1997). There are also emerging discussions of the ways in which culture and context can affect the meaning and consequences of sexual violence, such as in the context of codes of honor.

The stereotype of "real rape" (Esteal 1998) continues to undermine the intent underpinning legal reform. More recent attention to the attrition process reveals rates of prosecution and conviction are falling (Kelly et al. 2005). Thus, as the profile of reported rapes comes to more accurately reflect the realities established in social research, fewer and fewer cases result in a conviction. For example, in England and Wales in the mid-1970s, one in three reported rapes resulted in a conviction; in 2003, the conviction rate dropped to an all-time low of 1 in 19 (Kelly et al. 2005).

Whilst statute and theory may have moved on, attitudes and practices with respect to female and male sexuality retain many of the elements that prompted initial feminist critique. The dominant heterosexual culture continues to be one in which young women's ambivalence and uncertainty are viewed by young men as a challenge to be overcome, and women's sexual autonomy – not to mention sexual pleasure – is secondary. Thus the conditions in which coercive sex is commonplace are reproduced (Holland et al. 1997). Whilst young women undoubtedly aspire to be sexual subjects, and like their foresisters do resist sexual coercion, the context in which they act continues to be defined through powerful and essentialist notions of men's needs and desires. Whilst young women have greater space for action, some of these freedoms – such as being alone in public spaces, drinking alcohol – can be used to question their credibility should they be assaulted.

New challenges are evident in the emergence of attrition data, especially concerns about the failure of the criminal justice system to deal effectively with rape between persons who know each other. In this context the application of restorative justice practices (in particular the dropping of a criminal charge where the acts and harms are admitted) – currently being experimented with in South Australia and Tucson, Arizona – raises complex questions. Support from service users for "proactive" follow-up by agencies questions a number of orthodoxies in feminist practice that require more detailed research. In addition, how perpetrators/rapists are categorized and understood deserves revisiting, especially whether it is appropriate to refer to men who have met their victim only hours before the assault as "acquaintances." Does someone buying you a drink constitute "consensual contact"? Perhaps the context in which rapists target has changed with contemporary gender and sexual mores. The street and public places may simply be less successful "hunting" grounds for predatory men than clubs and pubs: and the latter may also provide a foundation for the most effective defense should they ever be charged – consent.

SEE ALSO: Compulsory Heterosexuality; Feminist Criminology; Gender, Social Movements and; Gendered Aspects of War and International Violence; Male Rape; Rape Culture; Rape/Sexual Assault as Crime; Sexuality, Masculinity and

REFERENCES AND SUGGESTED READINGS

Barstow, A. (2002) *War's Dirty Secret: Rape, Prostitution, and Other Crimes Against Women*. Pilgrim Press, Cleveland, OH.
Bart, P. & O'Brien, P. (1985) *Stopping Rape: Successful Survival Strategies*. Pergamon, Elmsford, NY.
Brison, S. (2002) *Aftermath: Violence and the Remaking of the Self*. Princeton University Press, Princeton.
Cahill, A. (2001) *Rethinking Rape*. Cornell University Press, Ithaca, NY.
Ehrlich, S. (2001) *Representing Rape: Language and Sexual Consent*. Routledge, London.
Esteal, P. (1998) Rape in Marriage: Has the Licence Lapsed? In: Easteal, P. (Ed.), *Balancing the Scales: Rape, Law Reform, and Australian Culture*. Federation Press, Canberra.
Estrich, S. (1987) *Real Rape: How the Legal System Victimizes Women Who Say No*. Harvard University Press, Cambridge, MA.
Gilbert, N. (1991) The Phantom Epidemic of Sexual Assault. *Public Interest* 103: 54–65.
Gordon, M. & Riger, S. (1989) *The Female Fear*. Free Press, New York.
Graycar, R. & Morgan, J. (2002) *The Hidden Gender of Law*. Federation Press, Annandale, NSW.
Hagerman White, C. (2001) Measuring Violence Against Women: The European Experience. *Violence Against Women* 7(7): 732–59.
Holland, J. et al. (1997) *The Male in the Head*. Tufnell Press, London.
Jewkes, R. & Abrahams, N. (2000) *Violence Against Women in South Africa: Rape and Sexual Coercion*. Crime Prevention Resources Center, CSIR, Pretoria.
Johnson, H. & Sacco, V. (1995) Researching Violence Against Women: Statistics Canada's National Study. *Canadian Journal of Criminology*. Special issue: Focus on the Violence Against Women Survey, 40: 281–304.
Jordan, J. (2004) *The Word of a Woman: Police, Rape, and Belief*. Palgrave, London.
Kelly, L. (1987) *Surviving Sexual Violence*. Polity Press, Cambridge.
Kelly, L., Lovett, J., & Regan, L. (2005) *A Gap or a Chasm: Understanding Attrition in Reported Rape Cases*. Home Office, London.
Kumar, R. (1993) *The History of Doing: An Illustrated Account of Movements for Women's Rights and Feminism in India, 1800–1990*. Kali for Women, New Delhi.

Lees, S. (1993) *Sugar and Spice: Sexuality and Adolescent Girls.* Penguin, Harmondsworth.

MacKinnon, C. (1989) *Towards a Feminist Theory of the State.* Harvard University Press, Cambridge, MA.

Matoesian, G. (1993) *Reproducing Rape: Domination Through Talk in the Courtroom.* University of Chicago Press, Chicago.

Regan, L. & Kelly, L. (2003) *Rape: Still a Forgotten Issue.* Rape Crisis Network Europe, Dublin. Online. www.rcne.com.

Rowland, D. (2004) *The Boundaries of Her Body: The Troubling History of Women's Rights in America.* Sphinx, Naperville, IL.

Schulhofer, S. (1998) *Unwanted Sex: The Culture of Intimidation and the Failure of Law.* Harvard University Press, Cambridge, MA.

Schwartz, M. (1997) *Researching Sexual Violence Against Women.* Sage, Newbury Park, CA.

Seith, C. & Kelly, L. (2003) *Achievements Against the Grain: Self-Defence Training for Women and Girls in Europe.* Child and Woman Abuse Studies Unit, London.

Sommerville, D. (2004) *Rape and Race in the Nineteenth-Century South.* University of North Carolina Press, Chapel Hill.

Tjaden, P. & Thoennes, N. (1998) Prevalence, Incidence, and Consequences of Violence Against Women: Findings from the National Violence Against Women Survey. *National Institute of Justice Centers for Disease Control and Prevention Research in Brief*, 1–16, November.

Walby, S. & Myhill, A. (2001) New Survey Methodologies in Researching Violence Against Women. *British Journal of Criminology.*

sexualities, cities and

David Bell

As part of a broader investigation of the connections between sexuality and space, researchers in a number of disciplines have explored the relationship between particular sexual practices and identities and urban space – either at a generic level or in terms of particular cities around the world. There are a number of intersecting strands to this work. First, there is research that explores the cultural construction of the city – the city as it is imagined and portrayed in popular culture – and that investigates how this construction shapes possibilities and limitations

for sexual practices and identities. For example, in terms of western gay male practices and identities, Kath Weston (1995) shows how US metropolitan centers were (and still are) constructed as places more open to male homosexuality, stimulating "the great gay migration" in the post-war United States. For other groups labeled as "deviant" the city may also be constructed positively, in terms either of its liberal atmosphere or of the possibility of anonymity. But this association can lead to the city itself being considered "deviant" or dangerous, and therefore as an unsafe place. This connection is forcefully articulated in relation to two issues: prostitution and (sexually transmitted) disease (STD). In nineteenth-century England, for example, moral panics about prostitution centered on city streets as danger zones, and moral regulation served to limit women's access to urban public space. In terms of disease, similar moral panics over STDs, most notably HIV/AIDS, have brought about policies to "clean up" parts of the city associated with certain sexual practices – perhaps most famously in New York City during Mayor Giuliani's administration.

A second important area of work is concerned with ideas about spaces within the city. In the first half of the twentieth century, researchers in the Chicago School of Urban Sociology investigated the urban geography of non-normative sexualities, mapping the varied "sex zones" used by different groups (Heap 2003). Later work also used the tools of urban ethnography to research the practices of "deviant" sexual cultures – most controversially in Laud Humphries's *Tearoom Trade: Impersonal Sex in Public Places* (1975), which utilized covert techniques in a study of male same-sex activity in public toilets. One issue both the Chicago researchers and Humphries discussed that has continued to be central to research on the city's sexual spaces is the distinction between public space and private space. Private space – usually thought to exist in the home – is often constructed as the only appropriate space for sexual expression. In contrast, public space is subject to intense scrutiny and regulation, and anything other than the "safest" forms of heteronormative sexual expression may be subject to formal or informal policing. This powerful divide has led to public space being seen as a crucial battleground in struggles over sexual politics. Some gay rights groups, for example, argue for the right to express their sexuality in public, staging protests to highlight discrimination. Moreover, the safety of the domestic home might not provide opportunities for sexual expression, if that expression is considered taboo within the moral economy of the family or household, so other spaces become centers of sexual practice and identity, including commercial spaces such as bars and clubs, and public spaces such as parks and streets. In the case of western gay male culture, for example, public spaces have historically played an important role, offering opportunities for men to meet away from the regulatory gaze of home and family – a role they continue to play today in western and non-western cities.

Related to the issue of public and private space comes the broader question of the politics of space. Access to space in the city is regulated in all kinds of ways, making claims on space an important political tactic. For marginalized sexual minorities, the symbolic and material claiming of space has been a central component of rights struggles. From the temporary claiming of space in a protest march to the permanent establishment of residential or commercial spaces, there are many manifestations of this aspect of the relationship between cities and sexualities. Some critics argue that *all* space is fundamentally constructed and coded as heterosexual, and that there are also normative "genderings" of space; these dominant codings and orderings of space limit possibilities for women and for sexual minorities. However, spaces of resistance to the dominant order can be carved out, and although some are highly ephemeral, others can become more permanently rooted in the city. In some large western cities, for example, particular neighborhoods have come to be associated with lesbian and gay communities – either as places where gay bars and clubs are concentrated, as in Manchester's gay village, or where there is a marked residential concentration of lesbian and gay households, supported by gay-owned or "gay-friendly" services, as in the Castro district in San Francisco. Other sexual minorities are not equally able to make such claims on cityspace, and have been unable (or unwilling) to develop neighborhoods or villages of their own. Nevertheless, districts like the Castro have historically been very important, in terms of making the lesbian and gay community visible, and also politically powerful (at least as regards local politics).

While claims on space in cities have been seen as important political markers, the spaces claimed are themselves seen by some people as contradictory. Marking out one neighborhood as "gay," for example, implicitly marks all other neighborhoods as "straight." Residential concentration also ghettoizes those who live there, and excludes those who do not. A visible gay neighborhood might be attractive not only to gay men and lesbians, but also to homophobic "queer bashers," or may be subject to excessive policing and regulation. Nevertheless, gay neighborhoods or villages have developed in a large number of cities (although their scale and scope vary considerably); in some cities this development has been encouraged by policymakers, especially since the so-called pink economy came to their attention. According to pink economy discourse, gay men (in particular) are affluent and like to spend their sizable disposable incomes on high-status lifestyle commodities. Attracting these high-spenders into the city therefore promises financial dividends. While the pink economy has been thoroughly debunked as an overhyped myth, there is still considerable commercial interest in some sexual minorities, gay men in particular – though this is considerably less than the commercial interest shown in heterosexuality.

The development of gay spaces in cities is only one of the many relationships between cities and sexualities. As Pat Califia famously wrote in *Public Sex: The Culture of Radical Sex* (1994), echoing the foundational work of the Chicago School, the city is a patchwork of "sex zones," some legitimate and dominant, others constructed as deviant or marginal. Considerable work has focused on exploring these sex zones, revealing the complex sexual ecology of the city. Part of that complexity comes from acknowledging specificity – moving away from generic discussions of "The City" to explore how particular sexualities relate to particular cities and cityspaces. This kind of attention to specificity has been tremendously important in highlighting that very different sexual spaces and cultures exist in different cities (and parts of cities); each city has its own map of sex zones.

While studies of the sexual life of cities have to date been dominated by work on large metropolitan cities and by a focus on particular sexual identities and communities – mostly homosexual – important work is increasingly exploring smaller cities (not to mention the rural) and other types of sexual expression, identity, community, and politics. One area of neglect has been an explicit and sustained investigation of the relationships between heterosexuality and the city – while there has been lots of work on gender, there has been much less explicitly about sexuality in this regard.

An area of growing interest and importance, in terms of more specific and situated studies of the relationship between cities and sexualities, concerns cities outside the contemporary West. Different times and different places have produced very different interconnections between urban space and sexual cultures. Historical studies, such as those collected in Higgs's *Queer Sites: Gay Urban Histories Since 1600* (1999), have much to teach us about these interconnections in the past, revealing long-forgotten urban sexual habits and habitats. Studies outside the West also reveal a multiplicity of distinct relationships between cities and sexualities, often in spite of the supposedly homogenizing forces of globalization. The study of globalization in relation to sexuality is also important for bringing issues of movement into focus: cities are spaces of flows, where people, goods, ideas, and images intersect as they circuit the globe. There is a growing interest in sexuality and movement, whether temporary or permanent, forced or elective. Rather than totalizing and fixing "The City" in space and time, therefore, work on cities and sexualities must necessarily be pluralistic, reflecting the full diversity of cities and sexualities.

SEE ALSO: Globalization, Sexuality and; Moral Panics; Prostitution; Sexual Citizenship; Sexual Identities; Sexual Politics; Sexual Practices; Sexualities and Consumption

REFERENCES AND SUGGESTED READINGS

Califia, P. (1994) *Public Sex: The Culture of Radical Sex*. Cleis Press, Pittsburgh.

Heap, C. (2003) The City as a Sexual Laboratory: The Queer Heritage of the Chicago School. *Qualitative Sociology* 26(4): 457–87.

Higgs, D. (Ed.) (1999) *Queer Sites: Gay Urban Histories Since 1600*. Routledge, London.

Weston, K. (1995) Get Thee to a Big City: Sexual Imaginary and the Great Gay Migration. *GLQ* 2 (3): 253–77.

sexualities and consumption

Yvette Taylor

Sexuality and consumption are interlinked in powerful and significant ways, perhaps even more so in contemporary, even "postmodern," times, shaping various material and subjective possibilities and impossibilities, as sexuality is displayed and regulated via consumption. Consumption refers to a wide variety of spending patterns and behaviors and is typically equated with "choice"; what we choose to buy, where and when, and how we choose to use purchasable commodities, ranging from mundane everyday goods and services to extravagant "one-off" specials, which seemingly reinforce the uniqueness of our own individual consumer choice. Crane (2000) explores fashion and its various and shifting meanings, symbolically, culturally, and economically, across time and place, drawing on data from England, France, and the United States. Crane claims that class has become a less salient aspect of identity, with less effect upon clothing practices, consumption, and signification, which she describes as a shift from classed practices to those based around "lifestyles." The concept of "subcultural" affiliation is invoked as a way of capturing the proliferation of clothing styles and choices, which, it is claimed, mark the changes from industrial class-based societies to "postmodern," "post-industrial" societies. The manifestations of class and gender are seemingly replaced by an erasure of fixed hierarchies, a blurring of certainty which these categories once represented, and a diffusion of meaning across and between other axes of "difference," particularly that of sexuality.

Yet to consume also implies a potential restriction in terms of what is being offered and to whom. Other market activities, such as employment, leisure activities, and citizenship, are related to consumption insofar as these afford possibilities for participating in certain markets, create and foreground certain "choices," while restricting and regulating individuals within multiple social domains. Heterosexuality is privileged, even expected, within many consumer spheres, but lesbian, gay, and bisexual sexualities are also increasingly affecting, and indeed affected by, marketization, as the notion of a ready, waiting, and willing "pink pound" implies (Chasin 2000; Hennessy 2000).

Sexuality, as an innately private and individual concern, has been interrogated and problematized by many feminist researchers, who have revealed its profoundly social and public regulation. While there has been longstanding attention to compulsory heterosexuality, as socially structured and institutionalized, others point to the increasing complexity, even fluidity, of sexual practices, identities, and regimes. The dichotomy existing around materialist versus queer conceptualizations of sexuality is strongly expressed through polarized critiques of sexuality and consumption (Jackson 2001). Here sexualities become either cynically commodified and thus inseparable from interconnecting inequalities, such as gender and class, or exist as evidence of potentiality and (market) possibility, affording diverse sexualities much cultural visibility.

Whether thought of as a resource or as a constraint, an equalizing force or a divisive battleground, it is difficult to ignore the ever-increasing spaces of sexual consumption, as manifest in the media (McRobbie 2004), in commercialized scene spaces, and even in the realm of citizenship. The interconnection between sexuality and consumption provides for a series of inclusions and exclusions, in the market and in the state itself, which has been a dominant theme in the literature on sexuality studies.

Chasin uncovers the linkage between the development of the "lesbian and gay movement" in the US and the growth of lesbian and gay "niche markets" that promise inclusion into the marketplace and the nation itself – but at a price. Within her account, social recognition is dependent on ability to consume as

identity becomes branded, commodified, and consumed. Lesbians and gays are integrated, even assimilated, as consumers rather than as citizens. Money then represents the prerequisite for participation as well as the boundary. Chasin's catchy (and cutting) title *Selling Out* conveys notions of failure and possible fraudulence, hinting at the ways in which sexual identities have been depoliticized, as they become only another consumer possibility. The skepticism aired resonates with many other critiques (Warner 1993; Hennessy 2000). Many theorists have examined consumption in relation to the construction and reconstruction of identity; Warner (1993) looks at the pivotal role of the market in the construction of queer sexualities and notes its exclusionary tendencies. Here the "institutions of culture building" are market mediated and include bars, discos, newspapers, magazines, phone lines, resorts, and urban commercial districts, which are only accessible to those with the requisite social, cultural, and economic capital (Bourdieu 1984; Skeggs 1999, 2001).

While popular discourses on the "pink pound" signal a new, consumer-based potential inclusion, many researchers have highlighted entrenched and compounded inequalities within this. Seemingly celebratory discourses on lesbians' and gay men's spending power invoke what Binnie (2004) describes as the "myth of the pink economy," which compounds the idea of a "special," even privileged, group who can more than afford their rights: here rights are equated entirely with spending power, which is a highly gendered phenomenon. Lesbians have rarely been addressed as consumers, which may be set to change as they are identified as potentially profitable, whether that is in terms of "new" leisure pursuits, fostered by improving incomes, or in the commercialization of, for example, civil partnerships. Nearly half of the countries in the European Union offer some legal recognition to same-sex couples, ranging from full civil marriage to domestic partnerships. An array of legal and commercial services has sprung up in response to this demand.

As sexuality becomes marketed and commodified as a "lifestyle option," many note that not all lifestyles are equally visible or validated. Similarly, the existence of commercialized scene spaces, thought of as refuges and "safe spaces" for sexual minorities, is not unproblematic and various theorists have given attention to inequalities operating within such commercialized space. Skeggs (1999, 2001) has shown that inequalities operate within leisure space, controlling entitlements to that space and affecting the appropriate "performance" (Taylor 2007b). Appearance in particular becomes the mechanism for inclusion and exclusion; a resource through which claims for legitimacy and entitlement are made whereby sexuality, gender, and class affect embodied presentations and a sense of entitlement versus a sense of exclusion. Having the money can buy access – having the right clothes, right style, and taste can indicate that entitlement to be there – but displaying sexual identity, and receiving affirmation, may require unaffordable presentations. Hennessy (2000) has critiqued discourses of consumer choice and the necessity to display a "designer identity" given that it may only be accessible to those materially poised to occupy the position, those with the ability and opportunities to engage in lesbian or gay male "chic."

Scene spaces are increasingly becoming leisurely spaces of consumption, where the claiming of a lesbian or gay identity is no longer necessary to "consume" such leisure space, but where the "intrusion" of a heterosexual presence into scene space is still far from unproblematic. Such intrusion, like the commercial scene space itself, appears to be highly gendered. Drawing upon longitudinal ethnographic research (1997) and research on violence, sexuality, and space in the UK, Skeggs (1999, 2001) highlights the contrast and tensions existing in scene spaces between a group of white working-class heterosexual women, whose identity is based on "dis-identification" (from being working class), and a group of lesbians who form their identity through visibility, recognition, and territorialization. Skeggs suggests that heterosexual working-class women enter commercialized scene venues in order to be safe from the male gaze, while their straight presence, or "lesbian masquerades," have negative consequences for others, namely lesbians and gay men.

Queer theory has been associated with the pursuit of a queer lifestyle, an "aestheticization of daily life" constructed through a "postmodern consumer ethic" (Hennessy 2000).

Fraser (1999) argues that queer theory's stance on visibility and recognition further marks a connection between identity and aesthetics, whereby queer becomes a brand name, an identity project assuming the form of aesthetic, consumer-based lifestyles (Featherstone 1991). The queer body, in displaying and signifying, is, from a queer perspective, seen to bestow a political value (Butler 1993). But within this are important ramifications for escalating class inequality, given that appearance can be another signifier upon which to denigrate working-class bodies and tastes, in which they (again) become "flawed consumers" who cannot pay and display in "proper," "tasteful" ways (Bourdieu 1984; Bauman 1998; Skeggs 1999, 2001). Aesthetics, and identity constructed via consumption of cultural goods, may mark the self as tasteful, authentic, and thus entitled (for example, to occupy queer space), or it may exclude and mark as wrong, unentitled, and inauthentic. When considering intersections between consumption and sexuality, materialist feminists would suggest that it has been difficult to fully utilize and appropriate the theoretical readings of queer. Although Judith Butler may usefully illuminate aspects of the operation of queer identity, this reading of performance and performativity may mean little to the everyday enactment of sexuality.

In contrast, Roseneil (2000) charts the cultural valorizing of the queer in popular culture, fashion, magazines, and television, which is taken as evidence of the "aspirational status of queer" rather than as the class-exclusive "aestheticization of everyday life," which materialist thought would name as a perpetuation and extension of current inequalities (Fraser 1999). Culturally, there is a proliferation of films and literature where femininity is fetishized and naturalized as objects of female desire (McRobbie 2004), while women can now choose the commodities and costumes from which to perform femininity, as part of their repertoire of self-identification. The burden faced is one of "having it all" whereby having it all, good career and good sex, becomes an imperative rather than a "choice." Pic 'n' mix relationships and "identity umbrellas" become necessities in building an experienced, endlessly adaptable, and refashioned self and multisexualism another sought-after and purchasable commodity. "Meterosexual" is becoming a new buzzword, apparently describing urban, fashion-conscious men who are not afraid to express an interest in fashion or beauty, areas typically thought of as the preserve of women and gay men. Nonetheless, multiplicity or "meterosexuality" does not necessarily translate into equality, and again choices are not equally available or validated on the (sexual) market. As one form of (male) sexuality is celebrated, other forms of (female) sexuality are problematized as excessive and simply wrong.

Romanticized representations seeking to reaffirm traditional femininity exist alongside representations that problematize and pathologize women's sexual behavior, appearance in public, especially leisure, space, and their uptake of a "laddish" drinking culture as resolutely "unfeminine" (McRobbie 2000; Harris 2004). A classed polarization between new celebratory (white and middle-class) femininities and sorrowful, pitiful, and excessive working-class sexuality, embodied in the pathological representations of the "teen mum," is articulated in the literature. Celebrations and denigrations of "new" femininity are challenged and resisted by the realization that gender, class, and sexual inequalities remain embedded within economic and social structures, something which materialist feminist approaches have been adept at highlighting.

Many feminist writers have explored young women's consumption of lifestyle magazines. McRobbie (2000) argues that contemporary femininity and masculinity are being reappraised with representations of sexuality now breaching traditional gendered boundaries of acceptance, whereas Tyler (2004) claims such "resources" bring managerial imperatives, such as efficiency and effectiveness, which must be incorporated into self-management of sexuality. Sexual pleasure may well be subject to rationalization, through a process of sexual "modernization," whereby issues of efficiency and outcome again come to the fore in the "sexual mode of production." Tyler (2004) maintains that the focus on and overinvestment in "good sex," weighted toward success, entitlement, and mobility, deflects attention away from gendered inequalities, such as women's continued familial dependence and exploitation in family and work realms, potentially separating out interconnections between sexuality, gender, and the household, emphasized in feminist research.

The restructuring of flexible global capitalism offers new research directions. Binnie (2004) unravels the links between sexuality, the nation-state, and globalization, critiquing previous studies for their heteronormative assumptions and attentions and instead choosing to "queer" globalization, providing a queer perspective on the subject. The prevalence of class inequalities contests the link between globalization and inevitable and progressive mobility, movement, and liberation. Not only are there enduring citizenship and immigration restrictions, perhaps felt less by the monogamous, high-earning couple, but the process of transnational movement is itself a highly gendered phenomenon. Maybe, as Binnie (2004) claims, we are all "sex tourists," tourism being a sexualized process, but gay men's tourism is often particularly problematized and pathologized as overtly, and deviantly, sexual. Thus a crucial reminder against collapsing important material and subjective differences and inequalities is highlighted in theorizing sexualities and consumption.

SEE ALSO: Advertising; Aesthetics; Consumers, Flawed; Consumption; Globalization, Sexuality and; Homophobia and Heterosexism; Postmodern Sexualities; Queer Theory; Sexual Markets, Commodification, and Consumption; Sexualities, Cities and; Shopping

REFERENCES AND SUGGESTED READINGS

Bauman, Z. (1998) *Work, Consumerism, and the New Poor*. Open University Press, Buckingham.

Binnie, J. (2004) *The Globalization of Sexuality*. Sage, London.

Bourdieu, P. (1984) *Distinction: A Social Critique of the Judgment of Taste*. Routledge, London.

Butler, J. (1993) *Bodies that Matter: On the Discursive Limits of "Sex."* Routledge, New York.

Chasin, A. (2000) *Selling Out: The Gay and Lesbian Movement Goes to Market*. Palgrave, Basingstoke.

Crane, D. (2000) *Fashion and its Social Agendas: Class, Gender, and Identity in Clothing*. University of Chicago Press, Chicago.

Featherstone, M. (1991) *Consumer Culture and Post-modernism*. Sage, London.

Fraser, M. (1999) Classing Queer: Politics in Competition. *Theory, Culture, and Society* 16(2): 107–31.

Harris, A. (Ed.) (2004) *All About the Girl: Culture, Power, and Identity*. Routledge, New York.

Hennessy, R. (2000) *Profit and Pleasure: Sexual Identities in Late Capitalism*. Taylor & Francis, London.

Jackson, S. (2001) Why a Materialist Feminism is (Still) Possible – and Necessary. *Women's Studies International Forum* 24(3/4): 283–93.

McRobbie, A. (2000) *Feminisms and Youth Culture*. Macmillan, London.

McRobbie, A. (2004) Notes on Postfeminism and Popular Culture: Bridget Jones and the New Gender Regime. In: Harris, A. (Ed.), *All About the Girl: Culture, Power, and Identity*. Routledge, New York.

Roseneil, S. (2000) Queer Frameworks and Queer Tendencies: Towards an Understanding of Postmodern Transformations of Sexuality. *Sociological Research Online* 5(3). www.socresonline.org.uk/5/3/roseneil.html.

Skeggs, B. (1999) Matter Out of Place: Visibility and Sexualities in Leisure Spaces. *Leisure Studies* 18(3): 213–32.

Skeggs, B. (2001) The Toilet Paper: Femininity, Class and Mis-Recognition. *Women's Studies International Forum* 24(3/4): 295–307.

Taylor, Y. (2007a) *Classed Outsiders: Working-Class Lesbian Life Experiences*. Palgrave, Basingstoke.

Taylor, Y. (2007b) "If Your Face Doesn't Fit. . .": The Misrecognition of Working-Class Lesbians in Scene Space. *Leisure Studies* 27.

Tyler, M. (2004) Managing Between the Sheets: Lifestyle Magazines and the Management of Sexuality in Everyday Life. *Sexualities* 7(1): 81–106.

Warner, M. (Ed.) (1993) *Fear of a Queer Planet: Queer Politics and Social Theory*. University of Minnesota Press, Minneapolis.

sexualities and culture wars

Glenn Lucke

The term "culture wars" came to prominence in the early 1990s, referring to conflicts in US society over abortion, religion in schools, acceptance of homosexuals, pornography, the judiciary, and the arts. Many of the flashpoints in the culture war derive from competing cultural assumptions about the body, particularly various aspects of sexuality. Activists in the culture war struggle to define what Americans believe a human to be and how human life is to be rightly ordered.

The origin of the term traces to German Chancellor Otto von Bismarck, who used *kulturkampf* in 1878 to launch a values campaign against Catholic and Jewish minorities in newly united Germany. Sociologist James Davison Hunter (1991, 1994) appropriated the concept as a tool for understanding the nature of contemporary cultural conflict in the US. In Hunter's work, culture wars concerns the activities of loosely clustered groups of elite knowledge workers who seek to impose their competing understandings of reality – both the way things are and the way things ought to be – on the rest of society.

Hunter's theory reflects the confluence of several strands of classical sociological theory, particularly the synthesis of Weber and Durkheim forged by Peter Berger (1967) regarding the sociology of knowledge and the sociology of religion. Humans construct reality in their social relations and productions, and this constructed reality becomes internalized "knowledge." Berger's key contribution was the concept of plausibility structures, social groups in which humans are embedded, that govern which ideas we find plausible or implausible. Thus, while humans experience reality as taken for granted, it is in fact socially constructed by the plausibility structures people inhabit.

Which social constructions will dominate society? Whose ideas and values will become plausible for the most people? These questions introduce the issue of power that is largely absent from Berger's synthesis. Thus, Hunter's culture wars theory also draws upon the insights of conflict sociology in the Marxist tradition to understand how power structures and relations affect the social construction of reality. In particular Hunter uses the work of Italian Marxist Antonio Gramsci, whose work in the sociology of knowledge contributed the idea of knowledge workers (elites) who have a disproportionate role in supplying the ruling ideas of a society. If in Marx's day the bourgeoisie were the ruling class by dint of their ownership of the means of production, Gramsci realized that knowledge workers were increasingly the ruling class by dint of their credentials and their relationship to the production of knowledge.

Hunter applies this understanding of elites as knowledge workers in trying to make sense of conflict in the US in the late twentieth century. Hunter notes that the old cultural cleavages – Christian versus Jew, Protestant versus Roman Catholic – no longer hold sway. In the contests over abortion, gay sexuality, and religion in the public sphere, he detects a realignment that has taken place as Christian and Jewish, Protestant and Roman Catholic elites form new, competing alliances. These new alliances of elites cut across the previous historic cultural cleavages.

The sociological questions of what has changed and why led to Hunter's signal (and much disputed) insight: that underneath the public contests about different aspects of sexuality are deep structures of moral authority. On the surface the conflict appears to be political: conservative versus liberal. Hunter contends that below the surface the knowledge worker activists generally cluster toward two poles: the orthodox and the progressives. The worldview of the orthodox moral universe is based on commitment to an external transcendent Being and the worldview of the progressives entails a tendency to recast values and historic faiths in light of prevailing cultural assumptions. While multitudes of viable positions exist between the two poles, Hunter suggests that many elites involved in contests over culture generally share either the orthodox or the progressive moral orientation. Those associated with the orthodox impulse include conservative Protestants, conservative Roman Catholics, and Orthodox Jews. Those associated with the progressive impulse include liberal Protestants, liberal Roman Catholics, Reform Jews, and secularists.

Debates between orthodox and progressive elites over aspects of sexuality, particularly abortion, homosexuality, sex education in schools, and pornography, generate significant controversy. The orthodox broadly enunciate principles found in their understanding of a Supreme Being, sacred texts, and historical church/synagogue teaching. These traditionalist religious perspectives largely militate against gay marriage and abortion rights, seeing the progressive

efforts as assaults on the nature of the family and a moral society. The progressives contend that the freedoms guaranteed by the US Constitution, not to mention enlightened thinking generally, mean extending full civil rights to gays and lesbians and maintaining a woman's right to choose in dealing with a pregnancy. Because these arguments are rooted in ultimate concerns, Hunter's account suggests that the competing elite knowledge workers do not appear to share much common ground. Given the stakes – defining how Americans will order society – the activists resort to inflamed rhetoric and power politics in a winner-take-all mentality.

Though Hunter's culture wars theory focused on elite knowledge workers and explicitly denied that most everyday Americans were involved in contests over culture, soon the media became fascinated with the notion that average citizens were combatants in the war. The perception that average Americans were caught up in the culture war was crystallized by a speech at the 1992 Republican National Convention by former presidential candidate Patrick Buchanan. He declared, "There is a religious war going on in our country for the soul of America. It is a cultural war, as critical to the kind of nation we will one day be as was the Cold War itself."

Increasingly, the media came to understand culture wars to refer to the opinions and/or values of everyday Americans. This impelled social scientists to investigate this notion as well as Hunter's claim that the cleavage was between two poles of moral authority. Three significant criticisms of the culture wars thesis emerged from various research initiatives: (1) public opinion really is not very polarized; (2) the orthodox/progressive dichotomy is too simplistic to account for the diversity of positions in contested culture; (3) the metaphor of "war" is overstated, sensationalistic, and thus inappropriate.

DiMaggio et al. (1996) use data from the National Election Survey and the General Social Survey (1972–94) to interrogate the notion that American public opinion is polarized. They find no increased polarization in American public opinion since the 1970s. Examination of between-group and within-group variance showed surprising convergence of opinion on most issues. The one exception to this was the central battleground of abortion, where opinion was polarized along the lines of the culture war concept.

Another project (Smith et al. 1997) engaged 128 evangelicals in two-hour in-depth qualitative interviews. Smith's team found that most evangelicals are oblivious to a host of culture war terms, issues, and personalities. Those respondents who were aware either believe such contests are wrong-headed or the respondents indicate that aspects of both orthodox and progressive positions/reasoning appeal to them.

Alan Wolfe's *One Nation After All* (1999) depends on 200 qualitative interviews and he finds that most middle-class Americans not only are not culture wars combatants, but also they believe much in common with other middle-class people. However, Wolfe agrees with the culture wars theory with respect to elite knowledge workers.

The culture wars thesis appeared to suffer cracks under the weight of these and other critiques. However, the 2000 presidential electoral map revived media discussion of culture wars. The election, so close that it came down to a few hundred votes in Florida, revealed a significant divide among the Red states (Bush supporters) and Blue states (Gore supporters). For the most part the Blue areas of electoral strength were in the vast population centers on the West and East coasts, with other centers near the Great Lakes. Bush's strongest support came from the South and Midwest, and predominantly suburbs, small towns, and rural areas. Election survey data revealed that the most robust variable for predicting voting behavior in Red and Blue states was frequency of church attendance: those who were most religious overwhelmingly voted Republican and those with the highest indicators for secularity voted overwhelmingly for Democrats.

However, social scientists began to point out that the presidential electoral results did not map onto cultural divides neatly or consistently. For example, politically liberal states like Massachusetts contain significant numbers of "orthodox" citizens, particularly Roman Catholics. Outside of a handful of states on either side, the rest of the states tilted Red or Blue by a small margin. Morris Fiorina et al. (2004) conducted an exhaustive review of the

culture wars literature, available polling data, and election returns to demonstrate that the US was emphatically not polarized. Fiorina's findings show that Americans are clearly divided, but *closely divided*. The largest cluster of citizenry lay near the middle, with a combination of orthodox and progressivist views. Fiorina contends that if a culture war means a polarized or polarizing public, then the culture wars thesis is false.

Culture war proponents point to 2004 as exemplary of the cultural conflict between orthodox and progressive activists. Not only were moral values the top issue cited by voters in the 2004 presidential election, but also issues of sexuality dominated the news. First, the Massachusetts Supreme Court and later the City of San Francisco legalized gay marriage for the first time, and hundreds of couples took advantage of their new right. Traditionalists swung into action, proposing a marriage amendment to the Constitution that would permanently ensure that marriage was between a man and a woman. Eleven states had similar amendments to their state constitutions on the ballot and the pro-traditional marriage side prevailed in all 11. Further, the Congress passed and the president signed a law that banned "partial birth abortion."

How does one make sense of the non-polarized opinion findings, yet still make sense of the remarkable cultural and political ferment in 2004 over sexuality battles? Most sociologists concur with Hunter's original statement that average citizens are not involved in these fights. A powerful minority of credentialed elites, many (but not all) of whom fit the generalizations about orthodox and progressive moral authority, are the key actors. Furthermore, where there is disagreement on most cultural issues, the divide is not large, except on sexuality issues like abortion and homosexuality. Some commentators see the common ground in popular opinion, coupled with the basic acceptance of abortion and increasing acceptance of homosexuality, as evidence that the progressives won the culture war a long time ago. In this view the skirmishes in which the orthodox prevail are last gasps of the once vibrant traditional culture.

The methodology used to examine the culture wars thesis has unfortunately mostly focused on popular opinion, when the thesis explicitly specified that elite knowledge workers were the combatants. Furthermore, most of the popular opinion research employs data sets collected for other projects. While sophisticated techniques (DiMaggio et al. 1996) can improve the utility of the existing data sets, the best way forward would be a research design that operationalized the culture wars thesis directly. Smith et al. (1997) did test moral questions directly, but their qualitative interviews with ordinary evangelicals did not test credentialed elites. A survey of knowledge workers in culture-producing institutions, coupled with in-depth qualitative interviews of the same, would allow sociologists to explore the moral universe of these elites and ways in which moral authority impacts their work on cultural issues.

SEE ALSO: Abortion as a Social Problem; Culture, Production of; Culture, Social Movements and; Moral Panics; Power Elite; Sex Panics

REFERENCES AND SUGGESTED READINGS

Berger, P. (1967) *The Sacred Canopy*. Doubleday, New York.

DiMaggio, P., Evans, J., & Bryson, B. (1996) Have American Attitudes Become More Polarized? *American Journal of Sociology* 102, 3 (November): 690–755.

Fiorina, M., Abrams, S., & Pope, J. (2004) *Culture War? The Myth of Polarized America*. Pearson Longman, New York.

Gramsci, A. (1971 [1949]) *Selections From the Prison Notebooks of Antonio Gramsci*. Trans. and Ed. Q. Hoare & G. N. Smith. International Publishers, New York.

Hunter, J. D. (1991) *Culture Wars: The Struggle to Define America*. Basic Books, New York.

Hunter, J. D. (1994) *Before the Shooting Begins*. Free Press, New York.

Nolan, J. (Ed.) (1996) *The American Culture Wars: Current Contests and Future Prospects*. University of Virginia Press, Charlottesville.

Smith, C., Emerson, O., Gallagher, S., Kennedy, P., Sikkink, D. (1997) The Myth of Culture Wars: The Case of American Protestantism. In: Williams, R. (Ed.), *Culture Wars in American Politics*. Aldine de Gruyter, New York.

Wolfe, A. (1999) *One Nation After All*. Viking, New York.

sexuality

Ann Cronin

A variety of different approaches to understanding sexuality have emerged over the last 150 years. One way of categorizing these approaches is to distinguish between essentialist and social constructionist models of sexuality. Essentialism prioritizes a biological explanation for sexuality and hence limits its definition of sexuality to the individual expression of human desire and pleasure. In contrast, social constructionism prioritizes the relationship between the individual and society to show that the meaning attached to sexuality is embedded in specific historical, political, and social practices. Attention is paid to the culturally and socially diverse ways in which sexual desires, practices, identities, and attitudes are conceptualized, categorized, deployed, and ultimately regulated through the social institutions and practices of different societies. Although sociology's historical silence on sexuality served to reinforce an essentialist and normative understanding of sexuality, contemporary sociologists of sexuality, while acknowledging the importance of biology, produce socially situated accounts of sexuality. Furthermore, sociology offers a critical analysis of essentialism. A diverse range of approaches are used to account for the social organization of sexuality, including the sociology of homosexuality, feminist understandings of sexuality, queer theory, and an examination of the relationship between masculinity and sexuality. While each approach highlights different aspects of the debate on sexuality, there are many similarities and connections between the different perspectives. Furthermore, attention is paid to the interaction of sexual identity with other salient social identities, such as gender, race and ethnicity, class, age, and nationality.

HISTORY OF SEXUALITY

The social construction of sexual identity based on a dichotomy of heterosexuality and homosexuality can be traced to processes that began in the nineteenth century. Foucault's (1979)

historical account of the social construction of sexuality in modern western societies challenges essentialist conceptualizations of sex and sexuality as transhistorical and stable categories. Foucault argues that since the eighteenth century the discursive invention of sexuality as a biological instinct has resulted in individuals and populations becoming subject to a new form of power: biopower, which assumes that sexuality is the key to understanding an individual's health, pathology, and identity. Initially directed at population control through the development of statistics and demography, the development of sexology – the science of sexuality – in the nineteenth century led to a separation of the "medicine of sex" from the "medicine of the body," which resulted in the construction and administration of scientifically based therapies. Within these therapeutic discourses, sex denoted the sexual act, while sexuality symbolized the true essence – the core identity – of the individual. Furthermore, distortion or perversion of the natural sexual instinct would lead to sexual abnormality and deviance. The task of sexology became one of developing schemes and categories of anomalies and perversions that were, in turn, applied to people's identities. Thus, for the first time, sexual behavior was discursively constructed to represent the true nature and identity of an individual. Same-sex sexual behavior was indicative of a homosexual identity; opposite-sex sexual behavior was indicative of a heterosexual identity. For Foucault, this resulted in the connection of the body, the new human sciences, and the demands for regulation and surveillance, so that power and pleasure (knowledge and sex) meshed with each other. Within this, homosexuality was regarded as a perversion, thus legitimating its regulation and surveillance, whether overtly as in the case of legal sanctions against male homosexuality, or covertly as in the invisibility of lesbianism and the promotion of marriage and motherhood.

While the sexologists favored a biological explanation for sexuality, it was Freud's psychoanalytic theory of sexual development that led to the psychological construction of different sexual identities in the first half of the twentieth century. Freud proposed a sequential systematic model, in which an individual progresses from an initial bisexuality, or polymorphous sexuality, in early childhood through to the development of mature sexuality, which is viewed as the achievement of a stable heterosexual identity. Within this, homosexuality is viewed as a temporary stage of development (usually occurring during adolescence) on the path toward heterosexuality. This implies that those who identify as homosexual in adulthood have "fixated" on an early and hence immature phase of sexual development; alternatively, they have, due to psychological disturbance, "regressed" to this early phase of sexual development. Either way, homosexuality is located within a discourse of deviance, psychopathology, and illness.

SOCIOLOGY OF HOMOSEXUALITY

In 1948 Alfred Kinsey and his colleagues published *Sexual Behavior in the Human Male* and in 1953 *Sexual Behavior in the Human Female*. Kinsey's large-scale study of human sexual behavior highlighted the discrepancy between the number of people who engage in same-sex behavior and the number who identify as homosexual. Kinsey developed a six-point continuum designed to encompass a variety of sexual behavior and feelings, ranging from exclusively heterosexual (1) to exclusively homosexual (6). In between are a range of feelings and behaviors that cannot be categorized as either exclusively heterosexual or homosexual, with bisexuality, a desire for both sexes, somewhere in the middle. Kinsey argued that individuals move between categories throughout their life, thus rendering invalid the use of discrete sexual identities. For Kinsey, the development of an exclusive homosexual identity was the outcome of society's rejection of the homosexual.

The birth of the Gay Liberation and Black Liberation movements, alongside the reemergence of the Women's Movement, in the 1960s signaled both a new form of political action and protest and provided the political stimulus for the academic research of oppressed groups in society (Plummer 1981). The Kinsey Reports and the development of the labeling perspective provided the theoretical catalyst for a sociology of sexuality, although initially it was focused mainly on sexual deviance, with a particular interest in prostitution and homosexuality.

Although Kinsey was a zoologist, his work resonates with sociologists using labeling theory and symbolic interactionism to challenge essentialist normative explanations of homosexuality. Starting from the premise that all sexual behavior is socially constructed, sociologists suggest that people who engage in same-sex behavior are labeled deviant due to the reactions of a hostile society; thus there is nothing intrinsically deviant about a homosexual identity.

McIntosh (1968) stated that the very concept of homosexuality as an individual condition should come under sociological scrutiny because labeling an individual "homosexual" acts as a form of social control. Firstly, it acts as a deterrent for possible newcomers and secondly, it acts as a device to segregate and reinforce difference in those identified as deviant, thus leading to the formation of a homosexual subculture, with its own rules, norms, and values. While not without its critics, McIntosh's work is generally regarded as a landmark in sociology for its introduction of the "homosexual category," which served as a basis for further work.

Gagnon and Simon (1973), broadening the debate to a general discussion on sexuality, used the concept of sexual scripts to explore how people internalize the sexual norms and values of society. The sociology of homosexuality, while remaining on the margins of the discipline, has made a major contribution to the understanding of the social organization of homosexual identity, culture, and community.

GENDER AND SEXUALITY

While feminism represents a diverse body of theory, radical feminist theorists have concentrated on the relationship between sex, gender, and sexuality to argue that women's sexuality and their reproductive capabilities are controlled and regulated by men through a system of patriarchy. Sex refers to the biological differences between women and men, while gender refers to the social construction of male and female roles. Although the two are interlinked, sex was regarded by early radical feminists as a biological given and hence unalterable. However, gender, the social meaning of femaleness and maleness, ensures the continuation of a patriarchal sex/gender system, which is reliant on male supremacy. Fundamental to this is the construction of a naturalized, passive,

female heterosexuality in opposition to an active male heterosexuality. Radical feminism deconstructs this "natural" relationship and through the slogan the "personal is political" highlights the relationship between women's personal lives and the patriarchal society they inhabit.

Both lesbianism and heterosexuality are theorized as political institutions aimed at regulating women's sexuality and contributing to their subordination. While for some feminists this ensures the continuation of unequal gender relations, others argue that sexuality actually constitutes gender; thus it should be viewed as a singular concept where the subordination of women is erotized in sexuality. However, this neglects other forms of male power that are not expressed through sexuality.

Faderman (1985) examines the relationship between the nineteenth-century sexological constructions of lesbianism as pathological with the demands of an emergent Women's Movement; while Rich (1980) argues that the compulsory nature of heterosexuality ensures that men retain their physical, economic, and emotional control over women. For feminists like Rich and Faderman, the institution of heterosexuality is dependent upon ensuring that the experiences of lesbians either remain invisible or are associated with disease and illness, thus limiting women's identification with this category. Feminists argue that the development of scientific theory and practice was used to maintain existing gender relations and deny women access to the public world. Rich proposes a new definition of lesbian existence: a lesbian continuum encompassing a wide range of women-identified experience, which moves beyond the clinical definition to deepen and broaden lesbian experience. Through deconstructing divisive labels of sexuality, women can unite to fight for women's liberation, regardless of the sex of the person they choose to have sexual relationships with.

The radical feminist understanding of sexuality sparked fierce debate among feminists, leading to the "sex wars" between "pro-sex" feminists who regarded radical feminists as being both essentialist in thinking and anti-sex. Lesbians argued that radical feminist theory desexualized lesbian relationships or impeded the formation of lesbian identity and community building; other feminists questioned the distinction between sex and gender. Some argue that heterosexuality is a "political regime" based on an artificial biologically based distinction between women and men, and is oppressive to both women and homosexuals. This analysis undermines the traditional understanding of the category of sex as being biologically defined and hence immutable and enables the examination of how sex difference contributes to the existing social order. Essentialist categories of woman, man, heterosexual, and homosexual are reconfigured as political categories to become critical sites of gender deconstruction.

While radical feminism urges all women to become lesbians in order to fight male domination, recent feminist work has argued that being heterosexual does not automatically mean women are being complicit in their own oppression. Some distinguish between the institution of heterosexuality and heterosexuality as individual practice and identity, in which women are able to operate agency and control. This distinction between the levels of structure and agency enables women to identify as heterosexual yet resist the institution of heterosexuality.

Partly as a result of both feminist and gay writing, some male sociologists have begun to examine the social construction of masculinity and its links to the social organization of sexuality. While diverse in its exploration of masculinity, a key focus has been the examination of the relationship between power and masculinity, which has been theorized under the concept of "hegemonic masculinity" and the related concepts of "subordinated" and "complicit" masculinities. Heterosexuality is regarded as being central to hegemonic masculinity, while homosexuality is regarded as being a subordinate masculinity.

QUEER THEORY

Queer theory emerged in the US in the 1980s, due firstly to the emergence of new political movements such as Queer Nation and ACT-UP, which initially developed in response to the failure of the right-wing American government to respond appropriately to the emerging AIDS epidemic; and secondly, the development of lesbian and gay studies programs in humanities departments. Epstein (1994) notes the following uses of the term: a linguistic

reclamation; a gesture signaling anti-assimilationist politics; a politics of provocation in which liberal boundaries are contested; reference to a more fully "co-sexual" politics between women and men; a way of moving beyond homosexuality/heterosexuality. That is, it is inclusive of all sexualities opposed to heteronormativity. Queer theory signals a social constructionist politics, which is characterized by a resistance to all sexual labels and categories; instead, it argues that there exists a fluidity of sexual expression.

Initially regarded with suspicion by sociology, partly due to its poststructuralist origins, sociologists have begun to examine the benefits of a mutually interactive relationship between queer theory and sociology (Seidman 1997). While sociology has concentrated on the construction of homosexual identities and communities, queer theory, through the work of Foucault and Derrida, has developed a radical agenda that concentrates on the dynamic relationship between the dualism homosexuality/heterosexuality. By focusing on the importance of this relationship it is possible to remove the sociological study of homosexuality from the "deviant ghetto" and permit a sociological examination of the heteronormative nature of all knowledge and social structures. Heteronormativity refers to the way in which the social organization of western societies is predicated on the belief that heterosexuality is biologically, psychologically, and sociologically superior to other forms of sexuality. Thus, heterosexuality does not simply refer to opposite-sex relationships but represents an axis of power and dominant mode for conducting intimate relationships, which in turn is linked to ideas concerning gender-appropriate sexual behavior. Heteronormativity as ideology and normative principle dominates both the legal system and the cultural system, thus legitimating differential treatment of those who stand outside of the heterosexual regime. The concept of heteronormativity increases our understanding of both the structural disadvantages of those who stand outside the heterosexual regime and the way in which institutionalized heterosexuality limits and constrains those who identify as heterosexual.

A theoretical concern with the borders that exist between sexual identities and communities has resulted in the deconstruction of all sexual identities, including politicized ones. For example, while recognizing that the very construction of the homosexual enabled the struggle for civil rights, claiming the label homosexual simultaneously reinforces the centrality of heterosexuality. This makes it impossible to locate oneself "outside" of dominant discourses, for to define oneself as standing outside the sexual norm means first placing oneself within dominant definitions of sexuality. Thus, many queer theorists examine how claiming a homosexual identity contributes to reinforcing the hetero/homo split (Namaste 1994).

Queer theory does not attempt to move beyond this "double bind" in current conceptions of sexuality. Instead, it concentrates on the creation, regulation, and resistance of sexual borders to show that sexuality and power are present in all aspects of social life and structures. Queer theory and practice signal important theoretical shifts, resulting in a critical distancing from the terms lesbian and gay; the term queer has become a catalyst for people disaffected by earlier work on sexual identity, which homogenized the experiences and interests of lesbian and gay men and assumed that sexual identity is both visible and static. Queer theory's poststructuralist approach challenges the foundationalist assumptions present in existing understandings of identity and uses this as a basis to question current notions of sexual identity, leading to a rejection of unifying concepts and an increasing emphasis on difference and plurality.

THEORY AND PRACTICE

Explanations for sexuality, whether they are biological, psychological, or sociological in origin, have a direct consequence on the way in which individuals understand and practice their own sexuality, as well as the laws, regulations, norms, and values that govern gender-appropriate sexual behavior. The stigmatization of homosexuality and its association with disease and deviance in the first half of the twentieth century had a detrimental effect on people who found themselves attracted to members of the same sex, a situation that was exacerbated by the social and legal sanctions surrounding same-sex lifestyles. In the UK, despite nearly two decades of active campaigning, the decriminalization of private homosexual acts between two men over the age of 21 did not occur until 1967. This was reduced to 18 in 1994 and finally achieved parity with the age of consent for heterosexuals (16) in 2001. Same-sex behavior between women has never been criminalized in the UK. Globally, lesbian and gay men have been subjected to both formal and informal discrimination in the workplace, educational institutions, military establishments, and health care, as well as being denied the benefits and rights accorded to heterosexual individuals. While there has been local or national reform over the last 30 years, many countries still discriminate against homosexual behavior and in some places it remains punishable by imprisonment or death. Likewise, while feminist campaigns have partially succeeded in exposing the complex relationship between gender and sexuality, women in many parts of the world remain in a subordinate position to men, and this is enacted either through the legal system or through the informal rules and regulations that govern the practice of sexuality. This includes the double sexual standard that still operates in many parts of the world, the high incidence of sexual violence against women, and sexual harassment in the workplace. Sociological interest in sexuality has helped to expose the discrimination and stigma faced by homosexuals, as well as providing a broader analysis of the social organization of sexuality in society.

SEE ALSO: Femininities/Masculinities; Hegemonic Masculinity; Heterosexuality; Homosexuality; Kinsey, Alfred; Labeling Theory; Lesbian Feminism; Queer Theory; Radical Feminism; Sex and Gender; Sexual Deviance; Sexual Identities; Sexual Politics; Sexual Practices; Sexualities and Consumption; Sexuality and the Law

REFERENCES AND SUGGESTED READINGS

Epstein, S. (1994) A Queer Encounter: Sociology and the Study of Sexuality. *Sociological Theory* 12: 188–202.

Faderman, L. (1985) *Surpassing the Love of Women.* Women's Press, London.

Foucault, M. (1979) *The History of Sexuality: An Introduction.* Trans. R. Hurley. Penguin, London.

Gagnon, J. H. & Simon, W. S. (1973) *Sexual Conduct: The Social Sources of Human Sexuality.* Aldine, Chicago.

Hawkes, G. (1998) *The Sociology of Sexuality*. Macmillan, London.

Katz, J. N. (1996) *The Invention of Heterosexuality*. Plume Penguin, London.

McIntosh, M. (1968) The Homosexual Role. *Social Problems* 16(2): 182–92.

Namaste, K. (1994) The Politics of Inside/Out: Queer Theory, Poststructuralism, and a Sociological Approach to Sexuality. *Sociological Theory* 12: 220–31.

Nardi, P. M. & Schneider, B. E. (Eds.) (1998) *Social Perspectives in Lesbian and Gay Studies*. Routledge, New York.

Plummer, K. (Ed.) (1981) *The Making of the Modern Homosexual*. Hutchinson, London.

Rich, A. (1980) Compulsory Heterosexuality and Lesbian Existence. *Signs* 5(4): 631–60.

Richardson, D. (Ed.) (1996) *Theorizing Heterosexuality*. Open University Press, Milton Keynes.

Seidman, S. (1997) *Difference Troubles: Queering Social Theory and Sexual Politics*. Blackwell, Oxford.

Weeks, J. (1985) *Sexuality and Its Discontents: Meaning, Myths and modern sexualities*. Routledge, London.

Williams, C. L & Stein, A. (Eds.) (2002) *Sexuality and Gender*. Blackwell, Oxford.

sexuality and the law

Leslie J. Moran

Reference to sexuality in the day-to-day operation of the law is coterminous with the emergence of sexuality as a category in the wider society. However, its explicit appearance in the official texts of law such as constitutions, codes of law, and statutes is relatively recent. For example, some of the most familiar legal terms associated with sexuality (e.g., buggery, sodomy, and indecency), phrases such as age of consent, or other key legal terms (e.g., justice, equity, marriage, spouse, parent, contract, libel, slander, property interest, and the right to privacy) make no explicit reference to sexuality. Sexuality is read into these legal concepts. An example of the emergence of sexuality as a legal term of art is the phrase sexual orientation. This phrase made its first formal appearance in the official texts of law in 1973.

One sign of an awareness of the pervasive significance of sexuality in the law is reflected in the move away from a preoccupation with criminal law in particular sexual offenses and the emergence of a more expansive exploration of sexuality across a wide range of areas of law, from property relations to access to fertility treatment, from taxation to hate crime, from domestic violence to international law, from the regulation of kinship to the regulation of business. Long dominated by work focusing on law in anglophone western liberal democratic states the agenda is expanding to include wider national and international contexts. For example, Carl Stychin and Didi Herman's edited collection *Sexuality in the Legal Arena* (2000) includes work on law in South Africa and Zimbabwe and studies of sexuality in international laws such as the European Convention of Human Rights and the UN's International Convention on Civil and Political Rights. Robert Wintermute and Mads Andenaes's edited collection *Legal Recognition of Same-Sex Partnership: A Study of National, European and International Law* (2001) includes essays that explore the impact of sexuality in the legal regulation of kinship relations in a wide range of national contexts (e.g., France, Germany, the Netherlands, Brazil, South Africa), as well as through a consideration of international law.

A search of electronic legal literature databases such as Hein online for material dealing with sexuality reveals that this body of work is dominated by material focusing on lesbian and gay sexualities. A much smaller body of work appears to focus on heterosexuality, with little appearing to examine bisexuality in a legal context (Moran 2006). Exploration of work on heterosexuality and the law reveals that much of that work focuses on lesbian and gay sexualities. For example, in Alison Young's *Femininity in Dissent* (1990), which studies the criminalization of female anti-nuclear protesters at Greenham Common in the UK, heterosexuality appears in an exploration of the media and criminal justice representation of the women protesters as lesbians. Andrew Sharpe's monograph *Transgender Jurisprudence: Dysphoric Bodies of Law* (2002) engages with heterosexuality in a series of judgments from the UK, Australia, and the US concerned with the struggle for legal recognition of transgender claims to establish their gender identity. A key finding of his analysis is the importance of heterosexuality in the jurisprudence of transgender and central to that heterosexuality is homosexuality and homophobia. Janet Halley's pioneering studies of the US Supreme Court decision of *Bowers vs. Hardwick* (1986) dealing with the constitutionality of state prohibition of consensual sex between adult males offers some of the best work using techniques of deconstruction to examine the constitution of heterosexuality through homosexuality as "other" (Halley 1993).

The dominance of work on gay and lesbian sexualities in studies of sexuality and the law is far from being a state of affairs unique to work on sexuality in law. As Jonathan Katz notes in his study *The Invention of Heterosexuality* (1995: 12), "talk of heterosexuality so often and so easily glides off into talk of homosexuality, leaving heterosexuality – once again – forgotten." Here Katz points to the difficulties of making heterosexuality as the norm an object of critical inquiry. But as Kitzinger and Wilkinson suggest in the introduction to their edited collection *Heterosexuality: A Feminist and Psychology Reader* (1993), the norm of heterosexuality is always present while, at the same time, it is that which most resists appearance. Work on gay and lesbian sexualities in law not only explores these particular sexualities in law, but also offers the most sustained scholarship on heterosexuality to date in that field. A key component of this work is its engagement with the nature, form, effects, and institutions of heterosexuality. Terms in this work that point to the relationship between heterosexuality and these other sexualities include homophobia, heterosexism, and more recently heteronormativity. However, the danger remains that through the focus on "lesbian" or "gay," critical reflection on "heterosexuality" may slip out of the frame. The challenge is to keep both the norm and the exception in the frame of analysis in order to expose and critique the (re)production of sexuality in law.

Scholarship on sexuality and law may take many different forms. The dominant mode of legal scholarship is known by the phrase "the black letter tradition." While it is an approach to law that has its roots in the western legal method, it also has wider global significance. The methodological preoccupation is with the language of the official texts of law and with an exposition of the "true" meaning of these texts.

Formally, this "truth" can only be established by reference to other official texts of law. These texts range from constitutions and other founding texts of the nation-state, such as a bill of rights, to legislation that flows from these founding texts. The latter may take the form of pieces of legislation, either created from time to time or introduced as codes of law offering a single catalog of the rules. In addition to establishing the true meaning of the language of law scholarship within, the black letter tradition also offers commentaries on the text of law: discovering meanings that appear to be formally absent from the text, finding endless consistencies and continuities of meaning, and explaining distinctions. This is a mode of legal scholarship that represents itself as being hermetically sealed from other scholarly disciplines and intimately associated with professional training for lawyers and formally devoid of politics. The methodology of this tradition of scholarship has been used to promote as well as deny legal recognition based upon a person's sexuality. Robert Wintermute's *Sexual Orientation and Human Rights: The United States Constitution, the European Convention and the Canadian Charter* (1995) is a good example of this type of legal scholarship. Wintermute offers an analysis of various legal terms such as equality, sexual orientation, and sex discrimination in several jurisdictional settings, including the US, Canada, and Australia. He explores the judicial interpretation given to these terms with a view to determining which legal category may best promote civil and human rights.

Other schools of legal scholarship (law in context, the law and society movement, sociolegal studies, critical legal studies, law and culture, legal history) and law-related scholarship such as criminology draw upon a wider range of methodologies, mainly (but not exclusively) associated with the social sciences and have a more interdisciplinary approach. They include a more expansive approach to legal phenomena, an interest in the wider operation of law in different institutional and everyday locations, and an explicit interest in the interface between law and economics, politics, psychology and the social, and cultural dimensions of law. The interdisciplinary dimensions of this work also draw attention to the fact that the study of law is not the exclusive preserve of legal studies, but may also be found in scholarship in other disciplines such as history, politics, psychology, literature, sociology, cultural studies, and so on (Moran 2002).

Davina Cooper's monograph *Sexing the City: Lesbian and Gay Politics Within the Activist State* (1994) provides a good example of work focusing on sexual politics in local government in the UK. Aileen Stein's *The Stranger Next Door: The Story of a Small Community's Battle Over Sex, Faith and Civil Rights* (2001) is a study of sexual politics in a small community in the Northwest of the US. This study explores sexuality and the law by way of the daily activities of individuals, in their relations with the central or local state and private institutions and in their everyday interpersonal interactions. Other work, such as Stephen Tomsen's *Hatred, Murder and Male Honour: Anti-Homosexual Homicides in New South Wales, 1980–2000* (2002), with its roots in criminological scholarship, explores sexuality through a study of police data on gay-related murder and examines not only the causes of violence in this context, but also the context in which it takes place, challenging a range of heterosexist assumptions that inform understandings of the nature of murder and the processes of investigation and criminal prosecution. Studies of the representation of law, laws, and legality in high and popular cultural contexts such as fine art, literature, music, film, television, video games, and so on are a new context in which work on sexuality in law has begun to emerge. Didi Herman's study, "Juliet and Juliet Would Be More My Cup of Tea": Sexuality, Law and Popular Culture" published in a collection of essays, *Law and Popular Culture* (2004), edited by Michael Freeman, explores the governance and regulation of sexuality in and through popular culture, in this instance television.

Some legal scholarship explores sexuality by reference to theories of law drawing upon a wide range of philosophical and metaphysical traditions. Here law is taken to be a repository of the founding ideals of human society, of its ethical and moral substratum. Morris Kaplan's study *Sexual Justice* (1997) is an example of this type of scholarship, using the work of philosophers such as Hegel, and Nietzsche and the more recent scholarship of Judith Butler to examine a range of legal issues

concerning sexuality. Nicholas Bamforth's *Sexuality, Morals and Justice* (1997) offers a sustained analysis of sexual equality by particular reference to moral philosophy. Ruthann Robson's *When Sappho Goes to Law School* (1998) draws extensively on the insights of feminist scholarship.

Some of the most exciting work on sexuality and the law is scholarship informed by queer theory, exploring the materiality of sexuality and challenging the essentializing dimensions of sexual identity politics in law. At best, queer theory offers a multidisciplinary set of tools drawing upon poststructuralist and post-Marxist political theory and cultural and literary studies. Margaret Davis's essay "Queer Property, Queer Persons: Self-Ownership and Beyond" (1999) is a brilliant example of the potential of queer theory. Her essay explores the nature of sexual identity by way of an analysis of themes of personality and property. Her work exemplifies queer theory's ability to expose the fundamental instability of what appear to be fixed categories of sexuality and to challenge and disrupt the sexual and gender hierarchies through which heterosexuality is given shape and form. Her analysis provides an example of work that challenges identity as the essence, core, or foundation of the subject. She reveals not only how deeply embedded these ideas are in western legal culture, but also how identity is implicated in and draws upon other fundamental legal ideas which might seem to be remote from it, such as property. Another important dimension of this essay is the way Davis explores the limits of queer theory, in particular the way it has rapidly been transformed from a technique of radical and progressive critique into just another (albeit new) identity category.

Other work drawing upon queer theory and its poststructuralist sources includes Carl Stychin's *Law's Desire* (1995), which offers a series of case studies of sexual politics in US legal disputes and one of the first engagements with queer theory in legal studies. Leslie Moran's *The Homosexual(ity) of Law* (1996) and Derek McGhee's *Homosexuality, Law and Resistance* (2001) offer a poststructuralist analysis of sexual identity in law, this time in the context of English law, developing a Foucauldian analysis. The former also has a strong historical focus and engages with the criminological literature on deviance and sexuality.

A different but related line of critical engagement within current legal studies of sexuality has focused on critiques of identity politics as "a politics of recognition." Susan Boyd's (1999) feminist-inspired work offers an example of legal scholarship exploring the challenge to identity politics raised by the "politics of redistribution." Her work also questions the point of departure that sets recognition and redistribution as two categories that are in a relation of either/or. Her exploration of these issues takes place in relation to debates within feminism and the politics of kinship recognition, more specifically struggles over women's rights in heterosexual and lesbian domestic relations.

The problematic reification of identity categories is another theme to be found in current work on sexuality in law. Here the concern focuses on the totalizing assumptions at work in sexual identity in general and "lesbian" or "gay" in particular as separate, distinct, and complete categories. Current work has examined the interface between sexuality and gender, race and ethnicity (Moran 2006). The impact of class, age, and disability on sexuality in law remains a neglected area of study. A new and exciting development has been an exploration of these issues in a postcolonial context (Kapur 1999; Hiu 2004).

Much remains to be explored, as the study of sexuality and the law is in its infancy. More research specifically examining the heterosexual norm needs to be undertaken in all contexts. In other respects, the future direction of research will in part be influenced by the context and location in which the research is being undertaken. For example, in several African states the preoccupation remains the impact of the criminal law, and sexual offenses in particular, on the lives of citizens and the absence of any civil and human rights relating to sexuality. In many western capitalist democracies sexuality in the arena of civil and human rights remains a dominant and still expanding theme. Sexuality in the context of kinship relations is another popular emphasis that is likely to grow in importance. In locations in which sexual citizenship has become more of a reality, studies of the impact of these changes not only upon the lives of individuals but on all aspects of society

will be important. As these reforms take effect, new agendas for empirical and critical work that explore the impact of these changes will emerge. For example, Shane Phelan's *Sexual Strangers: Gays, Lesbians and the Dilemmas of Citizenship* (2001) explores some of the problems associated with the emerging concept of sexual citizenship. Leslie Moran and Beverly Skeggs's *Sexuality and the Politics of Violence and Safety* (2004) explores some of the more troubling aspects of the sexual politics of criminal justice responses to the pervasive and damaging effects of sexual violence.

Another emerging agenda focuses on sexuality and law in a global context. One dimension of this is the global spread of sexual politics in relation to law. Carl Stychin's *Nation by Rights* (1998) and *Governing Sexuality: The Changing Politics of Citizenship and Law Reform* (2003) begin an exploration of the globalization of sexual politics and the impact of sexuality on civil and human rights in both national and international contexts. A second dimension of this global turn is the emergence of a body of work on sexuality in law that brings new theoretical insights into play, such as work influenced by postcolonial scholarship (Kapur 1999).

While the work on sexuality and law is methodologically diverse, much work remains preoccupied with the analysis of texts. While the type of texts is now more diverse (ranging from media reports of legal activities, to law reports and case files, to literature and film), work that has a strong empirical focus using both quantitative and qualitative methods or ethnographic work is less common. More empirical work needs to be undertaken to examine the rapidly changing sexual landscape of law and legal relations.

SEE ALSO: Globalization, Sexuality and; Heterosexuality; Homosexuality; Law, Sociology of; Queer Theory; Same-Sex Marriage/Civil Unions; Sexuality, Religion and

REFERENCES AND SUGGESTED READINGS

Boyd, S. (1999) Family Law and Sexuality: Feminist Engagements. *Social and Legal Studies* 8(3): 369–90.
Collier, R. (1997) After Dunblane: Crime, Corporeality and the (Hetero)Sexing of the Bodies of Men. *Journal of Law and Society* 24(2): 177–99.

Davies, M. (1999) Queer Property, Queer Persons: Self-Ownership and Beyond. *Social and Legal Studies* 8(3): 327–52.

Halley, J. E. (1993) The Construction of Heterosexuality. In: Warner, M. (Ed.), *Fear of a Queer Planet: Queer Politics and Social Theory.* University of Minnesota Press, Minneapolis, pp. 82–104.

Hiu, M.-C. (2004). "Censorship = Mission Impossible?" A Postcolonial Same Sex Erotic Discourse on Hong Kong Porn Law. *International Journal of Sociology of Law* 32: 39–63.

Kapur, R. (1999) "A Love Song For Our Mongrel Selves": Hybridity, Sexuality and Law. *Social and Legal Studies* 8(3): 353–68.

Mason, G. (2001) *The Spectacle of Violence.* Routledge, London.

Moran, L. J. (2002) Lesbian and Gay Bodies of Law. In: Richardson, D. & Seidman, V. (Eds.), *Handbook of Lesbian and Gay Studies.* Sage, London, pp. 291–311.

Moran, L. J. (2006) *Sexuality, Identity and Law.* Ashgate, Aldershot.

sexuality, masculinity and

Rebecca F. Plante and Michael S. Kimmel

Nowhere in our intimate lives is there greater expression of gender difference than in our sexual relationships. "She" may make love "just like a woman," as Bob Dylan famously sang, but "he" would make love just like a man. Though we often think that sexual orientation is the great dividing line in our sexual expression – that being gay or straight is all we need to know about a person's sexuality – the evidence points decisively the other way, toward an understanding that gender, not sexual orientation, is the dividing line along which sexual expression, desire, and experience is organized. Gay men and straight men think and act in sexually similar ways, as do lesbians and straight women. In that sense, sexually speaking, gay men and lesbians are *gender* conformists.

How do we explain the different sexualities of women and men? How different are men's and women's sexualities? Have men's sexualities changed over the last 100 years?

BEYOND BIOLOGY

Many people believe that the differences between male and female sexuality are the simple reflection of biological differences. Some point to different evolutionary imperatives, brain chemistry and organization, or endocrine differences to explain these differences. And while these are no doubt important, biological differences tend to *assume* the very questions we might seek to answer. For example, hormone levels may influence the intensity of the sex drive, but they do not predict its direction or the object of sexual desire. Evolutionary imperatives can be just as easily employed to find the opposite of contemporary US stereotypes. And biological models assume a uniformity *among* males and *among* females that is illusory; indeed, the really interesting variations are among women and among men, not small, sometimes barely perceptible, average differences between women and men.

To sociologists, sexuality is less the product of these biological drives and more a set of experiences constructed within a social, cultural, and historical context. Sex has a history and it varies not only between women and men, but across cultures and over time, and over the lifecourse. Sexual identities and sexual behaviors occur within these sociocultural parameters, and normative constraints and cultural expectations guide the individual experience and expression of sexual life. Most significantly, sexuality is constructed through the lens of gender. We tend to believe that sexual expression is gender expression; we imagine that gay men and lesbians are gender nonconformists.

THEORIES OF SEXUAL DEVELOPMENT

There are several explanations of how men learn hegemonic expectations; these theories could ostensibly be applied to most cultures. Gagnon and Simon's theory of *sexual scripting* argues that cultural, subcultural, and interpersonal standards for sexual and gendered conduct are socially constructed. Ideas about proper conduct and attitudes are gathered from prescriptive and proscriptive "scripts," the shoulds, ought to's, and don'ts of sexuality.

Social learning theory suggests that sexuality is learned through observation, modeling, and positive and negative reinforcement. So men's sexuality would be learned by observing models (family, friends, and mass mediated images) and coming to understand which behaviors and attitudes are culturally rewarded. This is in direct contrast to sociobiological theories, which posit that behavior is hormonal, innate, or essential. Therefore, men's sexuality would be ordained by non-social sources. This view contributes to the belief that men's sexuality is natural, simple, and easy to decipher.

Psychoanalytic theories, derived from Freud, argue that sexuality is a major force, or drive (*libido*), and that the ego functions to translate social mores for the irrational, pleasure-seeking id. Ego-strength is the ability of the ego to channel sexual energies (sublimation) and redirect them toward culturally constructive outlets. These theories would suggest that the social elements of sexuality and gender are created from or result from the natural aspects of biologically based sex.

However, most sociologists would agree that western societies privilege binary, dichotomized, gendered roles and distinctions; the sexual arena is an ideal place in which to exemplify and magnify differences. Research suggests that in the West and in much of the rest of the world, action, autonomy, competition, and aggression are thought to be desirable masculine qualities. When these values are linked to beliefs about biology, the groundwork is laid for the creation of masculine sexuality that expects men to take the initiative, be aggressive, and be knowledgeable.

SEXUALITY AND GENDER INEQUALITY

Theories of sexuality must not only account for the differences between women and men, and the variations among women and among men, but also must explain sexual and gender inequality. In addition to other predictors of social inequality (age, race, class, ethnicity), gender and sexual orientation provide both the grounding for identity and the basis for inequality.

Patriarchy, which refers to a society in which social power rests mostly in men's hands, can create a gender hierarchy in which men dominate or exploit women. The cultural value attributed to assertive, initiating, knowledgeable men is consequential. Rape, sexual assault, and child molestation are the darkest aspects of patriarchy, sexism, and gender inequities. Regardless of sexual orientation, men are expected to take charge and direct the action and interaction (but especially in heterosexual contexts). Certainly, in popular culture, men's sexuality is thought to be driven by efficient and irresistible forces and therefore resistant to social control.

Homophobia, defined as the fear of anyone or anything defined as gay or lesbian, is implicated in the construction of masculine sexuality. Conceptually, it can be better understood as a complex element of patriarchy and sexism, combined with hatred and fear of homosexuality. Homophobia disables intimacy for men. Masculine sexuality is organized around the underlying belief that women are inferior to men. The unfortunate misperception that gay equals feminine can result in the "sexual prejudice" that to be gay is to be "less than a man" (Herek 2005). Thus, some men's sexuality appears to be primarily organized around behavior and attitudes that prove heterosexuality. Many men suffer from the sociocultural contradictions of increasingly masculinized sexuality, which encourages risky and emotionally circumscribed interactions. Active pursuit of heterosex and overt sexual prowess confer status, particularly for young men.

ELEMENTS OF THE MASCULINE SEXUAL SCRIPT

With genitalia outside the body, men can feel as if their emotions and sexualities are wholly *externalized*, suggests Gergen (2001). In this way, bodies become mechanized, tool-like, exemplified by the occasional practice of referring to the phallus as an object (e.g., "The little head thinks for the big head," implying that phallic "behavior and logic" supersedes the brain). This can enhance a disjuncture for mind, body, feelings, and fantasies. Language and slang highlight this, such as "Little General," "love torpedo," "Herman the One-Eyed German," and "Woodrow." The crucial element of masculine sexuality is the penis, a visible and thus formidable symbol of *desire* and arousal. Men are expected to separate emotion from sexual action.

The mind/body separation, along with expectations of assertiveness and aggressiveness, can combine in volatile ways. Some men (and women) engage in "recreational" and/or risky sex. Recreational *sex* often requires a mind/body split so that feelings of intimacy, love, and tenderness can be dissociated from sexual encounters. This requires its participants to believe that sex is "just sex," and can be pleasurably enjoyed without emotional fallout, dashed expectations, and differences in participants' perceptions.

Sexuality for men has long included visual and written representations of people, positions, and practices, dating back to Greek and Roman eras. Pornography – materials that are sexually explicit and intended to cause sexual arousal – serves to eroticize particular cultural stories about sexualities. In modern western pornography men are depicted as powerful, lusty, sexual initiators with enormous phalluses that always perform reliably.

With the phallus as the largely undisputed focus of men's sexuality, sociocultural scripts assert that it is natural for the penis to be the main "tool" of men's sexuality. The corollary is that coitus (penile-vaginal intercourse) is the most natural sexual behavior. Coitus is "real sex," the only valid way to achieve pleasure. This taken-for-granted notion also reinforces the dominance of heterosexuality. This limits the cultural acceptance of non-genital and sometimes solo forms of expression, though masculine sexuality includes many such examples, including watching erotic dancing (stripping), going to sex/swing clubs, and many bondage/domination (or sado/masochism) activities.

Men are expected to master their bodies and sexualities. A spoof of the *Joy of Sex* (a popular sex how-to manual) depicted men as the workers of sex, wearing hard hats and wielding jackhammers (McConnachie 1974). The "job" of sex asserts that sex is performative, an opportunity for men to demonstrate their prowess. (Thus, men experience "performance anxiety" when they "can't get the job done.") Men are especially responsible for controlling all aspects of heterosex, from flirtation and first meeting to foreplay and everything else. Combined with

the seemingly overt nature of his desire (symbolized by an erection), a man is particularly expected to labor to arouse his female partners, whose desire is thought to be more hidden and mysterious.

Masculine sexuality, as natural and organic, is thought to encompass more knowledge of sex than does feminine sexuality. Men "naturally" know not only how to control their own orgasms but also their partners'. The taxonomy of what the *Diagnostic and Statistical Manual* (1994) calls *male sexual dysfunction* includes at least two orgasm-related issues: premature ejaculation and male orgasmic disorder (formerly "retarded ejaculation"). Both diagnoses rely on vague perceptions of what "normal" orgasm and ejaculation should be like – that it should be happening at just the right time. Masculine sexuality requires a man to be in control of his body at all times, moderating his arousal and responses so that he can orchestrate pleasure for his partner and/or display his skill.

Diagnoses of sexual dysfunction are not limited to orgasm issues – *erectile dysfunction* (ED) has powerful resonance for most men. The global market for erectile dysfunction pharmaceuticals is about US$3 billion. Given the expectation that masculine sexuality is focused on the penis and heterosexual coitus, it requires an erection under a man's control. ED challenges the belief that men's bodies are purely external, devoid of contextual, relational, or health-related influences. The popularity of erection control measures, including drugs, pumps, and implants, is testimony to the taken-for-granted assumptions that underlie masculine sexuality.

Masculine sexuality is especially thought to be subject to "the heat of the moment," a powerful force of libido and desire that inhibits rationality and planning ahead. Lust and desire combine with the cultural belief that sex should be spontaneous and powerful, in the moment, and free from restrictions imposed by prophylaxis and contraception. Heterosexually active men can counteract the heat of the moment by reassuring themselves, independently of specific sexual encounters, that female partners use contraception. This logic supports the argument that condoms interfere with the lusty, spur-of-the-moment impulses thought to be the most natural aspect of sex.

"Normative" male sexuality is therefore non-relational, objectifying, and phallocentric, more prone to various paraphilia, multiple partners, recreational sexuality, and a strict separation of sex and love. Normative male sexuality is thus an expression of gender inequality, a mechanism for its reproduction, rather than a resistance to it. Happily, as with all such normative constructions, norms are more fungible in practice, and individual men still have large latitude in negotiating and developing different (and individual) sexual expressions.

SEE ALSO: Femininities/Masculinities; Hegemonic Masculinity; Homosexuality; Male Rape; Patriarchy; Pornography and Erotica; Viagra

REFERENCES AND SUGGESTED READINGS

Connell, R. (2001) *The Men and the Boys*. University of California Press, Berkeley.
Gergen, M. (2001) *Feminist Reconstructions in Psychology*. Sage, Thousand Oaks, CA.
Herek, G. (2005) Beyond "Homophobia": Thinking About Sexual Prejudice and Stigma in the Twenty-First Century. *Sexuality Research and Policy: Journal of NSRC* 1(2): 6–24.
McConnachie, B. (Ed.) (1974) *National Lampoon The Job of Sex: A Workingman's Guide to Productive Lovemaking*. Warner Books, New York.

sexuality, religion and

Melissa M. Wilcox

Long perceived as major sources of social, political, economic, and even esoteric power, sexuality and religion are logical partners for sociological study. Although each is individually the subject of a significant subfield within sociology, in combination they have received less scholarly attention to date than they are due. Nevertheless, there is a significant body of work already in place on their many and varied connections – enough to point innovators in several fruitful directions. The key connections between these two powerful social institutions lie in religious ritual, social structure and social control, and boundary creation and maintenance.

RITUALS

Although much of the study of religion has focused on belief, to individual members of a religion practice is often most central. This holds especially true in the context of sexuality, which is generally practiced – or not – depending on the teachings of a religious group and the practitioner's position within that group.

Most salacious, though least common overall, are religious rites that involve sexual practice in some central way. Though many minority religious groups have been falsely accused of such ritual activity as part of attempts to discredit them, religions also exist that do make ritual use of human sexuality. In some cases these ritual practices are well within the social norm. Some cultures, for example, include sexual practices in their rites of passage from childhood to adulthood. It is worth noting that interpretations of such practices vary enormously; thus, sexual rites of passage are generally not viewed (primarily, at least) as a source of sexual pleasure but rather as a symbolically important part of social role transformation.

Socially normative sexual rites may also function metaphorically, on the time-honored esoteric principle that activities in the microcosm are echoed in the macrocosm. Some ancient Mediterranean cultures practiced a form of so-called "temple prostitution," in which a practitioner had sexual intercourse with a deity in the form of that deity's earthly representative – usually a priestess. Such intercourse, again, was not (primarily) for pleasure, and it was sometimes more symbolic than physical. Its purpose, rather, was to strengthen the bond between worshippers (or an entire people) and their deity, to encourage the fertility of the land, or to reenact a creation story. Within more esoteric traditions, such as Kabbalah (medieval Jewish mysticism), the sexual union of a married couple was interpreted as uniting the male and female aspects of the divine.

Other ritual uses of sexuality are intentionally transgressive. Perhaps the best known (and the most misunderstood) of these in the West today is Tantra, a set of religious beliefs and practices that arose in India as early as the seventh century CE and eventually came to influence sectors of Hinduism, Buddhism, and Jainism (White 2003). Over the course of the past century western esotericists have imported aspects of a fairly garbled understanding of Tantra into their own mystical teachings and marketed the result as "sex magic," "Tantra," or "Tantric sex" (Urban 2004). In its South Asian context, however, the sexual aspects of Tantra are but one part of a larger structure in which direct contravention of social norms is held to be the key to advanced religious practice.

More common than sexual rituals are ritual restrictions on and purifications of sexuality. These include the restrictions on sexual practices and practitioners so famously analyzed by Mary Douglas in *Purity and Danger* (1966). Many religions consider sexual activity and often sexual fluids to be extremely powerful; some interpret this power as a kind of pollution and some as a source of ritual power, whereas others see it simply as a potential source of interference in the ritual. Since religions concerned with pollution are usually also concerned with purity, special sexual regulations for religious practitioners are quite common. These may include engaging in purifying practices before religious rituals if one has had sexual intercourse, menstruated, touched one's genitals, given birth, masturbated, had nocturnal emissions, or, at the extreme, even thought about sex.

A number of important rituals regulate sexuality in the broader culture as well as within a religion. Marital rites are nearly ubiquitous, and often represent the social and religious sanction of sexuality between the people being married. Most religions treat sex within marriage and sex outside of marriage differently (such treatment also varies significantly by gender), and most see at least some forms of sexual activity as beneficial. A few, however, view human sexuality as a detriment to spiritual advancement, and enjoin either temporary or permanent celibacy on their most devout practitioners. Some, such as certain branches of Christianity, connect sexuality to evil, whereas others, such as renunciant strains of Hinduism and Buddhism, see it as a weakening of one's spiritual powers (Hinduism) or an unnecessary tie to an illusory and oppressive material world (Buddhism). A number of religions consider either women or (more commonly) men to be better suited to abstinence and therefore to advanced spiritual development; religion thus becomes an important determinant and carrier of gender roles as well as attitudes toward sexuality.

SOCIAL STRUCTURE AND SOCIAL CONTROL

Because religion concerns itself with ultimate reality, it is especially well suited as an agent of social control, but also as a locus for the deconstruction and reconstruction of the social order. Religious beliefs and practices shape sexual practices, beliefs, roles, identities, and norms; in essence, they are a key factor in the social construction of desire. Consider, for example, the stringent restrictions placed by many branches of Buddhism on contact between a nun or monk and a member of the opposite sex – or even, in the case of monks, certain types of men (Faure 1998). Catholic monastic orders warn against "special friendships" between members of the same sex; Orthodox Jewish synagogues and Muslim mosques keep the sexes separate; and many religions expect "modest" dress (however defined) during religious ritual. Each of these examples constructs desire implicitly, and suggests that sexuality and religion, while not necessarily enemies, are not quite compatible.

On the other hand, religion can also provide a site for powerful challenges to an existing social-sexual order. The symbolic deployment of the *hijab*, or headscarf, by Muslim women is one example of this. Worn in different styles – or not at all – depending on the country, the culture, and the individual woman, the polysemic *hijab* has come to represent simultaneously male repression, anti-imperialism, sensible fashion, and a feminist rejection of the male gaze. Other forms of social resistance that bring sexuality and religion together include new religious movements that experiment with sexual norms and family structure. In the US in the nineteenth century a flurry of new religious movements included the Shakers (founded in the eighteenth century), who practiced celibacy and lived in sex-segregated communal settings; the Church of Jesus Christ of Latter-Day Saints, which experimented with polygyny for several decades; and the Oneida Perfectionists, who practiced *coitus interruptus* as a form of birth control, experimented with eugenics, and considered non-procreative, heterosexual intercourse between members of the community to be a beneficial form of social interaction. Mid-twentieth century new religious movements in the US included The Family (Children of God), who practiced for a number of years an evangelical method known as "flirty fishing": using sex (usually between a female member and a male potential convert) as a recruitment tool.

An equally contested intersection of religion and sexuality is that of same-sex eroticism – particularly gay, lesbian, or bisexual identity – and the Abrahamic religions of Judaism, Christianity, and Islam. The status of same-sex eroticism in these religions has varied both across gender and over time. With contemporary western understandings of sexual orientation came a medicalized approach that removed same-sex eroticism from religious discourse. As scientific and public opinion shifted during the 1960s and 1970s, homosexuality returned to being an important subject of moral and therefore religious concern. Simultaneously, self-identified gay, lesbian, and bisexual Christians and Jews began organizing their own religious communities and demanding inclusion in heterosexually dominated organizations (Wilcox 2003). In response, efforts to resist the deconstruction and reconstruction of "tradition" have come not only from conservative, heterosexual-dominated organizations but also from a new set of organizations often run by self-identified "former homosexuals": the ex-gay movement, which argues that people with same-sex desires can be healed or can at least learn to live "as God wants them to" – that is, in procreative, opposite-sex marriages (Moon 2004).

In a number of societies sexual and gender norms are closely intertwined, with deviation from expected gender roles – especially on the part of men – implying an accompanying deviation from expected sexual roles. In most cases this has little to do with religion, but especially

in cultures where religion is diffuse, there is often overlap. Early Muslim cultures, for example, knew of *mukhannathūn*, "effeminate men," some of whom were associated with passive homosexuality, and this association strengthened in later centuries, though not without significant social and religious stigma (Rowson 1991; Murray & Roscoe 1997). In India, when a man assumes the identity of a *hijra*, he becomes a member of a third sex known to be sexually attracted to men but to live as women. Once a part of royal courts, *hijras* today are considered auspicious, especially on the occasion of a wedding or a birth, but are also social outcasts. Western cultures, lacking an auspicious model of gender-crossing or same-sex eroticism in their own dominant religion, have tended to romanticize the *hijra*s in recent years while forgetting the social stigma and often the poverty that attends their lives (Nanda 1990). Also romanticized, as well as appropriated and misunderstood, is the "two-spirit" person in indigenous North American cultures. Dubbed "berdache" (a derogatory term meaning male prostitute) by white anthropologists, two-spirit people in traditional cultures adopted the gender roles of the opposite sex and were referred to by a variety of terms in their respective cultures. Some indigenous traditions recognized this phenomenon only in the male-born, while several recognized it in those born female as well, and many did not recognize it at all. In some cultures a two-spirit person would also adopt the sexual role normative to the opposite sex, pairing with a same-sex but opposite-gender partner; in other cases the expected pairing for a two-spirit person was heterosexual (but homo-gender). Furthermore, while some indigenous traditions assigned a special religious status to the two-spirit person, this was not nearly as ubiquitous as contemporary gay and lesbian cultures have often implied. Today, traditional two-spirit identities appear to be relatively rare, although there is a pan-Indian two-spirit movement that includes both the same-sex attracted and the gender diverse (Jacobs et al. 1997).

In addition to sexual orientation, other forms of sexual identity may also be combined with religion. In religions where celibacy marks an advanced practitioner, the absence of sexual practice may itself be an important identity factor. Conservative Christian teens may find a part of their identity in the True Love Waits movement, which encourages celibacy until marriage. And as Hardacre (1997) and Underwood (1999) have convincingly demonstrated, a spate of tabloid articles and spiritualists' advertisements about "spirit attacks" from aborted fetuses may have played a complex role in women's identity negotiations amid changing gender norms and sexual standards in Japan during the 1980s. Marriage also brings up a number of identity issues surrounding religion and sexuality. The most prominent in most western countries at the moment may be the legalization and religious recognition of same-sex marriage, but questions of religious intermarriage and spousal conversion have been of concern in a number of religions for quite some time.

The topic of same-sex marriage points to the intersection of religion, sexuality, and politics – three social spheres whose overlap is particularly explosive and contested. Political organizing by religious groups in the US has increasingly focused on sexuality issues since the 1960s. Conservative religious movements were appalled by the 1973 Supreme Court decision in *Roe* v. *Wade*, which legalized abortion. Liberalization of divorce laws, the legalization and public availability of a variety of contraceptives, the decriminalization and demedicalization of homosexuality, sex education in public schools, pornography, and prostitution have all been issues that have drawn religious conservatives in the US and elsewhere to band together for political purposes. Religious liberals have also organized in recent years; one interesting example in the US is Soulforce, which uses direct-action tactics to protest policies that discriminate against lesbians, gay men, bisexuals, and transgendered people in religious groups. Also of concern globally is the rise of religious nationalism as a powerful political force, of which more below.

BOUNDARIES

Sexuality and politics intersect not only in secular spheres but also within religious organizations – and that intersection is increasingly global. As women, lesbians, gay men, and bisexuals demand inclusion and rise to leadership positions within an increasing number of religious groups, those groups with international membership are forced to grapple with questions of human sexuality whose answers are often culturally bound. Further complications are introduced by the recent history of western colonialism and the ongoing tensions of postcolonial and neocolonial relationships. Within Buddhism, debates over women's roles and sometimes over same-sex eroticism have been furthered by the differing perspectives of a growing population of western converts (some of whom are themselves religious leaders) and Buddhist leaders in historically Buddhist countries. The situation is even more complicated in the Anglican Communion, which began to evangelize in the southern hemisphere during British colonial rule and now includes a sizable and thus highly politically influential number of bishops from Africa and Southeast Asia. At recent conferences of the Anglican Communion, the ordination and episcopate of women, gay men, and lesbians have been central – and divisive – issues on the agenda (Rubenstein 2004).

Religion and sexuality played important roles in the formation of individual, group, national, and international boundaries long before gay and lesbian ordination, or even women's ordination, became a central topic of religious discussion. The creation and violation of personal sexual boundaries becomes a religious issue not only when religions are responsible for defining those boundaries, but also when religious leaders use their power and prestige to gain illicit sexual access to followers. Since both sexual harassment and rape are crimes of power, it stands to reason that some religious leaders, like other figures whose social standing is relatively unassailable, would be prone to such abuse. Examples abound across religions and time periods: medieval Japanese Buddhist texts praise the "love of boys," and describe not only secret communication codes between monks and novices but also strategies for coerced sex (Faure 1998). And despite the veneration of the female consort in South Asian Tantric texts, in practice the sexual rituals of Tantra can sometimes be more exploitive than enlightening for the women involved.

In 2002 sexual abuse scandals shook the Roman Catholic Church in the US. Of particular interest in this case are not only the allegations of sexual abuse, but also the intense interest of the media in sexual abuse committed on boys by celibate priests. A century and a half earlier, non-Catholics in the US had been horrified and titillated by false reports that Catholic priests were abusing young girls; that contemporary allegations of abuse of women, and allegations against religious leaders outside Catholicism (i.e., non-celibate leaders), fail to capture the public imagination in the same way says far more about sexual and religious preoccupations in the US than it does about the Catholic Church. Further analysis of representations of Catholicism and of the Vatican's draconian, homophobic response to the scandals would be immensely fruitful (Jordan 2003).

Religion and sexuality have conspired in the creation of boundaries and the construction of Others in ways that fundamentally shape the processes of colonialism, decolonization, and globalization. At the height of European colonialism many branches of Christianity worked hand in hand with colonial powers, not only accompanying military forces or in some cases paving the way through their evangelistic efforts, but also providing part of the justification for colonialism through their constructions of colonized peoples as religiously – and therefore culturally and intellectually – inferior. Important here is the religious and, later, academic construction of colonized peoples through sexual and gendered metaphors and stereotypes. A central aspect of missionary work in many colonies was the socialization of converts and schoolchildren into European sexual norms – a process that was integral to Christianization – and colonial laws often directly forbade sexual or related practices of which Christians of the period disapproved.

As countries around the world gained independence from European colonial powers, another important sexual and often religious symbol came to the fore: the use of the human body, and especially the bodies of women, as a metaphor for the nation (Friedland 2002). Religious nationalists in some former colonies decry western fashions for women (even as some nationalist men themselves sport western clothing) and insist on the careful control of women's sexual behavior as a way of regaining and maintaining the country's strength (impregnability?) and independence. A classic example of this phenomenon is the rhetoric produced by both India and Pakistan (but especially India) in the wake of widespread kidnappings and sexual violence following the partition of India in 1947 (Menon 1998). In the US, too, sexual and religious imagery intertwine in national metaphors. A particularly instructive case is the aftermath of the September 11 attacks. "God Bless America" became a frantically repeated invocation while news reports bemoaned the "traumatic penetration" of the country and conservative Protestant leader Jerry Falwell blamed abortion doctors, feminists, and homosexuals for the attacks.

Under conditions of globalization, the cultural tensions that arise between immigrant communities and their hosts also link religion and sexuality. Concerns over western sexual mores and sexual identities sometimes attend the immigration of westerners into non-western countries, and every immigrant community struggles some way with the differences in (often religiously based) sexual morality between the home culture and the host culture. Several European countries have recently become embroiled in what could be called "Muslim panics," fearing conservative Muslim influences on their societies and political systems. Many of those anxieties center around stereotypical perceptions of Islamic sexual and gender norms, driven in part (like some colonial sexual laws) by intense scrutiny of fairly rare events: in this case, especially "honor killings" and acid attacks directed against women believed to be threatening the family's honor, generally through a violation of strictly conservative sexual and gender norms. Some non-Muslim Europeans use the brush of honor killings to tar all of Islam, forgetting that, like any other world religion, Islam is widely culturally diverse. Sexualized Muslim panics are only the most recent case in which gender, religion, sexuality, globalization, and postcolonial/neocolonial dynamics intertwine; religion and sexuality are so often integrated that a complete analysis of either often requires attention to both.

SEE ALSO: Globalization, Sexuality and; Islamic Sexual Culture; Sex and Gender; Sexual Identities; Sexual Politics; Women, Religion and

REFERENCES AND SUGGESTED
READINGS

Faure, B. (1998) *The Red Thread: Buddhist Approaches to Sexuality*. Princeton University Press, Princeton.

Friedland, R. (2002) Money, Sex, and God: The Erotic Logic of Religious Nationalism. *Sociological Theory* 20(3): 381–425.

Goss, R. (2002) *Queering Christ: Beyond Jesus Acted Up*. Pilgrim Press, Cleveland.

Hardacre, H. (1997) *Marketing the Menacing Fetus in Japan*. University of California Press, Berkeley.

Jacobs, S.-E., Thomas, W., & Lang, S. (1997) *Two-Spirit People: Native American Gender Identity, Sexuality, and Spirituality*. University of Illinois Press, Chicago.

Jordan, M. D. (2003) *Telling Truths in Church: Scandal, Flesh, and Christian Speech*. Beacon Press, Boston.

Machacek, D. W. & Wilcox, M. M. (2003) *Sexuality and the World's Religions*. ABC-CLIO, Goleta, CA.

Menon, R. (1998) Reproducing the Legitimate Community: Secularity, Sexuality, and the State in Postpartition India. In: Jeffery, P. & Basu, A. (Eds.), *Appropriating Gender: Women's Activism and Politicized Religion in South Asia*. Routledge, New York, pp. 15–32.

Moon, D. (2004) *God, Sex, and Politics: Homosexuality and Everyday Theologies*. University of Chicago Press, Chicago.

Murray, S. O. & Roscoe, W. (1997) *Islamic Homosexualities: Culture, History, and Literature*. New York University Press, New York.

Nanda, S. (1990) *Neither Man Nor Woman: The Hijras of India*. Wadsworth, Belmont, CA.

Rowson, E. K. (1991) The Effeminates of Early Medina. *Journal of the American Oriental Society* 111(4): 671–93.

Rubenstein, M.-J. (2004) An Anglican Crisis of Comparison: Intersections of Race, Gender, and Religious Authority, with Particular Reference to the Church of Nigeria. *Journal of the American Academy of Religion* 72(2): 341–65.

Underwood, M. (1999) Strategies of Survival: Women, Abortion, and Popular Religion in Contemporary Japan. *Journal of the American Academy of Religion* 67(4): 739–68.

Urban, H. (2004) *Magia Sexualis:* Sex, Secrecy, and Liberation in Modern Western Esotericism. *Journal of the American Academy of Religion* 72(3): 695–731.

White, D. G. (2003) *Kiss of the Yoginī: "Tantric Sex" in Its South Asian Contexts*. University of Chicago Press, Chicago.

Wilcox, M. M. (2003) *Coming Out in Christianity: Religion, Identity, and Community*. Indiana University Press, Bloomington.

sexuality research: ethics

Moira Carmody

Sexuality research and sex research differ in a number of important ways. Sex research focuses on the mechanics of sex and is dominated by biomedical discourses and most often framed from an "objective" stance. Sexuality research, on the other hand, recognizes power relations between women and men, between heterosexual and homosexual, and between cultures, and therefore is inherently political (Connell & Dowsett 1993). Sexuality and the research of sexuality are embedded in cultural and historical contexts. Both are embodied experiences that consider the complex dynamic meanings and activities, cultural signs, politics, and ethics that impact on its realization or repression.

Power relations are embedded in every aspect of sexuality research. As Denzin in *The Research Act* (1989) has argued, when sociologists do research they inevitably take sides for or against particular values, political bodies, and society at large. This argument includes sexuality researchers, who focus on the most intimate aspects of people's lives. Within the divergent research traditions of sociology there are a number of approaches that reflect particular forms of knowledge about sexuality and ethics. These include functionalists such as Talcott Parsons, symbolic interactionists such as Gagnon and Simon, and Plummer, feminist theorists as diverse as Dworkin and Rubin, masculinity theorists such as Connell, and poststructuralist theorists such as Foucault. While each of these perspectives varies in how it conceptualizes sexuality and gender, they all reflect particular configurations of values, ethics, and society. How sexuality researchers frame their research projects will be influenced by their commitment to or rejection of these or other social theories.

Ethical considerations include the way the research question is constructed, the topic to be studied, and the people or issue being explored, the biography and relations among researchers, the values of the funding body and other actors, and the methodology chosen by the researcher. Laud Humphreys was strongly criticized for the use of deception in his methodology when following up men who engage in impersonal sex. Ethics also includes which individuals or groups are excluded from research and whether they represent marginal or more powerful groups. Lee, reviewing research on sensitive topics, highlights how sexuality researchers may experience "stigma contagion," coming to share the stigma associated with those being studied. Citing a range of authors, he highlights how researchers may experience stereotypical expectations about sex researchers or have their work and their advancement in the academy trivialized or seen as marginal to mainstream disciplines. Sexuality research therefore raises a diversity of ethical challenges for researchers in this field.

There are several ways that sexuality researchers can seek guidance to resolve research ethics. The benchmarks for guiding research with humans has a long history within medical sciences after the Nuremberg trials. Increasingly, social sciences are paying attention to this issue. Reference to codes of ethical practice such as those of the British Sociological Association (2002) or the American Sociological Association (1999) may provide a general overview. However, much of the academic surveillance of research is carried out by university ethics committees or internal review boards (US). It appears to vary significantly between disciplines, universities, and countries. The overriding concern in deciding what is ethical research is the balance between perceived harm to an individual involved in a research project and the perceived benefits to the individual and society in general. While as a guiding principle this is worthy, the operation of this principle can create particular difficulties for sexuality researchers. As Beck in *The Risk Society* (1992) has indicated, western societies are increasingly focused around a discourse of risk and risk management. When this is combined with ethics committees dominated by a positivist and biomedical model, sexuality researchers often find worthy projects questioned. This may include challenging the "objectivity" of qualitative methodology and sampling "bias" when sexual cultures or networks are the focus of study. Regulation may extend to a focus on reporting adverse impacts of research on participants rather than balanced reporting on both positive and negative outcomes. Underpinning these challenges is the conflict between different research paradigms or attempts to silence the voices of sexual minorities through assumptions of heteronormativity and institutionalized homophobia or sexism. These challenges and how sexuality researchers and ethics committees resolve them will significantly impact on the kind of research that gets funded and the construction of knowledge. A risk management model of research, while possibly protecting individual institutions against future litigation, does little to help sexuality researchers in developing transparent ethical research practices.

There is danger in researchers feeling that all the ethical issues have been dealt with once ethics committee approval is obtained. Codes of practice assume a fixed position and deny the dynamic nature of research and a conception of ethics where meanings are subject to negotiation and redefinition. However, ethical issues confront researchers in a number of areas, including relationships in the field, informed consent, use of the Internet, representation of data, and support for researchers.

Boundaries between the researcher and the researched may be blurred when exploring sexual cultures if the researcher is a member of that culture. This occurs in many aspects of sexuality research and is a continuing issue in HIV research. Disclosing personal details to enhance a connection with an informant could result in either feeling vulnerable or being exposed to harm. The erotic subjectivity of anthropologists in the cultures they study is explored in depth in an edited collection by Kulick and Wilson (1995). Interestingly, they had great difficulty finding heterosexual male anthropologists who were willing to write about how they resolve the ethics of these contacts. Feminist critiques of research have challenged the gender blindness of much research and some have argued for attempting to equalize the power relationships as a framework for shared political struggle. This can present ethical difficulties when researchers universalize the meaning of gender and how this relates to sexuality for other women within their own or other cultures.

Regulation of sexuality research may vary between institutional settings and countries and can raise significant risks of the researcher imposing first world research processes and interpretation of findings in a less developed setting. Sensitivity to cross-cultural differences may be acknowledged intellectually by research teams, but this may not provide ethical guidance in relation to personal and research relationships with participants. It may also result in a failure to recognize the ways in which sexuality and sex practices are understood in these settings and may "spoil the field" for future research efforts. There are positive and negative possibilities of participant observation in a range of settings where sex occurs, for example, if a researcher is investigating sex work, commercial sex venues, or sadomasochism (SM) communities. What ethical code do they call on to guide their relationships with other people in the setting or their own behavior? The risks are significant, not only physically but also professionally if not handled well, as Harry Wolcott recounts in *Sneaky Kid and its Aftermath* (2002).

Gaining informed consent from research participants is central to ethical research to ensure there is no coercion and that participants understand the meaning of consent. Some ethics bodies require written consent, but this can raise particular dilemmas for sexuality researchers. Participant observation research is a case in point. It may not be appropriate to pull out a consent form in a sex venue or when interviewing sex workers or young homeless people. In situations where people are justifiably suspicious of authority figures or "outsiders," the demand for written consent may work against gaining important knowledge from informants. Longitudinal studies may also present other dilemmas. Consent given at the beginning of a project may need to be revisited further into the project as participants' circumstances or researchers change.

Sexuality research using the Internet extends ethical issues into the virtual world. As this is a relatively new domain for sexuality research, there are to date only limited guidelines to assist researchers. Given the anonymity of cyberspace, it may be that respondents are less cautious in this context than in a face-to-face setting. Consent is complex in this setting and there needs to be a mechanism to ensure who is actually consenting and some way to verify their "identity." Privacy issues may also need to be addressed given the problems of computer hacking and software-sharing programs. The Internet may provide increased opportunities for researching individuals and groups who may be hard to recruit, for example, same-sex-attracted young people or groups with specific

fetishes. Research with under-age young people is often contentious. Yet important research with young people about sexuality could significantly add to community knowledge and lead to improvement in services targeted to their needs. However, fears of the sexual exploitation of children and young people make this an area that many ethics committees are reluctant to support without parental approval (Binik et al. 1999).

The interpretation of data and their dissemination raises another set of challenges for all researchers, including those in the field of sexuality. Decisions about what methodology will be chosen to analyze data not only impact on the rigor of the project but also highlight "the crisis of representation" facing all social science. Ethical decisions are reflected in the choice of theoretical approach, which part of the data to include and exclude, and what interpretation is made of findings. Postmodern approaches have challenged the "truth" claims of positivist research. This suggests the need to be very transparent about the partial nature of the stories told and to locate findings from the point of view of the "historically and culturally situated individual."

Sexuality researchers enter the field from a range of disciplines, including sociology, anthropology, criminology, psychology, history, cultural studies, and political science. The interdisciplinary nature of current sexuality research means that researchers often come to the issue with a range of expectations and experiences shaped by age, gender, sexuality, culture background, and (dis)ability. Their disciplinary background may provide some frameworks for guiding their behavior in relation to sexuality research. Research teams may provide an important context for ethical issues to be debated and resolved. However, many researchers work alone, or may be inexperienced or a long way from their home base. In addition, even experienced researchers may find themselves facing ethical and personal difficulties once the research project has commenced. While most ethics committees are focused on ensuring no harm is done to research participants and ensuring they have phone numbers for counseling or follow-up support, there is less formal acknowledgment of the need to prevent harm to researchers. This is relevant during fieldwork or afterwards when findings are published and they may come under intense scrutiny from disaffected individuals or organizations. Developing mechanisms of support during fieldwork, including debriefing and after the completion of projects, is fundamental to ethical research practice and necessary for new and inexperienced researchers, including postgraduates.

The development of ethical practice in relation to sexuality research requires a much more dynamic and complex process than a purely regulatory approach. The sensitive and intimate nature of sexuality research and the multiple sites and cultural contexts in which it is carried out suggest the need to encourage ethical subjectivity in researchers. Central to this would be a focus on reflexivity. Ethical subjects, following Michel Foucault, *Ethics: The Essential Works*, reflect on how we constitute ourselves as moral subjects of our own actions, and essential to this subjectivity is caring for others. Jeffrey Weeks proposes a sexual ethics based on radical pluralism. This approach moves away from an absolutist model of ethics. Instead, it suggests ethics need to be developed based on the social production of sexualities and the complex ways in which they are embedded in diverse power relations. Zygmunt Bauman (1993) argues for a postmodern ethics in which there is a greater awareness of making ethical choices in every part of life and the profoundly ambivalent nature of these choices. Plummer (2001) argues for a much clearer discussion of these issues amongst researchers that does not always rely on abstract principles but takes seriously the stories researchers provide of their own situated ethical problems and decision-making.

SEE ALSO: Ethics, Research; Observation, Participant and Non-Participant; Sexual Practices; Sexuality Research: History; Sexuality Research: Methods; Survey Research

REFERENCES AND SUGGESTED READINGS

Bauman, Z. (1993) *Postmodern Ethics*. Blackwell, Oxford.

Binik, Y. M., Mah, K., & Kiesler, S. (1999) Ethical Issues in Conducting Sex Research on the Internet. *Journal of Sex Research* 36(1): 82–90.

Connell, R. W. & Dowsett, G. W. (Eds.) (1993) *Rethinking Sex: Social Theory and Sexuality Research*. Temple University Press, Philadelphia.

Kulick, D. & Wilson, M. (Eds.) (1995) *Taboo: Sex, Identity, Erotic Subjectivity in Anthropological Fieldwork*. Routledge, London.

Plummer, K. (2001) *Documents of Life 2: An Invitation to a Critical Humanism*. Sage, Thousand Oaks, CA.

Punch, M. (1994) The Politics and Ethics in Qualitative Research. In: Denzin, N. K. & Lincoln, Y. S. (Eds.), *Handbook of Qualitative Research*. Sage, Thousand Oaks, CA, pp. 83–97.

sexuality research: history

Lesley A. Hall

Research on sexuality began as a complex and interdisciplinary endeavor. Although it was, like so many of today's fields, a product of the nineteenth-century belief in the power of rational scientific investigation, it was very much a latecomer. F. H. A. Marshall commented in his 1910 synthesis, *The Physiology of Reproduction*, that physiologists had made comprehensive studies of all other bodily functions, but reproduction had not been the object of sustained research. Marshall was thus obliged to bring together scraps of evidence from diverse sources, from anthropology via medicine to animal husbandry. Research on sexuality was similarly affected by a scarcity of materials and taboos against investigation, and the threat of prosecution for publication.

The lack of institutional and financial support, and the general unacceptability of the subject, meant that large projects using the research protocols emerging in medicine and the social sciences were an impossibility. Thus research into sexuality initially tended to be based in the analysis of phenomena brought to the investigator's attention (cases encountered by doctors, legal trials, self-observation, reports from friends and colleagues, letters from readers), and the collation of evidence gleaned from a wide variety of fields – history, literature, medicine, and the growing field of anthropology and ethnography. Theories might be engendered from impressionistic, limited, biased, and unrepresentative empirical materials. The subject was marginalized and stigmatized and did not lead to any of the usual professional rewards. Such research, therefore, was most often conducted by those who had some kind of personal motivation to pursue it.

The wider roots of the desire to investigate sexuality were several. The rise in urbanization and consequent opportunities for social mobility had led to the breakdown of traditional forms of control over sexual behavior. Prostitution was on a larger scale and much more visible in such conurbations. They also enabled previously isolated individuals, such as men who desired other men, to meet one another and to create subcultures based on identity. Darwin's theories of the role of sexual selection in evolution provided an important legitimating as well as analytical device for thinking about the subject. Venereal diseases were widespread and incurable. The rise of a social purity movement aimed at improving both the morality and the health of society made powerful representations for the benefits of talking about sexual matters rather than concealing them under a cloak of taboo. To provide proper knowledge of the workings of the body required that these should be understood, with healthy scientific information replacing old wives' tales and furtive smut. A developing women's movement destabilized accepted ideas about marriage and sexual morality and current notions of gender. All these elements were turning sexuality into something with social, rather than purely individual, resonances, while undermining assumptions about "the natural."

PRELIMINARY APPROACHES

Initially, specific problems were considered more or less in isolation. Concern over prostitution, and its concomitant of sexually transmitted diseases, led to interest in how and why women became prostitutes. Facilitated by the existing French system of regulation, sanitarian Jean-Baptiste Parent-Duchâtelet made a study of Parisian prostitutes, based on incarcerated women registered with the police, excluding casual and clandestine prostitution and the higher echelons. This major study was not published until after the author's death (1836). The British surgeon William Acton, in his own work on the subject (1858), deplored the fact that, because of both the differing organization of the trade and greater moral prudery, such a detailed study could not be undertaken in Britain. The American Abraham Flexner, in *Prostitution in Europe* (1919), revealed that covert, clandestine, and casual prostitution flourished even in countries which imposed regulatory systems of control and medical inspection.

Such studies were undertaken by men and focused on women, or a particular class of women, as a "problem," on whom they could turn a scientific and pathologizing gaze. The idea that the consumer of prostitution might also be a problem to be addressed was only raised later in the nineteenth century, by the feminist wing of the developing social purity movement, in a political, not merely moral, critique of social acceptance of male promiscuity. However, as studies on the subject continued to comment into the final decades of the twentieth century, the male purchaser of sexual services remained shadowy.

A rather different situation pertained in the case of men defined by the term coined by the Hungarian Kertebeny in 1869, "homosexual." While there were sporadic medical reports on cases involving men desiring other men, and a medico-forensic literature on "sodomy," the debate on homosexuality was generated, initially, by men trying to understand their own stigmatized desires, in many countries subject to brutal criminal penalties. Among the resources drawn upon were changing scientific understandings of the body and of anatomical development. The pioneering figure Karl Heinrich Ulrichs, initially under the pseudonym "Numa Numantius" and then in his own name, published a series of monographs on same-sex love in which he posited a theory of gender inversion (the female psyche in the male body, and vice versa) of congenital origin. He endeavored to gain medical allies, and influenced later work by the psychiatrists Richard von Krafft-Ebing and Carl Westphal, although he considered that their views were distorted by seeing an undue proportion of criminal or insane, rather than healthily functioning, homosexuals, leading merely to replacing concepts of homosexuality as sin or crime with a disease model.

While the evolution of ideas about the homosexual was a major concern in discussions of sexual "deviation" in the late nineteenth century, and has been the main focus of scholarship in the area, other phenomena which could not be assimilated to a post-Darwinian evolutionary model of the role of sexual selection in reproduction were also analyzed. French psychologist Alfred Binet invented the term "fetishism," given more extensive currency by Krafft-Ebing, who himself defined "sadism" and "masochism." Oosterhuis in *Stepchildren of Nature* (2000) reveals a significant subgroup of male masochists among Krafft-Ebing's patients and informants. A group generally marginal to these discussions was women (possibly because being a woman was already considered deviant or at least problematic). There was some discussion of the lesbian, though there were far fewer cases reported in the growing literature on homosexuality, but "masochism" was seen as innate to the female nature and thus only a problem when it manifested in men.

THE FIELD DEVELOPS

Around the turn of the nineteenth and twentieth centuries several writers began to pull together the various strands within which sexual matters were being analyzed – the public health and morality concern with prostitution and venereal diseases, the legal and medical debates on homosexuality, concerns over marriage and reproduction (inflected by the theory of eugenics adumbrated by Darwin's cousin Francis Galton), anthropological reports on other cultures, arguments for the desirability of general sexual enlightenment, medical cases, historical data – into broader syntheses. A leading figure in this new development was the British doctor and literary figure Havelock Ellis, who between 1897 and 1927 produced his massive seven-volume study, *Studies in the Psychology of Sex*, the first volume of which, *Sexual Inversion*, was prosecuted for obscenity, a traumatic event leading Ellis to have the rest of the series published in the US. Although Magnus Hirschfeld began as a homosexual rights activist anxious to repeal

or moderate the German laws on the subject, over his lengthy career as researcher, educator, and campaigner his copious writings covered a much wider range of sexual issues. He also created connections between isolated individuals in different countries working in the field by establishing journals, setting up an Institute for Sexual Science in Berlin (destroyed by the Nazis in 1933), and facilitating international networks through holding congresses. Iwan Bloch took a similar broad and deep view, in particular emphasizing the importance of historical understanding. Such figures laid a necessary foundation for further work by synthesizing materials from a diversity of sources to establish a picture of what was known about sexuality. A very different approach to the study of sex, emphasizing the depths of the psyche rather than the broad sweep of societies in time and space, was that evolved by Sigmund Freud and the early psychoanalytic movement. Freud made the significant observation that understanding the process by which heterosexuality developed was just as problematic as discovering the "cause" of homosexuality and that the relation between desire and its object was by no means a given.

Well behind investigation into the other endocrine secretions, work was undertaken on the sex hormones. The topic had been cast into some disrepute as a result of the Franco-American Brown-Sequard's sensationalized "rejuvenation" treatments of the 1890s, and respectability was further compromised by similar promises from Steinach and Voronoff in the interwar years. For several decades research remained predicated on the assumption that gender-specific ovarian and testicular hormones influenced sexual identity and functioning: this was discovered not to be the case by the late 1920s. With the development of biochemical assaying techniques, research moved into the realm of chemists in the laboratory – a degree of removal from the messy processes of the body and direct connection with sexual functioning which doubtless influenced the increasing scientific respectability of the field and its access to resources, but also led to a loss of connection with research into sex within its social context.

In the United States, the issues vigorously debated and discussed within American sex radical and reform movements of the mid-nineteenth century had been, if not silenced, seriously muffled by the rise of the movement for aggressive censorship of sexual materials embodied in Anthony Comstock. Thus initiatives such as Clelia Mosher's 1890s survey of women's experiences of and attitudes toward sex, unpublished until the 1970s, had no influence and established no tradition. For several decades Robert Latou Dickinson privately accumulated detailed information on the patients in his gynecological practice, including drawings (later photographs) of their genital anatomy. Prince A. Morrow brought European debates on the venereal disease (VD) problem and the ineffectuality of policing prostitutes to the US and tied these in to concerns over marriage. Research became legitimized by the arguments of improving marriage and reducing disease: studying what went wrong with sexual lives would assist in working out how to ensure things went right. A number of surveys were undertaken and several published: G. V. Hamilton's *A Research in Marriage* (1929), Katharine Bement Davies's *Factors in the Sex Life of 2200 Women* (1929), Robert L. Dickinson and Lura Beam's *A Thousand Marriages* (1931) and *The Single Woman* (1934).

It was in this context of the concept of strengthening marriage through better understanding of sex that Alfred Kinsey was able to inaugurate his mammoth enterprise of researching the sexual life of the human male and female. Focusing on behaviors rather than on emotions or attitudes, he collected a huge amount of material through face-to-face interviews with unprecedentedly huge numbers of men and women. The fruits of his researches were published as *Sexual Behavior in the Human Male* (1948) and *Sexual Behavior in the Human Female* estions about how representative they were, a factor of which Kinsey was well aware. He tried to obtain 100 percent responses from any group or community studied, made particular attempts to gain access to groups that might otherwise be underrepresented, and designated certain areas as necessitating future research projects. Kinsey's work remains controversial, but also still profoundly influential.

Kinsey and his team undertook, among other things, some direct study of sexual intercourse, but the researchers who fully broke this final barrier were William Masters and Virginia Johnson, who undertook extensive mapping of the processes of arousal and satisfaction using human participants in the laboratory, assisted by technological developments. Their work has been critiqued for its attempt to ignore context and social aspects of sexual interaction by selecting specifically for participants who were capable of functioning in the laboratory milieu, and, in the case of women, were readily orgasmic, and on this basis creating a one-size-fits-all model of the process of arousal, orgasm, and resolution.

Research into sexuality followed a path from the specific to the very general synthesis, succeeded by a branching out into new separate paths concentrating on distinct aspects (the physiological, the social, the psychological). Lack of coordination between different approaches has remained a problem.

SEE ALSO: Ellis, Havelock; Fetishism; Freud, Sigmund; Hirschfeld, Magnus; Homosexuality; Kinsey, Alfred; Krafft-Ebing, Richard von; Prostitution; Sadomasochism; Sexual Deviance; Sexuality Research: Ethics; Sexuality Research: Methods; Survey Research

REFERENCES AND SUGGESTED READINGS

Bland, L. & Doan, L. (Eds.) (1998) *Sexology in Culture: Labelling Bodies and Desires*. Polity Press, Cambridge.

Brecher, E. (1970) *The Sex Researchers*. André Deutsch, London.

Bullough, V. (1994) *Science in the Bedroom: A History of Sex Research*. Basic Books, New York.

Eder, F., Hall, L., & Hekma, G. (Eds.) (1999) *Sexual Cultures in Europe: National Histories*. Manchester University Press, Manchester.

Gathorne-Hardy, J. (1998) *Alfred C. Kinsey: Sex the Measure of All Things. A Biography*. Chatto & Windus, London.

Jones, J. H. (1997) *Alfred C. Kinsey: A Public/Private Life*. Norton, New York.

Oosterhuis, H. (2000) *Stepchildren of Nature: Krafft-Ebing, Psychiatry, and the Making of Sexual Identity*. University of Chicago Press, Chicago.

Porter, R. & Hall, L. (1995) *The Facts of Life: The Creation of Sexual Knowledge in Britain, 1650–1950*. Yale University Press, London and New Haven.

Robinson, P. (1989 [1976]) *The Modernization of Sex: Havelock Ellis, Alfred Kinsey, William Masters, and Virginia Johnson*, new edn. Harper & Row, New York.

Sengoopta, C. (2005) *The Glands of Life*. University of Chicago Press, Chicago.

Terry, J. (1999) *An American Obsession: Science, Medicine, and Homosexuality in Modern Society*. University of Chicago Press, Chicago.

Tiefer, L. (1994) *Sex is Not a Natural Act, and Other Essays*. HarperCollins, New York.

sexuality research: methods

Julia A. Ericksen and Eugene P. Ericksen

As Kinsey and others discovered to their cost, sex research is fraught with problems for researchers and must be managed carefully. In the US, Congress has cut or threatened the funding in recent decades for two national surveys of sexual behavior: a study of massage parlor workers and a study of sexual risk-taking, among other topics. And those who publish research invite trouble, as the University of Minnesota Press found when it published Judith Levine's *Harmful to Minors*.

Although researchers have been concerned about this problem for over 100 years, Kinsey was the first to discuss it explicitly. Worried abut guarding the confidentiality of the thousands of respondents who agreed to share their sex histories, he trained his hand-picked interviewers to learn the questions and write the answers in carefully guarded code, and he kept locks on all the materials in his institute. Even so, in 1954, when Congress investigated the Rockefeller Foundation to punish it for opposing the House Un-American Activities Committee, the only issue raised was their funding of Kinsey's research. As a result, the funding ceased.

While sociologists argue that we become sexual just like we become anything else, those who engage in sexuality research recognize that their work differs from that of others, for the reasons outlined above. These researchers have responded to the perceived dangers by careful management. Many sociologists of sexuality write theoretical articles, or use small numbers of qualitative interviews with carefully selected volunteer respondents, or undertake historical research using texts as their data source. Such studies cannot usually be generalized to the population of interest. Researchers who undertake quantitative work justify their carefully picked topics by citing compelling social reasons.

In addition, researchers have ignored methodological problems associated with asking sensitive questions for fear of inviting criticism discrediting their results. For example, there has been an enormous amount of research on voting behavior in the United States in response to the difficult problems associated with getting an accurate account of the vote and with predicting who will vote and how in forthcoming elections. Until recently, there has been no comparable body of research on sexual behavior surveys.

In the last decade or so the picture has changed, and major research centers have begun to undertake methodological research on sex surveys. In spite of Foucault's declaration that talk about sex led to self-policing, not to liberation, and even in the face of much discourse intended to control sexuality, most would agree that attitudes towards sexuality are more liberal and facilitate more open discussion of sexual behavior than previously. Surveys are one kind of open discussion about sex. In addition, the devastation caused by AIDS has provided ample justification for prying into the private lives of individuals.

Much of this research has been undertaken in the United States, and this is the focus of our discussion. However, a few examples of important research elsewhere should be mentioned. Here too, much of the impetus has been HIV transmission. When Congress cut the funding for a national survey of adults, the researchers at the University of Chicago were able to field a survey without support from the Robert Wood Johnson Foundation, but it was much smaller that originally planned. When the British government cut the funding for a similar survey, the Welcome Foundation funded a large national survey and a decade later the government funded a repeat. From the beginning, one of the researchers, Kaye Wellings, took an interest in data quality. A major research focus was behavioral change over time, so she used a series of techniques to ascertain whether reported changes in socially disapproved of behavior between 1990 and 2000 resulted from actual behavioral change. And at the Australian Research Centre in Sex, Health and Society, researchers interested in HIV transmission have explored such topics as how to measure sexual behavior in high-risk venues and the validity of self-reported condom use.

What follows is a brief description of some American research on some of the problems identified in sex surveys, and examples of attempts to solve these problems.

SELECTING THE POPULATION TO INTERVIEW

Kinsey refused to use probability sampling, even after its efficacy was explained to him, because he believed he could not interview respondents who were not volunteers and because he did not understand that the greatest variety was not the same as a representation of the population. Researchers now understand and use modern sampling techniques with great success. Survey response rates have declined as a result of caller ID and increased consumer weariness over telephone abuses, but they are not higher on sex surveys than other surveys. For example, the Chicago survey (the National Health and Social Life Survey) undertaken by Edward Laumann and colleagues at the National Opinion Research Center (NORC) in 1992, reported a 79 percent response rate, which compares favorably with between 75 percent and 79 percent for NORC's General Social Survey (GSS).

There are still major sampling issues, particularly in the lack of a national probability sample of men who have sex with men, because it is difficult and time consuming to sample rare populations, especially when the selection factor concerns behavior that is not always admitted to.

PROBLEMS WITH THE INTERVIEW

Several interviewing problems continue to challenge researchers. Kinsey believed erroneously

that respondents would be more willing to unburden themselves to middle-class white men with "non-ethnic" names. Today, most interviewers are women, and most experts regard women as better interviewers than men. With sex surveys, however, some argue that accuracy improves with interviewers of the same gender as respondents, particularly when asking about sensitive topics such as rape or anal intercourse. When AIDS first appeared, surveyors of gay men argued that self-identified gay male interviewers were more successful than women or heterosexual men.

The mere presence of an interviewer may affect response accuracy. When Laumann and colleagues (1994) asked respondents for the number of lifetime sexual partners, women reported an average of 3 male partners and men an average of 12 female. Both of these averages cannot be correct. One problem with asking this question is that it places a burden on respondents. For people with many partners, this question is difficult to answer. They may estimate rather than enumerate, particularly given interview time constraints. Those who enumerate may forget some partners, especially when constrained to give an answer quickly. Brown and Sinclair (1999) asked college students their total number of sexual partners, and then asked how the number was derived. When men and women used the same technique the distribution of number of partners was similar by gender, but enumeration produced lower tallies than estimation and men were more likely to estimate than women. Thus the authors concluded that the difference in results is not a product of intentional deception.

Not all researchers agree. Many recognize that reputational issues for men and women push the genders in opposite directions, such that some men deliberately overestimate their lifetime sexual partners and some women deliberately underestimate. If so, the more a respondent feels anonymous and unknown to even the interviewer, the more accurate the data should be. This was shown by Tourangeau and Smith (1996) in a comparison of computer-assisted personal interviewing with computer-assisted self-administered interviewing. Men using self-administered questionnaires reported fewer sexual partners than men listening to interviewers, and women reported more.

QUESTIONNAIRE DESIGN

Researchers recognize that respondents have to complete a number of tasks in answering a question. In addition to the issues of retrieval discussed above, they must comprehend the question. Since questions about sexual behavior are not part of everyday polite conversation, there may not be general agreement about the word meaning. When Bill Clinton stated that oral/genital sex did not constitute "having sex," about half the American population agreed with him. Furthermore, there are social class and educational variations in sexual terminology. Kinsey realized that less well-educated respondents would not understand "masturbation," so he used terms like "jerk-off" instead. However, since "jerk-off" would offend the better educated, he used masturbation where he deemed it appropriate.

Researchers today want to use the same words for all because wording changes affect answers, but problems of comprehension remain. Laumann et al. (1994) approached the masturbation problem with a written definition: "By masturbation, we mean self-sex or self-stimulation, that is, stimulating your genitals (sex organs) to the point of arousal but not necessarily to orgasm or climax." Thus, in order not to offend by using "jerk-off," they used several difficult words, one of which even got its own additional definition. And those who cannot understand such terms tend to be demographically concentrated. Binson and Catania found that although only 4 percent and 5 percent, respectively, said they had difficulty understanding "vaginal intercourse" and "anal intercourse," 20 percent and 25 percent of those with less than 12 years of schooling reported difficulty.

With sensitive questions, researchers may list alternative responses to a question so that the respondent can pick a category rather than reveal their actual answer. However, when social desirability is an issue, respondents may pick one of the central categories, on the grounds that this is going to appear average or normal. And the respondents may not volunteer information needed to understand their responses. For example, opinion questions on controversial topics may not record strength of the opinion. Schuman and Presser (1996) showed the importance of this in a study of attitudes towards abortion. In the GSS most respondents (58 percent) favored legal abortion for married women, but those opposing this right were much more likely to consider it to be a very important issue (49 percent) than those in favor (21 percent). In a follow-up study, 65 percent said they agreed with abortion on demand in the early months of pregnancy, but 70 percent of those opposed described their views as very strong or extremely strong, compared to only 25 percent of those in favor. Finally, almost 20 percent of women against abortion on demand had given money and/or written a letter for the cause, compared to just over 5 percent of those in favor. Even though most Americans support a woman's right to choose, activists are to be found substantially in the opposition.

Finally, researchers are sometimes unclear as to the question they want answering. When Kinsey asked questions about homosexuality, he asked about desire as well as about behavior because he assumed some people wanted to engage in same-gender sex but lacked the courage to act on their desires. Based on the result of these questions he placed each respondent on his scale from 0 (exclusively heterosexual) to 6 (exclusively homosexual). He assumed that desire could be added to behavior to provide an estimate of "natural" homoerotic behavior in a non-repressive society. Laumann and colleagues asked separate questions about behavior, about desire, and about identity and found differences in the incidence and distribution of each. Identity – that is, self-identifying as gay, lesbian, or bisexual – proved less frequent than the report of same-gender desire or behavior. Just over 10 percent of men and slightly fewer women reported any same-gender sexual activity or interest. Of these, only one quarter of the men and 15 percent of the women reported same-gender desire, behavior, and identity. Most women reported only desire, with some reporting desire and behavior and some reporting only behavior. The pattern was the same for the men, although men were less likely to report only desire and more likely to report only behavior. This becomes important when we consider that in studying AIDS, we should want to know which men have sex with other men, not which men consider themselves to be gay.

DATA ANALYSIS

Researchers now understand that their biases can influence the outcome of their data analysis, and they use sophisticated data analysis techniques to be more certain of their conclusions. Yet the questions they ask of the data reveal a point of view. Laumann and colleagues were careful to present their findings as evidence of the conservative nature of American sexual behavior, pointing out, for example, that the modal number of lifetime sexual partners was one and that married individuals reported the highest rates of sexual satisfaction. In doing so, they chose to emphasize the conservative sexual behavior of the majority of Americans instead of the libidinous minority. This was reassuring to researchers who had been accused of attempting to promote sexual hedonism in Americans by normalizing extreme behavior.

This brief description of modern practice suggests that a history of sexual behavior surveys is a history of the growing sophistication of researchers and the increasing certainty of their conclusions. In order for this to be the case, researchers would have to be neutral observers of sexual behavior, an unlikely proposition in a world where no one escapes pressure to monitor personal sexual standards and desires. In addition, sexual behavior would be independent of history and culture, and questions such as the proportion of gays in the population would be technical, not political, and they would not be historically specific. While survey improvements have produced more accurate reflections of historical moments, surveys do not divulge universal truths, only those relative to their time and place.

Surveys teach us not only about sexual behavior in America and elsewhere, but also about the beliefs shaping sexual behavior, and about the concerns driving researchers to ask questions. And as survey practice has improved, the ensuing descriptions of sexual practice not only provide a behavioral control, but they also normalize the desires of those who learn there are others like them.

SEE ALSO: Abortion as a Social Problem; AIDS, Sociology of; Health Risk Behavior; Interviewing, Structured, Unstructured, and Postmodern; Kinsey, Alfred; Methods; Random Sample; Sexuality Research: Ethics; Sexuality Research: History; Survey Research

REFERENCES AND SUGGESTED READINGS

Brown, N. R. & Sinclair, R. C. (1999) Estimating the Lifetime Numbers of Sexual Partners: Men and Women Do It Differently. *Journal of Sex Research* 36: 292–7.

Catania, J. A. (1999) A Framework for Conceptualizing Reporting Bias and its Antecedents in Interviews Assessing Human Sexuality. *Journal of Sex Research* 36: 25–38.

Copas, A. J. et al. (2002) The Accuracy of Reported Sensitive Sexual Behavior Change in Britain: Exploring the Extent of Change 1999–2000. *Sexually Transmitted Infections* 78: 26–30.

Ericksen, J. A. (1999) *Kiss and Tell: Surveying Sex in the Twentieth Century.* Harvard University Press, Cambridge, MA.

Laumann, E. O., Gagnon, J. H., Michael, R. T., & Michaels, S. (1994) *The Social Organization of Sexuality,* Appendix A. University of Chicago Press, Chicago.

Schuman, H. & Presser, S. (1996) *Questions and Answers in Attitude Surveys.* Sage, New York.

Sudman, S., Bradburn, N. M., & Schwartz, N. (1996) *Thinking About Answers: The Application of Cognitive Processes to Survey Methodology.* Jossey-Bass, San Francisco.

Turangeau, R. & Smith, T. W. (1996) Asking Sensitive Questions. *Public Opinion Quarterly* 60: 275–304.

sexuality and sport

Caroline Fusco

Michel Foucault (1978), one of the most influential historians of sexuality, argued that sex and sexuality became a pivot for the organization and control of life in the modern world, and that sex and sexuality are increasingly central to human affairs to the extent that much of contemporary life has been organized around these concepts.

Although the relation between sexuality and sport serves as a central structure for body/identity/gender meanings, sexuality was a neglected area of inquiry in sports studies until the mid-1990s. Sport has long been a site for the reproduction of difference, particularly the naturalization of sexual differences, but sexuality occupied a somewhat "absent presence" in sport sociological research until the late 1980s, when sports sociologists explicitly addressed this topic. Since that time, scholars in the sociology of sport have figured prominently in the critique of historical and cultural forms of sexuality and the ways that sport serves as a site for constructing and policing sexualities and both reproducing and resisting heterosexism and the heterosexualization of sport-related forms (Birrell & Cole 1994).

Although there are many sexual orientations (heterosexual, homosexual, bisexual, transgendered, transsexual, queer, etc.), the study of sexuality in physical education and sport has been characterized by the assumption that "sexuality" is non-normative; that is, the study of sexuality and sport has historically (and sometimes in the contemporary moment) been understood as the study of homosexuality or other "deviant" sexualities and sport. Such an approach assumes that heterosexuals do not have "a sexuality," and it has interfered with developing a fuller theoretical and empirical understanding of sexuality and sport.

Prior to the late 1980s, research on sport and sexuality was primarily framed within a socio-psychological framework and focused on the role conflict that women athletes experienced while participating in sports and the strategies they used to cope with the contradictions that arose between competing in sport – historically and socially constructed as a masculine practice – and their feminine gender role. Critics argued that all of this social psychologically oriented scholarship was based on the faulty assumptions that all women athletes were heterosexual, and that "feminine" always implied heterosexuality. These assumptions led researchers to overlook the experiences of women athletes who did not define themselves as heterosexual and identified as gay or lesbian. Lesbianism was thereby erased from women's sports. This "conspiracy of silence" meant that lesbian athletes were ignored, shunned, and constrained to remain invisible in sports, and the lesbian label was used to intimidate lesbians and heterosexual women. As a result, attempts by women athletes to challenge socially constructed gender relations in sport were undermined and sports continued to valorize heterosexuality.

Feminist theorists in the 1990s disrupted the conspiracy of silence by exposing homophobia in women's sport and physical education, and making visible the experiences of athletes, coaches, and physical education teachers who identified as gay or lesbian. Research identified the heterosexual and homophobic discrimination inherent in women's sports and validated a proliferation of accounts from lesbian athletes, coaches, and physical education teachers in North American schools that revealed how they are demonized and the identity-management strategies they must use to survive and resist systemic discrimination (Fusco 1998). Historical research has documented longstanding tensions between lesbians and heterosexual women in sport, and demonstrated that the institutionalization of homophobia in sport and physical education is grounded in sexology discourses popularized in the 1930s (Cahn 1994): these discourses heterosexualized women's physical activity by identifying beauty, sexual attractiveness, and male companionship as necessary affirmations of womanhood.

No single theory has informed scholarly work on sexuality and sport. Theoretical and methodological diversity has led to multiple questions about sexuality and sport. A combination of qualitative research strategies, surveys, and in-depth interviews has been used to present rich and often painful descriptions of the multiple realities of lesbians in sport. Theoretically, much of the early work on sexuality was based on liberal or radical feminist perspectives. *Liberal feminists* reported the oppression lesbians experienced; documented their feelings of being threatened, silenced, and excluded; and suggested that lesbian athletes, like other women athletes, wanted only to play and be recognized as athletes, not as lesbians. *Radical feminists* continue to critique this approach because it depoliticizes sport at the same time that it reproduces heterosexuality, gender normativity, and patriarchy in women's sport. Radical feminists document the links among sport, sexuality, and gender politics and make explicit the relationship between individual discriminatory behavior and institutionalized homophobia and heterosexism, which they argue maintains traditional gender roles, and bolsters masculinity while maintaining male privilege and control in sport. Most radical feminist scholars use a social constructionist framework (where sexuality is interpreted as socially and historically contingent) rather than an essentialist one (where sexuality is interpreted as a phenomenon common to all humans of every culture and time), and focus on the voices of lesbian athletes and their stories of oppression, silence, and marginalization. This approach has been informative, but it often ignores stories of lesbian agency, disruption, and radical resistance to the systemic heteronormativity of the sports world.

While the lesbian experience in sport has been thoroughly examined, little attention is paid to the experiences of gay men in sports. Pronger's *The Arena of Masculinity* (1990) remains the most comprehensive and theoretically rigorous examination of homosexuality in sport. Pronger reveals that the presumed masculine and heterosexual world of sport is also a potentially homoerotic world for gay men. Yet, because sport is an arena where male aggression and violence is encouraged, this homoerotic potential is stifled and violently suppressed. Masculinity in sports is solidified through the marginalization of homosexuality, which is vilified and mocked in songs and "drag" performances, while heterosexuality is confirmed in locker room banter that glorifies "heterosexual conquest." While silence surrounds lesbians in women's sport, there is near-complete denial about the presence of gay men in sport. The pervasive expectation that male athletes are heterosexual makes it almost impossible for gay men to come out in sports, and legitimizes threats of homophobic violence. The assumption that gay men do not participate in aggressive male sports confirms the two sex/gender classification system, which codes lesbians as masculine and gay men as effeminate. Therefore, men who compete in aesthetic sports are denigrated and labeled as gay, and this has led to a remasculinizing of these sports by emphasizing strength and power.

The two strands of theorizing that have emerged from initial investigations of homosexuality in sports are (1) sport as a site for reproducing aggressive hyper-heterosexual masculinity (Messner & Sabo 1994; Burstyn 1999) and (2) the erotic potential of men's sports and the ways that homophobia regulates the homosocial heterosexual milieu of men's sports and prevents them from slipping into homoeroticism (Pronger 1999).

Contemporary theorizing about gender, sex, sexuality, and sport demonstrates an increasing awareness and application of postmodern, poststructuralist, queer, postcolonial, and cultural geography theories to the study of sexuality and sport. Although each of these "new" theories provides a unique approach to the study of sexuality and sport, all of them are based on possibilities for rethinking sexuality and sport. Scholars using them are interested in the social, historical, and political discourses that produce sexuality and the ways that sexuality has consistently been marked as white, middle class, and able bodied. Liberal interpretations of sexuality as an essential, monolithic, homogeneous or fixed identity category are widely discounted as more scholars focus their attention on the intersectionality of gender, sexuality, race, and class (Collins 2004). Poststructuralists in sport studies deconstruct the discourses that organize sexuality, the body, and the sex/gender dimorphic system. Queer theorists explore the borders of sexual identities, communities, and politics and how categories such as heterosexual, gay, lesbian, and queer emerge, while also working to destabilize and disrupt the heterosexual/homosexual binary. While earlier scholarship incorporated certain epistemological and ontological assumptions about the categories "lesbian," "gay" and "heterosexual," queer theorists now question these essentialisms and suggest that all sexual identities are continually performed. According to Butler (2004), a democratic sexual society requires that people *undo gender*. While it is now recognized that a universal "homosexual" identity does not exist, early studies in the sociology of sport, which examined "lesbian" and "homosexual" experiences in sport, provided an important step in the analysis of sexuality and sport. They served as strategic and anti-oppressive scholarship that brought the experiences of lesbian and gay athletes out of the sports closet.

More recently, scholars using cultural geography have examined how heteronormative spaces of sport are a determinant of homosexual experiences. This research demonstrates that normative sport spaces can be disrupted through lesbian and gay presence. Scholars have particularly focused on the Gay Games as a potential site for queer disruption, despite some concern that the forces of commodity have coopted and normalized them. Likewise, recent decisions by the International Olympic Committee (IOC) to allow transsexual athletes to compete in the Olympic Games have garnered the attention of sports sociologists. The IOC's decision appears to acknowledge the continuum of sexualities espoused by queer theorists, and might be heralded as a move forward in human rights in relation to sexuality and sport. However, scholars are closely examining the regulations and requirements concerning transsexual athletes with respect to how this discourse remains embedded in the two sex/gender classification system. While the IOC appears to be recognizing transsexuals' rights to participate, scholars are skeptical that these policies will disrupt heterosexualized international sports.

While the homoerotic potential of men's sport has been explored, there is relatively little work on the homoerotic potential in women's sport. This is not surprising given that women are usually represented as objects of desire rather than desiring subjects. Overall, scholarship on lesbians and sport has de-eroticized lesbian desire by presenting a non-threatening image of lesbians to promote full inclusion as athletes and coaches. However, scholars increasingly recognize that this approach misses an important opportunity to challenge the constant affirmation and production of heterosexual desire in women's sports. At the same time, queer theorists call for new approaches that celebrate the body and acknowledge that sport is inherently erotic and sexual. However, sport as a cultural and social institution has set limits on the body and its desires and established boundaries that close off the possibility for pleasure and erotic desire (Pronger 1999). Scholars are exploring how these boundaries can be disrupted to create a physical culture in which Eros, rather than rationality, is celebrated. Concurrently, they are aware that the sexual objectification of women in sports; the sexual harassment of women, girls, and young boys in sport; the shame associated with homosexual abuse in men's sport; and the use of sexual games in ritualistic team hazing have been profiled in the media in ways that make people fearful of sexuality and the sexual and erotic potential of sport.

Despite the contentiousness of these issues, researchers continue to analyze the ways in which all forms of sexuality and gendered performances can be celebrated in sport in ways that do not ethically exploit, oppress, or cause harm to other beings.

SEE ALSO: Foucault, Michel; Gender, Sport and; Sex and Gender; Sexualities and Consumption; Sexuality; Sexuality, Masculinity and; Sport and the Body; Sport and Social Resistance

REFERENCES AND SUGGESTED READINGS

Birrell, S. & Cole, C. (Eds.) (1994) *Women, Sport, and Culture*. Human Kinetics, Champaign, IL.

Burstyn, V. (1999) *The Rites of Men: Manhood, Politics, and the Culture of Sport*. University of Toronto Press, Toronto.

Butler, J. (1999) *Gender Trouble: Feminism and the Subversion of Identity*. Routledge, New York.

Butler, J. (2004) *Undoing Gender*. Routledge, New York.

Cahn, S. (1994) *Coming on Strong: Gender and Sexuality in Twentieth-Century Women's Sport*. Free Press, New York.

Collins, P. H. (2004). *Black Sexual Politics*. Routledge, New York.

Foucault, M. (1978) *The History of Sexuality: An Introduction, Volume 1*. Vintage Books, New York.

Fusco, C. (1998) Lesbians and Locker Rooms: The Subjective Experiences of Lesbians in Sport. In: Rail, G. (Ed.), *Sport and Postmodern Times*. State University of New York Press, Albany, pp. 87–116.

Lenskyj, H. (2003) *Out on the Field*. Women's Press, Toronto.

Messner, M. & Sabo, D. (1994) *Sex, Violence and Power in Sports: Rethinking Masculinity*. Crossing Press, Freedom, CA.

Pronger, B. (1990). *The Arena of Masculinity: Sports, Homosexuality, and the Meaning of Sex*. St. Martin's Press, New York.

Pronger, B. (1999) Fear and Trembling: Homophobia in Men's Sport. In: White, P. & Young, K. (Eds.), *Sport and Gender in Canada*. Oxford University Press, Toronto, pp. 182–96.

Shadow Work (Ivan Illich)

Nicholas DeMaria Harney

Shadow Work (1981), written by the polymath ex-Catholic priest Ivan Illich (1926–2002), critiques what Illich sees as the contrived structures of desire present in modern commodity-intensive society. Shadow work refers to the "unpaid servitude" modern people tolerate to satisfy the desires that experts suggest they need. *Shadow Work* extends his earlier critiques of the way institutions and professions in the modern industrialized world dehumanize by creating needs and controlling the satisfaction of those needs. In a series of polemical books written in the 1970s, Illich argued that there was a tendency for institutions to develop in ways opposite to their original intent. For example, in *Deschooling Society* (1973) he argued that contemporary educational practices discouraged learning, and in *Medical Nemesis* (1976) care was neglected by the organizational imperatives of medical experts and institutions. He developed the principle of counterproductivity to label the transformation of a potentially positive ideal into a negative institutional arrangement because of the undesired externalities that came with the process of institutionalization. Illich was concerned with how technological advancement and "development" might work to destroy convivial human relationships, the human spirit, and the environment. In addition to critiquing modern institutions, experts, and expert knowledge, Illich critiqued the commodification of activities, transforming, for example, knowledge and learning into a possession rather than a way of being in the world.

Shadow Work followed on from *Towards a History of Needs* (1977) to evaluate how powerful groups created a "radical monopoly" over the satisfaction of human needs that these professionals defined for the public. *Shadow Work* connects the historical development of the commodification of speech by the standardization of a mother tongue at the expense of vernacular language and the destruction of the real, experiential learning inherent in everyday communication and speech with the emergence of a shadow economy. The professionalization of language for Illich opens up a realm of unpaid contributions that people make to manage society at the expense of vernacular domains, domains of subsistence and mutual self-help. This shadow work includes students cramming for exams, housework, commuting to work, shopping, and the myriad ways people prepare for, consume, and comply with professionally mediated services.

Illich's critique of the modern commodity-intensive society's substitution of exchange-values for use-values echoes Marx, Carlyle, and Polanyi in that he argues against any sense of the market or scarcity as "natural," rather that they are the result of choices. For him, commodity-intensive societies transfer people's autonomy and independence to rights guaranteed by techniques, tools, and arrangements offered by professionals and the desires they create for society. To combat this alienation, Illich suggests that people develop "vernacular values" based on reciprocity outside the market, subsistence, pragmatic restraint, conviviality, and autonomy to use technology and organize society to encourage greater liberty. Perhaps because much of Illich's work is polemical and he draws on a remarkable range of sources, he is not much cited today. Nevertheless, his work has relevance for the hypermediatized twenty-first century and contemporary research on non-monetized and non-commodified spaces in the globalizing world.

SEE ALSO: Commodities, Commodity Fetishism, and Commodification; Education; Institution; Language; Modernity; Professions, Organized; Technological Determinism

REFERENCES AND SUGGESTED READINGS

Elias, J. L. (1976) *Conscientization and Deschooling: Freire's and Illich's Proposals for Reshaping Society.* Westminster Press, Philadelphia.

Finger, M. & Asún, J. M. (2001) *Adult Education at the Crossroads: Learning Our Way Out.* Zed Books, London.

Gabbard, D. A. (1993) *Silencing Ivan Illich: A Fou-cauldian Analysis of Intellectual Exclusion.* Austin & Winfield, New York.

Illich, I. (1973) *Deschooling Society.* Penguin, Harmondsworth.

Illich, I. (1981) *Shadow Work.* Marion Boyars, Boston.

Shariati, Ali (1933–77)

Bryan S. Turner

Born in Mazinan, a desert village in the north-eastern province of Iran, Ali Shariati was a leading Iranian sociologist and Muslim intellectual, who published a number of influential books and a great volume of lectures, talks, and occasional articles. He contributed to the sociology of religion, but apart from his *On the Sociology of Islam* (1980a), his work is not widely known in western social science.

Shariati, who was greatly influenced by his father, a scholar and religious teacher, attended a teacher's training college and came into contact with young people from poor social backgrounds. As a student he became active in the nationalist movement of Mohammad Mossadeq, and, having received his bachelor's degree in 1959 from Mashhad University, he pursued graduate study in France, receiving his doctorate from the Sorbonne in 1964. On returning to Iran, he was briefly imprisoned on charges relating to his political activities in France. He began teaching at Mashhad University as an assistant professor of Islamic history, where his original interpretations of problems facing Muslim societies gained him a wide student audience. In 1967 at the invitation of Ayatollah Motahhari, he transferred to Tehran where he lectured at the Housseiniye Ershad Religious Institute, attracting even larger audiences. He was again imprisoned but popular and international pressure eventually secured his release in 1975. He remained, however, under close surveillance by SAVAK (the Iranian Security Agency). Shariati had many enemies but he was supported by Ayatollah Khomeini, and consequently he had a significant impact on the

Iranian Revolution. Because his movements were severely restricted, he migrated to England, but he was found dead in his apartment three weeks later in June 1977. It was generally assumed that he had been murdered by SAVAK agents (Rahnema 2004).

Along with Ayatollah Khomeini and Ayatollah Motahhari, Shariati was one of the principal architects of Islamic revolutionary thought as a direct response to the ideology of modernity, and as a challenge to the modernization policies of the Pahlavi dynasty (Chehabi 1990). During the reign of Mohammad Reza Pahlavi (1941–79), the overwhelming ambition to suppress communism meant that there was relative tolerance of Islamic discourse. In the 20 years before the Islamic Revolution, Islamic associations flourished among intellectual groups, and the urban population tripled and religious societies among the urban poor provided an important political network.

Shariati was intellectually influenced by both Marxism and radical Shi'ite theology. He was a critic of modernization, which he believed was a sinister means of seducing non-western communities into modernity. In order to export their own commodities, western powers have to destroy the self-sufficient domestic economy of traditional societies, and hence western modernity destroys traditional patterns of consumption. Although there are many critics of western imperialism, Shariati developed a deep and sophisticated understanding of the alienation of the self, or in his terms the "emptying" of the self, in which consumerism under neocolonial conditions brings about the eradication of cultural traditions and produces the authenticity of the self.

Shariati placed a substantial emphasis on the revolutionary role of intellectuals in defending culture against western consumerism, but he also criticized them for their distance from the mass of the population. In his book *Fatimah is Fatimah* (1971), he supported intellectuals in their quest for freedom and equality for the masses, but he condemned them for departing from their traditional religious roots, excoriating them for becoming "modernized pseudo-intellectuals." In his *The Intellectual and his Responsibility in Society* (1972), Shariati rejected secularism as a philosophy of the intellectual class, because religion, outside the West, is a bulwark against imperialism. Although the West had achieved modernity as a result of the Enlightenment, each society must find its own enlightenment in terms of its own culture and tradition. The West had imposed the Enlightenment without respect for the integrity of other cultures and its universalism had become a form of cultural imperialism. Intellectuals had to recognize the problem of living in what Shariati called a "dual society" in which only a small elite became modernized, leaving the mass of society in a state of poverty and disempowerment. For Shariati in *Whence Do We Begin?* (1975), only the religiously motivated intellectuals could bridge the gap between the educated, secularized elite and the masses.

The analysis of the self and subjectivity was central to Shariati's philosophy (Vahdat 2002). Shariati's sociotheology exhibited a tension between insisting that human free will is the defining characteristic of humanity and arguing that human subjectivity presupposes submission to God. Shariati tried to solve this dilemma by interpreting human existence as a journey away from material existence to a spiritual life. Humans are alienated in nature rather than from nature, and the spiritual life requires the radical subordination of the body to a spiritual purpose. The natural body is a "desolate abode" or a prison from which human beings must escape in order to realize their true essence. Contempt for the body is a precondition of the journey toward authentic subjectivity. Shariati recognized that this solution would always be partial and that human existence was a perennial conflict between autonomy and submission that he described as a condition of human bewilderment.

While Shariati was critical of Marx's sociology in his *Marxism and Other Western Fallacies* (1980b), he also borrowed extensively from Marx's vocabulary to describe this human bewilderment. Shariati was, like Marx, opposed to the liberal notion of individualism, and emphasized collective, not individual, agency. Islam recognized the agency of the mass of ordinary people, and Shariati developed the revolutionary proposition that the voice of the people is God. It was through this revolutionary theology that he came to affirm the needs of the "disempowered" – the mass of the population who suffered directly from colonial exploitation and marginalization. It was to the salvation of the disempowered and the cancelation of the forces of oppression that the message of the Qur'an was directed. Although Shariati emphasized the moral responsibility of the individual, the revolutionary role of Islam, the political responsibility of the intellectual, and the sovereignty of the people, he did not in his major political text, *Community and Leadership* (1979), advocate popular democracy, but instead he adumbrated the role of the charismatic imam who is neither elected nor selected.

Shariati's thought was a major intellectual contribution to one of the most significant revolutions of modern times. The originality of his thought was to combine existentialism, Marxism, and Islamic thought to produce a comprehensive criticism of western imperialism. Shariati developed a normative critique of modernization that emphasized the negative consequences of consumerism on an agrarian society under the control of an authoritarian government.

SEE ALSO: Colonialism (Neocolonialism); Globalization, Religion and; Islam; Religion

REFERENCES AND SUGGESTED READINGS

Chehabi, H. E. (1990) *Iranian Politics and Religious Modernism: The Liberation Movement of Iran Under the Shah and Khomeini*. Cornell University Press, Ithaca, NY.
Rahnema, A. (2004) *An Islamic Utopian: A Political Biography of Ali Shariati*. Tauris, New York.
Shariati, A. (1971) *Fatimah is Fatimah (Fatemeh Fatemeh Ast)*. Housseiniyeh Ershad, Tehran.
Shariati, A. (1972) *The Intellectual and his Responsibility in Society (Rushanfekr va Masuliyat-e Ou dar Jame-e)*. Housseiniyeh Ershad, Tehran.
Shariati, A. (1975) *Whence Do We Begin? (Az Koja Agbaz Konim?)*. Muslim Students.
Shariati, A. (1979) *Community and Leadership (Ommat va Imamat)*. Qalam, Tehran.
Shariati, A. (1980a) *On the Sociology of Islam*. Mizan Press, Berkeley.
Shariati, A. (1980b) *Marxism and Other Western Fallacies*. Mizan Press, Berkeley.
Vahdat, F. (2002) *God and Juggernaut: Iran's Intellectual Encounter with Modernity*. Syracuse University Press, Syracuse.

Shintoism

Tsuyoshi Nakano

Although there is no widely accepted definition of Shintoism even among Japanese scholars, the term could be defined tentatively as a Japanese traditional religious system based on so-called "Shinto." Shinto is generally believed to be indigenous to Japan. The term was coined by the combination of two words from Chinese – *shin*, originally from the Chinese character for "divine beings" or "gods" (*shen*), and *to*, originally from "way" (*tao*). Therefore, the literal meaning is "the way of the gods," which corresponds to the native Japanese reading of the term, *kami no michi*, or *kannagara no michi*. The term Shinto (*kami no michi*) first appeared in *Nihon shoki* (Chronicles of Japan compiled 720 CE), together with the term "Buddha's law," *hotoke no minori*. This was done in order to consciously designate traditional forms of worship of the emperor, which were inherited from ancestors, as these related to kami (god or gods; the same character as *shin*) and not to Buddhism. This indicates the large influence that rivalry with Buddhism had in the creation of the Shinto tradition from the outset.

Nevertheless, there are various theories concerning the establishment of Shintoism as a relatively independent religious system. One suggests the establishment of a centralized system of governance based on the legal codes of ancient Japan in the seventh or eighth century (Inoue 1998), and another holds that the idea of Shinto as an independent religion scarcely existed before the Meiji Restoration (Hardacre 1989). In any case, the Shinto tradition became an important religious source that was connected to agricultural rituals and festivals at the community level, and rites of passage at the personal level. Shinto is understood to have been a major religious and cultural influence that has provided a unique value orientation for the Japanese people. Therefore, in order to understand the divergent and yet uniquely Japanese sensitivities, attitudes, and mentalities of people and communities, a recognition and understanding of Shinto is essential.

According to statistics compiled every year by the Division of Religious Affairs of the Japanese Ministry of Education and Science based on reports from each religious body, at the end of 2001 the number of religious corporations (officially certificated and registered under Japanese law) related to Shinto was about 85,000, 46.7 percent of the total figure (Buddhist temples numbered over 77,000, 42.5 percent of the total; Christian churches 4,337, 2.4 percent of the total). Shinto adherents accounted for about 106,000,000, i.e., 49.7 percent, of the total number of religious adherents in Japan (Buddhists 95,000,000, 44.5 percent; Christians 1,800,000, 0.4 percent). The total number of religious adherents was twice that of the actual population of Japan, which means that most people are counted twice, by a Shinto shrine and by a Buddhist temple in each area. This kind of mixing of Shinto and Buddhist religious traditions is indicative of the traditional religious life of many Japanese people.

The National Police Agency also reported that nearly 90,000,000 Japanese visited a shrine on New Year's Day in 2004. According to more detailed public opinion surveys conducted by scholars and various newspapers, the percentage of respondents who said they visited a shrine on New Year's Day was 56 percent in 1979 and 61.7 percent in 1994. However, the rate of those who "believe" in Shinto was only 3.3 percent in 1979 (*Yomiuri Press*), and 4.4 percent in 1995 (*Jiji Press*). This indicates that Shinto in general is a religion of participation in traditional rituals and festivals at shrines, and is not a religion that constitutes an articulated system of beliefs, doctrine, and ethics.

The shrine (*jinja*) precinct is a sacred area with a gate (*torii*), ablution area, and sacred buildings, including the main sanctuary, which houses the symbol of the kami (*shintai*) and a worship area (*haiden*). At special times through the year, shrines become the focal point for community festivals (*matsuri*), which are held according to the tradition of each shrine in honor of its own kami. Nevertheless, there are also many common festivals, such as the Spring Festival (*Haru matsuri*), Autumn Festival (*Aki matsuri*), and the like. As individual rites of passage, family members sometimes visit the local shrine. After birth, for example, an infant is taken to the local shrine in order to be acknowledged and celebrated as a new member of the village or the community by its tutelary deity (or the local guardian god). Further celebrations include the Seven, Five, and Three Festival (*Shichigosan*), at which boys of 5 years of age and girls of 3 and 7 years of age are brought to the shrine. In addition, marriage rites are performed at shrines, though they are becoming less popular among the younger generation. Shinto is a "this-worldly" religion in the sense that it is interested in tangible benefits which will promote life in the human world.

The origin of basic forms of Shinto worship of gods is obscure. There is no founder, no sacred scriptures, nor any fixed system of doctrine. Instead, Shinto seems to originate from simple worship of kami-gami (gods), with rituals developing when people began to settle down to grow rice in the Yayoi era from 300 BCE to 250 CE. At least by the early historical period (third century CE), the clan (*uji*) system formed a certain ancestral worship, which was worship and rituals performed for gods of personal clans (*ujigami*). People also believed in other spiritual powers and beings which had the kami nature. Some kami were connected to specific geographical areas or lands; others were believed to reside within living beings and phenomena such as the sun, the moon, mountains, trees, thunder, fire, and wind. This religious culture was based on a kind of animism that prevailed in various parts of the world since ancient times. Shamans and diviners were regarded as important figures in operating and controlling these divine powers. The imperial (*tenno*) clan eventually gained power over other clans, especially in terms of rites and festivals that were connected with rice growing. Its supremacy could be attributed to a kind of shamanistic power, and following the famous work of Sir James Frazer, Japanese anthropologists agree that the Japanese emperor could be regarded as a shaman king or "priest-king" in origin.

Although each clan continued to maintain its own forms of ancestor worship and myths of origin, as the imperial clan gained greater supremacy its myths also gained ascendancy. These provided the dominant motifs into which the myths of the other clans were integrated. By the eighth century, these myths were collected and edited as two well-known volumes, *Kojiki* (Records of Ancient Matters)

of 712 CE and the above-mentioned *Nihon shoki*. These volumes laid important foundations for various ideas and themes of the cosmological view in Shinto. The universe was divided into three levels: the Plain of High Heaven (*Takama-ga-hara*); this Manifested World on the Earth (*Nakatsu-kuni*); and the Netherworld (*Yomotsu-kuni*). Moreover, beliefs in the creation of the world by *Izanagi* (male kami) and *Izanami* (female kami), the dominance of the sun goddess *Amaterasu Omikami* and the descent of the imperial line from *Amaterasu*, and in forces of life, fertility, pollution, and purification were established. The basic Shinto practices, dances, and chanting of *norito* (prayers) were formed in accordance with these myths as well. While the details of these themes are unique, they share a common structure with other typologies found in the Andromeda, Perseus, Oedipus, and Orpheus myths from ancient Greek mythology.

These records also indicate the hegemonic position of *Amaterasu Omikami*, and the myth that the imperial line directly descended from the sun goddess gradually became prominent. In addition, although the indigenous nature of Shintoism is often emphasized, it is obvious that Shintoism has transformed and hybridized with other religious traditions throughout history. This was particularly evident with its amalgamation with Buddhism and Confucianism, which became the ideology that legitimized the ruling of Japanese feudal societies by the imperial family. According to *Nihon shoki* and other sources, Buddhism was first officially introduced from Korea in the sixth century CE, and Empress Suiko declared she would adopt Buddhism as the principle of governing the country in 593. This was partly because it was regarded as having magical religious powers that would help govern the people and guard the nation. In this process of introduction, opposition, and amalgamation with Buddhism, Shinto itself became conscious of its own originality and tried to describe and develop its myths, forms of ritual, and certain doctrinal themes. The making of Shintoism as a religious system in Japan was formed through this process.

At the folk or community level, this syncretism is deeper and more intricate. In festivals and celebrations in traditional villages, a division of religious functions developed, with Buddhist temples usually taking charge of rituals relating to death such as funerals, while Shinto shrines were responsible for festivals, rites of passage, and agricultural rituals.

In spite of the National Seclusion policy in the Edo period (1603–1867), knowledge and information about western scholarship and science gradually filtered into Japan, especially after 1720 when Tokugawa Yoshimune (the shogun) lifted the ban on the importation of foreign books. By the early nineteenth century, Dutch studies (*rangaku*) and western studies (*yogaku*) were widely read throughout Japan.

At the beginning of the nineteenth century, as the School of National Learning (*Kokugaku*) emerged and then developed into Revival Shinto (*Fukko Shinto*), Shintoism was given more social importance not as a religion but rather as a political ideology. In the works of Hirata Atsutane, who emphasized a return to Shinto's original traditions, most religions such as Buddhism and Christianity were thought of as foreign. He and his contemporaries sought to discover an "original" Japanese religious tradition. As some of their ideas derived from other religious traditions, however, "original" tradition in this context should be understood as a result of cultural contact with other traditions and not as a purely original Japanese idea. Revival Shinto asserted that Shinto should return to its former position as the fundamental principle guiding the nation. Nevertheless, Revival Shinto can be seen as an expression of, or a reaction to, a cultural and colonial crisis brought about by the increasing influence of the West. This laid the foundation of a sweeping conservative anti-foreign movement, which gathered under the slogan "revere the emperor, expel the barbarians" (*sonno joi*).

By the Meiji Restoration in 1868, the Tokugawa shogunate was dismantled and replaced with a limited representative and monarch system under the Meiji Constitution (promulgated in 1889). Japan began building a modern nation-state partly to counter the colonizing threat posed by the West. The state's involvement in Shinto affairs increased and the formation of so-called State Shinto began. State Shinto was in a sense different from Shinto as it had originally developed. Although it included aspects of Shinto mythology and incorporated Shinto institutions and practices, the newly established Meiji government essentially invented State Shinto as a means to legitimize governmental authority and unify the people. The government incorporated all Shintoist rituals and observances and ordered all citizens to observe them, thus utilizing Shinto ceremonial events to promote nationalism. Thus State Shinto was a type of new national religion introduced by the government after the Meiji Restoration. However, the government itself did not regard State Shinto as a religion but as the Japanese "national cult" – one that included religious ideology and rituals and surpassed all other religions.

In addition, the qualifications of the emperor as head of state and his rights as sovereign did not have their source in the Constitution, although the form of government was a kind of constitutional monarchy according to its provisions (Chap. 1, Art. 4). The Imperial Prescript on the Promulgation of the Constitution declared: "The rights of sovereignty of the State, We have inherited from Our Ancestors." It was stressed that these rights had been derived neither from the people nor from the Constitution, but from an institutional charisma of a "lineal succession unbroken for ages eternal." Moreover, the stipulation in Article 3 of the Constitution that "the emperor is sacred and inviolable" granted the emperor a sacred, transcendental character. Thus the emperor possessed a mystical authority as a kind of divine king, or as the highest priest of the state, as well as possessing secular powers as sovereign of the state and as supreme commander of the military forces.

This politico-religious ideology was derived from an extreme interpretation of Shinto mythology, according to which the emperor was regarded as having descended from the supreme ancestral deity, the sun goddess *Amaterasu*, and was regarded as its manifest deity (*Akitsu kami*). This idea was based on, first, the assertion that the emperor, the land, and the people of Japan constituted one sacred invisible entity, and second, a system of related teachings, Shinto institutions, practices, and rites known as State Shinto, or National Shinto as it was called by the Allied Powers (Bunce 1948), or, as designated by W. P. Woodard (1972), a national cult.

Thus, the structure of the Japanese state as a whole was signified mystically or religiously by the ideology of the emperor system, and the government sought unification of the people in the nation and sought to control even their everyday religious life by utilizing this mystic ideology through State Shinto.

SHINTOISM SINCE 1945

On August 15, 1945, the Japanese government accepted the Potsdam Declaration of the Allied Powers and surrendered unconditionally. This defeat in World War II and the reform of the whole Japanese society through the Occupation by the Allied Powers led to radical changes in Japanese religions, especially in Shinto and its relation to the state.

The first directive relating to reform of the religious system, issued by the Supreme Commander for the Allied Powers (SCAP), was the so-called Civil Liberties Directive of October 4, 1945. In order to realize the objectives of freedom of thought, speech, religion, assembly, and respect for fundamental human rights, it required the abrogation and immediate suspension of the operation of all provisions of laws establishing or maintaining restrictions on those rights. However, the more important directive was the so-called Shinto Directive of December 15, 1945, which ordered clearly and in a shocking way the "abolition of State Shinto" and the "complete separation of religion and state."

The purpose of this directive was clear, namely, "to separate religion from the state, to prevent misuse of religion for political ends, and to put all religions, faith, and creeds upon exactly the same legal basis, entitled precisely to the same opportunities and protection." It forbade "affiliation with the government and the propagation and dissemination of militaristic and ultra-nationalistic ideology not only to Shinto but to followers of all religions, faiths, sects, creeds, or philosophies" (Shinto Directive, Article 2a). It therefore forbade "the sponsorship, support, perpetuation, control and dissemination of Shinto" by the state, abolished the Shrine Board (*Jingiin*) of the Ministry of Home Affairs, which was the representative agency of State Shinto within the administrative structure of the government, and prohibited all Shinto education and rites in educational institutions supported wholly or in part by public funds, the attendance of public officials in shrine worship or any other Shinto observances, and the use in official writings of terms with State Shinto, militaristic, and ultra-nationalistic connotations. In short, this meant in a very direct way the abolition of State Shinto and the disestablishment of state religion.

According to the policy, the Peace Preservation Law, in accordance with which many leaders of new religions had been thrown into prison during the war, was abrogated. The Religious Organizations Law (*Shukyo dantai ho*), which had been another instrument designed to restrict religious freedom, was replaced by the Religious Juridical Persons Ordinance (*Shukyo hojin rei*, Imperial Ordinance No. 719), promulgated on December 28, 1945. This ordinance set out working rules for the free establishment of religious corporations by mere registration with the appropriate government body. The laws obstructing religious freedom of religious groups were abolished, and by the amendments of this ordinance on February 2, 1946, even Shrine Shinto, now separated from the state and liberated from its control, was given the opportunity of continuing its existence as an ordinary religious corporation. Thus "equality of all religions before the law," which was one of the objectives of the Shinto Directive, became a reality. Finally, on November 3, 1946, the new Constitution of Japan was promulgated, coming into effect on May 3 of the following year. It codified "freedom of religion" and "separation of religion and state" in Articles 20 and 89.

The reform of the religious system by the Occupation administration effected great changes in Japanese society and religion. First of all, it brought about secularization of the Japanese state. Although the imperial system was retained, the emperor was no longer the head of the state nor the source of legitimacy for political rule, but was now regarded as a symbol of the unity of the whole nation. The new Constitution became the source of law and authority. For the first time, Japan became a constitutional democracy. The religious or mystical character of the state was disposed of, and freedom of religion was established as a "basic human right." In this free and democratic society, Shintoism continues to exist in several different forms:

1 Shinto of the Imperial Household (*Koshitsu Shinto*) focuses on rites for the spirits of imperial ancestors and is observed at imperial institutions. It is distinguished from other forms of Shinto partly because the emperor himself performs its ceremonies, and partly because it is believed that it retains the most archaic style of Shinto worship. But this Shinto is not open to the public.

2 Shrine Shinto (*Jinja Shinto*) is presently the form of Shinto that embraces the vast majority of Shinto shrines and adherents in Japan, administered by the Association of Shinto Shrines (Jinja Honcho). It is the most popular system of Shintoism now in Japan, which is upheld in a great many and varied local shrines with seasonal rituals and festivals held in honor of kami. It continues to emphasize the traditionally close relationship between Shinto and Japanese life and the need for national regeneration.

3 Sect Shinto (*Kyoha Shinto*) refers to 13 religious organizations which originated from new Shinto movements that arose from the social and economic distress toward the end of the Tokugawa period and the beginning of the Meiji period. They were mostly founded by charismatic figures and promised worldly benefits, such as wealth, success in life, and cures for sickness. Because the Meiji government did not want to incorporate these groups into the structure of State Shinto, it created a new classification of Sect Shinto, eventually recognizing them as offshoots of the mainstream Shinto tradition. Groups such as Kurozumi-kyo, Fuso-kyo, Ontake-kyo, Konko-kyo, and Tenri-kyo belong to this category.

4 Folk Shinto (*Minkan Shinto*) is a designation for the wide-ranging groups of superstitious, magico-religious rites and practices of the common people, embracing conceptions of spirits and souls, good and evil kami, divination of lucky or evil direction, and unlucky days. Folk Shinto does not stand in opposition to Shrine Shinto or Sect Shinto but might be considered as the substratum of those more organized forms.

PROBLEMS INVOLVING SHINTOISM

The post-war reforms established the principles of freedom of religion and the separation of religion and state. These principles have been widely accepted, for people remember how freedom was suppressed under State Shinto before and during the war. But with regard to their interpretation, questions have arisen as to whether "separation" is an absolute or relative term, to be understood as an end in itself or as a means of affirming religious freedom. There are a number of issues concerning the relationship between the state and religion, especially relating to Shintoism, in the post-war period.

State Support for and Official Worship at the Yasukuni Shrine

Before and during World War II, the Yasukuni shrine was an important national institution particularly for promoting hero worship and strengthening the fighting spirit of the nation. Enshrined within it are the spirits of many soldiers who died in war for the emperor or for the state since the Meiji period. Occupation policies dictated that the shrine be stripped of its militaristic elements and completely separated from the state. Consequently, the Yasukuni shrine was forced to sever its ties with the state yet it continued to exist on the same legal basis as other religious bodies, as one religious organization among others.

But with the peace treaty and the restoration of independence at the end of the Occupation in April 1952, a movement calling for state support to reestablish a special status for the Yasukuni shrine began. By the end of 1974 a bill supporting public funding of the shrine had been submitted unsuccessfully to the Diet on five separate occasions. Proponents of the movement eventually changed their strategy, and they began to lobby for the emperor and state officials to worship (*sanpai*) at the shrine in their official capacity, for foreign envoys to pay their respects, and for representatives of the Self-Defense Forces to offer formal worship there. In these and other ways, proponents sought to give people the impression that the shrine was already a de facto public institution, that is, a religious institution with special ties to the state. It was in this context that the movement for "official visits" (*koshiki sanpai*) emerged.

The event that particularly drew people's attention to the issues occurred on August 15, 1975, the thirtieth anniversary of the end of the Pacific War, when the then Prime Minister Miki Takeo visited the Yasukuni shrine. Although some of his predecessors had visited the shrine while in office, this visit was especially important as it highlighted two crucial issues: (1) whether it constituted a religious action by a government official that violated the Constitution, and (2) the complex problem of evaluating the war. Prime Minister Miki emphasized that he visited the shrine in a private capacity, but it is undeniable that his action opened the way for subsequent official visits. Thus it was that a later prime minister, Nakasone Yasuhiro, who was emphasizing the "end of the post-war period," made the first official visit to the shrine on August 15, 1985. He signed the register as "Prime Minister of the Cabinet" and made a donation of 30,000 yen from public funds.

Nakasone's visit provoked an unexpectedly strong barrage of protests from China and other Asian countries, and official visits to the shrine ceased for a time. However, Prime Minister Junichiro Koizumi reestablished this practice again on August 13, 2001, and since then has visited each year. Needless to say, a loud chorus of criticism against these visits arose from many Japanese people as well as other Asian countries, especially from China and Korea. It was even judged to be unconstitutional by the Fukuoka district court on April 7, 2004.

Although these visits ignited disputes over the distinction between the prime minister as a public figure or a private citizen and whether donations to the shrine's coffers constituted a religious act or were simply a matter of conventional etiquette, the more pressing issue is whether these visits give preferential treatment to one religion over others and serve to accord the shrine the status of a national institution. Moreover, these actions by leading conservative politicians are closely associated with the rise of religious nationalism in Japan, particularly when the Japanese Self-Defense Forces were being sent to Iraq and other areas.

The Emperor and Shinto Rituals

The post-war system that assigned a purely symbolic status to the emperor gave rise to yet another type of debate and lawsuit. In connection with the mourning service (*taiso*) held for Emperor Showa on February 24, 1989, questions arose as to the degree to which this ought to be a state ceremony. In order to forestall constitutional misgivings, it was finally decided that the *Taiso-no-gi*, a Shinto service of mourning for the emperor, would be carried out as an Imperial Household ceremony, but that the *Taiso-no-rei*, a separate Shinto rite, would be carried out as a secular state ceremony. A similar division was employed on November 12, 1990 when the new emperor's *Sokui-no-rei*, or Enthronement Ceremony, was handled as a state ceremony and the subsequent *Daijosai*, or Great Food Offering, as a private ceremony based on the Shinto of the Imperial Household. The central question in all these matters was the extent to which a rite could be a state ceremony without violating the principle of separation of religion and state.

A closely related question giving rise to intense debate was whether the *Daijosai* should be paid for with private funds from the Imperial Household's internal budget (*naiteihi*) or with public funds from the Imperial Palace budget (*kyuteihi*). The government, recognizing the religious character of this rite, decided that it would be an Imperial Household ceremony. But the government also recognized the "public character" of this rite and chose to use public funds from the Imperial Palace budget. This decision struck a balance between upholders of tradition, who wanted it to be a state ceremony, and public opinion, which called for strict application of the principle of separation of religion and state.

There are many other lawsuits that contest allegedly unconstitutional action on the basis of the principle of separation of religion and state. Most of these lawsuits, however, have to do with issues that grew out of pre-war and wartime State Shinto. One issue concerns the extent to which a religious organization is autonomous and the extent to which it is subject to judiciary intervention. The lawsuits mentioned above show clearly that the principle of separation of religion and state introduced by the Occupation has not taken firm root in Japan, and has yet to find a harmonious balance with traditional Japanese culture.

SEE ALSO: Animism; Buddhism; Civil Religion; Confucianism; Nation-State; Nation-State and Nationalism; Taoism

REFERENCES AND SUGGESTED READINGS

Bocking, B. (1996) *A Popular Dictionary of Shinto*. Routledge/Curzon, London.
Bunce, W. K. (1948) *Religions in Japan: Buddhism, Shinto, Christianity*. Report prepared by CIE in the GHQ of the Supreme Commander for the Allied Powers. Reprinted Greenwood Press, Westport, CT, 1978.
Gluck, C. (1985) *Japan's Modern Myths: Ideology in the Late Meiji Period*. Princeton University Press, Princeton.
Hardacre, H. (1989) *Shinto and the State, 1868–1988*. Princeton University Press, Princeton.
Hori, I. et al. (Eds.) (1972) *Japanese Religion*. Survey by the Agency for Cultural Affairs of the Japanese Ministry of Education. Kodansha International, Tokyo.
Inoue, N. (1998) *Shinto*. Shinyo-sha, Tokyo. (In Japanese.)
Inoue, N. & Ito, S. (Eds.) (2003) *Shinto: A Short History*. Curzon, London.
Kitagawa, J. M. (1966) *Religion in Japanese History*. Columbia University Press, New York.
Kitagawa, J. M. (1987) *On Understanding Japanese Religion*. Princeton University Press, Princeton.
Nakano, T. (1987) The American Occupation and Reform of Japan's Religious System: A Few Notes on the Secularization Process in Postwar Japan. *Journal of Oriental Studies* 26(1). Institute of Oriental Philosophy, Tokyo.
Nakano, T. (1991) Ecumenism and Peace Movements in Post-War Japan. *Religion Today* 7(1). King's College, London.
Nakano, T. (1996) Religion and State. In: Tamaru, Y. & Reid, D. (Eds.), *Religion in Japanese Culture*. Kodansha International, Tokyo, New York, and London, pp. 115–36.
Reader, I. (1998) *Simple Guide to Shinto, the Religion of Japan*. Global Books, London.
SCAP Government Section (Ed.) (1970) *Political Reorientation of Japan*. Reprinted by Greenwood Press, Westport, CT.
Tamaru, Y. & Reid, D. (Eds.) (1996) *Religion in Japanese Culture*. Kodansha International, Tokyo, New York, and London.
Woodard, W. P. (1972) *The Allied Occupation of Japan, 1945–1952 and Japanese Religions*. Brill, Leiden.

shopping

Sharon Zukin

As the public face of consumption, shopping includes an array of social, economic, and cultural activities connected with consumers' selection and procurement of goods and services. In contrast to consumption, which, historically, is synonymous with satisfaction of basic biological needs, shopping is a distinctly modern ensemble of actions, perceptions, and emotions. Shopping develops in a money economy, on a sophisticated industrial base, along with the integration of local places into larger markets providing a range of innovative, and often exotic, product choices. Choice is, indeed, a keyword of shopping, for the process of identifying needed or desired products and selecting among them magnifies the role of individual decision-making and taste. But collective norms and pressures are equally important. Whether the parameters of a man's, a woman's, or, increasingly, a child's shopping are set by money, access to information, or the example set by their peers, shopping expresses both individual desires and collective dreams.

Since Walter Benjamin (1999) wrote about the Parisian arcades, or mid-block shopping galleries, of the 1840s, social and cultural theorists have understood shopping to be an experience that envelops individuals in dreams of commodities. The physical sensation of being surrounded by goods, with their evocation of exoticism and novelty, suppresses criticism or rebellion; the design of the shopping space is calculated to impress and overwhelm. But shopping also provides an experience of sociality – being together with other people – in an apparently public space. Although the main point of shopping is to make purchases for individual use, families and friends do shop together, and age or peer groups meet – and examine each other – in shopping spaces. Shopping for necessities expresses solidarities among family members (especially mother and child) and intimate friends, while shopping in a local community – even among strangers – strengthens bonds of interdependence and place identity. But shopping also poses an implicit conflict. Increasingly under non-local, standardized, corporate control, shopping creates a public sphere in which consumers struggle to create an experience that they, themselves, value (Zukin 2004).

Only recently have scholars paid attention to shopping as a serious form of social action. Aside from marketing studies about what people buy and how they respond to the layout of stores, few researchers have suggested an institutional theory of how shopping develops, how it relates to both economy and culture, and how shoppers integrate their shopping experiences with overall ideology.

HISTORY OF SHOPPING

The earliest shopping dates back to ancient empires, when the density of residents, division of labor, and economic surplus in towns enabled them to establish marketplaces for exchanging the products of local farmers, urban artisans and craftspeople, and long-distance traders. Merchants gradually became a separate occupation from either traders or craftspeople; they kept a fixed stall at the market and, eventually, an indoor shop. After centuries of providing a limited range and number of products, some merchants used the emerging industrial system of mass production and access to bank credit to offer many different kinds of merchandise under one roof. Like the increasingly complex organization of the state, the nineteenth-century department store integrated a variety of specialized functions, and offered shoppers a world of goods.

Historically, shoppers have gone out to markets or stores, and come into direct contact with displays of goods to buy, as well as with merchants and other shoppers. But since the mid-nineteenth century, technological innovations, often supported by the state, have made it possible to view goods or images of goods at home, purchase them, and arrange for their delivery, all without going out in public. Beginning in the 1870s in the United States and Western Europe, mail-order catalogs connected retailers and warehouses in cities at the hub of transportation networks with consumers who lived in remote rural areas. Although individual entrepreneurs established these companies, and were closely linked to both manufacturers and banks, they depended on the state-run postal service to ship catalogs and on the railroads to transport goods. In the early 1900s regular parcel post deliveries throughout the USA encouraged the expansion of the mail-order business, while the widespread use of telephones enabled shoppers to place orders by calling, rather than visiting, local stores. By the 1970s, another pair of innovations – bank-issued credit cards and toll-free "800" telephone numbers – set loose an explosion of long-distance shopping, although it also increased consumer debt. And, by the 1990s, the diffusion of personal computers and public access to the World Wide Web allowed shoppers and stores to form a truly virtual, global market.

Even with "bricks and mortar" stores, the diffusion of automobile ownership and the construction of roads and highways during the twentieth century decentralized shopping as never before. Cars permitted shoppers to travel longer distances and transport a larger number of purchases on each shopping trip. Because new, post-World War II homes had modern refrigerators and roomy kitchen cabinets, shoppers were freed from the necessity of daily provisioning. By the same token, most postwar housing was built in suburbs that were zoned only for residences, which made shoppers dependent on automobile transportation for weekly shopping trips. These trips became family outings, and although they offered relief from the monotony and lack of public interaction that were typical of suburban life, they subjected family members to the routinization of supermarkets, chain stores, and ever larger shopping malls. Malls became, in effect, the most widely used public space in suburbs – even though they were privately owned and controlled, separated from streets by parking lots, and usually located in places accessible only by car.

Just as stores are compelled to respond to shoppers' changing needs and wants, so they also respond to rising costs of labor. For this reason, the clerks who served shoppers in traditional stores were gradually replaced, from the early 1900s, with self-service. Although steady customers in exclusive stores may still expect to be served by a salesperson who keeps track of their preferences, shoppers in most stores see all the merchandise displayed on shelves, racks, or counters before their eyes, feel and try on products without either help or interference from the staff, and carry their intended purchases, themselves, to central checkout lines. In some ways this makes shopping a more democratic experience, but it results in shoppers' frustration when they can't find what they want or need information. Transparent packaging, universal bar codes, and automation have also helped to reduce stores' labor costs while further routinizing the shopping experience.

TYPES OF STORES

From the earliest times, marketplaces have been bazaars of commercial display, theaters of social interaction, and even carnivals of transgression where men and women assume roles that may be unrelated to their everyday lives. Partly this reflects the magic that one perceives in desired objects to transform our lives, and partly it reflects the magic of a special place – the market – where strangers mingle, exchange information, and seek entertainment. By the late nineteenth century, the more carnivalesque or raucous aspects of markets had been tamed; not only did most shopping occur indoors, in stores, but corporate ownership, policing, and a greater number of middle-class women shoppers contributed to a more rigorous, though implicit, regime of social control. At the same time, the emergence of fixed prices, introduced by F. W. Woolworth's five-and-dime stores, eliminated the need to bargain and, in a sense, defined modern shopping. Elements of older marketplaces nonetheless survived in specific forms: public or farmers' markets, flea markets, and fairs.

During the nineteenth century, department stores, five-and-dimes, and mail-order catalogs created paradigmatic forms of shopping. Each brought an unprecedented array of products to large numbers of consumers and made shopping something of a universal experience. Unlike previous kinds of stores, including general or country stores, from which rural residents – mainly farmers – bought supplies, department stores, five-and-dimes, and mail-order catalogs catered to all social classes and ethnic groups, and treated them entirely as consumers rather than as producers. But the face-to-face interaction in stores did enforce social distinctions – often with terrible cruelty. Before the civil rights laws of the 1960s, department stores, especially in the South of the United States, would not permit black shoppers to try on clothes, and five-and-dimes restricted seats at their lunch counters to whites. Even now, salespeople in high-status stores may snub men and women of lower social classes. To avoid these everyday kinds of discrimination, some shoppers have always preferred to use mail-order catalogs or, these days, they shop on the Internet.

From the late nineteenth century, department stores expanded, modernized, and democratized the sense of luxury that shoppers had earlier experienced in small, custom shops and arcades (Leach 1993). They were the first big, multi-floor stores, and were usually located in the busy centers of cities' commercial districts, close to mass transit lines. Department stores borrowed theatrical techniques to heighten the aesthetic and emotional experience of shopping, dramatizing both window and interior displays with electric lights, colorful décor, mannequins, and tableaux. They also sought the collaboration of art museums in devising model rooms and special exhibitions. Not only were department stores visual feasts, they also kept shoppers in motion. Escalators brought them up to less-traveled departments, giving them a view of merchandise on each floor as they passed by. And in some department stores, shoppers descended to a "bargain basement" where especially low-priced goods were sold.

Department stores established special amenities to welcome women shoppers and to keep them longer in the store – from non-alcoholic tearooms and spacious rest rooms to fashion shows and infants' clothing departments. While women pressed for greater independence and the right to vote, department stores offered them a safe public space that they could use without being accompanied by men. This was especially important for women of the middle and upper classes.

The feeling of being surrounded by goods that could be bought and owned played to shoppers' imaginations. But if department stores were "dream worlds," as Rosalind Williams (1982) calls them, they relied on a strict, hierarchical business organization, with well-paid male merchants and managers at the top and low-paid, usually female sales clerks and African-American elevator operators at the bottom (Benson 1986). The five-and-dime store reproduced the same hierarchy – and the same dream-like experience – for an even broader public of shoppers. Five-and-dimes featured products that rich as well as poor could buy, all displayed on counters, and all priced at only five or ten cents. These stores helped to create the age of mass consumption for everyone.

The patterns set by department stores and five-and-dimes were expanded in the twentieth century by supermarkets, which sold many different kinds of food, as well as other goods, under one roof, and shopping centers, which featured an array of specialty shops as well as one or two department stores. By 1960, most Americans regularly drove to shop in these large places that were dominated by national chains, rather than walking to traditional, individually owned, local or corner stores.

During the 1950s, however, a new kind of store altered the shopping experience. To capture shoppers who were concerned about inflation, discount stores offered no-frills displays, few services or amenities, and guaranteed lower-than-usual prices. Dedicated, at first, to only a single category of merchandise – often, household appliances and electronics goods – discount stores soon branched out to include a wide range of products. Wal-Mart, which emerged by the 1990s as the largest, most successful discount chain, and, eventually, the largest private employer in the world, built upon the model of both the supermarket and the five-and-dime. Wal-Mart stores charged "low prices always" by holding their expenses down and pushing suppliers to do the same. For the first 20 years, discount stores sold only generic or no-name

brands, until Wal-Mart changed its strategy and offered nationally advertised brands at very low prices, often because these products were manufactured by low-wage workers in China. This shift changed the shopping experience, bringing rich and middle-class shoppers into the discount store alongside Wal-Mart's middle-income base, and made "aspirational" shopping for brand-name goods accessible to people of modest means. It is no wonder Wal-Mart expanded rapidly through the United States and into Mexico and China, though not without provoking serious complaints about its labor and environmental practices.

In the 1960s a different type of new, small store catered to an emerging group of teenage and young adult consumers. Copied from shops in London and Paris, *boutiques* soon spread to the United States and around the world. In contrast to department and discount stores, boutiques sold only a small range of products, beginning with fashion, and used these products to set out a definite, style-conscious point of view. Some boutiques specialized in the expensive clothing of a single, famous, international designer – and were among the first multinational chain stores. But many more boutiques just concentrated on a single kind of product or style, and were especially attractive to the young. During these years of cultural ferment, shopping became a vehicle for differentiating age groups and developing and diffusing "lifestyle," at least in the form of commodities that could be grouped together to suggest a common approach to life. Not just buying the products, but shopping in different kinds of stores became a form of peer groups' self-expression.

Reflecting the needs of consumer products companies rather than of consumers, another kind of store – the branded store, selling the various product lines of a single corporation – emerged during the 1980s. The model was set by The Gap, a national chain of moderate-price jeans and T-shirt shops, which, since the 1960s, had sold products of different suppliers under the manufacturers' labels. A corporate makeover defined a coherent visual identity for Gap stores, and unified all products that they sold under The Gap's own label. At the same time, the chain revised contracts with suppliers, so that all goods sold at The Gap were now identified with the chain rather than with independent or competing producers. Other stores followed The Gap's example, with Nike developing some of the most elaborate stores to showcase their athletic shoes, clothing, and equipment. Shopping then became an experience of communing with a specific brand, because of either the reputation of its products and designers, or the magic of its name.

Viewing individual consumers as the center of shopping focuses attention on need, desire, and identity as wellsprings of the willingness to shop. Yet every aspect of shopping – from places where people shop and displays of goods to buy, to the status cues of advertisements and the convenience of easy financial credit – is calculated to appeal. Abundance, novelty, low prices, and exclusive styles lure shoppers to loosen their self-control and engage in shopping more (Underhill 1999). Branding and creating an emotional experience in the store are bids to get shoppers' loyalty. From stores' and manufacturers' point of view, there is profit to be gained by prolonging shoppers' stay in a "buying mode." For this reason, modern retailers continually develop new amenities and amass a larger assortment of merchandise to engage shoppers and keep them involved. This is the strategy of every shopping site, from activity-filled malls to "sticky" retail websites. If shopping is reputed to be an entertainment experience, or promoted as a way of saving time, it is nonetheless exhausting, requires an increasing amount of attention, and intrudes into the privacy of our home. It intrudes as well into public spaces like art museums and Internet search engines, that have been, until recently, a refuge from creeping commodification.

SHOPPING AS A CULTURAL FIELD

Clearly, shopping is more than just an economic exchange of goods, and different from an individual effort to find commodities that express identity, achieve a higher status, or satisfy desire. It is really a cultural field in Pierre Bourdieu's sense (Ferguson 1998), including a range of cultural texts and social institutions. This cultural field is the interface between production and consumption, which helps to create both producers and consumers. Although the shopping experience centers on specific kinds of stores (or websites), where goods are displayed and bought, the entire field translates the product cycles of manufacturers, messages in magazines and advertisements, and credit policies of states and banks into individual cultural practices. Consumer guidebooks and product reviews play an important mediating role because they present authoritative judgments that legitimize and set rules for shopping, voicing the rational as well as the aesthetic values shoppers pursue. The individual is both socialized to shop and socialized by the activities, places, and texts that make up shopping.

Shopping, then, brings together the micro-level construction of individual identity and the macro-level development of modernity. This suggests future research focusing on questions that have already emerged about the modern public sphere: implications of shoppers' mobility and fascination with commodities; the uses of shopping in different societies to exclude social groups from, or create common access to, public space; the integration of shopping into rituals of solidarity in families, communities, and localities. As an attitude toward goods that, in a rich society, often emphasizes sensual pleasure and escape from everyday concerns, shopping is often interpreted as a behavior of excess, showing a lack of self-control bordering on narcissism. But this judgment neglects the anxiety that accompanies many shoppers' choices: keeping within the rigid limits of a budget, finding a comfortable store, and making the *right* choice.

Psychologists report that an abundance of choices – of products, services, and means of consumption – increases shoppers' anxiety (Schwartz 2004). For sociologists, the issue of choice should suggest research focusing on how the public is formed by the social practices of stores and by the consumer guides and magazines that play the role of cultural intermediaries, as well as on how public policies in a shopping culture are formulated and received.

SEE ALSO: Advertising; Commodities, Commodity Fetishism, and Commodification; Consumer Culture, Children's; Consumption, Cathedrals of; Consumption and the Internet; Consumption, Mass Consumption, and Consumer Culture; Consumption Rituals; Department Store; Shopping Malls; Supermarkets

REFERENCES AND SUGGESTED READINGS

Benjamin, W. (1999) *The Arcades Project*, trans. by H. Eiland & K. McLaughlin. Belknap Press, Cambridge, MA.

Benson, S. P. (1986) *Counter Cultures: Saleswomen, Managers, and Customers in American Department Stores, 1890–1940*. Indiana University Press, Bloomington.

Ferguson, P. P. (1998) A Cultural Field in the Making: Gastronomy in 19th-Century France. *American Journal of Sociology* 104: 597–641.

Leach, W. (1993) *Land of Desire: Merchants, Power, and the Rise of a New American Power*. Pantheon, New York.

Miller, D. (1998) *A Theory of Shopping*. Polity Press, Cambridge.

Miller, D. (2001) *A Dialectics of Shopping*. University of Chicago Press, Chicago.

Schwartz, B. (2004) *The Paradox of Choice: Why More is Less*. Ecco, New York.

Shields, R. (Ed.) (1992) *Lifestyle Shopping – The Subject of Consumption*. Routledge, New York.

Underhill, P. (1999) *The Science of Shopping*. Simon & Schuster, New York.

Williams, R. (1982) *Dream Worlds: Mass Consumption in Late Nineteenth-Century France*. University of California Press, Berkeley.

Zukin, S. (2004) *Point of Purchase: How Shopping Changed American Culture*. Routledge, New York.

shopping malls

Lauren Langman

The shopping mall is one of the most important social locations and symbols of contemporary consumer society and its cornucopia of goods. It is typically a "self-contained" social environment with an assembly of stores and shops, carts and kiosks, and surely various eateries located in food courts. Shopping malls are the points of intersection between a vast globalized system where the production of highly advertised goods is distributed to individual consumers. They are sites of practices that mediate between the globalized factories and stores that sell the merchandise and individual interactions and identities that are today ever more dependent on the consumption of "branded" goods (Klein 1999).

Insofar as mall shopping is more frequent than church attendance in the United States and consumerism has taken on a religious hue, malls have often been termed "temples of consumption" (Kowinski 1985). As special places apart from the "ordinary world," people celebrate the "superior power" of the globalized commodity system through rituals of consumption that affirm their identities and lifestyles, as they pursue beliefs that the "goods life" offers access to simulated heavens on earth.

HISTORY

From the earliest prehistoric times, people have traded goods with each other. With the rise of permanent settlements and merchant and artisan classes, certain times and social places were designated for trade, such as fairs, markets, and celebrations, making commerce spatially situated. Village squares and marketplaces were places where people might not only trade goods, but also exchange socially relevant information (aka gossip). Traditional markets were as much concerned with maintaining social ties and relationships as commerce.

This pattern of trade began to change after the Crusades, when silks, spices, and porcelain from the East became more readily available to Europe. When Marco Polo returned with tales of the Middle Kingdom, as trade with the Levant (Eastern Mediterranean) began to flourish, a series of events would lead to one of the most significant social transformations in history: the rise of a rational, industrial, market society that would culminate in a now globalized, capitalist modernity.

In the Paris of 1822, following industrialization and urbanization, arcades (covered passages of shops) came into being. Glass roofs create a new permutation of the "built environment": protection from the weather. Arcades catered primarily to the growing affluent middle classes and created what Benjamin (1999) called "phantasmagorias" of commodities. These new "dream worlds of the city" became backgrounds for the urban dandy with the conspicuous leisure to stroll through the city, and create the new experiences of urban life.

Later in the nineteenth century, throughout Europe, with a growing middle class working in urban centers and mass transportation improvements, came the department store, with its vast collections of goods from fashions to household items. The latest fashions were elegantly displayed on mannequins. Magnificent "rooms" of furniture were displayed with careful attention to the new forms of electric lights, colors, and arrangements (Leach 1989).

Following World War II, shopping malls began to sprout up throughout the US. Although some malls had been built in the 1920s, with the federally financed expressway system, stores went to the suburbs, where the people were. There were four central features of the new shopping malls: (1) huge parking lots, (2) established department stores became "anchors" for the mall, (3) many tried to develop a particular theme to make them "different" from other malls and make customers feel special shopping there, and (4) malls were private property that attempted to recreate nostalgic forms of "main streets" replete with casual interactions.

With globalization fostering certain kinds of urban-based jobs in finance, law, etc., there came the gentrification of many cities and their transformation into shopping/entertainment centers in the late twentieth century. High rise urban malls began to emerge, such as Water Tower Place in Chicago. Concurrently, mega malls such as the Edmonton Mall and the Mall of America were on the rise. Further, malls are now likely not only to consist of shops, but some may also have casinos, movie theaters, chapels, amusement parks, nightclubs, or even hotels for those who might travel long distances just to shop at some of the hundreds of stores – most of which are available everywhere.

SOCIOLOGY OF THE MALL

It is often surprising that there has been very little sociological research and theory about shopping malls and mall-specific behavior. One of the first sociologists to study malls was Gottdiener (2001), whose work influenced many other sociologists, such as Crawford (1992), Ritzer (1999), and Zukin (2004).

Functions of Malls

Malls are primarily places where consumer goods made anywhere in the world can be distributed to people according to their social locations (real and imagined) and membership in particular cultures of taste, fashion, and sophistication – aspects of what Bourdieu has called "distinction." Almost two-thirds of the goods sold in the US are purchased at malls.

There are two faces of mall functions: social and design. Mall design functions to disguise the exchange relation of producer and consumer by stimulating consumer fantasies (Gottdiener 2001). Malls are designed to lead consumers to walk through sequences of small and anchor stores, arranged on the basis of consumer behavior studies. Halls and fancy atriums are meant to add the leisure of a mall visit to support consumption maximization. In order to create symbolic differences between malls selling more or less the same goods, they are often "themed," given an overall motif connoting luxury, nostalgia or perhaps high tech fantasy (Gottdiener 2001). With the added symbolism provided by themes, malls now are not only about production and distribution, but also other phenomena related to goods and services: advertising, marketing, sales, individual taste, style, fashion (Ritzer 1999: 6). Despite their goal to be "different," the motifs that are considered "successful" in attracting customers to the malls are often repeated in other malls.

Malls as Social Locations

Perhaps the Arcades Project of Benjamin (1999) remains the most comprehensive classical attempt to frame the roofed passages as a new site of consumption with new modes of experiencing oneself and others. To Kowinski (1985), malls were spiritual places. Gottdiener emphasized the extent to which malls were exemplars of produced spaces that became essential moments of consumer society, exemplars of "theming," the creation of a coherent ambience in which symbolic differences attempt to give place a special leitmotif, and in turn loyalty to a specific place of consumption and location for the realization of the consumer-based self. For Ritzer (1999), malls, as "cathedrals of consumption," were places where the rationality of modernity was masked by a "re-enchantment of the world" to encourage consumption.

Some malls attempt to simulate public spaces for community events. For example, Christmas celebrations in shopping malls are typical, and may perhaps encourage some more shopping as well. Some malls encourage visits at Halloween by suggesting they are considered safer to do trick-or-treating for children rather than knocking on the door of a stranger's house (Chin 2001). Meanwhile, the parents may happen to buy things. People wandering about in malls are perceived more positively compared to those in outdoor public spaces, since the "controlled environment" of the mall is absent from the actual downtown urban space. This keeps out "unwanted people" and/or political ideas.

Shopping Mall Selfhood

Malls are the places that can be seen as sites where consumerism "colonizes the lifeworld of the self." One can buy the accoutrements of identity to fashion a "fantastic" subjectivity, including modes of gratifying self-presentations and appearances that awaken an often moribund self, and incorporation of one into consumption-based subcultures (Langman 1992), especially in a "branded" world when a "brand" is a synecdoche for a distinct, albeit imaginary identity and lifestyle (Klein 1999). Chin's (2001) study found that the consumer sphere in shopping malls is an almost imaginary world for African American girls from poor families, distracting them from threat and victimization from men and their childhood vulnerability at home. Malls are the places for subjective doing, being, and becoming, serving functional, existential, and imaginary purposes for the realization of consumer-based selfhood, often satisfying "needs" that are fostered by media-based programming and advertisement. "Being-in-the-mall," a fundamental ontological moment, results in being seen as a consumer and confirmed as one who can and does shop. For some people, being recognized as one who can and does buy an RL or DKNY jacket or a Rolex watch is often the best experience they have. The amount of money spent in the mall to buy is influenced by the degree of exposure to the consumer culture and limitations of buying power.

SOCIOLOGICAL RESEARCH OF MALLS

How do people experience malls? Although the research is often impressionistic rather that systematic, it has been suggested that malls provide an adventurous rush of new experiences; there is a feeling of leisurely "timelessness" where people seem not to be in a hurry. They give a cosmopolitan feeling of being somewhere "special" rather than in a kind of fortress. An important topic has been the extent to which malls as private properties are used as "public places," alternatives to schools or city centers, yet security guards often exclude political actions such as leafleting or petitioning and thus act to constrain free speech.

A number of research agendas have looked at specific features of malls, such as the impact of total closed circuit television (CCTV) surveillance as a disciplinary practice. Similarly, a topic that has warranted much attention has been the patterns of inclusion and exclusion. Malls generally don't want certain kinds of people: the poor, the unemployed (thought to be there not to buy but to steal), or the political. Those who are just likely to congregate and not buy much – aka teenage mall rats seeking hangouts – are observed closely or directed to inferior merchandise. Yet, at the same time, they are the primary consumers of certain kinds of fashions, music, videos, etc.

Most research on malls has been done by developers and marketers studying the demographics and psychographics of a potential consumer base. For example, Weiss (1988) has shown how American consumer patterns readily differ by zip codes, where people live. There are some 40 or more clusters of shoppers, some, like "young suburbia," are more likely to shop in malls than the more affluent, more educated, more urban "money and brains" or "new bohemians." Similarly, a great deal of marketing research has attempted to look at sales in terms of store location within the mall, store design, product placement, and even such things as lighting, scent, and the fashions of the sales staff as they impact consumers.

Malls present major challenges for social research, not the least of which is because of the many ways they can be studied, their historical evolution, impact on land use, class reproduction, job creation, or semiotic analyses of their design, décor, and ambience. Much less has been charted about malls as sites for social practices. Ethnographic studies typically require a stable population; mall shoppers typically come and go.

Some elites criticize the banality and commercialization of malls, yet consumption of various goods can and does provide some people with various pleasures, such as incorporation into peer groups – especially for the many people who do work that is both necessary and undesirable ("shadow work"). Malls provide realms where shopping is fun and buying or using goods provides valorized identities with agency and creativity.

FUTURE OF MALLS

In the past decade, the dominance of the mall as the primary site for the distribution of mass produced goods has faced at least two major challenges. Foregrounded by the growing inequality and wage stagnation, the stand alone "big box" superstores like Wal-Mart and Costco and Target have been growing rapidly. While such stores do not have as wide a range of goods and brands, they do offer "savings" on quantity purchases. The other threat to the mall has been the proliferation of "virtual malls" on the Internet. Most of the products available at the mall can be purchased online and often for less cost in time and money than going to the mall.

In order for malls to continue to stay in business, they will need to offer activities that cannot be easily done at home, as when movie theaters came to malls to take advantage of the empty parking lots in the evenings. Malls will need to offer people a lot more than goods to be able to sell them goods. For example, Edmonton Mall and the Mall of America include a number of amusements, such as rides for kiddies and sophisticated restaurants for parents. However, to expect malls to become full community and activity centers is probably asking too much considering their ability to exclude people, activities, and ideas. In a globalized world, the mall serves a central role in mediating advertising, fostering consumerism, and socializing the "emotion rules" and modes of experiencing the consumer self and the world.

SEE ALSO: Arcades; Consumption, Cathedrals of; Consumption, Landscapes of; Consumption Rituals; Consumption, Spectacles of; Department Store; *Flânerie*; Globalization, Consumption and; Shopping

REFERENCES AND SUGGESTED READINGS

Benjamin, W. (1999) *The Arcades Project*. Belknap Press of Harvard University Press, Cambridge, MA.

Bourdieu, P. (1984) *Distinction: A Social Critique of the Judgement of Taste*. Harvard University Press, Cambridge, MA.

Chin, E. M. L. S. (2001) *Purchasing Power: Black Kids and American Consumer Culture*. University of Minnesota Press, Minneapolis.

Crawford, M. (1992) The World in a Shopping Mall. In: M. Sorkin (Ed.), *Variations on a Theme Park: The New American City and the End of Public Space*. Hill & Wang, New York, pp. 3–30.

Gottdiener, M. (2001) *The Theming of America: Dreams, Visions, and Commercial Spaces*. Westview Press, Boulder.

Klein, N. (1999) *No Logo*. Picador, New York.

Kowinski, W. S. (1985) *The Malling of America: An Inside Look at the Great Consumer Paradise*. William Morrow, New York.

Langman, L. (1992) Neon Cages: Shopping for Subjectivity. In: R. Shields (Ed.), *Lifestyle Shopping: The Subject of Consumption*. Routledge, London, pp. 40–82.

Leach, W. R. (1989) *Consuming Visions: Accumulation and Display of Goods in America 1880–1920*. Norton, New York.

Ritzer, G. (1999) *Enchanting a Disenchanted World: Revolutionizing the Means of Consumption*. Pine Forge Press, London.

Weiss, M. J. (1988) *The Clustering of America*. Harper & Row, New York.

Zukin, S. (2004) *Point of Purchase: How Shopping Changed American Culture*. Routledge, New York.

shushin koyo

Ross Mouer

Literally translated as "end-of-life employment," *shushin koyo* is commonly rendered as "lifetime employment." The term has often been used out of context to refer to a practice of hiring employees at a young age and then continuously employing them until they die. This usage is associated with an emphasis on mutual commitment between the employer and the employee within a paternalistic framework. Some have argued that the employment relationship came out of the traditional sense of loyalty associated with the *samurai* in service to his master and the reciprocal obligations of the overlord to his retainers. Other factors commonly mentioned as supporting such a commitment at work include Japan's bureaucratic tradition in state-run enterprises, the interests of management in retaining skilled employees, and the need felt by many ordinary Japanese males after Japan's defeat in the Pacific War to reorient their strong sense of identity which had previously revolved around the nation-state.

More sanguine observers and ordinary Japanese have thought of *shushin koyo* in more practical terms as referring rather loosely to long-term or career employment. Labor turnover in Japan has been significant throughout the post-war period, and few think of *shushin koyo* as an actual practice, although many are cognizant that overall levels of labor mobility among Japanese firms may be lower than in many other industrialized economies (such as in America or Australia). They too will know that it is much lower in Japan's large firms than in its smaller ones. It has also been accepted that Japan's large firms have traditionally been better able to absorb the effects of economic downturns and to subsidize a certain degree of redundancy in such situations. Smaller firms have never had that margin and have had to behave in an economically more rationalistic manner. Nevertheless, recession and the further globalization of Japan's economy combined in the 1990s to increase the pressure on Japan's large firms to trim their workforce; some large firms went bankrupt and many others moved quickly to downsize and reduce fixed labor costs as a component of their overall operating costs. The unemployment rate in Japan rose from around 2.5 in the late 1980s to over 5 percent by 2000.

Debate about the actual practice of *shushin koyo* aside, many have argued that its greater importance has been as an ideal for many Japanese. Regardless of whether or not workers stayed with their firm for longer periods than workers in other countries, many argued that

the crux of the matter lies in understanding the cultural and social context in which employers would not unreasonably dismiss employees. The commitment on the part of the employer was reinforced in at least two ways. One was in the realization and belief that poverty was a serious issue in Japan immediately after the war when a consensus seemed to emerge that each standard household should be able to have at least one secure breadwinner. The other was that the shift from age to seniority as a criterion determining wages or salaries made sense if long-term employment was assured.

Long-term employment guarantees have tended to go hand in hand with the institutionalization of salary systems for most regular (male) employees. This tended to fix wage costs regardless of hours worked up to a point, an approach which tended to put pressure on many firms that struggled during recessionary times, and this was certainly the case since the 1990s.

It should be noted that the commitment to maintain employment for a household head did not necessarily extend to other members of the household. Before the mid- to late 1980s, Japanese women were often encouraged or even pressured to resign upon marriage, or upon reaching an arbitrary age (such as 30 or 31). The practice of hiring offspring (sons or daughters) varied, but the principle in most firms offering *shushin koyo* guarantees was that entry to the firm would be based on some notion of competitively demonstrated merit. Finally, employment associated with the *shushin koyo* guarantee was to begin immediately after graduation and extend to age 55 in most firms, an age not too far removed from the average life expectancy in the late 1940s and early 1950s.

As a set of cultural expectations, the notion of *shushin koyo* was central to the emergence in the 1960s of Japan's *sarariman* (salaried employee) as the key element in the formation of a new social class, and to the concomitant development of the mass culture associated with Japan having a broadly based middle class that initially spread across blue- and white-collar employment in Japan's large firms, and then came to include those employed in medium-sized and smaller firms (for more on Japan's middle class at that time see Vogel 1963). The stability for families that flowed from the *shushin koyo* guarantee fueled homeownership, successive waves of consumerism, and the materialism associated with the new lifestyle. As a way of life, the *sarariman* lifestyle incorporated a kind of womb-to-tomb tradeoff. For the *sarariman's* offspring this involved a commitment to doing their best at school and in a series of entrance examinations (*juken benkyo*). For many students this meant extra tuition in *juku* (private schools offering supplementary instruction) or *yobiko* (preparatory schools). For the cohort it meant over time a growing percentage of students attending private high schools and tertiary institutions. The pressure on students to start their salaried careers on the highest possible wage-age trajectory in the best possible firm reflected a credentialism which has over time led to decreasing intergenerational mobility and the reproduction of social class in contemporary Japan as described by Sato (2000) and others.

To obtain greater productivity at the firm level, management has over time developed a number of techniques to remove redundant employees. Most important is the fact that promotion has been more tightly linked to performance-based criteria in ways that determine the trajectory that each employee's age-wage curve follows. However, the major means of regulating fixed labor costs have been natural attrition through the fixed retirement age (known as *teinen*) and the freedom to decide the number of new graduates to be hired as replacements each April. In recent years there has been a tendency to hire fewer graduates as regular employees for *shushin koyo*-type positions and an increased reliance on part-time employees, freelancers, dispatched workers, and subcontractors. The move away from the idealized patterns of long-term employment has been reinforced by the movement of educated and otherwise skilled women into traditionally male domains, a reconstituting of career paths owing to equal employment opportunity legislation, the influx of migrant workers, multiculturalization, and the overall diversification of lifestyles (and hence the needs and motivations of employees). Taken together, these changes are altering the notion of *shushin koyo* as the dominant cultural practice associated with employment for male household heads.

One final issue connected to *shushin koyo* as a practice tied to a clear idea of *teinen* has been the rapid aging of the population, with the proportion of the population aged 65 and older increasing from 5.3 percent in 1955 to 17.3 percent in 2000. During the 1970s and 1980s this was partially accommodated in large firms by gradually moving the fixed retirement age up from 55 to 60. Since then many firms have introduced or formalized schemes for "rehiring" employees who had officially retired. Many also have informal means of redeploying retired employees in subsidiaries or subcontracting firms. While this often accommodated the needs of better-performing employees, those whose performance was below average often had to struggle as pensioners. Pension schemes are varied and complex, a factor adding anxiety to many Japanese employees over the decade preceding retirement. At the beginning of the twenty-first century many ideas are being discussed with regard to the financing of pensions and to their availability. One is to postpone access to pensions until a later age. Although this needs to be coupled to thinking about the fixed retirement age, it should be noted that by international standards a large percent of the Japanese population aged over 65 is still working. In 2000, 34.1 percent of Japanese men aged 65 and over (and 14.4 percent of women) were working. This compared with 16.9 and 9.1 percent in the US, 3.7 and 1.8 percent in France, and 10.7 and 2.8 percent in Italy (Japan Institute of Labor 2002: 17). At the same time, the increasing casualization of work in Japan is likely to see a growing disparity in retirement between (1) those who have been in the privileged *shushin koyo* sector as regular (male) employees in Japan's large established firms and enjoy the benefit of having a substantial component of their pension coming from a firm-linked private fund and (2) those who rely heavily on the state-funded component of their pensions.

SEE ALSO: Enterprise Unions; Japanese-Style Management; *Nenko Chingin*; Salary Men

REFERENCES AND SUGGESTED READINGS

Japan Institute of Labor (2002) *Japanese Working Life Profile: 2002 – Labor Satistics*. Japan Institute of Labor, Tokyo

Mouer, R. & Kawanishi, H. (2005) *A Sociology of Work in Japan*. Cambridge University Press, Cambridge.

Sato, T. (2000) *Fubyodo shakai Nihon: Sayonara sochuryu* (*The Unequal Society Japan: Farewell to the Mass Middle-Class Society*). Chuo Koron Sha, Tokyo.

Vogel, E. (1963) *Japan's New Middle Class*. University of California Press, Berkeley.

sibling relationships during old age

Ingrid Arnet Connidis

A growing interest in old siblings reflects the potential increase in their importance at a time when union dissolution is high and birth rates low. For many subjects, a definition merely begins the story. In the case of older siblings, defining the term and exploring different types of sibship remain compelling research challenges. Traditional definitions refer to the category of full siblings, related to one another through two biological parents. This restrictive definition excludes those who are half-siblings (related through one shared biological parent), adopted siblings (related through legal adoption), and step–siblings (related to one another through subsequent marriages of one or both biological or adoptive parents). In earlier times, acquiring step–siblings typically occurred after the death of one parent and subsequent remarriage of the other. Now, step–siblings are more likely to result from the remarriage of one or both parents following divorce. For most old persons today, these categories cover the vast majority of siblings; the future will bring an even broader array of adult sibling types in the wake of more marriage-like unions that also produce children.

Relatively little research concerns old siblings in their own right, but in recent decades research on siblings has finally extended beyond childhood. The bulk of studies tend to be psychological or developmental (Cicirelli 1995); to focus on university-aged adults; to address assumed traits of sibling relationships such as rivalry; or, when extended into middle age, to explore siblings largely in the context of caring for their parents rather than their direct relationships with one another. The variety of research on adult siblings, including cohort comparisons, suggests a general portrait of change in sibling ties over the life course and of a significant tie in later life.

The sibling bond is unique in the contradictory expectations that it include the obligations of family membership but, as a tie between relative peers, it should also be relatively voluntary (Allan 1977). This makes siblings an ideal relationship for exploring the *ambivalence* that characterizes family relationships at both the sociological and psychological levels (Connidis & McMullin 2002). Exploring sibling ties benefits from and in turn helps to extend the theoretical constructs of the life course and ambivalence (Walker et al. in press).

Sibling ties are very active in youth, then go through a period of relative dormancy, and eventually resurface once long-term relationships are established or disbanded, children are raised, and paid work is either stabilized or left behind, sometimes through job loss but usually through retirement. On the way to this more active phase in sibling relationships, various life transitions may rekindle bonds between siblings, as they reach out to and for one another. Life changes such as the illness or death of parents and other family members, divorce, widowhood, remarriage, and relocation nearby, often heighten sibling contact and support. Research on the negotiation of the sibling tie in the context of caring for a parent, particularly one without a partner, indicates the dynamics of family life and its interplay with larger social forces (Matthews 2002). Structured social relations based on gender, age, class, race, ethnicity, and sexual orientation play themselves out and are evident in studies *across* families (families of different races, classes, and ethnic background negotiate sibling ties differently) and *within* families (gender and sexual orientation influence the respective positions of siblings in the family network, including their relative responsibilities for particular obligations).

Even during times of relative inactivity as measured by contact, emotional closeness persists in the shared memories and reflections of siblings. The observed significance of reminiscence on old age adds a unique quality and value to sibling ties – typically the relationship that endures the longest in most of our lives. Women and single and childless persons have particularly involved sibling ties. Those who have fewer alternative attachments do not simply rely more heavily on their siblings; indications are that they also invest more heavily in them, directly as siblings and less directly as aunts and uncles (Connidis 2001). This means that older persons who have a sister or a single or a childless sibling are also more likely to sustain more active sibling relationships.

The greater involvement of sisters than brothers can be linked to both demographic trends and social structure. Because they live longer, women are more likely to either enjoy or require the company of someone other than a partner. This difference in availability is reinforced by socially constructed gender relations in which age remains a liability for old women who are interested in an intimate relationship (many are not). The stronger sister connections are also reinforced by a stronger culture of caring among women than men that is a further instance of socially structured gender relations.

An area of study that is likely to further our understanding of sibling ties particularly and family ties more generally is the extent to which divisions based on class occur *within* families when siblings are adults and no longer assume the same class position by virtue of their shared childhood. In the case of old persons, a related research question concerns the effect of timing – when sibling ties are acquired – on the long-term relationship between brothers and sisters. As well, many adults form close bonds with their partners' siblings that carry into old age; thus, siblings-in-law and their equivalent are important sibling types about whom we need to learn more.

SEE ALSO: Aging and the Life Course, Theories of; Aging and Social Support; Family Structure; Family Theory; Gender, Aging and; Life Course and Family; Life Course Perspective; Sibling Ties

REFERENCES AND SUGGESTED READINGS

Allan, G. (1977) Sibling Solidarity. *Journal of Marriage and the Family* 39: 177–83.

Cicirelli, V. G. (1995) *Sibling Relationships Across the Lifespan*. Plenum Press, New York.

Connidis, I. A. (2001) *Family Ties and Aging*. Sage, Thousand Oaks, CA.

Connidis, I. A. & McMullin, J. A. (2002) Sociological Ambivalence and Family Ties: A Critical Perspective. *Journal of Marriage and Family* 64: 558–67.

Matthews, S. H. (2002) *Sisters and Brothers/ Daughters and Sons: Meeting the Needs of Old Parents*. Unlimited Publishing, Bloomington.

Walker, A. J., Allen, K. R., & Connidis, I. A. (in press) Theorizing and Studying Sibling Ties in Adulthood. In: Bengtson, V. L. Acock, A. C., Allen, K. R., Dilworth-Anderson, P., & Klein, D. M. (Eds.), *Sourcebook on Family Theory and Research*. Sage, Thousand Oaks, CA.

White, L. K. & Reidmann, A. (1992) Ties Among Adult Siblings. *Social Forces* 7: 85–102.

sibling ties

Melanie Mauthner

Sibling ties are some of the most widespread and enduring intimate relationships. Located at the border of kinship and friendship, the sociology of siblings largely centers on childhood and old age, rivalry and social support. The role of sibling ties at other stages of the life course – youth and adulthood – and in relation to other topics such as mental illness, substance abuse, disability, and domestic violence (Sanders 2004) is neglected. Principally explored from an adult carer perspective and a policy and professional agenda rather than through a sociological lens, sibling ties are little understood. Exceptions include schooling, fostering, and adoption decisions, where the importance of sibling ties is recognized. Yet they continue to be viewed in relation to parent–child bonds rather than as relationships in their own right.

Until the 1980s the sociology of siblings was influenced by ideas from developmental psychology. Sibling ties were explored through a behavioral and cognitive lens with incest, eating disorders, aggression, and educational achievement as dominant themes. Other angles that characterized the field were the intensity and effects of sibling ties. Links between these elements and parental neglect and the endurance of sibling ties over time received a lot of attention. As a sphere of social interaction, support, and as a network even, empirical work was in its infancy until sociologists began to explore meanings of different types of adult sibling ties (Allan 1977).

Numerous factors account for sociological neglect of sibling ties until the 1980s. One was the preeminence in family studies of issues connected to marriage, reproduction, and parenting rather than to intimacy more generally, including lesbian/gay ties, friendship, and sibship. A second factor was the pervasive emphasis on the child as individual and on the mother–child bond rather than on the child as a member of a generational sibling group. Third, psychoanalytic notions of envy and the trauma of displacement after the birth of a sibling made it difficult to challenge either the rivalry or the deviance discourses (Coles 2003). Indeed, these continue to influence everyday understandings of hostility and misbehavior as perceived in sibling ties. A fourth factor was the absence of siblings' own narratives about what it means to be a sister or brother. This invisibility mirrored that of previously marginalized relationships in studies of domestic life among stepfamilies and nonheterosexual households. Fifth, there was a tendency to ignore sibling ties as constitutive of power relations and caring practices and socializing in themselves. In retrospect this silence appears ethnocentric for overlooking kin arrangements based on lateral rather than vertical connections.

Gradually, researchers instigated cross-disciplinary dialogues that placed sibling ties in social life firmly on the map (Zukow 1989). Attention shifted to social context, intra-household links, life events, and concepts such as negotiation and reciprocity. By the 1990s sociologists influenced by social constructionist and feminist perspectives started to investigate siblings as a social group (Walker et al. 2005). They examined the intrinsic value of their ties across the life course in order to understand patterns of transnational migration, family employment, and gendered identity. Ethnographies of sibling life and a sibling standpoint emerged (Song 1999; Mauthner 2002) as sociologists explored changing forms of intimacy in relation to residency, shared history, and belonging to familial cultures and ethnic communities.

There has been little sociological research on sibling ties, especially across the life course. Sibling ties now form part of sociological inquiry into the social relations of intimacy, care, and identity; no longer are they merely of concern in relation to instances of "clinical adaptation" (Lamb and Sutton-Smith 1982). For the topic of sibling sociology to grow, there is a need for a broader range of issues to be addressed and for more diverse theories and methodologies to be used, particularly more qualitative and longitudinal approaches. There is a need to investigate the complexity of the ties, the components of their longevity, and how they shape identity in psychic life. New interdisciplinary work attempts to define multiple meanings of "sibling," of sameness and difference, agency and interdependence, and of continuity and change by drawing on psychoanalysis, poststructuralism, and cultural geography.

A priority is to establish how competing discourses of rivalry, deviance, and care coexist in forming contested meanings of sibling ties. Other directions and topics ripe for investigation include more work exploring generational and historical dimensions, socio-legal aspects of sibling partnership and citizenship rights, sibling representations in popular culture, sibling experiences of asylum and resettlement, and memories of mental illness, adoption, and fostering. Sibling sociology is likely to encompass work on sibling identities shaped by previously overlooked sociodemographic variables such as ethnicity, class, and dis/ability. Greater methodological diversity will reveal the particularity and cultural specificity of sibling ties rather than their universal attributes. More research employing ethnography, memory work, and biographical methods will be useful. Thus, a new body of work documenting psychosocial elements of sibling ties for understanding identity and intimacy will emerge.

SEE ALSO: Kinship; Life Course and Family; Sibling Relationships During Old Age

REFERENCES AND SUGGESTED READINGS

Allan, G. (1977) Sibling Solidarity. *Journal of Marriage and the Family* 39: 177–84.

Coles, P. (2003) *The Importance of Sibling Relationships in Psychoanalysis.* Karnac Books, London.

Lamb, M. E. & Sutton-Smith, B. (Eds.) (1982) *Sibling Relationships: Their Significance Across the Lifespan.* Lawrence Erlbaum Associates, London.

Mauthner, M. (2002) *Sistering: Power and Change in Female Relationships.* Palgrave, Basingstoke.

Sanders, R. (2004) *Sibling Relationships: Theory and Issues for Practice.* Palgrave, Basingstoke.

Song, M. (1999) *Helping Out: Children's Labor in Ethnic Businesses.* Temple University Press, Philadelphia.

Walker, A. J., Allen, K. R., & Connidis, I. A. (2005) Theorizing and Studying Sibling Ties in Adulthood. In: Bengston, V. L., Acock, A. C., Allen, K. R., Dilworth-Anderson, P., & Klein, D. M. (Eds.), *Sourcebook of Family Theory and Research.* Sage, Thousand Oaks, CA.

Zukow, P. G. (Ed.) (1989) *Sibling Interaction across Cultures: Theoretical and Methodological Issues*, Springer-Verlag, New York.

sick role

Andrew C. Twaddle

The sick role was a formulation by Talcott Parsons that posited four institutionalized behavioral expectations that attached to people defined as "sick." For about three decades, from the early 1950s to about 1980, it was the central focus of many sociologists who studied medical care. It received a large amount of criticism as well as uncritical use and became passé when Parsons's theory fell out of favor and sociology turned toward a more critical and conflict-oriented approach to theorizing.

On the surface, it is quite simple and straightforward.

1 Sick people are expected to be *exempt from normal role obligations.* That exemption is limited and conditional. It is limited in the sense that one cannot claim exemption beyond some limit on one's own authority. At some point the right to exemption will have to be legitimated by someone with authority. It is conditional on the obligations of the sick role being fulfilled and by the "nature and severity of the condition."

2 Sick people are expected to be *"not responsible" for their condition* in the sense that they cannot get well by an act of motivation alone. The sick person "needs help" and has a claim on the larger community for care. It is important, in the light of subsequent criticisms, to note that this right does not attach to the onset of the condition, but to its continuation. Even if the condition arose because of the actions of the affected person, she still needs treatment to recover.

3 Sick people are expected to be motivated toward recovery, to *want to get well.* This expectation is an obligation that is one of the conditions for the two rights just noted. If the sick person seems to be motivated by secondary gain, the legitimacy of the two rights may be rescinded. They may become defined as not entitled to care or exemption from expectations attached to "normal" people.

4 Sick people are expected to *seek and cooperate with technically competent help.* This obligation limits the rights of the first two expectations, in part by being evidence of meeting the obligation of the third one. At some point, varying with the "nature and severity of the condition," sick people need the legitimation of a competent treatment agent in order to continue being entitled to care and to exemptions from normal expectations. In the light of subsequent criticisms, it is important to note that Parsons did not say that the "competent treatment agent" had to be a physician, but that physicians were the most commonly used.

There are some important contexts that are vital for understanding the sick role and which, when not taken into account, have led to considerable misunderstanding of the concept. First, the sick role applies only to those defined as sick, making it important to differentiate sickness from the related concepts of disease and illness on the one hand and other forms of "deviant behavior" on the other. Second, it was developed as a small part of Parsons's life's work, an attempt to generate a "general theory of action" under an "action frame of reference" that would unify the social sciences.

DISEASE, ILLNESS, AND SICKNESS

Sickness is a social identity, a defined incapacity for normal socially expected task and role performance. It is related to, but not the same as, disease, which is a physiological malfunction – an infection, mechanical breakdown, or degeneration resulting in reduced capacity and/or life expectancy. Nor is it the same as illness, a subjective feeling of health based on body state perceptions and/or feelings of competence. Disease has an organic basis, illness is social-psychological, but sickness is distinctively sociological.

Many critics have held that the sick role is more attuned to acute disease and not very appropriate for chronic disease (e.g., diabetes), on the grounds that the third expectation could not apply to people who are by definition not going to recover. Nor would it apply to trivial diseases (e.g., common cold) that do not result in professional consultations, stigmatized diseases (e.g., addiction, STDs, some mental illness) in which people are held responsible for their condition, or various permanent legitimate roles (sickly, handicapped, mentally retarded, etc.). If the focus is on incapacity as a source of nonconformity, disease and illness become contextual triggering and bargaining events. Distinctions between acute and chronic become less salient. At the same time, many characteristics of the "nature and severity" of the condition, including prognosis and the specific incapacities of individual cases, have been shown to modify behavioral expectations.

It is of at least passing interest that the biographical beginning of Parsons's work on the sick role, in addition to having an admired physician brother, was his own diagnosis with diabetes, a chronic disease.

ACTION FRAME OF REFERENCE

The sick role was a small part of Parsons's attempt to build a general theory of action. The most immediate context was, on one hand, his approach to the problem of social deviance and social control, which differentiated motivated and unmotivated deviance; crime and sickness as alternative forms of deviance; punishment and therapy as alternative responses to deviance; and the criminal justice system and the medical care system as alternative systems of social control. In this context, the sick role was an illustration of how sick people were different from criminals. Sickness was a designation for the condition where people deviate from social norms not because they "want to" but because they "can't help it." They lack the capacity for conformity and "need help, not punishment" to come into compliance.

Another important context was Parsons's concern with the modernization of societies along five axes he called pattern variables. He accepted the general view of sociological theorists that the rise of the business community was the hallmark of capitalism and the modern era. However, he posited that at the same time business was coming to dominance, the professions were rising to prominence. While they were also harbingers of modern society, they were distinct from business interests.

Professions and business were held to be similar with respect to the pattern variables except for one that distinguished self-interest and collectivity-interest. Here business was seen as self-interested, while the professions manifested collectivity-interest. Physicians were the prototype profession. Patients, and by extension clients of other professions, were people with problems they could not definitively identify or solve, hence they were dependent upon others with both expert knowledge and control of the means of treatment. In this state, they were vulnerable to exploitation and required a relationship in which they could trust the professional to work in their interest toward the collective goal of effecting a cure, if possible, or stabilization and control if cure were not an option. This was in stark contrast to the competitive *caveat emptor* ethos of business.

A third theoretical concern (much less developed with reference to the sick role) was the delineation of essential requirements for the continuity of societies, the "functional imperatives." Here Parsons held that maintaining, at some level, a healthy population was required for needed tasks and roles to be performed. It was hence important to make provision for some way of bringing sick people back to a capacity level that made the work of the society possible.

Most of the sociologists and others concerned with health, sickness, and medical care were (and are) more interested in variations within societies than in the characteristics of societies as global entities. Considerable documentation accumulated that the behavior of symptomatic and sick people varies along social class and ethnic lines and is strongly influenced by interaction patterns in families, neighborhoods, work settings, and friendship groups. From this work came an empirically based critique of the sick role along several lines; most important was that the concept did not focus on questions of core importance to most sociologists.

Another important dimension of the criticisms was the observation that most disease and illness episodes are relatively minor and self-limiting. Only a small minority ever comes to medical attention. Instead, people treat themselves, generating in the US a huge over-the-counter trade in remedies. In addition, many people use what is now called alternative medicine. The sick role was seen as too focused on the physician and the medical encounter.

The emphasis in the sick role formulation on the helplessness of the patient and her or his dependence on the physician for knowledge, skill, and access to resources was seen as underplaying the agency of patients. Interactions involved in the treatment of chronic disease are less likely to follow an activity–passivity model and more likely to be of a guidance–cooperation or mutual participation type. The one kind of patient most likely to be passively dependent, the critically "ill" in the intensive care unit, has seldom been studied.

It is worth noting that most studies of sickness behavior have been done on hospitalized low-income patients in the subsidized services of general hospitals. These are the conditions that maximize the social status and power differentials between physicians and patients, probably skewing the research toward the most insecure and deferential patients. If studies were done on the "gold coast" private services or in private medical receptions, we might see a different set of expectations operating (or not).

Work on sickness behavior has changed toward patient decision-making, using variants of the sickness career model which treats the sick role expectations as a set of parameters around which considerable variation is expected and incorporates other models, such as the health beliefs model and the concept of illness

behavior. It is an example of macro-micro theorizing.

People whose health status is in question interact with others who reflect the sick role expectations through the filters of their own social class and ethnic identities, as well as their specific relationship with the afflicted individual. A process of consultation and negotiation takes place around a series of questions that frame the career of the sick person: whether a change from "normal" has taken place; whether that change is significant; whether help is needed; the type of help needed; the treatment agent to be consulted; and the nature and degree of "cooperation" with treatment recommendations. With such an approach, it is possible to document the rich variety of human response to symptoms while understanding the structural impact of class and ethnicity and retaining the important insights of the sick role formulation.

In the last 30 years or so attention in medical sociology has shifted away from the social psychology of sickness and toward a focus on medical care systems and social conflict. The study of sickness, however, remains both theoretically and practically important and the sick role is still a meaningful framework for a part of that study.

SEE ALSO: Capitalism; Chronic Illness and Disability; Complementary and Alternative Medicine; Deviance; Health Behavior; Health Professions and Occupations; Health, Self-Rated; Illness Behavior; Illness Experience; Illness Narrative; Metatheory; Parsons, Talcott; Patient–Physician Relationship; Professions; Role; Social Control

REFERENCES AND SUGGESTED READINGS

Bury, M. (1991) The Sociology of Chronic Illness: A Review of Research and Prospects. *Sociology of Health and Illness* 4: 167–82.

Freidson, E. (1962) Medical Sociology. *Current Sociology* 10/11.

Freidson, E. (1970) *Profession of Medicine*. Dodd Mead, New York.

Gallagher, E. (1979) Lines of Reconstruction and Extension in the Parsonian Sociology of Illness. In: Jaco, E. (Ed.), *Patients, Physicians and Illness*. Free Press, New York.

Gordon, G. (1966) *Role Theory and Illness*. College and University Press, New Haven.

Parsons, T. (1951) *The Social System*. Free Press, Glencoe, IL.

Parsons, T. (1958) Definitions of Health and Illness in the Light of American Values and Social Structure. In: Jaco, E. (Ed.), *Patients, Physicians and Illness*. Free Press, New York.

Rier, D. (2000) The Missing Voice of the Critically Ill: A Medical Sociologist's First-person Account. *Sociology of Health and Illness* 22 (1): 68–93.

Twaddle, A. (1969) Health Decisions and Sick Role Variations. *Journal of Health and Social Behavior* 10: 105–15.

Twaddle, A. (1974) The Concept of Health Status. *Social Science and Medicine* 8: 29–38.

Twaddle, A. (1979) *Sickness Behavior and the Sick Role*. G. K. Hall, Boston; Schenkman, Cambridge.

Twaddle, A. (1982) From Medical Sociology to the Sociology of Health: Some Changing Concerns in the Sociological Study of Sickness and Treatment. In: Bottomore, T., Nowak, S., & Sokolowska, M. (Eds.), *Sociology: The State of the Art*. Sage, London, pp. 323–58.

Twaddle, A. & Hessler, R. (1987) *Sociology of Health*. Macmillan, New York.

Twaddle, A. & Nordenfelt, L. (1994) *Disease, Illness and Sickness*. Tema H, Universitet i Linköping, Linköping, Sweden.

significant others

Erica Owens

Significant others are those persons who are of sufficient importance in an individual's life to affect the individual's emotions, behavior, and sense of self. While in common parlance "significant other" has come to designate a romantic partner, sociologists' broader use of the term would include other relations such as family members and close friends or mentors. Through interactions with significant others, and perceptions of their responses to one's behavior, an individual gains a sense of who he or she is, and comes to understand how to act in a given context and role. Self-concept is based largely on our perceptions – whether accurate or not – of who we are in the eyes of those whose opinions matter to us.

The term "significant other" was coined by Harry Stack Sullivan, who identified significant others as those who directly socialize the person to whom they are significant. Sullivan (1940) and George Herbert Mead (1967) suggest that socialization relies upon a person's considering the other's view of himself or herself as important. Having positive feelings toward another will greatly increase the chances that this person will become significant, and thus serve as a reference for belief and behavior.

Mead was among the first to recognize the role of important others in the development and maintenance of identity. According to Mead, there is no inherent or core self present at birth. Rather, the self is a social product that develops in stages through the process of social interaction. The key to this process is the ability to take the role of the other party in an interaction, or picture what the other might do, think, or say within a given context. Taking the role of the other allows a person to make behavioral choices based upon these perceived responses, and thereby attempt to influence how he or she is perceived by others.

Very young children are incapable of this form of projection. Their first forays into social interaction involve simple imitation of others, without an understanding of the mechanics of the relationship between themselves and these others. As children develop greater understanding of the world around them, they enter the play stage of role taking behavior. During this stage a child has the ability to take the role of significant others, generally parents or caregivers. The young child has sufficient experience with these others, and sufficient emotional investment in their reactions to him or her, to make the cognitive leap required in playacting "mommy" or "daddy." To a casual observer, such play might seem unimportant. However, when a child pretends to be daddy and cautions a stuffed toy that if the toy is naughty it will be punished, this child is demonstrating the knowledge that under certain circumstances (naughty behavior) a given other (daddy) will likely react in a predictable way (punishment).

This process of understanding important others and applying this understanding to guide one's behavior is not without its dangers. The very importance of significant others magnifies the impact of their reactions toward the individual. For instance, Wiley (2003) suggests that parents who do not provide sufficient emotional support to the infant during identity development may do lasting damage to the integrity of the adult sense of self. Primary socialization is accomplished through a child's interactions with adults closest to him or her. The quality of this interaction will have lasting impact on whether the world is seen as a safe and welcoming place.

Parents who provide adequate support during the earliest stages of identity development provide a stronger basis for the perception of self, but continuing support from later significant others will be necessary for the individual to maintain self-esteem. The production of a positive self-concept, or a preferred self, is an ongoing project requiring the cooperation of others. Thus, the constant implicit threat that approval from significant others may be withdrawn helps to moderate behavior.

Deviance, or the violation of social norms, is discouraged partly by this threat of loss of significant others' approval. Whether the result is decreased or increased adherence to the norms of the larger culture depends upon the normative orientations of those others a person is trying to please. According to control theory, a person working to maintain close ties to people who adhere to conventional norms will be less likely to engage in behaviors that violate said norms. Conversely, differential association suggests that a person who wants to please significant others who engage in and approve of a form of deviance will be more likely to engage in deviance themselves. For instance, stealing may be discouraged ("If I got caught shoplifting my mom would kill me!") or encouraged ("Everyone in the gang is expected to shoplift, so I had better") depending in part upon the values held by significant others.

Tamotsu Shibutani (1962) explains this process further, through his discussion of reference groups and their function in social control. Reference groups are audiences for actions, even if the group being referenced is not physically represented through a member or members present to see the action. Every actor has a number of reference groups that serve as controls for behavior because the actor will try "to maintain or enhance his standing" in front of these groups (p. 132). Unfortunately, it may be difficult or impossible for a person to meet all of the behavioral norms of various competing groups. As people tend to conform to norms of those groups they find most compelling, and significant others tend to serve as representatives for reference groups, the closeness and sentiment felt between significant others greatly increases their influence over individual behavior.

The relationship between an individual and the persons he or she considers to be significant others is often, but not always, reciprocal. Husband and wife share a relationship that is reciprocally significant, as do mother and child. Each can reasonably be considered significant to the other. However, some relationships may be significant for one party and much less significant, or nonexistent, for the other. A popular coach may be a significant other for a large number of college athletes, none of whom need be individually significant to the coach in return.

SEE ALSO: Interpersonal Relationships; Play Stage; Primary Groups; Reference Groups; Socialization, Agents of

REFERENCES AND SUGGESTED READINGS

Mead, G. H. (1967 [1934]) *Mind, Self, and Society from the Standpoint of a Social Behaviorist.* University of Chicago Press, Chicago.

Shibutani, T. (1962) Reference Groups and Social Control. In: Rose, A. M. (Ed.), *Human Behavior and Social Processes: An Interactionist Approach.* Houghton Mifflin, Boston.

Sullivan, H. S. (1940) *Conceptions of Modern Psychiatry.* W. A. White Psychiatric Foundation, Washington, DC.

Weigert, A. J. & Gecas, V. (2003) Self. In: Reynolds, L. T. & Herman-Kinney, N. J. (Eds.), *Handbook of Symbolic Interactionism.* AltaMira Press, Lanham, MD, pp. 267–88.

Wiley, N. (2003). The Self as Self-Fulfilling Prophecy. *Symbolic Interaction* 26 (4): 501–13.

signs

J. I. (Hans) Bakker

The term "sign" is used in semiotics and hermeneutics as an umbrella (portmanteau) word covering all forms of gestures, ciphers, tokens, marks, indices, and symbols that convey human meaning. There have been many philosophical views expressed in the study of human meaning construction. Some thinkers trace the beginning of human cognition by the earliest *Homo sapiens* to the use of signs. The earliest religious thinkers emphasized some supernatural indicators of the true nature of reality; they understood "signs" in nature as messages. This led to necromancy and other forms of divination. The Chinese *Yi Ching* was initially based on the reading of tortoise shells. Victory in battle was often seen as a sign of the whim of the gods or of God's pleasure in ancient times. That which was not understood directly had to be fathomed on the basis of conjecture. Greek physicians utilized somatic signs to diagnose disease. They called this process semeiosis.

The idea of semiotic signs has gradually been extended to cover more and more features of reality. At the same time, secularization since the Scientific Revolution and the Enlightenment has made the notion that signs come from supernatural forces less acceptable. Classicist and theologian Friederich Schleiermacher utilized hermeneutics to translate and interpret both Plato and the Bible. He discovered that the way he carried out exegesis was no different for the pagan, secular texts than for the Christian, sacred texts. Hence, he postulated the possibility of a *general* hermeneutics. This idea was further developed by Wilhelm Dilthey, who thought of hermeneutics as a way of developing a "critique of historical reason" that would supplement Kant's three critiques. Dilthey's approach helped to provide a philosophical foundation for non-positivistic social sciences based on the study of human beings as moral and ethical actors whose outlooks and motivations could be understood (*Geisteswissenchaften* which used *Verstehen*). We can understand human actors because we ourselves are human, even though we may need to bridge a chasm of time or space (e.g., China in the tenth century). All human signs are human creations and therefore can be understood by human beings.

But hermeneutics lacked a more general epistemological foundation. That came with the work of Charles Sanders Peirce, founder of pragmatism and pragmaticism, considered by some to be the greatest American philosopher.

Peirce emphasized the way in which signs mediate between that which is being represented and that which is interpreted. While few follow Peirce's detailed arguments to the letter, the general thrust of Peirce's critique of Cartesian dualism makes it abundantly clear that an epistemology which focuses on the individual "subject" as an interpreter of "objects" is severely misleading. Peirce's correction of Descartes's epistemology parallels Einstein's extension of Newton's physics. For many practical purposes it is sufficient to simply think in terms of the subject's comprehension of time and space; but, for universal laws of physics, such as the law of gravity, such a limited framework will not do. Similarly, for many purposes a Cartesian dualism is adequate. It was important for the Scientific Revolution of the seventeenth century because the independent Cartesian subject looking through a microscope, eyeglass, or a telescope replaced argument based on the authority of the Roman Catholic Church's Thomist dogma. But a still wider perspective on human knowledge can be gained by questioning the "objectivity" of empirical observations based on inductive data gathering. A broader approach to knowledge requires a more sophisticated epistemology, one that includes an emphasis on the way in which a "sign" of some sort will always mediate between subject and object. Moreover, the isolated individual never exists in reality but only as a thought experiment (*Gedanken-experiment*). In reality all scientific understanding is based on communities of scholars (Cohen 2001).

By extension, the same is even true of everyday, commonsense reality, although we are usually not fully aware of it. We do not see the world; we only interpret stimuli with the aid of signs. Peirce had a complex typology of signs but the most important for sociology are icons, indices, and symbols. Icons are very specific images, such as those used on computer screens to indicate the location of a software application. Indices are signs which point to a more abstract level of reality. All descriptive statistics and statistical measures of association and correlation are indices. The most complex type of human sign is the symbol. A symbol can have many different meanings, depending on the context. George Herbert Mead's concept of the "significant symbol" is an echo of Peirce's general theory of signs. A symbol can only be significant to those who have learned to interpret it. It is very easy to misunderstand symbols. When a Roman Catholic sees a dove on a stained glass window he or she knows it represents the Holy Spirit; but the same Catholic seeing a swastika on a Buddha may not know that it represents good fortune. The Buddhist, in turn, may have no idea of the meaning of the dove. Our classification schemes and typologies are often highly symbolic even though we tend to assume that they are purely analytical and descriptive. This has led some philosophers (e.g., Wittgenstein) to argue that the real meaning of a sign is in its use, but others dispute that claim. To understand a "text" more clearly, we have to have an initial "vague notion" of what the key terms mean (Eco 1999: 275–9). That is, due to "intertextuality" we cannot escape a certain degree of circularity in examining signs.

The idea that we comprehend the world according to our "definition of the situation" can be extended to include the neo-Kantian notion that we perceive the world through a priori categories of understanding. Simmel took that one step further and argued that all a prioris are cultural. Today we would say that we are socialized into a culture. But the further specification of the true significance of any culturally constructed sign requires some awareness of the contexual mediating function of that sign. Theories put forward by Ferdinand de Saussure and C. S. Peirce have been further developed by other semioticians. But the key ingredient is awareness of the universal function in all human representation and communication of the sign. While theorists may differ concerning the precise operationalization of the concept of the sign, there has been considerable attention paid to signs in models of the process of semiosis by such divergent thinkers as Victoria Lady Welby, Mikhail Bakhtin, Charles W. Morris, Thomas S. Sebeok, Ferruccio Rossi-Landi, and Umberto Eco (Petrilli & Ponzio 2005).

SEE ALSO: Definition of the Situation; Language; Mead, George Herbert; Pragmatism; Saussure, Ferdinand de; Semiotics

REFERENCES AND SUGGESTED READINGS

Bouissac, P. (Ed.) (1998) *Encyclopedia of Semiotics.* Oxford University Press, New York.

Cohen, I. B. (2001) *Revolution in Science.* Belknap/ Harvard University Press, Cambridge, MA.

Dilthey, W. (1996) *Hermeneutics and the Study of History. Selected Works IV.* Princeton University Press, Princeton.

Eco, U. (1999) *Kant and the Platypus.* Harcourt Harvest, San Diego.

Petrilli, S. & Ponzio, A. (Eds.) (2005) *Semiotics Unbounded: Interpretive Routes through the Open Network of Signs.* University of Toronto Press, Toronto.

Schleiermacher, F. (1998) *Hermeneutics and Criticism.* Cambridge University Press, Cambridge.

Simmel, Georg (1858–1918)

Russell Kelly

Georg Simmel was born in Berlin on March 1, 1858 and died in Strasbourg in Alsace on September 26, 1918. He is generally recognized as an important sociological writer and teacher in Europe around 1900. He is less well recognized as an important philosopher of the same period. While he was a friend and contemporary of the German sociologist Max Weber, he was also a colleague and fellow teacher with the eminent philosopher Wilhelm Dilthey. Among the students and correspondents influenced by Simmel, four major figures in American sociology attended his lectures in Berlin: Albion Small, later head of department at the University of Chicago and founding editor of the *American Journal of Sociology*, George Herbert Mead, University of Chicago philosopher, W. I. Thomas, Chicago sociologist, and Robert Park, founder of the US research tradition known best as ethnography. In the famous "Green Book," *The Introduction to Sociology*, of 1921, Park and Burgess included more separate contributions from Simmel than from any other European sociologist. Simmel's influence from his teaching and his published papers on the development of sociology in the USA cannot be underestimated. Only his exclusion from Talcott Parsons's seminal *Structure of Social Action* cast a shadow for the period 1937 into the early 1960s. Since sociologists of the stature of Erving Goffman, Lewis Coser, and Kurt Wolff reclaimed Simmel's sociological work during the 1960s, his influence has been extended to virtually every area of the sociological spectrum.

FAMILY, BACKGROUND, AND CAREER

Simmel was born the youngest of seven children into a family of renowned chocolate makers, Felix & Sarotti. His father Ewald died in 1874 when Simmel was aged 16. His mother, Flora Bodenstein, was officially *Hausfrau* (housewife) to her seven children. Georg married Gertrud Kinel (aka as the author, Luise Enckendorff) in 1890 and his son Hans was born a year later. His daughter Angela was born in 1904 to his relationship with his student and colleague Gertrud Kantorowicz, writer and art historian.

Although born into a Jewish family, the Simmels had converted to Evangelical Protestantism. This was not unusual among the aspiring middle and upper-middle classes of respectable Prussian and Austro-Hungarian Imperial society in the nineteenth century. Access to state employment, social and professional contacts, and any form of royal patronage were all severely restricted if a person was officially Jewish. Many "modern" Jewish families took this option in Vienna, Budapest, Prague and, of course, Berlin. This is particularly relevant in Simmel's biography, as many subsequent writers have attributed his lack of recognition in Germany in his lifetime to anti-Semitism (Wolff 1950). This may not necessarily have been the case. During World War I, for example, Simmel abandoned all religious belief and any claim to a religious status.

After his father's death, Simmel's upbringing passed to the control of Julius Friedlander, a family friend and music publisher. After completing his *abitur* or college matriculation in Berlin in 1876, Simmel proceeded to study history and philosophy, and later art history, at the King Frederick William University in Berlin. Although usually described as the Berlin

University, this royal connection is particularly relevant to the son of a Jewish family. Had Simmel's Jewish background been that significant, his student career could not have been so successful. He studied history with Droysen and Mommsen, psychology with Lazarus, ethnology with Bastian, and history of philosophy with Zeller – all renowned professors of their day. In 1881, aged 23, Simmel publicly defended his first dissertation (*ordinarius*) on Kant's physical monadology (theory of substances). The success of his dissertation gave him the right to proceed to prepare his second dissertation (*habilitation*) and a requirement (and right) to teach in the department of philosophy while doing so. This dissertation was titled *On the Relationship between Ethical Ideals and the Logical and Aesthetic*. His degree was awarded on January 16, 1885.

His teaching included titles like Ethics, New Philosophical Theory, Sociology, and Social Psychology. As *Privatdozent* (associate lecturer), Simmel was paid according to the attendances at his lectures across the year, and on the balance of registered students and paying guests. His attractive style, performance, and topical content, directed towards his public rather than the registered students, maintained a regular audience of 150–200 between 1885 and 1898. Linked to his wife's daytime *salon* and his at-home tutorials, Simmel's courses became increasingly fashionable among Berlin intellectuals and their foreign visitors. Several notable sociologists of the next generation attended his lectures and tutorials. Americans on the post-graduation European tour and roving students from Eastern and Western Europe spread his influence and brought his ideas back to the USA or took them to their own country. His popularity and earnings, although not substantial, were the envy of some of his fellows and colleagues and were the source of some resentment.

Frequent attempts were made by Professor Wilhelm Dilthey and his colleagues in the philosophy department to sponsor Simmel for appointment to a full professorship. It is important to note that although universities sponsored faculty, professorships were awarded by the Prussian state and ministers were influenced in their decisions by external as well as internal pressures. The only concession was in 1900 when Simmel was awarded his *ausserordentlicher-*(Extraordinary) professorship. This allowed him to continue teaching and to use the title, but fell short of the full status of a professor who could recruit and supervise post-graduate students.

There are two explanations for his exclusion. One suggests that a reference from Schaefer describing "an Israelite through and through, in his external appearance, in his bearing and in his mode of thought" (Frisby 1992) was influential with its clearly racist substance. Equally, however, Schaefer and others were jealous and critical of his popularity as diminishing the status of his science and heavily critical of Simmel as a representative of the emerging discipline of sociology. The personal attack (and Dilthey's defensive references) were directed at sociology, at its radical and revolutionary potential, at its un- or anti-positivist, anti-empirical, and anti-scientific potential in Simmel's hands. His flamboyant appeal to foreigners and to women in attracting lecture audiences further weakened the case for Simmel as a serious academic.

Subsequent attempts to find him recognition outside of Berlin and Prussia, especially by his friend and colleague Max Weber, always stalled on the failure to secure promotion in Berlin. He was rejected for a second chair at Heidelberg and for the smaller university at Griefswald, although he was awarded a honorary doctorate in politics from Freiburg in 1911. Finally, in 1914, he was granted his full professorship at the University of Strasbourg, aged 56. Dissatisfied and unfulfilled, his health and his motivation went into rapid decline and he died of liver cancer in September 1918.

SOCIOLOGY OF KNOWLEDGE: *ERKENNTNISSETHEORIE*

Simmel's importance to sociology lies in his answer to his own question. "How is *gesellschaft* ?" was one of his first sociological essays and became the first chapter in his *Soziologie* (1908). He argued that sociology was not a science but more a method or methodology for exploring the ongoing and continuous processes of *socialization*, or what would be described today as *social interaction*. The data of social life were drawn from other disciplines like *Volkspsykologie* – a social and anthropological psychology –

and economics. Sociology's task was to use this data to describe and explain the processes of *sociation*. Simmel sought within these processes for the essentials of sociology, *formen*, or for the core of his formal sociology. All people in all societies interact and the forms of that interaction can be categorized. Simmel saw the task of his sociology as identifying the categories or types of interactions. This concept comes very close to the notion of "ideal type" associated with Simmel's friend and colleague, Max Weber.

Formen

Formen or *Lebensformen* are descriptions of processes of *sociation*, which allow the processes to be divided into types or categories. One example, for Simmel, was superordination and subordination, where his examples ranged from the simple leader and follower in a small nomadic or tribal group to the processes that made some relations between monarchs or princes and their people stable and some unstable. These *formen* become features of the work of others. One of the most fundamental of interactional processes still at the core of modern sociology is W. I. Thomas's "definition of the situation." Erving Goffman describes processes for self and identity management. Lewis Coser offers *social conflict* as another of the forms identified by Simmel under the heading of competition and conflict. But Simmel's notion of "Form" also has philosophical implications, as it is a "representation" expressed through and appearing in the interaction between persons, in intersubjectivity. More individual and interpersonal phenomena are identified as forms by Simmel, like jealousy or distrust. Jörg Bergmann (1993) followed the guide in his example of "secrecy," the form that underlies his studies of *klatsch* or gossip.

Form can best be recognized by the task it performs. Identifying forms involved Simmel in an extensive range of articles and papers. Each piece is in a sense a demonstration of the method at work, being a reflection on whatever the topic happened to be. How is society possible? What does art or culture do? Why is the family indispensable? Why is conflict between rich and poor inevitable? This same approach was introduced by Robert Park and W. I. Thomas as the ground for the work of the Chicago School in the 1920s and 1930s, from the early journalistic period through participant observation studies, to the more formal ethnographies of the 1960s to 1990s. It is also the style adopted by the more radical and experimental methods to be found in Harold Garfinkel's ethnomethodology, in the unique style of Erving Goffman, and in the widening array of projects listed under the heading qualitative research. Simmel's corpus is a set of demonstrations of *forms* that outlines the potential promised by the new science of sociology, unrestrained by commitments to set theories, methods, or perspectives. He opened avenues of inquiry that would take sociology more than a century to explore (Frisby 1992).

Dyad and Triad

One particular concept and focus originating in Simmel's work is the dyad (*Zweierverbindung* – literally, two hanging or binding together) and the triad (*Verbindung zu dreien* – three associating). Dyad and triad are translations that lose another important feature – the dynamic and processual nature of these forms. The dyad is unique as the only form that cannot exist without either of the two members whose associating is the pairing. For example, I cannot have an argument with myself, nor sustain that argument if the other party leaves and I become acutely embarrassed as I shout at the receding back of my opponent, drawing the attention of complete strangers.

Triads or larger groups can establish and continue their existence as a form with a constantly changing or revolving membership. New members can join while others leave or come and go. A discussion in a bar can continue all evening, long after the original group who set the topic up have left. A local soccer game can change personnel several times without interruption, but one, alone, cannot continue a game of chess. Simmel applies these notions in both directions, explaining the persistence of groups, large and small, on the one hand, while examining the internal features, stability, and fragility of monogamous marriage, on the other. Describing the dyadic form and the actions or behavior that constitute, maintain, and sustain it was fundamental to the development of not only sociology, but also psychology, and was the

origin of the discipline that is now social psychology.

Social Differentiation

From Karl Marx onward, the agenda for sociology had been set to account for processes of social change and revolution that rested on structures of social and economic inequality. Émile Durkheim and Max Weber, following Herbert Spencer and Social Darwinism, were seeking alternative explanations of order, stability or managed change, and how to achieve progress through evolution and development. Simmel's radical alternative to both these streams was to reject theories of social inequality or difference as a given structure imposed on the powerless by the powerful, or on the peasants by the landowners, or by princes on their subjects. Instead, he argues for social difference as a form describing exchanges between individuals, the totality appearing as a fixed structure. Changing the social interactions between individuals could radically transform what had previously looked like a fixed social structure. Marx, Durkheim, and Weber took it for granted that society existed and could be studied as a whole or in the constituent parts that they identified: actions, structures and systems, social classes, or social facts. Only Simmel started from the individual in interaction and "built" society from the bottom up. It was probably this radical individualism that opponents and critics saw as revolutionary and dangerous in Simmel's writing and teaching and in the development of sociology, and which led to his lack of promotion in the university.

Superordination and Subordination

In searching for a form in social interaction, Simmel identified the relation of leader and follower as occurring in many known societies. His description notes that there cannot be a leader without followers and that it follows from this that the leader, even in a relation of domination and coercion, still depends upon the dominated or subordinated for the relation to maintain. The follower is as essential to the existence of the interaction as is the leader for that *form* of interaction to sustain itself.

He examines all the logical variations of the relationship, concluding that the universality of the *form*, for example, would make socialism – where relations of inequality had been overwhelmed and absolute equality imposed – both idealistic and unstable, even impossible.

Conflict

Simmel argued that the analysis of conflict had moved on from that of the simplistic two-class conflicts of Karl Marx into the much more complex environment that was modern work in the modern city. The original relationship between early societies who had no other form of communication, interaction, or exchange had been war, direct physical conflict. More modern conflict relationships were institutionalized in contests between lawyers in courts. This brought to conflict two new dimensions. First, conflict was now bedded in a system of rules, norms, and laws that regulated conflict situations (e.g., rules of engagement in the Gulf War, Geneva Conventions on Human Rights, and International Courts). Second, conflict was a normal, expected phase or stage in any process of interaction, which could be resolved by the parties without destroying the relationship.

Lebensanschauung

Simmel's last major work, *Lebensanschauung* (Life-reflections), was published after his death. It has never been translated into English, probably because few sociologists felt it merited such attention. Simmel's return in this book to the individual in interaction as "self," as an aggregate process of the *forms* of sociation in which the individual engages, presages much of the fundamental work in philosophy and the emerging discipline of sociology. George Herbert Mead takes up the same themes from William James and, like Simmel, from Bergson in his lectures that became *Mind, Self and Society*. Martin Heidegger attributes some of the fundamental themes of his phenomenological philosophy to *Lebensanschauung*. Alfred Schutz and Aron Gurwitsch take the same starting points for *Phenomenology of the Social World* and *Studies in Phenomenology and Psychology*. Although Simmel is rarely quoted in the history of the concept of *self*, it would not be unfair to attribute the origins of the sociological version of the concept to these writings.

Otherwise, the book is a book of its times. Simmel had moved to Strasbourg, had doubts about his lack of fame as a leading sociologist, returned to philosophy, and begun to shift his position on supporting Germany's role in World War I. He abandoned all religious belief and was increasingly disillusioned with his student group, depleted by military service and with his colleagues at the university. The book reflects the spirit of pessimism that was to prove important to Germany's undoing as the twentieth century progressed. In the post-World War II spirit of optimism that marked the explosion of sociology in the 1960s, the *Lebensanschauung* was thus properly neglected and overlooked. With the refocus in the new millennium on micro-sociological processes, the book might receive the examination and detailed review that it warrants, if only to ensure historical accuracy.

OVERVIEW

Simmel was probably not the greatest sociologist of his generation. That tribute ought to go to Max Weber or Émile Durkheim. Nor can we claim that Simmel's writings are still key texts for the modern student. What can be said is that few sociologists at work today do not owe some methodological or theoretical debt which traces its origin back to *Soziologie*. The methodological stream known as qualitative research in sociology and across the range of social sciences was first promoted and demonstrated by Simmel in his teachings and writings. The focus on deviance, the outsider, and the stranger as they characterize urban and city life underwrite streams of work in urban sociology, the sociology of deviance, and the sociology of mental illness and its treatment. Micro-sociology, however its proponents might reject the label, symbolic interaction, sociology in the natural attitude or setting – all find their initial steps in Simmel's lectures and papers. Currently, the most profound debt is from cultural studies, where the attention of sociologists turns to fashion, art, sculpture, music, and performance set in the modern or postmodern world, following Simmel's early lead.

SEE ALSO: Collective Action; Cultural Studies; Dyad/Triad; Goffman, Erving; Groups; Knowledge, Sociology of ; Mead, George Herbert; Music; Secrecy; Self; Social Distance; Sociometry; Stranger, The; Symbolic Interaction; Weber, Max

REFERENCES AND SUGGESTED READINGS

Bergmann, J. R. (1993) *Discreet Indiscretions* (Klatsch: Zur Sozialform der diskreten Indiscretion). Trans. John Bednarz, Jr. Aldine de Gruyter, New York.

Frisby, D. (1992) *Sociological Impressionism: A Reassessment of Georg Simmel's Social Theory*, 2nd edn. Routledge, London.

Frisby, D. (Ed.) (1994) *Georg Simmel: Critical Assessments*, 3 vols. Routledge, London.

Park, R. E. & Burgess, E. W. (1921) *Introduction to the Science of Sociology*. Greenwood Press, New York.

Simmel, G. (1955) *Conflict and the Web of Group Affiliations*. Trans. K. H. Wolff & R. Bendix. Free Press, New York.

Simmel, G. (1992 [1908]) *Soziologie: Untersuchungen ueber die Formen der Vergesellschaftung*. Suhrkamp, Frankfurt am Main.

Simmel, G. (1994 [1922]) *Lebensanschauung: Vier metaphysische Kapitel*. Duncker & Humblot, Berlin.

Smith, G. W. H. (1989) Snapshots "Sub Specie Aeternitatis": Simmel, Goffman and Formal Sociology. *Human Studies* 12: 19–57.

Spykman, N. (1925) *The Social Theory of Georg Simmel*. University of Chicago Press, Chicago.

Wolff, K. H. (Ed.) (1950) *The Sociology of Georg Simmel*. Free Press, New York.

Wolff, K. H. (Ed.) (1959) *Georg Simmel, 1858–1918: A Collection of Essays*. Ohio State University Press, Columbus.

simulacra and simulation

Lauren Langman

For a number of sociologists, media theorists, and social critics, the current era, with its global market, advanced technologies, mass media and digital information, and the all-present marketing of goods and politics, must be seen as radically different from the industrial age of machine-based mass production. One of the central technological innovations of the industrial era was the capturing of visual images, sounds, and later media with both sound and picture. From the earliest photos, to records, and later movies and television, we have seen and heard endless reproductions. But, today, many argue that we live in a "postmodern" age dominated by an endless number of spectacular images, most of which are simulations, copies without an original source, imitations where the original never existed. With the proliferation of simulations, created images serve less to reproduce the reality that was seen or heard than to create various images that in turn create a new "reality" and new kinds of meanings. The "reality" of today, a world of fantastic dreams and images, is said to be largely a product of advertisers, marketers, and political consultants. They are the ones who create and disseminate the spectacles and simulations of "hyperreality." At some point in the late twentieth century, the prevalence of artificial images, staged events, and socially constructed "realities" had become so prevalent as to be considered "normal," "natural," and hardly worth more than a yawn. In retrospect, we might now call our times the age of simulation.

With the emergence of symbolic capacities and the intentional production of various grunts, groans, and sounds – distinct words – signifiers came to represent things, what was signified. Language, according to Saussure, was a system of signs through which the spoken word represented different kinds of objects, actions, and experiences. For most of history, communication has attempted to describe or "re-present" reality, or at least a particular version of reality ranging from the nature of the world, religious cosmologies, histories and law, and granary records to aesthetic expressions of one's self, desires, and meanings. Printing, mass literacy, and, more recently, mass-produced and mediated representations in newspapers, magazines, radio, film, and television transformed the way people experienced themselves and their world.

Classical social theory emerged before the mechanical reproduction of images and the proliferation of mass media. Marx had noted the importance of ideology in distorting and mystifying ruling-class interests to reproduce capitalist societies. Similarly, the fantastic nature of the "commodity form" hid the actual reality of class relationships. Weber saw the importance of written records for bureaucracies – the typical organizations of modern governments and, indeed, most formal organizations. But neither anticipated the world-transformative properties of mass media on politics and consumption.

The neo-Marxist Frankfurt School argued that mass media distorted and disguised reality to serve the interests of political elites. It argued that emotionally gratifying Nazi propaganda consisted of an endless barrage of spectacular images and simplistic slogans that mobilized support for Hitler. Meanwhile, denigrating images demonized the Jews, who were blamed by Hitler for Germany's problems as the Nazis promised retribution.

After the crises of 1939 that led to World War II, capitalism required expanding new markets. Consumer goods would provide that market – but the work ethic and frugality needed to be tempered in order to foster consumerism as a lifestyle. Thus consumer capitalism required the existence not only of affordable goods, but also of consumers who constantly "needed" to buy things. There was an increased role for advertising and marketing that moved from describing products to creating images in order to colonize consciousness and socialize people to buy commodities that provided meanings and gratifying, lifestyle-based identities. In the illusory world of crafted images, "authenticity" became a commodity to sustain consumerism.

The Frankfurt School then argued that the "culture industry" not only sold mass-mediated entertainment as a profitable commodity, but also fostered "one-dimensional" thought that dulled the capacity for critical reason. Dulled reason led people to accept the socially constructed versions of reality crafted by elite commercial interests or political elites. The "culture industry" provided escapism to distract people from important social issues; the shallowness of consumerism or the hypocrisy of political leaders was disguised. But for many scholars, critical theory was a "snobbish" expression of a cultural elitism that basked in pessimism.

The next generation of media/culture theorists, Guy Debord, Jean Baudrillard, Paul Virilio,

and Umberto Eco, might be called the "simulationists." They claimed that we now live in a world where mass-mediated communication and the mass production of simulations, fakes, and replicas do not so much represent and/or ideologically distort reality as "create" a new order of reality, a spectacular "hyperreality" based on images, simulations, and mythologies that have no connection with actual reality. Nor does this simulated reality hide "truth" behind appearances; rather, there are no "truths" other than the simulated images that now dominate our culture.

The French Situationists, a group of avant-garde Marxists, anarchists, and libertarians, were influenced by Dada and Surrealism. Debord (1977 [1967]) became their most elegant spokesman. They felt that the Soviet models of revolution and vision of society were deeply flawed and irrelevant to a consumer society dominated by endless spectacles. They argued that by the late 1950s we lived in a world characterized by continuous spectacle, extraordinary images and events that were systematically produced. Radio, television, film, music, industrial arts, fashions, athletic events, and festivals had become an all-powerful, hegemonic system sustaining elite privilege and rendering workers placid through consumption. Extraordinary representations mediated reality and the relations between people. For Debord, the spectacle had become an all-pervasive aspect of modern life, but this world of images served to justify the nature of capitalist society and ignore the "more fundamental" issue of how goods were produced – typically by exploited workers. For most people, the images of the new consumer society were its truth, while its "realities" of exploitation and domination were ignored. The spectacular images had displaced underlying realities and served to sustain the system.

The endless images and meanings of consumer society engendered "pseudo-needs" to consume, which, much like the drudgery of work under capitalism, fostered alienation and in turn powerlessness and passivity. The fetish of the commodity form now colonized everyday life; subjective experiences were imitations of experience. Being "human" became equated with buying and "having" things, and "having" was transformed into appearances. The domination of appearances, what seemed plausible or even true, isolated the present from history and maintained the status quo as an eternal today (Cubitt 2000). The spectacle had become the new form of domination.

The Situationists influenced the then young Jean Baudrillard, a neo-Marxist sociologist concerned with signification and consumption. But in 1972 he broke with the Marxism that he saw as a critique of now outmoded modern, capitalist, industrial production. He saw this as irrelevant to the new, postmodern, "semiurgical" society, one based on semiotics, the production and interpretations of meanings in which acts and objects served as "signs" that have relationships to each other to produce "texts." For Baudrillard (1994), this new order of seduction by images was increasingly based on simulation where simulacra preceded and created "hyperreality" rather than representing reality – accurately or otherwise. The "real" has imploded and been replaced by codes of reality. "The simulator's model offers us 'all the signs of the real' without its vicissitudes" (Baudrillard 1994). Producers of signs such as advertisers, politicians, or film stars attempt to manipulate the public by controlling the interpretive frameworks – the code. The code is an overarching mode of sign organization that influences the "correct" or widely accepted interpretation (Gottdiener 2001). The simulations or the model have become the determinant of the perception, experience, and understanding of the contemporary world.

Semiotics and simulation have displaced political economy in the postmodern era, in which there are no more "actual" events; only media events are significant. For example, wars now exist only to the extent that they are televised images of war. Charts or radar screens supplant actual blood, death, destruction, pain, and suffering. "Public opinion" has become more "real" than the people who offer it. Individuals have become simulations of self modeled after mass-mediated images, films, and ads that are articulated in spectacular self-presentations dependent on consumer products that convey the right images and meanings (Langman 1992). The masses are bombarded by images (simulations) and signs (simulacra) that encourage them to buy, vote, work, or play, but eventually they become apathetic (i.e., cynical) (Hawk n.d.). People are no longer concerned with knowing

the truth – the image is sufficient. This creates a world in which consumerism leads to the "goods life." Congenial, photogenic, yet often inept leaders are elected, disastrous policies appear brilliant, while a public exposed to thousands and thousands of media images shows little concern or outrage.

Virilio's (1986 [1977]) analysis of modern culture emphasized the history of warfare and the importance of speed in moving men, material, and information. The growing speed of media, from messenger-delivered notes to watching events unfold on television, or today emails and IMs that cross the globe, has led to a growing disconnection between images and the realities they would represent. This has, in turn, led to lapses in objectivity as well as subjectivity. Indeed, the speed of the succession of ephemeral images, without mass, bulk, or truth, has led to the erosion of freedom.

For Eco (1986 [1967]), "hyperreality" is the dominant trope of our age. His view of hyperreality is much like the spectacle for Debord and simulation for Baudrillard. Like them, he was one of the earliest writers to note the proliferation of the artificial, the fake, the imitation, and the replica as the new reality, the new "hyperreality" that was especially evident in Disneyland, Los Angeles, and Las Vegas, primary realms of recreations and themed environments that produce something better than the real. The US was seen as a land of fake history, fake art, fake nature, and fake cities where imitations do not so much reproduce reality as create a "better version" of a history without oppression, art without flaws, jungles without danger, and cities without crime, dirt, or even actual people. The Disney imitations of Main Streets, castles, (animatronic) people, animals, and monsters stand as the prototypic expression of an artificial realm of replicas. In the magical realms of Disney, fantasies are mass produced. This new theme park version of "hyperreality" can be seen in cities like Los Angeles, itself a center for the production of simulation. But the ultimate in simulation must be Las Vegas with its simulations of Egypt, Paris, Italy, and New York (Gottdiener 2001).

For Eco, the defining characteristic of our age is the emptiness of communication, perhaps best seen in the banter of sportscasters who engage in idle chatter for hours on end, who talk without there being anything to talk about. Such banter is without content or meaning – a total waste. But this style of form without substance has become the dominant trope of advertising, entertainment, and politics. Indeed, as Baudrillard suggested, there has been an implosion and the boundaries between these realms have withered.

To be sure, simulations, fantastic themes, and imaginary motifs in the service of consumerism may well provide corporations with profits by providing people with a myriad of gratifications. So too can simulation sustain political power. But there is a dark side to the proliferation of simulation – its celebrations of consumerism promise a gratifying identity, lifestyle, and even a reality that is always elusive. In the case of politics, often onerous policies can gain mass support. The use of radio and movies for propagandistic political purposes was essential to the rise of Hitler and support for his aggressive policies. Today, with television as the primary means through which most people are informed about the world, the ominous side of simulation and its capacity to dissimulate and misinform is greatly increased. Television, with its primary emphasis on the rapidly changing visual image, is especially well suited for entertainment. It does not so much represent reality as inform opinions. News and political information take the form of entertaining political spectacles and simulations. This is a major danger to freedom and democracy because of the passivity of viewing in general, the absence of counterfactual information, and the domination of the news programs by escapist distractions (Edelman 1987; Kellner 1992). With television's endless simulations and its creations of hyperreal worlds, there is a dulling of critical reasoning that fosters passivity at best, and cynicism at worst. Indeed, many question whether a free media and informed public can exist in the current world. All too often, it seems that the simulation and its realities are preferred.

A long tradition of intellectual work has been critical of representations that do not represent but instead distort and hide. Perhaps this began with Plato's critique of painting as an inferior form of representation. But in our current world, we might note that critics from the right such as Ortega, the left such as Adorno, or a democratic centrist such as Postman, have each in their own way been critical of the ways in which media images not only seduce, but also offer massive distortions of the actual ways the world functions by providing illusory utopias whose locations in hyperreality serve the powerful who remain in control of the realities of political economy.

SEE ALSO: Advertising; Commodities, Commodity Fetishism, and Commodification; Critical Theory/Frankfurt School; Culture Industries; Debord, Guy; Disneyization; Hyperreality; Implosion; Media; Postmodern Social Theory; Postmodernity; Semiotics; Simulation and Virtuality; Situationists

REFERENCES AND SUGGESTED READINGS

Baudrillard, J. (1975 [1972]) *The Mirror of Production*. Telos Press, New York.
Baudrillard, J. (1994) *Simulacra and Simulation*. University of Michigan Press, Ann Arbor.
Cubitt, S. (2000) *Simulation and Social Theory*. Sage, London.
DeBord, G. (1977 [1967]) *The Society of the Spectacle*. Black & Red Press, Detroit.
Eco, U. (1986 [1967]) *Travels in Hyperreality*. Harcourt Brace, New York.
Edelman, M. (1987) *Constructing the Political Spectacle*. University of Chicago Press, Chicago.
Gottdiener, M. (2001) *The Theming of America*. Westview Press, Boulder, CO.
Hawk, B. (n.d.) www.uta.edu/english/hawk/semiotics/baud.htm.
Kellner, D. (1992) *Television and the Crisis of Democracy*. Westview Press, Boulder, CO.
Langman, L. (1992) Neon Cages. In: Shields, R. (Ed.), *Lifestyles of Consumption*. Routledge, London, pp. 40–82.
Postman, N. (1986) *Amusing Ourselves to Death*. Penguin, New York.
Virilio, P. (1986 [1977]) *Speed and Politics: An Essay on Dromology*. Semiotext(e), New York.

simulation and virtuality

Sean Cubitt

The term *simulation* and its cognate *simulacrum* have a venerable history as the Latin translations of the Platonic *eidolon*. This is a copy of a copy, exemplified in Plato's *Republic* by a painting of a bed: the carpenter's bed is a copy of the Ideal; the painter's a copy of the carpenter's, and so at a distant remove from the reality of the Idea. The term *virtual* is almost as ancient, traceable to the Aristotelian distinction between potential and actual: the future is a field of infinite potential until it is realized, at which point it trades its potentiality for actuality. Both terms have double usages in contemporary social science, as theoretical tools and as descriptions of specific methods, both associated with computer modeling.

Simulation theory is most closely associated with French sociologist Jean Baudrillard. From his early work on consumerism to his first major books, *The Mirror of Production* (1973) and *Symbolic Exchange and Death* (1976), Baudrillard voiced the despair of his generation with the betrayal of the political movements of 1968. Drawing on the situationist Guy Debord's theory of the spectacle and on the renegade surrealist Georges Bataille's notion of symbolic economies, Baudrillard began to query the reality of an increasingly mediated world. Rather than a composite formation of individual or class actors, society was a self-replicating Code, a homeostatic system. In the most frequently cited statement of his position in mid-career he wrote of the simulacrum's four historical phases:

it is the reflection of a profound reality;
it masks and denatures a profound reality;
it masks the *absence* of a profound reality;
it has no relation to any reality whatsoever:
    it is its own pure simulacrum.
                        (Baudrillard 1994: 6)

By contrast with postmodern theorists of difference, Baudrillard's later work insists on a new historical condition of homogeneity from which the possibility of historical change has been eradicated: "The perfect crime is that of an unconditional realization of the world by the actualization of all data, the transformation of all our acts and all events into pure information: in short, the final solution, the resolution of the world ahead of time by the cloning of reality and the extermination of the real by its double" (Baudrillard 1996: 25). "Realization" and "actualization" indicate the Aristotelian roots of the later Baudrillard. The world as

material, and therefore as potential, has been lost in favor of an actual world composed of its transcription into data. And as data, the world acts as a homeostatic system realized "ahead of time," that is, before it could fulfill whatever other potentialities lay latent in it to evolve historically into something truly different.

Although, through its debt to Debord, simulation theory has roots in Marxism, and perhaps especially the Hegelian Marxism of Lukács, it is itself an anti-Marxism. Skeptical, even scathing, of the consumer society, Baudrillard nonetheless holds out no hope for social action to change the world. This is in part because social classes have been supplanted by their mediation in polling, leaving only silence and apathy as appropriate political strategies; and in part because, he claims, the traditional workplace core of Marxist organization has ceased to produce. Factories no longer manufacture goods, and social movements no longer seek to close them down or seize them. Instead, political groups seek to keep factories open and functioning, not for what they make, but so that they can provide jobs. People work in order to work, not to make things or to provide services. To claim a "right to work" is equivalent to demanding a "right to leisure," and both are equally simulations whose purpose is simply to reproduce the consumers of signs. Production itself, the core of Marx's *Capital*, has ceased to exist.

Other authors with an interest in simulation have shared this distrust of Marxism, especially the variants prevalent in 1968. Umberto Eco was a rigorous critic of the Italian Red Brigades as well as an ironic critic of North American consumerism in his *Faith in Fakes: Travels in Hyperreality* (1986). Urban planner and historian of warfare Paul Virilio, through his involvement with Henri Lefebvre, was a major participant in the May events in Paris in 1968, but in his career as essayist has increasingly expressed his distrust of the contemporary world in terms of radical Catholicism. Simulation theory has been particularly influential in media and leisure studies and in scholarship on contemporary warfare. It has found itself especially vulnerable to charges of monoculturalism, cultural pessimism, and an overly absolute periodization through which to distinguish the contemporary world from previous history.

The same cannot be said for the second usage of the term *simulation* in contemporary sociology, where it refers to the practice of modeling future scenarios through the use of computer programs such as geographical information systems. Typical uses consist of employing very large databases of past geographical, economic, and demographic trends from which skilled programmers can extrapolate likely future scenarios based on shifting key variables. This type of automated futurological social science is, indeed, the kind of activity which Baudrillard singles out for attention in *The Perfect Crime* as practice which reconfigures society as pure information, thus robbing it of its reality. The conflict arises over two key disagreements. Firstly, Baudrillard is a constructionist who believes that the datum is not given, while empirical social science believes that interpretation is epiphenomenal. Secondly, simulation theory is an extreme variant on the theory of representation, according to which no representation is adequate to the reality to which it refers: in the theory of representation, this results in partial representations which are open to bias, prone to agenda setting, and ideological. Simulation theory sees the inadequacy as absolute: representation depends on the absence of the represented, and thus overrides and obliterates the reality it refers to. Simulation as modeling, however, recognizes partiality as experimental tolerances or degrees of accuracy.

The term *virtuality* is often confused with simulation, especially in contexts where both are aligned with the less definite concept of hyperreality. It refers both to computer-generated quasi-realities and to the philosophical concept of potential existence. Although the word has attained general currency through its evocation of any connection to digital media, technically it refers to immersive systems capable of generating the illusion that the user is occupying a space which is in fact entirely or largely computer generated. Such systems include head-mounted displays, virtual environments with or without 3D-enhanced goggles or screens, and increasingly the domain of theme park rides. Because theme parks and other wholly designed environments (such as Forest Lawn cemetery and at least some heritage centers) are also emblematic topics in simulation theory, the confusion is unsurprising. Howard Rheingold's *Virtual Reality* (1991) and Michael Heim's *Metaphysics of Virtual Reality* (1993) and *Virtual Realism* (1998) presented immersive audiovisual media as pathways to enlightenment. In a key essay responding to such claims, roboticist Simon Penny (1994) asserted that virtual reality systems were the fulfillment of the European Enlightenment's dream of perfected individualism in a normalized Cartesian space. Although scientific and artistic experiments with immersive media continue, research now focuses on augmented reality, in which wearable computers allow data to be mapped over real-world perception, while the expected mass market in the games sector has been overtaken by the rise of network and mobile gaming as the major growth engine for the industry.

Outside research and educational and aesthetic uses, virtuality's main presence in the early twenty-first century is in mass spectacle. Thus the term is applied to such phenomena as Disneyland and similar theme parks, especially attractions whose spectacle, volume, and physical movement is sufficient to overwhelm participants, to IMAX and OMNIMAX theatrical screens, to the most lavish live theater, and to such urban phenomena as Las Vegas and downtown Tokyo. For the most part these spectacular venues involve participation in crowds rather than individuated interfaces, and confused spatial orientation rather than the Cartesianism of immersive technologies. For authors like Norman Klein (*The Vatican to Vegas: A History of Special Effects*, 2004) and Angela Ndalianis (*Neo-Baroque Aesthetics and Contemporary Entertainment*, 2004), the virtuality of immersive leisure technologies no longer appears as the precursor to new rationalist enlightenment, but as the heir to the European baroque's sensuous mysticism and celebration of power. In both instances, however, what can be discerned is a movement from the domination of nature to escape from it, both as environment and as human nature. Slavoj Žižek in *The Plague of Fantasies* (1997) sees this occurring on at least three levels: immersive virtual realities put "real" reality into question; biotechnologies and other real-world applications undermine the givenness of external reality; and the role-play of network-mediated communities disintegrates the reality and givenness of the self. This opens for Žižek two possible futures: a catastrophe in which the informational double of the world is lost and with it the function of the Other in the construction of desire and symbolization; and a utopia in which all symbolic conflicts, chief among them wars, are played out in virtual space with no real casualties at all. Either route might result in the redemption of real life from its own vanishing. At this juncture Žižek's virtuality appears to approximate Baudrillard's understanding of the stakes of simulation, but without Baudrillard's nihilistic reworking of Leibniz (i.e., why is there nothing rather than something?).

A similarly optimistic usage of "virtuality" derives from French philosopher Gilles Deleuze, a professed anti-Hegelian rather than an anti-Marxist (in contrast to the profoundly Hegelian Žižek). Defining the term in *Difference and Repetition*, another book from 1968, Deleuze uses a phenomenological example that comes close to his later readings of C. S. Peirce: the confused yet distinctive sounds of the sea. Such sounds are composed of differential relations among singularities, unique events, but are not yet distinguished as separate sounds. Such sensations are virtual as opposed to identified and distinguished sounds, which become actual in the process of becoming objects of perception. The virtual–actual opposition applied to social relations implies an atomistic field of differences, relationships, and points of singularity where they intersect to form, among other things, individual sensoria, all of which constitute a virtual domain of potentiality. The actualization of one specific potential deprives the virtual plane of its other possibilities, but also generates further potentialities, further virtuality. The concept seems close to both Ernst Bloch's conception of the future as not-yet existing, and to the idea of natality outlined in Hannah Arendt's introduction to her *The Human Condition* (1958).

The term has been taken up by numerous social thinkers. Hardt and Negri devote a chapter of *Empire* (2000) to the concept of virtualities as the desires of the multitudes and their productive capacity to transform them into reality. Thus defined, the virtual is both the affective motivation and the power to act "beyond measure," that is, outside the political and economic structures of dominance. Equally insistent that this virtual power is material and anti-dialectical, they assert the virtual as the boundless creativity of being. A similar use

appears in Luce Irigaray's concept of the virtual feminine, for example in *Sexes et parentés* (1987), where the project of becoming feminine is asserted to be an open-ended process of creation. This concept has been linked with Deleuze's virtuality in the work of Rosi Braidotti, for whom "Sexual difference, from being a boundary marker, has become a threshold for the elaboration and the expression of multiple differences, which extend beyond gender but also beyond the human" (Braidotti 2002: 261). Such virtual gender is at once immanent and embodied, singular but constitutionally articulated with multiple social relations. Like Baudrillard's simulation, such conceptualizations of virtuality deny that differences constitute a dialectic, and to that extent almost all simulation and virtuality theorists share a general anti-Hegelian or anti-Marxist stance, insisting on the fluidity of becoming rather than the mechanisms of conflict. Ironically, however, for two terms so frequently confused, simulation theory is strongly pessimistic and anti-realist (though practical simulation is both future-oriented and empiricist), while virtuality theory is equally strongly optimistic (although practical virtual reality is open to criticisms of nostalgic reconstruction of Enlightenment ideals).

SEE ALSO: Cyberculture; Deleuza, Gilles; Digital; Hyperreality; Information Society; Representation; Simulacra and Simulation

REFERENCES AND SUGGESTED READINGS

Baudrillard, J. (1983) *Simulations*. Trans. P. Foss, P. Patton, & P. Beitchman. Semiotext(e), New York.

Baudrillard, J. (1994) *Simulacra and Simulation*. Trans. S. F. Glaser. University of Michigan Press, Ann Arbor.

Baudrillard, J. (1996) *The Perfect Crime*. Trans. C. Turner. Verso, London.

Braidotti, R. (2002) *Metamorphoses: Towards a Materialist Theory of Becoming*. Polity Press, Cambridge.

Cubitt, S. (2001) *Simulation and Social Theory*. Sage, London.

Hardt, M. & Negri, A. (2000) *Empire*. Harvard University Press, Cambridge, MA.

Penny, S. (1994) Virtual Reality as the Completion of the Enlightenment Project. In: Bender, G. & Druckrey, T. (Eds.), *Culture on the Brink: Ideologies of Technology*. Bay Press, Seattle, pp. 231–48.

situationists

Alberto Toscano

The situationists were a collective of anti-capitalist thinkers, active from the late 1950s to the early 1970s, who theorized the alienated character of modern consumer society and its revolutionary overcoming. Plagued throughout its history by splits and expulsions, the Situationist International (SI) was formed in 1957 from a number of tiny avant-garde groups, including the Lettrist International and the Movement for an Imaginist Bauhaus. The SI published an eponymous journal from 1958 to 1969. Best known for its widespread cultural influence (from Baudrillard to punk rock) and role in the Paris events of May 1968, the SI counted among its ranks the Danish painter Asger Jorn, the Belgian writer Raoul Vaneigem, and the English art historian T. J. Clark. Its chief theorist was Guy Debord.

Undertaking a fierce critique of what they defined as the colonization of everyday life by capitalism, the situationists saw themselves as overcoming the limitations of the avant-gardes of Dadaism and Surrealism. Their name derives from the idea that capitalist culture could only be undermined through a deliberate practice – simultaneously aesthetic and political – of "constructing situations": "games of events" and "unitary ambiences" that would rupture the alienation or separation of the modern-day worker/consumer from his authentic desires and potentials, terminating his subjection to what Debord termed "the humanism of the commodity."

The project of constructing situations was both urbanistic and semiotic. In conjunction with Henri Lefebvre, whom they later denounced for his reformism, the situationists attacked the deadening effects of modernist urbanism and architecture, exemplified by Le Corbusier. They sought to counter this modernist planning of social life with the "psychogeographical" practice of *dérive*, a methodical practice of drifting through the fragmented space of the modern metropolis, experimenting with the city's effects on the behavior and desires of individuals. The ultimate horizon of such a practice was a "unitary urbanism" that would try to reactivate the sedimented potentials of the city and create spatial experiences freed from the domination of commodities. At the level of signs, the situationists advocated *détournement*, the subversive usage of the materials of capitalist culture. This was epitomized in the irreverent use of comic strips to communicate revolutionary messages during May '68. These strategies were linked, especially in the work of Vaneigem, to a politicization of pleasure and play as anti-systemic practices.

Relying heavily on Hegel, Feuerbach, the early Marx, and Lukács, Debord's *The Society of the Spectacle* (1995) proposed to update the categories of ideology critique to confront the novelty of advanced capitalism. Debord argued that the hegemony of capital over life had become virtually total, as capital was accumulated not just in the guise of material commodities but in that of "spectacles." According to Debord, the social relations underlying such spectacles were alienated in a manner far more severe than the one envisaged by Marx's account of commodity fetishism.

In his discussions of consumption and celebrity, Debord showed how capitalism can appear as an autonomous domain, both production and the image of that production. The spectacle – both as a sector of capitalism (the "media") and as the totality of alienated social relations – signals not just the subordination of men to the dictates of political economy, but also the simultaneous justification of such a state of affairs. In the spectacle, life itself vanishes into its separate or independent representation and capitalism perpetually celebrates its own existence. Even the most revolutionary of practices (situationist ones included) can be "recuperated" and made functional to the perpetuation of alienated life.

Reflecting more specifically on the geopolitical situation, Debord interpreted the Cold War as the complicit juxtaposition of a bureaucratic "concentrated spectacle" in the East and a consumerist "diffuse spectacle" in the West, and foresaw, on the eve of the collapse of historical communism, their unification in an "integrated spectacle." This diagnosis was linked to the situationists' virulent opposition not just to the Leninist and Stalinist visions of the party, but also to a host of revolutionary trends, from Maoism to third-worldism. Abhorring any notion of politics that would trade autonomy for representation (or for charismatic leadership), the situationists pledged allegiance to the tradition of workers' councils, which they regarded as the only form of organization that would not merely repeat or displace the alienation instituted by the spectacle.

The situationists' theory of contemporary society was accompanied by a bleak estimation of the human sciences. From urbanism to political science, from psychology to sociology, the situationists viewed the activity of such compartmentalized academic disciplines as, at best, a form of passivity deriving from the separation of intellectual from manual labor, and, at worst, a willful collusion with the reign of the spectacular economy. Though the situationists did make ample usage of notions originating in the human sciences, including sociology, it was only to the extent that such notions could be enlisted in a practical critique of alienation. Their aim was to identify those forms of life capable of breaking through the cultural "decomposition" and increasing "proletarianization" that affected the contemporary world. It is in this sense that the situationists focused, for instance, on the ambivalent role of leisure in contemporary society and the emergence of violent and unmediated forms of contestation (e.g., the Watts Riots of 1965). The goal was to accelerate the collapse of capitalism, not merely to interpret it. Or, as they put it in the SI editorial "Critique of Urbanism" (1961): "to envisage in terms of aggressivity what for sociology is neutral."

In line with Debord's frequent references to Machiavelli and Clausewitz, the thinking of the situationists, who repeatedly refused any fixed doctrine of "situationism," is best understood as a *strategic* critique rather than as any kind of dispassionate social analysis. The situationists sought to locate the faultlines in the ensemble of capitalist social relations and outline modes of living capable of constructing new, antagonistic desires that would resist their atomization and representation.

SEE ALSO: Alienation; Capitalism; Commodities, Commodity Fetishism, and Commodification; Consumption, Spectacles of; Debord, Guy; Everyday Life; Lefebvre, Henri; Leisure; Lukács, Georg; Marxism and Sociology; Media

REFERENCES AND SUGGESTED READINGS

Agamben, G. (2000) Marginal Notes on *Commentaries on the Society of the Spectacle*. In: *Means Without End: Notes on Politics*. University of Minnesota Press, Minneapolis.

Debord, G. (1995 [1967]) *The Society of the Spectacle*. Zone, New York.

Debray, R. (1995) Remarks on the Spectacle. *New Left Review* 1(214): 134–41.

Knabb, K. (Ed.) (1995) *Situationist International Anthology*. Bureau of Public Secrets, Berkeley.

McDonough, T. (Ed.) (2002) *Guy Debord and the Situationist International*. MIT Press, Cambridge, MA.

Plant, S. (1992) *The Most Radical Gesture: The Situationist International in a Postmodern Age*. Routledge, London.

RETORT (2005) *Afflicted Powers: Capital and Spectacle in a New Age of War*. Verso, London.

Vaneigem, R. (1983 [1965]) *The Revolution of Everyday Life*. Rebel Press, London.

Viénet, R. (1992 [1968]) *Enragés and Situationists in the Occupation Movement, France, May '68*. Autonomedia, New York.

slavery

Rodney Coates

Perhaps the oldest form of human oppression is that of slavery. Slavery, with its roots in antiquity (e.g., Egypt, Babylon, Assyria, Israel, and Greece), is defined as the forced labor of one group by another. The institution of slavery, where the slave was considered merely a piece of animate property or chattel, was first developed by the Greeks. Brutality, to include whipping, humiliation, and alienation, has been part of slavery from its inception. Slaves, stripped of their human dignity and title, were forced to abandon their family, culture, and personhood, as another owned their very being. Women, doubly exploited, were subject to sexual exploitation where they could be forced into prostitution or to submit to the sexual demands of their masters or their guests. Slaves during these periods, often accorded higher status, could be adopted and become legal heirs of the masters. Typically, these slaves were vested with special duties owing to their unique talents (such as teachers, actors, fighters, etc.). The modern system of slavery, a direct result of European imperialistic expansion, provided even harsher levels and degrees of exploitation, humiliation, and degradation.

The modern slave system beginning with the start of the Atlantic slave trade preserved many of the earlier exploitative conditions while creating unique variations of its own. Similar practices included the dehumanization and degradation of the slave in order to preserve order. Hence there were attempts to strip the slave of his identity, culture, and history, slaves were reduced to things (chattel property), and they were required to observe ritualistic etiquette and politically correct behaviors. These practices further served to reinforce the hegemonic structures of control and power. Modern slavery differed significantly in that it created race and racism to justify the institution. Slaves, not complacent, formed extensive networks of rebellion that greatly aided their attempts to revolt, escape, and contest the system.

The primary goal of modern slavery was to create a hyperexploitative system benefiting the master class. This institution is deemed hyperexploitative for it rested on the exclusive control of and the capacity to exhaust the total labor capacity of the slave. Hence, the average life expectancy of a slave was typically set at no more than 30 years of age. All of the produce, intellectual, physical, and even issue, were deemed to be the rightful property of the master. Death, escape, and the rarely utilized emancipation of the slave were the only release from this hyperexploitation. The fact that racial identity was integral to the system increased the likelihood that all persons of color, regardless of status (i.e., born free, emancipated, or escaped), were continually paranoid. Such paranoia was frequently manipulated (formally by race-specific laws, bands of disgruntled whites, or caprice) to ensure continued servile behavior of both free and non-free. Hence, slavery as a total institution shrouded persons of color regardless of status.

What few realize, when contemplating slavery, is the damage done to white and other forms of labor. Essentially slavery, with its capacity to hyperexploit labor, displaced other forms of labor where it was in competition. Those of lower class position, but in the same racial caste as the dominant master class, found their positions tenuously dependent upon the good will of the master class. That is to say, their labor value was unduly suppressed by the cheaper labor value supplied by the master class. In those areas where there was a shortage of slave labor, the value of lower-class white labor was lowered. Racism, in these situations, served to offset the lower value of lower-class white labor both psychologically and socially. Therefore, the slave could be humiliated, brutalized, and displaced by the lowliest of white workers. Inappropriate etiquette or politically incorrect behavior on the part of the slave could result in beatings, maiming, or even summary execution. Alternatively, in those situations where labor was in surplus, then white labor was actually displaced. Such displacement only aggravated the racial divide, while those white laborers forced to relocate tended to reproduce racial exclusionary or bifurcated labor systems wherever they settled. Racism, based upon these racial exclusions, far outlasted the system of hyperexploitation that produced them.

Sexual exploitation within slavery served multiple functions to include the sadistic pleasure of the master class, increased profit owing to issue produced, and of course the further humiliation of the slave.

Within the Americas three distinct slave systems developed. The distinctions between these systems derive from different cultural, political, and economic realities. These different realities, for want of a better terminology, are best described as those under the Spanish, French, and English sphere of influence. The major distinctions between these four slave systems had to do with the form of contact situation that prevailed. The most significant reasons for the differences among the European colonies have to do with the American Revolution among the English, and the influence of the Catholic Church among both the French and the Spanish. We shall briefly describe these three systems.

Spanish imperialist goals, fueled by vague and overly hyped claims of rivers and temples of gold, led to the first official European "settlements" in the Americas. These settlements, whose primary goal was to extract the claimed riches as fast as possible, soon led to disappointment as no rivers or temples of gold were found. Columbus and his men, undaunted, began to kidnap, imprison, ransom, and enslave the natives in their attempt to secure the illusive gold. Failing in this, the Spanish – still believing in hordes of gold just waiting for the plunder – sent more and more conquistadors to search out the prizes. With time, the only prize identified was the lush soils of the Amazon – and the Spanish colonial experience began. Maximization of exploitative goals led to, first, the enslavement of Native Americans, and later the importation of African slaves. The period of Spanish conquest, from 1519 to 1523, was characterized by extraordinary brutality and cruelty and decimated the indigenous population. Starting with a population of just over 4.5 million in 1519, the native population declined to 3.3 million in 1570 and to 1.3 million in 1646. The primary culprits for these declines were smallpox and typhus, wars of extermination, forced labor, brutal work conditions in the mines and on the plantations, tribute taxes, and cultural genocide. The decimation of the native labor force increased the demands for alternative labor sources. These alternative labor sources were soon supplied by the Dutch and Spanish merchants in the form of the African slave. The Spanish, with no intent on permanent settlement, did not encourage large numbers of Spanish women to immigrate. Thus, the gender imbalance increased the likelihood of sexual exploitation, prostitution, and the creolization of the population. Under rare circumstances, the Catholic Church stepped in and insisted upon the formalization of these unions in the guise of marriage. With time, the societies that came into being reflected these blended racial origins, generated by slavery, of Spanish, Natives, and Africans.

The French, eager to fill Napoleon's treasure chest and pay out mounting royal debt, entered the Americas with the express desire to maximize profits through trade. Their efforts in the Americas, centering in the Caribbean, Mid-South and West, brought them into immediate contact with the Native Americans. Almost from the start, they established rather friendly relationships. As with the Spanish, the French soon realized that their profits could be greatly enhanced with the creation of a colonial presence, and hence more permanent agricultural communities were established. In order to maximize these efforts, the French relied more and more heavily upon the African as the chief source of exploitable labor. Owing to the shortage of French women, again there was a heightened tendency to sexually exploit the African and Native American women. Thus prostitution, rape, and sexual abuse were often the result. Some of this sexual abuse was masked under the guise of formal marriages, which also served to provide access to greater resources among the indigenous population, legitimacy among the growing Creole population, and stability for the growing social structure.

The English, under the guise of freedom, initially promoted their imperialist expansion on the backs of lower-class Europeans. It is important to point out that among the English, the first group to experience slavery was not the Africans but the Irish. English rulers, beginning with Queen Elizabeth and continuing through Cromwell and King James, in a systematic attempt to destroy the Irish people and their culture forced several thousand Irish into slavery in the Americas. Thousands of other Europeans, similarly positioned at the bottom of European society, were forced to serve masters in this land of the free. Of interest is the fact that before African slavery was normalized, these individuals were collectively viewed as slaves. With the advent of African slavery, these slaves found their status significantly altered as they now became defined as servants. Still with the further passage of time, lower-status Europeans were allowed entry into the racial caste of whiteness. Whiteness accorded its participants the ability to discriminate against non-whites, hence we note the birth not only of racism but also of a racialized hierarchy. Both racism and this racialized hierarchy were functional in maintaining control over the slavocracy that later developed.

SEE ALSO: Apartheid and Nelson Mandela; Assimilation; Color Line; Diaspora; Holocaust; Interracial Unions; Melting Pot; One Drop

Rule; Race; Race (Racism); Racial Hierarchy; Reparations; Whiteness

REFERENCES AND SUGGESTED READINGS

Berlin, I. (1998) *Many Thousands Gone: The First Two Centuries of Slavery in North America*. Belknap Press, Cambridge, MA.

Fogel, R. W. (1994) *Without Consent or Contract: The Rise and Fall of American Slavery*. Norton, New York.

Franklin, J. H. & Moss, A. A., Jr. (2000) *From Slavery to Freedom: A History of African Americans*. McGraw-Hill, New York.

Genovese, E. D. (1976) *Roll, Jordan, Roll: The World the Slaves Made*. Random House, New York.

slurs (racial/ethnic)

John Moland, Jr.

A racial or ethnic slur is a remark or statement designed to defame, vilify, belittle, and insult members of a racial or ethnic group, usually by those who are not members of that racial or ethnic group (Rodale 1986: 1125). Examples of racial and ethnic slurs include expressions such as "miserly jew," "gook," "jap," "red savage," "mongrel," "half-breed," "sambo," "spook," "nigger," "coon," and "kike."

Racial and ethnic slurs reflect the attitudes and beliefs of individuals and groups, on both conscious and unconscious levels, to make another group, generally a group with less power, the target of the slurs. For this reason, there is for both the user and the target of the slurs a variety of psychological, emotional, and behavioral actions and counteractions. The choice of words used, and the force with which they are used, mirror the degree of animosity the users of the slurs will have toward the groups that are the targets of the slurs. Such slurs traditionally have meanings in the ideological underpinnings that buttress such slurs, for behind the use of slurs one would find beliefs in the biological, cultural, and moral inferiority of the victims of the slurs. Consequently, slurs are used to ascribe attributes of moral weakness, intellectual and academic weakness, and physical and behavioral peculiarities to members of the racial or ethnic group.

Historically, racial slurs used by white Americans toward black Americans depict black Americans as emotionally and intellectually immature, morally degenerate, and not being fully human. This can be seen in arguments used in the defense of slavery and segregation after the Civil War. Slurs against blacks were used in the sermons of white ministers, the speeches of politicians, and the writings of academicians to describe blacks in a very negative manner so as to justify the status quo. For example, the following slur appeared in the *Baptist Courier* of June 22, 1899: "The native African is a born liar and thief" (Owens 1971: 79). Senator Theodore G. Bilbo, a white supremacist and lay minister, was outspoken as a public official in his use of slurs to express his strong concern for maintaining segregation and "the purity of white blood." The intensity of his resentment of black Americans was demonstrated by the slur used in the title of his book, *Separation or Mongrelization* (1947). Table 1 presents examples of words used in expressing slurs against black Americans in the religious sermons, political speeches, and academic writings of white Americans.

From the perspective of *symbolic interaction*, the slur words provide qualitative data for examining the direct and indirect semantic differentials and far-ranging implications in the use of the slur. Each slur word generates a dichotomy of mutually exclusive characteristics for blacks and whites, with an implied logic and a possible course of action for the user of the slur as well as for those who are the targets of the slur. The slur, therefore, functions as a tool for the formulation of ideas, emotions, and actions toward those to whom the slur is applied. From this perspective, slurs provide an outlet for expressing emotions with the potential of serving as a rallying call to action. When the slur is used to describe an individual or group in strong negative terms, giving expression to feelings of hatred, then the slur symbolizes and arouses negative images, feelings, and emotions which the user assigns to the racial or ethnic background of those involved. When these negative qualities are intensely and saliently impressed

Table 1 Words used as racial slurs in sermons, speeches, and writing by white Americans

Black Americans	White Americans
Inferior	Superior
Blood (inferior)	Blood (superior)
Bestial, mongrel	Human
Uncontrolled sexual aggressiveness	Controlled sexual aggressiveness
Uncivilized	Civilized
Childlike, immature	Mature adult, paternal
Ignorant, incapable of learning	Intelligent
Lazy	Industrious
Immoral	Moral
Evil (bad, wrong)	Good (right)
Inherent thief	Honest
Inherent liar	Truthful
Heathen	Christian
Infidel	Believe in God
Cursed by God	Blessed by God
Perpetual servitude	Master

Sources: Bailey 1914: 93; Klineberg 1944: 5–12; Bilbo 1947: 49–58, 86–7, 198ff.; Broomfield 1965: 83–102; Wynes 1965: 16–17, 96ff.; Fredrickson 1971: 57–65; Owens 1971: 76ff.; Turner & Singleton 1978; Snay 1993: 56–60; Ambrose 1998: 45; MacCann 1998: xxviii–xxix.

upon the mind of the user, they become deeply internalized in the user's conduct and personality. The intense saliency of these features and the descriptive characteristic of the slur determine the nature and extent of interaction of the slur user with members of the targeted racial or ethnic group. The affective content of racial and ethnic slurs for the user include verbalized ideas, beliefs, and emotions. This constitutes part of the social psychological process which allows the user to maintain a coherent and meaningful view of the self and others in the context of the user's belief system, ideological perspective, and self-interest. In this sense, slurs demonstrate the power of words.

Racial slurs, as verbalized expressions of racist beliefs, result in the user constructing a circular logic in which social relations and interactions of blacks and whites are perceived only from a racist perspective of black inferiority and white superiority. By addressing and interpreting reality through slurs, social relations and group interaction are consequently limited and restricted to a linguistic framework that serves the vested interests of the user, which may be direct and/or indirect in its psychological, monetary, or other advantages for the user.

From the *social conflict* perspective, racial and ethnic slurs can be seen as mechanisms for expressing aggression toward an out-group through slandering, labeling, stigmatizing, and verbally "cutting to pieces" those of the ethnic and racial out-group. In this manner, the slur serves as an instrument or process for releasing aggressive hostility in in-group/out-group conflict situations. Such hostility is expressed in the use of slurs in anti-racial and anti-ethnic jokes (Middleton & Moland 1959: 61). The frequent use of racial and ethnic slurs in the rhetoric of institutional leaders and other members of the in-group creates in their minds and in the minds of listeners an almost permanent fixation of negative images of those in the racial or ethnic out-group. The stigma and label assigned to the out-group precede and dominate any contact or relationship in-group members have with those of the racial or ethnic out-group. This brings into play the *social control function* of slurs for in-group members. For example, white in-group members are aware of the slur "nigger lover" and the ridicule and rejection that one would experience if seen in frequent association with black Americans. In this manner, the slur serves a social control function by exerting strong pressure for conformity with conventional racial norms while promoting in-group solidarity. Finally, an important function of slurs for members of the racial or ethnic in-group (the users) is that of creating and reinforcing a sense of solidarity and intimacy within the group. It also provides the individual using the slur a sense of social approval and bonding with in-group members.

SEE ALSO: Discrimination; In-Groups and Out-Groups; Majorities; Race and Ethnic Etiquette; Racial Hierarchy; Scapegoating

REFERENCES AND SUGGESTED READINGS

Ambrose, D. (1998) Pro-Slavery Christianity in Early National Virginia. In: McKivigan, J. R. & Snay, M. (Eds.), *Religion and the Antebellum Debate Over Slavery*. University of Georgia Press, Athens, pp. 33–67.

Bailey, T. P. (1914) *Race Orthodoxy in the South and Other Aspects of the Negro Question*. Neale Publishing, New York.

Bilbo, T. G. (1947) *Take Your Choice: Separation or Mongrelization*. Dream Home Publishing, Poplarville, MS.

Broomfield, M. (1965) Dixon's *The Leopard's Spots*: A Study in Popular Racism. In: Wynes, C. E. (Ed.), *The Negro in the South Since 1865*. University of Alabama Press, Tuscaloosa, pp. 83–102.

Fredrickson, G. M. (1971) *The Black Image in the White Mind: The Debate on Afro-American Character and Destiny, 1817–1914*. Harper & Row, New York.

Klineberg, O. (1944) *Characteristics of the American Negro*. Harper & Row, New York.

MacCann, D. (1998) *White Supremacy in Children's Literature*. Garland, New York.

Middleton, R. & Moland, J. (1959) Humor in Negro and White Subcultures: A Study of Jokes Among University Students. *American Sociological Review* 24: 61–9.

Owens, L. L. (1971) *Saints of Clay: The Shaping of South Carolina Baptists*. R. L. Ryan, Columbia, SC.

Rodale, J. I. (1986) *The Synonym Finder*. Warner, New York.

Snay, M. (1993) *Gospel of Disunion: Religion and Separatism in the Antebellum South*. Cambridge University Press, New York.

Turner, J. H. & Singleton, R., Jr. (1978) A Theory of Ethnic Oppression: Toward a Reintegration of Cultural and Structural Concepts in Ethnic Relations Theory. *Social Forces* 56: 1001–18.

Wynes, C. E. (Ed.) (1965) *The Negro in the South Since 1865*. University of Alabama Press, Tuscaloosa.

Small, Albion W. (1854–1926)

Joyce E. Williams

Albion W. Small is known more for discipline-building in sociology than for contributions to sociological theory. He established the first department of sociology at the University of Chicago and served as its head from 1892 to 1924, and in that role influenced several generations of American sociologists. In 1895 he established the discipline's first professional journal, the *American Journal of Sociology*. He helped to found the American Sociological Society in 1905 and served two terms as its president. As with most of the first generation of sociologists in the US, Small's formal training was in philosophy and theology, but studies in Germany turned his attention to economics and interest theory. All of his work reflects an overarching concern with ethical interests. Small wrote and spoke about methodology, but not as we know it today. His own methodology was largely historical, economic, and political analysis. Nor did he clearly distinguish theory from methods. In his "Fifty Years of Sociology" (1916) under the subheading of theory, Small wrote about years of "wrangling about methods" along with the search for a single, theoretical explanation of society.

Influenced by Gustav Ratzenhofer and Ludwig Gumplowicz in Germany, Small's major contribution to sociological theory was his conceptualization of the social process, seen as developing, adjusting, and satisfying human interests. He viewed society as a process of social conflict, ultimately transformed by socialization and cooperative behaviors (Barnes 1948). His sociology was a classification of human interests and their significance in the social process, which he saw as a struggle of interest groups even though he believed strongly in solidarity. Small's text *General Sociology* (1905) focused on human interests and the social process, but made as many contributions to economics and political science as to sociology.

Small's writings reflect his struggle with cooperation and conflict. He taught a course on "The Conflict of Classes" and wrote *Between Eras: From Capitalism to Democracy* (1913), contextualizing class conflict in the rise of capitalism. Small's goal for sociology was to supply a secular theology for industrial capitalism. He combined a Marxian economic ethic with Christian social ethics, advocating a kind of Christian socialism based on rigorous empiricism. He saw subordination of self to society as the highest form of individual altruism. Much of his work was an attempt to unify character and social structure in an integration of self and society (Vidich & Lyman 1985). He provided a transition between systematizers such as Comte, Spencer, and Ward and subsequent generations of specialists. For Small, sociology provided the basis for an intelligent and efficient control of the social process and progressive improvement of human culture and social institutions. All of his work was about understanding the social process as a whole and about utilization of that process for social betterment.

SEE ALSO: American Sociological Association; Chicago School; Economic Development; Groups; Gumplowicz, Ludwig; Marx, Karl; Ratzenhofer, Gustav

REFERENCES AND SUGGESTED READINGS

Barnes, H. E. (1948) *An Introduction to the History of Sociology*. Phoenix Books, Chicago.
Odum, H. W. (1927) *American Masters of Social Science*. Henry Holt, New York.
Small, A. W. (1913) *Between Eras: From Capitalism to Democracy*. Intercollegiate Press, Kansas City, MO.
Small, A. W. (1916) Fifty Years of Sociology in the United States. *American Journal of Sociology* 21(6): 721–864.
Vidich, A. J. & Lyman, S. M. (1985) *American Sociology*. Yale University Press, New Haven.

Smith, Adam (1723–90)

D. A. Reisman

Adam Smith was born on June 5, 1723 in Kirkcaldy, a quiet fishing village north of Edinburgh. His father (whom he never knew) had been a Comptroller of Customs. He studied moral philosophy at the University of Glasgow, where his teacher, Francis Hutcheson, was emphasizing "the greatest happiness of the greatest number" even in the shadow of John Knox and Scottish Puritanism. Smith then spent six years at Oxford as a Snell Scholar. A crisis of faith, possibly brought on by an exposure to the epistemological skepticism of David Hume, led him to abandon his plan to become a clergyman.

Returning to Scotland in 1748, Smith lectured on literature (student notes from his course have been published as *Lectures on Rhetoric and Belles Lettres*) and from 1751–63 was Professor of Moral Philosophy at the University of Glasgow. His *Theory of Moral Sentiments* appeared in 1759. In it he argues that there is a social consensus on right and wrong which the sensitive social actor both absorbs and replicates. His theory of the "impartial spectator" who serves as the sounding board recalls the later ideas of G. H. Mead, while his appeal to "sympathy" or empathy that give the individual a way into others' feelings and thoughts looks forward to Weber on *Verstehen*.

Smith spent the years 1754–6 accompanying the young Duke of Buccleuch on his "grand tour" to Paris, Toulouse, Geneva, and other centers of European culture and thought. Smith met the French *philosophes* (including Turgot, Helvétius, and Rousseau) and also absorbed the great lesson of Physiocratic economics that the whole is an interdependent and a nature-driven circular flow. France in the last years of the *ancien régime* must have been an object lesson to him of how liberty could be suppressed by the Bastille, economical statesmanship by Versailles, and optimal allocation by tariffs and taxes.

Smith spent the next 10 years, in receipt of a pension from the Duke, doing research in Kirkcaldy. It was then that he wrote his great work, *An Inquiry into the Nature and Causes of the Wealth of Nations*. Published in 1776, it was an immediate success. It seemed to be defending the "invisible hand" of the free market against Mercantilist politicians and incompetent bureaucrats (including, significantly, the corporate hierarchy that Weber, Schumpeter, and Galbraith were to hold in high esteem) and to be saying that the instinctual drive to "truck, barter, and exchange" would be enough to produce rising living standards for all classes even without a Poor Law or a social welfare net.

Smith anticipates Marx in that he formulates a labor theory of value, implies that the class antagonisms of post-feudal industrialism would be based around the inputs of labor and capital, and demonstrates that the division of labor in the modern production-line system leaves the worker debased and alienated, "stupid and ignorant." His insights into conspicuous consumption resemble those of Veblen on the proof of status. They also demonstrate that he was envisaging a meritocratic, mobile society in which ascription would be challenged by achievement and the landed aristocracy would become increasingly irrelevant in a rapidly growing commercial society.

In 1778 Smith was appointed a Comptroller of Customs. He died in Edinburgh on July 17, 1790, aged 67, and is buried in the Canongate churchyard.

SEE ALSO: Economic Sociology: Neoclassical Economic Perspective; Ideology, Economy and; Liberalism; Mill, John Stuart; Moral Economy; Social Embeddedness of Economic Action

REFERENCES AND SUGGESTED READINGS

Pack, S. J. (1991) *Capitalism as a Moral System: Adam Smith's Critique of the Free Market Economy.* Edward Elgar, Aldershot.

Reisman, D. A. (1976) *Adam Smith's Sociological Economics.* Croom Helm, London.

Smith, A. (1976 [1776]) *An Inquiry into the Nature and Causes of the Wealth of Nations.* Clarendon Press, Oxford.

smoking

Jason Hughes

The word smoking has widely come to mean "consuming tobacco," and yet throughout history other substances – such as opium, cannabis, phencyclidine (PCP), and crack cocaine – have been smoked as a principal mode of their consumption. Equally, tobacco has been consumed in a multitude of ways other than through smoking. For example, prior to contact with Columbus, indigenous peoples of the Americas had variously chewed, snuffed (tobacco powder up the nostrils), drunk (tobacco juice), licked (applying tobacco resin to the gums and teeth), topically applied (to the skin), ocularly absorbed, and anally injected tobacco (Wilbert 1987). What we refer to as smoking should be understood first and foremost as a historically diverse set of practices surrounding the use of a range of drugs which, at various stages, did not necessarily involve the practice of smoking itself. That said, smoking today, as in pre-Columbian America, is by far the most widespread mode of consuming tobacco: the term refers to a phenomenon that has come to have enormous social, cultural, and economic significance. What follows is a broad and brief account of the sociocultural development of smoking divided into three main "stages": pre-Columbian smoking; modern smoking; and contemporary smoking. This focus on developments at the most general level serves to highlight the emergence of key themes in cultural uses and associations relating to the practice: a transition from understandings and uses of smoking as a practice to "lose control" and "escape normality" toward those in which smoking increasingly came to be used as a means of self-control and to return to "normality."

Sociocultural understandings and uses of tobacco among the indigenous peoples of the Americas in the pre-Columbian period varied considerably. However, characteristically, smoking held enormous spiritual significance; was highly ritualized; and involved more pronounced effects than those we would associate with present-day cigarette smoking. In formal ceremonial use, particularly shamanistic ritual, the strains and species of tobacco used and the practices surrounding consumption were such that smoking was capable of inducing hallucinogenic trances (Wilbert 1987: 134–6). Smoking was understood to offer a mode of transportation into the spiritual world through such altered states of consciousness; and in doing so it played a central role in indigenous American healing practices. Smoking marked many formal occasions: it was used to cement alliances between peoples, to symbolize peace, and to finalize agreements. Even recreational smoking was highly ritualized and involved the consumption of considerably stronger species and varieties than those associated with contemporary patterns.

The indigenous American esteem for tobacco smoking as a medical remedy was adopted by "modern" users – i.e., post-contact European smokers between the sixteenth and nineteenth centuries – with great enthusiasm. Some leading physicians of the time hailed tobacco as a panacea: a remedy for a range of ailments, from toothache to "cancer." While only the mildest and, to early Europeans, most palatable strains and species of tobacco were brought back from the "New World," even these, relative to those commonly in use today, were considerably more capable of producing intoxication. Indeed, concerns were expressed at the time that smoking, like drinking, may make workers unfit for labor (Brandt 1990). The practice rapidly became popular across Europe and had spread to many parts of Asia, Africa, and beyond by the end of the sixteenth century. Sociocultural uses and associations rapidly shifted from medical to recreational, and numerous treatises concerning the "abuse" of tobacco were written by physicians of the time who sought to retain tobacco as a medical remedy, rather than a drug of vice and the dissolute lifestyle with which it had by then come to be associated. Elite groups in European societies came to regard smoking as vulgar as it became "common." Following the French court in its capacity as a model-setting center for European upper classes, such groups switched from smoking to snuffing to distance themselves from what they considered to be their social inferiors. The practice of snuffing subsequently spread to all levels of society.

Contemporary patterns are epitomized by the resurgence of smoking, first in the spread of cigar smoking amongst affluent groups, and then through the emergence of the cigarette as a popular mode of consumption from the nineteenth century onwards. Smoking a cigarette, compared with indigenous American or even early European pipe smoking, involved relatively milder and more ambiguous effects. In part predicated upon such changes in its uses and effects, smoking came to be understood as a "psychological tool," a means to return one to normal from a range of dysphoric states linked to emotional arousal or underarousal. Compared to the ritualized and ceremonial use of tobacco of pre-Columbian smokers, and to a lesser degree the practices associated with "modern" smokers, "contemporary" smokers increasingly came to *individualize* the effects and functions of tobacco such that it could be used and understood as a means of self-control. The rise of cigarettes is also linked to processes involving the mass consumerization and feminization of smoking. Indeed, in the early twentieth century cigarettes became a symbol of women's emancipation – an association seized upon by tobacco companies of the time. Issues relating to the gender and class dynamics of smoking, health inequalities, and the marketing activities of tobacco corporations remain a topic of considerable sociological interest (see, e.g., Graham & Blackburn 1998; Pampel 2002). Also, particularly since the publication of findings from high-profile epidemiological studies in the 1950s and 1960s which linked tobacco consumption to fatal diseases, smoking has become increasingly *medicalized* – both understandings of smoking and, arguably, experiences of smoking and being a smoker; it has attained the status of an addictive disease in itself (Hughes 2003).

Thus, in short, the sociocultural development of smoking can be summarized as involving over the long term a series of interrelated shifts: from smoking to "lose control" toward smoking as a means of self-control, from ritualized smoking to more individualized smoking, from understandings of smoking as a panacea to its current status as a pandemic.

SEE ALSO: Addiction and Dependency; Consumption and the Body; Drug Use; Drugs, Drug Abuse, and Drug Policy; Health and Culture; Health Risk Behavior

REFERENCES AND SUGGESTED READINGS

Brandt, A. M. (1990) The Cigarette, Risk, and American Culture. *Daedalus* 119 (Fall): 155–76.

Gilman, S. L. & Zhou, X. (Eds.) (2004) *Smoke: A Global History of Smoking*. Reaktion Books, Hong Kong.

Goodin, R. E. (1989) The Ethics of Smoking. *Ethics* 99: 574–624.

Goodman, J. (1993) *Tobacco in History: The Cultures of Dependence*. Routledge, London.

Graham, H. & Blackburn, C. (1998) The Socio-Economic Patterning of Health and Smoking Behaviour Among Mothers With Young Children on Income Support. *Sociology of Health and Illness* 20(2): 215–40.

Greaves, L. (1996) *Smoke Screen: Women's Smoking and Social Control*. Scarlet Press, London.

Hughes, J. (2003) *Learning to Smoke: Tobacco Use in the West*. University of Chicago Press, Chicago.

Pampel, F. C. (2002) Inequality, Diffusion, and the Status Gradient in Smoking. *Social Problems* 49(1): 35–57.

Rabin, R. & Sugarman, S. (Eds.) (1993) *Smoking Policy: Law, Politics, and Culture*. Oxford University Press, Oxford.

Wilbert, J. (1987) *Tobacco and Shamanism*. Yale University Press, New Haven.

soccer

Richard Giulianotti and Dominic Malcolm

The game of association football, also known as soccer, involves two competing teams of 11 players. The players attempt to maneuver the football into the opposing team's goal, using any part of the body except the hands and arms. Only the goalkeeper is permitted to handle the ball, and then only within the penalty area surrounding the goal. The winning team scores most goals over a set time period, usually 90 minutes.

Association football is to be distinguished from those "football" codes that allow general ball handling and arm tackling, notably "American football," Australian Rules football, rugby union, and rugby league. Football is sometimes known as the "simplest game": its 17 basic laws and minimal equipment (a ball) ensure that games may be improvised and played in informal settings.

Football is the world's most popular team sport in participant and spectator numbers. The global governing body, the Fédération Internationale de Football Association (FIFA), estimated in 2000 that there are 250 million registered players, and over 1.4 billion people interested in football; a combined worldwide television audience of 35–40 billion watches football's premier tournament, the World Cup finals, played on a quadrennial basis. At the time of writing, FIFA boasts 205 member states, more than the 191 members of the United Nations, and, as a global organization, eclipsed only by the International Amateur Athletics Federation (IAAF) with 211 members.

Different kinds of football-related games have been played across the world, notably in China in the second century BCE and in medieval Tuscany. However, football developed into its modern form in Britain in the nineteenth century. "Folk football" games had been played in towns and villages since before medieval times, according to local customs and with few definite rules. In the early nineteenth century, industrialization, urbanization, and legal prohibitions restricted folk football but the game was taken up in English public schools and universities, partly as a mechanism for instilling discipline into pupils. The status rivalry between Rugby and Eton public schools was central to the initial codification of the separate and distinct forms of the game in the 1840s. These subsequently became rugby football and association football (of which American football, Canadian football, and Australian Rules football are subsequent refinements). In the 1840s, the "Cambridge rules" of football were established and applied, and in 1863 the game's rules were formally codified and printed and the (English) Football Association was formed. As the title of soccer's international federation indicates, to most of the world the game is known as football (or a local translation of the word, e.g., *Fussball* in German, *fútbol* in Spanish) rather than soccer. The word soccer is thought to have originated in the late nineteenth century at Oxford University, being a corruption of the term "association," and referring to a specific way of playing football, distinct particularly from rugby football.

The social and institutional aspects of football's global spread are of sociological interest. Football's international diffusion between the 1860s and 1914 was largely dependent upon British trade and educational influence overseas. In Europe, British migrant workers would form teams and attract challenges from local sides; or young local men would return from their education or peregrinations in Britain with a ball and rulebook to teach the game to their compatriots. In Latin America, British engineers, railway workers, sailors, teachers, and pupils were largely responsible for introducing local people to football. A similar story arises in Africa, though

British soldiers also introduced football in occupied territories such as modern-day Nigeria and South Africa. Thus football became more firmly established in the "informal" British Empire (and where the game was introduced by working- and merchant-class colonizers), in contrast with other British sports like cricket and rugby, which became popular in those countries formally subject to British imperial rule (and where sports were introduced by colonizers who were public school educated and held elite administrative roles in the host societies). Football was thus probably seen by non-British peoples as more "neutral" culturally, less compromised by imperialistic mores, as well as the most materially accessible form of modern sport.

Football associations were established in most nations in Europe and Latin America to oversee the game's organization. Notably in South America, these associations gradually shook off British influence, as a reflection of growing national pride and political autonomy. Driven particularly by the French, FIFA was founded by European associations in 1904, and continental governing bodies slowly followed: CONMEBOL in South America in 1916; UEFA in Europe, and AFC in Asia in 1954; CAF in Africa in 1957; CONCACAF in 1961; and the OFC for Oceania in 1965. Continental confederations organize tournaments and represent their members' interests inside FIFA. In true modernist style, the national football associations remain the basic political units within football's governance.

There are six dimensions of football that have attracted particular sociological interest: cultural differentiation; governance and politics; the cultural politics of race and gender; commodification; violence and hooliganism; and internationalism.

CULTURAL DIFFERENTIATION

Cultural differentiation falls into three broad domains:

1 Football is marked globally by intense club and supporter rivalries. At local level, particularly in major cities, heated "derby" fixtures arise, e.g., Boca Juniors versus River Plate in Buenos Aires. There are also strong regional rivalries, e.g., Bayern Munich versus Ruhr teams in Germany, or teams from north and south Italy; and major international rivalries, e.g., Brazil versus Argentina, England versus Scotland, Germany versus Holland. These rivalries habitually reflect and energize underlying intercommunal senses of cultural opposition and enmity. Allegiance to particular clubs and nations enables supporters to construct strong collective identities vis-à-vis these "others."

2 Neo-Durkheimians would argue that football has contributed substantially to modern nation building, especially in large or ethnically diverse developing nations like Brazil, Cameroon, and Nigeria. National electronic media allow citizens in remote regions to listen to or watch their "national" team in major international tournaments, so heightening cultural nationalism.

3 The globalization of football provides numerous illustrations of cultural "glocalization," whereby particular senses of cultural distinctiveness are constructed and expressed through the game. Particular clubs and nations establish favored playing styles or specific ways of administering their business. Each supporter community constructs particular "traditions" regarding its heroic players or the specific history of the club, thereby differentiating that club from its rivals.

GOVERNANCE

Governance falls into three broad domains:

1 Football's governing bodies undergo critical sociological scrutiny, notably regarding power struggles and corrupt practice. Major struggles have arisen between European and Latin American football officials over the control of FIFA, amidst substantial accusations regarding bribery and vote-fixing. The close ties between television networks and Latin American football associations have also attracted analysis.

2 Neo-Marxists argued that political elites have exploited football to germinate populist

domestic support for oppressive regimes, notably among military juntas in Latin America and in the old Soviet-bloc nations. These arguments too readily assume that performers and audiences can be duped by popular culture into supporting iniquitous regimes.

3 Sociologists in the UK have focused on the commercialization or "commodification" of football since the early 1990s. Particular attention has been paid to fan attempts to democratize club governance, such as through formation of independent supporters' associations or the more recent advent of "supporter trusts" that have gained control of some clubs. Greater awareness has arisen of alternative models of club governance in part through increasing public knowledge of the international game.

CULTURAL POLITICS OF RACE AND GENDER

Two general issues arise, regarding formal exclusion and cultural expressions of racism and sexism.

Historically, most nations have formally excluded non-white players from white-controlled football clubs and leagues. Even in polyethnic Brazil, non-white players were excluded until one club in Rio recruited blacks with great success in the 1920s. Post-war migration and African national independence have helped in the long term to secure anti-racism measures in FIFA and to promote non-white players in Europe.

Football has tended to provide a key space for the construction of particular forms of masculinity, thus women have always been excluded from full participation as players and officials. Whilst national and international women's football tournaments have been established since the 1970s, most notably in North America, and women's attendance at professional fixtures has risen in most parts of the world, in few instances do women make up over a quarter of football spectators. What advances have been made are driven partly by commercial motives, as football-related businesses tap new markets.

Overt and covert forms of cultural racism have gained greater analysis over the past 30 years. Overt racism is demonstrated through, for example, club refusals to sign players of particular ethnicity. Anti-racism campaigns have been inspired by top black players, and have been subsequently backed by football's governing bodies. Covert racism, such as not selecting non-whites for key playing positions, can be highlighted statistically but such actions are harder to contest in individual cases.

Overt sexism remains very evident, as masculine football cultures tend to deploy derogatory and objectifying language regarding women and gay men. Covert sexism continues in the highly gendered stratification of employees within sports institutions.

COMMODIFICATION

Four particular issues arise here.

1 Up to the 1930s, many European and Latin American football nations experienced hegemonic struggles over professionalization (i.e., the direct payment of players and coaches). More aristocratic and traditionalist forces favored player amateurism, partly to minimize or prevent mass participation and partly in attempts to retain control over the game. Business-minded football officials and marginalized social groups favored professionalism, eventually defeating the public school-influenced defenders of amateurism in the context of late twentieth-century capitalism.

2 More generalized concerns remain regarding social exclusion and alienation as germinated by football's increasing commercialization. Many social justice issues arise, e.g., higher admission prices may exclude poor but dedicated supporters; running football institutions as businesses may disenfranchise supporters politically from "their" game; high prices for football equipment or renting playing fields may alienate many and reduce young people's participation in the game; and inflated player salaries may sour the social relations between fans and players. What is perhaps most surprising is that it is only in the last 15 years that companies have

come to recognize the huge and inelastic demand for football, and sought to exploit this for economic gain.

3 Concerns have increasingly been voiced about the influence wielded by the media and corporations. Many argue that growing media control has led to fixtures being arranged to suit television viewers rather than fans who watch matches live, and that the media have also developed a particular kind of presentation which trivializes and spectacularizes football and thus detracts from aspects perceived to be the basis of the traditional appeal of the game. Allegations have even been made that sponsors now influence playing matters, most notably concerning Ronaldo's appearance for Brazil in the 1998 World Cup Final, and the role of Adidas in David Beckham's move from Manchester United to Real Madrid in 2003.

4 Intensified economic and cultural globalization generates major debates over neoliberalism within world football. The game is marked by intensified and unregulated flows in people (especially players), capital, media images, and commodities (notably merchandise). The largest and richest European markets come to dominate the world's leading football resources (notably top players), and can effectively corral the greatest corporate revenues and most numerous fans (that is, merchandise consumers) worldwide. These widening inequalities in world football are reinforced by the imposition of more general neoliberal policies in the developing world, resulting in the impoverishment of sporting clubs and leagues in Latin America and Africa.

VIOLENCE AND HOOLIGANISM

Violence and hooliganism fall into three broad domains.

1 "Football hooliganism" relates to a complex and culturally diverse phenomenon which in many instances is deeply rooted historically. For example, in Northern Europe, self-defining "hooligan" groups develop distinct subcultures characterized by the pursuit of status-seeking fights with similar fans that follow opposing teams. In Southern Europe and Latin America, fan violence is associated with "militant" supporters, known as *ultras* or *barras bravas*, who engage in culturally distinctive rituals of support.

2 The state contributes crucially to the construction of "hooliganism" through the (often violent) imposition of "security" in and around stadiums, and through juridical attempts to label and legally punish "hooligans."

3 Some football subcultures have ties to paramilitary movements and military conflicts. The Yugoslav civil war in the early 1990s involved several units drawn from football supporter organizations. Other violent conflicts with strong football connections have arisen in Nigeria, Mauritius, and the "Soccer War" between Honduras and El Salvador in 1969. More symbolically, fans of Glasgow's two leading teams, Celtic and Rangers, sing anthems that celebrate paramilitary movements in Northern Ireland.

INTERNATIONALISM

Internationalism falls into three main domains.

1 "Naïve internationalism" celebrates football's functionality in bringing peoples and nations together, promoting intercultural understanding and social harmony. This argument tends to ignore the historical evidence of conflict and violence within sport.

2 A "pragmatic internationalism" adopts a practical, social policy orientation toward football, notably in the developing world. Football is seen as having a positive practical function in the positive resocialization of traumatized peoples, such as former child soldiers in West Africa, and in helping to build peaceful social contact between warring communities, such as in Bosnia or Rwanda.

3 An emerging human rights perspective examines how the organization of sports like football in the developing world has impinged upon the personal liberties and freedoms of young people in particular. For example, coaches may enter into psychologically and

physically abusive relations with young players, in part by demanding long hours of labor from these child athletes.

Inevitably, these six sociological themes have received varied treatments by scholars from different nations and continents. In Britain, football hooliganism has been a major topic since the 1970s, with European nations (notably Italy and France) following in the early 1990s. In Scotland, religious sectarianism between supporters provokes a recurring debate. Whereas in England hostile debates between the advocates of various approaches have arisen, notably over explanations of violence in football, closer disciplinary ties exist between historians, sociologists, and anthropologists in many European nations (notably in Scandinavia, Italy, France, and Germany).

Since the early 1990s in the UK, the intensified commodification of football has received both critical and sympathetic sociological comments; the role of media corporations in advancing this process has attracted particular attention. Questions of social exclusion in football have focused particularly on ethnic minorities and, to a lesser extent, women in England.

In Latin America, anthropologists played the founding role in the social scientific study of football. Four major investigative questions have been apparent. First, how does football relate to distinctive national, cultural, and "racial" identities, particularly given the diasporic movements of players to Europe? Second, what "function" has football played in sustaining military juntas and *caudillo*-style politicians? Third, through the strong influence of Gramscian theory in Latin American sociology, how do football and other popular cultural forms encapsulate the resistant identities of marginalized communities? Fourth, how might Latin American football's endemic corruption be exposed and replaced by more transparent, democratic forms of governance?

Overall, the sociological analysis of football faces several methodological problems. A lack of systematic international collaborative research is still apparent, notably among many UK-based writers. Geopolitical and linguistic divisions remain between many sociologists, commonly separating Anglophone researchers, continental Europeans (North and South), and Latin Americans. European football researchers, such as those publishing in German and French, have shown stronger commitments to international dialogue, reflecting their greater empirical and conceptual grasp of globalization processes.

Three particular, substantive issues within football remain underexamined by sociologists. First, we require serious ethnographic studies of professional football clubs, although gaining access and funding to conduct such research is certainly problematic. Second, we need a proper sociological treatment of the technical and aesthetic aspects of football. Third, we require an adequate, cross-cultural analysis of the relationship between elite and grassroots football with particular attention to access and participation.

SEE ALSO: Consumption, Mass Consumption, and Consumer Culture; Consumption of Sport; Football Hooliganism; Globalization, Sport and; Nationalism and Sport; Sport; Sport and Capitalism; Sport and Culture; Sport, Professional; Sport and Religion; Sport as Spectacle; Sports Heroes and Celebrities; Sports Industry; Sports Stadia

REFERENCES AND SUGGESTED READINGS

Archetti, E. (1998) *Masculinities: Football, Polo, and the Tango in Argentina*. Berg, Oxford.

Armstrong, G. & Giulianotti, R. (Eds.) (1997) *Entering the Field*. Berg, Oxford.

Armstrong, G. & Giulianotti, R. (Eds.) (2004) *Football in Africa*. Palgrave, Basingstoke.

Brown, A. (1998) *Fanatics! Power, Identity, and Fandom in Football*. Routledge, London.

Dunning, E., Murphy, P., Waddington, I., & Astrinakis, A. (Eds.) (2002) *Fighting Fans: Football Hooliganism as a World Phenomenon*. University College Dublin Press, Dublin.

Fanizadeh, M., Hödl, G., & Manzenreiter, W. (Eds.) (2002) *Global Players: Kultur, Okonomie, und Politik des Fussballs*. Brandes & Apsel Südwind, Frankfurt.

Garland, J., Malcolm, D., & Rowe, M. (Eds.) (2000) *The Future of Football: Challenges for the 21st Century*. Frank Cass, London.

Giulianotti, R. (1999) *Football: A Sociology of the Global Game*. Polity Press, Cambridge.

Giulianotti, R., Bonney, N., & Hepworth, M. (Eds.) (1994) *Football Violence and Social Identity*. Routledge, London.

Goldblatt, D. (2003) *Football Yearbook 2003–4*. DK Publishers, London.

Hare, G. (2004) *Football in France: A Cultural History*. Berg, Oxford.

Hong, F. & Mangan, J. A. (2004) *Soccer, Women, Sexual Liberation: Kicking Off a New Era*. Frank Cass, London.

Murray, B. (1996) *The World's Game: A History of Soccer*. University of Illinois Press, Urbana.

Sugden, J. & Tomlinson, A. (1998) *FIFA and the Contest for World Football: Who Rules the People's Game?* Polity Press, Cambridge.

Walvin, J. (2000) *The People's Game: The History of Football Revisited*. Mainstream, Edinburgh.

social accountability and governance

Crawford Spence and Chris Carter

Recent accounting scandals such as Enron, Parmalat, and WorldCom have concentrated attention on the accountability and governance of corporations. Social accounting has been described and critiqued from a variety of positions, ranging from right-wing neoliberal critiques all the way through to Marxist and deep green critiques. The different positions taken on the desirability or otherwise of social accounting can be understood by considering the type of change that each theorist advocates. The majority of writing and work in the area has come from those who see social accounting as a means of bringing about evolutionary change in capitalism.

WHAT IS SOCIAL ACCOUNTING?

Social contractarian perspective: evolutionary change. Social accounting is generally understood as an attempt to investigate organizations more broadly. By scrutinizing the impact of the activities of organizations, social accountants seek to highlight the wider social and environmental costs of their operations. The rationale underpinning this approach is that corporations have a wider responsibility than merely making profits for shareholders. Social accounting has similarly been described as an "attempt to deconstruct conventional accounting, expose some of its more unpleasant characteristics and offer new accountings predicated on values wider than making rich managers and shareholders even richer" (Bebbington et al. 1999). The key master concept underpinning social accounting is *accountability*. Whereas conventional accounting (allegedly) serves to make an organization accountable to its financial owners, social accounting seeks to discharge accountability to other stakeholders. These are groups that are influenced by or can influence the social, environmental, and economic impacts of an organization (Gray et al. 1996). The principal argument behind accountability is that stakeholders have a *right* to information regarding the social and environmental effects of corporate economic activity. These rights to information may be enshrined in law, may appear in quasi-legal or voluntary codes of conduct, or may be moral in nature (Gray et al. 1996).

Enhanced corporate accountability would ultimately require companies to temper their relentless pursuit of profit and competitiveness by considering their interactions with a wider constituency of stakeholder groups. Indeed, the rendering transparent of an organization does not set the parameters to the vision of the social accounting project. Gray (2005) has argued that social and environmental accounts are an essential precondition to a healthy and functioning democracy, warning that the absence of such accounts leaves society relatively powerless when compared with the power of modern-day corporations. Thus something must happen once the accountability has been discharged. There is a radical intention in the social accounting project. The explicit intention is to increase democracy, but not necessarily as an end in itself. Underlying social accounting is a concern with the social dislocations and environmental degradation caused by organizations in advanced capitalism. Increased accountability, although morally desirable in itself, is also seen as a means to move toward a more socially and environmentally benign order.

Neoliberalism: radical change (right-wing). Critiques of social accounting emanate from a variety of theoretical positions. However, it has been very rare for those on the right to engage in the social accounting debate at all. One must return to Benston (1982) to find a critique of social accounting from a right-wing position.

On a practical note, Benston suggests that the measurement of "externalities" is problematic and therefore cannot be relied upon. Notwithstanding the practical considerations put forward by Benston (1982, 1984) and the logical inconsistencies therein (Schreuder & Ramanathan 1984), his arguments are primarily ideological: the primary responsibility of management is to shareholders and social accounting would impose unnecessary costs upon them. In any case, other stakeholders such as employees, customers, and creditors, Benston (1982) argues, are well served already by voluntary management reports. Social accounting may be useful with respect to corporate governance, exposing fraudulent dealings and misuses of shareholder assets by management. He holds that even the cost of an accounting standard would likely exceed the benefits to shareholders (see Benston 1984). As such, "the responsibility of accountants would be best served by their forbearance from social accounting" (Benston 1982).

Expedients: marginal change. Moving away from a radical right-wing position, another conception of what social accounting is and what it may do is offered by Parker (1986). Parker falls into what Gray et al. (1996) refer to as the "expedient" camp. Parker notes that social accounting means different things to different people. To "corporate defenders," it is a means of defense against critics of the corporation. To "corporate critics," it provides a constraint upon socially irresponsible behavior and a positive motivation for the corporation to act in a socially responsible manner. Parker argues that standards could moderate and regulate the competing purposes of these groups, i.e., allow corporations to manage their image whilst restricting reporting bias and thereby facilitating a more informed and protected society. Whilst those of radical left-wing persuasions would be horrified by the former, Parker sees the use of social accounting as an image enhancer as something that is actually good, as long as it is accompanied by the provision of substantive social accounting information. Although informed by a "suspicion of powerful private interests" (Parker 1991: 32), Parker's view emanates from an acceptance of the current essential structure of capitalist society (see Parker 1991: 27).

Marxian critique: radical change (left-wing). As long as one accepts the need for a more

sociodemocratic form of system, Benston's and Parker's views do little to disturb the rationale for social accounting. More shaking critiques of social accounting come from those theorists that put social justice (however this is defined; e.g., Puxty, 1986, 1991; Tinker et al. 1991) and ecological sustainability (e.g., Maunders & Burritt 1991) at the heart of their analysis. The essence of Tinker et al.'s position is that a better accounting can only come about after a change in structural conditions. The structure of society, and of capitalism in particular, is such that social accounting will be captured by vested interest groups and used to mask those vested interests. These structural inequalities, argue Tinker et al., are overlooked by Gray et al. by virtue of their commitment to pluralist thinking and "middle ground theorizing." The middle ground is characterized by Tinker et al. as concerned with "what is pragmatic and socially acceptable; not what is socially just, scientifically rational, or likely to rectify social ills arising from waste, exploitation, extravagance, disadvantage or coercion" (1991: 29).

Tinker et al. explain how the history of social accounting shows the middle ground shifting in specific directions, in response to definite social conflicts and struggles. This swaying in the tide minimizes and mystifies the structural inequalities of contemporary capitalism (1991: 36). Social accounting thus serves a political quietism function which "mask(s) the affinities of many right-wing positions and middle-of-the-road research" (p. 37). Gray et al.'s middle-of-the-road approach is therefore rejected. The middle ground is contested and unstable and Gray et al. refuse to examine the basic contradictions of the social system that cause this instability; Gray et al.'s approach has not been shown to be productive, Tinker et al. argue, and "the political quietism implicit in their viewpoint is empirically unsubstantiated" (1991: 47).

As an alternative, Tinker et al. advocate a critical accounting that speaks about social antagonisms and structural inequalities. The examples given by Tinker et al. are recasts of the accounting records provided by firms in terms of, in one case, the role that a mining company played in colonial exploitation and, in another, an analysis of General Motors' use of their annual reports as ideological weapons.

If there is any role for social accounting from a Marxist viewpoint, then one infers that it would be through external social audits. These are social accounts prepared about an organization by people outside of that organization. Examples of this particular type of social accounting are evident in the work of Social Audit Ltd. (see Medawar 1976) in the 1970s who, without the cooperation of the organizations whom they were auditing, constructed a series of detailed exposés of the social and environmental impacts of those organizations in the UK. In a similar vein, though with a much more Marxist slant, Counter Information Services compiled a series of *Counter Reports* of large multinational organizations in the 1970s (see Gray et al. 1987 for examples of these). Similar exercises have been carried out recently by Christian Aid and Friends of the Earth, who have produced "alternative" versions of social accounts of organizations such as Shell and Exxon.

Tinker et al.'s (1991) critique emanates from a view of society that focuses on conflict and power struggles. A similar viewpoint on social accounting is reached by Puxty (1986, 1991), who, following Habermas, argues that it owes its very existence to the needs of the powerful within society (1986: 103). This "capture" of social accounting is inevitable given the non-pluralistic makeup of society. Society has dominant interests. Social accounting does not dissolve these power relationships, as its proponents hope it might, but reenforces them: "Accounting is part of a system of distorted communication that reflects the social system. Any extension of accounting through the processes of that system can thus be no more than an extension of that systematic distortion" (Puxty 1986: 108). Puxty repeats these views through a later article where he "reject(s) the possibility of progress of society through current pluralist institutions, and corporate social information that might be generated through them" (1991: 41).

Deep green critique: radical change (ecological). Maunders and Burritt (1991) take a deep green perspective when considering how to account for the environment. They argue that any attempt to solve ecological problems through an accounting that is an extension of conventional accounting may be doomed to failure. This is because of the neoclassical ideological foundations on which conventional accounting rests: selfishness of maximizing individual utility; contrived consumer demand (wants over needs); and anthropocentrism. It is argued by Maunders and Burritt that a much more radical accounting is needed that actively challenges these cultural values.

These "radical" critiques variously place notions of social justice (Puxty 1986, 1991; Tinker et al. 1991; Cooper 1992) or environmental sustainability (Maunders & Burritt 1991) and/or Mother Earth (Cooper 1992) at the heart of their analyses. What is common to each of them is that they see social accounting, at least corporate *self*-reporting, as not a mere irrelevance but something that could actually exacerbate ecological problems and further entrench social inequality. Social accounting hides and disguises deeper structural inequalities that must be critiqued and transcended. As such, corporate social accounting is counterproductive. In seeking to disempower corporations, it actually seeks to bolster the interests of corporations. If there is any place for social accounting, then it must be through externally produced social audits. The problem, argues Lehman (1999, 2001), is in according a privileged status to corporations as the agents of change. Gray et al. seek to put corporations at the center of their theorizing as the entity that prepares the social/environmental analysis of its own operations. The radical left-wing critique curiously comes to the same opinion on social accounting as the radical right-wing critique. In Cooper's ecofeminist (and Marxist) critique of environmental accounting, she concludes that "in the present symbolic order accountants should not attempt to account for the environment" (1992: 37).

In the wake of accounting scandals and increasing concern over the environmental sustainability of the current economic orthodoxy, social accounting is likely to figure more widely in policy and academic debates. The contours of the debate on social accounting are currently configured around the responsibilities of corporations and the limits of reformist pluralism in the wake of corporate power.

SEE ALSO: Democracy and Organizations; Governmentality and Control; Power; Transnationalism

REFERENCES AND SUGGESTED READINGS

Bebbington, J., Gray, R., & Owen, D. (1999) Seeing the Wood for the Trees: Taking the Pulse of Social and Environmental Accounting. *Accounting, Auditing, and Accountability Journal* 12(1): 47–51.

Benston, G. J. (1982) Accounting and Corporate Accountability. *Accounting, Organizations, and Society* 7(2): 87–105.

Benston, G. J. (1984) Rejoinder to "Accounting and Corporate Accountability: An Extended Comment." *Accounting, Organizations, and Society* 9(3/4): 417–19.

Cooper, C. (1992) The Non and Nom of Accounting for (M)other Nature. *Accounting, Auditing, and Accountability Journal*, 5(3): 16–39.

Gray, R. H. (2002) The Social Accounting Project and *Accounting, Organizations, and Society*: Privileging Engagement, Imaginings, New Accountings, and Pragmatism Over Critique? *Accounting, Organizations, and Society* 27: 687–708.

Gray, R. H. (2005) Taking a Long View on What We Know about Social and Environmental Accountability and Reporting: Of Don Quixote, Placebos, and Capitalism. *Electronic Journal of Radical Organization Theory*.

Gray, R. H., Owen, D., & Maunders, K. T. (1987) *Corporate Social Reporting: Accounting and Accountability*. Prentice-Hall, Hemel Hempstead.

Gray, R. H., Owen, D., & Adams, C. (1996) *Accounting and Accountability: Changes and Challenges in Corporate Social and Environmental Reporting*. Prentice-Hall, London.

Lehman, G. (1999) Disclosing New Worlds: A Role for Social and Environmental Accounting and Auditing. *Accounting, Organizations, and Society* 24(3): 217–41.

Lehman, G. (2001) Reclaiming the Public Sphere: Problems and Prospects for Corporate Social and Environmental Accounting. *Critical Perspectives on Accounting* 12: 713–33.

Maunders, K. T. & Burritt, R. L. (1991) Accounting and Ecological Crisis. *Accounting, Auditing, and Accountability Journal* 4(3): 9–26.

Medawar, C. (1976) The Social Audit: A Political View. *Accounting, Organizations, and Society* 1(4): 389–94.

Parker, L. D. (1986) Polemical Themes in Social Accounting: A Scenario for Standard Setting. *Advances in Public Interest Accounting* 1: 67–93.

Parker, L. D. (1991) External Social Accountability: Adventures in a Maleficent World. *Advances in Public Interest Accounting* 4: 23–34.

Puxty, A. G. (1986) Social Accounting as Immanent Legitimation: A Critique of a Technicist Ideology. *Advances in Public Interest Accounting* 1: 95–111.

Puxty, A. G. (1991) Social Accountability and Universal Pragmatics. *Advances in Public Interest Accounting* 4: 35–45.

Schreuder, H. & Ramanathan, K. V. (1984) Accounting and Corporate Accountability: An Extended Comment. *Accounting, Organizations, and Society* 9(3/4): 409–15.

Tinker, T., Lehman, C., & Neimark, M. (1991) Falling Down the Hole in the Middle of the Road: Political Quietism in Corporate Social Reporting. *Accounting, Auditing, and Accountability Journal* 4(2): 28–54.

social capital

Rosalind Edwards

Social capital is a concept broadly referring to the ways people connect through social networks, common values within these networks such as trust and reciprocity, and how this constitutes a resource that equates to a kind of capital. Different theorists emphasize slightly different features within this broad definition.

Some perspectives pose social capital as a distinct form of "public good," embodied in civic engagement and having knock-on effects for democracy and economic prosperity. Putnam (2000) points to local communities in which a predominance of work-poor families and/or ethnic diversity has eroded positive social capital in favor of negative forms. Fukuyama (1995) argues that engagement in the private and voluntary sectors enhances economic prosperity, whereas strong kinship allegiances crowd out other economically beneficial social connections. Thus different forms of social capital are identified. Putnam highlights self-sustaining voluntary associations as generating the "bridging" form of social capital that enables people to "get ahead" – horizontal trust and reciprocal connections between people from different walks of life – as opposed to the "bonding" social capital among homogeneous people that allows them only to "get by." Woolcock (1998) has also added the notion of vertical "linking" social capital with formal organizations, with the state facilitating new local partnership networks.

Other work sees the family as a wellspring of social capital. Coleman (1988) argues that the family is where children have their human capital (notably, educational success) developed and are socialized into the norms, values, and sanctions of society. He argues that this nurturance is inherent in the structure of family relationships, which then affects the nature of local communities, and that social capital building is hindered where parents are "absent," as in lone-mother or dual-earner families.

Another perspective highlights social capital as intertwined with other capital assets: economic, cultural, and symbolic. These are transmitted and reproduced over time, within social groups and across generations, sustaining class privilege and power (Bourdieu 1986). Dominant social capital processes are seen as also having a "dark side," marginalizing or confining people on the basis of their ethnicity, gender, and age (Portes 1998; Morrow 1999; Molyneux 2002).

While engagement with the concept of social capital as a theoretical concept and policy instrument has been welcomed as signaling a shift towards engagement with social processes (Woolcock 1998; Schuller et al. 2000), there is some concern that this is occurring in a simplistic manner and is suffused with liberal economic rationality (Fine 2000). Other criticisms of the concept include the lack of consensus over its definition and hence difficulties in measuring it (Morrow 1999; Molyneux 2002), and the tautological nature of many conceptions of social capital processes (Portes 1998).

SEE ALSO: Bourdieu, Pierre; Capital: Economic, Cultural, and Social; Coleman, James; Social Capital and Education; Social Capital and Health; Trustworthiness

REFERENCES AND SUGGESTED READINGS

Bourdieu, P. (1986) The Forms of Capital. In: Richardson, J. E. (Ed.), *Handbook of Theory for Research in the Sociology of Education*. Greenwood Press, Westport.

Coleman, J. S. (1988) Social Capital in the Creation of Human Capital. *American Journal of Sociology* 94: S95–S120.

Fine, B. (2000) *Social Capital Versus Social Theory: Political Economy and Social Sciences at the Turn of the Millennium*. Routledge, London.

Fukuyama, F. (1995) *Trust, the Social Virtues and the Creation of Prosperity*. Hamish Hamilton, London.

Molyneux, M. (2002) Gender and the Silences of Social Capital: Lessons from Latin America. *Development and Change* 33(2): 167–88.

Morrow, V. (1999) Conceptualizing Social Capital in Relation to the Well-Being of Children and Young People: A Critical Review. *Sociological Review* 47(4): 744–65.

Portes, A. (1998) Social Capital: Its Origins and Applications in Modern Sociology. *Annual Review of Sociology* 24(1): 1–24.

Putnam, R. D. (2000) *Bowling Alone: The Collapse and Revival of American Community*. Simon & Schuster, New York.

Schuller, T., Baron, S., & Field, J. (2000) Social Capital: A Review and Critique. In: Baron, S., Field, J. & Schuller, T. (Eds.), *Social Capital: Critical Perspectives*. Oxford University Press, Oxford.

Woolcock, M. (1998) Social Capital and Economic Development: Towards a Theoretical Synthesis and Policy Framework. *Theory and Society* 27(2): 151–208.

social capital and education

Rafael Santana and Barbara Schneider

The concept of social capital has been widely used in educational research. However, researchers have yet to come to an agreement over what constitutes social capital and what its effects are on educational and other social outcomes. There are at least two distinct theories of social capital commonly used by educational researchers. The first, by James S. Coleman, conceptualizes social capital as the relational ties among individuals within a closed functional community (Coleman & Hoffer 1987; Coleman 1988, 1990). This perspective highlights the benefits of membership within a social system and emphasizes the functional form of social capital. The second, by

French sociologist Pierre Bourdieu, also emphasizes the interconnectedness of individuals within a social system but additionally highlights members' access to institutional resources as well as their consumptive behaviors that enable them to reproduce other forms of capital (Bourdieu 1986).

Coleman (1988) distinguishes social capital from human and economic capital by arguing that social capital is obtained through the relational ties of individuals in a social system, whereas human capital is increased through education and training, and economic capital is accrued through the reinvestment of capital for profit. Intangible, social capital is an abstract resource that actors use to facilitate certain actions that lead to productive outcomes (Coleman 1988). Social capital inheres in the relations among actors and is not lodged within any single individual but rather develops out of sustained interactions among actors.

Properties of social capital include (1) the degree of closure or interconnectedness of ties within a social network and (2) the density of social ties among its members. Coleman argues that a high degree of network closure enhances communication among members, thus strengthening ties. The density of social ties also facilitates the articulation of mutual expectations and obligations for network membership, which allows members to discern whether others are fulfilling their agreed-upon obligations. Shared norms, expectations, mutual obligations, and effective sanctions serve to strengthen social ties and give rise to another form of social capital, trustworthiness. Network members are regarded as trustworthy when they fulfill their obligations to others within the network. Networks characterized by high levels of trustworthiness are those in which members enforce agreed-upon norms through sanctioning unacceptable behavior.

For example, parents can draw on the social resources available within the network to monitor their children's behavior. The closure of the network and the density of the ties among parents and other adults in the network encourage the flow of information about their children's activities. If a child misbehaves in the presence of other adults in the community, they can be trusted to notify the child's parent of the child's behavior with the expectation that such misbehavior will be prevented by the parent in the future.

Offering an alternative perspective on social capital, Bourdieu argues that network collectivity is maintained through investment strategies that strengthen and ensure the durability of relationships binding individuals to each other. These investments and exchanges occur through ceremonies, ritualized meetings, and other social activities (Bourdieu 1986: 250). To Bourdieu, social capital is used to accrue advantages which are ascribed to social networks by virtue of their position within a social structure rather than from the inherent qualities of the relationships between individuals within the network. In contrast to Coleman, Bourdieu views social capital within the context of social stratification and reproduction, underscoring the benefits afforded to individuals located differentially within the social structure. As Portes (1998: 3) notes, Bourdieu's treatment of social capital is "instrumental, focusing on the benefits accruing to individuals by virtue of participation in groups and on the deliberate construction of sociability for the purpose of creating this resource."

Bourdieu defines social capital both as the social ties between individuals and the sum of resources that are available as a result of those ties. He suggests that actors operate within a social hierarchy, and individuals at varying positions in the social hierarchy will differ in their associated networks and in their access to social capital. For example, individuals of low social status may have ties primarily to other individuals of low status who can contribute only limited resources to the relationship. He notes, however, that individuals can increase their access to social capital by expanding their network of social relationships to others outside the primary network. This point is also developed by Granovetter (1973) and Burt (1992), who suggest that weak social ties within the network's structural configuration allow for greater individual mobility and more diverse channels for information and resources within and between networks.

Educational research more closely aligned with Coleman's conception of social capital tends to identify the productive, or positive, outcomes associated with increasing social capital within a social system, such as raising children's educational expectations, achievement, and attainment. On the other hand, scholars whose work relies more on Bourdieu's articulation of social capital emphasize the social structural implications of differential access to and use of social capital in reproducing inequalities in society.

SOCIAL CAPITAL THEORY AND ITS APPLICATION IN EDUCATIONAL RESEARCH

Educational researchers have examined both the various functions and forms of social capital within schools and its influence on student outcomes (i.e., achievement, attainment, and aspirations). According to Stanton-Salazar and Dornbusch (1995), institutional agents, such as counselors, teachers, and other students, are gatekeepers of resources and opportunities within schools, and students with access to these institutional agents are at a distinct advantage. Stanton-Salazar and Dornbusch report that Mexican American students with ties to institutional agents experience changes in their educational aspirations and expectations. Measuring social capital as the number of ties (strong and weak) students have with institutional agents (school, family, and non-family ties), they suggest that students may increase access to more diverse networks through strong and weak ties by maintaining Spanish use within the school. They conclude that bilingualism plays a prominent role in determining access to social capital for Mexican American students because they experience network advantages in accessing institutional support not available to Spanish-dominant immigrant students and English-dominant working-class students.

Maintaining one's own culture may increase the strength of ties within an ethnically or culturally determined network; however, assimilating into institutions such as schools may be necessary to develop weak ties to the institutional agents who offer guidance for academic success. For example, Portes (1998) argues that immigrants can adapt to mainstream culture while retaining positive aspects of their country of origin. He challenges the view that complete assimilation is the optimal mode of adaptation for upward social mobility in an English-dominated, nationalist environment.

Although high concentrations of black and Hispanic students within urban centers have been suggested to create a negative "culture of poverty" effect on achievement, Goldsmith (2004) finds that, in racially segregated schools, denser, more cohesive ties among students and teachers lead to higher educational expectations among Mexican American students than in schools that are more ethnically mixed or mostly white. Additionally, while agreeing with Coleman's (1988) suggestion that being in a single-parent family negatively affects students' achievement, Pong (1998) finds that social capital can counteract the negative effect of non-intact families on mathematics and reading achievement. In schools with high concentrations of students from single-parent families and stepfamilies, dense networks between single parents counteract the negative effects of these family forms on student achievement.

Scholars have taken an organizational perspective to explore the function that social capital plays in facilitating professional development among teachers. For example, Frank et al. (2004) argue that social capital within schools promotes the diffusion of teaching innovations between teachers and administrators. By observing and interacting with other teaching professionals, teachers and administrators are pressured to improve their pedagogical practices and also more easily benefit from the expertise of their colleagues. Frank et al. find that "change agents," that is, teachers who have already adopted new pedagogical techniques, should participate in local social capital processes that are related to the implementation of educational innovations and reforms. The authors recommend that change agents spend some of their professional development time interacting with other organizational members in order to share skills or cultivate new expertise.

Coleman (1988; Coleman & Hoffer 1987) argues that close relations between parents and students within the school produce increased student achievement. However, scholars have reexamined Coleman's work on the direct and positive effect that intergenerational closure has on student outcomes and found different results. Examining intergenerational closure among parents in public and private schools, Morgan and Sorenson find a negative association of closure with mathematics achievement, despite dense friendship networks. However, public schools characterized by closure among students, teachers, parents, and administrators were shown to positively affect student math achievement.

Trust between teachers, parents, and students is one of the most fundamental forms of social capital. Bryk and Schneider (2002) argue that within the school community, individuals are interconnected through a set of mutual dependencies which make them vulnerable to sanctions from other community members. Therefore, school members build relational trust in order to ameliorate the uncertainty that arises from their mutual vulnerability to each other. Relational trust, therefore, is derived from discerning the intentionality and discrete interactions that individuals have with each other in the community. Schools characterized by high levels of relational trust are much more likely to experience sustained improvement in student academic achievement, and teachers and administrators in these schools are likely to be more committed to students' learning.

Similarly, Goddard (2003) connects trustworthiness to both the structural and functional forms of social capital. Trust, measured as the relational networks that connect parents and community members, was found to have a significant, positive effect on students' likelihood of passing high stakes standardized tests. These trusting relationships were supported by norms that encourage learning within the school environment. Trust has also been found to be a key element in the development of leadership within schools. The relationships between teachers, administrators, and instruction specialists act as sources from which teachers obtain professional development and assistance. When developing leadership within the school, teachers can draw on trusting relationships with administrators and other teachers as sources of professional assistance. Trust, therefore, acts as a fundamental institutional resource for enhancing student learning and developing teacher professionalism.

Other research has examined the dynamic aspects of social ties and the ways in which these ties are mobilized for the achievement of goals (i.e., functional specificity; see Sandefur & Laumann 1998; Kim & Schneider 2006). Within schools, parents and teachers activate network connections to "broker" for their students. For example, Lareau (2003) demonstrates the different techniques employed by lower- and middle-class families in an attempt to improve student learning. These techniques vary by class and race, and produce both positive and negative student outcomes. Lareau finds that middle-class parents use a technique of concerted cultivation in order to foster their children's talents in leisure and academic activities. Working-class and poor parents, on the other hand, do not engage in this concerted cultivation, and instead trust the expertise and knowledge of educational professionals in directing their children's educational trajectories.

CRITIQUES OF SOCIAL CAPITAL IN SCHOOL RESEARCH: SUBSTANTIVE AND METHODOLOGICAL

Recent applications of social capital theory suggest that the formation of strong ties does not always have positive effects and can constrain the actions of network members (Portes & Sensenbrenner 1993). Intergenerational closure, for example, may promote normative behavior such as childrearing practices among working families (Parcel & Menaghan 1994), but it may also have a negative impact by inhibiting actions that could be beneficial, such as low-resource parents interacting frequently with their children's teacher. In other words, one form of social capital that works for a certain type of result may not work for other outcomes. Accordingly, Portes (1998: 15) identifies four negative consequences of social capital. Specifically regarding educational outcomes, strong norms may foster an environment of lowered expectations and behavior (defined as a downward leveling of norms).

Other scholars have also examined the deleterious effect of the negative or counterfeit social capital that teachers create with students. For example, though finding that positive student–teacher relations tend to positively affect student achievement, Ream (2003) concludes that teachers who cultivate and nurture social relations in the classroom for the sole purpose of maintaining classroom harmony do so at the expense of academic content. This negative social capital is epitomized by a teacher who excuses rather than sanctions misbehavior in order to maintain the already close relationship with a student. Although fostering positive relationships between teachers and students, this type of "defensive teaching" ultimately undermines academic achievement and serves to negatively affect academic progress.

Finally, research using social capital as a predictor of social outcomes has largely been descriptive and correlational rather than causal; causal links between social capital and its outcomes have been only weakly established. Some scholars, however, have attempted to remedy this lack of scientifically rigorous research by isolating the effects of social capital within the family on student academic achievement. Schneider and Coleman (1993) also look within the family and treat parental participation, family composition, maternal employment, and family activities as indicators of social capital. Characterizing social capital as a resource that facilitates action, these authors treat parental efforts and interventions in their child's schooling as positive influences in student learning. Despite the deficiencies in its use and definition, social capital continues to be a useful analytic concept for understanding relational ties and how they promote norms, sanctions, and trust between parents, students, teachers, and administrators.

SEE ALSO: Bilingual, Multicultural Education; Bourdieu, Pierre; Coleman, James; Cultural Capital; Education; Family Structure and Child Outcomes; Friendships of Adolescence; Friendships of Children; Parental Involvement in Education; Social Capital; Trust; Trustworthiness

REFERENCES AND SUGGESTED READINGS

Bourdieu, P. (1986) The Forms of Capital. In: Richardson, J. (Ed.), *Handbook of Theory and Research for the Sociology of Education*. Greenwood Press, New York, pp. 241–58.

Bryk, A. S. & Schneider, B. (2002) *Trust in Schools: A Core Resource for Improvement*. Russell Sage Foundation, New York.

Burt, R. (1992) *Structural Holes*. Harvard University Press, Cambridge, MA.

Coleman, J. S. (1988) Social Capital in the Creation of Human Capital. *American Journal of Sociology* 94: S95–S120.

Coleman, J. S. (1990) *Foundations of Social Theory*. Belknap Press of Harvard University Press, Cambridge, MA.

Coleman, J. S. & Hoffer, T. (1987) *Public and Private High Schools: The Impact of Communities*. Basic Books, New York.

Frank, K. A., Zhao, Y., & Borman, K. (2004) Social Capital and the Diffusion of Innovations Within Organizations: The Case of Computer Technology in Schools. *Sociology of Education* 77(2): 148–71.

Goddard, R. D. (2003) Relational Networks, Social Trust, and Norms: A Social Capital Perspective on Students' Chances of Academic Success. *Educational Evaluation and Policy Analysis* 25(1): 59–74.

Goldsmith, P. A. (2004) Schools' Racial Mix, Students' Optimism, and the Black–White and Latino–White Achievement Gaps. *Sociology of Education* 77(2): 121–47.

Granovetter, M. (1973) The Strength of Weak Ties. *American Journal of Sociology* 78(6): 1360–80.

Kim, D. H. & Schneider, B. (2006) Social Capital in Action: Alignment of Parental Support in Adolescents' Transition to Postsecondary Education. *Social Forces*.

Lareau, A. (2003) *Unequal Childhoods: Class, Race, and Family Life*. University of California Press, Berkeley.

Parcel, T. L. & Menaghan, E. G. (1994) Early Parental Work, Family Social Capital, and Early Childhood Outcomes. *American Journal of Sociology* 99(4): 972–1009.

Pong, S.-L. (1998) The School Compositional Effect of Single Parenthood on 10th-Grade Achievement. *Sociology of Education* 71(1): 23–42.

Portes, A. (1998) Social Capital: Its Origins and Applications in Modern Sociology. *Annual Reviews in Sociology* 24: 1–24.

Portes, A. & Sensenbrenner, J. (1993) Embeddedness and Immigration: Notes on the Social Determinants of Economic Action. *American Journal of Sociology* 98(6): 1320–50.

Ream, R. K. (2003) Counterfeit Social Capital and Mexican-American Underachievement. *Educational Evaluation and Policy Analysis* 25(3): 237–62.

Sandefur, R. L. & Laumann, E. O. (1998) A Paradigm for Social Capital. *Rationality and Society* 10(4): 481–501.

Schneider, B. & Coleman, J. S. (1993) *Parents, Their Children, and Schools*. Westview Press, Boulder, CO.

Stanton-Salazar, R. D. & Dornbusch, S. M. (1995) Social Capital and the Reproduction of Inequality: Information Networks Among Mexican-Origin High School Students. *Sociology of Education* 68(2): 116–35.

social capital and health

Craig B. Little

Social capital, according to the most widely accepted definition, refers to "features of social life – networks, norms and trust – that enable participants to act together more effectively to pursue shared objectives" (Putnam 1996: 56). Communities characterized by high levels of social capital have been hypothesized to benefit from lower crime rates, higher educational achievement, greater economic growth, and better health. Social capital generally incorporates the much older concepts of civic virtue and social cohesion. Research linking social cohesion and health dates back at least a century to Durkheim who demonstrated that populations with higher social integration have lower rates of suicide. Social theorists whose work serves as the foundation for the present interest in social capital include Pierre Bourdieu, James Coleman, and Robert Putnam. The appearance of social capital as a key word in research articles is relatively infrequent prior to 1980 and has grown enormously since the mid-1990s.

The core elements of social capital include measures of civic and social engagement (group memberships, political participation such as voting, community voluntarism, and time spent with friends) and indicators of trust (such as an agreement on a survey with the statement "Most people can be trusted"). The health indicators with which social capital has been shown to be correlated include both mortality data (infant mortality or life expectancy, for example) and morbidity statistics for various specific diseases. Assessments of the research evidence range from claims that the correlation is consistent and robust (Kawachi et al. 1997; Putnam 2000: 327) to reviews or studies that suggest that the relationship is both modest and variable among specific health indicators (Kennelly et al. 2003; Pearce & Davey Smith 2003; Morgan & Swann 2004).

The specific mechanisms to account for the relationship between social capital and health status remain to be established. One possible explanation is that people embedded in more intense social networks have greater access to money, transportation, home care, or other tangible assets that improve their health status or illness outcomes. Another is that people who are more socially isolated are more likely to engage in damaging health habits such as smoking, drinking, or overeating. It may also be the case that the social connections and supports inherent in social capital trigger physiological responses that buffer stress and, possibly, even stimulate a person's disease-fighting immune system. Recent evidence suggests that social capital, broadly defined as the quality of social relations, may mediate the relationship between inequality and health status (Marmot 2004: 188; Wilkinson 2005: 125). In this hypothesis, as social inequality increases in a society, the reservoir of social capital decreases, which, in turn, negatively affects people's health.

Broad agreement exists that research on the relationship between social capital and health is only at its beginning. Work to create greater conceptual clarity and more precise operational measures of social capital is necessary and continuing. Likewise, there is a need to search for evidence linking findings from large-scale epidemiological studies at the level of countries or states with the results from studies at the community and individual levels.

SEE ALSO: Bourdieu, Pierre; Coleman, James; Durkheim, Émile; Health Risk Behavior; Medical Sociology; Medicine, Sociology of; Social Capital; Sociology in Medicine; Stress and Health

REFERENCES AND SUGGESTED READINGS

Kawachi, I., Kennedy, B. P., Lochner, K., & Prothrow-Sthith, D. (1997) Social Capital, Income Inequality, and Mortality. *American Journal of Public Health* 87: 1491–8.

Kennelly, B., O'Shea, E., & Garvey, E. (2003) Social Capital, Life Expectancy, and Mortality: A Cross-National Examination. *Social Science and Medicine* 56: 2367–77.

Marmot, M. (2004) *The Status Syndrome: How Social Standing Affects Our Health and Longevity*. Henry Holt, New York.

Morgan, A. & Swann, C. (Eds.) (2004) *Social Capital for Health: Issues of Definition, Measurement, and Links to Health*. Health Development Agency, London.

Pearce, N. & Davey Smith, G. (2003) Is Social Capital the Key to Inequalities in Health? *American Journal of Public Health* 93: 122–9.

Putnam, R. D. (1996) Who Killed Civic America? *Prospect* (March): 66–72.

Putnam, R. D. (2000) *Bowling Alone: The Collapse and Revival of American Community*. Simon & Schuster, New York.

Wilkinson, R. G. (2005) *The Impact of Inequality: How to Make Sick Societies Healthier*. New Press, New York.

social change

Dusko Sekulic

Change can be defined as a "succession of events which produce over time a modification or replacement of particular patterns or units by other novel ones." Sociology as a discipline emerged in the middle of the nineteenth century as an attempt to explain not only the great waves of change sweeping Europe in the form of industrialization and democratization, but also the observed gap between European and colonized societies.

BASIC QUESTIONS

Whether something is changing or not depends on the perspective from which we observe. Recurrent fluctuations of prices or the unemployment rate do not change the nature of the market system; on the other hand, one of the characteristics of the market is constant push for changes in products, technologies, and social relations. How the market functions, the dominant actors, and the mediums of exchange evolve dramatically. However, from the more abstract perspective, we can argue that since capitalism emerged, it has not essentially changed, because its crucial regulatory institution, the free market, remains unchanged.

The second diagnosis of change or stability depends on the theoretical approach used to explain the causal mechanisms operating on the observed unit of analysis. Classical sociology was not only preoccupied with the explanation of the uniqueness of observed change,

for example the rise of capitalism in the West, but was also grounded on the assumption that some general principles and mechanisms producing all observed changes could be discovered. For Comte, such principles were the development of knowledge and ideas, for Marx, dialectics of productive forces and productive relationships, and for Lenski, development of technological capacities.

The third is the question of the tipping point. Is the change from 50 percent to 51 percent of employment in the service sector enough of a turning point that we can argue a new type of society (a post-industrial one) has emerged (Bell 1973)? Or at what point has the modern era ended and the postmodern arisen if we want to believe in the postmodernists' claim that we are living in a new "post-modern" era? At which point in time do the changes in the 1920s (the introduction of the assembly line, the application of "Taylorism") indicate the emergence of a new "Fordist" system (Kumar 1995)?

THEORIES OF SOCIAL CHANGE

Theoretical approaches to the question of macrosocietal change can be divided into two broad groups. In the first are theories starting from the assumption that underlying principles, general laws of social change, could be discovered. Although they differ in the acceptance of directionality or nonlinearity of change, they have in common the belief of "basic principles." On the other hand, we have theories rejecting this assumption and trying to explain particular historical events or configurations of factors characterizing group of events like revolutions or empires.

The first group of theories is based on the idea of evolution. According to that approach, the general mechanism of historical change can be described as going through certain stages driven by some inherent forces. These stages are the expression of some basic principle and are pointing in a certain direction. For Comte, societies go through three stages: a theological-military, a metaphysical-judicial, and a scientific-industrial stage. This "law of the three stages" obviously reflects the prevailing thought of the time, because similar formulations can be found earlier in Vico's *New Science* (1725): the age of Gods, the age of heroes, and the age of men.

In the two "discourses" Turgot presented at the Sorbonne in 1750, we can find the theory of three stages: religious, metaphysical, and scientific. In general, human development can be understood using the paradigm of growth; it is characterized by slow advancements from a less to a more developed state (Meek 1973). Similar formulations could be found in Saint-Simon. In his *Letters from an Inhabitant of Geneva*, he formulated the Law of Three Stages, later misappropriated and announced by Comte as an original discovery. According to this law, the nature of ideas determines and limits social arrangements.

Karl Marx can also be classified within the frames of classical evolutionary thinking. His evolutionism was of a particular kind, with class conflict being the main force producing change. This conflict perspective influenced later development of historical sociology, which is no longer based on evolutionist ideas. For Marx the mode of production of material life determines the general character of the social, political, and spiritual processes of life. It is not the consciousness of men that determines their being; on the contrary, it is their social being that determines their consciousness.

At a certain stage of their development, the material forces of production in society come into conflict with the existing relations of production. The stages of development are "primitive communism," slavery, feudalism, capitalism, and communism, with socialism as its first phase. This progression model was derived mostly from the analysis of European history. When Marx looked at other parts of the world, he introduced significant changes to it. For example, in the analysis of Asia, he introduced the concept of the "Asiatic mode of production." Its long duration derives from its "presupposition that the individual does not become independent vis-à-vis the commune; that there is a self-sustaining circle of production, unity of agriculture and manufacture" (Marx 1973 [1857–8]: 491).

Another subgroup of evolutionary theories is based on the idea of close resemblance of biological and social evolution. Herbert Spencer developed an evolutionary scheme for explaining historical change. The evolution of society can be understood by comparing it to the growth of an organism. Both increase in size and in structure, from a few like parts to numerous interrelated unlike parts: "matter passes from an indefinite, incoherent homogeneity to a definite, coherent heterogeneity" (Spencer 1964 [1862]: 394).

Spencer was the first to systematically use the concept of differentiation that became a key idea in evolutionary and functionalist theories. Social differentiation refers to a process whereby sets of activities performed by one social institution become split up among different institutions. Differentiation represents an increasing specialization of the parts of a society. For Spencer, differentiation was a necessary accompaniment of the growth in size of both biological and social aggregates.

Following Spencer, Émile Durkheim held that increasing dynamic density, the number of people in interaction with one another, is critical in determining social change. As dynamic density increases, societies are segmented into similar units that combine to form larger units. Such primitive, segmented societies are characterized by strong mechanical solidarity based on common belief and consensus. As societies industrialize and urbanize and become more complex, the increased division of labor destroys mechanical solidarity and moral integration. A new form of order arises on the basis of organic solidarity. This comprises the interdependence of economic ties arising out of differentiation and specialization within the modern economy, a new network of occupational associations such as guilds and professional associations that link individuals to the state, and the emergence within these associations of collectively created moral restraints on egoism.

Durkheim's evolutionism is clearly visible from his introductory explanations in *Elementary Forms of the Religious Life*: "Everytime we undertake to explain something human, taken at a given moment in history – be it religious belief, a moral precept, a legal principle, an esthetic style, or an economic system – it is necessary to go back to its most primitive and simple form, to try to account for the characterization by which it was marked at that time, and then to show how it developed and became complicated little by little, and how it became that which it is at the moment in question" (Durkheim 1947 [1912]: 3). In choosing the religion of Australian Aborigines, Durkheim assumed that he was studying religion in its most primitive and simple form. By studying the visible components, the culture and rites of primitive religion, he was able to analyze things that, in modern religions, are hidden by their complexity. Of course, underlying this scheme is an evolutionary assumption of the development of religion from simple to complex forms.

For both Spencer and Durkheim, the main mechanism producing social change is increased population density and the differentiation of society that follows. They both envisioned social change as leading to more complex social forms, but they rejected the idea that development goes through predetermined stages.

Modern evolutionary theory is less rigid in interpreting the stages of history. Nolan and Lenski in *Human Societies: An Introduction to Macrosociology* (1999) based their explanation of social change on the increased technological capacities of societies. New technologies of material production, as of information processing, send ripples of change through all aspects of social life. The evolution of societies is not predetermined but some general evolutionary patterns can be detected. Agrarian states are transformed into industrial societies but not the other way around. Lenski acknowledges that reversals are possible, but they are usually a consequence of some external cataclysm.

Cataclysmic events and environmental degradation are the topics of the evolutionary theory of Jarred Diamond. In his book *Collapse* (2005), he traces a fundamental pattern of catastrophe occurring when societies squander their resources, or ignore the signals of environmental degradation. Environmental damage, climate change, rapid population growth, unstable trade partners, and pressure from enemies are all factors producing the demise of societies. The indeterminate nature of new evolutionary theory is shown in Diamond with cases of societies that were able to find solutions for the same problems and persisted as a consequence. In his earlier work *Guns, Germs, and Steel* (1998), he shows how inequality among societies and subjugation of one society by others are rooted

in differing natural resources available to different people.

The second approach intertwined with evolutionism is functionalism. It regards change as the adaptation of a social system to its environment by the process of differentiation and increasing structural complexity. Society is viewed as a complex and interconnected pattern of functions, and change is explained as an epiphenomenon of the constant search for equilibrium. The dominant system structure is taken as the fixed point of reference against which other structures or latent consequences are seen as potentially disruptive. This means that deviance and strains of various kinds are residual in the model. They are not given full-fledged status as integral parts of the system as in the conflict model of social change. In response to the widespread critique of functionalism as static and not taking into account social change, Parsons developed in the 1960s his theory of sociocultural evolution in *Societies, Evolutionary and Comparative Perspective* (1966) and *The System of Modern Societies* (1971). Parsons's embrace of evolutionism read as repudiation of his statements from 1937: "Who now reads Spencer? . . . Spencer is dead" (Parsons 1949 [1937]: 3). For Parsons, evolution has a multidimensional character. Differentiation, the major Spencerian scheme, is the basic, although not the only, dimension of it. In Parsons's scheme, it is complemented by adaptive upgrading, cumulative learning leading to the establishment of ever more intelligent technologies and ever more comprehensive and deeper scientific knowledge.

Through evolutionary processes, societies move from a system of ascription to one of achievement. Groups excluded from contributing to the system must be freed for inclusion. A wider array of skills and abilities is needed to handle increased complexities. Higher stages of evolution are characterized by value generalization. The system of cultural ideas is increasingly abstracted from their concrete context of a particular place and time and is thus better able to serve as a measure of legitimation and criticism of any particular norm, institution, or action. Evolution, for Parsons, proceeds through a variety of cycles, but no general process affects all societies equally. Some societies may foster evolution, whereas others may be pervaded by internal conflicts or environmental constraints that impede the evolutionary process or even lead to the deterioration of the system. Although Parsons conceived evolution as occurring in stages (primitive, intermediate, and modern societies), he carefully avoided the impression of creating a unilinear theory of stages. For Parsons, evolution is not a linear process, although broad levels of advancement can be detected on a very abstract level with considerable variability of types.

The most sophisticated use of the structural differentiation concept in explaining social change is by Shlomo Eisenstadt (1964). His understanding of social change is based on the usage of concepts like "differentiated institutions," "crystalized roles," or "cultural orientations." In spite of this general approach for Eisenstadt, the direction and nature of change are not universal or explained by general principles and first causes. Change is always tied to concrete circumstances as defined within a particular society. Structural functional analysis is the only device for discovering particular historical configurations. Although his whole work is preoccupied with social change, the nature of change is most systematically analyzed in *Revolution and the Transformation of Societies* (1978).

The third group of theories emphasizes the cycles of growth and decay. The roots of this approach are in the works of philosophers like Arnold Toynbee and Oswald Spengler. The four volumes of *Social and Cultural Dynamics* (1937–41) by Pitirim Sorokin are a sociological version of philosophizers' cyclical analysis. He saw societies oscillating among three different types of mentalities; sensate, ideational, and idealistic. The first type emphasizes the role of senses in comprehending reality, the second more transcendental or religious principles, and the idealistic type combines the two principles. Change is produced by the internal logic of these systems, which push their mode of thinking until it reaches its end point and the system is transformed into another form.

The main position of modern historical sociology, which is regarded here as the fourth major type of general theory, is that there can be no single explanation for all the important transitions in human history. "History is informative to the degree that things are not instances of general categories, but are instead the product of causally connected series of events that produce unique configurations in each thing" (Stinchcombe 1978: ix). Historical changes must be located in their particular historical and cultural context and the main method used is historical comparison (Calhoun 1995, 1998). Max Weber was an important pioneer of this approach. He sees historical change as a concatenation of unique events and unrepeatable complexities. The rise of large-scale capitalism is the result of a series of combinations of conditions that had to occur together. This makes world history and major changes like capitalism the result of configurations of events so rare as to appear accidental. Weber's *Protestant Ethic and the Spirit of Capitalism* is very often interpreted as a simple causal statement that Protestantism caused the rise of capitalism in the West. De facto it is a much more complicated argument where Protestantism is only the last intensification of one of the chains of factors leading to capitalism.

Important contemporary work in that tradition includes Barrington Moore's *The Social Origins of Dictatorship and Democracy* (1966), which analyzes historical conditions producing dictatorships or democracies. There are three basic routes of change: the first is when feudal landowners become capitalist and ally themselves with the bourgeoisie. This route is most likely to produce democracy. When landowners enter capitalist markets but keep peasants on land, they increase their exploitation and enter into an alliance with state bureaucracy. This path leads to a fascist state. The final route is when landowners became absentee owners, which produces conflict and peasant revolts, mass mobilization, and social revolutions in different forms.

Theda Skocpol in *States and Social Revolutions* (1979) argues that revolutionary situations are the result of the emergence of politico-military crises of the state resulting usually from military defeats in the international arena. State collapse is the result of a fiscal/administrative crisis of the state, conflicts within the ruling elite, and popular revolt. The same line of thinking is developed in the geopolitical theory of historical change of Randall Collins developed in *Weberian Sociological Theory* (1986) and *Macrohistory* (1999). His main explanatory variable is the success of the state in the international arena. Internal legitimacy and external power prestige are connected.

SEE ALSO: Durkheim, Émile and Social Change; Evolution; Fordism/Post-Fordism; Functionalism/Neofunctionalism; Parsons, Talcott; Post-Industrial Society; Postmodernism; Social Change and Causal Analysis; Social Change: The Contributions of S. N. Eisenstadt; Social Change, Southeast Asia

REFERENCES AND SUGGESTED READINGS

Bell, D. (1973) *The Coming of Post-Industrial Society.* Basic Books, New York.

Calhoun, C. (1995) *Critical Social Theory: Culture, History, and the Challenge of Difference.* Blackwell, Cambridge, MA.

Calhoun, C. (1998) Explanation in Historical Sociology: Narrative, General Theory, and Historically Specific Theory. *American Journal of Sociology* 108: 846–71.

Chirot, D. (1994) *How Societies Change.* Sage, Beverly Hills.

Durkheim, É. (1947 [1912]) *The Elementary Forms of the Religious Life.* Free Press, Glencoe, IL.

Eisenstadt, S. N. (1964) Social Change, Differentiation, and Evolution. *American Sociological Review* 29: 375–86.

Kumar, K. (1995) *From Post-Industrial to Post-Modern Society.* Blackwell, Cambridge, MA.

Marx, K. (1904 [1859]) *A Contribution to the Critique of Political Economy.* Charles H. Kerr, Chicago.

Marx, K. (1973 [1857–8]) *Grundrisse.* Trans. M. Nicolaus. Penguin, Harmondsworth.

Meek, L. R. (Ed. and Trans.) (1973) *Turgot on Progress, Sociology, and Economics.* Cambridge University Press, Cambridge.

Noble, T. (2000) *Social Theory and Social Change.* Palgrave Macmillan, Basingstoke.

Parsons, T. (1949 [1937]) *The Structure of Social Action.* Free Press, Glencoe, IL.

Sanderson, S. K. (1990) *Social Evolutionism: A Critical History.* Blackwell, Oxford.

Spencer, H. (1964 [1862]) *First Principles of a New System of Philosophy.* DeWitt Revolving Fund, New York.

Stinchcombe, A. L. (1978) *Theoretical Methods in Social History.* Academic Press, New York.

Sztompka, P. (1993) *The Sociology of Social Change.* Blackwell, Oxford.

Vago, S. (2004) *Social Change.* Prentice-Hall, Upper Saddle River, NJ.

social change and causal analysis

Paul Bernard

Causal analysis means researching the processes through which causes produce their effects. This is particularly complex in the social sciences, which face challenges that do not affect the natural sciences (see Bernard with Boucher 2005). First, *social relations* are the real concern of the social sciences; variables can only indirectly represent these social relations through a characterization of the actors and objects involved in them (age, gender, or class categories, for instance, interacting in employment, family, or educational trajectories). Second, social relations are shaped in *historically* irreversible ways, at the microsocial level as well as at the meso level of institutions or at the macro level of societies. Finally, human actions depend on complex *intentions*; these largely have to be imputed when survey-based, quantitative variables are used, while they are explored more directly through qualitative, open-ended methods (see Bernard 1993 for a detailed discussion of how causal analysis can readily be used with both quantitative and qualitative types of data and methods).

Adapting causal analysis to these challenges in the social sciences means reformulating its basic rules. We cannot be looking for a set of necessary conditions which together form a sufficient condition for the effect to emerge; we are rather engaged in the invention of a usable *causal heuristics*. As Figure 1 indicates, the classic expression of causal rules reflects their use in the natural sciences (and to some extent in the more nomothetic of the social sciences, such as neoclassical economics and psychology), where quantities and general laws prevail. But in the more idiographic of the social sciences (such as sociology or political science), the reformulation of these rules as heuristic causality brings new meaning to the enterprise of linking causes to effects through processes.

First, researchers must identify *regularities*, quantitative or otherwise, involving the alleged "cause" and "effect"; there should be a discernible pattern linking them. Second, these

The three rules of classical causal analysis	The three corresponding rules of causal heuristics
Finding a statistically significant association between the alleged cause and effect	Observing regularities in the relation between the alleged cause and effect
Establishing a clear temporal sequence between the alleged cause and effect	Controlling for the ambient conditions of the relation between the alleged cause and effect
Introducing relevant control variables	Constructing a narrative focused on how the cause produces the effect

Figure 1 Classical causal analysis and causal heuristics.

regularities have to be checked systematically as to the contexts in which they prevail (or fail to appear). This is where relevant *control* variables are introduced, revealing such patterns as the following: both alleged cause and consequence depend on a common, antecedent "cause"; an intermediate variable serves as a "causal" conduit between alleged cause and consequence; and so-called interaction effects, where the pattern of relation between alleged cause and consequence changes under various conditions specified by the control variable.

Finally, and this is the most important rule, the researcher has to come up with a *narrative*, a telling of the story of the processes through which the cause (or causes) engenders effects, under certain specified conditions. These three steps are obviously iterative: researchers go back and forth, trying to inductively make theoretical sense of increasingly rich empirical patterns, and checking the theoretical implications of these interpretations against an ever broadening set of empirical findings (generalization); this was admirably explained by Arthur Stinchcombe (1968). Variables and their relations thus provide us with stenographic traces of social relations as they unfold through time; variables are markers for individual and collective actors and events upstream, which causally shape events, and indeed actors, downstream.

The narrative is of course key to how causal heuristics can meet the challenges of sociological analysis. Causal interpretations do rest on observed regularities and ambient conditions as indexed by control variables; but the focus of these interpretations should be on interacting individual actors, who shape their future in the midst of constraints and opportunities offered by their past. This shaping takes place in various contexts, at the micro, meso, and macro levels, in which actors are involved at specific historical junctures, according to their birth cohort. This view of human life, based on the increasingly widespread notion of *life course* (Marshall & Mueller 2002), brings together social relations, history, and intentionality.

To illustrate the uses of causal heuristics in the study of social change, two questions will be examined in more detail below. First, how do welfare regimes affect the life course of individuals? By welfare regimes, much more is meant than a simple collection of social policies; they designate the broad set of resilient institutional arrangements through which markets, states, families, and communities divide up among themselves and organize the work of producing and distributing well-being. Second, how do regimes themselves come about and change over time, partly under the influence of the mobilization of actors experiencing different trajectories?

REGIMES, LIFE CHANCES, AND THE LIFE COURSE

In a very influential book, Gøsta Esping-Andersen (1990) proposed a categorization of advanced capitalist societies into three types of institutional arrangements. These welfare regimes were: the social democratic regime, in the Nordic countries, in which the emphasis is on equality, giving the state a considerable role in sustaining universal social rights; the liberal regime, primarily in Anglo-Saxon countries, in which the liberty of economic actors is put forward, making markets the key institution and confining states to a more remedial role; and the conservative regime, in most Western European countries, in which the principle of solidarity dominates, with social insurance schemes often based on occupational categories and family affiliations.

The specific contours of such typologies and the labeling of welfare regimes have been intensely debated; some even argue that advanced societies are so different from one another in this respect that their situation can hardly be summarized in such a way. The issue of producing and distributing well-being is indeed closely related to that of social inequalities, and each society comes to grips with it in its own specific way, in the course of its history. This being said, typologies can be useful comparative tools under two conditions (Arts & Gelissen 2002). First, they must not be "sacralized": they are only meant to represent essential features, and to reveal the forest rather than the myriad individual trees. In fact, it is against the backdrop of broad types that the individual features of each society will stand out. Second, a typology is only helpful if it can be used to do something else. The question thus arises of whether welfare regimes have any consequences for the life chances and the life course of individuals.

There are abundant examples that they do. Welfare regimes are even drawing attention outside the circle of specialists in social policies as such. Health researchers such as Navarro and Shi (2001), for instance, examine the impact of the major policy traditions during the period 1945–80 (social democratic, Christian democratic, liberal, and ex-fascist, another set of labels for similar clusters of countries) in four areas: the main determinants of income inequalities, the level of public expenditures and health care benefits coverage, public support of services to families, and the level of population health as measured by infant mortality rates. The results indicate that countries more committed to redistributive and full-employment

policies, such as the social democratic, were generally more successful in improving the health of populations, and without loss of economic efficiency. An implicit causal chain is obviously evoked here, involving the level of inequality, social programs, and the resulting level of health.

Welfare regimes also have an impact on an issue of long standing in sociology, that of social mobility. DiPrete (2003) argues that the traditional comparative analysis of occupational mobility may not accurately describe cross-national differences in living standards changes over the life course. For one thing, occupational position may no longer be an appropriate index of belonging to a social class, in these times of contingent jobs and of individualization of trajectories. Moreover, industrial nations differ in the extent of labor force participation by women, stability of working hours, stability of households, and state tax and transfer policies, all factors that contribute to determining how well individuals will fare over their lifetime. Studies of living standards mobility in the liberal US, in conservative Germany, and in social democratic Sweden indeed reveal much greater similarity between the countries than do traditional studies of male occupational mobility, where the flexibility of the American society was featured. Note that the new factors brought to bear on the issue of the life course by DiPrete all reflect the influence of welfare regimes: this is obvious for taxes and transfers, but regimes also influence – as shown below – labor force participation, especially for women, the stability of professional careers, and indirectly the stability of families and households.

While both of these studies provide valuable narratives, they essentially rest their case on the broad association between regimes and typical life chances. Hicks and Kenworthy (2003) use more systematic causal modeling. They first apply factor analysis to 20 broad indicators of social policies in order to characterize 18 countries over the 1980s and 1990s. They can thus identify two dimensions along which these countries' policies differ: a "progressive liberalism" axis, characterized at its positive end by extensive, universal, and homogeneous benefits, active labor market policy, and government employment and gender egalitarian family policies; and second, a "traditional conservatism" axis featuring occupational and status-based differentiations of social insurance programs and specialized income security programs for civil servants, as well as generous and longlasting unemployment benefits, reliance on heavy tax burdens for employers, and extensions of union collective bargaining coverage. These two factors are then used in regression analysis as predictors of aggregate national socioeconomic outcomes. Progressive liberalism leads to income redistribution and greater gender equality in the labor market, while traditional conservatism leads to a weakened employment performance.

What can be learned from these three studies (and many others that could have been cited)? Encompassing macrostructures like welfare regimes clearly influence changes experienced by individuals in their lives, for instance in their health, in the evolution of their living standards, and in their chances of access to jobs, with gender differences playing a significant role. This finding in turn raises a new causal issue: where do welfare regimes come from?

HOW DO REGIMES COME ABOUT AND CHANGE?

As mentioned earlier, regimes correspond to the broad set of institutional arrangements through which markets, states, families, and communities divide up among themselves the production and distribution of well-being. They would not be regimes if they were not broad and resilient, and even self-reproducing. Such stability would seem to offer limited opportunities for the study of social change. But upon reflection, this is not necessarily so: explaining stability requires attention to the processes at play in preserving existing arrangements, just as explaining change requires attention to the processes at play to disrupt and transform them.

Saint-Arnaud and Bernard (2003) used an approach similar to Hicks and Kenworthy's, but they compared indicators for two time periods, the mid-1980s and the mid-1990s. They found that, for that interval at least, the clustering of advanced societies into regimes endured, in spite of the mounting pressures of globalization, which would hypothetically tend to dissolve the differences by making generous

welfare states fiscally unsustainable. In their search for an explanation of this resilience, they divided their indicators into three sets, concerning policies, outcomes, and civic participation (such as newspaper readership, voting, union membership, and trust). The same clusters of countries emerged in all three sets; this suggests that regimes, once established, so dominate the economic, social, and political scenes of the various countries that they give the same "texture" to their social situations, to their government programs, and to the civic commitment of their citizens. Why? Probably because policies influence outcomes, which in turn shape social and political mobilization, through civic literacy (Milner 2002); such mobilizations then lead to further confirmation of policy orientations and thus to the resilience of regimes. For instance, egalitarian policies would be confirmed and reinforced by a competent and mobilized citizenry, while the less egalitarian policies and situations of liberal countries would lead to less effective mobilizations in favor of policy changes.

This narrative of the processes linking policies, outcomes, and participation, while informative, is not being tested here with a specific causal analysis. Huber and Stephens (2001) take up that task in an impressive comparative effort that spans 18 advanced countries and 35 years of time series data; qualitative historical analysis is also called upon in about half of the cases, in order to confirm and enrich the interpretations coming out of quantitative modeling.

Their main thesis is that while the welfare state expanded during the 1960s and 1970s, it had to retrench in the 1980s and 1990s when austerity became the order of the day. Besides increasing economic pressures in the second period – in contrast with the continuing expansion in the first – two major factors were at play during the whole period: the political forces that dominated government, especially if they had sufficient time to put a strong imprint on the policies of the various countries, and the institutional structure, which can help or hinder discontinuities in policy directions.

The first factor is the more interesting from a causally narrative point of view. Huber and Stephens find that long-term government incumbency of social democratic parties, committed to equality and solidarity, leads to the construction of generous welfare states, with substantial entitlements, significant emphasis on the provision of public services – rather than only transfers – and redistribution through the tax and transfer system. Christian democratic parties, when they predominate, call for the support of all social classes, and this leads to substantive welfare expenditures. But they compete with the social democrats on the basis of religious appeal, and thus put forward the conciliation of various interests, not equality and redistribution. And their view of subsidiarity, where well-being is produced at the lowest possible level (families, then local communities, and only residually at the state level), restricts the expansion of publicly delivered services.

Why does long incumbency make such a difference? Not only because it allows a party in power to change many policies, but also because it changes the policy agenda and the policy scene themselves. According to Huber and Stephens, there is first a ratchet effect, such that the center of gravity of the policy agenda is shifted, and indeed defined in terms of the preferences embodied in previous policy innovations. Moreover, expectations are transformed, and certain policy alternatives that social actors might otherwise have found attractive are no longer considered by them. Opportunities are also foreclosed or opened by previous policy choices, sometimes to such a point that some political players are no longer present on the scene (for instance, employers of low-paid workers are absent in a country that has long had a high minimum wage). Finally, ideological hegemony sets in and makes an impression on the political ideas of most social classes.

One particular idea which has taken shape, and indeed redefined the agenda in social democratic countries, involves the labor force participation of women. Huber and Stephens point to the fact that the feminist movement, in alliance with unions and the labor movement, pushed for social and labor policies that would help women balance earning and caring roles. This has allowed an increasing number of women to join the labor force, thus further increasing their influence on the political scene, in a cycle of mutual reinforcement between policies and outcomes. The result is the development of services which at once help women participate, provide them with jobs in the public service that are better than would be the case in private services (though not as good as men's), and help increase the overall level of education and health in the population.

When they turn to the period of retrenchment of the welfare state, Huber and Stephens show that social democratic rule and Christian democratic rule cannot produce, in the 1980s and 1990s, the sort of growth in government expenditures that prevailed in the previous two decades. They may not be paying enough attention, however, to an emerging pattern which they themselves have pointed out in other parts of their analysis: while overall revenues and expenditures no longer grow, public services may well do, and they are particularly important to women's labor force participation because they help the family care for dependents.

RETRENCHMENT OR RECONFIGURATION: FROM WELFARE REGIMES TO SOCIAL REGIMES

In still unpublished research, Bernard and Boucher (2005) extend the method of factor-analyzing indicators of policies and outcomes to a broader set of dimensions and to more recent years (spanning the 1990s up to the early 2000s). They emphasize policies and outcomes having to do with services as well as transfers, and with the production of a healthy, well-educated, and work-ready population as well as with the coverage of traditional social risks.

The first factor in the analysis reveals an activation dimension, where policies are all aimed at making as many people as possible, and in particular women, active and productive in the labor market, with good health, basic education, and professional training. The second factor corresponds to a passive, welfare transfer dimension: programs essentially try to cover the risks of the many people who are unemployed, especially in the long run, or retiring early, voluntarily or not; and few women participate in the labor market.

At first sight, passive and active programs would seem to be polar opposites on a single dimension. But there is a third possibility: liberal countries tend to have fewer social programs of either kind. Indeed, the analysis reveals a growing competition between three models. First, a social democratic one, where programs are oriented toward high social investments, which are expensive but paid for by a population that participates heavily in the labor market. Second, a liberal model where labor market participation is also high, but without a substantial level of social investment: in fact, the dearth of social programs forces a large proportion of the population into employment, with those who can afford appropriate education and health care faring much better that those who can only rely on lean public services and transfer programs. Finally, continental Europe is at the crossroads, with fiscally unsustainable welfare programs that are not clearly oriented toward increasing labor market activity. The way this third group of countries evolves will pretty much decide the fate of the "European social model," and determine whether welfare regimes will generally retrench or be reconfigured.

One interesting aspect of this research that also surfaced, but not as explicitly, in the work of Hicks and Kenworthy, and in that of Huber and Stephens, is that welfare regimes no longer concern only welfare and traditional social risks. The redefinition of gender roles has become part of the reconfiguration of welfare regimes, and the latter are increasingly seen as part of production regimes, that is, of how capitalist societies manage, in diverse ways, their economy as well as their social problems. Research increasingly reveals the existence of "social regimes," where all dimensions of society and the economy become relevant to one another and must somehow, through clashes and debates, assume some coherence and become sustainable.

CONCLUSION

Causal analysis of social change is about determining and narrating how the macro structures of society shape the life chances and the life course of individuals. It is also about examining how broad social categories of individuals sharing a common fate can imagine and fight for changes in the organization of society, for instance in their welfare regimes. The causal analysis of comparative international data allows researchers to identify the contours of such regimes, to examine their effects on individuals,

and to identify the actors, institutions, ideas, and processes involved in their reproduction and in their transformation. Causal analysis guides us, empirically and theoretically, in examining how, as C. Wright Mills (1976 [1959]) put it, biographies and history interact.

SEE ALSO: Life Course Perspective; Social Change; Social Indicators; Stratification, Gender and; Welfare Regimes; Welfare State, Retrenchment of

REFERENCES AND SUGGESTED READINGS

Arts, W. & Gelissen, J. (2002) Three Worlds of Welfare Capitalism or More? A State-of-the-Art Report. *Journal of European Social Policy* 12(2): 137–58.

Bernard, P. (1993) Cause perdue: le pouvoir heuristique de l'analyse causale. *Sociologie et sociétés* 25(3): 171–88.

Bernard, P. & Boucher, G. (2005) Welfare State Retrenchment or Reconfiguration? A Tale of Activation. Presentation at the Annual Conference of the Society for the Advancement of Socioeconomics, Budapest, June 30.

Bernard, P., in collaboration with Boucher, G. (2005) Les chiffres pour le dire: les nouveaux instruments de l'heuristique causale. In: Mercure, D. (Ed.), *L'Analyse du social: les modes d'explication*. Presses de l'Université Laval, Quebec, 101–31.

DiPrete, T. A. (2003) Do Cross-National Differences in Household Standards of Living Mobility Parallel Cross-National Differences in Occupational Mobility? *Current Sociology* 51(5): 483–98.

Esping-Andersen, G. (1990) *The Three Worlds of Welfare Capitalism*. Princeton University Press, Princeton.

Hicks, A. & Kenworthy, L. (2003) Varieties of Welfare Capitalism. *Socioeconomic Review* 1: 27–61.

Huber, E. & Stephens, J. D. (2001) *Development and Crisis of the Welfare State: Parties and Policies in Global Markets*. University of Chicago Press, Chicago.

Marshall, V. W. & Mueller, M. M. (2002) Rethinking Social Policy for an Aging Workforce and Society: Insights from the Lifecourse Perspective. CPRN Discussion Paper No. W18, May.

Mills, C. W. (1976 [1959]) *The Sociological Imagination*. Oxford University Press, New York.

Milner, H. (2002) *Civic Literacy: How Informed Citizens Make Democracy Work*. University Press of New England, Hanover, NH.

Navarro, V. & Shi, L. (2001) The Political Context of Social Inequalities and Health. *Social Sciences and Medicine* 52(3): 481–91.

Saint-Arnaud, S. & Bernard, P. (2003) Convergence or Resilience? A Hierarchical Cluster Analysis of the Welfare Regimes in Advanced Countries. *Current Sociology* 51(5): 499–527.

Stinchcombe, A. L. (1968) *Constructing Social Theories*. University of Chicago Press, Chicago.

social change: the contributions of S. N. Eisenstadt

Eliezer Ben-Rafael and Yitzhak Sternberg

Social change is a major focus of S. N. Eisenstadt's sociological work. It runs as a thread that binds together many of his works, from his earliest studies on absorption of immigrants (1952) and empires (1963), through his explorations in Axial civilizations (see, e.g., 1986), up to his later works about multiple modernities (among others, 2003). A recurring theme in Eisenstadt's work is his emphasis on endemic factors – in-built tensions, contradictions, conflicts, and antinomies – as accounting for changes in, and transformations of, the social reality. In early formulations of this perspective, he already states that innovation and change are not external to institutional systems. They are aspects of the process of institutionalization and the working of social institutions (Eisenstadt 1965, 1968, 1970). He carries on this principle of dialectical transformation to his analyses of the dynamics of civilizations and modernity, which indeed once led Robert Bellah to describe Eisenstadt as a "non-Marxist Marxist."

From this standpoint, Eisenstadt elaborates typologies of social changes according to their scopes and impacts. He speaks of macro sociohistorical, civilizational, and epochal transformations, differentiating them from more restricted intra-epochal and intracivilizational changes. When he focuses on epochal transformations, he draws the distinction between major sociohistorical breakthroughs and secondary breakthroughs. Reflecting on Jaspers (1953), Eisenstadt argues that a major breakthrough in human history was the crystallization of Axial Age civilizations from 500 BCE to the first century of the Christian era. This worldwide transformation, he says, constituted some of the utmost breakthroughs in history, the central aspect of which was the surfacing of new ontological conceptions of a gulch between the transcendental and the mundane (Eisenstadt 2001: 1916). A most significant aspect of the dynamics of Axial civilizations was their potentiality to generate further internal transformations – i.e., secondary breakthroughs. Accordingly, the main outcome of one of the Axial civilizations in Western Europe was the development of modernity which, from there, was to expand and encompass the world (Eisenstadt 2001: 1918).

In comparison, Eisenstadt sees the great revolutions – such as the English Civil War, the American and French revolutions, and later the Russian and Chinese ones – as intra-epochal and less dramatic transformations. These revolutions, he contends, by no means constitute major processes of change, whether in premodern or modern times (Eisenstadt 1992: 397). Eisenstadt's unique contribution to the study of these revolutions is their understanding as part of the social transformations of epochal changes and dynamics, which incorporates them in his general civilizational analysis. The "kernels" of these revolutions, from this point of view, can already be found in the basic characteristics of Axial civilizations, and more specifically, in the ideological and structural components of their political process. However, it is only with early modernity (the chronology of which differs in different societies) that these dynamics generated revolutionary processes and that affinities tended to concretize between political developments pertaining to the Axial civilizations and the ideological and organizational forces embedded in revolutions (Eisenstadt 1992: 394).

On the other hand, a radical change like the Meiji Restoration of 1868 in Japan cannot be seen, according to Eisenstadt, as such a revolution, since appropriate historical civilizational kernels were lacking to the extent that, historically, Japan does not belong to an Axial Age civilization. More specifically, this analysis is grounded in the observation that in Japan, one could not find any autonomous religious order, group of intellectuals, or political party that formulated, and fought on behalf of, a universal utopian vision. This absence of such essential ingredients makes all the difference between the Meiji–Ishin and the great revolutions. In practical terms, the Meiji Restoration was intended to bring about the reconstruction of the Japanese nation, and did not raise any universalistic claim requiring propagation outside Japan (Eisenstadt 1992: 396, 390).

This linking of the concept of civilization with epochal transformations, and hence with a sociohistorical periodization, represents an important contribution to both social change theory and civilizational analysis (Arnason 2001). In this respect, this approach differs from other perspectives on civilization such as, among others, Fernand Braudel's (1980) spatial-synchronic analysis, which emphasizes long-term continuity; or the "classical" civilizational analyses, like Oswald Spengler's (1945) and Arnold Toynbee's (1965), which tend to evince recurring cyclical stages. Eisenstadt, in contrast, privileges a temporal-diachronic analysis that sets emphasis on sociohistorical epochal make-overs of civilizations. In this he also differs from approaches like Norbert Elias's (1994) that focus on sociohistorical, long-term civilizing processes; instead, he emphasizes discontinuities and divisions as accounting for the generation of new phases of development.

Hence, Eisenstadt's approach to the question of directionality in macro sociohistorical transformations cannot be understood as evolutionist. Although his civilizational analysis is prone to delineate vast periodic stages, it is clearly distinguishable from a linear evolutionist approach in the vein illustrated by Rostow (1960). Against evolutionary aspects in functionalism, Eisenstadt argued that considerable social changes do not always lead to greater differentiation between institutional spheres and developments. Transformations that, at first glance, delineate what might be thought of as "similar stages" of institutional development may be leading to divergent horizons (Eisenstadt 2003: 6–7). Eisenstadt insists on the multiplicity and variety that both Axial civilizations and modernity may adopt, side by side with their common characteristics (see also Tiryakian 2005). In brief, he calls attention to potential convergence as well as divergence. Above all,

he opposes evolutionary teleological approaches that overstate directionality toward convergence, such as Parsons's (1964) thesis on "evolutionary universals in society" or Fukuyama's (1992) vision of an "end of history."

As a derivative of his basic approach that underlines the importance of human agency and creativity, Eisenstadt contributes his own view regarding the "bearers" and initiators of social change by highlighting the crucial role of elites. Accordingly, for instance, the development and crystallization of Axial civilizations were made possible, in Eisenstadt's comprehension, only thanks to the emergence of a new type of elite that deeply differed from those that dominated pre-Axial Age civilizations. This new kind of elite consisted of individuals who were independent enough, intellectually, to elaborate and propose new cultural and social orientations, which they derived from new ontological conceptions (Eisenstadt 2001: 1917).

Though at a different level of analysis, this preoccupation with the influential in relation to social change was already present in Eisenstadt's early work about the absorption of new immigrants in Israel, where he insisted on the importance of elites in the construction of trust and solidarity (Eisenstadt 2003: 3). All in all, he contends, it is those groups that evince a high level of internal solidarity and trust that are best able to adjust in situations of change; elites, he pursues, play here a major role, not only in the building of cohesiveness within collectives but also in connecting this process with commitments to broader institutional and societal frameworks. This example shows how far Eisenstadt valorizes elites in connection with social change, and, moreover, that, in his mind, the very notion of social change is not bound exclusively to conflictual contexts. Change may also be bound to the building of social cohesion and it then much depends on the action of elites. Focusing on elites, and not on social classes, to be sure enables Eisenstadt to develop a more open explanatory framework for the appreciation of social change (see Eisenstadt with Curelaru 1971). This, however, does not mean that Eisenstadt can be identified, in this respect, with an elite-theoretician like Vilfredo Pareto (1963), who emphasizes recurring ahistorical cycles emanating from inter-elite and intra-elite conflicts. Eisenstadt's own underscoring of the importance of elites to social change remains bound to the specification of the social context of change and the historical processes wherein it takes place.

All in all, Eisenstadt's thought regarding the dynamics of social change, especially in relation to the study of civilizations and modernity, is best grasped through the concept of "program" (see also Boudon 1986, 2005). These dynamics that are grounded in basic characteristics, tensions, and antinomies inherent to the social order trace out paths of development and outcomes that cannot be known a priori and remain open to a variety of alternate trajectories. This scheme, in its general formulation, rejects any form of historical determinism and, on purpose, remains less specific than major alternate perspectives. In this latter respect, one may mention as examples the overwhelming weight granted to the relations of production and class structures in Marxism or to technology and productivity in the similarly close "technologist-productionist" model (see Kerr et al. 1962). In both these approaches, changes in key factors of the social structure account for changes in all other areas of social activity. In contrast, Eisenstadt, who by no means ignores the factors evinced by those outlooks, stresses the possibility that additional areas of activity also play an autonomous role in societal development.

In particular, his civilizational analyses attach much attention to the transformative potential of culture, and especially to the circulation of ideas and perceptions of the social order and, relatedly, to the confrontation of alternative intellectual and ideological horizons. Thus, for example, he insists on the impact, in the emergence and institutionalization of Axial Age civilizations, of new ontological conceptions that elaborated on chasms between transcendental and mundane orders (Eisenstadt 2001). In another example, where he compares the dynamics of Axial (China and Europe) and a non-Axial (Japan) civilizations, he insists on the significance of the combination of ideological elements and their institutional settings in the occurrence of political revolutionary processes in the former cases, while in the latter case there was a lack in universalistic missionary visions that can be traced back to its historical experience (Eisenstadt 1992: 395). Furthermore, the

"kernel" of great revolutions can be found only in Axial civilizations where the ontology of salvation was turned toward the mundane world – at least partially. In civilizations where the notion of salvation referred exclusively to the "other world," it is doubtful that the political arena might constitute a scene for struggles conveying a revolutionary signficance (Eisenstadt 1992: 395).

This openness of perspective is the rule regarding all topics investigated by Eisenstadt – youth cultures, empires, systems of social stratification, revolutions, historical civilizations, or the Israeli society. It is particularly salient in his work on modernity, where he elaborates an alternative approach to more closed models. Through the autonomy of action this perspective endows to men and women in their relation to society and the world, modernity sets people in a stance of reflexivity to their acts and goals. It opens the way to new behaviors and understandings of the social order as well as to new tensions and conflicts. On the other hand, modernity, it is also Eisenstadt's contention, does not collide head-on with religion and premodern traditions in every area of activity and regarding any topic of reflection. Modernity brings about radical changes in lifestyles and new challenges that may oppose religious and traditional patterns and premises, and require from them new formulations and expressions. It does not, however, necessarily combat them on essential existential questions or regarding symbolic aspects of collective endeavors. Hence, changes attached to the expansion of modernity may be derived from and be implemented through different, if not divergent, understandings of modernity, revealing the lasting traces of particular cultures, religious systems, and legacies. It is in the context, among other significant circumstances, of the diversity of such premodern traditions and the potential diversity of their influences on societies' turn to modernity that Eisenstadt speaks of the contemporary world in terms of multiple modernities. By this notion he means that contemporary modern or modernizing settings differ from each other not only by the forms that modernity takes on everywhere, but also according to foci, kinds and degrees of tensions that are endemic to those societies' experience. This opens the discussion of modernity to the widest range of possibilities, and it is as such that it definitely belongs, in a prominent place, to the comparative sociological literature of modernity.

In forging this view of modernity, Eisenstadt actually follows in the footsteps of both Marx (see Tucker 1978) and Weber (see Gerth & Mills 1948): he is close to the former when he focuses on social change as generated by dialectical processes endemic to social reality; he is closer to the latter when he sees social change in a broad comparative perspective where culture and views of the world do play a crucial role in the development of society. Moreover, and again like the founding fathers of sociology, Eisenstadt as well is by no means *neutral* toward the object of his investigations. One cannot mistake his liberal-pluralist outlook when, for example, he opposes "destructive" and "constructive" tendencies of modernity, nor when he contrasts totalistic and pluralistic societal arrangements of sociocultural divisions (see also Dahrendorf 2005). Eisenstadt stands here firmly on the ground of Weber, Durkheim, and Marx, for whom value-judgments and a priori convictions never hindered scientific achievements but, on the contrary, induced them to study and re-study the reality of society and the trends of its transformation (see Ben-Rafael & Sternberg 2003).

And, indeed, in this immense work that is Shmuel Eisenstadt's, the concept of social change holds the role of pivotal axis; it derives from, and concretizes the very openness of, his sociological perspective.

SEE ALSO: Authority and Legitimacy; Charismatic Movement; Civilizations; Civilizing Process; Elites; Globalization, Culture and; Globalization, Religion and; Modernity; Modernization; Revolutions; Social Change

REFERENCES AND SUGGESTED READINGS

Arnason, J. P. (2001) Civilizational Analysis, History of. In: Smelser, N. J. & Baltes, P. B. (Eds.), *International Encyclopedia of the Social and Behavioral Sciences*, Vol. 3. Elsevier, Amsterdam, pp. 1909–15.

Ben-Rafael, E. & Sternberg, Y. (2003) Divergent Commitments and Identity Crisis. In: Ben-Rafael, E. (Ed.), *Sociology and Ideology*. Brill, Leiden, pp. 119–34.

Boudon, R. (1986) *Theories of Social Change: A Critical Appraisal*. University of California Press, Berkeley and Los Angeles.

Boudon, R. (2005) Basic Mechanisms of Moral Evolution: In Durkheim's and Weber's Footsteps. In: Ben-Rafael, E. & Sternberg, Y. (Eds.), *Comparing Modernities: Pluralism versus Homogeneity* (In Homage to S. N. Eisenstadt). Brill, Leiden.

Braudel, F. (1980) *On History*. University of Chicago Press, Chicago.

Dahrendorf, R. (2005) Doubts about Pluralism. In: Ben-Rafael, E. & Sternberg, Y. (Eds.), *Comparing Modernities: Pluralism versus Homogeneity* (In Homage to S. N. Eisenstadt). Brill, Leiden.

Eisenstadt, S. N. (1952) *The Absorption of Immigrants*. Routledge & Kegan Paul, London.

Eisenstadt, S. N. (1963) *The Political System of Empires*. Free Press, New York.

Eisenstadt, S. N. (1965) The Study of the Process of Institutionalization: Institutional Change and Comparative Institutions. In: Eisenstadt, S. N., *Essays in Comparative Institution*. Wiley, New York, pp. 1–68.

Eisenstadt, S. N. (1966) *Modernization: Protest and Change*. Prentice-Hall, Englewood Cliffs, NJ.

Eisenstadt, S. N. (1968) Introduction. In: Eisenstadt, S. N. (Ed.), *Comparative Perspectives on Social Change*. Little, Brown, Boston, pp. xi–xxx.

Eisenstadt, S. N. (Ed.) (1970) *Readings in Social Evolution and Development*. Pergamon, Oxford.

Eisensadt, S. N. (Ed.) (1986) *The Origins and Diversity of Axial Civilizations*. SUNY Press, Albany, NY.

Eisenstadt, S. N. (1992) Frameworks of the Great Revolutions: Culture, Social Structure, History, and Human Agency. *International Social Science Journal* 44(3): 385–401.

Eisenstadt, S. N. (2001) Civilizations. In: Smelser, N. J. & Baltes, P. B. (Eds.), *International Encyclopedia of the Social and Behavioral Sciences*, Vol. 3. Elsevier, Amsterdam, pp. 1915–21.

Eisenstadt, S. N. (2003) *Comparative Civilizations and Multiple Modernities*, 2 vols. Brill, Leiden.

Eisenstadt, S. N. with Curelaru, M. (1971) *The Form of Sociology: Paradigms and Crises*. Wiley, New York.

Elias, N. (1994) *The Civilizing Process*. Blackwell, Oxford.

Fukuyama, F. (1992) *The End of History and the Last Man*. Free Press, New York.

Gerth, H. H. & Mills, C. W. (Eds.) (1948) *From Max Weber: Essays in Sociology*. Routledge & Kegan Paul, London.

Jaspers, K. (1953) *The Origin and Goal of History*. Yale University Press, New Haven.

Kerr, C. et al. (1962) *Industrialism and Industrial Man*. Heinemann, London.

Pareto, V. (1963) *The Mind and Society: A Treatise on General Sociology*. Dover, New York.

Parsons, T. (1964) Evolutionary Universals in Society. *American Sociological Review* 29(3): 339–57.

Plekhanov, G. V. (1956) *The Development of the Monist View of History*. Foreign Languages Publishing House, Moscow.

Rostow, W. W. (1960) *The Stages of Economic Growth: A Non-Communist Manifesto*. Cambridge University Press, Cambridge.

Spengler, O. (1945) *The Decline of the West*. A. A. Knopf, New York.

Tiryakian, E. A. (2005) Comparative Analysis of Modernity: 1203 and 2003. In: Ben-Rafael, E. & Sternberg, Y. (Eds.), *Comparing Modernities: Pluralism versus Homogeneity* (In Homage to S. N. Eisenstadt). Brill, Leiden.

Toynbee, A. J. (1965) *A Study of History*, 2 vols. Abridgement of Vols. 1–10 by D. C. Somervell. Dell, New York.

Tucker, R. C. (Ed.) (1978) *The Marx–Engels Reader*, 2nd edn. W. W. Norton, New York.

social change, Southeast Asia

Charles Hirschman and Jennifer Edwards

Southeast Asia consists of the 11 countries that lie between the Indian subcontinent and China. On the mainland of Southeast Asia are Myanmar (Burma), Thailand, Laos, Cambodia, and Vietnam. Insular Southeast Asia includes Indonesia, the Philippines, Brunei, Malaysia, and Singapore and most recently East Timor. While most of Malaysia (Peninsular Malaysia) is on the mainland, it is usually considered part of insular Southeast Asia because the Malay population (the majority ethnic population of Malaysia) shares a common language and religion with much of the Indonesian population. The city-state of Singapore (on an island connected by a mile-long causeway to Peninsular Malaysia) was historically part of Malaysia, but because of its unique ethnic composition (three-quarters of the population is of Chinese origin) it is more similar to East Asia than Southeast Asia.

While there are some common geographical and cultural features, diversity is the hallmark of the region. Incredible indigenous cultural variation has been overlaid with centuries of contact, trade, migration, and cultural exchange from within the region and from other parts of Asia, and for the past 500 years from Europe (for general overviews of the region, see Osborne 1997; Somers Heidhues 2000; Shamsul 2001; Wertheim 1968). The common characteristic of mainland Southeast Asia is Buddhism, although there are very significant variations across and within countries. Islam is the majority religion in Indonesia, Brunei, and Malaysia, and there are significant minority Muslim populations in Singapore, southern Thailand, and the southern Philippines. Christianity is the major religion of the Philippines, and there are small Christian minorities throughout the region. Hinduism is the major religion in Bali, an island in Indonesia, and among the Indian minority populations of Malaysia and Singapore. The lowlands of both mainland and insular Southeast Asia tend to be densely settled, and wet (irrigated) rice agriculture is the predominant feature of the countryside. Rural areas are knitted together with small and medium-size market towns. The major metropolitan areas of the region (Jakarta, Bangkok, Singapore, Manila, Rangoon, Kuala Lumpur, Ho Chi Minh City) are typically port cities or located along major rivers. Many of these towns and cities have significant Chinese minorities (often intermarried with the local population) that play an important role in commerce. Every country has remote highland and mountainous regions which are often populated by ethnic minorities.

In terms of land area, population size, and cultural and linguistic diversity, Southeast Asia is comparable to Europe. By the year 2000 the population of Southeast Asia exceeded 500 million – about 8 percent of the world's total. Indonesia is the fifth most populous country in the world, while the oil-rich sultanate of Brunei (located on the island of Borneo) is one of the smallest. The other large countries of the region, Thailand, Vietnam, and the Philippines, are more populous than all European countries except for Russia and Germany. The sea (South China Sea, the Indian and Pacific Oceans) surrounds much of the region, especially the immense Indonesian and Filipino archipelagos. While the sea can be a barrier, the ocean and the rivers of the region are avenues that have fostered local and long-distance trade throughout history. The same oceans can also be cruelly destructive forces, as evidenced by the enormous loss of life and of entire communities from the December 2004 Indian Ocean tsunami.

POLITICAL HISTORY

The contemporary political divisions of the region are largely a product of European imperialism, especially of the nineteenth century. Prior to European intervention, there were great regional civilizations – both agrarian states and maritime empires that waxed and waned over the centuries. The remains of temple complexes at Angkor (in Cambodia) and Pagan (in Burma) rival the architectural achievements of any premodern world civilization. Early western observers of the city of Melaka (a fifteenth-century maritime empire centered on the west coast of the Malayan peninsula) described it as more magnificent than any contemporary European city. These early polities were founded on intensive rice cultivation with complex irrigation systems and/or the dominance of regional and long-distance trade. The region has also been deeply influenced by contacts with the great civilizations of India and China. The cultural influences from outside have invariably been transformed into distinctive local forms in different Southeast Asian contexts. The ease of movement throughout the region seems to have shaped cultures that easily absorbed new ideas, immigrants, and a tolerance for diversity.

European influence began in the sixteenth century with the appearance of Portuguese and Spanish naval forces, followed by the arrival of the Dutch in the seventeenth century, and then by the British and French. In the early centuries of contact, European powers were able to dominate the seas and thereby limit the expansion of Southeast Asian polities, but rarely penetrated very far inland from their coastal trading cities. All of Southeast Asia was transformed, however, in the nineteenth century, as the industrial revolution in the West stimulated demand for mineral and agricultural products around the globe. New economic organizations of plantations, mines, and markets led to large-scale migration of people and capital to frontier areas and to the cities of Southeast Asia. There was an accompanying flurry of imperialist wars to grab land, people, and potential resources. In a series of expansions, the British conquered the area of present day Myanmar (Burma) and Malaysia, the Dutch completed their conquest of the East Indies (now Indonesia), and the French took the areas that formed their Indochina empire (present day Vietnam, Cambodia, and Laos). At the turn of the twentieth century, the United States defeated nationalist forces to take control of the Philippines just as the Spanish empire was crumbling. Siam (Thailand) was the only indigenous Southeast Asian state to escape the grip of colonialism.

The political history of the region has not been stable or evolutionary. As western countries moved toward more democratic social and political institutions over the first decades of the twentieth centuries, the colonists (British, Dutch, American, and French) constructed authoritarian dependencies in the tropics based on export economies and racial ideologies. Although there were stirrings of nationalist sentiment during the first half of the twentieth century, it was only after World War II that the nationalist forces were strong enough and the international environment favorable enough to bring political independence to the region. The critical turning point was the Japanese conquest and occupation of Southeast Asia from 1942 to 1945, which permanently shattered the myth of European superiority. The colonial powers returned after World War II, but encountered popular nationalist movements that demanded the end of colonialism.

Independence was negotiated peacefully by the Americans in the Philippines and the British in Burma and Malaysia, but nationalist forces had to wage wars of independence against the Dutch in Indonesia (1945–50) and against France in Vietnam (1945–54). The interplay of nationalist struggles, class conflicts, and East–West Cold War rivalry had a marked influence on political developments in the region. In almost every country there were radical and communist movements that held the allegiance of significant sectors of the population. In several cases, communist parties were part of the nationalist movement, but then departed (or were driven out of) the political arena as domestic and international tensions escalated. Vietnam was unique in that the nationalist movement was led by communists. After the French were defeated in 1954 and agreed to grant independence to Vietnam, the United States intervened to set up a noncommunist Vietnam state in the southern region of the country. After another 20 years of war and a million casualties, Vietnam was finally united as an independent state in 1975. Following 1975, tensions between the socialist states (Vietnam, Cambodia, and Laos) and the rest of the region were the major focus of international relations in the region, but by the late 1990s these rivalries had subsided.

Domestic political developments within individual countries of the region have been no less dramatic. Governments have oscillated between authoritarian and democratic forms with no clear linear trend. Behind the headlines of military coups, regional wars for autonomy, and "managed" elections, have been the complex political struggles among various contending groups defined by class, region, ethnicity, and kinship. These struggles have ranged from civil war to fairly open elections. Large-scale violence is not the norm, but massacres in Indonesia, Cambodia, and East Timor have been among the worst of such episodes in modern times. Popular civil protests against ruling elites in the Philippines and Burma have had significant domestic and international reverberations. Neither academic scholarship nor political reporting has offered broad empirical generalizations or convincing interpretations of the postwar political change in Southeast Asia.

Evolutionary – and sometimes revolutionary – social change continued throughout much of Southeast Asia in the 1980s and 1990s. After the collapse of the Soviet Union, the socialist countries in the region, including Vietnam, Cambodia, and Laos, moved rapidly toward more market-driven economies. Several other countries in the region experienced major political movements that led to changes in national leadership. The "people power" movement led to the end of the Marcos regime in the Philippines and a return of regular elections. Nonviolent mass street protests ended the string of military coups in Thailand and ushered in an era of open democratic governance. Popular protests also forced the end of the Suharto regime in 1998 and brought the first free elections in 45 years in Indonesia. The military junta continues to rule Burma in the early years of

the twenty-first century, but few expect it to last for many more years. Even in Malaysia and Singapore, perhaps the most stable countries in the region, change was in the air, when after several decades of rule, first Lee Kwan Yew in Singapore and then Mahathir Mohamed in Malaysia handed over power to appointed successors. After many years of instability, Cambodia experienced consecutive peaceful elections in 1998 and 2003.

The 1990s also witnessed the creation of the new state of East Timor. After a long history of political repression by Indonesia, the people of East Timor voted for independence in a UN supervised referendum in 1999. After a period of brutal retaliatory violence from Indonesian sponsored militias, East Timor was granted international recognition as an independent state in 2002.

SOCIOECONOMIC CHANGE

Southeast Asia has been one of the most economically dynamic regions in the developing world. Economic change has been accompanied by many other attributes of modernization, including the widespread availability of education, modern transportation, and the mass media during the post-Independence era. This is most evident for the original ASEAN (Association of Southeast Asian Nations) countries of Thailand, Malaysia, Singapore, Indonesia, Philippines, and Brunei (admitted in 1984). Several of these countries are often identified as second-tier Asian tigers (following the earlier model of the rapidly developing countries of South Korea, Taiwan, Hong Kong, and Singapore). Progress has been slower in the remaining Southeast Asian countries of Vietnam, Myanmar (Burma), Laos, and Cambodia, which were admitted to ASEAN in the 1990s.

Many indicators of development in Southeast Asia, including very low levels of mortality and almost universal secondary schooling, are approaching the prevailing standards of developed countries. Demographic research has revealed very rapid declines in fertility in several Southeast Asian countries, particularly in Singapore, Thailand, Malaysia, and Indonesia. If the current pace of decline continues, replacement-level fertility (two children per woman) should be reached in the near future (Hirschman & Guest 1990).

At the same time, however, there is wide variation within the region and within some countries on all of these indicators. Life expectancy varies by over 20 years across some of the ASEAN countries, with a low of 55 years in Laos and a high of 82 in Singapore. While Singapore and Malaysia are competing for high tech industry jobs, the majority of the population in Burma and Laos remains in subsistence agriculture.

The reasons for the success of some countries and economic stagnation in others are a matter of dispute. The East Asian model of state-sponsored export industrialization is widely discussed in policy and academic circles, but the parallels between East Asian and Southeast Asian economic development strategies are still a matter of considerable uncertainty. Although market-driven capitalism is part of the story, the role of the governments in managing their economies has also been integral to economic development in the region. What is striking about economic development in the region is the degree to which it has been carried out by fairly authoritarian states. The relationship between democracy and economic growth and development, argued to go hand in hand by modernization theorists, seemed to be challenged by the experience of Southeast Asian tigers towards the end of the twentieth century, but much research is left to be done on the causes and consequences of economic development and modernization in the region.

For much of the 1990s, most of Southeast Asia experienced rapid economic growth and the development of a middle-class population whose growing social and political influence has been widely discussed in the research literature (McVey 1992; Girling 1996; Embong 2001). For example, the reform political movements in Thailand, Indonesia, and Malaysia are thought to be one manifestation of the increasing role of the new middle class. The period of very rapid economic growth was halted in late 1997 by the "Asian economic crisis" that hit the region, and Thailand, Malaysia, and Indonesia in particular. The causes of the crisis are the subject of much debate, with the role of "crony

capitalism" and highly speculative financial markets widely considered to be important contributing factors.

Despite the economic crisis of the late 1990s, economic growth has resumed in the region, even for some of the poorer countries like Laos. Assuming that current socioeconomic trends continue, several countries in the region will probably follow Japan, Korea, and Taiwan along the path of development in the early decades of the twenty-first century.

SOCIOLOGICAL RESEARCH

Scholarship on Southeast Asia has often reached beyond the boundaries of the region to influence debates over social science concepts, theory, and models. Perhaps most influential has been the work on Indonesia by anthropologist Clifford Geertz. His evocative concepts of the "theatre state," "thick description," and "agricultural involution" have stimulated debate and research in several social science disciplines, including sociology. His model of agricultural involution (Geertz 1968) has been one of the most provocative developments in scholarship on Indonesia over the last generation. A strikingly bold thesis, agricultural involution is an attempt to explain how Java became one of the most densely settled populations in the world within a traditional agricultural economy. To address this question, Geertz presents an ecological interpretation of the evolution (involution) of Javanese social structure in the face of rapid population growth and Dutch colonialism within the constraints (and possibilities) of wet rice economy. The colonial system prevented industrialization and the development of an indigenous entrepreneurial class. The traditional rice economy, however, could absorb a larger population because additional labor inputs in the maintenance of irrigation facilities, water control, weeding, and harvesting yielded marginal increments in rice production. Over the decades, this refinement of traditional production technology (involution) led to an increasing rigidification of traditional Javanese culture that discouraged innovation and any efforts at social change – therefore reinforcing the structural limits of the colonial system. Even after independence when structural limits were lifted, the legacy of the past, as reflected in Javanese culture, remained.

Geertz's thesis remains highly controversial and many of its components have been confronted with negative evidence (for a review of the debate, see White 1983; Geertz 1984). For example, Geertz deemphasized social class divisions with his interpretation of "shared poverty" as the traditional social strategy. Most research has shown significant inequality of landholding and other socioeconomic dimensions in Javanese villages, although it is not clear if inequality is permanently perpetuated between families across generations. Even accepting many of the criticisms, agricultural involution is a seminal sociological model that should serve to generate empirical research on the historical development of Asian societies.

Moral Economy

A classic question in social science concerns the causes of revolution or rebellion. Neither Marxian theory, which emphasizes exploitation, nor relative deprivation theory seem to be satisfactory models to explain the occurrence of revolutions or rebellions. The most sophisticated sociological theory of peasant rebellion is based upon historical materials from Burma and Vietnam by political scientist James Scott (1976). Scott argues that peasants only rebel when their normative expectations of a minimum subsistence level are not met. These conditions are more likely to occur when capitalist market relations and colonial states erode traditional social structures and the reciprocal obligations of peasants and their patrons.

In a more recent study based upon fieldwork in a rural Malaysian village, Scott (1985) examines how class antagonisms are displayed in everyday life. Given that rebellion is a very rare event in most societies, Scott calls attention to political, social, and linguistic behaviors (weapons of the weak) that reveal the depth of antipathy and potential social conflict, but do not risk violent reaction from the state and powerful elites. In these two books and related publications, Scott has provided original interpretations of peasant political behavior in Southeast Asia and set a research agenda for

scholars of other world regions and, more generally, the development of social theory.

Status of Women

In addition to the theoretical concepts mentioned above, empirical generalizations have arisen from studies of Southeast Asian societies that have relevance far beyond the region. Empirically, the most common cultural characteristic across the region is the relatively high status of women in Southeast Asian societies, especially when compared to East Asia and South Asia. While women still face many social and cultural obstacles in Southeast Asia, the situation appears much different than the patriarchal societies of other Asian societies and the model of traditional female domesticity of many western societies. While there are a few matrilineal societies in the region, Southeast Asian kinship systems are typically bilateral, with equal importance attached to the husband's and wife's families. The patrilocal custom of an obligatory residence of a newly married couple with or near the groom's family is largely absent in Southeast Asia. The residence of young couples after marriage seems to be largely a matter of choice or dependent on the relative economic opportunities. There is no strong sex preference for children in Southeast Asia, and both girl and boy children are highly valued. Divorce, often initiated by wives, was part of the cultural fabric of several Southeast Asian societies, including Malaysia, Indonesia, and Thailand (Hirschman & Teerawichitchainan 2003).

The relatively positive status of women is also evident in earlier times. Historian Anthony Reid (1988: 146–72) reports that early European observers were struck by the active role of women in economic and political affairs in Southeast Asia. Traditional folklore also suggested that women play an active role in courtship and that female sexual expectations were as important as men's.

At present, women seem to be well represented in schools, universities, and in employment in all modern sectors of the economy in almost every country of Southeast Asia. There is only a modest scholarly literature on the higher status of women in Southeast Asia (Andaya 2001; Van Esterik 1982), and few efforts have been made to explain the links between traditional roles of women as productive workers in the rural rice economy and their relative ease of entry into the modern sector, particularly in manufacturing industries such as textiles. The impact of modernization and economic development on gender relations and on the status of women are important topics for future scholarship.

Cultural Pluralism

Cultural pluralism has been the focus of both historical and contemporary research on Southeast Asia. Historically, one of the defining features of the region was the relatively easy absorption of peoples, ideas, and cultural practices from elsewhere. In the twentieth century, however, assimilation into Southeast Asian societies became more difficult with the creation of political and social barriers. Some of the key sources of ethnic and religious conflict in the region are illuminated in Chirot and Reid's (1997) collection of essays that compare the experiences of the Chinese in Southeast Asia with those of Jews in Central Europe. The implications of religious and ethnic diversity in the region for democratization have also garnered scholarly attention (e.g., Hefner 2001).

In particular, the relationship between politics and Islam is a topic of growing regional research interest with implications far beyond the region. Even with their majority Muslim populations, Indonesia and Malaysia have managed to maintain relatively secular states in spite of challenges from opposition parties that espouse religiously oriented politics. Hefner (2000) challenges the widely asserted stereotype that democracy is unable to flourish in the presence of Islam.

CONCLUSION

A generation or two ago there was intense discussion and debate over the question of whether Southeast Asia was a region in more than a geographic sense. The question has pretty much been settled by historical and contemporary research (Wolters 1999; Reid 2003). In spite of the great political, economic, and sociocultural diversity in the region, there are many common cultural, political, and social forms. The similarity of family systems and the status of women throughout Southeast Asia suggest common historical and cultural roots among all the peoples of the region. The long history of migration from other regions, the ecological, cultural, and social differences between lowland and upland peoples, as well as the presence of linguistic and religious pluralism, have created multi-ethnic societies in every country in the region. Colonialism created many divisions that affected variations in the political and economic developments of Southeast Asian countries during the twentieth century. The study of these processes of modernization and social changes in politics, family structure, ethnic relations, and other social spheres makes Southeast Asia an extraordinarily interesting sociological laboratory for comparative research.

SEE ALSO: Colonialism (Neocolonialism); Gender, Development and; Modernization; Plural Society; Social Change; Transition from Communism

REFERENCES AND RECOMMENDED READINGS

Andaya, B. (2001) Southeast Asian Studies: Gender. In: Smelser, N. J. & Baltes, P. B. (Eds.), *International Encyclopedia of the Social and Behavioral Sciences*. Elsevier Science, Oxford.

Chirot, D. & Reid, A. (Eds.) (1997) *Essential Outsiders: Chinese and Jews in the Modern Transformation of Southeast Asia and Central Europe*. University of Washington Press, Seattle.

Embong, A. R. (Ed.) (2001) *Southeast Asian Middle Classes: Prospects for Social Change and Democratization*. Univeristi Kebangsaan Press, Bangi, Malaysia.

Geertz, C. (1968) *Agricultural Involution: The Processes of Ecological Change in Indonesia*. University of California Press, Berkeley.

Geertz, C. (1984) Culture and Social Change. *Man* 19 (December): 511–32.

Girling, J. L. S. (1996) *Interpreting Development: Capitalism, Democracy and the Middle Class in Thailand*. Southeast Asia Program, Cornell University, Ithaca, NY.

Hefner, R. W. (2000) *Civil Islam: Muslims and Democratization in Indonesia*. Princeton University Press, Princeton.

Hefner, R. W. (Ed.) (2001) *The Politics of Multiculturalism: Pluralism and Citizenship in Malaysia, Singapore and Indonesia*. University of Hawaii Press, Honolulu.

Hirschman, C. & Teerawichitchainan, B. (2003) Cultural and Socioeconomic Influences on Divorce during Modernization: Southeast Asia, 1940s to 1960s. *Population and Development Review* 29: 215–53.

Hirschman, C. & Guest, P. (1990) The Emerging Demographic Transitions of Southeast Asia. *Population and Development Review* 16: 121–52.

McVey, R. (Ed.) (1992) *Southeast Asian Capitalists*. Southeast Asia Program, Cornell University, Ithaca, NY.

Osborne, M. (1997) *Southeast Asia: An Introductory History*, 7th edn. Allen & Unwin, Sydney.

Reid, A. (1988) *Southeast Asia in the Age of Commerce, 1450–1680*. Vol. 1: *The Lands Below the Winds*. Yale University Press, New Haven.

Reid, A. (Ed.) (2003) *Southeast Asian Studies: Pacific Perspectives*. Program for Southeast Asian Studies, Arizona State University, Tempe.

Scott, J. C. (1976) *The Moral Economy of the Peasant: Subsistence and Rebellion in Southeast Asia*. Yale University Press, New Haven.

Scott, J. C. (1985) *Weapons of the Weak: Everyday Forms of Peasant Resistance*. Yale University Press, New Haven.

Shamsul, A. B. (2001) Southeast Asian Studies: Society. In: Smelser, N. J. & Baltes, P. B. (Eds.), *International Encyclopedia of the Social and Behavioral Sciences*. Elsevier Science, Oxford.

Somers Heidhues, M. (2000) *Southeast Asia: A Concise History*. Thames & Hudson, London.

Van Esterik, P. (1982) *Women of Southeast Asia*. Center for Southeast Asian Studies, Northern Illinois University, Dekalb.

Wertheim, W. F. (1968) Southeast Asia. In: Sills, D. (Ed.), *International Encyclopedia of the Social Sciences*, Vol. 1. Macmillian and Free Press, New York, pp. 423–34.

White, B. (1983) Agricultural Involution and its Critics: Twenty Years After. *Bulletin of Concerned Asian Scholars* 15 (April/June): 18–41.

Wolters, O. W. (1999) *History, Culture, and Region in Southeast Asian Perspectives*, rev. edn. Southeast Asia Program, Cornell University, Ithaca, NY.

social cognition

Chandra Mukerji

Studies of social cognition attempt to explain how thought or cognitive problem solving takes places in groups. While scholars generally agree that learning can be a collective activity, many are reluctant to accept that thinking itself could have a social dimension. Psychologists and cognitive scientists tend to consider thought as an internal brain activity. Sociologists generally avoid the problem by focusing on social behavior. When sociologists look at consciousness, they generally study how internal psychological processes have been shaped by external social demands. Media scholars examine patterns of persuasion, and political sociologists look at ideology and hegemonic practices. All agree that collective life proceeds through the mind as well as the body, but few consider social cognition or how thinking might take place through interaction (Scribner & Cole 1974; Longino 1990; Hutchins 1995; Turnbull 2000; Rosental 2003).

Scholars doing work in the sociology of scientific knowledge (SSK) have been the exception. Conducting fieldwork in laboratories, they have repeatedly found that ideas emerge through interaction. Researchers talk to one another about what they are seeing and how they understand their data (Bloor 1990; Longino 1990; Knorr Cetina 1999). Their thinking takes place in conversation and this fact is documented in the long list of authors in many scientific publications.

The problem for those interested in social cognition is to define the more general conditions under which such activity takes place (Latour 1993; Rosental 2003; Mukerji 2006). Ed Hutchins (1995), an anthropologist working in cognitive science, has been a leader in this field. He explains that social cognition can take place even when individuals are alone. He asks us to imagine a student sitting at a desk, doing a math problem. There is paper on the desk and a pencil in the student's hand. Where, Hutchins asks, is the thinking going on? The simple answer is in the brain. The student absorbs the problem, solves it internally, and puts the result onto the paper. But Hutchins argues that the calculations in fact take place on the paper as well as in the brain. The student uses cultural symbols to do the problem, and manipulates them in culturally prescribed ways, using techniques designed for pencil and paper. Many math problems are impossible to solve without writing them down. So, Hutchins argues, the thought is *both* in the brain and in the material world. The brain learns to do what the culture says can be done on paper, and the problem is solved where collective and individual life meet – at the desk or in the school room. The brain is not an autonomous source of ideas, but rather another part of the human anatomy that is trained to fit a culture. Just as people learn ways of walking, forms of sexuality, emotional states, languages, and work skills, so they also learn ways of thinking. And they practice them with others. The brain itself is trained as children grow to adulthood by the physical and cultural environment in which they are raised. Individual thought is not so individual after all.

Hutchins (1995) argues that collective forms of problem solving are even more evident in group life, and he demonstrates this in a series of studies of navigation. When pilots fly planes or sailors take their ship to sea, they routinely rely on the knowledge and cognitive skills of others. They enroll maps, gauges, observations, and instruments into the enterprise, forming what Latour has called "networks of people and things." The Pacific Islanders that Hutchins first studied, who navigate their canoes over long distances out of sight of land, determine their course collectively, watching the patterns of waves, tracking stars, watching for birds, and looking for currents in the color of the water. The measures are too diverse for any one individual to monitor effectively, so they work together to navigate the Pacific. US naval vessels with all their instruments also require distributed cognition. To determine a course, some sailors look at sonar screens while others follow wave and wind data or monitor the speed of the engine. These different but comparable actors similarly use multiple measures to solve problems of navigation, and use talk to integrate the information in useful ways.

Turnbull (2000) studies other instances and techniques of collective cognition. Like Hutchins, Turnbull is interested in the cognitive practices of indigenous people, focusing his attention on aboriginal groups in Australia. But he also studies western cartography and building practices. For example, he looks at the use of templates by medieval masons in building cathedrals. They could reproduce arches of a similar form without having to make novel measurements. With the templates, cathedrals that were erected over centuries gained continuity of form because new masons worked with the same cognitive tools as their predecessors. Turnbull looks

at maps in a similar way. Cultures may have such different mapping systems that one cannot translate information easily from one to another, but within their culture, maps help coordinate thought and sustain ways of life over time.

Mukerji (2006) also looks at social cognition and indigenous intelligence, but as part of historical sociology of early state power. She studies the construction of the Canal du Midi, one of the first navigational canals to make extensive use of locks. She is particularly interested in a group of indigenous women engineers who lived in the Pyrenees in the seventeenth century. They managed some of the most sophisticated waterworks of the period in these remote mountains where Roman settlers once built baths. Their skills in hydraulic engineering were derived from Roman precedents, but their provenance had been forgotten. The hydraulic techniques no longer served public baths, but public laundries. Because their skills were honed against the difficult landscape of the mountains, these indigenous workers had the very rare ability to cut contours with precision, and carry water over vast distances in rough country. Because of these abilities, they were employed as laborers on the Canal du Midi. They participated in a system of distributed problem solving with military engineers, academics, and artisans.

According to Longino (1990), the reluctance to see cognition as social is grounded on the philosophical assumptions of Descartes and his followers that for centuries privileged the individual knower in the pursuit of truth. Descartes defined outside influences as a source of confusion to anyone seeking knowledge. He argued that authorities can proffer illusions rather than point to the truth, so thinking independently is necessary for the pursuit of knowledge. Longino breaks with this tradition and makes a philosophical argument in favor of social epistemology, using the laboratory from SSK as her guide. She argues that group problem solving can be just as progressive as individual thought. Individuals as well as groups can cultivate illusions, but in fact, she says, the shared professional skepticism of scientists is a better means of dispelling than individual contemplation.

This position is compatible with what the developmental psychologists Scribner and Cole (1974) have argued about culture and learning. Following the precepts of the Russian psychologist Vygotsky, they contend that learning is a social activity, not simply a natural capacity of human brains. Literacy effects are not just abilities acquired in learning to decode and write messages, but rather effects of the schooling in which literacy is acquired. Rote memory and recitation may constitute literacy, but they do not produce the same kind of cognitive skills as critical reading. The reflexivity that psychologists usually associate with learning to read is really the product of the ways that texts are presented and interrogated in western societies. The collective practices of schools and families produce forms of consciousness that are social, not individual. Scribner and Cole argue that texts and other inscriptions are cognitive tools. They can be (but are not necessarily) used as intellectual scaffolding for developing higher forms of reasoning. Schools tell pupils how to understand and use these tools, and produce cultural forms of collective reasoning.

The notion of cognitive tools has proven particularly effective in interpreting the collective patterns of cognition in science. Scientific instruments constitute another type of cognitive tool that not only allows people to think in new ways, but to approach problems in similar fashions. Where the same instruments are used in multiple fields of study, they help to fashion a common way of working and thinking. Research that is very specialized can nonetheless contribute to collective shifts in knowledge because scientists share cognitive tools: not only types of measurements, but also mathematical models, or logics of research.

Hutchins, Cole, and researchers in the SSK tradition tend to focus on face-to-face interaction where people learn from one another or learn in tandem, but Mukerji, studying the Canal du Midi, also looks at how the state in this period cultivated and organized intelligence, using cognitive advantages to augment their institutional power. Military engineers, academics, and civil engineers were all cultivated and patronized by the royal treasury, and were obliged to serve on the king's projects. They came to the Canal du Midi when they were told to do so, combining their different expertise acquired as creatures of the state. The resulting social intelligence was a political asset, and used to improve the infrastructure of the kingdom.

Occupations have their own forms of intelligence that can be cultivated in seclusion or used in coordination with others. Large-scale organizations such as corporations or governments combine and use them in precise ways. The American sailors described by Hutchins, navigating navy vessels at sea, have duties defined by the naval hierarchy. Their skills are a product of this system, and so are their practices of collaborating. They are trained to help navigate collectively and to have the distinct skills needed for the job. Bureaucracies are not just socially rational systems of offices, but means for managing and exploiting human intelligence.

Currently, those who study social cognition do not question whether such a thing exists or not. The evidence for it seems strong. But it is still difficult to differentiate a pattern of *social* thought from a chain of command. In the former, group members share their ideas and find common solutions to problems together. In the latter, information is fed from the bottom to the people at the top, who do the thinking. More research is needed to make more precise descriptions of this. And more precise theories are needed to distinguish social cognition or distributed thought from other patterns of solving problems.

What is most intriguing in current research are the efforts to clarify what difference it makes that human beings can talk with one another and stabilize common understandings of things. Clearly, groups can sometimes accomplish through distributed cognition what individuals could not do on their own. The question is when and how this capacity is employed and how much of social life is founded on this ability.

SEE ALSO: Ethnomethodology; Frame; Framing and Social Movements; Information Technology; Knowledge, Sociology of; Kuhn, Thomas and Scientific Paradigms; Mannheim, Karl; Scientific Knowledge, Sociology of; Scientific Networks and Invisible Colleges

REFERENCES AND SUGGESTED READINGS

Bloor, D. (1990) *Knowledge and Social Imagery*. University of Chicago Press, Chicago.

Hutchins, E. (1995) *Cognition in the Wild.* MIT Press, Cambridge, MA.

Knorr Cetina, K. (1999) *Epistemic Cultures.* Harvard University Press, Cambridge, MA.

Latour, B. (1993) *We've Never Been Modern.* Harvester Wheatsheaf, New York.

Longino, H. (1990) *Science as Social Knowledge.* Princeton University Press, Princeton.

Mukerji, C. (2006) Women Engineers and the Culture of the Pyrenees. In: Smith. P. & Schmidt, B. (Eds.), *Knowledge and Its Making in the Early Modern World.* University of Chicago Press, Chicago.

Rosental, C. (2003) *La Trame de l'evidence.* Presses Universitaires de France, Paris.

Scribner, S. & Cole, M. (1974) *Culture and Thought.* Wiley, New York.

Turnbull, D. (2000) *Masons, Tricksters and Cartographers.* Harwood Academic, Amsterdam.

social comparison theory

Monica K. Miller and David Flores

Comparisons with other people play a significant role in social life, as they provide meaning and self-relevant knowledge. How people view their own circumstances, abilities, and behaviors varies according to the types of social comparisons they make. Although in his seminal work Leon Festinger (1954) did not offer a precise definition of social comparison, it is generally conceptualized as the process of thinking about the self in relation to other people. Individuals frequently make social comparisons because no objective comparison information is available; however, when both social and objective information is available, people are often more influenced by social information, as it is frequently more diagnostic than objective information. Further, many researchers believe that comparisons may be with real or imagined others, and do not require personal contact or conscious thought. Comparisons can also be made between one's own social group and another social group. Although comparison information can be encountered naturally in one's environment, most research has studied the types of comparisons that participants seek out intentionally.

There are many motivations for seeking social comparison information. First, comparisons provide information for self-evaluation. In situations lacking objective standards, people often look to similar others as an indicator of how well one has performed. For example, students often want to know how their test score ranks among their classmates' scores. Second, social comparison can serve self-improvement purposes, as is the case of younger children comparing themselves with older children when learning new tasks. A third goal is self-enhancement, which allows one to feel better about the self through comparison with someone who is worse off. Social comparisons are also made to inform future behavior. Customers at a bar observe other customers tipping the bartender, and take this as a cue that they should do the same. Finally, individuals seek comparisons out of a desire to affiliate with or gather information about others.

In order to achieve the goal of the comparison, individuals can be selective in their choice of a comparison target and strategic in their interpreting, distorting, or disregarding comparison information. Additionally, the presence of varying goals may lead to different types of comparisons. For example, cancer patients typically compare their coping and health with those less fortunate (i.e., a downward comparison), promoting a need for positive self-evaluation. However, patients also seek interactions with patients who are doing better than the self (i.e., an upward comparison), promoting the need for self-improvement.

Social comparisons evoke a variety of behavioral, cognitive, and affective reactions. Such reactions are largely thought to be brought about by a threat to the self-image, a sense of injustice, or some other uncomfortable state that results from a comparison. For instance, a worker who learns that he gets paid more than another worker can justify this inequity by either working harder or by reasoning that his work is more difficult than that of the lower-paid worker. This example indicates that people often can choose between behavioral and cognitive responses.

Affective responses have also been intensely studied. In general, a comparison with someone whose abilities, performance, or attributes are superior produces more negative affect and lower self-esteem than does a comparison with someone who is inferior. This is overly simplistic, however, and several caveats to this effect warrant consideration. First, in order to cause negative affect, a comparison domain must be important to one's self-image. Abraham Tesser's (1988) self-evaluation maintenance (SEM) model suggests that people want to maintain positive beliefs about themselves, and comparisons with superior others can have two different effects on self-views. SEM suggests that when a comparison other outperforms the self in a domain that is *not* relevant to one's self-image, the individual is not threatened and the comparison actually augments self-evaluation. In such a case the individual may feel proud to be close to someone who has performed so well. Alternatively, if the comparison other outperforms the self in a domain that *is* relevant to one's self-image, the individual is more likely to experience negative affect. Consequently, one option for an outperformed individual to reduce the threat of an unfavorable evaluation is to diminish the relevance of the comparison domain to his self-image.

Second, Tesser's SEM model suggests that the similarity of the comparison other to the self can affect one's reaction to a comparison. Before making a social comparison, individuals often consider the relevance of the other's situation to their own. Individuals favor comparisons with others who are members of their gender and in-group. This suggests that one way to avoid a negative social comparison is to alter the perceived similarity of the comparison other. By rationalizing that the comparison other is different from the self in some important way, the threat of being outperformed is reduced.

A third caveat is the perception of control that a person feels over the evaluative domain. In situations in which individuals feel a great amount of control, an upward comparison may actually lead to positive affect, as the comparison indicates that better outcomes are attainable. This is the case of cancer patients seeking companionship with patients who have recovered. If individuals feel that they have the ability to change their situation, these feelings of self-efficacy are likely to increase performance; however, without the perceived ability to change the situation, a person is likely to feel helpless.

The diversity of motivations, reactions to, and characterizations of social comparison has led researchers to employ a variety of methods in their study of the topic. There are three general methodological approaches to social comparison research (Wood 1996). The selection approach concerns what information is sought out for use in comparisons; the reaction approach focuses on the impact of provided social information; the narration approach concentrates on participants' reports about what information they use in their everyday lives.

The selection approach examines the processes involved in seeking social information. People often appear to select comparison others who are generally similar on some relevant factor, such as age or gender, though there are instances when a dissimilar other may be seen as most informative, such as when a person believes similar others may share one's own biases. As discussed earlier, an individual's motivations for making the comparison can influence selection of the comparison other. If multiple options for comparison are available, a person will strategically select a comparison other that helps reach the goal of the comparison, and might even construct a hypothetical other for comparison.

In order to study how individuals select a comparison other, researchers have employed a number of different methods. In the rank-order paradigm, participants are given their relative standing (e.g., they ranked third out of seven) and are then given the opportunity to see the score associated with other ranks. Typically, participants will first ask to see the extreme scores, and then ask to see the score associated with the ranks immediately above their own. Another approach provides the opportunity for participants to examine more than just the score the comparison other achieved; for example, participants have the chance to see the actual answers that other participants gave on their tests. Researchers measure how many of the other participants' tests the participant chooses to view. A final selection research method is the affiliation paradigm, which gives participants in a stressful situation the option of affiliating with fellow participants or non-participants. The choice to affiliate with other participants is seen as an interest in comparing reactions to the situation.

In addition to studying how participants select a comparison other, researchers also study how participants react to comparisons with others. In the reaction approach, social comparison is manipulated as the independent variable, and researchers assess the effects of social information on participants. Social comparisons can affect such variables as mood, jealousy, self-esteem, self-evaluation, and performance. Additionally, researchers study reactions to social information that is received during the course of participants' everyday lives. In such studies, some dimension of the social environment is correlated with an outcome measure. For example, students use social comparison information such as their class ranking to shape their career goals.

The final method of study, the narrative approach, concentrates on participants' descriptions and reports of comparisons made in everyday life. Methods used include asking participants to record their comparisons in a diary, directly asking participants about comparisons they make, and observing comparisons people make spontaneously during conversations.

Given the variety of responses, methods, and measurements involved with social comparisons, it is not surprising that the topic is marked by a number of controversies. One main disagreement involves what exactly constitutes a social comparison. Traditionalists assert that only a comparison with a specific person with whom one has had personal contact qualifies as a social comparison. An opposing view proposes that personal contact is not a necessary condition, and that any social information, including information about hypothetical and fictional comparison others, qualifies as social comparison.

Another debate involves whether a comparison must change an individual's self-evaluation to be rightfully considered a social comparison. Some researchers argue that a change in self-evaluation is a key criterion of a true social comparison, while others contend that this prerequisite excludes many phenomena that should justifiably be included. This latter view asserts that comparisons should not be defined in terms of effect, but rather social comparison occurs any time an individual is involved in the process of thinking about social information in relation to the self, regardless of consequences.

A large portion of the social comparison research has measured the selection of information by participants, thus treating comparison as a deliberate act. The question has been raised, however, as to whether social comparison is always intentional. Some researchers have proposed that, because people constantly face information about others, they may at times be forced to compare themselves to others, regardless of whether they desire to do so. Thus, comparisons may be encountered rather than selected. It has also been asserted that comparisons may sometimes be unconscious, suggesting that people may not be fully aware of some comparisons they make or the effects of these comparisons.

Social comparison research is also marked by controversy surrounding methodological issues. Some research methods require participants to report comparisons they make, and some researchers have questioned whether people can adequately do so. For example, people might make comparisons automatically, or may not be entirely aware of the steps taken in their comparison processes, thereby distorting self-reports. Furthermore, social comparison measures may be marked by social desirability effects, as participants might not admit to making social comparisons that violate norms or have unfavorable implications. Given the diversity that characterizes the processes of social comparison and the broad expanse of topics that it implicates, the fact that research in the field is marked by a number of issues of contention comes as no surprise.

Since its inception, social comparison has affected a diverse range of areas, including equity, affiliation, and social interaction. It has been used in a variety of fields including social psychology, clinical psychology, cognitive psychology, personality psychology, and sociology. Its wide-ranging application is evident in current research trends, including studies of marital and life satisfaction, and the eating behaviors and body image of adolescent girls. Researchers continue to apply social comparison theory to new topic areas, leading to an ever-expanding diversity of literature in the area.

SEE ALSO: Interaction; Self; Self-Esteem, Theories of; Social Psychology

REFERENCES AND SUGGESTED READINGS

Festinger, L. (1954) A Theory of Social Comparison Processes. *Human Relations* 7: 117–40.

Suls, J. & Wheeler, L. (Eds.) (2000) *Handbook of Social Comparison: Theory and Research*. Kluwer/Plenum, New York.

Suls, J. & Wills, T. A. (Eds.) (1991) *Social Comparison: Contemporary Theory and Research*. Lawrence Erlbaum, Hillsdale, NJ.

Tesser, A. (1988) Toward a Self-Evaluation Maintenance Model of Social Behavior. In: Berkowitz, L. (Ed.), *Advances in Experimental Social Psychology*, Vol. 21. Academic Press, San Diego, pp. 181–227.

Tesser, A. (2000) On the Confluence of Self-Esteem Maintenance Mechanisms. *Personality and Social Psychology Review* 4(4): 290–9.

Willis, T. A. (1981) Downward Comparison Principles in Social Psychology. *Psychological Bulletin* 90: 245–71.

Wood, J. V. (1996) Theory and Research Concerning Social Comparisons of Personal Attributes. *Psychological Bulletin* 106(2): 231–48.

social control

Darin Weinberg

The concept of social control entered the lexicon of academic sociology in the early twentieth century. It was articulated first in the pioneering work of Edward A. Ross, and then, a short time later, by a handful of some of the most distinguished figures in the early history of American sociology, including Ernest Burgess, Charles Horton Cooley, Robert Park, and W. I. Thomas. These scholars took a rather expansive view of the matter, suggesting the study of social control covered the sum total of institutions and practices by which societies regulate themselves. Concerned as it was with the great variety of social mechanisms that maintain social order in the widest sense, the earliest sociological research on social control was sometimes difficult to distinguish from efforts to define modern society as such or to specify the proper subject matter of sociology as a whole. While this broadly encompassing view of the concept's reach has sometimes been criticized, these sociologists cannot be held solely responsible for having cast the concept so generally. For in formulating their arguments regarding the meaning and importance of the concept of social control, these early American sociologists were responding to a much more established tradition of European social thought concerning the fundamental causes of social order in modern societies.

The conceptual problem of social order is usually traced to the English social philosopher Thomas Hobbes. Hobbes asked how individual human actors, guided by nothing but their own self-interests, might cohere in the form of an orderly, law-abiding society. His answer was that obedience to the law was a result of the self-interested human actor coming to recognize the poor prospects of his or her own survival in a lawless world. Precisely because we possess a natural instinct toward self-preservation, people produce and obey an absolute sovereign (whose sole right it is to set and enforce the law). Many have since argued that Hobbes formulated this argument in fear of the political upheaval occurring in Britain at the time he wrote and with a concern to give philosophical justification to a monarchy intent on violently subduing republican political revolt. Later social philosophers like John Locke argued, contra Hobbes, that human nature is not wholly selfish and that there is no need for the state to repress its free expression. However, as feudal Europe gave way to the industrial, American, and French revolutions it became progressively clearer to the social thinkers of the day that, quite regardless of the arguments of philosophers, the social order Hobbes defended was inevitably disintegrating. The classic sociological works of figures like Marx, Durkheim, and Weber can be understood as efforts to explain the nature of the new social order that was replacing feudalism and a specification of how this new social order cohered. Hence, for Marx, modern society cohered around what he called the capitalist mode of production; for Durkheim, it cohered due to the interdependencies introduced by a complex division of labor; for Weber, it cohered due to the emergence of large-scale institutions like the bureaucratic state and modern market. For these social theorists, the orderly maintenance of complex modern societies was to be explained largely as the result of their fundamental structural properties rather than the deliberate designs of the actors who comprise them.

While Edward Ross and his American followers embraced the classic European preoccupation with the question of how social order is maintained in complex modern societies, they distanced themselves from the structural explanations on offer from the likes of Marx, Weber, and Durkheim to posit an approach more grounded in the agency of social actors. For them, the question of social order, or social control, was a question of how modern societies might influence their members to see their own individual self-interests as more or less compatible with the collective interests of their society. Hence, the question of social control was precisely the question of how modern societies might remain orderly through the rational force of persuasion, rather than the brute force or coercion condoned by Hobbes. This question became fused rather early on with questions concerning the social problems of the city in what became known as the Chicago School of urban sociology. Early Chicago School sociologists believed the traditional forms of social control found in small towns and villages broke down in the city. While they shared this premise with European theorists like Ferdinand Tönnies, they differed in their desire to keep their research firmly grounded in the empirical world. Thus, whereas Tönnies was happy to make broad generalizations regarding premodern and modern societies, proponents of the Chicago School found too much variety and nuance both in the past and the present to remain comfortable with Tönnies's famous dichotomy between *Gemeinschaft* and *Gesellschaft*. Chicago School scholar Louis Wirth, for example, called for a more precise empirical attention to three variables that he felt distinguished cities that suffered comparatively more social problems from those that suffered less: population size, density, and heterogeneity. Wirth argued that as each of these increases, the close personal relationships found in smaller communities decrease. Because urban life is comparatively anonymous, big-city dwellers do not feel bound to honor each other, nor to sanction each other for breaking the law. This causes both increased social disorder and a need to delegate the work of social control to professionals in place of the self-policing community found in small towns. Because they cannot be as ubiquitous, professional agents of social control cannot be as effective in maintaining social order as is fuller community participation in this effort. Similar arguments were made by W. I. Thomas in defense of his influential theory linking what he called social disorganization, various urban social problems, and the breakdown of social control.

The early Chicago School's understanding of social control remains important to this day. However, it has been refined and rivaled by a variety of other approaches that bear discussion. In the first instance, one must note the important work done by C. Everett Hughes and his students on occupations and, more precisely, occupational socialization. Hughes departed from the emphasis early Chicago School researchers gave to the relationship between complex differentiated societies and social disorganization. Theorists like Wirth and Thomas tended to highlight the effective social controls small groups exercised over their members and the breakdown of these controls as groups grew larger. Hughes and his students noted that many of the mechanisms of social control one finds in smaller groups like families and villages were also operative in occupational groups. This insight served to introduce a higher level of empirical refinement into research concerning the non-coercive social control mechanisms at work in larger social groups and usefully to blur the line between what Cooley had called primary and secondary groups.

A somewhat higher level of theoretical refinement was introduced into the study of social control by Talcott Parsons and his students. Parsons argued that large-scale differentiated societies generate any number of mechanisms by which to manage the inevitable role strains and ambivalences introduced by the complexity of modern life. Parsons's structural functionalist approach maintained the early Chicago School's optimistic understanding of social control as the necessary work societies do upon themselves to sustain themselves. This line of theoretical development was radicalized considerably by ethnomethodology. Ethnomethodologists have sought to transform some of Parsons's theoretical premises regarding the regulative work that societies do upon themselves into questions for empirical inquiry. For example, in his famous "breaching experiments," Harold Garfinkel sent his students out into the world with instructions to deliberately disrupt the taken-for-granted meanings at work in various ordinary interactions. These experiments inaugurated a tradition of research that has revealed just how resilient, resourceful, and creative social actors can be when called upon to manage the diverse episodes of social disorder they encounter in the conduct of their everyday lives. Ethnomethodologists have discovered a vast collection of interactional techniques by which social control is exercised in both formal and informal social settings, ranging from laboratories to family dinners. This research has effectively demonstrated that social control should not be conceptualized as a set of intermittent interventions into our everyday lives, so much as a routine, pervasive, and indispensable feature of them. While remarkably different in their respective approaches to research, the emphases of Hughes, Parsons, and ethnomethodology are aligned insofar as they each remain decidedly focused on the collectively orchestrated aspects of social control and its role in creating and maintaining consensus, equilibrium, and collaborative activity. They are not as concerned to demonstrate how social control figures in the exercise of coercion and exploitation.

Conflict theories of social control have been vehemently opposed to the claims that social control can either be defined in contrast to coercive control or that it could ever reflect the freely achieved consensus of society as a whole. In place of the idea that social groups regulate themselves in pursuit of their collective interests, conflict theorists insist that modern societies are never as integrated or as harmonious as this imagery suggests. Because subgroups within society will inevitably hold different beliefs about what kinds of things merit regulation, actual social control efforts can never reflect the beliefs of everyone. Hence, social control will always entail more powerful factions within society regulating less powerful factions, not in the collective interest but in their own self-interest. Various research agendas emphasizing the coercive and self-interested dimensions of social control became prominent in the 1950s and 1960s. One such agenda, broadly known as labeling theory, was popularized by sociologists like Howard Becker, Erving Goffman, and Edwin Lemert. In expounding the labeling approach, Lemert, for example, wrote that while older studies of social control had "tended to rest heavily upon the idea that

deviance leads to social control, I have come to believe that the reverse idea (i.e., social control leads to deviance) is equally tenable and the potentially richer premise for studying deviance in modern society" (Lemert 1967: ix). According to labeling theorists, it is misleading to distinguish "social disorder" or "deviance" from the particular definitions of these concepts provided by specific agents of social control. This is because the activities of agents of social control like the courts, medical clinics, mental hospitals, and police forces are very often not only *responsive* to deviance, but actually define as deviance (and as meriting social control) activities that in other societies may not be seen as deviance at all. Hence, labeling theorists have argued that activities like drug use and homosexuality come to be seen as matters deserving of social control less because of breakdowns in social order than by virtue of the definitional or "labeling" activities of what Becker dubbed "moral entrepreneurs" and other elite members of society with a stake in seeing certain activities condemned and/or curtailed. The labeling perspective also highlights the negative consequences that can flow from labeling itself. For example, the idea of "secondary deviance" was devised to signal the fact that people labeled as particular kinds of deviants may come to be socialized by agents of social control to adopt roles attendant to the labels they have received. Thus labeled as a criminal or as learning disabled, for example, people might begin to adopt dysfunctional habits associated with these labels simply by virtue of the fact they have been so labeled.

The labeling perspective tended to highlight the stake had by particular professional groups or moral entrepreneurs in defining certain behaviors as deviant and subjecting them to social controls. This rather diffuse sense of the sources of various campaigns of social control was ultimately challenged by other conflict theorists who placed greater emphasis on centralized forms of power in modern societies, like the state and/or a relatively integrated dominant class. For these theorists, social control was still more nefarious than had been suggested by labeling theorists. Social control was now seen not just to impose the moral sentiments of one faction of society upon another, but to subdue class conflict and/or to facilitate the exploitation of the weak by the strong. Such research came in a variety of guises, but they all shared a much more sustained interest in macro-structural histories of modern societies. While some researchers focused on the nostalgic yearnings of a cultural elite whose power and authority were declining in the aftermath of industrialization, most took a more orthodox Marxist view of things. According to Marxist conflict theorists, social control is best understood as a collection of measures undertaken in the interests of the dominant economic class. This can include efforts to secure their ever-accumulating wealth through the use of evermore sophisticated police forces and carceral institutions; efforts to politically debilitate the working class through legislation restricting organized labor; the use of educational institutions and other approaches to disciplining the working class in order to make them at once less threatening to commerce and better suited to the labor needs of the dominant class; or efforts to diffuse the animosity and revolutionary potentials of the working class through mass cultural fare that serves to distract and pacify them and/or concessions in the form of state administered health and social welfare provisions. In short, social control is seen as a multifaceted project formulated and orchestrated by the economically powerful (or their hired minions) to ensure their retention of power and often to accumulate more.

While opposed to the reductionism evident in some Marxist analyses, the work of Michel Foucault has made immensely important contributions to our critical understanding of social control by refining our understanding of power. Marxist theorists of social control have very often been profoundly critical of the state and the multitude of other agencies through which the dominant economic class seeks to legitimate its putative stranglehold on the working class. But they have tended to preserve a distinction between the exercise of power and the exercise of knowledge. Whereas they have held that the use of power to control people is inevitably coercive, until Foucault, most Marxist theorists remained committed to the notion that the use of knowledge, or truth, to control people is noncoercive. Appeals to truth are appeals to the better nature of human beings, to their faculties of reason, and their amenability to influence

through genuine persuasion rather than coercive control. According to Foucault, this conception of the relationship between power and knowledge is highly problematic because it fails to appreciate the extent to which power, when it is exercised efficiently, is seductive rather than coercive. Foucault insisted that power is not merely repressive, but eminently productive, and that evidence of its repressive tendencies must be interpreted in light of the positive goals that it has prioritized over that which it has repressed. When it is most effective, social control is impossible to distinguish from self-control because those who are controlled are complicit in the control that is exercised over them and do not resist. Repression, then, ought only very rarely to be seen as an end in itself rather than a necessary cost of pursuing some putatively greater good. Moreover, power is not opposed to truth, but intimately connected to it. Foucault argued that all power is attended by a regime of truth through which its goals are formulated, and the means of achieving those goals are strategically devised and refined. This, for Foucault, was as true for science as it was for the military campaigns of powerful empires or for any other exercise of power. Finally, power and knowledge, or as Foucault wrote, power/knowledge, can be found in virtually any concrete regime of disciplined activity. In other words, the reality of power/knowledge is to be found in the endless actual practices in and for which it is summoned, consolidated, and developed. Foucault and his followers have called attention to the fusion of power and knowledge in such instances as the development of correctional facilities, formal educational institutions, the rise of professional military service, the development and rationalization of clinical expertise, public health measures, and, more broadly, the transformation of feudal courts into bureaucratic states. To highlight their role in the accomplishment of social control, Foucault referred to these various regimes as instances of what he called "governmentality," which he defined as "the conduct of conduct." For Foucault, while governmentality was certainly a form of social control exercised by governments, the scope of this concept also extended to wherever the "conduct of conduct" became an observable practice. It is something that bosses do with employees, parents do with children, teachers do with students, and that we as individuals do with our selves – as when we diet.

Toward the end of his life, Foucault's appreciation of the extent to which we as individuals play an active, rather than passive, role in the social control that is exercised over us was increasing. Of course, he remained cognizant of the fact that we are very deeply embedded in, and affected by, historically enduring regimes of power/knowledge of which we are often scarcely aware. However, he became more interested in the fact that our lives are projects that we ourselves do, at some level, craft and steer according to our own visions of the good. While these visions are by no means uninfluenced by our sociohistorical circumstances, they do not for that cease to be our own. Moreover, the forces by which we are socially controlled are not immune to our efforts to exert some influence upon them – modest though these efforts may often be. Rather than resigning himself to the notion that our collective fates must inevitably be coerced, Foucault seemed to be moving in the direction of the early Chicago School theorists of social control, who remained cautious and critical but, nonetheless, hopeful that the regulation of society could, in principle, be accomplished democratically and compassionately rather than coercively and exploitatively. And, along with many other contemporary students of social control, he was resolutely convinced that, while necessary as such, the regulation of society is, at present, considerably more coercive and exploitative than it has to be.

SEE ALSO: Chicago School; Conflict Theory and Crime and Delinquency; Cooley, Charles Horton; Crime; Crime, Social Control Theory of; Criminal Justice System; Deviance Processing Agencies; Disciplinary Society; Ethnomethodology; Foucault, Michel; Goffman, Erving; Governmentality and Control; Labeling Theory; Lemert, Edwin M.; Marx, Karl; Marxism and Sociology; Moral Entrepreneur; Organizations as Coercive Institutions; Park, Robert E. and Burgess, Ernest W.; Police; Power, Theories of; Primary Groups; Prisons; Regulation Theory; Secondary Groups; Social Disorganization Theory; Socialization

REFERENCES AND SUGGESTED READINGS

Becker, H. S. (1963) *Outsiders: Studies in the Sociology of Deviance*. Free Press, New York.
Burchell, G., Gordon, C., & Miller, P. (Eds.) (1991) *The Foucault Effect: Studies in Governmentality*. University of Chicago Press, Chicago.
Cohen, S. & Scull, A. (Eds.) (1985) *Social Control and the State*. Blackwell, Oxford.
Foucault, M. (1979) *Discipline and Punish: The Birth of the Prison*. Trans. A. Sheridan. Random House, New York.
Garfinkel, H. (1984 [1967]) *Studies in Ethnomethodology*. Polity Press, Cambridge.
Janowitz, M. (1975) Sociological Theory and Social Control. *American Journal of Sociology* 81(1): 82–108.
Lemert, E. M. (1967) *Human Deviance, Social Problems, and Social Control*. Prentice-Hall, Englewood Cliffs, NJ.
Meier, R. F. (1982) Perspectives on the Concept of Social Control. *Annual Review of Sociology* 8: 35–55.
Piven, F. F. & Cloward, R. A. (1971) *Regulating the Poor*. Random House, New York.

Social Darwinism

Bernd Weiler

Social Darwinism, a highly controversial and protean term, refers to the application of concepts and ideas to the social world which are allegedly derived from Charles Darwin's theory of evolution. Despite the fact that the so-called founding fathers of sociology tried to establish the autonomy of their discipline, the often unconscious reliance upon biological concepts and the interpretation of the social order as the outcome of a natural process were pervasive traits of late nineteenth and early twentieth-century social science. The term Social Darwinism first came into usage in the late 1870s and early 1880s and is, in its classic phase, commonly – and as some would immediately object wrongly – associated with such diverse theorists as Spencer and Bagehot in Great Britain, Sumner and Fiske in the US, Gumplowicz and Ratzenhofer in Austria, Lombroso, Ferri, and Niceforo in Italy, Broca, Topinard, and Lapouge in France, and Hellwald, Woltmann, Ploetz, and Ammon in Germany.

Modern historiographical debates about Social Darwinism, which date back especially to Hofstadter's seminal work *Social Darwinism in American Thought* (1944), have focused primarily on the question of the precise definition of the term and concomitantly on who should be classified as a Social Darwinist. Closely linked to this definitional issue are the methodological questions of the unit of analysis in Social Darwinism, as well as the overall significance and ideological connotations of Social Darwinism at the fin-de-siècle. Research has further revolved around the origins of Social Darwinism and the historical linkage between Darwinism and Social Darwinism. Finally, there remains the contentious issue whether, and in what form, the Social Darwinist tradition is still alive today.

Regarding the definitional issue of Social Darwinism, a term more often used in historiographical research than in the primary sources (Hodgson 2004), a "generalist" and a "restrictionist" approach can be analytically distinguished (Crook 1996). In the generalist definition, which corresponds more closely to the standard textbook accounts, Social Darwinism refers to the use of evolutionary, developmental, or progressivist ideas clothed in Darwinian terminology when analyzing social inequality. For the generalists, to classify somebody as a Social Darwinist it is not necessary for the person to explicitly rely upon the theory proposed by Darwin in his main works, *The Origin of Species The Descent of Man* (1871). In contrast to this broad definition, the restrictionists argue that the mere rhetorical use of catchphrases and metaphors such as "struggle for existence," "natural selection," "survival of the fittest," and "adaptation" does not make a social theorist a Social Darwinist. According to the restrictionists, the label should be reserved for those turn-of-the-century thinkers who consciously and explicitly applied the central elements of Darwin's composite theory to the analysis of social life. In this narrow understanding of the term, Spencer, the arch-Social Darwinist of the generalists, is classified as a Social Lamarckist because he, like many of his contemporaries, believed in the inheritance of acquired characteristics and also because he equated, contrary to Darwin, evolution with directed progress.

Neither would the Polish-born sociologist Gumplowicz qualify as a Social Darwinist because he explicitly rejected the transference of biological concepts to the field of sociology and was also a declared adherent of Agassiz's theory of the immutability of species. One might argue, however, that by opposing the categories of Social Darwinism and Social Lamarckism, one does not capture the complex web of actual interrelationships that existed between the two currents of sociobiological thought around 1900. It also needs to be emphasized that when Social Darwinists applied the idea of natural selection to social life, they seldom defined the unit of analysis in a precise manner. Not only did the elements in the "struggle for existence" range from individuals fighting each other to rival families, ranks, classes, societies, nations, and races, but also the analysis often shifted from one unit to the next. Furthermore, the units of analysis in Social Darwinist thought vary accordingly from biological, to economic, to cultural, and to political entities.

Intimately linked with these definitional issues is the question of the overall significance and the ideological connotations of Social Darwinism as an intellectual and a policy movement around 1900. Whereas the "orthodox" historiographical school of Social Darwinism, led by Hofstadter, argued that in America Social Darwinism was the dominant intellectual current of the Gilded Age, transcending the boundaries of academia and exerting a strong influence on business and politics, the "revisionist" school, based upon a narrower definition of the term and represented especially by Bannister, claimed that the significance of Social Darwinism as an intellectual movement had been greatly exaggerated (Bannister 1988; Hawkins 1998). Furthermore, whereas the orthodox school had linked Social Darwinism to conservative and liberal ideologies, the revisionist school emphasized the ideological use made of Darwin by the collectivist-oriented Left. From an ideological point of view Darwin's theory, despite emphasizing nature over nurture, has in fact proved to be quite multivalent, lending support to such diverse policy movements as liberal laissez-faire economics, protectionism, restricted immigration, imperialism, Left and Right eugenics, etc.

Research on the intellectual sources of Social Darwinism and on the relationship between Darwinism and Social Darwinism has shown that key elements of Social Darwinism, such as the Malthusian idea of a "struggle for existence," the idea of evolution, and the notion of a "survival of the fittest" (a phrase coined by Spencer several years before the publication of the *Origin*), predate Darwin's biology. In this context it has been argued that not only is Darwin's metaphorical language thoroughly Victorian, but also his whole theory represents – as Marx wrote to Engels in the early 1860s and Nietzsche in *The Gay Science* (1882) had already sarcastically noted – the transference of the experiences of the overcrowded, British industrial lower middle class into the realm of biology. According to this line of reasoning, Darwin's biological theory was able to exert a considerable influence on social thought because it was social in its origin and nature. The historical context of discovery, however, does not enable us to judge the validity of Darwinism or Social Darwinism. It should also be emphasized that as Darwin's evolutionary theory changed in the wake of the so-called Modern Synthesis, the complex relationship between Darwinism and modern social analysis needs to be reconsidered and recontextualized.

Social Darwinism, a polemical label that according to Bannister had been used from the beginning to denounce one's opponent, fell into disrepute after World War II because of its alleged connection to the ideology of National Socialism and Fascism. Reflecting upon the fact that such diverse intellectual and policy movements as the ethological work of people like Lorenz and Morris in the 1960s, Wilson's sociobiology and Dawkins's work on the *Selfish Gene* in the 1970s, Reagonomics and Thatcherite politics in the 1980s, Herrnstein and Murray's *Bell Curve*, and Pinker's evolutionary psychology in the 1990s have all been labeled or stigmatized as Social Darwinist, the ambiguity and ideological multivalence of the term still seem to prevail.

SEE ALSO: *Bell Curve, The* (Herrnstein and Murray); Biosociological Theories; Evolution; Malthus, Thomas Robert; Nature; Spencer, Herbert; Stratification and Inequality, Theories of

REFERENCES AND SUGGESTED READINGS

Bannister, R. C. (1988) *Social Darwinism: Science and Myth in Anglo-American Social Thought.* Temple University Press, Philadelphia.
Bellomy, D. C. (1984) "Social Darwinism" Revisited. *Perspectives in American History* N.S. 1: 1–129.
Clark, L. L. (1981) Social Darwinism in France. *Journal of Modern History* 53(1) (On Demand Supplement): D1025–44.
Crook, P. (1996) Social Darwinism: The Concept. *History of European Ideas* 22(4): 261–74.
Dickens, P. (2000) *Social Darwinism: Linking Evolutionary Thought to Social Theory.* Open University Press, Buckingham.
Hawkins, M. (1998) *Social Darwinism in European and American Thought, 1860–1945: Nature as Model and Nature as Threat.* Cambridge University Press, Cambridge.
Hodgson, G. M. (2004) Social Darwinism in Anglophone Academic Journals: A Contribution to the History of the Term. *Journal of Historical Sociology* 17(4): 428–63.
Hofstadter, R. (1992 [1944]) *Social Darwinism in American Thought.* Beacon Press, Boston.
Jones, G. (1980) *Social Darwinism and English Thought: The Interaction Between Biological and Social Theory.* Harvester Press, Brighton.
Peel, J. D. Y. (1971) *Herbert Spencer: The Evolution of a Sociologist.* Basic Books, New York.
Stocking, G. W., Jr. (1982 [1962]) Lamarckianism in American Social Science: 1890–1915. In: *Race, Culture, and Evolution: Essays in the History of Anthropology.* University of Chicago Press, Chicago, pp. 234–69.
Weikart, R. (1993) The origins of Social Darwinism in Germany: 1859–1895. *Journal of the History of Ideas* 54(3): 469–88.
Wilson, R. J. (Ed.) (1967) *Darwinism and the American Intellectual: A Book of Readings.* Dorsey Press, Homewood, IL.

social dilemmas

Jane Sell

A social dilemma is any setting in which there is a conflict between individual short-term incentives and overall group incentives. Social dilemmas are pervasive and appear in all levels of interaction, from small face-to-face interactions to large-scale global situations. The study of social dilemmas is prominent in all of the social sciences, and investigations have involved all types of methods ranging from case studies to experiments. Common examples of social dilemmas include the provision of public goods such as public education and international treaties and the maintenance of resources such as fisheries and other ecosystems.

There are many categorizations of social dilemmas. An important distinction is between a two-person (or actor) dilemma and multiperson dilemmas, termed N-person dilemmas. Other distinctions relate to the timing and structure of the incentives, and the relationship between cooperation (and the reverse of cooperation, defection) and group gains.

Two statements often used to frame the issues surrounding social dilemmas are Mancur Olson's *The Logic of Collective Action* (1965) and Garret Hardin's "The Tragedy of the Commons" (1968). Olson's book concerns public goods while Hardin's article addresses common property resources. Because both types of problems have an incentive structure that pits individual against group interest, they are considered social dilemmas; however, there are social psychological differences between the public good problem, which involves "giving up" individual resources for the group good, and the resource good problem of establishing individual restraint from using the resource.

Social dilemmas are often discussed in contradistinction to market settings. In market settings, exchanges occur because there are different preferences (revealed by the actor's behavior by observing what she gives up to consume the good). In perfectly competitive systems, the law of demand (ceteris paribus, the lower the price, the higher the demand) and the law of supply (ceteris paribus, the higher the price, the greater the supply) interact to yield an equilibrium. In this equilibrium, a profit-maximizing firm will produce the output for which price is equal to the marginal cost.

However, such market mechanisms are not present in social dilemmas. The basic reason they do not exist is that most social dilemmas are characterized by non-excludability: no member of the group can be excluded from consuming the good. Regardless of whether an individual actor has contributed, he or she is able to use the good. So, for example, regardless of whether individuals have helped a civil rights movement, they accrue benefits from the movement's gain. Or regardless of whether a nation practices sustainable development, it benefits from other nations' adherence to sustainable practices. It is not a market phenomenon that enables the exclusion of those who have not contributed.

From the perspective of game theory, a rational choice heuristic often employed in economics, social dilemmas and the basic principle of non-excludability create a particular dominant strategy. A dominant strategy is a strategy that is the best rational, individual strategy no matter what choices other actors make. So in most social dilemmas, the dominant strategy is to consume, but not contribute. In other words, it is individually rational to "free-ride" on others' contributions or sacrifices. However, if all actors are engaging in the same calculations, nobody will contribute and the good or resource will not survive. The civil rights movement will fail; sustainability will never be reached.

Given the incentive problems that are defining properties of social dilemmas, when are cooperation and solution of social dilemmas possible? We know that social dilemmas are sometimes solved. Examples include extraordinarily successful instances of the Zanjeras irrigation communities in the Philippines (first documented in 1630), cited by Ostrom (1990). On the other hand, there are many social dilemmas that have not been solved and have led to disastrous consequences. Examples include cases of genocide, and destruction of fragile ecosystems such as the Tigris–Euphrates alluvial salt marsh.

SOLUTIONS

What conditions are most likely to lead to solution of social dilemmas? Game theorists have concentrated on formal solutions that invoke mathematics involved in expected utility arguments. One very important formulation has been the folk theorem. The folk theorem (so called because it was a generally understood idea) posits a whole range of history-contingent strategies that allow for cooperation if, at some point, it is the case that an actor's cost of contributing exceeds the cost of contribution and the discount rate is sufficiently large such that contributing remains an individually rational strategy. From this point of view, social dilemmas can be solved rationally, although it is difficult to predict exactly how. That is, the folk theorem does not rule out many possibilities.

Many solutions to social dilemmas involve changing the basic structure of the dilemma and thereby affecting incentives. Such solutions include factors such as punishment mechanisms for not cooperating (one class of which includes "trigger strategies"), and incentives for cooperating.

Individual-level factors such as social motivation have been investigated and it has been demonstrated that some people, and indeed some cultures, appear more or less oriented toward cooperation (see Kopelman et al. 2002).

Other solutions to social dilemmas have focused on "social" factors, that is, factors affected by group interaction. Some of these solutions add additional costs or benefits that are social. So, for example, punishments might include the "loss of face" or shame for not cooperating. Incentives might include the acquisition of a positive reputation or honor that is bestowed upon the family. Two very powerful such factors are social identity and trust. Social identity is the sense of "we-ness" that accompanies shared significant social categories that indicate some extent of common fate. Trust is a more diffuse property, which may or may not relate to social identity, but does entail a sense of predictability of others' actions. If an actor trusts others to cooperate, and so acts on that basis, the original incentives of the social dilemma can be transformed and the dilemma solved.

Finally, there is the recognition that even if all the incentive problems associated with social dilemmas are solved, issues related to coordination remain. Clearly, coordination problems can sabotage the successful resolution of a dilemma. Ostrom (1990, 1998) details an interest in coordination by her attention to the "nested" nature of organizations or stakeholders. Communication lines among different levels of government must be clear and open. Local autonomy enables the tailoring of principles to the particular circumstances.

With such a tremendous range of interest in social dilemmas, it would seem that research accumulation would be apparent. But, it is an irony that literature on cooperation sometimes lacks cooperation. This is not a matter of obstinacy, but relates to issues of different assumptions, methods, and theories. For example, rich case study analyses are not often integrated into the formal, deductive analyses of game theory. A particularly promising suggestion for integration is the emphasis upon institutional rules and how such rules change the structure of the dilemmas and the strategies for their solution. These rules are most often used in political science, but they offer a framework by which to both conceptualize issues in a formal, mathematical sense and organize vast arrays of rich, in-depth data.

SEE ALSO: Collective Action; Ecological Problems; Game Theory; Rational Choice Theories; Social Identity Theory

REFERENCES AND SUGGESTED READINGS

Hardin, G. (1968) The Tragedy of the Commons. *Science* 162: 1243–8.

Kollock, P. (1998) Social Dilemmas: The Anatomy of Cooperation. *Annual Review of Sociology* 24: 183–214.

Kopelman, S., Weber, J. M., & Messick, D. M. (2002) Factors Influencing Cooperation in Common Dilemmas: A Review of Experimental Psychological Research. In: Ostrom, E., Dietz, T., Dolšak, N., Stern, P. C., Stonich, S., & Weber, E. U. (Eds.), *The Drama of the Commons*. National Academy Press, Washington, DC.

Olson, M. (1965) *The Logic of Collective Action: Public Goods and the Theory of Groups*. Harvard University Press, Cambridge, MA.

Ostrom, E. (1990) *Governing the Commons: The Evolution of Institutions for Collective Action*. Cambridge University Press, Cambridge.

Ostrom, E. (1998) A Behavioral Approach to the Rational Choice Theory of Collective Action. *American Political Science Review* 92: 1–22.

Sell, J. (1988) Types of Public Goods and Free-Riding. In: Lawler, E. J. & Markovsky, B. (Eds.), *Advances in Group Processes*, Vol 5. JAI Press, San Diego, pp. 119–40.

Sell, J., Chen, Z., Hunter-Homes, P., & Johansson, A. (2002) A Cross-Cultural Comparison of Public

Good and Resource Good Settings. *Social Psychology Quarterly* 65: 285–97.

Yamagishi, T. (1995) Social Dilemmas. In: Cook, K., Fine, G. A., & House, J. S. (Eds.), *Sociological Perspectives on Social Psychology*. Allyn & Bacon, Boston, pp. 311–35.

social disorganization theory

Barbara D. Warner

Social disorganization theory provides an explanation of the variation in crime rates among neighborhoods. It assumes that the basis of criminal behavior lies largely within the structural and cultural conditions of the neighborhood. Socially disorganized neighborhoods are defined as those not having the capacity to regulate behaviors and activities that are inconsistent with neighborhood values. This capacity to regulate behaviors is referred to as the level of social control. Recent social disorganization theory has particularly emphasized neighborhood levels of informal social control.

Social disorganization theory was originally developed by Clifford Shaw and Henry McKay in their book *Juvenile Delinquency and Urban Areas* (1942, revised 1969). In studying the distribution of delinquency among different areas of Chicago in the early 1900s, Shaw and McKay noticed several patterns. First, delinquency rates decreased as one moved from the center of the city outward. Second, a large proportion of "neighborhoods" (square mile areas) that had high rates of delinquency in 1900 continued to have high rates 30 years later. This was particularly remarkable because many of those neighborhoods had undergone tremendous ethnic change during that time period. Further, they found that neighborhoods with high levels of delinquency also had high levels of other problems such as adult crime, truancy, tuberculosis, and infant mortality.

Their approach to understanding variations in crime rates among neighborhoods was based on an ecological model that argued that distinctive features emerged in areas as a result of ecological differentiation arising from the growth of the city. As an end product of the process of city growth, areas within the city become differentiated in terms of physical, social, economic, and cultural conditions. Their research examined these characteristics in relation to rates of delinquency. The characteristics they found to be related to rates of delinquency were physical status (population increase or decrease), economic status (percentage of families on relief, median rental, home ownership), and population composition (percentage of foreign-born and African American families). Specifically, areas with decreasing population, low economic status, and higher percentages of foreign-born and African Americans were associated with higher rates of delinquency.

In explaining these relationships Shaw and McKay argued that low economic status, high levels of ethnic heterogeneity, and decreasing population led to a breakdown in the community's ability to articulate and reach shared goals. In turn, this led to weakened institutions (e.g., schools, family, and church) and therefore weakened informal social control. The inability of the community to informally control criminal behavior allowed for the development of a criminal subculture which, through cultural transmission or differential association, then led to increased rates of crime. To address these issues, Shaw and McKay argued for creating neighborhood programs carried out by local residents that would strengthen and unify the constructive aspects of community life.

From the 1940s through the 1960s there were several empirical tests of social disorganization theory that were, at least in part, supportive of the theory. However, there was also a growing recognition of problems in empirically testing social disorganization theory. These problems included the fact that studies examining social disorganization theory used official measures of crime (such as court records or arrest rates), and official measures of crime were argued to be biased in a way that would be consistent with the theory. For example, police may be more likely to make arrests in poor or ethnically diverse neighborhoods than they would in middle-class or all-white neighborhoods, leading to the appearance of higher rates of crime in the poorer or ethnically diverse neighborhoods. Hence, arrest rates were argued to be more likely to be reflective of police behavior than actual levels of crime. Second, it became increasingly clear that the main theoretical concept, social disorganization, was not measured separately from crime rates. Therefore, the main concept in the theory was not really being examined. Empirical tests only measured the extent to which measures of poverty, ethnic diversity, and residential mobility were related to crime, not whether the process or mechanism through which these factors were related was social disorganization.

Not until the 1980s was there systematic progress in addressing these issues. Arguably the most important study in the revitalization of social disorganization theory at the end of the twentieth century was one done by Sampson and Groves (1989). Previous to this study the intervening process of social disorganization that is hypothesized to link the community characteristics of poverty, residential mobility, and racial/ethnic heterogeneity to crime rates had not been empirically examined with a sufficiently large sample of neighborhoods to allow for reliable aggregate level multivariate analysis. Using data from the British crime survey, Sampson and Groves conceptualize social disorganization as the inability to bring about informal social control due to weak informal (kinship and friendship networks) and formal (organizational) associational ties. In this study they examine measures of social disorganization distinct from crime measures and use an unofficial measure of crime rates – specifically, victimization rates. The results of this study showed that low levels of both friendship networks and organizational participation, as well as the inability to supervise youth peer groups, were significantly related to rates of crime. Further, these intervening measures of social disorganization mediated much of the effect of the community structural characteristics (socioeconomic status, residential mobility, ethnic heterogeneity, and family disruption) on crime rates. This focus on friendship networks and associational ties as the basis for informal social control became known as the systemic model of social disorganization theory.

Since this time the concept of social disorganization has continued to be a fertile area of research, focusing on the differential capacity of communities to carry out informal social control, the different mechanisms of informal social control, and the different neighborhood structures that make informal social control possible. Some researchers have examined the structure and nature of friendship networks within neighborhoods as a necessary foundation for informal social control. Others have focused directly on levels of informal social control as defined by neighbors' willingness to intervene in inappropriate neighborhood behavior, or neighbors' levels of surveillance and guardianship within the neighborhood. Still other research has examined the impact of the absence of institutional resources, such as recreational facilities, or the presence of negative institutions, such as drinking establishments, on the ability of neighborhoods to exercise social control. More recently, Sampson et al. (1997) have developed a broader concept that combines the level of mutual trust among neighbors and their willingness to intervene as the mechanism necessary to bring about lower crime rates. They refer to this as collective efficacy.

While research within the systemic model has mainly focused on ties *within* the neighborhood, other researchers have addressed ties to external groups or institutions. The systemic perspective on neighborhoods views neighborhood structure as being comprised of private, parochial, and public ties. Private ties refer to intimate or kinship relationships. Parochial ties refer to friendship ties that are less intimate than private ties. These may be neighbors who participate in local organizations together or who occasionally discuss neighborhood or other issues. Both private and parochial ties refer to networks within the neighborhood. Ties within neighborhoods are viewed as essential for transmitting both expectations regarding appropriate behavior and informal sanctions when norms are violated. Public ties refer to linkages to persons, groups, or organizations, such as the police or other municipal organizations, external to the neighborhood, that can be activated to secure resources or services that affect the community's regulatory capacity. Public ties have been viewed as important mechanisms for neighborhoods to use to influence political decisions that may negatively impact on the community. For example, disadvantaged neighborhoods may be chosen for the placement of a variety of programs, such as drug treatment programs, needle exchanges, community correction facilities, or new public housing projects that may be viewed as having the potential to further destabilize the community. To the extent that neighborhoods are able to cultivate ties with public and private agencies or groups outside of their neighborhood, they may be better able to ward off decisions such as these, as well as acquire resources to remove abandoned or condemned buildings, clean up litter-strewn recreational areas, and remove prostitution hot spots or drug dealers. A study by Velez in *Criminology* (2001) finds public ties to decrease victimization, and further, that this relationship is most pronounced in disadvantaged neighborhoods.

Most of the current research examining social disorganization theory has focused on the structural aspects of social disorganization discussed above, and little attention has been paid to the cultural issues. However, with a growing number of ethnographic studies pointing to characteristics of oppositional or "street" culture in high-crime inner-city neighborhoods (e.g., Anderson 1999), more attention is turning to the potential role of neighborhood culture in a social disorganization model. In Shaw and McKay's original social disorganization model, culture had a prominent role. Shaw and McKay recognized the role of culture in terms of the variability among neighborhoods in the presence of delinquency values. Neighborhoods in which delinquent values were present provided conflicting value systems for youth and were viewed as an important motivation for criminal behavior. However, Kornhauser (1978) argued convincingly that such a cultural deviance model was inconsistent with the overall assumptions of a social control model of social disorganization theory. Nonetheless, Kornhauser did suggest that while the content of values did not vary across neighborhoods, the *strength* of those values within communities did vary. She referred to this as the attenuation of cultural values. This idea of attenuated culture has recently been examined by Warner (2003). Findings from this study suggest that neighborhood social ties increase cultural strength and cultural strength increases informal social control.

The availability of statistical packages that allow researchers to analyze multilevel and causal models has further enhanced the development of social disorganization theory. Because social disorganization theory argues that the roots of crime are within the neighborhood context itself and not simply the result of the types of individuals that comprise the neighborhood, multilevel models allowing for the examination of both aggregate and individual-level effects have become important tools in contemporary examinations of social disorganization theory. Similarly, because there are several posited processes through which community characteristics such as poverty, residential mobility, and ethnic heterogeneity affect crime rates, explicitly modeling the causal process, using structural equation models, has become important.

Community level studies of crime based in social disorganization theory are continuing to produce new insight into the causes and solutions to both property and violent crime. One of the biggest puzzles remaining from a social disorganization perspective is why neighborhood poverty or disadvantage continues to directly influence crime rates. While some of the effect of disadvantage is mediated by measures of social disorganization, most research also finds that a significant direct effect of disadvantage on crime remains. This finding suggests that there may be other neighborhood processes influencing crime rates that are not yet completely understood or effectively measured.

SEE ALSO: Collective Efficacy and Crime; Crime, Broken Windows Theory of; Crime, Hot Spots; Juvenile Delinquency; Social Control; Subcultures, Deviant; Urban Ecology

REFERENCES AND SUGGESTED READINGS

Anderson, E. (1999) *Code of the Street*. W. W. Norton, New York.

Bursik, R. J., Jr. (1988) Social Disorganization and Theories of Crime and Delinquency: Problems and Prospects. *Criminology* 26: 519–51.

Bursik, R. J., Jr. & Grasmick, H. G. (1993) *Neighborhoods and Crime: The Dimensions of Effective Community Control*. Lexington Books, New York.

Kornhauser, R. R. (1978) *Social Sources of Delinquency*. University of Chicago Press, Chicago.

Sampson, R. J. & Groves, W. B. (1989) Community Structure and Crime: Testing Social Disorganization Theory. *American Journal of Sociology* 94: 774–802.

Sampson, R. J., Raudenbush, S. W., & Earls, F. (1997) Neighborhoods and Violent Crime: A Multilevel Study of Collective Efficacy. *Science* 277: 918–24.

Warner, B. D. (2003) The Role of Attenuated Culture in Social Disorganization Theory. *Criminology* 41: 73–97.

social distance

Joyce E. Williams

Use of the concept of social distance dates back to Georg Simmel's discussion of the stranger in his *Soziologie* (1923). According to Simmel, the stranger represents the union of newness and remoteness as he moves out of one social circle and strives for acceptance in another. Robert Park (1924) popularized the concept of social distance as the grades and degrees of understanding and intimacy that characterize personal and social relations. Social distance is based on social norms that differentiate individuals and groups on the basis of race/ethnicity, age, sex, social class, religion, and nationality. The greater the social distance between individuals and groups, the less they influence each other.

It was Emory Bogardus (1925) who operationalized and measured social distance by first asking over 200 participants their willingness to admit members of 39 different racial and ethnic groups to the following: close kinship by marriage, as fellow club members, as neighbors, as workers in their same occupation, to citizenship in their country, as visitors only to their country, and as persons to be excluded from their country. The Bogardus Social Distance Scale is largely synonymous with the concept today. The scale is unidimensional and cumulative, assuming that at the highest level of acceptance the respondent would admit members of the designated group to all steps below that level. Although social scientists have applied variations of the social distance scale to social classes, and religious, occupational, and other groups for over three-quarters of a century, it has proved a reliable measure of the level of acceptance of one racial/ethnic group by another (Schaefer 2004). There is, however, some question as to whether it measures group status or social intimacy.

According to Bogardus, social nearness originates in favorable experiences and farness in unfavorable experiences. There is, of course, circularity in this logic: acceptance of members of another group is likely because of favorable experiences that are more likely to originate in social nearness as opposed to social farness. The concept of social distance subsumes individual characteristics in the characteristics of their group. Social nearness or farness originates with either a lack of knowledge, resulting in prejudice, about the group in question, or with knowledge that the group differs from your own in some identifiable way, such as appearance, beliefs, or behaviors. Both ignorance of a group or knowledge of their differences holds the potential for social conflict. Poole (1927) was the first to distinguish between social distance and personal distance, thereby offering an explanation of how individuals become "exceptions" to their groups. Social distance is dictated by social norms. Personal distance as in acquaintances, friendships, and love, on the other hand, is limited only by the possibilities of association between individuals or individuals and groups. While social or personal distance may not explain conflict, both can account for misunderstandings and ignorance that give rise to interpersonal and intergroup conflicts as well as social problems.

SEE ALSO: Groups; Prejudice; Race; Race and Ethnic Consciousness; Race (Racism); Simmel, Georg; Stranger, The

REFERENCES AND SUGGESTED READINGS

Bogardus, E. S. (1925) Measuring Social Distance. *Journal of Applied Sociology* 9: 299–308.

Ehrlich, H. J. (1973) *The Social Psychology of Prejudice*. John Wiley, New York.

Park, R. E. (1924) The Concept of Social Distance. *Journal of Applied Sociology* 8: 339–44.

Poole, W. C. (1927) Social Distance and Personal Distance. *Journal of Applied Sociology* 11: 114–20.

Schaefer, R. T. (2004) *Racial and Ethnic Groups.* Prentice-Hall, Upper Saddle River, NJ.
Simmel, G. (1923) *Soziologie.* Dunker und Humboldt, Munich.

social embeddedness of economic action

Enzo Mingione and Simone Ghezzi

The concept of embeddedness expresses the notion that social actors exist within relational, institutional, and cultural contexts and cannot be seen as atomized decision-makers maximizing their own utilities. Embeddedness approaches prioritize the different conditions within which social action takes place. They challenge the utilitarian, "undersocialized," neoclassical position, and the functional "oversocialized" position (where social conditions exist a priori to behaviors). The concept of embeddedness is based on several assumptions about society: the actor is not an atomized individual; immediate utility cannot explain the full meaning of social relations; logics underlying the formation of institutions and their norms of behavior cannot be removed from the contexts of social interaction within which these institutions exist; convergent trends of transformation result in diverse processes of adaptation, which evolve from specific social, cultural, and cognitive configurations.

These assumptions are present in Weberian approaches (methodological individualism) and become criteria for the ideal type reconstruction of the meaning of individual action. They are also present in structural approaches concerned with the dynamics of logics governing social behavior.

The concept of embeddedness that followed from the work of Polanyi (1944, 1957) was revisited by Mark Granovetter (1985) and has ever since been at the center of the theoretical and methodological debates within the so-called "new economic sociology" (Swedberg 1997, 2003). At the core of this approach a number of important contributions illustrate the importance of social networks, social capital, the

diversity of cultural and cognitive elements, and the social construction of markets (Burt 1992; Nee & Ingram 1998; Zelizer 1988, 1994).

DURKHEIM'S CONTRIBUTION: SOCIAL TIES, INSTITUTIONS, SOCIALIZATION

Even though it was Polanyi who introduced the term embeddedness, tools for analyzing the contextual diversity of social action were already present in classic works, especially those of Durkheim and Weber. The former theorizes the relevance of social ties and socialization processes; the latter brings into relief the tensions characterizing the processes of rationalization. Both conceive of the actor not as a utilitarian and atomized *homo oeconomicus*, but as a subject inserted in diversified networks and institutional contexts, the very subject matter of sociological analysis.

For Durkheim, the advent of modern industrial society is accompanied by a profound transformation in the ties that characterize social life. The increasing and more complex division of labor, industrialization, and urbanization progressively weakens ties of mechanical solidarity that regulate cooperation in the small and stable communities typical of the pre-industrial era. Durkheim opposes the idea that ties in modern society are the inevitable outcome of fragmented and diversified self-interests. The mechanical interplay of interests leads to conflict and anomie, to the breakup of society, and to the loss of opportunities for cooperation. Organic solidarity is therefore a relation of cooperation socially built upon an institutional process regulated by norms and rules within which the modern nation–state and labor organizations play a key role. This perspective may lead to an oversocialized position, but at the same time it may provide insights into the way in which social ties generate the institutional regulation of behaviors characteristic of different situations of embeddedness. Durkheim's contribution, to view socialization processes as a matrix of the different conditions of embeddedness, stems from this latter direction. Rules regulating social interaction are transmitted through learning, which takes place in situations of persistent diversity and ongoing change. Such situations determine not only new economic and technological opportunities, and consequently new regulative necessities, but also allow for different levels of individual freedom to next-generation cohorts.

MAX WEBER: PROCESS OF RATIONALIZATION AS A MATRIX OF DIVERSITY

To Weber, the interpretation of modern society relies on two linchpins: the notion of methodological individualism based on the motives of individual action; and the idea that modernity is characterized by complex processes of rationalization, which points to the increasing importance of rational action. Weber does not assume that social action is performed by atomized individuals maximizing utility, but rather by persons influenced by their social networks, specific habits and traditions, by shared values and culture. The diversity of social contexts produces substantial variations in "the interest of the actors as themselves are aware of them" (Weber 1978: 30). It is from this concern with diversity that Weber's contribution to the notion of embeddedness can be drawn.

Weber singled out two different forms of social interaction affecting social behavior in different ways: one form comes into being when two or more actors are related by a shared sense of membership in a delimited social group (the community); the second arises when actors share common interests (the association). Rationalization does not entail the extinction of community ties (*Vergemeinschaftung*), but it sets off an ongoing transformation of these same ties which inevitably cause tensions with associative relations (*Vergesellschaftung*). In particular, the pervasiveness of instrumental rationality is at odds with traditional habits. Change, therefore, does not lead to a uniform process of utilitarian individualism, but is the effect of variable forms of adaptation. Such forms constitute the main basis upon which the notion of embeddedness can be closely examined.

Weber's second major contribution regards the tensions present within rationalization processes, particularly between formal rationality and substantive rationality. The former pertains to market exchange and immediate utility, the latter may be seen as the foundation of redistributive logics. While rational behavior emerges from the tense interplay of these two forms of rationality, values determine the need for institutional regulation, the priority of the public good over the individual's immediate benefit.

"Formal and substantive rationality, no matter by what standard the latter is measured, are always in principle separate things, no matter that in many (and under certain very artificial assumptions even in all) cases they may coincide empirically" (Weber 1978: 108). Here, Weber indicates an important tool to empirically analyze the diversity present in the processes of social construction of regulative institutions.

The Protestant Ethic and the Spirit of Capitalism may be read as a pioneering work on sociocultural embeddedness. Weber notes how typical capitalist behavior – profit-orientation and emphasis on the importance of professional *beruf* (calling) – can only develop and extend in favorable cultural contexts fashioned by the Protestant ethic. Therefore, he reaffirms the idea that *homo oeconomicus* is not an atomized individual removed from his or her own cultural context, but rather that different sociocultural configurations (familial, ethnic, local, and religious conditions in which any individual is socialized) keep a decisive influence in orienting his or her social behavior.

POLANYI: PROCESS OF DISEMBEDDEDNESS AND REEMBEDDEDNESS

Polanyi argues that the diffusion of market-based relations is a socially disruptive process. The notion of embeddedness may thus be used to understand the logics underlying the formation and transformation of social institutions in contexts of market exchange. In market relations immediate self-interest prevails over other relationships, causing diversified processes of disembeddedness – as economic relations bring about social disruption – and concomitant processes of reembeddedness (i.e., new forms of regulation).

Polyani's historical approach in *The Great Transformation* (1944) denounces the disruptive effects of *laissez-faire* and emphasizes how serious tensions run through modern society.

Countermeasures (i.e., new regulative institutions) are established to keep at bay the negative impact of the diffusion of market relations. In particular, needs for new regulative principles occur in relation to the fictitious commodities – labor, land, and money –which are organized in self-regulating markets. For this very reason they are incompatible with social life and yet "essential to a market economy" (p. 73). It follows that capitalist societies, built upon commodification processes, are characterized by a double movement of disembeddedness and reembeddedness (the necessity to produce new social regulation in the markets of fictitious commodities). *The Great Transformation* does not contain a theoretical/methodological model to carry out sociological analysis on the various manifestations of embeddedness. Polanyi (1957), however, does outline a procedure employing the conceptual tools of anthropology, which is subsequently used to develop a sociological theory of embeddedness.

Polanyi identifies three types of exchange relations: reciprocity, redistribution, and market exchange. Reciprocal and redistributive exchanges are meaningful only in so much as they are conceived of as part of the social order. They express two diverse logics of social organization comprised of specific meanings and contents in different cultural and historical settings. The logic of reciprocity is built upon the collective interests of small groups with strong and close ties, defined as community relationships in sociological terms. In this form of exchange, rules favoring the reproduction of the social group prevail over the immediate self-interest of the individual. By contrast, the logic of redistribution stems from membership in a wider community and its internal power relations. In this setting of stable, hierarchically organized, and politically legitimated social relations resources are extracted from some individuals to benefit others.

At an abstract level market exchange is not compatible with society – the efficiency of competitive behavior occurs among atomized actors who are not enmeshed in social relations – and therefore appears to be guided by a universal logic devoid of social substance. Reciprocity and redistribution are viewed as embedded, while the market is disembedded. The problem of embeddedness in modern society is to explain

how it is possible to reconcile a growing number of market-based interactions with social order. If at the abstract level it is possible to hypothesize an interactive phenomenon which exists outside of any form of social organization, in reality systematic market exchanges cannot take place outside a favorable social context.

According to Polanyi the three different logics of exchange – present always in different combinations – provide society with needed institutions, and therefore with the various configurations of embeddedness. The disembeddedness resulting from increasing individualism constitutes the driving force in ongoing transformations affecting all social institutions: those founded on reciprocity (i.e., household, kinship), those based on redistributive principles (such as the expansion of welfare programs), and those which make the markets of fictitious commodities more compatible with society. The outcomes of this process vary according to the dynamic interaction at work in different historical, cultural, and cognitive contexts.

The notion of tensions singled out by Weber and Polanyi makes it more difficult to implement interpretive parameters, yet sociology should not retreat from such a challenge. The construction of institutions governing modern societies is understood as a contextual double movement – much more difficult to construe in terms of utility and immediate functionality. The disruption of sociality caused by growing individualism and the concomitant reconstruction of social ties to limit individualism itself explains the chronically unstable equilibrium of modern society.

SOCIAL CONSTRUCTION OF DIFFERENCES: INNOVATION AND PATH DEPENDENCY

The approaches based on embeddedness show how it is possible to interpret market-based societies without employing the reductive and asocial parameter of utilitarianism. It is true that utilitarian logics provide the easiest access to the atomized dimension of the individual, but these are socially meaningless because utilitarian behavior cannot occur without the concurrent presence of institutions, norms, and culture in society. Polanyi's critique of the self-regulating market, and Weber's idea of permanent tensions between formal rationality and tradition, and between formal and substantive rationality, stress this precisely.

In conclusion, an example regarding labor regulation serves to clarify embeddedness approaches. The market sets wages based on the competitive relation between the supply of the workforce and the demand of the employers within a logic of labor productivity. However, linking wages to productivity presents insurmountable difficulties when considering workers' social life. Their needs change because their life cycle and material condition change as well. For example, a working couple with small children inevitably goes through a concomitant decrease in productivity and an increase in social needs. Resorting to market self-regulation is not an effective solution: if the employer were to provide parental leave as well as a wage increase to the new parents, the company's competitiveness would be compromised and its future threatened. As a response to this problem, changes have occurred within the household through the devising of new strategies of adaptation; in addition, new forms of social protection have been introduced, such as the state regulation of parental leaves and childcare services.

The market, constrained by its own logic of competitiveness, cannot solve the labor disputes that are generated within it. Such disputes are being dealt with by the arrangement of adapting mechanisms, based on cooperative logics among which we may single out reciprocity (the family) and redistribution (the welfare state). The market enters the process of reembeddedness by mobilizing logics that allow for the stability of cooperation (consider the establishment of day-care programs provided by firms).

The process of adaptation changes across societies, even though they undergo similar pressures and economic trends. One of the steps suggested here to highlight the different conditions of embeddedness is path dependency analysis, that is, a historical selective process within which some embedded conditions are transformed into specific configurations of development.

Returning to the previous childcare example – as Esping-Andersen (1990) shows in his analysis of the different worlds of welfare capitalism – along different historical routes some social contexts develop a greater number of universal public services, whereas others give more importance to the private sector, and others more often resort to family care and to social network solidarity. Cultural and social diversity may be a source of social action or its very limitation. Adaptation continues to modify the various starting conditions through paths where choices and opportunities are given neither by individual utility nor by predetermined social institutions.

Path dependency suggests the historicized dimension of social analysis. The translation of such a historical dimension into research procedures is quite complex, yet essential. If the actor is not viewed as an atomized individual, he or she must therefore be located into different social, cultural, and cognitive contexts, which are the outcome of diversified historical processes of chance, innovation, and adaptation.

SEE ALSO: Community and Economy; Durkheim, Émile; Markets; Polanyi, Karl; Rational Choice Theory (and Economic Sociology); Weber, Max

REFERENCES AND SUGGESTED READINGS

Burt, R. (1992) *Structural Holes: The Social Structure of Competition.* Harvard University Press, Cambridge, MA.

Esping-Andersen, G. (1990) *The Three Worlds of Western Capitalism.* Polity Press, Cambridge.

Granovetter, M. (1985) Economic Action and Social Structure: The Problem of Embeddedness. *American Journal of Sociology* 91: 481–510.

Mingione, E. (1991) *Fragmented Societies: A Sociology of Economic Life Beyond the Paradigm of the Market.* Blackwell, Oxford.

Nee, V. & Ingram, P. (1998) Embeddedness and Beyond: Institutions, Exchange, and Social Structure. In: Brinton & Nee, V (Eds.), *The New Institutionalism in Sociology.* Russel Sage Foundation, New York, pp. 19–45.

Polanyi, K. (1944) *The Great Transformation.* Beacon, Boston.

Polanyi, K. (1957) The Economy as Institute Process. In Polanyi, K., Arensberg, & Pearson (Eds.), *Trade and Markets in the Early Empires.* Regnery, Chicago, pp. 243–69.

Swedberg, R. (1997) New Economic Sociology: What Has Been Accomplished, What Is Ahead? *Acta Sociologica* 40: 161–82.

Swedberg, R. (2003) *Principles of Economic Sociology.* Princeton University Press, Princeton.

Weber, M. (1958 [1904–5]) *The Protestant Ethic and the Spirit of Capitalism.* Scribner's New York.

Weber, M. (1978 [1922]) *Economy and Society: An Outline of Interpretive Sociology*, 2 vols. University of California Press Berkeley.

Zelizer, V. (1988) Beyond the Polemics of the Market: Establishing a Theoretical and Empirical Agenda. *Sociological Forum* 4: 614–34.

Zelizer, V. (1994) *The Social Meaning of Money.* Basic Books, New York.

social epidemiology

James House

Social epidemiology lies at the intersection between the traditionally biomedical field of epidemiology, which is concerned with understanding the distribution, spread, and determinants of disease in populations, and the parts of sociology and other social sciences concerned with understanding the role of social factors, forces, and processes in the epidemiology of health and illness of individuals and populations (Syme 2001). As a field, social epidemiology has been largely created over the past half century by the combined efforts of persons trained in sociology and related social sciences to study the nature, etiology, and course of physical and mental health and illness in human populations. In some cases, they ended up more as epidemiologists than sociologists (e.g., Leonard Syme and Saxon Graham). There were also a number of pioneering physician epidemiologists, mostly from England and the British Commonwealth (e.g., John Cassel, Michael Marmot, and Mervyn Susser) who recognized the importance of incorporating psychosocial factors into the epidemiology of human health and illness.

The result has been the development and growth of a major new and vibrant interdisciplinary field and the transformation of scientific and popular understanding of the nature of determinants of physical health and illness. From a hegemonic paradigm that, for about a

century through the 1950s, viewed physical health as largely a function of biomedical factors, physical health and illness are now understood by both scientists and lay persons as equally or more a function of social, psychological, and behavioral factors. Early understanding (e.g,. Freudian) of mental health and illness as being as much or more psychosocial as biomedical in nature, contributed importantly to the development of the social epidemiology of physical health and illness. Mental health epidemiology and treatment, in contrast, have headed in a more biological direction.

The 1950s have been aptly described as the high-water mark of the medical profession's dominance of the health care system and the preeminence of the biomedical paradigm of physical health and illness which had developed out of the great discoveries in bacteriology of the nineteenth century (Mishler 1981). Faith in biomedical science and practice was fueled by a sense of triumph in the development of vaccines, antibiotics, and other prophylactic agents, from antiseptics to pesticides to prevent or treat, and even virtually eradicate, many forms of previously fatal or highly debilitating infectious diseases, capped by the dramatic conquest of polio in the 1950s.

Even then, however, this biomedical dominance was already being challenged by several developments. First, as the prevalence and impact of infectious diseases waned, chronic diseases such as cardiovascular disease and cancer increased to "epidemic" proportions, virtually halting, from the mid-1950s to the early 1970s, the long-term increase in life expectancy in Western Europe and the US that had continued almost unabated since the eighteenth century. In contrast to most infectious diseases, the newly epidemic chronic diseases were produced by the interplay of multiple contingent "risk factors," no one of which was generally either necessary or sufficient to produce disease (House 2002). Initially, these risk factors were biomedical in nature (i.e., blood pressure, cholesterol), but they soon became environmental, behavioral, and psychosocial in nature.

Using methods similar to those used to identify biomedical risk factors, most notably the prospective cohort study, first health behaviors and lifestyles (from smoking to immoderate consumption of food and alcohol to lack of physical activity), then the Type-A or coronary-prone behavior pattern, and then a broad range of psychosocial factors – social relationships and supports, acute (or life event) and chronic stress, and psychological disposition, such as control/mastery/self-efficacy and anger/hostility – were shown to be consequential risk factors for morbidity and mortality from a wide range of causes (House 2002). Just over 40 years ago cigarette smoking was identified, on the basis of prospective epidemiological studies and laboratory research on animals, as a major risk factor for cancers of the lung and other sites, as well as for cardiovascular disease (DHEW 1964). Within 20 more years, Berkman and Breslow's (1983) analyses of the Alameda County Study, which Breslow had initiated in the early 1960s, combined with other research to expand the list of behavioral risk factors for health to include not only smoking, but also low levels of physical activity and immoderate levels of drinking alcoholic beverages and of food consumption/weight. The Alameda County Study also produced the first modern epidemiological evidence that lack of social relationships and support could be as risky as a cause of mortality as cigarette smoking, a finding repeatedly confirmed and generalized over the last two decades (House et al. 1988; Berkman and Glass 2000).

In the seminal decades of the 1960s through the 1980s, the identification by Friedman and Rosenman (1974) of the Type-A behavior pattern and its certification by the National Heart, Lung, and Blood Institute (Review Panel 1981) as a risk factor for coronary artery disease like smoking, high blood pressure, and cholesterol, was of major importance in legitimating social epidemiology in NIH and the broader biomedical arena. Subsequently, dispositional anger and hostility have been identified as the key toxic ingredient of the broader Type-A pattern (Smith 2001), and has joined a number of other psychological dispositions such as self-efficacy/mastery/control, optimism/pessimism, and depressive affect as potential consequential risk factors (House 2002).

Parallel to these developments in psychosocial risk factor epidemiology were two others that reinforced the importance of psychosocial factors, and hence social epidemiology, in understanding patterns of individual and especially population health. McKeown (1976) initiated a field of research showing that even the dramatic reduction in infectious diseases and consequent increases in life expectancy of the mid-eighteenth to early twentieth centuries occurred prior to, and hence could not be due to, the development of the germ theory of disease or its application in preventive vaccination or pharmacologic therapy. Rather, the bulk of the dramatic growth in human population and life expectancy over the period was attributable to broad patterns of economic development and attendant improvements in public health, nutrition, clothing, housing, and sanitation (Bengtsson 2001). Finally, the development of stress and adaptation theory in physiology (e.g., Cannon and Selye), psychology (e.g., Lazarus), and sociology and related social sciences (e.g., Levine and Scotch), along with subsequent developments in psychoneuroimmunology, provided explanations of how psychosocial risk factors got "under the skin" to cause physical illness and even death (House 2002; Taylor et al. 1997).

By the late 1980s, social epidemiology was increasingly well established within and between the biomedical and social sciences, focusing increasingly on uncovering new psychosocial risk factors and showing how interventions could be used to modify these risk factors and hence improve health. But social epidemiology and psychosocial risk factors to health also came increasingly to share in the problems of biomedical and environmental risk factors epidemiology: tendencies to proliferate disparate and scattered risk factors, each with small to modest effects and often a limited or disputable evidentiary base.

Over the last two decades, psychosocial risk factor epidemiology has come to be overshadowed and also positively transformed by a reemergent social epidemiology of socioeconomic and racial/ethnic disparities in health. The Black Report in England startled many in the early 1980s by showing that despite the operation of the National Health Service for a quarter of a century, occupational class difference in mortality and life expectancy had not diminished and had perhaps even increased in England and Wales between the late 1940s and mid-1970s (Black et al. 1982). This finding stimulated similar research and findings and a broader rediscovery of the strength and persistence of socioeconomic and also racial/ethnic disparities in health in the US, UK, and many other developed and developing countries.

These disparities generally outstripped those due to any single or small set of risk factors, reflecting the powerful tendency for the more health-damaging aspects or levels of almost any social, psychological, behavioral, and even biomedical risk factor to be more prevalent among disadvantaged socioeconomic and racial groups, even as the major disease threats to health and risk factors for them varied over historical time and social space. Socioeconomic and racial/ethnic health disparities prior to the mid-twentieth century were largely a product of differential exposure and susceptibility to infectious disease due to poorer nutrition, clothing, housing, sanitation, and other conditions of life and work. But as chronic diseases supplanted infectious diseases as the leading causes of morbidity and mortality by the later twentieth century, socioeconomic and racial/ethnic disparities in health came to be a function of differential experience of and exposure to these diseases and their risk factors. Indeed, over the course of the twentieth century, the increasingly leading cause of death – cardiovascular disease – and the major risk factor for it as well as cancer – cigarette smoking – went from being more prevalent and incident in the advantaged socioeconomic and racial/ethnic groups in the early twentieth century to being more incident and prevalent in less advantaged socioeconomic and racial/ethnic groups by the end of the century. Thus, socioeconomic and racial/ethnic stratification appear to operate as a fundamental cause or determinant of health via their influence on the experience of and exposure to virtually any and all risk factors for health in the past, present, or future (Link & Phelan 1995; House & Williams 2001).

In the first decade of the twenty-first century, understanding and hence alleviating socioeconomic and racial disparities in health has been identified as one of the (arguably *the*) most important goals for public health policy and research, and the most promising avenue for achieving continued improvement in overall population health (DHHS 2000). The most advantaged portions of the human population, both within and across societies, are increasingly approaching the biological limits of life expectancy and health, or what James Fries has termed the "compression" of mortality and morbidity against the biological limits of the human life span. Hence, the greatest opportunities for improving population health lie in bringing the health of the broad lower range of the population in terms of socioeconomic position and race/ethnicity increasingly closer to the biological optimum that the more advantaged are already starting to realize. In the case of the US, reducing socioeconomic and racial/ethnic disparities in health is also the necessary route to reversing the nation's declining relative position in the world in terms of population health indicators such as life expectancy and infant mortality.

Understanding the processes and mechanisms that generate socioeconomic and racial/ethnic health disparities and social and economic policy, as much or more than health policy, will be central to alleviating such disparities. The increased focus on such disparities is also essential to developing a more integrative causal theory of the determinants and consequences of psychosocial risk factors for health. Major challenges at this point, both theoretically and methodologically, are (1) to better understand the causal priorities and interconnections of socioeconomic position (SEP), race/ethnicity, and other major sociodemographic factors such as gender and age, with respect to each other and to health (e.g., how much of the cause flow is from SEP to health or vice versa, or how much of racial/ethnic and differences in health are a function of differences of SEP); (2) to delineate the social, psychological, behavioral, and biomedical processes and pathways linking SEP and race/ethnicity (and also gender and age) to health; and (3) understanding how all these factors and processes are influenced by broader social contexts, forces, and policies. Multilevel, life course, longitudinal studies and methods will be central to all of these goals.

Thus, only a half-century from its inception, social epidemiology has become increasingly central to broader health research and policy. All of this represents in many ways merely a reaffirmation, though on a much firmer conceptual, theoretical, and empirical base, of Rudolf Virchow's mid-nineteenth century insight that "Medicine is a social science, and politics nothing but medicine on a grand scale." Social epidemiological research and theory have come a long way since Virchow, and even from their more modern roots in the mid-twentieth century. They will be essential to twenty-first century efforts toward understanding and improving individual and population health and reducing social disparities in health.

SEE ALSO: Biosociological Theories; Disease, Social Causation; Health and Social Class; Mental Disorder

REFERENCES AND SUGGESTED READINGS

Bengtsson, T. (2001) Mortality: The Great Historical Decline. In: Smelser, N. J. & Baltes, P. B. (Eds.), *International Encyclopedia of the Social and Behavioral Sciences*. Elsevier, New York, pp. 10079–85.

Berkman, L. F. & Breslow, L. (1983) *Health and Ways of Living: The Alameda County Study*. Oxford University Press, Oxford.

Berkman, L. F. & Glass, T. (2000) Social Integration, Social Networks, Social Support, and Health. In: Berkman, L. F. & Kawachi, I. (eds.), *Social Epidemiology*. Oxford University Press, New York, pp. 137–73.

Black, D., Morris, J. N., Smith, C., et al. (1982) *Inequalities in Health: The Black Report*. Penguin, New York.

DHEW (US Department of Health, Education, and Welfare) (1964) *Smoking and Health: Report of the Advisory Committee to the Surgeon General of the Public Health Service*. US Department of Health, Education, and Welfare; Public Health Service; Center for Disease Control. PHS Publication No. 1103.

DHHS (US Department of Health and Human, Services) (2000) *Healthy People 2010*, 2nd edn. With *Understanding and Improving Health and Objectives for Improving Health*, 2 vols. US Government Printing Office, Washington, DC.

Friedman, M. & Rosenman, R. H. (1974) *Type A Behavior and Your Heart*. Knopf, New York.

House, J. S. (2002) Understanding Social Factors and Inequalities in Health: 20th Century Progress and 21st Century Prospects. *Journal of Health and Social Behavior* 23: 125–42.

House, J. S. & Williams, D. R. (2001) Understanding and Reducing Socioeconomic and Racial/Ethnic Disparities in Health. In: Smedley, B. D. & Syme, S. L. (eds.), *Promoting Health: Intervention Strategies from Social and Behavioral Research*.

National Academy Press, Washington, DC, pp. 81–124.

House, J. S., Landis, K., & Umberson, D. (1988) Social Relationships and Health. *Science* 241: 540–5.

Link, B. G. & Phelan, J. C. (1995) Social Conditions as Fundamental Causes of Disease. *Journal of Health and Social Behavior* 35, Extra Issue: 80–94.

McKeown, T. J. (1976) *The Role of Medicine: Dream, Mirage, or Nemesis*. Nuffield Provincial Hospitals Trust, London.

Mishler, E. G. (1981) Critical Perspectives on the Biomedical Model. In: Mishler, E. G., Singham, L. A., Hauser, S. T. et al. (Eds.), *Social Contexts of Health, Illness, and Patient Care*. Cambridge University Press, Cambridge.

Review Panel on Coronary-Prone Behavior and Heart Disease (1981) Coronary-Prone Behavior and Coronary Heart Behavior and Coronary Heart Disease: A Critical Review. *Circulation* 63: 1199–215.

Smith, T. (2001) Coronary-Prone Behavior, Type A. In: Smelser, N. J. & Baltes, P. B. (Eds.), *International Encyclopedia of the Social and Behavioral Sciences*. Elsevier, New York, pp. 2782–8.

Syme, S. L. (2001) Epidemiology, Social. In: Smelser, N. J. & Baltes, P. B. (Eds.), *International Encyclopedia of the Social and Behavioral Sciences*. Elsevier, New York, pp. 4701–6.

Taylor, S. E., Repetti, R. L., & Seeman, T. (1997) Health Psychology: What is an Unhealthy Environment and How Does it Get Under the Skin? *Annual Review of Psychology* 48: 411–47.

social epistemology

Steve Fuller

Social epistemology uses the resources of history and the social sciences to address normative questions surrounding the organization of knowledge processes and products. It seeks to provide guidance on how and what we should know on the basis of how and what we actually know. The subject matter corresponds to what John Dewey called "the conduct of inquiry" and what may appear today as an abstract form of science policy. Social epistemology advances beyond other theories of knowledge by taking seriously that knowledge is produced by agents who are not merely individually embodied but also collectively embedded in certain specifiable relationships that extend over large chunks of space and time.

The need for social epistemology is captured by an interdisciplinary gap between philosophy and sociology: philosophical theories of knowledge have tended to stress normative approaches without considering their empirical realizability or political consequences. Sociological theories suffer the reverse problem of capturing the empirical and ideological character of knowledge, but typically without offering guidance on how knowledge policy should be conducted; hence the debilitating sense of "relativism" traditionally associated with the sociology of knowledge. Social epistemology aims to consolidate the strengths and eliminate the weaknesses of these two approaches.

The phrase "social epistemology" was coined in the 1960s by the US library scientist Jesse Shera to name a field concerned with the "architecture of knowledge" in both its theoretical and practical senses, ranging from the organization of the sciences to the design of libraries and information retrieval systems. By the 1970s, in response to academia's complicity in the emergence of the "military-industrial complex," social epistemology was traveling under the banner of "critical science" (Ravetz 1971).

However, 1987 marks the introduction of the phrase into philosophy, as the title of a special issue of the revamped logical positivist journal *Synthese*, and the start of the first journal in the field, founded by Steve Fuller. That Anglo-American analytic philosophy – rather than a continental European school – formally introduced "social epistemology" is telling. Accounts of knowledge in the European traditions already presupposed a social dimension, which would have made "social epistemology" superfluous. From the nineteenth century onward, epistemologies descended from French positivism and German idealism have consistently stressed the systematic and collective character of knowledge. In contrast, Anglo-American philosophy has remained wedded to the individual – be it Cartesian or Darwinian – as the paradigm case of the knower. In this context, "social epistemology" is explicitly designed to redress the balance.

Social epistemologies may be compared in terms of the presumptive answers they provide to the following research questions:

- Are the norms of inquiry autonomous from the norms governing the rest of society?
- Is there anything more to a "form of inquiry" than the manner in which inquirers are arranged?
- Do truth and the other normative aims of science remain unchanged as particular forms of inquiry come and go?
- Is there anything more to "the problem of knowledge" than a matter of *whose* actions are licensed on the basis of *which* claims made under *what* circumstances?
- Is the social character of knowledge reducible to the aggregated beliefs of some group of individuals?
- Is social epistemology's purview limited to the identification of mechanisms and institutions that meet conceptually satisfying definitions of knowledge?

Social epistemologists inclined toward positive answers to these questions remain close to the Cartesian starting point of classical epistemology, which focuses on the individual's orientation to the truth. They rely sparingly on historical and social scientific findings, unless these are reasonably seen as part of the individual's stock of common knowledge, which is sometimes dignified as "folk epistemology" (e.g., Kitcher 1993; Goldman 1999). In contrast, social epistemologists inclined toward negative answers are more open to interdisciplinary and empirical approaches, often with the intention of making individuals sufficiently aware of the social context of their knowledge production that they revise their modes of inquiry altogether. An example would be to take to heart science's historic claim to universality by treating greater race, class, and/or gender inclusiveness in the community of inquirers as itself indicative of greater objectivity (Longino 1990; Harding 1991).

As the last example suggests, social epistemology does not deny the desirability of at least some of the classical ideals of epistemology. However, these ideals remain empty words without some clear strategy for overcoming the obstacles that block their successful institutionalization. Nowadays this sociological problem is perhaps most acute with respect to the autonomy of inquiry, given the openness of universities to extramural forces. Here social epistemology, under the influence of analytic philosophy, rightly upholds positivist strictures about the need to operationalize, proceduralize, and standardize key concepts that might otherwise have no clear meaning whatsoever.

SEE ALSO: Epistemology; Feminism and Science, Feminist Epistemology; Knowledge, Sociology of

REFERENCES AND SUGGESTED READINGS

Collins, R. (1998) *The Sociology of Philosophies*. Harvard University Press, Cambridge, MA.
Fuller, S. (1988) *Social Epistemology*. Indiana University Press, Bloomington.
Goldman, A. (1999) *Knowledge in a Social World*. Oxford University Press, Oxford.
Harding, S. (1991) *Whose Science? Whose Knowledge?* Indiana University Press, Bloomington.
Kitcher, P. (1993) *The Advancement of Science*. Oxford University Press, Oxford.
Longino, H. (1990) *Science as Social Knowledge*. Princeton University Press, Princeton.
Ravetz, J. (1971) *Scientific Knowledge and its Social Problems*. Oxford University Press, Oxford.

social exchange theory

Michael J. Lovaglia

Social exchange theory is an influential approach to the study of society, generating much recent research. Rather than a theory that explains precisely the nature of some social phenomenon, social exchange theory is an orienting strategy or perspective that shapes the way exchange researchers develop theories and conduct research (social conflict theory is another example of an orienting strategy). From the perspective of social exchange theory, society can be characterized as an exchange system in which social interaction consists of trade in valued resources. Resources exchanged can include any combination of consumable goods,

money, affection, attention, and perhaps most basically, information.

Early work that established the importance of exchange for developing social structure came from cultural anthropology that investigated patterns of exchange and gift rituals in tribal societies. The prototypical example is Bronislaw Malinowski's 1922 ethnography *Argonauts of the Western Pacific*, which documented a circular pattern of exchange (the Kula ring) among residents of a string of Pacific islands. Patterns of social exchange were proposed to enhance social solidarity and reduce intergroup conflict.

The increasing influence of social exchange theory in the twentieth century parallels the rise of utilitarian microeconomics as an explanatory framework for social development. Both approaches assume that individuals behave in ways they find rewarding. Whereas economics focuses on the exchange of goods for money in markets of equally positioned actors who have no history of previous exchanges, social exchange focuses on exchange more generally in networks of actors who may have quite different social positions and who have the opportunity to exchange with each other repeatedly. Rational choice theory has developed within sociology as a theoretical approach to individual decision-making related to social exchange theory but more heavily influenced by microeconomics.

In seeking to explain the relationships between individuals and groups, social exchange theory sits between sociological and psychological approaches. An emphasis on the relationships between individuals, and ultimately how patterns of those relationships affect outcomes, allows social exchange theory to address more macro-level sociological concerns. In particular, patterns of exchange relations constitute networks; thus social exchange theory has contributed to social network analysis and led to network exchange theory.

George Homans published *Social Behavior: Its Elementary Forms* in 1961, presenting a theory grounded in social exchange that is capable of explaining specific social phenomena and predicting outcomes of social interaction. Homans's theory blended ideas from behaviorist psychology and microeconomics to create foundational assumptions that could be used to generate predictions. Rewards, for example, are assumed to increase behavior while the marginal utility of increasing rewards declines due to satiation. Through the 1990s, Louis Gray, Irving Tallman and their colleagues have continued research on individual decision-making using a behaviorist approach with the development of their cost-equalization model.

Homans's behaviorist approach was criticized for the basic tautology that resulted in his theory: individuals are predicted to behave in ways that result in reward, but what individuals find rewarding is determined by how they behave. Moreover, Homans's espousal of methodological individualism as the proper means of studying society was resisted by many sociologists. He argued that social structure consisted of patterns of individual behavior; thus the study of society could be reduced to the study of individual behavior. Peter Blau's *Exchange and Power in Social Life* (published a few years after Homans's book) advocated the social exchange approach to develop a more macro theory of society.

In 1962, Richard Emerson's power-dependence theory continued to use behaviorist psychological principles of reward and satiation, but added ideas from John Thibaut and Harold Kelley's *The Social Psychology of Groups* about the social advantages conferred by access to alternative individuals capable of supplying valued resources. This new emphasis on exchange *relationships* was the sociological dimension that furthered theoretical progress. Emerson's theory established *power* (to acquire resources) as a central concern of social exchange theory. Power-dependence theory proposed that power differences result from exchange in two ways: (1) through individual decision-making as one actor placing more value on the rewards of an exchange relationship than does another, and (2) through a pattern of social relationships that gives one exchange partner greater access to alternative sources of reward.

In proposing social structure as an important source of power in exchange relationships, Emerson obviated the tautology inherent in using the internal values of individuals to explain their behavior. Instead, researchers could examine aspects of social structure that determine the distribution of resources in an exchange network. Rapid development of sociological theory and research on social exchange followed the 1972 publication of Emerson's article on social exchange in networks. Since then, the development of social exchange theory has been carried out in research programs that coordinate theoretical advance with empirical research supporting its validity.

Karen Cook, Toshio Yamagishi, and their colleagues continued Emerson's research program to investigate patterns of exchange relations in networks that determine the distribution of power among network positions. By systematically analyzing differences in relationships among positions and experimental tests of those analyses, Cook et al. (1983) discovered that more central positions in an exchange network were not necessarily advantaged, but could be either high power or low power depending on their direct and indirect connections to other positions. Their later work established trust in exchange relationships as a major area of research (Yamagishi, Cook, & Watabe 1998).

Markovsky et al. (1988) developed an algorithm to determine the power of positions in exchange networks of any size and shape. Network exchange theory uses graph theory techniques to count relationships as paths leading away from each position to quantify each position's power as a graph-theoretic power index (GPI) number. Later, with John Skvoretz, Michael Lovaglia, and others, network exchange theory continued to develop through a systematic program of theoretical development and experimental research. Two qualitatively different types of power were identified in exchange networks: strong power as quantified by the GPI, and a self-limiting variety of weak power that can be quantified by analyzing probabilities that individual positions will be included in an exchange (Markovsky et al. 1993). In 1995, network exchange theory researchers used the resistance equation from David Willer's elementary theory to transform probabilities of inclusion into exact predictions of the resources that different positions could acquire from exchange.

Beginning in the 1980s, Linda Molm has developed exchange theory to encompass coercion. Her research investigates reciprocal exchange as opposed to the negotiated exchanges often studied by network exchange researchers. In negotiated exchange, two individuals agree to trade one commodity for another. The assumption is that both parties gain from the transaction. No negotiation occurs in reciprocal exchange; instead, one party rewards or punishes another who then has the opportunity to reciprocate. Molm's (1997) statement of the theory and its supporting research proposes that punishment is more likely to be used when power differences are great and when rewards are used unjustly or ineffectively. These and other propositions of the theory are well supported by experimental research.

Edward J. Lawler developed a non-zero sum conception of power that continues to advance social exchange research. He proposed that to study power effectively, it is important to assess the total power of both individuals in an exchange relationship, as well as the relative advantage that one individual has over another. During the 1980s his work with Samuel Bacharach used a social exchange approach to investigate conflict resolution in negotiation and bargaining. Central to this approach is the idea that social exchange can reduce conflict. During the 1990s he developed a theory of relational cohesion. Working with Jeongkoo Yoon, he proposed and validated through experimental research that ongoing exchange relations can increase positive emotional bonds and thus social solidarity between exchange partners, but only to the extent that exchanges were perceived as equal. Large power differences reduced the emotional benefits of exchange relationships.

Research on social exchange continues to flourish. Social theories are influential in the discipline to the extent that they generate important research questions that are then answered through empirical investigation. For example, a longstanding question for social theory involves the intentionality of power use. Does the use of social power require that individual actors intend to use it? Willer and Skvoretz (1997) answered that question when they discovered that a passive actor in an exchange network, one who only accepts the best offer available but who makes no attempt to improve it, is capable of exercising as much power as one who actively seeks to maximize resources at others' expense. That is, the social power produced by the structure of an exchange network is independent of the intentions of those who occupy network positions. Social exchange theory is an influential research area because it continues to raise important questions and generate research capable of answering them.

SEE ALSO: Blau, Peter; Elementary Theory; Emerson, Richard M.; Homans, George; Malinowski, Bronislaw K.; Power-Dependence Theory; Power, Theories of; Rational Choice Theory (and Economic Sociology); Social Network Analysis; Social Networks

REFERENCES AND SUGGESTED READINGS

Cook, K. S., Emerson, R. M., Gillmore, M. R., & Yamagishi, T. (1983) The Distribution of Power in Exchange Networks. *American Journal of Sociology* 89: 275–305.

Emerson, R. M. (1962) Power-Dependence Relations. *American Sociological Review* 27: 31–41.

Emerson, R. M. (1972) Exchange Theory, Part II: Exchange Relations and Networks. In: Berger, J., Zelditch, M., & Anderson, B. (Eds.), *Sociological Theories in Progress*, Vol. 2. Houghton Mifflin, Boston, pp. 58–87.

Lawler, E. J. & Yoon, J. (1993) Power and the Emergence of Commitment Behavior in Negotiated Exchange. *American Sociological Review* 58: 465–81.

Lawler, E. J. & Yoon, J. (1998) Network Structure and Emotion in Exchange Relations. *American Sociological Review* 63: 871–94.

Lovaglia, M. J., Skvoretz, J., Willer, D., & Markovsky, B. (1995) Negotiated Exchange in Social Networks. *Social Forces* 75: 123–55.

Markovsky, B., Willer, D., & Patton, T. (1988) Power Relations in Exchange Networks. *American Sociological Review* 53: 220–36.

Markovsky, B., Skvoretz, J., Willer, D., Lovaglia, M. J., & Erger, J. (1993) The Seeds of Weak Power: An Extension of Network Exchange Theory. *American Sociological Review* 58: 197–209.

Molm, L. D. (1981) The Conversion of Power Imbalance to Power Use. *Social Psychology Quarterly* 16: 153–66.

Molm, L. D. (1997) *Coercive Power in Social Exchange*. Cambridge University Press, Cambridge.

Willer, D. & Skvoretz, J. (1997) Games and Structures. *Rationality and Society* 9: 5–35.

Yamagishi, T., Cook, K. S., & Watabe, M. (1998) Uncertainty, Trust, and Commitment Formation in the United States and Japan. *American Journal of Sociology* 104: 165–94.

social exclusion

Hilary Silver

Social exclusion is a rupturing of the social bond. It is a process of declining participation, access, and solidarity. At the societal level, it reflects inadequate social cohesion or integration. At the individual level, it refers to the incapacity to participate in normatively expected social activities and to build meaningful social relations.

The idea of social exclusion originated in France. It has many affinities with French Republican thought, especially the concepts of solidarity and the social bond. Its sociological pedigree is clearly Durkheimian, as Levitas (2000) has noted. However, the concept is also adumbrated in Georg Simmel's *The Stranger*, Norbert Elias's *The Established and the Outsiders*, *Stigma*, and Howard Becker's *Outsiders*. Social exclusion may also be conceived in terms of Max Weber's concepts of status groups and social closure.

Despite the concept's novelty and ambiguity, definitions of social exclusion abound. They vary by national context and sociological paradigm. Some scholars refer to an inability to exercise the social rights of citizenship, including the right to a decent standard of living. These approaches see social exclusion as synonymous with poverty and deprivation, and thus as an aspect of social stratification. Other approaches, especially in Britain, emphasize the importance of individual choice, for a person cannot be excluded if inclusion is accessible, but undesired. These perspectives emphasize exclusion from opportunities and thus conceive of the concept as one similar to discrimination. However, the original meaning of social exclusion stresses social distance, marginalization, and inadequate integration.

Social exclusion is most frequently defined in contrast to poverty. It is a relational rather than a redistributive idea. Although poverty can lead to social exclusion, as well as the reverse, one can easily imagine rich members of excluded groups. Thus, it is not strictly a question of insufficient material resources. As Touraine (1991) put it, exclusion is an issue of being in or out, rather than up or down. Because exclusion is about broken relationships, there are always two parties to consider: the excluders as well as the excluded.

Exclusion is also multi-dimensional, combining economic and social deprivation. However, analysts differ on whether exclusion is always a cumulative process of multiple, interrelated disadvantages. The UK's Social Exclusion Unit defines exclusion as "a shorthand label for what can happen when individuals or areas suffer from a combination of linked problems." Emphasizing joined-up social problems, especially when spatially concentrated, resonates with the idea of an "underclass." This is even more the case when, as Vleminckx and Berghman (2001) claim, exclusion implies entrapment or intergenerational transmission.

Certainly, research confirms that exclusion along one dimension may increase the risks of exclusion along other dimensions, but very few people are totally excluded from all social relations at once. There are many more people who are socially excluded in some respects than there are people excluded in all respects. Indeed, it is virtually impossible for human beings to exist totally outside societal influences.

Social exclusion may be considered as both a condition and a process, although it is most frequently treated in dynamic terms. Castel (1991), for example, eschews the term exclusion, preferring the notion of *disaffiliation*. Paugam (1991), another French sociologist, refers to a process of *social disqualification*. These authors consider exclusion along a continuum, with intermediate steps of vulnerability or precariousness.

There are many mechanisms of social exclusion: extermination, exile, abandonment, ostracism, shaming, marginalization, segregation, discrimination. Sometimes, even social assistance can produce exclusion. In general, groups deliberately use exclusion as a means of social control and boundary maintenance. It reinforces internal solidarity and may allow insiders to monopolize resources.

Although most scholars agree that social exclusion is multi-dimensional and has different forms in different social contexts, there is little consensus over what are the most important dimensions of social exclusion. Studies have so far examined the dimensions that are easiest to measure with available data. This has first and foremost meant extending poverty and unemployment indicators to take account of time and place. A. B. Atkinson, a British economist, proposed the initial exclusion measures for the European Union, most of which consisted of income and joblessness indicators (Atkinson et al. 2002). In the second EU Joint Inclusion Report these indicators were accompanied with education and health measures.

However, several sociological studies, especially in the UK, have tackled other social and political dimensions of exclusion. For example, Gordon et al. (2000) conducted a new *Poverty and Social Exclusion in Britain* survey for the Joseph Rowntree Foundation specifically for this purpose. In addition to income poverty and material deprivation, exclusion from the labor market and from public services, they examined four aspects of exclusion from social relations: socializing, social isolation, social support, and civic engagement. The researchers identified these aspects directly by asking Britons themselves what they considered "normal" social activities, whether they experienced constraints upon participating in them, and, if so, the nature of those obstacles. This and other studies (see Hills et al. 2002) reveal that income distribution and unemployment are weakly associated with sociability and community participation. Gallie and Paugam's (2000) research suggests material deprivation may even be positively related to social relations in Southern Europe.

The dimensions of social exclusion receiving the most recent attention concern the recognition and rights of racial and ethnic groups, especially of immigrants. This emphasis is largely due to the adoption of the 2000 EU "Racial Directive" on equal treatment irrespective of racial and ethnic origin, and the EQUAL program to fight labor-market discrimination. In 2005 the British Council of Brussels and other agencies released a European Civic Citizenship and Inclusion Index that uses uniform indicators to gauge the extent to which immigrants to a country have rights and obligations comparable to EU citizens. While these attempts to measure social dimensions of exclusion are important advances, many cultural, political, and social aspects of life lack good indicators. The Joint Report on Social Inclusion called for more attention to neglected types of disadvantage,

such as access to the Internet, housing, transportation, continuing education, and language acquisition. Further methodological advances are expected in the future.

Social exclusion has expanded its meaning over time to encompass more social problems and disadvantaged groups. In France, when the term originated in the 1960s, a group of "Social Catholics," especially the ATD-Fourth World movement headed by Father Joseph Wresinski, used the term to refer to the extremely poor of affluent and less developed countries living in the slums. In the 1970s, when René Lenoir (1974) used the term, the socially excluded referred to the handicapped, substance abusers, juvenile delinquents, and deviant groups. In the 1980s, as unemployment rose after the Oil Shocks, the term applied to youth and older unskilled workers whom deindustrialization displaced. As long-term joblessness, homelessness, and racism all became issues in the next two decades, they added yet more complexity to the meaning of social exclusion. A coalition of social movements concerned with these many issues demanded action, leading to France's anti-exclusion laws enacted in 1988, 1998, and 2005.

In the 1990s the European Union adopted the term. Leaders passed resolutions to fight social exclusion as part of the European Social Model, one that weds economic growth with job creation and social cohesion. Since 2001, member states of the EU have produced National Action Plans for social inclusion submitted to Brussels for coordination in a Joint Inclusion Report. The European Union will shortly consider the fight for social inclusion in the larger context of social protection. Already in 2005, the Joint Report on Social Protection and Social Inclusion coupled national progress reports on inclusion with benchmarks on pensions. The next Joint Report will further streamline the monitoring process, adding medical and other dimensions. As the EU expands from 15 to 25 members, new issues of social exclusion are likely to arise, such as discrimination against the Roma (gypsies) in Central and Eastern Europe. In sum, Brussels will probably determine the direction of the study of social exclusion for the near future.

Interest in social exclusion has expanded beyond Europe, although so far the concept has not caught on in the US. International agencies working in less developed countries have found the concept useful for studying the challenges of integration in pluri-ethnic societies, caste structures, religious cleavages, and indigenous peoples' rights. UN agencies and international development banks have funded programs to promote social inclusion in the global South.

Thus, political and policy considerations have been as important as sociological interests to the development of social exclusion as a subject of study. For example, Giddens (2000) discussed "social exclusion" in his book on *The Third Way* just as Tony Blair was adopting the idea. Esping-Andersen referred to the challenges of social exclusion in his 2002 book, *Why We Need a New Welfare State*. And France's full-fledged National Observatory for the Study of Social Exclusion produces annual research reports for the government.

Programs to fight social exclusion ideally take a comprehensive approach, progressively tackling multiple problems and tailoring solutions to a person's particular combination of needs. Solutions usually entail the participation of the excluded in their own inclusion. The European Social Funds have co-funded local projects that help rebuild social relations and "reinsert" excluded people in socially useful activities. These projects might include working in a subsidized job, taking a training course, or renovating housing for the homeless. They may not lift someone out of poverty, but they do reknit the social bond. Inclusion does not rely only on having a paid job in a for-profit business.

Finally, there are many critiques of the idea of social exclusion. Central among them is the argument that it distracts attention from social inequality and class conflict. The excluded have a wide range of problems and do not share interests that might cement them into a political force. In addition, inclusion is usually a euphemism for rejoining the labor force. Other critics point out the lack of a theory that identifies the causes and consequences of exclusion. There is not a zero-sum relationship in which greater exclusion means less inclusion. Rather, both processes are interrelated and can occur simultaneously. These and many other controversies will ensure the further development of the concept of social exclusion in the years to come.

SEE ALSO: Discrimination; Occupational Segregation; Outsider-Within; Poverty and Disrepute; Residential Segregation; Social Integration and Inclusion; Solidarity; Stigma; Stranger, The

REFERENCES AND SUGGESTED READINGS

Atkinson, A. B., Cantillon, B., Marlier, E., & Nolan, B. (2002) *Social Indicators: The EU and Social Inclusion*. Oxford University Press, Oxford.

Castel, R. (1991) De l'Indigence à l'exclusion: la désaffiliation. In: Donzelot, J. (Ed.), *Face à l'exclusion*. Esprit, Paris, pp. 137–68.

Commission of the European Communities (2005) *Joint Report on Social Protection and Social Exclusion*. COM 14, Brussels.

Esping-Andersen, G. (2002) *Why We Need a New Welfare State*. Oxford University Press, Oxford.

Gallie, D. & Paugam, S. (Eds.) (2000) *Welfare Regimes and the Experience of Unemployment in Europe*. Oxford University Press, Oxford.

Geddes, A. & Niessen, J. (2005) *European Civic Citizenship and Inclusion Index*. British Council, Foreign Policy Center and Migration Policy Group, Brussels.

Giddens, A. (2000) *The Third Way and Its Critics*. Polity Press, Cambridge.

Gordon, D. et al. (2000) *Poverty and Social Exclusion in Britain*. Joseph Rowntree Foundation, York.

Hills, J., Le Grand, J., & Piachaud, D. (Eds.) (2002) *Understanding Social Exclusion*. Oxford University Press, Oxford.

Lenoir, R. (1974) *Les Exclus: un français sur dix*. Seuil, Paris.

Levitas, R. (2000) What is Social Exclusion? In: Gordon, D. & Townsend, P. (Eds.), *Breadline Europe: The Measurement of Poverty*. Policy Press, Bristol, pp. 357–83.

Paugam, S. (1991) *La Disqualification sociale*. Presses Universitaires de France, Paris.

Silver, H. (1994) Social Exclusion and Social Solidarity: Three Paradigms. *International Labour Review* 133: 531–78.

Touraine, A. (1991) Face à l'exclusion. *Esprit* 169: 7–13.

Vleminckx, K. & Berghman, J. (2001) Social Exclusion and the Welfare State: An Overview of Conceptual Issues and Policy Implications. In: Mayes, D., Berghman, J., & Salais, R. (Eds.), *Social Exclusion and European Policy*. Edward Elgar, Northampton, MA.

social fact

Donald A. Nielsen

The concept of social fact was defined by the French sociologist Émile Durkheim, in his book on the *Rules of Sociological Method* (1982), as ways of feeling, thinking, and acting external to and exercising constraint over the individual. Durkheim's emphasis on social facts was part of his critique of psychological theories of human behavior and society. The concept of social fact is identified with Durkheim and his school, but is also relevant to the understanding of any social theory which views society as an objective reality apart from the individuals composing it. Such approaches can be distinguished from the theoretical perspectives of such figures as Weber, Mead, and others who emphasize social action, interaction, or individual definitions of reality.

According to Durkheim, social facts are collective phenomena and, as such, make up the distinctive subject matter of sociology. Social facts can be embodied in social institutions, such as religions, political forms, kinship structures, or legal codes. There are also more diffuse social facts; for example, mass behavior of crowds and the collective trends identifiable in statistical rates of social phenomena such as suicide and crime. Institutions are an especially central concern of sociology as a social science. Durkheim insisted that social facts should be treated as things. They are realities in their own right, with their own laws of organization, apart from the ways these facts might appear to the individual's consciousness. Durkheim thought that sociology would have no distinctive subject matter if society itself did not exist as an objective reality. Thus, sociology and psychology represent independent levels of analysis.

In *Suicide* (1897) Durkheim studied suicide rates as measurable manifestations of prior social facts. He argued that suicide rates were correlated with differing social circumstances and created a theory of four social causes of suicide, two of them endemic to modern society. Egoistic suicide emerged from a lack of integration of the individual into social groups, especially the family, the religious group, and the political community. Since familial, religious, and political ties were weakening in modern society, egoism was the most frequent contemporary cause of suicide. He suggested that the reintegration of the individual into society might be performed by strengthening the role of occupational or professional groups.

Anomic suicide resulted from the failure of another class of social facts, namely social norms, to regulate the individual's desires. It occurred especially during fluctuating economic circumstances, but could emerge in any setting where the individual's existing standards of conduct and expectations were radically disrupted. Durkheim emphasized that such social causes operated independently from the individual incidence of suicide and represented a level of social facts which could be understood only through a new science of sociology.

Durkheim and his school studied a wide range of social facts, including family and kinship, the division of labor, religion and magic, and the categories of human understanding such as time, space, and the person. Their emphasis on the factual character of society led Durkheim and his followers to examine what they called the social substratum of groups and the collective representations, or the collective psychology, shared by the average members of society. The former class of social facts, social morphology, was especially central to their work and involved the study of the number, distribution, and social organization of populations in space and over time. In this way, the Durkheimians combined the disciplines of geography, history, and demography into a holistic sociological analysis of the social substructure. Maurice Halbwachs focused especially on social morphology, although each member of the school, including Durkheim, adopted this approach to the study of social phenomena.

For example, Durkheim argued that the causes of changes in social facts must be located in historically antecedent social phenomena. In *The Division of Labor in Society* (1893) he examined the transformation of societies from mechanical to organic solidarity. Mechanical solidarity was based on a strong collective consciousness and organized around segmental groups, primarily extended kinship structures.

The result was a society based on the similarity among its individual members and social units. Organic solidarity was rooted in mutual interdependence of activities in the division of labor, where the collective consciousness became less strong and, thus, there appeared a greater individuation of thought and conduct. The cause of the change from mechanical to organic solidarity was found in social morphology; in particular, an increase in the overall population volume, an increase in society's material density (i.e., the number of people in a given territory), and an increased moral or dynamic density (i.e., communication and interaction among groups).

In a related study, *Seasonal Variations in Eskimo Society* (1904–5), Marcel Mauss used a similar approach. He found that major changes in religious ritual, law, family organization, economic life, and other features of Eskimo society resulted from the seasonal variation of population concentration and dispersion and their concomitant effects on moral density. Durkheim and Mauss argued, in their study of *Primitive Classification* (1901–2), that the main categories of thought and classification of objects in primitive societies reflected the social organization of those societies and should be understood apart from the individual's psychology. In his study of "The Preeminence of the Right Hand" (1909), Robert Hertz argued that the higher cultural value placed on the right hand was rooted in social and religious definitions of the sacred versus the profane, rather than in any biological asymmetry. Hertz's study laid the foundation for a growing literature on dual systems of classification which, in turn, gave an impetus to structuralist theories of culture and society.

Other social theories outside the Durkheimian orbit have also emphasized the role of objective social conditions or social facts. Marxist social theorists have focused on the ways in which forces and social relations of production confront individuals as objective conditions of existence. Marx argued that individuals make history, but do so under conditions independent of their individual wills. For Marx, social existence determines consciousness. Individuals are primarily to be seen as representatives of social classes or personifications of objective economic forces. When Marx does discuss social action, he emphasizes the role of collective actors in history, namely social classes like the bourgeoisie or the proletariat. This tension between objective factual conditions and collective voluntary action presented dilemmas for later Marxists.

A variety of functionalist and structuralist approaches have emerged from this early emphasis on the factual quality of social existence. Although Talcott Parsons's early study *The Structure of Social Action* (1937) developed an action frame of reference, he soon developed a macro-sociological, structural, and functional theory which muted his earlier emphasis on actors and social action. For example, in *The Social System* (1951) Parsons developed a general theory of social systems which focused on four basic functions which all social systems, including whole societies, needed to perform in order to continue as going concerns (i.e., adaptation to environment, goal attainment, social integration, cultural pattern maintenance). Parsons examined the interchanges among institutions (e.g., economy, polity, household, school, law, etc.) serving these functions and used this strategy to build increasingly inclusive theoretical systems, ones which could be applied to concrete sociological questions. For instance, in *Economy and Society* (1956) Parsons and Neil Smelser analyzed the economy as a social system and examined its internal organization along with its relations with other non-economic systems, while in *Family, Socialization and Interaction Process* (1955), Parsons and several collaborators discussed the family as a social system, including its structure of instrumental and integrative roles. On related grounds, Kingsley Davis and Wilbert Moore argued for the functional necessity of social stratification, while other functionalists such as Robert K. Merton turned to the study of social structures and their consequences. Merton distinguished between the manifest (i.e., intended and foreseen) and latent (i.e., unintended and unforeseen) functions of social arrangements. Merton's approach allowed him to examine various social phenomena of the "middle range" (e.g., conflict, bureaucracy, reference groups) which often slipped through the more holistic and systematic functionalism of Parsons.

More recent French social thought has produced a number of variations on Durkheim's
sociological objectivism. These include Lévi-
Strauss's structural anthropology, the historical
work of the *Annales* school, especially Braudel
and his followers, Foucault's investigations,
and the theorizing of Althusser. Lévi-Strauss
created structural theories of kinship, myth,
and culture by combining structural linguistics
with ideas drawn from the Durkheim school,
Marx, and Freud. His theories pitted structure
against history and argued for the centrality of
enduring structures of human cognitive and
social organization. Human expressions and the
actions of individuals were best seen as variants
operating within the confines of established
social and cultural structures. The second generation of *Annales* historians such as Fernand
Braudel pursued a similar agenda by rejecting
the study of history in terms of actors and events
and emphasizing structures of the *longue durée*,
including such things as enduring socioeconomic and civilizational structures and even
geography and climate. This approach is most
fully captured in Braudel's work on *The Mediterranean* (1949), but is also found in the work of
such *Annales* figures as Immanuel Le Roy
Ladurie, who has suggested that the study of
the economic and social impact of slow climatic
changes opens up the possibility of a "history
without people" (in this connection, it is worth
recalling that Durkheim rejected the idea that
climate had an impact on suicide rates). Michel
Foucault's work also diminishes the role of the
individual subject. His studies of madness, the
clinic, the prison, and changing systems of
knowledge reject the search for causal sequences
rooted in the actions of individuals or groups
and, instead, view actors and their actions as
instantiations of the words and deeds made possible by the reigning discourses. These structuralist tendencies are perhaps most fully expressed
in Louis Althusser's work. He rejects Marx's
early humanistic writings in favor of his later,
more objectivist scientific work, and ends by
forging a structural theory of society where
human agency is entirely eliminated and social
change occurs through a process of internal
contradictions within dynamic socioeconomic,
political, and legal structures.

The emphasis on social facts in sociology is
generally opposed by thinkers who see human

agency as central to our understanding of
society. This latter group includes Max Weber's
social action theory, the symbolic interactionist
theory of Herbert Blumer, the phenomenological perspective of Alfred Schutz, and several
related perspectives. For example, Weber's
work rests on the principle of "methodological
individualism," where objective social processes
can in principle be reduced to the actions and
interactions of individuals. In a similar vein,
symbolic interactionists see society as a process
and not an object. Schutz attempts to build
scientific concepts about society by starting
with the taken-for-granted conceptualizations
of individual actors. There have been efforts
by such figures as Peter Berger and Thomas
Luckmann, Anthony Giddens, and Pierre
Bourdieu to synthesize the positivist, objectivist
study of social facts derived from the Durkheimian, Marxian, structuralist, functionalist, and
related traditions with the study of social action,
interaction, and agency. However, these efforts
have not always been fully successful in doing
justice to both the objective social reality of
economy, society, and culture as well as the
equally robust reality of individual social action,
interaction, and response. This dilemma is
probably inherent to sociology as a social and
human science.

SEE ALSO: Althusser, Louis; Annales School;
Durkheim, Émile; Foucault, Michel; Function-
alism/Neofunctionalism; Marx, Karl; Marxism
and Sociology; Parsons, Talcott; Positivism;
Structuralism

REFERENCES AND SUGGESTED READINGS

Althusser, L. (1970) *For Marx*. Trans. B. Brewster.
  Vintage Books, New York.
Durkheim, É. (1982 [1895]) *The Rules of Sociological
  Method*. Trans. W. D. Halls. Free Press, New York.
Giddens, A. (1979) *Central Problems in Social Theory*.
  University of California Press, Berkeley.
Gilbert, M. (1992) *On Social Facts*. Princeton Uni-
  versity Press, Princeton.
Nielsen, D. A. (1999) *Three Faces of God: Society,
  Religion and the Categories of Totality in the Philo-
  sophy of Émile Durkheim*. State University of New
  York Press, Albany.
Ritzer, G. (1980) *Sociology: A Multiple Paradigm
  Science*. Allyn & Bacon, Boston.

social identity theory

Peter L. Callero

Social identity theory offers a social psychological explanation of intergroup prejudice, discrimination, and conflict. Its origins lie in the work of Henri Tajfel (Tajfel & Turner 1979) and his associates who have been instrumental in the development of a distinctly European approach to psychology. This approach is broadly concerned with the relationship between self and society. For Tajfel, the key to understanding prejudice, discrimination, and intergroup conflict is found in an individual's social identity as defined by group membership. Social identity theory rejects explanations based on individual defects of physiology, personality, or attitude. In this regard, it represents a challenge to more traditional psychological theories and has generated nascent interest among sociologists. Tajfel's experimental findings on group affiliation and personal bias were first published in the 1960s and, since then, social identity theory has generated an immense body of empirical research in support of its basic hypotheses. Over the years, social identity theory has been elaborated and extended to encompass issues of group leadership, organizational psychology, deviance, and political action. Today, social identity theory stands as one of the most influential theoretical perspectives within psychological social psychology.

MINIMAL GROUP PARADIGM

The empirical starting point for understanding social identity theory is found in a series of laboratory experiments that have come to be known as the minimal group paradigm. The objective in this early research was to identify the minimal conditions required to produce favoritism toward one group and discrimination against another. In the minimal group design, subjects are randomly assigned to one of two groups that they believe were established on the basis of a trivial preliminary test (e.g., whether one underestimated or overestimated the number of dots on a screen). The conditions are such that there is no history or prior knowledge of the group or of other group members, there is no interaction among or between group members, other group members cannot be heard or seen, no competition of any sort is ever established, and the only differentiating factor is the perception that there are two distinct groups. Results from studies using the minimal group paradigm consistently show favoritism toward one's own group and bias against another group (usually measured in terms of reward distribution to group members and member attitudes toward the in-group and the out-group). Thus, on the basis of a purely cognitive discrimination of groups as defined by simple category distinctions, the seeds of intergroup conflict are sown. Variations on the minimal group design have ruled out the effect of perceived similarity among group members and various other methodological artifacts. For Tajfel and his colleagues, the findings show that the mere categorization into groups can produce a distinctly consequential social identity, and that social identity based upon group membership is the psychological foundation of intergroup conflict. At the same time, Tajfel was quick to emphasize that the findings should not be interpreted to mean that material conditions, historical structures, and cultural traditions do not affect real-world conflict. In fact, these sociological forces are the context within which social identity operates.

SOCIAL IDENTITY

Social identity refers to an individual's subjective understanding of group membership. It is a cognitive category that includes emotional and evaluative associations. Social identity can be as simple and fleeting as a label employed in a psychology experiment or as complex and encompassing as national, religious, or ethnic affiliations. Unlike the symbolic interactionist tradition in sociology where self, identity, and personhood are seen as inherently social at all levels, social identity theory argues that group identity is formed psychologically and in opposition to one's personal identity.

In other words, the psychology of group behavior is assumed to be qualitatively different from the psychology of interpersonal behavior. While this ontological distinction provides social identity theory with the conceptual language needed to understand prejudice, discrimination, and conflict as ordinary, adaptive, and functional interactions of group behavior, critics have argued that it has led to the adoption of an overly restricted understanding of the social dimension of identity. Because social identity is seen as the cognitive mechanism that makes group behavior possible, understanding the motivations, contextual contingencies, and cognitive structures associated with the psychology of *groupness* has been a major focus of research.

As noted above, an enormous body of empirical research has found that an individual's commitment to a group is associated with positive bias toward the group, or in-group favoritism. In addition, the same expansive body of research finds that in-group favoritism is often associated with out-group bias such that members of other groups tend to be viewed in a stereotypical manner. In other words, the salience of a social identity (psychological commitment to a group) leads to prejudice, discrimination, and conflict between groups. But of course these basic associations are not universal. Not all group commitments for all individuals lead to the same type of bias. Perhaps the most valuable contribution of social identity theory is that it provides a framework for predicting when and how group bias occurs. The effects are highly contingent and so the explanations can be quite detailed and complex, but three major factors affecting the process are the salience of particular social identities, the objective features of a particular situation, and the individual's beliefs about the group.

When group membership in the form of a social identity is psychologically salient, it is said to affect perception, cognition, and behavior; predictions that have received substantial empirical support. But according to social identity theory, the salience of a group identity should not be viewed as a transsituational quality of the person. Rather, it is a process whereby specific social identities come to define the self in particular social contexts. Some social settings will allow for a fit between social identity categories stored in memory and the perception of self in relation to other group members. Categories that have optimal fit, and maximize

meaning for the actor, will become salient. For example, in a setting where groups are in conflict over financial resources, such as a collective bargaining table or a picket line, we would expect a worker's union identity to be salient. This in turn would be associated with positive generalizations about union members and negative generalizations regarding management. But even in this rather straightforward and simple example, the outcome is not determined since individual belief structures also intervene.

According to social identity theory, the two belief structures most important for understanding intergroup relations are those that address social mobility and social change. Importantly, these two beliefs are related in that they are said to represent different ends of a single continuum. An individual who believes in social mobility thinks that it is possible to achieve positive social regard by moving from one group of relatively low status to another of relatively higher status. This belief is based on the assumption of a relatively free and unrestricted social structure. In contrast, a belief in social change rests on the idea that positive improvement in one's social standing requires action as a group member. It is in effect a rejection of free and independent agency in favor of a more collective approach to changing the position of one's group. Because of its emphasis on solidarity with other group members, this end of the continuum is seen as corresponding to the psychological salience of a social identity.

MOTIVATION AND SELF-CATEGORIZATION

At its core, the social identity approach to group conflict is built upon the energizing forces of specific psychological motives. These include a motivation to enhance self-esteem, a motivation to maintain a distinct social identity, and a motivation to reduce uncertainty. Thus, it is hypothesized that the fundamental drive to achieve a favorable view of self leads individuals to associate with groups that will enhance self-regard. But since this cannot be achieved unless the group is recognizably distinct and clearly associated with positive sentiment, individuals are also motivated to affiliate with groups that offer *positive distinctiveness*. Moreover, as actors attempt to define and clarify knowledge about self and others, they are also driven by a need to reduce uncertainty. The cognitive processes associated with categorizing self and other are in turn viewed as effective strategies for reducing uncertainty. Although various hypotheses and contingencies linked to these motives have been studied at length, empirical support for the self-esteem motives has been mixed. This has contributed in part to a significant shift in emphasis over the last 20 years toward greater interest in developing the cognitive dimension of social identity theory.

During the 1980s Jon Turner and his colleagues (Turner et al. 1987) initiated the development of self-categorization theory as an extension and elaboration of social identity theory. Self-categorization theory addresses more specifically the cognitive structures and processes that define social identity and the psychology of group affiliation and commitment. For example, a key concept in self-categorization theory is that of *prototypicality*, or the degree to which a category member is representative of the category as a whole. A cognitive prototype is an actor's mental representation of the core defining attributes of a group. Research suggests that this is usually constructed from qualities of exemplary members, either through a disembodied ideal type or an actual group member who comes close to the imagined ideal. These stereotyped images are stored in memory and are altered in the social context of group comparison in order to enhance meaning. For example, under the principle of *metacontrast*, attributes of the prototype will change so as to maximize the difference between the in-group and the out-group. In this way, the self-categorization process functions to induce group solidarity, encourage social identity salience, and reduce self uncertainty by establishing shared beliefs through group membership.

SOCIOLOGICAL CONTRIBUTIONS

The distinguishing contribution of social identity theory is its explanation of the psychological foundations of intergroup prejudice, discrimination, and conflict. By assuming an ontological

break between interpersonal and group psychology, social identity theory departs from the more reductionist approaches to intergroup behavior. Since the 1980s social identity theory has seen tremendous growth and influence and must now be considered one of the most dominant theoretical perspectives in psychology. Nevertheless, at this point in time its standing among sociologists remains relatively weak. This is a partial consequence of institutional barriers, but it also reflects more basic epistemological differences between social psychologists in the two scholarly traditions. Because social identity theory assumes an ontologically independent person acting as either an individual or as a group member, its ability to provide an accounting of fundamental sociological processes is limited. Thus, the emergence of selfhood and identity from interpersonal interaction is not addressed within social identity theory, and historically situated macro forces of political economy, colonialism, and cultural imperialism can enter only as details of a specific situation. To the extent that social identity theory continues to rely primarily on laboratory experimentation focused on discovering and describing cognitive processes, it will unlikely develop a larger following among sociologists. Should, however, it begin to link these processes more directly with actual group conflict in real-world settings, it has the potential to contribute to interdisciplinary cross-fertilization.

SEE ALSO: Aggression; Authority and Conformity; Discrimination; Identity Theory; In-Groups and Out-Groups; Prejudice; Psychological Social Psychology; Self; Social Change; Social Cognition; Social Psychology; Status Construction Theory; Symbolic Interaction

REFERENCES AND SUGGESTED READINGS

Abrams, D. & Hogg, M. A. (Eds.) (1999) *Social Identity and Social Cognition*. Blackwell, Oxford.
Brown, R. (2000) Social Identity Theory: Past Achievements, Current Problems, and Future Challenges. *European Journal of Social Psychology* 30: 745–78.
Ellemers, N., Spears, R., & Doosje, B. (1999) *Social Identity*. Blackwell, Oxford.

Hogg, M. A. (2006) Social Identity Theory. In: Burke, P. J. (Ed.), *Contemporary Social Psychological Theories*. Stanford University Press, Stanford.

Tajfel, H. & Turner, J. C. (1979) An Integrative Theory of Intergroup Conflict. In: Austin, W. G. & Worchel, S. (Eds.), *The Social Psychology of Intergroup Relations*. Brooks/Cole, Monterey, CA, pp. 33–47.

Turner, J. C., Hogg, M. A., & Oakes, P. J. (1987) *Rediscovering the Social Group: A Self-Categorization Theory*. Blackwell, Oxford.

social indicators

Kenneth C. Land

Social indicators are statistical time series "used to monitor the social system, helping to identify changes and to guide intervention to alter the course of social change" (Ferriss 1988: 601). Examples are unemployment rates, crime rates, estimates of life expectancy, health status indices such as the average number of "healthy" days (or days without activity limitations) in the past month for a specific population, school enrollment rates, average achievement scores on a standardized test, rates of voting in elections, and measures of subjective well-being such as how satisfied individuals are with life as a whole. In addition to these specific indicators, recent work has led to the development of summary indices that combine a number of specific indicators into composite measures of the quality of life or well-being for a society as a whole or for specific segments or subunits thereof.

Associated with the term social indicators is a field of research that cuts across several social science disciplines (Land 1983). Three broad questions about social indicators are addressed here:

- Where did the field of social indicators come from? What is the historical development and intellectual history of social indicators?
- Can different categories of social indicators be distinguished? What are the major types?
- How are social indicators used? What are the functions of social indicators?

HISTORICAL DEVELOPMENTS

Social Indicators in the 1960s

The term *social indicators* was born and given its initial meaning in an attempt, undertaken in the early 1960s by the American Academy of Arts and Sciences for the National Aeronautics and Space Administration, to detect and anticipate the nature and magnitude of the second-order consequences of the space program, specifically the effort to launch a manned space flight to the moon and back, for American society. Frustrated by the lack of sufficient data to detect such effects and the absence of a systematic conceptual framework and methodology for analysis, some of those involved in the Academy project attempted to develop a system of social indicators – statistics, statistical series, and other forms of evidence – with which to detect and anticipate social change as well as to evaluate specific programs and determine their impact. The results of this part of the Academy project were published in a volume (Bauer 1966) bearing the title *Social Indicators*.

The appearance of this volume was not an isolated event. Several other influential publications commented on the lack of a system for charting social change and advocated that the US government establish a "system of social accounts" that would facilitate a cost-benefit analysis of more than the market-related aspects of society already indexed by the National Income and Product Accounts (Land 1983). The need for social indicators also was emphasized by the publication of the 101-page *Toward a Social Report* (US Department of Health, Education, and Welfare 1969) on the last day of Lyndon B. Johnson's administration in 1969. Conceived of as a prototypical counterpart to the annual economic reports of the president, each of its seven chapters addressed major issues in an important area of social concern (health and illness; social mobility; the physical environment; income and poverty; public order and safety; learning, science, and art; and participation and alienation) and provided an assessment of prevalent conditions. In addition, the document firmly established the link of social indicators to the idea of systematic reporting on social issues for the purpose of public enlightenment.

Generally speaking, the sharp impulse of interest in social indicators in the 1960s grew out of the movement toward collection and organization of national social, economic, and demographic data that began in western societies during the seventeenth and eighteenth centuries and accelerated in the twentieth century. The work of sociologist William F. Ogburn and his collaborators at the University of Chicago in the 1930s and 1940s on the theory and measurement of social change is more proximate and sociologically germane. As chairman of President Herbert Hoover's Research Committee on Social Trends, Ogburn supervised production of the two-volume *Recent Social Trends* (1933), a pathbreaking contribution to social reporting. Ogburn's ideas about the measurement of social change influenced several of his students – notably Albert D. Biderman, Otis Dudley Duncan, Albert J. Reiss, Jr., and Eleanor Bernert Sheldon, who played major roles in the emergence and development of the field of social indicators in the 1960s and 1970s.

Social Indicators in the 1970s and 1980s

At the end of the 1960s, the enthusiasm for social indicators was sufficiently strong and broad-based for Duncan (1969) to write of the existence of a Social Indicators Movement. In the early 1970s, this led to numerous developments, including the establishing in 1972, with National Science Foundation support, of the Social Science Research Council Center for Coordination of Research on Social Indicators in Washington, DC; research efforts to define and develop a methodology for the measurement of indicators of subjective well-being as measures of the quality of life (Campbell et al. 1976); the commencement of a US federal government series of comprehensive social indicators books of charts, tables, and limited analyses; the initiation of several continuing data series based on periodic sample surveys of the national population, such as the annual National Opinion Research Center's (NORC's) General Social Survey or the Bureau of Justice Statistics' annual National Crime Victimization Survey; the publication in 1974 of the first volume of the international journal *Social Indicators Research*; and the spread of social indicators/social reporting to numerous other nations

and international agencies, such as the United Nations and the Organization for Economic Cooperation and Development.

In contrast to the 1970s, social indicators activities slowed in the 1980s, as funding cuts or non-renewals led to the closing of the Center for Coordination of Research on Social Indicators, the discontinuation of related work at several international agencies, the termination of government-sponsored social indicators reports in some countries, including the United States, and the reduction of statistical efforts to monitor various aspects of society. Several explanations have been given for this turnabout. Certainly, politics and the state of national economies in the early 1980s are among the most identifiable proximate causes. Administrations that came to power in the United States and elsewhere based decisions more on a "conservative ideology" and less on current social data than had been the case earlier. And faltering economies producing large government budget deficits provided the incentive to make funding cuts. In addition, however, there was a perceived lack of demonstrated usefulness of social indicators in public policymaking. This was due, in part, to an overly simplistic view of how and under what conditions knowledge influences policy, a topic treated more fully below in discussions of uses of social indicators.

Social Indicators in the 1990s and 2000s

The 1980s ended with the question of "Whatever Happened to Social Indicators?" and the conclusion that the field had faded away. But, shortly after this conclusion was articulated, interest in social indicators revived and the field has been in an expansionary phase since the mid-1990s.

A key part in this expansion is a development that became vividly apparent in the 1990s: the widespread political, popular, and theoretical appeal of the quality-of-life (QOL) concept. This concept emerged and became part of the Social Indicators Movement in the late 1960s and early 1970s as doubts were raised in the highly developed western industrial societies about economic growth as the major goal of societal progress. The "social costs" of economic growth were cited, and there was increasing doubt about whether "more" should be equated with "better." The QOL concept which resulted from this discussion was posed as an alternative to the more and more questionable concept of the affluent society and entered discussions of social policy and politics as a new, but more complex, multidimensional goal.

As a goal of social and economic policy, QOL encompasses all (or at least many) domains of life and subsumes, in addition to individual material and immaterial well-being, such collective values as freedom, justice, and the guarantee of natural conditions of life for present and future generations. The social scientific and policy uses of the QOL notion have been paralleled in the private sector by the widespread use and popularity of numerous rankings – based on weighted scales of multiple domains of well-being – of the "best" places to live, work, do business, play, etc., be they cities, states, regions, or nations.

The theoretical appeal of the QOL concept as an integrating notion in the social sciences and related disciplines is, in part, due to the perceived importance of measuring individuals' subjective assessments of their satisfaction with various life domains and with life as a whole. For instance, during the last two decades of the twentieth century, QOL became a concept that bridged the discipline of marketing research and strategic business policy with social indicators. Marketing is an important social force – with far-reaching direct and indirect impacts on the prevailing QOL in a society – through consumer satisfaction and its impact on satisfaction with life as a whole. The intersection of marketing research with social indicators through the QOL concept led to the organization in the mid-1990s of the multidisciplinary International Society for Quality-of-Life Studies (for more information, visit www.isqols.org).

Another key development occurred in the field of social indicators in the 1990s and 2000s: the field entered a new era of the construction of composite or summary social indicators. Often these indices attempt to summarize indicators (objective and/or subjective) of a number of domains of life into a single index of the quality of life for the population or society as a whole or for some significant segment thereof (e.g., children and youth, the elderly, racial and minority groups, cities, states, or regions within the nation, etc.). They thus attempt to answer one of the original questions motivating the Social Indicators Movement: how are we doing overall in terms of the quality of life? With respect to our past? With respect to other comparable units (e.g., cities, states, regions, nations)? Many of the pioneers of the Social Indicators Movement in the 1960s and 1970s felt that the database as well as the theoretical foundations were not sufficient at that time for the development of composite indices and that efforts should, instead, be concentrated on conducting basic research on social indicators and the measurement of the quality of life and the development of a richer social database.

Since the 1960s, however, there has been a tremendous increase in the richness of social data available for many societies. There also has been an accumulation of studies and theoretical developments with respect to subjective well-being and quality-of-life studies. This has encouraged a new generation of social indicators researchers to return to the task of composite index construction. Some examples: (1) at the level of the broadest possible comparisons of nations with respect to the overall quality of life, the Human Development Index (United Nations Development Program 2004); (2) at the level of comparisons at the national level over time in the United States, the Fordham Index of Social Health (Miringoff & Miringoff 1999); and (3) for a specific subpopulation, the Child Well-Being Index developed by Land et al. (2001). The field of social indicators and quality-of-life research probably will see several decades of such index construction and competition among various indices – with a corresponding need for careful assessments to determine which indices have substantive validity for which populations in the assessment of the quality of life and its changes over time and social space.

TYPES OF INDICATORS

Policy/Welfare/Criterion Indicators

Based on the premise that social indicators should relate directly to social policymaking considerations, an early definition by economist Mancur Olson, the principal author of *Toward a Social Report*, characterized a social indicator as a "statistic of direct normative interest which facilitates concise, comprehensive and balance judgments about the condition of major aspects of a society" (US Department of Health, Education, and Welfare 1969: 97). Olson went on to state that such an indicator is, in all cases, a direct measure of welfare and is subject to the interpretation that if it changes in the "right" direction, while other things remain equal, things have gotten better, or people are better off. Accordingly, by this definition, statistics on the number of doctors or police officers could not be social indicators, whereas figures on health or crime rates could be.

In the language of policy analysis, social indicators are "target" or "output" or "outcome" or "end-value" or "criterions" variables, toward changes in which some public policy (program, project) is directed. Such a use of social indicators requires that (1) society agrees about what needs improving; (2) it is possible to decide unambiguously what "getting better" means; and (3) it is meaningful to aggregate the indicators to the level of aggregation at which the policy is defined.

In recognition of the fact that various other meanings have been attached to the term social indicators, the tendency among recent authors is to use a somewhat different terminology for the class of indicators identified by Olson. For instance, Land (1983) termed this the class of *normative welfare indicators*. Building on the Olson approach, MacRae (1985: 5) defined *policy indicators* as "measures of those variables that are to be included in a broadly policy-relevant system of public statistics."

Life Satisfaction and/or Happiness Indicators

Another class of social indicators has its roots in the work of Campbell et al. (1976), who argued that the direct monitoring of key social psychological states (attitudes, expectations, feelings, aspirations, and values) in the population is necessary for an understanding of social change and the quality of life. In this approach, social indicators seek to measure psychological satisfaction, happiness, and life fulfillment by using survey research instruments that ascertain the subjective reality in which people live. The result may aptly be termed *life satisfaction*, *subjective well-being*, or *happiness indicators*.

This approach led to many methodological studies exploring the utility of various survey and analytic techniques for mapping individuals' feelings of satisfaction with numbers aspects ("domains") of their experiences. These studies examine domains ranging from the highly specific (house, family, etc.) to the global (life as a whole). A large number of other studies and applications of these concepts and techniques have appeared over the past three decades and continue to appear – one or more studies of subjective well-being indicators can be found in almost any issue of the journal *Social Indicators Research* and the *Journal of Happiness Studies*.

The principle that the link between objective conditions and subjective well-being (defined in terms of response to sample survey or interview questions about happiness or satisfaction with life as a whole) is sometimes paradoxical and therefore that subjective as well as objective states should be monitored is well established in the social indicators literature. However, numerous studies of the measurement and psychodynamics of subjective well-being over the past three decades have led to a better understanding of this construct. While research continues and it would be incorrect to say that the debates have been settled, it appears that this construct may have both *traitlike* (i.e., a durable psychological condition that differs among individuals and contributes to stability over time and consistency across situations) and *statelike* (i.e., a condition that is reactive to situational differences and thus potentially amenable to influence by social context and public policies) *properties*.

With respect to the statelike properties of subjective well-being, Davis (1984) used an accumulated sample from several years of NORC General Social Surveys to document the responsiveness of happiness with life as a whole to (1) "new money" (recent changes in respondents' financial status as opposed to current income level), (2) "an old man/lady" (being married or having an intimate living partner), and (3) "two's company" (a household size of two as compared to living alone or families of three or more). Numerous other studies have found additional factors that are more or less strongly associated with variations in subjective well-being. But the relevance of intimate living conditions/family status almost always is replicated. The connection of subjective well-being to income levels has been a particularly intriguing problem for social indicators researchers ever since Easterlin's (1973) finding that income differences between nations predicted national differences in happiness but that the association of happiness with income within countries was much weaker. Easterlin's study has stimulated a large literature on the relationship of income to subjective well-being; for a recent review of this research literature, see Diener and Biswas-Diener (2002). Suffice it to say that the last word is not in on this subject and that the theoretical and applied importance of the relationship will continue to be a focus of research interest.

Descriptive Social Indicators

Building on the Ogburn legacy of research on social trends, a third approach to social indicators focuses on social measurements and analyses designed to improve our understanding of what the main features of society are, how they interrelate, and how these features and their relationships change. This produces *descriptive social indicators* – indices of the state of society and changes taking place therein. Although descriptive social indicators may be more or less directly (causally) related to the well-being goals of public policies or programs and thus include policy or criterion indicators, they are not limited to such uses. For instance, in the area of health, descriptive indicators might include preventive indicators such as the percent of the population that does not smoke cigarettes, as well as criterion indicators such as the number of days of activity limitations in the past month or an index of self-reported satisfaction with health.

The various statistical forms that descriptive social indicators can take were described by Land (1983). These can be ordered by degree of abstraction from those that require only one or two data series and little processing (e.g., an age-specific death rate) to those that involve more complicated processing into a single composite or summary index (e.g., years of life expectancy at age x, years of active or disability-free life expectancy at age x). Descriptive social indicators can be formulated at any of these levels of abstraction. Moreover, these

indicators can, at least in principle, be organized into demographic- or time-budget-based systems of social accounts.

FUNCTIONS OF INDICATORS

The Enlightenment Function

The Social Indicators Movement was motivated by the principle that it is important to *monitor changes over time* in a broad range of social phenomena that extend beyond the traditional economic indicators and that include *indicators of quality of life*. Many organized actors in contemporary society – including government agencies, organizations and activists interested in social change programs, scholars, and marketing researchers interested in market development and product innovations – monitor indicators in which they have a vested interest and want to see increase or decline (Ferriss 1988).

A second principle that has been part of the Social Indicators Movement from the outset is that a critically important role of social indicators in contemporary democratic societies is *public enlightenment through social reporting*. In brief, modern democracies require social reporting to describe social trends, explain why an indicator series behaves as it does and how this knowledge affects interpretation, and highlight important relationships among series.

It also is important to document the consequences that are reasonably attributable to changes in a series. This includes the systematic use of social indicators to *forecast trends in social conditions and/or turning points therein*. To be sure, the area of projection or forecasting is filled with uncertainties. Techniques range from the naïve extrapolation of recent trends to futuristic scenario construction to complicated model building with regression, time series, or stochastic process techniques. Demands for the anticipation of the future (at a minimum, for the description of "what will happen if present trends continue"), for foresight and forward thinking in the public and private sectors, and for the assessment of critical trends appear to be an intrinsic part of contemporary post-industrial societies. Thus, it is prudent to expect that the "anticipation" task will become an increasingly important part of the enlightenment function of social indicators.

As the decades of the 1990s and 2000s unfolded, the model of a comprehensive national social report in the tradition pioneered by Ogburn and Olson clearly had faltered in the United States, at least in the sense of federal government sponsorship and/or production. But the key ideas of monitoring, reporting, and forecasting were evident to greater or lesser extents in the production of continuing, periodic subject matter-specific publications by various federal agencies, including *Science Indicators* (published by the National Science Foundation), *The Condition of Education* (published by the Department of Education), the *Report to the Nation on Crime and Justice* (published by the Department of Justice), and numerous Bureau of the Census publications. Special topics involving groups of federal agencies also receive attention from time to time. For instance, the Federal Interagency Forum on Child and Family Statistics began in 1997 an annual publication on *America's Children: Key National Indicators of Well-Being*. In addition, the United States has numerous private research organizations, policy institutes, and scholars that continue to produce reports, monographs, and books interpreting social trends and developments in various areas of social concern.

In contrast to the situation in the United States, comprehensive social reports/social indicators compendiums continue to be published periodically in several other countries. Examples are the *Datenreport* series published biannually since 1983 by the Federal Republic of Germany, the *Social and Cultural Report* published biannually by the Social and Cultural Planning Office of The Netherlands, and *Australian Social Trends* published annually by the Australian Bureau of Statistics. Citations and summary reviews of these and other social indicators/social reports publications can be found in the quarterly newsletter and review of social reports, *SINET: Social Indicators Network News* (for access, see www.soc.duke.edu/resources/sinet/index.html).

The difference in the organization of social indicators/reporting work in the United States as compared to that in other countries is in part attributable to the lack of a central statistical office responsible for the coordination of all government statistical activities in the former. More generally, it is indicative of the fact that, despite the invention of the ideas of social indicators and comprehensive social reporting in the United States, the nation has lagged in their institutionalization. Whether a new round of legislative effort will eventually create the necessary institutional base remains to be seen.

The Policy Analysis Function

Policy analysts distinguish various ways of guiding or affecting public policy, including *problem definition, policy choice and evaluation of alternatives*, and *program monitoring* (MacRae 1985). The social reporting/public enlightenment approach to social indicators centers around the first of these, namely, the use of social indicators in problem definition and the framing of the terms of policy discourse. Indeed, studies of the actual use of social indicators suggest that this is precisely the manner in which they have affected public action. But policy analysts from Olson to MacRae always have hoped for more from social indicators, namely, the shaping of public policy and planning through the policy choice process.

Land and Ferriss (2002) noted that the following *model for directed social change* emerged during the 1990s concerning policy uses of social indicators in such areas as health, education, and the welfare of children and youth in the United States:

- *Identify trends in criterion indicators*, the direction or rate of change of which should be changed.
- *Gather together intelligence* from experiments, field research, or theory that suggests what should be done to bring about the desired change.
- *Launch a decentralized program to effect change in specific criterion indicators* by specific amounts, to be attained by a target date.
- *Monitor progress* by periodically assessing trends on the specific indicators, modifying strategies as needed.
- As initial goals are reached, *set new goals* for continued progress.

Land and Ferriss (2002) developed a more complete articulation of this scheme in the form of a sociological model that accommodates both the enlightenment and policy analysis functions of social indicators. They noted that identifying such goals and setting about altering their direction or rate of change is a process called *telesis*, which means "progress that is intelligently planned and directed; the attainment of the desired ends by the application of intelligent human effort to the means." The further development and application of this conceptual framework may provide the foundations for the policy analytic use of social indicators in the future.

SEE ALSO: Demographic Techniques: Population Projections and Estimates; Ecological Problems; Evaluation; Population and Development; Population and the Environment; Poverty; Social Problems, Concept and Perspectives; Urban Policy; Values: Global

REFERENCES AND SUGGESTED READINGS

Bauer, R. A. (Ed.) (1966) *Social Indicators*. MIT Press, Cambridge, MA.

Campbell, A., Converse, P. E., & Rodgers, W. L. (1976) *The Quality of American Life: Perceptions, Evaluations, and Satisfactions*. Russell Sage Foundation, New York.

Davis, J. A. (1984) New Money, An Old Man/Lady and "Two's Company": Subjective Welfare in the NORC General Social Survey. *Social Indicators Research* 15: 319–51.

Diener, E. & Biswas-Diener, R. (2002) Will Money Increase Subjective Well-Being? A Literature Review and Guide to Needed Research. *Social Indicators Research* 57: 119–69.

Duncan, O. D. (1969) *Toward Social Reporting: Next Steps*. Russell Sage Foundation, New York.

Easterlin, R. (1973) Does Money Buy Happiness? *Public Interest* 30: 3–10.

Ferriss, A. L. (1988) The Uses of Social Indicators. *Social Forces* 66: 601–17.

Land, K. C. (1983) Social Indicators. *Annual Review of Sociology* 9: 1–26.

Land, K. C. & Ferriss, A. L. (2002) Conceptual Models for the Development and Use of Social Indicators. In: Glatzer, W., Habich, R., & Mayer, K. U. (Eds.), *Sozialer Wandel und gesellschaftliche Dauerbeobachtung*. Festschrift for Wolfgang Zapf. Leske & Budrich, Opladen, pp. 337–52.

Land, K. C., Lamb, V. L., & Mustillo, S. K. (2001) Child and Youth Well-Being in the United States, 1975–1998: Some Findings from a New Index. *Social Indicators Research* 56 (December): 241–320.

MacRae, D., Jr. (1985) *Policy Indicators: Links Between Social Science and Public Policy*. University of North Carolina Press, Chapel Hill.

Miringoff, M. L. & Miringoff, M. L. (1999) *The Social Health of the Nation: How America is Really Doing*. Oxford University Press, New York.

President's Research Committee on Social Trends (1933) *Recent Trends in the United States*. McGraw-Hill, New York.

United Nations Development Program (2004) *Human Development Report 2004*. Oxford University Press, New York.

US Department of Health, Education, and Welfare (1969) *Toward a Social Report*. US Government Printing Office, Washington, DC.

social influence

Lisa Rashotte

Social influence is defined as change in an individual's thoughts, feelings, attitudes, or behaviors that results from interaction with another individual or a group. Social influence is distinct from conformity, power, and authority. Conformity occurs when an individual *expresses* a particular opinion or behavior in order to fit in to a given situation or to meet the expectations of a given other, though he does not necessarily hold that opinion or believe that the behavior is appropriate. Power is the ability to *force or coerce* rticular way by controlling her outcomes. Authority is power that is believed to be *legitimate* (rather than coercive) by those who are subjected to it.

Social influence, however, is the process by which individuals make *real* changes to their feelings and behaviors as a result of interaction with others who are perceived to be similar, desirable, or expert. People adjust their beliefs with respect to others to whom they feel similar in accordance with psychological principles such as balance. Individuals are also influenced by the majority: when a large portion of an individual's referent social group holds a particular attitude, it is likely that the individual will adopt it as well. Additionally, individuals may change an opinion under the influence of another who is perceived to be an expert in the matter at hand.

French and Raven (1959) provided an early formalization of the concept of social influence in their discussion of the bases of social power. For French and Raven, agents of change included not just individuals and groups, but also norms and roles. They viewed social influence as the outcome of the exertion of social power from one of five bases: reward power, coercive power, legitimate power, expert power, or referent power. A change in *reported* opinion or attitude (conformity) was considered an instance of social influence whether or not it represented a true private change.

French and Raven's original research was concerned with situations in which a supervisor influences a worker in a work situation. Subsequent scholarship has examined a wide variety of other social interactions, including families, classrooms, doctors and their patients, salespeople and customers, political figures, and dating couples. Work settings also continue to be a prominent topic for studies of social influence.

Since 1959, scholars have distinguished true social influence from forced public acceptance and from changes based on reward or coercive power. Social researchers are still concerned with public compliance, reward power, and coercive power, but those concerns are differentiated from social influence studies. Current research on social influence generally uses experimental methodology and tends to fall into five main areas: (1) minority influence in group settings, (2) research on persuasion, (3) dynamic social impact theory, (4) a structural approach to social influence, and (5) social influence in expectation states theory. Each is discussed below.

Minority influence is said to occur when a minority subgroup attempts to change the majority. For example, teachers often influence their students' beliefs, and political and religious leaders frequently influence the behavior of their followers. While some previous research has characterized the process of social influence as the majority riding roughshod over the minority, many scholars interested in minority influence believe that every member of a group can influence others, at least to some degree. Studies have found this to be particularly true when the minority group is consistent in what it presents to the majority.

In addition, the presence of minority groups within a larger group often leads to more creative thinking and better overall solutions on group tasks. Nemeth and Kwan (1987) demonstrated this in a study of four-person groups working on a creativity task. Individuals were given information that a majority (3 of 3) or a minority (1 of 3) of the other group members had come up with a novel response to the task at hand. Those who were in the minority condition actually produced more correct solutions to the task, indicating the strong effect of minority viewpoints.

Current research on persuasion, broadly defined as change in attitudes or beliefs based on information received from others, focuses on written or spoken messages sent from source to recipient. This research operates on the assumption that individuals process messages carefully whenever they are motivated and able to do so. Two types of theories dominate modern persuasion research: the elaboration likelihood model and heuristic-systemic models.

The elaboration likelihood model developed by Cacioppo, Petty, and Stoltenberg (1985) has been used most frequently (and very effectively) in therapeutic and counseling settings. It states that the amount and nature of thinking that a person does about a message will affect the kind of persuasion that the message produces. Aspects of the persuasion situation that have been shown to be important for this model include source, message, recipient, affect, channel, and context. Of particular importance is the degree to which the recipient views the message's issue as relevant to himself. This model has demonstrated its utility in persuading various people to make various types of healthier choices (e.g., cancer patients, those at risk from HIV/AIDS, teens at risk from tobacco use, etc.).

Heuristic-systemic models propose that argument strength will be most effective in persuading an individual when she is motivated and able to attend to the message (the "systemic" route). When the target individual is not motivated or is unable to attend carefully, persuasion will take place through more indirect means (the "heuristic" route), such as nonverbal cues or source credibility. Persuasion that takes place via the systemic route will be relatively permanent and enduring; persuasion through the heuristic route is more likely to be temporary.

Broader than persuasion, social impact theory, as developed primarily by Bibb Latane (1981), forms the basis for an active line of inquiry today called dynamic social impact theory. Social impact means any of the number of changes that might occur in an individual (physiological, cognitive, emotional, or behavioral) due to the presence or action of others, who are real, imagined, or implied. Social impact theory proposes that the impact of any information source is a function of three factors: the number of others who make up that source, their immediacy (i.e., closeness), and their strength (i.e., salience or power). Impact also may be attenuated by impediments to the operation of any of the three factors.

Dynamic social impact theory (Latane 1996) uses these ideas about social impact to describe and predict the diffusion of beliefs through social systems. In this view, social structure is the result of individuals influencing each other in a dynamic and iterative way. The likelihood of being influenced by someone nearby, rather than far away, (the *immediacy* factor noted above) produces localized cultures of beliefs within communication networks. This process can lead initially randomly distributed attitudes and beliefs to become clustered or correlated; less popular beliefs become consolidated into minority subcultures. Dynamic social impact theory views society as a self-organizing complex system in which individuals interact and impact each others' beliefs.

Like dynamic social impact theory, the structural approach to social influence examines interpersonal influence that occurs within a larger network of influences. In this larger network, attitudes and opinions of individuals are reflections of the attitudes and opinions of their referent others. Interpersonal influence is seen as a basis of individuals' socialization and identity. Social influence is seen as the process by which a group of actors will weigh and then integrate the opinions of significant others within the context of social structural constraints. The structure determines the initial positions of group members and the network and weight of interpersonal influences within the group.

Social influence network theory, as described by Friedkin (1998), has its roots in work by social psychologists and mathematicians, including French. The formal theory involves a two-stage weighted averaging of influential opinions. Actors start out with their own initial opinions on some matter. At each stage, then, actors form a "norm" opinion which is a weighted average of the other opinions in the group. Actors then modify their own opinion in response to this norm, forming a new opinion which is a weighted average of their initial opinion and the network norm. This theory utilizes mathematical models and quantifications to measure the process of social influence.

Expectation states theory provides another formal treatment of social influence. Rooted in the work of Bales (1950), which found inequalities in the amount of influence group members had over one another, researchers in this tradition have developed systematic models predicting the relative influence of task-oriented actors in group settings. Bales discovered that even when group members were equal on status at the beginning of the group session, some members would end up being more influential than others. The group would develop a hierarchy based on the behavior of the group members. When group members were initially unequal in status, inequalities would be imported to the group from the larger society such that, for example, age or sex or race would structure a hierarchy of influence.

Expectation states theory, as described in Berger et al. (1980), was originally proposed as an explanation for Bales's finding that groups of status equals would develop inequalities in influence. According to the theory, group members develop expectations about the future task performance of all group members, including themselves. Once developed, these expectations guide the group interaction. In fact, expectations both guide and are maintained by the interaction. Those group members for whom the highest expectations are held will be the most influential in the group's interactions.

Research in the expectation states tradition has developed into a burgeoning area within sociological social psychology. Scholars are continuing to expand the theory both theoretically and substantively. On the theoretical side, developments include the status characteristics branch, work on status creation, ideas about status interventions, and many others. More substantive or applied work has been conducted using expectation states approaches to social influence in settings such as classrooms, jury rooms, and the workplace. Status characteristics that produce influence have been identified and extensively studied, including sex, race, sexual orientation, and physical attractiveness.

Future work will need to integrate these approaches of minority influence, persuasion, social impact, the structure of social influence, and expectation states. While each approach has produced worthwhile knowledge thus far, a general model of social influence will need to incorporate group structures, the characteristics of the individuals in those structures, and the distribution of characteristics into majority and minority components.

SEE ALSO: Asch Experiments; Authority and Conformity; Expectation States Theory; Interpersonal Relationships; Reference Groups

REFERENCES AND SUGGESTED READINGS

Bales, R. F. (1950) *Interaction Process Analysis*. Addison Wesley, Reading, MA.

Berger, J., Rosenholtz, S. J., & Zelditch, M. Jr. (1980). Status Organizing Processes. *Annual Review of Sociology* 6: 479–508.

Cacioppo, J. T., Petty, R. E., & Stoltenberg, C. D. (1985) Processes of Social Influence: The Elaboration Likelihood Model of Persuasion. In: Kendall, P. C. (Ed.), *Advances in Cognitive-Behavioral Research and Therapy*. Academic Press, San Diego, pp. 215–74.

French, J. R. P., Jr. (1956) A Formal Theory of Social Power. *Psychological Review* 63: 181–94.

French, J. R. P., Jr. & Raven, B. (1959) The Bases of Social Power. In: Cartwright, D. (Ed.), *Studies in Social Power*. Institute for Social Research, Ann Arbor, MI, pp. 150–67.

Friedkin, N. (1998) *A Structural Theory of Social Influence*. Cambridge University Press, Cambridge.

Latane, B. (1981) The Psychology of Social Impact. *American Psychologist* 36: 343–56.

Latane, B. (1996) Dynamic Social Impact: The Creation of Culture by Communication. *Journal of Communication* 4: 13–25.

Moscovici, S., Mucchi-Faina, A., & Maass, A. (Eds.) (1994) *Minority Influence*. Nelson-Hall, Chicago.

Nemeth, C. & Kwan, J. (1987) Minority Influence, Divergent Thinking and the Detection of Correct Solutions. *Journal of Applied Social Psychology* 17: 788–99.

Raven, B. (1992) A Power/Interaction Model of Interpersonal Influence: French and Raven Thirty Years Later. *Journal of Social Behavior and Personality* 7: 217–44.

social integration and inclusion

Rainer Strobl

Social integration refers to the interrelation of elements in a social system. The term social system is used in a broad sense here. It describes a social unit with a relatively stable order that establishes a border between itself and its environment. In this sense groups, organizations, or even whole nation-states are examples of social systems. Traditionally, actors who are members of a social unit are regarded as the elements of a social system. However, in sociological works like Luhmann's *Social Systems* (1995) the elements are conceived more abstractly as actions or communications. This theoretical development reflects a social development of increasing functional differentiation and individualization with more demanding conditions for the coordination of the elements in a social system. In tribal societies the interrelation of elements is quasi-natural. It is granted by clear expectations in strict kinship systems. But already feudal societies need elaborate catalogues of rights and duties, albeit these are conceived as God-given and the individual is confronted with a clear set of norms in his social environment. With increasing functional differentiation in modern societies there is a decreasing involvement of actors as whole persons with all their abilities and social and psychological needs in a single social system. As a result, social integration is no longer self-evident and becomes both a social and a theoretical problem.

The pioneer in the study of social integration, Durkheim (1970) presents two ways for linking up elements of a social system and thus two types of social integration. On the one hand, his concept of mechanical solidarity stresses the traditional coordination of the elements in a social system through common values and beliefs. It implies tendencies common to all members of the society and the urge to conform to a "collective conscience." On the other hand, his concept of organic solidarity emphasizes a new form of integration through interdependence. It refers to the division of labor and the necessary cooperation of specialists. These two types of social integration are also known as normative and functional integration. Although Parsons (1967) approves of Durkheim's distinction between mechanical and organic solidarity, normative integration plays the dominant role in his work. It even encompasses functional integration and comes close to the notion of social order, which is a normative order in Parsons's theory. Although mechanical solidarity and organic solidarity are conceived as in Durkheim's work, Parsons emphasizes that organic solidarity also depends on common values and on norms of property, contract, market relations, etc. But unlike the norms of mechanical solidarity, these norms only set a framework for actors who then follow their individual interests. Apart from the mentioned two types of social integration there is another way of relating elements of a social system yet to be discussed: *conflict*. Georg Simmel demonstrated in "The Sociology of Conflict" (1903) that actors can be intensively linked by conflict. As soon as one gets involved in an escalating conflict more and more remarks and actions of the opponent become relevant in terms of intended discrimination or harm and are integrated into the system. Contrary to common belief, conflicts are social systems with a high degree of social integration. Thus, the opposite of social integration is not conflict but social disintegration. Conflicts arise if communication and interaction chains do not simply stop and disintegrate after the acknowledgment of a controversy, but begin to revolve around this controversy. Consequently, one has to acknowledge that there can be both too much and too little social integration.

Social integration has been discussed as being close to the general issue of social order. An additional aspect is how an element becomes part of an existing social system. In this connection *assimilation* and *inclusion* can be regarded as modes of incorporating new elements. Assimilation refers to the possibility of becoming a member of a social unit by the acceptance and adoption of a given normative system. In this way the assimilation concept is traditionally used in migration literature. In Gordon's (1964) well-known assimilation model the process starts with cultural and behavioral adaptation which opens access to cliques, clubs, and institutions on primary-group level and the possibility of intermarriage. According to Gordon, this should lead to identification with the host society and finally to an absence of prejudice, discrimination, and value and power conflicts. However, Gordon concedes that a certain phase may continue indefinitely and thus the final state may never be reached. Conforming to important normative standards of cliques, clubs, and institutions on primary-group level thus may grant access to functionally unspecific social systems and may fulfill the social and psychological needs of a person, but they cannot guarantee access to good jobs or good education in modern societies. In other words, assimilation refers to the sphere of the lifeworld. It involves the whole person who becomes a member of a group or community. Consequently, the person will be defined as a member of this group or community and her freedom to act will be restricted according to the normative system of this social unit. In this connection we can concede that once access is obtained there may start processes of negotiating social norms. Therefore, assimilation need not be conceived as a unidirectional process where (in the end) the minority has become a copy of the majority. But at least there is the idea of a cultural nucleus that has to be accepted (Alba & Nee 2003).

As in modern societies integration into the sphere of the lifeworld does not automatically lead to participation in function systems like the economy, science, the educational system, or the justice system, there has to be a mechanism for participation in these systems. This mechanism is called inclusion. *Inclusion* means that specific competences and actions of a person are relevant for a social system. Accordingly, no individual is completely integrated into only one function system (Luhmann 1995). The adoption of specific cultural norms is not a precondition for inclusion. Sometimes it is even the violation of norms that facilitates inclusion. An example is rap music. Some famous rap musicians violate diverse cultural and even legal norms. However, this behavior helps to make them relevant for the music industry and to include them into the economic system. The freedom for the individual to violate norms in some social areas and nevertheless be included in function systems is a result of the fact that only specific roles of an individual, or more precisely, only particular actions and communications contribute to the processing of a function system. For the economic system, it is the crucial question if someone can pay or not, for the justice system it is the difference between right and wrong, for science it is the difference between true and false, etc. Of course, the basic norms of the particular function system have to be accepted (e.g., the norms of property and contract in economy or theoretical and methodological standards in science). However, someone from abroad can be an important business partner without accepting the moral or cultural standards of the country and someone who is disrespectful towards his wife can have valuable scientific insights. The necessary condition for relevance in a function system is the availability of the respective media, such as money, knowledge, power, etc. On the other hand, a lack of money, knowledge, or power prevents inclusion in the particular system and implies the danger of exclusion from all function systems. People in this situation (e.g., illegal immigrants, the homeless) are not relevant as taxpayers, consumers, or voters and are reduced to social problems or completely lost from sight.

As participation in function systems is essential in modern societies, there are instruments to improve the abilities and resources of disadvantaged and excluded individuals. In particular, the institutions of the welfare state can be conceived as means to safeguard against exclusion and to re-include the excluded. Efforts to integrate migrants – improvement of legal status, language courses, financial support, etc. – also aim at the chances of inclusion. Assimilation, on the other hand, cannot be achieved by institutional actors because they typically address a person in the specific role of a client. However, the change of cultural habits and personal convictions would involve the whole person.

Therefore, this is beyond their capability. It may not even be desirable to support a strong commitment to family, friends or the local, religious, or ethnic community. This form of social integration may for example prevent a person from moving to another town for a job or from attending a university and thus turn out as an obstacle to inclusion. Therefore, to improve inclusion it may be necessary to loosen social integration into primary groups and to support normative disintegration to a certain degree. On the other hand, a strong commitment to the demands of the function systems and a neglect of the lifeworld may lead to dissatisfaction, emotional problems, or even psychosomatic symptoms. As function systems dominate modern societies, there are reasons for complaints about the colonization of lifeworlds. However, as Weber pointed out in *Economy and Society* (1968), integration into a group or a community can also go along with oppression and the restriction of chances in life. In traditional societies, those who are not willing or who are not able to conform to the norms of the family and the community often have to face massive sanctions. In this respect inclusion as a new form of social integration means more freedom for the individual. But in contrast to the clear-cut normative environment of traditional societies and groups, inclusion also means participation in different social systems with heterogeneous demands. In modern societies the individual is not undivided in the Latin meaning of the word, but divided into different roles and only specific actions and communications are relevant for the function systems and are included into their processing. From the perspective of the individual, there are no ready-made solutions for the integration of the included and excluded facets of his personality into a meaningful identity, as from the perspective of society there is no master scheme for the integration of the different subsystems into a consistent whole. Under these circumstances, assimilation to the rigid but clear norms of ethnic, religious, or political fundamentalism can become a tempting alternative. It will be a challenging task for future research to analyze the possibilities and risks for a compromise between the demands of lifeworld and function systems and for a balance between assimilation and inclusion.

SEE ALSO: Durkheim, Émile; Lifeworld; Marginality; Parsons, Talcott; Social Exclusion; Social System

REFERENCES AND SUGGESTED READINGS

Alba, R. & Nee, V. (2003) *Remaking the American Mainstream: Assimilation and Contemporary Immigration*. Harvard University Press, Cambridge, MA.

Durkheim, E. (1970 [1893]) *The Division of Labor in Society*. Free Press, New York.

Eisenstadt, S. N. (1954) *The Absorption of Immigrants: A Comparative Study Based Mainly on the Jewish Community in Palestine and the State of Israel*. Routledge & Kegan Paul, London.

Gordon, M. (1964) *Assimilation in American Life: The Role of Race, Religion, and National Origins*. Oxford University Press, New York.

Lockwood, D. (1976) Social Integration and System Integration. In: Zollschan, G. K. & Hirsch, W. (Eds.), *Social Change: Explorations, Diagnoses and Conjectures*. Wiley, New York, pp. 370–83.

Luhmann, N. (1995) Inklusion und Exklusion (Inclusion and Exclusion). In: *Soziologische Aufklärung 6: Die Soziologie und der Mensch*. Westdeutscher Verlag, Opladen, pp. 237–64.

Nassehi, A. (2003) Inklusion: Von der Ansprechbarkeit zur Anspruchsberechtigung (Inclusion: From Responsiveness to Entitlement). In: Lessenich, S. (Ed.), *Wohlfahrtsstaatliche Grundbegriffe*. Campus, Frankfurt am Main, pp. 331–52.

Parsons, T. (1967) Durkheim's Contribution to the Theory of Integration of Social Systems. In: *Sociological Theory and Modern Society*. Free Press, New York, pp. 3–34.

social justice, theories of

Karen A. Hegtvedt

Justice, in its many guises, is a fundamental principle ensuring order in social groups ranging from small, intimate circles of friends to large, diverse societies. Its counterpart, injustice, arises when expectations about distributions, procedures, or interactions are unmet. Such unmet expectations stimulate the potential for change, both trivial and profound. *Distributive justice* pertains to the fairness of the allocation of rewards or burdens to a circle of recipients. *Procedural justice* captures the fairness of the means by which distributions are made. *Interactional justice* refers to fairness in the treatment of individuals within a group. These formal definitions, however, beg the fact that what individuals perceive as fair is subjective. That subjectivity pervades the two general approaches of the sociological study of justice.

One approach analyzes the social injustices wrought by income inequality, racism, sexism, etc. Theories about differences between groups based on income, skin color, gender, etc. are addressed elsewhere in this encyclopedia. Such perspectives focus on the origins and consequences of the differences, and implicitly raise the specter of injustice in considering fairness of the distribution of resources to each group and the treatment of group members based on their (subjectively devalued or presumed inferior) characteristics. In a related vein, debates over the distribution of societal goods (e.g., health care, jobs, housing) and societal burdens (e.g., hazardous wastes, taxes) to different groups in society also constitute issues of social justice. Social movements, while caused by many factors and requiring resources and organization, may rally individuals with cries of injustice and signal changes to redress injustice.

The second approach, which is largely the focus of this entry, examines the intersection of individuals' objective circumstances, their perceived realities, and their behaviors in order to grasp what people believe is just and how they respond to perceived injustices. In pursuing this second approach, social psychologists have developed theoretical frameworks and cumulated empirical results to explain distributive, procedural, and interactional justice issues more broadly. Such explanations, in turn, may inform the study of social injustices.

DISTRIBUTIVE JUSTICE

Theoretical perspectives on distributive justice address in various ways three key questions: What is justice? Why do people differentially perceive injustice? How do people respond to perceived injustice? Most theoretical approaches focus singularly on one of these questions. Guillermina Jasso (2001), however, offers a theoretical framework for justice analysis that includes the building blocks to address all of the key questions.

Jasso identifies the following as abstract components of determining what is just: the observer, who makes judgments about justice, and the rewardees, who are recipients of whatever is being distributed (observers may also be rewardees). The theory focuses on the observer's beliefs about the just reward and its application to the rewardees, given their characteristics. The application results in a just reward function which, when summed over rewardees, ensures the just reward distribution.

Combining these abstract building blocks reflects prior theorizing on distribution rules and allocation preferences (e.g., Leventhal et al. 1980). Distribution rules specify how outcome levels should correspond with individual characteristics (i.e., just reward functions). Three basic principles are equality, equity, and needs. Distinct from the others, the equality principle ignores individual characteristics, focusing instead on the equality of outcomes. The equity principle assumes that contributions, status, effort, etc. constitute inputs that entitle actors to commensurate levels of rewards. Equity also typically implies a comparison of outcome to input ratios across individuals. The needs principle likewise emphasizes commensurability with outcomes.

Leventhal et al.'s expectancy-value perspective argues that various motivations (e.g., self-interest, fairness, expedience) coupled with expectations about which principle enhances the likelihood of achieving differentially valued goals (e.g., group harmony, productivity, group welfare) predict distribution rule preference. Although the theoretical framework recognizes different motivations, what is preferred shapes what individuals believe to be fair or, in Jasso's terms, the observer's beliefs about the just reward. The theory allows that situational circumstances do affect underlying motivations and the value of goals. For example, conditions emphasizing impartiality, attention to the welfare of others, emphasis on a currently blatantly unfair distribution, open discussion

of distribution principles, and/or politeness typically produce distribution preferences that differ from those associated with self-interest. Thus individuals' own concerns and circumstances influence what they believe to be just.

Recognition of variation in the social positioning of individuals is one means to explain why people differentially perceive injustice. Indeed, there tends to be an egocentric bias in what people believe is just, although situational factors (e.g., role demands, concern for others) and individual characteristics (e.g., gender, specific belief systems) may attenuate it (Hegtvedt & Markovsky 1995). In addition to objective circumstances and personal motivations, actors' subjective evaluations of what is just stem from perceptions about a given situation and comparisons invoked.

A number of empirical studies attempt to address how beliefs and perceptions affect evaluations of injustice. Drawing from attribution theory and notions about cognitive processing, individuals are more likely to weigh internally caused inputs (e.g., effort, ability), which are under the control of an actor, as a more suitable basis for deriving an equitable distribution than externally caused inputs. Schema about pay levels and pay processes also provide a standard for assessing justice.

Such standards are a form of non-social comparisons, but may stem from prior social comparisons. Early theoretical work in the expectation states tradition (Berger et al. 1972) highlighted the importance of both the status value of outcomes (not simply their consumatory value) as well as various types of comparisons. This status value formulation argues that people develop stereotyped ideas of how social characteristics go with particular rewards. These ideas constitute referential structures. Thus, when an individual assesses his or her reward level or outcome/input ratio, the comparison may be to that of another individual (i.e., a local comparison) or to that inherent in a referential structure representing what people with the given characteristics generally get. The latter comparison puts individual rewards into a broader perspective and raises the possibility of the combination of comparisons. Other comparisons include those to one's past (internal comparisons) or between one's group and another group.

Jasso (1980) captures mathematically the potential for variation in the magnitude of perceived injustice (i.e., degrees of under- and overreward) stemming theoretically from differences in cognitions and comparisons. The justice evaluation (J) represents the observer's judgment that someone (including self) is justly or unjustly rewarded. The formula for J defines the justice evaluation in terms of the comparison between the actual reward received and the amount considered just, which implicitly stems from the observer's motivations, perceptions, and comparisons, as discussed above. The formula includes a numerical coefficient that designates the reward as a good or as a bad, and that allows the transformation of the experience of the justice evaluation into an expressed evaluation. An array of observer–rewardee justice evaluations may create a matrix or index to capture the overall injustice in a group or society. Such an array may also distinguish variation in the experience of injustice, bolstering the subjectivity of the evaluation.

Evaluations of injustice are likely to engender emotional, psychological, and behavioral reactions. Adams' (1965) classic formulation of equity theory specifies non-mathematically how individuals are likely to respond to perceived injustice, while Jasso's (2001) more recent statement offers a mathematical approach. Adams suggested that individuals who feel unjustly treated are likely to feel distress, and as self-interested actors are likely to be motivated to eliminate unpleasant feelings and restore justice in the least costly manner. Homans elaborated on the concept of distress, arguing that under-rewarded actors are likely to feel anger while overrewarded ones may feel guilt. Although cumulated studies document the anger responses, the guilt response remains more equivocal. Likewise, research tends to support Adams's behavioral strategies for restoring equity (e.g., increasing inputs if overrewarded, increasing outcomes if underrewarded), but few studies address psychological mechanisms (e.g., cognitively altering the value of inputs and outcomes) or compare the conditions under which one strategy or another will be chosen. Adams's formulation is focused on individual-level reactions, while Jasso's further allows for the possibility of collective reactions.

Most theorizing and research in distributive justice pertains to individual-level phenomena, largely because it is individuals who assess whether or not injustice has occurred. As a result, perceptions of justice are sometimes confounded with feelings of deservingness and, ironically, equated with assessments of self-interest. Yet, as philosophical treatises on justice and the implicit moral underpinnings of social psychological approaches suggest, distributive justice ensures more than the welfare of an individual. Rather, it engenders beliefs that a fair distribution will benefit the collectivity more broadly by upholding consensual values and suppressing bias. The emphasis on the group, while somewhat lost in considerations of distributive justice, is the cornerstone of the key theoretical approaches to procedural and interactional justice.

PROCEDURAL AND INTERACTIONAL JUSTICE

Although the three key questions characterizing distributive justice research also apply to procedural justice, the development of this area is marked chronologically by several classic contributions. Thibaut and Walker (1975) first drew attention to the notion of procedural justice in the legal context. They argued that people are concerned about the procedures involved in decision-making, especially in conflict situations, because they affect outcome levels. Certain rules could ensure procedural justice (Leventhal et al. 1980): (1) consistency of procedures across persons; (2) suppression of bias; (3) accuracy of information; (4) mechanisms to correct bad decisions; (5) representativeness of the participants to a decision; and (6) ethicality of standards. Lind and Tyler (1988), however, documented that adherence to such rules is important to people independent of outcome levels and in a variety of contexts. As an alternative to Thibaut and Walker's "instrumental" approach to fair procedures, they offered a group value approach that has become the theoretical touchstone for both procedural and interactional justice, especially in the area of organizational research.

The group value approach assumes that people want to be valued members of their group and that they look to procedures within the group to provide them with information about their position in the group. To the extent that authorities employ fair procedural rules, such as giving individuals the opportunity to voice their concerns prior to a decision (e.g., allowing representativeness), they are likely to feel valued by the group. The use of fair procedures, moreover, solidifies the group structure and values, enhancing individuals' pride in their group. In addition, authorities who treat their subordinates in a trusting, respectful, and unbiased fashion are likely to be viewed as procedurally fair. In effect, Tyler and Lind (1992) recognize two forms of procedural justice: (1) the rules underlying the process of decision-making; and (2) the polite and dignified treatment of members of the group. Some researchers (Bies & Moag 1986) contend that the second constitutes a unique form: interactional justice.

Regardless of the labeling, a great deal of research specifies what rules appear to be procedurally fair, the relationship between procedural and distributive justice, and the implications of procedural injustice (see Tyler et al. 1997). Research indicates that people perceive rules such as consistency and representativeness as key to ensuring procedural justice. Also important to procedural justice evaluations are the reasons certain procedures are invoked. Providing a rationale for a decision allows evaluators to make more accurate attributions and demonstrates respect for their ability to understand why authorities made a certain decision.

Lind and Tyler (1988) emphasize the importance of procedures for understanding evaluations of distributive justice as well. Individuals are more likely to tolerate unfair or low outcomes if the procedures by which they were produced are perceived as fair. Two theoretical frameworks detail why this is so. Folger's (1986) referent cognition theory suggests that when people receive an unfair outcome, they examine the procedures or "instrumentalities" responsible for their outcomes. Comparisons between what actually happened and what could have happened (the referent cognitions) affect the perceived severity of the distributive injustice. Also relying upon cognitions, van den Bos et al. (2001) argue that people use whatever information they have to substitute for information

that might be more relevant but is missing (e.g., other people's levels of rewards). Their "fairness heuristic theory" argues that procedural information provides an individual with knowledge of his or her value to the group, which in turn underlies feelings of inclusion that affect acceptance or rejection of outcomes. When people have more information on outcomes upon which to make their distributive justice evaluations, they are less likely to rely upon procedural information. Thus it is in the absence of information that individuals use procedures as a heuristic.

Because of the importance of procedures in and of themselves, however, the group value model specifies reactions to procedural injustice or, more generally, the implications of procedural unfairness. Like reactions to distributive injustice, individuals who perceive procedural injustice may feel angry and dissatisfied, as well as develop a dislike toward the perpetrators of the injustice. Procedural unfairness also threatens compliance with rules and with authorities in a variety of settings. For example, in dealing with law enforcement officers, individuals are more likely to comply with their requests if they are treated in a polite, respectful manner. In organizational settings, procedural justice is likely to enhance organizational commitment and organizational citizenship behaviors (Colquitt et al. 2001). The forays of procedural justice researchers into more applied areas reinforce the role of basic theory in understanding issues of social justice.

RELEVANCE OF THEORIES TO SOCIAL JUSTICE

Although varying in levels of abstract and underlying theoretical assumptions (e.g., self-interest versus group value), the individual-level theories of distributive, procedural, and interactional justice may inform the study of social justice issues such as income inequality, racism, sexism, etc. Indeed, in the past, many studies have focused on the fairness of distribution of income or privileges across groups (Hegtvedt & Markovsky 1995). People in western societies tend to view inequality as fair by focusing on the importance of individual contributions.

This perception varies cross-nationally, however, depending upon strength of beliefs in the capitalistic economic system in comparison to beliefs in a welfare state. Similarly, justice theory has been brought to bear upon gender issues such as the fairness of the division of labor in the household. Like the role of belief systems in understanding perceptions of income inequality, gender roles attitudes tend to affect tolerance of inequality in the household division of labor. Understanding the ways in which people assess whether procedures or outcomes are fair or unfair may provide a basis for resolving conflicts occurring between different cultural and ethnic groups, especially as the demographics of these groups shift.

Theories of justice in social psychology have long assumed consensus on what is just or simply ignored the implications of different perceptions of injustice. However, as social injustices illustrate, such consensus is often illusive and the consequences profound for some groups. Several areas of research stemming from basic theoretical frameworks may contribute to a means to resolve social injustices. First, examination of social categorization processes and perceptions of similarity and dissimilarity may help to define the moral communities to which justice principles apply. Second, an understanding of the different interests and beliefs of groups may inform the likelihood and nature of conflict between groups (or individuals) and the potential role of a more general sense of justice (not simply justified self-interest) in resolving competing claims. And third, a shift away from the typical predictions of what the disadvantaged are likely to perceive, feel, and do toward determining when people who benefit from current societal procedures and distributions are likely to step beyond their own self-interests may inform understanding of social change and ultimately create a more consensual notion of justice.

SEE ALSO: Distributive Justice; Global Justice as a Social Movement; Globalization and Global Justice; Inequality/Stratification, Gender; Race and the Criminal Justice System; Social Movements; Stratification and Inequality, Theories of

REFERENCES AND SUGGESTED READINGS

Adams, J. S. (1965) Inequity in Social Exchange. *Advances in Experimental Social Psychology* 2: 267–99.

Berger, J., Zelditch, M., Jr., Anderson, B., & Cohen, B. P. (1972) Stuctural Aspects of Distributive Justice: A Status Value Formation. In: Berger, J., Zelditch, M., Jr., & Anderson, B. (Eds.), *Sociological Theories in Progress*. Houghton Mifflin, Boston.

Bies, R. J. & Moag, J. (1986) Interactional Justice: Communication Criteria of Fairness. In: Sheppard, B. H., Lewicki, R. J., & Bazerman, M. H. (Eds.), *Research on Negotiations in Organizations*. JAI Press, Greenwich, CT, pp. 83–99.

Colquitt, J. A., Conlon, D. E., Wesson, M. J., Porter, C. O. L. H., & Yee Ng, K. (2001) Justice at the Millennium: A Meta-Analytic Review of 25 Years of Organizational Justice Research. *Journal of Applied Psychology* 86: 425–45.

Folger, R.. (1986) Rethinking Equity Theory: A Referent Cognition Model. In: Bierhoff, H., Cohen, R. L., & Greenberg, J. (Eds.), *Justice in Social Relations*. Plenum, New York, pp. 145–63.

Hegtvedt, K. A. & Markovsky, B. (1995) Justice and Injustice. In: Cook, K., Fine, G. A., & House, J. (Eds.), *Sociological Perspectives on Social Psychology*. Allyn Bacon, Boston, pp. 257–80.

Jasso, G. (1980) A New Theory of Distributive Justice. *American Sociological Review* 45: 3–32.

Jasso, G. (2001) Formal Theory. In: Turner, J. H. (ed.), *Handbook of Sociological Theory*. Kluwer Academic/Plenum, New York, pp. 37–68.

Leventhal, G. S., Karuza, Jr., J., & Fry, W. R. (1980) Beyond Fairness: A Theory of Allocation Preferences. In: Mikula, G. (Ed.), *Justice and Social Interaction*. Plenum, New York, pp. 167–218.

Lind, E. A. & Tyler, T. R. (1988) *The Psychology of Procedural Justice*. Plenum, New York.

Sanders, J. & Hamilton, V. L. (Eds.), (2001) *Handbook of Justice Research in Law*. Kluwer Academic/Plenum, New York.

Thibaut, J. & Walker, L. (1975) *Procedural Justice: A Psychological Analysis*. Erlbaum, Hillsdale, NJ.

Tyler, T. R. & Lind, E. A. (1992) A Relational Model of Authority in Groups. *Advances in Experimental Social Psychology* 25: 115–91.

Tyler, T. R., Boeckmann, R. J., Smith, H. J., & Huo, Y. J. (1997) *Social Justice in a Diverse Society*. Westview Press, Boulder.

van den Bos, K., Lind, A. E., & Wilke, H. A. M. (2001) The Psychology of Procedural and Distributive Justice Viewed from the Perspective of Fairness Heuristic Theory. In: Cropanzano, R. (Ed.), *Justice in the Workplace: From Theory to Practice*, Vol. 2. Erlbaum, Mahwah, NJ, pp. 49–66.

social learning theory

Laura Auf der Heide

Social learning theory was developed in the 1950s by Albert Bandura as a direct response to strict behaviorism as a means for explaining how individuals learn about their social worlds. Instead of solely examining the result of the outside environment on individual behavior, social learning theory is concerned with the reciprocal influence of environmental cues on an individual's behavior and the impact of the individual's behavior on the environment. In addition, social learning theory places an emphasis on individuals' cognitive processes as they decide upon future courses of action. Thus, social learning theory takes a middle ground position between social psychological theories that stress either environmental or internal cognitive processes as the sole component of learning.

BEHAVIORISM

Social learning theory posits that people learn about their social worlds in two distinct ways. First, following in the tradition of behaviorism, individuals learn through direct experience with their environments, and the rewards and consequences that follow. Behaviorism espouses a phenomenon known as operant conditioning. In essence, through operant conditioning, behaviorists believe they can predict the future probability of behavior based on two types of contingency effects associated with a particular behavior. *Reinforcement contingencies* encourage an individual to keep repeating a task. *Punishment contingencies* serve to diminish a particular behavior. Similar to theories of social exchange and rational choice, behaviorism and social learning theory assume that individuals attempt to maximize their rewards and avoid punishments. For example, Carrie may learn that hitting her brother Bill is unacceptable when she is punished by her mother for that act. According to predictions of operant conditioning, Carrie should stop hitting Bill to avoid the negative sanction (punishment contingency). Similarly, Carrie might learn that putting her clothes in the hamper is good when her mother praises her for that act. Here we would expect Carrie to keep putting her clothes in the hamper in order to continue receiving praise (reinforcement contingency). Numerous experimental studies have shown that behavior can be effectively increased or decreased through the use of different contingencies.

OBSERVATIONAL LEARNING AND MODELING

In addition to recognizing the importance of direct experience on learning, social learning theory also stresses the importance of observational learning, or modeling, the actions of others. Social learning theory posits that individuals do not have to experience consequences directly to determine the value of a particular action if they have been able to observe the consequences somebody else has received for it. Thus, in reference to the first example above, if Carrie watches her older sister Margaret get in trouble for hitting Bill, she will learn that hitting Bill has negative consequences without experiencing the negative consequences for herself. Given this information, Carrie will likely not hit Bill in the future unless the reward for hurting him is greater than the punishment she receives from her mother. In reference to the second example, if Carrie sees Margaret get rewarded for putting her clothes in the hamper, she may model Margaret's behavior and put *her* clothes in the hamper to get a reward.

The concept of modeling is intrinsic to the discussion of observational learning. Whenever we learn by observing someone else's rewards/consequences, that person becomes a model for that behavior, whether we choose to reenact that behavior ourselves or not. In the above examples, Margaret served as Carrie's model. Bandura (1973) proposes that there are four necessary conditions for observational learning and modeling. *Attentional processes* highlight the importance of an individual's awareness of a model performing an activity. Thus, mere exposure to the model is not enough for an individual to learn from the model's behavior; one must also pay attention to the behavior. *Retention processes* refer to the individual's capacity for long-term memory of a model's behavior. It is a necessary component of the learning process that an individual be able to reproduce the model's behavior even when the model is not physically present; one primary way of retaining the learned behavior is through rehearsal. *Motor reproduction processes* occur when an individual enacts what she has learned. However, Bandura stresses that individuals can learn particular behaviors without having acted them out themselves. For instance, Carrie learned that hitting Bill had consequences for Margaret without having to hit Bill herself. Finally, *reinforcement and motivational processes* are integral to observational learning. Although individuals learn behavior from others, they are less likely to enact the behavior themselves if they have seen others get punished for the behavior. These four conditions specify *when* individuals are likely to learn from others. However, there are three conditions under which individuals may be more or less likely to imitate a model once these four conditions have been fulfilled.

DETERMINANTS OF MODELING

Bandura has identified three determinants that affect whether an individual will model what she has learned. First, the model's characteristics matter. Social learning theory recognizes that an individual's status, power, and competence at a task will greatly impact whether others choose to model her. This perspective has been developed formally as expectation states theory. In our society, people assume that individuals with high status, power, or competence must know the correct way of doing things; thus, social learning theory would predict that individuals with these characteristics will be modeled more often. Second, the attributes of the individual learning from the model (or the observer) determine whether she will be more likely to model the behavior. Research has demonstrated that those who lack confidence, have low self-esteem, and are more dependent are more often rewarded for imitating high-status people. Indeed, the status, power, and competence of the observer likely interact with the characteristics of the model to determine imitation: a low-status person will be more likely to model a

high-status person than the other way around. For example, research has shown that children model adults, but adults do not model children, a lower-status group. In addition to status characteristics, research shows that those who are more open to learning through modeling often obtain the greatest gains when learning new skills (Bandura 1977). Third, as mentioned above, the response categories associated with a model's behavior directly influence whether an observer imitates that behavior. This is especially true when an individual sees a model get rewarded or punished for a particular action. However, when a model receives a neutral response for her actions, or an observer is unsure of the response consequences for an action, then the observer will be more likely to focus on the status of the model when determining her future course of action. Thus, an observer will more likely imitate a high-status over a low-status model if she does not know the outcomes of the model's actions. Observers tend to continue imitating models as long as they receive rewards for that action. If they start obtaining bad reactions for their actions, then they will seek out a new model.

Adding observational learning to behaviorism's focus on operant conditioning was a great advance for social learning theory. However, both direct and observational learning still emphasize the environment when predicting the behaviors of individuals. Social learning theory extends this to include individual cognitions as part of the learning process. Given the assumption that individuals desire to maximize rewards and minimize punishments, social learning theory posits that they learn to regulate themselves in order to obtain desired rewards. Social learning theory holds that when observing the response consequences of others, individuals begin to understand the future consequences of various actions they could take. This knowledge, gained through observation of the environment, allows individuals to plan what actions will allow them to obtain desired rewards extrinsically, as well as influence them to intrinsically motivate themselves to achieve external rewards. Over the long term, research has shown that individuals are more influenced by intrinsic than extrinsic rewards (Bandura 1977).

APPLICATIONS OF SOCIAL LEARNING THEORY

Within sociology, social learning theory has been applied primarily to the socialization process, aggression, and deviance. As already detailed, social learning theory can be usefully applied to examine how children learn about their social worlds. Through processes of imitation and conditioning, children learn how to speak, how to interact with others, and how to adopt the norms and values of society. Some sociological research has attempted to extend social learning theory to learning across the life course, in such diverse areas as organizational behavior and social movements.

Perhaps in its most famous application, Bandura utilized social learning theory to study aggression. In contrast to the evolutionary perspective on aggression, which roots aggression in the individual's biological makeup and psychological functioning, and the frustration–aggression hypothesis, which posits that individuals behave aggressively when they encounter a stimulus that psychologically frustrates them, social learning theory examines how the *external* son's aggressiveness. In a series of well-known experiments, Bandura (1965) showed that children who watched models behave aggressively towards a blown-up Bobo doll were more likely to imitate the behavior when the model received a reward or a neutral response for the aggression. However, children who watched the model receive a punishment were statistically less likely to imitate the model's behavior. As a result of these experiments, Bandura concluded that the aggression individuals evidence in the present is directly contingent upon the amount of aggression they have learned in the past. Furthermore, Bandura posits that observational learning is more important than operant conditioning when children learn aggression. Social learning theory's views on aggression have been used to support claims that violence in multimedia outlets, especially movies, television, and video games, leads children to become more aggressive. This perspective has become more popular in the wake of children's violence in schools in the late 1990s.

Social learning theory has also been usefully applied in sociology to the study of crime and deviance in the form of the theory of differential association (Akers 1977). Akers's theory has four parts, two of which directly originate with social learning theory. First, the theory proposes that people associate with different groups (i.e., have differential association with groups), and as a result become exposed to the norms and values of those groups. Second, the groups with whom we choose to interact also provide us with significant definitions, symbols, and meanings. Most important to deviance, groups espouse definitions either favorable or unfavorable to delinquency. Third, like social learning theory, the theory of differential association predicts that individuals will engage in deviant acts if they receive positive reinforcement for them, and desist if they are punished for committing them. Most of the time, individuals will persist in deviant acts if the group reinforces that behavior. Finally, individuals imitate the behavior of individuals in their group, based on the three contingencies to modeling behavior specified above. Thus, if we see members of our group being delinquent, we see them receive positive rewards for that behavior, and they are high status in our eyes, we will be likely to imitate the deviant behavior. Although differential association was created specifically to explain deviant behavior, it could be usefully applied to most situations involving socialization to a particular group.

Classical tests of social learning theory, including Bandura's studies on aggression, employed experimental methodologies. However, more recent work using the social learning theory paradigm has successfully utilized survey instruments and interviews in an attempt to explain theoretical principles. Given social learning theory's attention to both individual and environmental phenomena, it is uniquely suited to explaining multiple facets of human behavior.

SEE ALSO: Aggression; Behaviorism; Crime, Social Learning Theory of; Deviance, Crime and; Expectation States Theory; Psychological Social Psychology; Rational Choice Theories; Social Exchange Theory; Socialization; Status

REFERENCES AND SUGGESTED READINGS

Akers, R. L. (1977) *Deviant Behavior: A Social Learning Approach*, 2nd edn. Wadsworth, Belmont, CA.

Akers, R. L. (1998) *Social Learning and Social Structure: A General Theory of Crime and Deviance.* Northeastern University Press, Boston.

Bandura, A. (1965) Influence of Models' Reinforcement Contingencies on the Acquisition of Imitative Responses. *Journal of Personality and Social Psychology* 1: 589–95.

Bandura, A. (1973) *Aggression: A Social Learning Analysis.* Prentice-Hall, Englewood Cliffs, NJ.

Bandura, A. (1977) *Social Learning Theory.* Prentice-Hall, Englewood Cliffs, NJ.

Bandura, A. & Walters, R. H. (1959) *Adolescent Aggression.* Ronald, New York.

Skinner, B. F. (1953) *Science and Human Behavior.* Macmillan, New York.

social movement organizations

Elizabeth A. Armstrong and Tim Bartley

Social movements organize people, resources, and ideas for social change. Many do this through formal organizations, and most sociologists recognize the social movement organization (SMO) as a key factor in the study of movements. SMOs can be defined as formal organizations that take the collective pursuit of social change as a primary goal. This concept is trickier than it may initially seem, since it relies on two concepts that are themselves difficult to define. Scholars generally define social movements as contentious forms of collective action operating at least partly outside institutionalized politics. Yet scholars disagree about how significant the desired change needs to be and what it means to work outside of institutionalized politics. Common definitions of organizations – as goal-directed, boundary-maintaining, and rule-governed groups – are somewhat less contentious.

Many social movement groups, both past and present, are clearly identifiable as SMOs – for example, the Student Non-Violent Coordinating Committee (SNCC), War Resisters League, Greenpeace, United Students Against Sweatshops, the National Gay and Lesbian Task Force, and many others. Other groups, however, are more ambiguous. Some groups

are insufficiently organized or change-oriented to be considered SMOs. For instance, Gay Liberation Fronts existed in many US cities in the early 1970s, but it is unclear if they ever cohered into formal organizations. In contrast, the AFL-CIO is highly organized, but at some points it has perhaps been too entrenched in "normal politics" to fit standard definitions of an SMO. Sociologists have not hit upon a simple formula for deciding what is and is not an SMO. In practice, they have often drawn on lay understandings – that is, treating a group as an SMO if its participants see themselves as building an organization that participates in a movement.

Organizations have not always been central to social movement research. Early theories saw mass activity as rooted in social *disorganization*. Studies of crowd behavior and mid-century "mass society" theories treated collective action as the result of alienation, social isolation, and authoritarian tendencies. Similarly, "strain theory" argued that social movements were caused by structural shifts that produced social disintegration and the breakdown of existing organizational and institutional structures.

The Civil Rights Movement had a profound impact on the study of social movements. Sociologists' sympathies with the movement contributed to the rise of theories that treated activism as rational political activity requiring resources and organization instead of irrational, spontaneous collective behavior. This shift moved SMOs to the center of the analysis, carried by two influential theories – resource mobilization and political process. Resource mobilization theory developed in part as a response to the professionalization of social movements in the later years of the Civil Rights Movement. McCarthy and Zald (1977) argued that the rise and fall of movements is best explained by the resources available for building and maintaining organizations, not by grievances, which were seen as relatively constant. The resource mobilization paradigm, more than any other approach, put the structure and strength of SMOs at the center of the analysis. Political process theory also drew attention to organizations, viewing social movements as "politics by other means" for those excluded from the formal polity (McAdam 1982). Researchers in this tradition have shown not only that political opportunities shape mobilization, but also that grassroots organizational infrastructures are critical, as illustrated by the important role that black churches and colleges played in the Civil Rights Movement.

Syntheses of resource mobilization and political process approaches solidified the SMO as a key focus of research. While the SMO was a novel focus in the early days of resource mobilization theory, it now occupies a central place in the sociology of movements.

INTERNAL DYNAMICS OF SMOs

Most research on the internal dynamics of SMOs engages with one of two strong theories of voluntary organizations. One strand focuses on Robert Michels's "iron law of oligarchy" (Michels 1962 [1911]), which argues that organizations inevitably evolve from democratic governance toward control by elites, from radical goals toward moderate ones, and from broad agendas for social change toward narrow dictates of organizational maintenance. Michels's critique of oligarchy inspired some new left and feminist activists in the 1960s to experiment with informal and anti-bureaucratic organizational forms, but these experiments often created new organizational problems. Freeman (1972) warned against a "tyranny of structurelessness" in which power coalesces in the hands of the few even in groups with little formal structure. Researchers and activists continue to puzzle over the conditions under which the iron law of oligarchy applies and how movements can subvert this process.

Michels's theory also inspired debates about the efficiency of formal organization – particularly hierarchical and bureaucratic organization – and its effects on movement outcomes. While Piven and Cloward (1979) suggested that formal organization depresses mass mobilization, Gamson (1975) argued that bureaucracy can help movements achieve their goals. This debate posed the question in a limited way: only two organizational forms were considered (bureaucracy versus no bureaucracy) and it was assumed that organizational forms were simply vehicles for achieving particular goals. Other research has moved past these limitations. Polletta (2002) argues that participatory democracy

within SMOs is politically effective under particular conditions. Participatory democracy has three main benefits: it builds group solidarity, enhances the development of innovative tactics, and develops leadership skills. Thus, participatory democracy works when costs of participation are high, the environment is uncertain, or when there are few people with developed leadership skills.

A second strand of research on the internal dynamics of SMOs responds to Olson's (1965) influential statement on the problem of "free-riding" in voluntary organizations. Olson argued that since self-interested individuals will tend to free-ride on the efforts of others, voluntary organizations will be doomed to failure unless they can provide excludable benefits (selective incentives) to their members. Sociologists have shown that organizations can also generate mobilization through "solidary" incentives, social networks, or the formation of a "critical mass." These studies have shed light on the determinants of movement participation, and have reminded social movement scholars that organization is a problem and a process, not merely a structure to be taken for granted.

ENVIRONMENTS AND FIELDS
OF SMOs

Scholars have developed several ways of thinking about how SMOs rely on broader environments. Resource mobilization theorists see the provision or withholding of resources – funding, space, staff, technical expertise, equipment – as the primary way environments affect the emergence, form, development, and survival of SMOs. SMOs are more likely to be founded, survive, grow, and achieve their objectives in resource-rich environments, and to struggle in resource-poor environments. Political process scholars have focused on how the structure of political opportunities shapes the formation, growth, survival, and success of SMOs. Specifically, they have shown that the state and other elite groups enable and constrain SMOs by providing positive opportunities for some kinds of organizations and establishing legal prohibitions against other kinds – typically, those with politically radical or otherwise undesirable ideologies or strategies. As a legitimate source of rules about what kinds of organizations are legal and will receive benefits from the state (i.e., tax exemption), the state effectively "channels" SMOs. Pressures from the state can also lead SMOs to become more bureaucratic, as tax breaks and governmental funding are often available only to organizations that can demonstrate that their internal structure is acceptable to the state. Institutional theory provides a third way to think about the relationship between SMOs and environments. Neo-institutionalists argue that SMOs, like other kinds of organizations, tend to adopt organizational forms that are culturally legitimate and taken for granted as appropriate.

Scholars have also expanded the focus to consider the structure and evolution of entire "fields" or "populations" of SMOs and the consequences for social movement outcomes. Influenced by population ecology theory, some social movement scholars have analyzed the interacting forces that cause populations of SMOs to grow or decline. Minkoff (1999) shows how SMOs constitute the environment for one another, such that the fate and impact of a particular SMO depends partially on its position within a population or field organization. SMOs in a field may compete for resources, cooperate on social movement actions, develop a division of labor, or provide resources and other forms of support to each other. The conditions under which cooperation or competition prevails are not fully understood.

Examination of the structure and evolution of movement fields has also shed light on the consequences of movement diversification. It has often been assumed that ideological differences in a social movement field reflect a lack of unity and thus indicate movement weakness. Yet ideological and functional diversity may enable movements to appeal to a larger constituency and to respond effectively to complex and rapidly changing political environments. Diversity in social movement fields also enables movements to benefit from "radical flank effects" and may even generate useful strategic innovation.

BEYOND THE SMO

Research organized around the concept of the SMO has generated insight into the problem of

how actors coordinate collective action. However, scholars have also found that the process of organizing a social movement is not fully captured by a focus on SMOs. The study of SMOs (as a noun) is only a part of the larger project of understanding social movement organization (as a process). Several strands of social movement scholarship shift the SMO out of the center of the analysis.

A cultural turn in social movement scholarship has reinvigorated interest in *why* people organize. While resource mobilization and political process approaches treated grievances as relatively unproblematic, cultural approaches argue that movements cannot be understood without attention to discourse, framing, and the crystallization of collective identities. This perspective sees SMOs as a site of the cultural work of movements – framing and building collective identities.

Clemens (1997) demonstrated that it is not just the quantity of organization that assists a movement; qualitative variation in organizational form also matters for the success of movements. Scholars have also emphasized that organizational forms are often selected not merely because of their perceived efficiency, but because of activists' ideological commitments or taken-for-granted assumptions.

The move beyond SMOs is also informed by the recognition that social movement activity is sometimes coordinated through networks, rather than or in addition to organizations. What we recognize as a social movement may actually be an extensive advocacy network, featuring SMOs but also including highly professionalized advocacy organizations, governmental or intergovernmental actors, and individual policy entrepreneurs. Some activists have adopted decentralized networks as an organizing principle, eschewing more traditional organizational vehicles. In the environmental movement, for instance, groups like EarthFirst!, the Rainforest Action Network, and the Indigenous Environmental Network all embrace a network model, albeit in varying ways and degrees.

Finally, scholars beyond the subfield of social movements have realized that the processes identified and described by social movement scholars are evident in other arenas of social life. Theories developed to explain SMOs are sometimes applied to other types of organizations, including businesses, industry associations, and universities. A synthesis of "social movements and organizational theory" (Davis et al. 2005) represents a deeper dialogue between these two subfields, which has the potential to generate new insights into the processes of organizing for change.

SEE ALSO: Civil Rights Movement; Collective Action; Collective Identity; Culture, Social Movements and; Framing and Social Movements; Institutional Theory, New; Mobilization; New Left; Oligarchy and Organization; Organizations, Voluntary; Political Opportunities; Political Process Theory; Resource Mobilization Theory; Social Change; Social Movements; Social Movements, Networks and; Social Movements, Participatory Democracy in; Social Movements, Recruitment to; Social Movements, Strain and Breakdown Theories of

REFERENCES AND SUGGESTED READINGS

Clemens, E. S. (1997) *The People's Lobby: Organizational Innovation and the Rise of Interest Group Politics in the United States, 1890–1925*. University of Chicago Press, Chicago.

Davis, G., McAdam, D., Scott, W. R., & Zald, M. (Eds.) (2005) *Social Movements and Organization Theory*. Cambridge University Press, New York.

Freeman, J. (1972) The Tyranny of Structurelessness. In: Jaquette, J. (Ed.), *Women in Politics*. Wiley, New York.

Gamson, W. (1975) *The Strategy of Social Protest*. Wadsworth, Belmont, CA.

McAdam, D. (1982) *Political Process and the Development of Black Insurgency, 1930–1970*. University of Chicago Press, Chicago.

McCarthy, J. D. & Zald, M. N. (1977) Resource Mobilization and Social Movements: A Partial Theory. *American Journal of Sociology* 82: 1212–41.

Michels, R. (1962 [1911]) *Political Parties: A Sociological Study of the Oligarchical Tendencies of Modern Democracies*. Free Press, New York.

Minkoff, D. C. (1999) Bending with the Wind: Strategic Change and Adaptation by Women's and Racial Minority Organizations. *American Journal of Sociology* 104: 1666–703.

Olson, M. (1965) *The Logic of Collective Action*. Harvard University Press, Cambridge, MA.

Piven, F. F. & Cloward, R. A. (1979) *Poor People's Movements: Why They Succeed, How They Fail*. Vintage, New York.

Polletta, F. (2002) *Freedom Is an Endless Meeting: Democracy in American Social Movements*. University of Chicago Press, Chicago.

social movements

James M. Jasper

Although scholarly definitions vary, common usage portrays social movements as sustained and intentional efforts to foster or retard social changes, primarily outside the normal institutional channels encouraged by authorities. *Sustained* implies that movements differ from single events such as riots or rallies. Their persistence often allows them to develop formal organizations, but they may also operate through informal social networks. *Intentional* links movements to culture and strategy: people have ideas about what they want and how to get it, ideas that are filtered through culture as well as psychology. Movements have purposes, even when these have to do with transforming members themselves (as in many religious movements) rather than the world outside the movement. *Foster or retard*: although many scholars have a Whiggish tendency to view movements as progressive, dismissing regressive efforts as countermovements, this distinction seems arbitrary and unsustainable (not to mention the unfortunate effect that different tools are then used to analyze the two types). *Non-institutional* distinguishes movements from political parties and interest groups that are a more regular part of many political systems, even though movements frequently create these other entities and often maintain close relationships to them. Most movements today deploy some tactics within mainstream institutions, and non-institutional protest is itself often quite institutionalized. Unsurprisingly, each of these claims about social movements has been subject to controversy and differences in emphasis.

UNDERSTANDING DISCONTENT

Theories of discontent have always reflected the historical forms protest was taking at the time, as well as each writer's own sympathies and political participation. In seventeenth- and eighteenth-century Europe, the collective expression of discontent was primarily understood through the lens of legitimate sovereignty. Economic and social dimensions of the emerging nation-state were not yet distinguished from the political, so protest both took the form of and was seen as a political act. The concept of the social movement was not yet possible. Contract theory, a primarily normative discourse, allowed thinkers such as Hobbes to argue against the legitimacy of most resistance to the state, and others such as Locke to defend revolutionary action in the face of predatory rulers. Thinkers of the time hardly noticed the activities of the lower classes.

With accelerated urbanization in the nineteenth century, European intellectuals increasingly took alarm at the regular rebellions of artisans, developing the concept of the mob to explain and disparage them. Crowds came to be seen as a form of madness that caused individuals to act differently than they would when alone – a view crystallized by Gustave Le Bon in the 1890s. Although based on little empirical research, the crowd image remained vital to a number of thinkers in the early twentieth century, including Durkheim, Freud, Weber, and Parsons. Only revolutionaries such as Marx viewed urban mobs favorably, wrongly insisting that they were part of the proletariat who would usher in a just society in the form of socialism (instead, most were the old working class of artisans whose way of life was disappearing).

More sophisticated versions of crowd theory appeared in the mid-twentieth century, largely in response to communism and fascism. Until the late 1960s, the dominant view of protest overemphasized the non-institutional dimension, lumping movements together with fads, panics, and other collective behavior. Explicitly or implicitly, crowds remained the heart of this vision: the kernel on which other forms of collective behavior were somehow built. Most analysts, drawing from Le Bon, feared crowds and movements and portrayed them pejoratively, although occasional interactionists pointed to their creativity instead (in a fruitful tradition stretching from Robert Park to Ralph Turner and Lewis Killian, and on through recent theorists such as David Snow and John Lofland). How movements were sustained and what were their goals received less attention, and only occasionally did theorists link movements to social change.

Suddenly everything changed. In the mid-1960s, social movements were everywhere, populated no longer by a dangerous working class but by familiar middle-class faces. In retrospect we can see various roots of this new activism: the emergence of a British and later an American new left; increasing international attention to the US Civil Rights Movement especially after the student sit-ins of 1960; the 1964 confrontation that spawned the Berkeley free speech movement; anti-colonial movements and revolutions around the globe. Theories soon appeared that were sympathetic to protestors.

An organizational or structural paradigm, steeped in Marxism, dominated research from the 1970s to the late 1990s, highlighting the sustained dimension of movements by portraying them as linked to the core political and economic institutions and cleavages of society. No longer grouped with fads, social movements were now nearly indistinguishable from political parties. They were thought to reflect deep structural interests, especially class but also gender, race, and (eventually) sexual preference. Structural assumptions discouraged the asking of "why" questions, as a desire for change or inclusion was assumed. So although movements were recognized as purposive, their purposes were taken for granted rather than empirically investigated. Attitudes and grievances assumed to be ever present were dismissed as causal factors of any importance. The essential question about movements was how they could overcome repression, especially by the state, in order to further their (already existing) interests. They were seen as insurgents or challengers, outsiders trying to gain entry into existing polities. (Scholars disappointed by the failure of most movements of the 1960s focused naturally on the structural constraints that they had faced.)

An American version of the new paradigm emphasized finances, often mobilized by paid, professional activists. Organizations require financial support, and the easiest way to attract this is by appealing to the privileged in society. Another is by gathering small donations from a large number of sympathizers, especially through direct mail. In the 1960s, a large social movement sector developed, with well-developed techniques for gathering funds, organizing shows of public support, and pressuring legislators (McCarthy & Zald 1977). These developments suggested a model of movements as similar to firms in markets, competing with one another for funds, members, and attention. This research tradition is often referred to as resource mobilization due to its emphasis on funding.

Another version of the structural paradigm focused on interactions between movements and the state, on the assumption that the state was usually the opponent as well as judge (under the Marxist assumption that states are instruments of the ruling class). Often dubbed "political process," this tradition emphasized the need for elite allies, cracks in state repression, state crises, and other windows of opportunity in the political environment. This perspective especially fit (because it was largely derived from) the study of European labor and American civil rights movements: efforts at inclusion by well-defined groups that lasted for decades. In Europe a more comparative version developed, highlighting ongoing state structures (Kriesi et al. 1995). Despite its healthy focus on a movement's external environment, this approach modeled that environment as a structure (open or closed, for example) rather than an arena of diverse strategic players, as relationships rather than interactions.

Alain Touraine and his many students crafted a different version of the structural paradigm, linking contemporary movements to social structure instead of concentrating on organizational forms. Whereas the central conflict of industrial societies, Touraine (1978) argued, pitted labor against capital in a struggle over the distribution of material goods, post-industrial societies saw conflicts over cultural understandings, especially the direction in which society's increasing self-control would take it. The technocrats of capital and government sought profit and efficiency, while protestors saw these as mere means to the deeper ends of cultural identities and political rights. Touraine's vision helped scholars recognize the significance of new movements such as ecology, feminism, or gay rights, invisible under traditional structural models. More recently, Touraine has admitted that Europe and the United States have become new kinds of capitalist societies more than the post-industrial societies he had prophesied. The technocrats won.

Alongside these macrosocial visions there emerged a more individualistic view of movements which were redefined accordingly as collective action. Rooted in neoclassical microeconomic theory, Mancur Olson (1965) and others cast doubt on the sustainability of movements, precisely by emphasizing the intentions of potential participants whose rationality consisted of constantly calculating whether to participate based on costs and benefits to themselves as individuals. Olson left little room for the attractions of collective solidarity and other incentives besides material benefits. As others have filled in some of these gaps, deriving solutions to the free-rider problem, the rational choice approach has become less and less distinct. Many of the solutions are the organizational challenges emphasized by the mobilization and process traditions.

At the turn of the millennium, the structural, Tourainian, and rational choice approaches faced deep problems, and appeared in articles most often as whipping boys for proffered alternatives. The main lacuna of all three was an inattention to cultural meanings, the socially constructed purposes and identities of social movement groups. Even Touraine, who emphasized struggles over cultural meanings rather than material rewards, too often derived those meanings from his theory of historical change rather than empirically from the movements themselves.

Accordingly, beginning in the late 1980s, considerable research and theory addressed the cultural dimensions of movements. Two concepts, frames and collective identity, dominated these efforts. David Snow, Rob Benson, and a series of collaborators did the most to theorize the nature of rhetorical frames, especially those used by activists to recruit others to their cause.

Inspired by identity politics in the United States, in the 1990s the concept of collective identity was increasingly used to get at cultural meanings not already covered by frames. At first, collective identities were seen as a mobilizing rhetoric built upon a structural position or discrimination, a form of cognitive liberation (McAdam 1982). Individuals imagined themselves members of some larger community, in whose name they acted. Only later was it realized that movements themselves can foster identities without any preexisting structural similarities – and identities can even form around movements, specific tactics such as nonviolence, or particular organizations (Jasper 1997). It also took time for scholars to recognize that emotional solidarities are just as important to identities as cognitive categories are.

Clearly and narrowly defined, frames and identities are important tools in our conceptual repertoire for understanding social movements, but there are additional ways to get at meanings (Jasper 1997; Goodwin & Jasper 2006). Analyses of ritual or of media coverage draw on well-established fields of anthropology and media studies. Narrative has also become popular, as stories are an important part of meetings and self-images in social movements. Although traditional narrative theory emphasizes the structuring plots of stories, others highlight the social context of storytelling. Rhetoric, which takes off from this latter point, highlights the interplay of orator and audience, building in not only interaction but intention and emotion. Like framing, naming is a key part of making sense of the world and of persuading others.

Emotions are a central component of culture, playing a role in all social movements. Basic affects like love and hate can pull a movement together or tear it apart. Reactive emotions such as anger, fear, and shock provide raw materials that organizers must transform into moral indignation. Moods such as resignation or cynicism can discourage recruits, just as those of confidence or exhilaration can attract them perhaps through the interaction rituals Collins (2001) describes. Emotions even figure in the outcomes of movements, which frequently aim to transform sensibilities such as compassion or justice.

EMERGENCE

The initial stirrings of a social movement are poorly understood. Given the sensibilities, ideas, values, and allegiances mixed together in different population segments, how does necessarily limited attention come to be focused on one set of issues rather than others? A newsworthy event or death of a loved one may shock people into attention. The zeitgeist may shift slightly, in an enormously complex way, bringing attention and sympathy to new arenas. News coverage also influences our emotional and moral attention. Typically, a small network of would-be leaders manages to set aside their normal lives to craft appeals to these understandings to recruit like-minded others (or they may be movement professionals whose work is to stimulate protest). Little is known about the first stirrings of a movement.

In contrast, extensive research has examined how individuals are recruited to an emerging or ongoing movement. Early arguments, focusing on individual psychology, had suggested that alienated, insecure, or dogmatic individuals joined social movements. The structural paradigm dismissed such speculation in favor of factors like biographical availability: the lack of spouse, children, or demanding jobs that frees people for the time commitment of participation. But the most important factor in explaining who joins and who does not may be whether the potential recruit already knows someone in the movement. In many movements, a majority of participants are recruited this way (Snow et al. 1980). In a process Anthony Oberschall dubbed bloc recruitment, entire networks can be coopted for new purposes, such as the fundamentalist congregations that became part of the movement to stop the Equal Rights Amendment for American women.

Researchers also turned their attention to the messages transmitted across networks, in other words the cultural aspects of recruitment. Snow and his co-authors suggested that recruiters and potential participants had to align their frames to achieve a common definition of a problem and prescription for solving it, with Snow and Benford (1992: 137) defining a frame as an interpretive schema that simplifies and condenses the world out there by selectively punctuating and encoding objects, situations, events, experiences, and sequences of actions within one's present or past environment. Although originally used to focus on the strategic and rhetorical interaction between organizers and recruits, frames have more often and less usefully been analyzed as static bundles of meanings that either work or do not work.

Recruitment requires more than cognitive agreement between organizers and their audiences. At least as important are the moral visions and emotions that propel people into action. Fear and anger must be transformed into indignation and outrage. Moral shocks are one way that people are drawn into action: when they learn something about the world that outrages them, discovering that the world is not as they had thought (Jasper 1997). The shock may come from a public event such as *Roe* v. *Wade* or from private sources like the death of a child through corporate negligence. These shocks can be so strong that people seek out protest groups even in the absence of social network ties. Emotions are an essential component of culture, and culture is an essential part of recruitment, whether it operates through social networks or other media.

In addition to people (both leaders and followers), an emerging movement usually needs some infrastructure to carry out its activities. It requires basic means of communication and transportation: a bullhorn to address a large crowd, a fax machine or Internet access to reach supporters, carpools to get people to a rally. It may also need a large meeting room. Financial support allows organizers to purchase what they need. In what was perhaps the high water mark of mobilization theory, Morris (1984) demonstrated the many contributions that black churches and other institutions made to the American Civil Rights Movement, from networks of preachers throughout the South and beyond to meeting halls in which ideas could be aired. Churches also provided cultural meanings, for instance Bible stories and religious songs, that could be used to convey the movement's message to a wide variety of Southern blacks.

In the late twentieth century, transnational social movements and their organizations spread rapidly in a world of globally improving communication and transportation (Keck & Sikkink 1998). It was hard to understand these international networks through the structural paradigm's focus on preexisting interests in a relatively homogeneous and well-networked population. This new work on globalization also portrays a world of many different kinds of players – local, national, and international nongovernmental organizations (NGOs), assorted state agencies, international institutions such as the United Nations or International Monetary Fund, diverse funding sources, various kinds of publics in complex interaction. Some perceive a shift in conflicts from institutions whose members are nation-states (World Bank, World Trade Organization, UN) to a more participatory public sphere of NGOs that cooperate directly as well as through the older organizations. The exchange of information and ideas lies at the heart of these newer networks.

DYNAMICS

But what do movements do? Tilly (1978) suggests that a society contains a repertoire of collective action, from which protestors inevitably draw, depending on local senses of justice, the daily routines and social organization of the participants, their prior experience with collective action, and the repression they are likely to face. Most social movements in a society will conduct the same activities, since that is what they have learned to do through trial and error. New tactics, outside the repertoire, may take opponents and authorities by surprise, but protestors themselves may bungle them due to lack of experience and know-how. At the extreme, those who face extreme surveillance and few legal rights are restricted to weapons of the weak such as sabotage, pilfering, poaching, or even jokes and gossip (Scott 1985).

The organizational forms which movements adopt have attracted much attention, perhaps because they are central to a structural paradigm. Piven and Cloward (1977) dissented from the common view that protest groups should accumulate resources, suggesting instead that these distract attention from the best strategy of downtrodden groups, radical insurgency and disruption. An organization, they warn, can all too easily begin to view its own perpetuation and expansion as goals alongside its original purpose. Others have countered that professionalized organizations can stimulate grassroots activity, and that they can allow movement ideas to survive long periods when they are out of favor. Jasper (2004) prefers to see the building of a stable protest organization as a dilemma, with risks and benefits to both doing it and not doing it.

What kind of organization to construct is another important strategic choice. Drawing on institutional theory, Clemens (1993) shows that organizational form is itself a message, presumably for both members and outsiders. In the American labor movement of the 1890s, fraternal forms of organizing downplayed economic interests and political confrontation, while more military forms like Coxey's Army elicited violent repression. Organizational forms, like other tactical choices, are a fundamental part of shaping a collective identity.

Most protest groups contain rival factions, which may have different goals or different tastes in tactics (Jasper 1997). Factions may develop as newcomers join a movement, demanding internal as well as external changes. Movements may grow more radical because new recruits want more action, or have identities based on being radical, although the structural account emphasizes rebuffs by the state as the key source of radicalization. Radical flanks can have advantages as well as disadvantages. Radical actions and ideas attract media attention, and sometimes garner quick concessions from opponents or authorities. Among disadvantages, foremost is the possibility that radicals will pull an organization or movement apart or that it will attract repression fatal to the cause.

Less research has addressed other features of what movements actually do on a daily basis: how they make decisions about tactics, seek allies, struggle with factions and unruly individuals, and balance their appeals to a number of different audiences. The structural emphasis on external allies and resources left little theoretical space to see how insurgents actually operated, especially when they had few resources. (Although Touraine, by bringing together representatives of different factions in a movement, was able to recreate their internal conflicts in his "sociological interventions.") Even the poorest can often generate internal resources, and most try to accumulate whatever resources they lack at the beginning of a conflict. Even without money and the resources it buys,

protestors can still be creative, doing things that catch their opponents off guard or take advantage of legal and political opportunities.

In a critique of classic research on organizing, Ganz (2000) derived a number of factors that made the United Farm Workers more inventive than its predecessors and rivals. These include leaders with diverse experience, salient local knowledge, personal commitment, diverse network ties (including strong ties to constituencies), and a diverse tactical repertoire. Organizations, Ganz found, were more creative when they had regular meetings open to diverse perspectives and with the authority to make decisions, had diverse resources (especially flowing up from the constituency itself), and were accountable to each other but also their constitutencies. Democratic or entrepreneurial selection of leaders worked better than more bureaucratic processes.

Under the influence of recent theories of agency, organizations can be seen as strategic players in fields of conflict with a range of other players, rather than reified as a movement facing either the state or a political environment. That environment is recognized as a farrago of friends, foes, bystanders, regulators, and others, each with its own goals, means, and internal conflicts. States and movements are both fanciful metaphors covering a variety of players. A more strategic perspective has the potential to explore the boundaries between movements and other political phenomena, finding both similarities and differences across institutional spheres.

In this strategic perspective Jasper (2004) highlights the choices that individuals and groups face by naming a range of dilemmas confronting movements, indeed all strategic players. Naughty or Nice, for example, gets at the diverse effects of disruption or violence, which are often widely unpopular but may inspire a panicked response and yield a quick victory. In the Extension Dilemma, organizers must decide how large a coalition or group to build: bigger ones have more resources at their disposal, but often at the expense of a consensus around goals or a clear collective identity. An emphasis on tradeoffs or choices like these is one way to insist on the agency of social movements even in the face of structural constraints.

EFFECTS

The effects of movements on policy, society, and culture have always interested scholars, as they provide much of the inspiration for studying movements in the first place. Scholars frequently exaggerate the impact of the movements they have spent so much time studying, especially as there are so many definitions and types of success to which to turn. Research in this area has also tended to have a normative flavor, as Whiggish scholars seek sources of progressive social change.

Gamson (1975) pointed to two forms of success: benefits for a movement's constituency and recognition for the protest group itself. The latter was based on a structural image of challengers attempting to gain access to a polity closed to them. An impact on public policy is the central or ultimate goal of many movements, but this effect is often hard to observe because politicians frequently deny it even while they sometimes advance a movement's goals. And indeed, a movement's effect is often to sensitize other actors in a political arena. Kriesi et al. (1995: 212) list internal impacts of identity and organization, and external impacts of four types: procedural, substantive, structural, and sensitizing.

Many factors determine a movement's influence. Rochon (1990: 108) lists size, novelty, and militancy, oddly ignoring resources. Size matters because it may affect resources, but also because in democracies protestors are also voters. Novelty gains media attention and discomfits opponents. Militancy, for instance violence and disruption, may also catch opponents and authorities off guard, but it runs the risk that the latter will organize a repressive strategy capable of suppressing the movement. This is Jasper's Naughty or Nice dilemma. Militancy, like most risky strategies, generally succeeds when a goal can be attained quickly and irreversibly.

All strategic choices can have ramifications. Social movements borrow heavily from each other, not least because activists often move from one to another. This is one reason that movements so often appear in waves, as a frame or tactic proves useful to a number of them. (Although the stronger concept of a cycle, in which one stage leads to the next, seems to have overreached the evidence.) Elisabeth Clemens showed that the early women's movement, by choosing one form of organization rather than another, often inspired changes in government as well. These groups introduced organizational logics from one sphere of life into another, inserting economic, charitable, and fraternal models into politics, and thereby helping to create today's pattern of interest group politics. New tactics spread rapidly.

Even when social movements have little impact on the world around them, they almost always affect their own members. A number of scholars have traced the consequences of participation in protestors' later lives, especially those active in the 1960s. Far from growing more conservative as they aged, this generation has maintained left-leaning sympathies and a well-documented inclination toward activism.

METHODS OF RESEARCH

Most studies of social movements, whether quantitative or qualitative, have been case studies. As with those who do area studies, scholars of movements must devote enormous time to mastering the diverse phenomena that comprise any social movement, usually composed of many diverse groups, different kinds of members, various kinds of tactics and events, interactions with a number of other strategic players, and so on. On the positive side, there is frequently a ready audience for reports on the many social movements that help compose our political landscape. On the negative, the same case is often used to develop new theories and concepts as well as to try them out empirically. For instance, every scholar who has written about political opportunities has discovered a different list of them, making it hard to discern the scope conditions of any of them.

Some scholars have tried to avoid this difficulty by looking at events instead of movements. Originally deployed in the study of riots, the use of events as units of analysis was especially helpful in the historical understanding of strikes and other contentious events for which newspaper reports but not richer information were available. Waves of events are useful for seeing the main product of organizing efforts, and for relating these activities to other political variables. The strength of this approach lies in tracking developments over time and checking correlations of protest with other variables such as unemployment or grain prices, but it remains largely wedded to newspaper accounts.

Protest events are hardly the only unit to be studied. Individuals can be interviewed in depth or randomly surveyed. Researchers can participate themselves, gaining introspective insights not otherwise available and which may be the most effective means for understanding emotions and some strategic choices. Organizations can be studied through a variety of methods, and the interplay of organizations is especially amenable to comparative analysis. Other methods are available for examining networks of individuals or organizations. All of the above can be studied through historical archives as well as contemporary means of gathering data. Computer simulations have also been used to test a number of impressions about movement organization. Gamson (1992) used focus groups to powerfully show the raw cultural materials available for organizing, the commonsense understandings that are as important as media framings of events. Fortunately, the study of social movements has proven open to a variety of techniques rather than being wedded to any kind of methodological purity (Klandermans & Staggenborg 2002).

To conclude, research into social movements shifts focus as movements themselves develop. Nineteenth-century riots inspired crowd theories. After mid-twentieth-century battles with fascism and communism, western analysts turned to mass society theories to explain political movements they feared. In the 1960s, sympathy for middle-class movements, especially of students who would later become academics, encouraged portraits of protestors as rational. A number of culturally oriented movements in the 1970s, often labeled new social movements to contrast them with the labor movement, helped to spawn cultural theories. Global networks of activists have inspired globally oriented theories. Future transformations will no doubt give us new portrayals and theories that we cannot yet imagine.

SEE ALSO: Civil Rights Movement; Collective Action; Collective Identity; Contention, Tactical Repertoires of; Crowd Behavior; Culture, Social Movements and; Emotions and Social Movements; Framing and Social Movements; Gender, Social Movements and; Global Justice as a Social Movement; Identity Politics/ Relational Politics; Mobilization; Moral Shocks and Self-Recruitment; New Left; New Social Movement Theory; Political Opportunities; Political Process Theory; Pro-Choice and Pro-Life Movements; Rational Choice Theories; Resource Mobilization Theory; Revolutions; Riots; Social Change; Social Movement Organizations; Social Movements, Biographical Consequences of; Social Movements, Leadership in; Social Movements, Networks and; Social Movements, Non-Violent; Social Movements, Participatory Democracy in; Social Movements, Political Consequences of; Social Movements, Recruitment to; Social Movements, Relative Deprivation and; Social Movements, Repression of; Social Movements, Strain and Breakdown Theories of; Transnational Movements

REFERENCES AND SUGGESTED READINGS

Clemens, E. S. (1993) Organizational Repertoires and Institutional Change: Women's Groups and the Transformation of American Politics, 1890–1920. *American Journal of Sociology* 98: 755–98.

Collins, R. (2001) Social Movements and the Focus of Emotional Attention. In: Goodwin, J., Jasper, J. M., & Polletta, F. (Eds.), *Passionate Politics: Emotions and Social Movements*. University of Chicago Press, Chicago.

Gamson, W. A. (1975) *The Strategy of Social Protest*. Dorsey, Homewood, IL.

Gamson, W. A. (1992) *Talking Politics*. Cambridge University Press, Cambridge.

Ganz, M. (2000) Resources and Resourcefulness. *American Journal of Sociology* 105: 1003–62.

Goodwin, J. & Jasper, J. M. (2006) The Cultural Approach to Social Movements. In: Klandermans, B. & Roggeband, C. (Eds.), *Handbook of Social Movements*. Kluwer, Dordrecht.

Jasper, J. M. (1997) *The Art of Moral Protest*. University of Chicago Press, Chicago.

Jasper, J. M. (2004) A Strategic Approach to Collective Action: Looking for Agency in Social Movement Choices. *Mobilization* 9: 1–16.

Keck, M. E. & Sikkink, K. (1998) *Activists Beyond Borders*. Cornell University Press, Ithaca, NY.

Klandermans, B. & Staggenborg, S. (Eds.) (2002) *Methods of Social Movement Research*. University of Minnesota Press, Minneapolis.

Kriesi, H., Koopmans, R., Duyvendak, J.-W., & Giugni, M. (1995) *New Social Movements in Western Europe*. University of Minnesota Press, Minneapolis.

McAdam, D. (1982) *Political Process and the Development of Black Insurgency, 1930–1970*. University of Chicago Press, Chicago.

McCarthy, J. D. & Zald, M. N. (1977) Resource Mobilization and Social Movements: A Partial Theory. *American Journal of Sociology* 82: 1212–41.

Morris, A. D. (1984) *The Origins of the Civil Rights Movement*. Free Press, New York.

Olson, M. (1965) *The Logic of Collective Action*. Harvard University Press, Cambridge, MA.

Piven, F. F. & Cloward, R. (1977) *Poor People's Movements*. Vintage, New York.

Rochon, T. R. (1990) The West European Peace Movement and the Theory of New Social Movements. In: Dalton, R. & Küchler, M. (Eds.), *Challenging the Political Order*. Polity Press, Cambridge.

Scott, J. C. (1985) *Weapons of the Weak*. Yale University Press, New Haven.

Snow, D. A. & Benford, R. B. (1992) Master Frames and Cycles of Protest. In: Morris, A. D. & Mueller, C. M. (Eds.), *Frontiers in Social Movement Theory*. Yale University Press, New Haven.

Snow, D. A., Zurcher, L. A., Jr., & Ekland-Olson, S. (1980) Social Networks and Social Movements: A Microstructural Approach to Differential Recruitment. *American Sociological Review* 45: 787–801.

Tilly, C. (1978) *From Mobilization to Revolution*. Addison-Wesley, Reading, MA.

Touraine, A. (1978) *La Voix et le regard*. Seuil, Paris.

social movements, biographical consequences of

Silke Roth

Personal and biographical effects belong to the unintended consequences of social movements. Participation in social movements changes people's lives, while social movements aim at social change (or its prevention), and even affect the lives of those who did not get involved in movements and countermovements.

A biographical perspective on social movements makes clear that social change and personal change are inextricably linked.

Biographical consequences of social movements can be observed at the micro, meso, and macro levels. The effects at the micro level concern the impact of movement participation on activists' life courses, the individual level of participants in movement activities. As numerous studies show, activists tend to remain committed to social change goals they pursue in social movements and that this commitment has significant effects in their work lives, political attitudes, and personal relationships (Evans 1979; Andrews 1991). Based on research on participants of the New Left, Giugni (2004: 494) summarizes the effects as follows: the former activists continue to hold leftist attitudes, define themselves as "liberal" and "radical," and remain active in social movements and other forms of political activity. They tend to be concentrated in teaching and other "helping" professions, have lower incomes then their age peers, and are more likely to have experienced an episodic or non-traditional work history. Furthermore, they are more likely to have divorced, married later, or remained single than their age peers. In addition, gender differences can be observed. For example, the participation in the Freedom Summer campaign of 1964 had different impacts on male and female life courses. Compared to their peers, male volunteers had jobs with less stability, prestige, and income, while female volunteers were less likely to be married or have children than their peers (McAdam 1992). Andrews (1991) found that lifelong commitment to socialism gave interviewees a purpose in life.

At the meso level, biographical consequences concern how social movements and movement organizations are shaped by the membership. Activists develop *tastes for tactics* (Jasper 1997), which have an impact on the participation in social movements and movement organizations as well as on the tactics employed and coalitions and networks formed. Roth (2003) argued that activists form bridging organizations in order to reconcile competing political identities that evolved in political socialization processes through the participation of social movements. Activists often move from one movement to the other and contribute to diffusion of strategies, tactics, and frames and engage in coalition building (Whittier 2004). The biographies of activists account for generational change in social movements and social movement organizations. Evans (1979) described how the women's movement emerged out of the Civil Rights Movement; Whittier (2004) discusses how movements influence each other, for example through spillover processes.

The consequences at the macro level concern the impact of social movements on the general population, for example changing norms with respect to education, employment, or marital status. Economic and demographic factors, as well as the social movements of the 1960s and 1970s, led to the transformation from a materialist to a post-materialist value system and changes in the life course. Consciousness-raising groups, as part of the women's movement, not only changed the self-definitions and worldviews of the participating women but also transformed society. McAdam (1999) argues that the links between the social movements of the 1960s and 1970s and the changes in life course patterns constitute a three-stage process. Initially, only activists reject normal life course trajectories in favor of alternatives like cohabitation, childlessness, and unstable work. In the second stage, the alternative lifestyle spreads to college campuses and countercultural neighborhoods, and finally, in the third stage, reaches young people in general.

The analysis of political generations can combine micro, meso, and macro levels of the biographical consequences of social movements. A biographical perspective on historical processes, cycles of protest, and political opportunity structures draws the attention to political generations (Mannheim 1952; Braungart & Braungart 1985) which share historical moments and process the past in a specific manner. Those active in the West German student movement of the 1960s as well as those active in the peaceful revolution of 1989 see their activism as a response to the involvement of their parents in National Socialism.

Giugni (2004) provides a critical assessment of the methodological shortcomings of the study of biographical consequences of social movements. Typically, the studies employed small samples which were non-representative and focused mostly on New Left activists. Further

problems include lack of control groups, small numbers of participants, and samples drawn from narrow geographical areas. In addition, often only a single point in time was measured. In order to disentangle aging or life cycle effects, cohort or generational effects, and period effects, panel designs should be employed. While aging and life cycle effects refer to various stages (youth, middle age, and old age) and different phases (education, work/career, marriage, parenthood) in one's life course, cohort and generational effects encompass sharing the experience of a historical event which has shaped this age group (e.g., World War II or the 1960s). Surveying the same group at various points in time (panel study) makes it possible to distinguish between the effects of a stage in one's life course and being born into a specific cohort or generation.

Biographical methods are especially well suited to studying the biographical impact of social movements at all three levels since they make it possible to study the process character of social action. Compared to other strategies of studying contentious politics, the life history method can assess subjective constructions and objective processes as well as developments in the private and public spheres and how they are interrelated. Life histories allow an understanding of individual developments as well as group phenomena and capture movement ideology, movement counterculture, organizational stories, and the dynamics of small networks. Instead of providing static images, life stories offer insight into processes (Della Porta 1992). Life histories enable the analysis of the sequences and patterning of life events and thereby contribute to a better understanding of the causes and effects of political affiliation as well as the interaction between the crystallization of consciousness and the mobilization of action, and social structures and networks that nourish (or fail to nourish) activist identities and beliefs during periods of political inactivity (Blee 1996: 687). Life histories provide a context for understanding the fluctuation and transient character of movement participation. Membership in a social movement organization is one practice within the trajectory of the life course; it has been preceded by former and parallel memberships and activities; it parallels developments in family and work careers. A life history approach promises to contribute to a better understanding of the social construction of the history, collective identity, alignment with social movements, and conceptualization of social movement organizations from the perspective of the membership (Della Porta 1992).

Since the mid-1990s, social movement research has seen an increasing integration of various research paradigms as well as a renewed interest in culture and emotions. Furthermore, research on revolutions and social movements has become more integrated. Globalization processes have affected theory formation by challenging North American and Western European experiences as paradigmatic. A perspective on the biographical consequences of social movements emphasizes that activists migrate from one movement to another and sustain multiple memberships over time. On the individual level, this points to processes of political socialization; on the organizational and movement level, this points to social movement interaction and diffusion processes (Roth 2003). Frames, strategies, and repertoires of action are transported from one movement to another through overlapping memberships and coalitions (Whittier 2004). Seidman (1999) explains the fact that gender issues became prominent in South Africa's democratic transition due to the fact that South Africans visiting Europe and North America either as students or exiles were often introduced to new feminist ideas. When they returned to South Africa, the exiles introduced feminist ideas in the democratic struggle, challenging earlier assumptions about women's role in politics. A focus on biographies of social movement activists contributes to a better understanding of social movement participation and development as well as to the analysis of diffusion processes.

SEE ALSO: Biography; Civil Rights Movement; Collective Identity; Culture, Social Movements and; Generational Change; Social Movements; Social Movements, Recruitment to

REFERENCES AND SUGGESTED READINGS

Andrews, M. (1991) *Lifetimes of Commitment: Aging, Politics, Psychology*. Cambridge University Press, Cambridge.

Blee, K. M. (1996) Becoming a Racist: Women in Contemporary Ku Klux Klan and Neo-Nazi Groups. *Gender and Society* 10: 680–702.

Braungart, R. G. & Braungart, M. (1985) Conceptual and Methodological Approaches to Studying Life Course and Generational Politics. *Research in Political Sociology* 1: 269–304.

Della Porta, D. (1992) Life Histories in the Analysis of Social Movement Activists. In: Diani, M. & Eyerman, R. (Eds.), *Studying Collective Action*. Sage, London, pp. 168–93.

Evans, S. (1979) *Personal Politics*. Knopf, New York.

Giugni, M. G. (2004) Personal and Biographical Consequences. In: Snow, D. A., Soule, S. A, & Kriesi, H. (Eds.), *The Blackwell Companion to Social Movements*. Blackwell, Malden, MA, pp. 489–507.

Jasper, J. M. (1997) *The Art of Moral Protest: Culture, Biography, and the Creativity of Social Movements*. University of Chicago Press, Chicago.

McAdam, D. (1992) Gender as a Mediator of the Activist Experience: The Case of Freedom Summer. *American Journal of Sociology* 97: 1211–40.

McAdam, D. (1999) The Biographical Impact of Activism. In: Giugni, M., McAdam, D., & Tilly, C. (Eds.), *How Social Movements Matter*. University of Minnesota Press, Minneapolis, pp. 119–46.

Mannheim, K. (1952) The Problem of Generations. In: Kecskemeti, P. (Ed.), *Essays on the Sociology of Knowledge*. Routledge & Kegan Paul, London, pp. 276–322.

Roth, S. (2003) *Building Movement Bridges: The Coalition of Labor Union Women*. Praeger, Westport, CT.

Seidman, G. (1999) Gendered Citizenship: South Africa's Democratic Transition and the Construction of a Gendered State. *Gender and Society* 13: 287–307.

Whittier, N. (2004) The Consequences of Social Movements for Each Other. In: Snow, D. A., Soule, S. A., & Hanspeter Kriesi, H. (Eds.), *The Blackwell Companion to Social Movements*. Blackwell, Malden, MA, pp. 531–51.

social movements, leadership in

Judith Stepan-Norris and Ben Lind

Social movement leaders act and make decisions on behalf of the movements they represent and therefore wield influence on the movement's trajectory. In this light, early scholarship addressed how leaders' personal qualities affect the character and actions of their movements. Mills (1971) notably identified union leader characteristics as telling of the distinctions between the American Federation of Labor and the Congress of Industrial Organizations. Stepan-Norris and Zeitlin (2003) extended this line of research by documenting the differential success of communist and non-communist leaders in collective bargaining accomplishments, union democracy, and attention to minority and women's rights. Similarly, Ganz (2000) partially credited the successful unionization of California's farmworkers (1960s–1970s) to the personal biographies, networks, and repertoires of leaders in the United Farm Workers Union.

Social movements provide leaders with selective incentives, and scholars have examined how they matter. McCarthy and Zald (1977) consider paid versus voluntary service as well as positions that provide career-building experience versus those that do not. Traditionally, positions that provide both salary and career experience are considered to be *professional* as opposed to *nonprofessional* leadership positions (Staggenborg 1988). Students of social movements have similarly categorized leaders according to their relationships with adherents of their respective social movements. Morris and Staggenborg (2004) proposed four types of movement leaders: (1) official title-bearing leaders of social movement organizations; (2) leadership team members who work with and advise top leaders (resembling McCarthy and Zald's definition of a cadre); (3) bridge leaders – movement activists who provide an intermediary between the top leadership and mass potential constituents and adherents (see Robnett 1996); and (4) local organizers who mobilize relatively small communities, but lack direct communication with top movement leaders. Kretschmer and Meyer (2005) identify a "platform leader" who maintains her position by clearly articulating a distinct position within a larger social movement.

Although much of the research focuses on how leaders affect social movements, some emphasize a more dialectical approach. Ganz (2000), for instance, proposed a model whereby leaders' biographies, personal networks, and collective action repertoires influence the strategic capacity and therefore the applied strategy of a movement. If their strategy utilizes effective and appropriate timing, targets, and tactics, it will produce successful outcomes for the movement that result in greater environmental effects – altering the biographies, networks, and repertoires of future movement leaders. McCarthy and Zald (1977) hypothesize that social movements that acquire increased funding have a tendency to procure professional leaders, who in turn are more likely to favor institutional tactics, coalition work, and formalization of their movement organizations. They also tend to avoid initiating new movements and introducing novel tactics when compared to social movements led by nonprofessionals (Staggenborg 1988).

In light of telling case studies regarding leadership in movements, most scholars acknowledge this topic remains under-theorized and in need of further research.

SEE ALSO: Collective Action; Leadership; Mobilization; Political Leadership; Resource Mobilization Theory; Social Movement Organizations; Social Movements; Social Movements, Participatory Democracy in

REFERENCES AND SUGGESTED READINGS

Ganz, M. (2000) Resources and Resourcefulness: The Strategic Capacity in the Unionization of California Agriculture, 1959–1966. *American Journal of Sociology* 105(4): 1003–62.

Kretschmer, K. & Meyer, D. S. (2005) Platform Leadership: Cultivating Support for a Public Profile. Working paper, University of California, Irvine.

McCarthy, J. D. & Zald, M. N. (1977) Resource Mobilization and Social Movements: A Partial Theory. *American Journal of Sociology* 82(6): 1212–41.

Mills, C. W. (1971 [1948]) *The New Men of Power: America's Labor Leaders*. A. M. Kelley, New York.

Morris, A. D. & Staggenborg, S. (2004) Leadership in Social Movements. In: Snow, D. A., Soule, S. A., & Kriesi, H. (Eds.), *The Blackwell Companion to Social Movements*. Blackwell, Oxford, pp. 171–96.

Robnett, B. (1996) African-American Women in the Civil Rights Movement, 1954–1965: Gender, Leadership, and Micromobilization. *American Journal of Sociology* 101(6): 1661–93.

Staggenborg, S. (1988) The Consequences of Professionalization and Formalization in the Pro-Choice

Movement. *American Sociological Review* 53: 585–606.

Stepan-Norris, J. & Zeitlin, M. (2003) *Left-Out: Reds and America's Industrial Unions.* Cambridge University Press, Cambridge.

social movements, networks and

Mario Diani

Since the interest in social movements started to develop in the 1960s, networks have been analyzed from two main perspectives. On the one hand, they have been treated as important facilitators of individuals' decisions to become involved in collective action, in the context of the debate inspired by Mancur Olson's seminal work on *The Logic of Collective Action.* On the other hand, analysts have looked at social movement networks as the structure of the links between the multiplicity of organizations and individual activists, committed to a certain cause. From this perspective, movement networks have been treated as the consequence, rather than the precondition, of collective action, a specific instance of the broader processes through which actors modify social structures through agency. More specifically, looking at the configuration of movement networks has provided observers with a clue to grasp the logics by which movement actors choose their partners, thus generating broader and complex organizational fields.

In their most basic sense, social networks consist of sets of nodes, linked by some form of relationship, and delimited by some specific criteria. Analysts of social movement networks have mostly used as nodes either the individuals mobilizing or sympathizing with a certain cause, or subscribing to certain alternative lifestyles, or the organizations promoting collective action on such issues and/or encouraging alternative cultural practices. They have looked at both direct and indirect ties. Direct ties are present when two nodes are directly linked in explicit interaction and interdependence – e.g., two activists who know each other personally,

or two organizations that jointly promote a rally. Indirect ties are assumed to exist between two nodes when they share some relevant activity or resource – e.g., interest in certain issues or in the same campaigns – yet without any face-to-face interaction.

Defining the boundaries of a social movement – i.e., classifying certain actors or events as part of a social movement dynamic or not – has proved most problematic. Many social movement analysts associate with a given movement all organizations sharing an interest in certain issues (e.g., the environment, or women's rights) or all organizations willing to adopt disruptive tactics, regardless of whether they are actually linked to each other. Others include in a movement only those nodes actually connected by some kind of relation. In particular, social movements have been conceived as the processes through which informal networks between a multiplicity of actors, sharing a collective identity, and engaged in social and/or political conflict, are built and reproduced. Identity plays a crucial role here as it connects actors to longer-term collective projects, thus making their relation different from that between actors engaged in purely instrumental coalitions.

In the beginning, social movement analysts mostly focused on the role of social networks as predictors of individual participation in collective action. Even in the early 1970s, many still regarded movement participants as individuals lacking a proper social integration, following the disruption of routine social arrangements brought about by radical processes of change and modernization. Interest in the link between social networks and movement participation developed precisely to challenge that assumption. By the 1980s, the notion that social movement participants are usually well integrated in dense systems of social relationships, that prior social ties operate as a basis for movement recruitment, and that established social settings are the locus of movement emergence, had become one of the most established findings in social movement research.

Social movement activists and sympathizers are usually linked through both "private" and "public" ties well before collective action develops. Personal friends, relatives, colleagues, and neighbors may all affect individual decisions to become involved in a movement; so may people who share with prospective participants some kind of collective engagement, such as previous or current participation in other movement activities, political or social organizations, or public bodies. Individuals may also be linked through indirect ties, generated by their joint involvement in specific activities and/or events, yet without any face-to-face interaction. These may range from participation in the same political or social activities and/or organizations, to involvement in the same subcultures or countercultures.

The impact of individual networks on individual participation has been tested in reference to different dependent variables. These have included presence or absence of participation; participation in specific types of activities (e.g., in conservation or political ecology groups); the continuation of participation over time; and the levels of risk associated with participation. Networks may provide opportunities for action through the circulation of information about ongoing activities, existing organizations, people to contact, and a reduction of the practical costs attached to participation. They may be the source of social pressure on prospective participants ("if you go, I will go too"), although cross-pressures are also possible, and so are people participating precisely because they expect others not to do anything. Networks may facilitate the development of cognitive skills and competences, and/or provide the context for the socialization of individuals to specific sets of values. They may also represent the locus for the development of strong emotional feelings.

It is disputed whether direct or indirect ties should operate differently, although in general social pressure is more likely to be exerted through direct links, while socialization to values or cognitive skills may also originate from involvement in similar organizational settings, regardless of strong involvement with specific individuals. Whether strong or weak ties should matter most is also a matter of debate: one would expect strong ties to matter more in the case of high-risk activities, but weak ties may facilitate the contacts between a movement organization and a constituency with more moderate or at least diversified orientations, and/or the diffusion or the spread of a movement campaign.

Another important illustration of the networks–movements connections is the view of movements as complex fields of interactions between multiple actors. This had already been noticed in the 1970s by scholars interested in subcultural and countercultural dynamics as well as in interorganizational relationships. However, this perspective has gained momentum since the 1980s, in parallel with the growing success of the network concept as a key to make sense of contemporary society, beyond classic dichotomies such as that between bureaucracy and markets, and with the renewed interest in agency in social theory. The spread of transnational contention and coalition building has further emphasized the interest in movement networks. All this has translated into growing attention to both interorganizational fields and subcultural and countercultural communities.

Looking at interorganizational fields reflects the fact that it is actually very difficult to think of movements as consisting of one organization. When this happens, as in the instances of the Bolshevik party in Russia or the National Socialist party in Germany, it usually means that the transition from movement to organization is complete. Movements indeed consist of multiple instances of interorganizational collaboration on campaigns of different intensity and scope. Direct ties between movement organizations include most prominently the exchange of information and the pooling of mobilization resources; indirect ties cover a broad range of possibilities, from shared personnel to joint participation in specific actions and/or events, from exposure to the same media, especially computer-mediated media, to shared linkages to third parties (whether private or public organizations).

Sometimes, relationships between groups and organizations are recurrent to the point that one can think, for a given social movement, of a distinctive "alliance structure" and "oppositional structure"; at other times this does not happen and ad hoc shifting coalition networks prevail. It is important to recognize the difference between a pure coalition, driven by instrumental principles, and a movement network. In both cases, networks facilitate the mobilization and allocation of resources across an organizational field, the negotiation of agreed goals, and the production and circulation of information.

However, it is the presence of a shared identity which qualifies a movement network vis-à-vis a coalition network, and draws its boundaries. As identity is not a given trait but is the product of incessant negotiations between social actors, which often involves ideological conflicts, movement boundaries are rarely stable. Their instability is also reflected in movement networks' internal segmentation, even though this may also depend on principles of division of labor or the diversity in issue agendas between different organizations.

At the same time, social movements, especially but not exclusively those challenging moral values and dominant cultural codes, also have a strong subcultural and countercultural dimension. Individual networks represent the backbone of broader social movement communities, where interpersonal ties involve the sharing of distinctive lifestyles or of broader cultural models. While social movement scholars have studied them mostly in reference to "new" social movements (e.g., gay and lesbian subcultures, alternative scenes, radical intellectual milieus), working-class communities continue to attract considerable attention from social historians and historical sociologists. To say the least, communitarian ties strengthen the identity and solidarity among movement activists and sympathizers. At the same time, though, they provide the specific locus of social conflict in those cases where the challenge is eminently on the symbolic side, where, in other words, at stake are mainly the definition of identities and the preservation of opportunities for the enactment of alternative lifestyles.

Thinking on networks and movements is likely to evolve along at least three lines. First, social scientists need to extend their conception of nodes in movement networks to objects other than individuals or organizations. In particular, protest events should be treated as network nodes. The whole idea of protest cycles presupposes interdependence between events, and so do the techniques of event history analysis increasingly used in this area of inquiry. The application of a network perspective could generate important insights on the innumerable mechanisms whereby events become linked to a social movement process. Organizations operate as ties by promoting and/or participating in multiple events; individual activists operate in

the same way; events may also be linked through symbolic means, e.g., by narratives that underline continuity between what would otherwise be largely independent and disconnected episodes of social conflict.

The time dimension should also be introduced more explicitly into the analysis of movement networks. Most studies of networks are based on data collected at one single point in time. More information is needed on how movement networks evolve over time, and how those changes affect patterns of collective action at large. Unfortunately, the data necessary to do those analyses are hard to locate, as systematic archives of social movement activity are rare. Nonetheless, some remarkable studies have indeed drawn upon archival records. Court records are another important source of network data, and have been used to account for recruitment to contemporary terrorist groups as well as for the traits of historical examples of contention. Newspaper reports offer a possible alternative, which has not been extensively explored yet. If data obtained in this way were confirmed to be a valid measure of actual ties, this would represent a major step forward toward network analysis of movements over long time spans.

Finally, research on networks and movements has increasingly explored the impact of virtual links, in particular those originating from computer-mediated communication, on collective action processes. The main question is whether "virtual," computer-mediated ties may replace "real" ties in the generation not only of the practical opportunities, but also of the shared understandings and – most important – the mutual trust which have consistently been identified as important facilitators of collective action. Available evidence is too sparse to be conclusive, and much more work is required to achieve conclusions that are at least as sound as those achieved, for all their limitations, in the study of the link between movement activity and "real" social networks.

SEE ALSO: Agency (and Intention); Alliances; Collective Action; Collective Identity; New Social Movement Theory; Protest, Diffusion of; Rational Choice Theories; Resource Mobilization Theory; Social Movements; Social Movements, Recruitment to; Social Network Theory; Subculture

REFERENCES AND SUGGESTED READINGS

Diani, M. (1992) The Concept of Social Movement. *Sociological Review* 40: 1–25.

Diani, M. (1995) *Green Networks*. Edinburgh University Press, Edinburgh.

Diani, M. & McAdam, D. (Eds.) (2003) *Social Movements and Networks*. Oxford University Press, Oxford.

Emirbayer, M. & Goodwin, J. (1994) Network Analysis, Culture, and the Problem of Agency. *American Journal of Sociology* 99: 1411–54.

Gerlach, L. (1971) Movements of Revolutionary Change: Some Structural Characteristics. *American Behavioral Scientist* 43: 813–36.

Gould, R. V. (1995) *Insurgent Identities: Class, Community, and Protest in Paris from 1848 to the Commune*. University of Chicago Press, Chicago.

Kitts, J. (2000) Mobilizing in Black Boxes: Social Networks and SMO Participation. *Mobilization* 5: 241–57.

Lemieux, V. (1998) *Les Coalitions: Liens, transactions et contrôles*. Presses Universitaires de France, Paris.

McAdam, D. (1988) *Freedom Summer*. Oxford University Press, Oxford.

Marwell, G. & Oliver, P. (1993) *The Critical Mass in Collective Action: A Micro-Social Theory*. Cambridge University Press, Cambridge.

Ohlemacher, T. (1996) Bridging People and Protest: Social Relays of Protest Groups Against Low-Flying Military Jets in West Germany. *Social Problems* 43: 197–218.

Osa, M. (2003) *Solidarity and Contention: Networks of Polish Opposition*. University of Minnesota Press, Minneapolis.

Van de Donk, W., Loader, B., Nixon, P., & Rucht, D. (Eds.) (2004) *Cyberspace Protest*. Routledge, London.

social movements, non-violent

Kurt Schock

Non-violent social movements rely primarily upon methods of non-violent action to promote change. Although most social movements concerned with personal transformation, lifestyle, and culture are non-violent, those concerned with political, social, and economic change that directly challenge the interests of the elite may be violent, non-violent, or a combination of the two. The focus here is on social movements that directly challenge elite interests, and that do so – by choice or due to limited options – only or primarily through methods of non-violent action, such as protest demonstrations, marches, boycotts, strikes, and civil disobedience. Of course, any social movement that directly challenges the interests of the elite, whether it is non-violent or violent, may be met with violence.

Non-violent action methods are actions that do not involve physical violence or the threat of physical force against human beings and that involve collective action in the pursuit of political, social, or economic objectives. Non-violent action occurs through (1) acts of omission, whereby people refuse to perform acts expected by norms, custom, law, or decree; (2) acts of commission, whereby people perform acts which they do not usually perform, are not expected by norms or customs to perform, or are forbidden by law or decree to perform; or (3) a combination of the two (Sharp 1973). These methods bring political, economic, social, emotional, or moral pressure to bear in the wielding of power in contentious interactions between collective actors (Sharp 1973, 1990; McCarthy 1990, 1997). Rather than viewing non-violent action as one half of a rigid violent–non-violent dichotomy, non-violent action may be better understood as a set of methods with special features that differ from both violent resistance and institutional politics, as well as from "everyday forms of resistance" (McCarthy 1990; Schock 2005).

Although non-violent action has been used in struggles against oppression throughout history, it was Mohandas Gandhi who was most influential in identifying nonviolence as a unique phenomenon with power different from and greater than that of violence, and developing the first comprehensive theory and praxis of non-violent resistance. Gandhi's philosophy and praxis of *satyagraha*, developed in the first half of the twentieth century, prescribes non-violent action in which people refuse to cooperate with laws and social relations perceived to be unjust and willingly suffer the consequences of noncooperation and civil disobedience. Along with noncooperation, *satyagraha* involves constructive programs, that is, building just, decentralized, non-coercive, and democratic social relations autonomous from state and market forces.

Over the course of the twentieth century, methods of non-violent action became a deliberate tool for social and political change, being transformed from a largely ad hoc strategy – based on either moral or religious principles, or a lack of violent alternatives – to a conscious, reflective method of struggle. There was a shift from informal and unorganized non-violent struggle to formal and organized non-violent struggle as expressed through social movements. By the end of the twentieth century non-violent action became a modular and global method for challenging oppression.

Major episodes of twentieth-century non-violent resistance include the Gandhi-led movement that challenged British rule in India (1919–47) and the Civil Rights Movement led by Martin Luther King, Jr. that challenged racial discrimination in the US South (1955–68). Various "waves" of non-violent social movements include a series of civic strikes against dictatorships in Latin America (1931–61); numerous protest movements in more developed countries in the late 1960s – exemplified by the student and anti-Vietnam War movements in the US and Australia, and the student-led insurrection in France in 1968; and a wave of "unarmed insurrections" throughout the "second" and "third" worlds from 1978 into the twenty-first century that challenged nondemocratic regimes, including those in Iran, South Africa, Chile, the Philippines, Indonesia, Nepal, Burma, China, and Ukraine. Non-violent social movements, beginning with the Solidarity movement in Poland in the early 1980s, contributed to the toppling of communist regimes in Eastern Europe. Moreover, these struggles contributed to the breakup of the Soviet empire and the end of the Cold War.

Various issue-related social movements have been almost exclusively non-violent. Throughout the twentieth century women's movements have fundamentally been concerned with the advocacy of non-violent methods and social relations. Women's movements have adopted non-violent action as both a tactical choice and a framing element, and have cultivated a social critique of violence – from domestic violence to war (Costain 2000). Labor movements in industrialized countries have historically depended on methods of noncooperation, especially the strike, to force concessions from capitalists and the state. The "new social movements" that emerged in western industrialized countries after World War II, such as the environmental and peace movements, have been almost exclusively non-violent. Indigenous people's movements throughout the world have also been primarily non-violent.

Many of the *violent* social movements of the twentieth century involved struggles for control of the state apparatus and/or struggles for self-determination, national liberation, or separatism. Although such conflicts will continue into the twenty-first century, many twenty-first century social movements have the goal of expanding democratic relations rather than controlling territory or the state – a goal that may be better attained through methods of non-violent action than through violence.

The beginning of the twenty-first century witnessed the emergence of a "movement of movements" implementing methods of non-violent action to expand global civil society and struggle for social justice. Globalization-from-below and global justice movements have relied almost entirely on non-violent action in their struggles against state and corporate-driven globalization. Throughout the Global South, land struggles have emerged that implement non-violent action to promote a more equitable distribution of land and sustainable development. Potential growth areas for non-violent social movements in the twenty-first century include challenging polyarchic or quasi-democratic relations and "manufactured consent," and promoting economic democracy throughout the world.

CHARACTERISTICS

Methods of resistance implemented by non-violent social movements fall into three classes: protest and persuasion, noncooperation, and non-violent intervention (Sharp 1973). Methods of protest and persuasion are symbolic expressions with communicative content intended to persuade the opponent, expose the opponent's illegitimacy, provide social visibility to unjust relations, illustrate the extent of dissatisfaction throughout a population, educate the public and third parties or catalyze their support, and overcome fear and acquiescence. These methods are often the crucibles in which frames are elaborated and disseminated, solidarity is forged, and people are mobilized to participate in other methods of non-violent action. These methods do not consist of the use of reason, discussion, or persuasion *exclusive of* direct contentious action. They include actions such as protest demonstrations, marches, rallies, public speeches, symbolic public acts, vigils, and political funerals.

Methods of noncooperation involve the deliberate withdrawal, restriction, or defiance of expected participation or cooperation. While these methods may have symbolic significance, they are also intended to disrupt the status quo and undermine the opponent's power, resources, and legitimacy. These methods may be social, economic, or political. Social noncooperation involves the refusal to carry out normal social relations, such as social boycotts, social ostracism, student strikes, stayaways, and offering sanctuary to dissidents. Economic noncooperation involves the suspension of existing economic relationships or the refusal to initiate new ones, such as labor strikes or slowdowns, economic boycotts, refusal to pay rent, debts, interest, or taxes, and the collective withdrawal of bank deposits. Political noncooperation involves the refusal to continue usual forms of political participation or obedience. A common type of political noncooperation is civil disobedience (i.e., the open and deliberate violation of laws or orders for a political purpose), such as the publication of banned newspapers or pamphlets, and the refusal to participate in the military or obey orders of state agents.

Methods of non-violent intervention are acts of interposition intended directly to disrupt continued subjugation or to develop alternatives to oppressive relations. Examples range from sit-ins, pickets, non-violent obstructions, non-violent sabotage, land occupations, and paralyzing transportation to developing alternative markets and creating parallel institutions during the course of contentious struggles. These methods can be subdivided into two types. *Disruptive* non-violent intervention upsets or destroys normal or established social relations. *Creative* non-violent intervention forges autonomous social relations (Burrowes 1996). Creative non-violent intervention is significant because in struggles against oppression it is not only necessary to reject participating in oppressive relations, it is also necessary to engage in positive action to build alternatives; that is, to implement constructive programs and parallel structures. The two types of non-violent intervention are mutually supporting and reinforcing: while disruptive non-violent intervention (and noncooperation) drains power from the oppressors, creative non-violent intervention generates power among the oppressed.

Non-violent social movements may produce change through various mechanisms, including conversion, accommodation, non-violent coercion, and disintegration (Sharp 1973, 1990). Conversion occurs when the opponent, as a result of non-violent action by challengers, adopts the challenger's point of view and concedes to its goals. Conversion may occur through reason and argumentation, or as a result of changes in the emotions, beliefs, attitudes, or morality of the oppressors. The likelihood of conversion increases the less the social distance there is between the oppressors and the oppressed. However, if the oppressors view challengers as outside of their moral order or as inferior, then they are more likely to be indifferent. Thus, gender, race, ethnicity, religion, and language may be characteristics that form the basis of dehumanizing ideologies that decrease the likelihood of conversion. In addition to social distance, physical distance or a lack of communication between the oppressors and the oppressed may also inhibit conversion. Conversion is commonly (mis) understood as the only way or the main way in which non-violent action produces change.

Through accommodation the oppressor grants concessions to the challengers, even though it is not converted to the challenger's point of view, is not forced to concede by the challenger's actions, and has the capacity to continue the struggle. An oppressor may accommodate a challenge when it perceives that the costs of ignoring or repressing are greater than the costs of giving in to some or all of its demands, views it as more of a nuisance than a threat, or calculates that by giving in to some or all of the challenger's demands the movement will be coopted thus preempting a more broad-based movement. While "coercion" is often associated with violence, coercion can also be affected through non-violent pressure. Through non-violent coercion, change is achieved against the oppressor's will as a result of the challenger successfully and non-violently undermining its power, legitimacy, and ability to control the situation. Non-violent coercion may promote change in one of three ways: (1) the challenge becomes too widespread to be controlled through repression, (2) the oppressor loses its willingness to repress, or (3) the movement's implementation of non-violent action creates situations whereby it is too disruptive for the opponent to function without significant alterations in its policies or structure.

Disintegration occurs when the opponent breaks down in the face of widespread non-violent resistance. That is, the challenge undermines the sources of the opponent's power to such an extent that there is no longer any effective institutional body to challenge or resist.

TYPES

Conceptual, if not empirical, distinctions can be made between social movements that implement non-violent action as a matter of principle and those that implement it for pragmatic reasons. Participants in principled or conscientious nonviolent social movements view nonviolence as a way of life and usually hold religious or ethical beliefs that prohibit using violence against others in most or all situations. In contrast, participants in pragmatic non-violent social movements perceive non-violent action as the most expedient method for promoting change. Nonviolence is viewed as a means for prosecuting conflicts and not necessarily as a lifestyle. Since conflict is viewed as a relationship of incompatible interests, conversion of the opponent's views is not expected, therefore other mechanisms of change come into play. The goal of these movements is to limit the opponent's options or undermine its power in order to promote change (Stiehm 1968; Burrowes 1996).

Distinctions can also be made between *reformist* and *revolutionary* non-violent social movements. In reformist non-violent social movements, particular policies are perceived as the cause of or the solution for social problems. Movements of this type tend to implement short to medium-term campaigns aimed at changing public policies within the existing political framework. Moreover, these movements do not usually involve constructive programs. In contrast, revolutionary non-violent social movements are guided by a structural analysis, and aim to change the basic structures of society. Particular campaigns, which may have a short to medium-term time frame, are conducted within the context of a long-term revolutionary vision and involve the implementation of constructive programs (Burrowes 1996).

The cross-classification of the principled-pragmatic dimension with the reformist-revolutionary dimension provides four types of non-violent social movements: pragmatic-reform, principled-reform, pragmatic-revolutionary, and principled-revolutionary. These categories are broadly descriptive rather than definitive and are not mutually exclusive (Burrowes 1996). Examples of pragmatic-reform movements include anti-nuclear and environmental movements in developed countries that target government and corporate policies. An example of a principled-reform movement is the American Civil Rights Movement that incorporated a religious perspective in its challenge to particular policies that upheld racial discrimination. Examples of pragmatic-revolutionary movements include the Eastern European revolutions of 1989 and the Palestinian Intifada (1987–90) that used non-violent methods against Israeli domination and occupation. An example of a principled-revolutionary movement is Gandhi's struggle in India directed at liberation from British rule and the development of constructive programs aimed to fundamentally transform social relations.

UNDERSTANDING NON-VIOLENT SOCIAL MOVEMENTS

A number of interrelated areas exist where research and theory building would increase our understanding of non-violent social movements: (1) correcting misconceptions about non-violent action; (2) rethinking history from a perspective of non-violent struggle and understanding the processes by which violence has been glorified throughout history; (3) reconceptualizing political power; (4) developing theories of non-violent revolution; and (5) theorizing the role of agency and strategy in non-violent resistance.

First, the ability to understand and explain the dynamics of non-violent social movements has suffered from numerous misconceptions about non-violent action. Some of these misconceptions include the inability to differentiate non-violent action from inaction or passive resistance; the view that non-violent action involves only actions that are legal or institutionalized; the view that non-violent action is a middle-class or bourgeois method for social change and that it can only produce moderate change; and the view that non-violent action works solely in democratic contexts and is ineffective in nondemocracies. For social scientific research on non-violent social movements to proceed it is essential that these and other misconceptions about non-violent action be identified and corrected (Schock 2003).

Second, while non-violent action has been used throughout history, it has received much less attention, relative to the exercise of violence, by social scientists, historians, politicians, and the media. An important task for research on non-violent social movements is to rethink history from a non-violent perspective (Sharp 1973; Wink 1992; Schell 2003). In addition to uncovering the history of non-violent action, social scientists must also explain why violence has been glorified throughout history. This would entail an attempt to understand the "myth of redemptive violence" (Wink 1992), the "mythology of terror" (Ackerman & DuVall 2000), and the glorification of violence in national myths and the socialization processes through which they are perpetuated.

Third, correcting misconceptions about non-violent action and uncovering the history of non-violent resistance will lead to a reconceptualization of the sources of political power. Schell (2003) makes a useful distinction between coercive power and cooperative power. Coercive power springs from the threat or use of violence, is based on fear, and flows downward from the state by virtue of its command of the instruments of violence. Cooperative power arises from the action in concert of people who willingly agree with one another. It flows upward from the consent, support, and non-violent activity of the people. While most political theory has assumed that violence, or coercive

power, is the final arbiter in politics, the increasing use and effectiveness of non-violent struggle has led to a questioning of this traditional assumption.

Fourth, the failure to understand the power and role of non-violent action in political change in the past has led to the failure to predict and understand non-violent political change in the present. In fact, it has been argued that we lack social scientific theories of non-violent revolution (Schell 2003). According to most social scientists, violence is one of the defining features of revolutions. Yet violence has historically been much more prevalent during the consolidation of power than in the toppling of the old regime or in the revolutionary transfer of power, and the consolidation of the new order does not necessarily have to be violent. Social scientists need to theorize more adequately the role of human agency and strategy in non-violent social movements. Social scientists have tended to emphasize structural theories of social movements and revolution. While useful, these theories may overlook the crucial role of agency, strategy, and tactics in promoting social change. Useful starting points include the works of Ackerman and Kruegler (1994), which delineate principles of strategic non-violent conflict, and Schock (2005), which identifies attributes of non-violent social movements that facilitate their resilience in repressive contexts and increase their leverage.

SEE ALSO: Anti-War and Peace Movements; Civil Rights Movement; Global Justice as a Social Movement; King, Martin Luther; Revolutions; Social Movements; Women's Movements

REFERENCES AND SUGGESTED READINGS

Ackerman, P. & DuVall, J. (2000) *A Force More Powerful: A Century of Nonviolent Conflict*. St. Martin's Press, New York.

Ackerman, P. & Kruegler, C. (1994) *Strategic Nonviolent Conflict: The Dynamics of People Power in the Twentieth Century*. Praeger, Westport.

Burrowes, R. J. (1996) *The Strategy of Nonviolent Defense: A Gandhian Approach*. State University of New York Press, Albany.

Costain, A. N. (2000) Women's Movements and Nonviolence. *PS: Political Science and Politics* 33: 175–80.

Galtung, J. (1989) Principles of Nonviolent Action: The Great Chain of Nonviolence Hypothesis. In: Galtung, J. (Ed.), *Nonviolence and Israel/Palestine.* University of Hawai'i Press, Honolulu, pp. 13–33.

McCarthy, R. M. (1990) The Techniques of Nonviolent Action: Some Principles of Its Nature, Use, and Effects. In: Crow, R. E., Grant, P., & Ibrahim, S. E. (Eds.), *Arab Nonviolent Struggle in the Middle East.* Lynne Rienner Publishing, Boulder, pp. 107–20.

McCarthy, R. M. (1997) Methods of Nonviolent Action. In: Powers, R. S. & Vogele, W. B. (Eds.), *Protest, Power, and Change: An Encyclopedia of Nonviolent Action from ACT-UP to Women's Suffrage.* Garland Publishing, New York, pp. 319–28.

Schell, J. (2003) *The Unconquerable World: Power, Nonviolence, and the Will of the People.* Metropolitan Books, New York.

Schock, K. (2003) Nonviolent Action and Its Misconceptions: Insights for Social Scientists. *PS: Political Science and Politics* 36: 705–12.

Schock, K. (2005) *Unarmed Insurrections: People Power Movements in Nondemocracies.* University of Minnesota Press, Minneapolis.

Sharp, G. (1973) *The Politics of Nonviolent Action,* 3 vols. Porter Sargent Publishers, Boston.

Sharp, G. (1990) *Civilian-Based Defense: A Post-Military Weapons System.* Princeton University Press, Princeton.

Stiehm, J. (1968) Nonviolence is Two. *Sociological Inquiry* 38: 23–30.

Wink, W. (1992) *Engaging the Powers: Discernment and Resistance in a World of Domination.* Fortress Press, Minneapolis.

Zunes, S., Kurtz, L. R., & Asher, S. B. (Eds.) (1999) *Nonviolent Social Movements: A Geographical Perspective.* Blackwell, Oxford.

social movements, participatory democracy in

Francesca Polletta

Participatory democracy refers to an organizational form in which decision-making is decentralized, non-hierarchical, and consensus-oriented. It can be contrasted with bureaucracy, in which decision-making is centralized, hierarchical, and based on a formal division of labor, as well as with majority vote. Participatory democratic organizations have been a prominent feature of many progressive movements, including radical pacifism, the Civil Rights Movement, the new left, feminism, environmentalism, anti-nuclear activism, and the anti-corporate globalization movement.

Participatory democratic organizations today claim a diverse lineage, with precursors in ancient Athenian democracy, the New England town hall, Quaker meetings, and Spanish Civil War affinity groups. The term itself was popularized in 1962 by the new left group Students for a Democratic Society (SDS). SDS leaders intended participatory democracy to describe a polity in which citizens were involved in public policymaking, not a mode of organizational decision-making. However, at the time, decision-making within SDS itself was collectivist and consensus-oriented, this despite the group's formal reliance on parliamentary procedure. The same was true of the militant civil rights group the Student Non-Violent Coordinating Committee (SNCC). For thousands of activists, participatory democracy soon became an organizational ethos. "Collectives" run on participatory democratic principles proliferated in the radical feminist and anti-war movements of the late 1960s (Rothschild 2000; Polletta 2002).

By the end of the decade, many young activists perceived the political system as intransigent, and they turned to building alternative schools, health centers, food coops, and publishing guilds, thus contributing to an enduring cooperative movement (Rothschild & Whitt 1986). With the rise of the anti-nuclear movement in Europe and the United States in the late 1970s, activists put participatory democratic movement organizations to use once again in overtly challenging the state, developing institutions of "affinity groups" and "spokescouncils" to coordinate mass actions involving thousands of people. More recently, participatory democratic forms have been prominent in the anti-corporate globalization and global justice movements (Polletta 2002).

For sociologists writing about the surge of collectivist organizations in the 1960s, the participatory democratic impulse reflected a youthful repudiation of authority that was at odds with the demands of effective political reform. Participatory democratic organizations were conceptualized as "expressive" or "redemptive" in contrast to their "instrumental" and "adversary" bureaucratic counterparts (Breines 1989). Since then, many scholars have instead adopted Breines's (1989) view of participatory democracy as animated by a *prefigurative* impulse. By enacting within the movement itself values of radical equality, freedom, and community, activists have sought to bring into being a society marked by those values. Far from anti-political, participatory democracy has been an attempt to transform what counts as politics.

Still, most scholars have seen participatory democracies as fragile. And indeed, some of the most famous participatory democratic movement groups, such as SDS, numerous feminist collectives, and the anti-nuclear Clamshell Alliance, collapsed after explosive internal battles about organizational decision-making. However, scholars have disagreed about the source of participatory democracy's fragility. One popular explanation centers on the form's inefficiency. Consensus decision-making takes time; decentralized administration creates problems of coordination; and a minimal division of labor sacrifices the benefits of expertise. These inefficiencies are manageable in an organization that is small or has little opportunity for political impact. But when participatory democratic groups grow in size or political stature and therefore face new demands for coordination and funding, such inefficiencies become intolerable. The result is often a battle between political pragmatists, who are willing to adopt a more centralized and hierarchical organizational structure, and purists who refuse such reforms. Ultimately, either groups bureaucratize, as did many feminist organizations in the 1970s and 1980s, or they collapse.

This account neglects the fact that participatory democracy can be efficient. Multiple lines of input facilitate tactical innovation; decentralized organization allows movements to tailor programs to local contexts; and rotating leadership can maximize political learning (see Rothschild 2000 on the instrumental benefits of collectivist forms in for-profit organizations). Moreover, the battles that have racked

participatory democratic groups have usually centered not on the inefficiency of the form but on the group's failure to live up to its professed egalitarianism. In line with this insight, some scholars have argued that participatory democracy's vulnerability is its inequity rather than its inefficiency. Michels (1958 [1915]) maintained that democratic organizations inevitably developed oligarchical structures as those occupying positions based on their expertise acquired a stake in retaining their positions. Participatory democrats refuse those imperatives and privilege democracy over expertise. That only means that the hierarchies are informal, scholars in this vein argue. The result is what Freeman (1973) calls the "tyranny of structurelessness," in which the elimination of formal structures of authority only makes it easier for informal cliques to rule freely. When members shut out of decision-making protest their marginalization, an organizational crisis is likely since participatory democracy provides no mechanisms for holding leaders formally accountable.

A third perspective holds that as long as members' interests are fundamentally congruent, they are unlikely to object to disparities in informal influence (Mansbridge 1983). But when members' interests conflict, which is likely to occur in all but the most homogeneous of groups, the consensus-based decision-making characteristic of participatory democratic organizations offers no way of adjudicating those conflicts. If minorities are not coerced to agree with the majority, then a stalemate is likely. After a series of such stalemates, an organizational crisis may ensue.

Although these explanations for participatory democracy's fragility have been advanced separately, one can imagine that one may be more applicable than the others depending on the circumstances, or that two or even all three dynamics may operate at the same time. For example, an influx of new members may increase organizational inefficiencies at the same time as it creates new conflicts of interest and heightens newcomers' perception of veterans as a controlling elite. But the three explanations also assume that there is a single form of participatory democracy across movements and historical eras. An alternative perspective holds that groups have enacted commitments to radical democracy, equality, even consensus, in very different ways. For example, Polletta (2002) argues that participatory democratic groups in the pacifist, civil rights, new left, and feminist movements of the 1950s and 1960s drew deliberative norms from relationships of friendship, religious fellowship, and tutelage. The familiarity of those interactional styles made participatory democracy fairly easy to practice but also made for distinctive organizational challenges. For example, groups that styled their democracies on friendship were more likely to encounter crises after an influx of new members than were groups that styled their democracies on religious fellowship, since the latter were more comfortable with an informal probationary period for new members. In a study of three antitoxics groups, Lichterman (1996) found that one group solicited members' input round-robin style for every decision, while another consistently deferred to the group's leader. Yet, both groups said that they made their decisions by consensus. Different versions of participatory democracy may reflect distinctive political traditions, modes of religious engagement, professional styles of collaboration, or class-based norms.

These kinds of institutional influences on how democratic commitments are enacted exist alongside the pressures exercised by funders and governmental agencies to shape what participatory democratic organizations look like. Funders often require explicit job descriptions and assessment criteria (Matthews 1994). The Internal Revenue Service's complex standards for retaining tax-exempt status push organizations to hire legal and financial experts (McCarthy et al. 1991). The accreditation groups that evaluate organizations' suitability for philanthropic funding encourage them to create conventional boards of directors (McCarthy et al. 1991). The result is that very few movement organizations today resemble anything like a pure form of participatory democracy (Bordt 1997). Instead, a hierarchy of offices is sometimes combined with informal consultation across levels, or decisions are divided into those requiring consensus and those not requiring it, and so on (Iannello 1992). Some research suggests that these hybrid organizations have been effective

in maximizing the tactical innovation and solidarity associated with participatory democracy while avoiding the form's inefficiencies, inequities, and potential for stalemate. Even groups whose commitment to consensus-based decision-making is paramount tend to accept supermajorities rather than unanimity for contentious decisions and they use a range of formal mechanisms unknown to 1960s participatory democrats, such as time limits on discussions and facilitators.

Several lines of research on participatory democratic organizations are promising. Rather than looking for the fundamental flaw in participatory democracy as an organizational form, several scholars have sought instead to identify the institutional conditions in which participatory democracies are likely to proliferate (Rothschild & Whitt 1986). Another valuable approach has been to identify the tasks that are furthered or impeded by particular organizational forms, tasks such as raising funds, innovating tactically, sustaining coalitions, and ensuring decision-makers' accountability (Staggenborg 1989).

A third area of promising research concerns the impacts of participatory democratic organizational forms. During historical periods or institutional arenas in which participatory democratic organizations are prominent, do they make inroads into the repertoire of institutionalized organizational forms? For example, Rothschild (2000) argues that widespread public support for workplace democracy reflects the popular valorization of terms such as "voice" and "empowerment" by the social justice movements of the 1960s and 1970s. What are the conditions in which particular versions of participatory democracy diffuse across movements? Some evidence suggests that a popular perception of participatory democracy as white and middle class may make it less appealing to activists of color and working-class activists (Polletta 2005). Finally, we know little about whether participatory democratic organizations exist in conservative movements and, if they do, if they are animated by goals other than prefigurative ones.

SEE ALSO: Anarchism; Democracy and Organizations; Global Justice as a Social Movement;

Globalization and Global Justice; New Left; Oligarchy and Organization; Social Movement Organizations; Social Movements, Leadership in; Women's Movements

REFERENCES AND SUGGESTED READINGS

Bordt, R. (1997) *The Structure of Women's Non-profit Organizations*. Indiana University Press, Bloomington.

Breines, W. (1989) *Community and Organization in the New Left, 1962–1968: The Great Refusal*. Rutgers University Press, New Brunswick, NJ.

Freeman, J. (1973) The Tyranny of Structurelessness. In: Koedt, A., Levine, E., & Rapone, A. (Eds.), *Radical Feminism*. Quadrangle, New York.

Iannello, K. P. (1992) *Decisions Without Hierarchy*. Routledge, New York.

Lichterman, P. (1996) *The Search for Political Community: American Activists Reinventing Commitment*. Cambridge University Press, New York.

McCarthy, J. D., Britt, D. W., & Wolfson, M. (1991) The Institutional Channeling of Social Movements by the State in the United States. *Research in Social Movements, Conflicts, and Change* 13: 45–76.

Mansbridge, J. (1983) *Beyond Adversary Democracy*. University of Chicago Press, Chicago.

Matthews, N. (1994) *Confronting Rape: The Feminist Anti-Rape Movement and the State*. Routledge, New York.

Michels, R. (1958 [1915]) *Political Parties: A Sociological Study of the Oligarchical Tendencies of Modern Democracy*. Trans. E. & C. Paul. Free Press, New York.

Minkoff, D. (2002) The Emergence of Hybrid Organizational Forms: Combining Identity-Based Service Provision and Political Action. *Nonprofit and Voluntary Sector Quarterly* 31: 377–401.

Polletta, F. (2002) *Freedom Is an Endless Meeting: Democracy in American Social Movements*. University of Chicago Press, Chicago.

Polletta, F. (2005) How Participatory Democracy Became White: Culture and Organizational Choice. *Mobilization*.

Rothschild, J. (2000) Creating a Just and Democratic Workplace: More Engagement, Less Hierarchy. *Contemporary Sociology* 29: 195–213.

Rothschild, J. & Whitt, J. A. (1986) *The Cooperative Workplace: Potentials and Dilemmas of Organizational Democracy and Participation*. Cambridge University Press, New York.

Staggenborg, S. (1989) Stability and Innovation in the Women's Movement: A Comparison of Two Movement Organizations. *Social Problems* 36: 75–92.

social movements, political consequences of

Edwin Amenta and Neal Caren

Scholars have increasingly turned their attention to the political or state-related consequences of social movements. Making sense of the state-related consequences raises specific and difficult conceptual and theoretical issues. Conceptually speaking, scholars have to address the meaning of "success" or "influence" for challengers. Theoretically, scholars need to address what, beyond some degree of mobilization and basically plausible claims-making, matters in explaining the state-related impacts of challengers. In comparison to mobilizing supporters, fashioning identities among them, or achieving recognition from targets, most macropolitical consequences of challengers are not as directly related to the efforts expended by challengers.

In designating the consequences of social movements, Gamson's (1990 [1975]) two types of success have been influential. Gamson considers success in new advantages, his first type, as meaning whether a challenger's goals or claims were mainly realized. Yet Gamson's concept of new advantages places limits on the consideration of possible impacts of challenges. It may be possible, notably, for a challenger to fail to achieve its stated program – and thus be deemed a failure – but still to win substantial new advantages for its constituents. This is especially likely for challengers with far-reaching goals. There may also be unintended consequences that influence beneficiary groups, and challengers may do worse than fail.

To address some of these issues, other scholars start with an alternative based on the concept of *collective goods*, or group-wise advantages or disadvantages from which non-participants in a challenge cannot be easily excluded (Olson 1965). Collective goods can be material, such as categorical social spending programs, but can also be less tangible, such as new ways to refer to members of a group. Social movement organizations almost invariably claim to represent a group extending beyond the leaders and adherents of the organization and most make demands that would provide collective benefits to that larger group (Tilly 1999). According to the collective benefit standard, a challenger can have considerable impact even when it fails to achieve what it is seeking. It also can address the possibility that challengers would have negative consequences or negligible ones, such as achieving a program that did not realize its intended effect to benefit constituents (Amenta 2006). Scholars working from this standard tend to refer to the consequences or impacts of social movements rather than successes or failures. From this perspective, the greatest sort of impact is the one that provides a group, not necessarily organizations representing that group, continuing leverage over political processes. These sorts of gains are usually at a structural or systemic level of state processes and are a kind of metacollective benefit, as they increase the productivity of all future collective action of the group. Gains in the democratization of state processes are perhaps the most important that social movements can influence.

Most collective action, however, is aimed at a more medium level – major changes in policy and the bureaucratic enforcement and implementation of that policy. Once enacted and enforced with bureaucratic means, categorical social spending programs, notably, provide benefits in such a manner (Amenta 2006). The beneficiaries gain rights of entitlement to the benefits, and legal changes and bureaucratic reinforcement of such laws help to ensure the routine maintenance of such collective benefits. Under these circumstances, the issue is privileged in politics, is effectively removed from the political agenda, and the political system becomes biased in favor of the group. A bureaucracy would have to be targeted and altered, if not captured, or new legislation would have to be passed rescinding benefits – a process that becomes more difficult as time passes as bureaucracies are reinforced and people organize their lives around the programs. Regulatory bureaucracies that are products of challenger mobilizations may push on their own to advance mandates in the absence of new legislation, as in the case of state labor commissions or in affirmative action. Through their policies, states can ratify or attempt to undermine potential collective identities or help to create new ones, sometimes on purpose, often inadvertently. Dividing

the process of creating new laws containing collective benefits into the agenda-setting, legislative content, passage, and implementation of legislation simplifies analysis and also makes it easier to judge the impact of challengers.

Gamson's second type of success, the "acceptance" (1990 [1975]) or "representation" (Cress & Snow 2000) achieved by challenging organizations, can also be related systematically back to states and collective benefits. To the extent that state action recognizing challenging organizations influences their form or resources, it also influences their potential to gain future collective benefits. Gamson's idea of acceptance may, however, be too broadly drawn to capture the sorts of representation sought by challengers attempting to influence democratic states. More important and plausible for state-oriented challengers is a version of Gamson's "inclusion," which would amount to the placing of challengers in state positions through election or appointment. Challengers can provide candidates for office or can stand as representatives of new political parties. As is the case for other, better politically situated groups, it is possible for social movement organizations to capture bureaucracies and run them in favor of their constituency. By gaining representation in legislative offices and bureaucracies, challengers can influence policies throughout the process, including placing programs on the agenda, helping to specify their content, aiding their passage, and supporting their enforcement. Movements may also attempt to gain recognition for altered or new movement organizations, which might include political parties, political lobbying, or educational organizations. Collective action may be intended to win or may result in winning higher-order rights through the state that advantage a group in its conflicts with other groups (Tarrow 1998). Labor movements, notably, often focus on the state to ensure rights to organize and engage in collective bargaining with businesses and business associations, and the state may be used as a fulcrum in transnational protest. Challengers blocked in one country may appeal to sympathetic organizations in others.

There are four main arguments designed to explain the impact of social movements on states. The first argument is that whatever aids a group's mobilization will lead to its making gains, as mobilization of various sorts will aid movements in whatever they do (McCarthy & Zald 2002). The mobilization of various resources is needed to engage in collective action, which is designed and expected to bring a certain amount of collective benefits. This line of argumentation is consistent with rational choice discussions of collective action problems, in that they view the main issue for social movements as overcoming free-rider disincentives to participation (Olson 1965). The ability to mobilize different sorts of resources is key for the impact of movements and mobilization of resources and membership has been shown to influence some state-related consequences in different research (McCarthy & Zald 2002). However, mobilization seems to be a necessary condition to have influence over states, as there seems to be no connection between size of a mobilized challenger and gaining new benefits (Kitschelt 1986; Gamson 1990 [1975]).

Second, specific strategies and goals of collective action and forms of challenger organization are more likely to produce influence. Gamson (1990 [1975]) found notably that limited goals, the use of "constraints," selective incentives, and bureaucratic forms of organization were more likely to produce new advantages. In contrast, goals and strategies aiming at "displacement" – in which a movement seeks to destroy or replace its opponent – were likely to fail. Others have advanced Gamson's argument about the importance of organization in social movement success by focusing on the sorts of social movement organizations likely to produce gains. It has been argued that resourceful movement infrastructures led to gains in policy implementation (Andrews 2001) and that innovative organizational forms can lead to gains for challengers and transformations of political institutions (Clemens 1997). Singled out for special attention are claims-making and framing. Cress and Snow (2000) argue notably that for a challenger to have an impact, it is necessary for it to employ resonant "prognostic" and "diagnostic" frames; to gain results, challengers need to identify problems and pose credible solutions to those problems that play to state actors and other third parties as well as to be able to mobilize participants.

A third argument attempts to take into account contextual influences by claiming that once a challenger is mobilized, the main thing influencing its impact is the political context or "opportunity structure." This line of argumentation has both systemic and dynamic components to it, and sometimes it is also argued that systemic political contexts greatly influence or determine the strategies of challengers. Kriesi and his colleagues (1995) take the most systemic view, arguing that the openness and capacity of states largely determine whether a state-related movement will have influence. When states have both inclusive strategies and strong capacities, challengers are most likely to achieve "proactive" impacts. Under weak states, by contrast, reactive impacts are more probable, as the state lacks the capacity to implement policies (see also Kitschelt 1986).

The more overarching arguments have been criticized, however, on the grounds that all manner of social movements with different strategies have developed within similar countries (Dalton 1995) and that within any country differences in impacts have varied over time. Arguments regarding systemic political contexts have also been criticized on the grounds that they take a too abstract view of states and political opportunity structures. Notably, focusing on the overall openness of polities and strength of states ignores conceptual and theoretical developments in political sociology literatures that have addressed the influence of polities and states in more fine-grained ways. Important factors include the polity structure, the democratization of state institutions, electoral rules and procedures, and state policies. These aspects of states influence forms of challenger representation, as well as the tactics of challengers. These arguments tend to drop the weak/strong state and open/closed polity dichotomies and refer to specific aspects of polity and political actors.

The centralization and division of power between each branch of government also has an impact on social movement organizations (Amenta 2006). An autonomous court system with veto power over the legislative branch, for example, may lead to an emphasis on legal mobilizations, which may shift focus away from more mass-based protests. Multiple points of access are a two-edged sword, however, as they also provide multiple points of veto. The level of democracy has important consequences for the forms that mobilization will take. Specifically, the greater the exclusion from the democratic process, the more likely non-institutional forms of protest will take place. Electoral rules may have the greatest impact on the relationship between social movements and the party system. Winner-take-all systems, such as in the US, discourage the formation and legitimacy of new political parties. Initiative and referendum procedures increase the likelihood that organizations will be single-focused. In addition, states can also provide a variety of resources for specific social movements that can vary from concrete items to legitimacy.

On the dynamic side, the political opportunity argument focuses on alterations in political conditions that improve the productivity of collective action of challengers. In their study of farm workers' mobilization and collective action, Jenkins and Perrow (1977) found that changes in the political context influenced their growth and impact, through the rise to power of favorable political regimes and through the support of liberal organizations like organized labor. In his study of the Civil Rights Movement, McAdam (1982) argued that favorable political conditions were necessary for its gains – which were based on tactical innovations. In short, according to the strongest form of this argument, mobilized challengers have impacts largely because they engage in collective action at the right time. This argumentation has suffered, however, in comparison with the systemic view of political contexts in being able to specify what constitutes a favorable context. The main candidates – polity openness, instability of elite alliances, the presence of elite allies for challengers, declines in capacities and propensities for repression – are drawn so widely as to be difficult to operationalize.

Finally, many scholars have developed different political mediation models of social movement consequences, which build on arguments concerning strategy, organizational form, and political contexts (Amenta et al. 1992; Skocpol 1992; Amenta 2006). The basic point of this argument is that the collective action of challengers is politically mediated. In a democratic political system, mobilizing relatively large numbers

of committed people is probably necessary to winning new collective benefits for those otherwise underrepresented in politics. So, too, are making plausible claims regarding the worthiness of the group and the usefulness of its program. Yet challengers' action is more likely to produce results when institutional political actors see benefit in aiding the group that the challenger represents. To secure new benefits, challengers will typically need help or complementary action from like-minded state actors, including elected officials, appointed officials, or state civil servants. And so challengers need to engage in collective action that changes the calculations of relevant institutional political actors, and challengers need to adopt organizational forms that fit political circumstances.

Political mediation arguments do not identify individual organizational forms, strategies, or long-term or short-term political contexts that will always or usually help challengers to win collective benefits. Instead the idea is that certain organizational forms and collective action strategies will be more productive in some political contexts rather than others. In her examination of organized groups throughout US history, Skocpol (1992) argues that to have influence the forms of challengers and other mass-based interest organizations need to fit the divided nature of the American political context, a systemic condition. US organizations need to have a wide geographical presence to influence Congress, which is based on district representation. The most extensive discussion of this sort suggests that challengers need to moderate strategies and forms to address political circumstances. The standard distinction between disruptive and assimilative strategies is dropped in favor of addressing variations in assertiveness of action (Amenta 2006), with assertive meaning the use of increasingly strong sanctions, something akin to Gamson's "constraints." If the political regime is supportive and the domestic bureaucrats are professionalized and supportive, limited protest based mainly on the evidence of mobilization is likely to be sufficient to provide increased collective benefits. By contrast, achieving collective benefits through public policy is likely to be more difficult if neither a supportive regime nor administrative authority exists.

Although this understanding of the political context is a dynamic one that takes into account changes in political contexts, it can also be related back to systemic and structural characteristics of political systems, notably political institutional conditions that make the establishment of a reform-oriented regime or bureaucratic capacities difficult. When the regime is opposed to the challenger or sees no benefit in adding its beneficiary group to its coalition and when state bureaucracies in the area are hostile or absent, the sorts of limited protest listed above are likely to be ignored or have a limited effect. As political circumstances become more difficult, more assertive or bolder collective action is required to produce collective benefits. Sanctions in assertive institutional collective action threaten to increase or decrease the likelihood of gaining or keeping something valuable to political actors – often positions – or to take over their functions or prerogatives. The institutional collective action of challengers works largely by mobilizing large numbers of people behind a course of activity, often one with electoral implications. This collective action may be designed to convince the general public of the justice of the cause and influence elected and appointed officials in that manner, but may also demonstrate to these officials that a large segment of the electorate is willing to vote or engage in other political activity mainly on the basis of a single key issue.

SEE ALSO: Collective Action; Framing and Social Movements; Political Opportunities; Political Process Theory; Political Sociology; Resource Mobilization Theory; Social Movement Organizations; Social Movements; Social Policy, Welfare State

REFERENCES AND SUGGESTED READINGS

Amenta, E. (2006) *When Movements Matter: The Townsend Plan and the Rise of Social Security.* Princeton University Press, Princeton.

Amenta, E., Carruthers, B. G., & Zylan, Y. (1992) A Hero for the Aged? The Townsend Movement, the Political Mediation Model, and US Old-Age Policy, 1934–1950. *American Journal of Sociology* 98: 308–39.

Andrews, K. T. (2001) Social Movements and Policy Implementation: The Mississippi Civil Rights Movement and the War on Poverty, 1965–1971. *American Sociological Review* 66: 21–48.

Clemens, E. S. (1997) *The People's Lobby: Organizational Innovation and the Rise of Interest Group Politics in the United States, 1890–1925.* University of Chicago Press, Chicago.

Cress, D. M. & Snow, D. A. (2000) The Outcomes of Homeless Mobilizations: The Influence of Organization, Disruption, Political Mediation, and Framing. *American Journal of Sociology* 105: 1063–104.

Dalton, R. (1995) Strategies of Partisan Influence: West European Environmental Groups. In: Jenkins, J. C. & Klandermans, B. (Eds.), *The Politics of Social Protest.* University of Minnesota Press, Minneapolis, pp. 296–323.

Gamson, W. A. (1990 [1975]) *The Strategy of Social Protest*, 2nd edn. Wadsworth, Belmont, CA.

Jenkins, J. C. & Perrow, C. (1977) Insurgency of the Powerless: Farm Worker Movements (1946–1972). *American Sociological Review* 42: 249–68.

Kitschelt, H. P. (1986) Political Opportunity Structures and Political Protest: Anti-Nuclear Movements in Four Democracies. *British Journal of Political Science* 16: 57–85.

Kriesi, H., Koopmans, R., Duyvendak, J. W., & Guigni, M. G. (1995) *New Social Movements in Western Europe: A Comparative Analysis.* University of Minnesota Press, Minneapolis.

McAdam, D. (1982) *Political Process and the Development of Black Insurgency, 1930–1970.* University of Chicago Press, Chicago.

McCarthy, J. D. & Zald, M. (2002) The Enduring Vitality of the Resource Mobilization Theory of Social Movements. In: Turner, J. H. (Ed.), *Handbook of Sociological Theory.* Kluwer Academic/Plenum, New York, pp. 533–65.

Olson, M. (1965) *The Logic of Collective Action.* Harvard University Press, Cambridge, MA.

Skocpol, T. (1992) *Protecting Soldiers and Mothers: The Political Origins of Social Policy in the United States.* Harvard University Press, Cambridge, MA.

Tarrow, S. (1998) *Power in Movement: Social Movements, Collective Action, and Politics*, 2nd edn. Cambridge University Press, Cambridge and New York.

Tilly, C. (1999) Conclusion: From Interactions to Outcomes in Social Movements. In: Giugni, M., McAdam, D., & Tilly, C. (Eds.), *How Movements Matter: Theoretical and Comparative Studies on the Consequences of Social Movements.* University of Minnesota Press, Minneapolis, pp. 253–70.

social movements, recruitment to

Steven E. Barkan and Steven F. Cohn

Social movements have long been an important basis of political participation in democracies and have achieved major political, social, and cultural changes. Although the influence of social movements depends largely on their ability to recruit members, it is by no means obvious why people choose to participate in them.

This question has been termed "the free-rider problem." As Mancur Olson's (1965) analysis indicates, people have limited time and energy and must choose to spend these resources in ways that most benefit themselves. Individuals join social movements because they believe that the movement's goals, if implemented, would yield significant benefits to themselves and/or to the attainment of values they cherish. Although these benefits motivate participation, there is an additional problem. If a movement has few participants, people desiring these benefits might believe that the movement could not succeed unless they joined the movement. Thus, joining the movement might represent a rational investment of their time, energy, and, often, money. However, if a movement already has a large number of participants, then it is unlikely that one more person's joining the movement would increase its chances of success. In that case, why would additional people join? If the movement is successful, they, along with the participants, would enjoy the fruits of this success; they would have gained all the benefits of participation without spending their own scarce resources of time and energy. In that case, they could use these resources to gain other benefits for themselves, while "free-riding" on the efforts of those already participating.

One possible response to this free-rider problem is that people who join social movements do not rationally calculate the costs and benefits of their joining. Analyses of social movements in the late nineteenth and early twentieth centuries indeed assumed that social movements were not rational enterprises and that those who joined them were, in fact, acting on the basis of irrational impulses. The most prominent proponent of this view, Gustave Le Bon (1897), a French theorist, said that people joined movements because they succumbed to crowd emotions and lost their ability to resist unconscious instincts. This general belief informed views of social movements well into the twentieth century, as these views stressed that movements represented an emotional and relatively unorganized response to a breakdown in social norms and social organization. Individuals were said to be attracted to movements because they were lonely and alienated owing to weak social ties and hence sought in movements a sense of belonging they otherwise lacked.

In recent years this non-rational model of social movements has fallen into disfavor. Social movements are now viewed as rational enterprises in pursuit of many kinds of political, social, and cultural changes, and their members are viewed as rational individuals favoring such changes. However, the success of recent efforts to demonstrate the rationality of social movement participants has reemphasized the importance of addressing the free-rider problem: if these people are rational, why do they participate at all? The contemporary literature on social movement recruitment and participation tries to answer this question.

Its dominant response derives from analogous work in complex and voluntary organizations, including labor unions. Organizations generally offer several types of resources to motivate recruitment and higher levels of participation after recruitment. These include (1) *coercion*; (2) *utilitarian incentives* such as paid income in work organizations and discounts for various goods and services in voluntary organizations; (3) *normative* (or *purposive*) *incentives* that appeal to the values, concerns, and ideologies of individuals and, in social movements, lead people to identify with a movement's goals and to believe that the movement is capable of achieving its goals; and (4) *social* (or *solidary*) *incentives* that make participation socially rewarding in terms of friendships and other personal contacts. Because social movement organizations (SMOs), like other voluntary organizations, typically lack the first two types of incentives, they must rely heavily on the latter two types to induce people to join them and to motivate higher levels of participation after joining.

In these respects, normative and social incentives act as *selective incentives* to induce self-interested people to devote time and energy to participation rather than to other potentially rewarding activities. An additional category of *organizational incentives* that lead people to feel a sense of belonging to the movement is also thought to be important for levels of post-recruitment participation.

In contrast to many types of voluntary organizations, normative incentives in social movements depend heavily on the movement's (or its SMOs') political ideologies and beliefs. These cognitions include the movement's grievances, goals, and strategies for change. Individuals whose own ideologies and beliefs are congruent with those of the movement are more likely to join it. In addition to these movement-specific ideologies, more general cognitions may also influence decisions to join. These include a liberal versus conservative belief system, a feeling of political efficacy, and religious ideologies. Movements and organizations that are liberal tend to attract liberal individuals, while those that are conservative tend to attract conservative individuals. People who are politically efficacious, that is, who believe that citizen participation generally, and their own particularly, can make a difference, are more likely to join than those who are politically alienated. Social movements and SMOs with a religious basis for their activities attract members whose religious beliefs coincide with those of the movement or SMO.

In all these respects, a movement's set of ideologies is thought to be an important, necessary condition for recruiting members, but it is far from a sufficient condition. The reason for this is simple: many more people agree with a movement's goals and other ideologies than ever participate in the movement or help it in any other way. This recognition has led the contemporary social movement literature to stress the importance of social incentives. In this view, people join movements because they have preexisting friendship and organizational ties that induce them to join. For example, agreeing to some friends' request to join them in a protest wins their appreciation, while declining their request may win their displeasure. In this respect, recruitment into social movements is no different from the many other activities in which social ties play an important role. Accordingly, a host of studies find that individuals with preexisting ties to movement members will be more likely to join a movement than those with fewer or no such ties. These ties appear to be especially important for recruitment into high-risk activism like the Freedom Rides in the US South that were a hallmark of the Civil Rights Movement in the 1960s. By challenging the earlier, non-rational model's assumption that social movements attract lonely and alienated individuals, the emphasis in contemporary work on friendship and organizational networks reinforces the rationality of social movement participation.

Turning to post-recruitment participation, individuals who develop friendships after joining a movement or SMO tend to exhibit higher levels of participation than those with fewer or no such friendships. In this regard, SMOs with a national membership face particular problems because their members are geographically isolated and usually have little contact with each other or with the national organization. To deal with this situation, some national organizations have developed a "federated" structure involving many local chapters. Because these chapters enable interaction and friendships among members who live near each other, they enhance commitment to the organization itself and promote higher levels of participation on its behalf.

Organizational incentives are the final type of resource offered by SMOs and are thought to be especially important for post-recruitment participation. These incentives take two forms, perceptions and communication. Members have various perceptions of their SMO. A first perception, *legitimacy*, involves members' willingness to trust SMO leaders and to support their decisions, even if the members might disagree with some of these decisions. Those with higher levels of perceived legitimacy are more likely to exhibit higher levels of post-recruitment participation. A second perception involves members' beliefs in the *effectiveness* of their SMO. Post-recruitment participation is generally higher among members who perceive stronger effectiveness. A final perception concerns members' *commitment*, including their sense of belonging, to their SMO and movement. Members who are more committed also exhibit higher levels of post-recruitment participation.

Communication with SMO leaders and staff also matters. In particular, members who are contacted more often by their SMO's leaders and staff or otherwise communicate with them are also thought to exhibit higher levels of post-recruitment participation than members with less or no such communication.

Future work on recruitment should address at least three problems in the literature. The first problem concerns potential deficiencies in the studies of recruitment. An ideal study would be predictive and would study a random sample of adults, predicting which factors would lead some of them to join a particular social movement. Because only a small proportion of adults become members of any given social movement, such a study would need an extremely large sample to have any statistical validity and would be astronomically expensive. Because of this, studies of social movement recruitment are limited in scope. Some studies are retrospective, asking current participants why they initially chose to participate. Results from these studies depend upon the assumption that current participants can accurately remember and will accurately report why they started to participate, and these studies often have no adequate control group of non-participants. Other studies are predictive but only in a limited context: for example, they study who among a set of people in a particular locality who favor the goals of a social movement rally actually choose to participate in the rally. As these difficulties suggest, the recruitment literature would benefit from better-designed studies, but, because of the nature of recruitment into social movements, such studies are difficult to devise.

A second problem in the recruitment literature concerns the many types of social movements. Many typologies of movements exist, but a common typology divides them, based on their goals, into political or social reform movements, religious movements, self-help movements, and cultural movements. Within each category there are many types of specific movements that have existed in many different nations and localities within nations and across many different decades and centuries. Although many studies of recruitment exist, they do not begin to match in number the sheer quantity of movements, and additional work on unstudied movements may shed new light on the dynamics of recruitment.

Finally, studies of recruitment obviously imply that one is being recruited into something. But what is this something? What does it mean to be a member of a social movement? If someone takes part in just one protest on behalf of a social movement, is that person a member of that movement? As this question suggests, people do not usually sign up for a movement in the way they sign up for many other activities. To compound this problem, some SMOs are organized in a very formal manner, with clear membership rolls and criteria for membership, while others are organized much more loosely, with unclear criteria for membership and only a loose understanding, if that, of who their members are. In the most informal SMOs, members may literally come and go, and it is not at all easy to identify their members. The lack of a clear understanding in movements and SMOs, and thus in the recruitment literature, of what it means to be a member confounds efforts to achieve a comprehensive understanding of recruitment, however important such an understanding is for the study of social movements.

SEE ALSO: Civil Rights Movement; Moral Shocks and Self-Recruitment; Resource Mobilization Theory; Riots; Social Movement Organizations; Social Movements, Biographical Consequences of; Social Movements, Networks and; Social Movements, Strain and Breakdown Theories of

REFERENCES AND SUGGESTED READINGS

Barkan, S. E., Cohn, S. F., & Whitaker, W. H. (1995) Beyond Recruitment: Predictors of Differential Participation in a National Antihunger Organization. *Sociological Forum* 10: 113–34.

Klandermans, B. & Oegema, D. (1987) Potentials, Networks, Motivations, and Barriers: Steps Towards Participation in Social Movements. *American Sociological Review* 52: 519–31.

Kornhauser, W. (1959) *The Politics of Mass Society*. Free Press, New York.

Le Bon, G. (1897) *The Crowd: A Study of the Popular Mind*. T. F. Unwin, London.

McAdam, D. (1986) Recruitment to High Risk Activism: The Case of Freedom Summer. *American Journal of Sociology* 92: 64–90.

Olson, M. (1965) *The Logic of Collective Action: Public Goods and the Theory of Goods.* Harvard University Press, Cambridge, MA.

Snow, D. A., Zurcher, Jr., L. A., & Ekland-Olson, S. (1980) Social Networks and Social Movements: A Microstructural Approach to Differential Recruitment. *American Sociological Review* 45: 787–801.

social movements, relative deprivation and

Mikaila Mariel Lemonik Arthur

The relative deprivation model aims to explain individuals' decisions to join or start social movements and is based on a certain set of psychological ideas (Gurr 1970). Relative deprivation itself refers to "the gap between what one has and what one expects" (Brusch 1996), particularly in comparison to some specific reference group. The concept of relative deprivation has its roots in the early "frustration–aggression hypothesis" of John Dollard, which suggested that when individuals respond to frustration and do not receive a response that relieves their frustration, such individuals will respond with aggression. Relative deprivation has been used as the mechanism to explain where this frustration emerges from.

Analysts of relative deprivation have specified a variety of dimensions of deprivation that individuals may experience. These include *aspirational deprivation*, or having increasing aspirations that are not realized; *decremental deprivation*, or when expectations are stable but available resources are declining; and *progressive deprivation*, or improvement in general social, economic, or power conditions which is followed by a sudden reversal of these trends. In general, in order to experience relative deprivation, an individual must not only experience desire, but also feel that she or he has a right to gain access to the sought-after resources. In addition, she or he must experience a perception that the likelihood of one's access's being blocked is quite high. The contradiction between this feeling of entitlement and this feeling of stymied progress forms a type of cognitive dissonance (Morrison 1971) which becomes activated through the appearance of a *structural strain* (McPhail 1971).

While many theorists of relative deprivation have confined their analysis to exploring when relative deprivation emerges and what form it takes, some have gone further to specify a mechanism whereby relative deprivation leads to collective action. The combination of feelings of relative deprivation with structural strain as noted above can lead individuals to come to see the sources of the blockages to their aspirations as *structural* blockages. Therefore, these individuals are led to seek structural solutions by working together as part of a similarly situated group – in other words, a social movement.

More sophisticated relative deprivation analyses include deprivation along with other factors, such as the balance of power between parties or resource mobilization. For instance, Korpi (1974) suggested that it is not only how deprived a group feels in terms of power resources that matters, it is also the rate of change in access to these resources relative to other groups, and that of the three types of deprivation, only progressive deprivation is likely to lead to situations of conflict. Similarly, Tilly (1973), while not writing specifically in the relative deprivation school, notes that violent collective action is particularly likely both when a group is gaining power relative to others and when they are losing it. Miller et al. (1977) propose another instance in which the experience of relative deprivation is likely to matter: in the case of uncertainty about the future. They note that only certain disaster is more frustrating than uncertainty. More specifically, models based on the notion of relative deprivation have been used to explain when revolution does and does not occur, how religious movements or cults come into being, and the timing of urban race riots.

The empirical evidence used to demonstrate relative deprivation is usually socioeconomic in nature and collected on aggregate levels, such as census data, even though deprivation itself is an individual experience. In addition, more recent empirical research has had difficulty confirming the usefulness of relative deprivation models. For instance, relative deprivation may be able to explain some small part of the variation in riots, but it is unable to explain why the majority of individuals who face relative deprivation do not act on this fact. However, even some analysts who are not fully impressed by the relative deprivation approach point to the likelihood that individual members of social movement organizations may talk about their reasons for forming or joining the movement in terms that can be conceived of as relative deprivation (Wallis 1975). Others have criticized the relative deprivation model because it cannot be tested empirically without some sort of evidence of feelings of deprivation prior to the collective action episode (Kent 1982). The model, therefore, is less commonly employed in sociological analyses of social movements today, though it continues to prove popular among psychologists.

SEE ALSO: Civil Rights Movement; Collective Action; Income Inequality and Income Mobility; Inequality and the City; Resource Mobilization Theory; Riots; Social Movement Organizations; Social Movements; Social Movements, Strain and Breakdown Theories of; Stress, Stress Theories

REFERENCES AND SUGGESTED READINGS

Brusch, S. G. (1996) Dynamics of Theory Change in the Social Sciences: Relative Deprivation and Collective Violence. *Journal of Conflict Resolution* 40(4): 523–45.

Gurr, T. R. (1970) *Why Men Rebel*. Princeton University Press, Princeton.

Kent, S. A. (1982) Relative Deprivation and Resource Mobilization: A Study of Early Quakerism. *British Journal of Sociology* 33(4): 529–44.

Korpi, W. (1974) Conflict, Power, and Relative Deprivation. *American Political Science Review* 68(4): 1569–78.

McPhail, C. (1971) Civil Disorder Participation: A Critical Examination of Recent Research. *American Sociological Review* 36(6): 1058–73.

Miller, A. H., Bolce, L. H., & Halligan, M. (1977) The J-Curve Theory and Black Urban Riots: An Empirical Test of Progressive Relative Deprivation Theory. *American Political Science Review* 71(3): 964–82.

Morrison, D. E. (1971) Some Notes Toward Theory on Relative Deprivation, Social Movements, and Social Change. *American Behavioral Scientist* 14(5): 675–90.

Tilly, C. (1973) Does Modernization Breed Revolution? *Comparative Politics* 5(3): 425–47.

Wallis, R. (1975) Comment. Relative Deprivation and Social Movements: A Cautionary Note. *British Journal of Sociology* 16(3): 360–3.

social movements, repression of

Jennifer Earl

The repression of social movements refers to attempts by groups, individuals, or state actors (e.g., militaries, national police, and local police) to increase the costs associated with social movement participation or otherwise limit social movement activity. Commonly studied forms of repression include police action at public protest events, such as arrests and police violence, military suppression of protest events, "disappearances" of activists, arrests and/or imprisonment of social movement participants, infiltration of social movements by government informants, covert counterintelligence programs against social movement organizations and participants, restrictions of free speech and assembly, assaults on human rights, and murders of social movement activists, among other tactics.

Recognizing that the above examples represent a wide variety of ways to suppress or control protest and social movements, scholars have sought to distinguish between different types of repressive actions. Two common distinctions that have been made are between overt and covert repression and between coercive repression and channeling. Researchers make these kinds of distinctions because they suspect that the dynamics and consequences of repression may differ depending on the kind of repressive tactic deployed.

The distinction between overt and covert is based on visibility of the repressive acts (or, at least, how visible they are intended to be). For instance, the Federal Bureau of Investigation (FBI) ran a series of covert counterintelligence programs against selected social movements from 1956 to 1971 in the United States. These programs used methods such as tapping phone lines, examining mail, and burglarizing dwellings and offices to gather information that was meant to affect the ability of social movements to survive and/or deploy certain tactics, without the public recognizing that the FBI was targeting these groups. In contrast to these covert tactics, other repressive actions are meant to be publicly visible (i.e., overt). An example of overt repression was the Chinese government's actions at Tiananmen Square in 1989, where the government used military tanks to crush protesters and move crowds.

The distinction between coercion and channeling is also important. Coercion involves violence, harassment, and surveillance while channeling occurs when laws, policies, or actions reward protest movements for using certain kinds of tactics (typically, more institutional and/or non-violent tactics) while discouraging others (typically, more radical, non-institutional, or violent tactics). Coercive repression is well known: the tanks in Tiananmen Square, South American death squads, and murders of civil rights activists in the US are all examples of coercive repression. In contrast, channeling focuses on the proverbial carrots that can lure protesters toward certain tactics and/or goals as well as the proverbial sticks that push protesters away from certain tactics and/or goals. For example, some have argued that US tax laws on non-profit status encourage social movement organizations to take more institutional action and less political action. If social movement organizations were to organize the use of violent tactics for political ends, for instance, their tax-exempt status could be threatened. Thus, social movements are channeled toward more conventional and less political action by the US tax code. Another well-studied example of channeling involves donations to social movement organizations. Some scholars have argued that philanthropists encourage moderate protest and discourage radical protest by funding moderate social movement organizations and defunding organizations that radicalize. Although empirical research suggests that funding can be reactive, scholars have not confirmed the extent to which defunding, in particular, actually occurs.

A less frequently invoked distinction between different kinds of repression involves who is "doing" the repression. The bulk of research on the repression of social movements has focused on the role of state actors (e.g., militaries, national police, and local police). However, this should not suggest that there are not important theoretical differences between state actors, nor should it suggest that private groups and/or individuals never repress social movements. Militaries charged with repression in authoritarian states are likely to differ from local police agencies, with respect to both how they distribute repression and the types of repressive actions they employ. In contrast to state action, groups such as the Ku Klux Klan (KKK), White Citizens Councils, universities, corporations, and the philanthropists discussed above have all been implicated in the repression of social movements. The KKK, for example, engaged in coercive repression against civil rights activists, and corporations have employed private security agents to disrupt strikes.

All three of these distinctions between various types of repression – covert versus overt, coercive versus channeling, and private versus public actors – are important because they bear on two fundamental questions that scholars have raised about repression: (1) how can researchers explain the level and types of repressive actions taken against different activists and social movements? and (2) how can researchers explain the consequences, or effects, of repression on activists and social movements?

EXPLAINING THE LEVEL OR TYPE OF REPRESSION

The vast majority of research that casts repression as a dependent variable has focused on explaining the level of particular types of repression without discussing tradeoffs between different types of repression. For instance, scholars may separately attempt to explain the number of protests at which police will be present, the number of political murders, or the severity of restrictions on free speech or free association in a country, but they have much less frequently examined how an increase in the severity of free speech and free association restrictions might affect the rate of political murders in the same country.

Scholars interested in explaining the prevalence, level, or severity of a particular type of repression tend to focus on a small set of causal explanations. The most widely researched and supported explanation is often referred to as a "threat" model of repression because it predicts that the more threatening a social movement, a social movement organization, or a protest activity is to the government and government elites, the more likely or severe repressive action will be. Because the emphasis is on threats to regimes, this approach has largely been used to explain repressive acts by governments or actors closely connected to the state.

Scholars working within a threat perspective have differed in whether they consider objective threats or subjective threats to be most important. Scholars who emphasize objective threats to a regime have been referred to as "rationalists" or "realists." Other scholars argue that governments and political elites do not always recognize existing threats, may misinterpret a non-threat as threatening, or may otherwise exaggerate or downplay objective threats. Scholars emphasizing the subjectivity of threats refer to the process by which states and/or political elites recognize and/or construct threats as "threat perception."

Whether concerned with objective or subjective threats, a range of particular factors has been identified as objectively threatening, or likely to be perceived as threatening, including: the mobilization of large numbers of social movement supporters and participants, the use of radical or violent protest tactics, and the embrace of radical or transformative ideologies, to list a few.

In addition to a threat model of repression, others primarily interested in repressive actions by states have argued that states are opportunists. That is, since scholars believe that states are interested in suppressing all challengers, weak challengers that appear vulnerable to repression will quickly become targets of repressive action. Weakness could be indicated by a range of characteristics, such as the social composition of social movement supports and/ or the level of resources a social movement has available.

Still others have attempted to explain the level or severity of repression with reference to the organizations and actors that are charged with carrying out repressive acts. For instance, recent research on the FBI's covert counter-intelligence programs in the 1960s and 1970s suggests that the organizational structure and decision-making processes of the FBI influenced what groups were targeted for action, the tactics that were used against targeted groups, and the extent to which different groups were consistently and heavily repressed. Others have made similar arguments about organizational and institutional characteristics of police forces in explaining police action at protest events.

In contrast to these approaches, which view repression as an outcome of some directional causal process, others have argued for a more emergent view of repression. Specifically, some researchers interested in processes of interaction between insurgents and authorities argue that general explanations of repression are problematic because many repressive outcomes are actually the result of situational interactions and thus cannot be predicted (e.g., police interact with protesters and out of that interaction emerges a police response to protesters).

Other scholars interested in interactions between activists and repressive agents have understood interaction to be less about situational interactions and more about the relationships over time between authorities and insurgents. Framing the interaction between authorities and insurgents as a predator–prey situation, these students of social movements have argued that causal consistencies may exist. Methodological techniques, such as biological predator–prey statistical models, allow these researchers to statistically diagnose feedback processes between authorities and insurgents. For instance, a general version of one of these models would specify that the actions of repressive agents at Time 1 affect some movement characteristic at Time 2, which in turn affects the actions of repressive agents at Time 3. Some researchers have expanded these techniques to consider how repressive actors, movements, and countermovements interact over time and thereby affect the rate and/or severity of repression.

THE EFFECTS OF REPRESSIVE ACTION

Quite aside from the question of how to explain repression, or changes in repressive levels over time, researchers have also engaged a second major research question on repression: what are the effects of repression on activists and social movements? Most of the research in this area has focused on the effects of repression on either the level of social movement activity or the tactics deployed by social movements.

Before discussing theories about the effects of repression, it is important to understand how this debate is related to major theories on social movements. Some interest in the effects of repression on the level of social movement participation has been generated by the connection of repression to arguments surrounding "political opportunities." In the political process approach to explaining social movement emergence, mobilization, and success, repression is thought to represent one type of political opportunity. Political opportunities are critical to political process theory because the theory's fundamental proposition is that favorable political opportunities have a direct (or curvilinear, according to some) relationship with movement emergence, movement mobilization, and movement success.

One could further specify, differentiating between stable and volatile political opportunities. Stable opportunities are often defined as being structural, and hence are called political opportunity structures (POS). Repressive capacities or structural controls on repressive agents (e.g., constitutional limitations on police power) are seen by some scholars as POS. Volatile opportunities vary over time and may be less structural. The prevalence of state repression at a given moment is often referred to as being a component of volatile political opportunities.

Political process theorists argue that repression dampens social movement mobilization and may encourage the use of more institutional, and less violent, social movement tactics. Sometimes framed as increasing the costs of movement participation, or the costs of deploying a particular tactic, the claim is that repression reduces the number of individuals willing to engage in protest at all, or at least the number of individuals willing to use particular protest tactics. Others interested in rational choice models of collective action, but not in political process or political opportunities, have agreed with this cost-based argument, suggesting that repression raises the costs of activism

and thus should reduce the overall amount of activism.

While supportive evidence of this claim has been found, evidence has also been found suggesting that repression radicalizes social movement participants. Thus, instead of diminishing protest or deterring the use of particularly aggressive tactics, many scholars have argued that repression encourages further protest and the use of non-institutional tactics.

Still other scholars have sought to reconcile these seemingly divergent empirical findings by arguing the repression has a curvilinear (or, alternatively, an inverted-U) relationship to movement participation and the use of confrontational tactics. For instance, if there was no repression, such a society might be so open to change that protest would be unnecessary. At the same time, if a society was under authoritarian control, the costs for activism might be exorbitant. Under this logic, one would expect protest where moderate repression is found, represented by an inverted-U relationship between repression and protest. This dizzying array of theoretical arguments is matched by a similarly large array of discordant findings: empirical evidence exists for direct, inverse, curvilinear, inverted-U, and null effects of repression on movement mobilization and tactical deployment. Thus, despite significant scholastic effort, substantial discord about the effects of repression still exists.

SEE ALSO: Contention, Tactical Repertoires of; Political Opportunities; Political Process Theory; Social Movement Organizations; Social Movements; Social Movements, Political Consequences of; Social Movements, Recruitment to

REFERENCES AND SUGGESTED READINGS

Barkan, S. (1984) Legal Control of the Southern Civil Rights Movement. *American Sociological Review* 49: 552–65.

Cunningham, D. (2004) *There's Something Happening Here: The New Left, the Klan, and FBI Counterintelligence.* University of California Press, Berkeley.

Davenport, C. (Ed.) (2000) *Paths to State Repression: Human Rights Violations and Contentious Politics.* Rowman & Littlefield, Lanham, MD.

Della Porta, D. & Reiter, H. (Eds.) (1998) *Policing Protest: The Control of Mass Demonstrations in Western Democracies.* University of Minnesota Press, Minneapolis.

Earl, J., Soule, S. A., & McCarthy, J. D. (2003) Protests Under Fire? Explaining Protest Policing. *American Sociological Review* 69: 581–606.

Hirsch, E. L. (1990) Sacrifice for the Cause: Group Processes, Recruitment, and Commitment in a Student Social Movement. *American Sociological Review* 55: 243–54.

Koopmans, R. (1993) The Dynamics of Protest Waves: West Germany, 1965 to 1989. *American Sociological Review* 58: 637–58.

Marx, G. T. (1974) Thoughts on a Neglected Category of Social Movement Participant: The Agent-Provocateur and the Informant. *American Journal of Sociology* 80: 402–42.

social movements, strain and breakdown theories of

Steven M. Buechler

Strain and breakdown theories seek to explain the causes of collective behavior and social movements. They implicitly presume that when social institutions are stable, collective behavior is unlikely. It is when institutions undergo strain or breakdown that the resulting social disorganization and decreased social control are more likely to foster collective behavior in the form of fads, crazes, riots, rebellions, movements, and revolutions.

The classical sociological spokesperson for this approach is Émile Durkheim, who diagnosed modern society as insufficiently integrated and subject to grave dangers of anomie and egoism. Put differently, chronic strains and acute breakdowns in social order could foster many types of antisocial behavior, including suicide (Durkheim 1951 [1897]). European crowd theorists then seized on notions of strain and breakdown to explain both the emergence and the stereotypically excessive and irrational nature of crowd behavior. Robert Park transplanted this perspective to the United States in the early twentieth century and laid the foundation for the collective behavior tradition.

Herbert Blumer definitively established collective behavior as a major subfield in US sociology. His work (Blumer 1951) posited strong links between strain or breakdown and a distinctive conception of collective behavior (including crowds, masses, publics, and movements) that emphasized its spontaneous, contagious, excitable, and often irrational character. Turner and Killian (1987) further developed this approach by analyzing emergent norms in collective behavior.

Several other variations of the collective behavior tradition emerged in the 1950s and early 1960s. Relative deprivation theory interpreted strain as a social psychological condition of cognitive dissonance that motivated collective behavior. Structural functionalists proposed an elaborate multistage model in which structural strain was a crucial factor facilitating the emergence of many different forms of collective behavior (Smelser 1962). Mass society theorists saw strain deriving from the lack of intermediate social groupings that fostered alienation, which in turn motivated participation in collective behavior.

From European origins in the 1890s through US sociology in the 1960s, strain and breakdown provided the preeminent explanations of the emergence of collective behavior and social movements. However, critics argued that this tradition viewed collective behavior in a distinctly negative way. While there were more differences between theorists than the critics acknowledged, the charge was that the tradition as a whole viewed collective behavior as irrational, disorganized, emotional outbursts that spread through contagion and threatened social order. This broad challenge was accompanied by more specific criticisms of strain and breakdown theories as too vague, not necessary, or not sufficient to explain collective behavior. These criticisms were part of a major paradigm shift prompted by the protests of the 1960s, the politics of younger sociologists, and their unwillingness to analyze these protests in the unfavorable terms of collective behavior theory.

Proponents of the new resource mobilization paradigm in the 1970s and early 1980s argued that the collective behavior tradition involved a priori, negative judgments of such behavior;

that collective behavior was too broad a category to be intellectually viable; that social movements required a different analysis than more fleeting forms of collective behavior; that movements were often rational, organized, enduring, and legitimate responses to injustice; and that movements were better explained in political than psychologically reductionist terms.

These critiques also rested on empirical investigation. Studies of 1960s urban riots found strain and breakdown theories to be vague and psychologistic, to obscure the political dimensions of these riots, to deny rational and strategic aspects of riots as a political tactic, and to obscure the actual roots of the associated violence. Work on European collective action also argued that violence is better seen as an interactive product of relations between authorities and protesters, and that protesters often act in a rational, purposive, political fashion when choosing tactics. In explanatory terms, these critics argued that the degree of solidarity among contenders is a much more precise predictor of the episodic nature of collective action than vague notions of strain and breakdown. These critics concluded that breakdown theories are logically and empirically flawed and that solidarity theories are universally preferable (Tilly et al. 1975).

Until the mid-1970s, strain and breakdown theories were still the prevailing explanation of collective behavior. Less than a decade later, they had all but disappeared with the paradigm shift from collective behavior to resource mobilization, and the consequent marginalization of strain and breakdown explanations.

Despite their marginalization, strain and breakdown theories persisted around the edges of this new subfield. One example may be found in studies of revolution. Working outside the mainstream resource mobilization paradigm, Goldstone (1991) identified similar dynamics in revolutions in the modern world involving state breakdown, revolutionary contention, and state rebuilding. State breakdown involves a conjunction of state fiscal distress, elite alienation and conflict, and high mobilization potential among the general populace. In this interactive model, all three elements must be present if a full revolutionary challenge is to unfold. The background causes of state breakdown are historically specific, but often involve demographic growth and population shifts which put new pressure on state resources (Goldstone 1991). Goldstone concludes that state breakdowns from 1500 to 1850 resulted from population growth which overwhelmed agrarian bureaucratic states and prompted fiscal instability, intra-elite conflicts, and popular unrest. In its emphasis on deterministic background factors and external variables, Goldstone's model is closer to the collective behavior tradition's emphasis on strain and breakdown explanations than it is to the more movement-centered resource mobilization model.

Another example of the persistence of strain and breakdown approaches is Piven and Cloward's (1992) argument that social structures normally limit opportunities for protest and diminish its force when it does occur. Thus, it is social breakdowns in society's regulatory capacity and everyday routines that provide rare but potent opportunities for mass defiance. But breakdown is not enough; people must also see their deprivations as unjust and mutable. Such insights are only likely when social distress is high or institutions are obviously malfunctioning. Societal breakdown thus not only disrupts regulatory capacity and everyday routines, it also raises consciousness about alternative social arrangements. Piven and Cloward (1992) further argue that strain and breakdown are especially critical for explaining non-normative protest in the form of mass defiance; the latter is a more basic challenge to power since it not merely pursues a specific agenda but does so in a way that challenges elite rule-making. The distinction is critical to the debate: breakdown is not a necessary precondition of normative group action but it is a precondition of collective protest, riot, and rebellion.

A final example of the persistence of breakdown theories is a recent specification that links breakdown and the quotidian nature of social life (Snow et al. 1998). The latter refers to taken-for-granted practices and routines that comprise habitual social action, alongside routinized expectations and the suspension of doubt about the social world and one's role within it. Disruptions of the quotidian make routine action problematic and undermine the natural attitude. This specification of breakdown dynamics can be combined with solidarity explanations since it is not the associational ties between people that break down but rather their taken-for-granted practices and beliefs. These three very different examples illustrate the persistence of strain and breakdown theories despite their marginalization by the resource mobilization perspective. For further examples, see Useem (1998).

While strain and breakdown theories have persisted in these ways, it can also be argued that they have actually returned to mainstream social movement theory under a new nomenclature (Buechler 2004). There is considerable conceptual overlap between what collective behavior theorists mean by strain or breakdown and what resource mobilization theorists mean by opportunity. What obscures this equation is the valuational bias of each set of concepts. The terms "strain" and "breakdown" inherently connote negative, problematic conditions to be prevented, avoided, or repaired. As these terms functioned in the collective behavior paradigm, they conveyed deeply embedded negative judgments about the appropriateness of collective behavior. And as Useem (1998) recently observed, breakdown theorists to this day are more likely to see social control in a positive light and protester action in a negative light. Thus, it was not just breakdown as a causal mechanism that provoked the ire of critics; it was also the halo of negative judgments that drew their fire.

The concept of opportunity was tailor-made for this debate. It provided the transvaluation sought by critics that allowed them to paint collective action in a positive light. In contrast to "breakdown," "opportunity" inherently signifies something to be sought, desired, seized, enjoyed, valued, and maximized. In addition, it preserved a way of talking about changes in background conditions that facilitate collective action. By substituting opportunity for breakdown, resource mobilization and political process theorists retained a powerful explanation for collective action while reversing the valuations placed on that action.

This concept has now found its place in social movement theory in a theoretical synthesis of political opportunities, mobilizing structures, and framing processes. While opportunity and breakdown are not the same thing, they do the same work in their respective theoretical traditions. Both refer to external, variable processes

that increase the likelihood of collective action. Put more polemically, a political process theorist might argue that to whatever extent strain and breakdown are causally relevant, that relevance is captured in the notion of opportunity structures. What is jettisoned are the negative connotations of traditional strain and breakdown theories. To the extent that opportunity has become a stand-in for strain and breakdown, it can be concluded that the latter never really disappeared from social movement theory.

SEE ALSO: Collective Action; Crowd Behavior; Durkheim, Émile; Emergent Norm Theory; Framing and Social Movements; Functionalism/Neofunctionalism; Political Opportunities; Resource Mobilization Theory; Revolutions; Riots; Social Movements; Social Movements, Political Consequences of; Social Movements, Relative Deprivation and; Solidarity, Mechanical and Organic; Strain Theories; Structural Functional Theory

REFERENCES AND SUGGESTED READINGS

Blumer, H. (1951) The Field of Collective Behavior. In: Lee, A. (Ed.), *Principles of Sociology*. Barnes & Noble, New York, pp. 167–222.

Buechler, S. (2004) The Strange Career of Strain and Breakdown Theories of Collective Action. In: Snow, D., Soule, S., & Kriesi, H. (Eds.), *The Blackwell Companion to Social Movements*. Blackwell, Oxford, pp. 47–66.

Durkheim, É. (1951 [1897]) *Suicide*. Free Press, New York.

Goldstone, J. (1991) *Revolution and Rebellion in the Early Modern World*. University of California Press, Berkeley.

Piven, F. & Cloward, R. (1992) Normalizing Collective Protest. In: Morris, A. & Mueller, C. (Eds.), *Frontiers in Social Movement Theory*. Yale University Press, New Haven, pp. 301–25.

Smelser, N. (1962) *Theory of Collective Behavior*. Free Press, New York.

Snow, D., Cress, D., Downey, L., & Jones, A. (1998) Disrupting the "Quotidian": Reconceptualizing the Relationship between Breakdown and the Emergence of Collective Action. *Mobilization* 3: 1–22.

Tilly, C., Tilly, L., & Tilly, R. (1975) *The Rebellious Century, 1830–1930*. Harvard University Press, Cambridge, MA.

Turner, R. & Killian, L. (1987) *Collective Behavior*, 3rd edn. Prentice-Hall, Upper Saddle River, NJ.

Useem, B. (1998) Breakdown Theories of Collective Action. *Annual Review of Sociology* 24: 215–38.

social network analysis

Barry Wellman

Social scientists have used the metaphor of "social network" for a century to connote complex sets of relationships between members of social systems at all scales, from interpersonal to international. Yet not until the 1950s did they start using the term systematically and self-consciously to denote patterns of ties that cut across the concepts traditionally used by social scientists: bounded groups (e.g., tribes, families) and social categories (e.g., gender, ethnicity).

Social network analysis has now moved from being a suggestive metaphor to an analytic approach to a paradigm, with its own theoretical statements, methods, and research findings. It has developed from diverse sources, including anthropological accounts of detribalized urban migrants, surveys of people's long-distance communities, political upheavals, Internet connectivity, and trade relations among nations. The Internet, inherently network-like, has so popularized the approach that *Business Week* named social network analysis "the hottest new technology" of 2003, and membership in network analysis' professional organization has doubled in four years.

Social network analysts reason from whole to part; from structure to relation to individual; from behavior to attitude. They argue that their social structural explanations have more analytic power than individualistic analyses that do not take relational patterns into account and that interpret behavior in terms of the internalized norms of discrete individuals. The structure of a network, the relations among network members, and the location of a member within a network are critical factors in understanding social behavior. Analysts search for regular structures of ties underlying often incoherent surface appearances, and they study how these social structures constrain network members'

behavior. Key concepts include network density, centrality, transitivity, tie strength, clustering, and structural equivalence.

Social networks are formally defined as a set of *nodes* (or *network members*) that are *tied* by one or more specific types of *relations*. In much research, these nodes are individual persons, but they can also be groups, corporations, households, blogs, nation-states, or other collectivities. Ties consist of one or more specific relations, such as financial exchange, friendship, hate, trade, web links, or airline routes. Ties vary in *quality* (whether the relation provides emotional aid or companionship), *quantity* (how much emotional aid; how frequent the companionship), *multiplexity* (sometimes called multi-strandedness: ties containing only one relation or several), and *symmetry* (resources flowing in one direction or both). The non-random structure of ties channels resources to specific locations in social systems, fostering inequalities.

Several analytic tendencies distinguish network analysis. First, there is no assumption that groups are the building blocks of society. While social network analytic techniques can discover the empirical existence of groups, the approach is open to studying less-bounded social systems. For example, researchers have mapped the structure of the World Wide Web on the Internet, showing how superconnectors shorten distances between websites.

Second, although social network data often include information about the attributes of individuals, such as age, gender, and beliefs, individuals are not treated as discrete units of analysis. Instead, analysis focuses on how the networks affect the individuals and ties embedded in them.

Third, social network analysis contrasts with analyses which assume that socialization into norms determines behavior and social structure. By contrast, network analysis looks to see the extent to which patterns of social relations affect norms and values.

Social network analysts gather data in many ways, such as ethnography, surveys, archives, and simulations. Their data collection emphasizes ties and the problematic nature of boundaries. Although analysts often visualize networks as point and line graphs, they analyze them as matrices that are more amenable to statistical and mathematical manipulation. Specialized programs, such as UCINet and Pajek, facilitate analyses.

Network analysts often study *whole networks*, all of the ties containing one or a few kinds of relations among the members of a population. These populations can be of different scales, from the members of a small office to Hollywood musicians to the vast blogosphere on the Internet. Multilevel and two-mode analyses facilitate the study of *networks of networks*, as when ties between persons also connect organizations. For example, analysts have studied interlocking corporate directorships (who sits on whose boards?) to describe ties among large organizations and to discover the structure of dominant institutions in western societies. Through manipulation of matrices representing who is connected with whom, analysts can discover densely knit clusters of heavily interconnected network members (and thus empirically identify true groups) or discover those network members whose *equivalent* relations show up in *blockmodels* as having similar roles in the social system.

Whole network studies are not always feasible because they require complete lists of all members of a population and all of their ties. Moreover, prior specification of population boundaries may not be appropriate for identifying clandestine networks or studying the diffusion of information, munitions, illicit drugs, and disease. In such situations, their interest is in tracing connections through unbounded networks and discovering clusters of ties.

Some network analysts study *egocentric* (or personal) networks, defined from the standpoints of egos (or *focal individuals*). Analysts typically use survey research to gather information about the networks' *composition* (e.g., percent gender), *structure* (e.g., the density of interconnection among members), and *contents* (e.g., the amount of support provided to egos). This is useful for studying far-flung communities, the provision of social support, and the mobilization of social capital.

Social network analysis has blossomed in recent years, with the paradigm appearing throughout the social science. It has a professional association, the International Network for Social Network Analysis, and three specialized journals: *Social Networks*, *Connections*, and the *Journal of Social Structure*. Network

rudimentary Internet software has proliferated, attempting to connect people who know each other directly and indirectly. In addition to sociology, network analyses are often found in management studies (mergers; organizational behavior); anthropology (kinship, urban relocation); geography (dispersion of network members); communication science (virtual community on the Internet); information science (information flows); political science (political mobilization); psychology (small groups; social support); social history (social movements); statistics (multilevel analysis); and mathematics (graph theory).

SEE ALSO: Community; Dependency and World-Systems Theories; Groups; Internet; Organization Theory; Power-Dependence Theory; Simmel, Georg; Social Capital; Social Exchange Theory; Social Movements; Social Network Theory; Transnational Movements; Weak Ties (Strength of)

REFERENCES AND SUGGESTED READINGS

Burt, R. S. (1992) *Structural Holes: The Structure of Competition*. Harvard University Press, Cambridge, MA.

Carrington, P., Scott, J., & Wasserman, S. (Eds.) (2005) *Models and Methods in Social Network Analysis*. Cambridge University Press, Cambridge.

Doreian, P., Batagelj, V., & Ferligoj, A. (2005) *Generalized Blockmodeling*. Cambridge University Press, Cambridge.

Freeman, L. (2004) *The Development of Social Network Analysis*. Empirical Press, Vancouver.

Lin, N., Burt, R. S., & Cook, K. (Eds.) (2001) *Social Capital: Theory and Research*. Aldine de Gruyter, New York.

Nohria, N. & Eccles, R. (1992) *Networks in Organizations*, 2nd edn. Harvard Business Press, Boston.

Nooy, W. de, Mrvar, A., & Batagelj, V. (2005) *Exploratory Social Network Analysis with Pajek*. Cambridge University Press, Cambridge.

Scott, J. (2000) *Social Networks: A Handbook*. Sage, Thousand Oaks, CA.

Scott, J. (Ed.) (2002) *Social Networks: Critical Concepts in Sociology*, 4 vols. Routledge, London.

Tilly, C. (2005) *Identities, Boundaries, and Social Ties*. Paradigm, Boulder, CO.

Valente, T. (1995) *Network Models of the Diffusion of Innovation*. Hampton Press, Cresskill, NJ.

Wasserman, S. & Faust, K. (1992) *Social Network Analysis*. Cambridge University Press, Cambridge.

Wellman, B. (Ed.) (1999) *Networks in the Global Village*. Westview Press, Boulder, CO.

Wellman, B. & Berkowitz, S. D. (Eds.) (1988) *Social Structures: A Network Approach*. Cambridge University Press, Cambridge.

White, H. (1992) *Identity and Control*. Princeton University Press, Princeton.

social network theory

Anne F. Eisenberg and Jeffrey Houser

The idea of social networks is prevalent in everyday vernacular language, ranging from the game "Six Degrees of Kevin Bacon" where players identify how any one actor is linked to the actor Kevin Bacon through no more than six different people, to the way in which people "network" with one another as an avenue through which they gain social capital, to how we describe our computers' ability to "talk" with other computers. The idea of social networks has an equally wide range of applications in sociology, from formal network theory to social network data analysis. The historical development of the sociological use of the idea of social networks originates with Durkheim and Simmel, and its breadth of use is reflected in contemporary theoretical and methodological developments and applications. In its different uses, from the vernacular to its historical development to its current developments, social network theory refers to the ways in which people are connected to one another and how these connections create and define human society on all levels: the individual, the group, and the institutional.

HISTORICAL DEVELOPMENT

The historical development of social networks as a sociologically important idea is represented by two main stages: its origins in the sociological work of Durkheim and Simmel, and its early development in the areas of social psychology. While Durkheim does not use the phrase social networks, it is obvious from his writings about religion, suicide, and the division of labor that he focused on how changes in the social world, such as those brought about by industrialization and capitalism, affected the connections between people. More to the point, he aptly illustrated how connections between people serve as the basis for human society. For example, in describing the shift from mechanical solidarity to organic solidarity he focused on several criteria, including the quality and quantity of individuals' connections to one another, as expressed by the idea of dynamic density, and by the level of the division of labor. Specifically, Durkheim argued that social relations in a society characterized by mechanical solidarity were meaningfully different from social relations in a society characterized by organic solidarity. He stated that all societies began with small communities of people who are all connected to one another in a familiar fashion. As the number of people within the community grew, social relations changed, leading to more organic forms of solidarity whereby people were connected to larger numbers of other people but in a less intimate way. This shift was also reflected in a change in the level of division of labor, with mechanical forms of solidarity having little to no division of labor and organic forms of solidarity having greater division of labor. Also, in his discussion of suicide, Durkheim focused on the role that integration played in maintaining social order. He defined integration in terms of how it allows for the interchange of ideas and feelings, as well as created shared moral beliefs and goals that prevented the excessive individualism that leads to egoistic suicide. Finally, Durkheim's discussion of religion centered on the role that religion plays in bringing a community of people together through their shared experiences, beliefs, and rituals. It is obvious that for Durkheim it is the meaningful connections between people that allow society to survive and flourish.

Simmel's work can generally be described as examining different aspects of individual lives and individuals' interactions. Similarly to Durkheim, while Simmel never directly used the phrase social networks, his writings focused on how interactions were affected by the way in which people are connected to one another in terms of an individual's social status, as well as the dynamics that occur as different people engage in interactions with one another. For example, in discussing how group size affected interactions, Simmel examined the qualitative change that occurs in interactions when the dyad becomes a triad. In the dyad, actors are connected by their total interdependence, while in a triad it is possible for a coalition to develop between two of the three actors. Simmel's focus on the different variables that affect our connections to one another is evident in a wide range of his discussions, from exchanges as a form of interactions, to group development, through a series of interactions among people, to the social characteristics (such as whether a person is a stranger) that affect the creation of connections between people.

The second stage in the historical development of social networks as a sociological idea occurs in the early work of sociologists specializing in social psychology. Early social psychologists, similarly to Simmel, discussed exchanges as a form of interactions by building on the ideas of anthropologists such as Frazer, Malinowski, Mauss, and Lévi-Strauss, as well as ideas associated with behaviorism in psychology. George Homans highlighted the basic principles of exchange theory, which focused on how connections between people were based on the need for exchanges to occur to fulfill each actor's needs. Peter Blau and Richard Emerson and his colleagues further developed Homans's ideas by explicating the conditions under which exchanges proceed (for the former) and how such exchanges might then create collective action between actors through different types of exchange networks (the latter). While Emerson was the only early social psychologist explicitly using the phrase social networks, it is evident from the work of Homans and Blau that their underlying themes examined the creation and maintenance of connections between people. These themes, and the phrase social networks, are developed further by contemporary theorists and empirical research applications.

CONTEMPORARY DEVELOPMENTS

The idea of social networks is used in a wide range of areas of study in sociology, from economic sociology to social psychology to political sociology, as well as representing a specific form of data analysis. From its historical development in social psychology, social networks appear in a number of contemporary social psychological theories. Cook and colleagues (1993), among others, extended Emerson's original formulation of exchange theory to examine issues such as the distribution of power in social exchange networks, how bargaining in social networks is affected by power distribution, commitment formation, and coalition formations. Each of these theoretical extensions of Emerson and Blau's work focuses on some aspect of social networks in terms of how connections between actors then affect further interactions and exchanges. Willer and colleagues (2002) developed network exchange theory (NET) to focus on exchange structures and power relations. NET provides explicit predictions about exchanges that may occur based on factors such as whether or not social networks are exclusively connected, the level of hierarchy and mobility that exists in any particular social network, and the order in which exchanges occur. These factors then allow Willer and colleagues to explore how collective action develops among actors in a social network. Finally, social psychologists such as Eisenberg (2002) and Ridgeway and colleagues (1994) interested in groups and group dynamics examine how social networks structure social interactions through social norms as reflected in status characteristics and the resulting group structure.

Network theory is a broader term that represents theoretical developments in all areas of sociology by focusing on the key idea of actors and how they are connected, whereby actors can be individuals or groups or social institutions. In other words, network theory allows us to examine the objective pattern of interactions represented by how actors are connected to one another. By examining how actors are connected to one another, sociologists gain insight into the structure of social interactions on the individual level as well as the structure of groups and institutions. For example, Granovetter (1973) used social networks to explain the importance of weak ties among people and how these types of ties affected exchanges. His work served as the basis for further work in economic sociology, such as explaining organizational survival in particular economic environments. Uzzi (1996) demonstrated how conformity to specific organizational norms increased an organization's likelihood for survival. Heckathorn (2002) used social networks to explain collective action in social movements by examining how particular networks of people developed into formal movement organizations. Additionally, social networks have been used to explain an array of social phenomena, including job mobility, the structure of groups of scientists, corporate networks, and consumer transactions.

Finally, social network also refers to a specific form of data analysis in which the researcher focuses on the ties among and between social actors. More importantly, social network analysis allows sociologists literally to draw a picture of the actors studied – from the dyad to the triad to the social movement. Social network analysis consists of basic concepts that emphasize how actors are connected to one another. For example, points and nodes identify specific actors (individual, group, organizational, or collectivities) who are then described in terms of their connections to others through either a simple graph figure or through a matrix representing particular ties. Once the social network has been so identified and described, it can then be analyzed in terms of the patterns and configurations of ties. This analysis includes examining the number of ties between any combination of actors, the direction in which resources flow for each set of ties, the strength of the ties, and the density of ties. Computer programs that provide both the descriptive and analytical are now readily available. These programs provide pictures of the social networks being studied, as well as the matrix of connections and calculations representing the patterns and configurations of ties. The reason social network analysis is becoming increasingly important in sociology is that describing and analyzing the social world in terms of objectively measured social connections allows us to avoid qualitative evaluations that lead to subjective, and possibly biased, understanding of specific social phenomena.

SEE ALSO: Elementary Theory; Exchange Network Theory; Social Network Analysis; Weak Ties (Strength of)

REFERENCES AND SUGGESTED READINGS

Blau, P. M. (1964) *Exchange and Power in Social Life*. Wiley, New York.

Cook, K. S., Molm, L. D., & Yamagishi, T. (1993) Exchange Relations and Exchange Networks: Recent Developments in Social Exchange Theory. In: Berger, J. & Zelditch, M., Jr. (Eds.), *Theoretical Research Programs: Studies in the Growth of Theory*. Stanford University Press, Stanford, pp. 296–322.

Durkheim, E. (1979 [1951]) *Suicide: A Study in Sociology*. Trans. J. A. Spaulding & G. Simpson. Free Press, New York.

Durkheim, E. (1984) *The Division of Labor in Society*. Trans. W. D. Halls. Free Press, New York.

Emerson, R. M. (1962) Power–Dependence Relations. *American Sociological Review* 17: 31–41.

Emerson, R. M. (1976) Social Exchange Theory. *Annual Review of Sociology* 2: 535–62.

Eisenberg, A. (2002) *Fringe Groups and their Fight for Legitimacy*. Dissertation, University of California, Berkeley.

Granovetter, M. (1973) The Strength of Weak Ties. *American Journal of Sociology* 91: 481–510.

Heckathorn, D. (2002) Development of a Theory of Collective Action: From the Emergence of Norms to AIDS Prevention and the Analysis of Social Structure. In: Berger, J. & Zelditch, M., Jr. (Eds.), *New Directions in Contemporary Sociological Theory*. Rowan & Littlefield, New York, pp. 79–108.

Homans, G. (1972 [1961]) *Social Behavior: Its Elementary Forms*. Harcourt Brace Jovanovich, New York.

Ridgeway, C. L., Johnson, C., & Diekema, D. (1994) External Status, Legitimacy, and Compliance in Male and Female Groups. *Social Forces* 72(4): 1051–77.

Rule, J. B. (1997) *Theory and Progress in Social Science*. Cambridge University Press, New York.

Simmel, G. (1950) *The Sociology of Georg Simmel*. Ed. K. H. Wolff. Free Press, New York.

Simmel, G. (1971) *On Individuality and Social Forms: Selected Writings*. Ed. D. L. Levine. University of Chicago Press, Chicago.

Turner, J. H. (2003) *The Structure of Sociological Theory*, 7th edn. Thomson Wadsworth, Victoria.

Uzzi, B. (1996) The Sources and Consequences of Embeddedness for the Economic Performance of Organizations: The Network Effect. *American Sociological Review* 61: 674–98.

Willer, D., Walker, H. A., Markovsky, B., Willer, R., Lovaglia, M., Thye, S., & Simpson, B. (2002) Network Exchange Theory. In: Berger, J. & Zelditch, M., Jr. (Eds.), *New Directions in Contemporary Sociological Theory*. Rowan & Littlefield, New York, pp. 109–43.

social order

Steven P. Dandaneau

Social order is synonymous with both society and social science. People do not regularly live in chaos, even when they are the denizens of postmodern societies that characteristically exacerbate the already chaotic tempo bequeathed by modernity. Regardless of whether it is edifying to accept, ritual and routine, not rebellion and revolution, absorb the lion's share of everyday energies. Likewise, apart from whether society is conceived theoretically as organism or system, language game or mode of production, interaction ritual or ethereal spectacle, the essential notion of "society" is scientifically and practically meaningful only when it refers to routinely observable phenomena about which lasting statements are possible. Without social order, social science would dissolve into the ephemeral study of ephemerality.

Probably no figure in the history of sociology more clearly represents the concern for theorizing the practical achievement of social order than Talcott Parsons. Parsons self-consciously built an integrated theory of social order through synthesis of previous ambitious attempts to grasp the totality of human society, including via the work of Herbert Spencer, Vilfredo Pareto, Émile Durkheim, Alfred Marshall, and Max Weber. Indeed, the last four are the principal subjects of Parsons's classic *The Structure of Social Action* (1937), which he famously inaugurated with Crane Brinton's question, "Who now reads Spencer?" And not just Spencer, but also Thomas Hobbes, Plato, and so many others. The "problem of order," as Parsons put it, is further systematized in the aptly titled *The Social System* (1951). This book outlined a model of society as a functionally differentiated set of institutions and cultural patterns. In such a society, social order is conceived as the aggregate equilibrium that is achieved when subsystems adapt to meet a priori societal needs. As determinative as this model appears, Parsons emphasized that, for him, social order was always already "precarious" and "problematical," not an "imperative" to be associated with theoretical, much less actual, "fascism."

Parsons's attention to the problem of order brought him many critics, including – as his own use of the fascism-word suggests – passionate and politically motivated critics. Among these are Parsons's own students and a striking number of sociology's leading lights. Among the sympathetic critics is his student, Robert K. Merton. While Merton's "middle-range" version of "structural functionalism" certainly shares Parsons's concern for social order, it recasts Parsons's theoretical focus on the societal totality in order to render it serviceable for empirical social research. Even such elementary concepts as Durkheim's anomie are in Merton's divining fundamentally revised to focus concern for the maintenance of social order away from the social totality and toward the various mid-range problems of social milieu.

Another student is Harold Garfinkel, whose "ethnomethodology" pursues the problem of order, not at the middle range but from the bottom up. Garfinkel advocates empirical analysis of the myriad everyday rules (the ethnomethods) that actors themselves use in creating orderly, predictable interactions. While this empirical approach differs fundamentally from that suggested by Parsons, the goal is the same. As Garfinkel stresses, his appropriation of Edmund Husserl's and Alfred Schütz's phenomenological insights is marshaled on behalf of "working out Durkheim's aphorism" that sociology's most fundamental data are concrete social facts. Thus, far from rejecting Parsons's focus on social order, both Merton and Garfinkel aim to render Parsons's problem of order amenable to empirical sociological research, although of significantly different types.

Parsons's more vociferous critics include C. Wright Mills and Alvin W. Gouldner, neither of whom were his students. Mills famously viewed Parsons's attempt to grasp an overarching social order as an instance of "grand theory," a pejorative meant to highlight the theory's ahistorical and empirically disconnected quality as well as call attention to its usefulness as ideological buttress for the specific faults of the mid-century United States of America. As immersed in Marx and Weber as was Mills, he could not countenance a social theory in which Marx played virtually no role and Weber appeared as a politically defanged shadow of himself. That is, Mills could not subscribe to a theory of social order virtually bereft of attention to power, politics, and social domination. Gouldner, for his part, pushed this criticism further, assessing the ideological roots of Parsons's theoretical system from Plato forward and announcing the need for a thorough rethinking of sociology's self-conception just as the discipline was in fact, depending on the perspective taken, decomposing through internal fragmentation or liberating itself from Parsons's theoretical straightjacket. Either way, sociology's focus on the problem of social order seemed to dissolve along with the identity of the discipline.

Although not typically conceived as such, Parsons's problem of social order remains an ongoing practical as well as theoretical problem. On the one hand, researchers' plates are full in pursuit of empirical analysis of postmodernity's acceleration, intensification, dispersal, and differentiation of social and cultural life, which may or may not ultimately facilitate the production of social order. Does the World Wide Web integrate globally, or divide humanity into disparate viewers of superficial information? Does the emergence of post-Fordist/Keynesian economic systems provide efficiency and facilitate meeting increasingly differentiated consumer demand, or globalize the crisis of overproduction without hope of an equally global Keynesian fix? Does the fact of planetary ecological crisis portend unprecedented forms of international cooperation, or will "the North" use its political, military, and economic power to suppress "the South's" demands for an equitable and democratically coordinated response? Will globalization result in genuinely pluralist societies, or will atavistic and ethnocentric responses undermine civility among culturally diverse populations? Will microtechnologies result in the further medical amelioration of disease and mortality, or will social order be subverted by viral contagions, organic or computer, endemic or laboratory-synthesized, unintentionally or by menacing design? Whereas social order in the eighteenth and nineteenth centuries was wracked by such massively disruptive forces as capitalist industrialization, urbanism, liberal democratic revolutions, and European colonialism, and whereas the twentieth century was dominated by such events as two world-embracing wars, worldwide ecological degradation, and the threat of nuclear apocalypse, the twenty-first century appears destined to continue to challenge the achievement of social order on terms as particular and general as human experience provides.

Thus, it is perhaps predictable that a leading contemporary social theorist such as Anthony Giddens would deemphasize his concern for social order as articulated in *The Constitution of Society* (1984) in favor of a more historically engaged reflexive modernization theory and pursuit of "third way" and, more recently, post-third way politics. Yet, it is also the case that perhaps the most influential contemporary inheritor of the Marxian tradition, Jürgen Habermas, has been profoundly influenced by Parsons and the autopoietic systems theory of another of Parsons's students, Niklas Luhmann. Additional streams of analysis of social order include those that derive from the towering achievement of Michel Foucault and his historical attention to the real-world Nietzschean interplay of knowledge and power, and that has resulted in such diverse treatises as Sheila Jasanoff and her colleagues' focus on "the coproduction of science and social order" and Jackie Orr's "genealogy of panic disorder," the latter, in fact, directly theorizing the historical intersections of Parsons, pills, and patriarchy.

SEE ALSO: Anomie; Autopoiesis; Ethnomethodology; Foucault, Michel; Luhmann, Niklas; Merton, Robert K.; Mills, C. Wright; Parsons, Talcott; Structural Functional Theory

REFERENCES AND SUGGESTED READINGS

Beck, U., Giddens, A., & Lash, S. (1995) *Reflexive Modernization: Tradition and Aesthetics in the Modern Social Order*. Stanford University Press, Stanford.

Foucault, M. (1984) Nietzsche, Genealogy, and History. In: *The Foucault Reader*. Ed. P. Rabinow. Pantheon Books, New York.

Garfinkel, H. (1967) *Studies in Ethnomethodology*. Prentice-Hall, Englewood Cliffs, NJ.

Garfinkel, H. (2002) *Ethnomethodology's Program: Working Out Durkheim's Aphorism*. Ed. and introduced by A. Warfield Rawls. Rowman & Littlefield, New York.

Giddens, A. (1984) *The Constitution of Society*. Polity Press, Cambridge.

Giddens, A. (Ed.) (2003) *The Progressive Manifesto*. Policy Network, Cambridge.

Gouldner, A. W. (1970) *The Coming Crisis of Western Sociology*. Basic Books, New York.

Habermas, J. (1975) *Legitimation Crisis*. Beacon Press, Boston.

Habermas, J. (1984) *The Theory of Communicative Action*, Vol. 1. Beacon Press, Boston.

Habermas, J. (1987) *The Theory of Communicative Action*, Vol. 2. Beacon Press, Boston.

Jasanoff, S. (Ed.) (2004) *States of Knowledge: The Co-Production of Science and Social Order*. Routledge, New York.

Luhmann, N. (1982) *The Differentiation of Society*. Columbia University Press, New York.

Merton, R. K. (1968) *Social Theory and Social Structure*. Free Press, New York.

Mills, C. W. (1959) *The Sociological Imagination*. Oxford University Press, Oxford.

Orr, J. (2006) *Panic Diaries: A Genealogy of Panic Disorder*. Duke University Press, Durham, NC.

Parsons, T. (1937) *The Structure of Social Action*. McGraw-Hill, New York.

Parsons, T. (1951) *The Social System*. Free Press, New York.

Parsons, T. (1977) *Social Systems and the Evolution of Action Theory*. Free Press, New York.

social pathology

Milena Büchs

The concept of social pathology applies the medical metaphor of pathology to describe and explain social problems. From this perspective those individuals and groups who deviate from social norms, or institutions that do not fit with core social norms, are "sick" or pathologic and a risk to the society's "health." Social pathology was a very influential model in nineteenth-century American and European sociological writings on social problems. The concept is closely related to those of social disorganization and deviance. However, social disorganization focuses on the malfunctioning of social institutions and structures rather than on the individual. The concept of deviance became popular in the 1950s. It was strongly influenced by the concept of anomie (Durkheim, Merton) and is similar to social pathology in that it focuses on the individual criminal. When the concept of social pathology became famous, many authors using this concept also applied Darwinist and evolutionary models to the analysis of society. They aimed to contribute to social progress and regarded every kind of behavior or social phenomenon that appeared as obstacles to social progress as pathologic and therefore inferior.

The concept of social pathology contains an inherent tension. On the one hand, it emerged at a time when sociologists such as Comte and Spencer sought to establish the field of sociology as a scientific discipline applying objective and scientific methods. This was one of the reasons why concepts from other scientific disciplines such as medicine and biology were employed to study society. On the other hand, social pathology is closely related to a nineteenth-century reform movement which applied normative views to the study of social problems. The perspective of social pathology defines social problems as those social phenomena that diverge from present social norms and morals. Social pathologists assumed that norms could be defined in an objective way, for example by setting universal standards of "health" or "normality."

One can distinguish different versions of the concept social pathology. These versions are also related to the development of the concept over time. Early versions, emerging in the second half of the nineteenth century, were closely related to the socioeconomic context of industrialization and urbanization. Many American social pathologists of that time are regarded as having held relatively moralistic and conservative values deriving from rural forms of social life (Mills 1943). Some authors used a biological or organic version of social pathology. Samuel Smith, for example, used an organic analogy in order to describe different social classes and their relationships. Smith (1911) saw phenomena such as crime and poverty as inherently related to each other and those affected by it as belonging to the "abnormal classes." Authors such as Lombroso and Ferrero (1895) developed the concept of the deviant person as a "born criminal." According to this concept, criminal behavior is caused by inherited mental or physical diseases. Another version of the concept regards a lack of socialization as the main reason for deviant behavior: here the criminal becomes "infected" by the bad morals around him or her. Both versions mainly supported (religious) education and medical treatment as the right methods to "cure" criminals. These early versions of social pathology had their heyday in the period before World War I, after which they declined slowly but steadily.

In the 1960s the concept of social pathology again became more frequently used. Social parameters were quite different and the concept became more popular among liberal social scientists who regarded whole social institutions as pathologic or as causing the pathological behavior of individuals (Rubington & Weinberg 1995). At this time, the concept of social pathology was also used to explain social and political disasters such as the Holocaust by Nazi Germany, the totalitarianism of the Stalin era, and the atomic bombs dropped on Hiroshima and Nagasaki by the US (Rosenberg et al. 1964).

Some authors in the same period also intended to apply the idea of social pathology in a more objective way. This was a response to the critique of social pathology which claimed that the concept in fact supported the culturally specific norms found in rural life such as piety and social stability, but disguised this by the use of pseudo-scientific methods (Mills 1943). Therefore, authors such as Kavolis (1968) developed what he called a "universal criterion" for the definition of pathologies. For him, the cross-culturally acknowledged criterion of social pathology was "destructive or self-destructive behavior" rather than deviance from culturally specific norms. Another difficulty in diagnosing social pathologies arises if one argues from Durkheim's functionalist point of view that deviance serves a social function and is therefore "normal."

Since the mid-1980s, constructivist approaches have become prominent in the study of social problems and the notion of social pathology is now rarely used. The constructivist approach does not agree that it is possible to define a cross-culturally accepted criterion of "normality." Rather, from the constructivists' perspective, social problems are those phenomena that are regarded as problems by the public, political movements, or politicians, all of whom may strive to change the situation by political action.

SEE ALSO: Criminology; Deviant Careers; Eugenics; Social Policy, Welfare State; Social Problems, Concept and Perspectives; Social Problems, Politics of

REFERENCES AND SUGGESTED READINGS

Kavolis, V. (Ed.) (1968) *Comparative Perspectives on Social Problems*. Little, Brown, Boston.

Lombroso, C. & Ferrero, W. (1895) *The Female Offender*. T. Fisher Unwin, London.

Mills, C. W. (1943) The Professional Ideology of Social Pathologists. *American Journal of Sociology* 49(2): 165–80.

Rosenberg, B. et al. (Eds.) (1964) *Mass Society in Crisis: Social Problems and Social Pathology*. Macmillan, New York.

Rubington, E. & Weinberg, M. S. (1995) *The Study of Social Problems: Seven Perspectives*. Oxford University Press, Oxford.

Smith, S. G. (1911) *Social Pathology*. Macmillan, New York.

Sutherland, E. H. (1945) Social Pathology. *American Journal of Sociology* 50(6): 429–35.

social policy, welfare state

Franz-Xaver Kaufmann

"Welfare state" and "social policy" are generalizing concepts legitimizing political intervention to protect the weaker members of society, to reduce social inequalities, and to promote human capacities for action and self-reliance. The contemporary welfare state is the institutional expression of a political system committing itself to human rights, including social rights. Social policy is the generic name for strategies to solve social problems by political intervention, as well as for an academic discipline dealing with such issues.

HISTORY

The idea that the king or the prince was responsible for the "security, welfare, and felicity" of his subjects was already part of premodern political ideology. In some countries (e.g., Prussia) there existed also a discernible set of policies aimed at promoting welfare (Dorwart 1971). In the UK, the poor laws of Queen Elizabeth I (1599–1601) drafted some basic features of social policy, i.e., the definition of a problem ("poverty"), a classification of recipients and selective treatment (workhouse versus asylum), their entrustment to local officers, and rules of financing. The followers of John Locke, Adam Smith, and Immanuel Kant, however, opposed such a comprehensive political authority. Responsibility for security alone should remain with government or (in continental Europe) the state, whereas individuals should be responsible for their own welfare and happiness.

In the modern sense, social policies and institutions of public welfare emerged in the nineteenth century in reaction to economic liberalism and the pernicious side effects of industrialization and urbanization, with Great Britain and Switzerland being the forerunners. The terms "social policy" and "welfare state" were first coined in Germany: *Social-Politik* on the eve of the revolutionary year 1848, and *Wohl-fahrtsstaat* by the social reformer Adolph Wagner in 1876. The most perspicacious social scientist in these matters was Lorenz von Stein. Drawing on Hegel's distinction between "the state" and "civil society" and inspired, like Karl Marx, by French socialists, from 1842 on he developed a dynamic theory of societal transformation leading inevitably to class struggle. But in contrast to Marx, he saw the way out not in revolution but in class compromise, mediated through a "monarchy of social reform" thought to be neutral toward class interests (cf. Stein 1964 [1850]). This class compromise should consist in the constitutional guarantee of private property in favor of the propertied class on the one hand, and in the protection and advancement of the working classes through education, free association, and "social administration" on the other.

In fact, in many European countries, things have evolved along the lines of Stein's argument, though mostly in a more democratic and corporatist way. Beginning with the September Agreement in Denmark (1899) and followed by Germany (1918), France (1936, 1968), Switzerland (1937), and Sweden (1938), agreements among employers' leaders and workers' associations have been made on a national basis with quite similar content: acceptance by trade unions of private industry and industrial authority on one hand, and acceptance by employers of obligatory collective bargaining and state intervention to protect workers on the other. These agreements proved more or less sustainable, but state intervention regulating labor protection, workers' rights, and social insurance, i.e., social policies, thus became accepted throughout Europe before World War II.

The welfare state's heyday came after World War II. The victorious powers were convinced that the ascendance of fascism and its atrocities was due mainly to the economic and social misery following World War I and the Great Depression. Thus the program for a more peaceful world, originating in the Atlantic Charter issued by Roosevelt and Churchill in 1941 and leading to the Organization of United Nations, included the proposal "to bring about the fullest collaboration between all nations in the economic field with the object of securing, for all, improved labor standards, economic advancement, and social security."

The ideological shift from social policies for industrial workers to a comprehensive set of welfare policies for all members of a society is documented in the 1944 Declaration of Philadelphia by the International Labor Organization (ILO), which became incorporated into the ILO's constitution in 1946. In this document is to be found for the first time the conviction that "all human beings ... have the right to pursue both their material well-being and their spiritual development in conditions of freedom and dignity, of economic security, and equal opportunity." Further, the document defines the major areas of welfare state policies. These ideas are echoed in Article 55 of the Charter of the United Nations Organization. Eventually, the UN's Universal Declaration of Human Rights in 1948 codified not only civil and political rights, but also economic, social, and cultural rights, to be promoted by national policies and international cooperation. The international implementation of the latter remained quite weak, however. The Economic and Social Council (ECOSOC) has remained a rather ineffective organ of the UN. Yet the plan of a welfare state was internationally established by these decisions and has taken shape through various regional declarations and covenants.

SCOPE

International comparative research on issues of the welfare state focuses mainly on systems of income maintenance or social security. This is admittedly the most expensive and widespread field of public intervention. But there are two other fields in which sociopolitical intervention is common, namely, labor protection (cf. Hepple 1986) and social services (cf. Alber 1995). From a functionalist perspective, it is thus possible to distinguish social policies in the realm of production (regulating working conditions, wages, labor markets), distribution (social security, taxation), and reproduction (social services: education, health, housing, personal services) (Kaufmann 2001).

In fact, some institutional arrangements providing protection of working conditions, income security, and social services have developed in almost all industrialized countries. But countries differ as to the extent of coverage of the population, the degree of political regulation or self-administration, the share of public, semi-public, non-profit, or private ownership, and financing from the general public budget, by specific but compulsory contributions, or by subsidized market prices. They differ moreover as to the legitimations and specific technologies of administrative intervention. All these features, which form the specific arrangement of public welfare production in a country, depend obviously on more general features of cultural orientations, the political system and the distribution of power, the structure and performance of the economy, and many other factors. So, from a comparative perspective, the object of inquiry is located in both the public and the private sphere, somewhere in between "state" and "civil society." It is much easier to describe "social policy" and "welfare state" from a specific national perspective. But these national self-descriptions are far from being convergent in a comparative perspective. Similarities and differences are themselves objects of inquiry.

The welfare state is a focus of research for many disciplines, from political philosophy (Walzer 1983; Goodin 1988) and history (Baldwin 1990; Ritter 1991) to economics (Atkinson 1983; Sen 1996) and even law. The bulk of research, however, stems from sociology and political science.

SOCIOLOGICAL APPROACHES

In the sociological discussion of the welfare state, the international context is seldom mentioned. This is one reason why concepts of the welfare state often remain rather loose and contested. Sociology mainly focuses on national developments in both national and comparative perspective, and most authors model their concept of the welfare state with respect to their own national or regional tradition. In the present context, only comparative and generalizing research is considered.

There is often an intrinsic correspondence between the choice of method for inquiry and the underlying concept of the welfare state. A widespread and very influential approach to comparative welfare state research operates with national or international statistics (Wilensky 1975). The statistical offices of the OECD and European Union (Eurostat) endeavor to standardize national figures to overcome the intricacies of comparison from heterogeneous national sources. This quantitative approach uses conventional definitions: the welfare state is often equated with social expenditure or its share in GDP. Moreover, all countries with available statistics are often included notwithstanding their institutional and ideological aspects.

A second approach starts from history and compares national developments of a limited number of welfare states in a more or less comprehensive way (Rimlinger 1971). This historical approach is quite flexible and contributes to an intrinsic understanding of various national cases, but it often lacks rigorous comparative dimensions and hence a clear basic concept of the welfare state.

More rigorous comparisons may be attained when the focus remains with particular institutional complexes of the welfare state such as the health system, old-age security, or labor protection. Such studies are often quite instructive for a certain field of social policy, but again fail to account for a comprehensive concept of the welfare state. The institutionalist approach may also focus on the impact of the political machinery upon the emergence of welfare states (Evans et al. 1985).

A thrust to more reflection of comprehensive differences of welfare states has been made by the typological approach. It began with the distinction by Richard Titmuss (1974) of the "institutional redistributive model," the "industrial achievement–performance model," and the "residual model" of social policy. This tripartite distinction is echoed by the welfare regime approach by Gøsta Esping-Andersen (1990) which links the institutional differences to the dominance of social democratic or conservative or liberal ideologies. This typology has provoked much debate and has proved fruitful by sensitizing the professional community to the complex character of welfare states and their institutional as well as cultural and ideological differences.

The debate about systematizing differences among welfare states obscured somewhat the question of what they have in common. A convincing answer came from general sociology: the growth and functional differentiation of modern societies erode traditional forms of all-embracing solidarity and lead to the emergence of increasingly selective forms of social organization and to growing individualization of life courses. It is therefore necessary to care politically for the inclusion of all individuals within the leading realms of life. This was already the underlying idea of the human rights movement. It was T. H. Marshall (1976 [1964]) who made it a sociological argument, which was then picked up under the heading of "inclusion" by Talcott Parsons and Niklas Luhmann.

This general perspective suggests that the emergence of a welfare state is a necessary concomitant of successful modernization. However, nations and political systems differ markedly in their relation to the economic system. Taking this difference as essential, one might distinguish between "state socialism" (e.g., the USSR), "welfare capitalism" (e.g., the US), and "welfare state," the latter "European model" being characterized by a continuous tension between state intervention and market forces as well as by class compromise (Kaufmann 2003).

The progress of research has not led until now to a dominating paradigm. The subject is complex and multifarious, so substantial approaches need to define first a specific perspective or, in a more advanced stage, the combination of a defined set of perspectives. Three overarching questions are to be found in comparative sociological and political research: (1) driving factors for the development and retrenchment of the welfare state; (2) functions of the welfare state; (3) evaluation and impact of welfare state provisions.

PROBLEMS

Historically, the emergence of welfare state institutions in Western Europe coincided with post-war prosperity and full employment. Between 1945 and 1973, the terms of trade were particularly favorable for Europe, due to the Bretton Woods monetary system linking all currencies to an implicit gold standard expressed by a stable relation to the US dollar. The breakdown of this monetary system and the first oil price shock of 1974 brought to an end these exceptionally favorable circumstances. From then on, the language of "crisis," stemming originally from Marxism, became common in discussions about the welfare state.

The extension of coverage and the creation of new insurances and services in the post-war period not only were eased by rapid economic growth, but also profited from the Cold War. There was an overlapping consensus among left and right in Western Europe that in order to survive as an economic system, capitalism had at least to be tamed and, moreover, be restrained to the realm of market economy. People's life chances should no longer be dependent entirely on market forces but should rely on public provision in the event of inability or impossibility of earning one's own living. There remained ample political dissension as to the extent of public protection, but no longer as to the principle of protection itself.

There was furthermore a certain naïve trust in the wholly beneficent character of social policies on the part of their champions. The egalitarian attitude that redistribution is good in itself was backed by Keynesianism, and the strong belief in the problem-solving capacities of politics remained unbroken, not only on the left. Doubts about the sustainability of this scenario then came not only from economists, but also from social scientists. Since the 1980s the deregulation of financial markets has made for intensifying international competition and the increasing bargaining power of capital.

Discourse about the crisis of the welfare state has many issues: crisis of financing, crisis of governability, crisis of legitimation, crisis of efficiency, and crisis of loyalty (cf. Offe 1984). Despite some evidence for particular deficiencies of existing arrangements of public welfare production, the basic idea of a self-enforcing crisis of the welfare state has so far proved to be wrong. There is ample evidence that in most European countries, the institutions of social protection and political responsibility for the basic welfare of all citizens meet sustained acceptance, despite growing economic difficulties.

The "welfare backlash" began with the governments of Margaret Thatcher and Ronald Reagan around 1980. Strong opposition to spending on welfare and social security did not spread throughout the industrialized world, though almost everywhere the tightening of public budgets, growing unemployment, and the perspective of rising demand due to demographic changes made for politics of welfare retrenchment. Empirical evidence shows that the political systems of various nations were coping quite differently with the challenges of unemployment, globalization, and demographic change (Scharpf & Schmidt 2000; Huber & Stephens 2001). By and large, the cutback movement was successful only in slowing down social expenditure, but did not destroy public responsibility for social welfare.

Substantial changes in priorities and methods of welfare provision did take place, however. A general trend is the change of emphasis from a "redistributive state" to an "enabling state" (Gilbert 2002). The class issue loses centrality, while other issues (e.g., regional and generational conflicts) gain in importance. The demographic perspective of aging and decline shifts emphasis from social security to education and family policies (Esping-Andersen et al. 2002; Castles 2004). A tradeoff between high standards of labor protection and unemployment is emerging in some countries. Moreover, the focus is switching from state provision of welfare to a mixed system of public, non-profit, and market provision ("welfare pluralism").

Though these shifts in emphasis are clearly against the established views of state- and class-centered welfare policies, it makes sense to preserve the term "welfare state" as long as political commitment to social rights for all and the power of the state with regard to the regulation of social services remain uncontested.

SEE ALSO: Poverty; Social Exclusion; Social Integration and Inclusion; Social Problems, Concept and Perspectives; Social Work: History and Institutions; State; State and Economy; Stratification and Inequality, Theories of; Welfare Regimes; Welfare State; Welfare State, Retrenchment of

REFERENCES AND SUGGESTED READINGS

Alber, J. (1995) A Framework for the Comparative Study of Social Services. *Journal of European Social Policy* 5: 131–49.

Atkinson, A. B. (1983) *Social Justice and Public Policy*. MIT Press, Cambridge, MA.

Atkinson, A. B., Rainwater, L., & Smeeding, T. M. (1995) *Income Distribution in OECD Countries*. OECD, Paris.

Baldwin, P. (1990) *The Politics of Solidarity: Class Bases of the European Welfare States, 1875–1975*. Cambridge University Press, Cambridge.

Castles, F. G. (2004) *The Future of the Welfare State: Crisis Myths and Crisis Realities*. Oxford University Press, Oxford.

Dorwart, R. A. (1971) *The Prussian Welfare State Before 1740*. Harvard University Press, Cambridge, MA.

Esping-Andersen, G. (1990) *The Three Worlds of Welfare Capitalism*. Polity Press, Cambridge.

Esping-Andersen, G., with Gallie, D., Hemerijck, A., & Myles, J. (2002) *Why We Need a New Welfare State*. Oxford University Press, Oxford.

Evans, P. B., Rueschemeyer, D., & Skocpol, T. (Eds.) (1985) *Bringing the State Back In*. Cambridge University Press, Cambridge.

Gilbert, N. (2002) *Transformation of the Welfare State: The Silent Surrender of Public Responsibility*. Oxford University Press, Oxford.

Goodin, R. E. (1988) *Reasons for Welfare: The Political Theory of the Welfare State*. Princeton University Press, Princeton.

Hepple, B. (Ed.) (1986) *The Making of Labour Law in Europe: A Comparative Study of Nine Countries up to 1945*. Mansell, London and New York.

Huber, E. & Stephens, J. D. (2001) *Development and Crisis of the Welfare State: Parties and Policies in*

Global Markets. University of Chicago Press, Chicago and London.

Kaufmann, F.-X. (2001) Towards a Theory of the Welfare State. In: Leibfried, S. (Ed.), *Welfare State Futures*. Cambridge University Press, Cambridge, pp. 15–36.

Kaufmann, F.-X. (2003) *Varianten des Wohlfahrtsstaats (Varieties of the Welfare State)*. Suhrkamp Verlag, Frankfurt a. M.

Marshall, T. H. (1976 [1964]) *Class, Citizenship, and Social Development*, 2nd edn. Greenwood, Westport, CT.

Offe, C. (1984) *Contradictions of the Welfare State*. Hutchinson, London.

Pierson, P. (2000) *The New Politics of the Welfare State*. Oxford University Press, Oxford.

Rimlinger, G. V. (1971) *Welfare Policy and Industrialization in Europe, America, and Russia*. Wiley, New York.

Ritter, G. A. (1991) *Der Sozialstaat: Entstehung und Entwicklung im internationalen Vergleich (The Welfare State: Origins and Developments in International Comparative Perspective)*, 2nd edn. Oldenbourg, Munich.

Scharpf, F. W. & Schmidt, V. A. (2000) *Welfare and Work in the Open Economy*, 2 vols. Oxford University Press, Oxford.

Sen, A. (1996) *On Economic Inequality*. Expanded edition with a substantial annexe by J. E. Foster & A. Sen. Clarendon, Oxford.

Stein, L. (1964 [1850]) *Geschichte der sozialen Bewegung in Frankreich von 1789 bis auf unsere Tage*, 3 vols. Wigand, Leipzig. (Abridged English version *The History of the Social Movement in France: 1789–1850*. Trans. and Ed. K. Mengelberg. Bedminster Press, Totowa, NJ.)

Titmuss, R. A. (1974) *Social Policy: An Introduction*. Allen & Unwin, London.

Walzer, M. (1983) *Spheres of Justice: A Defense of Pluralism and Equality*. Basic Books, New York.

Wilensky, H. (1975) *The Welfare State and Equality: Structural and Ideological Roots of Public Expenditures*. University of California Press, Berkeley.

social problems, concept and perspectives

Axel Groenemeyer

"Social problems" have formed a specialized field within sociology, especially in the US, at least since the end of the nineteenth century.

The European context has always been marked by the concept of the "social question," which was one of the principal sources for the development of sociology as a scientific discipline apart from philosophy, history, political science, and political economy. Unlike US sociology, in the European tradition the concept of social problems was not disseminated in the sociological literature until the end of the 1960s, when it appeared first in books and articles about social work. While the concept today is institutionalized in special sections of sociological associations and in some journals and textbooks, and its use has been spread in public and political discourse, European sociology has always privileged the concept of the social question, with greater emphasis on macrosociological reasoning and theory building. As a consequence, most of the literature using social problems as a theoretical concept is of US origin (Ritzer 2004; for handbooks in German and French, see Albrecht et al. 1999; Dorvil & Mayer 2001).

DEFINITIONS AND PERSPECTIVES OF SOCIAL PROBLEMS

The term social problem is used in public and political discussions and refers to very different social situations, conditions, and forms of behavior, like crime, racism, drug use, unemployment, poverty, exclusion, alcoholism, sexual abuse, and madness. However, especially in textbooks and journal articles, it also refers to premenstrual syndrome, ecological problems, stalking, exploitation of natural resources, traffic accidents, or even war, terrorism, and genocide. This diversity has been a challenge for sociological definitions and invites the question of identifying the feature that justifies classifying such phenomena under a common topic or theoretical perspective.

As a consequence, the scientific value of having the concept of social problem within sociology is contested, as it seems to be too vague and too broad to be useful for guiding the development of theories. Assessments such as those of Spector and Kitsuse (1987 [1977]) that "there is not and never has been a sociology of social problems" (p. 1) and of Best (2004) that the "social problem has not proved to be a particularly useful concept for sociological analysis" (p. 15) could find some justification.

The sociological use of the concept of social problems is connected with at least five different perspectives, outlined below.

Textbook eclecticism of social problems. The vagueness of the term is reflected in sociological textbooks and journals on social problems that offer a nearly endless list of various topics. These articles are the product of a vast amount of specialized sociological research on social problems that very often form special fields within (but also apart from) sociology, for example criminology, public health, or the sociology of poverty. In this textbook context, the concept of social problems is used as an umbrella for a wide range of situations and forms of behavior reflecting the public and political meaning of what is problematic within society and what should be treated, ameliorated, or controlled. The problematic character of such phenomena is taken for granted. Definitions of social problems, at least implicitly, follow various kinds of formulations that refer to everything that is defined in public (or by a certain number of people) as social problems: "social problem are what people think they are." This meaning of social problems is closely linked to the production of applied knowledge for public policy.

Sociology of social problems as applied sociology. Since its origin in American reform-oriented sociology at the beginning of the twentieth century and its connection to policy, the sociology of social problems is often treated as a field of applied sociology. This perspective is closely tied to the specialized fields of sociology, where the problematic character of social problems is the starting point for the production of knowledge about causes and forms of existing social evils and their social and political control. This is without doubt an important field of research within the sociology of social problems, but there is no common theoretical ground on which a theoretical concept of social problems could be justified. Nevertheless, social problems are the base for political programs, actions, and institutions evoking the fundamental problem of the relation between theory and policy and demanding a discussion of the role of values and normative theory within sociology.

Social problems as social harm and social disorganization. Whereas in these perspectives

the problematic character of social problems is taken for granted or defined by public opinion, there have always been attempts to define the object of the sociology of social problems on the basis of theoretical knowledge about the functioning of society. Social problems are those conditions and forms of behavior that undermine the functioning of important social institutions and cause harm to individuals and social groups. In this perspective – often labeled as "objectivist" – the common character of different social problems is seen in their common social structural sources, defined as social pathology, social disorganization, alienation and exploitation, unequal distribution of resources and power, or anomie. The discrepancy between cultural standards, norms, or values and the actual conditions of social life – Merton's (1976: 7) famous, quite formal definition of social problems – should be identified and analyzed by sociological inquiry, in principle without reference to "what people think" and as a "technical judgment" about the possibility of a better-functioning social system.

Social problems as the social question. In the context of European sociology, the concept of social problems has never had a prominent place. Its use is very often limited to problems seen as associated with social inequality and social integration or inclusion. In the European tradition of the social question, social problems are those behaviors and conditions that should be treated by the welfare state through social policy and social work. Unlike the American perspective of social disorganization, the tradition of the analysis of social problems related to the social question privileged a perspective of conflicts rooted in the social structure of modern societies (cf. Castel 2002 [1995]). In this sense the term social problem in the singular was introduced into US sociology in the nineteenth century, but very soon changed its meaning in a plurality of unconnected "social problems."

Social problems as social constructions. While in these perspectives social problems are treated as special objects of sociological inquiry, a constructionist perspective of social problems insists that social problems are not necessarily rooted in harmful social conditions and that the only thing the various phenomena have in common is that they are labeled as social problems. Social problems exist only as cultural definitions of public activities of grievances and claims (Spector & Kitsuse 1987 [1977]). Social conditions are dismissed as merely "putative," and sociological research focuses on the claims-making activities through which social problems become public concerns and political issues. Whereas in sociological research on causes, careers, and control of social problems their problematic character is often taken for granted, the constructionist perspective makes this question its central concern. The sociology of social problems adopts a sociology of knowledge perspective to analyze the strategies and discourses used by collective actors to bring issues onto the public and political agenda. In this perspective, sociology and scientific knowledge in general no longer have special status; their role is reduced to that of one claims-maker among others. As a consequence of this radical reformulation and change of paradigm, the "social problems approach" is identified no longer by its research objects but by its theoretical and methodological perspective.

THE EUROPEAN "SOCIAL QUESTION" AND AMERICAN "SOCIAL PROBLEMS"

The history of sociological reasoning has its starting point in the problematization of social conditions linked to the capitalist industrial revolution in Western Europe. In this context, social problems such as poverty, alcohol consumption, disease, and violence were seen as direct indicators of disorder of the social structure and crises of development. The central points of reference were social movements and ideas of social justice to assure national social inclusion and integration of modern societies. Social problems as social crises or social pathologies had been linked directly to questions of social inequality, and sociological reasoning of social problems formed a privileged way to uncover the central mechanisms of functioning and development of modern societies. These ideas are best expounded in the work of the founding fathers of sociology, Marx and Durkheim.

Nevertheless, the "social question" has always been a political question of social reform or social revolution, linked to the three dominant ideological streams: liberalism, conservatism, and socialism. Based on ideas of social justice, social integration, and social inclusion, national and collective political projects of the welfare state emerged to solve the conflicts of disintegrating capitalist economies.

This European tradition of welfare state orientation still marks an important difference from American sociological reasoning on social problems. Unlike the European tradition, American sociology was not confronted in the same way with fundamental social movements and their ideological orientations. Existing social movements were short-lived and concentrated more on single issues without problematizing the social structure as a whole. As a consequence, American sociology at the end of the nineteenth century adopted a reform-oriented perspective on isolated social problems (in the plural) and ideas of applied sociology to produce knowledge for treating these problems against the background of pragmatic philosophy.

The adoption of the concept of social problem and its rapid dissemination in European sociology in the 1970s from the US social context reflects a social change after World War II, marked by a rapid and extensive expansion of the welfare state and social services. In this context of economic prosperity, remaining social problems were individualized as deviant behavior to be treated by social work. The social question seemed to be solved and the idea of social problems seemed to be more appropriate for developing specialized sociological and professional knowledge to guide political reforms and interventions.

On the one hand, cultural pluralization and the development of new social movements in the 1960s and 1970s could explain the popularity of cultural relativism expressed by radical constructivist and postmodern perspectives in Europe. On the other hand, processes of globalization and internationalization, economic crises, and the spread of new poverty and growing social inequality from the 1980s on, together with an expansion of migration processes, brought back questions of social integration and exclusion to the sociological research agenda and strengthened the idea of a "new social question" as new challenges for the welfare state (Bourdieu 1993; Castel 2002 [1995]).

THEORETICAL ISSUES

Despite marked differences between the socio-logical traditions of understanding social pro-blems, there are common theoretical and conceptual perspectives and problems (for an overview, see Rubington & Weinberg 1995). While typologies of theoretical positions are arbitrary and misleading, very often there can be found a differentiation between "objective" or "realist" approaches and "constructionist" perspectives. These labels are misleading because, on the one hand, they involve the dan-ger of misinterpreting constructions of social problems as not being real social problems, and, on the other hand, they lead to the mis-interpretation of "objectivist" approaches in assuming that there is still a methodological position of naïve objectivism in sociology.

Social Problems as Social Harm and Social Disorder

An early version of describing social problems as harm and social disorder is *social pathology*. This perspective, still very common in political and popular discourse, is based on the idea of society as an organism. Social problems are indicators of a pathological state of society and/or are caused by pathological individuals. This idea found its roots in nineteenth-century sociology, where the success of medical treatment and hygiene formed the model for sociology as a medical profession of society. In this analogy, social pro-blems are seen as deviance from a normal and healthily functioning society, in which there is harmonious coordination between specialized subsystems. The identification of social pro-blems is not a problem, because the criteria underlying society as a well-functioning organ-ism are seen as evident and based on common-sense normative and moral ideas (fundamentally criticized as a backward conservatism by Mills 1943). However, the central arguments against the idea of social pathology are that values and norms in society are changing and have to be different for different groups in differentiated societies. Beyond this it is clear that many social conditions that mark "social health" in one field of society automatically cause harm to other fields, which also means that the pathological

functioning of one sector has to be analyzed as the condition for the healthy functioning of another sector (Rosenquist 1995).

Nevertheless, the sociology of social problems is always confronted by the question of how to analyze values and norms that inevitably form the base for constructing and identifying social problems in public as well as in sociology. Inas-much as the sociology of social problems takes existing definitions from public and political definitions of social harm as its starting point, it runs the risk of being normative. In a vast proportion of research in special fields of the sociology of social problems, the problematic character of the issue in this sense is taken for granted. This position very often corresponds with a perspective of applied sociology, where the problematic character of the issue has to be the starting point from which to develop and analyze political programs and interventions of social control.

A similar critique confronts the perspective of *social disorganization*, which was developed in the context of the Chicago School for analyzing deviant behavior and its spatial distribution in cities. Social problems are seen as indicators of, or as a result of, a breakdown of rules and social control in poor neighborhoods, caused mainly by processes of migration and rapid social change. Beyond criticisms of its normative base, the social disorganization perspective has been criticized for failing to specify the difference between deviance and social disorganization. Very often deviance is not a sign of disorganized neighborhoods or of a breakdown of norms and social control but is a result of a *cultural conflict* between local subcultures and the values of a majority society able to define common norms and values for the whole society. Within this perspective also, the problem of separating "normal" or even necessary and disorganizing social change is not solved.

The general form of argumentation with social disorganization also forms the base for the concept of anomie, developed by Durkheim (1902 [1893]). Here the disintegrating conse-quences of division of work and social differen-tiation in the processes of modernization result in "pathological" consequences, indicated by an extraordinarily high level of crime or suicides in modern societies. These perspectives of social disorganization and anomie experienced a renaissance after the 1980s in European sociology, especially for analyzing conflicts and social problems in relation to processes of migration and growing social inequality.

With the supremacy of *structural functionalism*, the idea of anomic developments became one of the leading sociological perspectives on social problems in US sociology in the 1950s and 1960s. Social problems are seen as functional disturbances of social systems and as a problem of social disintegration. The functioning of social systems and their stable reproduction became the central point of reference for identifying social problems. In Merton's (1971, 1976) classic formulation of this program, this identification is seen as a "technical" analysis of the possibility of a better functioning of a social system and not one of a political or normative judgment. In principle, social problems could be identified by sociological research without depending on their public or political definitions. This allows criticisms of existing public definitions of issues and claims as being ideological misconceptions of what in effect does not result in social harm, or diagnosing social developments as resulting in "latent social problems" not yet defined as social problems in public. The separation of problematic social conditions and of publicly recognized social problems thus defines, in principle, a critical program for a sociology of social problems, even if the idea of a "technical judgment" of social dysfunctions seems to present a perspective oriented by an organic view of a normally harmonious and well-functioning society already criticized in the approach of social pathology.

The differentiation of social problems as "social disorganization" and "deviant behavior" as different types of social problems has been developed in this context (Merton 1976). Social disorganization refers to the malfunctioning of the internal organization of a social system in providing stable role orientations, statuses, rules, and valid norms for the participant actors; it refers to the diagnosis of an absence or a breakdown of norms, whereas deviant behavior depends on the existence of a stable and accepted system of social norms and of actors motivated to obey them (Cohen 1959).

In the functional perspective, social disorganization is a consequence of rapid social change caused by technological, demographic, or cultural change to which some social systems react more easily than others. It could be interpreted as a cause of deviant behavior if a state of normlessness, contradictory, or conflicting expectations in a social system results in strain for individuals. But deviant behavior could also lead to social disorganization if mechanisms of social control and exclusion fail to reestablish social order. Very often social contexts described as disorganized have developed subcultural systems of values and norms that provide members with stable orientations, but are interpreted as deviant in relation to the social environment and the dominant system of values and norms in the society. In these cases, social systems could not be interpreted as disorganized; in a functional perspective, they could be described as disintegrated since subcultural social systems result in dysfunctional conflict for the system as a whole.

This concept seems to be too vague since it has not been able to provide "technical" criteria for the healthy functioning of a social system without reference to values, interests, and power apart from the absence of conflict, faulty socialization, and deviant behavior. As a consequence, this perspective has been criticized for failing to provide criteria to judge conflicts in pluralistic societies as disorganizing or as leading to necessary social change. The idea of social disorganization follows a utopian view of a society in harmonious balance. Implicit in this view is the misconception of social problems as being conditions that could and should be solved. Obviously, societies survive quite well even if they leave unsolved their major social problems, and typically the treatment or solution of one social problem means the creation of social problems in other fields of modern societies. Beyond this, Durkheim is known for his functional argumentation of social problems. Social problems and deviant behavior fulfill important functions for societies inasmuch as they provide sources of solidarity, mark limits of morality, symbolize examples of misconduct, or indicate necessary social change.

Whereas in perspectives based on the diagnostic of social harm the difference between social disorganization and deviant behavior is often interpreted as a difference between "structurally" and "behaviorally" caused social problems, it seems appropriate to interpret them as different kinds of social problem definition. For example, unemployment could be defined as a social problem related to the malfunctioning of the labor market, but it is also very widely seen as the malfunctioning of individuals who are either unwilling or unable to integrate into the labor market.

One central problem in the definition of social problems proposed by Merton is the identification of a "substantial discrepancy between widely shared social standards and actual conditions" (Merton 1971: 799). Even if Merton insists on identifying social problems on the basis of a "technical judgment" about the functioning of social systems, the identification of "social standards" and the diagnostic of a "substantial discrepancy" are finally based on the empirical registration of public opinion (Manis 1974). This could result in the problematic consequence of being unable to identify a social problem sociologically, for instance, if racial discrimination is found in a racist society, since in this case there is no "substantial discrepancy" between the shared racist standards and the actual racist conditions. We face the problem of having no standard beyond empirically measured public opinion to decide whether shared values in society are in fact ideological manifestations. This problem could only be resolved by stating the validity of a system of values – for instance, human rights – independently of publicly (and politically) shared social standards (Manis 1974). On this basis, the identification of "latent social problems" and the sociological critique of existing definitions of social problems remain important questions for the sociology of social problems.

This approach loses much of its power of persuasion when we ask why certain social harms or discriminations last over a long period without being identified as social problems by the public, or why definitions or interpretations of social problems change over time even if the social conditions remain nearly unchanged. Beyond this, the guidance of public interpretations of and attention to social problems fulfills important political functions and could be used as a means of achieving success in elections or to attract resources for public agencies or professional institutions. In this sense, social problems do not always have their origins in social developments but are rooted in political strategies of symbolic policy (Edelman 1977).

Social Problems as Social Construction

The "cultural turn" in sociology of the 1970s was caused at least partly by the adoption of ideas of symbolic interactionism and other microsociological approaches as criticisms of structural functionalism. This first happened in the field of sociology of deviance and social problems in the 1960s with the development of perspectives insisting on the idea that deviance and social problems in general are not qualities of social conditions or specific forms of behavior, but instead have to be analyzed as results of interactive processes of social definition and labeling. This idea was then radicalized in constructivist approaches based on the idea that social problems exist only as public "activities of individuals or groups making assertions of grievances and claims with respect to some putative conditions" (Spector & Kitsuse 1987 [1977]: 75). This has been a radical reformulation of the problem of defining and analyzing social problems.

Whereas sociological perspectives that define and analyze social problems as social harm insist on the fact that social structures and developments could result in problematic life conditions and behavior, for constructionist perspectives these social conditions are merely "putative" and a more or less rhetorical means of "claims-making activities": social problems are constructions that successfully attract public and political attention. As a consequence, the main questions to be analyzed are no longer about causes and social conditions that might explain the existence and affection of specific groups, but concern the processes of how social problems are successful in attracting public attention and become public issues with a special quality.

The approaches that follow ideas of social structure and social change as analytical bases for defining social problems – now labeled as "objectivist" – always had to face the problem of justifying a general concept of social problems that could unify very different social phenomena. With the new formulation of constructionist perspectives, this problem was solved in that different phenomena labeled as social problems could analytically be unified under the common question of what (and who) made them problematic and how they became public issues. The sociology of social problems consists in the reconstruction of activities and processes that explain the public mobilization for specific definitions of issues and themes within society and the establishment of social problem discourses. Social problems are specific forms of collective behavior which explain the significance given to the analysis of media representations, moral entrepreneurs, and social movements.

Whereas in so-called "objective" approaches scientific, especially sociological, knowledge has given an outstanding position to the analysis of social problems and their developments, in constructionist approaches this role is limited to that of one "claims-maker" among others. Constructionist perspectives insist that the role of sociology cannot be seen as criticizing existing constructions and their forms of public definition. Its role is reduced to that of a reconstruction of the processes by which such constructions became convincing for the public, and not to analyze their structural and social historical bases. In its radical form, this approach is limited to the analysis of rhetoric and counter-rhetoric on public issues.

Today, especially in the US context, the sociology of social problems is identified with the constructionist perspective, and a vast amount of social problem research is devoted to case studies of many different issues that at one time or another attracted public attention (see, e.g., Best 1989, 2001; Loseke & Best 2003). But, while it is very often identified as the only valuable perspective and forms the mainstream of social problem analysis, the constructionist perspective has its critics.

The most important criticisms from within constructionism have been developed by Woolgar and Pawluch (1985). In reconstructing constructionist case studies on social problems, they argue that the underlying argumentation of these analyses is marked by a contradictory use of the perspective of social construction. In framing their question, these case studies assume that the social conditions or the behavior in question remained more or less unchanged, while the social constructions of the problem in public have been changed. On the one hand they insist on the idea that social problems are social constructions, while on the other they base their argumentation on some "true" social conditions, what Woolgar and Pawluch criticize as "ontological gerrymandering."

Since then constructionist approaches have become highly differentiated (Holstein & Miller 2003; Loseke & Best 2003), but at the same time the idea of constructivism has become less clear and is very often reduced to the perspective that social problems are the result of the active behavior of interested groups and collective actors, who define and produce certain issues in a specific form. This is nowadays common sense within sociology; the main point of discussion is whether these "productions" are based on cultural and social resources that are rooted in social structures and embedded in social change in modern societies. But even if social problems are social constructions – as actually all objects of sociological research are – they are no less real in their consequences and effects; it makes no sense to talk about social problems as social constructions in opposition to "real" social problems. In this sense, the opposition of "objectivist" and "constructivist" approaches within the sociology of social problems is misleading, as it assumes that "objectivist" approaches are not able to analyze social problems as processes of cultural production.

As a reaction to the sociological hegemony of structural functionalism in the 1950s and 1960s, the constructionist perspective has been developed on the microsociological grounds of symbolic interactionism, ethnomethodology, and phenomenology. The European tradition of the social question as sociopolitical and macrosociological projects concerning social conditions and processes of social integration and social inclusion seems to have been completely dismissed from the American sociology of social problems.

SEE ALSO: Anomie; Deviance; Deviance, Constructionist Perspectives; Social Disorganization Theory; Social Movements; Social Pathology; Social Problems, Politics of

REFERENCES AND SUGGESTED READINGS

Albrecht, G., Groenemeyer, A., & Stallberg, F. (Eds.) (1999) *Handbuch Soziale Probleme*. Westdeutscher Verlag, Opladen.

Best, J. (Ed.) (1989) *Images of Issues: Typifying Contemporary Social Problems*. Aldine de Gruyter, New York.

Best, J. (Ed.) (2001) *How Claims Spread: Cross-National Diffusion of Social Problems*. Aldine de Gruyter, New York.

Best, J. (2004) Theoretical Issues in the Study of Social Problems and Deviance. In: Ritzer, G. (Ed.), *Handbook of Social Problems*. Sage, London, pp. 14–29.

Bourdieu, P. (Ed.) (1993) *La Misère du monde*. Seuil, Paris.

Castel, R. (2002 [1995]) *From Manual Workers to Wage Laborers: Transformation of the Social Question*. Transaction, New Brunswick, NJ.

Cohen, A. K. (1959) The Study of Social Disorganization and Deviant Behavior. In: Merton, R. K., Broom, L., & Cottrell, L. S., Jr. (Eds.), *Sociology Today: Problems and Prospects*. Basic Books, New York, pp. 461–84.

Dorvil, H. & Mayer, R. (Eds.) (2001) *Problèmes sociaux*. Vol. 1: *Théories et méthodologies*. Vol. 2: *Études de cas et interventions sociales*. Presses de l'Université du Québec, Sainte-Foy.

Durkheim, É. (1902 [1893]) *De la division du travail social: étude sur l'organisation des sociétés supérieurs*, 2nd edn. Alcan, Paris.

Edelman, M. (1977) *Political Language: Words that Succeed and Policies that Fail*. Academic Press, New York.

Holstein, J. A. & Miller, G. (Eds.) (2003) *Challenges and Choices: Constructionist Perspectives on Social Problems*. Aldine de Gruyter, New York.

Loseke, D. R. & Best, J. (Eds.) (2003) *Social Problems: Constructionist Readings*. Aldine de Gruyter, New York.

Manis, J. G. (1974) The Concept of Social Problems: Vox Populi and Sociological Analysis. *Social Problems* 21(3): 305–15.

Merton, R. K. (1971) Social Problems and Sociological Theory. In: Merton, R. K. & Nisbet, R. A. (Eds.), *Contemporary Social Problems*, 3rd edn. Harcourt Brace Jovanovich, New York, pp. 793–845.

Merton, R. K. (1976) The Sociology of Social Problems. In: Merton, R. K. & Nisbet, R. A. (Eds.), *Contemporary Social Problems*, 4th edn. Harcourt Brace Jovanovich, New York, pp. 3–43.

Mills, C. W. (1943) The Professional Ideology of Social Pathologists. *American Journal of Sociology* 49: 165–80.

Ritzer, G. (Ed.) (2004) *Handbook of Social Problems: A Comparative International Perspective*. Sage, Thousand Oaks, CA.

Rosenquist, C. M. (1995) The Moral Premises of Social Pathology [1940]. In: Rubington, E. & Weinberg, M. S. (Eds.), *The Study of Social Problems: Seven Perspectives*, 5th edn. Oxford University Press, New York, pp. 45–50.

Rubington, E. & Weinberg, M. S. (Eds.) (1995) *The Study of Social Problems: Seven Perspectives*, 5th edn. Oxford University Press, New York.

Spector, M. & Kitsuse, J. I. (1987 [1977]) *Constructing Social Problems*, 2nd edn. Cummings, Menlo Park, CA.

Woolgar, S. & Pawluch, D. (1985) Ontological Gerrymandering: The Anatomy of Social Problems Explanations. *Social Problems* 32(3): 214–27.

social problems, politics of

Axel Groenemeyer

SOCIAL PROBLEMS AND THE POLITICAL SYSTEM

In the sociology of social problems, surprisingly little attention has been paid to the state and the political system. Given the central importance of social problems as public issues and claims for political action and public policy, and their role in shaping social and political change, this neglect seems all the more surprising. Especially in newer US versions of constructing social problems – very often seen as the only valuable sociological perspective on social problems – they have been defined either as "claims-making activities" of collective social actors (Spector & Kitsuse 1987 [1977]) or as public discourses and rhetoric narratives (Ibarra & Kitsuse 1993). If the struggle for social problems were merely cognitive and symbolic, then the conflicts about their definition would have to be understood only as a system of contested narratives that result in new narratives. In these perspectives, references to power and conflict and to the political functioning of public issues and collective actors have attracted only little attention. But if the construction of social problems is based in the interests and values of collective actors, we have to ask how the struggle for public attention relates to the distribution of material, political, and symbolic resources. In this perspective, already the social construction of social problems by collective actors in society has to be analyzed as a social conflict, and in this sense as a fundamental political issue.

Not only in Western European democratic welfare states but also in all modern societies with a state-centered political system in general, the state has the legitimate monopoly on the means of violence and is the main target of "claims-making activities." Even if the treatment or claims of solutions for social problems sometimes are addressed to public associations or by private enterprises, the political system and the state are the ultimate arbiters of allocating valued goods and resources. The political system and the state are constituted by a system of organizations and institutions that shape public issues and social problems by providing opportunities for claims, by selecting and establishing administrative categories as quasi-official definitions of social problems, and by giving them the cultural power or by actively producing and promoting some definitions of social problems for political means and according to criteria of political strategies. In this sense, the political system is not only the more or less passive target of social claims and protest or the neutral arbiter of conflicting social groups within society, but is also a central, powerfully organized actor in the process of production and construction of social problems.

In modern societies, state activities and interventions accompany citizens throughout life, and from birth to death their lives are regulated and controlled by the state to an extent unknown in preceding epochs of social development, which allows us to speak of modern societies as politically framed and regulated societies. Despite processes of globalization and internationalization, nation-states and nationally organized political systems are still the main actors integrating societies with the claim of legitimate monopoly on the means of violence over a specified territory based on a unified system of laws and on the monopoly of taxation, which ensures the ability to make and enforce

binding decisions over citizens and social groups in the society.

This minimal definition of the state – classically developed by Max Weber (1972 [1922]) – refers to the state function of ensuring security of social and economic exchange. Ensuring social order could thus be seen as the fundamental purpose of states. If this function is not effectively fulfilled, states dissolve, as many examples of societies in civil wars show. In this context, the idea of security and of claims concerning security and safety became a central topic of claims-making activities.

However, the ideas of what should be the objective of states always have been highly contested. Whereas in liberal political discourses of the nineteenth century only the task of providing public safety and security of the law to ensure economic exchange was an accepted guideline for state activities, the idea of social security was developed, especially in Western European democracies, as an institutionalized and accepted state idea in the twentieth century. Very often nowadays these fundamental state functions are supplemented by the task of preserving natural resources and international obligations.

The ideas of the state constitute a political regime, institutionalized and organized within a nation-specific political system of representation, including established political parties, interest groups, and associations as well as social institutions and local organizations, with institutionalized access to centers of political decision-making. These qualifications of the state and the political system provide a cultural and political frame of reference for addressing specific social problems to the political system; the national traditions of state ideas, organized in nation-specific institutions, constitute a political opportunity structure for claims-making activities. The analysis of these processes demands a comparative perspective on social problems (Kitschelt 1986; Kriesi et al. 1992; Jenkins & Klandermans 1995).

In a classical liberal political perspective, social problems are interpreted as "inputs" for the political system, which raises the question of influence and power of social actors to promote specific definitions of social problems and to make them political issues. The success of establishing a specific definition of social problems or claims in this perspective depends on the capacity of mobilizing power and influence by social actors. The social issues and claims then are accepted, rejected, canalized, or redefined by specific mechanisms of selection and filters of the organizations within the political system. In this perspective, the success of claims-making activities depends on the system and forms of the organizations of the political system itself (Dunleavy & O'Leary 1987; Parsons 1995). System-theoretic approaches especially have radicalized this view in insisting that the political system constitutes an autonomous self-referential system with one set of rules, criteria, and rationalities that directly could not be influenced from outside. The classic model of social problems as "inputs" of the political system is supplemented or substituted by the idea of "withinputs," i.e., social problems may be discussed as social issues in public, but the organizations of the political system construct and produce them according to their own political rationalities, which are not directly linked to public definitions of the social problems and most of the time are completely different from what has been claimed by collective actors in society previously.

This perspective gives way to the idea that the organizations of the political system not only are passive receivers of social inputs from the society, but also are actively engaged in producing and constructing public issues and social problems according to the criteria of the system, like election strategies, gaining public support in interorganizational or party concurrence or accumulation of resources by presenting specific problem-solving capacities. In this sense, social problems are not only "inputs" or "withinputs" of the political system, but are "outputs" as well. Besides this, political interventions in social problems and their institutionalization not only produce official definitions of social problems, but also give rise to often unintended consequences for other systems and social groups as well as new social problems and opportunities for mobilization for claims in other areas. After all, it is important to notice that these consequences also appear when the politics of social problems are not directly addressed toward solving or at least treating social problems but merely follow a strategy of "symbolic politics" involving mobilizing

internal resources or political support from outside the political system.

Political theories that analyze the processes of "input" formations by social influence and power as well as the structure of the political system as "political opportunity structure" are treated at length elsewhere, so this entry will be limited to factors and explanations that are specific to the politics of social problems (see also Groenemeyer 1999; Blackman 2004).

FORMS OF CLAIMS AS POLITICAL ISSUES

The structure of the political system and its organizations influences the opportunity for collective actors in society to find support for social problems and public claims within the political system. Even if a public claim is accepted as a political issue, the political arena in which it is placed is important, as are the political actors and the strategy by which it is placed (Hilgartner & Bosk 1988). Becoming a political issue also means that the way in which the social problem has been constructed concerning its causes and effects – the "diagnostic frame" – as well as its solutions – the "prognostic frame" – are in some way compatible with the rationalities and interests of at least some organizations of the political system (Benford & Snow 2000).

There have been some attempts to develop typologies of claims and empirical hypotheses to treat these questions. One approach refers to the distributions of costs and utilities of public claims (Wilson 1973). Claims that benefit only a small group while their costs affect larger groups probably have less chance of being treated by the political system. This is one reason for the fact that collective actors are obliged to construct social problems in such a way that a significant number of people, or indeed the whole population, are affected by them.

Another classical approach developed by Lowi (1972) differentiated among "distributive policy issues," which refers to issues that demand the distribution of new resources, "redistributive policy issues" that demand a new distribution of limited resources, "regulatory policy issues" referring to claims without any distribution of resources, and "constituent policy resources," for which new political institutions must be established or already established institutions have to be reorganized. Each policy claim that, for example, affects an established distribution of limited resources could increase the level of conflicts with other social or political actors, whereas regulatory policies or interventions without direct distribution of resources are very often open for symbolic politics.

Another set of hypotheses, first proposed by Cobb and Elder (1972), concerns the process of political agenda building and the quality of claims: the higher the degree of specificity of an issue, its scope of social significance and its temporal relevance, and the lower its degree of complexity and the less it corresponds with preceding issues (categorical precedence), the higher is its chance of being accepted as a political issue within the political system.

However, these typologies are less clear when confronted with empirical cases of political issues and social problems. The specific form of the "diagnostic frame" of a social problem, and whether this suggests a "distributive" or a "redistributive" policy, is not a quality of the issue itself but the object of conflict about its meaning. In this sense, the form or quality of a public issue or social problem is itself the consequence of conflicts in the process of social and political constructions by the institutions of the political system.

The public construction of a social problem could intersect with other public issues resulting in a kind of concurrence on the scarce goods of public and political attention. Processes and strategies of mobilization for specific issues thus can also actively be used by political organizations to reduce the potential for conflict of other issues to ensure the capacities of the political system against public claims (Hilgartner & Bosk 1988). Besides this, it is also possible that some issues are linked together under a main topic to increase the possibility of public and political mobilization. But in general, the possibility of gaining public and political attention has to be seen as a fragile public good that has to be used with caution to avoid a "problematizing overdose."

These typologies and hypotheses are just some examples of what the sociology of social problems has to address concerning the agenda building of social problems in the political system. Currently, there seems to be no theory unifying this knowledge from different subfields of sociology, such as political sociology, the sociology of social movements, or the sociology of agenda setting by the media.

Whereas in these approaches the central questions are based on the idea of political opportunity structures provided or blocked for public issues and social problems by the structure of the political system, the organizations of the state and the political system also play an important role in actively constructing social problems, independently of claims-making activities within society. It is important to separate the processes of gaining attention and support for claims being constructed outside the political system from those processes of constructing social problems by the political system.

THE POLITICAL USE OF SOCIAL PROBLEMS

Whereas in modern societies with a welfare state the political program of coping with social problems seems to be institutionalized, at the same time, the extent of social problems seems to increase. Obviously, the majority of the most pressing social problems in modern societies are not solved without bringing the social and political order into a dangerous instability. This is not only a problem of the political system's regulating capacities but is also a central characteristic of pluralized modern societies. Very often, one solution for a social problem leads to other social problems and conflicts in other areas, or the institutionalization of one solution leads to increased political opportunities for new mobilizations and discourses on new problematic issues. Obviously for the political system, social problems fulfill other purposes than being solved, and political programs and intervention could fulfill other functions than those formulated in political discourses about social problems.

Modern societies and their political systems have developed a remarkable potential for survival and stability, despite the amount of unsolved problems, conflicts, and crises. If conflicts and social problems in modern societies normally are highly interconnected and collective actors are highly organized, then one would have to question the mechanisms of the political system to handle these claims without losing its own organizational capacities of action. As regards public claims and conflict, the political system in modern societies has normally developed a flexibility that also allows it to handle conflicts and claims strategically (Nedelmann 1986).

The acceptance of a specific definition of a social problem and its institutionalization not only means the success of public mobilization, it also constitutes resources for further conflicts about social definitions and constructions of issues. In this perspective, the success of political programs and interventions with regard to solving social problems directly very often seems to be of secondary importance. Especially in times of limited resources for social problem solving, and with regard to a constant overload of public claims, symbolic and rhetorical forms of political discourse assume central importance in the political system for ensuring its autonomy and its own capacities for action.

Starting from the assumption that the construction of social problems is always embedded in changing "cultural frames" (Tarrow 1998; Groenemeyer 2001) that give meaning to public claims, then regulating meanings and interpretive frames is one possibility for the organization of the political system to react to public claims. In this sense, the cultural base and definitions of social problems could become the object of strategic politics, and the political restructuring and manipulation of the cultural and moral milieux of social problem constructions could ensure the regulation of social conflicts. This cultural control of public claims could follow different strategies: manipulating the knowledge base of problem constructions so that alternative ideas and interpretations relating to the public claim are publicly disseminated; altering the affective loading of social problem constructions by increasing the complexity of issues and placing them within a scientific or professional agenda, which allows the reframing of morally loaded issues into technical ones; depoliticization of a social problem by denying its putative negative consequences; strategic mobilization of specific moral social contexts in order to mediate potential conflicts through reputable social institutions (e.g., religion or the courts). Support of

countermovements allows political organizations to weaken public support for a social problem and to become arbitrator in a social conflict. Publicly denying the reputation of claims-makers and their putative representatives also weakens public support for social problems; this could also be achieved by reframing a public claim into a private issue affecting specific interest groups. Sometimes it is also possible to decrease the public visibility of social problems to impede public mobilization.

The rhetoric and symbolic construction of politics refers to the manipulation of symbols signaling that something is done about the social problem: "words that succeed and policies that fail" (Edelman 1977; see also Gusfield & Michalowicz 1984). This does not mean that a definition of social problems and policies is possible without reference to symbols and specific cultural constructions, but these constructions are always the object of a cultural conflict before the background of specific interests, values, and strategic considerations, and the organizations of the political system and the state are at the forefront of this struggle with their own criteria and rationalities. The aim of sociological analyses always has to be the critical disentanglement of the involvement of specific interests and values in this political process of constructing social problems.

Whereas in this perspective interactions between collective actors in society and the organizations of the political system in gaining and preventing access to political decisions are at the center of sociological analyses, it is also important to mention the role of political organizations and the state in actively constructing social problems for their own purposes. The political acceptance of and support for specific constructions of social problems is not always the result of pressure from below. Very often it is the state, and not collective actors in societies, that plays the central role in promoting mobilizations and moralizations of social problems. Even in other policy areas, the integration of political organizations with collective social actors and professional associations in society has reached an extent where it becomes difficult to disentangle who is the central actor in constructing specific social problems.

Institutionalized arrangements and law-based procedures of the state not only present legal rules and patterns of resource distribution for social claims on social problems but also participate in creating a symbolic order and a system of reference for social constructions of social problems. The central aspect in this realm is the political construction of legal and administrative categories that entitle specific social groups to claims according to administrative and official definitions of the problem, or that allow the use of state power to control them. These administrative categories, i.e., of the penal law or of social benefits, create their own social reality, whose character as a consequence of a struggle over meaning and definition has been become invisible. Nevertheless, they also constitute an important and powerful cultural and social frame of reference for standards of normality and reasonableness relating to alternative social constructions of the social problem. In this sense, the sociology of social problems always has to be a historical and sociological analysis of the politics of social problems and their social control.

SEE ALSO: Agenda Setting; Framing and Social Movements; Political Opportunities; Politics; Social Movements; Social Problems, Concept and Perspectives; State

REFERENCES AND SUGGESTED READINGS

Benford, R. D. & Snow, D. A. (2000) Framing Processes and Social Movements: An Overview and Assessment. *Annual Review of Sociology* 26: 611–39.

Blackman, T. (2004) Social Problems and Public Policy. In: Ritzer, G. (Ed.), *Handbook of Social Problems: A Comparative International Perspective.* Sage, Thousand Oaks, CA, pp. 47–66.

Cobb, R. W. & Elder, C. D. (1972) *Participation in American Politics: The Dynamics of Agenda Building.* Johns Hopkins University Press, Baltimore.

Dunleavy, P. & O'Leary, B. (1987) *Theories of the State: The Politics of Liberal Democracy.* Macmillan, Basingstoke.

Edelman, M. (1977) *Political Language: Words that Succeed and Policies that Fail.* Academic Press, New York.

Groenemeyer, A. (1999) Die Politik sozialer Probleme. In: Albrecht, G., Groenemeyer, A., & Stallberg, F. W. (Eds.), *Handbuch Soziale Probleme.* Westdeutscher Verlag, Opladen, pp. 111–36.

Groenemeyer, A. (2001) Von der Sünde zum Risiko? Bilder abweichenden Verhaltens und die Politik sozialer Probleme am Ende des Rehabilitationsideals. In: Groenemeyer, A. (Ed.), *Soziale Probleme – Konstruktivistische Kontroversen und gesellschaftliche Herausforderungen,* Vol. 12. Centaurus, Herbolzheim, pp. 146–82.

Gusfield, J. R. & Michalowicz, J. (1984) Secular Symbolism: Studies of Ritual, Ceremony, and the Symbolic Order in Modern Life. *Annual Review of Sociology* 10: 417–35.

Hilgartner, S. & Bosk, C. L. (1988) The Rise and Fall of Social Problems: A Public Arena Model. *American Journal of Sociology* 94(1): 53–78.

Ibarra, P. R. & Kitsuse, J. I. (1993) Vernacular Constituents of Moral Discourse: An Interactionist Proposal for the Study of Social Problems. In: Miller, G. & Holstein, J. A. (Eds.), *Constructionist Controversies: Issues in Social Problem Theory.* Aldine de Gruyter, New York, pp. 21–54.

Jenkins, J. C. & Klandermans, B. (1995) *The Politics of Social Protest: Comparative Perspectives on States and Social Movements,* Vol. 3. University of Minnesota Press, Minneapolis.

Kitschelt, H. P. (1986) Political Opportunity Structures and Political Protest: Anti-Nuclear Movements in Four Democracies. *British Journal of Political Science* 16: 57–85.

Kriesi, H. et al. (1992) New Social Movements and Political Opportunities in Western Europe. *European Journal of Political Research* 22: 219–44.

Lowi, T. J. (1972) Four Systems of Policy, Politics and Choice. *Public Administration Review* 32: 298–310.

Nedelmann, B. (1986) Soziale Probleme und Handlungsflexibilität. Zur Bedeutsamkeit des kulturellen Aspekts sozialer Probleme. In: Oppl, H. & Tomaschek, A. (Eds.), *Soziale Arbeit 2000, Band 1: Soziale Probleme und Handlungsflexibilität.* Lambertus, Freiburg i. Br., pp. 13–42.

Parsons, W. (1995) *Public Policy: An Introduction to the Theory and Practice of Policy Analysis.* Edward Elgar, Aldershot.

Spector, M. & Kitsuse, J. I. (1987 [1977]) *Constructing Social Problems,* 2nd edn. Cummings, Menlo Park, CA.

Tarrow, S. (1998) *Power in Movement: Social Movements and Contentious Politics.* Cambridge University Press, Cambridge.

Weber, M. (1972 [1922]) *Wirtschaft und Gesellschaft. Grundriss der verstehenden Soziologie,* 5th rev. edn. J. C. B. Mohr, Tübingen.

Wilson, J. Q. (1973) *Political Organizations.* Sage, Beverly Hills.

social psychology

Anne F. Eisenberg

Social psychology is an approach to understanding human social relations that focuses on individuals and how their interactions impact social organizations and social institutions. Social psychological scholarship includes a wide range of theoretical perspectives, methodological tools, and substantive applications originating from diverse intellectual schools such as sociology, psychology, economics, education, and business. Contemporary social psychology is best understood by examining its range of theoretical perspectives, methodological tools, and substantive foci.

THEORETICAL PERSPECTIVES AND THEORETICAL IDEAS

The breadth and range of theoretical ideas in contemporary social psychology reflects the diverse intellectual origins of the various perspectives and approaches. Early discussions of social psychology focused on these distinctive intellectual origins by highlighting the differences between psychological and sociological social psychology. This representation of the field has been critiqued for its perpetuation of artificial boundaries that overlook significant connections between the shared subject matter of sociology and psychology. In 1980 Sheldon Stryker articulated three "faces" of social psychology: psychological social psychology, sociological social psychology, and symbolic interactionism. While each perspective represents unique theoretical ideas, they also inform one another and serve to create a comprehensive understanding of individual interactions and how they impact on the groups to which we belong as well as the environments in which group interactions occur. All three perspectives share a focus on the individual and individual interactions as the explanatory factor for all aspects of social life, such as the creation of stable group structures and the formation of successful social movements. The three theoretical perspectives in social psychology, known more generally as cognitive and intrapersonal, symbolic interactionist,

and structural, each represent different origins and intellectual affiliations and maintain a focus on different aspects of the individual and society.

Cognitive and Intrapersonal Social Psychology

Cognitive and intrapersonal social psychology originated with the work of experimental psychologists in Germany such as Wilhelm Wundt in the mid-nineteenth century and focuses on understanding how internal processes affect an individual's ability to interact with others. The internal processes most studied in this perspective are cognitive (memory, perception, and decision-making) and physiological (chemical and neural activity). Each approach examines a different aspect of how interactions are affected by these internal processes. The underlying basis of the cognitive and intrapersonal approach centers on how individuals store information in the brain in the form of schemas. Schemas represent the way in which people identify objects in their environment by labeling them, which then allows the objects to be categorized. The use of schemas allows individuals to process billions of bits of information from the environment, which then enables them to easily engage in interactions. The more accurate individuals' understanding of any given social situation, as determined by how well they label and categorize it based on information from the environment, the more successful and easy will be the interaction. The cognitive and physiological approaches in this perspective explore different aspects of the impact of schemas on interactions.

The cognitive approach examines how brain activity specifically associated with memory, perception, and decision-making processes affects an individual's ability to understand the information necessary for engaging in successful interactions. Additionally, this approach also explores how variations in cognitive processes lead to differences in individuals' ability to interact. The study of memory examines how people categorize events, situations, and others they have encountered previously, helping researchers understand the type of schema constructed and used in particular groups, cultures, and settings. Studying memory allows researchers to directly explore the connection between interactions and how they are labeled. Take as an example a person entering a room and observing two people interacting with each other. If she labels and categorizes the interaction as a romantic interlude between lovers, she is less likely to interrupt than if the interaction is labeled and categorized as a conversation between co-workers. Further, if the person entering the room identifies and labels one of the actors as a close friend, her interactions with the two people will be different than if they were simply co-workers. Theoretical ideas associated with understanding schemas and memory include stereotypes (the actual categories used in labeling people and situations) and self-fulfilling prophecy (where we act in such a manner as to confirm our initial impressions of people). In studying perception, researchers are interested in exploring how people's interpretation of information from the environment affects their interactions with others. The study of perception examines the meanings individuals associate with the categories in which events, situations, and people are placed. Key theoretical ideas associated with this approach to studying interactions from a cognitive social psychological perspective include the attributions people make when judging others' actions and the outcomes of those actions, and the errors in the attributions people make. Finally, decision-making research explores how schemas, memories, and perceptions contribute to the ways in which people make decisions ranging from what to wear in the morning to the level of risk they are willing to take in any situation. The decisions made directly impact whether or not an individual is willing to interact with one person as opposed to another, as well as the quality of the interactions that do occur.

While the cognitive approach examines those internal processes that impact on whether or not an interaction will occur as well as the quality of the interaction once it does occur, the physiological approach explores the ways that specific biological and chemical processes affect individuals' ability to create adequate and useful schemas, use their memory, perceive things accurately, and then make relevant decisions. The physiological approach in the cognitive and intrapersonal perspective is not normally included in discussions about social psychology, as at first glance its theoretical focus does not directly relate to social interactions. However, recent developments in this approach link it much more closely with the cognitive approach, thereby warranting its inclusion in this discussion. Cognitive and behavioral psychologists, along with neuroscientists, have conducted what are called "animal studies" for over 100 years. The goal of such research is to more accurately explain how particular chemical and biological processes directly impact on cognitive functioning. Technology is now allowing physiologically based researchers in psychology, neuroscience, and sociology to measure and examine the relationship between these chemical and biological processes and associated actions and interactions in humans. Early research in this area focused on non-human species due to the ethical issues associated with human experimentation. Newer technologies, such as the portable electroencephalogram (EEG) and the functional magnetic resonance imager (fMRI), allow researchers to study neural and chemical responses to individuals' actions and interactions. The implication is that such technologies will allow social psychologists to more accurately and directly measure social interaction.

Symbolic Interactionism

Symbolic interactionism originated from the work of George Herbert Mead and his students at the University of Chicago as well as the work of pragmatic philosophers. While Mead was formally associated with the psychology and philosophy departments at the University of Chicago, his classes on social psychology and social philosophy attracted a large number of students from the fledgling sociology department. One of the sociology students, Herbert Blumer, coined the term symbolic interactionism and other sociology students were instrumental in publishing Mead's ideas, after his death, concerning the individual. These ideas center on his discussions of the mind (what makes humans uniquely social creatures), self (how we become uniquely social creatures), and society (how our interactions are affected by social institutions). Mead wrote extensively about issues concerning more macro-level social

social psychology

phenomena such as the role of government in funding education and the role of education for socialization, but he is mainly recognized for his contributions to symbolic interactionism. Generally, the symbolic interactionist perspective in social psychology focuses on studying the meanings that underlie social interactions in terms of how they are created, how they are maintained, and how we learn to understand such meanings. Additionally, theorists writing within this perspective argue that individual interactions lead to the creation of formal social organizations and social institutions. Therefore, to understand society, it is necessary to understand the interactions that shape it and maintain it. There are three main theoretical approaches in the symbolic interactionist perspective, symbolic interactionism, phenomenological, and life course, each of which examines different aspects of these meanings and the self on which they are derived.

The symbolic interactionism approach is most closely related to Mead's original ideas concerning social psychology and focuses on exploring how meanings are created and maintained within social interactions with the self as the basis for such interactions. The underlying theme of this approach is that individuals create and manage meanings through the roles and identities they hold. It is important to note that each individual holds any number of roles and identities, depending on the people with whom they interact as well as the environment in which they find themselves. Classical symbolic interactionist studies include the work of Herbert Blumer, Charles Horton Cooley, and Manford Kuhn. Blumer elaborated on Mead's discussion of the social self examining itself as an object outside the individual, while Cooley focused on explaining the process in which the self recognizes itself as an object. Kuhn's discussions explored different dimensions of the self as a way of explaining individuals' ability to take on a variety of identities, depending on the situation and the other actors involved. Contemporary developments of these ideas are found in the work of Erving Goffman, Peter Burke, Sheldon Stryker, and their associates and students. Goffman's discussion of dramaturgy and the presentation of self, among other ideas, examined the ways in which individuals identified the role held in any particular

interaction and the expectations associated with that role. Stryker and others explored how roles are linked to individuals' identity and how meaningful these identities are to people. Burke and associates proposed a more formal theoretical explanation of how different parts of the self are associated with specific identities people hold.

The phenomenological approach originated from European sociology and philosophy, emphasizing the meanings themselves and how such meanings reflect unstated normative expectations for interactions. The underlying theme of this approach is that language, verbal and non-verbal, represents the informal and formal rules and norms that guide social interactions and structure society. The early work in phenomenology, as represented by the ideas of Alfred Schutz and Harold Garfinkel, differentiated between different aspects of how people create social reality as well as operate within already existing social reality. Schutz examined how language and communication represented an intersubjective process of reality creation and maintainance, while Garfinkel explored how people managed reality through the development of ethnomethodology. Contemporary developments of phenomenology are found in the work of theorists such as Howard Becker, Peter Berger, and Douglas Maynard. Through a series of studies, Becker explored the way individuals' interpretations of social interactions and social experiences reflect their own experiences and unspoken norms for behavior. Berger, along with Thomas Luckmann, is considered the American introduction to Schutz's ideas and phenomenology. Equally important, Berger and Luckmann also clearly demonstrated how everyday interactions and language create seemingly formidable social institutions and organizations. Finally, Maynard further developed ethnomethodology by focusing on conversation analysis as a way of understanding how social talk creates and represents reality.

The life course approach in symbolic interactionism focuses on how humans learn the meanings associated with interactions throughout their lifetime and the stages that reflect such learning processes. The underlying theme of this approach is that the norms, rules, and values that guide interactions and shape society change throughout individuals' lives, especially as they move into different social positions and environments. As a relatively newer approach in the symbolic interactionist perspective in terms of identifying as a unique approach, the key ideas can be traced to Mead's discussion about socialization and Georg Simmel's ideas about interactions within and between groups. Mead explained how humans become uniquely social creatures in his lectures about the self, where he describes a three-stage process (preparatory, play, and game) for humans to learn the norms, rules, and values of the group into which they are born. He argued that by the end of this process, people will have a fully developed self. Simmel's discussions concerning interactions and groups examined how individuals' interactions with one another changed as group size, group composition, and social environment changed. Contemporary theorists such as Glenn Elder, Roberta Simmons, and Dale Dannefer, and their students and colleagues, build on these ideas in similar ways. First, the contemporary approaches assume that socialization is a lifelong process that changes as individuals change. Second, theorists in the approach examine both individual-level factors and societal factors that contribute to the socialization process. Elder has focused on how socialization is consistent across cohorts of people, varying only in qualitative aspects related to differences in environments and resources. Simmons has examined how the socialization process itself varies depending on individuals' stage in life, and Dannefer has explored the ways in which groups with which people are associated play an important role in their continuing socialization throughout life.

Structural Social Psychology

Structural social psychology originated with the work of economists, psychologists, and sociologists interested in explaining social interactions more formally and mathematically with the goal of creating testable hypotheses. Structural social psychology assumes that social actors are driven by rational concerns centered on maximizing rewards and minimizing punishments. Another related assumption is that interactions based on rational calculations result in formally structured individual, group, and institutional interactions. This approach is related to cognitive and intrapersonal social psychology in the focus on developing formal theories to explain interactions and creating specific hypotheses for testing in experimental situations. More contemporary work in structural social psychology uses more diverse methods such as survey research and participant observation techniques. There are three main theoretical programs that represent this approach: power, exchange, and bargaining studies; social influence and authority studies; and status characteristics, expectation states theory, and social network studies. Each set of studies focuses on different aspects of describing and explaining the underlying structure of social interactions.

Power, exchange, and bargaining studies explore how social interactions can be described as exchanges between social actors with the assumption that individuals rationally calculate the costs and benefits associated with any particular interaction. Exchange studies began with the work of George Homans, Richard Emerson, and Peter Blau. Homans argued that interactions can be better understood as exchanges whereby actors engaged in interactions that brought specific benefits. His work also explored how the need for such exchanges leads to equilibrium between actor and the idea of distributive justice. Blau further specified this work by focusing on the social aspects of such exchanges in terms of how they rely on trust between actors that each person will fulfill his or her unspecified obligations. While Homans, Blau, and others discussed that power arises out of exchanges and that power is not necessarily equally distributed among actors, Emerson and his colleagues specifically explored the development of power, how it is managed by actors, and how power differentiation affects the possibility of future exchanges. More contemporary work building on these ideas is bargaining studies, which specifies how different types of power differentiation affect the bargaining that then leads to actual exchanges. Lawler and colleagues explored the type of bargaining that occurs prior to exchanges, as well as how differing levels of power among participants affect such bargaining. Molm and her colleagues examined how exchanges varied based on inequality of participants and the availability of other sources and actors.

The second set of studies that can be categorized under the structural social psychology perspective focuses on social influence and authority. The underlying theme of these studies is that there are several factors that encourage people to be influenced by others, including the status or position others hold in comparison to themselves and group encouragement of conformity. The classic studies in social influence include Stanley Milgram's research that examined the effect an authority figure in a position of power has on individual compliance. Milgram found that individuals overwhelmingly obeyed requests to complete a task that ostensibly required hurting another person. Seymour Asch's studies of group conformity demonstrated that individuals willingly change their answer or opinion when a majority in the group indicates a different answer or opinion. Contemporary ideas build on this base by examining the varying conditions under which compliance to authority occurs, and to what degree others can influence attitude change.

Status characteristics, expectation states, and social network studies examine how social interactions are based on socially and culturally derived expectations for behavior that people have of one another. These socially and culturally derived expectations are associated with assumed predictions concerning how successfully any individual will contribute to an exchange, or interaction, process. These predictions then determine which individuals are likely to be given the most opportunities for interaction and influence in a group. Originating with the work of Berger, Zelditch, and associates, status characteristics theory explicitly identifies two main types of social characteristics that have expectations for behavior associated with them – diffuse (such as race, gender, class, and ableness) and specific status characteristics (such as job experience, education, and relevant skills) – and it is usually associated with groups working toward achieving specific goals. Expectation states theory argues that those people who hold diffuse and specific status characteristics evaluated as more likely to successfully contribute to achieving group goals will be given a greater number of opportunities for interaction as well as greater social influence among other group members. More to the point, theorists argue, and have successfully demonstrated, that

specific and stable hierarchical group structures develop based on these expectations. Contemporary work in this area includes specifying the degree to which different status characteristics affect expectations as well as how such expectations develop and whether actors perceive that such expectations are just. Social network theory and elementary theory build on the ideas of these different approaches in structural social psychology by specifically examining how an actor's position, relative to another, affects social influence processes as well as the stability of group structure. The underlying assumption of social network theory is that social influence, power, and bargaining are all affected by the way in which actors are networked to one another. Markovsky, Willer, Cook, and their students and associates examine different aspects of how actors are connected to one another and how that affects other social processes.

As the above discussion indicates, the three theoretical approaches in social psychology all examine different aspects of individuals, their interactions, and how their interactions affect groups. Cognitive and intrapersonal social psychology focuses on internal processes that impact whether, and how successfully, interactions occur among people. The insights provided by this perspective help to explain how actors create meanings concerning interactions that then lead to the creation and maintenance of specific social institutions and organizations, as discussed by symbolic interactionists. Finally, structural social psychologists examine how the fluid interactions of symbolic life create formal group structures that then impact on people's interactions.

METHODOLOGICAL TOOLS

Social psychologists use a variety of research methods with which to explore and explain specific aspects of social interactions as well as test specific hypotheses concerning these social interactions. Each of the three different theoretical perspectives in social psychology is often associated with utilizing only one type of research method – for example, symbolic interactionists are usually associated with using interpretive methods similar to those used by anthropologists, and cognitive and intrapersonal as well as structural social psychologists are usually associated with using experimental methods. Such a simplistic view of social psychological research does not adequately reflect the breadth and diversity of research undertaken. The diversity of methods used by social psychologists and how they are used to examine specific aspects of individuals, their interactions, and the broader social environment in which they occur highlights the development of a mature scholarly area.

Interpretive Methods

Also known as "qualitative methods," interpretive methods are used to gain an in-depth understanding of social psychological phenomena, ranging from individuals to their interactions to the groups and environments in which such interactions occur. The type of interpretive research methods used by social psychologists include participant observation, unobtrusive research utilizing archival documents as representation of individuals and their interactions, and more extensive field research similar to ethnographic research commonly used by anthropologists.

Participant observation research in social psychology ranges from purely observational research to full participation while observing in selected social settings and environments. All types of participant observation research require the researcher to actually engage the setting in which the social interactions occur. Purely observational research consists of the researcher studying interactions in the environment in which they occur without the researcher becoming an active participant in the interactions themselves. An example of purely observational research in social psychology includes Kleinman's study of a holistic health center in which she attended all meetings, parties, and retreats as an observer only. The other way of doing participant observation research is to study interactions in the environment in which they occur with the researcher becoming an active participant on some level, ranging from engaging in interactions with the actors involved while identifying as a researcher who then exits the environment to return to her own environment, to the researcher who becomes a full

participant in the interactions and the environment without identifying as a researcher. In this approach to participant observation research, the researcher conducts short-term research as a fully immersed member of the interactions and environment, and then exits the environment after having conducted the research. An example of participatory participant research includes Adler and Adler's research with a men's college basketball team in which Peter Adler served as the coach and was an active participant of the group.

Unobtrusive research includes a variety of methods ranging from utilizing archival documents to in-depth case studies as well as personal experience, such as in autoethnography. These different methods share two commonalities; first, they focus on understanding how meaning is created and interactions are structured by examining representations of human relations and social life. Second, unobtrusive research does not require interaction with the social setting and its actors in order to understand the creation and maintenance of meanings underlying social life. Unobtrusive research is particularly useful when it is difficult to gain access to the individuals, interactions, or groups being studied. An example of such research includes Gubrium's study of the diaries of Alzheimer's patients and their caretakers.

Ethnographic research, typically associated with anthropological research, consists of the researcher becoming a full participant with the actors being studied in their environment for a lengthy period of time. Anthropologists argue that a minimum of one year is needed before the researcher becomes fully informed and aware of all aspects of the groups and culture being studied. Sociologically based ethnographers tend to focus on the quality of immersion in the culture and group being studied, arguing that deep immersion is possible in six months. While there are disciplinary and intellectual differences in determining what constitutes ethnographic research, identifying the purpose of ethnographic research is consistent among researchers. The purpose of ethnographic research is to gain an in-depth understanding of the unspoken and unwritten norms and values that guide individual interactions and group relations. Ethnographers agree that such understanding is only possible by literally living the life of the actors being studied. An example of ethnographic research in social psychology includes Maynard's study of prosecuting and defense attorneys.

Experimental Methods

Experimental methods in social psychology serve as a way to test specific theoretical hypotheses as well as to explore particular aspects of interactions. There are a range of experimental methods, from the quasi-experimental study which has fewer strict controls to the fully experimental study with formal control and experimental groups, as well as full control of all variables associated with the study. The full experimental study includes characteristics such as pre-study surveys, control and experimental groups, and post-study surveys. These studies are most concerned with testing specific theoretically derived hypotheses and thus seek to control all extraneous factors that may impact on the interactions. To do so, full experimental studies rely on random assignment of participants to the different conditions with the goal of increasing internal validity and reliability. Examples of such studies include the status characteristics and expectations studies conducted by Berger, Zelditch, Ridgeway, Hauser, and Lovaglia. The quasi-experimental study is a variation of the full experimental study whose goal includes theory testing as well as exploratory research. There are a range of variations of the full experimental study, from the more naturalistic studies where naturally occurring experimental and control groups are treated as case studies to the experimental studies where control groups and pre-study surveys are not used.

Survey and Interview Methods

Survey and interview methods used by social psychologists serve to test specific hypotheses as well as explore specific aspects of interactions, groups, and social institutions. Similarly to other areas in sociology, social psychologists use a range of survey tools and interview techniques including self-completing surveys, those conducted by the researcher, and in-depth interviews. It is worth noting that social psychologists often use surveys and interviews as

the second approach as a way of engaging in methodological triangulation. For example, pre- and post-study surveys are used in experimental studies where the participant will either complete the survey without the researcher present or be asked a series of questions by the researcher. Surveys are also used as the primary data collection tool for studies that examine self-esteem and self-concept definitions. Interviews are used by social psychologists to collect information to supplement field studies as well as to serve as the primary source of information. For example, in studying social networks of scientists, Eisenberg conducted in-depth interviews with participants who also completed a sociometric survey on their own. Many of the early studies conducted by the Chicago School of Sociologists used interviews and surveys to gain an in-depth understanding of issues such as inequality and racism.

SUBSTANTIVE FOCUS

Beginning students in social psychology are often surprised to learn the degree to which understanding the individual and her or his interactions allows them to also explain group dynamics, behavior in social organizations, whether a social movement will be successful, and the seeming durability of social institutions. Similar to the discussion of the methodological tools used by social psychologists, it is simplistic to describe the field as focused only on the individual. The substantive focus of social psychological theory and research ranges from individuals and their interactions to the groups in which they engage to the social organizations and social institutions that shape these interactions.

Individuals and Interactions

The study of individuals and their interactions seeks to explore, understand, and explain different aspects of the unique social quality of people. The range of topics includes understanding why prejudice and discrimination exist, the best way to persuade and influence people, and those topics typically found in social psychology texts – interpersonal attraction, helping and altruism, and aggression. The cognitive and intrapersonal perspective explains that the schemas individuals use to process the billions of bits of information from the environment are socially and culturally determined. Therefore, individuals' understanding of their environment is going to reflect the biases they are taught and their experiences. In other words, prejudice and discrimination are the direct result of the schemas people use and their perception of these different categories. This information, also, provides some indication of how to decrease prejudice and discrimination by challenging people's schemas and perceptions. The symbolic interactionist perspective in social psychology provides useful knowledge with which to understand interpersonal attraction. To ensure that their interactions are easy, people normally associate with individuals for whom the meanings of their roles and identities are similar to their own. Similarly, it has been shown that helping and altruistic behavior is likely to occur in situations when doing so strongly reflects individuals' values without causing them any harm. Finally, aggression can be explained by studying the power structure that exists among groups of people.

Other substantive topics include examining self-concept and self-esteem, which can affect whether girls suffer from anorexia nervosa, as well as emotions and how they impact interactions. Whether discussing married partners' perceptions of one another or predicting who might become foreperson of a jury based on group members' status characteristics, social psychology allows people to understand the interactions in which they engage as well as others' actions and interactions. More to the point, understanding the social psychology underlying individuals and their interactions allows people to become far more effective in their own lives. The teacher who avoids comparing students on the basis of their status characteristics is going to be a more effective teacher. The manager who successfully works with all of his or her employees regardless of the power differential between them will be more successful. And, the people who actively engage with people unlike themselves are less likely to be prejudiced. Finally, interactions are important in all areas of social life and can determine the success of an encounter between, for example, doctor/patient, teacher/student, parent/child, and among friends.

Groups

The study of groups highlights that the group environment affects individuals and their interactions. The range of topics for studying groups includes group conformity, group performance, and intergroup relations. Group conformity is a compelling topic as it addresses issues such as why people are willing to engage in illegal activity as part of a gang initiation ritual, or why college students binge drink to the point of death. Symbolic interactionist theory explains how interactions become habitualized within groups, thus creating norms and values for other interactions. Structural theory explains how these habitualized interactions are based on fulfilling members' needs as well as the stable power structure that will develop in the group. The needs to be fulfilled can range from material needs, such as actually being rewarded something tangible by the group to which individuals are associated, to social acceptance by other group members. Structural theory also explains whether any particular group is going to successfully complete its task due to the types of people in the group and the skills they bring to the group. For example, Olson discussed how the factors that affect individual interactions also affect group cohesiveness and therefore group performance. The group that is more cohesive is more likely to succeed at specific tasks than the group that is not as cohesive.

The broad substantive topic of intergroup relations examines how groups interact with one another and the factors that predict whether such interactions will be successful. Specific examples of such relations are the relationship between rival gangs, or even rival sports teams at any level. Some of the factors that impact on intergroup relations include the cohesiveness of each group as well as the strength of the group's social identity. Some researchers have explored the ability of gangs to avoid violence in terms of the social networks that connect the two groups and the similarity of each group's social identity. Symbolic interactionist theory identifies the importance of understanding the meanings other groups share and how they reflect a particular group culture. Structural theory explains why groups would want to cooperate with one another in terms of the resources to be shared and exchanged. The ability to understand group dynamics in terms of social networks, power distribution, and conformity allows individuals' to more successfully shape group interactions. Groups are important for the social psychologist because they represent the first place where we learn the meanings associated with social life as well as develop a fully developed self and self-identity.

Social Organizations and Social Institutions

In understanding individuals and their interactions, as well as how group membership affects those interactions, social psychologists are able to discuss and study social organizations and institutions. Some of the topics examined include social movements and whether they are successful as well as the idea of deviance as a social institution. Studying collective behavior and social movements includes examining motivations for joining in collective behavior as well as the organizations that develop out of members' interactions. Symbolic interactionist theory explains how people are more likely to join in collective action or a social movement when their own ideology and values match those of the social movement. Additionally, structural theory argues that people become members of a social movement when it provides a benefit beyond any specific cost. In other words, people's participation in a social movement is determined by social psychological factors.

Social psychological theory also explores social organizations as a form of social network that represents the likelihood of success for the organization. Symbolic interactionist theory explains how institutionalization formalizes the patterns of interaction among members of the organization or social institution, and structural theory discusses how power is distributed within the organization or institution. Understanding the social psychological factors that create, shape, and maintain organizations and institutions allows individuals to more successfully work within them. For example, the person who studies both the informal and formal social networks of the organization is more likely to successfully obtain the necessary resources for his or her tasks. Researchers have used these ideas to explain why some organizations will have a harder time surviving in a competitive market than other organizations. Finally, symbolic interactionists offer a compelling argument that since social organizations and social institutions are created out of individual interactions, it is possible to change such organizations and institutions.

CONCLUSION

Social psychology is an area of sociology that focuses on individuals and their interactions to explain a broad range of social relations and social phenomena. The area is diverse in terms of the theoretical ideas explored, the methodological tools used to test and explore these ideas, and the substantive foci that extend beyond individual interactions. In understanding the social psychology of everyday life, we can also create new realities in terms of ourselves, the groups to which we belong, and the social organizations and institutions that constrain our actions.

SEE ALSO: Asch Experiments; Attribution Theory; Blau, Peter; Blumer, Herbert George; Collective Action; Conversation Analysis; Cooley, Charles Horton; Decision-Making; Elementary Theory; Emerson, Richard M.; Ethnomethodology; Expectation States Theory; Experimental Methods; Goffman, Erving; Homans, George; Identity Theory; Interaction; Mead, George Herbert; Microsociology; Milgram, Stanley (Experiments); Norms; Observation, Participant and Non-Participant; Organizations as Social Structures; Phenomenology; Power, Theories of; Psychological Social Psychology; Role; Schütz, Alfred; Self; Self-Fulfilling Prophecy; Simmel, Georg; Social Cognition; Social Identity Theory; Social Movements; Social Network Analysis; Social Psychology, Applied; Socialization; Stereotyping and Stereotypes; Survey Research; Symbolic Interaction; Values

REFERENCES AND SUGGESTED READINGS

Adler, P. A. & Adler, P. (1987) Role Conflict and Identity Salience: College Athletes and the Academic Role. *Social Science Journal* 24: 443–55.

Asch, S. E. (1955) Opinions and Social Pressure. *Scientific American* 193: 31–5.

Berger, J., Cohen, B. P., & Zelditch, M., Jr. (1972) Status Characteristics and Social Interaction. *American Sociological Review* 37: 241–55.

Berger, J., Ridgeway, C. L., Fisek, M. H., & Norman, R. Z. (1998) The Legitimation and Delegitimation of Power and Prestige Orders. *American Sociological Review* 63: 379–405.

Berger, P. & Luckmann, T. (1966) *The Social Construction of Reality.* Anchor, New York.

Best, J. B. (1995) *Cognitive Psychology,* 4th edn. West, Minnesota.

Blau, P. (1964) *Exchange and Power in Social Life.* Wiley, New York.

Blumer, H. (1969) *Symbolic Interactionism: Perspective and Method.* Prentice-Hall, Englewood Cliffs, NJ.

Burke, P. J. & Reitzes, D. (1981) The Link Between Identity and Role Performance. *Social Psychology Quarterly* 44: 83–92.

Bush, D. & Simmons, R. (1990) Socialization Processes Over the Life Course. In: Rosenberg, M. & Turner, R. (Eds.), *Social Psychology: Sociological Perspectives.* Basic Books, New York.

Cook, K. (Ed.) (1987) *Social Exchange Theory.* Sage, Thousand Oaks, CA.

Cooley, C. H. (1902) *Human Nature and the Social Order.* Scribner, New York.

Elder, G. H., Jr. (1975) Age Differentiation and the Life Course. In: Inkeles, A., Coleman, J., & Smelser, N. (Eds.), *Annual Review of Sociology* 1.

Festinger, L. (1957) *A Theory of Cognitive Dissonance.* Stanford University Press, Stanford.

Gecas, V. & Burke, P. J. (1995) Self and Identity. In: Cook, K. S., Fine, G. A., & House, J. S. (Eds.), *Sociological Perspectives on Social Psychology.* Allyn & Bacon, Boston.

Goffman, E. (1959) *The Presentation of Self in Everyday Life.* Anchor/Doubleday, New York.

Gubrium, J. (1988) The Social Preservation of the Mind: The Alzheimer's Disease Experience. *Symbolic Interaction* 9: 37–51.

Kleinman, S. (1991) Fieldworkers' Feelings: What We Feel, Who We Are, How We Analyze. In: Shaffir, W. B. & Stebbins, R. A. (Eds.), *Experiencing Fieldwork: An Inside View of Qualitative Research.* Sage, Thousand Oaks, CA, pp. 184–95.

Lawler, E. J. & Bacharach, S. B. (1987) Comparison of Dependence and Punitive Forms of Power. *Social Forces* 66: 446–62.

Markovsky, B. (1998) Social Network Conceptions of Group Solidarity. In: Doreian, P. & Fararo, T. J. (Eds.), *The Problem of Solidarity.* Gordon & Breach, New York, pp. 343–72.

Maynard, D. (1984) *Inside Plea Bargaining.* Plenum, New York.

Milgram, S. (1963) Behavioral Study of Obedience. *Journal of Abnormal and Social Psychology* 67: 371–8.

Ridgeway, C. & Berger, J. (1986) Expectations, Legitimation, and Dominance Behavior in Task Groups. *American Sociological Review* 51: 603–17.

Stryker, S. (1980) *Symbolic Interactionism: A Social Structural Version.* Benjamin Cummings, Menlo Park, CA.

Zelditch, M., Jr. & Walker, H. A. (1984) Legitimacy and the Stability of Authority. In: Lawler, E. J. (Ed.), *Advances in Group Processes,* Vol. 1. JAI Press, San Diego.

social psychology, applied

Elmar Schlueter and O. Christ

As it is commonly used, the term applied social psychology refers to the application of social psychological methods, theories, principles, or research findings to the understanding or solution of social problems (Oskamp & Schultz 1998). Applied social psychology encompasses a range of theories intended to address the mechanisms of various social problems. In this regard, it can be considered a theoretically based form or praxis. One of the the most influential figures in this area is Kurt Lewin with his studies on intergroup relationships and the processes underlying intergroup conflict. But historically, applied social psychology has even deeper roots. Early applications of social psychological concepts can be traced to the experimental studies of Hugo Münsterberg (1914). Further senior pioneers of the field are Floyd Allport (1920) with his research on group influences, Muzafer Sherif's (1935) work on social norms, or Richard LaPierre's (1934) classic study on the relations between attitudes and behaviors.

The field of applied social psychology overlaps to a large extent with the disciplinary characteristics of social psychology, broadly defined as the scientific study of how people perceive, influence, and relate to other people. Notwithstanding this similarity, differences in the motivations underlying research in basic social psychology on the one hand, and research in applied social psychology on the other, can be detected.

Usually, research in basic social psychology starts with the primary intention to solve problems of theoretical significance only. For fulfilling this purpose, studies in basic social psychology can, but by no means need to, refer to applied settings. In short, basic social psychology's primary interest aims at solving theoretical questions and thereby contributing to the general knowledge base of social psychology.

Contrary to this, the focus in the realm of applied social psychology is toward the solution or improvement of real-life problems, as expressed above. Within this problem-oriented framework, theoretical perspectives are first and foremost utilized in order to achieve applied social psychology's major goal to improve certain social conditions. Nevertheless, in several instances pragmatic applications of social psychological concepts have led to important new theoretical insights as well. For instance, classical social psychological concepts such as the definition of the situation, self-fulfilling prophecy, or relative deprivation, or even influential theoretical approaches like dissonance theory originate from applied research settings. It is this reciprocal relationship between theory and problem orientation that Lewin (1951) emphasized: "Many psychologists working in an applied field are keenly aware of the needs for close cooperation between theoretical and applied psychology. This can be accomplished in psychology, as it has been in physics, if the theorist does not look towards applied problems with high-brow aversion or with a fear of social problems, and if the applied psychologist realizes that there is nothing so practical as good theory." Even today, the hybrid character of applied social psychology as being theory-based but oriented toward social problems can be seen as one of its most important features.

Studies applying social psychological knowledge address an increasingly broad range of substantive real-life topics. To illustrate this point, social psychological concepts have frequently been used for improving social problems tied to intergroup conflict, pro-environmental behavior, or health. More recent examples illustrating the ongoing expansion of the discipline focus on the consequences of part-time work or on the question of why some people adapt earlier to Internet usage than others. Frequently, such studies cross-cut academic boundaries to neighboring disciplines like applied sociology, criminology, communication sciences, or social work, to name just a few.

Because of the broad and heterogeneous substantive areas of application, it comes as no surprise that researchers using social psychological concepts revert to a wide methodological spectrum. For example, experimental and survey research, observational studies, and – to a somewhat lesser extent – qualitative approaches rank among the commonly used methodologies in the realm of applied social psychology. However, a key methodological characteristic of applied social psychology today is its focus on field research. Within such field settings, the modal research designs utilize experimental, quasi-experimental, or program evaluation approaches. The prominence of field research in applied social psychology can directly be attributed to the discipline's orientation toward real-life problems and the requirements stemming therefrom. For instance, sufficient external validity of study findings will often be achieved more easily in close to real-life situations as given in field studies than in the laboratory (for comprehensive overviews on the methods used in applied social psychology, see Edwards et al. 1990).

Three examples of applied social psychology follow. These examples refer to such substantial domains as the environment, intergroup relations at both national and international levels, and health behavior.

Typically, applications of social psychological knowledge with regard to environmental problems are concerned with the advancement of sustainable relations between human behavior and environmental contexts. This domain covers a broad range of issues such as common property resource management, effects of environmental stressors and problems, the characteristics of restorative environments, or the promotion of durable conservation behavior. Thus, in times of scarce resources and massive environmental pollution, using social psychological knowledge can provide answers on how to develop an ecologically sustainable society (Oskamp 2000). Many studies in this field explore environmental attitudes, perceptions, and values as well as devise intervention techniques for promoting environmentally appropriate behavior. Commonly used social psychological theories in this area are dissonance theory, norm activation theory, or the theory of planned behavior. Methodologically, such studies often draw upon various research methods ranging from experimental designs to large-scale survey studies.

A classic domain of applied social psychology is the field of intergroup relations and intergroup conflict. Several studies demonstrate the influence of social psychological concepts on programs for the improvement of intergroup relations, at both national and international levels (Pettigrew 2001). One famous illustration of the impact of applied social psychology on social change is racial desegregation in American schools. In the early 1950s, Kenneth Clark and other colleagues from social psychology drew up a social science appendix to the plaintiff's brief to the Supreme Court showing the detrimental effects of school segregation on colored children. This appendix was supported by the signature of 32 experts from different scientific fields. As a direct consequence, the US Supreme Court based its 1954 decision against school segregation explicitly on this report. Later evidence clearly showed the long-term positive consequences of school desegregation, even with sometimes mixed short-term effects. One particularly important social psychological concept in the field of school desegregation is the contact hypothesis (Allport 1954). Allport emphasized that intergroup contact per se would not necessarily improve intergroup attitudes and relations. Rather, only under certain conditions (e.g., equal status within the contact situation for members of all groups, cooperative rather than competitive activities) would contact lead to such positive effects. Although sometimes criticized, the contact hypothesis guided to a large extent research and practice of school desegregation. Further examples of applied social psychology in intergroup settings refer to third-party intervention in intergroup conflict such as the Israeli–Palestinian conflict in the Middle East. A figure of central influence here is Herbert Kelman, who has applied social psychological knowledge and methods to the peacebuilding process between Israelis and Arabs. For conflict resolution, he used small group

workshops in order to stress interactive problem solving (Kelman 1997). These workshops represent unofficial meetings between representatives with political influence (e.g., representatives of the parliament, journalists, and writers) from both conflict parties. The major intention of these workshops is, on the one hand, to cause individual change at the level of the workshop participants. Such processes can lead to attitude change, a more differentiated view of the other conflict party, a better understanding of the conflict dynamic, and new ideas for conflict resolution. On the other hand, in the long run, the workshops should cause structural changes at the macro level by influencing political debates and decision processes with new insights and ideas.

Another realm of applied social psychology is public health. Usually, such research focuses on people's beliefs, attitudes, and behavior that affect their health. Important social psychological concepts in the field of health are perceived control, stress and coping, social support, attribution, and self-esteem. These concepts stem from a broad range of classical social psychological theories like dissonance theory, attribution theory, social learning theory, and attitude–behavior theories, e.g., the theory of planned behavior (Taylor 2002). Many applied studies in this field deal with coping with chronic illnesses like cancer or HIV/AIDS. For example, applied social psychological research has shown that different patterns of coping with a chronic illness have either positive or negative impacts on the course of the illness.

Beside the examples presented, applied social psychology covers areas such as media and the Internet, sport psychology, organizational and industrial psychology, communication, and mediation. Comprehensive reviews of the substantive areas of applied social psychology are given in Oskamp and Schultz (1998) and in Sadava and McCreary's edited collection, *Applied Social Psychology* (1997).

Another important aspect of the field refers to the question of which basic principles guide researchers' decisions on which social conditions are considered problematic or not. As Sadava (1997) notes, such decisions refer ultimately to the personal values of those engaged with the application of social psychology. Notably, this value dependency implies that chances for a general consensus on which social situations need improvement are rather small. In modern societies, several different value systems usually exist, and often these value systems are diametrically opposed to one another. Therefore, different value perspectives might lead to opposing views on the need for improvement for one and the same topic. For instance, the desire to reduce environmental pollution by increasing the price of gasoline versus the freedom of consumers to choose the transport system they prefer, to name just one example. Applied social psychology is clearly not value free and classifications of which social conditions should be improved and which not are to a great extent contingent on the personal values of those applying social psychology.

However, the role of personal values in applied social psychological research requires further attention. Even if values might well influence the choice of a research problem, researchers need to be careful not to let them influence the objectivity of their research and the resulting findings. Clearly, this applies both to the methods to be used and to the interpretation of the empirical results.

Another aspect of the discipline refers to the normative question of on what grounds social psychology should be applied. One prominent perspective among scholars is to consider applied social psychology first and foremost as an empirical science. From this position, applied social psychology simply cannot respond to questions with a prescriptive character. But on a more general level, at least two alternative positions have been proposed. On the one hand, scholars advocate the well-being of the individual as an ultimate aim of all efforts in applied social psychology. Others have criticized this perspective for disregarding the possibility that the maximization of well-being for some individuals might well exert disadvantageous effects on the well-being of other individuals. To overcome this dilemma, the suggestion has been made that the well-being of humankind should be regarded as an appropriate goal of applied social psychology. A comprehensive approach to the question of which normative principles should guide the application of social psychological knowledge emphasizes that social psychology is most beneficial when it acts upon the recognition of every individual's dignity, when

respect, acceptance, and charity to one another are an integral part of it, and when applied social psychology likewise negates all forms of violence. This suggestion does not only refer to the purpose of applied social psychology. It also explicitly points to the process of how applied research in social psychology should be conducted. Perhaps this essentially humanistic suggestion fulfills its purpose best when it is considered as providing some form of general orientation rather than a definitive normative guideline.

SEE ALSO: Lewin, Kurt; Social Change; Social Problems, Concept and Perspectives; Social Psychology

REFERENCES AND SUGGESTED READINGS

Allport, F. H. (1920) The Influence of the Group Upon Association and Thought. *Journal of Experimental Psychology* 3: 159–82.

Allport, G. W. (1954) *The Nature of Prejudice*. Addison-Wesley, Reading, MA.

Bierhoff, H. W & Auhagen, A. E. (2003) *Angewandte Sozialpsychologie: Eine Standortbestimmung*. In: Auhagen, A. E. & Bierhoff, H. W. (Eds.), *Angewandte Sozialpsychologie*. Beltz, Weinheim.

Brown, R. & Gaertner, S. (Eds.) (2001) *Blackwell Handbook of Social Psychology: Intergroup Processes*. Blackwell, Oxford.

Edwards, J. D., Tindale, R. S., Heath, L., & Posavac, E. J. (Eds.) (1990) *Social Influence Processes and Prevention: Social Psychological Applications to Social Issues*, Vol. 1. Plenum, New York.

Kelman, H. (1997) Group Processes in the Resolution of International Conflicts: Experiences from the Israeli–Palestinian Case. *American Psychologist* 52: 212–20.

LaPierre, R. T. (1934) Attitudes vs. Action. *Social Forces* 13: 230–7.

Lewin, K. (1951) *Field Theory in Social Science: Selected Theoretical Papers*. Ed. D. Cartwright. Harper & Row, New York.

Münsterberg, H. (1914) *Psychology, General and Applied*. Appleton, New York.

Oskamp, S. (2000) A Sustainable Future for Humanity? *American Psychologist* 55: 496–508.

Oskamp, S. & Schultz, P. W. (1998) *Applied Social Psychology*, 2nd edn. Prentice-Hall, Upper Saddle River, NJ.

Pettigrew, T. F. (2001) Intergroup Relations and National and International Relations. In: Brown,

R. & Gaertner, S. (Eds.), *Blackwell Handbook of Social Psychology: Intergroup Processes*. Blackwell, Oxford.

Sadava, S. W. (1997) Applied Social Psychology: An Introduction. In: Sadava, S. W. & McCreary, D. R. (Eds.), *Applied Social Psychology*. Prentice-Hall, Upper Saddle River, NJ, pp. 1–9.

Sherif, M. (1935) A Study of Some Social Factors in Perception. *Archives of Psychology* 27(187): 53–4.

Taylor, S. E. (2002) *Health Psychology*, 5th edn. McGraw-Hill, New York.

social services

Lena Dominelli

Social services are provisions that respond to the needs of individuals, groups, or communities to improve social, emotional, and physical well-being not supplied by carers who are kin. Social services are difficult to define, but constitute part of the welfare state that is the domain of social work and its practitioners – social workers and those who assist them in their tasks, social care workers, home helpers, and a range of others who work to provide services backed by society including the state, voluntary agencies, and commercial enterprises. They cover all client groups across the life course – children, families, older people, disabled people, mentally ill people, offenders of all ages, in diverse institutional settings or local communities.

Social workers as the practitioners primarily responsible for delivering personal social services to individuals and families do so in a variety of settings. They have devised forms of practice to enable them to work effectively with service users. These have focused largely on casework, including clinical social work, psychological social work, and psychiatric social work; groupwork; and community work undertaken in a range of service settings within institutions and communities. Paying professionals to minister to individual need has its origins in the Gilbert Act or Poor Law Amendment Act of 1782, which approved of salaried "guardians of the poor."

Service delivery involves a range of providers – the state, voluntary agencies, religious authorities, and commercial enterprise, comprising the mixed economy of care. There was little coherence amongst these providers until the Seebohm Reforms of the 1970s ended this fragmentation through the creation of large bureaucratic organizations that unified provisions in social services departments under municipal control. Statutory services today come under the auspices of local authorities, but their dominance has been undermined by the marketization of service provision under the 1990 National Health Service and Community Care Act and the more recent reorganization of social services by client groups. These developments reinforce earlier competition between health and social work for authority over the provision of social services. The 1990 Act began the modern privatization of social service provision, initially for older people requiring institutional care. However, the quasi-market has now expanded to include services to children and offenders. The forces of globalization and the General Agreement on Trades and Services (GATS), which requires the privatization of health, social services, and education globally, will reinforce marketization.

Meanwhile, the number of multinational companies, especially American ones entering the British scene, has risen dramatically during the early years of the twenty-first century. As the private social agencies of old, these new ones are likely to cover the entire spectrum of social service provision. But there is one change that is likely to take place in the not too distant future: private social agencies are likely to assume delivery for the bulk of social service provision rather than simply supplement public ones as they did shortly after the implementation of the Beveridge Report, 1948 and the Seebohm Report, 1968. The proposed sale of 1,100 units on the Octavia Hill Housing Estate to non-state buyers in 2006 is symbolic of this move and the attendant loss of social housing for low-income earners is unlikely to be covered by either private or not-for-profit providers. Many sales of public assets have transferred funds from the public to the private sector.

That these social services are about caring for and about people raises a number of tensions that complicate their delivery. Amongst these are the care–control dilemmas; lack of professional status of those delivering services and authority; charitable giving or societal entitlements; state or market providers; and public or personal responsibility for their provision. Service boundaries are amorphous and constantly shifting as society changes the remit of those responsible for providing services by altering legislative fiats and social policies.

Social services provision has threads of continuity and discontinuity that can be traced back through centuries of the history of social work. This history is contested as struggles to delineate its boundaries as other professions including health claim some of the territory. Differences of opinion about causation and responsibility divide understanding of need and service provision. Commitment to interagency working means that different professionals can intervene in any one particular setting or client and without necessarily agreeing about the best way forward.

HISTORICAL CONTINUITIES AND DISCONTINUITIES

The reasons that people require social services have focused on personal inadequacies or structural causes. The former blame individuals for their plight; the latter examine social causation. Social changes rooted in economic exigencies have undermined the capacity of the family and kin to provide caring services for members requiring them. Although the monied classes have been able to purchase their social services in the marketplace, those on low incomes have done without unless kin, charities, or the state have assisted them. Charitable or philanthropic benevolence that relies on individuals and religious institutions has been meeting the needs of some in poverty for a period. This help has been predicated upon notions of personal pathologies and divided claimants into deserving and undeserving ones. The former have received stigmatized and inadequate forms of support; the latter have had to fend for themselves.

These tensions go back to the Elizabethan Poor Law, 1601, when the modern nation-state first began to provide meagre services through workhouses and outdoor relief. This institutionalized residential requirements and demanded

work in return for assistance. The workhouse and living in a particular parish have been consigned to the dustbin. Expressed differently, these conditions remain while being revised to accord with contemporary structures, expectations, and language. Only citizens can expect social services provisions under legally specified criteria and bureaucratically defined procedures. Additionally, services are conditional on the claimant agreeing to train to become more employable before an application for help is considered. While unemployed people have always been required to seek work, the state under New Labour has increased surveillance on compliance. It is now planning to introduce similar requirements on disabled people on Incapacity Benefit to reduce the number of claimants. These arrangements reflect a persistent strain between family and state or community support. The failure of such policies to move large numbers of people out of poverty and into gainful employment rather than the ranks of the working poor has been apparent since the New Poor Law Reform Act of 1834.

State social workers have constantly been caught in the trap of supporting individuals by stretching inadequate resources, balancing personal pathology with social causation, apportioning multiple loyalties amongst a range of stakeholders with diverse interests, trying to ensure that individuals acquire a sense of belonging and contributing to and having a place in society. Supporting individuals and groups in a holistic way is becoming increasingly difficult in a contemporary neoliberal context.

Professionals were not the only ones who challenged the assignation of claimants into deserving and undeserving categories. Claimants demanded change. Even in the days of poor relief, those receiving assistance demanded responses to need on their terms and recognition of the interplay between social causes and personal predicament when individuals could not help themselves. For example, pressures for changes that acknowledged such analyses amongst war veterans resulted in the Speenhamland Act of 1795 that enabled receipt of relief from the then local state in their own homes. Yet, Adam Smith, author of *Wealth of Nations*, like Charles Murray later, argued cogently for a laissez-faire approach to welfare to ensure that the state let the economy or market provide the mechanisms whereby individuals met their welfare needs. Smith's view was subsequently challenged by Karl Marx, who held capitalist social relations responsible for exploiting people to such an extent that they would be unable to rise out of poverty simply by selling their labor. Thus, demands for publicly provided social services were a byproduct of an economic system that constantly yielded people in need or casualties unable to care for themselves, and that remains the case today.

The Marxist tradition was taken forward by Christian socialists. Eventually, Marx's arguments underpinned the position of Fabian socialists, particularly Beatrice and Sydney Webb, who played leading roles in establishing the welfare state under the aegis of the Labour Party. This provided free school meals and medical care for school children, pensions to cover declining earnings in old age, and unemployment insurance to cover people lacking paid work. The commitment to social insurance retained the link between paid employment and entitlements and, based on men's employment careers, these promoted an institutional base that excluded those with different patterns of waged work and impacted badly on women, "black people," lone parents minding children at home, and those unable to work due to physical impairment or old age.

These debates continue to the present day and there is little agreement about whether individuals looking after their own welfare needs or state provisions produce the best outcomes. The American new right popularized arguments that the welfare state and social work "do-gooders" who side with clients are responsible for inducing a "culture of welfare dependency" that saps claimants of initiative and motivation to look after themselves. The failure of this approach is evidenced by large numbers of Americans living in poverty, without health insurance and unable to meet their own care needs. Additionally, inadequate public social services ensure that claimants are ping-ponged between different agencies as individuals go from one to another to secure services. Charles Murray, encouraged by the Thatcher government, attempted to make similar arguments in the UK. Yet, its welfare traditions and composition of claimant classes differ widely from those of the US.

The history of social work claimants shows an undying link between poverty, poor health, and individual hardship. The inability of individuals to pull themselves up by the bootstraps was exposed as far back as the nineteenth century by reformers like Edwin Chadwick, whose demands for public hygiene measures did more to enable working-class people to enjoy healthier lives, survive longer, and earn more money than self-help. However, the issue of low pay persists and is a key mechanism in excluding poor people from the marketplace where welfare resources can be purchased today.

The tension between personal pathological approaches and structural approaches to social services provision played a key role in the establishment of professional social work in the late Victorian era. The Charity Organization (COS) endorsed individual pathological explanations through its commitment to casework interventions that sought to establish a scientific basis to the social work profession. It was challenged by the Settlement Movement, which focused on structural explanations, particularly unemployment, low pay, and poor health amongst working-class people. The latter was responsible for replacing the "lady bountiful" image of social work with one of social responsibility in which workers cooperated with poor people, and lived and worked amongst them. The efforts of Octavia Hill, Samuel Barnett, and Henrietta Rowlands (Barnett's wife) promoted structural understandings of poverty and worked to meet needs within this framework. Social researchers including Charles Booth after 1886 provided empirical evidence of the role of economic change in locking people into poverty, presenting a picture that remains familiar.

More evidence of the link between structural economic decline and poverty appeared at the beginning of the twentieth century in the Poor Law Commission Report of 1905 and was highlighted when British mines failed to compete with better-equipped American ones that produced more tonnage per laborer. These arguments tally with findings made in the 1970s by Community Development Projects (CDPs), which were successors to the Settlement Movement's community-based approaches to poverty alleviation. CDPs exposed the ties between deindustrialization and deprivation in working-class communities throughout the UK, a debate now reinforced by critics of the New Deal and demands for human rights and social justice-based anti-oppressive social services.

Social services have provided a fraught and contested area of service provision and delivery that is full of contradictions that exclude marginalized groups who have little purchasing power on the market. Today's shift toward private provisions enables a new breed of entrepreneurs, many from overseas, to make fortunes out of a sector that the welfare state had once sought to remove from its ambit. Whether it can provide for those on low incomes or who are outside of the waged workforce remains to be seen. It has been unable to do so in the past and its failure was responsible for the development of welfare state-based social services in the first place. Meanwhile, as the rich enjoy the best social services the market can provide, poor people make do.

SEE ALSO: Capitalism, Social Institutions of; Caregiving; Carework; Civil Society; Gender, Work, and Family; Health and Medicine; Nation-State; Organizations; Practice; Social Network Analysis; Social Pathology; Social Work: History and Institutions; Social Work: Theory and Methods; Sociology in Medicine; Welfare Dependency and Welfare Underuse

REFERENCES AND SUGGESTED READINGS

Adams, R. (2003) *Social Policy and Social Work*. Palgrave, London.
Banks, S. (2002) *Values and Ethics in Social Work*. Palgrave, London.
Cnan, R., Wineburg, R. J., & Boddie, S. G. (1999) *The Newer Deal: Social Work and Religion in Partnership*. Columbia University Press, New York.
DuBois, B. & Krogsrud, K. M. (2002) *Social Work: An Empowering Practice*, 4th edn. Allyn & Bacon, London.
Dominelli, L. (1997) *Sociology for Social Work*. Macmillan, London.
Dominelli, L. (2004) *Social Work: Theory and Practice for a Changing Profession*. Polity Press, Cambridge.
Hill, M. (2000) *Local Authority Social Services*. Blackwell, Oxford.
Kendall, K. (2000) *Social Work Education: Its Origins in Europe*. CSWE, Alexandria, VA.
Kufeldt, K. & McKenzie, B. (Eds.) (2003) *Child Welfare: Connecting Research, Policy, and Practice*. Wilfred Laurier University Press, Waterloo, Ontario.
Payne, M. (2005) *Modern Social Work Theory*. Palgrave, London.

social structure

Stephen Hunt

The term social structure denotes a more or less enduring pattern of social arrangements within a particular society, group, or social organization. Nonetheless, despite its widespread usage, there is no single agreed concept of social structure that exists in sociology or related disciplines. An early attempt to theorize the notion of social structure was seen in the work of Lévi-Strauss, the French social anthropologist, who attempted to discover the universal rules that underpin everyday activities and custom through cultural systems (Lévi-Strauss 1967). Within sociology, however, the term has been employed in various ways according to the theoretical approach within which the concept is used. For instance, in one of the earliest uses of the term, Herbert Spencer related "social structure" to increasing differentiation and specialization of the biological organism as society "evolved."

Historically speaking, sociological theories exploring the concept of social structure are generally associated with macro or structural perspectives oriented to understanding the nature of social order, and in doing so stand in stark contrast to social action (or micro) approaches which seek meaning and motivation behind human social behavior. Social structural analysis has tended to be identified with two schools of thought. First, it is associated with the theoretical speculations of structural functionalists such as Talcott Parsons, for whom the major concern of the sociological enterprise was to explain how social life was possible. For Parsons (1951), the answer lay in the establishment of a certain degree of order and stability which is essential for the survival of the social system. Parsons identified cultural values as the key to stability. Value consensus provides the foundations for cooperation, since common values produce common goals. The value system permeated social structures which, in Parsons's schemata, constituted a fourfold system of functional prerequisites which give way to universal arrangements oriented towards adaptation, goal attainment, integration, and pattern maintenance. In Parsons's structuralist theory the notion of social structure also implied that human behavior and relationships are, to one degree or another, "structured," particularly in terms of rules, social status and roles, and normative values. Social behavior and relationships are thus patterned and recurrent. It follows that the structure of society can be seen as the sum total of normative behavior, as well as social relationships which are governed by norms.

Although remaining popular among North American academic schools of sociology for some time, social structure theory as espoused by structural functionalism was subject to scathing criticism from the late 1960s, not least of all in its apparent teleology and its normative theoretical stance, as well as strong objections related to the logic of the biological analogy. One observation was that social structures do not possess the relatively identifiable boundaries that clearly exist with biological organisms, nor do they possess the precisely identifiable homeostatic processes of organic structures. Although remaining largely within the structural functionalist school, Robert Merton also challenged what he termed the "postulate of universal functionalism," in particular, that all structures necessarily have positive social functions. Indeed some, notably religion, could have neutral or even detrimental effects on the social system (Merton 1949).

In Western Europe, in particular, functionalism has long been rivaled by Marxist schools of structuralism. Marx (1964) himself considered the importance of what he identified as the two dimensions of the social structure: the overarching economic substructure (or base) which for the most part determined the social superstructure comprised of the various institutions of society. In turn, the "hard" interpretation of Marxist thought came to identify the processes of dialectical and historical materialism as forging social structures concomitant with the economic base. In this elucidation the social superstructure was transformed into social structures that enforced class subjugation and exploitation.

The work of Gramsci, among others, weakened the hard interpretation of Marxist analysis and took it away from the significance of the economic base to the ideological and cultural superstructure, while retaining the notion of the hegemonic structural power of the state. Also further reducing the hard interpretation of Marx's structuralism was the school of thought typified by Poulantzas. In his poststructural theorizing the state is said to be "relatively" antonymous. According to Poulantzas, ruling interest is not necessarily *directly* related to the actions of the state at any given time. Rather, the state, in capitalist democracies, retains the flexibility and autonomy to sustain the politico-economic order in the long term and thus preserve the semblance of pluralism.

The emphasis on "agency," as compared to the rather deterministic framework of social structuralism, provided an alternative approach to understanding social behavior. Here the emphasis was on the motivational capacity of "actors" in dynamically structuring and restructuring the social world around them. Such an approach is usually identified with the work of Weber. However, while Weber is often interpreted as opposing structuralism in his critique of Marx, he provided the channels by which structuralist theory and social action could be reconciled without the determinism and teleology of the former (Weber 1922). This is perhaps exemplified by his work on bureaucracies and their dominant position as rationalized structures in the modern world. Such structures arose out of social (rational) action and, in turn, feed back and inform the experiences of social actors across numerous aspects of human life.

Criticisms of maco-level structuralist theories were to lead to the intellectual movement of poststructuralism which developed from the 1960s. Although initially derived from structuralist schools, theorists challenged assumptions concerning society and language as signifying coherent "systems." Through major exponents such as Derrida, Foucault, and others associated with schools of postmodernism, even earlier poststructuralist theory was itself "deconstructed" in order to understand how knowledge, linguistics, and centers of power came into existence in the first place.

SEE ALSO: Agency (and Intention); Economic Determinism; Functionalism/Neofunctionalism; Merton, Robert K.; Mesostructure; Poststructuralism; Social System; Structural Functional Theory; Structure and Agency

REFERENCES AND SUGGESTED READINGS

Lévi-Strauss, C. (1967) *The Scope of Anthropology.* Cape, London.

Marx, K. (1964) *The Economic and Philosophical Manuscripts.* International Manuscripts, New York.

Merton, R. (1949) *Social Theory and Social Structure.* Free Press, Glencoe, IL.

Parsons, T. (1951) *The Social System.* Free Press, New York.

Weber, M. (1922) *Economy and Society: An Outline of Interpretive Sociology.* Bedmester Press, New York.

social structure of victims

Koichi Hasegawa

Nobuko Iijima, a pioneer of environmental sociology both in Japan and internationally, applied her notion of the social structure of victims to the multidimensional and multilayered nature of the damage caused by pollution (Iijima 1976, 1979, 1984). The physical damage done to victims is relatively easy to discern, but this is only one aspect of pollution damage. Equally costly is the mental and social damage that occurs in the wake of the physical impact. Iijima attempted to describe comprehensively the complex structure of the suffering of victims, from physical suffering to worsening relationships between family members and neighbors who may be indifferent to the pollution problem or wish to keep it hidden. This approach reveals the flow-on effect of the physical damage. In fact, Iijima demonstrated how such suffering affects every aspect of a family's daily life, including loss of income and an increase in medical expenses, and often leads to family breakdown or the destruction of a family's living conditions. Through her research on Minamata disease, mercury poisoning of Canadian Indians, and drug-induced Subacute-Myelo-Optico-Neuropathy (SMON) disease, Iijima discovered that the structure of victims was very similar whether the damage was caused by a labor accident, a drug-induced disease, or an environmental hazard. The source of the pollution that caused Minamata disease was a factory already known as the site of numerous labor accidents. A systematic and institutional lack of care or consideration by industry and government for the safety of people's environment and the safety of working conditions nurtured the endemic problems that led to the Minamata outbreak.

Iijima's argument regarding the social structure of victims represented both a practical and a theoretical contribution to the field. In the case of drug-induced SMON disease, Iijima testified as to her research findings in court and her argument became the basis for the plaintiffs' demands for financial compensation for their sufferings, including the mental damage inflicted on them and the destruction of their daily lives.

More broadly, Iijima discussed the way that the sufferings caused by environmental damage were not evenly distributed in society, but reflected the disparities between majority and minority groups. Hence, in Japan, where small farmers and fishermen occupy the lowest strata of society, it is they who are most likely to suffer from environmental hazards. In this way, she found a kinship with US scholars of environmental justice and racism on African Americans and Native Americans, such as Bullard (1994).

In distinguishing between environmental sociology and medical and other social scientific studies of the environment, Iijima identified the description of the social structure of victims as the primary task of environmental sociologists.

SEE ALSO: Benefit and Victimized Zones; Environment, Sociology of the; High Speed Transportation Pollution

REFERENCES AND SUGGESTED READINGS

Bullard, R. (1994) *Dumping in Dixie: Race, Class, and Environmental Quality*, 2nd edn. Westview Press, Boulder.

Iijima, N. (1976) Wagakuni ni wokeru Kenko Hakai no Jittai (Current Status of Health Hazards in Japan). *Shakaigaku Hyoron (Japanese Sociological Review)* 26(3): 16–35.

Iijima, N. (1979) Kogai, Rosai, Yakugai ni okeru Higai no Kozo: Sono Doshitsu-sei to Ishitsu-sei (Similarities and Differences between Structures of Industrial Pollutions, Labor Accidents and Drug-Induced Diseases). *Kogai Kenkyu (Research on Environmental Disruption toward Interdisciplinary Cooperation)* 8(3): 7–65.

Iijima, N. (1984) *Kankyo Mondai to Higaisha Undo* (Environmental Problems and Victims' Movements). Gakubun-sha, Tokyo.

social support

Karen D. Lincoln

Social support has repeatedly been linked to a host of diverse social, economic, and health outcomes, including mortality (Berkman & Syme 1994), depression (Wethington & Kessler 1986), a variety of physical health problems, including heart disease (Kristenson et al. 1998), rheumatoid arthritis (Krol et al. 1993), and educational attainment and success (Hagan et al. 1996).

Social support, as a field of study, rose to prominence in the early 1970s and ushered in a groundswell of articles and books dealing with this topic. The burgeoning literature resulted in a plethora of definitions of the term. "Social support" usually refers to a process of interaction or exchange between individuals and significant others. Researchers have examined different *types* of support (e.g., emotional, informational, instrumental) and different *sources* of support (e.g., family, friends, neighbors, church members), as well as *functional* aspects (e.g., emotional support, sense of acceptance or belonging) and *structural* aspects (e.g., size, density, frequency of contact). House et al. (1988) recommended that studies of social support include measures representing more than one of these components in order to better understand how they relate to each other and to different outcomes. This approach has been widely adopted; however, many papers still rely on single measures of one component without a full understanding of the definition of support underlying their selection. Most empirical studies on this topic explore the associations between social support and health. A review of this broad literature over several decades leads to the conclusion that social support is beneficial to health. People with satisfying levels of support seem to cope better with stress and have better physical and mental health, compared to those who lack support.

Despite the volumes of research on social support, many questions of conceptual, methodological, and theoretical importance remain to be answered. This entry discusses the history, evolution, and current thinking in the field of social support, as well as directions for future research.

A hundred years ago, Durkheim's (1951) study of suicide made a significant contribution to the field of social support. He found that suicides were more prevalent among those with fewer social ties, which in turn produced a loss of social resources, a reduction in social constraints (based on defined norms and social roles), and ultimately resulted in poor psychological outcomes and increased risk of suicide. Almost a century later, extant reviews of the social support literature (Cohen & Wills 1985; House et al. 1988; Thoits 1995) conclude that social support, regardless of the way in which it is measured, is beneficial and has the potential to alleviate the deleterious effects of stress and other undesirable situations on physical, mental, and social outcomes.

Caplan (1974), Cassel (1974), and Cobb (1976) laid the foundation for work on social support and established the research issue that has since dominated the field: social support as a protective factor. They provided early definitions of the construct as well as ideas about the function of social support. Caplan (1974) and Cassel (1974) suggested that social support is feedback provided by significant others that *buffers* the adverse effects of stress and thus facilitates coping with difficult situations. Cobb (1976) was more precise in his efforts to provide a conceptual definition. He defined social support as information leading a person to believe that he or she is loved and cared for (e.g., emotional support), esteemed and valued (e.g., esteemed support), and belongs to a mutually supportive network (e.g., belonging support).

A decade later, Barrera (1981) emphasized that the term "social support" lacked adequate specificity and developed a classification scheme that has proved to be quite helpful in elaborating the diversity of definitions. Barrera identified three distinct categories of social support: social *embeddedness* (e.g., assessing the frequency of contact and connection with others), *perceived* social support (e.g., subjective evaluations of support availability and satisfaction), and *received* support (e.g., assessing the amount of tangible help that individuals actually provide).

Barrera's classification scheme contributed to the next wave of research that focused on comparing different dimensions of social support and their varied effects on particular outcomes. The consequences of perceived social support, especially emotional support, have most frequently been examined in the literature. The perception or belief that emotional support is available appears to have much stronger influence on outcomes than the actual receipt of social support.

Despite these advances, the social support literature continues to receive criticism. Many of these critiques coalesce around the definitions of social support as being too vague or too broad. Little consensus exists on how social support should be defined. This lack of consensus regarding the term is a major problem because it creates difficulty in measurement, as well as in assessing the status of research findings. The use of carefully chosen and more precise measures may help curtail the creation of more conflicting research findings about social support and have important benefits for summarizing study findings regarding the costs and benefits of social support.

Most conceptual models highlight the direct and stress-buffering effects of social support on outcomes. The *direct effects model* (Cohen & Wills 1985) assumes that social support has a direct effect and serves a health restorative role by meeting basic human needs for social contact regardless of the level of stress present. Thus, social support and stressors are largely independent of one another. Stressors have deleterious effects on health and other outcomes, while certain aspects of support, especially social integration and perceived support, are beneficial. Hence, these respective influences of support

and stressors are additive and, at least partly, offset one another. This generalized beneficial effect of social support occurs because social networks provide positive interactions, support, and affirmation that lead to an overall sense of self-worth, self-esteem, and positive affect.

Social support has also been studied widely as a psychosocial resource that potentially mitigates or buffers the deleterious psychological effects of stress on outcomes. Cohen and Wills's (1985) *stress-buffering model* proposes that social support buffers or protects individuals from the deleterious effects of stress. Many prior studies suggest that the effects of perceived support, and to a lesser extent those of received support, vary according to levels of stress. That is, support may be helpful mainly for persons who face high levels of stress, but may be much less important for others. Thus, the main role of social support in the stress-buffering model is to mitigate the otherwise deleterious effects of high stress. Supporting evidence for this model has been found in a variety of studies.

Discussions of social support increasingly focus on the need for theory as a guide to understanding the *mechanisms* by which social support affects health and other outcomes. This is a crucial next step to understanding how social support operates and ultimately developing a theory of social support. To accomplish this goal, researchers must (1) understand what the term social support means, (2) determine which dimensions or types of support play an especially important role in shaping the outcomes under consideration, and (3) identify the precise social mechanisms responsible for the observed effects.

There are several interesting new directions in recent research that may facilitate the goal of developing a theory of social support. First, a thorough examination of possible intervening factors can help us understand the mechanisms whereby social support operates to influence particular outcomes. Studies that examine the influence of measures of self-concept, such as self-esteem, personal control, or mastery, are promising. However, study findings to date have been inconsistent. Understanding the intervening mechanisms and supportive processes is a crucial next step to building theory in this area.

Another new and promising direction examines the negative side of social relationships. Negative interaction refers to unpleasant social exchanges between individuals that are perceived by the recipients as nonsupportive, critical, manipulative, demanding, or otherwise inconsequential to their needs. Research consistently shows that negative interactions exert a greater effect on health and well-being than measures of supportive interactions (for a review, see Lincoln 2000). In short, studies are beginning to show that there are important limitations on the degree to which social relationships benefit health and other outcomes. Consequently, a more complete understanding of social support requires a thorough examination of the negative as well as the positive aspects of interpersonal ties, as well as the stability, change, and effects in social relations over time.

Research designs have advanced from the cross-sectional correlational research that characterized early studies (Heller & Swindle 1983) to longitudinal designs that have appeared in recent studies (Barnes et al. 2004). A number of relatively underexplored questions remain, however, concerning the effects of factors such as stress and poverty, for example, on social support over time. Stressors such as financial problems and the death of a loved one are generally assumed to result in support mobilization rather than erosion or withdrawal. However, acute stressors are more likely to result in support mobilization in the short run, whereas chronic stressors may entail serious costs to the social network and thus erode support over time.

Most studies view social support primarily as an individual-level or interpersonal construct. However, community psychologists have identified the need for studies that treat social support as a system-level or community-level phenomenon that promotes social integration and perceptions of support. A focus on community- and systems-level factors is consistent with a sociological approach to the study of interactions among people and how social contexts influence these relationships. One example of this approach involves studies of social support in religious settings. Although this literature is not well developed, findings to date indicate that people who are members of formal religious organizations receive a sizable amount of emotional and tangible assistance (Taylor et al. 2004) from their fellow congregants. In addition to this line of research, more information is needed about the role of clergy in facilitating social support among parishioners. Research findings indicate that some people are more likely to consult members of the clergy than professional helpers (Taylor et al. 2004). However, more research is needed to understand what clergy actually do to assist people, whether they act as a conduit to professional helpers, and the types of problems they confront.

Questions remain about how social support operates among different populations. For example, more research is needed to understand the characteristics of social support networks among different age, gender, ethnic, racial, and SES groups. Little is known about whether extant measures of social support have the same meaning across different groups. The dramatic increase of older adults in the United States and worldwide highlights the importance of understanding social support among this population more than ever. Little is known about the effects of negative interaction across the life course or how those with limited support availability fare in terms of health and social outcomes. More discussion of policy implications of social support is needed. The widely accepted but recently challenged belief that some groups, such as African Americans, receive more social support than other groups has major implications for policies that affect long-term health care, poverty, and social insurance, particularly among populations with limited resources. For example, recent findings indicate that African Americans have a higher proportion of kin in their social networks (Ajrouch et al. 2001) and have smaller social networks compared to whites (Barnes et al. 2004). Whereas negative exchanges might be relatively uncommon among more distal network members (e.g., co-workers, neighbors), where few resources are transferred, they have been found to be fairly common among family members and when extensive support is provided. Consequently, African Americans may be more vulnerable to conflict within their networks compared to those with more multiplex networks (e.g., family, friends, neighbors, co-workers), as well as limitations in the availability or range of supportive resources.

Another promising new direction for future research is the use of computers and the Internet to provide and receive social support. This area of study views computer-mediated support groups as weak-tie networks that have the potential to provide support to those individuals who have limited or restricted opportunities to engage in supportive exchanges. Persons with functional limitations or loss of mobility, illness, advanced age, time constraints due to competing demands (e.g. caring for a disabled, aging, or ill family member), or who simply prefer social contact or discussing personal problems via cyberspace rather than face to face, may benefit from this form of support. This research is in its infancy and competing claims have been presented in the literature regarding the impact of Internet use on social support, with some studies suggesting that Internet use increases social interaction and support (Shaw & Gant 2002), while others suggest that it leads to decreased interaction and support, or has no effect (Noel & Epstein 2003). There is some disagreement as to whether the Internet has a positive or negative impact on social connection and well-being for older adults, in particular. Clearly, more work is needed in this area to determine who uses, who benefits, and what are the motives for using this form of exchange, as well as whether it is a replacement or supplement to face-to-face interactions.

The past few decades have made strides in clarifying the theoretical construct of social support and establishing how it is associated with different facets of social life. As more systematic research continues, future research will provide a more nuanced and contextualized understanding of the promise and limits of social support.

SEE ALSO: Aging and Social Support; Conjugal Roles and Social Networks; Durkheim, Émile; Emerson, Richard M.; Interaction; Interpersonal Relationships; Networks; Social Exchange Theory; Social Network Analysis; Social Network Theory; Social Support and Crime; Stress and Health; Symbolic Interaction

REFERENCES AND SUGGESTED READINGS

Ajrouch, K. J., Antonucci, T. C., & Janevic, M. R. (2001) Social Networks Among Blacks and Whites: The Interaction Between Race and Age. *Journals of Gerontology: Social Sciences* 56B: S112–S118.

Barnes, L. L., Mendes de Leon, C. F., Bienias, J. L., & Evans, D. A. (2004) A Longitudinal Study of Black–White Differences in Social Resources. *Journals of Gerontology: Social Sciences* 59B: S146–S153.

Barrera, M., Jr. (1981) Social Support in the Adjustment of Pregnant Adolescents: Assessment Issues. In: Gottlieb, B. H. (Ed.), *Social Networks and Social Support*. Sage, Beverly Hills, pp. 69–96.

Berkman, L. F. & Syme, S. L. (1994) Social Networks, Host Resistance, and Mortality: A Nine Year Follow-Up Study of Alameda County Residents. In: *Psychosocial Processes and Health: A Reader*. Cambridge University Press, New York, pp. 43–67.

Caplan, G. (1974) *Support Systems and Community Mental Health*. Human Science Press, New York.

Cassel, J. C. (1974) Psychosocial Processes and Stress: Theoretical Formulations. *International Journal of Health Sciences* 4: 471–82.

Cobb, S. (1976) Social Support as a Moderator of Life Stress. *Psychosomatic Medicine* 38: 300–14.

Cohen, S. & Wills, T. A. (1985) Stress, Social Support and the Buffering Hypothesis. *Psychological Bulletin* 98: 310–57.

Durkheim, E. (1951 [1897]) *Suicide*. Free Press, New York.

Hagan, J., MacMillan, R., & Wheaton, B. (1996) New Kid in Town: Social Capital and the Life Course Effects of Family Migration on Children. *American Sociological Review* 61: 368–85.

Heller, K. & Swindle, R. (1983) Social Networks, Perceived Social Support, and Coping with Stress. In: Felner, R., Jason, L., Moritsugu, J., & Faber, S. (Eds.), *Preventive Psychology*. Pergamon, New York, pp. 87–103.

House, J. S., Umberson, D., & Landis, K. R. (1988) Structures and Processes of Social Support. *Annual Review of Sociology* 14: 293–318.

Kristenson, M., Orth-Gomeer, K., Kucinskiene, Z., Bergdahl, B., Balinkyniene, I., & Olsson, A. G. (1998) Attenuated Cortisol Response to a Standardized Stress Test in Lithuanian versus Swedish Men: The LiVicordia Study. *International Journal of Behavioral Medicine* 5: 17–30.

Krol, B., Sanderman, R., & Suurmeijer, T. P. (1993) Social Support, Rheumatoid Arthritis and Quality of Life: Concepts, Measurement and Research. *Patient Education & Counseling* 20: 101–20.

Lincoln, K. D. (2000) Social Support, Negative Social Interactions and Psychological Well-Being. *Social Service Review* 74: 231–52.

Noel, J. G. & Epstein, J. (2003) Social Support and Health Among Senior Internet Users: Results of an Online Survey. *Journal of Technology in Human Services* 21: 35–54.

Shaw, L. H. & Gant, L. M. (2002) In Defense of the Internet: The Relationship between Internet Communication and Depression, Loneliness, Self-Esteem, and Perceived Social Support. *Cyberpsychology & Behavior* 5: 157–71.

Taylor, R. J., Chatters, L. M., & Levin, J. (2004) *Religion in the Lives of African Americans: Social, Psychological, and Health Perspectives.* Sage, Thousand Oaks, CA.

Thoits, P. A. (1995) Stress, Coping, and Social Support Process: Where Are We? What Next? *Journal of Health and Social Behavior* 35: 53–79.

Wethington, E. & Kessler, R. C. (1986) Perceived Support, Received Support and Adjustment to Stressful Events. *Journal of Personality and Social Psychology* 36: 87–96.

social support and crime

Ruth Triplett

In his 1994 Presidential Address to the Academy of Criminal Justice Sciences, Cullen (1994) argued that social support is an important organizing concept for criminology. Central to his argument about the importance of social support to criminological theory is Cullen's idea that social support is a concept that is actually present in many of today's criminological writings, including strain, labeling, feminist, and the works of the Chicago School. Cullen derives his definition of social support from Lin, who defines it as the perceived or actual instrumental and/or expressive provisions supplied by the community, social networks, and confiding partners.

For Cullen, there are a number of important dimensions surrounding this definition of social support. First, as one can see in the definition, two basic types of social support derive from one's relationships: expressive and instrumental. Expressive support is used to refer to the emotional support that one receives from relationships. An example of expressive support is when your spouse helps you release stress by listening to your complaints about work. Instrumental support refers to support from a relationship that leads the individual to achieve a goal. An example of instrumental support would be when parents provide money and a place to live for their children while they attend college.

A second dimension to social support is that it involves not only what is actually given as support, but the perception of support as well. Thus there may be a difference between what someone perceives they are giving and what another perceives they are getting. Third, social support occurs at different levels. It can be discussed at the individual level, given by a friend, at the community level, with communities varying in the extent to which they offer support, or even at the societal level, with some nations offering higher levels of social support than others. Finally, social support can be given formally, by agencies or institutions, or informally, by friends and family.

Cullen next argues that social support is related to crime at a variety of levels. At the macro level, Cullen relates varying levels of social support to crime at the societal and community level. For example, Cullen argues that the lower level of social support in the US is related to its higher rates of serious crime. Cullen also sees social support as varying across families, with some offering more support to their members than others. Finally, he sees social support having a direct effect on individuals' involvement in crime through both the giving and receiving of social support, and indirectly as it conditions the effect of other factors, such as strain.

When Cullen wrote his article on social support, he argued that there was much criminological research that already lent indirect support to the importance of social support in explaining crime. Since then, Cullen and other researchers have directly tested some of his ideas. In general, the research is supportive of the idea that social support is related to crime at a variety of levels. For example, at the individual level, Wright and Cullen (2001) have examined the relationship between parental support and delinquency. They found that control and support are both important aspects of parenting that significantly affect delinquency. In addition, they found a strong joint effect of control and support on delinquency. At the societal level, Pratt and Godsey (2003) found that social support is significantly related to national homicide rates and that the effect of inequality is stronger when social support is lacking, and diminished with its presence.

SEE ALSO: Feminist Criminology; Labeling; Social Disorganization Theory; Social Support

REFERENCES AND SUGGESTED READINGS

Cullen, F. (1994) Social Support as an Organizing Concept for Criminology: Presidential Address to the Academy of Criminal Justice Sciences. *Justice Quarterly* 11: 527–60.
Cullen, F., Wright, J. P., & Chamlin, M. (1999) Social Support and Social Reform: A Progressive Crime Control Agenda. *Crime and Delinquency* 45: 188–207.
Pratt, T. C. & Godsey, T. W. (2003) Social Support, Inequality and Homicide: A Cross-National Test of an Integrated Theoretical Model. *Criminology* 41: 611–44.
Wright, J. P. & Cullen, F. (2001). Parental Efficacy and Delinquent Behavior: Do Control and Support Matter? *Criminology* 39: 677–706.

social system

Stephen Hunt

There is a sense in which a "social system" may be defined as two or more people engaged in ongoing social interaction. What might be said to be the aspect of interaction which makes it specifically a "system" is that a high degree of regularity or recurrence is conducive to more or less permanent structural arrangements. This normatively defined categorization of a social system came to be largely identified with particular schools of sociology generally located within the framework of mid-twentieth-century structural functionalism and the speculative theories of its leading exponents.

Making an earlier contribution was Herbert Spencer (1820–1903), who drew an analogy between the social system and biological organisms. Spencer's speculation that all social systems "evolved" led him to develop a complex threefold scheme for categorizing social systems based on whether they displayed complex or simple structures and whether they were essentially stable or unstable. Firstly, a "simple" system is undifferentiated by sections, groups, or tribal formations. Secondly, a "compound" system amounts to an amalgamation of communities with a rudimentary hierarchy and division of labor. Thirdly, "doubly compound" systems are more complex still and united under one organized authority (Spencer 1971).

The major contributor to structural functionalism, Talcott Parsons, drew a complex blueprint of the social system applicable at all times and all places while allowing for the dynamics of complexity as societies evolved from pre-industrial to industrial forms (Parsons 1951). For Parsons, the social system was constituted by a number of interacting functional "parts" that arose to deal with universal prerequisites. The fulfillment of these prerequisites ensured the survival of the social system, as did adherence by social members to an overarching value system. Also ensuring the endurance of the system was the need of its constituent parts to evolve through the differentiation that was the hallmark of modernization.

In Parsons's schemata, a fourfold system of functional prerequisites gave way to universal structural arrangements: adaptation, goal attainment, integration, and pattern maintenance. Put succinctly, these universal social structural formations or "subsystems" realized these prerequisites through the following: economic activity (control over the environment), political arrangements (establishing goals and priorities), integration (the adjustment of potential or actual conflict), and the maintenance of value patterns (kinship structures and socialization processes). Parsons identified cultural values as the key to stability since value consensus integrates the various institutions or subsystems. Value consensus provided the foundation for cooperation given that common values engender common goals. In Parsons's model both value consensus and subsystem formations structured patterned and recurrent human actions and relationships, particularly in terms of rules, social status and roles, and normative values. Thus a social system constitutes the accumulative entirety of normative behavior.

According to Parsons, the very task of sociology was to analyze the institutionalization of the social system's value orientation. When values were institutionalized and behavior structured in terms of them, the result was a stable system or state of "social equilibrium." Such equilibrium was sustained by socialization, which constituted the means by which values are transmitted, alongside forms of social control, which encouraged conformity and discouraged social deviance.

Almost paradoxically, Parsons saw changes in the value system as the mechanism behind social evolution as well as the potential for disequilibrium. In short, change in one constitutive part (adaptation, goal attainment, integration, and pattern maintenance) was likely to engender change in another. Thus no social system was ever in a total state of equilibrium as it evolved toward more complex forms. Such evolution involved a general adaptive capacity as the social system increased its control over the environment. However, while economic adaptation might provide the initial stimulus for social evolution, it was changes in the value consensus that ensured that such change was forthcoming.

In identifying the evolutionary state of any given social system, Parsons outlined five key variables, which he referred to as cultural patterns "A" and "B." The former were synonymous with more simple forms, while the display of all or a majority of the latter constituted the cultural patterns of advanced societies. These patterns, for Parsons, entailed the following: (1) the change from ascribed to "achieved" status, which allowed social mobility according to merit; (2) the move from the diffuse and organic nature of social relationships toward the more utilitarian relationships of the modern world; (3) the transformation of the particularism engrained in social action into social acts according to universal principles; (4) the change from the affectivity of immediate gratification to deferred gratification; and (5) the evolution from a collective orientation toward self-orientation.

The logic implicit in the concept of a social system was criticized even from within the school of structural functionalism. In attempting to develop functionalist theory, Robert Merton (1949) focused upon the alleged efficacy of a number of underlying assumptions. In particular, Merton questioned whether any given subsystem or constituent element of the social system may be alternatively functional, dysfunctional, or non-functional. Thus, he advocated the necessity of evaluating their overall contribution to system survival. Secondly, he speculated whether the functional utility of the constituent elements of a social system is particularly integrative, especially in advanced industrial society.

There arose further critiques of Parsons's theoretical framework which were to undermine its credibility. An especially damaging criticism of the paradigm of a social system was derived from what might be interpreted as the teleology inherent in structural functionalism generally. While this school of sociology advanced the view that the constituent parts of the social system existed because they have beneficial consequences, it effectively treated an effect as a cause. Hence, the reductionist analyses of the dynamics of an abstract social system are logically unsustainable. Moreover, assessing the positive effects of these elements is often unquantifiable. Subsequently, the biological analogy on which the paradigm was initially based became perceived as flawed.

SEE ALSO: Functionalism/Neofunctionalism; Merton, Robert K.; Parsons, Talcott; Social Control; Social Structure; Socialization; Spencer, Herbert; Structural Functional Theory

REFERENCES AND SUGGESTED READINGS

Merton, R. K. (1949) *Social Theory and Social Structure*. Free Press, Glencoe, IL.
Parsons, T. (1951) *The Social System*. Free Press, New York.
Spencer, H. (1971) *Structure, Function, and Evolution*. Nelson, London.

social theory and sport

Jeffrey Michael Clair and Jason Wasserman

Despite acknowledgments of sport as a legitimate focus of sociological analysis from early thinkers such as Spencer, Simmel, Weber, Scheler, and Mead (Luschen 1980), the lack of theoretical development in sport studies has been well documented (Frey & Eitzen 1991), although there appears to be increased movement toward the generation and integration of more theoretically driven work.

Washington and Karen (2001) point out that Bourdieu's "Sports and Social Class" statement has focused much of our attention with these following key observations: (1) sports is a field relatively autonomous of society with a unique historical dynamic; (2) sport represents struggles between social classes; (3) sport shifted from an amateur elite practice to a professionally produced spectacle for mass consumption; (4) sport production and administration must be understood within the industrial political economy; (5) sports participation as exercise or leisure time depends on economic and cultural capital; and (6) sport practices vary by the conscious and unconscious meanings and functions perceived by various social classes.

Sport provides unique opportunities for understanding the complexities of everyday life. Bourdieu's (1991) original argument calls for theoretical inquiry that integrates macro and micro interests, bridging social structure and social psychological processes. Macro methodologies cover, for example: (1) concerns with developing sport as a science (Luschen 1980); (2) global politics (Strenk 1979);

(3) sociohistorical labor and leisure development (Zarnowski 2004); (4) the accessibility of sport to various classes and social mobility (Kahn 2000); and (5) the role of media in generating national identities (Lowes 1997). Micro orientations will focus inquiry on (1) sport preferences and participation (Miller et al. 2002); (2) socialization (McNulty & Eitle 2002); (3) self-esteem (Adler et al. 1992); (4) immortalizing the self through sport (Schmitt & Leonard 1986); and (5) sport play to display (Stone 1955).

Coakley (2004) explicitly addresses dominant theoretical perspectives and their relation to the study of sports, which are summarized in Table 1.

Still being a young field, the areas in need of theoretical attention are vast. While race, class, gender, and media studies have moved sport away from an "orphan speciality" status (Frey & Eitzen, 1991), other intriguing substantive areas remain fertile ground for development. Three areas which are particularly fruitful are the political nature of sport, sport as art, and the moral assumptions embedded in sport.

POLITICAL NATURE OF SPORT

Viewing sports as politics is not new. This connection has been referred to as "war without

Table 1 Dominant theoretical perspectives and their relation to the study of sport.

Theoretical paradigm	Focus in sport
Functionalist	Sport as producing positive social outcomes for social networks, physical and mental health, and benefits for non-sport related activities such as school, work, and family life.
Conflict	Political-economic forces that drive sport and the class-based relations that define it, such as the commercialization of sport, the influence of sport on economic inequality, etc.
Interactionist	Relations of sport participants examining the production of athlete identity, the meaning and significance of sport for athletes and spectators, and sport involvement processes from initiation of sport participation through retirement.
Critical	Power relations involved in sporting activities, such as how sport reproduces advantage or disadvantage, the relationship of sports to images of health compared to sickness or success compared to failure, etc.
Feminist	Gender relations embedded in sport, such as the construction of gendered identities within sport activity and the exclusion of girls and women in sports.
Figurational	Attempts to bridge the macro–micro divide by focusing on sports as embedded in a variety of multi-level social networks examining the evolution of sports in a historical network context.

weapons." Strenk (1979) points out how Nazis under Hitler and Fascists under Mussolini propagandized sport. The globalization process seems to have only increased the prominence of sport in politics. Examples of the obvious intersection of sport and politics include:

- The losers of world wars have been banned for several years from the Olympic movement (the US refused visas to East Germans for two decades).
- Egypt, Iraq, and Lebannon boycotted the 1956 Melbourne Olympics in protest of the Suez war. Spain, Switzerland, and the Netherlands withdrew over the Soviet invasion of Hungary, and China pulled out in a continuing demonstration against the International Olympic Committee recognition of Taiwan.
- South Africa was barred from the 1964 Tokyo Olympics.
- The Mexican government shot and killed students protesting the 1968 Olympics in Mexico City.
- Arab terrorists kidnapped and killed Israeli athletes in Munich in 1972.
- 32 nations boycotted the 1976 Olympics in Montreal because New Zealand maintained sports relations with South Africa.
- The US, followed by West Germany and Japan, boycotted the 1980 Moscow Olympics in protest of the Soviet invasion of Afghanistan. In return, the Soviet bloc boycotted the 1984 Los Angeles Olympics.
- North Korea, Cuba, Ethiopia, and Nicaragua boycotted the 1988 Seoul Olympics.
- Gabon, Congo, Honduras, and El Salvador have gone to war over the outcome of soccer games.
- The US and Russia attempted to proclaim superiority of their political and socioeconomic systems by winning the most Olympic gold medals.
- The US used table tennis to open relations with China.

Sports have been "justified since antiquity for providing soldiers with the physical training they would require in battle" (Semenza 2001). There is always binary opposition in battle. It is one team against another, one country against another, one individual against another, one alliance against another. Further, encounters in both sport and war are fundamentally a physical contest. Even competitors in sports where there is no direct physical contact between opponents understand their contest as one of warlike physical opposition. Finally, there are consequences for winning or losing. These may be concrete or symbolic, but they are clearly valued by competitors, as demonstrated by fierce competition and emotional reactions to winning and losing.

Gender also links sport and war. Male-gendered traits tied to physicality, power, and domination underlie both the good athlete and the good soldier. Generally, sports are not simply the random assertion of masculinity; rather, they are structured expressions of it, reflecting past, dominant, institutionalized representations of masculinity (i.e., war). Social theory can further illuminate similarities in sport and war, generating insight into current international political relations as well as reaching into the social psychological production of gendered identities.

SPORT AS ART

Athletes talk about a sense of effortless competency, a flow felt while playing where it all comes together – all the training, studying, and coaching. During this experience the mind seems to stop and there is expanded vision beyond thought. This is referred to as "being in the zone" or what we call a *creative action-rhythm*. It emerges from a twofold process: (1) *learning*, by first absorbing all that one can from books, practice, and coaches/teachers, and (2) *creative acting*, where one acts *out of* what was learned instead of merely imitating. This creative action-rhythm is the very essence of the true athlete as artist.

The dependence of sport on rules may suggest an opposition to creativity. But suppose the rules were restrictive and it was possible for them to remove the artistic, creative element of sport and that athletes merely applied what they had learned from their coaches. Would sport still be enjoyed by spectators? Would athletes still practice their crafts with passion and dedication? Imagine going to a basketball game where the players seldom did anything new. We would only tolerate it for young players, and then maybe only if the players were our own children. But reflect on how excited we are when a successful, dynamic, creative play occurs. These are actually the moments which give meaning to sport. These moments, when sport transcends physical mechanics and becomes emotionally salient, are what allow individuals to experience creative participation, even as spectators.

Young (1999) shares an interesting theoretical framework in this regard. Calling on Heidegger, he reminds us, "poetically dwells man upon this earth." This means, without art, he merely exists. Sport, like art, conjures emotion in the participant as well as the viewer. This emotion pulls us away from the maze of everyday details, demands, and decisions (Goffman 1961). This emotional experience is the essence of art and it is clearly found in sport.

Attending a sporting contest is itself seeking artistic expression (Young 1999). The game setting is far from the ordinary. Our team reveals the multicultural mix of our community, but is integrated. And although we sit in hierarchical seating, we experience union with one another, a manifest integrity of our community. We share a national anthem. We see our morality in the rules (e.g., fairness, earned accomplishment, etc.). The athletic activity, although subordinated to rules, encourages equality between competitors, but yet does not get in the way of artistic expression. We can see the virtues of skills. And however well planned and rehearsed, with the final outcome, we come to grips with being mortal. Through the athletic artistic expression, we are transported from our "average everydayness" into *Augenblick*, the "moment of vision" (Young 1999). The athlete helps us see the hero that is concealed in everyday characters. Social theory, particularly in the sociology of emotions, has much to contribute and gain from studying the creative, artistic, and emotional qualities of sport, and the meanings we bring and take away from our games (Duquin 2000).

MORAL ASSUMPTIONS EMBEDDED IN SPORT

Sport both embodies and impresses particular assumptions about human nature and a moral order. Particularly central to youth sports, the debate about the value of competition represents broader clashes over human nature itself. In a cyclical fashion, sport both assumes competition as an innate human quality and in turn teaches that this is the case. Like much western social, political, and economic theory, implicit in sport is the ideological assumption of a human will to power. The extent to which this is innate rather than cultural, if it is at all, remains unclear. There is evidence that this sort of orientation is primarily cultural (Sahlins 1972). Many traditional societies often do not overtly reflect this will to power. Thus, one might claim that it is the institutionalization and structure of sports, which most often follow a western, capitalist model of competition, that produce these tendencies. Sahlins (1972) similarly found that small, primitive societies tended to develop westernized power orientations only after being engulfed in larger, organized states. Sport is certainly one arena in which investigation into the matter may prove fruitful.

While emphasis on competition is still the pervasive ethos of sport, some youth organizations have consciously shifted away from a competitive model. For example, there are leagues in which everyone receives a participation trophy rather than just rewarding top-place teams and most valuable players. Coaches may be discouraged from emphasizing winning as a value, or even from showing too much enthusiasm for "successful" play (e.g., within the American Christian Upward Program). These organizations present an opportunity for sociology to address some competing hypotheses embedded in the ideologies of these typical and countertypical models of sport. Social theory ought to be able to contribute to and gain from the study of youth development, attitudes, and mental health by comparing these different models of sport, which seem particularly polarized concerning the value of competition.

We might compare the current diversity in the world to a prism. The nature of the prism's color spectrum is that there is no connectedness between colors, meaning there is no identifiable demarcating line that defines the end of one color and the beginning of another. It is essential to realize that one of the colors in the spectrum of global diversity is sport. Its boundaries blend and merge with the agenda and concerns of gender, race, ethnicity, religion, family, work, leisure, economic development, politics, global relations, etc. The selected literature cited here points to the possibilities of interdisciplinary social theory development.

SEE ALSO: Globalization, Sport and; Media and Sport; Politics and Sport; Sport; Sport, Alternative; Sport and Culture

REFERENCES AND SUGGESTED READINGS

Adler, P., Kless, S., & Adler, P. (1992) Socialization to Gender Roles: Popularity among Elementary School Children. *Sociology of Education* 65: 169–87.

Bourdieu, P. (1991 [1978]) Sport and Social Class. In: Mukerji, C. & Schidson, M. (Eds.), *Rethinking Popular Culture: Contemporary Perspectives in Cultural Studies*. University of California Press, Berkeley, pp. 357–73.

Coakley, J. (2004) *Sports in Society: Issues and Controversies*. McGraw Hill, Boston.

Duquin, M. (2000) Sport and Emotions. In: Coakley, J. & Dunning, E. (Eds.), *Handbook of Sports Studies*. Sage, London, pp. 477–89.

Frey, J. & Eitzen, D. S. (1991) Sport and Society. *Annual Review of Sociology* 17: 503–22.

Goffman, E. (1961) *Encounters*. Bobbs-Merrill, Indianapolis.

Kahn, L. (2000) The Sports Business as a Labor Market Laboratory. *Journal of Economic Perspectives* 14: 75–94.

Lowes, M. (1997) Sports Page: A Case Study in the Manufacture of Sports News for the New Press. *Sociology of Sport* 14: 143–59.

Luschen, G. (1980) Sociology of Sport: Development, Present State, and Prospects. *Annual Review of Sociology* 6: 315–47.

McNulty, T. & Eitle, D. (2002) Race, Cultural Capital, and the Educational Effects of Participation in Sports. *Sociology of Education* 75: 123–46.

Miller, K., Barnes, G., Melnick, M., Sabo, D., & Farrell, M. (2002) Gender and Racial/Ethnic Differences in Predicting Adolescent Sexual Risk: Athletic Participation versus Exercise. *Journal of Health and Social Behavior* 43: 436–50.

Reiss, S. (1990) The New Sport History. *Reviews in American History* 18: 311–25.

Sahlins, D. (1972) *Stone Age Economics*. Aldine, Chicago.

Schmitt, R. & Leonard, W. (1986) Immortalizing the Self through Sport. *American Journal of Sociology* 91: 1088–111.

Semenza, G. (2001) Sport, War, and Contest in Shakespeare's Henry VI. *Renaissance Quarterly* 54: 1251–72.

Stone, G. (1955) American Sports: Play and Display. *Chicago Review* 9: 83–100.

Strenk, A. (1979) What Price Victory? The World of International Sports and Politics. *Annals of the American Academy of Political and Social Science* 445: 128–40.

Washington, R. & Karen, D. (2001) Sport and Society. *Annual Review of Sociology* 27: 187–212.

Young, J. (1999) Artwork and Sportwork: Heideggerian Reflections. *Journal of Aesthetics and Art Criticism* 57: 267–77.

Zarnowski, F. (2004) Working at Play: The Phenomenon of 19th-Century Worker-Competitions. *Journal of Leisure Research* 36: 257–82.

social work: history and institutions

Sabine Hering

From the beginning of the nineteenth century industrialization and the rise of civil society created a new framework for human welfare: the fact that poverty caused by nature was replaced by poverty caused by social deprivation brought up the need for appropriate ideas and solutions that expanded the range of regional or national welfare strategies into an international perspective. "Social welfare" is not only the old-fashioned term for social work, but is also the more general term: social welfare continues to include in most parts of the world programs that promote the general welfare (e.g., social security) and involves other professions as well as social work. This entry details the main changes in the field of social welfare through the development and discussions of its international organizations.

The International Council of Social Welfare (ICSW) was founded in the context of the Conference for Social Welfare, held in Paris in July 1928. René Sand, one of the initiators of the conference and the ICSW, used to emphasize the "double origin" of the organization, pointing to the fact that it corresponds to the model of the American National Council of

Social Welfare (NCSW, founded 1874 as the Conference on Charity and Correction), as well as to organizations and networks in Europe whose activities go back to the middle of the nineteenth century – the *Congrès internationale de Bienfaisance* (1856–63) and the *Congrès d'Assistance publique et privée* (1889–1910).

Since the Enlightenment, the American Declaration of Human Rights and the French Revolution, together with the negative consequences of industrialization (e.g., poverty, slums), had given rise to public discussion about the "social question" and to new movements such as the Inner Mission of the Protestant church and the Settlements of the Social Utopians. The international peace movement, the movement for the abolishment of slavery, and the feminist movement inspired the political ideas of welfare strategies, as well as the declaration of the Geneva Convention initiated by Henri Dunant in 1864, which was the starting point for the International Red Cross. Discussions about prison reform also decisively influenced welfare discourses: the Congrès Penitentaire held in Frankfurt in 1846 and in Brussels in 1847 accelerated the discourses on welfare, education, and social reform, and led to the first attempt to gather information about poverty and the needs of the working class on an international basis, in order to inform the public about the necessity of social reforms.

Although the revolutionary activities in 1848–9 made these initiatives ineffective, there was a second departure in 1851–2 when the *Congrès d'hygiène public* raised questions of welfare in the context of social hygiene in Brussels. The main topics of these conferences were the housing shortage and the state of dwellings, disease, abolition of child labor, prostitution, and venereal disease.

Probably the first international welfare conference as such took place in Paris in 1856, the *Congrès internationale de Bienfaisance*. Nearly 300 participants from 20 countries came to the conclusion that there should be regular meetings in the future to create common standards of poor relief and charity for the most serious social problems: poverty and the lack of social hygiene. Discussion was dominated by questions of social insurance and social security, as well as the principles of self-help. The idea was to find a balance between the responsibilities of

the state and the resources of the clients (and the charity organizations which cared for them). Cooperation with conferences dealing with social science and statistics became closer, in order to accelerate political change in the field of social reform with "demographic evidence."

National and international political conflicts hindered the development of international social welfare for some years. It was not until 1889 that the pioneers of social welfare met again to form a new international association: the *Congrès d'Assistance publique et privée*.

In the meantime the efforts of the first wave of international exchange in the field of social welfare began to show results. In England in the 1860s the 1834 Poor Law was reformed, while a multitude of private philanthropic activities were united under the Charity Organization Society (COS) in 1869. In the US, Buffalo was in 1877 the first city to introduce the model of the COS into its local welfare system. By the end of the nineteenth century more than 100 larger cities in the US had followed this example.

In France the *Office Central des Institutions Charitables* performed comparable work. After 1871 the Third Republic emphasized the responsibility of the state for child relief and care for the elderly and mentally ill with new legislation, together with the importance of private charity. In Germany a district-oriented social system originally established in Elberfeld became influential (nationally and internationally) because it facilitated an effective relief structure based on semi-professional neighborhood support. In the 1880s the Bismarck Sozialsystem (including social insurance against illness, invalidism, and poverty among the aged) provided protection against the most serious social risks – an important step into the future, although it was in the beginning only intended for male industrial workers.

The *Congrès d'Assistance publique et privée* turned out to be the most important precurser of the ICSW. Until 1910 it furthered progressive ideas like female participation in public welfare activities, professional training, preventive measures against tuberculosis, child protection, and eugenics.

From the beginning of the twentieth century the influence of the feminist movement all over the world had become stronger, including within social welfare. While charity and municipal poor relief had been delivered exclusively by local authorities, priests, physicians, and other male citizens (occasionally assisted by nurses or nuns), social work was now defined as a typically female profession corresponding to "typical female attributes" like patience, compassion, and empathy. However, the "welfare takeover" by the feminist movement did not lead to more sense or sensitiveness in social work, but to more sensibility. It was obvious that the welfare system at the end of the nineteenth century urgently needed modernization, mainly in regard to the dark side of the industrial revolution and its numerous negative social consequences. Female pioneers at that time were especially interested in higher education and professional perspectives in order to take part in societal decision processes. They realized at once that social reform provided a wide area for systematic and serious activities, fitting perfectly into their ideas of public participation. Thus the feminization of welfare signaled the end of the predominance of individual charity and helped lead to the idea of social work as a profession.

The last and most important conference of the *Congrès d'Assistance publique et privée* (in Copenhagen in 1910) confirmed these ideas and focused the modern welfare system on three main principles: a balance between social insurance and social work, coordination of state and private welfare structures, and vocational training.

Although World War I furthered the processes of welfare modernization, as all countries had to cope with the welfare needs of an enormous number of widows, orphans, and disabled, international cooperation was again severely disrupted. The cancellation of a conference planned for 1915 in London was the beginning of an interruption to international welfare discourse that lasted until 1928. On the other hand, the terrible experiences of the war provided the impetus for the League of Nations (founded in 1920), the International Labor Organization (founded 1919), International Red Aid (founded 1921), the International League of the Red Cross (founded 1919) and the predecessor of the World Health Organization (the Health Committee, founded 1923), among other examples.

In this same period in the US, the NCSW became a great influence on the development of international structures in the field of social work. The main starting signal for the "great" International Conference of Social Welfare (the so-called *Quinzaine Social* held in Paris in 1928) came from the US, as did financial support for the preparatory work. These incentives of the NCSW and the efforts of the International League of the Red Cross (represented by Alice Masarykova from Czechoslovakia and the Belgian physician René Sand) enabled the largest welfare conference to take place. The idea of the conference was to create a survey of the development of social work all over the world, inviting welfare experts from as many nations as possible, who were supposed to describe the social systems in their countries. Soon, however, other organizations wanted to participate and urged the planning committee to widen the range of topics. In the end, there were five conferences united in the *Quinzaine*: the International Conference of Social Welfare itself, a revived *Congrès d'Assistance publique et privée*, the International Conference of Child Protection, the International Conference of Housing and Urban Development, and an exhibition on Settlements and Social Progress. Over 5,000 participants from 40 countries attended the conferences, the reports of which (published in French, English, and German) covered nearly 2,500 pages.

The most important result of the conference in Paris was the foundation of the International Council of Social Welfare as a worldwide platform for professional development and exchange. The participants decided that all the nations present should be members of ICSW, but only Belgium, Czechoslovakia, France, Germany, the UK, and the US were also represented on the executive board. With the exception of Japan and Chile, countries from Africa, South America, and Asia, as well as Australia, were excluded.

The next ICSW conference was held in Frankfurt in 1932 and focused on just one extremely topical social problem: the consequences of unemployment for the family. The conference proceedings showed unmistakably that there were very different political and professional positions "united" in the ICSW, varying from communist ideas of partnership to the attempt of some Catholic representatives to defend motherhood and family life against the temptations of modernization.

The third conference on "Social Work and the Community" took place in London in 1936. The most significant characteristic of these last pre-war proceedings was the venture of fascist countries like Germany and Italy to functionalize the term "community" for their idea of the *Volk*, in order to create eugenic standards for its perfection. There was no agreement in respect of this question, but nevertheless there was a certain sympathy for eugenic ideas in non-fascist countries.

The 1940 conference on "Youth Work and Youth Care" was prevented by World War II. In August 1946 the three former presidents of ICSW (Alice Masarykova, Mary van Kleeck, and René Sand) met to consider the future work of ICSW. Once again, they tried to reconstruct the organization so that it had close connections with the official international platform – this time, the United Nations. However, they had to take into account that other social organizations had already been established during the war to give help to refugees and other displaced persons. The United Nations Relief and Rehabilitation Administration (UNRRA) and the Intergovernmental Committee on Refugees (ICR) merged in 1948 to form the International Relief Organization (IRO). In contrast to ICSW, these organizations had adequate financial means and an enormous number of helpers. Furthermore, UNICEF and the WHO had already been instructed by the UN to develop activities in fields that had been under the direction of the ICSW before the war. Also of enormous influence was the Philadelphia Declaration of the ILO, which proclaimed that the worldwide struggle against poverty and for welfare was a human right independent of race, sex, or belief.

ICSW tried to reestablish itself within this framework of remarkable activities. Being mainly related to European traditions and networks, first attempts were hampered by the destruction of all kinds of infrastructure caused by the war and the new division between East and West. The first post-war conference was held in Scheveningen in the Netherlands in 1947 to discuss "Urgent Social Problems in the War-Stricken Areas of Europe" and was attended by only 168 representatives from 18 countries. Because of this very low rate of participation, conference members discussed not only the problems of effective help for millions of people in need, but also the question of their relation to the Council of International Voluntary Agencies (IVA, including the Quakers, Oxfam, and a number of other social organizations) and the UN. They realized that they urgently neeeded to establish closer connections to organizations in the US. They decided to hold the next conference in Atlantic City, combining the 75th anniversary of NCSW with their proceedings.

In the short period between Scheveningen and Atlantic City (1948) many of the national committees of ISCW, as well as the board, had largely recovered from the effects of the war. Although connections with members in Eastern Europe were broken, there was general agreement to carry on because the challenges were larger than ever. After Atlantic City, two items turned out to be of great importance for the future of ICSW as an international platform of relevance. First, it became obvious that "international" meant more than Europe and the US: ICSW had to be open to members on all five continents and consider them as equal partners. The second item was related to the remarkable increase of international social organizations, which required an efficient division of labor. ICSW had to serve as a platform for international discourses about social needs and support structures all over the world – excluding the political mandate for social work (held by the UN), the representation of the profession (held by the International Association of Social Workers), and all items of education and vocational training (covered by the International Association of Schools of Social Work).

ICSW defined itself in relation to the multitude of international NGOs in the field of social welfare as a partner for theoretical and methodical discourses and as a coordinator for common incentives. Meetings of ICSW – held for example in Madras (1952), Tokyo (1958), Rio de Janeiro (1962), and Jerusalem (1978) – included representatives from all over the world and showed that this idea worked. Furthermore, ICSW was able to face the most relevant topics of social welfare in each period after World War

II, discussing "Urban and Rural Development" (1962), "Social Welfare and Human Rights" (1968), "Social Development in Times of Economic Uncertainty" (1980), "Welfare in West and East" (1992) and "Global Governance" (2004).

Nevertheless it is impossible to relate the history of social welfare exclusively to the history of ICSW after 1945. The diversification of worldwide developments in the field of social work is too large to be interpreted within the framework of just one organization, even if the reflection of that diversification is one of the main activities of ICSW. In all emergent welfare states after World War II, social work was gradually established as a key profession charged with the implementation and the fine-tuning of an ever-denser net of social policy measures. Its discourses reflect a polarity between universalism, which is the legacy of early international activities, and the "indigenization" of methodological orientations. Along this spectrum, international conferences and activities remain a central feature of social work's professional orientation.

Looking back on the history of social work there is one important theme that connects the past to the present: the idea of "internationality," which has always been one of the basic guidelines of social work since its modernization in the nineteenth century. Social problems cross borders. Although every country has to find national answers to these international challenges, the seeds of a global perspective were sown at the first international meetings on social welfare.

SEE ALSO: Addams, Jane; Social Policy, Welfare State; Social Problems, Concept and Perspectives; Social Problems, Politics of; Social Services; Social Work: Theory and Methods; Welfare State; Women's Movements

REFERENCES AND SUGGESTED READINGS

Blankenburg, M. (1988) *Internationale Wohlfahrt. Ursprünge und Entwicklung des ICSW* (International Welfare: Origins and Developement of the ICSW). ICSW, Berlin.

Bruno, F. J. (1948) *Trends in Social Work – As reflected in the Proceedings of the National Conference of Social Work 1874–1946*. Columbia University Press, New York.

Conference Organizing Committee for the XIX International Conference on Social Welfare (Ed.) (1978) *Human Well-Being: The Challenge of Continuity and Change*. 50th Anniversary Publication.

Friedlaender, W. A. (1975) *International Social Welfare*. Prentice-Hall, Englewood Cliffs, NJ.

Hering, S. & Waaldijk, B. (Eds.) (2003) *History of Social Work in Europe (1900–1960): Female Pioneers and Their Influence on the Development of International Organizations*. Leske & Budrich Opladen.

Kendall, K. (1998) *IASSW – The First Fifty Years 1928–1978. A Tribute to the Founders*. International Association of Schools of Social Work, Alexandria, VA.

Lorenz, W. (1994) *Social Work in a Changing Europe*. Routledge, London.

Macdonald, J. (1975) *The International Council of Social Welfare: Yesterday, Today and Tomorrow*. New York.

Sand, R. (1931) *Le Service social à travers le monde – Assistance, Prévoyance, Hygiène*. Paris.

Stearns, P. (Ed.) (1994) *Encyclopedia of Social History*. Oxford University Press, New York.

Willemin, G. & Heacock, R. (1984) *The International Committee of the Red Cross*. The Hague.

social work: theory and methods

Silvia Staub-Bernasconi

Theory construction in social work which tries to bind together theory and methods and to introduce the notion of social work as discipline and profession departs from an "open triangle" consisting of theory as an interrelated conceptual system, research, and practice, or applied social science plus social work values and skills linked in a dynamic way (Lovelock et al. 2004: 3). Thus it is a basic scientific undertaking to connect the following elements: a theory of the individual as a biological, psychic, and social being and as a member of different social systems; a theory of society and culture and the interaction between the individual and society/culture; a policy or program as a scheme for changing problematic situations; and a set of people, among them professionals, in different forms of social organization (social services, social movements, networks, etc.) committed to carrying this change through with the help of specific methods.

Looking at the history of ideas in social work (Soydan 1999), one has to start with the contributions of two classical theorists: Mary Richmond and Jane Addams, who paved the way for the two main theoretical traditions of social work focusing on individuals and/or society. Mary Richmond focused on the individual, his or her personality and unmet needs, and the social environment upon which the individual depends for need satisfaction. Seeking the main causes of social problems within the individual, her change program was therefore oriented to the individual – as in professional casework – in order to remedy social problems. Jane Addams's theoretical focus was basically on the structure and culture of society and their influence upon the individual. She developed a normative vision of integral democracy that promoted freedom and participation, but also social care and justice for all. In addition she realized that it was essential to develop social change programs on the basis of scientific knowledge and genuine research. For Addams, the causes of social problems had to be sought in societal structures and their cultural legitimation. The work of change therefore had to be directed at these conditions. Thus one had to fight – along with political parties and other organizations and professions – for the institutionalization of new laws of social security, especially for the protection of children and women in abusive work conditions, or one had to change the actual social rules or ideologies that allowed exploitation in the workplace, discrimination against women, and legitimation of wars on nationalistic grounds that made heros out of soldiers. This approach to individual and social change was reflected in a multilevel conception of social work activities that encompassed activities on the individual, family, community, regional, state, and international levels.

The split of theory and action between Richmond and Addams into a micro and macro approach, together with the implicit or explicit claim of exclusiveness by both parties, is not unique in the history of human and social sciences, and persists to the present day. Yet, there are mediating positions, too, the most prominent being the internationally consensual definition of social work as follows: "The social work profession promotes social change, problem solving in human relationships and the empowerment and liberation of people to enhance well-being. *Utilizing theories of human behavior and social systems, social work intervenes at the points where people interact with their environments.* Principles of human rights and social justice are fundamental to social work."

THEORETICAL AND PRACTICAL APPROACHES: THE FOCUS ON INDIVIDUALS

After the pioneer contributions of Richmond and Alice Salomon in Germany, *psychodynamic concepts* became the first strong explanatory theory for many practice concepts (see Payne 1991).

Psychoanalytic social work. Florence Hollis adapted psychoanalytic theory for social work practice by developing the notions of a sustaining relationship and techniques to reduce anxiety, low self-esteem, and lack of confidence. She added procedures of environmental work with people relevant to the client (family members, employers, landlords). The role of the social worker is as an interpreter of feelings, promoter of insights, provider or creator of resources, and mediator or protector (of children). Although there may be things wrong with society, the social worker's main task is to help the individual to cope with problems in developing a realistic – anxiety-free – perspective of his or her situation and adapting to it. The professional seeks social reform here as a separate activity.

Behavioral theories and methods derive from the work of experimental behavioral psychologists which criticized the diffuse, untestable conceptions of psychoanalytic theory. The behavior of clients is seen as coping with frustration and aggression in different role settings. Action-oriented concepts are classical conditioning by stimulus-response, the techniques of operant conditioning, and social learning. The social worker has to manage contingencies that affect the relationship between the behavior of an individual and its (un)desired social consequences. The main goal is adequate role behavior as parent, pupil, employee, and so on.

Cognitive theories work on the assumption that people construct their own versions of reality and problems through what they have learned. Stimuli are transformed by a process of awareness, description, and interpretation into overt behavior. There can be conflicts between self-conceptions, perceiving self through others, and intentional self. The task of the social worker is to support strategies of learning such as discrimination, concept formation, value finding, and problem solving, sustained by a diary and tasks (homework). The social worker confronts the client with her divergent thinking, pointing out inconsistencies and faulty and alternative modes of thinking, with the aim of finding a more rational way to solve problems.

Task-centered social work seeks to replace psychodynamic social work based on a "time-consuming" supportive relationship with a rationally planned, "short-term therapy" that has a clear time limit. It rejects any specific psychological or sociological base for its methods, because no theory can adequately explain the range of problems that social work has to deal with. Central to this approach is what the client presents or accepts as problems and what he wants to change in his life, as well as the establishing of a contract about the desired outcome, the amount of contact and time limits, and the arrangement of incentives for success.

Strength development. Strength or resilience is seen as a product of facing adverse life events and traumatic situations which can be used as a resource for actual problem solving. Strengths-focused listening is the main method, i.e., observing until, through mutual discovery, events and themes can be found that mobilize the courage to try new behavior.

An integrated – systemic – view would combine these approaches in such a way that it would become clear that individuals have emotions, cognitions, values, self-concepts, and so on that all influence how they cope with life tasks and social problems. The last two approaches coincide with the beginning of the

neoliberal hegemony favoring methodologicial "fast-food versions" (James, in Lovelock et al. 2004).

THEORIES AND METHODS: INTERACTION OR NETWORKS BETWEEN INDIVIDUALS

As these theories start with a conception of the individual as a member of families, groups, communities, and organizations, it is possible to speak of the beginning of systems theory in social work. Yet, their focus is mostly on communication patterns, leaving aside an elaborated systemic theory of individual and society. Many of them focus on symbolic interaction and role expectations, especially in relation to processes of stigmatizing, scapegoating, and exclusion (Mead, Goffmann). These interaction processes describe the behavior and problems of social work clients with their social environment as a result of the possible stigmatizing effects of social workers in "people-processing organizations."

A prominent approach in family treatment is *transaction analysis*, which comes from psychodynamic theory and focuses on the ego states in one person (as child, parent, adult) interacting with those in another person. When transactions involve different ego states, problems and misunderstandings arise. The role of the social worker is to analyze and change communication patterns which make the other feel bad, incompetent, powerless, and inferior. Further techniques are reframing, family sculpting, role-playing, videotaping, homework assisgments, and mediation (Kirst-Ashman & Hull 1993).

Social work with *groups* bases its interventions on the structure, culture, and dynamics of groups. The role of the social worker can be task oriented, more supportive/therapeutic, or action oriented. The last-named role can lead to economic, social, and cultural activities in the larger community.

Another set of theories conceptualizes resources of social and cultural environments in order to construct supportive social networks or organizations in a community, e.g., for the creation of new jobs suited for long-term unemployed, disabled, and minority members who have no chance of getting a job in the mainstream economy.

THE INTERFACE BETWEEN SOCIAL WORK AND SOCIAL POLICY

From the 1960s to the 1980s, "radical social work" – neo-Marxist, structural, feminist, anti-racist, anti-oppressive, or anti-discriminatory – emerged as a distinctive theoretical and practice approach. It criticized psychological explanations, which privatized social problems instead of transforming them into public issues, blamed the victim, and cut service users off from collective action by treating them individually. This was accompanied by a radical critique of the social welfare system for the overspecialization of its social agencies, for sharing mainstream ideologies and bureaucratic rigidity, and for selectively working with those who were easiest to help; in short, for simply being a servant of the ruling class. The general theoretical hypothesis was that service users – the poor, unemployed, women, ethnic minorities, and so on – would act rationally in their own interests once they understood that the true origins of their problems lay not in themselves but in exploitative and oppressive social structures and cultural codes (Leonard 1975; Galper 1980). Thus, social workers should not waste their energy changing clients' behavior to make it conform to standards of so-called normality. "Structural theory" extended the approach to all forms of overlapping and mutually reinforcing injustices in relation to class, gender, race, disability, sexual orientation, and religious and ethnic minority status (Mullaly 1997). Furthermore, the power relationships between social agency, social workers, and their clients became a target of critical reflection.

The role of social work is seen in three different ways: (1) as part of the oppressive capitalist system which has to control the working class, unwed mothers, minorities, and so on and make them fit for work; (2) as advocate of social change, promoting consciousness-raising and supporting community organization and collective action; and (3) as both agent of capitalist, paternalistic, and racist society and as willing or unwilling leader of change by transmitting new perspectives, knowledge, knowhow, and power sources to the marginalized for organizing themselves to reach their goals. Following this last line of reasoning, the role of social work is to:

- organize shelter for victims of oppression and violence, help them to regain dignity in listening to their accounts, assess their power resources, and support them to carry through their claims for social justice (for black empowerment, feminist empowerment, etc.);
- transform private troubles into public issues by building cooperatives at the community level and participating in social action;
- introduce human rights, especially social justice, into the culture and practice of social agencies according to the international code of ethics for social work (Staub-Bernasconi 1991, 2003;Reichert 2003).

INTERACTION BETWEEN INDIVIDUAL AND SOCIETY: FOUR WAVES OF SYSTEMS THEORY

General systems theory. The first system theorist in social work (Hearn 1958) used biological and cybernetic concepts such as homeostasis, entropy, equifinality, and feedback. Essential for growth was the maintenance of a "steady state" between the individual and social systems, avoiding states of entropy (disorder). Critics argued that the chosen concepts reflected a mechanistic, non-human nature of people, especially the concept of "steady state," which could legitimize patriarchal domination and violence in families.

Ecosystems perspective. Germain and Gitterman (1996) used the notion of ecosystems not as a theory but as a metaphor to focus on transactions within and across systems. For them, problems arise when there is a poor fit between a person's environment and her needs, capacities, rights, and aspirations. Change endeavors focus on transactions instead of an isolated improvement of the social functioning of individuals. The life model of social work practice (Germain & Gitterman 1996) stands for the following action principles: active partnership based on mutuality and reciprocity, assessment of life stressors in passing from one system to another (family to school, school to work), and assessment of strengths and capacities, using an "ecomap" as a pictorial representation of micro, meso, and macro systems in concentric circles and their resources, in discussion with the client. The social worker's role is to create supportive community networks. At the organizational level (school, work, social service institutions), advocacy should be aimed at changing policies if they work against client interests. This requires skills such as coalition-building, positioning, lobbying, and testifying.

Complex systems theories. Complexity theorists (Warren et al. 1998) argue that it is not stability but change – as a form of "deterministic chaos" – that is the normal feature of systems, amplified by self-reinforcing feedback with possible snowball effects and moments at which the system switches from one pattern of complexity to another. Thus social workers have to assess and use these moments to help the system to switch in the direction of social work goals. The criticism here is again that chaos theories emerged originally in math, physics, thermodynamics, and cybernetic engineering, and thus have limited application in human and social sciences. Proponents of the systems theory of Luhmann state that social problems are generated by the exclusion of people from social systems such as the family and educational, economic, political, and cultural systems; thus a new autonomous social welfare system became institutionalized which works with the excluded for their reinclusion or, if this is not successful or possible, for the management of the excluded.

The *systemic paradigm* of social work (Staub-Bernasconi 1991, 1995; Hollstein-Brinkmann & Staub-Bernasconi 2005; Obrecht 2005) sees systems theory as a chance for a unifying (meta) theoretical foundation of social work under the general idea of "integrated pluralism." It acknowledges that the reduction of systems theory to physics, biology, and cybernetics was a theoretical mistake, but that it paved the way to a more adequate, non-reductionist systemic view. The main focus is on understanding the structure and dynamics/transactions of and between biological, psychic, and social/cultural systems, and on building the transdisciplinary explanatory base for social work.

Social work practitioners face individuals with needs, cognitions, wants, hopes, plans, and learning capacities who are faced with (un) responsive, discriminating, and oppressive social systems and cultural environments, from the family to world society. Transactions between

individuals as members of social systems can be cooperative, competitive, conflictive, or destructive. It is the latter that lead to social problems. Social work practitioners point to vulnerable individuals and groups deprived of resources, power, justice, and dignity under the overarching perspective of unfulfilled human needs and human rights violations (Staub-Bernasconi 2003). The general goals of social work are the well-being of the individual and the social reform of social systems, relying on human rights, especially social justice, as regulative ideas laid down in the UN Manual on Social Work and Human Rights and the Global Accreditation Standards for Education and Training in Social Work of 2004. Methods can comprise the theoretical base and procedures of resource identification, production, and allocation; consciousness-raising; ego-strengthening; changing cognitive structures, values (i.e., self-conceptions, prejudices), interpretations, and plans; task-focused learning and behavioral training to attain specific goals; networking and mediation in relation to an unresponsive social environment; intercultural communication; empowerment, advocacy, anti-discriminatory work, and democratic participation; and finally, all the methods and techniques of influencing public and political social policy as well as legislative discourse and legislation to provide access to individuals, groups, and members of vulnerable social categories to societal resources and power.

SEE ALSO: Addams, Jane; Marginality; Marginalization, Outsiders; Social Change; Social Justice, Theories of; Social Policy, Welfare State; Social Problems, Concept and Perspectives; Social Problems, Politics of; Social Work: History and Institutions; System Theories

REFERENCES AND SUGGESTED READINGS

Dominelli, L. (2002) *Feminist Social Work: Theory and Practice.* Palgrave, Basingstoke.

Galper, J. (1980) *Social Work Practice: A Radical Perspective.* Prentice-Hall, Englewood Cliffs, NJ.

Germain, C. & Gitterman, A. (1996) *The Life Model of Social Work Practice: Advances in Theory and Practice,* 2nd edn. Columbia University Press, New York.

Healy, K. (2005) *Social Work Theories in Context: Creating Frameworks for Practice*. Palgrave Macmillan, New York.

Hearn, G. (1958) *Theory Building in Social Work*. University of Toronto Press, Toronto.

Hollstein-Brinkmann, H. & Staub-Bernasconi, S. (Eds.) (2005) *Systemtheorien im Vergleich. Versuch eines Dialogs*. VS-Verlag, Wiesbaden.

Kirst-Ashman, K. K. & Hull, G. H. (1993) *Understanding Generalist Practice*. University of Chicago Press, Chicago.

Leonard, P. (1975) Towards a Paradigm for Radical Practice. In: Bailey, R. & Brake, M. (Eds.), *Radical Social Work*. Edward Arnold, London.

Lovelock, R., Lyons, K., & Powell, J. (Eds.) (2004) *Reflecting on Social Work: Discipline and Profession*. Ashgate, Aldershot.

Mattaini, M. A., Lowery, C. T., & Meyer, C. H. (Eds.) (1998) *The Foundations of Social Work Practice*. NASW Press, Washington, DC.

Mullaly, B. (1997) *Structural Social Work: Ideology, Theory, and Practice*. Oxford University Press, Toronto.

Obrecht, W. (2005) Ontologischer, Sozialwissenschaftlicher und Sozialarbeitswissenschaftlicher Systemismus: Ein integratives Paradigma der Sozialen Arbeit. In: Hollstein-Brinkmann. H. & Staub-Bernasconi, S. (Eds.), *Systemtheorien im Vergleich. Versuch eines Dialogs*. VS-Verlag, Wiesbaden, pp. 93–172.

Payne, M. (1991) *Modern Social Work Theory: A Critical Introduction*. University of Chicago Press, Chicago.

Reichert, E. (2003) *Social Work and Human Rights: A Foundation for Policy and Practice*. Columbia University Press, New York.

Simon Levy, B. (1994) *The Empowerment Tradition in American Social Work: A History*. Columbia University Press, New York.

Soydan, H. (1999) *The History of Ideas in Social Work*. Venture Press, Birmingham, AL.

Staub-Bernasconi, S. (1991) Social Action, Empowerment, and Social Work: An Integrative Theoretical Frame of Reference for Social Work. *Journal of Community and Clinical Practice* 14, 3/4 (October): 35–51.

Staub-Bernasconi, S. (1995) *Systemtheorie, soziale Probleme und Soziale Arbeit: local, national, international*. Haupt, Bern, Stuttgart, and Vienna.

Staub-Bernasconi, S. (2003) Soziale Arbeit als (eine) Menschenrechtsprofession. In: Sorg, R. (Ed.), *Soziale Arbeit zwischen Politik und Wissenschaft*. LIT, Münster, pp. 17–54.

Warren, K. et al. (1998) New Directions in Systems Theory: Chaos and Complexity. *Social Work* 4: 357–72.

social worlds

Adele E. Clarke

The term social worlds is used in the social sciences in two main ways. One is as a generic reference to a specific situation or social context, and the second is explicit social worlds/arenas theory within the theoretical tradition of symbolic interactionism.

In its generic form, the term social world usually refers to the relatively immediate milieu of the individuals or collectivities being studied. It is conventionally understood as pointing at the specific contexts of the situation in which those individuals and/or collectivities are to be found. For example, reference may be made to the social world of antique collectors, professional baseball, or surfing. The usage is somewhat similar to the concept of subculture. However, (sub)cultural studies generally focus on the subculture per se (who the members are, what they do, how and why they do it, etc.), such as "Deadhead" or "Trekkie" fandoms. The generic use of social world usually points outward from the individuals or collectivities being studied to their salient contexts as a means of explicitly situating them in sociocultural space and time.

In symbolic interactionist theory over the past century, a series of concepts has been built up around the core concept of social world. Here as elsewhere, interactionists have taken a general term, elaborated it conceptually, and integrated it with related sensitizing concepts to form a theoretical/analytical framework useful in empirical research.

Early Chicago School studies focused on "social wholes": communities of different types (e.g., ethnic communities, elite neighborhoods, impoverished slums), distinctive locales (e.g., taxi dancehalls, the stockyards), and signal events of varying temporal durations (e.g., a strike). The sociological task was to make the *group* the focal center and to build up a knowledge of the whole by examining it in concrete situations. Instead of emphasizing shared culture as anthropologists of the time did, these early works in the Chicago tradition focused on shared territory or geographic space and the encounters and interactions of human groups that occurred within these environments or ecologies.

These inventories of social spaces often took the form of maps. Many traditional Chicago School studies were undergirded by an areal field model – a "map" of some kind done from "above," such as a city map modified to show ethnic, racial, elite, and other specific neighborhoods and/or work areas, etc. Relationality was a featured concern and the communities, organizations, and kinds of sites and collectivities represented were to be viewed both in relation to one another and within their larger contexts. Blumer (1958) was a key early paper that drew upon this framing.

In the 1950s and 1960s, researchers in the interactionist tradition reframed the study of social wholes by shifting to studies of work, occupations, and professions, moving from local to national and international groups. Geographic boundaries were dropped as necessarily salient, replaced by *shared discourses* (again, not culture) as boundary making and marking. Perhaps most significantly, they increasingly attended to the relationships of those groups to other social wholes, the interactions of collective actors and their discourses.

Sociologists Tamotsu Shibutani (1955), Rue Bucher (1962), Anselm Strauss (1978), and Howard Becker (1982) then initiated explicit social worlds theory development – the high modern version of studies of social wholes. Social worlds (e.g., a recreation group, an occupation, a theoretical tradition) generate shared perspectives that then form the basis for collective action, while individual and collective identities are constituted through commitments to and participation in social worlds. Commitment was understood as both predisposition to act and as part of identity construction. Social worlds are *universes of discourse* and principal affiliative mechanisms through which people organize social life.

Strauss argued that each social world has at least one primary activity, particular sites, and a technology (inherited or innovative means of carrying out the social world's activities) and, once underway, more formal organizations typically evolve to further one aspect or another of the world's activities. People typically participate in a number of social worlds simultaneously

and such participation usually remains highly fluid. Becker asserted that *entrepreneurs*, deeply committed and active individuals, cluster around the core of the world and mobilize those around them. Shibutani viewed social worlds as identity and meaning-making segments in mass society, drawing on distinctive aspects of mass culture, with individuals capable of participation in only a limited number of such worlds.

Every complex social world characteristically has *segments*, subdivisions or subworlds, shifting as patterns of commitment alter, reorganize, and realign (Bucher 1962; Baszanger 1998). Two or more worlds may intersect to form a new world, or one world may segment into two or more worlds. Larger *arenas* of concern are constituted of multiple social worlds focused on a given issue and prepared to act in some way, usually in struggles for power, authority, and legitimacy within that arena and beyond. In arenas, various issues are debated, negotiated, fought out, forced, and manipulated by representatives of the participating worlds and subworlds (Strauss 1978).

What this means methodologically is that, if one seeks to understand a particular social world, one must understand all the arenas in which that world participates and the other worlds in those arenas and the related discourses, as these are all mutually influential/constitutive of that world. The *boundaries* of social worlds may cross-cut or be more or less contiguous with those of formal organizations. This fluidity and the action focus fundamentally distinguish social worlds theory from most organizations theory (Clarke 1991). Society as a whole, then, can be conceptualized as consisting of layered mosaics of social worlds, arenas, and their discourses.

As part of Chicago School interactionism, social worlds/arenas theory is a conflict theory. There typically exist intraworld differences as well as the more conventionally expected interworld differences of perspective, commitment, and inscribed attributes. For Strauss, *negotiations* of various kinds – persuasion, coercion, bartering, educating, discursively and otherwise repositioning, etc. – are strategies to deal with such conflicts and are routinely engaged. Strauss (1993) also called this *processual ordering* tive and emergent aspects of interaction.

Key sociological differences emerge when researchers focus on studying the social world's work activities, organization, and discourses rather than studying individuals or organizations. Placing work–action in the analytic foreground facilitates the analysis of social worlds qua worlds. Here social worlds and arenas become the units of analysis in studies of collective action and discourse.

There can also be *implicated actors* in a social world, actors silenced or only discursively present – constructed by others for their own purposes (Clarke 2005). This concept provides a means of analyzing the situatedness of less powerful actors and the consequences of others' actions for them, and raises issues of discursive constructions of actors. There are at least two kinds of implicated actors. First, there are those implicated actors who are physically present but are generally silenced, ignored, or made invisible by those in power in the social world or arena. Second, there are those implicated actors *not* physically present in a given social world but solely discursively constructed. They are conceived, represented, and perhaps targeted by the work of those others; hence, they are discursively present.

Star and Griesemer (1989) developed the concept of *boundary objects* for things that exist at junctures where varied social worlds meet in an arena of mutual concern. Boundary objects can be treaties among countries, software programs for users in different settings, and even concepts themselves. The object is "translated" to address the multiple specific needs or demands placed upon it by each of the different worlds involved. Boundary objects are often very important and hence can be sites of intense controversy and competition for the power to define them. The study of boundary objects can be an important pathway into often complicated situations, allowing the analyst to study the different social worlds through their distinctive relations with and discourses about the boundary object in question.

Drawing upon Bucher's (1962) insights, interactionists have examined fluidity and change within social worlds and arenas by extending social movements analysis to include studies of reform movements of various kinds undertaken by segments or subworlds within professions, disciplines, and work organizations.

Such reform movements can cut across whole arenas. Fujimura (1996), who studied the molecularization of biology, called such larger-scale processes *bandwagons*. In many arenas, reform movements have centered on processes of homogenization, standardization, and formal classifications – things that would organize and articulate the work of the social worlds in that arena in parallel ways (Bowker & Star 1999). (This contrasts with theories of organizational isomorphism.)

Extending Strauss's work on articulation, Fujimura (1996) introduced the concept of *doable problems*. Doable problems require successful alignment across several scales of work organization. In her example in science, this included (1) the experiment as a set of tasks; (2) the laboratory as a bundle of experiments and other administrative and professional tasks; and (3) the wider scientific social world as the work of laboratories, colleagues, sponsors, regulators, and other players all focused on the same family of problems. Doability is achieved by articulating alignment at all three scales simultaneously to meet the demands and constraints imposed: a problem must provide doable experiments, be feasible within the parameters of immediate constraints and opportunities in a given laboratory, and be viewed as worthwhile and supportable work within the larger scientific social world.

The concept of *staged intersections* – one-shot or short-term events in which multiple social worlds in the arena come together – is Garrety's (1998) particular contribution to social worlds/arenas theory. The key feature of staged intersections is that despite the fact that the same representatives of those worlds probably will never come together again, the events can be highly consequential for the future of all the social worlds involved, for the arena, and beyond. They can be what Strauss termed turning points in trajectories.

The social worlds/arenas framework has recently been used as the conceptual infrastructure of a new mode of grounded theory for qualitative research called situational analysis (Clarke 2005). Here, making maps of social worlds and their arenas is part of the data analysis, providing portraits of collective action at the meso level. The key analytic power of social worlds/arenas theory, so rooted in Chicago social ecologies, is the elasticity of the various concepts to analyze at multiple levels of complexity.

SEE ALSO: Mesostructure; Networks; Public Realm; Reference Groups; Symbolic Interaction

REFERENCES AND SUGGESTED READINGS

Baszanger, I. (1998) *Inventing Pain Medicine: From the Laboratory to the Clinic*. Rutgers University Press, New Brunswick, NJ.

Becker, H. S. (1982) *Art Worlds*. University of California Press, Berkeley.

Blumer, H. (1958) Race Prejudice as a Sense of Group Position. *Pacific Sociological Review* 1: 3–8.

Bowker, G. C. & Star, S. L. (1999) *Sorting Things Out: Classification and Its Consequences*. MIT Press, Cambridge, MA.

Bucher, R. (1962) Pathology: A Study of Social Movements Within a Profession. *Social Problems* 10: 40–51.

Clarke, A. E. (1991) Social Worlds Theory as Organizational Theory. In: Maines, D. (Ed.), *Social Organization and Social Process: Essays in Honor of Anselm Strauss*. Aldine de Gruyter, Hawthorne, NY, pp. 119–58.

Clarke, A. E. (2005) *Situational Analysis: Grounded Theory After the Postmodern Turn*. Sage, Thousand Oaks, CA.

Fujimura, J. H. (1996) *Crafting Science: A Socio-History of the Quest for the Genetics of Cancer*. Harvard University Press, Cambridge, MA.

Garrety, K. (1998) Science, Policy, and Controversy in the Cholesterol Arena. *Symbolic Interaction* 21(4): 401–24.

Shibutani, T. (1955) Reference Groups as Perspectives. *American Journal of Sociology* 60: 562–9.

Shibutani, T. (1986) *Social Processes: An Introduction to Sociology*. University of California Press, Berkeley.

Star, S. L. & Griesemer, J. R. (1989) Institutional Ecology, "Translations" and Boundary Objects: Amateurs and Professionals in Berkeley's Museum of Vertebrate Zoology, 1907–1939. *Social Studies of Science* 19: 387–420. Reprinted in Biagioli, M. (Ed.) (1999) *The Science Studies Reader*. Routledge, New York, pp. 505–24.

Strauss, A. L. (1978) A Social Worlds Perspective. *Studies in Symbolic Interaction* 1: 119–28.

Strauss, A. L. (1993) *Continual Permutation of Action*. Aldine de Gruyter, New York.

socialism

Lloyd Cox

Socialism refers to doctrines and practices sharing a pattern of family resemblances centered on collective property, social equality, cooperation, and communal forms of economic and political association. Beyond these shared attributes, socialism as doctrine and practice is characterized by immense diversity and competing claims to authenticity, which belie the frequent eliding of socialism with Marxism. This internal diversity was already present when the term was first used in English in the 1820s and in French and German in the 1830s, as well as in earlier political and religious movements that anticipated future socialist practices.

Although it is sometimes suggested that socialist forms of organization constituted the original human condition prior to the emergence of agriculture and urbanization in the Near East (8,000–10,000 BCE), the genealogy of socialism in its contemporary senses can be traced to early modern Europe. Early Christian-inspired radical movements, such as the Levelers and especially the Diggers in seventeenth-century England, and the Anabaptists in sixteenth- and seventeenth-century Central Europe, propounded ideas that had a clear socialist resonance, as did Babeuf during the French Revolution, with his "Conspiracy of the Equals." Socialist ideas received a more systematic elaboration, however, in the works of three early nineteenth-century thinkers – Claude Henri de Rouvroy, Comte de Saint-Simon (1760–1825), François-Charles Fourier (1772–1837), and Robert Owen (1771–1858).

While all three have routinely been grouped under the unifying label of "utopian socialist," this tells us more about the mid-nineteenth-century reception of their ideas than it does about the distinctive content of their socialism. They all shared an antipathy to individualism, a desire to replace competition with cooperation, and a belief that a positive science of society and human nature was possible, which could be a guide to social organization. But they differed significantly over the concrete detail of the social forms that they advocated, how they could be realized, and the understandings of human nature on which they were based. Saint-Simon and Fourier rejected the Enlightenment view propounded by Rousseau and others that human nature, while inherently good, noble, and rational, had been corrupted by modern society in general and private property in particular. Instead, they argued that human nature was typified by fixed personality types, which could only be brought into more harmonious coexistence by cooperative social arrangements. By contrast, Owen endorsed the view that human nature was malleable and shaped by objective circumstances. The latter could and should, therefore, be arranged in ways that contribute to the perfectibility of humankind. Cooperation and solidarity should replace competition and individualism, thus ensuring human happiness and collective harmony. This vision was given practical effect in England in Owen's New Lanark textile mill and other cooperative communities that were established according to his principles.

Socialist ideas gained a more widespread currency in England, France, and the German-speaking states during the 1830s and 1840s. Accelerated industrialization and urbanization, and the social problems that they brought in their wake, gave rise to various radical movements for social reform and transformation. These included early working-class organizations, cooperative movements, trade unions, and Chartism, plus a range of anti-modernist groupings that sought refuge in projects for the reconstruction of premodern communalism. It was in this milieu of social and political ferment that Marx and Engels began developing their distinctive brand of what Engels would later refer to as "scientific socialism."

Marx and Engels did not begin their intellectual careers as socialists, much less communists. Their early anti-clerical, radical democratic politics only gave way to a more explicitly socialist position with the elaboration of a distinctive perspective on history, capitalism, and class. According to the materialist conception of history, history involves the progressive unfolding of distinct stages, each defined by a dominant set of production relations. Revolutionary transformations of society had in the past, Marx and Engels contended, always resulted in the emergence of new class-divided societies, but on a more advanced material plane. It was only with

the advent of capitalism, and its relentless drive to improve labor productivity through technological innovation and intensified exploitation of the modern proletariat, that the material and political preconditions for socialism were laid.

Marx famously declined to systematically outline any blueprints for the socialist future that he envisaged. He was not, he once wrote, in the business of writing recipes for the kitchens of the future. Nevertheless, passages scattered in his political writings offer important insights into his views on socialism and the transition from capitalism to socialism. In his reflections on *The Class Struggles in France, 1848–1850*, for example, he concluded that the abolition of capitalism would necessitate a transitionary political form that he labeled as the "dictatorship of the proletariat." In the immediate aftermath of capitalism's overthrow, Marx reasoned, the new proletarian ruling class would need to exercise power ruthlessly over all other classes whose actions and interests threatened a return to the old social order. But it could not do so by simply claiming the capitalist state machinery as its own. This had to be destroyed and replaced by state institutions of a new type.

The Paris Commune of 1871 – where for over two months Parisian workers seized power in the French capital – offered Marx a rare glimpse of the institutions that might constitute such a new state type. In particular, he endorsed the Commune's fledgling efforts to overcome the capitalist division between political and economic life. This was manifested in universal suffrage and the election of workers to local and national delegations of workers' deputies, which combined executive, legislative, and judicial functions. These representatives were to be accountable and recallable at short notice, and to be paid no more than the workers whom they represented. They would contribute to the administration of a society in which the means of production was taken into common ownership, where the hierarchy of bureaucratic ranks and privileges within the state was abolished, and where the standing army was to be replaced by a national workers' militia with short terms of service.

The other main source for Marx's ideas on post-capitalist society is his *Critique of the Gotha Programme*, written in 1875 but not published until 1891. In it, Marx criticized the program that came out of the conference that unified the two main wings of German socialism. Here he made a distinction between a first (lower) and second (higher) phase of communism, a distinction that later came to be recognized as one between socialism and communism. In the first phase, society would remain stamped with its capitalist origins, including the residues of class relations and attitudes. As such, this transitionary stage would be one in which a state was still necessary to ensure proletarian rule, while the distribution of the social product would be in accordance with labor expended rather than differentiated individual needs – a right of inequality given the unequal endowment and needs of individual workers. With the further development of the productive forces and the transcendence of the last vestiges of capitalism, the state would wither away and social need would become the main criterion determining distribution in the higher phase of communism. All of this could only be accomplished if an initial national proletarian revolution was internationalized.

In the decades following Marx's death in 1883, his particular brand of socialism was the subject of fierce controversies both within and outside socialist circles. From the outside, Max Weber and other liberals criticized what they viewed as the illiberal implications of socialism in general and Marxism in particular. For Weber, socialism would entail an accentuation of the worst bureaucratic features of modernity. It would remove competing sources of authority within society, concentrating all power in the hands of state officials. In so doing, individual autonomy would be severely curtailed, and the key mechanisms ensuring economic dynamism under capitalism – interfirm competition and entrepreneurial initiative – would be removed. The result would be human servility combined with economic stagnation, tendencies of socialism that many liberals after Weber viewed as being confirmed by the history of the Soviet Union and all other societies created in its image. Socialism was, as the title of Hayek's book would later assert, *The Road to Serfdom* (1944).

The nature of socialism and the means by which it could be realized were also key areas of debate within socialist movements. In Germany in the 1890s, this took the form of the so-called

"revisionist" controversy between defenders of Marxist orthodoxy and those who argued that the Social Democratic Party's theory had to be revised to bring it into line with its reformist practice, and with the changed conditions of contemporary capitalism. Eduard Bernstein, the key advocate of revisionism, claimed that many of the defining propositions of orthodoxy had been falsified by economic and political developments. In particular, the increased dispersal of property ownership through the growth of joint-stock companies, the rise of state-led social insurance that ameliorated the conditions and insecurities of workers, and the growing parliamentary influence of organized labor all contributed to social improvements that obviated the need for socialist revolution. Rather, socialism could and should be realized through the movement of incremental reforms, pursued through parliaments, which improved the lot of workers in the present rather than through a violent revolution in search of an uncertain utopian future.

This pragmatic, social reform-oriented socialism was not confined to Germany. It found its corollaries in progressivism in the United States, laborism in Australasia, the establishment of reformist socialist parties in France and Italy, and Fabianism in Britain (under whose direct influence Bernstein had come while living in England). Fabianism had emerged in the 1880s, and found(ed) an institutional embodiment and medium for its ideas through the establishment of the Fabian Society and the London School of Economics. The Fabian Society was the prototypical left-wing think tank, and went on to become affiliated to the British Labour Party. Its principal early figures included George Bernard Shaw and Sydney and Beatrice Webb, for whom systematic social research provided a means of illuminating and publicizing poverty and disadvantage, which could then be addressed through state-sanctioned social reforms. As such, they pioneered the traditions of sociologically informed public policy, and public policy-inspired sociology, which came to inseparably link sociology and socialism in the minds of many politicians, scholars, and lay people.

During their travels around the turn of the nineteenth and twentieth centuries, Sydney and Beatrice Webb had been particularly impressed by the social reforms that they encountered in the seven British colonies that were on the verge of becoming the national states of Australia and New Zealand. They were not the only ones. The French socialist Albert Meitin had written in glowing terms of Australasia's pragmatic *Socialism Without Doctrines*, while the American socialist Henry Damerest Lloyd had espoused a "New Zealandization of the world," in reaction to industrial and social arrangements that he viewed as exemplary. Such observers were expressing an enthusiasm for institutions and reforms that in their eyes established "already existing socialism" long before that phrase had been coined. State-led industrial arbitration and conciliation systems, relatively high wages for workers, early suffrage for women, and the beginnings of a social safety net in the form of invalid and old-age benefits were just some of the innovations that fired the socialist imagination.

The early formation of mass workers' parties in Australasia's white settler societies contrasted with their absence in the US. It was not so much that socialism was absent in the US – Edward Bellamy, progressivism, the Industrial Workers of the World (Wobblies), and the American Socialist Party itself confirm that socialist doctrines and practice were very much present in the US in the decades before World War I – as that it failed to find expression in the formation of a mass workers' party. Consequently, Sombart's question as to why socialism fails in the US retains its relevance today. Many answers have been proffered. These include ones emphasizing the dominant individualistic ethos in the US, born of the necessity of self-reliance in a frontier society; the greater opportunities for upward mobility than was the case in Europe; the damaging consequences of slavery and its political epilogue on working-class solidarity; the greater religiosity of the US population, with their contempt for socialist atheism; the militancy and effectiveness of US economic and political elites in suppressing many forms of collectivism; and the association of socialism with the immigrant Central Eastern European intellectuals and workers who were early propagandists and agitators for socialism. As was often lamented, socialism failed to "Americanize." This was exacerbated by the Bolshevik Revolution and its aftermath.

The seizure and consolidation of state power in Russia by the Bolsheviks in and after 1917 was pivotal to the subsequent history of international socialism. Its consequences were several. First, the USSR came to be associated with socialism per se, by both supporters and critics of the new regime. Supporters argued that the socialization of the main means of production, the subordination of market mechanisms to central planning, and the state's monopoly over foreign trade and domestic finance were the sources of rapid industrialization from the early 1930s and a growing equality of consumption. Critics, on the other hand, suggested that this was fanciful reasoning as it ignored the basic facts of bureaucratization, continued inequality, growing political repression, and the extinction of democracy, all of which discredited the very idea of socialism. Second, the Russian Revolution was significant in that it was instrumental in establishing (in 1919) an organization ostensibly committed to world socialist revolution – the Third or Communist International. The Comintern came to dominate communist parties around the world (for which the histories of the French, Italian, Spanish, and Greek communist parties, for example, bear ample witness), with the latter being increasingly subordinated to the needs of Soviet foreign and domestic policy. This was bound up with the third critical consequence of Soviet power for socialism, namely, that the Soviet Union helped to establish a series of regimes in its own image in Eastern Europe. These came to be equated with "already existing socialism," an ideologically defined political bloc that constituted one part of the Cold War structural divide. Finally, Soviet power was significant for socialism insofar as it was the site for the elaboration and practice of "socialism in one country," which Stalin developed from the mid-1920s, and which can be viewed as a key episode in the marriage of socialism with nationalism.

During the decades of decolonization after World War II, this coupling of socialism with nationalism would become a central feature of so-called third world socialism, from China and Vietnam to Nicaragua and Cuba. In Cuba, for instance, what had in the main been an anti-imperialist, nationalist movement, combining sectors of the national bourgeoisie, intelligentsia, workers, and the peasantry within a popular front for national liberation (July 26

Movement), moved increasingly leftward under the pressure of internal and external circumstance. By the early 1960s, Castro had nationalized the commanding heights of the Cuban economy, implemented central planning and a radical program of land reform, and consolidated one-party rule, albeit one that had greater popular support than the ruling regimes of Eastern Europe and the Soviet Union itself. This support was at least in part built on the social successes of Castro's regime. Despite a crippling US economic blockade, which has still not been lifted, Cuba established itself as a leader amongst Latin American countries in terms of health, education, and other social indicators. The 1991 collapse of the Soviet Union and hence Soviet support, however, has jeopardized these achievements.

On the other side of the Cold War divide, the Keynesian-inspired welfare states of Scandinavia, Western Europe, and Australasia provided the main modernist alternatives to Soviet-style socialism. Premised on Keynesian countercyclical demand management, economic nationalism, a commitment to full employment, political pluralism, and a significant degree of decommodification in the provision of social services, the welfare state blurred the boundaries between capitalism and socialism. For a time, it seemed that the five great evils of modern society that Beveridge identified in 1940s Britain – want, ignorance, squalor, disease, and idleness – could be transcended by the judicious application of social(ist) policy within what remained essentially capitalist economies. The relative economic and political success of that model, combined with its redistributive potential, was reflected in its widespread endorsement on the left and toleration on the right. Market socialism, or socialism with markets, became the dominant model advocated by a generation of democratic socialists in the three decades following World War II.

But the welfare state was not without its detractors. These became more vociferous from the early 1970s, with the emergence of stagflation and increased social and industrial unrest in the heartlands of modern welfare capitalism. Marxists argued that the welfare state contributed to the economic, political, and ideological reproduction of capitalism without significantly mitigating inequality or exploitation. At the same time, it enhanced the state's surveillance over the working class, thus constituting a powerful instrument of social control. The "welfare" state remained essentially a capitalist state, pseudo-socialism at best, despite what Marxists would acknowledge were progressive social reforms. Socialist feminists are similarly skeptical of the welfare state's socialist credentials. They point to the implicit gendered assumptions on which many welfare policies are based, not least of which are family and work policies frequently aimed at manipulating female fertility in the cause of particular demographic outcomes. Moreover, they are clear that the welfare state has had very different outcomes for middle-class and working-class women, typically enhancing the welfare of the former while functioning as a mechanism of social monitoring and control over the latter. For socialist feminists, socialism will only retain a progressive content and promise if it is based on an understanding of the patriarchal forms on which modern capitalism is founded.

The other main critique of the modern welfare state is as much a criticism of socialism and collectivism more generally. From the 1970s through to the new century, a resurgent economic liberalism affirmed the economic and political bankruptcy of the welfare state and socialism. Socialism in all of its variants was regarded as being inherently predisposed to economic stagnation, and restricting of human liberty. The collapse of eastern bloc state socialism in the early 1990s was presented as confirmation of this diagnosis, with an end of socialism and end of history triumphalism marking sociological and political discussion in the last decade of the twentieth century. Capitalism was now the only game in town, and debate would revolve around the forms that it should take rather than an alternative to it.

This triumphalism was the corollary of and contributor to the contemporary "crisis of socialism," which much of the left has bemoaned for the past two decades. While this crisis is real enough, being felt in the spheres of institutions, theory, and practice, there are fledgling signs of socialist renewal. Most importantly, socialist ideas and ideals have infused much of the antiglobalization and environmentalist movements that have grown in recent years. Regardless, it is clear that the problems of social inequality, injustice, and deprivation that gave rise to socialism in the first place are still with us, which makes it premature to eulogize the death of socialism.

SEE ALSO: Anarchism; Capitalism; Citizenship; Communism; Decolonization; Engels, Friedrich; Environmental Movements; Global Justice as a Social Movement; Individualism; Laborism; Marx, Karl; Nationalism; Property, Private; Revolutions, Sociology of; Socialist Feminism; Socialist Medicine; Utopia

REFERENCES AND SUGGESTED READINGS

Beilharz, P. (1994) *Postmodern Socialism: Romanticism, City, and State*. Melbourne University Press, Melbourne.
Castro, F. (1972) *Revolutionary Struggle, 1947–1958*. Cambridge, MA, MIT Press.
Cole, G. D. H. (1953–60) *A History of Socialist Thought*, Vols. 1–5. Macmillan, London.
Hayek, F. A. von (1944) *The Road to Serfdom*. Dymock's Books, Sydney.
Lenin, V. I. (1932) *State and Revolution*. International Press, New York.
Lipset, S. M. & Marks, G. (1999) *It Didn't Happen Here: Why Socialism Failed in the United States*. Norton, New York.
Marx, K. (1959) *Critique of the Gotha Programme*. Foreign Languages Press, Moscow.
Marx, K. (1972) *The Class Struggles in France, 1848–1850*. International Publishers, New York.
Marx, K. (1998) *The Communist Manifesto*. Verso, London and New York.
Sassoon, D. (1996) *One Hundred Years of Socialism: The West European Left in the Twentieth Century*. New Press, New York.
Stalin, J. V. (1972) *Economic Problems of Socialism in the USSR*. Foreign Language Press, Peking.

socialist feminism

Ann Cronin

Socialist feminism, which draws on aspects of Marxist feminism and radical feminism, emerged in the 1970s as a possible solution to the limitations of existing feminist theory. While Marxist feminism cites capitalism as the cause of women's oppression, radical feminism argues that women are oppressed through the system of patriarchy. Marxist feminism has been criticized for its inability to explain women's oppression outside of the logic of capitalism, and radical feminism for producing a universalistic, biologically based account of women's oppression, which pays insufficient attention to patterned differences between women. Socialist feminism attempts to overcome these problems through the production of historically situated accounts of women's oppression that focus on both capitalism and patriarchy.

In Mitchell's (1975) psychoanalytic model, capitalism – the economic system – is allocated to the material level; patriarchy – the rule of law – is allocated to the ideological level and assumed to operate at an unconscious level. While Eisenstein (1984) retains Mitchell's conceptualization of capitalism, she reassigns patriarchy to the conscious cultural level and dismisses any distinction between the two, leading to the term "capitalist patriarchy." In contrast, Hartmann (1979) produces a materialist understanding of patriarchy and capitalism as two distinct but interactive systems which center on men's exploitation of women's labor. Challenging Eisenstein's single-system theory, Hartmann states that patriarchy predates capitalism and exists beyond its boundaries; thus, it is inappropriate to regard them in terms of a single system.

The allocation of patriarchy to either the material, cultural, or ideological level does not permit an analysis of the pervasive nature of patriarchal structures across all three levels. Simultaneously, it assumes that all social structures can be reduced to the workings of either capitalism or patriarchy, whilst assuming there is a symbiotic relationship between the two. A focus on paid work dismisses radical feminist concerns with sexuality and violence.

Walby's (1990) dual-systems approach attempts to overcome these problems through a historically and socially defined understanding of patriarchy as a system of six interrelated structures (paid work; household production; culture; sexuality; violence; the state), which in contemporary society are in articulation with capitalism and racism. This model enables Walby to chart the dynamic nature of patriarchy over the last 150 years, including the move from a private to a public form of patriarchy.

SEE ALSO: Feminism; Gender Ideology and Gender Role Ideology; Liberal Feminism; Patriarchy; Psychoanalytic Feminism; Radical Feminism; Socialism

REFERENCES AND SUGGESTED READINGS

Eisenstein, H. (1984) *Contemporary Feminist Thought*. Allen & Unwin, London.
Hartmann, H. I. (1979) Capitalism, Patriarchy, and Job Segregation by Sex. In: Eisenstein, Z. R. (Ed.), *Capitalist Patriarchy*. Monthly Review Press, New York.
Mitchell, J. (1975) *Psychoanalysis and Feminism*. Penguin, Harmondsworth.
Ramazanoglu, C. (1989) *Feminism and the Contradictions of Oppression*. Routledge, New York.
Walby, S. (1990) *Theorizing Patriarchy*. Blackwell, Oxford.

socialist medicine

Mark G. Field

The term socialist medicine applies to a health care delivery system designed to provide preventive, diagnostic, clinical, rehabilitative, educational, and custodial services to a designated population free of charge at the time of the service. The prototype of socialist medicine is also known as Soviet socialized medicine.

At a time when health care is being recognized as a basic human right, Soviet socialist medicine has often been cited as a model for the universal provision of health care. The nature and structure of Soviet socialist medicine reflected the ideological and political orientation of the Soviet regime. There were two major ideas underlying the health care system of the former Soviet Union. One was that illness and premature mortality were primarily the product of a flawed system (capitalism) and its exploitation of the working class. This exploitation exposed workers to a series of pathogenic elements that affected their health and well-being: poor pay, child labor, long working hours, miserable housing conditions, inadequate nutrition, and a noxious social environment (Engels 1958). Thus, capitalism was indicted as the major etiological factor in illness and early death. Only socialism (and eventually communism) would eliminate the sources of most socially caused ill health.

The second idea was that the provision of health care under capitalism meant that workers were, in most instances, deprived of access to such care because they could not afford it. The removal of that payment by the patient meant the elimination of the barrier to health care. Under socialist medicine, it was society (i.e., the polity) that would henceforth shoulder the responsibility for the provision of health services to the entire population. The Soviet Union was the first country in the world to promise universal and free health services as a constitutional right (Sigerist 1937, 1947). This would also permit physicians to stop being engaged in a "commercial" transaction and enable them to treat patients without being fettered with questions of money. By the same token, hospital and other health institutions would also offer free services at the expense of the state. The promise of gratuitous and universal (though not necessarily equal) medical care to the entire nation was one of the few redeeming factors of an otherwise bleak totalitarian regime. It was often held as an example to emulate worldwide, and served as important propaganda for use at home and abroad.

The term used in the Constitution for health care is *zdravookhranenie*, a Russian-language combination of two words meaning health and protection, a duality already visible in Greek mythology. Aesculapius, the God of Medicine, had two quarrelsome daughters, Hygiea and Panacea. Hygiea was the goddess of health through healthy living (thus of prevention and preservation). Panacea was the goddess of cure, but eventually the demand for Panacea's services grew so much as to exceed her capacity to help everyone and soon outstripped many people's ability to obtain needed services.

The history of Soviet socialist medicine can be divided into two phases. In the first ten years after the revolution of 1917, the ideology of Hygiea and Marxism prevailed. The basic assumption, noted above, was that the establishment of socialism, and eventually communism, would eliminate most sources of illness and early death through an overall improvement in the living and working conditions of the workers, and eventually the entire population. The situation changed radically after Stalin assumed total power at the end of the 1920s and launched a massive program of industrialization and militarization, domestically financed primarily through enforced savings at the expense of the population (particularly the peasantry). Under these circumstances, an improvement of the standard of living of the population gave way to the transformation of the economy. Panacea took over with the responsibility of treating the population to ensure the maximum productivity and military strength. The principle of free care at the time of service, however, remained in force. It was accompanied by a rapid increase in the number of physicians (mostly women) and an expansion of medical facilities, as well as a gradual stratification in health care according to rank, residence, or occupation (Field 1957).

Health personnel at all levels became state-salaried employees. It was therefore not an insurance scheme in which subscribers paid a "dedicated" premium to reimburse physicians and hospitals. It was not an indemnity scheme, a copayment or deductible arrangement, nor a private, religious, or charitable organization. It became a state public service, just like education in most countries. Furthermore, the concept of the physician as an autonomous professional practitioner was not part of socialist medicine, nor was there a corporate body of professionals able to politically influence the state or legislation (Jones 1991). The education of health personnel, at all levels, was carried out in state-funded schools, the hospitals were financed by the state, and medical and related research was carried out in state-supported institutes. Health and related services became a responsibility of the polity (Field 1967).

The Soviet scheme of socialist medicine was meant to serve both the state and the population; in theory the development of the health care system was integrated with the planning of the economy. What this meant was a high degree of control over the whole area of health care, implemented through a large and centralized bureaucratic machine headed by the Ministry of Health Protection USSR, itself under the control of the Communist Party, the supreme ruling organization of the Soviet Union. Under the national ministry, counterpart ministries in the constituent republics, and health departments down to the local levels of the governmental structure were responsible for health matters in their jurisdictional areas. Each unit of the health system was under the dual authority of the ministry (vertical control) and the corresponding governmental units (horizontal control). In general, the ministry and its units provided instructions and suggestions, and the health departments determined the tasks for their area of responsibility and received financial (tax-generated) support from their corresponding governmental unit.

The health care system was so organized that, in theory, every person knew where to turn for initial or primary care. There were basically two general networks of health institutions, plus a series of departmental or special establishments to serve specific segments of the population, leading in essence to a differentiated health care system reflecting the stratification of Soviet society.

Access to primary health care was provided to the general population on a *territorial* basis in outpatient polyclinics, and an *occupational* one. In the first case, it was the individual's home address that determined the outpatient polyclinic and the physician(s) to whom he or she was assigned. That polyclinic was the portal of entry into the health care system. There was thus little or no choice of physician or facility. In the second case, industrial organizations had their own physicians and facilities (the larger the unit, the more sophisticated its medical system) and workers were assigned to health care and to a physician on the basis of their department or shop. Outpatient clinics were affiliated with hospitals where individuals could be referred. In most urban areas, a system of emergency services was established with ambulances that could be summoned with a telephone call. The population in the countryside, by contrast, was in general poorly serviced; in many instances the primary caregiver was a *feldsher*, or physician assistant, not a physician.

In addition to the two above mentioned networks, there were departmental health care systems that serviced a specific organization, for example the armed forces, railroads, research institutes, and even department stores. Finally, there was a special set of high-quality special medical institutions reserved for the members of the elites and their families, the quality and the amenities of these institutions depending on the rank of the individual, and headed by the Kremlin Medical Unit. A promotion or demotion was accompanied by a change in one's medical category.

The ideological justification (or rationalization) for inequality was that in a period of scarcity determined by the "building of socialism," medical care was universal but available on a priority basis determined by the importance of the role of the individual. Only under far-distant communism would all people be treated equally, medically or otherwise.

The idea that society was responsible for the health of its members was, in itself, a progressive one, and an expression of social solidarity. The Soviet Union was, as mentioned above, a pioneer in this matter. But health care was so interwoven with the fabric of Soviet society that it suffered some of the same general problems that led to the collapse of the Soviet Union.

The provision of financial support on the part of the polity to operate and manage all aspects of health care is a double-edged sword: on the one hand, it can be considered as positive, since society has the power to appropriate funds for any purposes it chooses. On the other hand, what the state giveth it also taketh away. The financing of health care then becomes part of national priorities, a "line item" that must compete with many other demands, especially, in the Soviet case, national defense. In times of crisis, or change of priorities, health care is often underfunded in the light of more pressing needs, particularly since it does not produce material wealth but, on the contrary, absorbs resources. The funding of health care was often based on what the Soviets themselves called the *residual principle*; after all the line items had been taken care of, whatever was left went to health. And that was clearly insufficient. At the time the USSR broke down, it is estimated it received about 2 percent of the gross national product, down from the 6 percent it enjoyed 30 years earlier. The impact on services and health facilities and upon vital indices was catastrophic.

Health personnel in general were poorly paid, often less than regular industrial workers. Medicine was not a prestigious occupation, and its heavy feminization in a sexist society kept its status low. There was little incentive or competition among personnel, since the rewards remained the same regardless of quality, depending primarily on seniority (Knaus 1981). Because of the poor remuneration, patients often felt compelled to bribe health personnel either before the service (particularly in surgery) or after, to show gratitude and ensure future attention. Individuals, as noted, could not make a *dedicated* contribution, such as an insurance premium, that gave them a personal stake or guarantee for better care or attention. The health care system became heavily centralized, bureaucratized, subject to corruption, and rigid in responding to emergencies (as in the case of Chernobyl). In addition, the bureaucratic element often seeped into the physician–patient relationship.

The low priority given to the rural population, as a rule, meant very poor quality of health care for the peasantry. Efforts on the part of the regime to assign doctors to the countryside were often unsuccessful because the law stipulated that spouses should not be separated, and since most doctors were women, they were able to escape the assignment.

The lack of adequate funding meant that most health facilities lacked maintenance, equipment, supplies, and in the countryside, even running water. Patients often had to bring their own food, medications, sheets, blankets, and even in some instances, X-ray films. Pharmaceuticals were often in short supply or not available.

The Soviet system emphasized quantitative indices at the expense of quality. For example, hospitals were financed according to the number of beds, so that "beds" were added without the necessary infrastructure, and in buildings inappropriate for medical care.

Soviet socialist medicine broke down when the Soviet Union collapsed. Cuba is the only country that has such a system at the beginning of the twenty-first century. In short, the Soviet environment did not provide the necessary support for socialist medicine as originally conceived. Verdict: noble purpose, grandiose scheme, inadequate financing, flawed execution, mixed results.

SEE ALSO: Communism; Health Care Delivery Systems; Socialism; Socialized Medicine

REFERENCES AND SUGGESTED READINGS

Cockerham, W. C. (1999) *Health and Social Change in Russia and Eastern Europe*. Routledge, New York.

Davis, C. M. (1989) The Soviet Health System: A National Health Service in a Socialist Society. In: Field, M. G. (Ed.), *Success and Crisis in National Health Systems*. Routledge, London, pp. 233–62.

Davis, C. M. & Feshbach, M. (1980) Rising Infant Mortality in the USSR in the 1970s. US Department of Commerce, Washington, DC.

Engels, F. (1958 [1848]) *The Condition of the Working Class in England*. Macmillan, New York.

Field, M. G. (1957) *Doctor and Patient in Soviet Russia*. Harvard University Press, Cambridge, MA.

Field, M. G. (1967) *Soviet Socialized Medicine: An Introduction*. Free Press, New York.

Field, M. G. & Twigg, J. L. (Eds.) (2000) *Russia's Torn Safety Nets: Health and Social Welfare During the Transition*. St. Martin's Press, New York.

Jones, A. (Ed.) (1991) *Professions and the State: Expertise and Autonomy in the Soviet Union and Eastern Europe*. Temple University Press, Philadelphia.

Knaus, W. A. (1981) *Inside Russian Medicine*. Everest House, New York.

Pidde, A., Krivosheev, G., & Kiselev, A. (2003) Bringing the Russian Health Care System Out of Its Crisis. *Sociological Research* 42: 81–96.

Ryan, M. (1981) *Doctor and the State in the Soviet Union*. St. Martin's Press, New York.

Sigerist, H. E. (1937) *Socialized Medicine in the Soviet Union*. Norton, New York.

Sigerist, H. E. (1947) *Medicine and Health in the Soviet Union*. Citadel Press, New York.

Solomon, S. G. & Hutchinson, J. F. (Eds.) (1990) *Health and Society in Revolutionary Russia*. Indiana University Press, Bloomington.

socialization

Sal Zerilli

The concept of socialization figures prominently in sociology, underlying many of the discipline's major claims about the nature of society and social relations. Sociologists have used socialization to examine the possibility of society, the nature of social order, the reproduction of social organization, the formation of personal identities, and mechanisms of social control and deviance. The concept has also played an important role in studies of families, schools, professions, organizations, peer groups, and subcultures. In general terms, socialization is a generic concept embracing the ways people acquire the general competencies required for participation in society. At the societal level, socialization helps explain how and the extent to which large numbers of individuals come successfully to cooperate and adapt to the demands of social life (Long & Hadden 1985). At the organizational level, it summarizes processes by which newcomers to social groups and organizations are transformed from outsiders to participating members. At the personal level, it refers to the social and cultural shaping and development of the mental, emotional, and behavioral abilities of individuals.

Sociology's major conceptions of socialization have shifted over time. At the turn of the twentieth century, sociologists employed the concept to address the Hobbesian question of how social order is possible given the egoistic, asocial nature of individuals (Wentworth 1980). This understanding of socialization was crystallized in prominent early conceptions of socialization as the channeling and molding of human nature into a collective unity. Socialization was seen generally at this time as the transmutation of naturally independent beings into social creatures. This way of thinking was eventually superseded by an understanding of socialization as the individual's internalization of the social and cultural constituents of the self. This dominant formula of socialization-as-internalization helped render questions of human nature marginal to sociological interests in the subject. Sociologists have generally come to believe that social and cultural processes permeate, even constitute, the minds and bodies of individuals. Wentworth (1980) argues that sociological thought on socialization over the last 50 years has focused almost exclusively on the social aspects of individuals, and that sociologists have tended to frame these as fully constituted by society and culture. Today, sociologists regularly argue that socialization is how the individual becomes fully human or a "person."

Sociology offers three main theoretical orientations to socialization: a functional, an interactional, and a critical perspective. Structural functionalists such as Talcott Parsons and Robert Merton view socialization as a process of role-learning by which people come to adopt prescribed orientations to life which limit the ends to which they may aspire, as well as the means they can use to achieve them. Parsons claimed that role-learning was society's primary mechanism for integrating individuals into the patterns of interaction that constitute the major institutions of society. From this perspective, socialization is essentially the imprinting of cultural patterns on the personalities of individuals, or how society inculcates in its members the skills and orientations required for participation in social life. As such, successfully socialized individuals learn to function in society by interacting with others in accordance with the social roles and positions they occupy. This is a deep process leading people to treat external value standards and norms as definitive and expressive of their identity. The functionalist position was heavily influenced by Durkheim's theory of society and Freud's model of internalization. This position has declined steadily in prominence since its heyday in the 1950s and 1960s. Its influence can still be detected in the tendency of sociologists to equate socialization with the internalization of elements of society and culture, and through continuing sociological interests in role-learning.

Structural functionalism has been criticized for exaggerating society's control over individuals and for portraying people as utterly passive recipients of social influence. The symbolic interactionist perspective leans in the opposite direction by emphasizing the individual's active role in the socialization process. Symbolic interactionism traces its lineage to pragmatist philosophers such as George Herbert Mead and John Dewey, and sociologists of the Chicago School such as Herbert Blumer and Everett Hughes. For symbolic interactionists, the crux of socialization is the formation of self-concepts in the context of social relationships mediated by shared symbols. Selves are said to emerge and develop as individuals mutually construct versions of reality through communicative processes based on shared symbols, especially language. By learning how to communicate with shared meanings and symbols, individuals come to incorporate the responses of others into their actions and self-understandings. Selves emerge and develop as individuals gain experience of (1) imagining their own demeanor from the standpoint of others, (2) interpreting and evaluating these perceptions in the light of shared attitudes, and (3) adjusting their actions accordingly. Interactionists hold that people do not automatically internalize or respond to others' perceptions, attitudes, and understandings, but rather have the ability to evaluate and select from them. There are many strands of symbolic interactionism in contemporary sociology. Taken together, they exert a significant influence on sociological understandings of socialization.

Symbolic interactionism and structural functionalism have been criticized for underplaying the role of power and inequality in social life. Though they offer different perspectives on the process, critical orientations to socialization in sociology, such as Marxism and feminist theory, are unified by deep concerns with power imbalances in society and the reproduction of structures of inequality. Proponents of these perspectives generally agree that socialization is a primary mechanism of social control. Pierre Bourdieu's critical view of socialization has gained prominence in contemporary sociology. For Bourdieu, socialization is the acquisition of "habitus," which he characterizes as individuals becoming deeply habituated to the customary ways of behaving, thinking, and feeling common to other members of their social worlds. The process is one in which members who share similar positions in society inculcate in each other deeply ingrained patterns of subjective adjustments to external social conditions. For example, Bourdieu and Passeron argue in *Reproduction in Education, Society, and Culture* (1977) that schools institutionalize, honor, and transmit the cultural values and knowledge of the dominant classes in society. As a result, the background experiences and knowledge acquired by working-class students through family socialization (i.e., their habitus) do not translate easily into academic success. Many of these students adjust their aspirations and self-conceptions in the light of the obstacles these dynamics present to them in school. Their resulting poor performances and withdrawal from school culture not only serve to powerfully inhibit their chances of upward mobility, but also reinforce widespread acquiescence to economic subordination. In this way, the schools play a fundamental role in the reproduction of class inequalities. Bourdieu's ideas have found a receptive audience in contemporary sociology and exert a wide influence in many fields, most notably in studies of education in poor and working-class communities.

Many disciplines share sociology's interest in socialization. Perhaps the most influential of these fields has been Freudian psychoanalysis. The classic Freudian model of socialization posits a civilizing process at odds with human nature. The process is one in which the innate sexual urges and aggressive drives of humans are tamed and channeled into socially acceptable forms of conduct and ways of thinking. For example, Freud argues in *Civilization and its Discontents* (1961) that social forces work to transform the individual's raw drive for sexual gratification into feelings of warmth and affection for others. These same forces also redirect the individual's natural aggressiveness towards others back on himself in the form of a self-disciplining, guilt-dispensing conscience. The individual's personality develops from the manner in which she manages the resulting internal conflict between natural drives and internalized social inhibitions. Psychological defense mechanisms (e.g., sublimation) play a critical part in socialization and personality formation insofar as they enable individuals to satisfy natural urges in socially approved ways. The classic Freudian model of socialization stresses how the locus of moral regulation of action is transferred from society to the self through the individual's internalization of external authority. Many contemporary psychoanalysts subscribe to object relations theories which shift the theoretical focus from the social channeling of natural drives to people's need for relatedness to others, as well as the manner in which people develop the internal imagery of self, other, and relationship of self to others that guide them through life.

Freudian ideas exerted a deep influence on anthropological understandings of socialization (Singer 1961). In the 1920s, anthropologists influenced by psychoanalysis began to examine the cultural antecedents of individual personalities (Clausen 1968). Prior to this period, anthropologists paid relatively little attention to the relationship between personality and culture, favoring instead factual surveys of the characteristics of given cultures in and of themselves (Bidney 1967). The psychoanalytic impetus inspired many anthropologists to examine how culture stamps itself on individuals, how individuals internalize cultural elements, and how the personality develops from this enculturation process (Wentworth 1980). Well-known examples of anthropology's culture and personality orientation include Malinowski's *Sex and Repression in Savage Society* (1927), Mead's *Coming of Age in Samoa* (1928), and Benedict's *Patterns of Culture* (1934). Many contemporary anthropologists forgo questions of personality development while maintaining the discipline's quintessential concern with how distinctive patterns of culture are preserved, understood, and transmitted across generations. Much of the work on socialization in cultural anthropology is steeped in a social constructionist paradigm that rejects psychoanalysis in favor of studying how people transmit and acquire meanings, practices, and methods of reality construction, as well as the ecological, institutional, and economic forces impinging on these processes.

Psychologists have generated an array of orientations to socialization, most of which emphasize aspects of individual development. Cognitive psychologists such as Piaget (1926) and Kohlberg (1981) envision socialization as a process of development in which new experiences spur the individual to move through qualitatively distinct stages of cognitive and moral growth. For behavioral psychologists, socialization is the learning of patterns of behavior through conditioning or through regular participation in recurring interactional activities such as observing and imitating (Bandura and Walters 1963). Blending behavioral psychology and psychoanalysis, many personality psychologists contend that the individual's personality is firmly established in early life through behavioral reinforcements and punishments (Zigler et al. 1982). Cultural psychologists such as Vygotsky (1978) and Bruner (1990) view socialization as an ongoing interplay between culture and cognition in which people internalize aspects of their sociocultural environments, giving many aspects of the mind cultural origins. Psychological thought on socialization has generally been limited to childrearing and child development and specifically focused on direct encounters between children and major agents of socialization (Slaughter-DeFoe 1994).

Sociological research on socialization is organized around substantive domains, such as families, schools, media, and work. Much of this research frames socialization as a mediating process between self, social organization, and broader social conditions.

Families, especially parents, are often framed as principal agents of socialization. Family socialization has often been conceptualized as children learning their parents' beliefs, values, worldviews, and behaviors. Some researchers argue that families serve as seedbeds of a child's basic orientations to society, and that parental social attitudes serve as powerful predictors of children's attitudes throughout life. Families are also seen as important sites for socialization into social identities. Many researchers suggest that children learn to conceptualize themselves in gendered, religious, political, racial, and class terms in and through routine interactions with parents, siblings, and members of the extended family. Feminist scholars argue persuasively that family socialization into traditional gender roles is pervasive and harmful to boys and girls, and detrimental to gender relations in democratic societies. Increasingly, sociologists are concerned with the implications of changing family forms for child development. Some researchers who compare children raised by single parents or stepfamilies to children raised by "both original parents" suggest that socialization in single-parent families and stepfamilies is generally disadvantageous for children (McLanahan 1999). This is a hotly debated issue, in and out of sociology.

Studies of socialization in educational settings tend to highlight how socialization extends beyond the official academic curriculum. School settings provide many students with their earliest encounters with institutional evaluations of their competencies as people, sometimes with significant effects on their self-conceptions. A prominent theme here is that teachers' expectations of students' academic growth exert a powerful influence on the intellectual gains students actually make. Schools are also known to place students into evaluative categories that affect the way teachers treat students and how

students treat each other. Such labels not only inform the self-concepts of children, they also help students to draw distinctions between themselves along several lines, including racial, class, and gender lines. Scholars have shown how even routine activities in schools, such as line formations and teasing, can reinforce gender stereotypes and inequalities. A body of research influenced by Bourdieu holds that social-class positions are reproduced in the way schools value or devalue the cultural and economic backgrounds of students. Some have argued that schools train poor children for low-status jobs by emphasizing respect for authority, conformity, and submissiveness. The hierarchical and disciplinary nature of social relations in schools is thought to replicate the division of labor in the economy, with the effect of schools training compliant workers for job markets. Poor and working-class students have also been shown to develop cultures of resistance that reflect and reinforce class inequalities. Recently, scholars have argued that race, class, gender, and culture interact in educational settings in subtle ways that lead students to reproduce in their own lives the objective conditions they face in society (MacLeod 1995).

People acquire much of their knowledge of the social world from mass media. Some theorists argue that the images and information disseminated by media overpower people's conceptions of reality to the point of obliterating distinctions between fact and fiction. People's relationship to "reality" is said to be fundamentally altered by the mediating images of television, cinema, Internet, and print media. A prominent theme suggests that consumption of television, magazines, and music reinforces unrealistic, negative, or stereotypical images of gender, sexuality, race, and ethnicity. Many scholars suggest that frequent media use leads men and women to develop distorted, often unhealthy, images of their own bodies and selves, as well as the bodies and selves of others. Research on television viewing patterns suggests that children not only learn values, attitudes, and behaviors by watching television, but that they also imitate many of these televised behaviors. Some scholars argue that images of violence lead some viewers to become aggressive and violent themselves. Alternatively, research on computer technologies suggests that they can serve as liberating resources for self-socialization, enabling children and adults to more freely experiment with alternative versions of their personal identity. Another way media affects socialization is by serving as surrogates for face-to-face interaction. The full implications of this apparent decentering of face-to-face interaction in social life remains unclear and under-studied. Some scholars examining socialization and learning in complex organizations speculate that new communication technologies present "ontological barriers" to the teaching and learning of tacit and embodied knowledge.

One exception to the discipline's tendency to focus on children in socialization studies is the research on professional socialization and work-setting socialization, which focuses on adults. Research on professional socialization highlights how adults learn the skills and knowledge required for both the professional roles they hope to eventually assume and the current demands of the role of apprentice. A body of research shows how, in helping one another cope with the demands of the student role, peers undergoing professional socialization collectively regulate, even block and minimize, the influence of socialization on themselves. The research on adult socialization into work roles and workplaces emphasizes how individuals change from outsiders to participating members of organizations. This transition is often portrayed as an intense process of resocialization during which individuals are pressured not only to learn the new demands of the job, but to relinquish many of the attitudes, values, and behaviors they acquired in previous settings. This research also indicates that work has pervasive effects on the adult's emotional, intellectual, and psychological functioning and identity. Longitudinal studies suggest that occupational experiences lead to broad changes in psychological functioning and personality over time. Sociologists also portray professional socialization as a long process connected to innovations in technology and market dynamics that push working adults to hold a variety of jobs during their careers.

Two public debates about the implications of societal change for socialization beg for more attention from sociologists. First, sociologists recognize how emerging technologies are reshaping many aspects of how people relate to each other, but more research is needed on the affects of new media and computer technologies on child socialization. Second, although sociologists pay considerable attention to societal changes in family formations, they have conducted comparatively few studies of the long-range implications of social changes in families for personal development. A more academic challenge for sociologists comes from the flood of empirical and theoretical developments in other social sciences, some of which challenges basic sociological assumptions about socialization. For example, Andrew Meltzoff's research indicates that newborns can intentionally imitate the basic facial gestures of adults even though they cannot have taken the position of the adult on themselves to know that they have a face with which to imitate (Katz 1999). This research calls into question sociology's longstanding cognitive bias in socialization studies, and invites phenomenological examinations of the role of the body in socialization and development. If sociologists conducting research on socialization were to engage theory and research outside of the discipline in a sustained way, they would be better able to inform public debates over the relative influence of nature versus nurture in human development.

SEE ALSO: Developmental Stages; Mass Media and Socialization; Resocialization; Socialization, Adult; Socialization, Agents of; Socialization, Anticipatory; Socialization, Gender; Socialization, Primary; Socialization and Sport

REFERENCES AND SUGGESTED READINGS

Bandura, A. & Walters, R. H. (1963) *Social Learning and Personality Development*. Holt, Rinehart, & Winston, New York.

Bidney, D. (1967) *Theoretical Anthropology*. Schocken Books, New York.

Bruner, J. (1990) *Acts of Meaning*. Harvard University Press, Cambridge, MA.

Clausen, J. (Ed.) (1968) *Socialization and Society*. Little, Brown, Boston.

Corsaro, W. (1997) *The Sociology of Childhood*. Pine Forge Press, Thousand Oaks, CA.

Gecas, V. (1992) Contexts of Socialization. In: Rosenberg, M. & Turner, R. (Eds.), *Social Psychology:*

Sociological Perspectives. Transaction Publishers, News Brunswick, NJ.

Katz, J. (1999) *How Emotions Work*. University of Chicago Press, Chicago.

Kohlberg, L. (1981) *The Philosophy of Moral Development*. Harper & Row, San Francisco.

Long, T. & Hadden, J. (1985) A Reconception of Socialization. *Sociological Theory* 3(1): 39–49

McLanahan, S. (1999) Father Absence and the Welfare of Children. In: Hetherington, E. M. (Ed.), *Coping with Divorce, Single Parenting, and Remarriage*. Erlbaum, Mahwah, NJ.

Mac Leod, J. (1995) *Ain't No Makin' It: Aspirations and Attainment in a Low-Income Neighborhood*. Westview Press, Boulder.

Mortimer, J. & Simmons, R. (1978) Adult Socialization. *Annual Review of Sociology* 4: 421–54.

Piaget. J. (1926) *The Language and Thought of the Child*. Kegan Paul, London.

Singer, M. B. (1961) A Survey of Culture and Personality Theory and Research. In: Kaplan, B. (Ed.), *Studying Personality Cross-Culturally*. Harper & Row, New York.

Slaughter-De Foe, D. (1994) *Revisiting the Concept of Socialization: Caregiving and Teaching in the 90s – A Personal Perspective*. Center for Urban Affairs and Policy Research, Northwestern University, Evanston, IL.

Vygotsky, L. S. (1978) *Mind in Society: The Development of Higher Psychological Processes*. Harvard University Press, Cambridge, MA.

Wentworth, W. (1980) *Context and Understanding: An Inquiry into Socialization Theory*. Elsevier, Oxford.

Zigler, E., Lamb, M., & Child, I. (1982) *Socialization and Personality Development*. Oxford University Press, Oxford.

socialization, adult

Joseph A. Kotarba

Socialization refers to the process by which people learn and internalize the attitudes, values, beliefs, and norms of our culture and develop a sense of self. The concept of socialization is among the most important in sociology, because it attempts to illustrate and explain the tremendous impact living in society has on shaping the individual. The individual becomes a human being through socialization, and what it means to be an individual evolves over the life course.

Sociologists and psychologists have traditionally agreed that socialization occurs in stages. Early theories of socialization, largely reflecting cultural beliefs about development in the early twentieth century, focused on self and moral development up to what we today know as adolescence. Mead's theory of the self, for example, posited three stages: infancy, play, and game stages. The final game stage occurs during adolescence when the individual is able to learn and respond to the community's norms and standards and act accordingly in everyday life. Mead assumed that the socialized self acquired through adolescence generally remains stable throughout the remaining life span.

Symbolic interactionist thinkers following Mead have attempted to refine his theory to account for the apparent changes in the adult self-concept present in modern society. Shibutani (1961) adapted Merton and Kitt's (1950) structural notion of *reference group* to interactionist thinking to illustrate how adults can be expected to be members of various groups which in turn serve as audiences to the self. In effect, the adult learns to be different selves to accommodate the multiple complex situations that mark modern life. Zurcher (1977) devised the concept of the *mutable self* to argue that contemporary adults must be able to negotiate numerous self-concepts, since the requisite social skill today is being able to change who we are rapidly and gracefully.

STAGES IN ADULT SOCIALIZATION

Social psychological theories of adult socialization analytically divide adulthood itself into stages. Erikson (1982) identified three developmental stages in adult life that focus on a series of crises that must be resolved. During early adulthood (approximately age 20–40) people must manage conflicts between family life and work. They are socialized to pursue the roles of spouse and parent, yet during the same period are expected to earn a living and pursue a career. Consequently, they are faced with reconciling the conflict between spending time with spouses and children and establishing a career. In American society, traditional sex-role expectations have made this dilemma particularly difficult for women.

Middle adulthood (approximately age 40–60) is characterized by conflict between *generativity and stagnation*. Erikson argued that adults in this age range are aware that they are getting older and that ultimately death is in their future, yet they may want to feel a sense of rejuvenation. They may change jobs or otherwise pursue some of their youthful ambitions. If unable to do so, they run the risk of becoming depressed and stagnant and of acting much older than their chronological age. Late adulthood (from age 60 on) provides the final challenge of attempting to achieve a sense of integrity and satisfaction with one's life while not sinking into despair over impending death. Erikson contended that during this stage adults tend to wrestle with the conflict between being satisfied with their accomplishments in life and despairing over missed opportunities and could-have-beens.

Levinson et al. (1978) identified three distinct stages in the life of an adult: early adulthood (about age 17–45), middle adulthood (approximately age 45–65) and late adulthood (age 65 on). Levinson contended that the midlife decade (age 35–45) marks one of the most crucial stages of adult development. During this period, a midlife transition occurs that involves important changes in biological and psychological functioning, as well as in social status. It marks an important turning point in which individuals reappraise their life goals, assess their accomplishments or failures, and consider the possibilities of a better or worse future. Levinson concluded that it is virtually impossible for a person to go through the midlife transition without experiencing at least a moderate crisis.

More recent thinking on adult socialization sees gender as a critical dimension to social, psychological, and moral development. Gilligan (1982) argues that men tend to rely heavily on rules and abstract ideals when determining right from wrong – what she calls a justice perspective on morality. Women develop more of a care and responsibility perspective, preferring to use personal experience and social relationships as important criteria in developing moral judgments about social situations. Gilligan argues that scholars and laypeople alike should not view women's reasoning as inferior to that of men. Sheehy (1976) proposed a set of adult developmental stages for both men and women. Sheehy described the *trying twenties* as a time of making a break from parents, selecting mates, and starting careers: a time of high expectations, hopes, and dreams. The *catch thirties* are the years when bubbles often burst and people realize their mates and jobs are not exactly perfect. This difficult period is characterized by high divorce rates and sudden career changes. The *forlorn forties* follow, when adults enter their midlife crises. Sheehy described these as dangerous years during which the dreams of youth must be reassessed. It is common for men to become dissatisfied with their jobs and to want to stay home; it is a time when women who have not worked outside the home become dissatisfied and want to take jobs.

SOCIALIZATION EXPERIENCES

In his classic statement, Brim (1968) suggested six situations in adulthood that typically involve socialization experiences or responses. These situations do not necessarily follow a life cycle logic, although the physical and psychological effects of aging can precipitate them. First, individuals may place demands on themselves to change the people in their lives, the lifestyles they lead, and the values to which they adhere. Second, individuals may experience changes in roles or statuses, such as the movement from "church member" to "church elder." Third, individuals may experience changes in occupation, either in change or entry. Fourth, individuals may experiences changes in the family, through events such as death and divorce. Fifth, individuals may experience geographic mobility, such as that related to retirement or immigration. Sixth, individuals may experience downward mobility, as a result of poor health, widowhood, and so forth.

Contemporary research has generally supported Brim's model of situations in adulthood that typically involve socialization experiences or responses. Social, cultural, economic, and political changes over time, however, have changed the content of the situational categories. As adults increasingly remain a part of mainstream society, they place increasing demands on a wide range of social institutions. For example, adult education is expanding rapidly, to the degree education policymakers refer to *andragogy* as adult learning and *geragogy* as older adult learning (John 1988).

In summary, traditional models of adult socialization have been strongly influenced by biological models of development. Early life was posited as growth and gain, whereas adulthood and later life were posited as periods of loss and decline (Labouvie-Vief & Diehl 1999). More recent thinking sees adult socialization as a very complex, non-linear, and somewhat situational phenomenon involving a tradeoff between growth and decline. Neugarten's (1974) classic categories of young-old and old-old are less definitive today when the trend is for old-old people in our society increasingly to stay at work or seek work, either to prolong a productive life or to adapt to (often negatively) changing economic conditions for the elderly.

ADULT SOCIALIZATION IN EVERYDAY LIFE

Sociologists of everyday life contend that the process of becoming an adult in our society is rich, ongoing, and worthy of detailed ethnographic analysis. Studies of adult socialization are no longer limited to traditional elderly settings. Since aging in our society no longer requires radical change in lifestyle, at least as one's health remains functional, the culture individuals acquire during a lifetime can be very functional in later adulthood. Kotarba (2006), for example, explores the many ways baby boomers continue to use rock 'n' roll music and culture as resources for refining their sense of self as they occupy the role of parents, lovers, and others. They shape and modify the musical values they acquired during adolescence to fit the needs of later adulthood, so that they may continue to attend rock 'n' roll music concerts but may prefer comfortable seating in the shade near the stage as opposed to more adventurous lawn seating. They may also convert their taste in rock 'n' roll to adult-friendly styles such as country music or the blues. Fontana (1977) examines everyday life in various retirement communities in the American West to show how varied life after work can be. His basic finding is that people generally construct lifestyles in retirement that reflect their pre-retirement lifestyles. If they developed a sense of self that involved high levels of social interaction and community involvement, they will continue that way – barring inevitable health and occasionally financial problems.

Health remains a major concern for aging adults. The sources of information on what is illness, how to care for and prevent illness, and – most relevant to this entry – how to integrate issues of health and illness in one's sense of self are increasing rapidly. For example, the Internet is not only a source of information on health for those adults for whom communication at home is preferred, but also increasingly a place to locate drugs and other health materials and services (Fox & Rainie 2000).

CURRENT ISSUES

Along with scholars from other disciplines, sociological gerontologists are interested in developing new and innovative ways to conceptualize rapid changes taking place in adult socialization among the elderly. The elderly are significant because, for the first time in western history, they are the most likely of all age groups to die, as Hochschild (1978) noted when she referred to them metaphorically as society's "death lepers." The elderly are demographically elusive because the can be found in many different kinds of places – segregated retirement communities, senior centers, and nursing homes – where, incidentally, less than 5 percent reside. The elderly are socialized into being elderly from an increasing number of audiences-to-the-self: earlier life experiences, friends and family, the mass media through portrayals of the elderly such as the immense coverage given to former president Ronald Reagan at the time of his death, and interest groups such as the AARP.

SEE ALSO: Gerontology: Key Thinkers; Socialization; Socialization, Agents of; Socialization, Anticipatory; Socialization, Gender

REFERENCES AND SUGGESTED READINGS

Bengtson, V. (1996) *Adulthood and Aging: Research on Continuities and Discontinuities.* Springer, New York.

Bly, R. (1990) *Iron John: A Book About Men.* Addison-Wesley, Reading, MA.

Brim, O. (1968) Adult Socialization. In: Clausen, J. A. (Ed.), *Socialization and Society.* Little, Brown, Boston.

Erikson, E. (1982) *The Lifecycle Completed.* Norton, New York.

Fontana, A. (1977) *The Last Frontier.* Sage, Beverly Hills, CA.

Fox, S. & Rainie, L. (2000) *The Online Health Care Revolution: How the Web Helps Americans Take Better Care of Themselves.* Pew Charitable Trusts, Washington, DC.

Gilligan, C. (1982) *In a Different Voice.* Harvard University Press, Cambridge, MA.

Hochschild, A. (1978) *The Unexpected Community.* Prentice-Hall, Englewood Cliffs, NJ.

John, M. T. (1988) *Geragogy: A Theory for Teaching the Elderly.* Haworth, New York.

Kimmel, M. (2004) *The Gendered Society.* Oxford University Press, New York.

Kotarba, J. A. (2006) *I'm just a Rock 'n' Roll Fan: Popular Music Experiences in Middle Age.* Left Coast Press, Walnut Creek, CA.

Labouvie-Vief, G. & Diehl, M. (1999) Self and Personality Development. In: Cavanaugh, J. & Whitbourne, C. (Eds.), *Gerontology: An Interdisciplinary Perspective.* Oxford University Press, New York.

Levinson, D. J. et al. (1978) *The Seasons of a Man's Life.* Knopf, New York.

Mead, G. H. (1934) *Mind, Self and Society.* University of Chicago Press, Chicago.

Merton, R. K. & Kitt, A. (1950) Contributions to the Theory of Reference Group Behavior. In: Merton, R. K. & Lazarsfeld, P. F. (Eds.), *Studies in the Scope and Method of "The American Soldier."* Free Press, Glencoe, IL.

Neugarten, B. L. (1974) Age Groups in American Society and the Rise of the Young-Old. *Annals of the American Academy of Political and Social Science* 415: 187–98.

Sheehy, G. (1976) *Passages.* Dutton, New York.

Shibutani, T. (1961) *Society and Personality.* Prentice-Hall, Englewood Cliffs, NJ.

Zurcher, L. (1977) *The Mutable Self.* Sage, Beverly Hills, CA.

socialization, agents of

Delores F. Wunder

Socialization is the process whereby individuals learn and internalize the attitudes, values, and behaviors appropriate to people living in any given society. Socialization ensures that an individual will develop a social identity (or self) and have the motivation and knowledge to perform the roles she may need throughout the course of her life.

It is a basic tenet in sociology that humans do not have "instincts." (In sociology and biology an instinct is a complex pattern of behavior that is genetically determined.) Humans have some basic reflexes (such as startling when frightened), but no real instincts. Because of this lack, people have to learn virtually everything to get along in life. We call this learning "socialization." Socialization is the process of social interaction through which people acquire personality and learn the ways of their society. It is an essential link between the individual and society.

Socialization is a lifelong process. It never really ends, not until death. At every stage of our lives, we confront new situations and have to learn new ways of doing things, new values, or new norms. The really crucial time of socialization is infancy and early childhood. That is when you learn the language of your group and come to understand the norms and values important to your family and society.

Agents of socialization enable us to become aware of all the various things we need to know. Agents of socialization are significant individuals, groups, or institutions that provide structured situations in which learning takes place. This continuing and lifelong socialization involves many different social forces that influence our lives and affect our self-images. These agents of socialization include the following.

The family. Family is by far the most significant agent of socialization. It is within the family that the first socializing influence is encountered. Families teach the child the language of their group, acceptable gender roles, and important values. In addition, families give children their geographic location (northerners, westerners, rural or urban), and they determine their religion, race, and ethnic group. In modern societies, most early socialization takes place within the nuclear family. In more traditional families, the extended family may be equally important. But either way, children learn the behavior characteristics of their family members and community. A family's social class and parents' occupations also influence the way children are reared and their gender and role expectations. It is important to acknowledge that children are not just passive recipients of socialization; they are active agents, influencing and altering the family, too.

School. In some societies, socialization takes place almost entirely within the family. But for children in modern industrial societies, school is an important, formal agent of socialization that influences most individuals for well over a decade. Schools teach not only selected skills and knowledge but also additional things, such as the importance of a good diet and exercise. There is often a "hidden curriculum" as well. This includes obeying authority, being punctual, not being absent unless you are ill or have a legitimate excuse, and following rules. Personality characteristics of self-discipline and dependability are encouraged. (Business and industry prefer employees with those attributes and so they are taught in schools for the future workforce.) Mass education also promotes feelings of nationalism and the need to be a good citizen. American schools teach ideals of equality and equal opportunity. Some traditional societies do not include formal schools for everyone. If so, school is not an agent for those groups. For them, the family is far more important.

Peers. The peer group is a friendship group of roughly equivalent age and interests, who are social equals. They are an important agent all over the world, but particularly for teens and young adults. Peer groups can ease the transition to adulthood. In the modern world, peer relations are even more important than they may have been in earlier times. Peer groups often remain important throughout much of a person's life. They tend to be more egalitarian than some of the other agents and influence a person's attitudes and behavior. Peer groups have great influence on how children socially construct and experience gender meanings in the classroom, playground, and informal social groups.

Mass media and technology. In modern societies, these are important agents of socialization. In the United States, over 98 percent of households have at least one television set and many have several. Even in less advanced societies, the media are increasing in importance, particularly the various electronic media. Research has investigated whether violence on television (or in movies) encourages violent behavior among viewers (particularly among children). The findings are not conclusive, but most people believe that people's attitudes and values are affected by what they see and hear in the media. A positive influence is the fact that televisions and commercials can introduce young people to unfamiliar ideas, lifestyles, and cultures.

Public opinion. In every culture, what people think about controversial issues is an important agent of socialization. But in reality, not everyone's views are equally influential. Better-educated, wealthier, well-connected people often carry much clout. In societies where the mass media are important, that may greatly influence public opinion, too. This agent influences appropriate gender roles, notions of right and wrong, and beliefs about controversial topics such as abortion or gay marriages.

Religion. Religion is important and relevant for some people, but in the modern world religion is losing some of its power and influence as an agent of socialization. For those that follow religious tenets, the norms influence people's values, the desired size of families, the likelihood of divorce, rates of delinquency, behaviors considered appropriate (or not), and a host of other things. Religion has a role in social integration, social support, social change, and social control.

Workplace. The workplace is also an agent of socialization. Among other things, it teaches us that the work women do is often valued less than the work men do. Until recently, women employees were concentrated into routine, poorly paid occupations. Women's opportunities were often blocked by gender stereotypes. Work also teaches us appropriate values, work ethic (or lack of it), and appropriate attire. In modern societies, full-time employment confirms adult status and awards us a personal identity. In a culture that has few rites of passage, that is important. Every society has "work," but in modern societies where work and home are separate, "going to work" involves more of a transition than in traditional societies.

The state. The state has recently been added to the list of agents of socialization. We recognize the state's growing impact on the life course. Increasingly, outside agencies like nursing homes, mental health clinics, and insurance companies have taken over functions previously filled by families. The state runs many of these institutions or licenses and regulates them. In a sense, the state has created new rites of passage, such as the age a person can legally drive, purchase and consume tobacco and alcohol, marry without parental consent, or officially retire.

Total institutions are an important agent of resocialization for some people. Total institutions are places where residents are confined for a set period of time and kept under the influence of a hierarchy of officials (e.g., the military during basic training or officer training or a prison or mental institution). Every aspect of life is controlled, from the time you get up until you go to bed. The goal of a total institution is to resocialize individuals, to totally change them and make them into something new (and presumably "better").

Socialization, and what the agents of socialization teach, differs from one society (or subculture) to another. These differences include such basics as the following.

Treatment of children. Do we allow them a great deal of freedom (both physically and psychologically) or are we more rigid in our demands? Some cultures (such as in the United States) give infants a great deal of space, with large cribs and perhaps the run of the house when they are old enough to crawl and toddle. Other societies swaddle and restrain infants for their first year of life.

What we consider fit to eat and drink. The human body can digest and get nourishment from many different substances, but what we consider "fit" or suitable to consume varies greatly by culture. Some cultures (such as some Native American tribes or some Asians) appreciate puppy meat, while others are appalled at even the thought of eating dog. Traditionally, the French have thought diluted wine suitable for children to drink with meals, but probably most Americans find the thought of serving alcohol to children inappropriate.

What we "see" or notice in our environment. In some societies in Africa, people "see" only two or three colors while Americans (thanks to Crayola boxes with 120 colors) can distinguish between a dozen shades of blue. Children who never have the opportunity to see photos, movies, or television often cannot "see" things when given just two dimensions. We "learn" to see as young children and it may be difficult if we encounter these things later in life.

Crying and display of emotions. In American society, "big boys don't cry," but males are allowed to display anger by swearing or expressing pain with a grimace. But some Native Americans, living in what we now consider the United States, had rites of passage where both pain and anger were suppressed. We are taught by the various agents of socialization when crying, anger, or anguish is appropriate (or not).

Knowledge and what we learn. In some more primitive societies, people count only to 10 or 20 (using fingers and toes). Anything above that number is designated as "many." But in western, advanced societies many people learn advanced mathematics. In the western world we learn to read from left to right, from the top of the page going down. In other parts of the world we read from the top to bottom, or from right to left. Agents of socialization teach us these things.

SEE ALSO: Mass Media and Socialization; Organizations as Total Institutions; Resocialization; Socialization; Socialization, Adult; Socialization, Anticipatory; Socialization, Gender; Socialization, Primary; Socialization and Sport

REFERENCES AND SUGGESTED READINGS

Cooley, C. H. (1902) *Human Nature and the Social Order*. Scribner, New York.
Elkin, F. (1984) *The Child and Society: The Process of Socialization*, 4th edn. Random House, New York.
Erikson, E. (1982) *The Lifecycle Completed*. Norton, New York.
Hochschild, A. (1978) *The Unexpected Community*. Prentice-Hall, Englewood Cliffs, NJ.
Kellner, D. (1995) *Media Culture*. Routledge, London.
Mead, G. H. (1934) *Mind, Self, and Society*. University of Chicago Press, Chicago.
Strand, P. S. (2000) Responsive Parenting and Child Socialization: Integrating Two Contexts of Family Life. *Journal of Child and Family Studies*.
Zurcher, L. (1977) *The Mutable Self*. Sage, Beverly Hills, CA.

socialization, anticipatory

Gordon Shepherd

Anticipatory socialization refers to preparation for status changes and role transitions and, as such, is an important aspect of most forms of human socialization over the entire life course. While socialization in general may be defined as the social process in which groups transmit their culture and individuals simultaneously acquire self-concepts and personality characteristics, anticipatory socialization directs particular attention to those situations where individuals are likely either to be induced to change or prepare themselves for change in conformity or opposition to a set of normative standards.

The concept of anticipatory socialization was introduced by Robert K. Merton and Alice S. Kitt in their 1950 article "Contributions to the Theory of Reference Group Behavior," in which they amplified the theoretical implications of *The American Soldier*, a large-scale empirical study of military recruiting and training published in 1949. Merton and Kitt developed the concept to explain variations in the conformity of enlisted personnel to official military values and their subsequent promotions in military rank. They then generalized the concept as a key mechanism for understanding the relationship between reference group identification and social mobility in social systems. Merton and Kitt initially defined anticipatory socialization as the process in which individuals adopt the values of a group to which they aspire but do not belong. Merton subsequently refined the definition in 1968 to include not only nonmembership reference group aspirations but also, more generally, social statuses to which individuals aspire and which they are likely to attain. This allowed Merton to include in his analysis the structural concepts of normatively defined status sequences and role gradations which function to facilitate anticipatory socialization, producing greater continuity over time for both groups and individuals rather than disjunctive status changes.

Anticipatory socialization may occur in both formal and informal settings. In formal settings, organizations deliberately recruit new members and programmatically attempt to shape their attitudes and values in conformity with organizational goals. Anticipatory socialization is especially prominent in organizations that sponsor opportunities for upward mobility in a status hierarchy. In general, anticipatory socialization is characteristic of achievement-oriented, open systems which function in competitive environments. Merton and others have argued, however, that the major focus of analysis should be on the informal aspects; that is, situations in which role preparation occurs but which do not require specialized training personnel or didactic learning. Even in schools or training organizations, informal anticipatory socialization takes place outside the formal agenda and curriculum. Individuals respond more or less unwittingly to cues from an assortment of role models or reference others and draw implications for future role behavior, becoming oriented toward statuses they do not yet occupy.

Anticipatory socialization in formal settings draws attention to the agents of socialization, the group interests they represent, and the methods they use to shape the attitudes and values of novices who aspire to pursue organizational careers. The agents of socialization and the normative models which they project are important to the understanding of informal anticipatory socialization as well, but attention also is drawn to the individual agency of those being socialized and the choices they make in selecting reference groups and corresponding career paths over the life course. Personal agency is particularly significant in pluralistic social systems that offer individuals a wide range of life choices, in contrast to highly traditional or closed systems in which individuals have relatively few status or role options from which to choose. Thus the nature of the larger social structure in which groups and individuals function has a major impact on both formal and informal modes of anticipatory socialization.

Informal anticipatory socialization is an implicit part of the subject matter of both developmental psychology and the sociology of the life course. In both disciplines the patterned transition between various age statuses is a central topic of analysis. In developmental psychology, maturational and cognitive changes are discussed in conjunction with the various modes of socialization to which individuals are exposed. There is a large literature on both the intended and unintended effects of different parenting styles on personality development in childhood. Considerable attention also has been given to the sometimes mutually reinforcing, sometimes competing influence of siblings and other family members, play groups, peer cultures, and the effects of an increasing array of mass media in contemporary society in the process of anticipatory socialization for adult roles during childhood and adolescence.

In addition to the various agents and methods of anticipatory socialization, two socialization outcomes in particular have received major attention: gender role identification and occupational career orientations. The term "differential socialization" is often used when referring to these outcomes. Differential socialization in these contexts means that individuals typically are socialized differently depending on their sex and social class. Numerous studies have documented the ways in which females are systematically defined and treated differently than males by parents, siblings, peers, teachers, and various role models or reference others portrayed in books, television, movies, computer games, music videos, advertising, and other agencies of mass culture. The net effect of these influences is to reinforce identification and compliance with gender role expectations in the process of development. Similarly, research initiated by Melvin Kohn demonstrates the way in which parents' social class and own occupational experience are correlated with their approach to childrearing in anticipation of the occupations they project their children will most likely pursue in life. Working-class parents typically are more successful in jobs when they observe organizational rules and consequently tend to emphasize conformity to external authority in raising their children. In contrast, middle-class parents typically are more successful in jobs when they take the initiative, work effectively without close supervision, and get along well with co-workers. Consequently they are more likely to reinforce self-expression and self-control in their children. In societies where public schools track and sort students into vocational or college-bound cohorts, the link between social class and anticipatory socialization for occupational careers is especially evident.

While many empirical studies have incorporated anticipatory socialization as an explanatory variable, little has been done to develop the concept theoretically since Merton's pioneering work. One interesting exception is Kazuo Yamaguchi's exposition of rational choice models of anticipatory socialization and, in particular, his development of a related theoretical concept which he calls anticipatory non-socialization. In contrast to different types of anticipatory socialization involved in the process of role entry and status attainment, anticipatory non-socialization concerns decision-making processes that rational actors engage in when exiting current roles or withdrawing their investments from previous commitments and social relationships.

SEE ALSO: Developmental Stages; Game Stage; Identity: Social Psychological Aspects; Mass Media and Socialization; Mobility, Horizontal and Vertical; Play Stage; Reference Groups; Socialization; Socialization, Adult; Socialization, Agents of; Socialization, Gender; Socialization, Primary; Status Passages

REFERENCES AND SUGGESTED READINGS

Kohn, M. L. & Schooler, C. (1969) Class, Occupation, and Orientation. *American Sociological Review* 34: 659–78.

Merton, R. K. & Rossi, A. S. (1968) Contributions to the Theory of Reference Group Behavior. In: Merton, R. K. (Ed.), *Social Theory and Social Structure*. Free Press, New York, pp. 215–48. [Previously published as Merton, R. K. & Kitt, A. S. (1950) Contributions to the Theory of Reference Group Behavior. In: Merton, R. K. & Lazarsfeld, P. F. (Eds.), *Continuities in Social Research*. Free Press, Glencoe, IL.]

Shepherd, G. & Shepherd, G. (1998) *Mormon Passage: A Missionary Chronicle*. University of Illinois Press, Champaign.

Williams, L. S. (2002) Trying on Gender, Gender Regimes, and the Process of Becoming Women. *Gender and Society* 16: 29–52.

Yamaguchi, K. (1998) Rational-Choice Theories of Anticipatory Socialization and Anticipatory Non-Socialization. *Rationality and Society* 10: 163–99.

socialization, gender

Deana A. Rohlinger

As children grow up they develop a sense of who they are, how they should relate to others, and the role they play in a larger society. The lessons children learn and the processes through which cultural norms are passed from one generation to the next is known as socialization. The focus on gender socialization highlights that there are roles, or cultural expectations and norms, which are associated with each sex category ("male" or "female"). Sociologists make distinctions between sex and gender. While sex is based on biological categories, gender is the result of cultural processes that construct different social roles for men and women. Gender socialization, then, is the process through which boys and girls learn sex appropriate behavior, dress, personality characteristics, and demeanor.

While gender socialization is lifelong, many sociological theories focus on early childhood socialization. Four such perspectives are the psychoanalytical, cognitive development, social learning, and social interaction perspectives.

The most famous psychoanalytical explanation of gender socialization is Sigmund Freud's identification theory. Freud argued that children pass through a series of stages in their personality development. During the first two stages (the oral and anal stages), boys and girls have similar behavior and experiences. Around age four, however, boys and girls become aware of their own genitals and that members of the opposite sex have different genitalia. It is during this phallic stage that children begin to identify and model their behavior after their same-sex parent, thus learning gender appropriate behavior, although this process differs for boys and girls. At an unconscious (and precognitive) level, a boy's love for his mother becomes more sexual, and he views his father as a competitor, a feeling that is frightening because of the father's imagined retribution. Fearing his own castration, the boy begins to identify with his father, who he regards as powerful since he still has a penis, and models his father's behavior. The process is different for girls. Like boys, girls initially identify with their mothers. However, upon viewing male genitalia, a girl believes that she has been castrated and develops the desire for a penis. This desire causes the girl to shift her love to her father, but to identify with her mother in an effort to find ways to win her father's penis. Eventually, she recognizes that she can only have a penis symbolically, through intercourse and childbirth. However, her continued penis envy causes her to adopt gender appropriate behaviors and to desire men.

While Freud's theory has been largely discredited, sociologists have drawn on it to extend psychoanalytical explanations of gender socialization. Nancy Chodorow (1978) drew on Marxist theory and psychoanalytic object-relations theory to argue that gender socialization processes are key for the reproduction of the capitalist economy. She argued that identification is more difficult for boys than for girls because boys need to psychologically separate themselves from their mothers and model their fathers, who are largely absent from the home as a result of the breadwinner-homemaker division of labor. This results in boys being much more emotionally detached than girls, who do not experience this psychological separation. Instead, mothers and daughters maintain an intense relationship, and during their interactions the female gender role is transmitted from one generation to the next. Ultimately, gender roles are reproduced and the next generation is socialized when these children are grown and try to recreate the families in which they were raised. Men work outside the home as their fathers had done, and women desire children in order to recreate the bonds of their youth and find emotional fulfillment. Chodorow argued that the socialization of children into traditional gender roles, where women are responsible for child rearing and men for earnings, reproduces a family structure that benefits a capitalist economy because the breadwinner expectation keeps men working at unsatisfying and often exploitative jobs. Moreover, because of their powerlessness in the labor market, men exert control over their families and reinforce traditional gender roles. This, in turn, ensures that men will continue to sell their labor in the market, despite their dissatisfaction, and that women will stay at home raising the next generation of workers and mothers. Chodorow's theory of socialization has been criticized for being limited to white, middle-class families in western democracies, and thus unable to explain how children from other family structures and other cultures acquire gender roles.

The second perspective points to cognitive development as a way to explain gender socialization, arguing that socialization occurs as children try to find patterns in the social and physical world (Piaget 1954; Bem 1993). From this perspective, children's earliest developmental task is to make sense of a seemingly chaotic world. As they observe and interact with their environment, they develop schema, or organizing categories. Because children rely on simple cues to understand the world and because there are clear differences in how women and men look and act, biological sex provides a useful schema. Children first label themselves, and then apply the schema to others in an effort to organize behaviors into distinct gender categories. Schema, however, are not static. Children's understanding of gender roles changes as they grow older and reflect increased complexity in their cognitive development. Thus, very young children are more rigid and stereotypical in their understanding of gender appropriate behaviors than older children, adolescents, and adults.

Critics highlight three problems with the cognitive development perspective. First, while the perspective suggests that children develop gender identities between the ages of three and five, a body of research indicates that the development of gender identities occurs much sooner. Second, while the cognitive development perspective assumes that children's use of sex and gender schemas are undifferentiated by sex, girls generally are more knowledgeable about gender than boys and are more embracing of cross-gender behavior. Third, this perspective ignores the social world in which children are embedded. Children's understanding of gender identities is not limited to mental development, but also stems from interactions with peers, parents, and teachers.

The social learning perspective (Bandura 1986) posits that gender socialization is learned. This theory draws on the psychological concept of behaviorism to argue that children learn gender by being rewarded for gender appropriate behavior and punished for gender inappropriate behavior. Rewards and punishments may be direct. For example, a parent may

directly admonish a boy for wanting to purchase a doll with his birthday money, but praise a girl for the same choice. Children also learn gender appropriate behavior through indirect rewards and punishments as when they observe peers, parents, and other adults model the behaviors that will elicit praise or opprobrium. The main problem with the social learning perspective is that it assumes children are passive recipients of gender socialization messages rather than agents who actively seek out and evaluate information.

The social interaction perspective offers a fourth approach to gender socialization. This perspective has deep sociological roots. In 1902, sociologist Charles Cooley argued that individuals develop a sense of self by imagining how they appear to others, interpreting others' reactions to their actions, and developing a self-concept based on these interpretations. Thus, a person's sense of self, which he called "the looking glass self," is an ongoing process embedded in social interaction. From this perspective, interaction forms the basis of gender socialization.

One set of interactions integral to gender socialization are those between parents and children. More often than not, parents tend to interact with boys and girls in ways that reinforce traditional gender roles. For example, while on average there are no sex differences among one-year-olds' attempts to communicate, adults respond to boys and girls differently. Parents respond to boys when they demand attention by being aggressive, crying, whining, and screaming, and they respond to girls when they use gestures, gentle touching, or words spoken in nondemanding tones. Such parent–child interactions have long-term effects on girls' and boys' communication styles, leading to boys with more assertive styles and girls with more talkative and emotive styles. Parents also tend to encourage physical play and roughhousing in boys and vocal-interaction games with girls. These differences affect how girls and boys handle interpersonal strife and conflict later in life, with boys more likely to resort to physical confrontations and girls attempting to "talk out" their problems. Traditional gender roles also are introduced and reinforced through the kinds of toys parents provide their children. Dolls, doll houses, and miniature home appliances encourage girls to be nurturing and engage in domestic tasks such as cooking, cleaning, and childcare, while blocks, construction vehicles, and science kits encourage boys to engage in construction, invention, and exploration which will provide skills useful in a competitive corporate world. In short, gender socialization occurs through parent–child interactions that reinforce traditional notions of gender in which girls are emotional and nurturing and boys are physical, aggressive, and competitive.

Social institutions are crucial to gender socialization. Parent–child interactions like those described above do not occur in isolation, but are embedded in the social institution of the family. Other social institutions important to gender socialization in childhood are school, sports, and mass media. In the educational system, a "hidden curriculum" refers to the values that are not explicitly taught in the classroom but are still part of the schools' unacknowledged lessons. This curriculum reinforces traditional conceptualizations of how girls and boys look and act through the use of course material, examples used in class, and activities that separate and pit boys against girls. These messages are buttressed through interactions with teachers and peers. Teachers, for example, reinforce gender roles by encouraging girls and boys to develop different skills (encouraging boys to excel at math and science and girls to excel in humanities and social science) and by differently praising their school work (commending boys for substantive content and girls for the neatness of their work). Children also divide themselves along gender lines in the lunch room, claim different spaces of the playground, and often sanction individuals who violate gender norms (Thorne 1993).

Sports are important to socialization because they teach children about cooperation, competition, and gender. For boys, the sports arena becomes a site where masculinity is performed. A boy's success at sports is seen as more masculine by other boys, which generates prestige in his peer group, while boys who fail are ridiculed and labeled "sissies" or "girls" (Messner 1992). Rewarding boys for "acting masculine" on the sports field has lasting consequences because it teaches boys that they must publicly prove their masculinity to others. This, in turn, encourages boys to develop

instrumental relationships, or relationships in which something of value may be acquired, rather than meaningful relationships based on mutual emotional fulfillment. Most sports sociology has focused on how sports affect the gender socialization of boys. However, since the passage of Title IX in 1972 in the US, the participation of girls in sports has increased dramatically. It remains to be seen how sports will affect the gender identities and socialization of girls.

Mass media are one of the most powerful tools of gender socialization because television, magazines, radio, newspapers, video games, movies, and the Internet are ubiquitous in American culture. Like other social institutions, mass media reinforce traditional gender roles. Magazines targeted at girls and women emphasize the importance of physical appearance as well as finding, pleasing, and keeping a man. While boys' and men's magazines also focus on the importance of physical appearance, they also stress the importance of financial success, competitive hobbies, and attracting women for sexual encounters (rather than lasting relationships). These supposed "masculine" and "feminine" characteristics and behaviors are reinforced across the media system, from video games and movies that show athletic heroes rescuing thin and busty damsels in distress, to television programs that depict women as housewives, nurses, and secretaries and men as lawyers, doctors, and corporate tycoons. Print media also play an important role in socialization. In children's literature, for example, boys typically are the protagonists, who use strength and intelligence to overcome an obstacle. When girls are included in stories, they are typically passive followers of the male leader or helpers eager to support the male protagonist in his plan. This state of affairs is undergoing change, however. An increasing number of television shows (*Zena: Warrior Princess, Buffy the Vampire Slayer, Alias,* and *Veronica Mars*), movies (*Laura Croft: Tomb Raider* and *Elektra*), and books (*Harry Potter*) have crafted new visions of masculinity and femininity. It remains to be seen if these images take hold and affect gender socialization processes.

In sum, sociologists offered a variety of theories to explain gender socialization. The most fruitful to date has been the social interaction perspective because it recognizes that gender is an ongoing process and that gender roles are produced and reproduced in social institutions. A great deal of theoretical and empirical work remains to be done, however. Much of the scholarship on gender socialization has examined middle-class, white heterosexuals. Thus, sociologists need to examine how their theories and data apply across class, race, ethnic, and sexual boundaries.

SEE ALSO: Gender, Development and; Gender Ideology and Gender Role Ideology; Sex and Gender; Socialization; Socialization, Agents of; Socialization, Primary

REFERENCES AND SUGGESTED READINGS

Bandura, A. (1986) *The Social Foundations of Thought and Action: A Social Cognitive Theory.* Prentice-Hall, Englewood Cliffs, NJ.

Bem, S. L. (1993) *The Lenses of Gender.* Yale University Press, New Haven.

Burke, P. (1991) Identity Processes and Social Stress. *American Sociological Review* 56: 836–49.

Chodorow, N. (1978) *The Reproduction of Mothering.* University of California Press, Berkeley.

Messner, M. (1992) Boyhood, Organized Sports, and the Construction of Masculinity. In: Kimmel, M. & Messner, M. (Eds.), *Men's Lives*, Macmillan, New York, pp. 161–76.

Piaget, J. (1954) *The Construction of Reality in the Child.* Basic Books, New York.

Thorne, B. (1993) *Gender Play: Girls and Boys in School.* Rutgers University Press, New Brunswick, NJ.

West, C. & Zimmerman, D. (1987) Doing Gender. *Gender & Society* 1: 121–51.

socialization, primary

Leslie Wasson

Socialization is the process by which humans learn the ways of being and doing considered appropriate and expected in their social environments. We call it primary socialization when the individual is a newly born member of society and is therefore experiencing this process for the first time. Primary socialization

has the social psychological characteristic of primacy, meaning that its position as first in the acquisition of social knowledge renders it a filter and a foundation for the subsequent information internalized by the fledgling social being. Primacy also makes early socialization remarkably resilient, in that it is much more difficult to change primary habits and beliefs than those learned later in the life course.

With regard to symbolic interaction, primary socialization becomes the initial set of significant symbols by which the individual interprets the perceived social world, formulates a conception of personal identity or identities, and through which he or she communicates understanding and desire with others. Through the symbolic structure of language, coupled with non-verbal communication and other cultural cues, the individual negotiates an understanding of the agreed-upon realities of social settings with significant others in their environment.

An early social philosophy of childhood portrayed the newborn social participant as a tabula rasa, or a blank slate upon which society then inscribed an identity. Later theorists, however, questioned the passivity of this model of child socialization. In his discussion of the origins of the self, George Herbert Mead (1934) drew upon the "looking-glass self" model formulated by Charles Horton Cooley (1902). Cooley's socialization process entailed the individual engaging in a cycle of observation of the reactions of others to a behavior and the subsequent adjustment of that behavior to match perceived expectations. Unlike Cooley, however, Mead located the self as more than a passive reflection of social observation and response. Mead's novice social being was an active participant and negotiator in the socialization process, and his conceptualization of this agency has influenced subsequent theorizing on the subject.

There may be some biological preconditions for primary socialization to be effective. The work of Piaget (1954), for example, on the development of cognitive abilities in young humans indicates that at least some of the physical elements of human life must be present in order for the social aspects to persist. Although any stage theory should be treated with caution, Piaget's schema indicates that a child may not be capable of socialization beyond a certain point if physical development is inadequate.

Ancillary implications include a consideration of the primary socialization difficulties encountered by persons born with disabilities, although their acquisition of social competency may also be influenced by social expectations of their ability.

Some recent efforts to expand primary socialization include the use of music to stimulate cognitive development even prior to birth, and the use of American Sign Language as a communication medium with babies who are not yet physically able to speak coherently. Although more data collection is under way, early results indicate that non-verbal forms of socialization are effective at much earlier ages than previously believed.

Children require sociability in order to thrive. Kingsley Davis (1947) and others (Spitz 1945, 1946; Curtiss 1977) who studied children raised in isolation provide evidence of the essentiality of interaction with human others for the full development and ongoing physical well-being of the child. Children who are denied interaction in the extreme fail to thrive emotionally, mentally, and physically. It appears that the causality between the physical and the social in human development is complex.

Primary socialization involves learning, and humans are capable of a complex set of learning behaviors. Learning processes that may occur during primary socialization may include operant conditioning to environmental or social contingencies, observational learning (imitation), and internalization of social and emotional norms and values. The content of primary socialization is likely to include language and other forms of communication, identities and role-taking, negotiation and meaning construction, and cultural routines. Contemporary researchers such as Strand (2000) distinguish between developmental and behavioral research on the socialization of young children.

Humans emerge at birth fairly unfinished. They go through a long period of dependency and require years of training in order for socialization to be perceived as successful. Anthropological research describes a myriad of human arrangements to which children are socialized, giving credence to a view of humans as remarkably flexible in their adaptation to material conditions. For the individual, primary socialization serves the very important function of making the world predictable and easing interaction with others.

Primary socialization performs important functions for any society. Since society exists before the individual arrives, primary socialization allows new members to be integrated into existing social arrangements. This primary socialization process also makes possible the perpetuation of culture via intergenerational transmission. In primary socialization, therefore, the earliest agents of socialization are crucial to the fundamental construction of new social beings. In most cases, the foremost agents of primary socialization are parents, especially mothers. Changes in the composition of families in contemporary society, however, such as single-parent households, grandparent parenting, and day care for working families, may create a shift in the source and character of primary socialization.

SEE ALSO: Cooley, Charles Horton; Mead, George Herbert; Looking-Glass Self; Resocialization; Socialization; Socialization, Adult; Socialization, Agents of

REFERENCES AND SUGGESTED READINGS

Cooley, C. H. (1902) *Human Nature and the Social Order.* Scribner, New York.

Curtiss, S. (1977) *Genie: A Psycholinguistic Study of a Modern Day "Wild Child."* Academic Press, New York.

Davis, K. (1947) Final Note on a Case of Extreme Isolation. *American Journal of Sociology* 3(5): 432–7.

Elkin, F. (1984) *The Child and Society: The Process of Socialization*, 4th edn. Random House, New York.

Mead, G. H. (1934) *Mind, Self, and Society.* University of Chicago Press, Chicago.

Piaget, J. (1954) *The Language and Thought of the Child.* Meridian, New York.

Simons, L. G., Simons, R. L., Conger, R. D., & Brody, G. H. (2004) Collective Socialization and Child Conduct Problems. *Youth and Society* 35(3): 267–93.

Spitz, R. (1945) Hospitalism. *Psychiatric Study of the Child* 1: 53–72.

Spitz, R. (1946) Hospitalism: A Follow-Up Report. *Psychiatric Study of the Child* 2: 113–17.

Strand, P. S. (2000) Responsive Parenting and Child Socialization: Integrating Two Contexts of Family Life. *Journal of Child and Family Studies* 9(3): 269–81.

socialization and sport

Jay Coakley

There is a long tradition of research on socialization and sport. The roots of this research are grounded in theories that explain the role of play in child development, in Progressive-era notions that team sports constituted an environment in which valuable lessons could be learned, and in popular twentieth-century assumptions that playing sports was an inherently character-building experience.

Empirical studies of socialization and sport were initiated in the 1950s as the first cohort of baby boomers in North America inspired parents as well as developmental experts to seek optimal conditions for teaching children, especially boys, the skills needed to succeed as adults in rapidly expanding, competitive, national and global economies. The structured experiences embodied in competitive sports were seen by many people in Western Europe and North America – especially suburban parents in the United States – to be ideal contexts for adult-controlled socialization of children. It was assumed that sports taught young people lessons about teamwork, competition, achievement, productivity, conformity to rules, and obedience to authority. Consequently, organized youth sports and interscholastic sports grew dramatically, although the pace of this growth varied by nation and regions within nations.

The growth of organized sports for young people sparked questions about the benefits of sport participation and how to attract and retain participation. Those who asked these questions were often associated with organized sport programs, and they usually had vested interests in recruiting participants and promoting their programs by linking sport participation to positive developmental outcomes. Scholars in physical education were the first to use these questions as a basis for research, and their studies were usually designed to examine sport participation as an experience that shaped social and personal development in positive ways. Most of these studies found correlations between sport participation and positive character traits, although research designs were generally flawed and provided little information about the dynamics of specific socialization experiences in sports compared to other activities (Stevenson 1975).

Research on socialization and sport has also been done in psychology and anthropology, as well as sociology. Psychological studies have focused on the socialization effects of sport participation on personality characteristics, moral development, achievement motivation, sense of competence, self-esteem, and body image. Anthropological studies have focused on the role of play, games, and sports in the formation of value orientations in particular cultural contexts, especially those in pre-industrial societies. Sociological studies, published mostly by scholars in North America, have focused on three main topics: (1) socialization into sport, dealing with the initiation and continuation of sport participation; (2) socialization out of sport, dealing with termination and changes in sport participation; and (3) socialization through sport, dealing with participation and multiple facets of social development.

Through the mid-1980s most sociological research on socialization and sport was grounded in structural functionalism or forms of Marxism, neo-Marxism, and conflict theory. This research was based on the assumption that socialization was a process of role learning through which people internalized values and orientations enabling them to participate in established social systems. It was also based on the assumption that sport was a social institution organized in connection with the social system of which it was a part.

Since the mid-1980s most research has been grounded in a combination of interactionist and critical theories. The approach used in these studies assumes that: (a) human beings are active, self-reflective decision-makers who define situations and act on the basis of those decisions; (b) socialization is a lifelong process characterized by reciprocity and the interplay of the self-conceptions, goals, and resources of all those involved in social interaction; (c) identities, roles, and patterns of social organization are socially constructed through social relations that are influenced by the distribution of power and resources in particular cultural settings; and (d) sports are cultural practices with variable forms and meanings (Coakley 2004).

This shift in the theoretical approaches and the assumptions used to guide research on socialization and sport is represented in the ways that scholars have studied socialization into sports, out of sports, and through sports.

SOCIALIZATION INTO SPORTS: BECOMING INVOLVED AND STAYING INVOLVED

Research based on an internalization-social systems approach clarified that socialization into sport is related to three factors: (1) a person's abilities and characteristics, (2) the influence of significant others, including parents, siblings, teachers, and peers, and (3) the availability of opportunities to play and experience success in sports. Most of this research utilized quantitative methods and presented correlational analyses, but it provided little information about the social processes and contexts in which people make participation decisions and in which participation is maintained on a day-to-day basis at various points in the life course.

Research based on an interactionist-social process approach has focused on the processes through which people make decisions to participate in sports; the ways that gender, class, race, and ethnic relations influence those decisions; the connections between participation decisions and identity dynamics; the social meanings that are given to sport participation in particular relationships and contexts; and the dynamics of sport participation as a "career" that changes over time. This research, often utilizing qualitative methods and interpretive analyses, indicates that sport participation is grounded in decision-making processes involving self-reflection, social support, social acceptance, and culturally based ideas about sports. Decisions about sport participation are made continually as people assess opportunities and consider how participation fits with their sense of self, their development, and how they are connected to the world around them. These decisions are mediated by changing relationships, the material conditions of everyday life, and cultural factors, including the sport-related social meanings associated with gender, class, race, age, and physical (dis)abilities.

SOCIALIZATION OUT OF SPORTS: CHANGING OR TERMINATING SPORT PARTICIPATION

Research on changing or terminating sport participation is difficult to characterize in terms of the theoretical and methodological approaches used. Even the terminology used to describe socialization out of sport has been confusing. References have been made to attrition, disengagement, desocialization, withdrawal from sport roles, dropping out, nonparticipation, burnout, transitions, alienation, "social death," exits, retirement, and involuntary retirement (i.e., being "cut" or denied access to participation opportunities). Studies have focused on many issues, including the relationship between participation turnover rates and the structures of sport programs, the attributes and experiences of those who terminate or change their sport participation, the dynamics of transitions out of sport roles, the termination of participation in highly competitive sport contexts as a form of retirement or even as a form of "social death," and the connection between declining rates of participation and the process of aging.

Prior to the mid-1970s, socialization out of sports was not a popular research topic. Changing or terminating sport participation was treated more as a fact than a problem. It became a problem when baby-boom cohorts younger than 13 years old declined in size and growth trends in organized programs slowed relative to the rapid increases that characterized the 1960s. Additionally, many parents in the 1970s had come to define participation in organized sports as important for the development and social status of their children. A growing emphasis on physical fitness in post-industrial nations also heightened general awareness that physical activities, especially the strenuous activities involved in sports, were important to health and well-being. And finally, there was an emerging system of elite sport development that depended on an expanding pool of developing young athletes nurtured through a feeder system of youth sports and interscholastic teams. As the vested interests in participation grew, so did research on the processes related to terminating and changing participation in sports.

This research indicates that terminating or changing sport participation occurs in connection with the same interactive and decision-making processes that underlie becoming and staying involved in sports. When people end their active participation in one sport context, they often initiate participation in another context – one that is more or less competitive, for example. Terminating active participation due to victimization or exploitation is rare, although burnout, injuries, and negative experiences can and do influence decisions to change or end participation. Changes in patterns of sport participation often are associated with transitions in the rest of a person's life, such as moving from one school to another, graduating, initiating a career, marriage, and becoming a parent. And for people who end long careers in sports, adjustment problems are most common among those who have weakly defined identities apart from sports and lack the social and material resources required for making transitions into other careers, relationships, and social worlds.

SOCIALIZATION THROUGH SPORTS

The belief that sport builds character has its origins in the class and gender relations of mid-nineteenth century England. Although the history of beliefs about the consequences of sport participation varies by society, the notion that sport produces positive socialization effects has been widely accepted in most western industrial and post-industrial societies, especially England, Canada, and the United States. For nearly a century the validity of these beliefs was taken for granted and promoted by those associated with organized competitive sports in these countries. It was not until the 1950s that people began to use research to test the validity of these beliefs.

Most research between the 1950s and the late 1980s consisted of atheoretical, correlational analyses presenting statistical comparisons of the attributes of "athletes" and "nonathletes," usually consisting of students in US high schools. The dependent variables in these studies included academic achievement, occupational mobility, prestige and status in school cultures, political orientations, rates of delinquency and deviance, and various character traits such as moral development. Because few of the studies used longitudinal, pre-test/post-test designs, research findings were usually qualified in light of questions about "socialization effects" (i.e., the attributes that were actually "caused" by sport participation) versus "selection effects" (i.e., the attributes that were initially possessed by those who chose to play organized sports or were selected to play by coaches and program directors). Additionally, most of these correlational studies simply divided all respondents into so-called "athletes" and "nonathletes," thereby ignoring their participation histories and the confounding effects of participation in a wide range of activities offering experiences closely resembling those offered by playing on school-sponsored varsity teams.

McCormack and Chalip published a key article in 1988 in which they critiqued the methodological premises of research on socialization through sports. They noted that most researchers mistakenly assumed that (a) all sports offered participants the same unique experiences, (b) all sport experiences were strong enough to have a measurable impact on participants' characters and orientations, (c) all sport participants passively internalized the "moral lessons" inherently contained in the sport experience, and (d) that sport participation provided socialization experiences that were unavailable through other activities. These assumptions led researchers to overlook that (a) sports are social constructions and offer diverse socialization experiences, (b) participants give meanings to sport experiences and those meanings vary with the social and cultural contexts in which participation occurs, (c) the personal implications of sport participation are integrated into people's lives in connection with other experiences and relationships, and (d) sport participation involves agency in the form of making choices about and altering the conditions of participation. Focusing strictly on socialization outcomes led researchers to overlook the processes that constituted the core of socialization itself. Therefore, their studies missed the tension, negotiation, misunderstanding, and resistance that characterize lived sport experiences.

These assumptions and oversights gave rise to a body of literature containing contradictory and confusing findings often leading to the conclusion that little could be said about socialization through sports. However, research initiated during the 1980s and 1990s, often guided by interactionist and critical theories, began to focus less on socialization outcomes and more on the social processes associated with sport participation and the social and cultural contexts in which sport experiences were given meaning and integrated into people's lives. The findings in this research indicated that:

- Sports are organized in vastly different ways across programs, teams, and situations offering many different socialization experiences, both positive and negative, to participants.
- People who choose to play sports are selected to participate by coaches, and those who remain on teams generally differ from others in terms of their characteristics and relationships.
- The meanings that people give to their sport experiences vary by context in connection with gender, race/ethnicity, social class, age, and (dis)ability, and they change through the life course as people redefine themselves and their connections with others.
- Socialization occurs through the social interaction that accompanies sport participation, and patterns of social interaction in sports are influenced by many factors, including those external to sport environments.
- Socialization through sport is tied to issues of identity and identity development.

These findings indicate that sports are most accurately viewed as sites for socialization experiences rather than causes of specific socialization outcomes. This distinction acknowledges that sports and sport participation may involve powerful and memorable experiences, but that those experiences take on meaning only through social relationships that occur in particular social and cultural contexts.

Since the late 1980s an increasing number of studies related to sports and sport culture have viewed socialization as a community and cultural process. Using various combinations of critical theories, cultural studies, and poststructuralism, researchers have undertaken textual and semiotic analyses in which they focus on sports as sites where people construct and tell stories that can be used to make sense of their lives and the worlds in which they live. In the process, culture is produced, reproduced, reformed, or transformed. Much of this research analyzes media-based discourses by deconstructing the images and narratives used in connection with sports and the personas of sport figures, especially high-profile athletes.

This research acknowledges that sports and the discourses that constitute them have become one of the more influential narratives in twenty-first century culture. They are implicated in struggles over meanings, processes of ideological hegemony, and the expansion of global capitalism and consumer culture. One of the goals of this research is to understand sports in ways that contribute to informed and progressive explanations of the political, economic, and social issues that influence people's lives.

SEE ALSO: High School Sports; Identity, Sport and; Play; Socialization; Socialization, Agents of; Socialization, Gender; Youth Sport

REFERENCES AND SUGGESTED READINGS

Andrews, D. L. (Ed.) (2001) *Michael Jordan, Inc.: Corporate Sport, Media Culture, and Late Modern America*. State University of New York Press, Albany.

Baker, A. & Boyd, T. (Eds.) (1997) *Out of Bounds: Sports, Media, and the Politics of Identity*. Indiana University Press, Bloomington.

Coakley, J. (1993) Sport and Socialization. *Exercise and Sport Sciences Reviews* 21: 169–200.

Coakley, J. (2004) *Sports in Society: Issues and Controversies*. McGraw-Hill, New York.

Coakley, J. & Donnelly, P. (Eds.) (1999) *Inside Sports*. Routledge, New York.

Fine, G. A. (1987) *With the Boys: Little League Baseball and Preadolescent Culture*. University of Chicago Press, Chicago.

Fishwick, L. & Greendorfer, S. (1987) Socialization Revisited: A Critique of the Sport-Related Research. *Quest* 39: 1–9.

Foley, D. E. (1990) *Learning Capitalist Culture*. University of Pennsylvania Press, Philadelphia.

Helanko, R. (1957) Sports and Socialization. *Acta Sociologica* 2: 229–40.

Kenyon, G. & McPherson, B. D. (1973) Becoming Involved in Physical Activity and Sport: A Process of Socialization. In: Rarick, G. L. (Ed.), *Physical Activity: Human Growth and Development*. Academic Press, New York, pp. 303–32.

Shields, D. L. & Bredemeier, B. L. (1995) *Character Development and Physical Activity*. Human Kinetics, Champaign, IL.

SIRLS Sport and Leisure Database (1989) Annotated Bibliography: Socialization in Sport. *Sociology of Sport Journal* 6: 294–302.

Stevenson, C. L. (1975) Socialization Effects of Participation in Sport: A Critical Review of the Research. *Research Quarterly* 46: 287–301.

socialized medicine

Sarah Nettleton

Socialized medicine is a system of health care delivery in which care is provided as a state-supported service. The term was introduced in 1954 by an American academic – Almont Lindsay – on a study visit to the United Kingdom. On his return to the US, he published a book called *Socialized Medicine in England and Wales* (Lindsay 1962), describing the history, organization, and structure of the National Health Service (NHS). However, the term "socialized medicine" is one that tends to be used by "observers" (particularly North American observers) of the UK health service and it is less commonly heard within the UK itself (Webster 2002: 1). This may be because the British NHS is considered by many analysts to be a unique example of socialized medicine. Indeed, it is often described as "a socialist island in a capitalist sea." In this respect it forms part of a welfare system which rests on collective provision, social justice, social equality, and democracy in order to mitigate the adverse effects of capitalism. The fundamental principles of the NHS are therefore: that it should be publicly funded (predominantly by taxation); health care should be universal and be provided on the basis of health "need" rather than the ability to pay; and services should be comprehensive in that they should include preventive health services as well as treatment for those who are ill.

The NHS was established by the Labour government that had won a landslide victory after World War II and came into operation on July 5, 1948 as a result of the NHS Act passed in 1946. The Minister of Health, Aneurin

Bevan – said to be the architect of the NHS – described it as "the biggest single experiment in social service that the world has ever undertaken" (quoted in Webster 2001: 171). It is unique. Other European countries and Canada developed variations on compulsory social insurance schemes. Sweden's universal system, established in 1955, perhaps best approximates the UK system, although it required higher levels of direct payments from patients (Webster 2001).

But to what extent can the NHS be regarded as an example of "socialized medicine"? A definitive definition of the term socialized medicine that would be required in order to answer this question is not easy, in that it would invariably fail to capture the diversity of debates associated with socialism or, more accurately, socialisms (Ginsburg 1998). However, a comparison between the initial proposals for the NHS and its subsequent design may offer some clues.

Following the two world wars there was a general consensus that health care provision in the UK was partial, chaotic, ineffective, and inequitable. Experiences during World War II not only threw these facts into sharp relief but also provided civil servants, policymakers, and practitioners with opportunities for delivering more effective "emergency" services. Proposals for a new system of health care came from the influential Socialist Medical Association, the British Medical Association (BMA), and the thinktank Political and Economic Planning. The proposals were very popular with the public and the ideas formed the basis of the 1944 White Paper (that is, a government document that sets out legislative proposals) entitled *A National Health Service*. There was to be a comprehensive, universal service provided on the basis of need and divorced from the ability to pay, provided by the state which, in turn, would employ doctors on a salaried basis. The service would be run by local authorities and located in hospitals and health centers. Before the Act was passed, however, Bevan had to modify his plans as a result of the opposition and skepticism of the medical profession. The profession's trade union – the BMA – was anxious about its clinical freedom, and negotiated a number of concessions. Bevan is regarded as a smart political operator because he managed to capitalize on a division within the profession between those who provided specialist secondary hospital care and those who provided primary generalist care (known in the UK as general practitioners or GPs). In particular, the latter would not be employed on a salaried basis and retained their status as independent practitioners being paid on a capitation basis, whilst the former could continue with their private medical practice alongside their NHS work. Bevan gave explicit reassurance that their clinical freedom was sacrosanct, and quietly dropped the plan for health centers. In addition, instead of implementing the unified, centrally controlled, and locally run system, a tripartite structure was introduced which meant that the hospitals, local authorities, and primary care GPs, dentists, etc. were run separately. This latter concession led to insurmountable problems in terms of coordination of services. Thus the ideal of socialized medicine resulted in a compromise, not least as a result of the need to win over the powerful profession of medicine. Such compromises continued; as the health policy analyst Rudolf Klein (2002: 230–1) notes, the political history of the NHS is one of a series of conflicts between governments and the medical profession. In particular there have been conflicts over pay, private practice, and the structure of the NHS.

In recent decades this has changed. Throughout the 1980s ideologically conservative governments dominated British politics; they challenged the medical profession and altered the internal dynamics of the NHS. The NHS was established in a period of political consensus and commitment to social welfare and collectivism. Forty years later when the government led by Mrs. Thatcher was in office, the mood was for consumerism, individualism, marketization, and privatization. It is perhaps remarkable, therefore, that such a libertarian political leader proclaimed that "the NHS is safe with us" (Thatcher cited by Klein 2002: 119). The NHS remained funded predominantly out of public funds, services remain predominantly free at the point of use (although charges for drugs and services first introduced in the 1950s have increased), and health care practitioners are predominantly employed by government-funded institutions. In this respect it adheres to the principles of socialized medicine. Privately financed health care and private health

care insurance remain at the margins. The margins, however, may be getting wider. Attempts to alter the internal structures of the NHS and to establish new opportunities for private finance initiatives may shift the extent to which it remains a collective and communal service. According to the official historian of the NHS Charles Webster (2002: 258), it is misguided to represent Bevan's health service as some kind of obsolete command and control system. He suggests that politicians would do well to endorse Bevan's conception of the NHS as a triumphant success, wherein the merits of collective provision outweigh the pernicious consequences of commercialization.

SEE ALSO: Health Care Delivery Systems; Health and Medicine; Socialist Medicine

REFERENCES AND SUGGESTED READINGS

Klein, R. (2002) *Politics of the NHS*. Prentice-Hall, London.
Ginsburg, N. (1998) The Socialist Perspective. In: Alcock, P., Erskine, A., & May, M. (Eds.), *The Students' Companion to Social Policy*. Blackwell, Oxford, pp. 78–84.
Lindsay, A. (1962) *Socialized Medicine in England and Wales: The National Health Service 1948–1961*. University of North Carolina Press, Chapel Hill.
Webster, C. (Ed.) (2001) *Caring for Health: History and Diversity*. Open University Press, Buckingham.
Webster, C. (2002) *The National Health Service: A Political History*. Oxford University Press, Oxford.

society

Larry Ray

The concept of society is both core to sociological analysis and subject to wide-ranging dispute that is often informed by the theoretical disputes within the discipline. When in 1987 the British prime minister Margaret Thatcher said in an interview "There is no such thing as society. There are individual men and women and there are families," many sociologists offered a robust defense of the concept. But one British sociologist subsequently stated: "Thatcher might have been right [in her claim] ... or at least the riposte from the sociological community was not fully justified" (Urry 2000). This illustrates an uncertainty within the discipline as to the appropriateness of the concept, especially in a globalized age in which the idea of discrete societies bound by national borders has been widely questioned. Ironically, however, in the rest of her interview Thatcher went on to emphasize the importance of reciprocal social obligations and bonds between people – things that many sociologists would regard as central to the idea of society.

However, the idea of society as a generalized term for social relations is relatively new and appeared, like sociology, during the transition from pre-industrial to industrial society. Implicit concepts of the social can be identified much earlier, for example in Platonic and Aristotelian philosophy, but premodern philosophies did not generally differentiate "society" from the political organization of the state. It is only in late seventeenth- and early eighteenth-century European social thought that the term society begins to be applied to the ensemble of social relations. The use of the adjective "social" to mean "pertaining to society as a natural condition of human life" derives from Locke (1695). This use of the concept of society is based in the delineation of "civil" from "political" society, which in turn reflected the increasing complexity of social life with the transition from feudal to modern society. The principle of the feudal state as the property of the sovereign slowly gave way to the principle of impersonal rule bound by juridical rules, while the state underwent a process of differentiation into administrative, judicial, and representative functions. Civil society theorists such as Adam Ferguson celebrated the new commercial social order, the rise of public opinion, representative government, civic freedoms, plurality, and "civility." Thus, society came to depict a realm of contractual and voluntary relationships independent of the state, which in turn became merely one area of social activity among others. Society was increasingly conceptualized as a realm of life no longer emanating from a political center, but rather the site of diffuse voluntary associations, in which individual self-interested actions result in an equilibrium of unintended consequences.

However, the liberal Enlightenment understanding of these processes as realms of individual liberty conflicted with Catholic conservative reactions to the 1789 French Revolution and its aftermath. For conservatives such as de Bonald and de Maistre, enlightened individualism and the revolution had destroyed the organic bases of society that lay in sacred moral authority and the institutions of church, monarchy, and patriarchal family. Although not sociologists, their ideas set the scene for the organic functionalist theories of society of Comte, Durkheim, and later Parsons and Luhmann. For Durkheim, society is an internally differentiated yet functionally integrated system whose operations could be understood only from the point of view of the whole. This complex system is an entity *sui generis*, that is, a discrete reality that cannot be reduced to or explained with reference to another ontological level such as biology or psychology. For systems theory, core problems of society are those of achieving sufficient internal integration to persist over time and boundary maintenance, that is, preserving borders between internal and external systems. This concept underpins systemic functionalist analysis, although mechanisms of integration are viewed differently in different theorists – moral integration in Durkheim; a more complex process of adaptation, goal attainment, integration, and latency in Parsons; and complexity reduction in Luhmann.

This approach has been criticized from at least two perspectives. First, Marxist and other critical theories have emphasized the centrality of power, exploitation, and conflict as central organizing principles in society such that "society" is a field of contestation around class, gendered, and racialized structures. Moreover, these structures operate to some extent "behind the backs" of acting subjects such that they are not immediately accessible to conscious reflection. From this point of view, "society" has only an illusory unity which critical analysis deconstructs to reveal patterns of hegemonic domination and resistances.

Secondly, individualistic theories drawing on liberal pragmatism appear in writers such as Simmel, Mead, Becker, and Goffman. They approach "society" as at best a metaphor for an aggregation of human interactions rather than an entity *sui generis*. Indeed, Simmel would have had much sympathy with the view that we should not speak of "society" in abstraction from the forms of association that connect individuals in interaction.

This central issue has been core to many debates in sociological theory – that is, how to comprehend society both as social action and as a system of interrelated practices with unintended consequences. One can say that "society" refers to all forms of mutual and intersubjective communication in which the perceptions and behavior of actors are oriented to those of others. These may be specific others – such as family members, colleagues, friends, rivals, enemies, and authority figures – or they may be generalized others in the form of internalized expectations derived from cultural, moral, practical, and communicative practices. These intersubjective networks can exist on a multiplicity of levels – personal and impersonal; local and global; within regions, nations, and across borders. They exist across a continuum between informal and voluntarily entered relationships (such as friendship), through formal institutional interactions (e.g., in workplaces and with officials), to highly coercive ones such as prisons. Social relationships at each of these levels can be constituted by expressive (affective) orientations or by instrumental ones. Relationships can be highly personal and influenced by the particular characteristics of others or highly impersonal and formalized encounters, such as a money exchange or phoning a call center. "Society" thus refers to the complex patterns of social relationships that will be sustained through time and space, although encounters may be anything from fleeting to lifelong and proximate to distant. Any social interaction though will summon up or, as Giddens (1979) puts it, "instantiate" vast amounts of tacitly held, taken-for-granted background cultural knowledge about how to perform and attribute meaning to social interaction. This means that as well as situated interactions and communications, "society" also refers to the latent structures of linguistic, affective, cultural, and normative rules that are deployed piecemeal in any actual interaction. Systems of power and domination also inhere within these structures, although they can be accessed and subject to

critical reflection and practice through intersubjective communication.

SEE ALSO: Civil Society; Functionalism/ Neofunctionalism; Globalization; Social Worlds; Society and Biology; Sociology

REFERENCES AND SUGGESTED READINGS

Giddens, A. (1979) *Central Problems in Social Theory*. Macmillan, London.

Locke, J. (1695) *Essay Concerning Human Understanding*, 2nd edn.

Ray, L. J. (1999) *Theorizing Classical Sociology*. Open University Press, Buckingham.

Thatcher, M. (1987) Talking to *Women's Own*. *Women's Own* (October 3).

Urry, J. (2000) Mobile Sociology. *British Journal of Sociology* 51(1): 85–203.

society and biology

Adrian Franklin

Society and biology is one of the new transdisciplinary fields of sociology that emerged in the 1990s. Owing to its strong links with genetic research, medicine, health, agriculture, environment, and science and technology, it has developed a number of important research centers, such as Bios (Center for the Study of Bioscience, Biomedicine, Biotechnology, and Society) at the London School of Economics, the Center for Biology and Society at Arizona State University, the Center for Science Studies at the University of Lancaster, and the Department of Biology and Society at the University of Amsterdam.

In the 1990s it became clear, from work in the areas of the sociology of health, the sociology of the body, and science and technology studies, that it was no longer possible to conceive of a sociological domain that was separable from the biological even if biological processes and social processes could be distinguished as different (Newton 2003a, b). Critically, social phenomena operate in material and biotic contexts in which important transfers of materials, information, prehensions, and inscriptions take place. Anthropologists, for example, are just beginning to take notice of and understand the natural construction of society as well as the social construction of nature (see Franklin 2002: ch. 4).

Foucault argued that power, surveillance, and control operate on and through the human body. However, our very conception of biology and "life itself" has enormous implications for how we think of ourselves socially. Sarah Franklin argues that we can identify three shifts in the way life itself has been considered in modern societies.

First, in the nineteenth century nature was *biologized*. According to this view, life originates in narratives of evolution and natural selection. It became possible to think of human difference in biological terms (such as race). Equally, individuals could be explained in conception stories of eggs and sperm, and of genetic blueprints. These were "the facts of life."

Second, biology itself became geneticized in the latter half of the twentieth century, and now social issues surrounding human behavior, pathology, and risk were geneticized: social planning and management now involved *genetic* assessment. Social life oriented itself to genetic genealogy and referenced "genetic parents," "genetic relatedness," "genetic risk," "genetic identity," and "genetic variation." Concern over genetic inheritance gave way to socially significant technologies of control such as genetic screening, the human genome project, and human gene therapy. The discourse of genetics, then, was an important language to describe not only the human condition, but also the condition of life itself, and technologies emerging in the human world were transferred to new concerns with environmental change and the future of reproduction generally. Life had been reduced to information.

Third, geneticization became inseparable from its instrumentalization or the uses that could be made of it. In addition to being able to make new life and change existing life at will (theoretically), geneticization made possible completely new forms of property and power. More can be done with genes, such as the capitalization of life itself. The commodification of genomics drove international scientific competition to claim biotechnical market share but also expertise in the management and

surveillance of genetic risk. Patents were now possible for new life. As Franklin (2000) put it, "emergent definitions of genetic risk, and their attendant techniques of detection and intervention, are indexical of changing relationships between health and pathology, disease and cure, technoscience and the body, humans and animals, and the regulation of public health. In turn, such altered understandings contextualize the ways in which life itself can be owned, capitalized and patented."

Nature becomes biology, becomes genetics, through which life itself becomes reprogrammable information across time, space, and "species" (which become irrelevant?). Franklin asks us to think about *Jurassic Park* as an example of the emergent genetic imaginary. However, it is not just life that changes but *being*. Creatures such as Dolly the Sheep, "Oncomouse," and Jefferson the Calf were not born but *made*; they were not beings but "done-tos." More social life will focus on accumulation strategy deals between corporate wealth generation and molecular biology. And as this happens, sociologists are beginning to ask whether society itself will become recombinant.

Tim Newton argues, however, that genetic technologies and future technologies to tackle hitherto uncontrolled natural forces such as weather and volcanic activity will dissolve finally the very distinction between biology and society: "What remains of interest is how far human techno-linguistic skill will enable us to increasingly plasticize biological and physical processes and 'short-circuit' seemingly millennial natural stabilities. Are we moving toward plastic bodies (with 'clonable' parts) and a pliable world where we will be able to play with *all* the times of nature? If we move toward the latter scenario, current differences between natural and social times will increasingly erode" (2003a: 27–8).

In the meantime, the sociological study of society and biology will monitor not only social change emerging from new technologies and their implications, but also its *contested* nature in the realm of biopolitics. Nikolas Rose says that "the biological existence of human beings has become political in novel ways" (2001:1). He traces the history of biopolitics, beginning with the nineteenth to mid-twentieth centuries when those in power sought to discipline individuals, through health and hygiene regimes and breeding programs, "in the name of the population." Further into the twentieth century the massive political apparatus of health would not have been possible without the increasing health aspirations of the people themselves. This alliance between state and people shifted in the second half of the twentieth century from an emphasis on avoiding sickness to an emphasis on attaining well-being (an optimization of health, but also of beauty, fitness, happiness, sexuality, and more). As Rose says: "selfhood has become intrinsically somatic – ethical practices increasingly take the body as a key site for work on the self" (2001: 18). This biopolitics merges with what he has called ethopolitics or the politics of life itself: "the ethos of human existence – the sentiments moral nature or guiding beliefs of persons, groups, or institutions – have come to provide the 'medium' within which the self-government of the autonomous individual can be connected up with the imperatives of good government. In ethopolitics, life itself, as it is lived in its everyday manifestations, is the object of adjudication" (2001: 18). Because of this, the salience of biology and society is not just important for sociology, it is the basis on which important life choices must be made by most of the individuals it studies.

SEE ALSO: Actor-Network Theory; Actor-Network Theory, Actants; Animal Rights Movements; Biosociological Theories; Gender, the Body and; Genetic Engineering as a Social Problem; Human Genome and the Science of Life; Nature; Science and Culture; Society

REFERENCES AND SUGGESTED READINGS

Franklin, A. S. (2002) *Nature and Social Theory*. Sage, London.
Franklin, S. (2000) Life Itself: Global Nature and the Genetic Imaginary. Online. www.comp.lancs.ac.uk/sociology/soc048sf.html.
Franklin, S. (2001) Are We Post-Genomic? Online. www.comp.lancs.ac.uk/sociology/soc047sf.html.
Newton, T. (2003a) Truly Embodied Sociology: Marrying the Social and the Biological. *Sociological Review* 51(1): 20–42.
Newton, T. (2003b) Crossing the Great Divide: Time, Nature, and the Social. *Sociology* 37(3): 433–57.
Rose, N. (2001) The Politics of Life Itself. *Theory, Culture, and Society* 18(6): 1–30.

sociocultural relativism

John Curra

INTELLECTUAL AND SOCIAL CONTEXT

While the word "culture" was first used in 1877 by Edward Tylor to describe the totality of humans' behavioral, material, intellectual, and spiritual products, it was Franz Boas who gave the term one of its most distinctive elaborations. Unlike some other anthropologists (e.g., Malinowski), Boas refused to devalue cultures regardless of how primitive they might appear to outsiders. For Boas, the principal task was to describe accurately and understand completely the cultures of the world, not to rank them from good to bad. Students of Boas, especially Benedict and Herskovits, carried on his legacy, especially his commitment to cultural relativity. They adopted cultural relativity as a principal way to generate respect and tolerance for human diversity, while defending indigenous peoples from threats to their collective and individual well-being.

Sociocultural relativism is a postulate, a method, and a perspective. One implication of the postulate of relativity is that actions and attributes vary from time to time, place to place, and situation to situation. If anything "real" or "objective" exists in the social world, it is the intrinsically situational nature of both rules and reactions and the dynamic, negotiated nature of social order (Becker 1973). A second implication of the postulate of relativity is that collective *definitions* of actions and attributes are elastic and also vary from time to time, place to place, and situation to situation (Cohen 1974). Things that are mightily upsetting to one generation may be trivial to the next (or vice versa), and a particular trait of an individual can be admired by friends but despised by enemies (Goode 2001: 37). The concept of relativism is based on the fact that at certain times and places, acts and attributes that an outsider might find distressing or wrong are not defined as such by individuals living in those times or places (Goode 2003). Sociocultural relativism is a method, too. It demands an actor-relevant approach in which social scientists take the role of their subjects and understand the world through the subjects' eyes. While this does not guarantee freedom from ethnocentrism, it does make this bias less likely. In Goffman's (1961: 130) words, "the awesomeness, distastefulness, and barbarity of a foreign culture can decrease to the degree that the student becomes familiar with the point of view to life that is taken by his [her] subjects." Sociocultural relativism requires that you put yourself in the shoes of another, maybe even an adversary's, in order to understand why someone might wear those shoes at all (Fish 2001). Sociocultural relativism is also a perspective, as it is possible to find relativism or nonrelativism in human experience depending on how an observer's eye is slanted. If you are looking for vacillation, drift, and indeterminacy, they are easy to find in this constantly changing, multiplex world of ours; if, however, you are looking for stability and constancy, you can find them, too. Not all sociologists consider themselves relativists, but *all* sociologists must wrestle with the ethical, philosophical, logical, theoretical, and empirical issues that surround a discussion of sociocultural relativism.

Respect for diversity must be tempered with the knowledge that some conditions can neither be easily overlooked nor dismissed as an example of the equivalency of human cultures. We have neither a convincing moral code that can be applied to all places and times nor any theory that makes it possible to understand human experience separate from its social context (Hatch 1997). Nonetheless, situations will be found in which it is impossible to maintain an attitude of indifference. Sociocultural relativists do not have to believe in the absolute equivalency of values, norms, or customs and blindly accept whatever they find. Romanticizing diversity blunts our ability to recognize the genuine

tragedy, pathos, and harm that deviant social practices can produce.

Marx had relativistic leanings, apparent in his claim that economic forms are transitory and historical, and he was opposed to any fixed or determinate view of nature. However, the first extensive application of sociocultural relativism is found in Durkheim's *Rules of Sociological Method* when he contrasts the "normal" with the "pathological." He asks us to imagine a society of saints, a "perfect cloister of exemplary individuals" (Durkheim 1938: 68–9). Crimes like murder, rape, robbery, and drug addiction would not exist in this virtuous place, but crime would still be found even though it would seem minor to individuals from the less-than-saintly society. Durkheim was contending that it is the *attitude* about, and *reactions* to, some act (i.e., how it is judged and punished) by observers that is principally responsible for its categorization as criminal. Acts may be viewed as offenses even though they are not harmful in any essential or intrinsic way, as is found in proscriptions against allowing a sacred fire to die down or mispronouncing a ritual formula. Even when a crime *is* indeed harmful to a society, the intensity of the reaction may be disproportionate to the harm done (Durkheim 1933: 72). Deviance as an analytical and empirical category may be near universal, but the particular form that deviance takes most assuredly is not (Ben-Yehuda 1990: 11).

A relativizing motif is a driving force of sociological consciousness, and sociologists call into question what most other people take for granted. One of sociology's strengths is that it can make sense of groups and relationships in a world in which values have been radically relativized (Berger 1963: 48). Sociologists uncover and critically evaluate the pretensions and propaganda individuals use to hide, distort, or legitimize what they are doing. They shift from one perspective to another, ranging from the impersonal and remote transformations of the wider society to the inner experiences of individuals in order to understand the interconnections between the two. Sociologists participate mentally in the experiences of individuals differently situated from themselves no matter where or when they are found. Sociocultural relativism can help us to understand the experiences of people in groups and subcultures *within* the boundaries of any one society, as well as the experiences of people drawn from different societies and cultures.

PATHOLOGY, BASIC HUMAN RIGHTS, AND SOCIOCULTURAL RELATIVISM

To describe some culture, social arrangement, group, or human being as "sick" may be convenient, but it does little, or nothing, to further our understanding of human experience. Things do not have to be categorized as pathological for them to be recognized as harmful or to admit that humans and their societies would be better off without them. Sociologists are inclined to think that the concept of pathology fails to illuminate actual happenings and needs to be rejected. The principal defect of pathologizing diversity is that it fails to explain correctly the phenomenon under review (Matza 1969: 44). It fails to recognize the functionality and durability of deviance.

Even as the notion of pathology was being purged from sociology, it was being replaced by a notion of intrinsic harm and a normative definition of deviance. The global concern with basic human rights, principally in response to the horrors of the Holocaust and World War II, was formalized in the Universal Declaration of Human Rights (UDHR) of the United Nations (1948). Before World War II, human rights protections were viewed as a domestic, not international, project. The atrocities of the war, especially the Holocaust, changed things. It became clear that individuals were at a disadvantage when faced with governmental power, and they needed more protection against abuse than the legal system of any one nation could provide. The UDHR was sanctioned by each member country of the United Nations in 1948, and it continues to be viewed as a standard against which human decency should be measured. It forbids murder, torture, and slavery, even while it authorizes freedom of conscience, speech, and dissent. Specific sections of the document confirm the rights to employment and fair working conditions; to health, food, and security; to education; and to participation in the cultural life of the community. These human rights claims are based on principles of fairness, rightness, justice, or equity that should in principle extend to people in all parts of the world.

A normative approach to basic human rights is not without its problems. Mills's critique of the ideology of "social pathologists" (specialists on social problems and deviance) was thoughtful and thought provoking. His discussion offers a cautionary note to any normative approach that defines harms in terms of universal social norms. Norms, Mills (1943) instructed, reflect the interests, experiences, and resources of the people who fashion them, not a universal morality or global consensus. Norms do not simply create and channel human behavior, they also serve as the standards against which deviation is defined and measured. To the extent that norms are ideological, so are definitions of right and wrong or proper and improper. The push for universal human rights is difficult to justify in the face of substantial cultural and religious diversity, and profound doubts exist about the workability of implementing uniform moral standards cross-culturally (Zechenter 1997). Rights and harms must be understood from a study of particular social-historical groupings and their relationships with other social groupings, not from the application of abstract, self-contained sets of rules.

We must be careful not to be duped by what may be called "expedient relativism." This exists when elites in sovereign nations justify everything they do, no matter how harmful it is, by insisting that they should be allowed to do whatever they want. Countries that violate the human rights of their populations most often are the ones whose leaders are most likely to justify their actions by appealing to sovereignty and cultural relativity. They defend practices such as corporal or capital punishment, the abuse of women (including genital mutilation), sexism and racism, and political violence by claiming that their critics are ethnocentric or indifferent to their local customs. The concept of relativity, which was developed to encourage an awareness of, and respect for, human diversity has returned to haunt the social sciences. It is used to legitimize the subjugation of indigenous groups, women, and minorities and to excuse human rights abuses.

RELATIVITY OF DEVIANCE

Sociocultural relativism has kindred ties with Matza's (1969) idea of "natural deviation." Naturalism is an approach that views the human actor as a self-conscious, reflexive being who engages in meaningful activity. Naturalism rejects determinism, and its only obligation is to offer a correct rendition of worldly activities. It combines observation with empathy, intuition, and experience, while it views humans as individuals who intentionally create the world within which they live. "The growth of a sociological view of deviant phenomena involved . . . the replacement of a correctional stance by an *appreciation* of the deviant subject, the tacit purging of a conception of pathology by new stress on human *diversity*, and the erosion of a simple distinction between deviant and conventional phenomena, resulting from more intimate familiarity with the world as it is" (Matza 1969: 10). The difficulty in defining deviance is due neither to flaws in the concept of deviance nor in sociocultural relativism. The difficulty lies in the unruly nature of society and the indeterminacy of interpersonal relationships. Definitions of deviance are naturally ambiguous because deviance lacks inherent or essential characteristics, and human relationships are characterized by both drift and defiance. We have a right to our views of proper and improper but, if we are studying deviance, we have to pay attention to how such judgments are constructed and vary through time and space. How visitors to some culture or group react to some act, attribute, or condition is a completely separate issue from how its members do (Goode 2003).

Sociocultural relativists are inclined to view deviance as a relationship instead of a condition that some people have that others lack (Curra 2000). Social control can actually cause deviance by categorizing acts, attributes, and actors as deviant and helping to mold deviance into a pattern or career (Becker 1963: 25–39). Goffman (1961) showed that rules and reactions regularly produce counter-rules and resistance, which inevitably produce new categories of "deviance" and "deviant" because resistance to authority is usually defined as a serious matter by those who do not want their authority challenged. Cohen (1974) noted that social definitions continually work to ensure that all positions on a continuum from good to bad are always filled, so some individuals will always be classified as worse than other individuals. The wickedness of the villain, like the virtue of the saint, may have to be invented. Parsons (1951) made it clear, at least as clear as he could, that social control agents assigned the status of "deviant" to individuals and "deviance" to acts because it helped to support and sustain the normative order, as well as masking or disguising legitimate social conflicts over proper and improper motivational orientations and behaviors. In creating an "other," groups may manufacture a scapegoat that can be used to explain away continuing or worsening social problems.

Becker's writings synthesize the sociological concept of deviance with sociocultural relativism. In fact, relativism is at the core of the interactionist or labeling approach to deviance. With his ideas of "sides" (Becker 1967), "sentimentality" (Becker 1964, 1967), "hierarchies of credibility" (Becker 1967), and "moral entrepreneurs" (Becker 1963), Becker was able to draw attention to the role played by labeling, power, and audience reactions in producing careers of deviance. By moving away from the inclination of many other theorists to define deviance in terms of intrinsic qualities of actions and attributes, Becker gave a new spin to the sociology of deviance. Groups of people create deviance as they act together; no individual can create deviance alone. Social control agents, as Goffman (1961) showed with both precision and elegance, have both personal and bureaucratic reasons to create labels and apply them to individuals. If individuals refuse to follow rules or resist the labels being applied to them, control agents will view the resistance itself as a problem and in need of correction. In this way, deviance grows exponentially to the number of institutions established to deal with it (Sumner 1994).

Lemert's idea of "putative" deviance allowed sociologists of deviance to clarify the parameters of sociocultural relativism in regard to *warranted* or *unwarranted* definitions and reactions. "The putative deviation is that portion of the societal definition of the deviant which has no foundation in his [her] objective behavior. Frequently these fallacious imputations are incorporated into myth and stereotype and mediate much of the formal treatment of the deviant" (Lemert 1951: 56). Reactions to deviance can be disproportional, and individuals can be falsely accused (Becker 1963). Members of a society may come to believe that the threats from deviance are greater than they actually are (Goode & Ben-Yehuda 1994). Objective mole-hills can be transformed into subjective mountains (Jones et al. 1989), and moral enterprises can evolve into moral panics (Goode & Ben-Yehuda 1994).

Becker's concept of sentimentality shows that what is deviant depends on whose view is being taken. He borrowed the term from Freidson's (1961) study of physicians and their patients. Freidson was willing to give credibility and authority to patients' views of their physicians, even when these views were at odds with what physicians thought of themselves. Becker defined sentimentality as a disposition on the part of a researcher to leave certain variables in a problem unexamined or to refuse to consider alternate views or distasteful possibilities (Becker 1964). We are sentimental particularly when we refuse to consider the merits (or lack thereof) of *both* conventional and unconventional social actors only because we do not want to face the possibility that some cherished sympathy of ours might be shown to be untrue (Becker 1967). Putative deviance, coupled with "unsentimentality," can serve as an excellent foundation upon which to identify and, if necessary, condemn inhumane practices and, more important, the sociocultural features that produce them in the first place. If sociocultural relativists believe in anything universal, it is their belief in human potentialities and their confidence that individuals can be better than they are.

SEE ALSO: Boas, Franz; Cultural Relativism; Deviance, Absolutist Definitions of; Deviance, Constructionist Perspectives; Deviance, Reactivist Definitions of; Labeling Theory; Moral Entrepreneur; Moral Panics; Social Pathology

REFERENCES AND SUGGESTED READINGS

Becker, H. (1963) *Outsiders: Studies in the Sociology of Deviance*. Free Press, New York.

Becker, H. (1964) Introduction. In: Becker, H. (Ed.), *The Other Side: Perspectives on Deviance*. Free Press, New York, pp. 1–6.

Becker, H. (1967) Whose Side Are We On? *Social Problems* 14: 239–47.

Becker, H. (1973) Labeling Theory Reconsidered. In: *Outsiders: Studies in the Sociology of Deviance*. Free Press, New York, pp. 177–212.

Ben-Yehuda, N. (1990) *The Politics and Morality of Deviance: Moral Panics, Drug Abuse, Deviant Science, and Reversed Stigmatization*. State University of New York Press, Albany.

Berger, P. (1963) *Invitation to Sociology: A Humanistic Perspective*. Anchor/Doubleday, Garden City, NY.

Cohen, A. (1974) *The Elasticity of Evil: Changes in the Social Definition of Deviance*. Blackwell, Oxford.

Curra, J. (2000) *The Relativity of Deviance*. Sage, Thousand Oaks, CA.

Durkheim, E. (1933) *The Division of Labor in Society*. Trans. G. Simpson. Free Press, New York.

Durkheim, E. (1938) *The Rules of Sociological Method*, 8th edn. Trans. S. Solovay & J. Mueller. Free Press, New York.

Fish, S. (2001) Condemnation Without Absolutes. *New York Times*, October 15, p. A23.

Freidson, E. (1961) *Patients' View of Medical Practice*. Russell Sage Foundation, New York.

Goffman, E. (1961) *Asylums*. Doubleday/Anchor, Garden City, NY.

Goode, E. (2001) *Deviant Behavior*, 6th edn. Prentice-Hall, Upper Saddle River, NJ.

Goode, E. (2003) The Macguffin that Refuses to Die: An Investigation Into the Condition of the Sociology of Deviance. *Deviant Behavior* 24: 507–33.

Goode, E. & Ben-Yehuda, N. (1994) *Moral Panics: The Social Construction of Deviance*. Blackwell, Oxford.

Hatch, E. (1997) The Good Side of Relativism. *Journal of Anthropological Research* 53: 371–81.

Jones, B., Gallagher, B., III, & McFalls, J., Jr. (1989) Toward a Unified Model for Social Problems Theory. *Journal for the Theory of Social Behavior* 19: 337–56.

Lemert, E. (1951) *Social Pathology: A Systematic Approach to the Theory of Sociopathic Behavior*. McGraw-Hill, New York.

Matza, D. (1969) *Becoming Deviant*. Prentice-Hall, Englewood Cliffs, NJ.

Mills, C. W. (1943) The Professional Ideology of Social Pathologists. *American Journal of Sociology* 49, 165–80.

Parsons, T. (1951) *The Social System*. Free Press, New York.

Sumner, C. (1994) *The Sociology of Deviance: An Obituary*. Continuum, New York.

United Nations (1948) *Universal Declaration of Human Rights*. Adopted and Proclaimed by

General Assembly resolution 217 A (III) of 10 December 1948. Online. www.un.org/Overview/rights.html.

Zechenter, E. (1997) In the Name of Culture: Cultural Relativism and the Abuse of the Individual. *Journal of Anthropological Research* 53: 319–47.

socioeconomic status, health, and mortality

Richard G. Rogers and Jarron M. Saint Onge

The World Health Organization broadly defines health as "a state of complete physical, mental, and social well-being and not merely the absence of disease or infirmity" (WHO 1948). Health can be assessed in a number of ways, but generally includes subjective health, physical impairment, vitality and well-being, and chronic disease. Health is a measure of the quality of life, whereas mortality defines the risk of death and can be used to measure length of life. Socioeconomic status (SES) exerts a profound influence on all dimensions of health and mortality. Individuals who are situated in elevated positions in the social hierarchy tend to experience superior levels of health and survival.

Mortality captures the extreme consequences of socioeconomic disadvantage and in some cases reflects the ultimate state of poor health (Rogers et al. 2000). Mortality outcomes are a useful way of understanding the negative effects of socioeconomic disadvantage. For example, while death rates in the general population have fallen overall, more advantaged groups have experienced greater declines in mortality, which has resulted in increased mortality disparities between socioeconomically advantaged and disadvantaged groups (Pappas et al. 1993).

SES MEASURES AND RELATIONSHIPS

SES is usually conceptualized to include multiple dimensions (knowledge, employment, and economic status) and is often indexed by educational and occupational attainment and income. Individuals who are employed, with higher levels of education, and with greater incomes tend to enjoy better health and lower mortality than socioeconomically disadvantaged individuals. SES is measured in a variety of ways, depending on data availability and the specific research questions posed.

Education is regarded as the most important dimension of SES. It is typically measured categorically by highest degree attained, with the assumption that qualitative differences exist between those with less than a high school degree, a completed high school degree, and advanced degrees. Educational attainment usually occurs prior to employment, may be a prerequisite for occupational advancement, engenders a broader world perspective, contributes to a sense of personal control, is related to healthy behaviors, and provides the requisite knowledge and skills to obtain health information (Mirowsky & Ross 2003).

Education has a graded effect on health and mortality, with higher educational levels contributing to better health and survival prospects. Figure 1 shows this education gradient for both sexes. The gap in life expectancy between high and low levels of education is larger for males than females. And the returns to education are substantial: a 25-year-old male with less than a high school degree can expect eight fewer years of life than a comparably aged male with an advanced degree. Increased education adds years to life.

Income can be measured for the individual or family. Family incomes are noteworthy because families can pool resources to provide for all members and they benefit from economies of scale. Methods of measuring income include per capita income, poverty rates, income-to-needs ratios, and various consumption thresholds. Income can also be measured through relative comparisons. Whereas incomes can directly affect health through access to health care and opportunities for healthy lifestyles, income inequality can indirectly affect health outcomes and mortality through underinvestment in social spending, erosion of social cohesion, and stress. For example, reduced social spending can limit life opportunities for less privileged groups by means of public goods such as education. The disintegration of social cohesion may increase levels of mistrust and reduce civic attachments, thereby limiting important social buffers to mortality. Finally, income inequality can

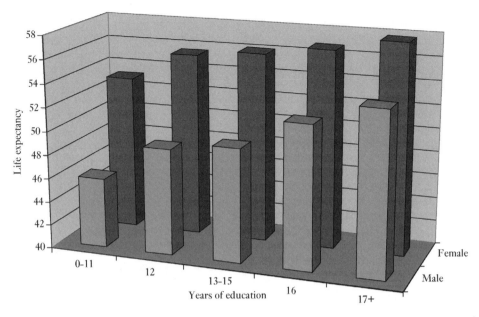

Figure 1   Education-specific life expectancies at age 25 by sex, USA.
Source: Derived from Richards & Barry (1998) and based on 1990 data.

increase stress and frustration levels by means of relative deprivation in which perceived disparities contribute to potential health problems.

Recent research has expanded measures of economic status. Diversified income portfolios, higher levels of wealth, home ownership, and a lack of credit card debt predict better health and lower mortality. Income portfolios demonstrate that individuals derive income from multiple sources, such as job income, self-employment income, interest income, dividend income, pensions, and Social Security. Additional income streams help individuals buffer against the loss of any single income source, and higher levels of wealth can translate into better health at older ages.

Researchers have begun to examine the associations between SES and health and mortality among individuals with limited socioeconomic resources. In an innovative analysis, Krueger and colleagues (2004) examined the effects of Food Stamp receipt on mortality. Food Stamp aid can improve health and reduce mortality by directly providing access to adequate nutrition, while also indirectly allowing households to allocate other earnings to such factors as health

care, education, job training, or simply paying bills, which could reduce stress, and thereby improve health and survival. Not all eligible individuals participate in the Food Stamp program, but those who participate experience reduced risks of death.

Assessing the causal direction between income and health is complicated: does low income produce poor health or vice versa? In some instances, sick, ill, and frail individuals may suffer job demotions and pay reductions. But the overwhelming evidence supports the strong and persistent effects of income on health. Low income increases the likelihood of poor health and contributes to higher risks of death.

Compared to individuals who are not in the labor force, employed individuals are generally healthier, in part, because they have access to income, workplace camaraderie, workplace health factors such as gyms and exercise programs, and health insurance. This employment benefit is termed the healthy worker effect. Again, causality is difficult to assess: poor health also impedes the likelihood of employment.

Specific occupations affect health behaviors, health risks, and mortality. For instance,

Academy Award winners can expect to live 3.9 years longer than less recognized actors and actresses (Redeimeier & Singh 2001). Others, using measures of occupational status, such as the Nam-Powers Occupational SES Scores (OSS), or indicators of occupational prestige, such as Duncan's Socioeconomic Index (SEI), show that mortality and morbidity decrease with increased status and prestige.

FUNDAMENTAL CAUSES AND PATHWAYS

There are many explanations for the existence of health disparities by SES. Explanations can be examined through both resource- and non-resource-dependent characteristics. According to Jonathan Feinstein (1993), resource-dependent characteristics include, for example, income and wealth, whereas non-resource characteristics are composed of psychological, genetic, and cultural factors. Additionally, the non-resource dependent characteristics depend on life span experiences and differential access to health care services.

Bruce Link and Jo Phelan (1995) make a persuasive case that higher levels of SES translate into behaviors that minimize the risks associated with morbidity and mortality. Compared to individuals with lower SES, individuals with higher SES are more likely to engage in healthy behaviors – exercise, abstention from smoking, more nutritious diets, use of seatbelts, avoidance of drug use or excessive alcohol consumption – which translate into lower risks of death from such causes as cardiovascular disease, many forms of cancer, diabetes, accidents, and homicide.

Researchers have demonstrated that poor SES conditions in infancy and childhood may predispose individuals to later health problems. Poor SES conditions early in life may expose individuals to additional infectious diseases, environmental hazards, or stress that may contribute to health problems in middle and older ages.

A stress paradigm may also explain deleterious health effects. Individuals with lower SES are more likely to suffer greater environmental and social insults, such as discrimination and social subjugation, which contributes to higher psychological and physiological stress. Higher stress can translate into detrimental health behaviors, including drug and alcohol dependence, which result in increased risks of chronic conditions, functional limitations, and mortality. Lower SES individuals also have fewer resources to deal with these stressors, which further exacerbates their poor health and survival prospects.

Contextual or structural components may lead to deleterious negative health outcomes. Lower SES individuals have less access to health information and healthy foods, and are less able to implement health recommendations. Additionally, the marketing and location of fast food restaurants target lower SES groups and lead to poorer diets. Lower SES groups are more likely to be exposed to violence, crime, disorder, and fear that adversely affect health and mortality.

FUTURE DIRECTIONS IN RESEARCH, THEORY, AND METHODOLOGY

Although a vast literature on SES and health and mortality exists, a number of questions warrant further investigation. Researchers have shown strong associations between education, measured as formal years of schooling completed, and health outcomes. The use of more refined measures of education might provide additional insight into what it is about education that is health enhancing. Is education merely a proxy for ability or IQ or is it the knowledge, skills, training, and certification that education confers that leads to better health outcomes? There may be measurable differences between individuals who obtain a high school diploma, a GED, or who do not graduate but all of whom obtain 12 years of formal schooling. In addition, many individuals acquire extensive on-the-job training. Others may not accrue additional years of formal education but instead dedicate substantial time and effort to, and gain important insight through, workshops and seminars. Further, some individuals, especially in professional positions, are required to maintain levels of certification. Formal years of education is a crude measure of the multiple aspects of knowledge attainment that may influence behaviors that either enhance or impede good health.

Some researchers are investigating an expanded array of occupational characteristics that may also be related to health and mortality. Jencks et al. (1988) have proposed new measures of job desirability. They have asked individuals to rate their job relative to others based on such characteristics as educational requirements, hours worked, on-the-job training, level of supervision, repetitiveness, and job dirtiness. Some jobs are more physically demanding, requiring twisting, turning, vibrating, and bending. Other jobs may expose workers to hazards such as chemical exposure to insecticides, pesticides, solvents, and acids, or to radioactive material, risk of fire, or risk of accidents.

Longitudinal panel data, life course conceptual frameworks, and related analytic techniques allow the assessment of time-varying covariates, or changes in statuses over time, and the effects on later health outcomes. For example, we need to know more about how job loss, income shocks, job transitions, or temporary layoffs affect health and mortality. Also, individuals do not live in social isolation; they are nested within families, households, neighborhoods, and communities. Future analyses must examine these multilevel dynamics. For instance, families often make employment decisions for family members. Thus, families may endeavor to optimize the health of all family members rather than focus on selected family members. Finally, new research on social capital and social networks may also provide valuable insight into health and mortality.

SEE ALSO: Biodemography; Gender, Health, and Mortality; Health Risk Behavior; Health and Social Class; Healthy Life Expectancy; Life Chances and Resources; Mortality: Transitions and Measures; Race/Ethnicity, Health, and Mortality

REFERENCES AND SUGGESTED READINGS

Feinstein, J. S. (1993) The Relationship between Socioeconomic Status and Health: A Review of the Literature. *Milbank Quarterly* 72(2): 279–322.

Jencks, C., Perman, L., & Rainwater, L. (1988) What Is a Good Job? A New Measure of Labor-Market Success. *American Journal of Sociology* 93(6): 1322–57.

Krueger, P. M., Rogers, R. G., Ridao-Cano, C., & Hummer, R. A. (2004) To Help or to Harm? Food Stamp Receipt and Mortality Risk Prior to the 1996 Welfare Reform Act. *Social Forces* 82(4): 1577–1603.

Link, B. G. & Phelan, J. (1995) Social Conditions as Fundamental Causes of Disease. *Journal of Health and Social Behavior* Extra Issue: 80–94.

Mirowsky, J. & Ross, C. E. (2003) *Education, Social Status, and Health.* Aldine de Gruyter, Hawthorne, NY.

Pappas, G., Queen, S., Hadden, W., & Fisher, G. (1993) The Increasing Disparity in Mortality between Socioeconomic Groups in the United States, 1960 and 1986. *New England Journal of Medicine* 329(3): 103–9.

Redeimeier, D. A. & Singh, S. M. (2001) Survival in Academy Award-Winning Actors and Actresses. *Annals of Internal Medicine* 134(10): 955–62.

Richards, H. & Barry, R. (1998) US Life Tables for 1990 by Sex, Race, and Education. *Journal of Forensic Economics* 11(1): 9–26.

Rogers, R. G., Hummer, R. A., & Nam, C. B. (2000) *Living and Dying in the USA: Behavioral, Health, and Social Differentials of Adult Mortality.* Academic Press, New York.

World Health Organization (1948) Preamble to the *Constitution of the World Health Organization.* Online. www.who.int/about/definition/en/.

sociolinguistics

J. K. Chambers

Sociolinguistics is the systematic study of the social uses of language. It proceeds by observing the way people use language in different social settings. People adjust their vocabulary, sounds, and syntax depending upon who they are speaking to and the circumstances of the conversation. Such adjustments are often linguistically subtle and socially meticulous and largely subconscious. They are not taught or consciously learned, but are part of the innate linguistic competence of all normal people.

Philosophers have always recognized that socialization is the primary function of language. In 1690, Locke wrote: "God, having designed man for a sociable creature, made him not only with an inclination, and under a necessity to have fellowship with those of his kind, but furnished him also with language, which was to be the great instrument and common tie of society." Yet linguistic research into its social significance is relatively recent, having emerged as an international movement only in the second half of the twentieth century. Sociolinguistics extends social science methods to the venerable study of language, which since Plato has been conceived as the abstract study of the combinatorial possibilities of parts of speech (syntax) and speech sounds (phonology). Around 1960, linguists began tracking social variables in speech acts, such as the age, sex, and social class of the participants, and correlating them with dependent linguistic variables.

Variation in language is socially motivated and linguistically insignificant. To take a simple example, it is possible in English to say either *John doesn't need any help* or *John doesn't need no help*. Those two sentences convey the same linguistic meaning and both are readily understood by anyone who speaks the language. Linguistically, they are perfect paraphrases. Socially, however, they are not equivalent at all, with the former deemed to be correct, educated, standard usage, and the latter, though it differs by only one small word, deemed to be incorrect, uneducated, or rustic.

Variables with widely held social evaluations, like double negatives (and *ain't* for *isn't*, *hisself* for *himself*, and *we wasn't* for *we weren't*), are said to stigmatize. Most variables carry more subtle social evaluations. William Labov (1966), in the seminal sociolinguistic masterwork, showed that New Yorkers, who variably pronounce /r/ in certain contexts, so that *cart*, *pork*, and *bird* are sometimes pronounced "r-less," like *caht*, *pohk*, and *boid*, carry complex biases. Labov's subjects, when asked to guess the occupations of speakers based on tape-recorded samples of their speech, guessed "TV personality" for one woman, but on hearing another sample, unwittingly spoken by the same woman, they downgraded her to "receptionist"; the second speech sample was identical to the first except that it contained one r-less pronunciation. Moreover, the New Yorkers made that judgment regardless of whether they themselves usually used r-less pronunciations.

Hallmarks of the sociolinguistic enterprise are (1) the identification of linguistic variants correlated with social factors, (2) the incorporation of style as an independent variable, and (3) the apparent-time apprehension of linguistic changes in progress. All represent innovations in language studies due to sociolinguistics (Chambers 2002).

Social factors largely determine the linguistic realization of speech acts. Janitors speak differently to lawyers in the office block than they do among themselves, and vice versa. Young mothers meeting by chance at the local doctor's office chat to one another more familiarly than they do to elderly neighbors in the same situation. Men and women in sex-exclusive domains such as locker rooms tend to slant both the topics of their conversation and their speech styles in different ways. These responses are partly predictable in terms of the social attributes of the participants.

Social class, age, and sex are overriding determinants of linguistic variation, but others also play roles. Ethnicity figured crucially in the development of sociolinguistic concepts because close study of African American varieties became a testing ground and sounding-board at the inception of the new discipline (as summarized in Rickford 1999). American sociolinguists like Labov, Walt Wolfram, and John Baugh demonstrated beyond any doubt that African American varieties, notwithstanding more than a century of disparagement by cultural arbiters, were as systematic, rule-governed, and complex as mainline Philadelphia speech or any other English dialect, or for that matter any human language from Latin to Laotian.

In modern industrial societies the speech of the educated middle class in capital cities tends to gain acceptance as the national norm and get codified (in somewhat idealized form) in dictionaries, grammar books, and usage guides. Working-class varieties typically differ from the standard dialect both grammatically and phonologically, and the differences are socially stratified, so that they become greater down the social hierarchy, with lower working class more different from the standard than middle working class, and so on. Within social classes, women tend to use fewer stigmatized and nonstandard features than men, a robust difference that apparently holds in all complex societies. The age groups at the social extremes also tend to differ most from the standard, with the oldest groups preserving some features that have become archaic or old-fashioned in the dialect, and adolescents accelerating changes and adopting innovations at a greater rate than their elders.

Most variation is a matter of degree rather than kind. Only stigmatized variants like multiple negatives occur as absolute differences, in that they almost never occur in middle-class speech but do occur in working-class speech. Most variants typically occur with graded frequencies in all the social classes. For instance, the common English variable known as (ng), which indicates variant pronunciations of present participle endings as *walking* vs. *walkin'*, *running* vs. *runnin'*, and *telling* vs. *tellin'* (phonetically, a final velar nasal vs. alveolar nasal), is graded throughout the social hierarchy (as summarized in Chambers 2003: 121–6). A study in Norwich, England, showed lower-middle-class people used the *walkin'* variant 18 percent of the time in casual conversation, while upper working class used it 72 percent and lower working class 91 percent in the same circumstances. Consistent with sex patterns, women always use it less than men of the same social class: for instance, upper-working-class Norwich women use it 66 percent of the time, but the men who are their brothers, husbands, and neighbors use it 79 percent of the time. Consistent with the acceleration of variation by adolescents, a study in Sydney, Australia, showed that working-class teenagers used the *walkin'* variant 26 percent of the time, but their parents and grandparents only 4 percent of the time.

Style cuts across the social variables and adds a second dimension to linguistic variation (Schilling-Estes 2002). Stylistic adjustments in more casual contexts usually result in an increase in the frequency of vernacular variants, and vernacular variants are generally the ones that characterize working-class speech. So, in terms of the *walkin'* variant, middle-class speakers use it more frequently among friends in recreational situations than among colleagues at business meetings. Casual styles thus bear some of the characteristics of social-class speech lower on the social hierarchy, but since the adjustments take the same direction for all social classes the styles remain stratified, with little or no overlap between the classes. This recurring pattern shows that a speech community is defined not because its members speak the same

as one another, but because they share the communal norms.

Adjustments in style are usually explicable in terms of self-monitoring. As social settings become more casual, participants become less self-conscious about their behavior. Linguistically, they use more vernacular variants. This explanation presupposes that the vernacular is more natural than standard speech, more relaxed, and presumably more deeply embedded in the language faculty. Under special circumstances, stylistic adjustments are highly self-conscious, as when a white adolescent adopts African American features with his peers (called "crossing," Rampton 1995), or an adult with social airs adopts features of the higher social class (called "aspirers," Chambers 2003: 101–5). Self-conscious adjustments like these attract attention and are sometimes subject to criticism, whereas style-shifting toward the vernacular in casual settings generally goes unnoticed.

Understanding language change constitutes perhaps the greatest advance in language study that is a direct consequence of sociolinguistic methods. Labov noticed consistent differences in the speech of people in different age groups, and postulated that the differences represented changes in progress, such that the younger people were using features that were supplanting the ones used by older generations. Prior to sociolinguistics, historical linguists had studied change in what is called "real time," by comparing two (or more) states of a language at different periods. Studying change in "apparent time," by comparing two (or more) age groups in the same period, reveals its dynamics and introduces the possibility of determining how the change is progressing, which groups are leading it, and how it is spreading socially (summarized in Bailey 2002).

The apparent-time hypothesis assumes that people acquire their accents and dialects in their formative years, say, by age 20, and retain them throughout their lifetimes. The speech of 80-year-olds thus reflects the language norms of the community some 60 years earlier. Generally, the hypothesis holds, as shown in tests whereby apparent-time results have been subjected to real-time comparisons, by linguists revisiting a community 20 or more years later. The apparent-time hypothesis provides a framework that yields, as Weinreich et al. (1968) put it in a seminal article, "a theory of language change that bypasses the fruitless paradoxes with which historical linguistics has been struggling."

Nevertheless, as a hypothesis, it must be applied prudently and tested rigorously. It can be disrupted, for instance, by individuals going against the grain of their social cohort, like the aspirers mentioned above, and one subcategory of individuals can defy communal norms in predictably ways (discussed as "oddballs and insiders," in Chambers 2003: 93–115). A type of linguistic change that disrupts the apparent-time hypothesis is "age-grading," the regular adjustment of linguistic features as maturity emblems (Bailey 2002: 324; Chambers 2003: 206–11). For instance, Japanese boys use honorific markers characteristic of women and only gradually adopt the adult male system as adolescents; an apparent-time study would thus show differences between boys and men, indicative under ordinary circumstances of change in progress, but a real-time study of those boys 10 years later would reveal them perfectly aligned with the adult males, evidence that no change had taken place in communal norms.

Sociolinguistics has discovered nuances such as social subcategories and age-graded changes in coming to grips with the manifold ways in which interacting variables of class, sex, age, ethnicity, and style affect the way people speak. For the first time, a branch of linguistics studies grammar and phonology as they are enacted in the service of communication. Sociolinguistics is necessarily variant, continuous, and quantitative, and in all those respects it differs from older branches of linguistics. For centuries, thinking people have recognized, at least tacitly, that our speech expresses who we are and how we relate to the social setting, as well as what is on our minds. The social uses of language are so deeply engrained in our human nature that they were thought to be beyond human comprehension, as were consciousness and genetic coding. Like them, when sociolinguistics came into being in the second half of the twentieth century, its very existence represented an assault on the presumed limits of knowledge. Also like them it made rapid progress, a consequence undoubtedly of the fact that there was everything to learn. It is now firmly established as a core area in the study of language.

SEE ALSO: Language; *Langue* and *Parole*; Quantitative Methods; Sex and Gender; Social Structure

REFERENCES AND SUGGESTED READINGS

Bailey, G. (2002) Real and Apparent Time. In: Chambers, J. K., Trudgill, P., & Schilling-Estes, N. (Eds.), *The Handbook of Language Variation and Change*. Blackwell, Oxford, pp. 312–32.

Chambers, J. K. (2002) Studying Language Variation: An Informal Epistemology. In: Chambers, J. K., Trudgill, P., & Schilling-Estes, N. (Eds.), *The Handbook of Language Variation and Change*. Blackwell, Oxford, pp. 3–14.

Chambers, J. K. (2003) *Sociolinguistic Theory: Linguistic Variation and Its Social Significance*, 2nd edn. Blackwell, Oxford.

Labov, W. (1966) *The Social Stratification of English in New York City*. Center for Applied Linguistics, Washington, DC.

Locke, J. (1997 [1690]) *An Essay Concerning Human Understanding*. Ed. R. Woolhouse. Penguin, London.

Rampton, B. (1995) *Crossing: Language and Ethnicity Among Adolescents*. Longman, New York.

Rickford, J. R. (1999) *African American Vernacular English*. Blackwell, Oxford.

Schilling-Estes, N. (2002) Investigating Stylistic Variation. In: Chambers, J. K., Trudgill, P., & Schilling-Estes, N. (Eds.), *The Handbook of Language Variation and Change*. Blackwell, Oxford, pp. 375–401.

Weinreich, U., Labov, W., & Herzog, M. I. (1968) Empirical Foundations for a Theory of Language Change. In: Lehmann, W. P. & Malkiel, Y. (Eds.), *Directions for Historical Linguistics: A Symposium*. University of Texas Press, Austin, pp. 95–188.

sociological imagination

Christopher Andrews

The term "sociological imagination" comes from a book with that title by American sociologist C. Wright Mills (2000 [1959]) and describes an understanding of one's own position and experiences as reflective of broader social and historical forces. According to Mills, the sociological imagination is more than just a theoretical concept or heuristic device: it is a "promise." The promise of the sociological imagination is to allow individuals to understand their place in the broader social and historical context. As Mills says in the first sentence of *The Sociological Imagination*, people today increasingly feel that their private lives are a series of "traps" (p. 3). The promise of the sociological imagination is to understand the nature of these traps and to determine if they are in fact private in nature, or if, as Mills suggests, their actual origin lies with broader social and historical forces.

In this regard, the sociological imagination provides a "fruitful distinction" between individual and social problems. Some problems faced by individuals simply reflect those which threaten individually held values or lifestyles, and are problems whose origin and resolution, according to Mills, lie in the personal sphere (p. 8). Other problems, however, reflect broader social or public issues. While the individual may experience these problems subjectively or first hand, the sociological imagination prompts one to imagine or speculate as to how such problems may be tied to broader structural or historical trends.

The "promise" of the sociological imagination involves the linking of "personal troubles" to "public issues" (p. 8). Described by Mills as a form of "self-consciousness," the sociological imagination directs attention to the linkages between "the personal troubles of milieu" and "the public issues of social structure" (pp. 7–8). "Troubles" reflect one's personal problems and are "private matter[s]" undeserving of sociological attention, whereas "issues" reflect problems that transcend the private sphere of the individual, and are therefore "public matter[s]" (p. 8).

One example offered by Mills concerns unemployment. When one person is unemployed, he notes, it is a personal matter. However, when a significant number of people are unemployed, it becomes a public issue concerning a lack of economic opportunity. Thus, broad social and historical trends, such as deindustrialization, produce outcomes felt and experienced by individuals as private or "personal troubles," masking their structural origins. The key, therefore, is in linking experiences such as unemployment to broader social and historical

trends (e.g., deindustrialization). When many people experience similar personal troubles or find themselves in a similar set of "traps," it suggests structural rather than personal origins.

In this respect, the sociological imagination is reflective of a broader sociological preoccupation with the micro–macro linkages of society. For Mills, many of the individual, or micro-level, problems that people face in fact reflect broader structural, or macro-level, phenomena. Thus, by focusing on these macro-level or structural arrangements, one can grasp a better sense of one's own life experiences or "biography." Rather than individuals blaming themselves for their own problems, Mills offers the sociological imagination to the American public as a way of linking personal troubles and the "traps" of daily life to larger social and historical trends. As Mills suggests, many of the pressing problems in our daily lives are problems of social structure; the key is in linking individual outcomes or "biographies" to broader social structures and structural trends.

In viewing one's own life or "biography" as reflective of larger social and historical forces, Mills saw those focused on the intersection of history and biography as being directed toward three key questions concerning (1) the structure of society, (2) its relation to other past or contemporary societies, and (3) the types of people such a society produces. Accordingly, the sociological imagination in practice denotes a focus on the nature of social institutions, the way in which they interact and change over time, and the effect they have on the outlook, attitudes, and orientations of individuals.

Mills himself arguably utilized the sociological imagination in much of his own work. With Hans Gerth (1953), Mills explored how certain types of institutions create or select for certain traits and personalities, such as authoritarianism. In *White Collar* (2000 [1951]), Mills documented how the shift from entrepreneurship and small businesses toward corporations and bureaucracy brought about changes in how individuals defined "success" and experienced work, while *The Power Elite* (2000 [1956]) linked the increasing concentration of power or "ascendancy" of the executive branch to growing political disillusionment and the emergence of a "mass society."

SEE ALSO: Micro–Macro Links; Mills, C. Wright; Social Problems, Concept and Perspectives; Social Structure

REFERENCES AND SUGGESTED READINGS

Gerth, H. & Mills, C. W. (Eds.) (1953) *Character and Social Structure*. Harcourt, Brace, & World, New York.

Horowitz, I. (Ed.) (1967) *Power, Politics, and People: The Collected Essays of C. Wright Mills*. Oxford University Press, New York.

Mills, C. W. (2000 [1951]) *White Collar*. Oxford University Press, New York.

Mills, C. W. (2000 [1956]) *The Power Elite*. Oxford University Press, New York.

Mills, C. W. (2000 [1959]) *The Sociological Imagination*. Oxford University Press, New York.

Mills, K. (Ed.) (2000) *C. Wright Mills: Letters and Autobiographical Writings*. University of California Press, Berkeley.

Rose, A. M. (1969) Varieties of Sociological Imagination. *American Sociological Review* 34: 623–30.

sociology

Gerard Delanty

Sociology is a form of social inquiry that takes wide-ranging forms. As is the case with many disciplines, it is contested and there is no generally accepted definition of what constitutes sociology. But we should not draw the conclusion that the contested and diverse nature of sociology amounts to the absence of any sense of self-understanding and that the discipline has lapsed into irreversible fragmentation. Sociology can be partly defined by citing examples of what sociologists actually do, but it can also be defined by referring to some of the major intellectual statements of the discipline, such as classic works or theoretical and methodological approaches that are characteristically sociological. To begin, it is helpful to look at sociology in terms of its subject matter, its approach, and some of the classical works that have shaped the discipline.

Many disciplines have a clearly defined subject matter, although very often this is due to the absence of methodological scrutiny and uncritical consensus, as in the general view that "the past" is the subject domain of historians while political scientists study "politics." Sociologists generally have a tougher time in defending their territory than other disciplines, even though they unhesitatingly take over on the territory of others. Sociology's subject domain can arguably be said to be the totality of social relations or simply "society," which Durkheim said was a reality *sui generis*. As a reality in itself the social world is more than the sum of its parts. There has been little agreement on exactly what these parts are, with some positions arguing that the parts are social structures and others claiming that society is simply made up of social actors and thus the subject matter of sociology is social action. The emphasis on the whole being greater than the sum of the parts has led some sociologists to the view that sociology is defined by the study of the relations between the different parts of society. This insight has tended to be reflected in a view of society as a movement or process. It would not be inaccurate to say that sociology is the social science devoted to the study of modern society.

In terms of theory and methodology, sociology is highly diverse. The paradigms that Thomas Kuhn believed to be characteristic of the history of science are more absent from sociology than from other social sciences. Arguably, anthropology and economics have more tightly defined methodological approaches than sociology. As a social science, sociology can be described as evidence-based social inquiry into the social world and informed by conceptual frameworks and established methodological approaches. But what constitutes evidence varies depending on whether quantitative or qualitative approaches are adopted, although such approaches are not distinctively sociological. There is also considerable debate as to the scientific status of sociology, which was founded to be a social science distinct from the natural sciences and distinct from the human sciences. The diversity of positions on sociology today is undoubtedly a matter of where sociology is deemed to stand in relation to the experimental and human sciences. While it is generally accepted that sociology is a third science, there is less consensus on exactly where the limits of this space should be drawn. This is also a question of the relation of sociology to its subject matter: is it part of its object, as in the hermeneutical tradition; is it separate from its object, as in the positivist tradition; or is it a mode of knowledge connected to its object by political practice, as in the radical tradition?

A discipline is often shaped by its founding figures and a canon of classical works. It is generally accepted today that the work of Marx, Weber, and Durkheim has given to sociology a classical framework. However, whether this canon can direct sociological research today is highly questionable and mostly it has been relegated to the history of sociology, although there are attempts to make classics relevant to current social research (Shilling & Mellor 2001). Such attempts, however, misunderstand the relation between the history of a discipline and the actual practice of it. Classic works are not of timeless relevance, but offer points of reference for the interpretation of the present and milestones in the history of a discipline. For this reason the canon is not stable and should also not be confused with social theory: it was Parsons in the 1930s who canonized Weber and Durkheim as founding fathers; in the 1970s Marx was added to the list – due not least to the efforts of Giddens – and Spencer has more or less disappeared; in the 1980s Simmel was added and in the present day there is the rise of contemporary classics, such as Bourdieu, Bauman, Luhmann, Habermas, and Foucault, and there are recovered classics, such as Elias. It is apparent from a cursory look at the classics that many figures were only later invented as classical sociologists to suit whatever project was being announced. The word "invented" is not too strong here: Marx did not see himself as a sociologist, Weber was an economic historian and rarely referred to sociology as such, and Foucault was a lapsed psychiatrist; all of them operated outside disciplinary boundaries.

The impact of Foucault on sociology today is a reminder that sociology continues to change, absorbing influences from outside the traditional discipline. The range of methodological and theoretical approaches has not led to a great deal of synthesis or consensus on what actually defines sociology. Since the so-called cultural turn in the social sciences, much of sociology takes place outside the discipline itself, in cultural studies, criminology, women's studies, development studies, demography, human geography, and planning, as well as in the other social and human sciences. This is increasingly the case with the rise of interdisciplinarity and more so with post-disciplinarity, wherein disciplines do not merely relate to each other but disappear altogether. Few social science disciplines have made such an impact on the wider social and human science as sociology, a situation that has led to widespread concern that sociology may be disappearing into those disciplines that it had in part helped to create (Scott 2005).

ORIGINS, TRAJECTORIES, AND NATIONAL TRADITIONS

Sociology today still remains in the shadow of its origin. As Levine (1995) has pointed out, sociology has always continued to return to its history and all the major schools have elaborated trajectories of their own history. So the story of the emergence of sociology is often inseparable from the attempt to define sociology.

In the most general sense sociology arose as a mode of knowledge concerned with the moral problems of modernity. The origins of sociology go back to the discovery of the existence of the social as a specific reality independent of the state and the private domain of the household. The eighteenth century marks the emergence of social theory as a distinctive form of intellectual inquiry and which gradually becomes distinguished from political theory. The decline of the court society and the rise of civil society suggested the existence of the social as a distinctive object of consciousness and reflection. Until then it was not clear of what "society" consisted other than the official culture of the court society. By the eighteenth century it was evident that there was indeed an objective social domain that could be called "society" with which was associated the public. This coincided with the rise of sociology.

One of the first major works in the emergence of sociology was Montesquieu's *The Spirit of the Laws*, which brought about the transformation of political theory into sociology. The central theme in this work, which was published in 1748, was that society is the source of all laws.

Society was expressed in the form of conditioning influences on people, shaping different forms of life. Durkheim claimed that the notion of an underlying spirit or ethos that pervades social institutions was a resonating theme in modern sociological thought from Montesquieu – a tread that is also present in Weber's *The Protestant Ethic and the Spirit of Capitalism*. *The Spirit of the Laws* demonstrated the sociological notion that social laws are socially and historically variable, but not to a point that human societies have nothing in common. According to Montesquieu, who was acutely aware of the diversity of societies, they differ most notably according to geographical factors, which have a conditioning influence in norms, morals, and character. His empirical method demonstrated a connection between climate and social customs and gave great attention to the material condition of life. It was this use of the empirical method to make testable hypotheses that Durkheim admired and which had a lasting influence on French sociology to Bourdieu and beyond.

Although generally regarded as one of the founders of modern political philosophy, Rousseau anticipated many sociological theories. He was one of the first to identify society as the source of social problems. In the *Discourse on the Origin of Inequality*, published in 1755, he argued that inequality is not a natural characteristic, but a socially created one for which individuals themselves are not responsible. The notion of the "general will" – itself based on Montesquieu's "spirit of the laws" – influenced Durkheim's concept of collective representations. The general will signified the external normative and symbolic power of collective beliefs. But Rousseau's enduring legacy is the theory of the social contract, which can be seen as an early notion of community as the basis of society and the state as a political community. In his most famous work, *The Social Contract*, published in 1762, he postulated the existence of the social contract to describe the social bond that makes society possible.

The discipline of sociology has been strongly influenced by the French sociological tradition, for in France social science – where the term first arose – was more advanced as an officially recognized activity. Auguste Comte coined the term sociology to refer to the science of social

order and which he believed to be the "queen of the sciences." Comte's plea for a positivistic sociology must be seen in the context of the age, where social inquiry was largely associated with the speculative approaches of Enlightenment intellectuals and the officers of the restored *ancien régime*. Against the negative critiques of the intellectuals, Comte wished sociology to be a positive science based on evidence rather than speculation. But his legacy was his notion of sociology as the queen of the sciences. In this grandiose vision of sociology, the new science of modernity not only encapsulated positivism, but it also stood at the apex of a hierarchy of sciences, providing them with an integrative framework. While few adhered to this vision, the idea that sociology was integrative rather than a specialized science remained influential and has been the basis of the idea of sociology as a science that does not have its own subject matter but interprets the results of other sciences from the perspective of a general science of society. From the nineteenth century this general conception of sociology became linked with the problem of the moral order of society in the era of social and political unrest that followed the French Revolution. This is particularly evident in the sociology of Durkheim, whose major works were responses to the crisis of the moral order. This was most acutely the case with *Suicide*, which was one of the first works in professional sociology, but was also the central question in the *Division of Labour in Society*. Thus it could be said that the French tradition reflected a general conception of sociology as the science of the social problems of modern society.

Attention must also be paid to the Scottish origins of sociology, which go back to the moral philosophers of the Scottish Enlightenment, who can be regarded as early sociologists in that they recognized the objectivity of society (Strydom 2000). This tradition, too, provided a basis for a tradition of sociology as a general social science of modernity. Adam Ferguson's *Essay on the Origin of Civil Society*, published in 1767, emphasized the role of social conflict and in terms very different from John Hobbes's account of conflict and individual egoism. For Ferguson, conflict between nations produces solidarity and makes civil society as a universal norm possible. He recognized that society is always more than the sum of its parts and can never be reduced to its components. In marked contrast to the prevailing ideas of the age, Ferguson argued that the state of nature is itself a social condition and that sociality is natural. John Millar's *Origin of the Distinction of Ranks*, published in 1770, contained one of the first discussions of social class and can be seen as a pioneering work in historical sociology. Millar and Ferguson were particularly interested in the historical evolution of society, which they viewed in terms of a model of progress. But it was in the writings of Adam Smith that the notion of progress was most pronounced. Smith developed moral philosophy into a theory of political economy coupled with a theory of progress that was influential for over a century later. Society progresses in four historical stages, he argued, which can be related to stages – hunting, pastoral, agricultural, and commercial – in the development of the means of subsistence. Commercial society is based on private property and the economic pursuit of individual interest. Smith argued, however, that the well-being of commercial society and indeed the very fact of society is due to a collective logic – which he called an "invisible hand" – at work, which ensures that individual actions function to serve collective goals. Although Smith came to personify laissez-faire capitalism, his concerns were largely philosophical and must be understood in the intellectual and political context of the age. Like the other moral philosophers in Scotland, Smith was acutely aware of the contingent nature of the human condition, which could never be explained by natural law. Moral norms and the rules of justice must be devised in ways that function best for the needs of society and in ways that will reduce evil and suffering. In this respect Smith, Ferguson, and Millar established a vision of sociology as a moral science of the social world, the outcome of which was that the social and the natural were separated from each other and sociology became the science of the social.

From its early origins in Enlightenment thought, sociology emerged along with the wider institutionalization of the social sciences from the end of the nineteenth century. In France, as already noted, it was most advanced and the Durkheimian tradition established a firm foundation for modern French sociology,

which was based on a strong tradition of empirical inquiry. In Germany, where sociology emerged later, it was more closely tied to the humanities. While in France sociology had become relatively independent of philosophy, in Germany a tradition of humanistic sociology developed on the one side from the neo-Kantian philosophy and on the other from Hegelian Marxism. While Weber broke the connection with psychology that was so much a feature of the neo-Kantian tradition, German sociology remained strongly interpretive and preoccupied with issues of culture and history. Weber himself was an economic historian primarily concerned with the problem of bureaucracy, but increasingly came to be interested in comparative analysis of the world religions and the relation between cultural and moral meaning with economic activity. His work was testimony to the belief that social inquiry can shed light on moral values that are constitutive of the social condition. Where German sociology as represented by Weber was concerned with the problem of subjective meaning, French sociology was animated by the concern with social morality. For this reason it is plausible to argue, as Fuller (1998) claims, that sociology has been a kind of secular theology. Underlying both the German and French traditions has been a vision of sociology – distilled of Comtean positivism – as a general social science of modern society.

According to Talcott Parsons in one of the classic works of modern sociology, *The Structure of Social Action* (1949), Hobbes and Locke articulated the basic themes of sociology, namely the problem of social order. But we cannot speak of a British sociological tradition before the Scottish Enlightenment thinkers mentioned above. Hobbes and Locke have been claimed by political theory and were not influential in sociological thought. Modern British sociology initially emerged from the work of such Victorian liberal reformers as J. S. Mill and Herbert Spencer. Although Spencer broke from Mill's utilitarianism, his biological evolutionism led to a restrictive approach that has now been largely discredited. British sociology has on the whole been shaped by a vision of sociology as a social science concerned with specific issues. By far the dominant trend has been a view of sociology concerned with class and social structure. The social relations and associated social institutions – class mobility, work and industry, education, poverty, and social problems – that defined sociology for several decades were of course closely linked to industrial society and the kind of political values it cultivated. Modern British sociology was strongly influenced by Marxism. Another significant British tradition in sociology was one allied to social policy, as reflected in the tradition associated with Hobhouse and the London School of Economics, where sociology and social policy were closely related. To this tradition belongs T. H. Marshall and what broadly can be called policy-relevant social science. In the British tradition the continental European vision of sociology as a general social science has mostly been absent. However, it must be noted that much of modern British sociology was the product of continental European traditions that had come to Britain since the 1930s. Sociologists such as Norbert Elias and Karl Mannheim who came from Germany and John Rex from South Africa gave to British sociology a varied character that was not encapsulated in a specific tradition. In addition, of course, there was the Marxist tradition, beginning with Marx himself in exile in London. Nevertheless, British sociology tended to reflect a view of sociology as in part having a special subject matter: class and social structure.

There is little doubt that the international prestige of sociology in the twentieth century would not have been possible were it not for the tremendous expansion and institutionalization of the discipline in the US. American sociology arose out of economics and was professionalized relatively early, with the foundation of the American Sociological Society by Albion Small and others in 1905. The Society, renamed American Sociological Association in 1959, in fact was a break-away movement from the American Economic Association. Small, Charles Horton Cooley, and William Thomas were the most influential figures in shaping American sociology, which was closely related to the American philosophical tradition of pragmatism at least until the 1940s. Comparable to the British reformist concern with social policy, pragmatism reflected a belief in the public role of social science. Early American sociology was thus shaped in the spirit of scientific knowledge assisting in solving social problems (Lynd 1939).

The twentieth century, however, saw a growing professionalization of American sociology, which shed its reformist origins. On the one side, a strong tradition of empirical sociology developed which was largely quantitative and often value-free to a point that it ceased to be anything more than hypothesis testing. On the other side, a tradition of grand theory associated with Parsons developed, but it rarely intersected with the empirical tradition. Existing outside these traditions was the remnant of the early pragmatist tradition in the sociology of symbolic interactionism, stemming from George Herbert Mead.

This short survey of some of the major national histories of sociology tells us that no one national tradition has prevailed and within all these national traditions are rival traditions. This has led some critics to complain that sociology has somehow failed. Horowitz (1993) complains that sociology is in crisis due to its specialization and also due to its over-politicization. Sociology is decomposing because it has lost its way. The great classical visions of sociology no longer prevail and the discipline has lost its integrity. Much of what is called sociology is merely untheoretical empirical case studies, he argues. Such pessimistic views often depend on whether one believes that sociology is based on a single method or vision that can provide a foundation for the discipline. But this may be too much to demand. It is certainly the case that a single school or method has not emerged to define the discipline, but this could also be said to be the case for much of the social and human sciences. It would be an over-simplification to characterize the history of sociology as a process of decomposition or fragmentation of an inner unity guaranteed by a discipline. The classical tradition was not a unified one and much of this has been reflexively constituted by a discipline that changes in response to changes in the nature of society.

INSTITUTIONALIZATION OF SOCIOLOGY

Sociology has been shaped in three major phases: the pre-institutional period prior to the early twentieth century, the era of institutionalization and disciplinary specialization, and the current period of post-disciplinarity. As discussed, sociology arose out of different national traditions of social science. In the nineteenth century only Comte, Spencer, and later Durkheim used the term sociology to describe their particular mode of social inquiry. Even with Durkheim this was a pre-institutional period. Durkheim's chair was in educational thought and much of early sociology was a development out of economics, psychology, philosophy, law, or history. In this early phase the disciplinary identity of sociology was formed to a large extent by the question of its scientific status. Durkheim's *Rules of the Sociological Method*, published in 1895, provided the first systematic outline of sociology as a scientific inquiry. Weber's essay "Objectivity in Social Science and Social Policy," published in 1904–5, provided an additional statement of what social scientific objectivity consists (Weber 1949). In these accounts, despite their different perspectives and backgrounds, sociology was established as an empirical science based on objective factual knowledge. Both accounts (perhaps Weber more so) were aware that the scientific status of sociology was a limited one, as is apparent from Weber's neo-Kantian styled attempt to qualify the limits of objectivity. But social science could nonetheless attain objective knowledge. This was a debate that continued up to the 1960s, when the neo-positivist philosophies of science espoused by Carl Hempel and Ernst Nagel provided new justifications for sociology to claim scientific status. The result of some of these efforts was to reduce the scope of sociology to testable hypotheses in order to uncover the laws of society (Adorno et al. 1976). While sociology was pulled in the direction of the natural or experimental sciences on the one side, on the other it remained allied with the human sciences. This bifurcation of sociology led to an uncertain relation to social and public policy, with the result that sociology tended to enter the period of institutionalization relatively depoliticized.

The institutionalization of sociology coincided with the formation of disciplines in the twentieth century. As a profession, one of the early statements was Weber's address "Science as a Vocation" in 1918, which although addressed to the wider question of a commitment to science as a different order of commitment than to politics, has been recognized as one of the major expressions of the professionalization of sociology (Weber 1970). The notion of *beruf* invoked referred to both the idea of sociology as a profession and as a vocation whose calling required certain sacrifices, one of which was not to seek in science answers to fundamental moral questions. As a science, sociology is concerned with providing explanations about social phenomena and in Weber's view it also has a role to play in guiding social policy.

In its formative period sociology had to compete with the natural sciences. As social science gained general acceptability as an area distinct from both the human sciences and the natural sciences, sociology found that its greatest challenges came in fact from the more established of the social sciences (Lepenies 1988). In Britain the prestige of anthropology overshadowed sociology. The older disciplines, geography and economics, as well as political science tended to command greater prestige than sociology, which never held the same degree of reliance to the mission of the national state. It must be borne in mind that much of social science owed its existence to its relation to the state: it was the science of the social institutions of the modern state.

The institutionalization of sociology did not fully commence until the period following World War II, when the discipline expanded along with the rise of mass higher education. The professionalization and institutionalization of sociology was marked by the foundation of academic journals such as the *American Journal of Sociology*, founded in 1895, and the later *American Sociological Review*. Professional associations such as the American Sociological Association and the British Sociological Association, founded in 1951, greatly enhanced the professionalization of sociology as a discipline, which subsequently underwent a process of internal differentiation with new subfields emerging, ranging from urban sociology and industrial sociology to political sociology, historical sociology, and cultural sociology. By the 1960s sociology became increasingly taught in secondary schools and in the 1970s it became an A-level subject in British schools. The 1960s and 1970s saw a tremendous expansion in the discipline in terms of student enrollments and teaching and research careers. In this period sociology became recognized by governments as a major social science and many chairs were created. Sociological research became recognized by the principal national research foundations and acquired prestige within the university system. In the US there are over 200 sociology journals, a professional associational membership of some 14,000, and more students major in sociology (25,000) annually than in history and economics (Burawoy 2005a). As sociology became one of the major social sciences in universities throughout the world, it became increasingly seen as the most comprehensive science of society. This was viewed by some as a source of the strength and relevance of sociology, but in the view of others it was in danger of becoming a pseudo-science, lacking subject specialization, since when sociologists specialize they cease to be sociologists. Neo-positivist philosophies attempted to check the dangers of over-generalization, while the growing politicization of the discipline that came with its widening social base led to fears that sociology was too closely linked to radical causes, such as Marxism.

Many influential sociologists openly questioned the institutionalization of sociology. If the first era was one of the struggle for the institutionalization of the discipline, the phase that drew to a close in the 1970s was one that was marked by calls for the political engagement of sociology with everyday life. Gouldner (1970) argued that sociology needs to be reoriented to be of relevance to society. In his view, sociology went through four main phases: sociological positivism in nineteenth-century France, Marxism, classical European sociology, and finally American structural functionalism as represented by Parsons. Contemporary sociology must articulate a new vision based on a completely different sense of its moral purpose. For Gouldner, this had to be a reflexive sociology and one that was radical in its project to connect sociology to people's lives. The purpose of sociology is to enable people to make sense of society and to connect their own lives with the wider context of society.

This turn to a reflexive understanding of sociology had been implicit in C. Wright Mills's *Sociological Imagination*, which was published in 1959 and was widely read in the 1960s and 1970s. Sociologists such as Mills and Gouldner were opposed to the depoliticized kind of sociology that was emerging in the US. They wanted to recover the moral purpose of sociology that had become lost with its institutionalization in specialist subfields. Mills provided a definition of sociology that continues to be relevant: "The sociological imagination enables us to grasp history and biography and the relations between the two within society. That is its task and promise" (Mills 1970: 12). This conception of sociology was as much opposed to general theory as it was to administrative social research. Mills was primarily inspired by the American pragmatic tradition, which predisposed him to be critical of social science that was cut off from the practical purposes of improving social well-being.

The vision of sociology articulated by Mills was not too far removed from the continental European conception of sociology as a diagnosis of the age. In this tradition, which was represented by a broad range of sociologists, such as the Frankfurt School and the humanistic tradition of western Marxism, sociology was connected to social renewal and was primarily a critical endeavor. As represented in the programmatic thought of Theodor Adorno, sociology must recover its mission in philosophical thought as a mode of critical thinking. For Adorno, the rise of neo-positivism had a detrimental effect on sociology, which had the promise to become the leading critical science of what Daniel Bell and Alain Touraine in their respective works called the "post-industrial society." Habermas (1978) outlined the basis of a view of sociology as concerned with critical knowledge tied to an interest in human emancipation.

Since the 1970s, which saw the expansion and institutionalization of sociology as a discipline, the question of the scientific status of sociology became less important. Although major methodological differences continued to divide quantitatively oriented sociologists from those in the humanistic tradition, sociology had become too broad to unite under a common method. With the consolidation of the discipline, sociology developed in many directions. The large-scale entry of women into sociology in the 1980s inevitably led to different concerns and feminist approaches emerged around new research fields, which on the whole tended to orient sociology in the direction of cultural issues concerning identity, gender, and biographies. The shift from industrial to post-industrial societies and the growing impact of globalization have led to a series of shifts in the subject matter of sociology. Without a common method, a cumulative theoretical tradition, the result has been that sociology has been drawn in different directions. While this has led to some weaknesses, it is also a source of strength. Today, sociology has many different approaches which together constitute an influential body of methodologies and theories that have made considerable impact on the wider social and human sciences.

As a discipline acutely aware of the overall reality of society and the historical context, sociology has been more versatile than many sciences. This has been especially the case with regard to the "cultural turn" of which postmodernism has been one expression. Sociologists have been very prominent in developing new frameworks that have greatly advanced the scientific understanding of the social world. One only has to consider the influence of sociologists such as Ulrich Beck on the idea of the risk society, Pierre Bourdieu on the habitus and the forms of capital, Anthony Giddens on structure and agency, Jürgen Habermas on modernity and the theory of communicative action, Edward Soja on space, Bruno Latour on science and technology, Niklas Luhmann on systems theory, Manuel Castells on the information society, Roland Robertson on globalization, and Bryan Turner on citizenship. Sociology, in particular social theory, played a leading role in the reorientation of human geography around space. Much of urban geography today is simply the rediscovery of sociological approaches to the city. The shift in anthropology from the study of primitive societies to modern western societies has made it more or less indistinguishable from sociology. Anthropology, which enjoyed greater prestige in the past, has suffered a far greater crisis in its self-understanding than sociology. In this context the rise of cultural and contemporary history as well as cultural studies can be mentioned as relatively new interdisciplinary subject areas that have been closely linked to sociology.

This, however, comes at a price. Much of sociology today is outside of sociology. As sociology becomes more specialized on the one side, and on the other more influential, the result is that it easily loses a specific identity. Thus, the sociology of crime has influenced criminology

where most specialized research on crime now occurs and which is not essentially sociological but interdisciplinary. Norbert Elias in 1970 complained of "pseudo-specialization" and the retreat of sociologists into sub-areas; but he noted what was occurring in sociology was something that had already happened in other disciplines. It would only be a matter of time, he wrote, before the "fortress will be complete, the drawbridges raised." Like many continental European sociologists, Elias held to the Comtean vision of sociology having the distinctive feature of a general science. Despite Elias's resistance to specialization, sociology did undergo specialization and it may be suggested that social theory took over the general conception of sociology (Delanty 2005b). But the resulting kind of specialization that sociology underwent led to fears that sociology cannot in fact be a specialized science, since what it does is merely to open up the ground for specialized interdisciplinary areas elsewhere. Thus, specialized sociological research occurs only outside the actual discipline – it is a question of sociologists without sociology. While some see this as the end of sociology, others see it as a new opportunity for a post-disciplinary sociology, which should not retreat into the false security of a discipline. John Urry (1981), for instance, argues that sociology does not have a specific disciplinary area in terms of a method or subject matter and it has often been (and necessarily so) "parasitic" on other sciences. Consequently, it should cease to think of itself as a science of society and enter the diffuse territory of post-disciplinarity (Urry 2000). This is a contentious position and there have been several recent defenses of sociology, such as the notion of a public sociology advocated by Ben Agger (2000) and Michael Burawoy (2005a, 2005b) and the various attempts of John Scott (2005) and Steve Fuller (2006) to revive the sociological imagination. On the other side, there is a position advocated by John Goldthorpe (2002) that confines sociology to a narrow methodologically grounded science. Is it a choice of "disciplinary parochialism" or "imperialism," as Andrew Sayer (2000) asks?

CURRENT CHALLENGES

It is evident that the challenges facing sociology are no longer those that it faced a century ago; it is no longer a question of the scientific status of the discipline and the need to demarcate a space between the natural sciences on one side, and on the other the human sciences. Some of the major debates of the second half of the twentieth century will continue to be important, but will not define the field of sociology, such as the micro-macro link, agency and structure, quantitative versus qualitative methods, the nature of theory and its relation to empirical research, the question of normative critique, the status of evidence and the limits of explanation, etc. Three major debates have emerged in recent times which capture the current situation of sociology more fully than these methodological and theoretical issues: the question of the subject matter of sociology in light of globalization; the question of disciplinarity; and the debate about the public function of sociology.

As the science of society, sociology has always been a contested inquiry. Many of the major disputes have been about the nature of method and the scope of social science more generally. The debate about the subject matter of sociology has mostly resolved around issues of the know-ability of the social world. In recent years an additional challenge has emerged around the very conception of the social (Gane 2004). To a large degree this has been due to major changes in the very definition of society. While much of classical sociology on the whole took society to be the society of the nation-state, this is less the case today. It should be pointed out that while the equation of classical sociology with national societies has been exaggerated, there is little doubt that sociology arose as the science of the modern industrial nation-state. The comparative tradition in sociological analysis, Weber's historical sociology, and much of Marxist sociology is a reminder of the global concerns of sociology. However, as an institutionalized social science, sociology has mostly been conducted within national parameters. By far the greatest concentration of sociological research in the second half of the twentieth century has been in the US, where sociology has been the science of social order and national consensus. While the national institutional frameworks continue to be primary in terms of professional accreditation, teaching, funding, and research, the global dimension is coming more to the fore. International sociological associations such as the International Sociological Association and the European Sociological Association now offer rival contexts for sociological research.

It is true too that much of what might be called global sociology is merely the continuation of the comparative tradition, which can be located within an "international" view of sociology. But this would be to neglect a deeper transformation which is also a reflection of the transformation of the social itself. While many social theorists (e.g., Urry 2000) have argued that the social is in decline and others that the social does not coincide with the notion of society, conceived of a spatially bounded entity, it is evident that notwithstanding some of these far-reaching claims the social world is undergoing major transformation and the notion of society is in need of considerable reevaluation (Smelser 1997). Exactly how new such developments are will continue to be debated. A strong case can be made for seeing current developments as part of a long-term process of civilizational shifts and transformation in the nature of modernity. It is no longer possible to see the social world merely in terms of national structures impacting on the lives of individuals. Such forces are global and they interact with the local in complex ways. The turn to globality in contemporary sociology is not in any way an invalidation of sociology, even if some of the classical approaches are inadequate for the demands of the present day. Indeed, of all the social and human sciences, sociology – with its rich tradition of theory and methodology – is particularly suited to the current global context. Just one point can be made to highlight the relevance of sociology. If globalization entails the intensification of social relations across the globe, the core concern of sociology with the construction and contestability of the social world has a considerable application and relevance.

This leads directly to the second challenge, the question of disciplinarity. According to the Gulbenkian Commission for the Restructuring of the Social Sciences: "To be sociological is not the exclusive purview of persons called sociologists. It is an obligation of all social scientists" (Mudimbe 1996: 98). Does this mean the end of sociology? Clearly, many have taken this view and see sociology disappearing into new inter-disciplinary areas and that it can no longer command disciplinary specialization due to its highly general nature. This is too pessimistic, since the Gulbenkian Commission report also points out that the same situation applies to other sciences: history is not the exclusive domain of historians and economic issues are not the exclusive purview of economists. In the era of growing interdisciplinarity, sociology is not alone in having to reorient itself beyond the narrow confines of disciplinarity. Political scientists hardly have a monopoly over politics. Sociology now exists in part within other disciplines, in particular in new post-disciplinary areas which it helped to create, but it also exists in its own terms as a post-disciplinary social science. In the present day it is evident that sociology takes disciplinary, interdisciplinary, and post-disciplinary forms.

While much of sociology has migrated from sociology to the other sciences, sociology today is also increasingly absorbing influences from other sciences. A survey of the discipline's most influential works noted that a large number have been written by non-sociologists (Clawson 1998). This is nothing new: from the very beginning sociology incorporated other disciplines into itself. Of course, this is not without contestation, as in the debate about the influence of cultural studies – itself partly a creation of sociology – on sociology (Rojek & Turner 2001). Sociology is well positioned to engage with other sciences and much of modern sociology has been based on a view of sociology as a science that incorporates the specialized results of other sciences into its framework. As Fuller (2006) argues, today this engagement with other sciences must include biology, which can now explain much of social life. Sociology must engage with some of the claims of biology to explain the social world and offer different accounts. In this respect, then, interdisciplinarity and post-disciplinarity need not be seen as the end of a sociology, but a window of opportunity for sociology to address new issues.

One such issue is the public function of sociology. The specialization of sociological research by professional sociology has led to a marginalization of its public role. Michael Burawoy argued this in his presidential address to the ASA in 2004 and opened up a major debate on the future of sociology (Burawoy 2005a, 2005b; Calhoun 2005). Public sociology and professional sociology have become divorced and need to be reconnected, he argues. Public sociology concerns in part bringing professional society to wider publics and in shaping public

debates and it may lead to a reorientation in professional sociology as new issues arise. However, as Burawoy argues, there is no public sociology without a professional sociology that supplies it with tested methods and theoretical approaches, conceptual frameworks, and accumulated bodies of knowledge. Public sociology is close to policy-relevant sociology, which is a more specific application of sociology to problems set by the state and other public bodies. Public sociology is wider and more discursive and takes place in the public sphere. Burawoy also clarifies the distinction between public and critical sociology. The latter concerns a mode of self-reflection on professional sociology and is largely conducted for the benefit of sociology, in contrast to public sociology. Critical sociology has a normative role to play for the discipline. While critical and professional sociology exist for peers, public and policy sociology exist for wider audiences. Of course, many of these roles overlap, as is apparent in the connection between critical and public sociology.

According to many views, one of the functions of sociology is to raise social self-understanding. Adorno (2000), for instance, held that while sociology may be the study of society in some general sense, society as such is not a given or a clearly defined domain that can be reduced to a set of "social facts" in Durkheim's sense. Rather, society consists of different processes and conflicting interpretations. Sociology might be defined in terms of the critical analysis of these discourses in a way that facilitates wider public self-reflection. This is a view of sociology reiterated by Mills (1970) and Habermas (1978). In different ways it is present in Scott's (2005) and Fuller's (2006) cautious defense of a disciplinary sociology. This means that sociology must be relevant; it must be able to address major public issues (Agger 2000). Inescapably, this means sociology must be able to ask big questions. The success of sociology until now has been in no small part due to its undoubted capacity to address major questions, in particular those that pertain to everyday life.

CONCLUSION

Sociology is the only science specifically devoted to the study of society in the broad sense of the term, meaning the social world and the open field of the social. Like many of the social and human sciences it does not have a clearly defined subject matter. This situation often leads to the assumption of a crisis. Sociology today is often faced with three broad choices. One is the classical vision of a field that is based on the interpretation of the results of other sciences from the perspective of a general science of society guaranteed by a canonized sociological heritage. Second, those who reject the first as too generalist, parasitic, and lacking a clearly marked out specialized field argue that sociology must confine itself to a narrow territory based on a tightly defined conception of sociological research and disciplinary specialization. Third, those who reject the highly specialized understanding of sociology and resist the generalist understanding of sociology tend to look to post-disciplinarity, whereby sociology is not confined to the traditional discipline and occurs largely outside sociology.

These are false dilemmas, despite the fact that there are major challenges to be faced. Interdisciplinarity is unavoidable today for all the sciences, but it does not have to mean the disappearance of sociology any more than any other discipline. It is also difficult to draw the conclusion that sociology exists only in a post-disciplinary context. However, it is evident that sociology cannot retreat into the classical mold of a general science. Sociology is a versatile and resilient discipline that takes many forms. One of its enduring characteristics is that it brings to bear on the study of the social world a general perspective born of the recognition that the sum is greater than the parts.

SEE ALSO: Aging, Sociology of; AIDS, Sociology of; American Sociological Association; Biosociological Theories; Body and Cultural Sociology; British Sociological Association; Computational Sociology; Death of the Sociology of Deviance?; Durkheim, Émile; Economic Sociology: Classical Political Economic Perspectives; Economic Sociology: Neoclassical Economic Perspective; Economy (Sociological Approach); Environment, Sociology of the; Existential Sociology; Family, Sociology of; Figurational Sociology and the Sociology of Sport; Financial Sociology; Globalization; Institutional Review Boards and Sociological Research; Knowledge, Sociology of; Law, Sociology of; Marx, Karl; Marxism and Sociology; Mathematical Sociology;

Medical Sociology; Medical Sociology and Genetics; Medicine, Sociology of; Microsociology; Military Sociology; Neurosociology; Political Sociology; Rational Choice Theory (and Economic Sociology); Religion, Sociology of; Revolutions, Sociology of; Rural Sociology; Scientific Knowledge, Sociology of; Simmel, Georg; Society; Sociological Imagination; Sociology in Medicine; Taste, Sociology of; Weber, Max; Work, Sociology of

REFERENCES AND SUGGESTED READINGS

Abraham, J. H. (Ed.) (1973) *Origins and Growth of Sociology*. Penguin, London.

Adorno, T. W. (2000) *Introduction to Sociology*. Sage, London.

Adorno, T. W. et al. (1976) *The Positivist Dispute in German Sociology*. Heinemann, London.

Agger, B. (2000) *Public Sociology*. Rowman & Littlefield, New York.

Berger, P. (1966) *Invitation to Sociology: A Humanistic Approach*. Penguin, London.

Berger, P. & Luckmann, T. (1967) *The Social Construction of Reality*. Penguin, London.

Bourdieu, P. & Wacquant, L. (1992) *An Invitation to Reflexive Sociology*. University of Chicago Press, Chicago.

Burawoy, M. (2005a) For Public Sociology. *American Sociological Review* 70(1): 4–28.

Burawoy, M. (2005b) The Return of the Repressed: Recovering the Public Face of US Sociology, One Hundred Years On. *Annals of the American Academy* 600 (July): 68–85.

Calhoun, C. (2005) The Promise of Public Sociology. *British Journal of Sociology* 56(3): 355–63.

Calhoun, C., Rojek, C., & Turner, B. (Eds.) (2005) *Handbook of Sociology*. Sage, London.

Clawson, D. (Ed.) (1998) *Required Reading: Sociology's Most Influential Books*. University of Massachusetts Press, Amherest.

Cole, S. (Ed.) (2001) *What Went Wrong With Sociology?* Transaction, New Brunswick, NJ.

Delanty, G. (2005a) *Social Science: Philosophical and Methodological Foundations*, 2nd edn. Open University Press, Buckingham.

Delanty, G. (Ed.) (2005b) *Handbook of Contemporary European Social Theory*. Routledge, London.

Durkheim, E. (1982) *Rules of the Sociological Method*. Macmillan, London.

Fuller, S. (1998) Divining the Future of Social Theory: From Theology to Rhetoric via Social Epistemology. *European Journal of Social Theory* 1(1): 107–26.

Fuller, S. (2006) *The New Sociological Imagination*. Sage, London.

Gane, N. (Ed.) (2004) *The Futures of Social Theory.* Continuum, New York.

Giddens, A. (1996) *In Defence of Sociology.* Polity Press, Cambridge.

Goldthorpe, J. (2002) *On Sociology.* Oxford University Press, Oxford.

Gouldner, A. (1970) *The Coming Crisis of Western Sociology.* Basic Books, New York.

Habermas, J. (1978) *Knowledge and Human Interests*, 2nd edn. Heinemann, London.

Horowitz, I. (1993) *The Decomposition of Sociology.* Oxford University Press, Oxford.

Lepenies, W. (1988) *Between Literature and Science: The Rise of Sociology.* Cambridge University Press, Cambridge.

Levine, D. (1995) *Visions of the Sociological Tradition.* University of Chicago Press, Chicago.

Lynd, R. (1939) *Knowledge for What? The Place of Social Science in American Culture.* Princeton University Press, Princeton.

Mills, C. W. (1970 [1959]) *The Sociological Imagination.* Penguin, London.

Mundimbe, V. Y. (Ed.) (1996) *Open the Social Sciences: Report of the Gulbenkian Commission on the Restructuring of the Social Sciences.* Stanford University Press, Stanford.

Parsons, P. (1949) *The Structure of Social Action.* Free Press, New York.

Rojek, C. & Turner, B. (2001) Decorative Sociology: Towards a Critique of the Cultural Turn. *Sociological Review* 48: 629–48.

Sayer, A. (2000) For Postdisciplinary Studies: Sociology and the Curse of Disciplinary Parochialism and Imperialism. In: Eldridge, J. et al. (Eds.), *For Sociology.* Sociology Press, Durham.

Scott, J. (2005) Sociology and its Others: Reflections on Disciplinary Specialization and Fragmentation. *Sociological Research On Line* 10 (1).

Shilling, C. & Mellor, P. (2001) *The Sociological Ambition.* Sage, London.

Smelser, N. J. (1997) *Problematics of Sociology.* University of California Press, Berkeley.

Strydom, P. (2000) *Discourse and Knowledge: The Making of Enlightenment Sociology.* Liverpool University Press, Liverpool.

Urry, J. (1981) Sociology as a Parasite: Some Vices and Virtues. In: Abrams, P. et al. (Eds.), *Practice and Progress: British Sociology, 1950–1980.* Allen & Unwin, London.

Urry, J. (2000) *Sociology Beyond Societies.* Routledge, London.

Weber, M. (1949 [1904–5]) Objectivity in Social Science and Social Policy. In: *The Methodology of the Social Sciences.* Free Press, Glencoe, IL.

Weber, M. (1970) Science as a Vocation. In: Gerth, H. & Mills, C. W. (Eds.), *From Max Weber.* Routledge & Kegan Paul, London.

sociology in medicine

Carey L. Usher

Sociology in medicine is the label given to the collaborative work between sociologists and medical or health personnel within medical institutions or health care organizations. This distinction represents the applied work of medical sociologists in the pure versus applied dichotomy of the social sciences. In its most extreme form, sociology in medicine encompasses sociological work aimed at the provision of technical skills and problem solving for the medical community while neglecting contributions to the parent discipline.

Medical sociology, like its parent discipline, experienced dual roles early in its institutionalization. The distinction between applied and pure work in medical sociology arose in conjunction with the desire for a communication network that would identify the activities and affiliations of medical sociologists in the United States. Sociology in medicine and sociology of medicine were the names designated for applied and pure work, respectively, by Robert Straus in 1957. Sociology in medicine represents the thrust toward reform, advocacy, and application, with which medical sociologists responded to the call for inclusion of clinical research in the social components of health and illness. During the 1950s and 1960s, the roles of the social sciences in health care organizations experienced significant increases due to expansion of medical schools, increased private and public supports for medical research and training programs, and significant proportions of funds granted for establishment of social science units within schools of medicine, public health, and nursing. The primary aim of medical sociology during this time was to serve medicine, with a large majority of medical sociologists employed by health science schools, and only 30 percent holding appointments in traditional sociology departments. The ascendancy of sociology in medicine was short lived, however, as the effects of the Cold War, which equated sociology with socialism, decreased the influence of sociology on public health issues and policy. The role of the medical sociologist in medicine decreased, while academic work in medical sociology, or sociology of medicine, began to increase. During the 1980s, increasing opportunities for nonacademic sociology applications were recognized by the American Sociological Association. Sociology in medicine again became an exciting career choice for medical sociologists, although they were now competing with other health-related researchers for funding in medical institutions.

The work of the sociologist in medicine is intended to be directly applicable to health issues, and consists of teaching and research activities focusing on disease processes or factors influencing patients' responses to illness, with the goal of improving diagnosis and treatment. Sociology in medicine may examine doctor–patient relationships, various therapeutic situations, or social factors that affect and are affected by specific health disorders. The sociologist in medicine may also have responsibilities of educating health science students in the sociology of health and illness. The major contributions of sociology in medicine have been to medical education, social epidemiology, and knowledge of utilization and compliance. Sociologists in medicine seek to answer questions of interest to their sponsors and institutions rather than to the discipline of sociology.

Sociology in medicine, then, treats sociology as a supporting discipline to medicine, which involves achieving the goals of medicine while neglecting those of sociology. For this reason, sociology in medicine has been severely criticized since its inception. Sociologists in medicine are less compelled to defend the significance of their work, theoretical or otherwise, to the academic community than are conventional sociologists. The demands placed upon the sociologist in medicine are for practical applications rather than sociological significance. Therefore, sociology in medicine has consistently battled with the question of whether or not it is real sociology. Aside from the criticisms of its parent discipline, sociology in medicine has historically faced problems within its working environment as well. Communication, status, and relationship issues have surrounded sociology in medicine since the first tenure-track position was created for a sociologist in a medical school in 1953. Howard Freeman and Leo Reeder, as early as 1957, point out the difficulty the sociologist in medicine has in attaining co-worker status with the physician, stating that all PhDs working with MDs face a continual threat of relegation to subordinate status. Communication and understanding have been problematic as well, as neither the sociologist nor the physician would freely discard discipline-specific, esoteric rhetoric to adopt that of the other.

When the distinction was made between pure and applied work of medical sociologists, the predominant opinion of sociologists was that the two were incompatible. Academic sociologists believed sociologists in medicine showed more loyalty to the medical institution than to their parent discipline, and did not contribute to the discipline. Those working in medicine, however, considered themselves to be quite practical sociologists, as their work was directly applicable to human health, and they had less restricted access to research funds than did conventional sociologists. The opinion of incompatibility has changed dramatically and will continue to change in the future. Robert Straus, who as we saw named the distinction in 1957, wrote in 1999 that it is possible for the medical sociologist to do both pure and applied work at the same time. Many medical sociologists consider the structural position of the scholar to be irrelevant today, and have called for a renaming of the work of medical sociologists. Rather than distinguishing between sociology *in* medicine and sociology *of* medicine, the work of medical sociologists may be aptly called sociology *with* medicine.

SEE ALSO: Health and Medicine; Medical Sociology; Medicine, Sociology of

REFERENCES AND SUGGESTED READINGS

Bloom, S. (1986) Institutional Trends in Medical Sociology. *Journal of Health and Social Behavior* 27: 265–76.

Cockerham, W. C. (2004) *Medical Sociology*, 9th edn. Prentice-Hall, Upper Saddle River, NJ.

Freeman, H. & Levine, S. (1989) *Handbook of Medical Sociology*, 4th edn. Prentice-Hall, Englewood Cliffs, NJ.

Freeman, H. & Reeder, L. (1957) Medical Sociology: A Review of the Literature. *American Sociological Review* 22: 73–81.

Levine, S. (1987) The Changing Terrains in Medical Sociology: Emergent Concern with Quality of Life. *Journal of Health and Social Behavior* 28: 1–6.

Straus, R. (1957) The Nature and Status of Medical Sociology. *American Sociological Review* 22: 200–4.

Straus, R. (1999) Medical Sociology: A Personal Fifty Year Perspective. *Journal of Health and Social Behavior* 40: 103–10.

sociometry

Barbara F. Meeker

The word "sociometry" was coined by Jacob Levi Moreno (1889–1974). Moreno, one of the pioneers of psychotherapy, is also credited with developing psychotherapeutic techniques such as psychodrama and role playing. As he used it, sociometry was a way of uncovering the underlying emotional structure of a small group by asking group members which other members they would choose or reject as partners in specific roles such as roommate or fellow team member for a work project. Moreno believed that if group activities were set up according to these preferences, the task performance and morale of the group would be maximized and individual group members would experience satisfaction, empowerment, and personal growth. Jointly with Helen Hall Jennings (Moreno 1934), he applied his methods to the assignment of girls to residential cottages in the New York Training School for Girls, concluding that the predicted positive results did occur. Moreno also founded a journal named *Sociometry* to promote his research. This journal eventually became one of the official journals of the American Sociological Association where it has been for many years the primary outlet within sociology for social psychological research in general. Reflecting this more general interest, it changed its name and is now the *Social Psychology Quarterly*.

Within research sociology, "sociometry" refers to the measurement aspect of Moreno's concept, not to its use as a principle for organizing groups. It also refers to results about interpersonal attraction and group structure and cohesion that have been found using sociometric techniques, and to statistical and mathematical techniques for analyzing sociometric data. Typically, in a sociometric study respondents are asked in a paper-and-pencil survey to name their best friends, or the three or five others they like best, or to rate the name of each other group member on how much the other is liked, admired, respected, or other evaluation; these ratings may extend into negative sentiments such as dislike. Some may include behavioral ratings (such as how often the respondent talks to or works with the other). In a historical reflection of Moreno's intentions, these ratings are referred to as "choices." Analyzing choices identifies social isolates (individuals neither giving nor receiving choices); mutual pairs (two individuals each choosing the other); pairs with unreciprocated choices; transitive triads (three individuals all choosing each other); sociometric stars (an individual receiving more choices than others); and cliques (a set of individuals making positive choices within the set but no choices or negative choices outside). These patterns can be displayed as a diagram called a sociogram, in which points represent individuals and arrows represent their choices. Influential early use of sociometry includes Theodore Newcomb's study of the development of friendships in two college dormitories and George Homans's emphasis on interpersonal sentiments as basic building blocks in a theory of individual and small group behavior.

A large body of research in natural settings as well as in laboratories shows that the principles that affect the formation and maintenance of sociometric choice are: (1) propinquity (or proximity) – bonds of attraction form between individuals who encounter each other in daily life; thus, sociograms show choices between people who live in adjoining rooms in dormitories, have offices next to each other, sit in adjacent seats in a classroom, etc., or marriages that occur between persons from the same neighborhood; (2) reciprocity – attraction tends to be mutual, people choose others who they think choose them; (3) perceived similarity – individuals choose others they think share socially important characteristics, attitudes, or values; and (4) status – individuals choose others who have high prestige within the group. The principles of reciprocity and perceived similarity produce mutual attraction and increase the number of reciprocal pairs, while the principle of status produces one-way or unreciprocated choices as persons with higher status are more often chosen.

Cognitive balance theory, especially as formulated by Fritz Heider (1958), has been used by many students of sociometry. Heider proposed that a basic principle of individual cognitive organization is that people seek to agree with others whom they view positively and to disagree with others whom they view negatively; these are *balanced states* and are assumed to be stable and to provide personal satisfaction. On the other hand, when an individual finds that she or he disagrees with a positively valued other, or agrees with a negatively valued other, this is an *imbalanced state* which produces dissatisfaction and a motivation to change at least one bond, that is, imbalanced states are unstable. This explains both reciprocity and similarity as types of cognitive balance and also predicts that relationships among three or more persons will become transitive and positive bonds will form in larger structures transitively.

Sociometric structure also concerns the relationship among behavior, attitudes, and interaction. Informal interaction tends to occur between persons who have positive bonds and such persons tend to influence each other and hence to become similar. Thus, a sociogram can give predictions about the flow of gossip, attitude change, formation of group or organizational culture, and boundaries of cliques or conflict groups within organizations. An example of an application is work examining effects of school integration on the interracial friendships of students (Hallinan & Smith 1982).

The formal properties of consistency and transitivity appeal to mathematically inclined sociologists, overlapping with rapidly developing work in social networks and using the mathematics of graph theory.

SEE ALSO: Attraction; Cognitive Balance Theory (Heider); Friendship: Interpersonal Aspects; Interpersonal Relationships; Networks; Social Influence; Social Psychology

REFERENCES AND SUGGESTED READINGS

Doreian, P. & Fararo, T. (Eds.) (1998) *The Problem of Solidarity: Theories and Models*. Gordon & Breach, Amsterdam.

Hallinan, M. T. & Smith, S. S. (1982) *The Effects of Classroom Racial Composition on Students' Interracial Friendliness*. Center of Education Research, Madison, WI.

Heider, F. (1958) *The Psychology of Interpersonal Relations*. Wiley, New York.

Homans, G. C. (1950) *The Human Group*. Harcourt, Brace, & World, New York.

Moreno, J. L. (1934) *Who Shall Survive? A New Approach to the Problem of Human Interrelations*. Beacon House, Boston.

Newcomb, T. M. (1961) *The Acquaintance Process*. Holt, Rinehart, & Winston, New York.

solidarity

Rodney Coates

Solidarity, defined as the perceived or realized organization of individuals for group survival, interests, or purposes, may result from either external threats or internal needs. Solidarity, reflecting various dimensions and forms of organizing, may best be described in Durkheimian terms as ranging from organic to the inorganic. That is to say, we may describe solidarity that derives from some intrinsic characteristic of the participants or from extrinsic characteristics. When we speak of intrinsic characteristics, related to organic solidarity, we typically include such types as family, racial/ethnic groups, national and to some extent religious affiliation. Alternatively, inorganic solidarity, related to the more voluntary, associational characteristics of such organization, suggests greater volition on the part of its members. When we speak of inorganic solidarity we typically make reference to neighborhood associations, clubs, political organizations, and the like. Given the more transient nature of today's populations, religion and national identity may also fall into this latter category for obvious reasons associated with mobility and personal choice. Depending upon type, solidarity comes into being for multiple reasons. Social and political movements, community organizing, and social activism rely upon the ability of respective leaders to organize and solidify significant groups for the purposes of social action. The capacity of groups to solidify is directly associated with their capacity to organize about significant issues, events, visions, and/or threats. Thus the capacity to solidify is evidence of the capacity to survive, thrive, persist, and promote group interests, viability, and/or vitality.

While it is possible, for heuristic purposes, to distinguish between organic and inorganic solidarity, in reality such distinctions are blurred. Hence successful social movements, political or social activism, and collective actions often depend upon multiple types and methods for generating solidarity. Hence, if we were to discuss the successful Civil Rights movements in the United States of the 1960s, or that led by Mahatma Gandhi in India – we clearly see the overlapping of family, religion, political, civil, ethnic/racial, and social groups. More simply, we would see the cultural, social, and political elements within specific societal contexts solidifying about specific issues, visions, and interests. These complex moments of heightened solidarity, so critical for social, political, and cultural activism, are rare examples of multiple forms, dimensions, and levels of solidarity coalescing at the national and often international levels.

Differing forms of solidarity (to include dimensions, levels, and types of solidarity) may be associated with different types of groups, institutions, or organizational components. Hence, along the organic continuum and within the family, issues of kinship and major life events such as marriage, births, deaths, reunions, holidays, celebrations, and so on form the basis of specific events that may evoke episodes of solidarity. These events, repeated over time, and depending upon frequency, intensity, and level of interaction, produce a sense of family solidarity. Thus we can talk about solidarity in the family as being a process experienced over these various and collective life events.

Alternatively, within religious or other cultural institutions, we can likewise talk about events which serve to enhance, inspire, or evoke episodes of solidarity. Such events typically revolve around the ceremonial, but may also include the commemorative, induction of new members, proselytizational, and other significant life events of members which have been serialized within the cultural institution (e.g., typically marriage, birth, coming of age, and so on find expression within religious and other

cultural institutions and also serve as solidifying events). Religious and other cultural institutions also provide, encourage, and to a great extent require vision and visionary leaders that serve to express institutional-wide ideas, values, and purpose which not only transcend the everyday events and issues of its members, but also give members a sense of collective identity, thus encouraging solidarity. These visions and visionaries, occurring periodically through the institutional memories of members, serve to produce and sustain group cohesion. Collectively, then, within religious and cultural institutions, the ceremonial, those life events that are commemorated, and visions and visionary leaders provide the organizational glue that accounts for solidifying events. These events over time are what we refer to when we speak of solidarity within religious and cultural institutions.

Often solidarity is held out to various groups (e.g., racialized, gendered, political) as if it were some actuality that can be achieved. As such, and given the reality that it is often presumed to be associated with specified dominant groups, it only manifests itself oppositionally. Solidarity, for heterogeneously large groups, presumes a level, form, and/or quality of unity which is prevented by the very nature of heterogeneously large groups. What solidarity that does come into being tends to be experienced not universally but partially by specific sections of groups whose interests, goals, and/or opportunities are perceived to be challenged, effected, or affected. More generally and typically, members of groups seek to organize or mobilize as a consequence of perceived organization or mobilization by external groups, forces, and/or threats. Consequentially, solidarity is not an event but a process that is never quite complete and is dependent upon such things as perceived threat, advantage, and disadvantage to which and by which organizational resources are expended. The nature of these organizational resources is defined by the resource base(s) of the group, the historical progression or context to which the group owes its existence, and the ability of group members to effectively acquire, access, and mobilize resources and members for the purposes of obtaining levels of solidarity.

The problem inherent in a constant insistence upon solidarity is that such calls may be at the expense of legitimate, necessary, and important conflict. Conflict, differences of opinion, and critical discussions require opposing perspectives, the ability to be heard, addressed, and exist. The notion that solidarity somehow eliminates or minimizes such critical dialogues fails to understand the nature of group dynamics. Solidarity, as a relative construct, therefore exists to the extent that group members feel free to express critical differences, identify alternative strategies, and explore multiple frames of references. The extent to which relative solidarity becomes a reality is determined to the extent that agendas, priorities, and goals can be identified which garner significant group support, to which members are willing to devote their individual resources. Further, to the extent that the understanding of solidarity advanced here does not preclude multiple agendas, goals, and interests within and overlapping various groups, we may speak of a more elaborate conceptualization (i.e., one which is not monolithic but pluralistic) that is being envisioned.

Ideally, solidarity is achievable across the full spectrum of group members. In reality, solidarity tends to be tenuously associated with specific threat levels, opportunities, and member interests. Specific external inducements, threats, and/or events can serve as catalysts to solidarity initiatives, but these initiatives tend to be uniquely experienced and structured by the internal dynamics of the specific groups. Hence, solidarity episodes may be identified, catalogued, and understood within specific historical contexts for specific groups.

When we observe these solidarity episodes across time, i.e., within specific historical contexts, we may note increasing or decreasing levels of solidarity associated with what we may call social movements. Social movements, here being defined as increased group cohesion aimed at effecting system changes within societal or community contexts, are successful to the extent that solidarity events are sustainable over multiple events and/or episodes. The effectiveness of these social movements is directly associated with the appearance of solidarity, but in actuality may be associated with the ability of group leaders to control external impressions. The implication of this is that solidarity is more about impression management than actual (perceived or otherwise) levels of solidarity.

It is in the interests of group leaders to present the impression of high levels of solidarity as this gives credence to their legitimacy and credibility. This is especially true for social movement leaders, whose political currency is tied to these impressions and who are keenly aware how notions of solidarity impact upon their effectiveness as leaders, both within and external to the group. Hence, such things as marches, meetings, and various types of protests are selectively used to demonstrate the level of solidarity, leaders' ability to encourage solidarity, and their ability to promote specific issues and/or advance specific agendas as a result. What this also suggests is that numbers, counts, and levels of involvement become highly subjective and contested pieces of information as they are related to perceptions of levels of solidarity, leadership capacity, and group viability.

SEE ALSO: Accommodation; Acculturation; Agency (and Intention); Alliances (Racial/Ethnic); Assimilation; Black Feminist Thought; Charismatic Movement; Civil Rights Movement; Class Consciousness; Diversity; Durkheim, Émile; Ethnic Enclaves; Ethnicity; Feminism; Feminism, First, Second, and Third Waves; Indigenous Movements; King, Martin Luther; Leadership; Race; Race (Racism); Social Movements; Social Movements, Leadership in; Solidarity, Mechanical and Organic

REFERENCES AND SUGGESTED READINGS

Amit-Talai, V. & Knoles, C. (Ed.) (1996) *Re-Situating Identities: The Politics of Race, Ethnicity, and Culture.* Broadview, Canada.

Coates, R. (Ed.) (2004) *Race and Ethnicity: Across Time, Space, and Discipline.* Brill, The Netherlands.

Du Bois, W. E. B. (1995) *The Souls of Black Folks.* Signant, New York.

Elias, N. & Scotson, J. L. (1994) *The Established and the Outsiders: A Sociological Enquiry into Community Problems,* 2nd edn. Sage, London.

Fauye, E. (Ed.) (2000) The Working Class and Urban Public Space. *Social Science History* 24(1), special issue.

Hacker, A. (1992) *Two Nations: Black and White, Separate, Hostile, Unequal.* Ballantine, New York.

Markoff, J. (2005) *The Dark Side of Democracy.* Cambridge University Press, Cambridge.

Olzak, S. (1992) *The Dynamics of Ethnic Competition and Conflict*. Stanford University Press, Stanford.

Ostrom, E. (1990) *Governing the Commons: The Evolution of Institutions for Collective Action*. Cambridge University Press, Cambridge.

Scott, J. C. (1985) *Weapons of the Weak: Everyday Forms of Peasant Resistance*. Yale University Press, New Haven.

Scott, J. C. (1990) *Domination and the Arts of Resistance: Hidden Transcripts*. Yale University Press, New Haven.

solidarity, mechanical and organic

Anne M. Hornsby

French sociologist Émile Durkheim (1858–1917) coined the terms mechanical and organic solidarity to describe two types of social organization, that is, ways in which individuals are connected to each other and how they identify with the groups and societies in which they live. Social solidarity is a state of unity or cohesion that exists when people are integrated by strong social bonds and shared beliefs and also are regulated by well-developed guidelines for action (values and norms that suggest worthy goals and how people should attain them). In his first book, *The Division of Labor in Society* (1893), Durkheim argued that social solidarity takes different forms in different historical periods and varies in strength among groups in the same society. However, reflecting the popularity of social evolutionary thought in the late nineteenth century, Durkheim summarized all historical forms of solidarity into a traditional–modern dichotomy. Mechanical solidarity is a simple, pre-industrial form of social cohesion and organic solidarity is a more complex form that evolves in modern societies.

In developing his mechanical–organic distinction, Durkheim drew on the organicist thinking that influenced many intellectuals of his generation, where human societies are analyzed with analogies to biological organisms. A single cluster of embryonic cells, where each cell is initially identical in structure and function, develops by dividing into separate clusters with cells changing form and specializing into kidney cells, skin cells, etc. Over time they form organs that have distinct boundaries but must be interdependent for the functioning of the whole organism. By analogy, settlements of small kinship groups are scattered across territories and organized similarly. Over time these simple societies disappear as rural and urban areas emerge, cities grow, and a complex division of functions appears within cities.

Specifically, mechanical solidarity occurs in small, simple organisms, where people live in small groups and each group is likely to perform all the functions needed to survive (familial, economic, political, religious, etc.). There is no specialization or differentiation of function. Each person feels and lives a similar connection to group life because everyone's experience of the world comes from a religiously based common culture that reproduces in each person the same ways of thinking, feeling, and acting. By mechanical, Durkheim does not mean machine-like or artificial. He means that the conditions of life are the same for everyone so there is little diversity in people's experiences and ideas. Individuals do not have a sense of identity separate from being a member of a family, clan, or a warrior caste. Consequently, "the ideas and tendencies common to all the members of the society are greater in number and intensity than those which pertain personally to each member" (Durkheim 1964: 129).

Organic solidarity occurs in complex organisms composed of specialized parts, each of which performs distinct functions to support the whole. No one household, neighborhood, town, or economy can produce everything its members need to survive. Economies begin to depend not only on the family but also on educational institutions to produce dependable workers with a range of needed skills. A complex division of labor has developed, where there are many different occupations, a great diversity of racial and ethnic backgrounds, and a wide range of religious beliefs and political views. Such diversity of people, groups, and institutions is organized into distinct yet interdependent roles and functions. Moreover, a cultural concept of the individual and individualism emerges, and people are integrated by social exchange among free individuals in market economies.

Durkheim grew up as the son of a rabbi in the long-established and tightly-knit Jewish community of Alsace-Lorraine. He left his traditional world to pursue his studies in the cosmopolitan world of Paris. Many scholars have observed that Durkheim's personal experiences of tradition and modernity inspired his lifelong interest in the nature and condition of solidarity in contemporary democratic society. The central question Durkheim posed in *The Division of Labor* is what is the basis of social solidarity in modern societies where there is a great diversity of people living in vastly different settings? How do the parts of a modern society (individuals, groups, institutions) become more interdependent while at the same time becoming more distinct from each other?

His argument is summarized in a well-known statement: "Social life comes from a double source, the likeness of consciences and the division of labor" (Durkheim 1964: 226). Here, Durkheim identifies the two key variables that distinguish mechanical and organic solidarity, which continue to be important variables in sociology today: (1) the extent (degree of complexity) of the division of labor, by which he means differentiation of distinct functions or roles, such as the historical separation of economic production from family and kinship systems, and the organization of economic production into differentiated occupational groupings and industries; (2) the extent to which members of a society share a collective consciousness (i.e., all the ways of thinking, feeling, and acting that are common to a group or society). (The extent of collective consciousness means the number and intensity of the values, beliefs, norms, emotions, and activities that are shared.)

In mechanically organized societies the division of labor is absent or weak, and the collective consciousness contains a large number of clear, powerful beliefs, values, and traditional practices shared intensely by all members. In contrast, organic societies have a complex division of labor and a smaller number of more ambiguous and thus less constraining ideas and practices that everyone shares. A complex division of labor and great diversity of people creates the condition where the collective consciousness becomes more abstract by virtue of including only values and norms that are meaningful to

everyone. Durkheim notes that perhaps the only value widely shared and strongly held in modern western societies is individualism – the inherent dignity, worth, and freedom of the individual. As the collective consciousness becomes more abstract because shared ways of thinking, feeling, and acting are far fewer in number and are more ambiguous, society is less able to regulate all behavior.

Exactly how does the evolution from mechanical to organic solidarity occur? Durkheim argues that physical and social density increase, which generates competition among people, resulting in differentiation of roles and institutional functions. Population size increases and is distributed across a territory differently due to improvements in transportation and communication that link people and villages more easily. Villages and towns grow, cities emerge, and as urbanization increases, each person has more contact with a great many more people. This increase in social density – the actual pattern of who interacts with whom, how, and with what frequency – stimulates competition for jobs and other resources. From competition emerges a more complex division of labor, where people find occupational niches, firms find market niches, and different zones of a city specialize in different functions.

In short, social ties are based on difference instead of likeness. Everyone is more interdependent, in worlds separated yet linked by specialization. Durkheim concludes that "even where society relies most completely upon the division of labor ... the members are united by ties which extend deeper and far beyond the short moments during which the exchange is made. Each of the functions that they exercise is, in a fixed way, dependent upon others, and with them forms a solidary system" (Durkheim 1964: 227).

In *The Division of Labor* Durkheim argued that as specialization and interdependence of function increase, the extent and intensity of collective consciousness recede in importance as a source of social solidarity. Together, both changes produce a different type of society. In subsequent work, however, Durkheim became less convinced that the collective consciousness recedes in importance in modern societies. Over time his work focused more on the pre-rational basis of solidarity (i.e, the moral and emotional effect of social ties), especially how groups produce ideologies through mechanisms such as ritual practices (Collins 1994: 190, 204). Durkheim did not discuss mechanical and organic solidarity per se after *The Division of Labor*. Yet over his lifetime he continued his interest in both manifestations of the structural relations among people: the evolution of institutions and the symbolic and emotional components of social life that unify groups and societies.

SEE ALSO: Collective Consciousness; Division of Labor; Durkheim, Émile; Durkheim, Émile and Social Change; Norms; Tradition; Values

REFERENCES AND SUGGESTED READINGS

Alexander, J. & Smith. P. (Eds.) (2005) *The Cambridge Companion to Durkheim*. Cambridge University Press, Cambridge.

Bellah, R. N. (Ed.) (1983) *Émile Durkheim on Morality and Society*. University of Chicago Press, Chicago.

Collins, R. (1994) *Four Sociological Traditions*, 2nd edn. Oxford University Press, Oxford.

Durkheim, E. (1964 [1893]) *The Division of Labor in Society*. Trans. G. Simpson. Free Press, New York.

Lehmann, J. M. (1993) *Deconstructing Durkheim*. Routledge, New York.

Lukes, S. (1973) *Émile Durkheim: His Life and Work*. Penguin, London.

Sombart, Werner (1863–1941)

Alan Sica

Werner Sombart was born in the small Protestant town of Ermsleben (Harz region) and died in Berlin, an event fully recorded in the *New York Times* with obituary and editorial (May 20 and 22, 1941). His father, Anton Ludwig Sombart, was from seventeenth-century Huguenot stock and personified what Sombart's friend Max Weber would call in 1905 the Protestant ethic, and what Sombart himself named the bourgeois

spirit. The elder Sombart was elected *Burgermeister* of Ermsleben in 1848, and became rich as an industrialist and estate owner through the sugar trade. Not satisfied simply to enjoy his wealth, he co-founded the famous *Verein für Sozialpolitik*, an influential organization of concerned citizens that sponsored social research prescribing government policy, particularly pertaining to the liberation of agricultural workers from virtual serfdom on large estates. Bismarck invited him to become minister of agriculture, but he declined owing to poor eyesight.

Despite his own eye disease and nascent tuberculosis in youth, Werner Sombart was able to use his family's great wealth to study economics and humanities at Pisa (1882), Berlin (1893), and Rome. His Berlin dissertation on the ancient Roman *Campagna* (1888) (substantively similar to Weber's) was directed by Gustav Schmoller, the leading exponent of sociohistorical economics. It remains an impressive scholarly achievement by virtue of the way primary documents from the Roman state archives were examined. Sombart's first professional position was as a city lawyer for Bremen, which he was loath to leave after 2 years when offered a professorship (partly through the machinations of his father) at remote Breslau in 1890. (Max Weber unsuccessfully applied for the very position in Bremen which Sombart had vacated.)

Sombart's first classes treated the Communist Manifesto and *Capital* (Vol. 1), to which he had been drawn after becoming radicalized, not by reading social science, but instead the fiction of Emile Zola. He decided at this early date to commit his prodigious scholarly energy to the study of the proletariat and the nature of capitalism as they evolved in unison throughout history. Like today's sociologists, he toured worksites in order to understand the proletarian's plight, a practice which did not sit well with his hidebound academic colleagues, who already regarded him as "a young and conceited person." Thus, from this unusual background of familial wealth and connections, childhood disease and poor early school performance, wide travel, and passionate interests in literature, economics, and history, plus the usual linguistic capacity of mandarins of his period, Sombart perfected a style of living and writing which throughout his life shocked his staid peers while thrilling readers and auditors. He was known as a dandy among the more straitlaced, yet was able through sheer force of style to write books that sold 30,000 copies, some in cheap editions to the working class. C. Wright Mills, writing about Veblen, quoted from Bernard Shaw's *Man and Superman* – "he who has something to assert will go as far in power of style as its momentousness and his conviction will carry him" – which could as well be applied to Sombart (quoted in Grundmann & Stehr 2001). Once again in the history of social thought, a son of privilege dedicated himself utterly to the interpretation of life among the lower orders (as with Weber, Simmel, and Lukacs), and for reasons not entirely clear, perhaps even to himself.

Beginning with the belief that Marx was "the greatest social philosopher of the nineteenth century," Sombart elaborated his predecessor's arguments. For some years his fellow leftist intellectuals fully expected him to succeed Marx as the foremost analyst of capitalism. The widespread belief that he was heir apparent to the leftist tradition began early, after he published a brilliant analysis of Marx's *Capital* (Vol. 3) at the age of 31. This 40-page work (Sombart 1894) has won steady encomia ever since it appeared, beginning with Engels's celebrated remark in a letter from 1895: "It is the first time that a German professor has made the effort to try to understand from his writings what Marx really has been saying" (published in an appendix to *Capital*, Vol. 3). Yet eventually he became impatient with the proletariat – which he knew first-hand – for its inability to transcend its quotidian self-definition by becoming an effective agent of social change, and found others to admire, principally among the leaders of National Socialism. Nor could he accept Marx's utopian tendency, substituting for it the hardnosed English and German view of economic life – perhaps due to a sobering realism that sprang from witnessing his father's efficacious business activities. (He also rejected full-scale political work and "self-sacrifice" when invited by his friend Ferdinand Tönnies to join the Social-Democratic Party in 1893, partly at least for fear of losing his job and jeopardizing his young family's welfare.) In brief, he wanted to substitute an evolutionary for a revolutionary brand of Marxist theory and practice, and he enunciated this viewpoint

before other leftist thinkers, like Eduard Bernstein, had done so. By 1900 he was speaking regularly to large trade-union audiences and had been publicly branded as a Marxist, despite the fact that by 1908 he announced in print that most of Marx's ideas about capitalism's dynamics he found unsupportable when measured against the evidence of economic history. Some critics argue that Sombart peaked as a scholar and thinker when quite young, and the older he became and the larger his audiences, the poorer his analysis and the less credible and admirable his political allegiances became.

Sombart's lingering fame in the anglophone sphere is mostly due to a short book, *Why is There No Socialism in the United States?* (1976), which he would have regarded as ancillary to his major project. It is ritually cited by authors discussing "American exceptionalism," but there is little evidence that it is any longer read with the sort of care lavished, say, on Weber's *The Protestant Ethic and the Spirit of Capitalism* (1930). And ever since Sombart's death, his magnum opus *Der moderne Kapitalismus* (1902 and thereafter) – never fully translated into English (Sombart 1967b) – has been eclipsed in importance by two briefer works, *The Jews and Modern Capitalism* (1913) and *Luxury and Capitalism* (1967a). In the former work he imaginatively argues that the Jews, due to their moneylending and trading skills, were pivotal in the formation of capitalism, a point which caused some proud, early Jewish reviewers to embrace the book. But others, due perhaps to Sombart's thoroughgoing support of the Nazis in later years, find his argument anti-Semitic because he juxtaposes rationalist Jewish economic practices against Germanophilic industrial behavior, all to the detriment of the former. In taking this position he was quite self-consciously extending Tönnies's 1887 argument about the forgiving warmth of *Gemeinschaft* versus the urban chill common to life within *Gesellschaft*. And Sombart (unlike Weber or Tönnies) explicitly attributed the former to "real" Germans and reserved the latter, unhappy condition to the influence of Jewish commercial practices and the worldview that went along with it. Later critics insist that Sombart's notion of Judaism is fantasy, a result of his lack of Hebrew and consequent misunderstanding of the religion's social and sacred practices. The canonical comparison is with Weber's

Ancient Judaism (1952), which had held up well even after decades of study.

More useful today, however, is Sombart's book on luxury, which some scholars believe is more suited for the explanation of contemporary consumerist culture than is Veblen's more famous sister-tome, *The Theory of the Leisure Class* (1899). Sombart held that the desire for what Veblen wonderfully called "conspicuous consumption" played a vital role in the birth of capitalism, beginning with courtiers wishing to outdo each other in the presence of their sovereigns. Veblen regarded this as a pathological condition, but Sombart, anticipating the late twentieth century, saw in it the roots of capitalist behavior, and as such not in itself ethically or morally questionable.

Werner Sombart's legacy is a troubled one, to be sure. On one hand, he wrote a multi-volume study of capitalism which for sheer detail and historical sweep has no rivals, after Marx's own works. Yet it has often been noted that his use of data lacked precision and his powerful prose style swept him, and his unsuspecting readers, into unsupportable claims. His occasional anti-Semitic remarks coupled with a longstanding support for *Deutschtum* (chauvinist Germanness) via the Nazi party have naturally made him permanently anathema to many readers. Yet some scholars argue (e.g., Stehr and Grundmann in Sombart 2001) that he deserves continued study. They see him as a potent counterbalance to the ideas of Weber, Simmel, and others in that luminous circle, whose principal scholarly preoccupation was the explanation for capitalism's wild success in Europe and America, and also for its corrosive nature and high social costs across the globe.

SEE ALSO: Capitalism; Culture, Economy and; Global Economy; Political Economy; Weber, Max

REFERENCES AND SUGGESTED READINGS

Grundmann, R. & Stehr, N. (2001) Why is Werner Sombart not Part of the Core of Classical Sociology? *Journal of Classical Sociology* 1(2): 257–87.

Sombart, W. (1894) Zur Kritik des ökonomischen Systems von Karl Marx. *Archiv für soziale Gesetzgebung und Statistik* 7: 555–94.

Sombart, W. (1913 [1911]) *The Jews and Modern Capitalism*. Trans. M. Epstein. T. F. Unwin, London. Reissued Collier Paperbacks, New York, 1962.

Sombart, W. (1967a [1913]) *Luxury and Capitalism*. Trans. W. R. Dittmar. University of Michigan Press, Ann Arbor.

Sombart, W. (1967b [1915]) *The Quintessence of Capitalism*. Trans. & ed. M. Epstein. Howard Fertig, New York.

Sombart, W. (1976 [1906]) *Why is There No Socialism in the United States?* Trans. P. Hocking & C. Husbands. Macmillan, London; M. E. Sharpe, White Plains, NY.

Sombart, W. (2001) *Economic Life in the Modern Age*. Ed. N. Stehr & R. Grundmann. Transction Publishers, New Brunswick, NJ.

Veblen, T. (1899) *The Theory of the Leisure Class*. New York.

Weber, M. (1930 [1905]) *The Protestant Ethic and the Spirit of Capitalism*. Trans. T. Parsons. Charles Scribner's Sons, New York.

Weber, M. (1952 [1917]) *Ancient Judaism*. Trans. H. Gerth & D. Martindale. Free Press, New York.

Sorokin, Pitirim A. (1889–1968)

Edward Tiryakian

By any objective criteria of contributions to macrosociology, Pitirim Aleksandrovich Sorokin ranks alongside such twentieth-century figures as Max Weber, Émile Durkheim, and Talcott Parsons. His pioneering contributions in the comparative-historical study of revolutions, social mobility, cultural sociology (considerably in advance of the "cultural turn" of sociology), rural-urban sociology, and the sociology of altruism are lasting landmarks with a prime focus on the hows and whys of what he designated as sociocultural change.

As Coser (1977: 489) has noted, there is considerable overlap in the general structural-functional perspective of Sorokin and Parsons regarding the significance of culture, values, and meaningful symbols in social organization (both consequently highly critical of economic reductionism, as in later rational choice theory). Yet these departmental colleagues differed as to the course of social change in the period of late modernity. Sorokin came to reject a linear view of social change, opting for a more cyclical and critical perspective; Parsons in later writings on social change and the value system of modernity took a more optimistic perspective of current western cultural orientations becoming globally accepted.

During the length of a long, productive career, Sorokin filled many roles as a sociologist: he was an entrepreneur in founding departments of sociology at Petrograd University on the eve of World War I and at Harvard in 1931 (where Robert K. Merton was the first graduate student to enrol and became his early collaborator); he engaged in "public sociology" as a student activist in prerevolutionary and revolutionary Russia, and again in the last decade of his life in his opposition to the Vietnam War; like C. Wright Mills at Columbia, he was highly critical of the "establishment," including the "power structure" of the United States and of the dominant, reductionist methodology of the profession. Sorokin readily took on the role of prophet in various writings on the cultural crisis of modernity, and experienced a double exile – an exile from his native Russia after being banished by Lenin for obstructing the Bolshevist Revolution (a fate he shared with his contemporary Georges Gurvitch, who became a leading figure in French sociology after World War II), and a second symbolic exile from American mainstream sociology after World War II. His "banishment" came to an end with his election after a write-in campaign to the presidency of the American Sociological Association in 1964, and perhaps as important, symbolically in 1969 when the radical students protesting the Vietnam War adopted the recently departed Sorokin as their icon at the ASA meetings in San Francisco by having a special session on "Sorokin Lives!"

EARLY RUSSIAN PERIOD

Born in a remote rural ethnic enclave of Russia, Sorokin came of age in a period marked by modernization as well as by agrarian and urban unrest, culminating in the failed revolution of 1905 and the successful revolution of 1917.

Noted as a brilliant student, Sorokin developed his interests in law and criminology (his doctoral dissertation was *Crime and Punishment*) and broadened them to sociology. He was a participant-observer of the revolutionary setting, later making use of his observations at close hand of how people behave towards one another in extreme situations, including the condition of mass food deprivation (*Hunger as a Factor in Human Affairs*, eventually translated into English). His political involvement led to various arrests subject to capital punishment, but his academic reputation and scholarly publications provided the grounds for clemency from Lenin, subject to Sorokin's permanent exile.

Not all or even the majority of his writings of this period have been translated (see the selections in Sorokin 1998). Beside providing him with a treasure house of observations on collective behavior and social movements, the ruptures of World War I and Revolutionary Russia provided Sorokin with materials to reject the naïve positivism associated with an evolutionary and linear view of change.

EARLY AMERICAN PERIOD: 1920s

Coming to the University of Minnesota and a more tranquil academic life, Sorokin brought to American sociology an important comparative-historical perspective in major volumes dealing with rural-urban differences and convergences (Sorokin & Zimmerman 1929), stratification and mobility (Sorokin 1927), and schools of sociological theory in terms of their major premises and orientations.

In *Principles of Rural-Urban Sociology* Sorokin noted that the city plays predominantly the role of innovator, the countryside that of the preserver of existing national culture. The heterogeneity of the population and a greater percentage of foreign-born inhabitants generates a more "international" character to city culture, while rural classes have a greater development of patriotism, which as a particular attachment to one's region and place of birth becomes a part of personality. Urban dwellers, with greater mobility and heterogeneity, are more prone to atheism and secularism; rural societies have a better chance of preserving the integrity of their national culture in times of foreign political sub-jugation and to regain their political independence than highly urbanized societies. These observations of Sorokin and Zimmerman were borne out in African colonial rule and Eastern Europe under communist rule.

Although much more is to be found in this massive comparative study, for the purpose at hand it may be noted that (in contrast to other perspectives prevalent at the time, which looked at rural society with nostalgia as a setting of virtue and *Gemeinschaft* only) the perspective deployed is one of even-handedness concerning rural–urban differences. There is not, in other words, an idealization of rural life and "small town" community. The volume also looked at dynamic aspects of the modern rural-urban setting rather than as set in fixed poles. As important sociologically as the differences of rural and urban are their interchanges, with increasing urbanization of the rural world and also with the "ruralization" of the city world (a dialectical process which a later generation recognized as gentrification and suburbanization, and yet later as the global–local interplay).

MIDDLE AMERICAN PERIOD: 1930s AND 1940s

In addition to launching and chairing the Harvard department of sociology, Sorokin produced a four-volume magnum opus, *Social and Cultural Dynamics* (1991), the most comprehensive sociological analysis of the institutional components of civilizations understood as dynamic cultural systems. Other publications in this period apply the theoretical perspective of a decaying "sensate" phase of civilization to diagnoses of the global crisis of the later 1930s, culminating in World War II (*Crisis of our Age*, 1941; *Man and Society in Calamity*, 1942). In a different vein, Sorokin published a methodological treatise having affinity with phenomenology (*Sociocultural Causality, Space, Time*, 1942) and a comparative study of the two countries that became the superpowers of the postwar era (*Russia and the United States*, 1944). While aware of some obvious differences, Sorokin in the latter study also pointed out important similarities and structural bases of compatibility.

LATE AMERICAN PERIOD: 1950s AND 1960s

This bitter-sweet period of Sorokin's career was marked initially by an increased estrangement from the profession (*Fads and Foibles in Sociology and Related Sciences*, 1956) and a very critical orientation to cultural and political aspects of American society (*The American Sex Revolution, Power and Morality: Who Shall Guard the Guardians?* 1959). His "critical" writings, published well in advance of critical sociology, tended to be dismissed by the profession, with grudging accolades given to more "mainstream" works (*Sociological Theories of Today*, 1966). However, the accolades became more pronounced in his last decade, and a certain reconciliation of Sorokin with the profession is best manifest in his ASA presidential address "Sociology of Yesterday, Today and Tomorrow" (published in the *American Sociological Review*, December 1965).

His most creative activities in this last period were devoted to setting up the Harvard Research Center in Creative Altruism, which generated several important volumes (see the discussion in Johnston 1995). These relate to Sorokin's view that sociology needs to provide from empirical data possibilities of social reconstruction emphasizing creativity, love, and normative ideals as alternative to prevalent emphases in popular culture and in research on what in a comparative-historical perspective are malevolent features of the human condition.

MAJOR THEMES OF SOCIAL CHANGE

For Sorokin, echoing the insight of Heraklitus, the social order is characteristically in flux. The social order is given its orderliness by the cultural integration of its component parts, which are themselves institutions and systems of ideas (political, economic, philosophical, cultural). These parts of a complex whole sociocultural system (a civilization) are grounded in a basic worldview of ultimate reality, with three primary modes of apprehending reality as truth. First, reality may be taken to be given by the senses and the objects of the senses: this Sorokin termed *sensate* reality. Second, in contrast, ultimate reality may be seen as lying beyond the senses and their time-space coordinates; it is apprehended by intuition, intuitive experience, a moment of "enlightenment" and the like, recognized in various cultural and religious traditions, from Plato to Zen Buddhism. This Sorokin termed *ideational*. Third is a combination or synthesis of the first two by means of the faculty of reason and rational thought – what Sorokin called *idealistic*.

All three cognitive modes are present in any complex social order, though in any period of the existence of a social system one mode may have salience over the other two. But because all three are features of social organization, in order to have a comprehensive understanding of the structure and dynamics of social reality – of the comportment of social actors and of inevitable changes in social organization – sociology must be an "integralist sociology," that is, it must have a multidimensional methodology that can treat social reality in all three modes. Stated in different terms, an adequate methodology for sociology is one that is empirical (Sorokin utilized quantitative data in various studies), rational, and interpretive.

However integrated sociocultural systems and their component parts may be, there is no perfect, permanent integration – humans can imagine a perfectly integrated society (as in socialist and other totalitarian systems), but history shows that change is prevalent and that the major factors producing change are internal factors (Sorokin's *principle of immanent change*). Over time, the cultural premises exhaust their creative capacity of integration, and in periods of decay (or decadence), normative disarray is reflected in social pathological behavior, from anarchy and civil wars to world wars and genocides.

Drawing from his early observations on the Russian scene, but also from secondary sources of other settings, Sorokin proposed that in periods of crisis and at the end phase of a given system of cultural integration, particularly the modern one of a late sensate period, there is the phenomenon of *polarization*. Instead of the modal "average" conduct of morality, the majority may be drawn to acts of violence and brutality against others, but a creative minority will engage in acts of abnegation, sacrifice, and altruism.

Lastly, Sorokin's perspective on change is a rejection of a linear view of change in favor of a *principle of limit*. There is a limit to how far in extent a given cultural mentality can go, and there is only a finite number of immanent possibilities available to a given sociocultural system. Hence, the historical process can be observed through various indices to have recurrent rhythms and patterns, rather than being unidirectional.

In brief, long-term change is cyclical with a *longue durée* of the dominant mentality, whose exhaustion results in crises of malintegration manifest in social disorders and wars. In essential respects, Sorokin's analysis of change in late modernity converges with and amplifies Durkheim's theory of anomie.

CONCLUSION

Sociology has at various times "discovered" major figures of the past, as their overlooked or forgotten writings take on new relevance with changing societal conditions: Karl Marx, Georg Simmel, and Norbert Elias come to mind as receiving new "upgrades" in the decades after World War II. Sorokin is a prime candidate for "upgrade status," with his focus on civilizational change as a unit of macrosociology (a theme accentuated by the "clash of civilizations" replacing the clash of superpowers), with his studies of by-products of social deterioration in an era of the accelerating decline of sensate culture (witness Internet pornography, "reality" TV shows, and other anomic manifestations of popular culture), and with his comparative-historical research on the creative and beneficial aspects of altruistic behavior. The "postmodern condition," however elusive this may be, is one of flux and ambiguity. The rosy optimism of a "new international order" at the end of the Cold War has given way to a more sober realism of late modernity in the face of new cycles of genocide and warfare. In this period of transition, Sorokin's integralist sociology offers methodological guidance for dealing and researching with emerging sociocultural phenomena, and his studies of altruistic behavior (which he designated as the study of "amity"), well in advance of current emerging research on philanthropy, point to a possible new paradigm of modernity, a new "idealistic" period, though not a new utopia.

SEE ALSO: Anomie; Durkheim, Émile; Gurvitch, Georges: Social Change; Parsons, Talcott; Phenomenology; Revolutions

REFERENCES AND SUGGESTED READINGS

Coser, L. A. (1977) Pitirim A. Sorokin. In: Coser, L. A., *Masters of Sociological Thought*, 2nd edn. Harcourt, Brace, Jovanovich, New York, pp. 464–508.

Johnston, B. V. (1995) *Pitirim A. Sorokin: An Intellectual Biography*. University Press of Kansas, Lawrence.

Sorokin, P. A. (1925) *The Sociology of Revolution*. J. B. Lipincott, Philadelphia.

Sorokin, P. A. (1927) *Social Mobility*. Harper, New York.

Sorokin, P. A. (1942) *Man and Society in Calamity*. E. P. Dutton, New York.

Sorokin, P. A. (1956) *The American Sex Revolution*. P. Sargent, Boston.

Sorokin, P. A. (1991 [1937–41]) *Social and Cultural Dynamics*, revd. edn. Transaction Books, New Brunswick, NJ.

Sorokin, P. A. (1998) *On the Practice of Sociology*. Ed. B. V. Johnston. Heritage of Sociology series. University of Chicago Press, Chicago.

Sorokin, P. A. & Zimmerman, C. C. (1929) *Principles of Rural-Urban Sociology*. Henry Holt, New York.

sovereignty

Stephen D. Krasner

The term sovereignty has been used in many different ways. The most important and widely understood distinction is between internal (domestic) and external (international) sovereignty. Internal sovereignty refers to the existence of an authoritative decision-making structure within a political entity, a structure that is both legitimated and effective. External sovereignty refers to the autonomy or independence of a political entity and its associated authority structure from external control or interference.

INTERNAL OR DOMESTIC SOVEREIGNTY

Internal sovereignty is associated with the principle that within each political entity there is a structure capable of making authoritative determinations. In its modern formulations this idea is rooted in the work of Bodin and Hobbes, both of whom wanted, above all, to create a basis for domestic political order in the face of religious conflicts that were undermining the major states of Europe. Bodin's *Six Books of the Commonwealth* was motivated by the religious wars in France and was a rebuttal of the claim made by some Huguenot theorists for the right to rebel. Bodin himself was almost killed in the St. Bartholomew's Day massacre of 1572. For Bodin, the basic goal of government was to ensure order, and order could not be preserved if there was a right of rebellion against the sovereign. Bodin recognized that the sovereign could be a tyrant and he accepted the possibility that such a tyrant could be killed by outsiders, but he rejected in principle the right of domestic resistance.

Hobbes published the *Leviathan* at the end of the English Civil War, the bloodiest conflict in per capita terms for Britain until World War I and one of whose victims was the British king. Hobbes's basic contention was that once individuals had entered into the social contract, they had given up any right of rebellion. The alternative to the Leviathan, the sovereign, was the state of nature in which life was "nasty, brutish, and short." Both Bodin and Hobbes believed that there must be some one final point of authority within the state, an idea never realized in practice and perhaps even inimical to domestic order because of the dangers presented by the arbitrary exercise of power. Locke's idea of the state as a fiduciary trust for the citizens who did have the right of rebellion if that trust was violated has proven a more durable formula for establishing stability. Regardless, however, of whether domestic sovereignty is organized in some single hierarchy or based on a separation of powers, the basic claim of internal or domestic sovereignty is that decent human existence requires an independent authority structure capable of providing order and, ideally, justice and prosperity as well.

Domestic or internal sovereignty has never been taken for granted. Issues of order and justice, which informed the work of the great political thinkers of the past, continue to be the concern of modern scholars. In the contemporary environment there are huge variations in the quality of domestic sovereignty or governance. In the modern industrialized countries of North America, Western Europe, and East Asia economic prosperity has grown, life expectancy has increased, and the lives of most individuals are secure. Domestic sovereignty works. In other parts of the world, however, there are populations in many countries that suffer under failed, weak, incompetent, or abusive national authority structures. Life expectancy is declining. Public services are not delivered. Per capita income is falling. Civil war is endemic. In the most extreme cases, any semblance of an effective national or even regional authority structure may have collapsed. Internal or domestic sovereignty has failed.

EXTERNAL OR INTERNATIONAL SOVEREIGNTY

External or international sovereignty refers to a way of organizing political life among political entities. In its ideal typical form external sovereignty is defined by three characteristics: territory, autonomy, equality. A sovereign state has a defined territory. A sovereign state is autonomous or independent; no external actor has authority within the state's territorial boundaries and each sovereign state accepts the autonomy of other sovereigns. Finally, sovereign states are formally equal. Although they obviously vary with regard to size, population, resources, and wealth, every sovereign state has the right to sign treaties with others and to be free from interference by external actors. With regard to equality, sovereign states are analogous to individuals in a liberal society; each state is regarded as having a basic set of rights regardless of other attributes.

Conventional analyses by international lawyers and by international relations scholars as well have treated international or external sovereignty as fundamental for any adequate understanding of the modern international system. The sovereign state system has been seen as emerging from the Peace of Westphalia of 1648, which ended the Thirty Years' War. In his classic "The Peace of Westphalia, 1648–1948," Leo Gross wrote that the "Peace of Westphalia, for better or worse, marks the end of an epoch and the opening of another. It represents the majestic portal which leads from the old world into the new." For Gross, the Peace marked the end of the hierarchical medieval system within which the emperor and the pope stood at the pinnacle of religious and secular authority.

For the conventional perspective, once sovereignty was accepted at Westphalia it became increasingly embedded over time. Conventional sovereignty became the foundation upon which international law was based. Law was the result of treaties or customary behavior undertaken by sovereign states, each of which was free to choose its own course of action. For international relations scholars, especially those associated with realism, the dominant perspective for American political scientists from the 1950s through the 1990s, sovereignty was the fundamental assumption upon which their analyses were based: outcomes in the international system were the result of the distribution of power among states, each of which was assumed to be independent from all others. For many scholars, as well as policymakers, international or external sovereignty came to have a taken-for-granted quality.

Conventional understanding of international and domestic, of external and internal, sovereignty is complementary. An autonomous territorially based political unit capable of entering into agreements with other such units on an equal basis, the key to international sovereignty, must also be a unit in which there is a domestic authority structure capable of guaranteeing that international commitments can be honored.

ALTERNATIVES TO SOVEREIGNTY

Sovereignty can be contrasted with other ways of organizing political life. Traditional tribal groups claimed authority over their members but did not have a defined territory. Authority relations were defined in terms of individuals rather than territory. Colonies had specific territory but they did not have autonomy; final authority rested with the colonizing state. In the traditional sinocentric world, imperial China was regarded as superior to other political entities; these other entities, tributary states, sent periodic tribute missions to China (missions that were often as much concerned with trade as with deference), and China sent investiture missions to tributary states when new rulers were chosen; but in most other ways tributary states were effectively independent.

SOVEREIGNTY IN PRACTICE

Observers have always recognized that in practice domestic or internal sovereignty can be problematic because domestic authority structures can break down. There is also now increasing recognition of the fact that external sovereignty as well can not be taken for granted. External or international sovereignty can work in practice only if two fundamental rules are observed by states. The first rule, a corollary of the idea that each state is supposed to be independent or autonomous, is that no state should intervene in the internal affairs of another. The inhabitants or rulers of each state can create whatever domestic authority structures they want free from outside interference. The second rule is that there should be mutual recognition among juridically independent territorial entities. Mutual recognition allows states to enter into international agreements on the basis of formal equality. In the contemporary world, it also provides membership in international organizations and, for poorer states, access to the resources of international financial institutions. The official representatives of recognized states are accorded special privileges such as diplomatic immunity.

Both of these rules, the rule of non-intervention and the rule of mutual recognition, assume the absence of any final authority structure in the international system. Indeed, it is the absence of such a final authority that distinguishes a world of sovereign states from an imperial system in which there is a final arbiter for all political entities. If, however, there is no final authority in the international system, why would we expect that the rules of non-intervention and mutual recognition would be honored? One possibility is that these rules, which define a logic of appropriateness for the

international system, are so taken for granted that political leaders cannot conceive of violating them. This possibility, however, is not consistent with the empirical evidence.

The rule of non-intervention has frequently been violated. For example, during the Cold War, the Soviet Union and the United States both sought to promote their own model of domestic authority in other states. In Western Europe after the war, the United States used both financial resources and military threats to weaken the position of the Communist Party in Italy. In what became West Germany and in Japan, the occupying powers led by the United States pressed for the creation of authority structures based on democracy and capitalism. The Soviet Union, for its part, supported or imposed communist regimes in the countries of Eastern Europe that its army occupied at the end of World War II. In the developing world, both the Americans and the Soviets supported political leaders who, at a minimum, would shun the other side. In Korea and Vietnam the United States intervened to prevent a communist regime from assuming control of the entire country, an enterprise that was successful in Korea but not in Vietnam. The United States sent troops into the Dominican Republic and Grenada to prevent what American political leaders perceived to be the dangers of a communist takeover. In Afghanistan the Soviets intervened, ultimately unsuccessfully, to prevent the overthrow of a communist regime.

The inescapable tension at the core of international or external sovereignty is that a logic of consequences may dictate a different behavior than a logic of appropriateness. The international system is characterized by power asymmetries, differing interests, and the absence of any final authority. The core interests of powerful states have repeatedly been threatened by the nature of domestic political regimes in weaker states. To lessen this threat, political leaders in powerful states have moved to change the domestic authority structure in weaker ones. If the interests of powerful states are furthered by intervening in the internal affairs of weaker ones, there is no authority that can prevent such policies from being implemented. Violations of the rule of non-intervention are not an aberration but rather an enduring characteristic of the sovereign state system.

In the post-Cold War environment failures of internal or domestic sovereignty, violations of basic human rights, and the threat of transnational terrorism have created new tensions between a logic of appropriateness and a logic of consequences. Genocidal developments have led major countries to condemn developments in some countries, for instance Rwanda, and to intervene in others, for instance Kosovo. Concerns about terrorism motivated wars against Afghanistan and Iraq. Transitional administrations with executive authority, usually authorized by the United Nations Security Council, have been created in a number of countries since the end of the Cold War, sometimes for short periods, such as in East Timor, and sometimes for much longer periods, as in Bosnia, where the high representative, a Western European essentially appointed by the major European powers, continued to make key political decisions for many years after the signing of the Dayton accords in 1995. Thus, while ideological differences between the Soviet Union and the United States during the Cold War created tensions between the logic of appropriateness associated with external sovereignty and the logic of consequences driven by the desire of the superpowers to support regimes that mimicked their own domestic authority structures, in the post-Cold War period failures of domestic authority and the dangers of terrorism have led to similar tensions.

In an environment as complex as the international system, strains between logics of appropriateness and consequences are inevitable. In their relations with each other powerful states with effective domestic sovereignty may honor the rules of international sovereignty because such behavior is consistent with a logic of consequences. But in relations between powerful states and weak states with either poor or abusive domestic governance, logics of consequences driven by material interests will trump logics of appropriateness. Both internal and external sovereignty have not been, and cannot be, taken for granted.

SEE ALSO: Authority and Legitimacy; Colonialism (Neocolonialism); Global Politics; Imperialism; Nation-State and Nationalism; Organizations as Social Structures; State

REFERENCES AND SUGGESTED READINGS

Bodin, J. (1967 [1583]) *Six Books of the Commonwealth*. Barnes & Noble, New York.
Gross, L. (1948) The Peace of Westphalia, 1648–1948. *American Journal of International Law* 41: 20–41.
Krasner, S. D. (1999) *Sovereignty: Organized Hypocrisy*. Princeton University Press, Princeton.
March, J. G., with the assistance of Heath, C. (1994) *A Primer on Decision Making: How Decisions Happen*. Free Press, New York. (See pp. 57–60 for a discussion of the distinction between logics of consequences and logics of appropriateness.)
Skinner, Q. (1978) *The Foundations of Modern Political Thought*. Vol. 2: *The Age of Reformation*. Cambridge University Press, Cambridge, pp. 284–8.
Weiler, J. H. H. (1991) The Transformation of Europe. *Yale Law Journal* 100: 2479–980.

space

Leslie Wasson

Space has many faces: the bubble of individual space, the private spaces we maintain for our personal lives, the situated space defined for social interactions, the public spaces of wider social activity, and space as a scarce distributed resource in the organization of human social life. A sociological examination of space might look at one or more of these aspects. Although some theorists use the terms space and place interchangeably, they are not the same concept. A place is a social organization of space to which we have attached a particular meaning, and in which certain activities are more likely to occur. Space is the physical distance among the elements of which that place is constituted.

Hall's groundbreaking text *The Hidden Dimension* (1966) treats space as a sociological category of experience. For Hall, as for other well-known theorists of space such as LeFebve (1991), space is ordered by human custom and definition. The reverse is also observed: the design or definition of a space can affect the sort of activities and meanings that occur within it. Hall cites the transitory character of late industrial society, and ties it to conflict among the unspoken cultural assumptions about space, time, and other abstract concepts. His exploratory study raises many subtopics, such as proxemics, which is the individual's need for space between people in order to interact, and which varies by culture. He also suggests an examination of the city, wherein he delineates three kinds of spaces: fixed-feature, semifixed-feature, and informal spaces.

INDIVIDUAL SPACE OR PROXEMICS

Individuals carry an invisible bubble of space around them in order to feel comfortable interacting with others. The size of this cushion of space varies from one individual to another, and also varies across cultures. For example, a person in one of the Arabic cultures needs to get very close, about 1 foot away, in order to communicate effectively. In other cultures, about 4 feet is the acceptable communication distance. Most Americans need about 30 inches (Sommer 1969). The implication for diplomatic missions and everyday conversation is that others may be perceived as either too pushy or too cold and distant for reasons that have nothing to do with the content of their communications, and much to do with the amount of intervening space.

PRIVATE SPACE: HOMES

There is, according to conventional wisdom, no place like home. Home is the essential private space. Douglas (1991) suggests that homes need not be large, but that a home begins by bringing some space under control. She characterizes the private space of the home as being regarded with a mixture of resistance and nostalgia. The sociological interest in this construction of meaning, however, is that home as a private space may or may not be "fixed" in its location or attributes. As Levinson and Sparkes (2004) find in their study of Gypsy culture and space, when previously nomadic people leave their home on the road and start living in houses they may experience a loss of cultural identity.

Homes are domestic spaces. They reflect the interests, roles, and statuses of the men, women, children, and pets who are their inhabitants (Walker 2002). Walker provides the example of the space allocation and semiotic relations of the rooms in a Victorian house, and ties that architecture to the prevailing assumptions about age, gender, and social roles of the time.

SITUATED SPACE

Spaces of any kind are subject to a variety of social definitions. This variety is not infinite, but spaces can be flexible to different definitions of the situation and accompanying interactions. A small space beneath a kitchen table may be room for feet and legs, a cave or a castle to a young person, or the land of bountiful opportunity to the family dog. For the situational attributes of space, an excellent starting source would be Goffman (1959), who describes the settings and spaces of everyday life as stages for scripted social interactions. Lessons from the world of architecture and design indicate that more flexible spatial frames can lead to greater participation in sociability, as participants engage in the process of fine-tuning a space to a more transient situated meaning that suits their needs of the moment.

PUBLIC SPACES

Oldenburg (1999) demonstrates the importance of everyday community spaces to the construction of social relationships and meanings. His examination of the "third spaces" that people spend time in after home and work highlights the importance of semi-private and public spaces in providing meaning and continuity to human life. Historians and political scientists have examined the roles of taverns and coffee houses as community facilitators and sites for political discourse and organization. Milligan (1998) looks at what happens to the definition of a community place when it is moved into a new space. Community bonds forged in the crucible of one intense social space lose their integrity when those facilities and their limitations are no longer extant. Du Bois (2001) provides examples from his consulting work as an applied sociologist of space-sensitive designs that encourage social interaction in nursing homes, bars, and other public spaces.

HUMAN SPACES AND URBAN GEOGRAPHY

Although space as a form of social organization has been studied most thoroughly by human geographers (Tuan & Hoelscher 2001), their studies have had a significant influence on sociological research. Jones (2001) proposes that sociology could and should be done in concert with the design professions who create human habitations. He provides a rationale based on many classic sociological studies of cities, beginning with the Chicago School. Subsequent researchers and theorists have examined the relationship between behavior and environment in both directions, from the perspective that all social interactions are guided or constrained by their physical contexts, to the proposition that all physical designs occur partly as a result of social processes.

Many studies of the use of space in human communities focus on urban settings. Some research examines the contestation of the finite commodity of public space in crowded urban conditions, and the marginalization of some public spaces over others (Madanipour 2004). Also, some research indicates that the homogenization of public urban spaces discourages intercultural communication (Rahder 2004). This can be an unproductive use of scarce space in crowded and diverse city settings, as it silences the participation of some groups. Kitchin (1998) explores social responses to disability as a spatialized political economy combined with social constructivism in which spaces are defined to exclude certain kinds of people and limit their visibility.

Space in suburban communities can influence interaction patterns as well. Gans (1967) described the layout of space in the early Levittown communities and suggested how this kind of organization affected the interactions of the residents. Rural sociologists might include space, in the form of isolation and transportation issues, in research on dispersed households or agricultural communities. They might also examine the transformation of food-producing agricultural space into housing developments.

There may be a growing view of residential sprawl as a loss of open space and therefore a decline in the quality of life of a community. Such a perception can result in social movements and legislation attempting to limit uncontrolled or unplanned development (Romero & Liserio 2002). Communities with abundant space may negotiate a balance between the individual tendency to spread out more or less evenly over available space versus distinctions in the allocation of location, acreage, and square footage by social status. Communities with more limited space may experience competition and rising prices that place ownership or even tenancy beyond the means of a significant percentage of their population.

Related to the idea of urban or suburban space is the political theory concept of "civic spaces," which contribute to the exercise of shared governance in a democratic society. An example of this might be Speaker's Corner in Hyde Park in London. To complicate matters, occasionally a convergence will occur between civic or political spaces and sacred religious spaces, as in Jerusalem. Such a contest of meanings may result in conflict over the space and its use.

CONFLICT AND CONTROVERSY OVER SPACE

Competition over desirable space has a long history. Many wars have been fought over territory. Much of American history is a tale of expansion into larger spaces perceived as unoccupied or marginally tenanted by their native caretakers.

There is some ethnocentric bias in defining anything as "open" space. Spaces that are not already saturated with urban or suburban forms of development are assumed to be empty and therefore available. Some ecological writers in the popular press, for example, suggest that conserving land by evicting its indigenous residents is illogical and unethical, and also potentially disruptive of an existing ecological balance. With an ever-expanding global population and dwindling non-renewable resources, this competition over space, and the emergence of social movements aimed at preserving it, may increase.

Cyberspace may be viewed as a nearly infinite virtual commodity in the age of computers, but not all human interaction has the benefit of Internet access. Space may indeed be the final frontier, but perhaps not the space above us. In a rapidly globalizing world, we may find it more pressing to address the space around us and between us.

SEE ALSO: Chicago School; Cities in Europe; City Planning/Urban Design; Definition of the Situation; Dramaturgy; Goffman, Erving; Identity Theory; Lefebvre, Henri; Levittown; Place; Suburbs; Urban Space

REFERENCES AND SUGGESTED READINGS

Douglas, M. (1991) The Idea of a Home: A Kind of Space. *Social Research* 58(1): 287–307.

Du Bois, W. (2001) Design and Human Behavior: The Sociology of Architecture. In: Du Bois, W. & Dean Wright, R. (Eds.), *Applying Sociology: Making a Better World*. Allyn & Bacon, Boston, pp. 30–45.

Gans, H. J. (1967) *The Levittowners: Ways of Life and Politics in a New Suburban Community*. Pantheon Books, New York.

Goffman, E. (1959) *The Presentation of Self in Everyday Life*. Doubleday, Garden City, NY.

Hall, E. T. (1966) *The Hidden Dimension*. Anchor Doubleday, New York.

Jones, B. (2001) Doing Sociology With the Design Professions. In: Du Bois, W. & Dean Wright, R. (Eds.), *Applying Sociology: Making a Better World*. Allyn & Bacon, Boston, pp. 23–9.

Kitchin, R. (1998) "Out of Place," "Knowing One's Place": Space, Power, and the Exclusion of Disabled People. *Disability and Society* 13(3): 343–56.

LeFebvre, H. (1991) *The Production of Space*. Trans. D. Nicholson-Smith. Blackwell, Oxford.

Levinson, M. P. & Sparkes, A. C. (2004) Gypsy Identity and Orientations to Space. *Journal of Contemporary Ethnography* 33(6): 704–34.

Madanipour, A. (2004) Marginal Public Spaces in European Cities. *Journal of Urban Design* 9(3): 267–86.

Milligan, M. (1998) Interactional Past and Potential: The Social Construction of Place Attachment. *Symbolic Interaction* 21(1): 1–33.

Oldenburg, R. (1999) *The Great Good Place: Cafes, Coffee Shops, Bookstores, Bars, Hair Salons, and Other Hangouts at the Heart of a Community*, 3rd edn. Marlowe, New York.

Rahder, B. (2004) The Uncertain City: Making Space(s) for Difference. *Canadian Journal of Urban Research* 13 (supplement): 37–55.

Romero, F. S. & Liserio, A. (2002) Saving Open Spaces: Determinants of 1998 and 1999 "Antisprawl" Ballot Measures. *Social Science Quarterly* 83(1): 341–52.

Sommer, R. (1969) *The Behavioral Basis of Design*. Prentice-Hall, Englewood Cliffs, NJ.

Tuan, Y.-F. & Hoelscher, S. (2001) *Space and Place: The Perspective of Experience*. University of Minnesota Press, Minneapolis.

Walker, L. (2002) Home Making: An Architectural Perspective. *Signs: Journal of Women in Culture and Society* 27(3): 823–35.

spatial mismatch hypothesis

Ted Mouw

The spatial mismatch hypothesis argues that the movement of jobs away from central city areas, combined with constraints on geographic mobility imposed by continued residential segregation, limits the employment prospects of inner-city minorities. The basic story is straightforward: as jobs decentralize to the suburbs or beyond, black workers find it difficult to move to where the jobs are because of racial residential segregation, resulting in a "mismatch" between the jobs and black workers that raises unemployment and/or lowers wages. The spatial mismatch hypothesis has been widely discussed since it was first proposed in the late 1960s as an explanation for black–white differences in unemployment rates. At the same time, there are longstanding and unresolved debates in the literature regarding the magnitude of the effect that it has on racial differences in unemployment and wages.

John Kain (1968) was the first to attempt to empirically test the spatial mismatch hypothesis. He used data on employment location from the 1950s to divide Detroit and Chicago into 98 workplace areas. He then regressed the share of black employment in the workplace area on the share of the population and the spatial distance from the black ghetto area and found a strong relationship between black employment share and distance from the ghetto. He estimated that the geographic mismatch between workers and jobs resulted in a loss of about 22,000 jobs for Chicago and 9,000 for Detroit.

Despite changes in residential segregation and job decentralization since Kain's initial formulation, the basic story behind the spatial mismatch hypothesis is still relevant today. Residential segregation between blacks and whites has declined slowly over the past two decades, but is still high, suggesting that in many metropolitan areas the geographic mobility of black workers is constrained. The evidence on employment decentralization suggests that the general trend over the past several decades has been one of job loss and decentralization in large urban areas as jobs moved toward the suburbs or left the metropolitan area entirely. John Kasarda (1995) shows that between 1980 and 1990, employment growth was much higher in suburban counties of metropolitan areas than in their central cities. Recent data indicate that this pattern held during the economic boom of the 1990s; between 1992 and 1997, for example, central cities experienced an increase in employment of 8.5 percent, compared to 17.8 percent in their suburbs. Steven Raphael and Michael Stoll (2002) calculate segregation indices between workers and jobs using data on population and employment by zip codes and argue that the mismatch between black workers and jobs declined slightly during the 1990s, but that blacks are still significantly more isolated from employment than whites.

CRITIQUE

In a prominent critique of the spatial mismatch hypothesis, David Ellwood (1986) tests the effect of average commuting time on youth (ages 16–21) unemployment in Chicago. He finds little effect of commuting time on neighborhood unemployment rates, and concludes that it is "race not space" that is of central importance in understanding the high unemployment rate of black workers.

Keith Ihlanfeldt and David Sjoquist (1990) argue that Ellwood's results are misleading because of the small sample sizes that he used to calculate neighborhood commuting times and because he did not estimate separate equations for black and white workers. They estimate the effect of average travel time on youth unemployment using micro-level census data for Philadelphia, Chicago, and Los Angeles, and find results consistent with the spatial mismatch hypothesis.

A one standard deviation increase in average commuting time for black youth in Philadelphia (3.7 minutes) is associated with a predicted reduction of employment rates of 4 to 6.3 percentage points. Overall, Ihlanfeldt and Sjoquist estimate that spatial job accessibility explains about 33–39 percent of the racial difference in unemployment among 16- to 19-year-olds who are not enrolled in school.

In general, most tests of the spatial mismatch hypothesis use neighborhood black unemployment rates as the dependent variable and some measure of distance to jobs as the central independent variable. The empirical question is whether neighborhoods with better spatial access to employment have lower unemployment rates for black workers. Two important difficulties in assessing the magnitude of the spatial mismatch effect, however, are the measurement of the spatial proximity of employment and the problem of endogeneity posed by selective migration.

THE MEASUREMENT OF EMPLOYMENT PROXIMITY

In order to calculate spatial job proximity, one needs to measure how far the average job seeker in each neighborhood has to travel to find employment opportunities. Recent research has done this in two ways. A number of studies use the average travel time for employed black workers in each neighborhood as a measure of spatial accessibility. A problem with this is that an unemployed person's travel time may be longer because nearby jobs may already be filled with local workers. An alternative is to use data on the spatial location of jobs and calculate the number of "nearby" jobs for each neighborhood. There are two measurement difficulties with this approach. First, one must take the number of competing workers into account. Hence, the jobs to workers ratio is a better measure of job availability. Second, one has to take the two-dimensional spatial data on the location of jobs and workers and transform it into a measure of job accessibility. Raphael (1998) and Ted Mouw (2000) both borrow the "gravity model" of commuting behavior from the transportation literature to calculate spatially weighted indices of job accessibility (as well as the size of the competing labor force), where "near" jobs are given more weight than "far" jobs based on the analysis of actual commuting behavior. Using data from the San Francisco metropolitan area, Raphael (1998) calculates changes in the proximity to jobs between 1980 and 1990 and controls for the size of the competing labor supply. In regressions of youth unemployment rates that combine both black and white workers, Raphael estimates that changes in job proximity explain about 29 percent of the racial gap in unemployment. Nonetheless, when he estimates these models separately by race, job proximity is statistically insignificant for black workers, reflecting a small sample size (N = 367).

Mouw (2000) estimates a "fixed effects" model of the spatial mismatch hypothesis by calculating changes in job proximity and adult unemployment rates between 1980 and 1990 in Detroit and Chicago. Data on job location from the 1980 and 1990 Census Transportation Planning Packages (CTPP) are used to calculate spatial measures of job proximity. The data document the substantial decentralization of employment that occurred during the 1980s in Detroit; within a 10-mile radius around the average black worker's home there was a net loss of about 100,000 jobs between 1980 and 1990.

ENDOGENEITY

In addition to the problem of calculating job access, estimates of the spatial mismatch hypothesis may be biased if workers sort themselves into different neighborhoods based on unobserved characteristics that affect labor market outcomes. If housing prices and neighborhood quality tend to increase with distance from the city center, then more "successful" workers may end up living closer to suburban areas of employment growth. To the degree that this is true, proximity to regions of suburban job growth may be the result of labor market outcomes rather than the cause. Recent research on the spatial mismatch hypothesis has studied unemployment of teenagers rather than adults as a way to get around this problem of endogeneity. If teenagers live at home, then their residential location might be considered an exogenous factor uncorrelated with unobserved

labor market factors that would affect their ability to get a job. Even in this case, however, the decision of a teenager to work full-time instead of being in school is probably correlated with his or her parents' socioeconomic status, and hence this research is not immune to questions about endogeneity. Examples of this approach are Ihlanfeldt and Sjoquist (1990) and Raphael (1998).

An alternative approach is to study changes over time. As mentioned above, Mouw (2000) used "fixed effects" models of changes in neighborhood unemployment and job proximity between 1980 and 1990. Provided neighborhood selectivity – i.e., the tendency for workers to sort themselves into neighborhoods on the basis of their labor force characteristics – has remained constant over the time period, fixed effects models represent an alternative way to get around the problem of endogeneity in residential location. Based on his results, Mouw concluded that a 10 percent drop in job proximity would result in an increase in the black unemployment rate of 5.6 percentage points in Detroit and 2.9 percentage points in Chicago.

In another approach to the problem of endogeneity, Jefferey Zax (1991) and Zax and Kain (1996) studied the effect of a single firm's decision to move from downtown Detroit to the suburbs, about 8 miles away. The advantage of studying a single firm is that it represents a "natural experiment" to observe the effect of distance on employment. By studying employment records for racial differences in quit rates, Zax and Kain (1996) concluded that the resulting spatial mismatch between the location of the firm and the residences of their black workers forced about 11 percent of the black workers to quit after the relocation. While this research is persuasive, studies of a single firm cannot assess the magnitude of job decentralization as a whole or follow the employment outcomes of those workers who quit the firm.

Recent quasi-experimental evidence from government-funded housing programs, the Gautreaux program and Moving to Opportunity (MTO), has been used to assess the spatial mismatch hypothesis. In both of these programs, inner-city black residents were given housing vouchers to allow them to move to different neighborhoods in their metropolitan area. In the Gautreaux program, voucher recipients were randomly assigned to either suburban or urban neighborhoods in Chicago. James Rosenbaum (1995) showed that, in the Gautreaux program, respondents who moved to suburban neighborhoods had higher post-move employment rates than urban movers. Nonetheless, the suburban movers did not have significantly higher employment rates than before they moved (64.3 percent employed pre-move and 63.8 percent employed post-move; see Rosenbaum 1995: 237). The MTO program is a large-scale housing mobility experiment conducted in five cities. Families were randomly assigned to an "experimental" group and offered vouchers to live in a low-poverty neighborhood, a "Section 8" group that was given vouchers with no geographic restrictions, and a control group that did not receive vouchers. Five years after random assignment, there is no statistically significant difference in employment rates or earnings between the experimental and control groups. Nonetheless, Jeffery Kling et al. note that these MTO results do not directly contradict the spatial mismatch hypothesis, as an analysis of employment growth by zip code suggests that the experimental group was not living in regions of higher job growth than the control group (employment in the control group zip codes increased by 5 percent compared to 4.9 percent in experimental group zip codes).

Overall, research during the past decade, with better measurement and methodological approaches than earlier research, has found substantial evidence to support the spatial mismatch hypothesis. Ihlanfeldt and Sjoquist (1998), for example, found that 21 of the 28 studies they reviewed that were published between 1992 and 1997 reported findings consistent with the spatial mismatch hypothesis. Nonetheless, the modest size of the effects in most studies indicates that the spatial mismatch hypothesis cannot be the only explanation of the black–white employment gap. Individual cities may differ greatly in their degree of "spatial mismatch" between workers and jobs, and even in Detroit, which because of high levels of racial residential segregation and job loss would seem to be the poster child for the mismatch hypothesis, a recent empirical estimate (Mouw 2000) suggests that the large-scale decentralization of employment during the 1980s explained no more than 30 percent of the 1990 racial gap in unemployment rates.

SEE ALSO: Discrimination; Economic Geography; Exurbia; Gentrification; Hypersegregation; Labor Markets; Race; Residential Segregation; Rustbelt

REFERENCES AND SUGGESTED READINGS

Ellwood, D. T. (1986) The Spatial Mismatch Hypothesis: Are There Teenage Jobs Missing in the Ghetto? In: Freeman, R. B. & Holzer, H. J. (Eds.), *The Black Youth Employment Crisis*. University of Chicago Press, Chicago, pp. 147–90.

Fernandez, R. (1994) Race, Space, and Job Accessibility: Evidence from a Plant Relocation. *Economic Geography* 70: 390–416.

Fernandez, R. & Su, C. (2004) Space in the Study of Labor Markets. *Annual Review of Sociology* 30: 545–69.

Holzer, H. J. (1991) The Spatial Mismatch Hypothesis: What Has the Evidence Shown. *Urban Studies* 28: 105–22.

Ihlanfeldt, K. & Sjoquist, D. L. (1990) Job Accessibility and Racial Differences in Youth Employment Rates. *American Economic Review* 80: 267–76.

Ihlanfeldt, K. & Sjoquist, D. L. (1998) The Spatial Mismatch Hypothesis: A Review of Recent Studies and Their Implications for Welfare Reform. *Housing Policy Debate* 9: 849–92.

Kain, J. F. (1968) Housing Segregation, Negro Employment, and Metropolitan Decentralization. *Quarterly Journal of Economics* 82: 165–97.

Kain, J. F. (1992) The Spatial Mismatch Hypothesis: Three Decades Later. *Housing Policy Debate* 2: 371–460.

Kasarda, J. (1995) Industrial Restructuring and the Changing Location of Jobs. In: Farley, R. (Ed.), *State of the Union: America in the 1990s*. Russell Sage Foundation, New York, pp. 215–67.

Kling, J. R., Liebman, J. B., Katz, L. F., & Sanbonmatsu, L. (2004) Moving to Opportunity and Tranquility: Neighborhood Effects on Adult Economic Self-Sufficiency and Health from a Randomized Housing Voucher Experiment.

Mouw, T. (2000) Job Relocation and the Racial Gap in Unemployment in Detroit and Chicago, 1980–1990. *American Sociological Review* 65(5): 730–53.

Raphael, S. (1998) The Spatial Mismatch Hypothesis and Black Youth Joblessness: Evidence From the San Francisco Bay Area. *Journal of Urban Economics*.

Raphael, S. & Stoll, M. A. (2002) Modest Progress: The Narrowing Spatial Mismatch Between Blacks and Jobs in the 1990s. In: *The Brookings Institution Living Census Series*. Brookings Institution, Washington, DC.

Rosenbaum, J. E. (1995) Changing the Geography of Opportunity by Expanding Residential Choice: Lessons from the Gautreaux Program. *Housing Policy Debate* 6.

Zax, J. S. (1991) The Substitution Between Moves and Quits. *Economic Journal* 101: 1510–21.

Zax, J. S. & Kain, J. F. (1996) Moving to the Suburbs: Do Relocating Companies Leave Their Black Employees Behind? *Journal of Labor Economics* 14: 472–504.

spatial relationships

Martin Hess

Traditionally, the analysis of spatial relationships has been considered to be the domain of geography, whereas the academic discipline of sociology was concerned about the relationships between societies and social actors. Following a period of regional geography approaches in the first half of the twentieth century that had emphasized territorial differentiation as being at the core of human geography, this view has been subsequently contested. Rather than space being conceived of as a Kantian a priori for human existence and action (absolute space), the focus of many human geographers began to shift towards the analysis of spatial relationships between objects and events, thus introducing the concept of relative space.

During the 1960s and 1970s this concept underpinned an emerging strand of spatial science studies, with mathematical space superseding physical space to the extent that more and more human geographers became concerned about the "spatial fetishism" of the discipline (Gregory 2000). This is not to say that social interaction never has been a subject of geographical enquiry. But the prevalent tendency of treating social relationships as purely spatial relationships at the time was increasingly criticized, calling for a different ontology of space as being socially constructed and shaped by human practices (relational space).

As an increasing number of human geographers have adopted such a social science perspective, at the same time there has been an increasing awareness among sociologists of the spatiality of social structures and social action, to the extent that it sometimes has been called the spatial turn in social sciences. This alleged spatial turn and the related dialogue between sociology and geography recently have become most pronounced in the subdisciplines of economic sociology and economic geography (Grabher 2006); however, according to commentators from both sides there still is too little serious engagement in sociology with issues of space and place and how they shape and are shaped by social interaction (Tickamyer 2000; Peck 2005).

When analyzing spatial relationships, we need to make a distinction between different aspects of the notion of space as discussed above. On the one hand, space is seen as an arena in which social interaction takes place. On the other hand, space has to be conceived of as being relational, and therefore is much more than a mere "container" for human activities (Pries 2005). The analogy of a football match may serve as a good illustration of these two conceptualizations: while a football match is played out on a pitch within a confined, Eucledian space (the spatial "container"), it ultimately is the spatial relations of players on both sides and their interactions that define the match and its outcome.

Among social theorists, Anthony Giddens is one of the relatively few academics in sociology to have theorized space (see Giddens 1984). For example, Giddens (1990) argued that in premodern times the spatiality of social relations was very much place-bound, as well as time and space being linked together in particular places. With the decoupling of time and space in the modern age, Giddens argues, space and place have become separated as social interaction is now possible through spatial relations beyond the place or locality. One of the consequences of modernity – highlighted by what has become the catchword of globalization –is thus the dislocation or disembedding of spatial relationships.

The notion of embeddedness is very often at the center of debates about the relationships between sociology and geography, between social and economic relations and spatial relations

(Peck 2005; Grabher 2006). Based on Karl Polanyi's seminal work about the relationships between markets and societies, embeddness has become a key concept in some social sciences, particularly through the work of American economic sociologist Mark Granovetter. Unlike the schools of thought that apply a methodological individualism approach, Granovetter (1985) conceptualizes economic action as being embedded in a set of ongoing social relations. This relational view of human action – albeit silent on the spatial nature of these social relationships – has been adopted by geographers who have used it in particular at the local and regional scale of analysis.

This emphasis of localized social interaction and embeddedness is mirrored in other branches of social science (e.g., the sociologies of everyday life), where social relations are assumed to be based on face-to-face contact and thus spatial proximity is paramount. However, such a reading of locally embedded social relationships runs the risk of becoming an over-territorialized concept by privileging one geographical scale over others (Hess 2004). This is problematic for a number of reasons. First, it tends to create a false dichotomy of place and space, where social interaction is either "in here" (the place) or out there (the space). Second, it does not fully recognize the multi-scalarity of sociospatial relations. Third, it often fails to acknowledge the importance of embedded ties beyond the locale.

As Massey (2004) rightly observes, in academic as well as in policy discourses place is considered to be more "real," more "grounded," and thus often seen as much more meaningful than space, which denotes the outside: an abstract spatiality outside place. Such a perceived antagonism of place vs. space often comes hand in hand with questions of power and identity, whereby the latter is often seen as being created through spatial relations on the local level, and, according to Massey, through a process of "othering" – negatively defining local identity by regarding others (non-locals) as outsiders. Likewise, place is often regarded as powerless in a globalized world, where power is overwhelmingly exercised outside the place, in a global arena.

A relational view of sociospatial interaction, however, will take seriously the multiple forms of identity that characterize individuals and communities, as becomes clear by – for instance – having a look at global cities like London. There, as elsewhere, most identities are shaped simultaneously by local–non-local social relations, creating relational spaces of belonging as in the case of transnational communities. Likewise, places are by no means powerless vis-à-vis global actors out there, but part of much wider networks of power within which a locale is not automatically condemned to passivity. Spatial relations across the scalar spectrum thus require an understanding of spatial scale not as something mutually exclusive or separable like the different shells of a Russian doll, but as intrinsically interwoven.

As we have seen, space is an integral conceptual part in the analysis of social relations. And over the last few years there was certainly progress in the development of more elaborate multi-scale or multi-level concepts, the lack of which has recently been criticized by Tickamyer (2000). A case in point is the emergence of work in social sciences that is informed by actor-network theory (ANT). Although ANT is too critical of concepts that are concerned with social relations in space and time at the expense of non-human agents, it has nevertheless contributed to a less deterministic analysis of spatial relationships, applying an understanding of space as topological stratifications and linking time and space in dynamic, heterogeneous relations (Hess 2004). In their theorization of space, Mol and Law (1994) develop a threefold typology of space and spatial relations, echoing previous discussions of multi-scalarity and multiplicity: regions, networks, and fluid spaces. In their work there is still the acknowledgment of territories as regions in which objects are clustered together and social relations may be concentrated. These regions, however, are crisscrossed by networks as topological spaces, where distance is a function of social and cultural relationships rather than designating physical proximity. Finally, there are fluid spaces, characterized by "liquid continuity" and constituted by mobile agents (Hess 2004).

The nature of spatial relationships and how to conceptualize them are still subject to ongoing debates in human geography. But it seems that their analysis is no longer considered to be the sole domain of this academic discipline, with sociology and economics, among others, sharing for instance an interest in questions about spatial inequality that has long been at the core of much research, yet with an often unsatisfying or insufficient reflection on the spatiality of social interaction and the social construction of spatial relations (Gregory & Urry 1985). As it is, there is still much work left to do within and beyond academic disciplines if we want to improve our understanding of how space is folded into social relations through human practices and interactions (Harvey 1996).

SEE ALSO: Actor-Network Theory; Community; Economic Geography; Glocalization; Identity Politics/Relational Politics; Networks; Place; Space; Time-Space

REFERENCES AND SUGGESTED READINGS

Dicken, P., Kelly, P., Olds, K., & Yeung, H. W. (2001) Chains and Networks, Territories and Scales: Towards an Analytical Framework for the Global Economy. *Global Networks* 1(2): 89–112.

Giddens, A. (1984) *The Constitution of Society*. Polity Press, Cambridge.

Giddens, A. (1990) *The Consequences of Modernity*. Polity Press, Cambridge.

Grabher, G. (2006) Trading Routes, Bypasses, and Risky Intersections: Mapping the Travels of "Networks" between Economic Sociology and Economic Geography. *Progress in Human Geography* 30.

Granovetter, M. (1985) Economic Action and Social Structure: The Problem of Embeddedness. *American Journal of Sociology* 91(3): 481–510.

Gregory, D. (2000) Space, Human Geography and. In: Johnston, R. et al. (Eds.), *The Dictionary of Human Geography*, Blackwell, Oxford, pp. 767–73.

Gregory, D. & Urry, J. (Eds.) (1985) *Social Relations and Spatial Structures*. Macmillan, London.

Harvey, D. (1996) *Justice, Nature and the Geography of Difference*. Blackwell, Oxford.

Hess, M. (2004) "Spatial" Relationships? Towards a Reconceptualization of Embeddedness. *Progress in Human Geography* 28(2): 165–86.

Massey, D. (2004) Geographies of Responsibility. *Geografiska Annaler* 86(B1): 5–18.

Mol, A. & Law, J. (1994) Regions, Networks and Fluids: Anaemia and Social Topology. *Social Studies of Science* 24: 641–71.

Peck, J. A. (2005) Economic Sociologies in Space. *Economic Geography* 81(2): 129–75.

Pries, L. (2005) Configurations of Geographic and Societal Spaces: A Sociological Proposal between "Methodological Nationalism" and the "Space of Flows. *Global Networks* 5(2): 167–90.

Tickamyer, A. R. (2000) Space Matters! Spatial Inequality in Future Sociology. *Contemporary Sociology* 29(6): 805–13.

speaking truth to power: science and policy

Javier Lezaun

"Speaking truth to power" refers to the belief that scientists, unimpeded by economic self-interest or partisan bias, will deliver honest and often uncomfortable truths to those in positions of power.

It is the foundational claim of the sociology of science that only certain types of social structure enable scientists – or, rather, science as a social institution – to reach the truth and present it with due authority. In a series of pioneering articles, written at a time when science was actively enlisted in the service of the state and made subservient to totalitarian projects, Robert K. Merton (1938, 1942) argued that a self-governed science was most congenial to the aims and principles of a free society, and that this autonomy was best guaranteed by the distinctive "ethos" of its practitioners, which he characterized by the norms of universalism, communitarism, disinterestedness, and organized skepticism. Capable of regulating itself through these normative principles, science was entitled to demand freedom from external influences and pursue unhampered the acquisition of fundamental knowledge.

Merton's depiction of a self-regulating science as the pillar of a democratic society and the best guarantee of uninterrupted scientific and technological progress reinforced the case of those scientists and politicians who, in the aftermath of World War II, believed that the state should continue its active support of science but ought to leave the management of resources and the setting of research agendas to the scientific community. A peculiar "social contract" between

science and the state was established following
the demobilization of science. This consensus
was embedded in new institutions, like the
National Science Foundation, through which
government continued to provide enormous
amounts of funding for basic scientific research,
conducted mostly in academic institutions, but
abstained from intervening directly in the setting
of research priorities or the evaluation of the
knowledge being created.

Thus, the model of science as a community
driven by an ethos of disinterestedness, organized skepticism, and universalism allowed the
drawing of a sharp boundary between science
and the state. It is this balance of separation
and mutual dependency between science and
politics that has become the central object of
investigation of the sociology of science ever
since.

Starting in the 1970s, sociologists and historians began to explore more closely the historical
origins of the "ethos of science" and to question
the degree to which it informed the actual practice of science. Studies of both the paradigmatic
American case (Price 1965) and the contrasting
experience of totalitarian regimes shed light on
the historical imbrications of science and political power. These works were either skeptical of
the idea of an autonomous science, driven solely
by the curiosity of its practitioners, or at least
put this image in a historical and comparative
context. They expressed an uneasiness over the
subjugation of science to the objectives of its
patrons and the emergence of the infamous
"military-industrial-scientific complex." The
image of a "basic," or "pure," science, innocent
and deaf to the interests of power and in a
position to provide useful advice to policymakers, appeared increasingly untenable, and
sociologists began to question the demarcations
of the scientific and political realms.

In other words, what *kind* of truth does
science speak to power, and how does its close
engagement with state and market affect the
scientific community? Detailed analyses of
the role of scientific and technical expertise in
policy debates highlighted the inability of
science to bring technical closure to policy discussions, and showed how the truths that
science speaks to power are often shaped and
informed by the powers it hopes to speak to.
The work of Dorothy Nelkin (1979) and others

showed that groups of scientists, committed
from the start to different policy options rather
than disinterestedly searching for the independent truth, used their expertise to shore up their
positions and to challenge alternative views that
were themselves supported by equally confrontational scientific advocates. The scientification
of policy leads to an intensification of differences rather than to their smooth resolution.

Similarly, Collingridge and Reeve (1986)
showed how the desire to influence policy,
and the consequent obligation to address the
concerns and interests of policymakers, brings
science to violate the very conditions – autonomy, clear disciplinary boundaries, and a low
level of criticism of scientific claims – on which
its ability to produce clear answers and unquestioned consensus is predicated. The result is
almost paradoxical: to speak truth to power,
science must abandon many of the normative
and institutional conditions that protect its
autonomy and efficiency. Science cannot deliver consensus when it is oriented toward questions posed by external actors, and on terms
defined by those actors, and its legitimacy
suffers as a consequence.

The intimacy of science and politics gives rise
to forms of knowledge production and validation that differ significantly from the model
offered by Mertonian sociology. Terms such
as "regulatory science," "trans-science," or
"mandated science" convey the sense in which
science is increasingly a hybrid product, constituted by the constraints of political and economic agendas; they also express a desire to
distinguish these hybrids from the paradigmatic
"pure" or "basic" science, the kind of unen-
cumbered truth-finding enterprise from which
the social authority of science still derives. This
"boundary work," through which science shores
up its autonomy and authority, has been a constant theme in the sociology of science (Jasanoff
1987; Guston 1999). In a similar vein, science's
ability to provide public truths to powerful institutions becomes more a matter of rhetoric and
"staging" (Hilgartner 2000) than of revealing
self-evident truths.

When science speaks truth to power, then, it
often has to answer the questions that power
poses to it, and the truths it can speak are of a
particular kind – they are a form of knowledge
deeply attuned to the logic and demands of the

policymaking process. The complexity of political issues, most conspicuously in the regulatory arena, where matters of fact and technical assessment are inextricably linked to political and societal choices, turns science into a more complex, less pure, and less autonomous social institution. Some may think this threatens its integrity; others believe that it enriches it, and reintegrates science into the fabric of politics.

SEE ALSO: Big Science and Collective Research; Controversy Studies; Expertise, "Scientification," and the Authority of Science; Military Research and Science and War; Science/Non-Science and Boundary Work; Scientific Norms/Counternorms

REFERENCES AND SUGGESTED READINGS

Collingridge, D. & Reeve, C. (1986) *Science Speaks Truth to Power: The Role of Experts in Policy Making*. Frances Pinter, London.
Guston, D. (1999) Stabilizing the Boundary between US Politics and Science. *Social Studies of Science* 29: 87–112.
Hilgartner, S. (2000) *Science on Stage: Expert Advice as Public Drama*. Stanford University Press, Stanford.
Jasanoff, S. (1987) Contested Boundaries in Policy-Relevant Science. *Social Studies of Science* 17: 195–230.
Merton, R. K. (1973) "Science and the Social Order" (1938) and "The Normative Structure of Science" (1942). In: *The Sociology of Science: Theoretical and Empirical Investigations*. University of Chicago Press, Chicago.
Nelkin, D. (Ed.) (1979) *Controversy: Politics of Technical Decision*. Sage, Beverly Hills.
Price, D. K. (1965) *The Scientific State*. Harvard University Press, Cambridge, MA.

Species-Being

Rob Beamish

Species-Being (*Gattungswesen*), a controversial Feuerbachian-inspired term refashioned in Marx's critique of Hegel's idealist philosophy, is central to Marx's conception of alienation.

Hegel had argued the form and substance of knowledge developed historically. The conscious mind (*Geist*) initially experiences reality as external and separate; true knowledge seems to reside in that alien reality. Exploring that world, consciousness becomes self-consciousness as mind progressively grasps the complex, dialectical subject/object basis of knowledge. An increasingly comprehensive intellectual Spirit (*Geist*) emerges, culminating in an Absolute form. Overcoming the original perception of separation – alienation – Mind's full potential is actualized in grasping the totality of Absolute Being.

Hegel's philosophy buttressed nineteenth-century Prussia's narrow, intolerant state. Ludwig Feuerbach's *Essence of Christianity* – a democratically inspired critique of the supreme religious Absolute – challenged the state's Hegelian foundation. In religion, the powers of humankind are alienated from it, extrapolated, made infinite, and then impose themselves as an Absolute Being. Feuerbach's anthropologically based critique of theology undermined idealism by emphasizing humankind's material Being as a species (*Gattungswesen*) – the real, existent, identifiable, characteristics of humankind that religion hypostatized.

Species-Being in Marx emanates from his critiques of Hegel and Feuerbach. Following Feuerbach, Marx began with real, active humans, but "inverting" Hegel's idealism produced a dramatically different conception of Species-Being. Hegel, Marx (1975) argued, "grasped the self-creation of humankind as a process, objectification as loss of object [*Vergegenständlichung als Entgegenständlichung*], as alienation [*Entäußerung*] alienatation." Hegel "grasped the essence of labor and objective [*gegenständlichen*] humankind," but only as mental (*geistige*) labor.

For Marx, humankind was a materially active, social being, compelled to produce (labor) in order to exist. Production (labor) – the ontological basis to praxis – changes and develops humankind's knowledge, conditions of being, and social arrangements. Labor, the material mediation of subject and object, is the ontological basis for humankind's mental, creative, social, and material development. This is humankind's Species-Essence. Species-Being is not a set of fixed natural characteristics – our species' Being is materially active, interactive, and creative, producing our material life, thereby changing our circumstances.

Mind developed through intellectual subject/object mediation with Hegel; with Marx, human life develops in the material practice of subject/object mediation – labor. Humankind's Species-Essence or Being is the praxis of such development.

Under conditions of private property, humankind's fundamental Species-Being – its creative laboring activity – is dominated by an external reality. Rather than developing workers, the externalization process creates products, a process, and a system that confronts and stultifies their physical, emotional, social, and political development. Labor's alienated products confront the producers and oppose them. Only by overturning private property can humankind's Species-Being fully flourish in freedom.

SEE ALSO: Alienation; Feuerbach, Ludwig; Hegel, G. W. F.; Labor; Marx, Karl; Praxis

REFERENCES AND SUGGESTED READINGS

Avineri, S. (1968) *The Social and Political Thought of Karl Marx*. Cambridge University Press, Cambridge.

Gould, C. (1978) *Marx's Social Ontology*, MIT Press, Cambridge, MA.

Hegel, G. W. F. (1977) *Phenomenology of Spirit*. Trans. A. Miller. Clarendon Press, Oxford.

Marx, K. (1975) Economic and Philosophical Manuscripts. Trans. G. Benton. In: *Karl Marx: Early Writings*. Penguin, London, pp. 279–400.

Spencer, Herbert (1820–1903)

Jonathan H. Turner

Herbert Spencer was the most widely read sociologist of the nineteenth century, but by the second decade of the twentieth century his influence had declined dramatically, prompting Talcott Parsons in 1937 to ask "who now reads Spencer?" Today, very few sociologists read Spencer, who, through sociology's biased eyeglasses, is seen as a political conservative and as a crude functionalist. This contemporary conception of Spencer is not only incorrect but, more fundamentally, it also keeps present-day sociologists from realizing the power of Spencer's ideas. The other classical figures in sociology have been canonized, with each generation of sociologists continuing to read the canon with the same dedication as biblical scholars. In contrast, Spencer is ignored, to the detriment of the cumulative sociological theory (Turner 1985). Nowhere is Spencer's genius more evident than in the topic of social change. Spencer developed several models of social change. One is a stage model of societal evolution from simple to complex forms; another is a dialectical model emphasizing the transformative effects inherent in the centralization and decentralization of political power; still another explores "selection" as a force behind social change; and a final model deals with the rise and fall of empires and interstate systems.

Before reviewing these models, it is wise to deal with the functionalism that runs through Spencer's sociology. Spencer argued that all superorganic systems composed of relations among organisms must address three fundamental problems: *operation* or the need to secure resources (production) and to generate new members (reproduction); *regulation* or the coordination and control of system units through power and cultural symbols; and *distribution* or the movement of resources, commodities, people, and information. These three "functional requisites" are critical to understanding all of Spencer's sociology, as we will come to appreciate.

THE STAGE MODEL OF SOCIETAL EVOLUTION

Like all functional theorists, Spencer saw differentiation as a master social process as societies move from simple to complex forms. As populations grow, structural differentiation ensues in order to support the larger "social mass" (an ideal that Spencer first developed in *The Principles of Biology*, 1864–7). Structural differentiation occurs along three axes corresponding to the functional requisites: operation (production and reproduction), regulation, and distribution. The first node of differentiation is between new kinds of productive and reproductive structures, on the one side, and regulative structures revolving around the consolidation and centralization of power. Later, as differentiation continues, new kinds of distributive structures (markets and infrastructures for transportation and communication) emerge. For Spencer, then, long-term evolution revolves around continued differentiation of structures within each of the axes and between these three axes. In the 2,000-plus pages of *The Principles of Sociology* (1874–96), Spencer provides a wealth of empirical detail (taken from his monumental 16-volume *Descriptive Sociology*) in describing each stage of evolution. He denotes each stage in terms of the degree of "compounding" from simple to more complex societal formations: simple without political leaders (e.g., hunting and gathering); simple with political leaders (Big Man hunting and gathering as well as horticultural systems); double compound (agrarian societies); and treble compound (industrial societies). If he had lived through the twentieth century, he would have no doubt described post-industrial societies as the new level of compounding. Spencer's description of these stages of evolution is by far the most sophisticated of the nineteenth century, and it certainly rivals any description on the stages of societal evolution in the twentieth and twenty-first centuries. This stage model is largely descriptive, but evolutionary stages are all driven by dynamics outlined in Spencer's other models of social change.

THE DIALECTICAL MODEL OF SOCIAL CHANGE

Probably the most important pages in *The Principles of Sociology* are those devoted to the analysis of "militant" and "industrial" societies. Spencer made this distinction in order to examine the dynamics of power (as it is consolidated and centralized along the regulative axis of differentiation); and this analysis of power is woven throughout the pages of *The Principles of Sociology*. In fact, Spencer is a theorist of power more than any other topic – an emphasis that goes against the perception of Spencer as a stage-model functionalist. For Spencer, once power emerges in human societies at *any* stage of evolution, it reveals an inherent dialectic between highly centralized (militant) and more decentralized (industrial) forms. There is, Spencer argued, a tendency for systems with highly centralized power to sow the seeds for their transformation to a more decentralized profile, and conversely, decentralized political systems establish the conditions for the centralization of power. Societies thus cycle between centralized and decentralized patterns of political power. Let us start with a society revealing centralized power (militant). Power in such systems is used to regulate operative (production and reproduction processes) and distributive structures to a very high degree, while at the same time increasing the level of inequality as elites with power usurp resources for their own privilege and for sustaining the administrative and coercive structures necessary for tight control of a population. Such regulation generates problems of productive stagnation and market contraction, as well as resentments over growing inequality. The result is for liberal ideologies stressing freedom from such control to emerge, leading actors involved in production, reproduction, and distribution as well as those in lower social classes to exert political pressure for less regulation and redistribution of elite privilege. The end result is a more decentralized political system that, in turn, sets into motion its own set of dialectical forces. Decentralized power allows for increased differentiation within and between the operative and distributive axes, but as this differentiation occurs, problems of coordination, control, and conflict escalate, leading to the formation of conservative ideologies emphasizing the need to control the emerging chaos; and eventually these ideological pressures and the social movements that they inspire cause the consolidation and centralization of power which, over time, will set into motion pressures for decentralization of power. Thus, long before Vilfredo Pareto's analysis of the circulation of elites, Spencer had developed a far more sophisticated model of dialectical change.

SELECTION AS A TRANSFORMATIVE DYNAMIC

Nine years before Darwin published *On The Origin of Species*, Spencer (1851) coined the famous phrase "survival of the fittest," and unfortunately his sociology has been tainted by this view of human social organization. But a sympathetic reading of Spencer leads to a more favorable view of what this phrase means in his sociological reasoning. For Spencer, the social world is driven by social selection within and between societies. When populations grow, competition for resources increases, with the more fit securing resources and the less fit dying out or finding new resource niches. This is the argument that Durkheim would adopt 20 years later in *The Division of Labor in Society* (1893); and of course, it is the basic point of emphasis in all contemporary theories of human ecology. Spencer also used this phrase to describe war between societies. Indeed, Spencer viewed war as a powerful force in the evolution of societies from simple to complex forms. He argued that the more complex and differentiated society typically wins a war, absorbing the conquered society (often repressively). Yet, with each round of conquest of the simpler society by the more complex, all human societies become more differentiated. Thus, an important force behind the long-term trend toward differentiation of societies has been war and conquest of the simple by the more complex.

Spencer also developed another view of selection as a transformative force. For Spencer, populations often encounter problems of adaptation that require the invention of new structures. For example, if a population grows, it requires new kinds of productive and regulative structures to feed and control the larger population, but if such structures cannot be developed, a society "dissolves" or "de-evolves." Here, then, is another kind of selection in which new organizational problems and logistical loads facing a population generate selection pressures for new structures if the population is to survive in its environment. If individual and collective actors find a way to respond to these selection pressures, the development of these new structures increases the level of differentiation in society and makes it more adaptive to its environment (an idea that Talcott Parsons was later

to develop into the notion of "adaptive upgrading," apparently unaware of Spencer's reasoning 100 years earlier). The most important selection pressures arise from the functional needs for operation, regulation, and distribution. That is, as populations grow or confront problems internally or in their environment, the selection pressures almost always revolve around developing new structures for resolving problems of production, reproduction, regulation, or distribution.

THE MODEL OF EMPIRE FORMATION AND DISINTEGRATION

Spencer was one of the most important early geopolitical theorists, although most sociologists remain unaware of his analysis of intersocietal dynamics. When populations grow, Spencer argued, they mobilize power; and often this power is used to conquer neighboring populations (frequently under selection pressures to secure more resources to support the growing population). As neighboring societies are conquered, the logistical loads for regulation and control increase. The result is for governments to impose ever more taxes in order to support the administrative and coercive bases of power that are needed to maintain control. As government imposes additional taxes, it increases the level of inequality in the expanding empire, thereby generating another kind of logistical load for control. Conquest thus generates enormous pressure on polity to control the larger population, conquered territories, and problems inherent in inequality. As a polity copes with these selection pressures, it often conquers more territory to secure needed resources, but in doing so, it only increases the logistical loads: more people must be controlled; larger territories must be governed; ethnic diversity and diverse cultures of the conquered must be managed; and the threats arising from growing inequality must be repressed. Eventually, these logistical loads and the selection pressures that they generate cannot be managed, leading to the collapse of the empire and the devolution of societies back to simpler forms. The history of the world, Spencer felt, was very much a history of these dynamics, as empire formation increased societal complexity, only to be undone by the logistical loads inherent in all empires and the need to concentrate power. These inevitable dynamics led Spencer to oppose British colonialism. For, at the height of the British Empire, Spencer argued that colonialism concentrated too much power in the hands of elites, increased tension-generating inequalities, diverted capital (in the long run) from production, and eventually imposed logistical loads that would lead to the collapse of the empire.

It is impossible to communicate the sophistication of Spencer's analysis. Moreover, Spencer had professional historians and ethnographers develop the large database in *Descriptive Sociology* to illustrate his theoretical models (the largest database ever created in the nineteenth century, and one that served as the model for George P. Murdocks's Human Relations Area Files). Indeed, when *The Principles of Sociology* was first published, readers complained about what they saw as too much descriptive data, but Spencer wanted the reader to be sure that each analytical point in his theoretical models could be assessed with data from a wide variety of societies – from the simplest hunter-gatherer society to the England of his time. The great tragedy is that Spencer is often viewed as an "armchair theorist" who had no contact with data but, in fact, Spencer paid professionals to collect the largest database ever assembled by a sociologist. And, while he was an armchair theorist in that he did not collect the data himself, his sociology avoided speculative ideas that could not be assessed with data. The models of social change summarized above represent only one theme in Spencer's sociology, but their sophistication should encourage other sociologists to mine this classic work.

SEE ALSO: Division of Labor; Durkheim, Émile; Ecological View of History; Evolution; Functionalism/Neofunctionalism; Historical and Comparative Methods; Institution; Political Sociology; Social Change; Structural Functional Theory

REFERENCES AND SUGGESTED READINGS

Durkheim, É. (1947 [1893]) *The Division of Labor in Society*. Free Press, New York.

Parsons, T. (1966) *Societies: Evolutionary and Comparative Perspectives*. Prentice-Hall, Englewood Cliffs, NJ.

Perrin, R. G. (1993) *Herbert Spencer: A Primary and Secondary Bibliography*. Garland, New York.

Spencer, H. (1867 [1864–7]) *The Principles of Biology*. Appleton-Century, New York.

Spencer, H. (1880 [1862]) *First Principles*. A. L. Burt, New York.

Spencer, H. (1888 [1851]) *Social Statics*. Appleton-Century, New York.

Spencer, H. (2002 [1874–96]) *The Principles of Sociology*. Transaction, New Brunswick, NJ.

Turner, J. H. (1985) *Herbert Spencer: A Renewed Appreciation*. Sage, Beverly Hills, CA.

spirituality, religion, and aging

Robert C. Atchley

Religion and spirituality are enduring aspects of the human condition. Some of the earliest human records were accounts of the spirituality and religious culture of the day. Religion and spirituality have also fueled human conflict for thousands of years. Our concern here is how religion and spirituality interact with aging: how aging affects religion and spirituality, and how religion and spirituality affect aging.

Religion is a social institution concerned with ultimate questions such as the meaning and purpose of life, the existence of a higher power, coping with the reality of suffering and death, the existence and nature of an afterlife, and what it means to lead a moral life. Religions are also social organizations that meet not only the need to join with other believers, but also various social needs such as comfort, aid, and social support. Most American adults are associated with a local congregation of a major faith. There are hundreds of religions with widely varying answers to life's ultimate questions. Religious beliefs are among the most deeply held, and religion can be a source of both comfort and conflict. There are also people who attach no significance to religion. Religiousness is an individual attribute – the extent to which a person has internalized a religious culture and uses it to make decisions in their life.

Spirituality is an experiential, inner aspect of consciousness. It is the capacity to experience the sacred directly. Such experience can be cognitive, emotional, and/or motivational. For many people, the sacred can be experienced in an enormous variety of situations: nature, in relationships, in music, dance, and art, in religious devotions, in inspirational texts and orations.

The inner experience of spirituality and socially constructed religion are related for most people, and for some people are inseparable. But there are also people who consider themselves spiritual who disavow religion and still others who find neither term applies to them.

In the US, a large majority of elders have had a lifelong identification with their religion and are long-time members of their local religious group. Local religious groups are the most common type of community organization membership for middle aged and older people. About half of the general population attends religious services at least twice a month. Frequency of attendance increases with age up to age 60 and then declines gradually thereafter. Informal religious behavior such as reading scripture, personal prayer or meditation, or participation in religious study groups also increases with age and is especially important for disabled elders. Religious involvement is particularly important for African Americans and women.

Local religious groups and regional and national denominations vary considerably in how they approach the needs of aging and older members. Some consciously work to maintain integration of older members in the life of the religious community by taking steps such as recruiting elders for leadership positions, making special efforts to provide transportation to elders, and mobilizing the religious group to attend to the special needs of frail elders. Other local religious groups may do very little to encourage continued participation or attend to the needs of their older members, even in situations where the proportion of older religious group members is rapidly increasing. Religious groups are not immune to the agism that permeates their culture.

More than 90 percent of adults express a religious preference, and a large proportion of older adults believe that their faith has grown stronger over time. Life stage appears to be related to spiritual development. In middle age, many adults begin to address seriously the issue of life's meaning. They may find that conventional superficial answers to this question are increasingly unsatisfying. During this stage, many adults embark on a quest that may involve systematic study and reflection, which in turn often gives a sense of deepening understanding. Tornstam's (1994) theory of gerotranscendence holds that as people move into later adulthood, they begin to develop a more universal and less personal stance toward the meaning of life. By old age, many people take more enjoyment from their inner life, feel greater connection to the entire universe, and are less afraid of death.

Experiences of spirituality begin in childhood for many people and contain an element of transcendence in the sense that the experience transports the individual from his or her conventional perceptual field to being able to see things in a wider context. It could be said that spirituality is a direct experience of the source of spirit, the life force that animates all being. Spiritual practices such as prayer, meditation, or making sacred music and art aim to cultivate a deeper awareness of spirit within the individual. For most people, spirituality is integrated with religious values, beliefs, and attitudes, but some see themselves as spiritual but not religious. A lifetime of spiritual practice makes a difference. From middle age onward, people may find that many years of spiritual practice and life experience combine to soften the edges of their religious ideas and create a more inquiring, spacious, and tolerant attitude toward other faiths. Spiritual development seems to lead toward more interest in common ground among religions and peaceful coexistence. One of the unfortunate results of age segregation in large urban communities is the loss of everyday interaction with spiritual elders, people whose high degree of spiritual development can be an important source of wisdom within the community.

Involvement in organized religion, subjective religiousness, and spiritual experience are associated with greater physical and mental well-being and longevity. People affiliated with religions that prohibit tobacco, alcohol, and drug consumption tend to be healthier and live longer than others. As people age, the degree of participation in both formal and informal religious activities has been associated with better health and greater life satisfaction.

In general, the greater the degree of religiousness, the better people's health and subjective well-being. The greater the religiousness, the lower the prevalence of anxiety, fear of death, and loneliness. Highly religious people also cope better with grief. Religious beliefs and spiritual orientations are the very prevalent resources for coping with negative aspects of life, especially in old age. The more serious the problem, the more likely that people will use religious coping. However, religiousness can also be maladaptive if it isolates elders from others, if it defines negative aspects of aging as resulting from sin, or if elders seek support from their congregations and do not get it.

Sociologically, the subject of aging, religion, and spirituality represents a relatively new field of inquiry, filled with important questions begging for better answers. There can be no doubt that those who see themselves as religious and/ or spiritual have a different, often better, experience of aging compared with those who do not. But better analytical description is needed of what happens, how, and why. In addition, we need better maps of how aging people relate to various types of religious organizations and better understanding of the effects of specific religious and spiritual beliefs and practices over time. Major challenges facing research in this area include incomplete theory development, difficulty in constructing measures that are valid across faith groups, and coping with the enormous diversity of religious beliefs and practices and their potential interactions with aging.

SEE ALSO: Aging, Sociology of; Religion, Sociology of

REFERENCES AND SUGGESTED READINGS

Atchley, R. C. (2000) Spirituality. In: Cole, T. R., Kastenbaum, R., & Ray, R. E. (Eds.), *Handbook of Aging and the Humanities*, 2nd edn. Springer, New York.

Atchley, R. C. (2004) Religion and Spirituality. In: Atchley, R. C. & Barusch, A. S. (Eds.), *Social Forces and Aging*, 10th edn. Wadsworth, Belmont, CA, pp. 294–315.

McFadden, S. H. (1996) Religion, Spirituality and Aging. In: Birren, J. E. & Warner Schaie, K. (Eds.), *Handbook of the Psychology of Aging*, 4th edn. Academic Press, New York, pp. 162–80.

Moberg, D. O. (2001) Spirituality in Gerontological Theories. In: Moberg, D. O. (Ed.), *Aging and Spirituality: Spiritual Dimensions of Aging Theory, Research, Practice and Policy*. Haworth, New York, pp. 33–51.

Tornstam, L. (1994) Gero-Transcendence: A Theoretical and Empirical Exploration. In: Thomas, L. E. & Eisenhandler, S. H. (Eds.), *Aging and the Religious Dimension*. Auburn House, New York, pp. 203–29.

sport

John W. Loy and Jay Coakley

Sport is an embodied, structured, goal-oriented, competitive, contest-based, ludic, physical activity. Given the multitude of sport forms and the vast variety of specific sports, ranging from rural, primitive athletic folk games of old, to new urban, hi tech, extreme sports, this definition is unlikely to satisfy one-and-all. It does, however, (1) highlight the major social characteristics of modern sport; (2) suggest the specification of the embodied structural properties and social processes underlying the social development of modern sport; and (3) provide a set of common features for examining the magnitude and complexity of sport as a social phenomenon at different levels of analysis, including sport as a unique game occurrence, sport as a particular type of ludic activity, sport as an institutionalized game, sport as a social institution, and sport as a form of social involvement (Loy 1968).

SPECIFIC CHARACTERISTICS OF MODERN SPORTS

Sport is Embodied

The degree of physicality varies by sport, but the body constitutes both the symbol and the core of all sport participation (Hargreaves 1986). The essence of embodiment in sport is that sporting activities involve many kinds and degrees of physicality, including physical activity, physical aggression, physical combat, physical exercise, physical presence, physical prowess, physical recreation, physical sexuality, physical training, and physical work. In short, sporting bodies represent a range of desiring bodies, disciplined bodies, displaying bodies, and dominating bodies.

Sport is Structured

There are at least four ways in which sport is highly structured. First, all sports (whether informal or formal) are *rule governed* by either written or unwritten rules. Second, most sports are *spatially circumscribed* by the sites of their venues, whether they be arenas, courts, fields, pools, rings, rinks, stadiums, or tracks. Third, most sports are *temporally circumscribed* as illustrated by designated time periods such as innings, halves and quarters; or number and time of bouts and rounds; or allocated attempts within a specific time period. Indeed, to prevent indefinitely long sporting encounters sports have instituted tie-breakers, "sudden death" playoffs, and "shorter versions" of selected sports (e.g., one-day cricket matches). Fourth, modern sports tend to be *formally administered*, whether by local clubs, universities, professional teams, or sport federations.

Sport is Goal Oriented

Individuals, teams, and organizations are typically goal directed in sport situations, especially in terms of the perennial overriding goal of winning. Athletes and coaches alike continually attempt to achieve various standards of excellence. And numerous forms of self-testing and contesting take place in all sporting encounters. The sporting media constantly stresses the theme of being Number 1 in terms of games won, points earned, medals obtained, rank on the money list, most career victories, or number of Grand Slam titles.

Sport is Competitive

A key feature of all forms of sport is physically playful competition. Such competition may be between individuals or teams, and may involve either an animate object of nature (e.g., a bull in a bullfight), or an inanimate object of nature (e.g., climbing the highest mountain in the world), or it may be focused on competition against an "ideal standard" (Loy 1968). A spectator typically perceives three basic forms of competition (McPherson et al. 1989: 16): First, *direct competition* where two opponents, either individuals or teams, directly confront one another, as for example, in boxing or football. Second, *parallel competition* wherein participants compete against one another indirectly by taking turns as in bowling or golf; or contesting in separate spaces, as for example, separate lanes in swimming events or track sprints and hurdle races. Third, there are forms of competition which are largely *competition against a standard* such as trying to make a qualifying time for an Olympic running event, or attempting to set a world automobile speed record on the Bonneville Salt Flats in Utah.

Sport is Contest Based

Many, if not most, sporting encounters are contests, that is, competitive activities characterized by two or more sides (individuals, teams, or larger organizations), agreed upon rules, and criteria for determining the winner, with a non-reciprocal outcome. As defined below, most sport contests are either agonal games or sporting matches.

Sport is Ludic

Even the most highly professionalized forms of sport possess some play-like elements. Two ludic or play elements inherent in all sports are *artificial obstacles* and *realized resources*. Individuals and groups are confronted in daily life by obstacles they must attempt to overcome. Unfortunately, individuals and groups often do not have the required resources to cope adequately with the specific obstacles that they confront. Contrarily, in the context of sports, individuals and groups artificially create obstacles to overcome, be it a hurdle in a steeplechase or the height of a pole vault. And unlike real-life situations, individuals and teams in sport situations are typically provided with the needed resources (e.g., coaching, equipment, training, etc.) to cope with their artificially created obstacles.

Sport, as defined and described above, represents a particular type of ludic activity and thus is closely related to the social phenomena of play and games.

COMMON CHARACTERISTICS OF LUDIC ACTIVITIES

Like play and games, sport is ancient, ubiquitous, and diverse.

Antiquity and Ubiquity

Play precedes culture and humankind: some mammals exhibited play activity about 65 million years ago. Human play is a universal activity found in all institutional sectors of society. Similarly, games, at least games of physical skill, have been found in all societies, past and present (Chick 2004). Although games are not as old as play, archeologists have discovered gaming artifacts that are several centuries old. Today, board games like chess and new electronic video games are pervasive throughout the world.

In turn, sports are at least as old as the first recorded Olympic victor in Greece in 776 BCE. Although sports are particularly characteristic of modern societies, and while the phenomenon of sport is not found in all past societies, many contemporary sport forms have long cultural traditions and historical legacies.

During the past century sport has become a social phenomenon of great magnitude and complexity, having both positive and negative consequences for individuals and groups throughout the world. The ubiquity of sport is illustrated by Boyle's (1963: 3–4) observations about American sport in the early 1960s. He explains that sport pervades all spheres of social life and influences everything from values, status, and race relations to business, fashions, and ideas about heroes. The pervasiveness of sport in society today is best indicated by the mass media that covers sundry forms of sport throughout the world on a daily basis.

Diversity

There seems be to be an infinite number of play forms worldwide. And there are hundreds, if not thousands, of different game forms throughout the world. In turn, the great variety of sports throughout history and in very different cultures and diverse geographical regions of the world amply attests to the diversity of sport. Moreover, it is evident that modern sports have diverse historical roots and social derivations.

First, some of our contemporary sports are derived largely from relatively primitive, fundamental movement activities such as climbing, diving, kicking, jumping, running, swimming, throwing, vaulting, and weightlifting. Many events of our modern Olympic Games are based on such basic fundamental movement activities.

Second, several forms of modern sport have their roots in early survival activities and often represent transformations of work practices to play practices. Noted examples of such sport forms are fishing, hunting, skating, sledding, and skiing. Sporting activities such as dog racing, horse racing, pigeon racing, and rodeo events may also be assigned to this category, as they represent the transformation of human use of domestic animals for work to purposes of play.

Third, still other forms of sport today represent modifications of ancient martial arts and military exercises. Readily recognizable examples include archery, boxing, fencing, javelin throwing, and wrestling.

Fourth, less directly, but no less importantly, a number of modern sports have distant roots in ball games, dances, and ceremonies associated with the religious practices of traditional, preliterate societies. Lacrosse is perhaps the most prominent example of a modern sport having its origins in religious ritual.

Fifth, some contemporary sports are the patent result of individual invention. Classic examples are basketball (invented by Canadian James Naismith in December 1891 while a student at the YMCA Training College in Springfield, Massachusetts) and volleyball (invented by William G. Morgan in 1895 while serving as physical education director at the YMCA in Holyoke, Massachusetts).

Sixth, other modern sports represent a continuum of development from informal (if often brutal) play, to formal competitive play, to athletic folk games, to recreational and representational sports. For example, it may be reasonably argued that selected forms of folk-football (Elias & Dunning 1986) led to the development of soccer (Chick 2004), which led in turn to the development of rugby (Dunning & Sheard 1979), and in turn to the development of intercollegiate gridiron football (Riesman & Denny 1951), and finally the emergence of both American and Canadian versions of professional gridiron football.

Although modern sports may differ markedly from their original folk forms they nevertheless possess significant residual sporting traditions, styles, and practices (Ingham & Loy 1993).

BASIC DIFFERENCES OF LUDIC ACTIVITIES

On the one hand, physically competitive play, agonal games, and elite sports are similar in that they typically involve competition between two or more sides, with agreed upon rules, criteria for determining the winner, and the outcome largely based on the display of superior physical skill. Because they share the same basic features, play, games, and sport are often treated as one and the same. For example, tennis is considered a sport, but we play a game of tennis, and the person who wins the most games and takes the most sets wins the match. A tennis match is, of course, a contest, like a boxing match or a wrestling match. And tennis matches are an official sport of the modern Olympic Games.

On the other hand, play, games, and sport differ in degree, if not in kind, in terms of formalization, reciprocal activity, and non-reciprocal outcome. *Formalization* refers to the formal structure of ludic activities in terms of social, spatial, and temporal organization as well as the rules that govern them. Play is generally informal in terms of both structure and rules, whereas most games are more highly structured and have more formal rules. In turn, sports are extremely structured, with some having large volumes of published official rules.

Reciprocal activity denotes the degree of interaction among rival participants and the degree of sociability among both playful friends and foes. Informal competitive play ranks high in terms of reciprocal activity; face-to-face games involve at least moderate degrees of interaction; while sports tend to show the lowest degrees of sociability, especially among opponents at the elite and professional level.

Non-reciprocal outcome refers to the degree to which the end result of a ludic encounter is zero-sum, with only one winner or side taking all. Among play, games, and sport there is an inverse relationship between reciprocal activity and non-reciprocal outcome. Traditional play places little emphasis on non-reciprocal outcomes, most games give moderate emphasis to such outcomes, while nearly all sports clearly stress the importance of non-reciprocal outcomes. The most extreme examples of non-reciprocal outcomes are found in terminal contests such as bullfights, cockfights, dogfights, and, most critically, war.

Specific similarities and differences among play, games, and sport are denoted by the following definitions of ludic action and typology of ludic activities.

DEFINITIONS OF LUDIC ACTION

Ludic, from the Latin term *ludus*, refers to any play-like and/or game-like expressive activity. *Agonal*, from the Greek term *agon*, refers to any contest involving struggles of physical prowess. *Physical prowess* denotes the display of athletic ability in terms of varying degrees of skill (accuracy and coordination), strength, speed, and stamina (endurance). *Play* is a voluntary, expressive activity, which is both uncertain and unproductive, characterized by spontaneity, pretense, and non-linearity, which focuses on process rather than product, and which can be initiated and terminated at will. *Competition* denotes active efforts by individuals or groups to reach a goal, to achieve a superior position, or to win a prize or title. *Physically playful competition* represents earnest struggles for supremacy in agonal games or sporting matches. *Contests* are competitive activities characterized by two or more sides (individuals, teams, or larger organizations), agreed upon rules, and criteria for determining the winner, with a non-reciprocal outcome. *Matches* are contests between opposing individuals. *Sporting matches* typically involve individual demonstrations of physical superiority in terms of speed, strength, stamina, accuracy, and coordination (Weiss 1969). Although some team sports may be called matches (e.g., cricket matches and soccer matches) they are classified here as agonal games. *Games* are playful contests whose outcome is determined by physical skill, strategy or chance, employed singly or in combination. *Agonal games* are games whose outcome is largely determined by the demonstration of superior physical prowess in combination with superior tactics and strategy. *Sports* represent institutionalized agonal games or sporting matches.

These definitions are summarized in the following typology of ludic activities:

1 *Non-play contests* (e.g., deadly fights, duels, wars)
2 *Non-contest play* (e.g., drama, humor, music)
3 *Playful contests* (e.g., puzzles, riddles, spelling bees)
4 *Non-sport games* (e.g., bridge, checkers, chess)
5 *Sporting matches* (e.g., boxing, tennis, wrestling)
6 *Agonal games* (e.g., basketball, ice hockey, soccer)

THE FUN FACTOR IN LUDIC ACTIVITIES

Given the plethora of play forms in culture and the pervasiveness of games and sports throughout the world, one must ask why these ludic activities are so attractive and appealing for participants and spectators alike. Perhaps the primary answer is given in Huizinga's (1955) assertion that *fun* is "the essence of play." He contends, however, that "the *fun* of playing, resists all analysis, all logical interpretation." Huizinga may be correct, but some sociological reasons can be given as partial explanations for why play, games, and sport are fun. For example, sociability, euphoric interaction, quest for excitement, and emotional dialectics may in large measure account for the fun factor in ludic activities.

SOCIABILITY

Simmel (1950) views sociability as the play-form of human association and proposes that the principle of sociability rests on maintaining reciprocity in the values offered and received in interaction. Henricks (2003) observes that, for Simmel, the distinctive characteristics of sociability are fourfold. First, sociability is simultaneously connected to and disconnected from everyday life. For example, in "real-life" situations, individuals must confront serious obstacles without the resources needed to overcome them, whereas, in ludic activities, individuals create artificial obstacles to overcome and all participants are provided the resources to meet the challenge of the obstacles adequately.

Second, the dynamics of sociability involve depersonalizing participants. The masks worn by gridiron football players, the costumes worn by participants at fancy balls or children on Halloween, and the personas assumed by professional wrestlers ensure the playing of distinctive roles while keeping personal matters to a minimum.

Third, sociability calls for cooperation and tactfulness. For an expressive configuration of positive affect to hold, the instrumental concerns and ego-demands of the participants must be minimized, equalized, or ruled as irrelevant (Ingham & Loy 1973). As Goffman (1967) notes, in order to maintain the expressive frame of sociability, it is expected that participants will make efforts to support the feelings and face of interaction partners, and that these efforts will be made spontaneously and without second thought because participants mutually identify with each other's emotions and feelings.

Fourth, sociability is fostered by the social equality of participants. For example, Loy (1968) notes that the contestants in a game act as if they were equals, and status distinctions related to income, occupation, education, and race are not considered relevant through the contest. Ingham (2004) observes that games are democratic, and sociability is sustained only when intrinsic outcomes are available to all participants and when extrinsic gains are perceived as shared.

EUPHORIC INTERACTION

Goffman (1961) refers to the pleasurable sociability provided by gaming encounters as "euphoric interaction." He argues that the bases of fun in games are twofold: an uncertain outcome and sanctioned display. "A successful game would then be one which, first had a problematic outcome and then, within these limits, allowed for a maximum possible display of externally relevant attributes" (p. 68). Goffman's two primary bases of fun in games are an inherent part of the structural dynamics of modern sport. In order to ensure an *uncertain outcome* in sporting contests, a variety of efforts are made to establish equality between opposing sides. Efforts to establish equality of competition typically focus on the factors of age, gender, size, and skill. For example, youth sport teams typically represent age groups, and at the level of elite sport, men and women seldom compete against one another. Examples of controlling for size are restricting competition according to weight class for boxers and wrestlers, while examples of control for skill level are the handicap systems developed in golf and bowling to help equate the contestants. Chance also plays a role in efforts to ensure equality for purposes of ensuring an uncertain outcome, as for example, flipping a coin to determine which team begins play, or randomly drawing a number for a lane in a running or a swimming event.

Sanctioned display is another important structural feature of sports for generating excitement. The display of bodily excellence in terms of various forms of athletic ability and physical prowess provides pleasurable excitement to participants and spectators alike. However, too much extraneous display, in the form of taunting and other player antics, can greatly detract from the pleasurable excitement of a ludic activity. As Stone (1955) pointed out, play and display are precariously balanced in sport, and once that balance is upset, the whole character of sport in society may be affected. Furthermore, the spectacular element of sport, may, as in the case of professional wrestling, destroy the game.

It is evident that Goffman believes that sanctioned display and a problematic outcome lend excitement to game encounters by creating tensions. Elsewhere he implies that a third element also generates tension in a game encounter, namely, "what is at stake." The value of the stakes that players compete for, in combination with the value of the stakes that players risk, adds excitement to any ludic activity. Gaming encounters with *high stakes* involve what Goffman calls "action," referring to engagement in activities that are consequential, eventful, and problematic, which are undertaken for what is felt to be their own sake, and wherein participants may put their very lives "at risk" (Goffman 1967: 185). A world championship poker game or a bullfight are ready examples of ludic activities providing exciting tension because the stakes are high.

QUEST FOR EXCITEMENT

While Simmel speaks of pleasurable sociability, and Goffman talks about euphoric interaction, Elias and Dunning (1986) analyze sport and leisure in terms of what they call "quest for excitement." They distinguish between "real excitement," such as that associated with seriously critical situations in everyday life, and "mimetic excitement," characteristic of sporting encounters. They propose that sport situations are structured in such a way as "to stir the emotions, to evoke tensions in the form of a controlled, a well-tempered excitement without the risks and tensions usually connected with excitement in other life-situations" (pp. 48–9). Elias and Dunning discuss a number of tension balances built into sport situations, which are designed to evoke tensions related to mimetic excitement. They place particular emphasis on the controlled expression of emotions related to aggression, conflict, danger, risk, and violence.

With reference to the structural dynamics of team sports they stress the importance of "interdependent polarities" for generating tension balances in sporting encounters. For example, they cite the overall polarity between competing teams; and the tension balances between offense and defense, cooperation and competition within teams, and the external control by sport authorities versus the internal control of players (pp. 202–3).

EMOTIONAL DIALECTICS

The theorizing of Elias and Dunning about "quests for excitement" can be considered an important example of what Sutton-Smith has termed "emotional dialectics." As Goodger and Goodger (1989) have summarized the work of Elias and Dunning: "It is not a case of there being a special type of relationship between the content of mimetic events and that of critical situations that they appear to resemble (for example, a sporting contest and a 'real-life' struggle), but rather there is a relationship between affects simulated by mimetic events and those simulated by real-life events, the affects in the former resembling those in the latter in a 'playful and pleasurable fashion.'" In a somewhat similar vein, Goffman (1961) discusses "subversive ironies" and the "function of disguise" in his interactional analysis of "fun in games." Fun, he explains, occurs when participants abide by rules of irrelevance and are careful to conceal reality to the point that it does not disrupt encounters.

Like Huizinga, Sutton-Smith (2003) thinks the primary purpose of play is having fun. Further, like Elias and Dunning, he believes fun in play provides mimetic excitement. In turn, like Goffman, he believes play offers contexts for subversive irony and treats play as a parody of emotional vulnerability. In reference to what have variously been called involuntary emotions, reflexive emotions, or survival emotions, Sutton-Smith focuses on what he calls the six primary emotions of anger, fear, shock, disgust, sadness, and joy. In proposing a dialectical hypothesis, he suggests that these emotions must be exercised (as in play) because they are fundamentally required for survival in the face of emergencies, but must also be constrained in the familial emotional contexts of contemporary social life. However, Sutton-Smith also recognizes that there are times when the expression of these emotions surpasses normative limits and results in "excessive noise, riots and hooliganism."

The preceding account supports the Goodgers's (1989) supposition that people have a basic, socially induced desire to experience "enjoyable excitement." But Ennis (1967) observes that societies face a sociological challenge when determining how such a motivational state can be institutionalized when it is grounded in the sense that all institutional enclosures are being broken or transcended. Some insight into how society institutionalizes this motivational state is given in accounts of both ludic institutionalization and sportification.

LUDIC INSTITUTIONALIZATION

Ingham (1978) aptly calls the transformation of play and games to modern sport the process of ludic institutionalization. He suggests the process can be understood most clearly if it is viewed in terms of multidimensional continua in which play and sport constitute the polar extremes. This enables one to see that sport involves ludic activity that is, to relatively extreme degrees, regulated, formalized, instrumentalized, regimented, and estranged. In general, what have been variously called traditional games, folk sports, or folk athletics fall at the expressive end of the continuum; whereas, what has been variously called elite sport, top-level sport, or professional sport falls at the most instrumental end of the continuum. However, even the most instrumental forms of ludic action possess some play-like elements; thus, modern sports can be placed on a truncated expressive-instrumental continuum. For example, "recreational sports" (e.g., street or playground pickup games), largely based on the principles of play, pleasure, and participation, represent expressive sporting activities; whereas "representational sports" (e.g., intercollegiate and professional sport), largely based on the principles of performance, profit, and prestige, represent instrumental sporting activities.

In sum, the ludic institutionalization of sport is best understood in terms of the tension balances associated with the expressive and instrumental dimensions of sport. Current analyses of the sportification process reflect thoughtful examinations of the expressive and instrumental dimensions of modern sport.

SPORTIFICATION

The transformation of modern sports from primarily expressive activities to largely instrumental *sport*

activities reflects the process of sportification. More specifically, as Renson (1998) notes: "Sportification is depicted as a universal hegemonic trend of standardization and globalization of sport practices." The global sport monoculture of representational sport denoted by the concept of sportification is also reflected in Heinila's (1998) concept of the "totalization of sport" and Donnelly's (1996) concept of "prolympism." Heinila (1998) argues that due to the totalization process, international sport has been transformed from contests between individuals and/or teams to contests between nation-states that have unequal resources to produce elite athletes and teams. In a similar manner, Donnelly (1996) documents the articulation of professionalism and Olympism as the two dominant sport ideologies of the twentieth century. He demonstrates how these formerly very different alternative codes of sport merged into a single organic hegemony. Donnelly argues that prolympism is self-reinforcing, in that it marginalizes alternatives and becomes a standard against which other forms of physical culture are assessed.

BASIC QUESTIONS AND SOCIAL PROCESSES

The degree of sportification of any particular sport can be usefully examined by answering four questions in terms of four related social processes: (1) What is the *social structure* of the sport? What are the kinds and degrees of *rationalization* characteristic of the sport? (2) What is the *social thought* about the sport? What are the ideologies and rationales put forth to *legitimize* the sport? (3) What are the kinds and degrees of *social participation* in the sport? What are the kinds and degrees of *democratization* characteristic of the sport? (4) What is the *social diffusion* of the sport? What are the kinds and degrees of *globalization* of the sport?

These questions direct attention to specific social parameters, polarities, foci, and social processes that aid the assessment of the degree and kind of sportification for a particular sporting activity or sport form, as shown in Table 1.

RATIONALIZATION OF SPORT

The most fundamental characteristic of the monolithic social structure of elite international or representational sport is its instrumental rationalization. The totalization of international sport and the prolympism of representational sport indicate that for the principles of performance, profit, and prestige, virtually every basic component or element of sport has been rationalized to the ultimate degree for reasons of efficiency and effectiveness. Examples of the key elements of representational sport and the specific processes underlying their rationalization are shown in Table 2.

LEGITIMIZATION OF SPORT

Both recreational and representational sport have been legitimized in a variety of ways at various historical periods of different societies. Table 3 lists some of the selected rationales that have been used to justify the social significance of modern sports. As is also indicated in the table, modern sports must continually confront problems of delegitimatization, such as the use of illegal performance-enhancing drugs.

DEMOCRATIZATION OF SPORT

A notable historical trend of the sportification process has been the increasing democratization of modern sports. For example, the early modern Olympic Games were noted for their elitism, sexism, and racism. Today, few Olympic events are closely linked to social class per se,

Table 1 The sportification process

Social parameters	Social focus	Social binary	Social process
Social structure	Efficiency	Expressive/Instrumental	Rationalization
Social thought	Efficacy	Legitimate/Illegitimate	Legitimization
Social participation	Equality	Inclusion/Exclusion	Democratization
Social diffusion	Equatorial	Export/Import	Globalization

Table 2 The rationalization of sport

Element	Focus	Process
Players	Personnel	Resource allocation
Rules	Regulation	Formalization
Equipment	Technology	Innovation
Skills	Training	Specialization
Strategies	Knowledge	Complexity
Outcomes	Records	Quantification
Spectators	Fans	Spectatorship
Administrators	Organization	Bureaucratization
Owners	Profits	Entrepreneurism
Rewards	Salaries	Professionalization
Rights	Equity	Unionization
Publicity	Media	Mass communication

Table 3 Legitimization and delegitimization of sport

Legitimization of sport	Delegitimization of sport
Personal development	Blood sports
Social development	Bribery
Health and wellness	Cheating
Military preparedness	Doping
Community spirit	Drug abuse
National prestige	Gambling
Patriotism	Game fixing
Escapism	Hazing
Entertainment	Sexual harassment
Corporate profits	Violence

Table 4 Democratization of sport

Opposing social categories	Discriminatory process
Able vs. Disabled	Ableism
Young vs. Old	Agism
Class vs. Mass	Elitism
White vs. Black	Racism
Men vs. Women	Sexism
Straight vs. Gay	Homophobia
Rich vs. Poor	Statusism

Table 5 Globalization of sport

Forms of globalization	Sporting examples
Economic globalization	IOC corporate sponsors
Political globalization	IOC host city bidding
Cultural globalization	Media empires and satellite telecasts of events
Global migration	International professional athletes
Global tourism	Sport ecotourism
Global slavery	Third world labor for sporting goods
Global terrorism	1972 Munich Olympic massacre; Athens spends est. $1.5 billion on security for 2004 Olympic Games

there is a marked increase of women participants and events in which they can compete, and many Olympic athletes, both male and female, are persons of color. Further, games and sports have been developed for special populations (e.g., the Special Olympics, the Paralympics, the Gay Games, and various "Senior" Games). Table 4 highlights the major forms of social discrimination that scholars, journalists, and cultural critics have addressed in the sportification process over time.

GLOBALIZATION OF SPORT

It is difficult to determine precisely the general emergence of the globalization of sport, but as evidenced by the diffusion of British sports throughout the world, the development of international sport federations, and the establishment of the modern Olympic Games, by the beginning of the twentieth century sport was already a worldwide phenomenon (McIntosh 1971: 95). Today, we can find examples of nearly every different form of globalization within the world of sport, as shown in Table 5.

COUNTER-REACTIONS TO THE SPORTIFICATION PROCESS

Broadly viewed, a strong case can be made that the sportification process has or will result in a monolithic global sport culture. On the other hand, folk sports and forms of recreational sport survive in the face of powerful global economic and cultural processes. This illustrates that sporting practices are dynamic ongoing activities always subject to change and transformation in connection with local and global actions. For example, traditional sporting activities are constantly being modified as the conditions of play are negotiated through relationships and processes that involve a combination of players, managers, administrators, owners, media personnel, and spectators. All sports are historically produced and socially constructed. And while the most prominent cultural forms of sport embody systems of dominant meanings and practices, new sports and sporting practices are continually being invented which may generate forms of resistance and/or offer alternative structures and subcultures. In this sense, sports constitute contested cultural and social terrains.

A case in point is what are currently called extreme sports or variously known as adventure sports, alternative sports, action sports, panic sports, X sports, or whiz sports. These sports are typically characterized by risk, speed and vertigo, and a desire by participants to maintain control of their bodies and physical activities without the intrusion of formalized administrative structures and hierarchical supervision. Many participants in such sports express a rhetoric and follow norms that are anti-establishment and often transgressional in their nature (Rinehart 2004). These sports might be considered as modern folk sports, given their grassroots origins and local variations. At the same time, some of these new and alternative sport forms have been captured in the "iron cage of play" of the monolithic global sport culture. Their technology and popular appeal among young men and women with money to spend has attracted the attention of mainstream sporting bodies and commercial enterprises, including media organizations and sponsors. As some participants resist commercial cooptation and others maintain parallel forms of non-commercial, participant-controlled activities, there are questions to be asked about the dynamics of cultural production and transformation (Honea 2004) and about sport as a game occurrence, a ludic activity, an institutionalized game, a social institution, and a form of social involvement. In this sense, sport constitutes a pervasive social phenomenon of great magnitude and complexity that continues to attract the attention of sociologists and other scholars.

SEE ALSO: Globalization, Sport and; Leisure; Play; Sport and Capitalism; Sport as Catharsis; Sport and Culture; Sport and Ethnicity; Sport, Professional; Sport and Social Capital; Sportization; Sports Heroes and Celebrities; Sports Industry

REFERENCES AND SUGGESTED READINGS

Boyle, R. H. (1963) *Sport – Mirror of American Life*. Little, Brown, Boston.

Chick, G. (2004) History of Games. In: McNeil, W. H. (Senior Ed.), *Berkshire Encyclopedia of World History*. Berkshire Publishing, Great Barrington, MA, pp. 798–802.

Donnelly, P. (1996) Prolympism: Sport Monoculture as Crisis and Opportunity. *Quest* 48: 25–42.

Dunning, E. & Sheard, K. (1979) *Barbarians, Gentlemen, and Players: A Sociological Study of the Development of Rugby Football*. Robertson, Oxford.

Elias, N. & Dunning, E. (1986) *Quest for Excitement: Sport and Leisure in the Civilizing Process*. Blackwell, Oxford.

Ennis, P. H. (1967) Ecstasy and Everyday Life. *Journal for the Scientific Study of Religion* 6: 40–8.

Goffman, E. (1961) *Encounters: Two Studies in the Sociology of Interaction*. Bobbs-Merrill, Indianapolis.

Goffman, E. (1967) *Interaction Ritual: Essays on Face-to-Face Behavior*. Anchor Books, Doubleday, Garden City, NY.

Goodger, J. & Goodger, B. C. (1989) Excitement and Representation: Toward a Sociological Explanation of the Significance of Sport in Modern Society. *Quest* 41: 257–72.

Gruneau, R. (1999) *Class, Sports and Social Development*. Human Kinetics, Champaign, IL.

Hargreaves, J. (1986) *Sport, Power and Culture*. Polity Press, Cambridge.

Heinila, K. (1998) *Sport in Social Context*. University of Jyvasykla Press, Jyvaskyla, Finland.

Henricks, T. S. (2003) Simmel: On Sociability as the Play-Form of Human Association. In: Lytle, D. E. (Ed.), *Play and Educational Theory and Practice*. Praeger, Westport, pp. 19–32.

Honea, J. (2004) Youth Cultures and Consumerism: Sport Subcultures and Possibilities for Resistance. PhD Dissertation, Colorado State University, Fort Collins.

Huizinga, J. (1955) *Homo Ludens: A Study of the Play-Element in Culture*. Beacon Press, Boston.

Ingham, A. G. (1978) American Sport in Transition: The Maturation of Industrial Capitalism and Its Impact on Sport. PhD dissertation, University of Massachusetts, Amherst.

Ingham, A. G. (2004) The Sportification Process: A Biographical Analysis Framed in the Work of Marx [Engels], Weber, Durkheim and Freud. In: Giulianotti, R. (Ed.), *Sport and Modern Social Theorists*. Palgrave, Basingstoke, pp. 11–32.

Ingham, A. G. & Loy, J. W. (1973) The Social System of Sport: A Humanistic Perspective. *Quest* 19: 3–32.

Ingham, A. G. & Loy, J. W. (Eds.) (1993) *Sport in Social Development: Traditions, Transitions, and Transformations*. Human Kinetics, Champaign, IL.

Loy, J. W. (1968) The Nature of Sport: A Definitional Effort. *Quest* 10: 1–15.

McIntosh, P. C. (1971) *Sport in Society*. C. A. Watts, London.

McPherson, B. D., Curtis, J. E., & Loy, J. W. (1989) *The Social Significance of Sport: An Introduction to the Sociology of Sport*. Human Kinetics, Champaign, IL.

Renson, R. (1998) The Cultural Dilemma of Traditional Games. In: Duncan, M. C., Chick, G., & Aycok, A. (Eds.), *Diversions in Fields of Play*. Ablex Publishing, Greenwich, CT, pp. 51–8.

Riesman, D. & Denney, R. (1951) Football in America: A Study in Culture Diffusion. *American Quarterly* 3: 309–25.

Rinehart, R. (2004) Extreme Sports. In: Cross, G. S. (Ed.), *Encyclopedia of Recreation and Leisure in America*. Charles Scribners' Sons, New York, pp. 318–21.

Simmel, G. (1950) *The Sociology of Georg Simmel*. Trans. K. H. Wolff. Free Press, New York.

Stone, G. P. (1955) American Sports: Play and Display. *Chicago Review* 9: 83–100.

Sutton-Smith, B. (2003) Play as a Parody of Emotional Vulnerability. In: Lytle, D. E. (Ed.), *Play in Educational Theory and Practice*. Praeger, Westport, pp. 3–17.

Weiss, P. (1969) *Sport – A Philosophic Inquiry*. Southern Illinois University Press, Carbondale.

sport, alternative

Joy Crissey Honea

Many sports can be considered alternatives to dominant sport forms, but the term alternative sport has generally been used in sociology to refer to a group of activities that meet a particular set of organizational criteria. Alternative sports initially existed outside of formal sports organizations and participants were primarily young people who, for one reason or another, did not fit into the world of traditional youth sports such as baseball and football. Though they differ greatly from one another, Robert Rinehart (2000) suggests that alternative sports can be loosely defined as: (1) participant controlled and directed, rather than organized through a governing body or other official organization; (2) individually focused, emphasizing personal achievements; (3) focused less on competition than traditional sports; and (4) generally possessing an insider requirement. That is, they are more likely than traditional sports to encompass their own subculture – one that stands in opposition to the dominant culture. In other words, skateboarders, for example, are not just people who happen to ride skateboards, but are "skaters," expected to participate in a lifestyle associated with involvement in the sport.

Some alternative sports were originally titled "extreme." This appears to have meant that they involved risk-taking that more mainstream sports did not (like BASE jumping or cliff diving). The term was appropriated by the media and applied to any sport that was not generally considered a sports staple on television in the 1990s, and the label has by and large been abandoned by participants and, to some degree, by the media. Increasingly, mass media narratives refer to alternative sports as "action sports."

Throughout the 1990s, alternative sports became increasingly popular. All-sports cable television networks like ESPN and Fox Sports have been instrumental in exposing the sports to the public, particularly targeting the attention of young males (aged 12–34) in their coverage. These sports are now featured on ESPN, ESPN2, ESPNews, ESPN Classic, and ABC. The best-known alternative sporting events are ESPN's annual X Games and Winter X Games, which feature a varying array of sports including skateboarding, snowboarding, inline skating, motocross, bicycle motocross (BMX), ski boarding and snow mountain biking. The X Games premiered in 1995 (originally titled the eXtreme Games). ESPN reported that between 1994 and 1998 its audience for alternative sports increased 119 percent and that the 2003

X Games were expected to reach more than 110 million homes in 145 countries and territories worldwide. Corporate sponsors have also gotten into the action and previous X Games sponsors include AT&T, Coors, Nike, Taco Bell, Mountain Dew, Chevrolet, VISA, and Snickers. According to a recent newspaper article, sales of skateboard shoes exceed $1.4 billion annually, more than the total regular season game receipts of major league baseball, and skateboarder Tony Hawk's series of video games earned him a $20 million advance from Activision while his clothing line brings in $50 million annually.

Participation rates also reflect the increasing popularity of alternative sports. According to a survey conducted by the National Sporting Goods Association (NSGA), between 1996 and 2001 participation rates for snowboarding increased 72 percent and skateboarding participation rates increased 106 percent. These two historically alternative sports had the highest growth rates of all sports surveyed. For example, baseball, a more traditional sport, had a growth rate of only 8 percent and two other traditional sporting activities had declining participation rates – football was down 4 percent and basketball was down 12 percent.

The rapid increase in popularity of these sports has led researchers to examine why they are attracting so many (especially young) people and what they offer that perhaps mainstream sports do not. NSGA Vice President of Information and Research Thomas B. Doyle points out that snowboarding participation rates have tripled since 1990, while alpine skiing rates dropped more than 30 percent, and adds that skateboarding has experienced phenomenal growth since 1995, when it hit a low of only 4.5 million participants. Doyle contends that the growth of these two sports may reflect the fact that young people often choose activities that set them apart from adults. He suggests that traditional sports like skiing may have become too mainstream to be of great interest to adolescents and young adults.

Sociologists have addressed the claim that traditional sports are too mainstream for young people today and have examined what has historically attracted individuals to alternative sports. Beal (1995) analyzed the subculture status of alternative sport in her study of skateboarding in the early 1990s. Using Gramsci's theory of hegemony, she examined the competing potentials of sport as an enforcer of dominant ideology and as a site of social resistance. Her findings indicated that members of the skateboarding culture she studied held beliefs about their sport that stood in contrast to the ideals of commercial sport. They were generally non-competitive, process-rather than goal-oriented, and emphasized participant control of sporting events. She determined that, to some degree, the skaters were successful in resisting outsider control of their sport. Rinehart and Grenfell (2002) studied a group of BMX riders and examined the differences between the participants' experiences of riding at a self-made bicycle track and at a corporate-sponsored "park." They found that the riders often preferred the home-made course, as it was truer to the original values of the sport, including participant control and informal organization.

Rinehart (2000) has studied a variety of alternative sports and their associated subcultures and has addressed the conflicts that arise as the sports become increasingly commercialized. He argues that participants' desire to have their sports legitimated and to prosper individually from their participation leads them to take part in commercial events like the X Games, but there they encounter conflicts with corporate and media sponsors who have different ideas about how to organize and present the sports. Rinehart contends that, while athletes participate in commercial events like the X Games, they simultaneously resist outsider definitions of what and who they are. He concludes that control over the presentation of alternative sports is significant because those who own and control the presentation of these events control not only the economics, but also the very core or "soul" of these sports.

What is emerging within alternative sport subcultures are struggles between corporate culture producers who are attempting to organize and present these sports like mainstream sport forms and the participants themselves, who seek to maintain some control of their sports and of the "authentic" roots of their cultures as they become commercialized. Beal and Weidman (1998), for example, found that skateboarders were indeed resisting outsider definitions of their culture and were participating in the production of their culture by influencing the advertising industry in its marketing strategies toward skaters. Within snowboarding, Crissey (1999) found that Winter X Games participants were dissatisfied with ESPN's organization and presentation of their sport and engaged in symbolic forms of resistance to the commercialized nature of the event. Snowboarders refused to be interviewed, criticized the judging format, and called the competition "a joke." However, this resistance did not appear to be having much success, as the opposition was largely in the form of verbal complaining rather than organized action directed at change. In addition, their complaints were certainly not broadcast by ESPN or affiliates and the participants were essentially supporting the commercialized version of their sports by participating in the X Games events. The snowboarders appeared to be ambivalent about the role of commercial interests. Kleinman (2003) comes to a similar conclusion in his analysis of professional skateboarders, who expressed both positive and negative sentiments toward the commercialization, or "mainstreaming," of their sport.

Commercialization can be both beneficial and detrimental for alternative sports and their adherents. While commercialization results in organizational changes such as outsider control, increased competition, and extrinsic rewards for performances, it also provides new opportunities for participants including monetary rewards, product endorsements, new facilities, and video and television appearances. The most current data indicate that while athletes dislike the organizational changes and the commercial versions of their sports, they recognize that the newfound popularity and media coverage of their activities have opened new avenues for involvement in alternative sports, in terms of both sport participation and business ventures. For example, public and privately funded skateboard parks can now be found in many cities and towns, ski resorts now cater to snowboarders by building terrain parks, and the most talented athletes can earn income through contests, corporate sponsorships, and media performances. Though many alternative sport participants continue to view participation in the commercial version of their activities as "selling out," there is evidence of an increasing acceptance of the mainstream status of alternative sports and attempts to capitalize on their current popularity through participant-owned businesses that market equipment and apparel, host demonstrations and contests, and produce videos of sport performances.

While commercialization and social resistance are the most common targets for analysis, researchers have also examined other aspects of alternative sports and their subcultures. For example, sociologists have studied gender relations within alternative sports to determine how alternative sports either reinforce or challenge dominant gender roles. Alternative sports are overwhelmingly a male activity. Approximately 17 percent of skateboarders, 20 percent of surfers, and 30 percent of snowboarders are female. At ESPN's X Games, arguably the most publicized current alternative sporting event, only 15 percent of the competitors in 2000 were female. Of the three most popular events, skateboarding, BMX, and inline skating, only inline skating featured a women's division, and there were six female competitors as compared to 20 in the men's division. While some competitors and ESPN organizers attribute the disparity to a genuine lack of interest on the part of women, many female participants call it sexism.

Male participants in alternative sports often attribute the lack of female involvement in their sports to the difficulty of the activities – claiming, for example, that BMX requires exceptional upper body strength. Advocates of women's participation in these sports contend that it has little to do with physical ability or lack of interest and much more to do with discouragement from male participants. Beal (1995) found that, in her study of skateboarding, girls and women were marginalized as a result of discouragement by male skateboarders and trivializing terminology such as referring to female skaters as "Skate Betties." Although four of her 41 participants were female, Beal found that, within skateboarding, girls and women were most frequently relegated to the role of girlfriend or supporter of male skaters.

Although the marginalization of female athletes occurs in both traditional and alternative sport, gender relations are not identical across the two sport forms. Beal (1996) points out that male skateboarders construct an alternative masculinity that, while continuing to privilege males, rejects the "jock mentality" of traditional sports. Within snowboarding Kristen Anderson (1999) argues that the alternative nature of snowboarding means that the construction of gender in the sport is different than it is in mainstream, organized sports. She asserts that male snowboarders construct the sport as a masculine practice through a variety of social practices including sporting a "street punk" style of dress, adopting an aggressive and superior attitude, emphasizing the danger of their sport, and stressing their heterosexuality. Because alternative sports like snowboarding are individualistic, loosely organized, and controlled by the participants, standard methods of constructing and enforcing gender are less readily available to male participants than they are in the organized world of mainstream sports, especially team sports, where gender borders can easily be patrolled through the sex segregation of teams.

Other areas of inquiry within alternative sport include issues of identity, subcultural membership and cultural production, and, particularly within skateboarding, the use of urban space. Sociologists interested in the use of public space have studied how skateboarders utilize urban locations for purposes other than what was intended, and, in this way, "disrupt" city space. Methodological approaches in the study of alternative sport have been largely qualitative, employing methods such as participant observation, interviewing, and content analysis of sport media. Future analyses of alternative sports are likely to continue to explore the strategies commercial interests use to "mainstream" these sports, the changes that occur as they become mainstream (as is currently the case within snowboarding), and forms of social resistance employed by participants as they seek to retain some control over the future of their sports. Quantitative data are also needed to assess the reasons for the popularity of alternative sports among participants and to investigate possible future directions for these sport forms.

SEE ALSO: Gender, Sport and; Identity, Sport and; Popular Culture; Sport; Sport and Culture; Sport and Social Resistance

REFERENCES AND SUGGESTED READINGS

Anderson, K. L. (1999) Snowboarding: The Construction of Gender in an Emerging Sport. *Journal of Sport and Social Issues* 23(1): 55–79.

Beal, B. (1995) Disqualifying the Official: An Exploration of Social Resistance Through the Subculture of Skateboarding. *Sociology of Sport Journal* 12(3): 252–67.

Beal, B. (1996) Alternative Masculinity and its Effects on Gender Relations in the Subculture of Skateboarding. *Journal of Sport Behavior* 19(3).

Beal, B. & Weidman, L. (1998) The Skateboarding Image: An Analysis of the Industry's Impact on the Participants' View of Authenticity. Paper presented at the annual meeting of the International Sociology of Sport Association, in conjunction with the World Congress of Sociology. Montreal, Quebec.

Borden, I. (2001) *Skateboarding, Space and the City: Architecture and the Body.* Berg, Oxford.

Crissey, J. (1999) Corporate Co-optation of Sport: The Case of Snowboarding. Unpublished Masters Thesis. Colorado State University, Ft. Collins, CO.

Heino, R. (2000) What Is So Punk About Snowboarding? *Journal of Sport and Social Issues* 24(2): 176–91.

Kleinman, A. (2003) Post X-Games Skateboarding: An Exploration of Changes in the Skateboarding Subculture. Unpublished Masters Thesis. Temple University, Philadelphia.

Muggleton, D. (2000) *Inside Subculture: The Postmodern Meaning of Style.* Berg, New York.

Rinehart, R. E. (2000) Emerging Arriving Sport: Alternatives to Formal Sports. In: Coakley, J. J. & Dunning, E. (Eds.), *Handbook of Sports Studies.* Sage, London, pp. 504–20.

Rinehart, R. E. & Grenfell, C. (2002) BMX Spaces: Children's Grassroots Courses and Corporate Sponsored Tracks. *Sociology of Sport Journal* 19: 302–14.

Rinehart, R. E. & Sydnor, S. (Eds.) (2003) *To the Extreme: Alternative Sports, Inside and Out.* State University of New York Press, Albany, NY.

Wheaton, B. & Beal, B. (2003) "Keeping it Real": Subcultural Media and the Discourses of Authenticity in Alternative Sport. *International Review for the Sociology of Sport* 38(2): 155–76.

sport, amateur

Bruce Kidd

Amateurism in sport is at once ideology, a network of sports organizations, and a system of athletic eligibility. First articulated in Victorian England – there is absolutely no substance to the

International Olympic Committee's oft-made claim that amateurism governed the athletics of ancient Greece – amateurism melded the upper-class desire for social hierarchy with the middle-class belief in education, self-discipline, and social responsibility. The amateur ideal has always been to improve individuals and society by instilling the values of hard work, team sacrifice, and fair play, and inspiring community pride through inspirational performances. Amateurism resonated with the aspiration to "rational" or "improving" recreation that led urban reformers and the respectable working class to start public libraries, adult education classes, community orchestras and theater companies, public playgrounds, and children's summer camps.

In sport, amateurs sought to enforce adherence to their beliefs through a system of eligibility known as the amateur code. The first codes required competitors to be gentlemen, excluding women, workers, and, in some countries, aboriginals and persons of color simply on the basis of their status. As sports organizations became more meritocratic, in the face of growing working-class political power, the spread of democratic ideas, and the outstanding performances of black and aboriginal "professional" athletes, amateur governing bodies replaced the ascriptive code with rules that required participants to adhere to the value of disinterested play. The adoption of amateurism in 1894 by the newly formed International Olympic Committee (IOC) for its quadrennial Olympic Games gave enormous affirmation and clout to this system of regulation and, in many countries, linked it strongly to nationalism. By World War I (1914–18), the principal test of eligibility in most international, national, and local governing bodies, including educational and faith-based leagues, was whether an athlete had accepted monetary benefit from his participation or had ever played with or against a professional (i.e., someone who had accepted pay for play).

Although the prohibition against remuneration discouraged working-class participation, especially during periods of high unemployment, it encouraged those who could afford to participate to combine athleticism with education and careers and realize the ideals. Not surprisingly, amateurism drew its greatest strength from the male urban middle class. It resonated with their belief in education, self-discipline, and social order, and enabled them to win most of the prizes. In many countries, the advocacy of amateur sport also contributed to the development of more universal programs of sport development in state schools and municipal recreation departments. But when strictly enforced, the amateur rules had telling consequences. Those deemed to have violated them were usually banished from amateur competition, without any of the basic rights of "natural justice" or due process. When the aboriginal American Jim Thorpe, who won the pentathlon and decathlon at the 1912 Olympics in Stockholm by overwhelming margins, was reported to have received $25 a month for playing baseball, he was stripped of his medals and records. Numerous other athletes met the same fate at the hands of international, national, and local amateur officials. In many countries, the definition of an amateur, and its interpretation and enforcement, often divided clubs, coaches, athletes, and entire sports into warring factions. Not surprisingly, during the heyday of amateurism, the public and scholarly discourse was almost entirely preoccupied by these debates.

By the 1960s, the pressures against a strict financial definition of amateurism had grown to the point where they threatened to split the entire network of Olympic and amateur sports organizations worldwide. The rapid post-war growth of spectator sports in the capitalist world gave athletes the incentive to train and compete on a full-time basis and sporting goods manufacturers and event impresarios the revenue with which to pay them, while the state-financed victories of Soviet-bloc athletes in international competitions gave western sports leaders the rationale for liberalization. In 1974, the IOC dropped the term "amateur" from its eligibility code and gave member International Federations the right to set the terms of participation. By 1983, virtually all prohibitions against athletes receiving remuneration were dropped in Olympic sports. These changes were accompanied by new scholarship, which focused on the "social control" represented by amateurism and "rational recreation" and the socioeconomic status of those who benefited.

While amateurism has disappeared as a code of eligibility, the ideas it represents remain as strong as ever. The amateur ideal continues to provide motivation and legitimation for the vast network of public and voluntary sports organizations in the developed world, as any award banquet speech or appeal to private or government sponsors will attest. Beginning in the early 1990s, the amateurs' claim that sport can serve as a vehicle for education, health, and citizenship has also begun to inform a new wave of "rational recreation" for children and youth "at risk" in the ravaged areas of the developing world, and in international development assistance, particularly at the United Nations. In 2003, the General Assembly endorsed the idea of sport as a major tool of development and peace, and declared 2005 the International Year of Physical Education and Sport. Even the Olympic Movement has retained the structure of amateur regulation in the strict prohibitions against performance-enhancing drugs it now enforces through the World Anti-Doping Organization. Not all of these interventions are progressive, as concerns about the "assimilative reform" implicit in such well-publicized programs as "Midnight basketball" in US inner cities make clear. There is much social scientists can contribute to our understanding of these changes and continuities through an analysis of the auspices of contemporary forms of amateurism and the impacts upon/resistance by the peoples involved.

SEE ALSO: Olympics; Sport; Sport, College; Sport, Professional; Sport as Work

REFERENCES AND SUGGESTED READINGS

Allison, L. (2001) *Amateurism in Sport: An Analysis and a Defence*. Frank Cass, London.
Bailey, P. (1978) *Leisure and Class in Victorian England: Rational Recreation and the Contest for Control, 1830–1885*. Routledge & Kegan Paul, London.
Morrow, D. (1986) A Case Study in Amateur Conflict: The Athletic War in Canada, 1906–08. *British Journal of Sport History* 3(2): 173–90.
Pitter, R. & Andrews, D. L. (1997) Serving America's Underserved Youth: Reflections on Sport and Recreation in an Emerging Social Problems Industry. *Quest* 49(1): 85–99.

sport and the body

Pirkko Markula

Given the centrality of the body in sport performance, it might be assumed that the corporeality of athletes has been an essential facet of sport sociological analysis. Despite its vital role, however, the body has occupied "an absent presence" in this research and only since the late 1980s have sport sociologists expressed a growing interest in this topic.

This rather late awakening to the social construction of the body can be attributed to the persistent mind-body dualism that has had a deep impact on how the sociology of sport and sport studies view themselves as academic disciplines. The break of sport sciences from physical education reflected the move away from the bodily experience into an intellectual understanding of sport and a validation of sport as a scientific discipline. Opting for the science route, in its early phase from the mid-1960s to the early 1980s, sport sociology was dominated by structural-functionalist theorizing that focused on examining human beings as role actors within social structures ignoring the embodied actor. However, in the late 1980s and during the 1990s, along with other social sciences, the "non-body bias" started to lift and there was an increased awareness of the importance of studying how the sporting body has been constructed within power relations.

Examinations of the sporting body have evolved through several theoretical traditions. Inspired by the work of Norbert Elias, several sport sociologists have looked at how the (male) sporting body has become more civilized when molded through different figurations of power over time. This has evolved into further process sociological examinations of interrelationships between the body, power, and identity construction.

Interpretive sociology, particularly the dramaturgical work of Erving Goffman, has inspired sport scholars to examine the presentation of the body in its everyday context. In addition, phenomenological approaches have been used to examine how the lived body is experienced within the sporting context.

Critical cultural studies examine how the body has been shaped by the ideological construction of sport and by the dominant groups that maintain the current structure of sport. In addition, researchers using this approach have drawn attention to how different bodily identities – such as gendered bodies, lesbian/gay bodies, disabled bodies, ethnic bodies, and aging bodies – have been constructed within commercialized, globalized sport. They have also examined how a body can act as site of agency to resist the dominance of the powerful groups in sport.

More recently, the work of French poststructuralists such as Pierre Bourdieu and particularly Michel Foucault have become increasingly visible tools to examine the social construction of the sporting body. Bourdieu's work has enabled sport scholars to locate the body within the context of social fields where different sport practices construct distinctive habitus for its participants. Foucault's understanding of the body as a material site of disciplinary, discursive practices has been used to examine sport as a technology of domination. However, there is also an expanding literature on how the body might act as practice of freedom from the truth games that dominate sport and subvert the ethics of self-care. Feminist sport research, particularly, has contributed to growing Foucauldian interpretations of sporting bodies (Markula 2004).

Against this theoretical backdrop, several major topics emerge. One of the major premises for the current investigation of the sporting body as socially constructed is not just about how it is shaped but also about how individual bodies are shaping the power relations in sport. From the modernist perspective, the sporting body is seen as a contradiction: simultaneously being constructed by and constructing the dominant ideologies of sport. Sport, therefore, has been identified to act as a social field that has potential to liberate such oppressed identities as women, lesbian/gay people, disabled, aged, minority ethnicities, or economically underprivileged groups, but who simultaneously conform to the current dominant ideologies of sport. Similarly, different sports, such as male contact sports, have been identified as particular sites for oppressive bodily practices, whereas other sports, such as women's team/contact sports or women's bodybuilding, have been analyzed as sites for liberation from the structures of power.

Poststructuralist/postmodern theorists aim to expand the possibilities for the body's ability to change the existing power relations by assuming the embodied human being as an anti-essentialist self who, instead of struggling to resist against power that someone else exclusively holds, assumes a certain amount of power themselves. In this scenario, power relations turn from something to be resisted and eventually overturned into a potential source of creative and positive change through bodily practices. These examinations have also transgressed the boundaries of "traditional" definitions of sport to examine bodily dimensions of such popular phenomena as extreme and adventure sports, "trash sport" events such as the performances by World Wrestling Enterprise (WWE), and the fitness industry within the increasingly global economy of leisure.

While sport scholars have used a variety of methods, their examination of the sporting bodies can be located within two broad categories: textual readings of the sporting body and the sporting body as experienced by the athletes. The textual readings range from the representation of women athletes' bodies in the media, to the signification of celebrity athletes in the current socioeconomic climate. Individual bodily experiences have been mapped primarily by interviewing athletes within a diverse range of sports and at diverse levels of sport. These studies have focused on such bodily issues as violence, physicality, the impact of injury in a sporting career, body-image, disordered eating, sexuality, sexual harassment, sport for disabled, and becoming disabled through sport. Several researchers have also embarked on interview studies to determine whether a particular sporting body can be interpreted as a transgressive body. In addition to interviewing, ethnographic studies have been conducted to trace the social construction of sporting bodies within such contexts as bodybuilding, boxing, the fitness industry, sport spectatorship, football hooliganism, football industry, adventure sports, WWE, women's ice-hockey, and rugby union. There is also a growing literature of autoethnographically based examinations of bodily experiences. These studies trace, through the authors' personal experiences, how the physically active body has been lived into existence within the structures of power.

The sporting body has been examined from diverse theoretical perspectives using multiple methods to create a rich and varied body of literature. This multiplicity is likely to characterize future research on the social analyses of sporting bodies. However, there appears to be a theoretical trend toward the postmodern/poststructuralist analysis of the body. Therefore, while the modernist body as ideologically constructed into such categorical identities as gender, class, race, or sexuality will persist as part of sociological examination of the sporting body, the performative, postcolonial, queer, cyborg, and embodied postmodern body that is fragmented and in constant flux in the hyperreal, global economy of the sign will feature strongly in future research, as scholars expand their research horizons to further transgress the definitional boundaries of sport. In addition, the storied bodily writing continues to challenge social science research texts through their engagement in performance and performative writing.

SEE ALSO: Body and Cultural Sociology; Disability Sport; Drugs/Substance Use in Sport; Gender, Sport and; Sport; Violence Among Athletes

REFERENCES AND SUGGESTED READINGS

Coakley, J. (2004) *Sports in Society: Issues and Controversies*. McGraw-Hill, Boston.
Cole, C. L. (2000) Body Studies in the Sociology of Sport. In: Coakley, J. & Dunning, E. (Eds.), *Handbook of Sports Studies*. Sage, London, pp. 439–60.
Featherstone, M., Hepworth, M., & Turner, B. S. (1991). *The Body: Social Process and Cultural Theory*. Sage, London.
Gruneau, R. (1993). The Critique of Sport in Modernity: Theorizing Power, Culture, and the Politics of the Body. In: Dunning, E. G., Maguire, J. A., & Pearton, R. E. (Eds.), *The Sports Process: A Comparative and Developmental Approach*. Human Kinetics, Champaign, IL, pp. 85–110.
Hall, M. A. (1996) *Feminism and Sporting Bodies*. Human Kinetics, Champaign, IL.
Klein, A. (1993). *Little Big Men: Bodybuilding Subculture and Gender Construction*. State University of New York Press, Albany.
Markula, P. (2004) Tuning Into One's Self: Foucault's Technologies of the Self and Mindful Fitness. *Sociology of Sport Journal* 21(3): 302–21.
Rail, G. & Harvey, J. (1995) Body at Work: Michel Foucault and the Sociology of Sport. *Sociology of Sport Journal* 12: 164–79.
Shilling, C. (1993). *The Body and Social Theory*. Sage, London.
Sociology of Sport Journal (2001) Special issue on disability and sport. 20(1). Online. www.humankinetics.com or www.sagepub.co.uk.

sport and capitalism

Rob Beamish

As an analytic term, capitalism refers to the economic system that began to emerge in thirteenth-century Europe and extends into the present. Sport is an abstraction that denotes a variety of cultural practices that occur and develop within the context of specific socioeconomic formations. "Sport" and various sports exhibit several particular tendencies and characteristics when they occur within capitalist socioeconomic formations.

As an economic system, capitalism is a mode of "providing for material wants, animated by a definite spirit, regulated and organized according to a definite plan and applying a definite technical knowledge" (Sombart 1930: 196). The spirit of capitalism is based upon a historically unique approach to acquisition, specific attitudes about unfettered competition, and the use of instrumental reason (Weber 1927: 352–68). Acquisition under capitalism is not directly or centrally related to human need; it is focused on money (capital) and its potentially unlimited accumulation. As a result, each economic unit competes to extend its sphere of acquisition as far and as advantageously as possible, using all available means (within the existing penal code).

Instrumental reason pervades the capitalist system, as all economic units plan (usually long term), calculate the best means for acquisition, carefully manage all resources, and develop and employ technology to enhance profitability and competitiveness (Borkenau 1934). Most important, the "strict adaptation of means to ends, one of the essential ideological props of capitalism, permeates the totality of culture and leads in the course of time to a purely utilitarian valuation of human beings, objects, and events" (Sombart 1930: 198). Within the spirit of capitalism, everything is viewed as a means for accumulation. People are labor power or consumers; nature is a repository of resources; perfecting the business enterprise dominates the working day; progress is the creation of new wants, advances in technology, reductions in costs, and increases in the speed of capital circulation.

Within this socioeconomic context, all of the key issues related to sport and capitalism arise. Sport becomes a market opportunity for owners or promoters to purchase the skills of individual athletes to produce an athletic spectacle that can be sold to live spectators, sponsors, and various media. Athletes are workers engaged in labor processes that are tightly controlled by their employers and the corporations employing them accumulate the profits. In addition, just as the education system develops future workers, youth sports and schools provide opportunities for young athletes to feed into professional sport. To mitigate the excesses of the drive for acquisition and the unbridled application of instrumental reason in industries centered upon maximizing human physical performance in a competitive, zero-sum, environment, local, regional, and national governments have more or less successfully regulated different aspects of sport (Houlihan 1991).

The ascendance of town over country as the center of economic activity characterized the early emergence of capitalism. The associated shift in population facilitated the transformation of rural folk and traditional pastimes and games into urbanized, rule-bound games and sport forms that could be carried out in defined and confined spaces, creating the conditions for commercialized sport (Ingham & Beamish 1993; Kidd 1996). While amateur sport and tradition tempered the ascendance of capitalized sport forms, the exclusion of workers, the existence of paying spectators, traditions of gambling and gaming, interest among various media, and the spirit of entrepreneurialism

created opportunities for open competitions and professional sport.

The early pursuit of sport-entertainment revenues pitted promoters and owners against each other, as they bid for the best athletes to produce the most commercially appealing spectacles. To prevent their own self-destruction, owners in many sports formed leagues which acted as cartels to control costs, prevent economic competition internally, and to set prices in the marketplace (Beamish 1988). Though illegal in other forms of commerce, a 1922 Supreme Court decision granted baseball immunity from American anti-trust laws – a decision that had tremendous repercussions for all professional sports. The 1922 *Federal Baseball Club of Baltimore, Inc.* v. *National Baseball Clubs* decision centered on the control of players through the "reserve system." In their efforts to gain the freedom of movement all other employees enjoy, the players in North America used labor laws, the courts, and engaged in open conflict with league owners. After a number of court challenges, it became apparent that athletes' interests could be best defended through unionization and collective bargaining. The leagues in which the players had the most leverage unionized first – basketball in 1954 and hockey in 1967. Organized in 1956 and recognized in 1968, the owners used replacement players in 1987 to break the National Football League Players Association (NFLPA). The NFLPA was recertified 6 years later. From the Brotherhood of Professional Base Ball Players (1885) through to the American Baseball Guild (1946), the attempts to organize baseball players did not succeed until 1965 (signing its first collective agreement in 1968).

Once drastically underpaid and toiling under conditions set completely by owners, collective bargaining has balanced owner–player power relationships so that today's professional athletes in most North American sports receive an increasingly fair share of the tremendous revenues they generate for their teams and leagues. While players' salaries dwarf those of regular working people, their remuneration is consistent with the television celebrities they have become and the revenues accruing to the near-monopoly conditions established by team owners.

Pierre de Coubertin launched the modern Olympic Games as a sport spectacle that would inspire and reestablish traditional values in opposition to the crass materialism and decadence of nineteenth-century capitalism. From their inauguration in 1896 through to the present, commercial interests and nationalist political objectives – seen especially in the Nazi Games of 1936 and the Cold War confrontations between 1952 and 1989 – the Games have become as commercialized and profit driven as any other professional sport in the modern era. The International Olympic Committee's 1974 decision to revise the "Eligibility Code" in the Olympic Charter removed the last vestiges of amateurism and any barriers that genuinely separated the Games from other professionalized sport forms (Beamish & Ritchie 2004). The dominant instrumental rationality of the contemporary Games has led to significant questions about child labor, the neglect of athletes' rights, performance-enhancing substance use, and financial and ethical corruption (Hoberman 1992; Voy & Deeter 1991). As a movement that began as the antithesis of the capitalist spirit, the Olympic sports now rank among those that are the most deeply entrenched in the drive for acquisition, accumulation, the use of instrumental reason, and a purely utilitarian approach to human athletic performance.

Oppositional forms like "extreme sports" and other alternative sport forms have sprung up to resist the logic of capital, but they are quickly incorporated into the marketplace and begin to display the same ethos as mainstream, commercial, and high-performance sport.

SEE ALSO: Capitalism; Drugs/Substance Use in Sport; Gambling and Sport; Political Economy and Sport; Sport, Alternative; Sport as Work; Sports Industry

REFERENCES AND SUGGESTED READINGS

Beamish, R. (1988) The Political Economy of Professional Sport. In: Harvey, J. & Cantelon, H. (Eds.), *Not Just a Game: Essays in Canadian Sport Sociology.* University of Ottawa Press, Ottawa, pp. 141–59.

Beamish, R. & Ritchie, I. (2004) From Chivalrous "Brothers-in-Arms" to the Eligible Athlete: Changed Principles and the IOC's Banned Substance List. *International Review for the Sociology of Sport* 39: 355–71.

Borkenau, F. (1934) *Der Übergang vom feudalen zum bürgerlichen Weltbild.* Librairie Félix Alcan, Paris.

Hoberman, J. (1992) *Mortal Engines: The Science of Performance and the Dehumanization of Sport.* Free Press, New York.

Houlihan, B. (1991) *Government and Politics of Sport.* Routledge, London.

Ingham, A. & Beamish, R. (1993) The Industrialization of the United States and the "Bourgeoisification" of American Sport. In: Dunning, E., Maguire, J., & Pearton, R. (Eds.), *The Sports Process.* Human Kinetics, Champaign, IL, pp. 169–206.

Kidd, B. (1996) *The Struggle for Canadian Sport.* University of Toronto Press, Toronto.

Sombart, W. (1930). Capitalism. In: Seligman, E. & Johnson, A. (Eds.), *The Encyclopedia of the Social Sciences*, Vol. 3. Macmillan, New York, pp. 195–208.

Voy, R. & Deeter, K. (1991) *Drugs, Sport and Politics.* Leisure Press, Champaign, IL.

Weber, M. (1927) *General Economic History.* Free Press, Glencoe, IL.

sport as catharsis

Michael L. Sachs

The word catharsis comes from the Greek *katharsis* or *katairein*, which means a cleansing or a purging. *Webster's Dictionary* definition reads: "A discharge of pent-up emotions so as to result in the alleviation of symptoms or the permanent relief of the condition." Catharsis essentially refers to a release or discharge or cleansing of emotions, generally with the purpose of relieving the stress that develops from holding these emotions within the individual. English and English (1958) talk about "the relaxation of emotional tension or anxiety by any kind of expressive reaction." We often refer to the cathartic nature of sport (and exercise), relieving stress or tension that might build up, or serving as a release for anger and hostility (that may be seen as acceptable on the playing field or in the arena).

In exercise and sport settings the concept of catharsis may actually be seen as encompassing two possible areas. The most "popular" is the use of sport as a means to express one's anger or hostility in a setting where such behavior is sanctioned. The less commonly thought of application of catharsis is the use of exercise and sport as a stress reducer, a reliever of the stresses and tensions that may build up in an individual.

In considering the most popular use of the term, the thinking is that some individuals have elevated levels of anger or hostility (we all have differing levels of many different personality traits, some more socially acceptable than others). While expressing these emotions overtly is generally considered anti-social or even illegal, depending on how and where the expression occurs, the playing field or arena often offers a site where expressing certain emotions is permissible, and even desirable. This is likely to be the case when emotional expression facilitates competitive success. Given the importance in our society of success in the form of winning, coaches in some sports, such as those involving heavy contact, prefer players who express emotions related to aggression and motivation.

Many theories are related to this notion that catharsis is especially valuable for releasing aggression through sport. Instinct theories often assume that we have innate instincts to be aggressive, and catharsis allows us to release them in socially acceptable ways. Little empirical evidence supports this theory, despite its intuitive appeal to many people. The frustration-aggression theory suggests that, as the name implies, aggression is manifested when frustration is caused by failure to achieve a goal. But again, little research supports a sport/aggression link because frustration does not always result in aggression, and aggression may be manifest even when frustration does not appear to be present. Indeed, aggressive acts may increase during the course of a sport event rather than decrease in the later stages of the event due to catharsis.

Other theories that apply to aggression (social learning and a revised frustration-aggression theory which incorporates elements of the original frustration-aggression hypothesis as well as social learning theory) are available, but they have similar weaknesses: some individuals may find exercise and sport settings cathartic in relieving anger/aggression, while others do not

(or even find themselves learning to increase aggressive acts). The general public tends to support the notion that aggressive actions, by athletes and/or spectators, have a cathartic effect. However, research supports the exact opposite: engaging in or viewing aggressive actions often leads to increased levels of aggressive feelings and actions. Additionally, learning theory suggests that for those whose aggression facilitates success (winning), emotions related to aggression are reaffirmed and legitimized rather than being purged or cleansed as catharsis theory would predict.

In psychoanalysis, therapeutic approaches (following the lines of Freud) dealt with recalling traumatic events in one's past and venting these experiences, reaching a point of understanding these emotions, and then cleansing/draining these pent-up feelings to achieve symptom relief. Some schools of therapy incorporate the potential healing power of cathartic experiences. This potential may be seen in considering the second use of the term, as a stress reliever. Herein we find a more frequent application of the concept of catharsis, although most exercise and sport participants would not use the term in this way. Many sport participants see physical exercise and sport as stress relievers (although in some competitive situations stress/pressure may be perceived to increase). This is an appropriate hypothesis, and when considering catharsis more metaphorically (or more broadly) it is easy to see that exercise and sport participation could reduce the physical and even cognitive manifestations of tension and stress. Exercise and sport are ideal for this function, especially when stripped of their competitive elements, allowing one to focus on the process of physical activity and the potential joy that comes with human movement. Other activities such as yoga and meditation may be helpful as well. There are, of course, undesirable stress-reducing activities, such as drinking alcoholic beverages and using recreational drugs. Exercise and sport, however, are preferred, because they produce physical and psychological benefits in addition to the stress release/catharsis role they may serve.

SEE ALSO: Health and Sport; Play; Sport and the Body; Violence Among Athletes; Violence Among Fans

REFERENCES AND SUGGESTED READINGS

Bandura, A. (1977) *Social Learning Theory*. Prentice-Hall, Englewood Cliffs, NJ.

Berkowitz, L. (1993) *Aggression: Its Causes, Consequences and Control*. Temple University Press, Philadelphia.

Bohart, A. C. & Stipek, D. J. (Eds.) (2001) *Constructive and Destructive Behavior: Implications for Family, School, and Society*. American Psychological Association, Washington, DC.

English, H. B. & English, A. C. (1958) *A Comprehensive Dictionary of Psychological and Psychoanalytical Terms*. David McKay, New York.

Hays, K. F. (1999) *Working It Out: Using Exercise in Psychotherapy*. American Psychological Association, Washington, DC.

Sachs, M. L. & Buffone, G. W. (1984) *Running as Therapy: An Integrated Approach*. University of Nebraska Press, Lincoln.

sport and the city

Kimberly S. Schimmel

As even a casual observer may recognize, the phenomenon of contemporary sports bears little resemblance to that of the fairly recent past. At the turn of the twentieth century, sports were occasional and unregulated events played by members of local sports clubs. In the late 1950s and early 1960s, an individual's association with sport might have been limited to participant, spectator, or consumer of sport news mainly through radio or newspaper. However, as sports became meaningful to more than just the people who played them, the emergence of crowds at local sport club contests provided the opportunity for risk-taking entrepreneurs to turn games into profit-making ventures. In a relatively short time, traditional agrarian pastimes became today's urban commercial spectacles. Voluntary participation was replaced by binding contractual arrangements, and small hometown rivalries gave way to regional and international urban mega-events produced for global television audiences.

Historians agree that the urbanizing landscapes and expanding capitalist economic system that transformed the societies of Europe and North America fueled the evolution of contemporary sport. The mass production of agricultural and material goods necessary to sustain and stimulate urban growth disrupted traditional patterns of work, leisure, and land use. In large cites such as London and New York, immigrants with widely diverse sporting backgrounds adjusted to the routine of congested urban-industrial culture, which created both the demand and the means for the development and growth of sports. Cities were the sites of the dense populations, transportation networks, technological innovations, discretionary incomes, and entrepreneurial spirit necessary for the success of commercial sports. Additionally, cities were the focus of concerns for health, morality, and community, which continually served as rationales for promoting sports to urbanites. Through numerous case studies, sport historians have documented how the development of sport and the development of cites was intertwined. David Nasaw (1993), for example, shows how cities were not just the problems for which sports were an answer; only cities had the necessary conditions and elements to sustain the rapid growth of sports. Other scholars, including Melvin Adelman and Steven Hardy, considered sports as both cause and effect in the development of physical structures, social organizations, and ideologies in Boston and New York between 1820 and 1915.

A dominant theme in the social science literature on sports and the contemporary city is an examination of the ways sports have come to be valued not for their own sake, but as a means to some other desirable end. City governments, for example, support inner-city "midnight basketball" leagues in an effort to reduce crime rates. In many cities, sport is advertised as a way to generate a sense of civic pride or to create a civic identity. In cities around the globe, sport stadium and infrastructure construction is promoted to have both tangible and intangible benefits for city residents. The tangible benefits are connected to urban regeneration through the belief that sport facilities will attract elite sport teams and events that stimulate the local economy and create jobs. In turn, this investment in sport-related construction is thought to enhance the quality of life for urban community residents. However, many social scientists view with deep caution any notion that sports can act as a solution to general urban problems. While sports may create a sense of attachment that is important at an interpersonal level, these scholars point out that sports does not significantly change the economic, social, and political realities of everyday urban life. Many scholars who study sport-related urban development, for example, refute the claim that this type of civic investment provides real benefits for the city as a whole. Empirical evidence shows that while some groups in a city may profit, others are actually burdened. As has been the case since the rise of sport in an urban-industrial context, ethnic assimilation, class conflict, control of urban space, and race and gender relations are inseparable from the promotion of contemporary sports.

SEE ALSO: Leisure; Sport and Capitalism; Sport, Professional

REFERENCES AND SUGGESTED READINGS

Adelman, M. (1986) *A Sporting Time: New York and the Rise of Modern Athletics, 1820–1870*. University of Illinois Press, Urbana.

Bale, J. (2001) *Sport, Space and the City*. Routledge, New York.

Gratton, C. & Henry, I. P. (Eds.) (2001) *Sport in the City: The Role of Sport in Economic and Social Regeneration*. Routledge, New York.

Hardy, S. (1982) *How Boston Played: Sport, Recreation, and Community 1865–1915*. Northeastern University Press, Boston.

Hardy, S. (1997) Sport in Urbanizing America: A Historical Review. *Journal of Urban History* 23(6): 675–708.

Nasaw, D. (1993) *Going Out: The Rise and Fall of Public Amusements*. Basic Books, New York.

Riess, S. (1989) *City Games: The Evolution of American Urban Culture and the Rise of Sport*. University of Illinois Press, Urbana.

sport, college

D. Stanley Eitzen

Organized sport competition and institutions of higher education are inseparable in the United States. But the intertwining of the two as found in the US is not present in other countries. In European and Scandinavian countries, for example, intercollegiate sports competition is virtually nonexistent. Rather, there are club sports outside of the school system where young people in teams compete against other clubs. Canada fits somewhere between the European way and the American system. Jay Coakley and Peter Donnelly describe the Canadian system as one where interuniversity sports are a normal, but not highly significant, part of student life. There just are no parallels with the highly publicized "big-time" sports programs in US universities. However, sport in the Canadian schools is akin to other levels of university sport in the US, such as the NAIA level of competition (2004: 453). In short, sports are social constructions. In this sense, sport and education can be organized and played in many ways.

College/university sport in the US is organized into six divisions, five administered by the National Collegiate Athletic Association (NCAA) and one by the National Association of Intercollegiate Athletics (NAIA) (Coakley 2004: 494–6). These divisions reflect athletic budget size, level of competition, rules, and the availability of athletic scholarships. The NCAA Division I is subdivided into three categories: 117 schools with big-time football programs (I-A), 123 schools with smaller football programs (I-AA), and 85 schools without football teams but with big-time basketball programs (I-AAA). Division II and Division III with 270 and 410 schools, respectively, have smaller programs with smaller budgets and few, if any, full-time athletic scholarships. The NAIA has about 300 relatively small schools with meager athletic budgets.

To illustrate the differences, the range in athletic budgets is from $70 million at Ohio State University to less than $400,000 at small liberal arts colleges. Large universities may field as many as 18 varsity sports for men and women, while small colleges may have only a few varsity sports, supplemented by a number of club sports. In Division I schools, sports have multiple coaches who are separate from the educational part of their schools, while coaches in Division III and NAIA schools often teach academic classes and may coach two or more teams. The Division I schools are popular on a regional and sometimes a national basis because of television and other media coverage, while schools in other Divisions play in relative obscurity. And, most significant, at the big-time level, student athletes, with few exceptions, are athletes first and students second. At the lower levels, they are students first with the athlete role second. Throughout the world there is no equivalent to the highly commercialized system where athletics supersedes education, as found in the US version of big-time college football and basketball.

Big-time college sport involves many contradictions. The overarching contradiction is that sport is organized as a commercial entertainment activity where educational goals have been compromised. At the heart of this contradiction is that institutions of higher learning allow the enrollment and subsidization of ill-prepared and uninterested students, solely for the purpose of winning games, enhancing the visibility of the university, and producing revenue. This occurs even at the most prestigious institutions where athletes are admitted below the standards applied to others (Shulman & Boyer 2001). Add to this mix demanding coaches who require so much for practice, watching film, travel, weightlifting, and meetings. The athletic subculture also discourages athletes from identifying primarily with the student role (Adler & Adler 1991; Curry 1991).

Positively, college football and basketball offer entertainment, spectacle, excitement, festival, and excellence. Negatively, educational goals have been superseded by the quest for revenue. Because winning programs receive huge revenues from television, gate receipts, fees for seating, bowl and tournament appearances, boosters, and even legislatures, many sports programs are guided by a win-at-any cost philosophy, which leads to a second contradiction.

This contradiction is that while higher education should be a model of ethical behaviors, the enormous pressures to win result on occasion in scandalous behaviors. Sometimes there are illegal payments to athletes. Education is mocked by recruiting athletes unprepared for college studies, altering transcripts, having surrogate test-takers, providing phantom courses, and by not moving the athletes toward graduation. As a result, the graduation rates of male athletes in the revenue-producing sports of football and basketball are relatively low compared to other athletes and to the general student population.

To this contradiction related to ethics add problems associated with the exploitation of athletes. This abuse of athletes takes several forms (Eitzen 2003). One form of abuse is that athletes' freedoms are restricted. Once athletes sign a contract to play for a school, they are bound to that institution. They make a four-year commitment to that university, yet the school makes only a one-year commitment to them. If an athlete wishes to play for another big-time school, he is ineligible for one year. Yet, if a coach wants to cut an athlete from a team, the school is merely bound to provide the scholarship for the remainder of that school year. Furthermore, the right to privacy of athletes is invaded routinely, for example, with mandatory drug testing and bed checks, social controls not applied to other students. Some coaches insist that their athletes not engage in political protest. Some prohibit athletes from associating with individuals or groups that they deem undesirable, and some demand dress codes, organize mandatory leisure time activities, and even inflict their religious beliefs on their athletes. Another form of abuse, although by no means a universal trait of coaches, involves instances of physical and mental cruelty toward athletes. This may take the form of intimidation, humiliation, and even physical aggression.

A third contradiction found in big-time athletic programs is that while universities promote diversity and equity, they have historically denied women and minorities equity in athletics. Using African Americans as an example, they were denied athletic participation in most colleges and universities until the 1950s. Now they are the majority of players in the revenue-producing sports of football and basketball, but are underrepresented as head coaches (in 2004, only five of the 117 Division I-A head football coaches were African American), athletic directors, athletic trainers, and directors of sports information.

Another area of concern in big-time college sports is the dominance of male elite sport. Title IX, which Congress passed in 1972, mandated gender equity in school sports programs. While women's intercollegiate sports programs have made tremendous strides toward that goal, they lag behind men's programs in participation, athletic budgets, athletic scholarships, and coaches' salaries. Moreover, a majority of women's teams are coached by men and the top administrators of athletic departments are overwhelmingly men. If participation in sport is educational in and of itself, a common rationale that university administrators advance in support of college sport, then these educators are caught in a contradiction because many of them willingly accept, and sometimes actively resist, changes to correct the present maldistribution of resources, scholarships, and opportunities for women's sport.

A fourth contradiction is that although big-time sports are revenue producing, for most schools they actually drain money away from academics. This occurs when more scholarship moneys are given to students with athletic abilities than to students with cognitive abilities, and when athletic budgets are supplemented with generous sums from student fees and subsidies from the academic budgets.

Another contradiction involves the influence of money on decision-making as the power to decide tends to leave the university and flow toward the sources of revenue. Television money dictates schedules. Prominent donors may influence the hiring and firing of coaches. When a football coach makes over eight times more money than the university president and when the coach has a powerful constituency outside the university, the athletic "tail" often wags the university "dog," thus subverting the independence of colleges and universities (Sperber 1990: 35).

A final contradiction is that although the marketing/sales side of big-time sport is big business, the production side is an amateur extracurricular activity in which athletes are "paid" only with an "education" (e.g., room, board, tuition, fees, and books). This limitation is to keep the activity "amateur." Economist Andrew Zimbalist (1999: 6) describes this unequal system as like no other industry in the United States, since it manages not to pay its principal producers a wage or a salary. Meanwhile, individuals, schools, and corporations make huge amounts of money off of these "amateurs" (Sack & Staurowsky 1998).

Dealing with these contradictions presents challenges to university administrators. The most commonly suggested reforms are based on a goal of achieving educational objectives and include the following:

- Athletic departments must not be self-contained corporate entities that are separate from the university; rather, they should be placed under the control of university presidents.
- Presidents must monitor athletic programs for illegalities such as recruiting violations, dehumanizing behaviors by coaches, and other unethical acts.
- Athletic departments must also be monitored by an external body other than the NCAA, which has a fundamental conflict of interest.
- Limits should be placed on coaches' income (e.g., no more than the college president).
- Athletes should be paid a living wage.
- Only those athletes who have the potential to compete as students should be admitted – no special admissions and no special curricula for athletes.
- Student athletes must make satisfactory progress toward a degree.
- Time demands on athletes should be kept within reasonable bounds and strictly enforced.
- A comprehensive athletes' bill of rights should be established to ensure a non-exploitive context (Eitzen 2003: 131).
- Moneys from student fees and discretionary funds from the administration, as well as from legislatures, should be funneled exclusively to women's sports and to minor men's sports to achieve greater equity.
- The expenditures for football should be reduced by limiting scholarships and the size of teams, reducing the number of coaches, and eliminating costs unrelated to the health and education of athletes.
- The financial spending race should be stopped by placing limits on the amount that can be spent on capital expenditures for athletics.

In light of these suggestions for reform, administrators have three choices. First, they can retain the current system with all of its contradictions. Second, they can remove the hypocrisy by accepting a semi-professional team that is separate from the educational mandate, but this choice assumes that universities should sponsor commercial entertainment activities outside the sphere of education. A third possibility is to shift to a sports system such as that found at the NCAA Division III level or among the NAIA schools where athletic programs are more likely in harmony with educational goals.

What will happen? If history is a guide, university presidents involved in big-time programs will push the NCAA for cosmetic changes, but they will balk at meaningful structural changes and passively allow athletic programs to do what they have to do to win.

SEE ALSO: Deviance, Sport and; High School Sports; Socialization and Sport; Sport; Sport, Amateur

REFERENCES AND SUGGESTED READINGS

Adler, P. A. & Adler, P. (1991) *Backboards and Blackboards: College Athletes and Role Engulfment.* Columbia University Press, New York.

Coakley, J. (2004) *Sports in Society: Issues and Controversies,* 8th edn. McGraw-Hill, New York.

Coakley, J. & Donnelly, P. (2004) *Sports in Society: Issues and Controversies,* 1st Canadian edn. McGraw-Hill, Ryerson, Toronto.

Curry, T. J. (1991) Fraternal Bonding in the Locker Room: A Profeminist Analysis of Talk About Competition and Women. *Sociology of Sport Journal* 8(2): 119–35.

Eitzen, D. S. (2000) Slaves of Big-Time College Sports. *USA Today: The Magazine of the American Scene* 120 (September): 26–30.

Eitzen, D. S. (2003) *Fair and Foul: Beyond the Myths and Paradoxes of Sport,* 2nd edn. Rowman & Littlefield, Lanham, MD.

Sack, A. L. & Staurowsky, E. J. (1998) *College Athletes for Hire: The Evolution and Legacy of the NCAA's Amateur Myth.* Praeger, Westport, CT.

Shulman, J. L. & Boyer, W. G. (2001) *The Game of Life: College Sports and Educational Values.* Princeton University Press, Princeton.

Sperber, M. (1990) *College Sports, Inc.: The Athletic Department vs. the University.* Henry Holt, New York.

Sperber, M. (2000) *Beer and Circus: How Big-Time College Sports is Crippling Undergraduate Education.* Henry Holt, New York.

Zimbalist, A. (1999) *Unpaid Professionals: Commercialism and Conflict in Big-Time College Sports.* Princeton University Press, Princeton.

sport and culture

David Rowe

For sociologists subscribing to a hierarchical model of culture, sports may be regarded as its antithesis: a bodily practice, of little cultural consequence, gazed on by passive spectators for the enrichment of the leisure and media industries. The neglect of sports as a sociological subject until relatively recently may be attributed to a common resistance within intellectual culture to engagement with the corporeal realm of popular pleasure. However, the increasing prominence of (especially electronically mediated) sports, a more open-minded attitude within sociology to what has often been dismissed as "mass" or "low" culture, and the influence of interdisciplinary approaches (especially cultural studies) has created space for a developed cultural sociology of sport. This shift by no means signals a theoretical, conceptual, and methodological consensus concerning sports and culture in the discipline, but, rather, a new willingness to explore their relationship within a sociological framework.

One obstacle to a sociological engagement with sports and culture is establishing an agreement on the defining characteristics of the objects of analysis, a particular problem given their diversity and dynamism. Precisely what constitutes sports and culture presents, in itself, grounds for dispute, alongside contending evaluations of their relationship. In broad sociological terms, sports can be conceived as the social institution developed out of the rationalization and commercialization of physical game contests that has occurred since the mid-nineteenth century (notably, first, in Britain), and culture as the shifting ensemble of symbols, signifying practices, and texts that give expression and meaning to the social world of which sports is an increasingly significant part. The twin focus of this entry, then, is on the place and influence of sports within the wider sociocultural sphere, and on the specific, rapidly developing characteristics of sports as a "subset" of society and culture as a whole.

SPORTS AND THE "CULTURAL TURN" IN SOCIOLOGY

Many sociologists have noted – and often regretted – the "cultural turn" in sociology that has produced, among other subdisciplinary shifts, an increasing interest in sports. Prior to the 1960s there was a tendency for sociologists to be suspicious of the everyday subjects that appeared epiphenomenal to the main sociological determinants – class structures, state relations, and so on. However, analyzing culture, especially in its popular form, became a more compelling activity in the light of what can be called "culturalization" and "mediatization" – the heightened social, economic, and political importance of the making of meaning and the circulation of symbols, especially through popular media such as television, radio, magazines, newspapers, and recorded music. Stuart Hall (1989: 128) makes this point eloquently in proposing that, in the late twentieth century, a "New Times" had emerged that demanded new perspectives. For Hall, culture is no longer, and probably never has been, the epiphenomenal symbolic superstructure determined by the material socioeconomic base. Culture is now deeply material in its productive processes, and the material world is permeated by cultural practices and meanings.

Sociologists in the post-World War II era began to find the objectivist tradition of mainstream sociology (and the streak of puritanic rationalism that it often displayed) overly austere and lacking in contemporary relevancy. The influence of youth culture, for example, now registered in subcultural and deviancy theory, and the popularization and personalization of politics (encapsulated in the catchcry "the personal is the political") taken up by feminist and postcolonial scholars also resonated within sociology. More sociologists felt licensed to embrace everyday life as a legitimate starting and reference point for their investigations of the social. Addressing popular cultural subjects like rock music, television consumption, and sports enabled a more reflexive mode of analysis that conceived culture as dialectically constitutive of structural relations, not as the predetermined outcome of them. New strands of social theory, such as postmodernism, and interdisciplinary perspectives like cultural and media studies, challenged the grand narratives of sociological theory and the integrity of its disciplinary boundaries. The distanced, all-seeing eye of macrosociology was criticized for producing a universalist regime of knowledge that obscured its own historically conditioned, subjectivist limitations. The cultural turn enabled (mainly male) sociologists who were "closet" sports aficionados (fans), as well as those who had felt victimized by sports (through compulsory physical education at school or by the ideologies embedded in the sports media), to interrogate, critically and self-reflexively, their own and others' cultural tastes and consumption. Adopted excessively, such an approach can be condemned as unscientific, impressionistic, narcissistic, and self-indulgent. But with appropriate attention to the enduring questions and techniques of sociology, it is able to illuminate the ways in which contemporary culture (aided and abetted by capital and state formations) is both shaped by and profoundly influences the social.

Taking sports seriously as culture, therefore, was a crucial step in a more general reinvigoration of sociological inquiry. Instead of seeing sports and other forms of popular culture simply from, say, a functionalist perspective – and thereby necessarily emphasizing its adaptive and integrative ramifications for the social whole – it became possible to explore sports as a social domain of contending ideologies and values with a disparate range of relations to social reproduction and change. Similarly, from an orthodox conflict (including Marxist) sociological perspective, sports tended to be seen as a straightforward product of social class relations, especially those involving commodification and "false consciousness," but a less mechanical engagement with sports as culture offers a more dialectical, complex understanding that is less reliant on a single, central axis of domination and subordination.

The analysis of sports in traditional macro-sociological terms can still be productive, but a culturalist approach, appropriately informed by social theory, is able to draw on a richer, more contingent theoretical repertoire as well as a more intimate, ethnographic insight into how sports culture is "lived" as everyday practice. This intellectual project does not necessitate the abandonment of formative sociological questions of structure, agency, and power, but helps to "rehabilitate" and extend them into hitherto neglected areas of growing prominence. In this regard, sports, by a series of measures, can be seen to be a pivotal element of contemporary society and culture. Its raw popularity as spectacle alone makes it so – for example, it has been estimated that the cumulative audience for the 2002 Korea/Japan World Cup of association football was 28.8 billion viewers; that 9 out of 10 people in the world with access to television watched some part of the Sydney 2000 Olympic Games; and that there was 35,000 hours of dedicated broadcast coverage of the 2004 Athens Olympic Games among 220 countries. Such "mega-media" sports events are profoundly instructive about cultural change in (post)modernity.

THE RISE OF SPORTS CULTURE AND THE CULTURAL SOCIOLOGY OF SPORTS

Over the last three centuries, occasional physical folk play and game contests have become codified, scheduled practices, and the love of the game (the "amour" at the root of "amateurism") has progressively given way to professional spectator sports. The relatively modest remuneration of sportspeople (mostly male) that followed the decline of the class-based, aristocratic ideal of the "sporting gentleman" involved first the payment of expenses and lost wages by those who had to exchange their labor power to live; then payment for play that was usually insufficient to provide a living wage; and, later, reasonable returns for "sportswork" for the duration of the usually short and uncertain career of the professional athlete. But, just as in other areas of the labor market where income inequality grew

between fellow workers in the same industry and between industries, so the emerging cultural "sale-ability" of sports has produced "superstars" compensated at extraordinary levels. Conspicuous examples of celebrity athletes include the African American basketballer Michael Jordan, surveyed in the 1990s as the world's most recognizable individual, and English footballer David Beckham, whose high profile, like Jordan's, derives from "leveraging" his sports standing for a diverse range of pecuniary purposes. The restructuring of the athletic labor market into a tiny minority of the "super rich," a larger but still small group of modestly rewarded professionals, and a vast number of aspiring professional athletes with little prospect of success, reflects a "structure of culture" in sports that now aligns it closely to the broader entertainment industries.

Even those (the majority of active sportspeople, although not of the whole population) who play sports but earn little or no income from it are part of a large sports industry supplying facilities, clothing, training, and equipment. Thus, professional athletes represent the alluring face of contemporary sports, behind which lies the "industrial" engine that produces it – including sponsors, advertisers, media companies, sports agencies, peak sports organizations, management, equipment and clothing manufacturers, privately and publicly funded sports educators, administrative and training bodies, and research scientists. Systematic planning, design, and operation are central to contemporary sports, while retaining a crucial symbolic element of a spontaneous culture of play.

Sports is, then, both symptom and cause of a much larger sociocultural shift, as the highly localized cultural practices of spatially fixed settlements such as villages and small towns have become concentrated in large urban centers, only for sports to be redispersed in mediated form through their dissemination as images and sounds. This symbolic sports communication, in turn, has become a pivotal means by which national cultural identity can be constructed through the sports press, and public service and commercial broadcasting. Mediated international sports events are extraordinary opportunities for internal and external representations of nation, an inherently ideological practice demanding close sociological interrogation, not least because of its apparent innocence. This brief sketch reveals how mediated sports culture can attract the interest of sports sociologists, who have found its terrain richly productive, pursuing questions surrounding social relations, economics, politics, ideology, and culture within and beyond the sports world.

Dimensions of Sports and Culture

The major dimensions of the sports–culture relationship concern the impacts of the industrial development of sport, the social ideologies that circulate within the "media sports cultural complex" (Rowe 2004: 4), and the positioning and influence of sports within the wider sociocultural sphere. In relation to sports and industry, the developments outlined above can be regarded as important elements of the penetration of the logic of capital into everyday culture. Inducing, from the mid-nineteenth century onwards, spectators to pay to enter the controlled space of the sports stadium in order to watch paid athletes perform, is a significant instance of the industrialization of leisure time and practice. The combination of the incipient sports industry and the betting and hospitality industries proved an effective way of facilitating the congregation of large crowds and the expenditure of the discretionary income that organized labor secured from the owners of capital. A class-cultural dimension to the sports industry reproducing wider social structural relations is an important feature of its historical formation. For example, cricketers were divided by class into (amateur) gentlemen and (professional) players well into the twentieth century, and horse racing – the "sport of kings" – displayed a hierarchy extending from the member's enclosure down to the "punters" restricted to the open areas of racecourses. As the sports industry has grown and "massified," these overt class-cultural distinctions have been less sharply drawn, but they have not been eradicated. For example, the "bourgeoisification" of contemporary sports stadia, including expensive seating, corporate boxes, and high-class catering, has ensured that quality of access and service provision are governed by socioeconomic circumstances. Similarly, the sports labor market is stratified and segmented, with privileged access to individual expensive sports (such as golf and tennis) more readily available to the already privileged, while in team sports there are patterned divisions of labor that commonly restrict leadership positions to the socially advantaged (the practice of "stacking").

Although these spatialized aspects of sports culture remain important – major stadia, for example, are invested with the kind of quasi-spiritual qualities that lend support to the proposition that sports is a secular religion – the most important force in the development of sports over the last century has been its increasingly intense relationship with the media. Without the media, sports would be hampered by the restrictions of time and space, with itinerant caravans of sports people displaying their wares in different towns, cities, and countries. This practice is, of course, still evident, but in economic terms it is much less significant than another, more flexible process: the symbolic transportation of the unique sports event to the domestic hearth. The simultaneous development of the sports and media industries has been, although not without some tensions, synergistic. The development of sports was limited while it relied on the staging of events for the exclusive pleasure of those present. Correspondingly, the commercial media could not flourish without regular, popular uses for their communicative infrastructure enabling exposure of large audiences to the advertisers who underwrote their print and electronic texts. In sports, with its large, passionate audiences, regular, relatively inexpensive and "long-form" programming, and capacity to function in both news and entertainment genres, the media found an ideal industry partner. As a result, sports became an integral component of contemporary culture, inescapable for all citizens regardless of their cultural tastes because of the efficiency and reach of the sports media.

Because of its intimate involvement with the media, sports is a highly effective bearer of social ideologies disguised as natural, self-evident truths. The sports industry is imbued with a highly performative ethos, with its outcomes organized around measurable qualities and outcomes – winning and losing, faster and slower, stronger and weaker, and so on. When coupled with an ideology of transparent meritocracy (those who succeed deserve and can be seen to do so) and a mythology of a sports world that stands aloof from the "ordinary" world, sports culture can be seen to offer a microcosm of a simpler, fairer universe. In this sense, there is a close articulation between sporting values and neoliberal ideology. But sports culture also contains within it anti-modernizing values reliant on tribalism and collective identity. Sports as cultural practice is arbitrary and trivial in that it consists of rule-governed physical game contests onto which meaningful significance is projected by participants and spectators. The often nostalgic (and, indeed, sometimes atavistic) forms of identification on which sports draws its cultural power may, then, release reactionary impulses that are inimical to the "disembedding" that is constantly attempted by modernism and neoclassical economics. For example, as discussed below, the spatial relocation of a sports team (economically classified as a franchise), as has occurred with many gridiron and ice hockey teams in the USA, or the attempted takeover of a sports club, can stimulate anti-market, anti-capitalist sentiments among sports fans. Such ideological tensions within sports mean that its institutional analysis cannot be reduced to an assumed capture by a commercial ethos. Instead, sports can be seen as a social site – albeit one that is heavily scored with ideologies of dominance – in which the cultural interplay involves social ideologies that are both reinforced and contested.

These ideologies in and of sports do not only involve, directly, matters of capital and labor. The (re)construction of the nation through international sports competition can reinforce, in some instances, racism and xenophobia, but also challenge the power of globalizing processes to erase the specific qualities of the local. Sports culture displays a discourse that is split between universalism (humanity united by the love of and respect for the game) and particularism (humanity fractured into competing, partisan clusters that support one team – sometimes violently – against national, racial, and ethnic others). The critical task of sports sociology is to analyze, "without prejudice," these fissures and tensions within sports culture.

The linkage between nationalism and gender – the "masculinization" of citizenship criticized by feminists – suggests the potential role of sports in the cultural "enforcement" of the societal gender order. Sports, like many other cultural forms, is marked at many levels by sex and gender, although there are few forms of culture that have been so clearly and consistently divided by sex (reflected most obviously by sexually segregated competitions). The social construction of sexual difference in sports – its gendered complexion – is an important subject when analyzing the ideological reinforcement of notions of masculine superiority and exclusion.

Sports, both with regard to participation and spectatorship, is historically a key aspect of masculine culture. According to the "objective" performative measures of sports, men dominate in terms of athletic records, athlete remuneration, and spectator interest. Over the last century, in which women have challenged men in many domains – such as the workplace, representative government, and the home – sports has tended ideologically to reproduce male (pre) dominance. Those sports prizing the qualities in which men have an advantage (biologically inherited and socially learned) with regard to strength, speed, and aggression (as opposed to, say, style, subtlety, and cooperation), have consistently been the most valorized in sports culture.

However, the logic of capital accumulation has simultaneously eroded this gender segregation, as the saturation of the male and the neglect of the female spectator markets have been recognized. The commercial importance of television sports spectating, in particular, has prompted systematic strategies to attract the female viewers who also make many of the purchasing decisions on household products. Sports broadcasts are now increasingly tailored to mixed-sex audiences, but greater recognition of women as viewers has not been matched by higher status in sports. Thus, apart from a small number of elite sports, such as tennis and golf, and relatively infrequent multi-sports events, like the Olympic and Commonwealth Games, the gendered culture of sports is largely one of males and females watching predominantly male sports (such as the football codes of soccer, rugby, gridiron and league, and other major team sports such as basketball, ice hockey, and baseball). Male viewing of female sports is routinely accompanied in sports journalism and commentary by their sexual objectification, and an emphasis on their performative inferiority (in relation to men), maternal and marital status, and dependency on males. This assertion of "hegemonic masculinity" is also applied to other men, especially those who are homosexual, and is expressed in sexist and homophobic insults in sports (such as "playing like a girl/ queer"). Again, however, the gendered repositioning of sports marketing has fostered the sexualization and reconstruction of sporting masculinity, leading sportsmen (such as David Beckham) who adopt a more flexible, (post)modern masculine style, to become subjects of popular debate concerning new forms of manliness.

By such means, the space of sports culture can operate as a forum for wider social debate about change and continuity. Recurrent sports scandals, intensively covered by the media, are especially prominent vehicles for collective reassessments both of the institution of sports and the societies of which it is a part. For example, financial impropriety (such as betting-related match fixing in association football and cricket, or secret inducements to the International Olympic Committee members who decide on which city is to host the Summer and Winter Olympic Games) and the use of performance-enhancing drugs in sports (for example, in Olympic athletics and weightlifting, and Tour de France cycling), provoke intense debates about the corruption of sports by commerce and the associated privileging of ends over means. Personal indiscretions by sports stars, ranging from the criminal (such as rape) to the individual-ethical (like infidelity), also discursively bridge the sports and wider social worlds, enabling the airing of issues that concern both the corrosive effects of celebrity culture and the everyday dilemmas confronting "ordinary" people that are held in common with sports stars. Sports culture, from this perspective, can be regarded as a vivid symbolic canvas onto which grand pictures of contemporary society are drawn, often with reference to idealized representations of the past.

Sports discourse and language is also highly influential in framing the wider society in its own image – the "sportification" of society. As noted above, there is an apparently simple competitive logic within sports that conjures up a world of clearly defined competitors, rules, and outcomes. As a result, sports metaphors, such as those involving "level playing fields," regulatory "hurdles," and "races" for company acquisitions and profit goals, have insinuated themselves into business discourse, not least in news bulletins. Similarly, political discourse in representative liberal democracies is suffused with the language of sports, with electoral contests, parliamentary debates and policy disagreements routinely framed in the language of sports encounters. Advertisers also often "pitch" products and services in sporting terms, with companies and consumers represented as "teams" and "oppositions," and the visual imagery of sports used to depict producers and consumers. The ideological implications of representing diverse organizations, relations, and practices as analogous to sports phenomena require skeptical sociological examination given their symbolic reduction of complex social, economic, and political processes to simple, imagined sports contests and outcomes.

Such ideological deployments of the culture of sports also impute to it a "purity" of contest (based on talent, tactical acumen, and diligence) that is highly contestable. For example, success in international sports, while often represented as reflecting national character and physique, is also deeply influenced by the resources provided by capital and the state to support the sporting effort. Success in sports, as in commerce and politics, is the product of the mobilization of existing (often inherited) social advantage; "behind-the-scenes" maneuvering, not all of which is legal or ethical; and contingencies (favorable or unfavorable conditions). The idealization of sports draws misleading, ideologically loaded contrasts between it and other domains of social practice. For this reason, sports sociologists and their counterparts in cultural studies, gender studies, postcolonial studies, and so on, have counseled skepticism when the "lessons" of sports have been extended to other social spheres.

Nonetheless, the resilience and influence of sports culture cannot be underestimated. Elements of sports culture constantly threaten to spill out into the wider sociocultural spaces. For example, viewers of television – the medium that, despite "post-broadcasting" challenges by new media technologies such as the Internet, remains the most popularly significant form of contemporary culture – have increasingly been presented within the high-profile television genre of "reality TV." Formats such as *Survivor*, *(American) Idol*, and *Big Brother* are profoundly influenced by sports and sports television. They all involve, like sports, "actuality" coverage of contestants in competition with each other for a prize, shot from multiple angles, points-of-view, and speeds. The contests require strategic and tactical maneuvers akin to sports contests, with competing teams and individuals, and performative tasks and goals. There is also, like sports, fan participation, including expressions of approval or disapproval of contestants, and large, staged real-time events with boisterous audiences. In other words, it can be argued that sports has not only, as is often claimed, taken on the values and practices of entertainment but, by means of a cultural feedback loop, it now influences other major forms of popular culture. Indeed, sports has challenged the prime place of rock music as the principal source of popular cultural "cool" style in the last two decades.

Central to popular culture is the figure of the fan, and sports is a key arena in which a dynamic interplay between culture and commerce in fandom can be discerned. The sports fan is often represented in sports sociology as something of a victim of powerful commercial forces, stripped of agency by the capture of their pastime by capital and the state. The media, in particular, are often accused of taking over sports, with television reducing its physical practice to sedentary spectacle, and shaping sports contests to fit the demands of audience maximization and broadcast schedules. Sociologists have also been critical of the media's imputed seizure and deformation of sports discourse. Because sports is a cultural form that can be readily adapted to fill cultural space throughout the media – including live, replayed, and edited broadcasts, quiz shows, news bulletins, feature films, documentaries, newspaper sections, photo-essays, magazines, novels, and biographies – sports culture can appear reducible to a simple, unidirectional relationship between a range of media producers and passive cohorts of media sports consumers. However, this is a misleading account of how popular culture is made, remade, and used that relies on totalizing and static analyses of cultural relations.

While there is a corresponding danger of romanticizing the resistive agency of the fan, sports culture displays many examples of fandom in action that do not correspond to orderly and guided consumption. Fans are by no means inherently progressive – indeed, as was noted earlier, sports culture is often deeply nostalgic and characterized by xenophobia, leading on occasions to racially motivated abuse and violence. The inequitable gender order described above that is structured into the formal institutions of sports can also be viewed as a common feature of "informal" sports fandom – for example, in the many exclusive, homosocial fan groupings in association football, or in some crowd chants and behavior towards women in sport stadia. In this regard, though, sports culture can be seen to be connected to wider social structures, practices, and values – it would be profoundly unsociological to imagine otherwise. Reactionary behavior and values are not the preserve of sports, but it provides a vivid popular theater in which all forms of signifying practice – whether socially progressive or regressive – can be accentuated and "writ large." Indeed, the pivotal presence of the media creates circumstances in which sports spectators are not just watchers, but also the self-consciously watched, and so can be performing, like the professional athlete, for each other, for others present, and for the vast, unseen television audience. The mediated spectacles that are so central to sports culture are, then, opportunities for spectators to be key participants as essential producers of the atmosphere ("ambience") of the sports event.

Sports fandom, then, exhibits a number of responses to the transformation of sports and the society of which it is a part. For example, the aforementioned "bourgeoisification" of sports, through which spectatorship is systematically subjected to a commodifying, "civilizing" leisure consumer influence intended to replace earlier unruly, proletarian, and aggressively masculine forms of sports fandom, has provoked some (mostly male) sports fans to protest against its sanitization. The unhappiness of some fans with what they see as clichéd and compromised professional sports journalism has also encouraged the emergence of "fanzines," which range from technically rudimentary publications with small circulations to more sophisticated, widely read, idiosyncratic magazines that take both sports journalism and the sports industry to task for their lack of consideration for grassroots fans.

Fan activism can also take on more formal political dimensions, as in the case of lobbying by the Independent Manchester United Supporters Association against the attempted takeover in 1999 of Manchester United Football Club by the dominant force in English football television, the Rupert Murdoch-controlled BSkyB. The British government accepted the view, put by these football supporters, the fans of other clubs, and the non-Murdoch media, that such a move would overly concentrate power in football, reduce economic competition in the football industry, and have deleterious social effects by disadvantaging smaller football clubs and so their local communities. Here it can be seen that sports culture is a test bed for both economic and social debates, with the proponents of the takeover arguing that the primary locus of the association football industry was no longer national but international (in this case European), and that city-based fans look beyond the nation to new, transnational communities (in this case involving supporters of equivalently elite clubs from Italy, Spain, Holland, and other countries). The deregulation of the football labor market through the so-called 1995 "Bosman ruling," and its associated freedom of labor migration within the European Union, challenged received ideas of local and national sports, just as the extension of the functions of the European Union, the operation of the World Trade Organization, and other transnational arrangements and agreements have caused wider anxieties. The highly charged area of sports, therefore, can symbolize and articulate in a concrete, dramatic fashion often abstract notions of transnational regulation and national identity.

In the same year that many Manchester United fans agitated against a takeover of the club, in the United States fans of the Cleveland Browns gridiron team (supported by its local elite), following the owner's relocation of the franchise to Baltimore, successfully lobbied the National Football League to award it an expansion team, allow it to retain its key signifiers (name and colors), and even to provide a loan to renovate its stadium. Not all such activist campaigns are successful and, indeed, most of them are defensive rather than proactive in nature, but they reveal that sports culture is in part created by affective, identity-based communities and coalitions that are sometimes able to influence developments in sports, rather than the product of a monolithic "sportsbiz" with an unstoppable commodifying momentum.

Thus, sports fans sometimes identify themselves as citizens who demand respect for the rights of "cultural citizenship" associated with sports. This extension of the concept of citizenship to the cultural domain reflects the strengthening of the broad processes of "culturalization" and "mediatization" discussed above. It registers in the successful petitioning of many governments to enshrine access to prime free-to-air television sports (as opposed to its delivery only through paid subscription) as part of a citizen's cultural entitlement and heritage, and in the reluctance of peak sports bodies like the IOC to allow sports broadcasting exclusivity to "pay" television operators. It is also evident in agitation to provide citizens' access to sports infrastructure – including community sports facilities, elite institutes of sport, and high-quality sports stadia – to be guaranteed by state subvention. Furthermore, opposition to sports sponsorship promoting and advertising unhealthy products (such as tobacco) and support for the use of sports in health promotion campaigns (such as the landmark "Sport for All" and "Life. Be In It" campaigns) have prompted positive and negative intervention in sports by the state. Thus, as sports culture has become increasingly pervasive in social life, it has taken on a range of features, including athletic display, carnivalesque fandom, commercial deployment, and state regulation.

The participants in this culture are, in some form, almost of necessity the entire population, which is confronted daily by sports, willingly or not. The omnipresent signs of sports in public and media space ensure that, to a degree, contemporary culture has been "sportified." These circumstances have stimulated more discerning, interactive forms of sports fandom and consumption. For example, new media technologies have reduced the power of a small number of television companies and their producers to determine when and how a televised sports event can be seen. Digital broadcasting has made it possible for viewers to make many of their own spectatorial decisions, such as which match to watch in a tennis tournament, which camera angles to use, and what statistical data to summon. The advent of the Internet, furthermore, has created multifarious opportunities for fans to access written sports texts and still and moving images, thereby eroding the centralized power of large media corporations. However, such choices can only be made by those affluent enough to invest in the requisite equipment and services (apart from those provided freely or cheaply by public service broadcasters), thereby indicating that debates about empowering sports fans cannot be isolated from broader questions of social equity and access.

SPORTS AND CULTURE: INTO THE FUTURE

The sociological analysis of sports and culture has to deal adequately with the size, complexity, scope, and volatility of its immediate subject, and then to seek to encompass its deep intrication with the sociocultural world as a whole. This is no mean task, and, as Crawford (2004: 111) has noted in relation to sports fandom and consumption, there has been a strong temptation to concentrate on out-of-the-ordinary phenomena and to advance already-constructed theories founded on binary notions of hegemony and resistiveness. Crawford complains that little serious attention has been given to the mundane, everyday experience and consumption of sport, with researchers drawn to unrepresentative groups of especially ardent fans, whose very conspicuousness makes them relatively easy to research. Thus, he argues, sports researchers have tended to conceive sports fandom as an artifact of a theoretical predisposition that neatly divides it into dichotomous clusters of passive sports consumers and actively resistant sports fans. This observation is a reminder of Raymond Williams's famous dictum that "culture is ordinary." Sports culture, it might be observed, is now an ordinary element of social life, punctuated by extraordinary moments, both of which offer multiple opportunities to research the dynamics of increasingly heterogeneous, evanescent social formations.

Sociological inquiry into sports and culture is, then, an exacting exercise. It has been limited, once belatedly commenced, by inherited dualistic theoretical frameworks, with a functionalist assessment of social adaptation and integration posited against a conflict theory-based (often Marxist-inflected) critique of sports culture. Each tradition has produced its own variants and developments, with those emphasizing the more benign ritual dimensions of sports culture challenged by assertions of its repressiveness, although sometimes conceding that sport can be a site of popular cultural "productivity" where structures and ideologies of dominance are countered by (self-reflexive or unconscious) communities of resistance. The theories and methods adopted in this field of research and scholarship have tended to reflect these divergent positions. Disciplinary debate is crucial to the health of sociology, but the divergent approaches of political economy, ethnography, discourse analysis, textual interpretation, and so on evident in analyses of sports culture have often resulted in an unproductive series of parallel, disconnected conversations.

In current and anticipated trends, though, there are some signs of more auto-critical and less predictable approaches to sports and culture. These are less likely to imply that sports culture can be hermetically sealed from its global, national, and local social context, and are more attuned to the specific, contingent ways in which sports culture can exert its influence on wider society. This research and scholarship demands a closer attention to what constitutes sports, how it is mediated, and the diverse, structurally influenced ways in which it is encountered and used by human subjects in their various social locations and relational networks. The overwhelming available evidence is that sports is an increasingly important component of culture and society in nations with conspicuously different histories. The global "club" of sports is no longer exclusive (there are, for example, currently 202 National Olympic Committees across five continents), but the power that can be wielded within sports culture is highly variable and clearly related to other resources of power (including economic, military, and geopolitical). The form that sports culture takes in different national and transnational contexts is both highly diverse and globally connected, and demands a rejuvenated, theoretically rigorous, historically informed, and culturally attuned sociology of sports and culture.

SEE ALSO: Body and Cultural Sociology; Identity, Sport and; Media and Sport; Sport, Alternative; Sport Culture and Subcultures; Sport as Spectacle; Sports Heroes and Celebrities

REFERENCES AND SUGGESTED READINGS

Andrews, D. L. & Jackson, S. J. (Eds.) (2001) *Sport Stars: The Cultural Politics of Sporting Celebrity.* Routledge, New York.
Bernstein, A. & Blain, N. (Eds.) (2003) *Sport, Media, Culture: Global and Local Dimensions.* Frank Cass, London.
Birrell, S. & Cole, C. L. (Eds.) (1994) *Women, Sport, and Culture.* Human Kinetics, Champaign, IL.
Birrell, S. & McDonald, M. G. (2000) (Eds.) *Reading Sport: Critical Essays on Power and Representation.* Northeastern University Press, Boston.
Boyle, R. & Haynes, R. (2000) *Power Play: Sport, the Media and Popular Culture.* Pearson Education, Harlow.
Cashmore, E. (Ed.) (2000) *Sports Culture: An A–Z Guide.* Routledge, London.
Crawford, G. (2004) *Consuming Sport: Fans, Sport and Culture.* Routledge, New York.
Hall, S. (1989) The Meaning of New Times. In: Hall, S. & Jacques, M. (Eds.), *New Times: The Changing Face of Politics in the 1990s.* Lawrence & Wishart, London, pp. 116–34.
Hargreaves, J. (1986) *Sport, Power and Culture.* Polity Press, Cambridge.
King, A. (2003) *The European Ritual: Football in the New Europe.* Ashgate, Aldershot.
Martin, R. & Miller, T. (Eds.) (1999) *SportCult.* University of Minnesota Press, Minneapolis.
Miller, T. (2001) *Sportsex.* Philadelphia, Temple University Press.
Miller, T., Lawrence, G., McKay, J., & Rowe, D. (2001) *Globalization and Sport: Playing the World.* Sage, London.
Roche, M. (2000) *Mega-Events and Modernity: Olympics and Expos in the Growth of Global Culture.* Routledge, New York.
Rowe, D. (1995) *Popular Cultures: Rock Music, Sport and the Politics of Pleasure.* Sage, London.
Rowe, D. (2004) *Sport, Culture and the Media: The Unruly Trinity,* 2nd edn. Open University Press, Maidenhead.
Tomlinson, A. (1999) *The Game's Up: Essays in the Cultural Analysis of Sport, Leisure and Popular Culture.* Ashgate, Aldershot.
Wenner, L. A. (Ed.) (1998) *MediaSport.* Routledge, New York.
Whannel, G. (1992) *Fields in Vision: Television Sport and Cultural Transformation.* Routledge, London.
Whannel, G. (2001) *Media Sport Stars: Masculinities and Moralities.* Routledge, London.

sport culture and subcultures

Peter Donnelly

Research and theoretical approaches to sport culture and subcultures in the sociology of sport fall into three overlapping periods: (1) early interest in sport subcultures from an interactionist perspective; (2) a transition period during which more critical theoretical approaches to culture and subcultures and more rigorous methodological approaches emerged; and (3) a wholehearted embrace of "cultural studies" and the consequent fragmentation of approaches to sport culture and subcultures. These changes were accompanied by parallel theoretical and definitional concerns about the meaning of culture and subculture.

Following the example of sociologists such as Howard Becker and Everett Hughes, some of the earliest work in the emerging subdiscipline of sociology of sport concerned sport subcultures. Weinberg and Arond's (1952) study of boxers preceded studies of professional baseball players, professional wrestling, pool hustlers, ice hockey players, and the various jobs involved in horse racing. These were followed by a series of striking comparative studies of, for example, hockey players and Hollywood musicians, professional wrestlers and physicians, and female gymnasts and professional wrestlers.

These studies of occupational subcultures were grounded in the US tradition of subcultural research. Definitions of culture had not really developed beyond Tylor's (1871) "complex whole which includes knowledge, belief, art, morals, law, custom, and any other capabilities acquired by man as a member of society." Culture was that which humans passed along socially, rather than biologically; subcultures were sub-units of the larger culture; and even Fine and Kleinman's (1979) attempt to "rethink" subculture maintained a basic interactionist definition in which "the referent group" encourages potential members to take on the cultural characteristics of a particular subculture. The original subcultural research in sociology, focusing on youth and deviance, had spread from "deviant careers" to other occupations and avocations, and Arnold (1972) provided justification for the study of sport subcultures by arguing that they "have a sociological importance in and of themselves." Arnold proposed that membership in such "achieved" (as opposed to ascribed) subcultures provided an alternative identity status as the institutional significance of work decreased.

Ingham (1975) signaled the critical shift in the sociology of sport subcultures by combining Marx, Weber, and Goffman in his analysis of "occupational subcultures in the work-world of sport." His work was contemporary with a "cultural turn" in both sociology and the sociology of sport. Culture was no longer something relatively inert, "meanings and ways" that were passed from generation to generation; rather, it was a social construction, a site of struggles, something that was produced, reproduced, and resisted – and subcultures could now be seen as both the engines of cultural production and the battlegrounds for contesting culture. As Bourdieu (1993) pointed out: "The field of sporting practice is the site of struggles in which what is at stake, *inter alia*, is the monopolistic capacity to impose the legitimate definition of sporting practice and the legitimate function of sporting activity."

Thus, in sport, these struggles were fought over the "meanings and ways" of what was now being recognized as a dominant sport culture – a culture that was outcome, achievement, and record oriented; a culture that was characterized by homogenizing principles of governance and commercial interest. In the dominant sport culture, sport was rationalized and utilitarian – it was for the purposes of entertainment and/or to encourage civic/national pride; it was to demonstrate the effectiveness of a political ideology (e.g., Olympics during the Cold War); it was for the purposes of health (in the new era of privatized/personal conceptions of health); and it was primarily for socialization – character,

work habits and discipline, individual achievement and teamwork, etc.; or even just to occupy the time of those considered to be "dangerous" or "youth-at-risk" (e.g., "midnight basketball" for the social control of urban youth).

Studies of sport subcultures slowly began to incorporate these changes, influenced both by Geertz's (1973) "thick description," which produced richer and more nuanced ethnographies, and by the more politicized ethnography and subculture theory that was developing at the Centre for Contemporary Cultural Studies in England. Although the broader notion of "career" was still at the root of most research, there was also the beginning of a change toward socialization and identity factors in sport subcultures, an interest in class cultures and sport, and the beginning of a focus on sport subcultures as sites of cultural production. Gruneau (1981) pointed out that the study of sport subcultures now concerned how "subcultures, with their various 'establishment' and 'countercultural' emphases, have been constitutively inserted into the struggles, the forms of compliance and opposition, social reproduction and transformation, associated with changing patterns of social development." Bishop and Hoggett (1987) similarly argued that sport and leisure subcultures are crucial sites for the transmission, resistance, and negotiation of the dominant values of the larger society.

Research during this second period maintained an interest in careers – extending that interest to the life cycle of a career in sports, and to processes of socialization and desocialization or retirement from participation (for a collection of studies representing this type of research, see Coakley & Donnelly 1999). Identity issues also began to emerge in terms of how individuals developed appropriate subcultural identities and how those identities are negotiated and accepted (or not) by other members.

Further evidence of transition during this period concerns what are now referred to as alternative or extreme sport subcultures – they were "alternative" to the dominant sport culture, openly rejecting many of the "meanings and ways" noted above. Earlier research on sports such as surfing and rock climbing had focused on the activities as deviant subcultures; research emerging at this time began to reinterpret the alternative nature of such subcultures as "resistance" rather than "deviance." This work also led to recognition of the ephemeral nature of resistance to the dominant sport culture, and the ways in which activities such as freestyle skiing, skateboarding, and snowboarding were subject to commercial and media pressures, and to incorporation by the dominant sport culture. The life cycle of freestyle skiing, from its "hot dog" origins, resisting all of the trappings of mainstream sport, to almost complete incorporation into the international skiing federation (FIS) and recognition as an Olympic sport, represents a classic example of such resistance and incorporation (Donnelly 1988). Using Raymond Williams's approach to hegemony and resistance, Donnelly (1993) also showed how alternative cultural formations were evident in both residual and emergent contexts.

Recent research on sport culture and subcultures represents a completion of the shift toward cultural studies evident in the transition period, and an increasing fragmentation of approaches to subcultures parallel to the broader fragmentation of approaches to sociology following the postmodern turn. In addition to an increasing interest in identity work in sport subcultures, there has been increased interest in (and opposition to) the idea of a global sport culture, increasing amounts of research on fan culture and celebrity culture in sports, and a substantial focus (given the embodied nature of sports) on body culture. Research in the sociology of the body now covers a wide range of bodily practices, including sports. As Bourdieu (1993) pointed out, the definitional struggles associated with sport also extend to defining the "legitimate body" and "legitimate uses of the body." Definitional concerns have also reappeared with regard to the concept of subculture itself, with some contending that "subworld" represents a better descriptor than "subculture" of the cultures that emerge around sports; they argue that "subculture" implies a condition of domination and subordination that does not exist in some sport "subworlds." And theoretical issues range from concerns that some researchers have overused the concept of resistance to the point that it no longer has a political impact, to concerns that studies of subcultures imply a homogeneity of culture where heterogeneity is widespread.

Recent research suggests that sport sociologists will continue to be interested in fan culture, celebrity culture, and body culture in sports, and interest in alternative sport subcultures is increasingly popular. To the extent that sport subcultural research continues to shed light on the historical processes by which *a* way of playing a sport becomes *the* way of playing the sport; on the ways that cultural meanings and ways are produced in sport subcultures; and on the ways in which sport subcultures are involved in larger processes of resistance, social reproduction, and social transformation, such research will continue to be of interest to sociologists. The recent reemergence of interest in class cultures in sport suggests that this is still the case.

SEE ALSO: Sport and Culture; Sport as Spectacle; Sport as Work; Sports Heroes and Celebrities

REFERENCES AND SUGGESTED READINGS

Arnold, D. (1972) The Social Organization of Skydiving: A Study in Vertical Mobility. Paper presented at the Pacific Sociological Association annual meeting, Porland.

Bishop, J. & Hoggett, P. (1987) Clubbing Together. *New Socialist* (Summer): 32–3.

Bourdieu, P. (1993 [1978]) How Can One Be a Sportsman? In: *Sociology in Question*. Sage, London, pp. 117–31.

Coakley, J. & Donnelly, P. (Eds.) (1999) *Inside Sports*. Rouledge, London.

Donnelly, P. (1985) Sport Subcultures. *Exercise and Sport Sciences Reviews* 13: 539–78.

Donnelly, P. (1988) Sport as a Site for "Popular" Resistance. In: Gruneau, R. (Ed.), *Popular Cultures and Political Practices*. Garamond, Toronto, pp. 69–82

Donnelly, P. (1993) Subcultures in Sport: Resilience and Transformation. In: Ingham, A. & Loy, J. (Eds.), *Sport in Social Development: Traditions, Transitions, and Transformations*. Human Kinetics, Champaign, IL, pp. 119–45.

Fine, G. A. & Kleinman, S. (1979) Rethinking Subculture: An Interactionist Analysis. *American Journal of Sociology* 85: 1–20.

Geertz, C. (1973) *The Interpretation of Culture*. Basic Books, New York.

Gruneau, R. (1981) Review of "Surfing Subcultures of Australia and New Zealand. *ICSS Bulletin* 21: 8–10.

Ingham, A. (1975) Occupational Subcultures in the Work-World of Sport. In: Ingham, A. & Loy, J. (Eds.), *Sport in Social Development: Traditions, Transitions, and Transformations*. Human Kinetics, Champaign, IL, pp. 355–89.

Tylor, E. B. (1871) *Primitive Culture*. John Murray, London.

Weinberg, S. & Arond, H. (1952) The Occupational Culture of the Boxer. *American Journal of Sociology* 57: 460–9.

sport and the environment

Otmar Weiss

Everything outside the boundaries of the subsystem *sport* is considered to be its environment, and this can be influenced and altered by sport or, conversely, can itself influence sport. Examples of the latter are to be observed, for instance, in the effects on athletic performance of certain climatic qualities of the environment of Mexico City (tropical uplands) during the Olympic Summer Games 1968, or of Lagos (humid tropical lowlands) during the Pan-African Games in 1973. In the sociology of sport it is principally the first-mentioned influence – sport on the environment – that is the subject of discussion and study, and in particular the integration of sport in ecosystem structures is at the centre of consideration.

Since the United Nations Conference on Environment and Development (UNCED) in 1992, the guiding principle of sustainability has been internationally recognized. This principle says that nature must be protected from overexploitation so that it will be available to future generations in sufficient quality and quantity. And it is also a guideline for sport (e.g., when choosing the location for sports grounds). Here it is important to exploit areas which can stand ecological strain, and to spare sensitive areas (Schemel & Erbguth 2000: 13–22). This principle not only applies to the construction of buildings and development of sports grounds, but also to the practice of outdoor sports. Originally looked upon as harmless leisure activities, they are now being subjected to harsh criticism. For

even though sport is a secondary problem compared with the main causes of environmental destruction (agriculture, industry, settlements, and traffic), it is nevertheless imperative to reconsider various aspects of the subject "sport versus environment."

Noxious emissions and pollution caused by sports tourism and by athletes and spectators traveling to and from events must be mentioned in this context. There is also the construction of stadia, hotels, roads, etc., all too often in otherwise unspoiled countryside, and sometimes exclusively for one single big event, such as the Olympic Games. A further matter for discussion is the huge consumption of energy at big athletic events, and all the effects of various individual sports, such as alpine skiing, on the environment. Every year 120 million tourists and athletes go to the European Alps. This figure makes it clear that the compatibility of sports and leisure activities in the Alps with nature and the environment must be subjected to scrutiny in the light of the principle of sustainability. Building ski lifts not only means the loss of trees and the natural appearance of the local landscape, but, above all, also results in damage to vegetation cover due to the use of crawler-type vehicles, which also brings up the question of erosion. Then there is the damage caused by each individual: the noxious emissions produced during travel to and from the mountains, garbage, ski wax and waste water left on site, vegetation damaged by skiing off-piste or when there is too little snow to protect it (Weiss et al. 1998). This is discussed more often since 1990 due to recent climatic changes. On the other hand, all the alpine ski pistes and slopes together only represent a total of 0.9 percent of the entire area of the Alps (Baetzing 1997: 215), so that damage to mountain regions is in effect very slight.

The effects of sport on the environment need not necessarily be negative. Opinions can be subjective and often differ greatly. Laying out a golf course, for instance, will probably be regarded by conservationists as a negative alteration to the natural environment. Golfers, on the other hand, will look upon it as conservation of the countryside. This is mainly due to differences in the appreciation of nature. For those who understand "natural" to mean "unspoiled" or "untouched," sport appears to be a threat to the environment, for it brings mountain bikers, joggers, hikers, riders, skiers, and other sports-people into regions hitherto unused by human beings. However, if humans are seen as a legitimate part of a common habitat together with flora and fauna, then specially bred plants, flowerbeds, paths, or skiing pistes are all part of nature. From this point of view, sport has a positive effect on the environment, in that it gets human beings out of their over-heated living rooms and air-conditioned cars and (following Rousseau) back to Nature.

SEE ALSO: Sport; Sport and Capitalism; Sport and the City; Sportization; Sports Stadia

REFERENCES AND SUGGESTED READINGS

Baetzing, W. (1997) *Kleines Alpen-Lexikon.* Umwelt-Wirtschft-Kultur, Munich.
Schemel, H.-J. & Erbguth, W. (2000) *Handbuch Sport und Umwelt.* Ziele, Analysen, Bewertungen, Loesungsansaetze, Rechtsfragen, Aachen.
Weiss, O., Norden, G., Hilscher, P., & Vanreusel, B. (1998) Ski Tourism and Environmental Problems: Ecological Awareness among Different Groups. *International Review for the Sociology of Sport* 33(4): 367–80.

sport and ethnicity

C. Richard King

Ethnicity has proven fundamental to sport. It has long determined who has played, what participation and performance has meant, treatment by fans, media representations, and presentation of self.

Ethnicity is closely related to race. In fact, the two concepts are often confused with one another and used interchangeably, because both provide means to classify and organize observable differences among people. It is important, however, to distinguish between them, particularly in the context of sport. Whereas race describes the use of biological features, especially skin color, to understand people and define social groups, ethnicity refers to the use of cultural characteristics, including language, nationality, country of origin, and custom, to make sense of others and create social groups. While the physicality of sport rightly directs attention to issues of race and racism, the relationships between ethnicity and sport afford keen insights into the formation of identity, community, and society.

ETHNIC IDENTITY

Through sport, ethnic groups define who they are or aspire to be, the values that matter to them, and what distinguishes them from other people. In a very real sense, sport has facilitated the creation of imagined communities: athletic performance and circulation of it through print, visual, and electronic media encourage individuals to identify and connect with others, seeing themselves as part of a common people, or ethnic group. The capacity to play and watch sport has proven to be especially meaningful for ethnic minorities, particularly when great performance offers a foundation for pride and celebration.

In many instances, a particular sport becomes emblematic of a people. Baseball, for example, is said to be America's pastime and as American as mom and apple pie. Similarly, hockey has come to be closely associated with Canadian identity and rugby with what it means to identify oneself as a New Zealander. And ethnic groups, particularly native peoples, increasingly have sought to revive historic sporting practices as a means to reinvigorate heritage and culture.

In other cases the style of play becomes a means to claim or refuse a particular ethnic identity. In the US, the flamboyance, creativity, individuality, and flair associated with the black urban culture has transformed contemporary sport and society, providing African American and Euro-American athletes and fans an important reservoir for the presentation of self and the nurturance of social networks. Negative public perceptions of this style of play and its association with urban blackness have also caused gatekeepers to affirm the values defining whiteness through controlling transgressive expressions. Similarly, the hard and fast style of cricket cultivated in the West Indies not only radically changed the sport, but it also became a powerful affirmation of ethnic identity. Increasingly, corporations and sport teams, mindful of ethnicity and style, have capitalized upon ethnicity to attract fans and sell products.

Increasingly, over the course of the twentieth century, sporting spectacle offered important occasions for ethnic and national groups to present themselves. The opening ceremonies of the Olympic Games provide an excellent illustration of this pattern. In 1936 the Nazi regime used the Summer Olympics in Berlin to articulate a muscular, romantic vision of Germanness, while giving material expression to its anti-Semitism. The Summer Olympics in Mexico City in 1968 witnessed a much more oppositional statement when African American athletes raised their fists in a black power salute on the award stand, affirming an ethnic identity too long marginalized and demonized. The Calgary Winter Olympics in 1988 were also the scene of ethnic protest. The Lubicon Lake Cree Band used the ceremonial torch run passing through Saskatchewan in advance of the games to bring attention to their ongoing land claim disputes and the destruction of their culture.

It would be a mistake, however, to think of the assertion of ethnic identity through sports to be a matter of choice free from the constraints of history or power. In fact, a range of factors, including cultural expectations, political access, social location, and education, delimit the capacity of ethnic groups to articulate an identity audible to all. Making matters worse, stereotypes, bias, and misconceptions often influence public understandings of athletes and athletics. Indeed, research shows that media coverage, beginning with the emergence of modern sport in the nineteenth century, has displayed a propensity to frame players in ethnic terms. In the US, Canada, Australia, and Great Britain, for instance, the media have lamented the minimal work ethic and discipline of athletes of color, while emphasizing their natural abilities, and in turn, have praised white athletes for their hard work, intelligence, and leadership abilities.

In many ways, Tiger Woods offers a striking example of the limits and possibilities of ethnic identity in sport. The celebrated golfer has sought to be identified and accepted as *Cablinasian*, a term he created to encapsulate his multi-ethnic heritage. Supporting Woods's hybridity, Nike ran a series of ads in which kids from a number of distinct ethnic groups proclaimed, "I'm Tiger Woods." Most journalists, commentators, and fans, however, worked hard to assign a singular identity to Woods. Many observers sought to claim Woods, taking him as an example of African American or Asian American excellence and a source of ethnic pride. Media coverage, in turn, frequently presented the golfer in terms that broke with conventional understandings of blackness, but when Woods was not successful, stereotypes of the black athlete became more common.

ETHNIC RELATIONS

While many commentators and fans have pointed to sport as a prime example of multiculturalism and social progress, athletics actually is a much more complex arena of ethnic relations, at once highly visible, saturated with power, and often very contentious. Sport often emerges as a borderland or middle ground that has promoted efforts to assimilate ethnic minorities, encouraged ethnic groups to challenge the precepts and practices of mainstream society, and prompted countless cultural borrowings and social reinventions.

Sport socializes. Sport teaches. It conveys important ideas about the social order. When incorporated into school, physical education and extracurricular athletics have proven important to the efforts of multi-ethnic states to deal with perceived social problems. Through sport societies seek to nationalize those deemed foreign – immigrants, indigenous peoples, and other ethnic minorities. In the US (and Canada), boarding schools were established in the late nineteenth century for Native Americans. Over time, athletics became increasingly important to efforts to Americanize indigenous peoples, or as it was often put at the time, "kill the Indian, to save the man." Educators hoped to instill a competitive spirit, discipline, morality, and manliness. In time, they would come to see sports as a powerful public relations tool that might elevate public perceptions of Native Americans, easing the process of assimilation as it eroded misconceptions and prejudices. As Native American boarding schools began to fall out of favor in the 1920s, the post-revolutionary Mexican government sought to use physical education for similar ends, namely to unify a multi-ethnic country around shared values.

In contrast to its northern neighbor, the effort was not focused on eradicating Indianness. Instead, it amplified ethnic difference, incorporating indigenous practices into the physical education curriculum to forge the hybrid, mestizo nation it envisioned Mexico becoming. Importantly, in both of these examples, athletics in education target ethnic minorities, affixing the problems of broader society on their backs.

In neither case did sport ease ethnic tensions or misunderstandings; however, in both instances sport proved to be especially transformational precisely because the play of sport simultaneously changes individuals and invites differently situated players in turn to change it. Encouraging interaction among different ethnic groups, sport offers a space in between, a meeting ground in which ideas, practices, games, pleasures, and possibilities can be shared, exchanged, and borrowed. Ethnic minorities often adapt individual sports to their own ends. In addition to the play of cricket and basketball previously discussed, the introduction of cricket to the Trobriand Islands is instructive here. Missionaries hoping to acculturate Trobrianders and offer them a substitute for warfare taught them to play cricket. Much to the missionaries' chagrin, however, the islanders rewrote the rules of the sport and used matches as occasions to perform traditional rituals and magic. Dominant ethnic groups remake games played by marginalized groups as well. After watching and playing it for years, Canadians appropriated lacrosse from Native groups, taking a traditional sacred cultural complex and turning it into a rationalized and secular sport that looked quite different. Later, lacrosse organizations in Canada banned First Peoples from participating in sanctioned matches. At the same time, sport has allowed marginalized ethnic groups to survive in hostile social environments. On the one hand, many immigrants play games brought with them. Latino soccer leagues in urban areas in the US allow participants to establish important social networks, find work and community, and maintain connections with homelands. On the other hand, ethnic groups often turn to sport in unbearable social circumstances, such as Japanese Americans in internment camps during World War II.

In highly stratified societies, where the distribution of rights and resources turns on ethnicity, there are limits to the creativity and freedom afforded by sport. Indeed, as in other social domains, sport has long exhibited pronounced ethnic inequality. Ethnicity has been the basis for exclusion from competition. It is common knowledge that indigenous peoples were barred from lacrosse in Canada, African Americans could not participate in baseball, football, and myriad other sports in Jim Crow America, Jews were marginalized in athletics under the Nazi regime, and Asian immigrants could not play as equals in Great Britain. Even more commonly, ethnic minorities have endured discrimination in position assignment and coaching opportunities, while suffering persecution as they have taken the field and played the game. At the same time, the marginalization and underdevelopment of ethnic communities frequently translates into extremely limited social and economic opportunities. Ethnic minorities regularly turn to sport as a means to achieve a better life. In fact, the history of sport in virtually every country throughout the world parallels its history of immigration; successive waves of immigrants enter into particular sports, only to be replaced a generation later by a subsequent, more newly arrived ethnic group. Only a small fraction of athletes ever achieve their dreams of playing professional sport, suggesting that it is an uncertain path to upward mobility which misdirects energies and aspirations and in turn furthers the underdevelopment of marginalized communities.

Finally, sport is a site of social struggle and ethnic resistance. The ongoing controversy over the use of American Indian names, images, and symbols in sport provides an excellent example. For nearly a century, Native American mascots have reflected and reinforced dominant notions of masculinity, citizenship, and history. Over the past 35 years, a multi-ethnic coalition, led by American Indians, has challenged such symbols, asserting that they misappropriate, misuse, and misunderstand indigenous culture and history. They have protested and petitioned, pressing educational institutions and professional teams to change their mascots. In many ways, the controversy has derived in part from efforts to defend traditional formulations of identity in the US, especially its foundations in ethnicity (whiteness), gender (masculinity), nation (Americanness), and history (the myth of the frontier). It also reflects deep interpretive differences. Whereas supporters insist that mascots foster respect and are meant to honor Native Americans, opponents assert that they denigrate Native Americans, perpetuating historical patterns of discrimination and dispossession. Moreover, supporters stress text (honor, intention), while opponents emphasize context (history and racism).

Ethnicity has been central to athletics since the emergence of modern sport in the nineteenth century. It has proven particularly important for the articulation of ethnic identity and the shape of ethnic relations. As sport becomes increasingly global and mass mediated, the relationships between ethnicity and sport undoubtedly will become more intense and intricate.

SEE ALSO: Ethnic Enclaves; Ethnic Groups; Ethnicity; Identity, Sport and; Nationalism and Sport; Postcolonialism and Sport; Race and Ethnic Consciousness; Sport and Culture; Sport and Race

REFERENCES AND SUGGESTED READINGS

Bloom, J. & Willard, M. N. (Eds.) (2002) *Sport Matters: Race, Recreation, and Culture*. New York University Press, New York.
Cronin, M. & Mayall, D. (Eds.) (1998) *Sporting Nationalisms: Ethnicity, Immigration, and Assimilation*. Frank Cass, Portland.
Eisen, G. & Wiggins, D. K. (Eds.) (1994) *Ethnicity and Sport in North American History and Culture*. Greenwood Press, Westport, CT.
King, C. R. & Springwood, C. F. (2001) *Beyond the Cheers: Race as Spectacle in College Sports*. State University of New York Press, Albany.
MacClancy, J. (Ed.) (1996) *Sport, Identity, and Ethnicity*. Berg, Oxford.

sport, professional

Jim McKay

According to the ideal type suggested by Freidson (2001), sport does not exhibit all of the characteristics of a profession. Unlike archetypal high-status professions (e.g., medicine) in which the practitioners rather than governments or markets exert significant control over their labor, professional athletes work in cartels and oligopolies where they must respond to the demands of owners, managers, coaches, sponsors, consumers, and the media. Thus it is more appropriate to say that like many institutions, sport exhibits particular *professionalizing tendencies* (e.g., specialization, relying strongly on expert knowledge). However, these professionalizing propensities can only be understood if they are located in a complex of five other interdependent and mutually reinforcing processes that have shaped modern sport from youth leagues to the international level: commercialization, commodification, bureaucratization, globalization, and governmentalization (Gruneau & Whitson 2001; Miller et al. 2001; Ingham 2005).

Modern sport has been transformed into a multibillion-dollar global industry that employs millions of professional athletes, administrators, coaches, scientists, and lawyers. Paying this labor force would be impossible without the income that sporting organizations generate from gate receipts, the sale of media rights, and contracts with sponsors from the business world. It is crucial to emphasize that commercialization, commodification, and mediatization are not simply economic phenomena. For instance, commercialization and commodification simultaneously both constitute and are constituted by discourses in the sporting media. At a more general level, Rowe (2004: 95–6) refers to the *culturalization* of all institutions, noting that despite being progressively more commodified and commercialized, "sports events have become the most important, regular manifestations of . . . national culture."

Commercializing and commodifying sport occurred in tandem with the replacement of part-time volunteers in informal community organizations by national and international bureaucracies administered by full-time professionals holding degrees in business, economics, marketing, public relations, and management. Thus sport has gone from being discussed around the kitchen table to being managed by the executive office (McKay 1997). For example, virtually all private and public sporting organizations now have an executive director overseeing managers who monitor their business, operational, and strategic plans.

The Olympics, various World Cup events, and the Super Bowl are some of the most popular entertainment events in the world. One outcome of the integration of sport into the global entertainment industry has been the creation of "celebrity athletes," in whom multinational corporations invest vast sums of money in the form of endorsements and sponsorships. Like other sought-after and mobile professionals, elite athletes and coaches have become "flexible citizens" who switch nations and even nationalities for commercial purposes. Like most global processes, this one is based on the capacity of powerful nations to exploit disadvantaged ones.

The commercialization, commodification, bureaucratization, and globalization of everyday life have been facilitated by governmentalization, the process by which capitalist states have steadily calibrated and managed the conduct of their citizens. Citizens today are the objects of myriad private and public strategies that frame health, well-being, lifestyle, fitness, quality of life, and "at risk" behavior as a matter of individual responsibility (Rose 2001: 5–7). This important shift in biopower means that professional experts have become increasingly authoritative in spheres that were not traditionally subjected to direct intervention by private and public agencies. Thus most nations now have government departments responsible for the national planning and funding of "amateur" sport, which are often linked with health, lifestyle, and physical education programs (McKay 1997; Howell & Ingham 2001).

In this regime of biopower, professional athletes have become classic "somatic individuals": both participants in and targets of "molecular politics," with their technologies of self-government articulating favorably with the emphasis by professional experts in both the private and public spheres that individuals must accept responsibility for managing their lives (Rose 2001). Thus cyborg-athletes gradually subject their bodies to a plethora of legal and illegal performance-enhancing techniques. Moreover, all of the above processes have transcended their origins in capitalist states and now pervade virtually *all* formal organizations worldwide.

There are immense qualitative and quantitative differences between organized sport when it was the pastime of mainly Victorian gentlemen amateurs and the current hegemonic "power and performance model" (Coakley 2004: 110–12), which features the professionalizing developments outlined above. Although these professionalizing trends cannot eliminate all other forms of sport, alternatives seemed destined to occupy a marginal status, given that they exist in a context in which there is heavy reliance on the knowledge of professional experts who continually try to improve athletic performance by the tiniest fraction. Like life in effectively all formal organizations, the tradeoff for the rewards that flow from submitting to this professionalizing regime is the unremitting "government of the soul" (Rose 1999).

SEE ALSO: Media and Sport; Sport, Amateur; Sport as Work; Sports Heroes and Celebrities

REFERENCES AND SUGGESTED READINGS

Coakley, J. (2004) *Sports in Society: Issues and Controversies.* McGraw-Hill, New York.

Freidson, E. (2001) *Professionalism: The Third Logic.* Polity Press, Cambridge.

Gruneau, R. S. & Whitson, D. (2001) Upmarket Continentalism: Major League Sport, Promotional Culture, and Corporate Integration. In: Mosco, V. & Schiller, D. (Eds.), *Continental Order? Integrating North America for Cybercapitalism.* Rowman & Littlefield, New York.

Howell, J. & Ingham, A. G. (2001) From Social Problem to Personal Issue: The Language of Lifestyle. *Cultural Studies* 15: 326–51.

Ingham, A. G. (2005) The Sportification Process: A Biographical Analysis Framed by the Work of Marx, Weber, Durkheim, and Freud. In: Giulianotti, R. (Ed.), *Sport and Modern Social Theorists.* Palgrave Macmillan, Houndmills.

McKay, J. (1997) *Managing Gender: Affirmative Action and Organizational Power in Australian, Canadian, and New Zealand Sport.* State University of New York Press, Albany.

Miller, T., McKay, J., Lawrence, G., & Rowe, D. (2001) *Globalization and Sport: Playing the World.* Sage, Thousand Oaks, CA.

Miller, T., Rowe, D., McKay, J., & Lawrence, G. (2003) The Over-Production of US Sports and the New International Division of Cultural Labor. *International Review for the Sociology of Sport* 38: 427–39.

Rose, N. (1999) *Governing the Soul: The Shaping of the Private Self*, 2nd edn. Routledge, London.

Rose, N. (2001) The Politics of Life Itself. *Theory, Culture, and Society* 18: 1–30.

Rowe, D. (2004) *Sport, Culture, and the Media: The Unruly Trinity*, 2nd edn. Open University Press, Buckingham.

sport and race

Ben Carrington

Sport and race have been in complex articulation since the nineteenth century, yet a *critical* sociology of sport and race has only developed substantially since the 1990s. In the 1960s a few academic studies and journalistic accounts examined segregation and racial discrimination in sport, but these were largely descriptive. Two exceptions to this were C. L. R. James's critical reading of the role of cricket in shaping West Indian political identity in the anti-colonial struggles of the 1950s and 1960s, and Harry Edwards's important account of the radicalization of the black athlete in the context of America's Civil Rights Movement of the 1960s and black nationalist politics of the 1970s. In the 1970s and 1980s sport sociologists began to investigate continuing racial discrimination in sport with a liberal focus on issues of equity and opportunity, normally using quantitative methods to measure the degree of meritocracy in sports. More recently, scholars have used cultural studies approaches to examine questions of representation and ideology in sport media texts, and ethnographic methods to understand racial identity construction in sport and its intersections with class, nation, gender, and sexuality.

SPORT AND RACE AS SOCIAL PHENOMENA

"Sport" and "race" are sociologically problematic because, at first sight, both appear to be aspects of human life that are immediately knowable and products of a natural physicality that precedes socialization. "Race," the division of humanity into biologically discrete groups based on phenotypical markers, is commonly believed to be the result of an inherent, fixed, and natural distinction between actually existing groups. But sociologists and biologists alike have demonstrated that the supposed "natural" division of humanity is unrelated to underlying genotypical distinctions. Instead, racial distinctions are based on arbitrarily chosen physical features, such as skin color and hair texture, that are used to demarcate people into groups. Thus, "race" is a complex system of representation learned through socialization, and then acted upon as if these distinctions were "real." In short, "race" appears to be a biological fact of absolute physical difference when it is actually a socially constructed and culturally reproduced set of ideas and beliefs.

Similarly, "sport" appears to be a purely physical activity that is separate from the wider divisions and structures of society. Although we might immediately recognize the social conditions of education, cultural capital, and aesthetic discernment that frame the production and consumption of other cultural forms, sport is commonly seen as an activity that is "simply" physical and open to all regardless of class, gender, race, or sexuality. Barriers in sports, it is believed, exist only in connection with the physical abilities and motivation of individuals. This view of sport as "free" from structural constraints means that sport's role in maintaining and reproducing power relations is underestimated.

Sociologists of sport have sought to explain how the sports we choose to play, the ways that we play them, the meanings we give to and take from them, and the material and social rewards associated with participation and success are intimately related to the structure and organization of societies. Given this, it requires great sociological imagination to go beyond such everyday understandings to reveal how both race *and* sport, far from being universal, naturally occurring phenomena, are actually the result of temporally bound and historically specific human action. In short, the interrelationship between race and sport is a deeply sociological articulation with profound political consequences for how we generally understand racial difference and who has access to sport itself.

RACIAL SCIENCE AND EMPIRE

There is an interesting historical parallel between the emergence of the scientific foundation for ideas of racial difference and the formation of organized, codified, competitive sport. Racial science – the scientific belief in the inherent superiority of white Europeans – developed into a coherent set of ideas during the nineteenth century. In Britain this was the period when sports such as rugby football, cricket, and soccer were institutionalized, as emerging governing bodies formalized rules and assumed authority over how these sports should be played.

The nineteenth century was also the high point for European imperialism, when the idea of race emerged to justify conquest and exploitation. Countries such as Britain sought to maintain their power over their colonies in Africa, South and East Asia, and the Caribbean by a twin process of undermining and destroying local cultures while attempting to "civilize" native peoples by the imposition of British customs and ways of life. In this context of imperialist expansion, buttressed by notions of inherent white European supremacy, sport came to be seen as a way of educating and socializing colonized peoples into more civilized forms of modernity. Cricket served this purpose in the English-speaking Caribbean, South Asia, Central and Southern Africa, and in the white settler colonies of New Zealand and Australia. The notion of "cricket, the classics, and Christianity" was seen by British Victorian elites as a way to bring order and civilization to the British Empire – at once a form of control over the masses and a way to inculcate them into the values and norms of an imperial notion of Britishness.

Elsewhere, soccer was "exported" by Europeans to Africa, Asia, and Central and South America. In this context, indigenous games and pastimes, suppressed since the first European expeditions overseas in the fifteenth and sixteenth centuries, faded away or were gradually replaced with new sporting imports. For example, the game of *ulama de cadera*, or hip *ulama* – *ulama* meaning "ball game" – was once popular throughout Mesoamerica, but began to die away after the Spanish outlawed what they perceived to be a pagan game with inappropriate rituals,

such as decapitation for the losers. The game itself, which is similar to volleyball but requiring the use of the hip rather than the hand, dates to around 1500 BC. Although it still survives in parts of Mexico, it is no longer central to Mexican culture, except as a focus for anthropologists, archeologists, and tourists. Soccer is now the national sport of Mexico, as it is throughout most of Central and South America, and most Mexicans have no idea of what *ulama*, one of the world's oldest sports, actually involved.

SPORT, RACE, AND THE STRUGGLE FOR FREEDOM

At the start of the twentieth century notions of white European supremacy were simply assumed to be an objective, unquestionable fact. While Africans were often seen to be "animal-like" in their nature, it was still assumed that whites were intellectually and physically superior to all other "races of man." The newly emerging international sports arenas were one public space where this obvious superiority was seen to be confirmed. Given the importance of sport in reproducing dominant forms of hegemonic masculinity, it is not surprising that boxing, and heavyweight boxing in particular, came to be regarded as one of the prime avenues for demonstrating the attributes of white male strength, power, and courage. The symbolic significance of black and white athletes competing against each other in public *as equals*, and the fear of black success in the sporting arena, was such that sporting encounters began to take on wider political significance.

In this context Jack Johnson's successes in the boxing arena heralded a pattern of racial contestation that was to structure relations on the world's sporting fields for over a century. In 1908 Johnson became the first black World Heavyweight Champion. Given the racial politics of the Jim Crow era, Johnson's victory caused widespread consternation within wider white society and jubilation among blacks. The search then went out for a "great White hope" to reclaim the mantle of masculine supremacy from the black Texan. In order to prevent such threats to the symbolic racial order, the so-called "color line" was redrawn when Johnson eventually lost his title which once again prevented black boxers from competing against whites. The later achievements in the 1930s, 1940s, and 1950s of African American athletes such as the boxer Joe Louis, the athlete Jesse Owens, the baseball player Jackie Robinson, and the tennis player Althea Gibson, were subsequently seen by black people throughout the African diaspora as victories in the struggle for freedom from racial oppression.

Sport as a form of political resistance can be seen in the example of cricket in the Caribbean. While the imposition of European sporting forms led to both the extinction of indigenous games and an attempt at colonial governance over local populations, these very same conditions led to sports becoming a site for cultural contestation and ideological struggle. Campaigns for equality within the game of cricket thus paralleled wider struggles for freedom and emancipation from colonial rule. Thus, the campaign to allow a black player to captain the West Indies national cricket team – previously only white West Indians were deemed intelligent enough to assume such leadership roles – was achieved in 1960 when the captaincy was finally given to Frank Worrell. Increasingly, from the 1950s onwards, former colonized countries gained their independence, giving further impetus to the symbolic significance of international sporting competitions, especially against their former colonial masters.

The politics of protest through sport continued into the 1960s and 1970s as sport became an important vehicle through which racial oppression and injustice could be highlighted. The "black gloved" protest at the 1968 Mexico Olympics by Tommie Smith and John Carlos similarly drew attention to the human rights abuses that were taking place in America and elsewhere. Their simple but powerful protest also portrayed the ideological role of black athletes who were now able to compete in international arenas for western countries; when athletes succeeded on the field they were hailed as heroes at the same time that black people were denied full rights as citizens. The radical black athletes of the 1960s, best personified perhaps in the figure of Muhammad Ali, revealed the previously ignored racial politics of sport. This enabled a generation of black athletes to speak out, as previous generations dared not do,

against discrimination in sports and society at large.

Nowhere was racial oppression more explicit than in the apartheid regime of South Africa, where a minority white population held complete power and control over the country's majority black African population. The 1977 Gleneagles Agreement led to a sporting boycott of the regime. This called attention to the suffering of South Africa's black population and it assisted the anti-apartheid movement by exerting political pressure on the South African government. By further isolating South Africa from normal international relations, the boycott contributed to apartheid's eventual collapse in the early 1990s. Thus, sport – in Caribbean cricket squares, American sporting arenas, and South African rugby pitches, among other sites – has been central to the wider story of black diasporic struggles for freedom throughout the twentieth century.

STEREOTYPES AND THE RETURN OF RACIAL SCIENCE IN SPORT

A persistent legacy of nineteenth-century racial science is the ideology of absolute racial difference and its alleged effects on human behavior. While notions of a direct biological link between race, intelligence, and the propensity to commit criminal acts has been effectively critiqued, the belief that a person's "race" is linked to abilities on the sports field remains strong. For example, using limited and often contradictory evidence, it continues to be asserted that "West African blacks" are genetically predisposed to power and speed events such as sprinting and jumping, while "East African blacks" are meant to have special properties that allow them to dominate endurance events like long-distance running.

Stereotypes attributing to black people natural advantages compared to whites when it comes to running and jumping have affected structural and strategic dimensions of sports. Sociological research since the 1970s has shown how "stacking" – the disproportionate placing of black athletes into certain positions assumed to be more suited to their "natural" abilities – has occurred in many sports from American football to rugby league and rugby union. Linked to stacking is the concept of "centrality," which suggests that certain positions are more important to a team's chances of winning as these require players to make cognitive decisions, as opposed to merely reflexive or instinctive physical reactions to opponents' movements. These "central" positions are thus seen to be more suited to white players who have a greater ability to "read the game," thus relegating black players to positions believed to require pure physical ability and little if any cognitive ability. In American football, for instance, this supported a stacking pattern in which there was a disproportionate number of white quarterbacks and black wide receivers. This pattern reproduced a racial ideology focused on innate biological differences and led people to overlook socially produced conditions in which coaches and school teachers selected and encouraged players from different racial backgrounds to play in certain positions. Even when stacking patterns have become less apparent, the race logic used in the sports media recategorizes players by, for example, suggesting that "new" black quarterbacks are somehow more "athletic" than their white counterparts, and play in a more "physical" way.

Black success in certain elite sports is often "explained" by these alleged natural differences, further reifying the idea of race. This undermines black athletic excellence by implicitly linking it with an inherent genetic disposition shared by the entire "black race" and ignoring the dedication, hard work, and ability of individual athletes who happened to be racialized as black. Such stereotypes persist in the face of evidence to the contrary. For example, the record-breaking times of British long-distance runner Paula Radcliffe or the "superhuman" achievements of the American cyclist Lance Armstrong are often seen by scientists and journalists in terms of dedication and their almost fanatical commitment to training to compete at the highest level. Rarely is white achievement in sport explained by biological or genetic racial attributes. This preserves the myth of black athletic superiority as well as ideological notions of "natural" racial difference. This illustrates the power of hegemonic racial ideology in framing how people interpret success or failure in the world's sporting arenas and how the discredited legacy of racial science continues to inform sports science discourse today.

SPORT AND RACE TODAY

Success in sport has been one way for subordinated racial and ethnic minority groups to register protests and fight discrimination in the wider battles for recognition and inclusion. In the 2000 Sydney Olympics, for example, Cathy Freeman became the first Australian Aborigine to win an Olympic gold medal, and was widely seen as a symbol of Australia's attempts to come to terms with its racist treatment of Aboriginal peoples. A century after Jack Johnson's arrival on the international boxing scene, black athletes now compete successfully in sports such as tennis and golf that were previously the preserve of whites only. The achievements of sportsmen and women of color have only recently been recognized as part of the wider struggle for racial justice and equality.

A danger is that the perceived level playing field of sport can serve an ideological function by leading people to assume that western societies in particular have achieved a meritocracy that transcends the structural correlates of a racialized social order. Similarly, rather than using their position to speak out on issues of racial injustice and social inequality, contemporary millionaire black celebrity athletes often align themselves with commercial programs bringing them monetary rewards. However, research continues to show that, despite diversity on many playing fields, the power positions in the structure of sport organizations are controlled by white men who coach, manage, and own teams. Similarly, the abuse of athletes of color by spectators and occasionally by fellow players and managers continues to be a feature of domestic and international competitions in sports such as soccer. The myth of race is sustained by the apparent "obviousness" of racial difference in sports performance, while the continuance of racism is often disavowed.

The centrality of sport as a cultural practice in many nations and the pervasiveness of ideas about racial difference mean that the complex articulation of "race" and "sport" will persist well into the twenty-first century. Critical research on the ways that sports serve as sites for "race-related" identity formation for all racialized minorities as well as majority white populations is needed in order to develop more nuanced and effective anti-racist strategies.

Research into non-English-speaking contexts is also required to explain the many forms of racism that exist alongside the local and national context of particular sporting cultures.

SEE ALSO: Colonialism (Neocolonialism); Color Line; Postcolonialism and Sport; Race; Race and Ethnic Consciousness; Race (Racism); Sport and Ethnicity

REFERENCES AND SUGGESTED READINGS

Bass, A. (2002) *Not the Triumph but the Struggle: The 1968 Olympics and the Making of the Black Athlete.* University of Minnesota Press, Minneapolis.

Beckles, H. & Stoddard, B. (Eds.) (1995) *Liberation Cricket: West Indies Cricket Culture.* Manchester University Press, Manchester.

Bloom, J. & Willard, M. (Eds.) (2002) *Sport Matters: Race, Recreation and Culture.* New York University Press, New York.

Booth, D. (1998) *The Race Game: Sport and Politics in South Africa.* Frank Cass, London.

Carrington, B. & McDonald, I. (Eds.) (2001) *"Race," Sport and British Society.* Routledge, London.

Edwards, H. (1969) *The Revolt of the Black Athlete.* Free Press, New York.

Guttmann, A. (1996) *Games and Empires: Modern Sports and Cultural Imperialism.* Columbia University Press, Columbia.

Hartmann, D. (2003) *Race, Culture and the Revolt of the Black Athlete: The 1968 Olympic Protests and Their Aftermath.* University of Chicago Press, Chicago.

Hoberman, J. (1997) *Darwin's Athletes: How Sport Has Damaged Black America and Preserved the Myth of Race.* Mairner Books, Boston.

Ismond, P. (2003) *Black and Asian Athletes in British Sport and Society: A Sporting Chance?* Palgrave, Basingstoke.

James, C. L. R. (1994 [1963]) *Beyond a Boundary.* Serpent's Tail, London.

Mangan, J. A. & Ritchie, A. (Eds.) (2005) *Ethnicity, Sport, Identity: Struggles for Status.* Routledge, London.

Marqusee, M. (2005) *Redemption Song: Muhammad Ali and the Spirit of the Sixties.* Verso, London.

Melling, P. & Collins, T. (Eds.) (2004) *The Glory of Their Times: Crossing the Colour Line in Rugby League.* Vertical Editions, Skipton.

Miller, P. & Wiggins, D. (Eds.) (2004) *Sport and the Color Line: Black Athletes and Race Relations in Twentieth-Century America.* Routledge, London.

Shropshire, K. (1996) *In Black and White: Race and Sports in America.* New York University Press, New York.

Vasili, P. (2000) *Colouring Over the White Line: The History of Black Footballers in Britain.* Mainstream Publishing, Edinburgh.

Williams, J. (2001) *Cricket and Race.* Berg, Oxford.

sport and religion

Tara Magdalinski

Sport and religion have a conflicted relationship. At times, sport has served the objectives of religious authorities and has been imbued with a morality and philosophy derived from religious doctrine. At others, it has been rejected for its secular, corporeal emphasis and its capacity to divert attention from godly activities. Sport has been utilized as a means to evangelize and to convert non-believers, and yet it has also represented a threat to the social and moral order. As such, religion has had an indelible impact on modern sport, and sport has been both embraced and rejected by religious authorities across the centuries.

The Ancient Greek Olympic Games is perhaps the most renowned example of the inclusion of physical contests in a religious festival. The Ancient Olympics emerged from the ritual celebration of Zeus, the king of the Ancient Greek pantheon of gods, with the first event, the stade, recorded as part of the festivities in 776 BC. In other regions, religious or ritualized practices influenced athletic contests, including the ancient Mayan culture in Central America, where priests presided over ball games on playing grounds adjacent to their temples. In Japan, the ritualized aspects of sumo wrestling borrow extensively from the national religion, Shinto. Christianity, however, has most influenced modern conceptions of sport.

The relationship between Christianity and physical activities has not always been congenial. The Christian church has regarded sport with suspicion, owing to its emphasis on the profane body and its potential to lure its followers away from their godly responsibilities. While the Catholic Church included many popular physical activities into its religious and festive occasions, the rise of Puritanism in the sixteenth and seventeenth centuries heralded an era where many sporting activities were regarded as sinful. While the Puritans did recognize the political and military utility in many physical endeavors, recreations popular among the peasant classes were prohibited as they were invariably accompanied by drinking and gambling and other dubious pursuits. Nevertheless, since the mid-nineteenth century, there has been a shift in the relationship between the two institutions, beginning with the incorporation of games in the education of the elite classes in the English public schools. The inclusion of a physical education curriculum to complement the intellectual and moral training already in place elevated sport from a mere corporeal activity to one with a moral and ethical philosophy. In short, sport was employed specifically to teach boys qualities that would transfer to other aspects of life, and as such became a training ground to produce morally and physically competent civic leaders.

Using sport to construct generations of strong, fit, Muscular Christians was the mission of many organizations that feared the feminization of the male youth as a result of industrialization and urbanization. The closer relationship between religious and sporting ideologies was in part responsible for the reconfiguration of Jesus from effeminate and fragile to strong and robust, a more inspiring athletic figure. This mission is apparent in both early Christian organizations that provided sporting opportunities for its members, such as the Young Men's Christian Association, as well as in contemporary evangelism that utilizes sport and sporting organizations as a means to preach to and/or convert adherents.

Since the rapid expansion of the sports industry through the twentieth century, it has not been uncommon to hear popular commentators refer to sport *as* a contemporary religion. In this conception, stadia are said to be *ersatz* cathedrals, while athletes fulfil the role of modern deities. Harry Edwards (1973) pointed to the close structural relationship between sport and religion, identifying saints and gods, ruling patriarchs, high councils, scribes, shrines, houses of worship, symbols of faith, and seekers of the kingdom as features of both. His typology is, on one level, appealing, though he himself regarded sport as quasi-religious rather than an outright religion. Yet the similarities he identified have inspired a number of authors to declare categorically that sport is a religion, though this controversial statement is not without its opponents.

In arguing that sport is an actual religion, researchers have examined the emotional and devotional aspects of sport and suggest that sport holds meaning for fans in a way that traditional religions are unable to do. The structural similarities between sport and religion, as identified by Edwards, are not solely what define sport as a religion, but rather the passion, commitment, agony in defeat, and elation in victory reveal a transcendent experience in followers that provides sacred, communal moments between players and fans. For them, a religion delivers a sense of ultimacy, and sport is capable of providing a means of ultimate transformation that alters people's lives.

Others are not convinced, but recognize that there is more than a coincidental relationship between sport and religion. These researchers argue that sport is similar in structure to a revealed religion and that the two share many ritualized and sacred aspects. But sport itself is also regarded as religious as it represents in tangible form epic human and spiritual struggles, the quest for perfection, an intrinsic drama, and the explication of moral attributes. The ritualized engagement with and in sport, it is argued, serve to deliver a religious experience to their participants, feeding a "deep human hunger" (Novak 1976).

Sport may also be considered a folk religion, which can be understood as the result of shared moral ideals as well as behaviors, and emerges from daily life experiences to provide a means to integrate society, legitimate national values, and communicate societal ideologies. In this conception, sport is accepted as a product of its social, political, and economic context and as an institution that is complicit in reproducing these ideologies. In declaring sport to be a folk religion, researchers recognize its mythic, collective, and historical elements, without necessarily suggesting it is a transcendental experience.

By contrast, those who challenge sport's elevation to the status of a religion argue that the objects of each institution are not consistent, and thus to equate the two would be to ignore fundamental philosophical differences. Religion, they suggest, is derived from the divine realm, while sport is firmly located in the human experience. One offers truths about life beyond our own experience; the other is simply a corporeal activity embedded in the profane. There is concern that to equate the two might secularize religion and diminish its value.

Essentially, the argument that sport is not a religion rests on the recognition that the intentions underpinning the two institutions vary significantly. Rather than examining sport and religion in terms of structure, it is perhaps more revealing to analyze each from the inside out. Such an analysis reveals the key difference to be the role of religion to proffer answers to, or explanations about, the mysteries of human existence. Sport has no such stated purpose, and even the most ardent sports fan would disagree that devotional activities will reveal anything about people's lives, destinies, or significance. Sport may well embody and reflect social values and ideologies, they argue, but it does not offer any deeper meanings about this world beyond the activity itself.

For others, the contention that sport is a religious experience is problematic. The mere physical act of playing or watching sport, they suggest, has little relationship to rituals of worship. At the same time, they identify a difference between having a religious experience when playing sport and playing sport for the actual purpose of glorifying a god. While these researchers may recognize that many of the rituals, passions, and even myths within sport can take on a religious-like significance for participants, they maintain that the actual sporting performance is not a religious act. Thus the symbolic links between physical movement and the expression of a religious doctrine are questioned. As such, some have suggested it is best to examine the moments when sport and religion serve each other's interests rather than trying to define one as the other.

A final way of examining this phenomenon is to regard sport as a cultural vehicle through which religious communities may disseminate their faith or reinforce their beliefs to their existing members. This approach suggests that sport may not be divine in and of itself, but as an institution that reproduces cultural meanings and values, it might also serve the interests of religious groups. Cultural activities that rest upon ritualized performances are significant ways to reproduce hegemonic ideologies, and sport is no exception. There are numerous examples where sport has been used as one of a number of cultural means to reinforce the collective identity of a religious community. In South Africa, the Muslim population of Cape Town used rugby as an avenue through which their religious and cultural identity could be consolidated. While not using sport as a direct means to proselytize, rugby nevertheless provided social opportunities for members of the community to interact and reaffirm their sense of belonging. Similar outcomes can be seen among Jewish Americans who used physical recreations as both a means to maintain their faith and cultural heritage, and also to integrate themselves into a new national community. In this way, sport contributes to the reproduction of the religious community's social arrangements, particularly in new or rapidly changing cultural contexts as members engage in repetitive, ritualistic cultural practices.

The use of sport has not been as pronounced in Eastern or traditional indigenous religions as it has in the Judeo-Christian religions, though there is certainly much evidence that movement cultures are incorporated into religious or sacred practices. The primary point of divergence for many Eastern philosophies, such as Hinduism and Buddhism, is a rejection of the material world in preference for the attainment of a higher spiritual order. An emphasis on the body merely for the sake of gaining material rewards in the secular world is antithetical to the quest for enlightenment, and as such, modern, rational, quantified sport does not serve a purpose in the transcendence of the material world and the development of spiritual awareness.

The relationship between sport and religion has been influenced by differing perceptions of the body, the significance of sporting practices in the expression of religiosity, as well as the structure of both institutions. Christianity has had the most pronounced impact on the philosophy of modern sport, though the various Christian churches have not always regarded sport as a suitable activity for their followers. The emphasis on the corpus was thought to be at the expense of the spiritual, a division that remained until the rise of the Muscular Christian movement in the nineteenth century, which provided a new model of the sport/religion nexus, one that led to the proliferation of evangelist practices in sport throughout the twentieth and early twenty-first centuries. The popularity of modern sport and the devotion that fans display to their teams has led some to regard sport as a contemporary religion, one that holds more meaning for their followers than traditional religions; however, this standpoint has been challenged by those who regard the inherent natures of sport and religion to be fundamentally different.

SEE ALSO: Civil Religion; Identity, Sport and; Politics and Sport; Popular Religiosity; Religion, Sociology of; Socialization and Sport; Sport; Sport and Ethnicity

REFERENCES AND SUGGESTED READINGS

Edwards, H. (1973) *Sociology of Sport*. Dorsey Press, Homewood, IL.

Higgs, R. (1996) *God in the Stadium: Sports and Religion in America*. University of Kentucky Press, Lexington.

Hoffman, S. J. (Ed.) (1992) *Sport and Religion*. Human Kinetics, Champaign, IL.

Magdalinski, T. & Chandler, T. (Eds.) *With God on their Side: Sport in the Service of Religion*. Routledge,London.

Novak, M. (1976) *The Joy of Sports*. Basic Books, New York.

Overman, S. J. (1997). *The Influence of the Protestant Ethic on Sport and Recreation*. Avebury, Aldershot.

sport and social capital

Jean Harvey

The literature on sport and social capital is scarce and discussions are fragmented because there are disagreements about the definition of social capital, the role of sport in contributing to social capital, and the forms of social capital that may be generated in the sphere of sport.

Three major approaches to social capital exist in the social science literature. The most dominant is the functional approach, as represented in the work of political scientist Robert Putnam. For Putnam (1993: 167) social capital consists of "features of social organization, such as trust, norms, and networks, that can improve the efficiency of society by facilitating coordinated action." Putnam (2000) argues excessive individualism in the US has reduced civic engagement and participation in the electoral process, both of which are marks of declining social capital. This, in turn, undermines the efficacy of public institutions. In the case of sports, declining participation in sport clubs and volunteerism is a sign of declining social capital.

Within Putnam's framework, three forms of social capital are distinguished: (1) bounding, referring to the relations within homogeneous groups, like sport teams or clubs; (2) bridging, referring to relations across horizontal social divisions, such as across teams within a league; and (3) linking, referring to ties between different strata of society, for example citizens from all social classes who are fans of their local pro football club. Putnam's work has been criticized (Dyreson 2001), especially by those who argue that the evidence on aggregate measures of social capital and civic engagement may obscure "a more complex reality" and that "the overall picture is of shifts in civic engagement more than losses, and of only moderate net losses at worst" (Curtis et al. 2003).

A second approach is based on the work of Pierre Bourdieu. For Bourdieu (1986: 249), social capital is "the aggregate of the actual or potential resources which are linked to the possession of a durable network of more or less institutionalized relationships of mutual acquaintance and recognition or, in other words, membership in a group." Moreover, Bourdieu explains that the amount of social capital possessed by an agent depends on a combination of the number of network connections one can mobilize, plus the economic, cultural, and symbolic capital possessed by those comprising the network connections. Bourdieusian studies of sport and social capital are rare, although several scholars who use the two other approaches often refer to his work.

The third approach regroups a wide variety of network-based approaches to social capital. Those who use this approach build on

Bourdieu's emphasis on social capital as a resource. For example, Lin (2001: 25) defines social capital as "the resources embedded in social networks accessed by actors for actions." Within this general social network approach, some researchers are more interested in the networks themselves (the structure of relations within the networks), whereas others focus on the relational aspects of the networks (the resources available and accessible).

Most sport scholars use the functional definition of social capital, although they do not all adopt a functionalist theoretical framework. Jarvie (2003), Maguire et al. (2002), and Smith and Ingham (2003) have focused on the role of sport in the regeneration of community social capital. They argue that there are ways in which sport can positively contribute to community social capital, although it cannot be assumed that sport always increases social capital all the time.

Smith and Ingham (2003) highlight this situation in their exploration of public discussions (i.e., town meetings) over the development of professional sport stadia in the US. Their findings demonstrate that the public subsidization of professional sport stadia does not contribute to or re/generate the sense of a "community-as-a-whole, but indeed may further divide residents depending upon their situated interests." Dyreson (2001) also notes that there are situations in which sport can promote division, excessive competition, and unhealthy practices among people and communities.

Some scholars are examining sport through the lens of network-based social capital. Alegi's (2000) study of soccer in Africa illustrates Bourdieu's theory of social capital as resources grounded in network connections, namely with people who are in positions of power or in a position to change things. Alegi examined the importance of soccer to the social experiences of black African workers, entrepreneurs, and political leaders and analyzed how people subject to systemic discrimination and without political rights used soccer as a site for developing social networks based on community identities at a national, regional, and local level. Specifically, while black African workers and youth were generally not interested in seeking personal mobility in the political sphere, they often turned to soccer for self-advancement

combined with the "charitable uplift of their community." Litwin (2003) used a network-based approach to confirm that physically active older adults are more socially connected. Furthermore, the older adults in diverse networks consisting of connections across the spheres of friends, neighbors, and family were most likely to engage in physical activity.

Overall, research on social capital supports the notion that sport can enhance social capital as well as erode it. Future research will explain the circumstances under which these outcomes occur.

SEE ALSO: Social Capital; Sport and Culture; Sport and Social Class; Sport and Social Resistance

REFERENCES AND SUGGESTED READINGS

Alegi, P. C. (2000) Keep Your Eye on the Ball: A Social History of Soccer in South Africa, 1910–1976. Doctoral dissertation, Boston University, Boston.

Bourdieu, P. (1986) The Forms of Capital. In: Richards, J. G. (Ed.), *Handbook of Theory and Research for the Sociology of Education*. Greenwood Press, New York, pp. 241–58.

Curtis, J., Baer, D., Grabb, E., & Perks, T. (2003) Estimation des tendances de l'engagement dans les associations volontaires au cours des dernières décennies au Québec et au Canada anglais. *Sociologie et Sociétés* 35(1): 115–42.

Dyreson, M. (2001) Maybe It's Better to Bowl Alone: Sport, Community and Democracy in American Thought. *Culture, Sport, Society* 4(1): 19–30.

Jarvie, G. (2003) Communitarianism, Sport and Social Capital: "Neighborly Insights into Scottish Sport." *International Review for the Sociology of Sport* 38(2): 139–53.

Lin, N. (2001) *Social Capital: A Theory of Social Structure and Action*. Cambridge University Press, Cambridge.

Litwin, H. (2003) Social Predictors of Physical Activity in Later Life: The Contribution of Social-Network Type. *Journal of Aging and Physical Activity* 11: 389–406.

Maguire, J., Jarvie, G., Mansfield, L., & Bradley, J. (2002) *Sport Worlds: A Sociological Perspective*. Human Kinetics, Champaign, IL.

Putnam, R. (1993) *Making Democracy Work: Civic Traditions in Modern Italy*. Princeton University Press, Princeton.

Putnam, R. (2000) *Bowling Alone: The Collapse and Revival of American Community*. Simon & Schuster, New York.

Smith, J. M. & Ingham, A. G. (2003) On the Waterfront: Retrospectives on the Relationship between Sport and Communities. *Sociology of Sport Journal* 20(3): 252–74.

sport and social class

Alan Tomlinson

Sport is a significant contributor to relations of social class in that people in elite groups have the resources to organize and maintain games on their own terms and in spaces inaccessible to others. This ultimately serves to reproduce social and economic distinctions and preserve the power and influence of those who control resources in society. The growth of modern sports cannot be fully understood unless this key influence and core dynamic is fully recognized.

In it most general sense, social class refers to the social and cultural expression of an economic relationship. Classes are made up of individuals located and identified by (1) their contribution to economic production, (2) their access to and control over resources, and (3) their distinctive class cultures and lifestyles. In modern societies social classes are based on the individual's and the group's place in the industrial and economic process, with the most significant measures of class distinction being wealth and occupation. Explaining the relationship between these indices of class position and other sources of status and identity has long been a focus of sociological theory and research. For example, at the end of the nineteenth century, Veblen (1953) stressed that people in the ruling class recreated imagined lifestyles of the elites from previous times and constructed a life of leisure that set themselves apart from lower classes and less privileged groups. Veblen explained that the accumulation of wealth and conspicuous consumption in sport and leisure were inextricably linked. As the leisure and consumer economies of the twentieth century consolidated and expanded, this link would become increasingly important for social classes that could balance work–leisure choices, and not just for those who could afford to dispense with paid work or employment altogether.

HISTORICAL CONTEXT

Forms of inequality and exploitation characterized the civilizations of the ancient world, where participation and spectatorship in Greek festivals and Roman games were based upon position and rank in the social and economic order. In the European Middle Ages, when the military rationale of the jousting tournament receded, it was maintained by despotic rulers as a spectacular public display of power and a form of theater in which participation and spectatorship were based on social status and class position.

In comparable ways, a structure of social differentiation based on class characterized the emergent social order of the West's early modern period as industrialization and urbanization reshaped the basis of society and culture. Ascribed status, leaving little option for social mobility, was superseded by achieved status that, in theory, held the promise of a change in status, according to the individual's economic position and potential. Social standing came to be defined in terms of what people did to make a living and how they publicly displayed their acquired economic status rather than in terms of inherited status and prescribed opportunities (Sugden & Tomlinson 2000). Yet, in practice, social class, defined in terms of economic status and its associated cultural dimensions, reproduced the status quo and contributed to the consolidation of power relations and cultural distinctions.

Seminal social histories of sports in Britain – association football/soccer (Mason 1980), rugby football (Dunning & Sheard 1979), and cricket (Birley 2003) – have vividly demonstrated how the emergence and the evolution of modern sports forms were rooted in class relations. Association football in its amateur form was championed by the middle and upper classes, and developed in its professional form by the working class and lower middle classes. The attitudes and beliefs embodied in the ethos of particular sports expressed class-based status and values. The middle classes, for instance, believed that the amateur code of the game built character, strengthened the body, discouraged drinking, and unified social classes (Mason 1980: 229). Rugby football's "Great Schism" of 1895 saw the split between the Northern English mass spectator form of the game, and the amateur, Southern English-based Rugby Football Union (Dunning & Sheard 1979: 198–200). Class patronage shaped many forms of sports provision, in the US and advanced societies generally. Marxist-influenced accounts have had a widespread impact upon how such class dynamics and relations have been theorized.

NEO-MARXIST ACCOUNTS

Miliband (1977) noted that the development of a Marxist sociology of sport was not an outstandingly urgent theoretical imperative, but added that neither was it the most negligible of tasks. Marxist and neo-Marxist analysts of sport have been concerned mainly with two themes: sport's ideological role and sport's potential as contestation and resistance.

Marx said nothing about sport or its relationship with social class, but neo-Marxists have explored the nature and histories of class dynamics and class struggles. Thompson's (1968) historical interpretation of the making of the English working class describes how sport and leisure often were sites for class struggle, as the social forces that pioneered the development of capitalism emerged and sought to shape the ideological and cultural production of the new age. The establishment of capitalism and the inexorable rise of an industrial and commercial bourgeoisie demanded a disciplined and reliable labor force. A priority for the new ruling class was the reformation of the working rhythms of those whose experience of labor was based in rural rhythms past and seasonal cycles. Necessarily, the non-work habits of the masses formed part of the equation of reform, for what people did in their spare time had implications for how they related to the process of production. Thompson showed how an emergent bourgeoisie in England used its influence both in government and within the church to carry out a legal and moral crusade against the recreational habits of the lower orders. He also explained that new

labor habits were established through the imposition of time discipline, a division of labor, the supervision of labor through the use of fines, money incentives, and bells and clocks, the words of preachers and teachers, and the suppression of fairs and sports (Thompson 1967). The incipient working class did not willingly surrender long-established customs and leisure practices. Such reforms succeeded only through processes of resistance and struggle between classes and class fractions. For example, Delves's (1981) study of the decline of folk football in the English city of Derby illustrated how new cross-class alliances – the emergence of newly dominant class fractions with common interests in commerce, change, and reform – accounted for the demise of the traditional form of folk football, and the rise of horse racing – a more regulated, enclosed, civilized, and profitable form of sport.

SPORT CULTURES: CLASS, HABITUS, AND REPRODUCTION

Bourdieu (1978) notes that sports emerged in exclusive English public schools, where the sons of wealthy, powerful, and aristocratic families appropriated popular games and changed their function to suit their interests. He connects the rationalization of games into modern sport forms with a class-based philosophy of amateurism that expressed the moral ideal and the ethos of the most powerful segments of the bourgeois class. To play tennis or golf, to ride or to sail, was, as Bourdieu argues, to bestow upon the participant what he called gains in distinction. Sports in which lower-middle-class or working-class people participate develop as spectacles created for the people as mass commodities. Sports, therefore, are not self-contained spheres of practice, and it is class habitus that defines any meaning conferred on sporting activity, and any social value that is associated with the sporting practice. From this perspective, then, sports participation is not a matter of personal choice or individual preference; it depends upon the financial resources available to the potential participant, the social status of those prominent in that activity, and the cultural meaning of a sport and the individual's relationship to those meanings.

Far from being an open sphere of limitless possibilities, sport is a social phenomenon and cultural space that operates in Weberian terms as a form of social closure, in which potential entrants are vetted and excluded to suit the incumbent gatekeepers. At the same time, the inner world of the sports culture is tightly monitored and controlled, as in golf or tennis club membership committees, and in other sports institutions in which formal or informal entry requirements are barriers to open participation. The recruitment and induction processes into such clubs are operational expressions of and examinations in cultural capital. For example, entrance into a tennis club requires that newcomers must communicate competently with the gatekeepers of a club; read the social interactions and etiquette and conventions of a club; comply with the dress code; be equipped with relatively sophisticated technology; and have the ability to play at an acceptable level of competence. This apparently open choice is in reality a possibility or trajectory based upon what Bourdieu recognizes as the power of economic and cultural capital, so that class variations in sporting practice can be understood as shaped by not just the basic financial costs of an activity, but also by the perceived benefits that will accrue, either immediately or later, to the participant. Sporting practices, and associated physical and body cultures, are therefore aspects of the class habitus. Practices, in the Bourdieuian framework, are articulations of habitus.

Bourdieu is sensitive to the fact that classes are not monolithic. He argues that there can be divisions within classes and these too can be reflected in sports. An interesting example that he uses is that of the gender dimension of the class habitus that produces a sexual division of labor that in turn affects participation in particular sporting activities. But in general, for Bourdieu, the analysis of sport is a form of class analysis. Sport acts as a kind of badge of social exclusivity and cultural distinctiveness for the dominant classes; it operates as a means of control or containment of the working or popular classes; it is a potential but unlikely source of escape and mobility for talented working-class sports performers; it articulates the fractional status distinctions which exist within the ranks of larger class groupings; and it reveals the capacity of the body to express social principles and cultural meanings, for physical capital (Wacquant 1995) to connect with forms of economic and cultural capital. Bourdieu described his study *Distinction* (1986) as an attempt to think through Marx and Weber's rival conceptions of class and status, and his major achievement was to connect the study of class position and concomitant lifestyles and statuses. The lesson here for the sociologist of sport is to recognize the need for a complementary and integrated analysis of both the class dimensions of a sport and its associated lifestyle dimensions.

CONCLUSION

Studies of sport continue to pose the question of how important social class is as an influence upon participation and/or spectatorship. A Canadian study (White & Wilson 1999) reports the primary influence of socioeconomic status upon sport spectatorship; a Scandinavian study (Thrane 2001) questions this, disputing any linear influence of household income upon spectatorship, and claiming a further complexity by seeking to measure the influence of education, cultural capital, and sport participation. Unsurprisingly, the more that is measured, the more confusing the picture gets. However, analyzing data from the US General Social Survey in 1993 and drawing upon Bourdieu's concept of cultural capital, Wilson (2002) is much more analytically unequivocal: cultural capital enables people to do more sport, and social class provides the knowledge, tastes, skills, and preferences that motivate individuals towards particular types of sport consumption.

An overemphasis upon the potential of sport to offer social mobility to a few can distort this picture of sport's reproductive capacity. It is often thought that working-class males take up boxing in order to get out of the ghetto. Some do; a few more may. But Sugden's (1987) insightful ethnography of the Burnt Oak boxing gym shows how for the majority who will not graduate to the professional ranks, boxing is a form of exploitation, giving them little more than survival skills, honing skills and fueling hope, but confirming their ghetto culture.

In societies such as Britain sport participation in a general sense has demonstrated a relative stability. National participation figures are notoriously difficult to unravel in completely reliable ways, but it is clear that there was no boom in participation during the 1990s. In fact, sport participation rates and the patterns of participation between different social groups have remained largely unchanged since the early 1970s, with the exception that more women now participate in fitness activities (Rowe 2003). The 2002 General Household Survey in Britain showed enormous differences between groups classified by socioeconomic criteria: 20 percent of adults in the higher occupational cum economic groupings did keep fit; for those not working, or long-term unemployed, it was 4 percent; 59 percent of the former group took part in at least one physical activity in the 4-week reference period compared with 30 percent of those in routine jobs. One in 10 of the top occupational group had played golf, the same figure for running/jogging; only 1 in 50 of those in routine jobs had participated in these activities (Fox & Rickards 2004).

National studies confirm such persisting patterns of class-based inequality; local and regional studies provide parallel confirmation, as in analyses of urban space and sport and leisure consumption. Twenty-first century consumer society without doubt offers numerous opportunities for the expression of experimental identities, for a kind of project of the self to which sport can be one contributing source, as work on lifestyle and extreme sports has shown. Cultures can and do change, but as Williams (1977) noted, in subtle ways in which the dominant, residual, and emergent elements sometimes intermesh. Dominant cultures resist transformation though, and in this wider context sport, at its various levels of performance, participation, and spectatorship, continues to show how class habitus and cultural capital remain major determinants of everyday practices and cultural institutions.

SEE ALSO: Political Economy and Sport; Sport and Capitalism; Sport and Culture; Sport and Social Capital; Sport as Work

REFERENCES AND SUGGESTED READING

Birley, D. (2003) *A Social History of English Cricket.* Aurum Press, London.

Bourdieu, P. (1978) Sport and Social Class. *Social Science Information* 17(6): 819–40.

Bourdieu, P. (1986) *Distinction: A Social Critique of the Judgement of Taste.* Routledge & Kegan Paul, New York.

Delves, A. (1981) Popular Recreation and Social Conflict in Derby, 1800–1850. In: Yeo, E. & Yeo, S. (Eds.), *Popular Culture and Class Conflict 1590–1914: Explorations in the History of Labour and Leisure,* Harvester Press, Brighton, pp. 89–127.

Dunning, E. & Sheard, K. (1979) *Barbarians, Gentlemen and Players: A Sociological Study of the Development of Rugby Football,* New York University Press, New York.

Fox, K. & Rickards, L. (2004) *Sport and Leisure: Results from the Sport and Leisure Module of the 2002 General Household Survey.* TSO, London.

Giddens, A. (1993) *Sociology.* Polity Press, Cambridge.

McIntosh, P. (1993) The Sociology of Sport in the Ancient World. In: Dunning, E. C., Maguire, J. A., and Pearton, R. E. (Eds.), *The Sports Process: A Comparative and Developmental Approach.* Human Kinetics, Champaign, IL, pp. 19–38.

Mason, T. (1980) *Association Football and English Society 1863–1915.* Harvester Press, Brighton.

Miliband, R. (1977) *Marxism and Politics.* Oxford University Press, Oxford.

Rowe, N. (Ed.) (2003) *Driving Up Participation: The Challenge for Sport (Academic review papers commissioned by Sport England as contextual analysis to inform the preparation of the Framework for Sport in England).* Sport England, London.

Sugden, J. (1987) The Exploitation of Disadvantage: The Occupational Sub-Culture of the Boxer. In: Horne, J., Jary, D., & Tomlinson, A. (Eds.), *Sport, Leisure and Social Relations.* Routledge & Kegan Paul, London, pp. 187–209.

Sugden, J. & Tomlinson, A. (2000) Theorizing Sport, Social Class and Status. In: Coakley, J. and Dunning, E. (Eds.), *Handbook of Sports Studies.* Sage, London, pp. 309–21.

Thompson, E. P. (1967) Time, Work Discipline and Industrial Capitalism. *Past and Present* 38: 56–97.

Thompson, E. P. (1968) *The Making of the English Working Class.* Penguin, London.

Thrane, C. (2001) Sport Spectatorship in Scandinavia: A Class Phenomenon? *International Review for the Sociology of Sport* 36(2): 149–63.

Veblen, T. (1953) *The Theory of the Leisure Class: An Economic Study of Institutions.* New York, Mentor.

Wacquant, L. (1995) Pugs at Work: Bodily Capital and Bodily Labour among Professional Boxers. *Body and Society* 1(1): 65–93.

White, P. & Wilson, B. (1999) Distinction in the Stands. *International Review for the Sociology of Sport* 34(4): 245–64.

Williams, R. (1977) *Marxism and Literature*. Oxford University Press, Oxford.

Wilson, T. C. (2002) The Paradox of Social Class and Sports Involvement: The Roles of Cultural and Economic Capital. *International Review for the Sociology of Sport* 37(1): 5–16.

sport and social resistance

George H. Sage

Social resistance is a social phenomenon in which disadvantaged, exploited, and dominated groups contest the dominating practices that nation-states, social institutions, social organizations, and traditional cultural practices have constructed. Resistance and acts of agency – meaning the capability of individuals to construct and reconstruct their world – against abuses of power, discrimination, inequality, social injustice, and autocratic control are pervasive features of human history. There are always ongoing struggles against domination through various forms of social resistance. As British social theorist Robin Williams (1977) asserted, dominance "does not just passively exist . . . It has continually to be renewed, recreated, defended, and modified. It is also continually resisted, limited, altered, challenged by pressures not at all its own" (p. 112).

Individual resistance and human agency are the means through which individuals change social processes and structures and build alternatives. When social resistance is carried out under the auspices of an organized group, this is referred to as a social movement. Research on social movements most often focuses on the social and psychological characteristics of those who participate in the movement, the relations between the leaders and other participants, and the social and political outcomes of the organized resistance.

Resistance movements use violent and/or nonviolent tactics. Several of the most common forms of resistance are boycotts, civil disobedience, guerrilla warfare, and passive resistance. Social scientist James C. Scott (1990) asserts that opposition and resistance of subordinate groups is frequently "found neither in overt collective defiance of powerholders nor in complete hegemonic compliance, but in the vast territory between those two polar opposites" (p. 136).

Sporting practices have typically been vehicles of cultural reproduction, but they have also been avenues for the expression of various forms of social resistance and agency. Athletes and others associated with sport have resisted dominant models of sport in subtle and not-so-subtle ways. In doing so, they have contradicted, modified, and transformed definitions and modes of control in sporting practices. Several areas of research in which social resistance struggles have taken place in sport are illustrated in the following selected examples.

Issues of race and gender have given rise to social resistance in sport. African American athletes have challenged the sport establishment over racism in sport in a variety of ways. For almost a century after the abolition of slavery, blacks were excluded from participation and attendance at most mainstream American sports. As one form of resistance to being barred from mainstream sport, blacks formed their own teams and leagues. The so-called Negro baseball leagues flourished for more than 40 years in the first half of the twentieth century. All-black basketball teams and leagues succeeded in many cities of the Northwest and Midwest during this same era. Black boxers resisted formidable barriers to their boxing careers and several, such as Jack Johnson and Joe Louis, became world champions. More recently, heavyweight boxing champion Muhammad Ali refused to serve in the military and participate in the Vietnam War, saying that he didn't have anything against the North Vietnamese.

In the 1990s, black and white athletes and coaches boycotted several sport events because of racist policies or practices of the sponsors. They also increased the pressure on the sport establishment for greater African American representation in coaching and managing. Sport has become a medium for demonstrating black pride through hairstyles and handshakes and other rituals carried out in connection with sport events, thus affirming black capabilities, and challenging the subordination imposed by the politically and socially powerful within American society.

Gender differentiation has been powerfully constructed through sport and the culture of sport. Historically, one of the most persistent and widespread forms of discrimination was the lack of access to sport opportunities for females. Social attitudes and conditions made female athletes an anomaly until the 1970s. Before that, girls and women who participated in competitive sports faced social isolation and censure. Even into the late 1980s, public attitudes supported sport as a male preserve in most nations around the world.

With the women's movement as an ideological foundation, resistance to traditional restrictions to female involvement in sport began in earnest in a few nations. At the youth sports level, girls and their parents began to question the rules and regulations of youth sport organizations. In the Unites States, for example, they challenged baseball's Little League "boys only" policy by registering to play on Little League teams. They challenged policies of public recreation departments that sponsored only boys' sports teams, and insisted that girls be allowed to play on these teams or that an equal number of girls' teams be created.

Women were a major force resisting the sport inequities for females in US high schools and colleges that were conspicuous and widespread before the 1970s. They were successful at securing the passage of the Education Amendments Act of 1972. A key provision in this act, Title IX, required that educational institutions receiving federal funds must provide equivalent programs for males and females. Similar forms of resistance have occurred internationally and in other nation-states.

In recent years sport-related political protests have been waged on behalf of various causes. Between 1970 and the overthrow of the white government in South Africa in the early 1990s, unpopular American government and corporate support for South Africa and its apartheid policies led many sport groups to successfully resist the participation of South African athletes in sporting events in the US. Indeed, sport resistance was one of the most important sites for condemning the South African apartheid government.

Athletes and activist groups, even nations, have occasionally chosen sporting venues for social resistance to demonstrate against political policies and practices. In the 1968 Summer Olympic Games in Mexico City, African American Olympic medal-winners Tommie Smith and John Carlos raised their gloved fists during the playing of the national anthem to protest racism in the US and racial oppression around the world.

In the 1970s and 1980s, nation-state boycotts plagued the Olympic Games. African nations boycotted the 1976 Olympics because New Zealand's rugby team had played in South Africa. The United States and several other western nations refused to compete at the Moscow Olympics in 1980 because of the Soviet invasion of Afghanistan. The Soviet Union and its Eastern Bloc partners countered by boycotting the 1984 Olympics in Los Angeles.

In the United States protesters have used major sporting events to stage protests against war, racism, sexism, nuclear proliferation, and environmental pollution. Speeches, distribution of literature, and placard displays typically take place outside the sports venue, while demonstrations occur inside during pre-game or half-time. Intercollegiate athletes themselves have engaged in a type of resistance that James C. Scott calls low-profile resistance and infrapolitics. Because they do not receive a salary or wage for their labor – they receive an "athletic scholarship" – they have forged an underground economy, frequently accepting under-the-table payments and improper benefits from coaches, boosters, and sports agents. Although their actions are not intended to have structural ramifications, they are struggles for social justice in the distribution of wealth that is generated from their labor.

One form of social resistance involves withdrawing or evading the dominant canon of a social practice, which in contemporary sport is a highly competitive organized sport culture. Outdoor activities such as hiking, rock climbing, rafting, hang gliding, skydiving, skateboarding, scuba diving, and so forth where participation has priority, have boomed among a clientele seeking alternatives to organized, commercial, and corporate forms of sport. This phenomenon is worldwide. Many participants create alternative norms and relations that emphasize participant control of the physical activity and open participation rather than rule-bound, high-level competition.

There are several categories of these alternative sports forms – "action" sports, "whiz" sports, "adventure" sports – often overlapping into a rather ill-defined category called extreme sports. Most of these activities do not attract masses of spectators, so the fanfare associated with mainstream sports is not missed. One sport sociologist claims these forms of sport "are about sharing the experience and about community" (Rinehart 2000: 504) – characteristics that attract many of the participants.

Social resistance represents an important precursor for social transformation. This can occur when groups of people use sport to resist certain social attitudes, practices, and laws in an effort to raise public consciousness and bring about social change. For example, to call public attention to prejudice and discrimination against homosexuals and to improve public attitudes about them, in 1982 leaders of the gay and lesbian community planned to create and hold a Gay Olympic Games in San Francisco. The event was quickly crushed by a lawsuit from the United States Olympic Committee (USOC), claiming that the use of the word Olympics violated a trademark the USOC was granted under the Amateur Sports Act of 1978. Nevertheless, resistance quickly emerged within the gay and lesbian community. The name of the event was changed to the Gay Games and the first Gay Games were held in 1982. They have been held every four years since then in different cities throughout the world. The Gay Games have helped to transform the attitudes of many "straight" people towards homosexuals, and have had a transformative effect for many members of the gay community, giving them a sense of empowerment, enhanced self-esteem, and opportunities to display socially valued physical skills in a visible context.

Social resistance has extended to apparel and equipment used by sports participants. In the global economy, product manufacturing is a major driving force. A key aspect of the global economy is a system of manufacturing and division of labor known as the export processing system. In this system, product research, design, development, and marketing take place in industrially developed countries, while the labor-intensive, assembly-line phases of product manufacture are relegated to developing countries. The finished product is then exported for distribution in developed countries of the world.

Sporting goods manufacturing is one of the most flourishing export-processing industries, and Nike was one of the pioneering sporting goods corporations in foreign export-processing. During the 1990s, 16 major investigations were made of factories producing Nike footwear in Asian countries. The reports uniformly found appalling working conditions in Nike's factories: local industrial safety laws were violated and workers' rights were nonexistent. Between 1992 and 1996, as global understanding and consciousness grew about Nike's Asian factories, a mass chord of horror and outrage spurred collective actions and launched what became the Nike social movement. This resistance movement was composed of an international coalition of organizations. Their goal was to create enough public outrage against Nike that governments, businesses, unions, religious organizations, and human rights groups would bring pressure on Nike to change its labor practices and improve conditions in the factories. The Nike social movement severely damaged the Nike brand name and reputation for millions of people throughout the world. In 1998 the Nike CEO announced plans for what he called New Labor Initiatives, which was a plan for significant reform in the company's labor practices. These reforms likely came about as a direct result of the Nike social movement campaigns.

SEE ALSO: Agency (and Intention); Social Movement Organizations; Social Movements; Sport; Sport, Alternative

REFERENCES AND SUGGESTED READINGS

Ballinger, J. & Olsson, C. (Eds.) (1997) *Behind the Swoosh: The Struggle of Indonesians Making Nike Shoes*. Global Publications Foundation, Uppsala.

Jasper, J. M. (1997) *The Art of Moral Protest: Culture, Biography, and Creativity in Social Movements*. University of Chicago, Chicago.

Meyer, D. S., Whittier, N., & Robnett, B. (2002) *Social Movements: Identity, Culture, and the State.* Oxford University Press, New York.

Rinehart, R. E. (2000) Arriving Sport: Alternatives to Formal Sports. In: Coakley, J. & Dunning, E. (Eds.), *Handbook of Sports Studies.* Sage, Thousand Oaks, CA, pp. 504–19.

Scott, J. C. (1990) *Domination and the Arts of Resistance: Hidden Transcripts.* Yale University Press, New Haven.

Shaw, R. (1999) *Reclaiming America: Nike, Clean Air, and the New National Activism.* University of California Press, Berkeley.

Tilly, C. (2004) *Social Movements, 1768–2004.* Paradigm Press, Boulder.

Wiggins, D. & Miller, P. B. (Eds.) (2003) *The Uneven Playing Field: A Documentary History of the African American Experience in Sport.* University of Illinois Press, Urbana.

Williams, R. (1977) *Marxism and Literature.* Oxford University Press, Oxford.

sport as spectacle

David L. Andrews

The spectacle, in the form of an imposing public display, is not simply a benign cultural form, because it can seldom be separated from "noncoercive strategies of power and persuasion" (Cary 2005). This is often overlooked when considering contemporaneous high-profile sporting events staged for the entertainment of spectating publics (e.g., the NFL Super Bowl, Olympic Games, or FIFA World Cup), which, despite their celebratory sporting veneer, routinely communicate the values and ideologies of the dominant corporate capitalist order. The sport spectacle has, of course, long been a vehicle for the expression and/or performance of dominant cultural practices and sensibilities. This can, at least partially, be attributed to the fact that the visceral intensity of competition-based physical culture possesses an almost unrivaled capacity to capture the interest and imagination of publics located within divergent historical and social contexts. Moreover, the very practice of bearing witness to (or spectating) particular displays of competitive physicality has played an important role in establishing the sociocultural import of some physical activities over others. Thus, the Olympic festivals of ancient Greece, the gladiatorial contests of ancient Rome, and even the folk football rituals of pre-industrial Europe (such as the Florentine *calcio*) were only fully constituted as socially, culturally, and indeed politically significant practices through the presence and involvement of massed ranks of spectators, whose numbers dwarfed those of active participants.

As resonant focal points for popular identities, desires, and fears, physical cultural spectacles have frequently become appropriated by particular social groupings looking to advance their own political and ideological agendas. This is perhaps best exemplified in what Juvenal famously described as the "circuses" of violent entertainment staged within Rome's vast amphitheaters as a means of appeasing the baser sensibilities of the Roman populace. As well as providing a diversion for the underworked (due to the presence of an extensive slave populace) yet disenfranchised (due to the nature of the Republic's constitution) Roman masses, these games also constituted a highly visible site for the Roman elite to exhibit their economic and political power. Roman luminaries thus regularly sponsored ever more extravagant, bloodthirsty spectacles (including gladiatorial combat, elaborate and voluminous human sacrifices, the mass slaughter of animals, and even carefully staged naval battles) as a means of securing the popular approval of Rome's excitement-seeking plebian classes.

While the emergence of modern spectator sport in the late nineteenth and early twentieth centuries incorporated considerably less savage forms of competitive physicality than their ancient antecedents, they did nonetheless perform similar sociopolitical functions. By codifying sporting practice (regulated participation) and sanctioning cathartic release (mass spectatorship), the patrician-industrialist power bloc ensured that sport helped constrain working bodies to the demands and discipline of the industrial workplace, while simultaneously contributing to the commercialization of what was a burgeoning urban leisure culture. Thus, within the modern industrial era, and specifically its newly defined realm of leisure time, institutionalized sport became an increasingly important site of "surveillance, spectacle, and profit"

(Miller & McHoul 1998). As Brookes (2002) reiterated, the instantiation of modern sport during the nineteenth century both disciplined and commodified popular physical culture, through the standardized regulation of sporting "time, space, and conduct," which provided opportunities for aspirant participants, entrepreneurs, and spectators alike.

While most industrializing nations began developing their own inventory of spectacular sporting events at this time, the modern Olympic Games, originating with the 1896 Athens Olympiad, rapidly became sport spectacle of truly global proportions. The global spectacularization of the Olympic Games was expedited through successive phases of technological advancement in the mass communications industry (i.e., newsreel, radio, television, and Internet innovations) that allowed the Olympic spectacle to engage, and inform, both internal and external audiences alike. Initially advanced as a festive celebration of sporting excellence, fair play, amateurism, and internationalism, the modern Olympic Games soon became appropriated by, and an expression of, the prevailing power structure within the host nation. Thus, the Games have become forums for the (inter) national display and attempted validation of specific political-economic orders, such as those associated with British imperialism (London, 1908), German fascism (Berlin, 1936), USSR communism (Moscow, 1980), US capitalism (Los Angeles, 1984), and US neo-imperialism (Salt Lake City, 2002). Interestingly, within many recent Olympic celebrations (Salt Lake City, 2002, excluded), the Games have been spectacularized – particularly through the performance of defining national cultural characteristics within Olympic opening ceremonies, and the utilization of specific national geographies as event locations and facilities (Hogan 2003; Tomlinson 1996) – as mechanisms of place-marketing for potential tourist visitors to the host cities. In this manner, Barcelona (1992), Sydney (2000), and Athens (2004) are all illustrative of the commercial processes through which the Olympic Games have become implicated within, and veritable motors of, what are the overdetermining forces and networks of global (consumer) capital.

In the second half of the twentieth century sport was conclusively and apparently irreversibly integrated into the commercial ferment of the dominant consumer capitalist order. Of course, many sporting entities, such as Major League Baseball (MLB), the National Basketball Association (NBA), the National Football League (NFL), and the National Hockey League (NHL), originated as professional, putatively commercial, ventures. However, until relatively recently, most occupied a space at the periphery of the commercial marketplace, with utility maximization (sporting performance) routinely taking precedence over – frequently to the exclusion of – profit maximization (financial performance). The commercialization and commodification of sport – what Walsh and Giulianotti (2001) describe as a continuing process of converting "the social meaning of a practice or object into purely financial terms" – reached a heightened level of intensity with the contemporaneous advancement of the profit-driven corporation as the naturalized, and largely unquestioned, model of social organization. Sporting *bodies* (sport organizations, events, leagues, teams, athletes, etc.) thus became incorporated into the structures, values, and directives of late capitalist culture. Put simply, a conjuncture within which "everything ... has become cultural; and culture has equally become economic or commodity oriented" (Jameson 1998). Within this context, an expansive economy of highly managed and marketed sport spectacles has become an important "correlative" to a consumer society in which consumption (of commodities and services) has become the generative core (Kellner 2003: 66). Since contemporary capitalism's culturally inflected regime of accumulation is prefigured on the operationalizing of the mass media (simultaneously as both core commercial product and commercializing process), sport's evolution has become inextricably tied to the rhythms and regimes of an expanding media-industrial complex. Thus, from the mid-twentieth century onwards, the emergence and rapid diffusion of commercial television has played a crucial role in the enlarging presence, and intensifying influence, of mass-mediated, mass-entertainment oriented, commercial sport spectacles. Moreover, the relentless rise of commercial television as a major conduit to both the *commercialization of culture* and the associated *culturalization of the economy* has revolutionized the sport economy:

escalating fees from the selling of broadcast rights and media sponsorships having become, for many professional sports, teams, and events, the single most important source of revenue generation (Bellamy 1998). Thus, there is a growing tendency for media organizations and corporate sponsors/advertisers to exert monopoly-like control over sport organizations (Jary 1999). In other words, there has been a conclusive "institutional alignment of sports and media in the context of late capitalism" (Real 1998).

Of course, the demands of understanding the spectacular economy of contemporary sport culture lead, somewhat predictably, to Debord's (1990, 1994) theorizing on the society of the spectacle. However, as Tomlinson (2002) warned, all too frequently Debord's provocative treatise on the transformations in relations between capitalism, technology, and everyday life is the subject of little more than superficial invocation. Within examinations of sport, this is routinely done through reference to the proliferation of mass-mediated spectacular sporting events as if they, in and of themselves, encapsulate the complexities of spectacular society. In Tomlinson's terms, this trite appropriation belies an "interpretive shorthand" used by academics, whose passing references to Debord signify an acknowledgment of the mediated spectacle "without any fully developed sense of the conceptualization of the spectacle." The tendency toward reifying the spectacle is soon eviscerated through actual recourse to Debord's theses which exhume the layered complexity and multidimensionality of the spectacle, and its position and function within spectacular society: "The spectacle appears at once as society itself, as a part of society and as a means of unification" (Debord 1994: 12). According to Debord, the upper-case Spectacle (mediated mega-event) and the lower-case spectacle (relentless outpourings of the corroborating and/or parasitic culture industries and processes) provide both the monumental and vernacular architecture of a spectacular society, in which the spectacle as capitalist product and process realizes a situation in which the "commodity completes its colonization of social life" (p. 29). Kellner (2003: 66), this time with specific reference to the dualism of the sport spectacle, similarly observed that "postindustrial sports have transformed traditional (and in some cases, non-traditional) practices into

media spectacles in such a way that exemplifies the broader processes of cultural commodification associated with the rise of a mass media-driven consumer society."

SEE ALSO: Debord, Guy; Olympics; Sport and Capitalism; Sport Culture and Subcultures; Sport and Culture; Sport as Work; Sports Heroes and Celebrities

REFERENCES AND SUGGESTED READINGS

Bellamy, R. V. (1998) The Evolving Television Sports Marketplace. In: Wenner, L. A. (Ed.), *Mediasport*. Routledge, London, pp. 73–87.

Brookes, R. (2002) *Representing Sport*. Arnold, London.

Cary, J. (2005) Spectacle. In: Bennett, T., Grossberg, L., & Morris, M. (Eds.), *New Keywords: A Vocabulary of Culture and Society*. Blackwell, Oxford, pp. 335–6.

Debord, G. (1990) *Comments on the Society of the Spectacle*. Trans. M. Imrie. Verso, London.

Debord, G. (1994) *The Society of the Spectacle*. Trans. D. Nicholson-Smith. Zone Books, New York.

Hogan, J. (2003) Staging the Nation: Gendered and Ethnicized Discourses of National Identity in Olympic Opening Ceremonies. *Journal of Sport and Social Issues* 27(2): 100–23.

Jameson, F. (1998) *The Cultural Turn: Selected Writings on the Postmodern 1983–1998*. Verso, New York.

Jary, D. (1999) The McDonaldization of Sport and Leisure. In: Smart, B. (Ed.), *Resisting McDonaldization*. Sage, London, pp. 116–34.

Kellner, D. (2003) *Media Spectacle*. Routledge, London.

Miller, T. & McHoul, A. (1998) *Popular Culture and Everyday Life*. Sage, London.

Real, M. R. (1998) Mediasport: Technology and the Commodification of Postmodern Sport. In: Wenner, L. (Ed.), *Mediasport*. Routledge, London, pp. 14–26.

Tomlinson, A. (1996) Olympic Spectacle: Opening Ceremonies and Some Paradoxes of Globalization. *Media, Culture and Society* 18(4): 583–602.

Tomlinson, A. (2002) Theorizing Spectacle: Beyond Debord. In: Sugden, J. & Tomlinson, A. (Eds.), *Power Games: A Critical Sociology of Sport*. Routledge, London, pp. 44–60.

Walsh, A. J. & Giulianotti, R. (2001) This Sporting Mammon: A Normative Critique of the Commodification of Sport. *Journal of the Philosophy of Sport* 28: 53–77.

sport and the state

Jacques Defrance

Since the end of the nineteenth century the dynamics of the sport–state relationship are best understood by taking into account (1) the dramatic growth of sport relative to other forms of physical activity (gymnastics, traditional games, etc.) and (2) socially significant changes in the operation and status of the state.

Sport is a competitive form of physical activity, codified to ensure equal opportunities of victory to competitors and guarantee physical security in contests. This mode of physical game, a unique feature of industrial and parliamentary societies, emerged first in England during the eighteenth and nineteenth centuries (Elias & Dunning 1986). Between 1880 and 1900 it had become common in western industrial societies and territories controlled by the British Empire (Mangan 1985) and it became worldwide after the era of decolonization in the 1950s and 1960s.

The British state, under which modern sport was invented, was also the first to adopt a parliamentary form of government. As these developments occurred, British society also was characterized by relatively stable internal social relationships (i.e., during the eighteenth and nineteenth centuries). However, as organized forms of competitive sports spread during the twentieth century, they were appropriated and incorporated into diverse social formations and different state structures, including those that were socialist, fascist, corporatist, liberal, etc. These recent historical developments raise a series of questions about sport and the state. Through what processes did states acquire power over sports (Harvey et al. 1993)? What functions were fulfilled by sports in different political systems? How are institutionalized forms of sports shaped and developed as autonomous activities in different types of states? What relations are formed between institutionalized versions of sports and public powers?

Scholars in the social sciences have raised these questions only since the 1960s. Although research on the state is common among scholars in political philosophy, law, sociology, and political science, is has only recently been undertaken by scholars in the sociology of sport.

There have been English, French, and German-speaking scholars with interests in political economy and the sociology of sport who have published research and theoretical essays on the relationship between sporting institutions and the state. This work varies with the underlying conception of the state used by scholars. Some have employed a Marxist or neo-Marxist definition of the state and focused attention on the nature of the state, domination by the bourgeois classes (employers, capitalist class, leisure class), and the role of class power in the reproduction of the social order in general and institutionalized forms of sport in particular. This approach is structural and theoretical. Other scholars have done empirical analyses of the state, including its agencies and policies related to sport. They have provided sociohistorical accounts of the making and transformation of the contemporary state through the twentieth century (Houlihan 1991; Callède 2000). They have focused on nationalism, imperialism, and the form of the nineteenth-century state, and then on the forms of the state that emerged in connection with advanced capitalism and the formation of public welfare policies during the twentieth century. Less functionalist than Marxist analyses, these studies have revealed a less monolithic state and produced typologies of state forms.

Among sociological traditions that deal with relations between sport and the state, only figurational theory produces specific insights on the making of the modern state and the place of sport in this process (Elias & Dunning 1986). The civilizing process that occurred during the fifteenth through nineteenth centuries in Western Europe assumed an associated process of state formation and the state's monopoly over the exercise of legitimate violence. Norbert Elias's analysis of the civilizing process in eighteenth-century England shows that the English inner political space was pacified through a civilizing spurt, in which political elites agreed to challenge each other for access to governmental offices by using non-violent strategies. Two factions of the upper classes struggled to gain power through the use of rhetoric and persuasion in a parliamentary system, rather than using coercive force. At the same time, political elites transformed their pastimes into sports, that is, into rule-governed competitive games in which opponents, regulated by the norms of civility, compete for victory without destroying each other. Elias uses historical data to show that the quest for domination in the realm of the state and on playing fields is grounded in a competitive disposition shared by those elites attracted to both political involvement and sporting activity. This theory also takes into account that as social space has divided into separate spheres through the twentieth century, it has broken the direct class-based links between political activity and sporting practice. Chris Rojek addressed this divergence and proposed a complementary analysis to the work done by Elias and Elias and Dunning (Dunning & Rojek 1992).

Scholars using forms of critical theory have studied the growing involvement of political bodies in capitalist and socialist industrial nations/states in sport since the beginning of the Cold War. The sociology of culture and political sociology have been used as frameworks for developing explanations of the ways that government involvement have influenced sporting practices and the development of elite-level sport in the USSR, the US, Japan, and Europe. A "pluralist" sociological model is employed by some political scientists who analyze diverse management methods across the nations, and the social functions that sport fulfills for contemporary political powers (Meynaud 1966).

Work based on a Marxist model defines the state as an apparatus dominated by the bourgeoisie, whose control is gained through a struggle among different groups competing for power (hegemony theory). This work shows the ways that sport fits into state policies, market mechanisms, and commercial entertainment regulated by the state (Cantelon & Gruneau 1983; Hargreaves 1986). It highlights the similarity between the sport-related values of physical efficiency and competition, and capitalist norms of productivity and economic competition, all of which are fostered by the state (Brohm 1978). Much of this work is conceptually limited, but it has pointed out the contradictions between (1) the development of a sporting culture which attracts popular classes (soccer in Europe, football in the US, hockey in Canada), (2) the domination of bourgeois values in the sporting ethic and the control exercised by dominant classes over sport organizations, (3) the state, and (4) the corporations that sponsor sport.

In England and North America, hegemony theorists, inspired by Gramsci, and sociologists using cultural studies frameworks, have studied the ways that the working classes construct and interpret sporting practices according to their ideological and material interests. Similar work has been done by sociologists analyzing the sporting field and habitus; they identify the historical circumstances in which members of lower classes have succeeded in using the symbolism of sport to support protest and opposition to dominant economic and political norms. The state usually assists mainstream sport organizations in condemning protesters and marginalizing grassroots sport forms. However, in the US, for example, there have been cases of collective protests, such as those by African Americans in the 1960s and women in the 1970s, when the state enacted legislation to make discrimination by race and sex illegal in sports (e.g., in 1972, Title IX of the Equal Education Amendments to the Civil Rights Act made discrimination by sex illegal in schools receiving federal funds).

When scholars have analyzed sport and its functions in international political relationships they have focused on the ways that the state promotes or restricts international sporting relationships. They examine the autonomy of sporting powers and the degree of politicization in the sphere of sport. This work has examined foreign affairs and diplomacy, but has ignored other aspects of relations between sport and the state.

The material support given by the state to sport, mostly during the 1960s, enhanced the legitimacy of sport in many societies. As a result, sport and sport-related values were introduced into the school curriculum in several European countries and Canadian provinces such as Quebec. The sociology of education and culture, therefore, has focused some attention on the conditions under which a bond is established between the state and sports organizations in order to impose a sporting culture in school. Some research has tried to identify the ways that state agencies are influenced by sport-related lobbying interests that work in and through committees for school reform, with representatives of sport industries, or under the leadership of coaches' associations and elected representatives. The receptiveness of public officials to sporting interests indicates a spurt of "sportization" in connection with the state. Conversely, the situation in some countries shows state interference in sport in the form of government control and a corresponding lack of autonomy in the sporting field. This was the case in the USSR with the socialist sporting system (Riordan 1977), in the Fascist regime in Italy and Germany in the 1930s, and it is still the case in nations with authoritarian regimes and military dictators (e. g., some African nations and Western Asian kingdoms). Partial forms of government control exist in strongly centralized democracies like France, where the state manages sporting centers (e.g., the National Sporting Center in Paris established in 1942), creates state-guaranteed diplomas (state certificate for sporting educators established in 1962), and employs and finances technical staff in sporting federations, among other things.

In the US there is another type of articulation between the (federal) state and the sporting field dominated by men's professional leagues (such as the National Football League and Major League Baseball). Until the 1960s, the state seldom intervened in sports, except when a dispute between officials or other parties threatened the system, or when a scandal or unsavory events occurred and received public attention. The state then played a regulatory role in reconciling conflicting interests and providing equal opportunity to practice sports; it also mediated conflicts that interfered with winning medals in international competitions such as the Olympic Games. When the economic stakes associated with sports increased dramatically during the 1960s and 1970s, and when a dispute subverted the process of selecting athletes for national teams, the federal government intervened and restructured the organization of amateur sports. Like other states, the US government has influenced sports through its economic and fiscal policies (Johnson & Frey 1985).

Studies on sport and the state increased through the 1970s and early 1980s, when public sports policies reached their peak. They decreased afterwards, when neoliberal policies reduced state interventions in all social and cultural domains, including sport. At that point, research in the sociology of sport began to focus on the professionalization and commodification of sport, and other issues in which public policies do not play a major role.

The revival of state theory in political science served as an incentive for research based on Marxism during the 1960s, and research focusing on welfare policies as state-funded social programs were reduced during the 1980s. Functions of the state, as a normalizing, regulating, and repressive agent, were reexamined during the 1990s and 2000s.

The concepts used to study the state have come from the political sciences, history, and the sociology of social relationships and conflicts. Although scholars need to clarify concepts such as "the state," (sporting) "ideology," "public policy," and "domination," they have used the theories of Marx, Weber, Durkheim, Elias, Giddens, and Bourdieu in their research on sport and the state. Some research has helped us understand details in decision-making processes and the financing of sport, but many questions remain unanswered. A clear definition of a frame of analysis for the "world of sports," conceived as precisely as the models of the state, would permit the development of a more coherent body of research, as it is proposed by the theory of "fields," borrowed from Pierre Bourdieu (Defrance 1995). Comparative studies are needed to explain the relationships between sport and various state forms, such as those organized around religious power, those established alongside a strong industrial capitalist sector, those that have been militarized for a long time, and others.

Questions related to the culture of the state personnel (qualified occupations in public administration) and their perception of sport should be examined to understand the public administration of sport, as well as when and where it prevails over private administration. The specific transformations of the neoliberal state since the 1980s form a new topic in the analysis of sports policies. During this period, the issue of controlling sport doping practices has become a topic that enables scholars to study alliances and oppositions between public and private powers in the governance of contemporary sports.

SEE ALSO: Figurational Sociology and the Sociology of Sport; Nationalism and Sport; Political Economy and Sport; Politics and Sport; Sport and Capitalism; Sport and Culture; Sportization

REFERENCES AND SUGGESTED READINGS

Brohm, J. M. (1978) *Sport: A Prison of Measured Time*. Ink Links, London.

Callède, J. P. (2000) *Les Politiques sportives en France: eléments de sociologie historique*. Economica, Paris.

Cantelon, H. & Gruneau, R. (Eds.) (1983) *Sport, Culture and the Modern State*. University of Toronto Press, Toronto.

Defrance, J. (1995) L'autonomisation du champ sportif, 1890–1970 *Sociologie et Société* 27(1): 15–31.

Dunning, E. & Rojek, C. (Eds.) (1992) *Sport and Leisure in the Civilizing Process*. Routledge, London.

Elias, N. & Dunning, E. (1986) *Quest for Excitement: Sport and Leisure in the Civilizing Process*. Blackwell, Oxford.

Hargreaves, J. (1986) *Sport, Power and Culture*. Polity Press, Cambridge.

Harvey, J., Defrance, J., & Beamish, R. (1993) Physical Exercise Policy and the Welfare State: A Framework for Comparative Analysis. *International Review for the Sociology of Sport* 28(1): 53–64.

Houlihan, B. (1991) *The Government and Politics of Sport*. Routledge, London.

Johnson, A. T. & Frey, J. H. (Eds.) (1985) *Government and Sports*. Rowman & Allanheld, Totowa, NJ.

Mangan, J. A. (1985) *The Games Ethic and Imperialism: Aspects of the Diffusion of an Idea*. Viking, New York.

Meynaud, J. (1966) *Sport et politique*. Payot, Paris.

Riordan, J. (1977) *Sport in Soviet Society*. Blackwell, Oxford.

sport as work

Peter Donnelly

If work and sport are referred to in the same breath, it is usually as opposites. Although it is now commonplace to refer to professional sports as a business, perhaps some resentment about the salaries of some professional athletes in some sports (as opposed to, for example, a more widespread acceptance of corporate salaries/bonuses, and incomes in the entertainment industry) is related to this sense that sport is not work. Along with leisure, recreation, games, and play, sport is usually considered as part of the non-serious side of social life. However, there are many ways that sport is and has become work-like, and a number of ways that sport is related to work.

Consider, for example, how sport has become a metaphor for work. Even in children's sports we continually find references to "work out," "work rate," "hard work," and "getting the job done." Taylorism, the scientific management and measurement of work, found its way into coaching and training principles in sports in the twentieth century, as coaches emphasized discipline, routine, and repetitive systems of training. As sports became both ideologically and commercially important following World War II, the emphasis on outcome (product) in the form of "win at all costs"/ends-justify-the-means approaches became widespread. By the 1980s a system of early talent identification and intensive and specialized training for young athletes was widespread, making the experience of sports work-like for many children, and leading some sociologists to refer to such involvement as "child labor" (Donnelly 1997).

The utilitarian idea that sport for its own sake was not justification enough and that sport and recreation ought to have a rational purpose first became evident in the nineteenth century, when it was assumed that the function of sport was to build character. Eventually, sport took on a larger socializing purpose. Riesman (1978) highlighted this when he observed: "The road to the boardroom leads through the locker room." Seeley et al. (1956) described how sports prepared upper-middle-class boys in a Toronto neighborhood for the "career." The somewhat contradictory, but career-necessary skills of individual achievement and teamwork were exemplified in sports, and sports created opportunities for bonding and networking. Berlage's (1982) corporate socialization research involved a series of studies of boys' sports in upper-middle-class suburbs of New York City. However, feminism added a new interpretive dimension to her research, highlighting the relationship between the "glass ceiling" and sport participation. Lacking experiences in team sports,

Berlage noted, prevents women from being more successful in the corporate world.

The socialization theme was also evident in the work of several European neo–Marxist sociologists of sport in the 1970s. They argued that sport in capitalist societies was practiced in such a way as to enculturate work discipline in participants and spectators. However, their argument went further, pointing out that in the relations of production of sport, working athletes (amateur and professional) were alienated from both the process and the product of their labor (Rigauer 1981). As with alienated labor more generally, sport participation held no instrinsic satisfaction for athletes who did not own the profits of their labor. These ideas were picked up in North America, where similar arguments were made with regard to college athletes (in the US) and professional athletes.

Occupational analyses of sport have addressed both direct involvement – athletes, coaches, and officials – and the numerous ancillary occupations associated with sport.

Some of the earliest studies in the sociology of sport were of professional wrestling and horse racing. Subsequent studies focused on careers such as university coaches and referees. These studies used an interactionist/interpretive approach and often focused on "career contingencies." A critical and cultural shift in the field of subcultural research in the late 1970s led to a combination of interactionist and more critical sociologies (e.g., Ingham 1975), leading to a cultural studies approach to occupational subcultures in sports.

Ancillary occupations (e.g., sport agents, sport lawyers, sport scientists, and those engaged in the administration and marketing of sports) have received less sociological attention. However, there are growing bodies of research on clinicians involved in sports medicine; and on sports journalism, including newsroom studies, television production ethnographies, and the struggles of female journalists to cover sports. Another set of ancillary occupations involves those who work in the manufacture of sporting goods and clothing, and the construction of sports facilities. The manufacturing group has been the focus of research deriving from the anti-Nike campaigns (Sage 1999) and more recently the focus has returned to child labor in the sporting goods industry, and to the

trafficking of child athletes (Donnelly & Petherick 2004). However, the majority of work in sports is carried out by unpaid volunteers – without them, a significant number of organized sports events would not occur. Although research on volunteers is just beginning, there is a small but important body of research on the ways in which women's unpaid labor facilitates the sport participation of men and children (Thompson 1999).

The final form of work that has generated interest in the sociology of sport has been termed identity work. Research shows how individuals becoming involved in sports actively work to construct appropriate athletic identities (Donnelly & Young 1988). More recently, interest has shifted to class and gender, and to studies of racial, ethnic, and national identities, exploring the relationships between sport and attempts to produce, reproduce, and maintain relevant identities.

The Beijing Olympics may provoke more interest in fair labor practices in sports; there is growing interest in the work of sports clinicians, and in workplace health and safety/injury issues related to sports; research has begun to focus on sport volunteers and ideas of social capital and community; and studies of identity work will continue as researchers turn to Bourdieu's theories to analyze the ways that individuals work to maintain class distinctions through sports.

SEE ALSO: Identity, Sport and; Leisure; Sport, Amateur; Sport and Capitalism; Sport Culture and Subcultures; Sport, Professional; Sport and Social Capital; Sport and Social Class; Sports Heroes and Celebrities

REFERENCES AND SUGGESTED READINGS

Berlage, G. (1982) Are Children's Competitive Team Sports Socializing Agents for Corporate America? In: Dunleavy, A., Miracle, A., & Rees, R. (Eds.), *Studies in the Sociology of Sport.* Texas Christian University Press, Fort Worth, pp. 309–24.

Donnelly, P. (1997) Child Labour, Sport Labour: Applying Child Labour Laws to Sport. *International Review for the Sociology of Sport* 32(4): 389–406.

Donnelly, P. & Petherick, L. (2004) Workers' playtime? Child Labour at the Extremes of the Sporting Spectrum. *Sport in Society* 7(3): 301–21.

Donnelly, P. & Young, K. (1988) The Construction and Confirmation of Identity in Sport Subcultures. *Sociology of Sport Journal* 5(3): 223–40.

Ingham, A. (1975) Occupational Subcultures in the Work-World of Sport. In: Ball, D. & Loy, J. (Eds.), *Sport and Social Order*. Addison-Wesley, Reading, MA, pp. 355–89

Riesman, D. (1978) Cited in "Comes the Revolution." *Time* (June 26): 54–9.

Rigauer, B. (1981) *Sport and Work*. Columbia University Press, New York.

Sage, G. (1999) Justice Do It! The Nike Transnational Advocacy Network: Organization, Collective Actions, and Outcomes. *Sociology of Sport Journal* 16(3): 206–35.

Seeley, J., Sim, R. A., & Loosley, E. (1956) *Crestwood Heights*. University of Toronto Press, Toronto.

Thompson, S. (1999) *Mother's Taxi: Sport and Women's Labor*. State University of New York Press, Albany.

sportization

Joseph Maguire

The sportization process involved a shift towards the competitive, regularized, rationalized, and gendered bodily exertions of achievement sport that, in turn, connected to wider changes at the level of personality, body deportment, and social interaction. This process entailed regulating violence, developing formalized sets of rules and governing bodies, and shifting body habitus. Despite the existence of European rivals in the form of German and Swedish gymnastics, and although some older folk pastimes also survived, it was male achievement sport, emerging out of England, that was to affect people's body habitus on a global scale. Resistance to and reinterpretations of this body culture have been evident throughout the ongoing sportization process.

The initial sportization of British/English pastimes occurred in phases. There was a seventeenth- and eighteenth-century phase in which the principal pastimes of cricket, fox hunting, horse racing, and boxing emerged as modern sports. A second, nineteenth-century phase followed in which soccer, rugby, tennis, and track and field assumed modern forms and during which school-based sport developed (Elias & Dunning 1986). A third sportization phase during the late nineteenth and early twentieth centuries paralleled wider globalization processes and was shaped by a series of global flows. Modern sport rapidly diffused globally along the lines of the formal and informal British Empire. At this stage, the content, meaning, and control of sport reflected British/European male values. The fourth phase lasted from the 1920s through to the 1960s, when sportization processes, though still powered by western values, increasingly reflected "American" notions of sport and was further consolidated across the non-western parts of the globe. Beginning in the late 1960s, there emerged a fifth phase of sportization containing two seemingly contradictory features: the increasing standardization of what counts as sport – through media sport and the Olympic movement – combined with new varieties of body cultures and movements that challenge the hegemony of modern achievement sport (Maguire 1999).

There is a series of structured processes that have permeated the five phases of sportization (Maguire et al. 2002). While the reach and spread of each of these structured processes has varied over time and across space, they now constitute modern achievement sport – the context within which people experience global sport (Guttmann 1994; Van Bottenburg 2001). The pattern and development of these structured processes also reflects and reinforces prevailing established/outsider relations and the power geometry within specific societies. These structured processes involve the following.

First, there is the emergence and diffusion of achievement sport accompanied by the decline of both western and non-occidental folk body cultures. Modern achievement sport has marginalized indigenous games. Although such practices have not disappeared, and may, in some societies, be undergoing revival, the overall trend is for folk games to become residual features of body cultures (Renson 1998).

Second, global sport reflects a gendered ideology and content, making it a "male preserve" whose levers of power are still handled by men (Hargreaves 1994).

Third, sportization involved the development of physical practices that entail schooling the body. There have been shifts from nineteenth- and twentieth-century forms of "drill," European forms of gymnastics and dance, Physical Training, and Physical Education to late twentieth-century practices associated with Human Movement Studies, Sport Science, and Kinesiological Studies. The state, through its compulsory schooling policies, has thus played an active role in the reinforcement of global sport (Maguire 2004a).

Fourth, from its inception through its current high-tech manifestations, modern achievement sport has reflected and reinforced the medicalization, scientization, and rationalization of human expressiveness. The athlete is increasingly seen as an enhanced, efficient machine, adhering to a sport ethic associated with the "ultimate" performance. The logic at work may well be leading the athlete towards genetic modification and a cyborg coexistence (Hoberman 1992).

Fifth, global sport has impacted the habitus of people across societies and the habitats in which they live. Over time, as sport practices moved from small to large scale, from low intensity to high intensity forms, and from "natural" materials to synthetics, the athlete, spectator, viewer, and employers became consumers of scarce resources and threats to the environment (Maguire et al. 2002).

Sixth, the global diffusion of sport has reflected the ongoing balance of power within and between nations, and today the sport power elite have maintained their grip on power and been joined by a range of representatives from large media and sponsoring corporations (Miller et al. 2001). Demands for democratic control and transparency and accountability in decision-making remain unfulfilled, while academic stakeholders are frozen out of the sport policy process.

Seventh, both in the making and ongoing formation of global sport we see the reinforcement and enhancement of global inequalities within the West and between the West and non-occidental societies. Here, questions concerning cultural power, civilizational struggles, and wider globalization processes arise (Maguire 1999; 2004b).

SEE ALSO: Gender, Sport and; Globalization, Sport and; Postcolonialism and Sport; Sport; Sport and the Body; Sport and the Environment; Sports Heroes and Celebrities

REFERENCES AND SUGGESTED READINGS

Elias, N. & Dunning, E. (1986) *Quest for Excitement: Sport and Leisure in the Civilizing Process.* Blackwell, Oxford.

Guttmann, A. (1994) *Games and Empire: Modern Sports and Cultural Imperialism.* Columbia University Press, New York.

Hargreaves, J. (1994) *Sporting Females: Critical Issues in the History and Sociology of Women's Sports.* Routledge, London.

Hoberman, J. (1992) *Mortal Engines: The Science of Performance and the Dehumanization of Sport.* Free Press, New York.

Maguire, J. (1999) *Global Sport: Identities, Societies, Civilizations.* Polity Press, Oxford.

Maguire, J. (2004a) Challenging the Sports-Industrial Complex: Human Sciences, Advocacy and Service. *European Physical Education Review* 10: 299–322.

Maguire, J. (2004b) Body Cultures: Diversity, Sustainability, Globalization. In: Pfister, G. (Ed.), *Games of the Past – Sports for the Future?* Academia Verlag, St. Augustin, pp. 20–7.

Maguire, J., Jarvie, G., Mansfield, L., & Bradley, J. (2002) *Sport Worlds: A Sociological Perspective.* Human Kinetics, Champaign, IL.

Miller, T., Lawrence, G., McKay, J., & Rowe, D. (2001) *Globalization and Sport.* Routledge, London.

Renson, R. (1998) The Reinvention of Tradition in Sport and Games. In: Doll-Tepper, G. & Scoretz, D. (Eds.), *Ancient Traditions and Current Trends in Physical Activity and Sport.* ICSSPE: Berlin, pp. 8–13.

Van Bottenburg, M. (2001) *Global Games.* University of Chicago Press, Chicago.

sports heroes and celebrities

Steven Jackson

The terms hero and celebrity have increasingly become used interchangeably, but they are fundamentally different. According to Daniel Boorstin, "*The celebrity is a person who is known for his well-knownness ... The hero was distinguished by his achievement; the celebrity by his image or trademark. The hero created himself;*

the celebrity is created by the media. The hero is a big man [*sic*]; the celebrity is a big name" (1992: 57, 61). Thus, there are some clear distinctions between the two concepts and the challenge is to ascertain how and why they have become conflated. First, we must examine the meaning, significance and types of heroes and why sport remains such an important site for their identification and development. In turn, we need to understand how changes in wider society have tended to shift attention, status, and rewards from heroes to celebrities.

Heroes/heroines have existed throughout human history. From ancient Greece and Rome through the Middle Ages and the Renaissance to the twenty-first century, societies and cultures have created, defined, bestowed, and otherwise recognized what is known as a hero (Klapp 1949). In Browne's (1990) view, heroes highlight the potential and possibility of humans by expanding and/or conquering the physical, psychological, social, spiritual, and altruistic limits of human beings.

And while there are many cultural arenas in which individuals have emerged as heroes, sport has always been one of the key sites. There are likely many reasons for this, but in particular sport, as a cultural practice and institution, offers the opportunity for the demonstration of physical superiority in a system with clear rankings and rewards, the display of courage, commitment, and sacrifice, and the chance to represent a particular group, community, or nation. In a contemporary commercial context the latter point is quite important, given that "Only sports has the nation, and sometimes the world, watching the same thing at the same time, and if you have a message, that's a potent messenger" (Singer 1998; cited in Rowe 1999: 74).

Even a cursory look at the diversity of sport heroes, both historical and contemporary, indicates that they emerge from a wide range of personal achievements, social backgrounds, and cultural contexts. In effect, there are different ways by which heroes emerge. Although the typology that follows is not exhaustive, it may aid in understanding the process of how different individuals became heroes. Although the categories are not mutually exclusive, one becomes a hero in one of four ways (Ingham et al. 1993). First, a person can perform an extraordinary superhuman feat. In actual fact

heroes are often people who perform ordinary things but at a much higher level and with much greater consistency than the average. A few people who fit this category might include Sir Donald Bradman, Babe Didrikson, Jessie Owens, Paavo Nurmi, Pelé, Nadia Comaneci, Michael Jordan, Wayne Gretzky, Carl Lewis, Tiger Woods, and Lance Armstrong.

Second, one can become a hero by being the first to achieve a particular and unexpected standard. Such a category would include people like Sir Roger Bannister who, in 1954, was the first person to break the 4-minute mile; or Sir Edmund Hillary who, along with Tenzing Norgay, was the first to climb Mount Everest, the highest point on earth, in 1953.

Third, one can become a hero through risk-taking, personal sacrifice, and/or saving a life. There may be no better example of this type of hero than Canadian Terry Fox. Diagnosed with cancer and with part of his right leg amputated, Fox set out to run across Canada in what he called the Marathon of Hope. Sadly, his run ended after 3,339 miles because the cancer spread to his lungs. Terry Fox died at age 22 on June 28, 1981. Still his life and mission are celebrated annually. Each September 13 marks the Terry Fox Run and to date his foundation has raised over $360 million.

Fourth, a person can become a hero by virtue of a particular performance within a specific sociohistorical context: being the right person at the right time (see Ingham et al. 1993). One example of this type is John Roosevelt (Jackie) Robinson, who, facing enormous racial discrimination and other social barriers in 1947, became the first "black" athlete to play Major League Baseball.

The world still has heroes, but something has changed in terms of the type of people that society celebrates and rewards. Increasingly, status appears to be something that is *manufactured* versus *achieved* and heroes are being marginalized by celebrities, stars, and idols (cf. Andrews & Jackson 2001; Dyer 1979; Gamson 1994; Rojek 2001). While there are no simple answers to explain this transformation, consideration must be given to the emergence of the society of the individual, a greater scrutiny of private lives embodied in an exploitive tabloid culture, and a world driven by consumption, advertising, and marketing. As a consequence, "everyone is involved in either producing or consuming celebrities" (Rein et al. 1997: x). Arguably, the most powerful vehicle in this shift are the media, whom Leo Braudy (1997: 550) calls the "arbiters of celebrity." The media are global, immediate, and increasingly interconnected, resulting in a virtual saturation of celebrity culture linked to sport, music, fashion, movies, and reality television.

Ultimately, we are left with a challenge to gain a better understanding of the social and political function of contemporary heroes and celebrities. In part, this will require an examination of who has the power to define heroes and celebrities, under what conditions, and in whose interests.

SEE ALSO: Celebrity Culture; Media and Sport; Sport; Sport and Capitalism; Sport and Culture; Sport Culture and Subculture; Sport, Professional; Sport as Spectacle; Sports Industry

REFERENCES AND SUGGESTED READINGS

Andrews, D. & Jackson, S. (Eds.) (2001) *Sport Stars: The Politics of Sporting Celebrity*. Routledge, London.

Boorstin, D. (1992) *The Image: A Guide to Pseudo-Events in America*. Random House, New York.

Braudy, L. (1997) *The Frenzy of Renown: Fame and Its History*. Vintage, New York.

Browne, R. B. (1990) *Contemporary Heroes and Heroines*. Gale Research, Detroit.

Carr, E. (1961) *What is History?* Penguin, London.

Dyer, R. (1979). *Stars*. BFI Publishing, London.

Gamson, J. (1994) *Claims to Fame: Celebrity in Contemporary America*. University of California Press, Berkeley.

Ingham, A. Howell, J., & Swetman, R. (1993) Evaluating Sport Hero/ines: Contents, Forms and Social Relations. *Quest* 45: 197–210.

Klapp, O. (1949) Hero Worship in America. *American Sociological Review* 14(1): 57–63.

Rein, I., Kotler, P., & Stoller, M. (1997) *High Visibility: The Making and Marketing of Professionals into Celebrities*. NTC Business Books, Chicago.

Rojek, C. (2001) *Celebrity*. Reaktion Books, London.

Rowe, D. (1999) *Sport, Culture and the Media: The Unruly Trinity*. Open University Press, Buckingham.

sports industry

Dominic Malcolm

Sport became an industry at the point at which events (matches, races, bouts) ceased to be oriented solely toward participants and became largely organized so that they could be consumed by spectators. In perhaps the earliest sociological analysis of this process, Gregory P. Stone (1955) argued that consequently "play" (unscripted, spontaneous) became overshadowed by "*dis*play" (prearranged, staged, spectacular); that is to say, in some respects industry or commercialism is the very antithesis of sport. This critique still lingers amongst those who might be termed "purists," but it must now be recognized that whilst on the one hand sport has become an industry just like any other, on the other hand, and particularly in terms of the demand for sport, it has a number of distinctive or peculiar features.

Contemporary analysis of the sports industry can be subdivided into four mutually interdependent parts: sports teams and leagues; the media; sponsors and manufacturers; and sports celebrities. A brief initial examination of the development of the sports industry, however, will be used to demonstrate the long lineage of these commercial processes, and therefore to correct the prevalent, false, assumption that they are unique to contemporary sport.

Aspects of a sports industry can be seen in the "sports-like" activities of ancient Rome, but it is more useful to trace the development of the sports industry back to eighteenth-century Europe, and England in particular. At this time, tavern owners and innkeepers started to exploit existing sports events to increase trade. The more entrepreneurial would provide facilities for playing cricket, quoits, horse-racing, cock-fighting, and so on. As the eighteenth century progressed, tavern owners started to charge admission fees to supplement the profits made through the sale of refreshments and lodgings. Subsequently, the emergent ruling bodies of sport (e.g., the Jockey Club, the Marylebone Cricket Club) established their own permanent facilities (i.e., Newmarket Race Course, Lords Cricket Ground) to contain the 10,000-plus spectators that could be attracted to the major sporting events of eighteenth-century England.

The development of the sports industry in England progressed relatively unrestricted until the advent of amateurism in the middle of the nineteenth century. Boxers, cricketers, and jockeys were often sponsored by a wealthy aristocrat who would employ talented sportspeople, nominally as household servants or for work on his estate but, in fact, principally on account of their sporting skills. The first professional sports team was William Clarke's All-England XI, a cricket team which toured England playing "exhibition" matches from 1846 to 1870. A number of imitators soon followed. Churches and factories were subsequently influential in establishing works teams. These teams came to represent towns and cities and thus became key sites of identity formation in a time of industrialization-led geographical mobility. Public demand for regular and meaningful fixtures, fueled by the emerging publishing industry that grew up around sporting contests, led to the establishment of the Football Association (FA) Challenge Cup in 1871 and the English Football League, consisting of 12 clubs from the English Midlands and the north, in 1888. In 1895, rugby clubs in the north of England broke away from the staunchly amateur English Rugby Football Union (RFU), ultimately forming a professional version of the game, rugby league. English counties first competed for a cricket championship in 1873 (Holt 1989).

Whilst the emergence of a sports industry in America was initially slower, the lack of a strict adherence to amateurism enabled it to subsequently develop rather more rapidly. During the 1860s sports entrepreneurs enclosed grounds, assembled "all-star" teams, and charged entry fees. Initially, baseball was strongly influenced by the amateur ethos, but by the time the National Baseball League (NBL) was formed in 1876, commercialization and covert professionalization were well established. Albert Spalding, a significant driving force in the development of the NBL, had the year before moved from the Boston Red Stockings to the Chicago White Stockings because he was offered a well-paid job in a grocery which entailed minimal duties and thus the chance to play regular baseball. Spalding subsequently went on to organize promotional baseball tours to England and develop baseball-related merchandise such as balls, uniforms, and bases. The antecedents of today's sports industry were well established in nineteenth-century Britain and America (Wiggins 1995).

SPORTS TEAMS AND LEAGUES

The appeal of sport, and therefore the economic viability of the sports industry, is said to depend on "uncertainty of outcome," i.e., its unpredictable, unscripted nature. It is on this basis that anti-competitive practices (the draft system, collective merchandising, and revenue-sharing agreements) and legal exemptions from antitrust laws exist in many US sports (and to a lesser extent under EU law). US leagues are organized as monopolies – or cartels – with no automatic mechanism for the removal of weaker clubs and their replacement by stronger teams. By limiting the extent to which the individual teams compete against one another for fans, media revenues, and merchandise sales, the league is in a stronger position to eliminate competition from rival leagues. The peculiar feature of sport in the US is that competitions are oriented toward the economic benefit of all the teams in the league, rather than forwarding the interests of individuals and individual teams (Gratton & Taylor 2000).

Somewhat ironically, after decades in which team sports have not been particularly profit-oriented (economists have traditionally described English professional football clubs as utility maximizers rather than profit maximizers), the leagues and sports clubs of Europe have, in some regards, "out-commercialized" their American role models. Pyramids of leagues exist to enable weaker teams to be replaced by stronger ones. Leading clubs have successfully sought to consolidate their own economic position, at the expense of teams with less popular support, using as leverage the threat of withdrawal from existing competitions and the establishment of their own private league and cups. Recently developed European football competitions (e.g., the European Champions League in football) structure prizes and revenue-sharing to favor the clubs from the wealthiest leagues. Currently, broadcasting rights are sold by the league or competition as a whole, but if clubs were to negotiate individually, some, and Manchester United in particular, would be likely to profit considerably. To this end, some clubs (e.g., Manchester United) have established their own television stations. Whereas most American sports organizations are privately owned but reliant on publicly funded or owned stadia, mainland European (football) clubs have traditionally been membership clubs owning their own facilities (though an increasing number have established commercially oriented, more streamlined, executive boards in the last decade). Traditionally, English sports clubs have been privately owned but in an attempt to release capital and increase spending power, many have become publicly listed companies on the London Stock Exchange. A consequence of this is that clubs now have a legal obligation to prioritize the interests of shareholders, and inevitably this leads to a more direct pursuit of profit.

THE MEDIA

It is often said that the relationship between the media and sport (but strictly speaking the sports industry) is symbiotic. Media companies pay large amounts for the right to broadcast particular sports events because the programs are cheap to produce, attract relatively large audiences, and because the demographics of the viewers they attract (e.g., young males with large disposable incomes) appeal to sponsors who, in turn, are willing to pay large fees for the right to advertise during the broadcast. The sports industry needs the media both as a source of income and as a means of publicity. The balance of power between the sports industry and media companies varies from sport to sport and between countries. However, certain common patterns of the ways in which the media have shaped sport in recent years are identifiable (Wenner 1998).

First, media companies request that events are scheduled at particular times in order to appeal to the largest viewing audience. The establishment of Monday night football in the US is a classic example. Similarly, whilst

English football matches have traditionally been held on Saturday afternoons, increasingly television has (successfully) requested matches to be rescheduled to Sundays, Monday nights, and Saturday mornings in order to maximize viewing figures (which itself has led to the expansion of the phenomenon of sports consumption based around bars and inns). International sporting events, such as the Olympics, are most heavily influenced by the media of economically dominant countries, i.e., the US. Second, it has been claimed that media companies have forced changes to the structure of the sports themselves. Boxing contests were reduced from 15 to 12 rounds, it has been argued, to enable television companies to more conveniently package bouts within a 1-hour time slot. Rule changes have increasingly protected quarterbacks in American football to encourage a more open passing game. Free throws in basketball have been minimized to speed up the action. Third, accompanying these structural and timing changes have been changes in presentational style. The use of loud music, video, cheerleaders, and mascots all serve to make the behavior of sports crowds more orchestrated, and thus more amenable to broadcasters' desires and production needs. Whilst there is a tendency to exaggerate the media's influence (sports are not fixed in time, and rules are not inherent or unalterable but have continually been refined for various purposes), commercial interests currently play a larger part in rule reformation than at any stage in the past (Sewart 1987).

Some sports events combine some or all of these characteristics and essentially become "TV made" (e.g., Kerry Packer's cricket "circus" in Australia, indoor soccer leagues in America, professional wrestling competitions). Television programs such as *Gladiators* illustrate the media's ideal format for sports but, tellingly, as Stone earlier argued, the demands of spectacularization are sometimes entirely antithetical to play, for they destroy the uncertain element that is the basis of the appeal of sport. This has led television companies to pursue a new strategy, the purchase of sports clubs, for this is now seen as the most effective way in which broadcasters can exert control over "genuine" sporting events which enjoy enduring and widespread popularity.

SPONSORS AND MANUFACTURERS

Sponsors of sport can be divided into two groups, those whose products are intrinsically sport related, and those whose aren't. For the latter group, sport is seen as a useful tool through which to promote products because of the supposedly health-promoting and character-building qualities of sport. The mass and youth appeal of sport is similarly attractive to sponsors and the male dominance of sports spectatorship has led numerous beer manufacturers to sponsor leagues and teams. In recent years tobacco companies have used sports sponsorship (most notably motor racing) to overcome legal restrictions on their ability to advertise. A classic example of what has been called the "sport–media–production complex" is the coalition of the National (American) Football League (NFL), Anheuser Busch (makers of Budweiser beer), and British television company Channel 4 (Maguire 1990). Their mutual interests converged in an attempt to increase the popularity of American football in the UK, overcome the British perception of American beers as unmasculine, and aid a newly established broadcaster to develop a distinct profile and market. Despite the triumvirate's success in the 1980s, the subsequent decline of American football in the UK again shows the limits of the industry's ability to manipulate popular demand.

There is, however, a more natural link between sport and companies producing sports-related products, but it is only since the 1980s that the demand for sports-related goods – such as sports shoes – has become big enough (i.e., as high-performance sports gear has become high fashion) to justify the levels of expenditure required to sponsor major sports events. Nike are thought to have changed the rules for sports marketing by paying huge endorsements to tie athletes to using their equipment ($90 million for basketball's Lebron James, $450 million for the right to run Manchester United's merchandise and kit operation) and "in-your-face," aggressive advertising linking their products to the athletic success of a few high-profile individuals. Nike, more than most, have had to deal with accusations about their dependency on exploited Asian labor, but this seems to have had little impact on sales and profits (Sage 1999).

SPORTS CELEBRITIES

It is the convergence of the interests of sponsors such as Nike, media/television companies, and sports organizations that means that when we look at the sports industry we must recognize the role of sports celebrities (Andrews & Jackson 2001). The sports industry idealizes images of sports celebrities so that they become general objects of glamour and fantasy in popular culture. Nike's endorsement deal with basketball superstar Michael Jordan led the "Air Jordan" sports shoe to become the highest-selling sneaker of all time, and helped bolster the popular appeal of the NBA. But these interdependencies also fed Jordan's celebrity status, which in turn served as a site for the production of particular (largely racial) ideologies. Sociologists have also highlighted how, in tennis, the Anna Kournikova sports industry produces ideologies relating to gender and how Nike's work with self-starred "Cablinasian" golfer Tiger Woods has sought to promote a color-blind, multicultural America of the future, which in turn has helped open up lucrative new markets for golf equipment in Asia.

But perhaps at the pinnacle of this sports celebrity industry is English footballer David Beckham, about whom an increasing quantity of academic literature has appeared (Cashmore 2004). Beckham ties all these themes of the sports industry together: a sport which has in the last decade exploited satellite television technology to increase exposure and generate ever-increasing income; a player for the wealthiest soccer clubs in the world (Manchester United, Real Madrid); huge endorsement contracts with Adidas, Brylcream, and others; and, underlying his success and celebrity status, the production of various class and sexuality discourses. But more than this, unlike Michael Jordan whose celebrity was a largely North American phenomenon, Beckham, by virtue of playing the only truly global sport, is perhaps the most globally recognized sports celebrity.

The sports industry started as a local financial venture, with locally based sports celebrities like Albert Spalding. As the Beckham case shows, the contemporary sports industry has expanded to be global in scale, hunting out new audiences and markets for merchandise, filling increasing amounts of television airtime, and creating new sources of revenue for sports teams, sports media, sports sponsors, and sports celebrities.

SEE ALSO: Consumption, Mass Consumption, and Consumer Culture; Media; Media and Sport; Sport, Amateur; Sport and Capitalism; Sport and Culture; Sport, Professional; Sports Heroes and Celebrities

REFERENCES AND SUGGESTED READINGS

Andrews, D. L. & Jackson, S. J. (2001) *Sports Stars: The Cultural Politics of Sports Celebrity*. Routledge, London.

Cashmore, E. (2004) *Beckham*, 2nd edn. Polity Press, Cambridge.

Gratton, C. & Taylor, P. (2000) *Economics of Sport and Recreation*. Routledge, London.

Holt, R. (1989) *Sport and the British*. Oxford University Press, Oxford.

Maguire, J. (1990) More Than a Sporting Touchdown: The Making of American Football in England, 1982–1990. *Sociology of Sport Journal* 7(3): 213–37.

Sage, G. (1999) Justice Do It! The Nike Transnational Advocacy Network: Organization, Collective Actions, and Outcomes. *Sociology of Sport Journal* 16(3): 206–35.

Sewart, J. (1987) The Commodification of Sport. *International Review for the Sociology of Sport* 22(3): 171–90.

Stone, G. P. (1955) American Sports: Play and Display. *Chicago Review* 9: 83–100.

Wenner, L. (Ed.) (1998) *Mediasport*. Routledge, London.

Wiggins, D. K. (1995) *Sport in America: From Wicked Amusement to National Obsessions*. Human Kinetics, Champaign, IL.

sports stadia

John Bale

Sports do not require stadia, but in their commodified form they have come to be seen as necessities. In contemporary discussions of the sports stadium two broad themes have attracted the attention of both sports scholarship and public opinion: (1) activity and organization within the stadium, and (2) extra-stadium effects and implications. Academic approaches to these themes are considered in turn.

The sports stadium is an ambiguous architectural form. It has been read and written from various perspectives. With its rows of numbered seats, its geometrically segmented form, and the all-prevailing video-surveillance equipment, the modern stadium has been read as an example of container architecture analogous to a prison. Such a reading draws on the ideas of Michel Foucault. It is undoubtedly a secure place to house large numbers of bodies and, in times of unrest, stadia occasionally have been used as places of incarceration. The gaze of the police and video camera is, at the level of the "playing field," matched by the gaze of the referee or umpire. The controlled character of stands and bleachers is matched by the spatial positioning and constraints on those who entertain the entertained. The spectators and the players each have defined positions in stadium space. The stadium, then, is a facility for displaying dominance and power. A Marxist view would add that it is a modern site of "bread and circus" (Brohm 1974) in the production of "docile bodies." This is not to say, however, that resistance from both spectators and players has been eliminated, as numerous studies of deviance and hooliganism testify (Dunning et al. 2002).

The Foucauldian model can be read as a malign, pessimistic view of power. An alternative, slightly more benign perspective is to see the stadium as a theater. Elias and Dunning (1986) write that the drama as a game of soccer unfolds has something in common with a good theatrical play. The play has a script; sports have their game plans. A major difference, however, is that the modern theater crowd remains passive compared with that of the sports stadium, though this was not always the case. And there is a logical case for making the sports crowd more like that of the theater. After all, it is well known from studies of the home field advantage that the crowd has an impact on sporting performance, hence contributing to an unfair advantage. Some postmodernists have suggested, therefore, that crowds should be excluded from stadium sports events (Bale 2003).

A widely used third metaphor is that of the garden: a stretch of grass (nature) in the middle of the city (culture). This view is encouraged by the notion that there is more to the stadium experience than watching a game (Raitz 1995). The color, the playfulness, the noise and smell are said to make the stadium visit a sensory experience or a carnival. Of course, there is nothing "natural" about a football, baseball, or cricket field. Indeed, the progress of "turf science" has produced grass surfaces that are often almost indistinguishable from nylon carpets. Nevertheless, the garden metaphor is revealing in that, like the garden, the stadium is a melding of horticulture and architecture, and of dominance and affection. Arguably the prime advocate of the stadium as garden is Bartlett Giamatti (1989), who sees the stadium as an adult version of the kindergarten. And it worth recalling how many stadia are still called gardens and parks, despite the absence of flowers, trees, and foliage.

It is also possible to read the stadium as a reduced mirror image of the city (Bromberger 1995), with its segmented spectator space and sense of community. Different research, then, reads and writes the stadium in different ways.

A second broad approach to "stadium studies" is to explore the wider impact that the stadium has on urban or rural space. The social, economic, and geographical impact of stadia in urban areas has been the subject of considerable research. Residents and business in close proximity to stadia may receive both indirect benefits and disadvantage from such proximity. Quality of life can be reduced for such residents on game days as noise, crowds, and various forms of pollution may be imposed upon them. These are the stadium negative externalities. Contrariwise, some businesses such as bars and vending depend greatly on stadium events for revenue. From a social perspective the presence of a local stadium and its occupants can generate bonding and place pride (Bale 2001).

Stadium relocation – implying the migration of the clubs and teams that play in them – has become a widespread phenomenon in the United States. It is widely believed that the construction of such new stadia adds to urban image, status, and economic regeneration. It is further argued that the new spending associated with such facilities creates an economic multiplier effect that boosts local or regional wealth. The evidence for such positive effects of stadium development is mixed, but the general

view is that the benefits of such developments are often negative (Baade 1995).

Stadia are increasingly becoming multifunctional facilities or "entertainment centres" rather than monofunctional spaces, dedicated to a specific sport. The diversity of stadium activities is driven by the need for revenues and profits, hence the need for intensive use of space. The ambiguous nature of domed stadiums, for example, with retractable roofs, and associated banqueting, hotel, conference, and restaurant facilities, makes it clear that these places are not just for sport. The Toronto Skydome (Kidd 1995) represents an early example of such a structure, and Ritzer (2005) has identified recently constructed, large stadiums as "cathedrals of consumption."

SEE ALSO: Sport; Sport and Capitalism; Sport and the Environment; Sport, Professional; Sport as Spectacle; Sports Industry

REFERENCES AND SUGGESTED READINGS

Baade, R. (1995) Stadiums, Professional Sports, and City Economies: An Analysis of the United States Experience. In: Bale, J. & Moen, O. (Eds.), *The Stadium and the City*. Keele University Press, Keele, pp. 277–94.

Bale, J. (2001 [1993]) *Sport, Space and the City*. Blackburn Press, Caldwell, NJ.

Bale, J. (2003) A Geographical Theory of Sport. In: Møller, V. & Nauright, J. (Eds.), *The Essence of Sport*. University Press of Southern Denmark, Odense, pp. 81–92.

Brohm, J.-M. (1974) *Sport: A Prison of Measured Time*. Ink Links, London.

Bromberger, C. (1995) *Le Match de football*. Éditions de la maison des sciences de l'homme, Paris.

Dunning, E., Murphy, P., Waddington, I., & Astrinakis, A. (Eds.) (2002) *Fighting Fans: Football Hooliganism as a World Social Problem*. University College Dublin Press, Dublin.

Elias, N. & Dunning, E. (1986) *Quest for Excitement: Sport and Leisure in the Civilizing Process*. Blackwell, Oxford.

Giamatti, B. (1989) *Take Time for Paradise: Americans and their Games*. Summit Books, New York.

Kidd, B. (1995) Toronto's Skydome: The World's Greatest Entertainment Centre. In: Bale, J. & Moen, O. (Eds.), *The Stadium and the City*. Keele University Press, Keele, pp. 175–96.

Raitz, K. (Ed.) (1995) *The Theater of Sport*. Johns Hopkins University Press, Baltimore.

Ritzer, G. (2005) *Enchanting a Disenchanted World: Revolutionizing the Means of Consumption*, rev. edn. Pine Forge Press, Thousand Oaks, CA.

stalking

Emily Finch

No single definition of stalking exists. This is probably because, despite certain commonalities, there is no prototypical case upon which a definition could be founded. Although some types of behavior are common in many stalking cases – silent/abusive telephone calls, unwanted gifts and letters, surveillance – each case involves an idiosyncratic combination of these and other diverse types of behavior that renders a definition based on the conduct involved somewhat nebulous. Other than this, definitions have isolated factors such as the relationship between the parties or the motivation behind the behavior, but again, these are so diverse and wide-ranging that it is impossible to formulate a definition that captures the full spectrum of stalking cases. Although the various attempts at definition differ, a common theme exists that facilitates the identification of core characteristics: repeated and unwanted intrusions into the life of another that engender a negative reaction in the recipient.

Stalking emerged as a pressing and prevalent social problem during the 1990s. Its emergence was incremental as stalking developed through a series of manifestations before becoming embedded in the public consciousness. Initially, stalking rose to prominence in the United States as a problem experienced by celebrities as overzealous fans resorted to desperate measures to make contact with the object of their affections. Gradually, it became apparent that stalking was not just a celebrity problem but something that affected "ordinary people" too, although this was generally viewed as occurring in the context of a turbulent or terminated domestic relationship. It was for this reason that stalking became viewed for a time as inherently associated with domestic violence. It underwent a further metamorphosis as non-relational stalking

rose to prominence. This manifestation of stalking, in common with celebrity stalking, had connotations of irrational obsession and mental illness as it became clear that stalkers could develop an obsession based on only tenuous contact with the victim. Although the evolutionary period of stalking gave rise to some divergent constructions, it finally emerged as a problem that was based upon repeated, unwanted, and unwelcome intrusion into the victim's life irrespective of the identity or relationship of the parties involved.

Even after the emergence of stalking as a social problem and the development of a shared social understanding of its nature, there were impediments to the formulation of an appropriate and effective legal response. Definitional difficulties thwarted some of the earliest attempts at the introduction of stalking legislation due to the formidable challenge of creating legislation that differentiated between stalking and lawful conduct. It became clear that an unfortunate paradox existed in relation to a legal regulation of stalking. If stalking involved conduct that was inherently unlawful such as damaging property or causing harm/injury, for example, the police were able to intervene without the need for reliance on stalking legislation. Frequently, however, the stalker would engage exclusively in lawful conduct such as sending gifts or waiting for the victim in a public place, so any attempt at the criminalization of stalking needed to find a means of distinguishing between such conduct undertaken for lawful reasons and that undertaken as part of a campaign of stalking. How is the law to encapsulate the amorphous distinction between the single-minded pursuit of the object of desire that occurs in stalking cases and which mirrors the socially acceptable pursuit of one's true love in a way that criminalizes the former without undermining the legitimacy of the latter?

Ogilvie (2000) attributes this definitional dilemma to the "paradoxical status of stalking as simultaneously being an exemplar of conformity and criminality." This acknowledges that stalking frequently involves behavior that would not be regarded as deviant or unacceptable if it were to occur in a different context. Sending flowers to a loved one can be distinguished from sending flowers to a total stranger, but even this is not unacceptable if it is welcomed by the recipient as a romantic gesture. Context is everything in stalking cases. Unlike the majority of criminal offenses, stalking frequently involves no breach of normative conventions; rather, it often involves lawful conduct that engenders a negative reaction in the recipient. As such, the response of the recipient of the conduct is legally transformative; a positive or indifferent response allows the conduct to retain its lawful nature whilst an adverse response brings the conduct within the remit of stalking and hence within the reach of the regulation of the law.

Stalking is particularly problematic in the complex context of sociosexual relationships in which pursuit and persistence is socially acceptable, even desirable. Mullen et al. (1999) believe that the apparent increase in stalking in the late twentieth century can be attributed in part to the more transient nature of relationships, which can leave individuals feeling isolated and rejected and thus engender desperation to find a partner. The intensity of these feelings and the pressure to achieve social acceptability by the formation of a romantic relationship can lead individuals to engage in overexaggerated or excessive romantic gestures; what Ogilvie (2000) describes as an "amplification of normative conformity." If this coincides with an anxiety-induced inability (or reluctance) to recognize the often subtle social cues that delineate the parameters of acceptable behavior at the early stages of a sociosexual relationship, then the initiator of the conduct may be unaware that his attentions are unwelcome. Differential understanding and interpretations of the same events by different actors are frequently the basis of accusations of stalking. In a culture in which the authorities play an increasing role in what was previously considered to be the private realm of interpersonal relationships and in which there is an expectation of the state's protection from all that is adverse and unpleasant in society, the primacy of the recipient's interpretation and the consequent criminalization of such events were an almost inevitable development.

SEE ALSO: Crime; Deviance; Deviance, Crime and; Domestic Violence; Mental Disorder; Social Problems, Concept and Perspectives; Victimization; Violence

REFERENCES AND SUGGESTED READINGS

Mullen, P., Pathe, M., Purcell, R., & Stuart, G. (1999) Study of Stalkers. *American Journal of Psychiatry* 156: 1244.
Ogilvie, E. (2000) *Stalking: Legislative, Policing, and Prosecution Patterns in Australia*. Australian Institute of Criminology Research and Public Policy Series No. 34. Australian Institute of Criminology, Canberra.

standardization

Darin Weinberg

Standardization is a procedure used in science to increase the validity and reliability of research. It is predicated on the principle that truly objective scientific findings ought to be noncontradictory and replicable and that the most efficient technique for facilitating both internal consistency and replication is to ensure that the various aspects of research design and conduct (e.g., measurement instruments, methods of data collection, methods of analysis) do not clash either within the confines of a particular study or from one study to the next. Standardization is thought to fortify scientists against the biases that may otherwise be introduced into research by things like their own personal characteristics and/or the characteristics of the particular social contexts within which research is conducted. The concept of standardization is used in two distinct but related senses in science. In a purely descriptive sense, the standardization of research methods secures uniformity in the scientific enterprise by establishing a certain lingua franca within which to conduct meaningful and productive dialogue and debate. Standardized methods facilitate confidence among researchers conforming to them that they and others who also conform are gathering new knowledge about the same empirical phenomena. In the second sense, standardization is less descriptive than prescriptive. Hence one seeks to standardize scientific research methods not only to make them uniform among scientists studying the same things, but also to ensure that a certain level of excellence is maintained. In this sense, scientists seek to standardize research methods not only to keep standards uniform but also to keep them "high." In the social sciences, the concept of standardization has become particularly important in survey research. Considerable efforts are made to both promote the uniform adoption of particular question formats and other kinds of measurement instruments across studies and to ensure uniformity of procedure amongst interviewers working on the same study. Critics of standardization sometimes argue that procedures that ensure scientific findings can be replicated, or reproduced at different times and in different places, are not the same as procedures that might ensure that those findings are in fact valid. These critics argue that the preoccupation with replicability can easily mistake reliable findings for valid ones. Other critics suggest that standardization inevitably entails a level of veiled coercion as proponents of different standardized procedures wrangle with one another for supremacy. Still others suggest that standardized research methods impose an artificial framework on the collection of data that can introduce distortions into our data. These critics suggest that a more naturalistic and spontaneous approach to data collection may facilitate a more nuanced sensitivity to the nature of phenomena under investigation. More recently, sociologists of science have shown that standardized procedures must inevitably be applied in real-world research situations that require discretionary assessments as to whether those procedures have been implemented properly. Because these discretionary assessments themselves can never be fully reduced to standardized protocols, we must remain cognizant of the fact that standardization can never completely eliminate the influence of specific individuals and specific social contexts on the conduct of scientific research.

SEE ALSO: Demographic Techniques: Decomposition and Standardization; Experimental Design; Quantitative Methods; Reliability; Replicability Analyses; Science, Ethnographic Studies of; Survey Research; Validity, Qualitative; Validity, Quantitative

REFERENCES AND SUGGESTED READINGS

Cicourel, A. V. (1963) *Method and Measurement in Sociology*. Free Press, New York.
Fowler, F. J., Jr. & Mangione, T. W. (1990) *Standardized Survey Interviewing: Minimizing Interviewer-Related Error*. Sage, Newbury Park, CA.
Lynch, M. (1993) *Scientific Practice and Ordinary Action: Ethnomethodology and Social Studies of Science*. Cambridge University Press, Cambridge.
Maynard, D. W., Houtkoop-Steenstra, H., Schaeffer, N. C., & van der Zouwen, J. (Eds.) (2001) *Standardization and Tacit Knowledge: Interaction and Practice in the Survey Interview*. Wiley Interscience, New York.
Timmermans, S. & Berg, M. (2003) *The Gold Standard: The Challenge of Evidence-Based Medicine and Standardization in Health Care*. Temple University Press, Philadelphia.

standardized educational tests

Mark Berends and Albert Boerema

Standardized tests are tests that are administered under controlled (or "standardized") conditions – specifying where, when, how, and for how long test-takers may respond to questions. The test questions provide a way to gather, describe, and quantify information that assesses performance on particular tasks to demonstrate knowledge of specific topics or processes. Standardization is important to compare individuals or groups and involves a consistent set of procedures for designing, administering, and scoring the test. The aim of standardization is to ensure that test-takers are assessed under the same conditions, assuring that their test scores have the same meaning and are not influenced by differing conditions. Such standardized tests occur over the life course, with a range of uses including determination of school readiness, achievement throughout the schooling progress for students, accountability for districts, schools, teachers, and students, capabilities for college, and achievement as employees in the workforce.

Standardized tests, as a part of the wider educational, psychological, and sociological testing and assessments, have a long history within the United States. They represent one of the most important contributions of behavioral and social science to society, even though tests have been used in a myriad of proper and improper ways (AERA 1999). Their history is deeply rooted in a United States culture that is: empirically oriented and data-driven; focused on change, which is assumed to be progress; embraces a belief that evidence can provide general guidance for efficient action; and straddles the choices that give individuals certain advances versus choices that serve the larger society (Baker 2001).

As described by *Standards for Educational and Psychological Testing* (1999) – an authoritative document on standards for measurement – there are four important facets of testing standards: (1) technical standards for test construction and evaluation; (2) professional standards for test use; (3) standards for particular applications; and (4) standards for administrative procedures. For a standardized test to be technically adequate, it should meet standards of validity and reliability, whether the test is norm-referenced or criterion-referenced.

Reliability is the degree to which the results of an assessment are dependable and consistently measure particular student knowledge and/or skills. Reliability also refers to the consistency of scores over time, across different performance tasks or items intended to measure the same thing, or consistency of scores across different raters. That is, reliability statistics can be computed to measure (1) *item reliability* – the relationship between individual test items intended to measure the same knowledge skills; (2) *test/retest reliability* – the relationship between two administrations of the same test to the same student or students; or (3) *rater reliability* – the extent of agreement between two or more raters. If assessments are not reliable, they cannot be valid.

Validity refers to both the extent to which a test measures what it is intended to measure and the appropriate inferences and actions taken based on the test scores. If a math test can only measure a subset of the domain of math skills, how confident are we that students are good at math if they perform well on a math test? How

confident are we that the proficiency level accurately portrays proficiency in mathematics? Within the current policy environment of the United States, if an assessment is to be valid, it should be aligned with the standards it is intended to measure and it should provide an accurate and reliable estimate of the students' performance relative to the standard.

In addition to the importance of standardized tests being reliable and valid, they can be either norm-referenced or criterion-referenced. A *criterion-referenced* test is linked to specific performance standards or learning objectives. One interprets scores on criterion-referenced tests based on the degree to which students demonstrate achievement of the specific learning standards and not how students perform compared to other students. On a criterion-referenced test, it is possible that all students (or no students) will perform well on the specific learning objectives or standards. Of course, the percentage of students who will perform well on specific learning objectives depends on how ambitious those performance standards are (Linn 2003).

In contrast to criterion-referenced tests, *norm-referenced tests* are tests that compare student performance to a larger group. Typically, this larger group, or norm group, is a national sample representing a large and diverse cross-section of students that allows comparison of a particularly student's performance to the performance of others. The scores on norm-referenced tests allow comparisons between the norm group and particular students, schools, districts, and states. All of these tested groups can be rank-ordered in relation to the norm group. Thus, norm-referenced tests are typically used to sort students rather than measure proficiency of specific learning objectives or standards.

Standardized testing has played a number of important roles in educational settings. These tests have been used for placement in instructional groups (e.g., ability groups or tracks), measuring achievement, assisting in making career and postsecondary educational choices, determining acceptance of applicants to colleges and universities, and monitoring the performance of educational systems.

Intelligence testing to guide ability grouping was one of the early uses of standardized testing (Cronbach 1975). The perceived need for ability grouping arose as two factors – students staying in school longer and the large waves of immigration to the US at the turn of the twentieth century – created a wider range of student ability in high school classrooms. These changes had an impact on college-bound students whose progress was held back, according to some ability grouping proponents, by the large number of students who did not seem to be academically gifted.

Following from the work of Binet in development of what were called "mental tests," Terman developed a screening tool to identify students who were viewed as not prepared for the intellectual challenges of typical schooling with such labels as "feebleminded" or "retarded" (Resnick 1982). These early tests were administered individually to students to determine whether they should be removed from normal instruction. Wholesale use of intelligence testing was introduced by the military during World War I, when tests were developed to identify potential officers. The successful use of standardized testing by the military encouraged further development of tests and non-military use, such as determining placement of students in homogeneous instructional ability groups (Resnick 1982). In the 1950s, there was a resurgence of intelligence testing for the purpose of grouping as a result of implementing the comprehensive high school with differentiated tracks (Linn 2000).

A second use of standardized testing has been the measurement of student achievement levels in a variety of academic domains. Examinations had long been used to determine student progress and set standards for high school graduation, but as the number of students increased it became the necessary to establish standardized criteria. The National Education Association adopted recommendations to standardized evaluation in 1914. At the time of World War I, there had been a rapid increase in the number of achievement tests, numbering more than 200 available for use in the primary and secondary schools (Resnick 1982). Later, a related use of achievement testing was the implementation of minimum-competency testing for high school graduation in the 1970s and early 1980s (Linn 2000, 2001).

Standardized testing played a third role as it was used by school guidance departments to assist students in job or career selection and in making decisions about attending postsecondary institutions. Testing in this area included assessing student aptitudes, interests, and skills to guide decision-making between career and educational options. One aspect of this innovation was the move to keeping cumulative student records to document continued individual development (Resnick 1982; Linn 2001).

Determining whether students were academically prepared for college and university entrance is a fourth use of standardized tests. In 1899, the College Entrance Examination Board was created to "establish, administer, and evaluate examinations, in defined subject areas for entrance to participating colleges" (Resnick 1982: 187). After World War I, the Scholastic Aptitude Test (SAT) was developed to provide a standardized test that was not based on a specified curriculum, such as one from a college preparatory school. The focus on aptitude rather than curriculum was seen as being more equitable. In addition, the SAT introduced the use of multiple choice rather than essay-type questions. Performance on the SAT and the American College Test (ACT), which was introduced in 1957, became a major component in the decision to accept students into most postsecondary institutions in the US.

A final important role of standardized testing, and possibly one of the earliest, was to compare schools and monitor their performance. As early as the 1840s a set of common questions was used in Boston to determine student progress. The result of this testing had little effect on students or teachers, but provided the Superintendent with a way to hold schools within the district accountable to common standards of student and teacher performance (Resnick 1982). This practice of using student achievement tests to hold schools accountable grew and continued through the rest of the nineteenth century, and is certainly prevalent today (Linn 2001).

New interest in the use of standardized testing occurred as a result of the 1965 federal Elementary and Secondary Education Act (ESEA). Standardized achievement tests became the means of monitoring and evaluating the use of these funds (Linn 2000; Koretz 2002). The 1983 *A Nation at Risk* report on the state of American education added a new impetus for the use of standardized testing in evaluating the performance of schools. While the testing arising from the ESEA focused on educational equity, the new emphasis after *A Nation at Risk* was overall performance of the American educational system relative to international education systems.

Most recently, the 2001 ESEA reauthorization, the No Child Left Behind Act (NCLB), increased the importance of standardized testing to new levels in the US. This wave of standardized testing has moved the focus to establishing content standards, the setting of performance (or proficiency) standards for all students, and the addition of high-stakes assessments for schools, educators, and, in some jurisdictions, students (Linn 2000, 2003; Linn et al. 2002).

In the foreseeable future, there are several avenues of research that are currently underway or likely to be carried out.

First, research should continue to examine reasonable projections for schools making adequate yearly progress toward learning objectives. The current federal law of NCLB increases the testing requirements and establishes accountability standards for states, districts, and schools in that they need to make measurable adequate yearly progress (AYP) for all students and subgroups of students defined by socioeconomic background, race/ethnicity, English language proficiency, and disability. There is currently wide variation in the rigor of both standards and tests so that students measured to be proficient vary widely from state to state. Over the next few years, researchers could continue to analyze data from different states to examine which schools make large gains on state assessments to understand what ambitious, yet reasonable, goals might be established for AYP (see Koretz 2002; Linn et al. 2002; Linn 2003).

Second, research needs to focus great attention to the tradeoffs that schools and teachers deal with under NCLB by examining how instructional resources are devoted to students at different points in the achievement distribution. For example, by focusing educators on the task of bringing all students to a minimum level of proficiency, it is possible under NCLB that schools will divert attention and resources from students who already meet this standard. In addition, schools may divert resources away from students who are so far below the standard because schools perceive little chance of bringing them to the proficient level. However, such consequences are not inevitable. It may be possible to avoid negative distributional effects if schools instead make more efficient use of their resources, but additional research is needed to address this important issue.

Third, researchers should continue to examine how school principals and teachers actually use test score results for improvement (Goldring & Berends 2006). Schools are typically inundated with data and many teachers and principals are not trained in statistics and measurement to thoroughly understand how to use test score results for improving the conditions of schools and classrooms. Further research into the capabilities and capacity of schools to use data in effective ways for improving students' test scores would be beneficial for accountability systems that require shared responsibility (Linn 2003).

Finally, researchers should explore different ways to use tests to hold schools accountable. The current research suggests that test-based accountability does not always work as intended, but there is no adequate research base to offer a compelling alternative to policymakers and educators. Koretz (2002: 774) describes the current situation as one in which "the role of researchers is like that of the proverbial custodian walking behind the elephant with a broom. The policies are implemented, and after the fact a few researchers are allowed to examine the effects and offer yet more bad news." Alternative accountability approaches would expand beyond just tests to examine a mix of incentives for teachers, changes in instructional practice, quality of examining standardized test score gains and growth for students in addition to proficiency levels, and alignment of instruction to standards to tests (see Porter 2002). Together, empirical analyses of these elements incorporated into various programs, policies, and interventions may provide not only alternatives, but also better information about the system of student learning.

SEE ALSO: Education; Educational Inequality; Intelligence Tests; Meritocracy; Opportunities for Learning; Schooling and Economic Success; Standardization; Stratification and Inequality, Theories of; Validity, Quantitative; Variables; Variables, Dependent; Variance

REFERENCES AND SUGGESTED READINGS

American Educational Research Association, American Psychological Association, and National Council on Measurement in Education (AERA) (1999) *Standards for Educational and Psychological Testing.* American Educational Research Association, Washington, DC.

Baker, E. L. (2001) Testing and Assessment: A Progress Report. *Educational Assessment* 7(1): 1–12.

Cronbach, L. (1975) Five Decades of Public Controversy Over Mental Testing. *American Psychologist* 30: 1–14.

Goldring, E. & Berends, M. (2006) *Leading with Data: A Path to School Improvement.* Corwin Press, Thousand Oaks, CA.

Koretz, D. (2002) Limitations in the Use of Achievement Tests as Measures of Educators' Productivity. *Journal of Human Resources* 37(4): 752–77.

Linn, R. L. (2000) Assessments and Accountability. *Educational Researcher* 29(2): 4–16.

Linn, R. L. (2001) A Century of Standardized Testing. *Educational Assessment* 7(1): 29–38.

Linn, R. L. (2003) Accountability: Responsibility and Reasonable Actions. *Educational Researcher* 32(7): 3–13.

Linn, R. L., Baker, E. L., & Betebenner, D. W. (2002) Accountability Systems: Implications of Requirements of the No Child Left Behind Act of 2001. *Educational Researcher* 3–16.

Porter, A. C. (2002) Measuring the Content of Instruction: Uses in Research and Practice. *Educational Researcher* 31(7): 3–14.

Resnick, D. (1982) History of Educational Testing. In: Wigdor, A. & Garner, W. (Eds.), *Ability Testing: Uses, Consequences, and Controversies, Part II: Documentation Section.* National Academy Press, Washington, DC, pp. 173–94.

state

Boris Frankel

Few concepts are as central to social analysis and political practice as the state. Many assume that the state is synonymous with the elected government. All the non-elected state administrators, coercive apparatuses, and sociocultural institutions that constitute modern states are often ignored. Despite the crucial nature of state power, major political and methodological disputes remain over the nature and role of the state and how to acquire and maintain state power. Some argue that state institutions are interwoven with social and economic relations in society. Others view the state as distinct from non-state institutions because they perform coercive, taxing, judicial, and other administrative roles that private institutions cannot perform. Despite the privatization of various state industries and services, there is little prospect that the state will be abolished and that all its current roles will be performed by private businesses. Sociologically and politically, Marxists argue that class and power relations in society hold the key to understanding state institutions and the way states maintain ruling-class power, ideology, and cultural practices. Conversely, liberals and conservatives claim that society is made up of rich and poor individuals rather than a ruling class dominating other classes. Hence, they see the state as independent of class divisions in society. Weberians also argue that states are autonomous of class relations in society and have their own bureaucratic rationality and political and military agendas. Regardless of the political perspective, state theorists are also divided between those who formulate ideal types and models such as the "feudal state," the "capitalist state," or the "advanced liberal state," and those who reject ideal types and stress the historical uniqueness of each state.

Without a notion of state institutions it is difficult to explain how stateless societies (such as indigenous communities) differ from societies with elaborate forms of military, fiscal, and administrative state power. Revolutions, imperialism, world wars, welfare states, and numerous other developments would be unintelligible if the vital roles played by state institutions were ignored. State theory has always been intimately related to particular historical and political developments. Political philosophers from Aristotle to Machiavelli analyzed political power in city-states and empires. Between the fifteenth and eighteenth centuries, religious conflict and secular opposition to religious authority led to a redefinition of church–state relations. Absolutism gave rise to liberal ideas about state sovereignty and property rights, constitutional checks on tyranny, and the belief in a "social contract" between rulers and citizens. Hobbes, Locke,

Rousseau, and Hegel produced differing conceptions of the relationship between civil society and state institutions. States were either conceived as embodying the highest spiritual, legal, and political values, or as a constant threat to the freedom and privileges of citizens. The eighteenth- and nineteenth-century political economists – from Adam Smith to Karl Marx and J. S. Mill – helped lay the foundations of contemporary liberal and Marxist analyses of the role of states in developing capitalist societies.

By the late nineteenth century, two parallel trends were evident in state theory. The formal legal-constitutional state theorists produced numerous books outlining national constitutions and various laws (Dyson 1980). However, little was written by these nineteenth and early twentieth-century constitutional formalists on the *informal* structures of state power, such as "backroom" machinations and bureaucratic processes. By contrast, between the 1880s and the 1930s a combination of new political movements and academic analyses established the foundations of contemporary state theory. Politically, the rise of labor, socialist, and communist parties on the one side, and various conservative and fascist parties on the other, thrust the whole issue of state power on to center stage. From an anti-socialist and anti-liberal perspective, the "new Machiavellians" or elite theorists Mosca and Pareto celebrated the cunning of foxes and the brute force of lions as necessary to winning and holding state power (Bottomore 1964). The elite theorists later became admirers of Italian Fascism, which made a cult of state power. Lenin (1917) also criticized parliamentary-road strategies favored by socialist and labor movement parties as naïve. According to Lenin, socialists should not place too much faith in formal liberal constitutional processes and ignore the power of state repressive apparatuses (the army, police, and bureaucracy). Repressive apparatuses can defend capitalism by obstructing or overthrowing a socialist party should it win a parliamentary majority. The Italian Communist leader Antonio Gramsci (imprisoned by the Fascists in the 1920s) analyzed the complex relationship between capitalist states and civil society. Capitalist hegemony required both coercion and consent via an elaborate set of cultural and educational practices, values, and socioeconomic relations. The visible state in the industrial capitalist West, Gramsci (1971) argued, could not be captured by revolutionaries (as Lenin had done in the largely agrarian Russia of 1917) if the less obvious "earth-works" (shoring up the state) of cultural and social hegemony remained largely intact. Fifty years later, neo-Marxist state theorists used Gramsci's work to reconceptualize contemporary state–civil society relations.

State coercion and consent were also central in the work of Weber. He differentiated between traditional forms of spiritual and princely authority or legitimacy and the development of an impersonal legal-rational authority that underpinned modern organizations – especially bureaucracies of the modern state. Weber defined the modern state as an organization that has "a monopoly of the legitimate use of physical force." Although state authorities do not like sharing armed power with other groups in nation-states, Weber's definition is limited in that many state officials tolerate both non-state criminal organizations and illegitimate coercion and corruption within state armed forces and police. Various state administrations and secret police have practiced state terrorism and illegal torture without the knowledge of citizens or other branches of government, thus mocking the notion of a monopoly of "legitimate violence." The legitimacy or illegitimacy of a whole state system (rather than the popularity or hatred of a particular party or individual in government) requires an understanding of how state power is maintained. Some states rely heavily on repressive power, while others prefer voluntary adherence to the law and social norms. Anarchists and other anti-statists regard all states as illegitimate and advocate a non-hierarchical stateless society. Freedom for the individual or community from abusive hierarchical state power may be desirable, but it remains unclear whether cooperative stateless societies can carry out complex administration, production, and distribution at local, national, or global levels.

Between the 1930s and 1950s liberals became increasingly divided over theories of democracy and the modern state. Conservative liberals continued to favor a laissez faire, "minimal state" that primarily defended private property rights against demands for social equality.

The Great Depression of the 1930s, followed by the defeat of fascism in 1945, led various Keynesian liberals and "social market" liberals to champion new interventionist welfare states and international economic steering bodies such as the International Monetary Fund. Nevertheless, most liberals believe parties or individuals in government might pursue sectional interests, but view the state as neutral, serving all citizens impartially. Marxists, however, argued that it was impossible for the state to be a neutral umpire in a class-divided society. Despite their differences, Marxists agreed that without capitalist state institutions private market forces would be unable to manage society, sustain profitability, or, equally importantly, defend capitalism against working-class and other opposition. In the US a new generation of liberal pluralist theorists had fused the insights of the elite theorists, Weberian sociology, and neoclassical economics into a redefinition of democratic government. The two-party system, they argued, was a choice between competing elites. Liberal representative democracy was no longer based on a relationship between the state and the rational individual. Instead, the mass media and interest groups helped frame policy agendas. The "new class" of managers, bureaucrats, and technocrats now ran private corporations and government, rendering obsolete the world imagined by both classical liberal individualism and Marxian class analysis (Bottomore 1964). Paradoxically, the new political science dominant in American and other western universities during the Cold War resulted in state theory almost disappearing between the late 1940s and the late 1960s. While western modernization theorists wrote many works on how newly decolonized or "undeveloped" African, Asian, and Latin American countries could take the correct path to "state-building," few scholars paid attention to state institutions in the West. It was widely assumed that state power was crucial in totalitarian communist societies. However, in the West, systems theory and American pluralism reduced states to neutral structures akin to a black box, with inputs (interest group pressures) that produced outcomes (policies and decisions). What happened inside the box or the state was not entirely clear. Yet American pluralists vigorously asserted that there was no ruling class or power elite as

claimed by orthodox Marxists and radical critics such as Mills (1956). Against a background of mass protest movements in the late 1960s and 1970s, a renaissance in state theory occurred as new state theorists broke the deadlock between pluralists and radicals by refocusing on state institutions.

The various Althusserian, Frankfurt School, Gramscian, capital-logic, and other schools of neo-Marxist state theory rejected both elite theory and the liberal claim of a classless society and state neutrality by documenting the pro-capitalist material and immaterial roles played by state institutions. The *material* roles ranged from vital infrastructure (roads, ports) through to numerous state subsidies for industry and other state-funded contracts and benefits without which private businesses could not function or earn high profits. The *immaterial* roles included everything from states undertaking the education and training of labor, research, and development necessary for new products, through to promoting and securing pro-market values and ideology in the public sphere. Capitalist states were also defined by what they could not do. Private capitalists strongly opposed replacing market competition with state planning or nationalizing private companies. The neutrality of the state was also challenged by pointing to the inequity of taxation and budgetary allocations at the expense of workers and those dependent on state benefits. State repressive apparatuses constantly protected private property and maintained commodity production and capital's dominance over labor, while little was done to protect workers, consumers, and the environment from abuses perpetrated by businesses and government departments.

Most neo-Marxists rejected simple orthodox Marxist mechanical notions of the state as a superstructure determined by the economic base. Poulantzas's (1969) critique of Miliband's (1969) work on the capitalist state highlighted the "relative autonomy" of the capitalist state from market forces and the structural role state officials had to perform. Individual office holders or managers in state apparatuses may have bourgeois or working-class family and school or economic backgrounds. What counted were the structural roles each had to perform as part of the capitalist state, regardless of social background. Marx and Engels's definition of the capitalist state as "the executive committee of the bourgeoisie" or the "ideal collective capitalist" was seen as simplistic by many neo-Marxists (Frankel 1979). The idea that the capitalist state embodied the *collective will* that eluded capitalists because of perennial conflicts and competition was replaced by neo-Marxist emphasis on the *contradictory* nature of state institutions. Capitalist states were arenas of class struggle. If labor movements and other social protest movements were strong, parties sought electoral support and state officials implemented policies to placate demands for better welfare services or such things as environmental pollution regulations. O'Connor (1973) and Habermas (1975) analyzed the economic and social contradictions flowing from the capitalist state promoting the private accumulation of wealth while simultaneously trying to disguise or legitimate this class-based set of policies. Poulantzas (1973) emphasized the divisions between the finance, industrial, merchant, and other fractions of capital and how these ongoing divisions among capitalists gave rise to particular state policies that antagonized sections of business depending on which fraction or fractions were dominant. Offe (1975) stressed the formal methods of acquiring state power via election or appointment to office as opposed to the informal bases of power exercised by private capital upon which state administrators depended for fiscal revenue and the smooth running of society. If governments pursued policies designed to redistribute wealth to non-capitalists or other social justice strategies, they risked investment strikes by capitalists, destabilization, and other hostile reactions. Reform governments encountered obstacles ranging from obstructive behavior by hostile senior state bureaucrats through to military *coups d'état*, as happened to the Allende government in Chile in 1973. The extensive growth of state activity in all spheres of socioeconomic life during the twentieth century meant that state institutions were not just political-administrative structures separate from, or intervening in, "the economy." State institutions at local, regional, and national levels employed up to a third of the workforce, sustained millions of pensioners, the sick, and unemployed on state income, and generally accounted for a significant proportion of investment and

economic life in capitalist societies. According to Offe (1975), where state officials are preoccupied with "allocating" state resources in a routinized manner – that is, any activity that involves fixed rules and sanctions – then the Weberian notion of bureaucracy has a degree of applicability. But where state officials are involved in "productive" state activity – administering and creating policies and practices in a whole range of areas such as health, education, and so forth – then the Weberian notion of bureaucracy as "routinization" is grossly inadequate and inappropriate. Most state employees also do not conform to the Weberian notion of independent bureaucrats standing between capital and labor. Instead, millions of state workers lack power and share many characteristics with white- and blue-collar workers employed by capitalists, such as poor work conditions and insecurity of employment (Frankel 1983).

The neo-Marxist renaissance in state theory also stimulated interest in the state by feminists who focused on the *patriarchal state*, which reproduced male dominance and worked against the interests of women in all spheres of social policy and power relations (Chappell 2003). Environmentalists also analyzed the absence of a *green state* or an *ecological state* (Eckersley 2004). Like Marxists and feminists, environmental theorists rejected the liberal notion of a neutral state and highlighted the manner in which capitalist and communist states endangered ecological sustainability. The demise of Keynesian policies and the rise of neoliberalism since the late 1970s ushered in analyses of changes from the *corporatist state* (tripartite agreements between capital, labor, and government) to the *contract state* of privatization and the importation of market practices into state institutions and services. Ascendant market values and greater global corporate power have ironically coincided with the unpopularity of Marxist theories of the capitalist state. Post-Marxist followers of Foucault (1991), for instance, reject class analyses of the capitalist state in favor of studies of "governmentality" and "advanced liberal" technologies of power. The Foucauldians often appear more concerned with surveillance and accountability rather than explaining how neoliberal states sustain social inequality and pro-market policies.

Despite numerous state theories, many misconceptions and problems remain. It is common for radicals, liberals, and conservatives to speak of complex state institutions as if they were a homogeneous actor or subject, like Machiavelli's Prince, capable of moral, immoral, or amoral behavior and having a "collective mind" or political will. Similarly, others simplistically conceive of state institutions as instruments that can be wielded by a ruling class or elite outside the state (Frankel 1983). Despite numerous cases of cronyism and corruption and the complicity of state officials and presidents in corporate collapses or the promotion of special favors, the complex sociopolitical relations embodied in state institutions make them more than mere instruments. Economistic Marxists conflate the political with the economic. Yet state institutions also embody residues of pre-capitalist legal, religious, racial, and sexual values and practices, as well as contemporary cultural and social policies that are not derivative of the conflict between capital and labor (Frankel 1983). Capitalist relations currently coexist with republics, monarchies, communist states, military dictatorships, theocracies, and federalist, unitary, and other state institutional forms. Boundary problems are also very confusing, as no two Marxists or liberals, for instance, can agree on what constitutes the state, "civil society," or "the economy" and whether they overlap or are separate spheres. Althusser (1971) placed almost all the institutions of "civil society," such as family, media, and school, inside the "ideological state apparatuses," thus making the notion of the state all inclusive. Blurred state/society boundaries are also evident in the "party-state" of fused political and state officials, or the "para-corporatization" of non-state associations to provide social welfare services on the cheap, or expensive public–private partnerships of combined state and capitalist economic and social activity that earn businesses high profits. The orthodox Marxist notion of capitalist repressive apparatuses also fails to explain how the military led revolutions or staged *coups d'état* ranging from Egypt to Portugal. Moreover, there is no agreement among state theorists on how large a state-run public sector can become in a capitalist society and how many egalitarian reforms are possible before the capitalist state ceases to defend and reproduce capitalist social relations.

Finally, state institutions are not equivalent to a particular nation-state. Globalization and the emergence of supra-states such as the European Union exacerbate the confusion over state–society "boundary problems" and raise questions about the future power and role of existing state institutions (Jessop 2002).

SEE ALSO: Anarchism; Civil Society; Culture, the State and; Liberalism; Marxism and Sociology; Nation-State; Nation-State and Nationalism; Patriarchy; Sport and the State; State and the Ecnonomy

REFERENCES AND SUGGESTED READINGS

Althusser, L. (1971) *Lenin and Philosophy and Other Essays*. New Left Books, London.

Bottomore, T. (1964) *Elites and Society*. Penguin, London.

Chappell, L (2003) *Gendering Government*. UCB, Vancouver.

Dyson, K. (1980) *The State Tradition in Western Europe*. Martin Robertson, Oxford.

Eckersley, R. (2004) *The Green State: Rethinking Democracy and Sovereignty*. MIT Press, Cambridge, MA.

Foucault, M. (1991) Governmentality. In: Burchell, G. et al. (Eds.), *The Foucault Effect: Studies in Governmentality*. University of Chicago Press, Chicago.

Frankel, B. (1979) On the State of the State: Marxist Theories of the State after Leninism. *Theory and Society* 7(1, 2).

Frankel, B. (1983) *Beyond the State?* Macmillan, London.

Gerth, H. & Mills, C. W. (Eds.) (1946) *From Max Weber*. Oxford University Press, New York.

Gramsci, A. (1971) *Selections From the Prison Notebooks*. Lawrence & Wishart, London.

Habermas, J. (1975) *Legitimation Crisis*. Beacon Press, Boston.

Jessop, B. (2002) *The Future of the Capitalist State*. Polity Press, Cambridge.

Lenin, V. I. (1951 [1917]) State and Revolution. In: *Marx Engels Marxism*. Foreign Language Publishers, Moscow.

Miliband, R. (1969) *The State in Capitalist Society*. Weidenfeld & Nicolson, London.

Mills, C. W. (1956) *The Power Elite*. Oxford University Press, New York.

O'Connor, J. (1973) *Fiscal Crisis of the State*. St. Martin's Press, New York.

Offe, C. (1975) The Theory of the Capitalist State and the Problem of Policy Formation. In: Lindberg, L. et al. (Eds.), *Stress and Contradiction in Modern Capitalism*. D. H. Heath, Lexington.

Poulantzas, N. (1969) The Problem of the Capitalist State. *New Left Review* 58.

Poulantzas, N. (1973) *Political Power and Social Classes*. New Left Books, London.

state and economy

John L. Campbell

The literature on the relationship between states and economies is vast. This entry focuses exclusively on states and economies in advanced capitalist societies. In this context, sociologists tend to follow Max Weber in viewing nation-states as organizations consisting of administrative, legislative, judicial, and military apparatuses that govern a finite territory, ultimately through the use of force if necessary. They tend to view economies as systems of material production that are organized around market exchange and the pursuit of profit, and that are embedded in a variety of surrounding institutions, including political ones. Research in the area of state and economy has focused on several questions. How does the economy affect the state? How does the state affect the economy? How are state–economy relations organized? How are state–economy relations changing?

HOW DOES THE ECONOMY AFFECT THE STATE?

To address this question, sociologists have often researched why government promulgates the regulatory, macroeconomic, and other business-related policies it does. For example, pluralists argue that a wide variety of economic actors, including representatives from business and labor, but also consumers, environmentalists, and others, struggle to influence the policymaking process. Policymakers tend to respond most favorably to those groups who have the most resources, organizational skills, and access to policymakers. If labor is strongest in this regard, then states pass legislation protective of workers; if business is strongest, then states pass legislation that is protective of corporate interests; if consumers are strongest, then states pass legislation that regulates product safety and quality.

However, some scholars maintain that the business community has a significant advantage in this political competition because it has more resources than other groups in society and so is generally able to capture, dominate, or otherwise influence the policymaking process to its advantage. For instance, according to this view, business leaders are able to make comparatively large contributions to politicians' electoral campaigns. This affords them greater access to politicians and therefore greater opportunity to influence the policymaking process than other groups enjoy, who have less money to contribute.

Taking a view that focuses more on the structural constraints imposed on states by economies than on the influence of instrumentally oriented economic actors per se, other researchers claim that policymaking is inevitably biased in favor of business interests. This is because policymakers have little choice but to promote continued business investment and economic growth. For instance, regardless of how much pressure the business community or others put on policymakers, states must ensure that the economy continues to operate smoothly, that unemployment remains relatively low, and that inflation remains in check. Otherwise, political leaders will be voted out of office, tax revenues will dry up, and the state will suffer political and fiscal crises.

Still other observers argue that states enjoy far more autonomy over economic policymaking than any of these other perspectives acknowledge. Some go so far as to suggest that states are predatory in the sense that their rulers are driven to maximize the revenue their states extract from the economy in order to increase their own power. In the extreme, self-interested rulers may extract so much revenue that it saps the vitality of the economy altogether.

These debates have provoked an enormous amount of empirical research (e.g., Evans et al. 1985). Much of this has focused on the development of welfare states insofar as they provide the social policies upon which economies depend, such as unemployment compensation, pensions, health care, job training, and education (Hicks 1999). Less attention has been paid to identifying the determinants of tax policies (but see Campbell 1993). This oversight is surprising because welfare spending would be impossible without sufficient revenues to finance it and because tax policy itself has significant effects on the economy, as we shall see later. And sociologists have largely ignored the formation of general macroeconomic and monetary policy, subjects that have traditionally been the province of economists and political scientists.

HOW DOES THE STATE AFFECT THE ECONOMY?

Regardless of who or what influences state policymaking, the state always influences the economy in several ways (Lindberg & Campbell 1991). First, governments provide and allocate *resources* to business through direct subsidies, infrastructure investment, and procurement, which create incentives for firms to engage in many kinds of behavior. As noted earlier, welfare and tax policy also affect the economy. For instance, welfare spending can affect the availability and quality of labor in the labor market and the amount of money firms need to spend on health insurance and pension benefits for their workers. State spending can also affect the sorts of research and development in which firms engage and the types of products they manufacture.

Second, states establish and enforce *property rights* and regulate firms in ways that affect not only their behavior, but also their organization. Anti-trust law, for instance, influences whether firms form cartels or merge to create vertically and horizontally integrated firms. Similarly, dairy cooperatives were commonplace in many European countries during the early twentieth century, but were illegal under anti-trust law in the US and were therefore relatively rare until Congress passed legislation in 1922 legalizing them. Tax law is another form of property rights insofar as it determines the amount of profit firms can retain and the amount of earnings workers can keep. Tax policy also influences, among other things, whether consumers buy or save, whether firms invest or return profits to stockholders, and whether workers seek to improve their skills through education.

Third, the *structure* of the state apparatus affects business. For example, decentralized states provide different opportunities for firms to relocate their operations within national borders than do centralized states. In decentralized states like the US, where there is wide variation across subnational governments in tax, labor, and other types of business law, these variations may create incentives for firms to relocate their operations from one part of the country to another. Different laws of incorporation were one reason why US firms tended to incorporate in New Jersey during the late nineteenth and early twentieth centuries. And differences in labor law were one reason why US textile manufacturers moved from their mills from the northeast to the southern part of the country later on. Variations like these are less common in more centralized states like France or Japan.

Fourth, nation-states engage other nation-states in *geopolitics*. Such international activity often impacts national economies. Notably, when war breaks out, economies can be devastated or revitalized, as occurred in Western Europe and the United States, respectively, during World War II. But even during peace time, geopolitics can have significant effects. The development of common markets, such as the North American Free Trade Agreement and the European Union (EU) are two important examples. In both cases, the states involved agreed to open their borders to increased levels of trade, capital mobility, and labor migration. In the EU, this eventually led to the adoption of a common European currency that replaced several national currencies. It also led to hundreds of EU directives that were designed to harmonize the business environment across member countries.

HOW ARE STATE–ECONOMY RELATIONS ORGANIZED?

The complex relationships between states and economies take different institutional forms in different societies. Generally speaking, scholars recognize three types of state–economy relationships in capitalist countries (Katzenstein 1978). First is the *liberal* model where the state tends to maintain an arm's-length relationship from the economy, grants much freedom to markets, pursues relatively vigorous anti-trust policy to ensure market competition, relies heavily on broad macroeconomic and monetary policies to smooth out business cycles, and tries not to interfere directly in the activities of individual firms. The US is often cited as the typical example of the liberal model.

Second is the *statist* model. Here countries like Japan, France, and South Korea come to mind. In these countries the state is much more involved in the economy and exercises much greater influence over individual firms, such as by providing finance and credit directly to them. Occasionally, the government owns and runs firms in key infrastructural industries such as railways, telecommunications, and energy, although since the 1980s statist countries have privatized many of these firms.

Third is the *corporatist* model, typically found in the Scandinavian countries, Germany, Austria, and Switzerland. In this model the state promotes bargaining and negotiation among well-organized social partners, notably centralized business associations and labor unions, in order to promulgate economic and social policies that benefit all groups in society. In Germany, for example, national legislation passed after World War II ensured that labor would be represented on corporate boards of directors and would be able to establish works councils that would facilitate bargaining between managers and workers over issues like investment, plant closings, shop floor relations, and the introduction of new production technologies. The state also organized centralized bargaining between employers' associations and unions over wages, benefits, and in some cases prices.

In sum, government can be an arm's-length regulator, a strong economic player, or a facilitator of bargained agreements. But regardless of which model we refer to, it is important to understand that the state and economy are *always* connected in important and complicated ways. And this has always been true, even in the most *laissez-faire* examples. For example, in the US during the nineteenth and early twentieth centuries the state was pivotal in providing corporate charters, infrastructure, subsidies, property rights, and a variety of other supports for the economy's development. Furthermore, during the early days of industrialization when capitalism was first emerging in Europe, the state played an important (albeit rudimentary) role in defining property rights, regulating

business, and providing at least minimal protection to workers. According to Karl Polanyi (1944), this was necessary in order to prevent capitalist self-interest and the pursuit of profit from getting out of hand to the point where it hurt workers, consumers, and the environment so much that it would have led eventually to capitalism's self-destruction.

Variations in how state–economy relations are organized matter in terms of the ability of firms to compete successfully and the ability of states to manage macroeconomic problems, such as inflation and unemployment. However, there is much disagreement as to which variation is best. Many economists and conservatives maintain that the liberal model is the best because it ensures relatively unbridled market activity, which, following neoclassical economics, is the most efficient and surest way to achieve positive economic performance. Many political scientists and sociologists tend to favor the other two models, reasoning that coordinated economic activity will more effectively mitigate market failures and social ills like inequality and poverty.

Recently, some scholars have shown that each variety of capitalism has its own strengths and weaknesses. For instance, liberal economies enable firms to compete by making decisions quickly, keeping costs low, and moving capital rapidly from sector to sector and region to region. The other varieties enable firms to compete by producing high-quality products and by ensuring a high degree of cooperation between labor and management. Why? Because governments in statist and corporatist countries tend to provide a well-educated labor force, ensure bargaining and negotiation between business and workers, and offer generous welfare supports to facilitate the sort of economic restructuring that enables business to be competitive internationally (Hall & Soskice 2001).

HOW ARE STATE–ECONOMY RELATIONS CHANGING?

Since the mid-1970s, economic activity has become increasingly globalized. In particular, capital has gained the ability to move from one country to another faster than ever and in greater volume than ever. This has generated much concern that the ability of firms to shift investments rapidly from one country to another has undermined the institutional differences associated with the three models of capitalism discussed earlier. Many have warned that states will need increasingly to compete against each other to retain and attract capital investment. To do so, it is argued, they will have to realign their institutional arrangements with the liberal model. In other words, they will have to grant firms more autonomy to do as they please without having to worry about the interests of government, labor, or other actors. As a result, states will have to reduce taxes, welfare spending, and the regulatory burden on business. If they fail to do so, then capital flight will result and precipitate a host of economic problems, including plant closings, job loss, unemployment, and poor economic growth. Ultimately, according to this view, state sovereignty is at risk to the extent that the only way to control capital in such a globalized environment is for nation-states to relinquish some of their powers to regulate economic activity to international organizations, such as the World Trade Organization, the European Union, and the like.

During the 1990s this became a popular argument among politicians who sought to roll back business regulation, welfare spending, and taxes. Nevertheless, researchers have shown that there is little sign of institutional convergence on the liberal model, or that serious economic problems result for countries that fail to adopt it (Hicks & Kenworthy 1998; Swank 2002). Instead, the relationship between state and economy and the institutional basis by which business competes continue to evolve along a variety of trajectories. There are several reasons why.

To begin with, states are not helpless in the face of increased global economic pressures. After all, states are partly responsible for the rise in international trade and capital mobility because they have deliberately lowered barriers to trade and investment. As such, they can surely reverse these trends if they want. States can also block these sorts of reforms if political forces are strong enough to resist change. This happens, for example, when well-organized labor unions and social democratic parties defend welfare spending from its political opponents. And even when states make concessions in one area, such as by lowering corporate profit taxes, they can compensate in other areas, such as by devising new taxes on Internet commerce or cross-national financial transactions (Campbell 2003).

Second, institutional change tends to proceed in path-dependent ways. Even when governments try to mimic institutional practices observed elsewhere, they typically translate them into local contexts in ways that do not fully supplant current practices (Campbell 2004: ch. 5). So, for example, even though the Japanese state privatized its national telephone company in 1984, it also developed a powerful regulatory ministry to supervise many aspects of the new private firm's operations, including pricing and technology development. These state capacities were much more in line with Japan's traditional statist model than the alternative liberal model. In other words, Japan *reregulated* rather than *deregulated* the industry.

Third, firms do not compete just on the basis of costs. Even if they can find cheaper labor or lower taxes somewhere else, they do not automatically move their operations there if they recognize that they enjoy other competitive advantages where they are currently doing business. For instance, firms operating in the Scandinavian countries may face much higher taxes and labor costs than their competitors elsewhere, but they enjoy other off-setting advantages like a well-educated workforce, peaceful labor–management relations, excellent infrastructural support, and more. The point is that even though capital may have become increasingly mobile internationally, firms recognize that they can compete on the basis of comparative *institutional* arative *cost* advantage. Thus, when firms recognize this they will often defend against attempts to undermine these institutional advantages. Although German firms pay relatively high wages and benefits to their workers as a result of the institutionalized bargaining described earlier, they have resisted recent calls to dismantle these arrangements precisely because they understand the advantages that accrue from them, such as very cooperative labor–management relations that facilitate high-quality production and the ability to be flexible in the face of the rapidly changing market demands that are associated with globalization. These are things that have bolstered Germany's international competitiveness for decades and many firms want to preserve this.

This is not to say that state–economy relations will not change in the face of globalization. As noted earlier, the point is that the institutional environments within which economic activity takes place – including the institutionalized relationships that link state and economy – will continue to evolve as they have for decades. But variation among institutional types of capitalism will likely persist for a very long time.

SEE ALSO: Global Economy; Globalization; Law, Economy and; Political Economy; State; State and Private Sector Employees

REFERENCES AND SUGGESTED READINGS

Campbell, J. L. (1993) The State and Fiscal Sociology. *Annual Review of Sociology* 19: 163–85.

Campbell, J. L. (2003) States, Politics, and Globalization: Why Institutions Still Matter. In: Paul, T.V., Ikenberry, G. J., & Hall, J. A. (Eds.), *The Nation State in Question*. Princeton University Press, Princeton, pp. 234–59.

Campbell, J. L. (2004) *Institutional Change and Globalization*. Princeton University Press, Princeton.

Crouch, C. & Streeck, W. (1997) *Political Economy of Modern Capitalism*. Sage, Thousand Oaks, CA.

Evans, P., Rueschemeyer, D., & Skocpol, T. (Eds.) (1985) *Bringing the State Back In*. Cambridge University Press, New York.

Hall, P.A. & Soskice, D. (Eds.) (2001) *Varieties of Capitalism*. Oxford University Press, New York.

Hicks, A. (1999) *Social Democracy and Welfare Capitalism*. Cornell University Press, Ithaca, NY.

Hicks, A. & Kenworthy, L. (1998) Cooperation and Political Economic Performance in Affluent Democratic Capitalism. *American Journal of Sociology* 103: 1631–72.

Katzenstein, P. J. (Ed.) (1978) *Between Power and Plenty*. University of Wisconsin Press, Madison.

Lindberg, L. N. & Campbell, J. L. (1991) The State and the Organization of Economic Activity. In: Campbell, J. L., Hollingsworth, J. R., & Lindberg, L. N. (Eds.), *Governance of the American Economy*. Cambridge University Press, New York, pp. 356–95.

Polanyi, K. (1944) *The Great Transformation*. Beacon Press, Boston.

Swank, D. (2002) *Global Capital, Political Institutions, and Policy Change in Developed Welfare States*. Cambridge University Press, New York.

Weiss, L. (1998) *The Myth of the Powerless State*. Cornell University Press, Ithaca, NY.

state and private sector employees

Rolf Becker

Public employment is a significant characteristic of modern welfare states. After the building of nation-states, professional employment in the state sector has become for an increasing share of citizens an indicator of modernization and democratization in most of the western countries (Weber 1920–1). While in the early phases of industrializatiozn and modernization public employment has been characterized in terms of bureaucratization and the privileged status of a minority of the labor force, employment in the state sector became the pioneer of the post-industrialization of social stratification (Esping-Andersen 1990). In the twentieth century, the dominance of traditional tasks of the state sector such as military, police, public administration, and production of common goods (electricity, railway, and water supply) has shifted to social services and welfare production. As in any large-scale organization in the private sector, a division of labor and well-defined areas of competencies are basic characteristics of the state. A segmentation of specific welfare programs as well as segmentation within state employment is brought about (Mayer & Schoepflin 1989).

This development arising in the nineteenth century has been accelerated by the expansion of the welfare states in the post-war era of the twentieth century. The rapid increase of public employment is the most visible direct effect of the welfare state expansion in the post-war era (Table 1). In the modern western nations, in particular during the "golden era of the welfare state" from the 1960s until the end of the 1970s, at least 20 percent of employed individuals are public employees (Rose et al. 1985). After 1980, political changes in the government, economic crisis, and declining ability to finance labor-intensive welfare programs led to decreasing shares of public employment over total employment. In most contemporary mixed economies, the welfare state is still one of the largest employers: public employment grew faster than private employment during the post-war decades and

Table 1   Growth in public employment (in % of employed persons)

Country	Pre-1850	Pre-1914	Pre-1939	ca. 1950	ca. 1960	ca. 1970	ca. 1980	ca. 1990	ca. 1999
UK	2.4	7.1	10.8	26.6	24.3	27.6	31.4	19.5	12.6
France	5.0	7.1	8.9	17.5	23.3	23.2	29.1	20.4	21.3
Germany	7.2	10.6	12.9	14.4	16.0	21.2	25.8	15.1	12.3
Italy	2.2	4.7	7.8	11.4	13.4	19.8	24.4		15.2
Sweden				15.2	16.6	25.6	38.2		
Finland							25.3	23.3	24.3
USA	0.8	1.4	7.9	17.0	17.6	19.8	18.3	14.9	14.6

Source: Rose et al. (1985); OECD (2001).

contemporary public employees make a major claim upon tax revenues.

The social democratic welfare states (e.g., Sweden, Finland, Norway, Denmark) have expanded their labor-intensive welfare programs (education and health) and are followed by the state-corporatist welfare states (e.g., Germany, France, Austria) in which economic programs dominated until the 1960s and 1970s. One of the major aims of the expansion of the social democratic welfare state was the reduction of social inequality by the guarantee of long-term employment and income in the state sector. In state-corporatist welfare states, the generous alimentation of civil servants is a significant tradition in such systems. The rationality of this alimentation is the exchange of political loyalty of employees and the maintenance of their privileged social status and position in the social stratification. In this respect, this exchange between the modern state as employer and public employees results in the maintenance of existing social inequalities to the advantage of civil servants. Liberal welfare states (e.g., US, UK, Canada, Australia, Switzerland) as well as rudimentary welfare states (e.g., Italy) provide a minimum of public support of individuals and their families, and social welfare is oriented toward market processes. These countries employ citizens mainly in the state-defining programs including police, law enforcement, and military defense.

The growth of public employment is linked to political decisions related to several programs and the shift of public employees to these programs (Table 2). In terms of the type of welfare state, most of the public employees produce goods and services in the social welfare program. The number of public employees producing common goods in state-defining programs has been diminished to a greater degree than the number of public employees in economic activities. The byproduct of this shift among the state programs is the increase in female employment in the state sector (almost 50 percent of the employees are female) and the recruitment of qualified employees offering skilled services. In most of the western welfare states, the state sector employs a higher proportion of educated personnel than the private sector. Government can even employ a majority of highly educated graduates. The post-war expansion of labor-intensive social programs is the chief cause of a high level of public employment of qualified manpower and reflects the self-consumption of the output of educational expansion initiated by the state itself.

As a side-effect, the expansion of the welfare state and increase of public employment has had an important impact on the careers of state employees and their position in social stratification compared to employees in the private sector (DiPrete & Soule 1988). In particular, the employment and career prospects of qualified women have been advanced by the state as employer (Becker 1993). Similar to private employees in the internal labor market of large-scale firms, for the state employee there are privileged working conditions with special occupational status and labor contracts, guarantee of employment, early recruitment in hierarchical systems of career lines, formal regulations of careers by certificates and seniority, rigid and stable structure of careers and mobility patterns

Table 2 Growth of public employment and the functional distribution of public employment

Country	1950	1960	1970	1980
Sweden	*15.2*	*16.6*	*25.6*	*38.2*
Social welfare	30.8	37.3	52.2	53.1
Economic activities	37.7	33.0	27.3	25.3
Defining activities	24.6	19.5	15.6	13.7
Other	6.9	10.2	4.9	7.9
Germany	*14.4*	*16.0*	*21.2*	*25.8*
Social welfare	30.8	29.3	32.4	37.8
Economic activities	50.1	43.3	37.8	31.8
Defining activities	17.4	24.4	25.2	24.7
Other	1.7	3.0	4.6	5.7
USA	*17.0*	*17.6*	*19.8*	*18.3*
Social welfare	23.9	35.8	45.1	48.8
Economic activities	15.5	17.4	15.6	17.5
Defining activities	54.2	41.2	30.7	28.0
Other	6.4	5.6	8.6	5.7

Source: Rose et al. (1985), own calculations.

in career lines, and more independence from individual characteristics (Grandjean 1981). In the course of increasing the importance of internal labor markets in the private sector, the differences between the private and state sectors in terms of such organizational and institutionalized working conditions (DiPrete & Soule 1986; Erikson & Goldthorpe 1992) are probably diminishing. However, studies of career and income trajectories in the private and public sectors demonstrate remaining differences (Visher 1984; Carroll & Mayer 1986; Becker 1993). On the one hand, there is less empirical evidence for the self-selection of individuals with a specific personality and habitus (rule orientation, unconditional obedience, dogmatism, risk avoidance, need for security) into the state bureaucratic sector (Grunow 1991), but some indications that there is an intergenerational reproduction of state employees (Becker 1993). For Norway and Germany, we have empirical evidence for consecutive birth cohorts that the relationship between social origin and entrance into the state sector has become closer in the course of educational expansion and expansion of labor-intensive service in the state sector. On the other hand, because of their privileges, state employees are not interested in job shifts from the state sector into the private sector during their working life (Becker 1993). However, in contrast to the employees in the private sector, they have lower rates of upward mobility and remain longer in their jobs and in the same organization.

SEE ALSO: Bureaucratic Personality; Class, Status, and Power; Labor Markets; Post-Industrial Society; State; State Regulation and the Workplace; Welfare State

REFERENCES AND SUGGESTED READINGS

Becker, R. (1993) *Staatsexpansion und Karrierechancen. Berufsverläufe im öffentlichen Dienst und in der Privatwirtschaft*. Campus, Frankfurt am Main.

Carroll, G. R. & Mayer, K. U. (1986) Job-Shift Patterns in the Federal Republic of Germany: The Effects of Social Class, Industrial Sector, and Organizational Size. *American Sociological Review* 51: 323–41.

DiPrete, T. A. & Soule, W. T. (1986) The Organization of Career Lines: Equal Employment Opportunity and Status Advancement in a Federal Bureaucracy. *American Sociological Review* 51: 295–309.

DiPrete, T. A. & Soule, W. T. (1988) Gender and Promotion in Segmented Job Ladder System. *American Sociological Review* 53: 26–40.

Erikson, R. & Goldthorpe, J. H. (1992) *The Constant Flux: A Study of Class Mobility in Industrial Societies*. Clarendon Press, Oxford.

Esping-Andersen, G. (1990) *The Three Worlds of Welfare Capitalism*. Polity Press, Cambridge.

Grandjean, B. D. (1981) History and Career in a Bureaucratic Labor Market. *American Journal of Sociology* 86: 1057–92.

Grunow, D. (1991) Development of the Public Sector: Trends and Issues. In: Kaufmann, F.-X. (Ed.), *The Public Sector: Challenge for Coordination and Learning*. Walter de Gruyter, Berlin, pp. 89–115.

Mayer, K. U. & Schoepflin, U. (1989) The State and the Life Course. *Annual Review of Sociology* 15: 187–209.

OECD (2001) *Highlights of Public Sector Pay and Employment Trends*. Paris: HRM Working Party Meeting. Working Paper PUMA/HRM (2001) 11.

Rose, R. (with Page, E., Parry, R., Peters, B. G., Cendali Pignatelli, A., & Schmidt, K.-D.) (1985) *Public Employment in Western Nations*. Cambridge University Press, Cambridge.

Visher, M. (1984) The Workers of the State and the State of State Workers: A Comparison of Public and Private Employment in Norway. PhD thesis, University of Wisconsin-Madison.

Weber, M. (1920–1) *Wirtschaft und Gesellschaft*. Siebeck (Mohr), Tübingen.

state regulation and the workplace

Holly J. McCammon

Workplaces are highly regulated spaces. As Edelman and Suchman (1997) state, they "are immersed in a sea of law." In regulating the workplace, the state attempts to control the behaviors of employers, managers, and workers using a system of incentives and penalties and a variety of policy tools. In the US, the government has at least some say – and often much say – over discrimination in the workplace, union activities, workplace safety, wage levels, hiring practices, work hours, employee leaves, plant closings, and compensation for injuries at work. The two main areas of workplace regulation in the US are employment law and labor law. Employment law encompasses anti-discrimination law, affirmative action policy, and equal pay law. Labor law, on the other hand, regulates trade union organizing, collective bargaining between workers and employers, and strike action by workers. Both areas have received substantial attention by researchers in sociology as they try to make sense of the law's development over time and its impact on employment relations.

EMPLOYMENT LAW

The 1960s were a watershed in US employment law. In 1963 the Equal Pay Act was passed, requiring employers to pay men and women equally for equal work. And in 1964, in response to the Civil Rights Movement, Congress enacted the Civil Rights Act, which greatly broadened the state's ability to restrict race and sex discrimination, including in the workplace. Prior to this time, workplace discrimination against women, African Americans, and other minorities was commonplace. Employers routinely refused to hire blacks, ethnic minorities, and women for a variety of jobs, and even when hired these social minorities were segregated into occupations and jobs deemed culturally "appropriate" for them (Hodson & Sullivan 2002). Title VII of the new law made it unlawful for employers to treat employees differently because of their "race, color, religion, sex, or national origin." The law also established the Equal Employment Opportunity Commission (EEOC) to oversee the law's enforcement. Title VII fundamentally altered the cultural environment of workplaces by instituting due process rights. But as Reskin (2001) points out, enforcement of Title VII has often depended on the perseverance of the victims of discrimination to carry their cases forward. This stems primarily from underfunding of the EEOC. In addition, the nature of Title VII and of EEOC procedures obscures the intersectionality of discrimination by requiring that plaintiffs choose among their social identities when filing cases (Crenshaw 1989). The unique experience of a black woman, for instance, can be overlooked if, as the law requires, she must identify herself as *either* female or African American to file her case.

Another key development in anti-discrimination law in the 1960s was the passage of Executive Order 11246 in 1965 by President Lyndon Johnson. This affirmative action policy, as it has come to be known, requires that a company doing business with the federal government "take affirmative action to ensure" that employees and applicants for jobs are not discriminated against with regard to "race, color, religion, or national origin." In 1967, Executive Order 11375 included "sex" in its affirmative action provisions. Affirmative action policies are thus proactive workplace regulation, mandating that companies with governmental contracts establish workplace policies that give preference, particularly in hiring, to qualified female and minority applicants in order to address the effects of past discrimination. The policies, however, have been controversial and support for them has declined over time among whites (Sears et al. 2000). Moreover, many workplace policies have called for only minimal adjustments in hiring and promotion practices and thus have had a limited impact in reducing occupational race and sex segregation (Reskin 1998). But research indicates that the policies have helped some workers, particularly women and minority men seeking professional and managerial positions, where most affirmative action programs have been targeted (Tomaskovic-Devey 1993). Research also shows that the effectiveness of affirmative action depends on the organizational resources devoted to the programs, the commitment of company leaders, and the duration of the programs' existence within a business (Konrad & Linnehan 1999).

Research on anti-discrimination law has also explored the impact of these policies on race and gender wage inequality. Wage data document that an earnings gap continues to exist between men and women and among racial and ethnic groups, with white men being substantially advantaged (Padavic & Reskin 2002). Various studies, however, indicate that the 1960s shift in employment law helped to narrow the disparity. McCrone and Hardy (1978) find that the racial wage gap declined significantly under Title VII. Burstein (1979), using indicators of EEOC funding and the number of lawsuits decided in favor of the plaintiff, shows that women's and minority wages increased with greater agency enforcement, resulting in greater equality. A number of US states have enacted comparable worth or pay equity laws that go beyond the 1963 Equal Pay Act and stipulate (for public employers but as yet not for private employers) that compensation systems must pay workers equally for comparable, and not just

identical jobs. The US federal government, however, has not yet enacted comparable worth legislation. Instead, federal comparable worth law has developed as a result of wage discrimination suits filed within the courts (Guthrie & Roth 1999).

A more global perspective finds affirmation of equality in the workplace in both the United Nations' Declaration of Human Rights and its International Covenant on Economic, Social, and Cultural Rights (see especially Article 7). The International Labor Organization as well states in its Declaration of Philadelphia that "all human beings, irrespective of race, creed or sex, have the right to pursue both their material well-being and their spiritual development in conditions of freedom and dignity, of economic security and equal opportunity." Most western countries today have adopted such principles in their body of law. Some recent developments include Northern Ireland's Fair Employment Act of 1989 (which places restrictions on discrimination based on religious affiliation) and Germany's Frauenförderungsgesetz of 1994 and Israel's Civil Service Act of 1995, both of which provide for fair gender representation in government service (Ben-Israel 2001). Other nations have also made important strides in establishing equal employment law. China enacted a law to protect women's right to employment, and India and Belize now have policies to prevent sexual harassment in the workplace (United Nations Office of Public Information 2000).

US LABOR LAW

If the decade of major change in US employment law was the 1960s, in labor law it was the 1930s. In 1935 during the Depression, Congress passed the National Labor Relations (Wagner) Act, which institutionalized a system of collective bargaining and provided workers with a legal right to organize unions and to strike. The law also established the National Labor Relations Board (NLRB) to adjudicate workplace disputes. The US Supreme Court upheld the constitutionality of the new law in 1937. Prior to this time and largely through the courts, the government had regularly impeded attempts by workers to organize unions and mount strikes.

Both state and federal judges routinely issued labor injunctions to end strikes and enforce "yellow-dog" contracts or contracts which a worker signed to gain employment but in which he or she was also compelled to agree not to join a union. The courts' use of injunctions significantly restricted the collective activities of labor (McCammon 1993b). In 1932, just before enactment of Wagner, the Federal Anti-Injunction Act was passed. The anti-injunction law was a response to labor and legal reformers who called for an end to the courts' constraints on labor's actions. The anti-injunction act barred the federal courts from issuing injunctions to halt strikes; however, it did not go so far as to protect the right of workers to strike. This came with Wagner. The Wagner Act, a New Deal law, was passed in a period of acute unemployment and economic stagnation, but also one of increasing labor militancy. Workers struck to force employers to recognize their unions. But even with passage of Wagner, strikes continued, largely because employers ignored Wagner, refusing to recognize unions and participate in collective bargaining. Not until the Supreme Court affirmed the law in 1937 did employment relations gradually begin to calm.

The 1937 decision of the Supreme Court redirected the actions of employers away from attempts to repeal the law and away from open resistance to unionization in the workplace and instead toward establishment of bargaining relations with organized labor. In short, a new legal regime of employer–labor relations was instituted (Bowles & Gintis 1982). Prior to the New Deal era, the government's legal policy concerning worker collective action was generally one of "repressive intervention," as it wielded the injunction to halt worker actions (McCammon 1993a). With passage of Wagner and the Supreme Court's affirmation of it, however, the state's legal policy became one of "integrative prevention." The law granted workers legal rights in their interactions with employers, viz., the right to organize, bargain, and strike. But the law also constrained these rights. The subsequent development of labor law after passage of Wagner, with the enactment of the Labor Management Relations (Taft-Hartley) Act of 1947 and a number of pivotal Supreme Court decisions (e.g., *Lincoln Mills*, 1957; "Steelworkers Trilogy" cases, 1960; *Boys Markets*, 1970; *Buffalo Forge*, 1976), meant that unionization and collective bargaining were increasingly regulated and the circumstances in which workers could strike became particularly limited (Wallace et al. 1988). While strikes over wages between labor contracts were legally permissible, strikes over issues that challenged employer control in the workplace were typically defined as illegal.

Moreover, the developing law provided employers with important tools for resisting worker organizing and collective action (Gross 1995). During union certification elections, for example, the law grants long delays between the filing of a petition for a union and the actual election, and whereas employers have free speech rights to communicate their opposition to a union with employees while employees are at work, union access during working hours is greatly restricted (Bronfenbrenner 1994). The law also allows employers to hire permanent replacements for striking workers, so that strikers may not be able to retain their employment. And although the law does not permit employers to discharge workers for attempting to unionize, the law's minimal penalties for such action can make the strategy viable for some employers (Comstock & Fox 1994). Surveys suggest that employer intimidation of unionizing workers is more common among low-wage, minority, and female workers (Comstock & Fox 1994). A number of researchers provide evidence that these provisions in labor law are at least in part responsible for the decline in the labor movement in the US today (Sexton 1991). Given that unions have played a significant role in increasing working-class wages and augmenting the size of the middle class in the US, their decline and the role of state regulation in that decline are likely to be important contributors to rising economic inequality in the US today.

Antagonistic labor–employer relations are not limited to the US, but most Western European nations generally have a history of more harmonious relations. Collective bargaining exists in the UK and France similar to that in the US, although strikes are more common in France when bargaining breaks down (Hodson & Sullivan 2002). In Germany, Norway, and Sweden, workers have greater power in workplace decision-making, through works councils (composed of workers and management) in unified Germany and automonous work groups in the Scandinavian countries (Servais 1998). Arthurs (1998), however, suggests that in most western nations collective bargaining laws are no longer being strengthened as these countries' economies adapt to competitive pressures in the global economy. He points out that only in "newly reconstructed states," such as South Africa, South Korea, and in Central and Eastern European nations, have labor's legal rights been augmented in recent years.

SEE ALSO: Affirmative Action; Labor–Management Relations; Labor Markets; Labor Movement; Law, Economy and; State and Economy; State and Private Sector Employees; Work, Sociology of; Workplace Diversity

REFERENCES AND SUGGESTED READINGS

Arthurs, H. W. (1998) Collective Labour Law of a Global Economy. In: Amicorum, L. & Blanpain, R. (Eds.), *Labour Law and Industrial Relations at the Turn of the Century*. Kluwer Law International, The Hague.

Atleson, J. B. (1983) *Values and Assumptions in American Labor Law*. University of Massachusetts Press, Amherst.

Ben-Israel, R. (2001) Equality and Prohibition of Discrimination in Employment. In: Blanpain, R. & Engels, C. (Eds.), *Comparative Labour Law and Industrial Relations in Industrialized Market Economies*. Kluwer Law International, The Hague.

Bowles, S. & Gintis, H. (1982) The Crisis of Liberal Democratic Capitalism: The Case of the United States. *Politics and Society* 11: 51–93.

Bronfenbrenner, K. L. (1994) Employer Behavior in Certification Elections and First-Contract Campaigns: Implications for Labor Law Reform. In: Friedman, S., Hurd, R. W., Oswald, R. A., & Seeber, R. L. (Eds.), *Restoring the Promise of American Labor Law*. ILR Press, Ithaca, NY.

Burstein, P. (1979) Equal Employment Opportunity Legislation and the Income of Women and Nonwhites. *American Journal of Sociology* 44: 367–91.

Comstock, P. & Fox, M. B. (1994) Employer Tactics and Labor Law Reform. In: Friedman, S., Hurd, R. W., Oswald, R. A., & Seeber, R. L. (Eds.), *Restoring the Promise of American Labor Law*. Industrial Relations Review Press, Ithaca, NY.

Crenshaw, K. (1989) Demarginalizing the Intersection of Race and Sex. *University of Chicago Legal Forum* 139: 139–52.

Edelman, L. B. & Suchman, M. C. (1997) The Legal Environment of Organizations. *Annual Review of Sociology* 23: 479–515.

Gross, J. A. (1995) *Broken Promise: The Subversion of US Labor Relations Policy, 1947–1994*. Temple University Press, Philadelphia.

Guthrie, D. & Roth, L. M. (1999) The States, Courts, and Equal Opportunities for Female CEOs. *Social Forces* 78: 511–42.

Hodson, R. & Sullivan, T. A. (2002) *The Social Organization of Work*. Wadsworth, Belmont, CA.

Konrad, A. M. & Linnehan, F. (1999) Affirmative Action: History, Effects, and Attitudes. In: Powell, G. N. (Ed.), *Handbook of Gender and Work*. Sage, Thousand Oaks, CA.

McCammon, H. (1993a) From Repressive Intervention to Integrative Prevention: The US State's Legal Management of Labor Militancy, 1881–1978. *Social Forces* 71: 569–601.

McCammon, H. (1993b) "Government by Injunction": The US Judiciary and Strike Action in the Late 19th and Early 20th Centuries. *Work and Occupations* 20: 174–204.

McCrone, D. & Hardy, R. (1978) Civil Rights Politics and the Achievement of Racial Economic Equality. *American Journal of Political Science* 22: 1–17.

Padavic, I. & Reskin, B. (2002) *Women and Men at Work*. Pine Forge Press, Thousand Oaks, CA.

Reskin, B. (1998) *The Realities of Affirmative Action in Employment*. American Sociological Association, Washington, DC.

Reskin, B. (2001) Employment Discrimination and Its Remedies. In: Berg, I. & Kalleberg, A. L. (Eds.), *Sourcebook of Labor Markets: Evolving Structures and Processes*. Plenum, New York.

Sears, R. R., Sidanius, J., & Bobo, L. (Eds.) (2000) *Racialized Politics*. University of Chicago Press, Chicago.

Servais, J. (1998) Industrial and Workplace Relations. In: Amicorum, L. & Blanpain, R. (Eds.), *Labour Law and Industrial Relations at the Turn of the Century*. Kluwer Law International, The Hague.

Sexton, P. C. (1991) *The War on Labor and the Left: Understanding America's Unique Conservatism*. Westview Press, Boulder, CO.

Tomaskovic-Devey, D. (1993) *Gender and Racial Inequality at Work*. Industrial Relations Review Press, Ithaca, NY.

Tomlins, C. L. (1985) *The State and the Unions: Labor Relations, Law, and the Organized Labor Movement in America, 1880–1960*. Cambridge University Press, Cambridge.

United Nations Office of Public Information (2000) *Fact Sheet No. 6: Women and the Economy*. United Nations Office of Public Information, New York.

Wallace, M., Rubin, B. A., & Smith, B. T. (1988) American Labor Law: Its Impact on Working-Class Militancy, 1901–1980. *Social Science History* 12: 1–29.

Woodiwiss, A. (1990) *Rights v. Conspiracy: A Sociological Essay on the History of Labor Law in the United States*. Berg, New York.

statistical significance testing

Andrew Poggio and John Poggio

The act of reasoning from factual knowledge or evidence is a process ubiquitous in the lives of individuals. In order to make good decisions and function effectively, one must make distinctions between events that are likely to occur and those that are not. If the morning sky is dark and threatening, one logically concludes that the forecast is for rain and thus one carries an umbrella. A student attends class on the assumption that the professor will be there. Most of the decisions a person makes involve subjective estimates of the probability of various events occurring based on specific observations. Statistical inference uses probabilistic reasoning in a more objective and precise fashion and allows the researcher to account for chance error in drawing inferences from a small set of observed data to a larger set of unobserved data.

Suppose a researcher is interested in the attitude of taxpayers toward the use of state dollars for subsidizing a federally mandated education program. It would not be possible to question every taxpayer in the country, therefore the researcher would want to survey the attitudes of a random sample of taxpayers to infer characteristics about the population. The fundamental goal of statistical inference is simple: based on information obtained from a sample of elements, the researcher draws conclusions about a population by inferring that what is observed in the sample reflects what one might expect to be true in the population. While convenient, when one deals with sample data and not data from the entire population, one cannot describe the population characteristics with complete certainty so any statement about the population is somewhat risky. Had the investigator only surveyed a group of five citizens, for example, the ability to generalize the findings from these few individuals interviewed would be low as the observed difference in attitudes could be due to chance alone with such a small sample.

The adequacy of statistical inferences depends on how well the sample represents the population. If one is uncertain of how representative a sample is, then the individual should be equally uncertain about inferring any results to a specific population. The key to solving problems of statistical inference is to answer the question, "How likely is the occurrence of sample events when the sample is assumed to be representative of the population?" Or, stated another way, "What kind of sample results can be expected from chance alone?" These are questions of probability that are pertinent to the statistical inference process. Thus, one assigns probabilities to the inferences. Probability allows the researcher to make decisions with predetermined levels of confidence.

A hierarchical relationship exists between the research process and the statistical inference process. The research process is all-encompassing and provides the framework for general research activities. Statistical inference imposes a logical reasoning methodology on the research process, resulting in inferences about population characteristics based on sample data. Statistical reasoning and procedures for making inferences about populations from sample data are defined by the hypothesis-testing process and confidence intervals. Statistical hypothesis testing, also known as significance testing, is the most widely used statistical inference approach by behavioral and social science researchers.

HYPOTHESIS TESTING

The goal of statistical inference is to be able to infer something about the truth of a hypothesis without collecting data from an entire population. Hypothesis testing allows the researcher to make this inference, but one must start with some hypothesized value of a population characteristic. In hypothesis testing, the statistical hypothesis identifies an *assumed* value or relationship about a population. The exact population characteristic value is not known, so a hypothesis is formulated about it. One assumes that the hypothesized population value is correct (null hypothesis) until the sample data provide contradictory evidence. The null is rejected if an event can be shown to be *highly unlikely* to occur if the hypothesis is assumed true. That is, if the sample result is contrary to what is expected when the hypothesis is assumed true, then the hypothesis is rejected as a possibility. "Highly unlikely" refers to a specified statistical significance level, or *alpha* (α) level. As one will not be able to be certain of any inferences when sampling from a population, probabilities are assigned to the inferences. The level of significance is set prior to data analysis and is the probability criterion level for rejecting the null hypothesis. For example, if the difference between the sample value and the hypothesized parameter is due to random chance fewer than five times in a hundred (i.e., $\alpha < .05$, or a 5 percent level of significance), then the results are statistically significant. Researchers in the social and behavioral sciences typically select low alpha values (e.g., .01 and .05, most commonly) to protect against concluding that an observed result is true when it could have occurred by chance.

Hypothesis testing is a sequential process that typically involves five steps. Illustrative examples, definitions of certain terminology, formulas, and other discussions regarding the logical aspects of the process facilitate understanding and appreciation of the procedure but are beyond the scope of this entry. Further treatment of the topic is available in many sources as standard statistics texts discuss hypothesis testing in detail (see Blalock 1979; Glass & Hopkins 1996; Shavelson 1996; Levin & Fox 2006).

The hypothesis-testing steps outlined below are described through references to the simple situation of testing differences between group means. It should be noted, however, that the thinking and reasoning behind the steps are the same whether one is dealing with these types of situations or very sophisticated multivariate problems. Hypotheses will differ depending on a particular study (e.g., one may want to hypothesize differences in group means, variances, and proportions, or in terms of correlations), yet the same general steps are employed and the logic guiding the process is the same.

Step 1: Identification of the hypotheses, which are represented statistically using population parameter symbols such as the mean, proportion, indices of variability, and correlation, for example. The convention of labeling the statistical hypothesis to be tested (the null) is H_O. Possible alternative hypotheses are labeled H_A. A null hypothesis is a statement of equality, that is, no difference or no relationship exists between population parameters. The alternative hypothesis, or research hypothesis, is the null's complement, a statement of inequality. The alternative is formed by specifying a direction of the difference from the hypothesized value, so H_A is formed by using the symbols for "does not equal" ($\neq$), "less than" ($<$), or "greater than" ($>$). The alternative does not state a specific alternative value for the population parameter as the process does not test a hypothesized alternative. The following illustration translates a simple research question into verbal and symbolic hypotheses:

Research question: Does assertiveness training help make people more assertive?

Verbal H_O: There exists no difference between the mean level of assertiveness between persons who have received training and those who have not

Symbolic H_O: $\mu_{training} = \mu_{no\ training}$

Verbal H_A: The mean level of assertiveness is greater for people who have received training than for those who have not.

Symbolic H_A: $\mu_{training} > \mu_{no\ training}$

The alternative hypothesis in this example specifies the direction of the difference between the means. This is a one-tail hypothesis, whereas an alternative in which the direction of the difference is not specified is called a two-tailed hypothesis, meaning it can be significant in either direction.

Step 2: Specification of the a priori level of significance (α) to be used, that is, the criteria for rejecting H_O. The extent to which the sample value coincides with expectations is defined by the probability of the sample value occurring as a result of random sampling from the hypothesized population. The researcher can set any probability level as a criterion for rejecting H_O. As decisions based on probabilities will not be correct 100 percent of the time, it is always possible that an error has been made in the statistical inference resulting from the decision on whether to reject H_O. The level of significance defines the degree of improbability deemed necessary to cast doubt on the null hypothesis to warrant its rejection. The probability level chosen as a criterion for rejecting H_O directly affects the potential for making specific kinds of errors in the inferential process. When a criterion level is set for rejecting the null, one is actually identifying the *potential* probability of committing a Type I decision error. For a discussion of these potential errors and a consideration of factors influencing the choice of significance level, see below.

Step 3: Determination of the region(s) of rejection by identifying the critical value resulting from the α level set for testing H_O. The critical region is an area under the normal probability distribution; thus, critical values (z) are obtained from the normal distribution. The area of the curve to the left of the lower critical value and to the right of the upper critical value is the region of rejection. Consistent with the level of significance adopted, it is chosen so that if the obtained value of the statistic (test statistic, *step 4*) falls within the region, rejection of the null hypothesis is indicated. For example, for a two-tailed hypothesis ("does not equal"), a z must exceed 1.96 or be less than –1.96 to be significant at the α = .05 level. The critical value for a one-tail test (α = .01) is 2.33 or –2.33 depending on the direction of the alternative hypothesis.

Step 4: Calculation of the sample statistic value needed to test the null hypothesis. The term *test statistic* refers to the statistic employed in the testing of H_O. In conducting research and engaging in hypothesis testing, a sample is drawn from a population and a summary statistic, such as a mean, is obtained. Direct comparison between the sample value and the hypothesized population value is not an appropriate procedure as the sample data will deviate somewhat from the population characteristics. Rather, one must convert the sample value to a standard test statistic. Common test statistics include z, t, F, and χ^2. The framework for testing statistical hypotheses is similar for each of these tests. While a discussion of each test statistic is beyond the scope of this entry, examples as well as formulas for computing various tests of significance can be obtained from the same sources listed previously.

Step 5: Decision regarding the null hypothesis. The decision process in hypothesis testing is straightforward as it involves a comparison of the observed sample standard score to the critical value determined by the α level. If the test statistic falls in the region of rejection, the null hypothesis is rejected and the inference is made to accept the research hypothesis. If the test statistic does not fall in the critical region, the null fails to be disproved and no inference can be made.

CONFIDENCE INTERVALS

Statistical inference under the significance testing paradigm uses a sampling plan to select a single representative of some population, or a point estimate, which is often a mean. However, there is another approach to statistical inference: interval estimation. Rather than using a single value as a direct estimate of a parameter, interval estimation establishes a range or interval to which a level of confidence (typically 95 or 99 percent) can be attached that the interval contains the parameter. Establishing a range for the population mean based on the sample data with an upper and lower bound intuitively provides more information about the mean; however, in terms of accuracy of the estimate, interval estimation and point estimation are identical as both are based on the same information.

When the value specified by the null hypothesis is not contained in the confidence interval, the result is statistically significant. Standard notation for confidence intervals is to let the confidence level equal the quantity $1 - \alpha$. Thus, if α = .01, the confidence level is .99 or 99 percent. To construct the interval, the upper and lower limits are found using the formulas (when σ is known):

Upper limit $= \overline{X} + (z_{1-\alpha/2})\, \sigma_{\overline{X}}$

Lower limit $= \overline{X} - (z_{1-\alpha/2})\, \sigma_{\overline{X}}$

where $\sigma_{\overline{X}} = \sigma/\sqrt{n}$

The proper interpretation of a confidence interval reflects the sampling concept of the sampling distribution (discussed in the next section): over repeated random samplings of size n, the probability is that $(1 - \alpha)$ percent of all of the confidence intervals that could be constructed around the sample means will contain the population mean. Interval size relates directly to estimate precision: the smaller the range, the more precise the interval estimate of the population mean. Additionally, with greater confidence comes a wider interval, meaning that a 99 percent interval will encompass a wider range than a 95 percent interval. Sample size and the amount of variability in the population affect the precision of interval estimates by affecting the size of the standard error. Both factors improve estimator precision by making the standard error smaller.

SAMPLING DISTRIBUTIONS

Inferences are made from a single event, single experiment, or single set of sample results. Assuming a model of randomness, one is usually interested in determining how probable a result is by chance for the single event or sample. To make this determination, the researcher needs to know something about how the sample outcomes are distributed in general. A *sampling distribution* is the relative frequency distribution of a statistic of all possible samples of size n that could be selected from the population. Fortunately, the characteristics of sampling distributions for various sample statistics have been derived by statistical theory. Sampling distribution characteristics describe theoretical models to indicate a sample statistic's precision in estimating a population parameter of interest.

Different sampling distributions are possible; every sample statistic has one and each is defined by its shape, mean, and standard deviation. Characteristics of a sampling distribution of means, for example, are expected and predictable from mathematical theorems. One such theorem, the *central limit theorem*, identifies

these three characteristics that describe fully the expected distribution of sample means resulting from random samples of size n.

Shape: The sampling distribution approaches normality as sample size increases and for a very large n is approximately normal.

Measure of central tendency: The mean of a sampling distribution of means $(\mu_{\overline{x}})$ for samples of any size n equals the population mean (μ).

Measure of variability: The standard deviation of means $(\sigma_{\overline{x}})$ in a sampling distribution is known as the standard error of the mean, which reflects the amount of variability among the sample means.

Figure 1 illustrates distributions of various-sized random samples. Suppose one were drawing random samples of size 16, 49, and 100 from a population with $\mu = 50$ and $\sigma = 10$. Figure 1 shows how the theoretical sampling distribution of means would appear. As n is increased, the standard error becomes smaller and the more closely the sample means cluster around μ: that is, the sampling distribution approximates a normal curve more closely.

TYPE I/TYPE II ERRORS AND POWER

Earlier, it was said that the α level selected directly affects the potential for making specific kinds of errors in the inferential process. Examining the consequences of one's decisions resulting from hypothesis testing, it is clear that only two decisions regarding H_O can be made: one can reject it or not. Consequences of this decision relate directly to the true state of affairs concerning H_O – whether H_O is true or whether it is false as a description of the population characteristic. Table 1 identifies the consequences (correct decision or error) of rejecting or not rejecting H_O given the truth about the null.

A Type I error – a decision to reject H_O when H_O is true – can only occur when the null hypothesis is true. When α is set as the criterion for rejecting H_O, one is actually identifying the potential probability of concluding that a difference exists where really one does not. Type II error (β) refers to a decision to not

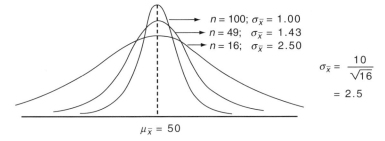

$n = 100;\ \sigma_{\bar{x}} = 1.00$
$n = 49;\ \ \sigma_{\bar{x}} = 1.43$
$n = 16;\ \ \sigma_{\bar{x}} = 2.50$

$$\sigma_{\bar{x}} = \frac{10}{\sqrt{16}}$$

$$= 2.5$$

$\mu_{\bar{x}} = 50$

Figure 1   Distributions of various-sized random samples.

Table 1   Consequences of the hypothesis test

	True State of Affairs	
	H$_o$ *True*	H$_o$ *False*
Decision:	Type I	Type II
Reject H$_o$	Decision Error (α)	Correct Decision ($1 - \beta$)
Do Not Reject H$_o$	Correct Decision ($1 - \alpha$)	Decision Error (β)

reject H_O when H_O is false. In many instances, Type I error is the more severe error as change is likely to be implemented upon finding a significant result. Therefore, one usually sets the probability criterion level for rejecting H_O by chance quite low (typically .05 or lower) in social science research.

If one decides to reject H_O, one of two potential consequences results: an error (Type I) or a correct decision. The α probability level is only relevant and applicable if H_O is really true. If one decides to reject the null and H_O is really false, this is a correct decision. The probability of this outcome is called the *power* of a statistical test (rejecting H_O when the null is truly false) and equals $1 - \beta$. Manipulating several design factors can increase the power when testing the null hypothesis so that if H_O is false, the probability of rejecting it is high. Factors affecting power include: increasing sample size and sampling from a more homogeneous population (reduces standard error resulting in a more precise estimate), using a one-tailed test (a directional hypothesis results in greater power than a two-tailed test), and using a larger α level. The latter factor will result in greater power in testing H_O when H_O is false; however, when

H_O is true, the Type I error rate is larger due to the increased α. Therefore, many researchers are reluctant to use a larger significance level in an attempt to increase power.

MEANINGFUL DIFFERENCES: STATISTICAL VS. PRACTICAL SIGNIFICANCE AND EFFECT SIZE

Statistical significance is often confused with practical or substantive significance. When a null hypothesis is rejected, a difference between two means has been found, but the magnitude or importance of the difference does not necessarily follow. Given large samples, any difference will likely be significant in statistical terms. A misconception of significance testing is that a smaller significance level (α) indicates a stronger treatment effect or that somehow this indicates a more important result. However, a statistically significant outcome does not imply that a difference is large or of substantive importance. To determine if a difference is substantively trivial, researcher judgment (simply examining results) should play a role in addition to available empirical procedures.

In recent years, *effect size* reporting has become a popular empirical method for reporting the magnitude of a difference between means: that is, the size of a statistically significant result. In comparing distributions, the researcher will typically find the standard deviations to be similar, though not identical. In such situations, the standard deviations can be pooled for the purposes of appraising the magnitude of the difference between two means. Effect size (d) is the index that quantifies a mean difference in terms of pooled standard deviation units. One convention defines effect sizes $d = .20$ as small, $d = .50$ moderate, and $d = .80$ large (Cohen 1988). The need for judgment regarding practical significance should not be abandoned at this point as any sample difference is subject to sampling variation, especially in the cases of small sample size.

SEE ALSO: Confidence Intervals; Descriptive Statistics; Effect Sizes; Hypotheses; Measures of Centrality; Quantitative Methods; Statistics

REFERENCES AND SUGGESTED READINGS

Blalock, H. M., Jr. (1979) *Social Statistics*. McGraw-Hill, New York.
Cohen, J. (1988) *Power Analysis for the Behavioral Sciences*. Erlbaum, Hillsdale, NJ.
Glass, G. V. & Hopkins, K. D. (1996) *Statistical Methods in Education and Psychology*, 3rd edn. Allyn & Bacon, Boston.
Levin, J. & Fox, J. A. (2006) *Elementary Statistics in Social Research*, 10th edn. Allyn & Bacon, Needham Heights, MA.
Shavelson, R. J. (1996) *Statistical Reasoning for the Behavioral Sciences*, 3rd edn. Allyn & Bacon, Needham Heights, MA.

statistics

Wayne Gillespie

Censuses are used to enumerate a population and its characteristics. Statistics are mathematical calculations derived from this information or data that are collected and recorded in a numeric or quantitative format. Quantitative methods such as these have been used to describe human populations for hundreds, even thousands, of years. Censuses, or the numbering of people, occurred throughout the ancient world. For example, the Romans conducted censuses in order to determine household income for political (i.e., voting) and taxation purposes. The Han dynasty census from 2 CE China is the earliest, intact census surviving from ancient times; it shows that the population of this dynasty exceeded 57 million. Another notable census is the *Doomsday Book*, which was compiled in 1086 after the Norman invasion of England to determine the amount of wealth obtained from the conquest. Sometimes censuses are conducted on the dead as opposed to the living. In 1662, John Graunt reported the number of deaths in London over the preceding 30 years. He even analyzed mortality trends by gender, season, and location. Graunt eventually published the first "life tables," used to compute life expectancy. In 1693, Edmund Halley refined Graunt's calculations to correctly compute life expectancy (Heyde & Seneta 2001). Censuses of human populations are still conducted throughout the modern world. The first census in the United States was taken in 1790, and censuses are done every 10 years in the US (US Census Bureau 2005).

Censuses are useful in describing an entire population, but they can be costly and time consuming. Probability sampling and statistical analysis allow for information to be generalized from a smaller group of people to the general population from which the group was selected. The primary advantage of statistical analysis is that compiling information on entire populations is not necessary. Rather, by drawing from probability theory, statistics allow researchers to estimate the attributes of populations from the characteristics of samples.

Statistics is an applied mathematical science, but not necessarily a subfield of mathematics; as Moore and Cobb (2000) noted, statistics values mathematical understanding but only as a means to an end, not as an end unto itself. Indeed, statistics has application in many seemingly disparate fields such as biology, education, public health, and sociology. In their text on statistical reasoning in sociology, Mueller et al. defined the concept of statistics in two related manners: "(1) the factual data themselves, such as vital statistics, statistics on trade, production, and the like; and (2) the methods, theories, and techniques by means of which the collected descriptions are summarized and interpreted" (1970: 2).

The discipline of sociology emerged in tandem with the development of the field of statistics in the nineteenth century. Adolphe Quetelet (1796–1874) was a Belgian astronomer who became deeply interested in the application of statistical principles to human populations. He used probability theory to explain the consistency in the number of crimes from year to year, as well as to describe the characteristics of the "average" man (Mueller et al. 1970). For example, Quetelet used statistics to devise the first body mass index, known as the Quetelet Index, which is still used today as an indicator of obesity. Quetelet even organized and presided over the First International Congress of Statistics in 1853 (Heyde & Seneta 2001). According to de Heer et al. (1999), Quetelet's two important contributions toward social statistics were his concept of the average man and his fitting of the normal curve to social phenomena.

Positivism was the first major paradigm in sociology, and it relied on statistical methods, such as those advanced by Quetelet, combined with Auguste Comte's (1798–1857) positive philosophy and later Émile Durkheim's (1858–1917) structural functionalism. This variant of early sociology was concerned with patterning social science after natural science and identifying laws of human behavior and social facts. The positivist approach is inherently quantitative, and it has been criticized for reducing complex social behavior to statistical probabilities and undermining human free will (Mueller et al. 1970). It is this penchant toward determinism that is the greatest criticism of both positivism and statistics.

Current statistical methods rely on laws or rules of probability. The estimation of population parameters from sample statistics is possible through probability theory. Probability is the numerical representation of the likelihood of an expected outcome occurring over multiple trials. It is the ratio of the number of expected outcomes (i.e., successes) to the total number of possible outcomes (Blalock 1972). There are at least three rules of probability that inform statistics (Ritchey 2000). The first rule notes that probabilities are bound between 0 and 1, or between 0 percent and 100 percent. The second rule is called the addition rule. When two mutually exclusive outcomes are expected, then the probability of either of these events occurring is equal to the sum of the probabilities of the individual outcomes. However, when these events are not mutually exclusive, the probability of either the first or second outcome occurring is equal to the sum of their separate probabilities with the probability of their joint occurrence subtracted. The third probability rule is known as the multiplication rule. When two outcomes are statistically independent, the occurrence of the first event does not influence or predict the second. When two outcomes are statistically independent, the probability of both events occurring at the same time is equal to the product of their separate probabilities. However, when two outcomes are not statistically independent, the probability of both events occurring simultaneously is the same as the product of the probability of one event and the conditional probability of the other.

These rules of probability are important to statistics because many statistical tests assume that there is independence between events or outcomes, and that conditional probabilities do not need to be used. As Blalock pointed out, "it is assumed that there is independence of selection within a sample – the choice of one individual having no bearing on the choice of another individual to be included in the sample" (1972: 142). Random sampling, where every subject has an equal chance of being selected into the sample, is required to meet the assumption of independence.

Probability theory is used to produce sampling distributions. Sampling distributions are infinite since they involve repeated sampling (i.e., random samples repeatedly drawn from a population). A sampling distribution is another mathematical representation derived from repeated sampling that describes all possible event outcomes and the probability of each one (Ritchey 2000). It is important to note that sampling distributions are hypothetical, theoretical distributions, and researchers never attain a sampling distribution through empirical trials. Yet, when statistics are calculated for each of these samples and then graphed, it results in a bell-shaped or normal distribution. The normal distribution is one of the fundamental concepts in statistics, and it is expressed as the central limit theorem. According to this principle, regardless of the shape of the raw score distribution of a characteristic measured at an interval or ratio level, the sampling distribution of means will be more or less normal in shape as the sample size increases.

Probability and sampling provide the theoretical basis for statistics from a mathematical perspective. However, many of these rules and laws are implicitly assumed. The field of social statistics, in practice, is probably more concerned with the levels of measurement and the various types of statistical tests rather than the laws and rules that make such analysis possible in the first place (Blalock 1974). Indeed, the level at which social phenomena are measured dictates the type of statistical test that can be calculated. Once a characteristic is measured, and the characteristic shows variation, then it is called a variable. Variables are measured at four levels: nominal, ordinal, interval, and ratio. Ratio measurement is the most precise because the distance between values is both equal and known, and variables measured at the ratio level may contain a true zero, which signifies the total absence of the attribute. As with variables expressed at the ratio level, interval-level variables are continuous, and the distance between values is also both known and constant. However, for variables measured at the interval level, no true zero point exists; the zero in interval-level data is arbitrary. Variables measured at the nominal and ordinal levels are categorical. With ordinal-level data, the response categories are both mutually exclusive and rank-ordered. The categories of a variable measured at the nominal level have no relationship with one another; they simply signify the presence or absence of a particular quality. It is important to note that these levels of measurement are cumulatively related to one another; for example, a ratio scale possesses all the properties of an interval scale, included in an interval scale are all the properties of an ordinal scale, and the ordinal scale has all the properties of the nominal level.

Blalock (1972: 21) observed that "the use of a particular mathematical model presupposes that a certain level of measurement has been attained." Statistical tests are generally univariate, bivariate, or multivariate in nature. Univariate statistics involve the description of one variable. If the variable was measured at a nominal level, then it is possible to report the mode (i.e., the most commonly occurring value), proportions, percentages, and ratios. When the variable is measured at the ordinal level, it becomes possible to calculate medians, quartiles, deciles, and quartile deviations. Then, at the interval and ratio levels of measurement, univariate procedures include means (i.e., the arithmetic average), medians (i.e., the midpoint), variances, and standard deviations. Measures of central tendency include the mode, median, and mean; measures of dispersion or the spread of the values for a given variable are typically reported as a quartile, percentile, variance, or standard deviation.

Bivariate statistics involve tests of association between two variables. Again, the level of measurement determines the appropriate bivariate statistic. For example, when both the dependent variable (i.e., the effect or the characteristic that is being affected by another variable) and the independent variable (i.e., the cause or the characteristic affecting the outcome) are measured at a nominal level, then the chi-square statistic is most commonly used. Unfortunately, the chi-square test only reveals if two variables are related; in order to determine the strength of a bivariate relationship involving two nominal variables, other statistics such as lambda or phi are used. When the dependent variable is measured at an interval or ratio level, and the independent variable is categorical (i.e., nominal or ordinal), then it becomes necessary to compare means across the categories of the independent variable. When the independent variable is dichotomous, the t-test statistic is used, and when the independent variable contains more than two categories, an analysis of variance (ANOVA) must be used. When both variables are measured at an interval or ratio level, then statistical tests based on the equation for a line, such as Pearson's correlation and least-squares regression, become appropriate procedures. Multivariate statistics often test for the relationship between two variables while holding constant a number of other variables; this introduces the principle of statistical control.

Examples of multivariate techniques include multivariate analysis of variance, multiple linear and logistic regression, factor analysis, path analysis, structural equation modeling, hierarchical linear modeling, and meta-analysis (Grimm & Yarnold 1998).

Blalock (1972) identified five steps that all statistical tests have in common. First, assumptions concerning the population and the ability of the generalizations from the sample must be made. The assumptions also influence the formal stating of hypotheses (e.g., the null hypothesis is a statement of no association, and the research hypothesis is the alternative to the null). Then, the theoretical sampling distribution must be obtained or the probability distribution of the statistic must be rendered. Next, an appropriate significance level and critical region for the statistic must be selected. Fourth, the test statistic must be calculated. Lastly, based on the magnitude of the test statistic and its associated significance, a decision about the acceptance or rejection of hypotheses must be made. In many ways, hypothesis testing is the apex of statistical methods because it combines statistical theory with empirical, mathematical calculations to describe social phenomena and determine relationships between social facts.

SEE ALSO: ANOVA (Analysis of Variance); Demographic Data: Censuses, Registers, Surveys; Descriptive Statistics; Factor Analysis; Hierarchical Linear Models; Hypotheses; Measures of Centrality; Meta-Analysis; Multivariate Analysis; Path Analysis; Positivism; Quantitative Methods; Random Sample; Regression and Regression Analysis; Statistical Significance Testing; Structural Equation Modeling

REFERENCES AND SUGGESTED READINGS

Blalock, H. M. (1972) *Social Statistics*, 2nd edn. McGraw-Hill, New York.

Blalock, H. M. (Ed.) (1974) *Measurement in the Social Sciences: Theories and Strategies*. Aldine, Chicago.

de Heer, W., de Leeuw, E. D., & van der Zouwen, J. (1999) Methological Issues in Survey Research: A Historical Review. *Bulletin de Méthodologie Sociologique* 64: 25–48.

Grimm, L. G. & Yarnold, P. R. (1998) *Reading and Understanding Multivariate Statistics*. American Psychological Association, Washington, DC.

Heyde, C. C. & Seneta, E. (Eds.) (2001) *Statisticians of the Centuries*. Springer Verlag, New York.

Moore, D. S. & Cobb, G. W. (2000) Statistics and Mathematics: Tension and Cooperation. *American Mathematical Monthly* 107(7): 615–30.

Mueller, J. H., Schuessler, K. F., & Costner, H. L. (1970) *Statistical Reasoning in Sociology*, 2nd edn. Houghton Mifflin, Boston.

Ritchey, F. J. (2000) *The Statistical Imagination: Elementary Statistics for the Social Sciences*. McGraw-Hill, New York.

US Census Bureau (2005) Facts About the Census Bureau. Online. www.census.gov/main/www/aboutus.html.

status

Vasiliki Kantzara

Status, originally a Latin word, means state of affairs, condition of a person as defined by law and in social sciences; it denotes standing in society. In sociology, the notion of status or social status designates location and position of collectivities – communities, groups, or strata – in the social hierarchy of honor and prestige. Positions are distinguished from one another in terms of differentiated duties and rights, immunities and privileges, and usually are associated with a lifestyle or a consumption pattern. In their turn, these distinguishing traits are attributed a hierarchical value that generally represents the scale of social worth in society.

Status as a concept denotes both the evaluation process entailed in achieving a position and the granted location in the social hierarchy. Individuals attain status mainly in two ways: status is achieved and is ascribed (Linton 1936). It is achieved on the basis of personal effort, which is represented in educational titles and income earnings. Status is ascribed on the basis of characteristics that seem given, such as a person's age, ethnicity, or gender. In addition, status has an interrelational aspect, that is, the honor or prestige achieved needs to be granted or attributed so that one may argue that a high status is truly attained. Groups and individuals strive to maintain or increase their acquired status, while they may strongly resist status loss.

THEORETICAL FOUNDATION OF STATUS

The term status captured the imagination of social scientists and particular sociologists, for they thought that the term could explain the constitution of social order and the position and relation of individuals to this order. The latter is emphasized in Linton's approach, the former in Weber's.

Ralph Linton, a social anthropologist in the US, employed the term status in the 1930s, referring to status as "a position in a particular pattern" (1936: 113). The status of an individual is, for Linton, the "sum total" of all the statuses a person occupies. A status is distinct from the person and it is defined as a collection of duties and rights, which form the static aspect of a position. When duties and rights are put into effect, they constitute the "dynamic" part of status, that is, the role involved in a position. These obligations and rights derive primarily from custom rather than law. Until about that time, the term status was largely employed in a legal sense, that is, rights and duties conferred to a person by law. Status in Linton's sense departs from this definition as the social position of an individual is viewed in terms of the degree of attributed prestige, esteem, and respect rather than in terms of possessing wealth and power (Zelditch 1968: 250).

Max Weber defined status as "a quality of honor or a lack of it" (1974: 405). Honor is furthermore differentially attributed, constituting a system of social stratification that is based on custom and communal values. In Weber's view, status groups differ in an important respect from classes. Classes are based upon the economic order, being an essential part of this order (pp. 180–1), and status groups are based on and are part of the social order, which is formed by customs and legal arrangements.

Status groups may be tight or less tight – "amorphous" – communities and are distinguished entities, as they are characterized by a common consumption pattern and a lifestyle. These social groups, furthermore, claim rights and privileges for their members and strive to increase their status, while defending acquired rights. In this, status groups may come into conflict with other social groups or may exercise a closure strategy by controlling, for instance, the admission of new members to their ranks.

Status groups are in Weber's view part of the stratification system and are "knitted" into the economic order. In the long run, status groups and classes are interlinked and interconnected: a highly valued status group will acquire wealth and power, and a wealthy class will eventually acquire a high status (Weber 1974: 180–94; Scott 1996). Later, Benoit (1966), drawing on Weber, described this tendency as a "status conversion mechanism."

Weber's approach has been significant for the social stratification paradigm in social sciences. In the US, his approach has been influential, albeit without the social conflict component of his theory (Turner 1988). Linton's approach is important in that it has laid the basis for approaching status at the level of individuals. Subsequent theorizing and research on status throughout the twentieth century focused on varied aspects and dimensions of the term. From these researches and theories three broad areas can be discerned. First, a considerable amount of research has investigated the importance and relevance of social status to stratification by exploring the status of occupations. Second, status has been examined in relation to interaction and its outcomes within groups, exploring inequality in face-to-face interaction. This approach is known as the expectation states theory. Third, status consistency or inconsistency has been the focus of some approaches that sought to explain variation of holding different statuses at an individual level.

SOCIAL STATUS AND OCCUPATIONAL STRATIFICATION

In social sciences, it is viewed that in modern western societies the status of an individual derives primarily from one's occupation, as it is considered the main avenue of acquiring immunities, privileges, honor, and wealth, and is an indicator of authority and power. Its significance becomes evident in some studies that relate achieved status and occupation to levels of self-esteem.

The significance of occupation in determining an individual's position in the social hierarchy underlies the paradigm that focuses on occupational stratification. In this paradigm, it was thought that measuring the standing of occupations would provide an answer to questions and issues relating to social stratification and upward social mobility (Bendix & Lipset 1966). It has been largely assumed that achievement in western societies can overcome ascription and barriers posed, for instance, by social origins or gender (Treiman 1977). Ideally, in an open society, supposedly even the highest positions are open to every aspiring individual worthy of such a position.

Research in this area was directed to exploring occupational status or prestige (Reiss 1961; Treiman 1977) by measuring the standing of occupations. The terms status, social status, occupational status, and occupational prestige are used interchangeably and sometimes synonymously (Kantzara 2001). Research has been mainly quantitative and the main criteria or "variables" employed are education, occupation, and income, best known as the socioeconomic index.

The occupational stratification paradigm has produced numerous indices that depict the "images" and the hierarchy of occupational status as well as the changes it undergoes. This variation within a country as well as in comparative studies has made it difficult to sustain the main argument that social stratification is "invariant," obeying "laws" that the sociologist has only to uncover. Certain tenets and arguments of this paradigm have been criticized and challenged (Burawoy 1977), while research from this perspective continues to this day.

STATUS AND GROUP INTERACTION

Status order within groups is the primary focus of the expectation states theory or status characteristics theory. This theory constitutes a theoretical program comprising different but related research programs. It is based on the work of Bales and others, who found that in small task-oriented groups, inequalities could be observed in relation to members' participation and influence (cited in Berger & Zelditch 1998: 97–8). Expectation states theory sought to elaborate on these findings and explore some of the conditions in which a status order emerges or is maintained. Concepts such as status characteristics, status organizing processes, and path of relevance are employed in order to analyze patterns of evaluation and status order in small task-oriented groups (Berger & Zelditch 1998; Ridgeway 1992).

Research has focused more particularly on the status characteristics of individuals, such as their age, ethnicity, and gender and the relation of these traits to judging individuals' degree of competence, quality of work performance, or the degree of influence these actors exercise in making decisions in small groups. The research results are based on experiments conducted in these groups. There is sufficient evidence that the assumed status of individuals plays a major role in the evaluation of competence and the quality of one's work performance; that is, the higher the status, the higher the positive evaluation of work performance regardless of whether it is qualitatively better. States expectation theory is an ongoing research project that has already passed through various stages within the disciplines of social psychology and sociology (Berger & Zelditch 1998).

STATUS CRYSTALLIZATION OR CONSISTENCY AND INCONSISTENCY

Focusing on an individual level, some authors have referred to the phenomenon of status consistency or inconsistency. These terms broadly denote that an individual's achieved status in one area converges or on the contrary may differ from ascribed or achieved status in another area.

In cases where status in one area converges with status in another, some authors suggest that an individual's status is crystallized or consistent. Lenski's approach attempted to formulate this proposition with a mathematical equation (cited in Smith 1996). The equation has been challenged to a great extent, but not the content of the argument. Lenski's work is based on that of Benoit, who discusses status equilibration and status conversion mechanisms, drawing on Weber's approach. The terms denote that different "types" of status tend to reach a common level; that is, an individual's high status in the economic hierarchy will match the achieved status in the "political hierarchy" and this in turn will be equivalent to the status in the "hierarchy of prestige" (Benoit 1966: 80).

Merton (1966), who takes up Linton's definition of status and role, suggests that when an individual puts into effect different roles that have conflicting obligations, we witness a status inconsistency. Merton suggests that society usually develops adaptive mechanisms to mitigate these conflicts. In addition, individuals may avoid role conflicts by exercising "self selection," which means that they usually avoid occupying positions that cause role conflicts.

Hughes, on the other hand, discusses status contradictions and dilemmas people face when they interact with those who are in a status-inconsistent position. Such cases, Hughes suggests, can be seen in occupations where the expected traits of professionals do not match with those in reality: a "black" doctor and a woman engineer were common examples in his time of status dilemmas. The solutions given include segregation, in two ways: (1) the individuals who differ are "put out of sight," so that, for instance, clients or co-workers do not come into contact with them; (2) the individuals in question are directed to occupations that are thought to suit best their race and gender, that is, a "black" sociologist will eventually teach "race studies" and a woman engineer will design household appliances (Hughes 1971: 142–9). This approach also touches upon the issue of the interrelational aspect of status – to attain it, it needs to be granted (Kantzara 2001) – and "status passage."

CURRENT RESEARCH

Status both in Weber's and in Linton's sense has in a variety of ways greatly influenced theorizing in social sciences in general and in sociology in particular. Since the 1970s, the concept has also been increasingly employed to document the position and relative ranking or standing of disadvantaged social groups on the basis of gender or ethnicity. In sociology of education, for instance, studies from a Weberian perspective explore and explain the changes in educational systems as an outcome of conflicts between rival status groups aspiring to control education and access to certain benefits. Additionally, the term status is employed to explain advantage or underachievement in education. Currently, however, status is mostly employed descriptively as shorthand for social position, as for instance women's status, or indicating a current state of affairs, as in the term health status.

It seems that status as a term has ceased to be at the center of theorizing in social sciences. However, the relevance of the concept for investigating the constitution of society has not diminished in importance. Status could be employed as an analytic concept in exploring and explaining social hierarchy, stratification, or inequality, which is still very relevant in the face of such social tendencies as increased diversity on the one hand and homogenization on the other. The relation of status to social identity and citizenship is a promising area of research as well. The latter relation is apparent in cases where various or competing social groups pursue and demand equal rights, and most importantly demand the application of equal rights for their members. In practice, it is witnessed that depending on context, prestige and standing still largely define the unequal distribution of rewards, whether financial, political, or cultural, and unequal access to social goods and services.

SEE ALSO: Class, Status, and Power; Ethnicity; Inequality/Stratification, Gender; Role; Status Attainment; Status Construction Theory; Status Passages; Weber, Max

REFERENCES AND SUGGESTED READINGS

Bendix, R. & Lipset, S. M. (Eds.) (1966) *Class, Status, and Power: Social Stratification in Comparative Perspective*, 2nd edn. Free Press, New York.

Benoit, E. (1966 [1944]) Status, Status Types, and Status Interrelations. In: Biddle, B. J. & Thomas, E. J. (Eds.), *Role Theory: Concepts and Research*. J. Wiley, New York, pp. 77–80.

Berger, J. & Zelditch Jr., M. (Eds.) (1998) *Status, Power and Legitimacy: Strategies and Theories*. Transaction Publishers, New Brunswick, NJ.

Burawoy, M. (1977) Social Structure, Homogenization, and "The Process of Status Attainment in the United States and Great Britain." *American Journal of Sociology* 82(5): 1031–42.

Hughes, E. C. (1971) *The Sociological Eye: Selected Papers.* Aldine-Atherton, Chicago.

Kantzara, V. (2001) An Act of Defiance, an Act of Honour: Gender and Professional Prestige among Teachers in Secondary Education in Greece. PhD Thesis, University of Utrecht.

Linton, R. (1936) *The Study of Man.* Appleton-Century, New York.

Merton, R. K. (1966) The Social Dynamics of Status-Set and Status Sequences. In: Biddle, B. J. & Thomas, E. J. (Eds.), *Role Theory: Concepts and Research.* J. Wiley, New York, pp. 74–6.

Reiss, A. J., Jr. (with Duncan, O. D., Hatt, P. K., & North, C. C.) (1961) *Occupations and Social Status.* Free Press of Glencoe, New York.

Ridgeway, C. L. (Ed.) (1992) *Gender, Interaction, and Inequality,* Springer-Verlag, New York.

Scott, J. (1996) *Stratification and Power: Structures of Class, Status and Command.* Polity Press, Cambridge.

Smith, R. D. (1996) The Career of Status Crystallization: A Sociological Odyssey. *Sociological Review Online* 1(3): 37.

Treiman, D. J. (1977) *Occupational Prestige in Comparative Perspective.* Academic Press, London.

Turner, B. S. (1988) *Status.* Open University Press, Milton Keynes.

Weber, M. (1974 [1948]) *From Max Weber: Essays in Sociology.* Trans. & Ed. H. H. Gerth & C. Wright Mills. Routledge & Kegan Paul, London.

Zelditch, M., Jr. (1968) Social Status. In: Sills, D. L. (Ed.), *International Encyclopedia of Social Sciences* 15: 250–7.

status attainment

Claudia Buchmann

Status attainment research begun by sociologists in the United States more than three decades ago laid the foundation for the study of the transmission of socioeconomic advantage from one generation to the next (also called intergenerational social mobility). Status attainment research seeks to understand how characteristics of an individual's family background (also called socioeconomic origins) relate to his or her educational attainment and occupational status in society. It developed a methodology – usually path analysis and multiple regression techniques with large survey data sets – to investigate the intergenerational transmission of status.

In the classic study, *The American Occupational Structure* (1967), Peter Blau and Otis Dudley Duncan used national-level data obtained from the 1962 Current Population Survey from the US Census Bureau and presented a basic model of the stratification process in which father's education and occupational status explain son's educational attainment, and all three variables, in turn, explain son's first job and subsequent occupational attainment. They found that the effect of son's education on son's occupational attainment was much larger than the effect of father's occupation on son's occupational attainment; thus they concluded that in the United States in the mid-twentieth century, achievement was more important than ascription in determining occupational status.

David Featherman and Robert Hauser replicated the Blau and Duncan study in their book *Opportunity and Change* (1978), and found many of the same results. They found evidence of mobility both within generations (intragenerational mobility) and between generations (intergenerational mobility). Most mobility was rather short in distance and occurred primarily in the middle of the occupational hierarchy. They also found more upward mobility than downward mobility. Combining the findings of Blau and Duncan, Featherman and Hauser, and follow-up studies, status attainment research has determined that there has been a long-term decline in the importance of family background in determining an individual's occupational status.

Around the same time that Blau and Duncan were writing *The American Occupational Structure,* William Sewell and colleagues at the University of Wisconsin began publishing papers that addressed questions regarding the relative impacts of family background and schooling on subsequent educational and occupational attainments (Sewell et al. 1969). A notable aspect of the "Wisconsin model" of status attainment was its focus on social psychological factors, such as aspirations and motivation, in conjunction with family socioeconomic status in determining student achievement. In this regard, the Wisconsin model attempted to specify the mediating mechanisms by which family origins influenced individual educational and occupational outcomes. The Wisconsin model of status attainment demonstrated that "significant others," including parents, friends, and teachers, strongly affect the educational and occupational expectations of male high school students. Subsequent research found that peers and parents help shape students' ambitions and attitudes toward schooling, both of which are mediating factors in later educational attainment and achievement. Generally, parents are more influential as definers of behavior while peers are important as both modelers and definers of behavior. Most of these studies include controls for socioeconomic status, parental education, and the student's academic ability or achievement, all of which have the effect of increasing aspirations. While Blau and Duncan specified father's occupation and education as separate influences, the Wisconsin researchers usually combined these measures, along with mother's education and family income, into a single measure of socioeconomic status. Despite these measurement differences, both models concluded that socioeconomic status strongly determined educational attainment.

The now classic research by Blau and Duncan and the Wisconsin model of status attainment established a framework for the study of family background on educational and occupational attainment in a wide range of contexts. By the early 1980s, more than 500 papers had attempted to replicate or extend their basic findings (Campbell 1983).

Human capital models in economics, in which family background and schooling decisions determined education and earnings outcomes, also contributed to this growing field.

While some studies applied the status attainment model to nationally representative samples in the United States, others examined status attainment processes in very different countries and contexts. Building on the foundation laid by status attainment research in the United States, studies have examined the role of social origins in determining educational and occupational status and mobility in a range of countries; other research has investigated how intergenerational mobility changes over time with large societal changes, such as the expansion of formal schooling, the industrialization of society, or the transition from socialism to capitalism.

Some comparative status attainment research sought to examine another hypothesis offered by Blau and Duncan. On the basis of their findings from the United States, Blau and Duncan predicted that as societies industrialize, achievement processes become more important and ascriptive processes become less important in determining educational and occupational attainment. They tested this hypothesis for the United States by comparing the experiences of different birth cohorts but they found no clear trend over time. Donald Treiman (1970) expanded upon these ideas to provide a detailed explanation of the mechanisms by which industrialization should promote greater mobility. As societies develop, urbanization, mass communication, and industrialization should lead to greater social openness and a shift from particularistic to universalistic bases of achievement. As a result, the direct influence of father's occupational status on son's occupational status, as well as father's educational and occupational status on son's educational attainment, should decline, while the direct influence of son's educational attainment on his occupational status should increase. During the 1970s and 1980s, researchers set out to test these propositions. Most studies examined historical or regional differences within a single society and few found support for the industrialism thesis. To date, the evidence regarding how the impact of social origins on educational and occupational attainment varies with industrialization remains inconclusive, largely due to the lack of cross-national survey data for a wide range of countries.

International studies of social mobility have contributed greatly to our understanding of how family socioeconomic status shapes educational and occupational outcomes. The influence of the Blau–Duncan model is clearly evident in this international research; most studies conceptualize socioeconomic status as either father's education and occupation or a composite measure of these and other family background factors. Some researchers have had to alter this approach due to data limitations or considerations of the local context, but still, the systematic approach to the measurement of family background is striking. As a result of these efforts, status attainment models now exist for many nations in all regions of the world.

In status attainment research, occupational status is typically measured via scales that have been developed to generalize the prestige associated with occupations across a wide range of societies. The earliest of these was the Socioeconomic Index (SEI) scale formulated by Duncan for the United States and subsequently modified by other researchers for other countries. Comparative stratification researchers have devoted considerable effort to developing internationally comparative scales of occupational prestige and testing their reliability cross-culturally. Two of these scales, the Standard International Occupational Prestige (SIOP) scale and the International Socioeconomic Index (ISEI) of occupational status, have been used extensively in international research. Although most prior research relied on paternal occupational status in constructing this measure, recent empirical evidence indicates that mother's occupational status has a strong impact on educational outcomes, independent of father's education and occupational status. Such findings, combined with the increasing prevalence of women's full-time labor force participation throughout the world, suggest that mother's occupational status should be included as a measure of family background in future status attainment research. The inclusion of mother's education has been more common, perhaps because early status attainment research indicated that mother's education had positive effects on children's schooling, net of father's education and occupational status. In many cases, maternal and paternal education are highly correlated and researchers use one or the other as a measure of parental education. In contexts where mothers spend more time with their children or where males are typically absent from the household, it is reasonable to expect that mother's education should have a stronger impact than father's education, and researchers have used mother's education as the measure for parental education. Another strategy has been to use the sum of both parents' schooling.

As in the case of occupational status, scales have been developed for measuring educational attainment with the goal of ensuring comparability cross-nationally. CASMIN and ISCED are two such scales. The International Standard Classification of Education (ISCED) was originally developed by UNESCO and is regularly used by UNESCO and other international organizations for reporting national education statistics. The CASMIN categories were developed as part of a project known as "Comparative Analysis of Social Mobility in Industrial Nations." Walter Mueller and his colleagues at the University of Mannheim, Germany developed CASMIN with the express purpose of facilitating comparative research on social stratification and mobility. ISCED and CASMIN are similar in that they focus on the levels of education completed: elementary, secondary, and tertiary education, and specify some subdivisions at each level. The CASMIN scale goes a step further to distinguish general or academic credentials from vocational credentials. These scales have facilitated international comparisons of educational systems and educational stratification.

Status attainment research constitutes one of the largest bodies of empirical research in the study of social stratification. It reshaped the study of social mobility by focusing attention on how aspects of individuals' socioeconomic origins relate to their educational attainment and occupational status in society. Nonetheless, critics have noted several limitations with this line of research. First, status attainment research does a better job of explaining the social mobility for white males than females or minorities. Second, this line of research has limited explanatory power because, even for white males, status attainment models can explain only about half of the variance in occupational attainment. This indicates that even the most complex status attainment models still do not get very close to approximating the even more complex reality of the attainment process. Third, in its focus on individual characteristics, status attainment research has tended to neglect the role of structural factors in determining individual educational and occupational outcomes. Changes in the economy or changes in the opportunity structure of occupations caused by large-scale policy changes (e.g., equal employment opportunity policies) are just two examples of factors that create societal shifts that can impact status attainment processes at the individual level. Since the 1990s, more research has expanded status attainment research to account for such social structural or organizational factors that may play a role in individual mobility.

SEE ALSO: Capital: Economic Cultural, and Social; Intergenerational Mobility: Methods of Analysis; Mobility: Horizonal and Vertical; Mobility: Intergenerational and Intragenerational; Occupational Mobility; Status

REFERENCES AND SUGGESTED READINGS

Blau, P. M. & Duncan, O. D. (1967) *The American Occupational Structure*. Wiley, New York.
Campbell, R. (1983) Status Attainment Research: End of the Beginning or Beginning of the End? *Sociology of Education* 56: 47–62.
Featherman, D. L. & Hauser, R. M. (1978) *Opportunity and Change*. Academic Press, New York.
Sewell, W. H., Haller, A. O., & Portes, A. (1969) The Educational and Early Occupational Attainment Process. *American Sociological Review* 34: 82–92.
Treiman, D. J. (1970) Industrialization and Social Stratification. In: Laumann, E. (Ed.), *Social Stratification: Research and Theory for the 1970s*. Bobbs-Merrill, Indianapolis, pp. 207–34.

status construction theory

Cecilia L. Ridgeway

Status construction theory focuses on the collective development of widely shared status beliefs about apparently nominal social differences among people, such as sex or ethnicity (Ridgeway 1991; Webster & Hysom 1998; Ridgeway & Erickson 2000). Status beliefs associate greater respect and greater competence at socially valued tasks with people in one category of a social difference (e.g., men, whites) than with those in another category of that difference (women, people of color). A typical reaction to the recognition of social difference is for people in each category to assume that their own group is "better." When status beliefs develop about a recognized social difference, however, they transform simple difference into an evaluative hierarchy so that the distinction

becomes a status characteristic in society. The distinctive aspect of status beliefs is that those in the social category that is favored by the status beliefs and those in the less favored category both come to hold similar beliefs that "most people" view the favored group as better than the other group. Status construction theory describes one set of processes by which such beliefs could come to be accepted as a matter of social reality by those they disadvantage and by those they advantage. In this way, beliefs become roughly consensual in society. The theory claims that the processes it describes are sufficient to produce widely shared status beliefs but are not the only way such beliefs might develop in a society or collectivity.

Status construction theory developed in the 1990s in the context of two well-established bodies of theory and research. Several decades of research on status hierarchies among individuals in groups, especially research associated with expectation states theory, had documented that interpersonal influence and deference are largely driven by differences in the status characteristics of the individuals involved (Berger et al. 1977). How social differences became status characteristics, however, was unknown.

While this micro tradition of theory and research examined status between individuals, macro approaches to status, beginning with Max Weber, focused on status as a relationship between social groups in society. Status between individuals and status between groups are linked by the widely held status beliefs that both represent the social standing of groups in society and cause group differences to manifest as status characteristics in interpersonal settings. Status construction theory attempted to connect these two bodies of work by offering an account of the development of status beliefs about social differences.

The theory is a micro–macro theory that focuses on the aggregate effects that emerge from interpersonal encounters between socially different actors when these encounters have been framed and constrained by macrostructural conditions. The theory takes as a starting point the existence of a socially recognized but not yet consensually evaluated categorical distinction. An assumed scope condition is that members from the groups created by the distinction are to some degree interdependent in that they must regularly cooperate to achieve what they want or need. Under these conditions, status construction theory, drawing on its roots in expectation states theory, argues that the local contexts in which people from different categories encounter one another become arenas for the creation, spread, and maintenance of status beliefs about categorical difference.

The theory's basic arguments can be summarized as follows (Ridgeway & Erickson 2000). In interdependent encounters between categorically different people, interpersonal status hierarchies are likely to develop among the participants just as they do in most cooperative, goal-oriented encounters. Such interpersonal influence hierarchies develop implicitly, through multiple small behaviors that the participants rarely scrutinize. Since the actual origins of their influence hierarchy are obscure to them but their categorical difference is salient, the theory argues that there is some chance that the participants will associate their apparent difference in esteem and competence in the situation with their categorical difference. If the same association is repeated for them in subsequent intercategory encounters, the theory argues that it will eventually induce them to form generalized status beliefs about the categorical distinction.

Once people form such status beliefs, they carry them to their next encounters with those from the other group and act on them there. By treating categorically different others according to the status belief, belief holders induce at least some of the others to take on the belief as well. In effect, they "teach" the others the beliefs by acting on it. This in turn creates a diffusion process that has the potential to spread the new status belief widely in the population.

Whether the new status belief does in fact spread widely and which categorical group it casts as higher status depend on the structural conditions that shape the terms on which people from each group encounter one another (Ridgeway 1991; Ridgeway & Balkwell 1997). Of central interest is whether structural conditions result in an unequal distribution between the groups of some factor such as material resources or technology that is helpful in gaining influence in intercategory encounters. The unequal distribution of such a "biasing factor" means that in intercategory encounters, there

will be a systematically greater likelihood that people from the group with more of the factor will emerge as the influential actors in the situation compared to people from the group with less of the factor. As a consequence, the set of intercategory encounters in the population will continually foster more status beliefs favoring the structurally advantaged group than favoring the other categorical group. As these beliefs spread and diffuse through future encounters, beliefs favoring the structurally advantaged group will eventually overwhelm counterbeliefs and become nearly consensual in the population. From this reasoning, the theory argues that if a biasing factor is unequally distributed between categorical groups, status beliefs favoring the structurally advantaged group will emerge and spread to become widely shared in the population.

As this description shows, the theory consists of two sets of arguments. The first addresses processes through which participants form status beliefs in micro-level encounters between categorically different actors. The second set of arguments addresses the role of structural conditions in determining the aggregate consequences of belief formation in micro encounters.

In its initial formulation, status construction theory focused on one specific structural condition, a correlation between superior material resources and membership in a particular categorical group (Ridgeway 1991). Since Max Weber, sociologists have observed that a common precondition for the development of status beliefs about two social groups is that people in one group become, on average, richer in material resources than those from another. In its first statement, the theory delineated a set of processes through which this precondition gives rise to status beliefs about the group distinction. This statement brought together Peter Blau's (1977) theory of how social difference affects the likelihood that people encounter one another with expectation states theory's arguments about the influence hierarchies that would be likely to develop in encounters of various social composition. The analysis shows that "doubly dissimilar" encounters between people who differ in both material resources and the categorical distinction are especially important for the systematic development of status beliefs.

Although other intercategory encounters may induce status beliefs, it is only in doubly dissimilar encounters that material resources systematically bias the development of influence hierarchies so that these encounters reliably produce more status beliefs favoring the materially advantaged group. Doubly dissimilar encounters are the least common type of intercategory encounter according to Blau's association arguments. However, through the diffusion process, these encounters feed a steady surplus of beliefs favoring the materially advantaged group into the population. Such beliefs overwhelm the cultural confusion of conflicting local beliefs, allowing widely shared status beliefs to emerge.

Two sorts of evidence support the initial formulation of the theory. Laboratory experiments suggest that people do form status beliefs favoring the materially advantaged group after two repeated doubly dissimilar encounters, as the theory predicts (Ridgeway et al. 1998). In these experiments, participants formed beliefs that most people would see the typical member of the materially advantaged group as higher status, more respected, and more competent, but not as socially considerate, as those in the other group. Participants formed these beliefs even when the beliefs cast their own categorical group as less respected and competent, although more considerate, than the other group.

In addition, computer simulations of the diffusion process provide logical support for the theory's arguments about how structural conditions shape the aggregate consequences of encounters. These simulations show that the emergence of nearly consensual status beliefs would be a logical consequence under a variety of assumptions about the strength of the correlation between categorical membership and superior resources, the strength of homophily bias in associations, and the relative sizes of the categorical groups (Ridgeway & Balkwell 1997).

Subsequent developments revealed that the theory's initial focus on the effects of inequalities in material resources was unnecessarily narrow and that the theory could account for the development of status beliefs under a broader range of structural conditions. The logic of the theory was shown to imply that an inequality in the distribution between two categorical groups of any factor, not just material resources, that biases the development of influence hierarchies in encounters will lead to the emergence of status beliefs about the categorical distinction

(Ridgeway et al. 1998; Webster & Hysom 1998). Webster and Hysom (1998) used this more general formulation of the theory to show how the social distribution of moral approval based on sexual orientation acts as a structural biasing factor that fosters the formation of status beliefs about homosexuality.

The viability of this more general formulation of the theory depends on the assumption that people form status beliefs simply from the repeated, consistent association of categorical difference with participants' relative influence in intercategory encounters. Further laboratory experiments showed that this does occur and that participants form these status beliefs even when the beliefs represent their own group as lower status and less competent than the other group (Ridgeway & Erickson 2000).

The above studies offer evidence that people form status beliefs about salient social differences from their cooperatively interdependent encounters with different others. For widely shared status beliefs to emerge about a categorical distinction, however, people must also be able to spread their newly acquired status beliefs to others by acting on those beliefs in subsequent encounters with those who differ on the distinction. Two laboratory experiments have examined this aspect of the theory (Ridgeway & Erickson 2000). The first showed that when participants had two repeated experiences of being treated in a status-evaluated way, i.e, either deferred to or treated assertively, by a nominally different other, the participants formed status beliefs about the nominal distinction that corresponded to the way they were treated. A second study showed that participants acquired status beliefs not only when they were directly treated according to such beliefs themselves, but also when they witnessed the status-evaluated treatment of someone like themselves by someone different. These studies suggest that intercategory encounters have the potential to propagate newly forming status beliefs widely through the population.

Status construction theory and the research that supports it suggest that interactional contexts are relatively powerful contexts for transforming nominal social differences into status differences. Yet despite this, not all socially recognized differences become status differences. Recent developments in status construction theory examine in greater detail the processes of belief formation in encounters in an effort to discern how the processes of belief formation can sometimes be interrupted and undermined in local contexts so that widely shared beliefs do not emerge.

This recent elaboration of the theory argues that for participants to form status beliefs, not only must the influence hierarchies in their encounters be consistently juxtaposed with a salient categorical distinction, but the apparent correspondence between influence and difference must also seem socially valid to the participants (Ridgeway 2006). The stronger the appearance that the correspondence between difference and influence is consensually accepted by others, rather than resisted or challenged, the more socially valid it will seem, and the more likely it is that clear status beliefs will form. Legitimated authority will also make the correspondence seem socially valid, facilitating the formation of status beliefs. Supporting these arguments, experimental evidence shows that challenges to consensus undermine the formation of status beliefs, while the support of authorities strengthens status beliefs. These results suggest that widely shared status beliefs are most likely to emerge about a categorical distinction when structural conditions not only advantage one categorical group in gaining influence in intercategory encounters, but also constrain the ability of those in the structurally disadvantaged group to display resistance to that influence.

Status construction theory has framed its principal arguments in terms of the creation of new status beliefs. The theory also claims, however, to speak to the maintenance of existing status beliefs, particularly over changes in the initial social conditions that created them (Ridgeway 1991). According to the theory, if structural conditions described by the theory, such as an inequality in resources between the categorical groups, are currently present, then status construction processes will be sufficient to maintain status beliefs about that categorical distinction. This will occur whether or not these processes played a role in the actual historical origin of the status beliefs. Status construction processes, then, may cause status beliefs based on race, gender, or other social differences to persist in contemporary societies even though the original historical cause of those status

beliefs has disappeared. This aspect of status construction theory has been used in combination with other arguments to account for the persistence of gender status beliefs in western societies over major transformations in the socioeconomic organization of gender relations in those societies, such as those associated with industrialization or the movement of women into the paid labor force.

SEE ALSO: Blau, Peter; Class, Status, and Power; Expectation States Theory; Micro–Macro Links; Status; Status Attainment; Weber, Max

REFERENCES AND SUGGESTED READINGS

Berger, J., Fisek, M. H., Norman, R. Z., & Zelditch, M. (1977) *Status Characteristics and Social Interaction*. Elsevier, New York.

Blau, P. M. (1977) *Inequality and Heterogeneity: A Primitive Theory of Social Structure*. Free Press, New York.

Ridgeway, C. L. (1991) The Social Construction of Status Value: Gender and Other Nominal Characteristics. *Social Forces* 70: 367–86.

Ridgeway, C. L. (2006) Status Construction Theory. In: Burke, P. (Ed.), *Contemporary Social Psychological Theories*. Stanford University Press, Stanford.

Ridgeway, C. L. & Balkwell, J. (1997) Group Processes and the Diffusion of Status Beliefs. *Social Psychology Quarterly* 60: 14–31.

Ridgeway, C. L. & Erickson, K. G. (2000) Creating and Spreading Status Beliefs. *American Journal of Sociology* 106: 579–615.

Ridgeway, C. L., Boyle, E. H., Kuipers, K., & Robinson, D. (1998) How Do Status Beliefs Develop? The Role of Resources and Interaction. *American Sociological Review* 63: 331–50.

Webster, M. & Hysom, S. J. (1998) Creating Status Characteristics. *American Sociological Review* 63: 351–79.

status passages

Michael J. McCallion

The term status comes from the Latin word meaning "to stand," which helps to clarify how the term has come to be used in sociology as constituting a basic analytic unit in a social system (society), denoting a *position* that an individual holds (stands) in a particular institution or social structure. The concept of status had wide currency in the post-World War II heyday of structural functionalism (Parsons 1951), and generally referred to a collection of specific institutional rights and duties (Linton 1936). The enactment of these rights and duties, on the other hand, was considered an individual's "role," the more dynamic aspect of status. Status passages, therefore, refer to persons passing from one status to another (e.g., from being single to married).

Gennep (1960) enduringly inscribed in the social scientific community's consciousness the phenomenon of status passages, in particular, age-based status passages (e.g., adolescence to adulthood). Although Gennep was an anthropologist, sociologists used his work to explain various societies' methods for moving people from one status to another. Although sociologists have studied these transforming procedures, it could be argued that they have been overly influenced by Gennep's work in assuming that most status passages are regularized, scheduled, and prescribed. Certainly, many status passages have these characteristics and sociologists have spent considerable effort in studying these within occupations (careers) and organizations (mobility), as well as how these status passages affect self-identity. But it was not until Strauss published "Some Neglected Aspects of Status Passages" (1968) and Glaser and Strauss's book *Status Passage* (1971) that various other properties or characteristics of status passages were theorized and studied. Among the other properties of status passages, Glaser and Strauss list the following:

- The passage may be desirable or undesirable (getting married or becoming a prisoner).
- The passage may be inevitable (birth to childhood).
- The passage may be reversible to some degree (job demotions).
- A passage may be repeatable or nonrepeatable (being sick).
- The person "passing" may do so alone or collectively (with any number of persons).
- It follows that when people go through a passage collectively, they may not be aware

that they are all passing through together (large school classes).
- Persons involved may or may not be able to communicate with the others (junior executives being simultaneously demoted).
- The person making the passage may do so voluntarily or have no choice in the matter (commitment to a mental institution).
- Degree of control during the passage by the one making the passage and others who oversee it (father not allowing his son to obtain a driver's license).
- The passage may require some special legitimation by one or more authorized agents (a physician and being sick).
- The clarity of the signs of the passage may vary from great to negligible (a con man turning one into a mark or parents not knowing their daughter is getting married).
- The signs of passage may be clear or disguised by relevant parties (which are also signs of control).
- The centrality of the passage to the person, that is, how much difference it makes to him or her (similar to desirability, above).
- The length of time or duration of a status passage.

Glaser and Strauss admit this is an incomplete list of properties. Nevertheless, these properties sensitize the researcher to the broader and more dynamic nature of status passages. Indeed, Glaser and Strauss argue that they have developed a formal theory of status passages, which is a theory developed for a formal or conceptual area of sociological inquiry which transcends any one substantive or empirical area of investigation.

Since the work of Glaser and Strauss, status passages have come to be viewed as dynamic, constantly shifting, changing, and in motion rather than as static. This dynamism is evident in the fact that status passages involve not only the "passagee" but various "agents" who assist or hinder the passage. These agents are sometimes called coaches, sponsors, teachers, guides, gurus, parents, and so forth who assist the passagee particularly during the transitional or liminal phase of the status passage, for this is when the passagee is betwixt and between statuses and, consequently, most vulnerable. For example, an individual passagee has left the single life status (engaged to be married), but has not yet been fully initiated into married life. Equally important is the fact that the relationships involved and developed during the status passage underscore the social nature of such passages, that is, they are not traversed alone.

Accordingly, from a sociological perspective, status passages reveal the fundamentally social nature of human life. Successfully or unsuccessfully negotiating a status passage assumes that agents/others have been integral to the status passage (whether bane or blessing). The status passage can vary in terms of how much individuality or collectivity is involved, but there is always some degree of the "other" involved in a status passage. Although status passages are most often researched at the social psychological level, the broader social dimension is evident as well in the fact that society-at-large legitimates certain statuses into which one may pass. Individuals do not make up statuses and then passages to go through to obtain them without "others" recognizing and legitimizing them as such (Stone 1970).

As indicated above, most recent studies have been at the social psychological level in that they have focused on how individuals have completed the passage into a host of professional occupations (MacNeil 1997; Bradby 1990), been converted to a particular religion (Snow & Machalek 1984; McCallion & Maines 2002), pass through the life course (Glaser & Strauss 1968), attain the status of deviant (Becker 1963), and many others. What have been under-researched are the broader levels of the social and cultural. For example, do various societies have more or less extensive status passages, more or less opportunity to undergo a status passage, and, if so, why? If more extensive, for example, does this indicate that the particular society is more rigid and closed or flexible and open – a question sociologists and historians have examined for years. And if there are more opportunities, are the status passages strong or weak, short or long? The basic sociological question that still needs further research is under what social conditions are there more or less, weak or strong, long or short, fewer or more opportunities for status passages? Why are some churches (Catholic), for example, maintaining lengthier status passages than others (Protestants)?

Status passage research can reveal much about a society and its culture, especially in terms of socialization, social mobility, social structural arrangements, and identity salience. Further research on status passages, therefore, could advance sociological theory about these matters, as well as how societies work at the more macro level.

SEE ALSO: Aging and the Life Course, Theories of; Cognitive Dissonance Theory (Festinger); Collective Consciousness; Durkheim, Émile; Generalized Other; Interaction Order; Networks; Norms; Reference Groups; Resocialization; Ritual; Role-Taking; Sacred/Profane; Social Control; Socialization; Socialization, Adult; Socialization, Agents of; Socialization, Anticipatory; Status; Status Attainment; Symbolic Interaction; Youth/Adolescence

REFERENCES AND SUGGESTED READINGS

Becker, H. S. (1963) *Outsiders: Studies in the Sociology of Deviance*. Free Press, New York.

Bradby, M. (1990) Status Passage into Nursing: Undertaking Nurse Care. *Journal of Advanced Nursing* 15: 1363–9.

Gennep, A. van. (1960 [1908]) *Les Rites de passage* (Rites of Passage). Trans. M. Vizedom & G. Chafee. University of Chicago Press, Chicago.

Glaser, B. G. & Strauss, A. L. (1968) *Time for Dying*. Aldine, Chicago.

Glaser, B. G. & Strauss, A. L. (1971) *Status Passage: A Formal Theory*. Aldine, Chicago.

Linton, R. (1936) *The Study of Man*. Appleton-Century, New York.

McCallion, M. J. & Maines, D. R. (2002) Spiritual Gatekeepers: Time and the Rite of Christian Initiation of Adults. *Symbolic Interaction* 25(3): 289–302.

MacNeil, M. (1997) From Nurse to Teacher: Recognizing a Status Passage. *Journal of Advanced Nursing* 25: 634–42.

Parsons, T. (1951) *The Social System*. Free Press, Glencoe, IL.

Snow, D. A. & Machalek, R. (1984) The Sociology of Conversion. *Annual Review of Sociology* 10: 167–90.

Stone, G. P. (1970) Appearance and the Self: A Slightly Revised Version. In: Stone, G. P. & Farberman, H. A. (Eds.), *Social Psychology through Symbolic Interaction*. Wiley & Sons, New York, pp. 187–202.

Strauss, A. L. (1968) Some Neglected Aspects of Status Passages. In: Becker, H. S. et al. (Eds.), *Institutions and Persons*. Aldine, Chicago, pp. 265–71.

Strauss, A. L. (1971) *The Contexts of Social Mobility: Ideology and Theory*. Aldine, Chicago.

steering, racial real estate

Gregory D. Squires and Jan Chadwick

Racial real estate steering occurs when home-seekers are guided by housing providers to communities where their race is already highly concentrated. So as racial minorities are channeled to integrated or predominantly non-white neighborhoods and whites are shown homes primarily in white communities, steering contributes directly to the segregated housing patterns that have long persisted in urban communities and the many costs associated with that separation.

Steering can take several forms. Information steering occurs when minority homeseekers are shown or given information on fewer homes or neighborhoods than non-minority homeseekers. Segregation steering occurs when minorities are shown homes in areas with larger minority populations than areas shown to non-minorities. And class steering occurs when neighborhoods shown to minority homeseekers are of lower socioeconomic status than those shown to non-minorities. Several actors in the housing industry engage in steering. Mortgage lenders and insurance agents often provide less information and offer fewer, more expensive, and lower-quality products to non-white households or residents of non-white communities than they do for whites and predominantly white communities. These practices influence the location and range of housing options for minority families. However, racial steering is most closely associated with the practices of real estate agents who are often the gateway to housing opportunities, which often differ for white and non-white families.

Historically, steering was virtually required by law and widespread industry practice in many communities. Early in the twentieth century steering took the form of restrictive zoning laws that apportioned particular city neighborhoods for different racial groups. Blacks and other minorities were prohibited by law from living in certain neighborhoods of several cities, North and South. When these policies were ruled unconstitutional by the Supreme Court in the 1917 case of *Buchanan v. Warley*, they were replaced by the racially restrictive covenant. These covenants generally took the form of deed restrictions stating that the property could not be occupied by members of certain ethnic groups. They were promulgated and often instigated by real estate agents and mortgage brokers who would encourage entire neighborhoods to participate. The National Association of Real Estate Boards (NAREB) promoted this practice by stating in its code of ethics up until 1950 that "a realtor should never be instrumental in introducing into a neighborhood ... members of any race or nationality ... whose presence will clearly be detrimental to property values in that neighbhorhood" (Massey & Denton 1993: 37). While judicial enforcement of racially restrictive covenants was declared unconstitutional in 1948, and the words "race" and "nationality" were eliminated from NAREB's code of ethics in 1950, the practice of steering between already established segregated neighborhoods has continued.

Racial steering has been motivated by several factors. Real estate agents generally serve selected neighborhoods within metropolitan areas and rely heavily on word-of-mouth advertising to recruit new clients. Many fear loss of business if they introduce a minority family into a white neighborhood. Historically, some agents feared strong reprisals from area residents if they introduced a household that could have a "detrimental" effect on the neighborhood. Some maintain they are simply responding to the preference of renters and buyers who prefer to live in homogeneous neighborhoods. And others no doubt still assert that they are helping to maintain property values by steering homeseekers to such communities.

A combination of statutes, court cases, and regulations has declared racial steering to be unlawful. In 1968 Congress passed the federal Fair Housing Act (Title VIII of the Civil Rights Act of 1968), prohibiting discrimination on the basis of race, color, national origin, sex, or religion, and in 1988 persons with disabilities and families with children were added as protected classes. While the law does not specifically use the word "steering," case law has generally found steering to be in violation of section 3604(a) of the Act, which states that it is unlawful "to otherwise make unavailable" housing because of a protected class status. Both rental and sales steering have been successfully challenged in court, and not always by actual homeseekers who were steered. In *Trafficante* v. *Metropolitan Life Insurance Co.* (1972), the white plaintiffs claimed that they had been injured because they had lost the social benefits of living in an integrated community; they had missed the business and professional advantages which would have accrued if they had lived with members of minority groups; and they had suffered embarrassment and economic damage in social, business, and professional activities from being stigmatized as residents of a "white ghetto." Other significant steering cases included *Gladstone, Realtors* v. *Village of Bellwood* (1979) and *Havens Realty Corp.* v. *Coleman* (1982) where the court gave standing under the Fair Housing Act to other local residents and investigators with fair housing centers who claimed that steering by real estate agents was destroying the racial balance of their neighborhood or community and denying residents the benefits of integrated living. In the 1985 case of *Heights Community Congress* v. *Hilltop Realty, Inc.*, the Sixth Circuit held that a real estate agent who engaged in intentional racial steering violated the Fair Housing Act. Perhaps more significantly, the court held that even if the statements made by the agents about the racial makeup of the neighborhoods were truthful, if the effect of the statements was to discourage people of particular races from considering those neighborhoods, it violated the Act.

In addition to the statutory and case law, when the Fair Housing Act was amended and strengthened by the Fair Housing Amendments Act of 1988, the US Department of Housing and Urban Development (HUD) promulgated regulations prohibiting steering, which it defined as any effort to "restrict or attempt to restrict the choices of a person by word or conduct in connection with seeking, negotiating for, buying or renting a dwelling so as to perpetuate or tend to perpetuate, segregated housing patterns, or to discourage or obstruct choices in a community,

neighborhood or development." These regulations state that unlawful steering includes but is not limited to: (1) discouraging any person from inspecting, purchasing, or renting a dwelling because of the minority status of the person, or the minority status of the persons in a community, neighborhood, or development; (2) discouraging the purchase or rental of a dwelling because of a protected class reason by exaggerating drawbacks or failing to inform any person of desirable features of a dwelling or of a community, neighborhood, or development; (3) communicating to any prospective purchaser that he or she would not be comfortable or compatible with existing residents of a community, neighborhood, or development because of a protected class reason; or (4) assigning any person to a particular section of a community, neighborhood, or development, or to a particular floor of a building, because of a protected class reason.

Even with the passage and strengthening of the Fair Housing Act, studies have shown that racial steering continues. These studies generally take the form of a housing audit and utilize "matched paired testing" where white and minority testers posing as homeseekers are identically matched on all relevant housing-related characteristics (e.g., income, occupation, housing preference) and sent to visit real estate offices. While many local housing audit studies have been conducted, the most comprehensive national audits have been sponsored by HUD and conducted by the Urban Institute. In 1979, 1989, and 2000, national paired-testing studies were conducted. Due to methodological differences, it is not possible to draw comparisons between the 1979 research and the two subsequent studies. But the latter two studies, each of which covered more than 20 metropolitan areas, do permit some conclusions about the changing nature of housing discrimination.

The key finding from the 1989 and 2000 studies is that overall discrimination has dropped considerably, but still remains a central feature of the nation's urban and metropolitan housing markets. The share of black and Hispanic homebuyers and renters experiencing discrimination dropped from approximately one-third of all homeseekers in 1989 to about one out of every five in 2000. However, these studies understate the actual level of discrimination, for several reasons. The studies included only housing units that were advertised in major daily newspapers. Homes in minority neighborhoods are less likely to be advertised in these outlets than are homes generally. This is also the case for homes in exclusively white neighborhoods where racial discrimination may be the most explicit. And testers did not follow up their initial contact with housing providers, so the study did not capture behavior that occurs during subsequent visits, after an offer is made, or when insurance or mortgage loans are applied for in the homebuying process. Consequently, the 2000 study reports a conservative estimate of the actual level of discrimination that occurs in the housing market (Turner et al. 2002).

Despite the lower incidence of racial discrimination overall in 2000 compared to 1989, the frequency of racial steering actually increased. For example, the percentage of tests in which whites were shown homes in communities that had a higher white population than the communities in which black testers were shown homes increased from 7.5 percent in 1989 to 11 percent in 2000. When whites and Hispanics were paired, the share of white-favored tests on this measure increased from 7.4 percent to more than 14.7 percent. However, steering most commonly occurred through informal, unsolicited comments directed to white homeseekers about the racial composition of selected neighborhoods. Among these comments were the following:

> "I would not recommend (area), it's totally black. And I don't like (area), it's pretty mixed."

> "There are lots of Latinos living there ... I'm not supposed to be telling you that, but you have a daughter and I like you."

> "(Area) is very mixed. You probably wouldn't like it because of the income you and your husband make. But I don't want to sound prejudiced."

> "(Area) is different from here; it's multicultural ... I'm not allowed to steer you, but there are some areas that you wouldn't want to live in." (Galster & Godfrey 2003: 19, 23).

If racial discrimination has declined in recent years, it persists at very high levels in the nation's urban and metropolitan communities.

And steering has increased. Steering, along with other forms of discrimination, contributes to the ongoing segregation of American cities and its many social costs. Segregation nurtures the concentration of poverty, and particularly the concentration of poor minorities. Housing values and the wealth accumulation associated with homeownership are undercut for racial minorities because of their continued isolation from more favored neighborhoods. Consequently, racial minorities are disproportionately trapped in neighborhoods where school achievement is lower, crime rates are higher, and most public services and private amenities are of lower quality or not available at all.

But fair housing enforcement appears to be working. Reductions in discrimination during the 1990s suggest that the efforts of HUD and other law enforcement authorities, along with the work of non-profit fair housing organizations around the country, are having the intended effect. During the 1990s lawsuits filed by non-profit housing centers generated more than $180,000,000 for plaintiffs. But the fair housing agenda remains unfinished. Racial steering is clearly one of the issues that should be the focus of future enforcement efforts. Persisting high levels of discrimination (even if lower than in previous years) indicate that equal housing opportunity, though the law of the land, is not yet the reality.

SEE ALSO: Blockbusting; Hypersegregation; Inequality and the City; Race (Racism); Redlining; Residential Segregation; Restrictive Covenants

REFERENCES AND SUGGESTED READINGS

Cashin, S. (2004) *The Failure of Integration: How Race and Class are Undermining the American Dream.* Public Affairs, New York.

Galster, G. & Godfrey, E. (2003) By Words and Deeds: Racial Steering by Real Estate Agents in the US in 2000. Paper presented at the Urban Affairs Association Annual Meeting, Cleveland, OH (March).

Goering, J. & Squires, G. D. (Ed.) (1999) Commemorating the 30th Anniversary of the Fair Housing Act. *Cityscape: A Journal of Policy Development and Research* 4(3): 1–220.

Gotham, K. F. (2002) *Race, Real Estate, and Uneven Development: The Kansas City Experience, 1900–2000*. SUNY Press, Albany, NY.

Logan, J. R., Stults, B. J., & Farley, R. (2004) Segregation of Minorities in the Metropolis: Two Decades of Change. *Demography* 41(1): 1–22.

Massey, D. S. & Denton, N. A. (1993) *American Apartheid: Segregation and the Making of the Underclass*. Harvard University Press, Cambridge, MA.

Turner, M. A., Ross, S. L., Galster, G. C., & Yinger, J. (2002) *Discrimination in Metropolitan Housing Markets*. US Department of Housing and Urban Development, Washington, DC.

Yinger, J. (1995) *Closed Doors, Opportunities Lost: The Continuing Costs of Housing Discrimination*. Russell Sage Foundation, New York.

stepfamilies

Marilyn Coleman and Lawrence H. Ganong

Stepfamilies are common throughout the industrialized world. In the US nearly everyone marries, and about half of the marriages include at least one previously married partner (US Census Bureau 2000). Most divorced people in other western countries also either remarry or cohabit, but at lower rates than in the US. About half of the remarriages involve adults who have children.

Because not all remarriages involve parents, remarriages and stepfamily formation are not the same. A stepfamily is a cohabiting or legal union of two adults, at least one of whom has a child or children from previous relationships. According to Fields (2001), about 17 percent of all children in the US live in a stepfamily household, usually with a stepfather and mother. An estimated 30 percent of children in the US will live in a stepfamily household before they become adults. A large number of children who live primarily with a single mother also visit a remarried or cohabiting father.

Although stepfamilies have been common throughout history, they have not been studied until relatively recently. Until past the midpoint of the twentieth century, remarriage was considered the solution to a social problem. When divorce rather than bereavement became the most common precursor to remarriage and stepfamily formation (around 1974), stepfamily formation became viewed as a social problem. This view appeared to stimulate both research and clinical work (Ganong & Coleman 2004). Most stepfamily research has been done since 1990 (Coleman et al. 2000). These studies offered marked improvement over previous work: samples were more representative, large-scale longitudinal studies were launched that allowed us to examine family process, more observational research was conducted, measurement was greatly improved, and there was increased use of theory. However, little attention has yet been paid to racial, ethnic, or SES diversity.

The most frequently studied phenomena have been the effects on children of living in stepfamilies. These studies generally have reported that stepchildren, on average, are slightly more at risk for externalizing and internalizing behavior problems, do less well in school, and are less likely to form stable couple relationships as adults than are children who grow up living with both parents. However, the differences between stepchildren and children in first-marriage families tend to be small, and most stepchildren (about 80 percent) function normally on psychological, cognitive, and interpersonal outcomes. The research emphasis primarily has been on documenting problems in stepfamilies – sometimes called a *deficit comparison* approach. In recent years, more researchers have begun to explore how and why some stepfamilies function well and others do not, using what has been called a *normative adaptive* approach.

Numerous reasons for problems in stepfamilies have been offered, but one of the more widely known is Cherlin's (1978) seminal work that described families formed after remarriage as *incomplete institutions*. Cherlin argued that stepfamilies lack institutionalized guidelines and support in solving family problems, and as a result they have more problems than do first-marriage families. Research in general has lent some support for this hypothesis. A contributing factor to the incomplete institutionalization of stepfamilies is *nuclear family ideology*. This means that there are strong cultural biases that families *should* live in nuclear families, and those who do not conform to this model are deficient and/or deviant. The nuclear family ideology creates social stigma that appears to result in many stepfamilies attempting to hide their status and to act as if they were a nuclear family (e.g., stepchildren using their stepfather's surname even though it is not their legal surname), which may only further contribute to their feelings of isolation or being different. Negative media images and language negatively stereotyping stepfamilies and stepfamily members (e.g., "the parks system is the stepchild of city government") continue to be a problem as well. Stepparents are motivated to adopt stepchildren, in part, to convert a step-relationship legally into a parent–child relationship, thereby avoiding stigma and acquiring norms for guiding their relationship.

People who remarry differ from those in first-marriage families in several ways. For example, individuals who remarry are older, engage in shorter courtships, and are more likely to have children from previous relationships. They also are more likely than couples in first marriages to marry someone who is different from themselves in various ways (age, race, religion, SES). In the US, whites are more likely to remarry than other racial groups, divorced adults tend to remarry other people who have been divorced, and men remarry more quickly and at a higher rate than women. On average, people in the US remarry within 4 years of divorce. Additionally, individuals cohabit or remarry quickly, often within months of beginning a relationship. Approximately 75 percent of remarried couples cohabit before legally remarrying; increasingly, couples in all western cultures are cohabiting in lieu of legal remarriage. We know little about how decisions to remarry or cohabit are made.

Until the late 1970s, clinicians basically treated stepfamilies as though they were the same as first-marriage families, which, perhaps not surprisingly, resulted in stepfamily members reporting that therapy was not helpful. Early work by clinicians such as Goldner, Sager, and John and Emily Visher identified a number of ways in which stepfamilies are different from first-marriage families. For example, stepfamilies are more complex than nuclear families and this complexity either can be exciting and challenging or it can be overwhelming to family members. Contributing to this complexity is the fact that children often belong to two households. They typically have their primary residence with their mother and stepfather, but increasingly also are likely to spend significant amounts of time with their father and stepmother. Because of this often legally mandated sharing of children between the two households, if stepfamilies are to function well, they need to have permeable boundaries that allow children to move in and out of the household comfortably.

Stepfamilies' histories differ from those of nuclear families. In nuclear families the parents have been together from the beginning and over time they have developed roles, rituals, family rules, and other patterns of behavior to which children are socialized. Stepfamilies, however, can form any time in a child's lifetime, from infancy to adulthood. Adults in stepfamilies do not have the luxury of gradually developing family routines and rituals together before they socialize children. Instead, adults and children in stepfamilies find they must negotiate their new household rules and routines while they are learning how to live together. Without clear and frequent communication, the opportunities for hurt feelings and oppositional behavior are great. Children seldom appreciate new rules, especially if they come from the stepparent. They also may miss the rituals from their previous family household and be unenthusiastic about developing new ones, especially when the stepfamily household is first formed.

Still another way that stepfamilies differ from first-marriage families is that the parent–child bonds are older than the spousal bonds. This means that at least during the early formation of the stepfamily, the parent–child bond is likely to be the closest one. As a result, it is often difficult for the stepparent to feel a part of the family early in the stepfamily's life. Fortunately, over time, most stepparents develop step-relationships and find functions that they can fulfill in the household. For example, a stepparent may become the math homework expert or the tennis-teaching expert in the family. Stepparents who try to fill more traditional parental roles such as disciplinarian are more likely to find their efforts meet with resistance. Clinicians suggest that the genetic parent should be the main disciplinarian for quite some time and that the stepparent should enforce household rules, such as bedtime, in much the same way that a babysitter might enforce them. If the stepparent takes on the role of disciplinarian too soon, without a relationship being formed with stepchildren, coalitions are likely to form between the children or between the parent and the children. Such coalitions weaken the couple bond and seriously hamper stepfamily functioning and stability.

Finally, legal relationships between stepparents and stepchildren either do not exist or are ambiguous. This means that a stepparent does not have the legal authority to check a child into the emergency room if there is an accident. It also means that if the parent and stepparent divorce, the stepparent no longer has any rights regarding the stepchild. If the parent does not want the child to see or keep in touch with the stepparent, the stepparent must abide by the parent's wishes. The effect that the lack of a legal relationship has on the stepparent–stepchild bond has not been fully explored, but some scholars have speculated that it might hinder efforts by stepparents to develop close relationships with stepchildren.

Evolutionary scholars posit that it is not the lack of a legal relationship that contributes to stepparents investing less emotionally in their stepchildren, it is the lack of a genetic tie that results in low investment. Their view is that men who treat their stepchildren well do so only to impress the children's mother rather than out of an interest in the children's well-being. Evolutionary scholars propose that individuals want to protect and invest in their own offspring, so stepchildren are at much greater risk of child abuse and neglect than children living with both parents. There is evidence that children who live in a household that includes an adult who is not their genetic parent are at greater risk of abuse than those who live with their genetic parents only, but stepparents (usually stepfathers) are categorized with mothers' boyfriends, uncles, grandfathers, and a host of other adults who share the mother's home. There also is speculation that there are fewer barriers to reporting a stepfather or other household member for child abuse than for reporting a parent. Regardless, some stepchildren are abused by stepparents, and this has caused a few social scientists to accuse parents who remarry of engaging in child abuse by placing their children at risk! This argument is an

extreme overreaction that perpetuates harmful stereotypes that may negatively contribute to stepfamily process. Other, perhaps more plausible reasons for stepchildren faring slightly less well than children in first-marriage families have to do with stress (the cumulative effect of multiple family changes and transitions), poor-quality parenting by parents who are too stressed to competently monitor their children, and conflicts (between divorced parents and within stepfamily households).

In addition to differences between nuclear families and stepfamilies, there are numerous differences among stepfamilies. Stepfamily configurations are diverse. For example, stepfather families are different from stepmother families, and they both differ from complex households in which both adults are stepparents to each other's children. Additionally, it makes a difference if a stepfamily is formed following the death of a parent, following parental divorce, or if the parent had never been married. The sibling configuration within stepfamilies makes a difference as well. Some stepfamily households contain only full siblings, often the children of the mother. Blended stepfamily households contain children from previous relationships of both adults. These children are stepsiblings that share a residence but have no genetic ties. Many stepfamily households have at least one half-sibling. These children are a product of the remarried couple, and they share one genetic parent in common with the other children in the household. To add further complexity, some stepfamilies may have children living with them as well as with the other parent. If a stepfamily adult has shared physical custody of children from prior relationships, children move in and out of the stepfamily household. Stepfamily variations seem almost endless and this complexity has created tremendous research challenges.

In spite of the challenges, there has been an increase in studies in the past decade. However, more longitudinal studies are needed to explore how stepfamily processes change over time. We also need more within-group studies to replace the deficit-comparison approach so that we gain a better understanding of how strong stepfamilies function. Additionally, we need qualitative studies that provide in-depth understanding of stepfamily members' experiences. We lack information about family processes in cohabiting stepfamilies. Although there has been a large number of studies on residential stepfather/stepchild relationships, stepmothers and nonresidential stepparents have received little attention from researchers. Stepsibling relationships, relationships between stepchildren and stepgrandparents, and mother–child relationships in stepfamilies have been overlooked as well. Finally, researchers need to continue to develop more innovative designs that capture the complexity of remarriage and stepfamilies.

SEE ALSO: Childhood; Cohabitation; Divorce; Family Diversity; Family, Men's Involvement in; Family Structure and Child Outcomes; Stepfathering; Stepmothering

REFERENCES AND SUGGESTED READINGS

Cherlin, A. J. (1978) Remarriage as an Incomplete Institution. *American Journal of Sociology* 84: 634–50.

Coleman, M., Ganong, L., & Fine, M. (2000) Reinvestigating Remarriage: Another Decade of Progress. *Journal of Marriage and the Family* 62: 1288–307.

Fields, P. (2001) Living Arrangements of Children 1996. *Current Population Reports*, pp. 70–4. US Census Bureau, Washington, DC.

Ganong, L. & Coleman, M. (2004) *Stepfamily Relationships*. Kluwer/Plenum, New York.

Papernow, P. (1993) *Becoming a Stepfamily*. Jossey-Bass, San Francisco.

Visher, E. B. & Visher, J. S. (1996) *Therapy with Stepfamilies*. Brunner/Mazel, New York.

stepfathering

Rosalind Edwards with Lucy Hadfield

Stepfamilies are becoming increasingly common in contemporary developed societies, with the vast majority (in heterosexual families) comprising a stepfather who has partnered and formed a (married or cohabiting) household with a biological mother and her resident children. The rise in stepfather households, however, occurs in an institutional context where legislation in many countries has shifted towards the view that bringing up children, and financial responsibility for them, primarily and unchangeably rests with biological parents. In contrast, and despite their prevalence, the institutional position of stepfathers is largely one of invisibility, or at least ambiguity, with few defined rights and responsibilities.

Stepfamilies are usually considered to involve particularly complex family forms and relationships. Work that has developed typologies of different forms of stepfamilies, focusing on gender of the stepparent, marital status, step- and biological children's residence and access patterns, and so on, draws attention to the diversity of stepfamilies. As a body of literature, however, the evidence on the implications of this diversity, in terms of stepchildren's development and relationships between stepfathers and stepchildren, is equivocal. Further, a continuous theme of work on the topic is that there is normative uncertainty around the practice of stepfathering, focusing on how much of a father figure stepfathers can, are, or should be. This is especially the case because stepfathers now often have to negotiate their practice alongside the involvement of a nonresident father. In this respect, issues of context, including gendered expectations of fatherhood in general over time and social class, are coming increasingly to the fore.

One key preoccupation of studies is the effect of stepfathers on children's behavior and attainment. This usually draws on survey data, and has largely been conducted within the psychological and therapeutic fields, drawing on clinical inventories or family systems theories, as well as cohort-based social studies. Family structure is examined in relation to the outcomes for children's psychological adjustment, educational achievement, "transition" points such as leaving school and home, sexual activity and parenthood, and involvement in criminal activity. The age of the child when a stepfather enters the household and the child's gender in relation to the stepfather are often highlighted as factors. The evidence, however, provides equivocal messages. For example, boys are said to be especially affected negatively by having stepfathers, but there are also problematic issues of sexuality in stepfathering girls in early adolescence (for assessments of the literature, see Gorell Barnes et al. 1998; Hughes 1991). Another inconclusive facet is the issue of whether or not stepfathers are more likely than biological fathers to abuse their stepchildren (Daly & Wilson 1998).

Overall, the relationship between stepfathers and their stepchildren is seen as a difficult one to manage, primarily because it is built on a third person, the mother. On the one hand, stepfather–stepchild relationships are characterized as ones of conflicting loyalty. Stepfathers are said to be subject to resentment and jealousy about the time and attention children require impinging on their own time and relationship with their partner, as well as on the part of the children over sharing their mother (Robinson & Smith 1993). On the other hand, there is also some evidence that stepfathers can understand their coupledom with the children's mother as a foundation for building relationships with their stepchildren (McCarthy et al. 2003). The mother's involvement in facilitating the mode of stepfathering practice, and the stepchildren's own perceptions and reactions, are also issues here.

Another potential cause of conflict of loyalties relates to the fact that many stepfathers have their own biological children, either from a previous relationship and with whom they have contact, or in their stepfamily household from their current relationship. Again, the evidence is contradictory, with some concluding that stepfathers feel more commitment to their biological children and others concluding that having their own biological children enhances stepfathers' ability to take on a fathering identity in relation to their stepchildren (Marsiglio 1995).

This leads into another key preoccupation of the literature: the extent to which stepfathers are father figures to their stepchildren. In turn, this raises issues of the historically situated constitution of fathering. Lack of clarity in quite what stepfathering consists of is often related to a shift towards a less clear formulation of norms concerning fathering in general, in particular whether or not it is ascribed and status bound or achieved and socially constructed. Ascribed fatherhood is rooted in the biological tie and its accompanying social status as a father, which in itself is seen to constitute the essence of fatherhood. Within this status, fathering practice is related to the gendered division of labor between married parents wherein fathers are breadwinners, disciplinarians, and emotionally distanced, and mothers are nurturing carers. In contrast, fathering as an achieved relationship is rooted in what are considered to be new expectations that fathers should actively engage with their children as physically and emotionally involved carers. The emphasis has shifted from fatherhood as an institutional status to fathering as an engaged relational form; a transition from ascribed to achieved.

Stepfathering is not necessarily captured in this idea of a transition from ascribed to achieved fathering because both concepts are underpinned by the biological tie. For this reason, researchers often make a distinction between biological and social fathering, with stepfathers falling into the latter category in that they act as fathers in the social sense. This does not tell us about the content of social fathering, however. For example, the practice of stepfathering may work towards ascribed fatherhood in all but biology.

There are two main strands of work attempting to throw light on this issue, using different methodologies but both working within a constructionist approach to stepfathering practice. The first and dominant strand comprises survey data. This can examine stepfathers' identity and the extent to which they seek and maintain "affinity" with their stepchildren, with the evidence here equivocal again. On the one hand, nonresident fathers are said to impinge on stepfathers' ability to take on a fathering identity, in that they have the ascribed breadwinner and authority role undermined by the nonresident fathers' input. On the other hand, there is also evidence that stepfathers can take on a father identity alongside the biological father rather than feeling in competition with or undermined by them (Marsiglio 2004). Survey data is also used to assess stepfathers' behavior, focusing on patterns of parental employment, family activities, and practical involvement in childcare and child rearing. Here shifts over time can be detected, from a social practice akin to ascribed fatherhood towards one that represents more involved achieved fathering (Ferri & Smith 1998).

The second strand is relatively small, but comprises grounded qualitative studies that provide a valuable insight into the subjective aspects of stepfathering. A feature of this work is the extent to which stepfathers feel their stepchildren to be "their own." Some research, taking a developmental approach, attempts to posit "timescales" governing stepfathers' integration into, and involvement in, their stepchildren's lives, but again the evidence for a distinct pattern is contradictory, and in some views the search for it is misplaced (Gorell Barnes et al. 1998). More interpretive work attempts to draw out the images and factors informing stepfathers' orientation towards their stepchildren. In this respect, several studies across different national contexts indicate that working-class stepfathers are more concerned with a social practice in which they can feel and act the same as biological fathers, while middle-class stepfathers are more likely to place an emphasis on the primacy of biological fatherhood, meaning that they cannot take on a full fathering role (Edwards et al. 2002). The interplay between economic and material circumstances, and culture over time, may well be an issue here, and is one that deserves further attention, including in relation to ethnicity.

SEE ALSO: Divisions of Household Labor; Family Diversity; Family, Men's Involvement in; Family Structure and Child Outcomes; Fatherhood; Gender Ideology and Gender Role Ideology; Stepfamilies; Stepmothering

REFERENCES AND SUGGESTED READINGS

Burgoyne, J. & Clark, D. (1984) *Making A Go Of It: A Study of Stepfamilies in Sheffield*. Routledge and Kegan Paul, London.

Daly, M. & Wilson, M. (1998) *The Truth About Cinderella: A Darwinian View of Parental Love*. Weidenfeld and Nicolson, London.

Edwards, R., Bäck-Wiklund, M., Bak, M., & Ribbens, McCarthy, J. (2002) Step-fathering: Comparing Policy and Everyday Experience in Britain and Sweden. *Sociological Research Online* 7(1). www.socresonline.org.uk/7/1/edwards.html.

Ferri, E. & Smith, K. (1998) *Step-Parenting in the 1990s*. Family Policy Studies Centre, London.

Gorell Barnes, G., Thompson, P., Daniel, G., & Burchardt, N. (1998) *Growing Up in Stepfamilies*. Clarendon Press, Oxford.

Hughes, C. (1991) *Steparents: Wicked or Wonderful? An Indepth Study of Stepparenthood*. Avebury Press, Aldershot.

Ihinger-Tallman, M. & Pasley, K. (Eds.) (1994) Stepparenting: Issues in Theory, Research and Practice. Greenwood Press, Westport, CT.

McCarthy, J. R., Edwards, R., & Gillies, V. (2003) *Making Families: Moral Tales of Parenting and Step-Parenting*. Sociology Press, Durham.

Marsiglio, W. (1995) Stepfathers with Minor Children Living at Home: Parenting Perceptions and Relationship Quality. In: Marsiglio, W. (Ed.), *Fatherhood: Contemporary Theory, Research and Social Policy*. Sage, Thousand Oaks, CA, pp. 211–29.

Marsiglio, W. (2004) *Stepdads: Stories of Love, Hope and Repair*. Rowman & Littlefield, Boulder.

Robinson, M. & Smith, D. (1993) *Step By Step*. Harvester Wheatsheaf, Hemel Hempstead.

stepmothering

Marilyn Coleman and Lawrence H. Ganong

Stepmothers are women who marry or cohabit with partners who have children from prior unions. This broad definition of stepmothers includes women from a variety of roles and who live in diverse family constellations – those who have children of their own as well as women that are childless or childfree, women in lesbian relationships, and it includes stepmothers who reside with their stepchildren all of the time, some of the time, or never. Women who live with their stepchildren are called *residential* stepmothers and those who do not live with their stepchildren, or who spend only part of each year living with their stepchildren, are called *nonresidential* stepmothers. Some women that fit the broad definition of stepmothers, such as women cohabiting with fathers whose children live elsewhere, and some lesbian partners, do not see themselves as stepmothers, and, in fact, are seldom included in studies of stepmothers. Given the diversity of stepmothers' situations, it is unfortunate that the majority of studies have been limited to married stepmothers and most researchers have not distinguished between residential and nonresidential stepmothers.

Anyone who is familiar with children's fairy tales such as Cinderella and Hansel and Gretel knows that stepmothers are not a new phenomenon; there have always been large numbers of stepmothers. However, throughout most of human history, stepmothers were women who moved in with a father and his children after the death of the children's mother. In the past, stepmothers often were considered mother substitutes; in fact, fathers often were motivated to wed because they needed help with childcare after the death of their wives. In the last century, better control of disease, especially infections related to childbirth, resulted in fewer early deaths of mothers and less need for stepmothers as substitute mothers. Fewer early maternal deaths, combined with increases in divorce, resulted in divorce replacing death as the precursor to remarriage in the 1970s, a trend that continues (Ganong & Coleman 2004). Consequently, stepmothers now are not replacements for deceased mothers, but are additional family members.

In western societies fathers are seldom awarded physical custody (at least, sole physical custody) of their children after divorce, so the vast majority of stepmothers do not live with their stepchildren on a daily basis. These nonresidential stepmothers may have adult stepchildren whom they barely know, they may have minor-aged stepchildren who visit them on occasion, or they may have stepchildren who visit regularly and frequently. According to Nielsen (1999), over 90 percent of the estimated 13 million stepmothers in the US are nonresidential, and it is reasonable to expect similar percentages of nonresidential stepmothers in other western societies.

Because mothers most often have physical custody of their children after divorce, there are about five times more residential stepfathers than residential stepmothers. Not surprisingly, the majority of stepfamily research has focused on stepfathers and stepfather–stepchild relations, in part because they are easier for researchers to find (Coleman et al. 2000; Ganong & Coleman 2004). As a result, a lot more is known about stepfathers than is known about stepmothers.

Clinicians (Bernstein 1989; Visher & Visher 1979) and some researchers (MacDonald & DeMaris 1996; Sturgess et al. 2001) have indicated that stepmothers struggle more with their roles within stepfamilies than do stepfathers. Clinicians and the few researchers who have studied nonresidential stepmothers have found that these women are involved in the lives of their stepchildren, but they struggle with ambiguous expectations and feel frustrated with the lack of support from their partners (Ambert 1986; Church 2004; Morrison & Thomson-Guppy 1985; Weaver & Coleman, in press).

Stepmothers are stressed by not knowing how they should interact with their stepchildren. As additional adults, nonresidential stepmothers report actively avoiding acting as if they were the mother to their stepchildren out of fear of usurping the inviolate role of the biological mother (Church 2004; Weaver & Coleman, in press). One nonresidential stepmother in Weaver and Coleman's study described herself as enacting "a *mothering* but not a *mother*" role. However, when she described her behaviors in the stepfamily (taking care of the stepchildren, cooking for them, helping them with homework) it was difficult to tell how these behaviors differed from what a mother would do. Nonetheless, this stepmother was typical of others in her efforts to distinguish what she did from what her stepchildren's mother would do for them. Because of cultural expectations that women should be responsible for the quality of their family's relationships, stepmothers are in a difficult position. They are not the mothers of their stepchildren, yet to be a good woman, they are responsible for their stepchildren's well-being, at least during the time they share a household. This is an ambiguous position at best, and one that many stepmothers report feeling ambivalent about. Church (2004) found that one way stepmothers deal with this is by identifying more strongly with their spousal/partner role than with their parenting role. This enables them to avoid competing with the mother and attempting to meet the nearly impossible expectations that assuming the mother role would require.

Stepmothers who reproduce with the father of their stepchildren are not as close with their residential stepchildren as are stepmothers who do not produce a half-sibling for the stepchildren (Ambert 1986) and they are less satisfied with being a stepmother (MacDonald & DeMaris 1996). The role of mother is so important (Hayes 1996) that it likely predominates over the stepmother role in stepfamily households.

Women who become stepmothers to grown (adult) stepchildren struggle less with issues about how to relate to their stepchildren. They often attempt to be friends with stepchildren or take a peripheral position to that of the father. Vinick (1998) found that women who became stepmothers later in life often played an important role in promoting the reestablishment of relationships between their husbands and their stepchildren. Nonresidential fathers often lose contact or maintain only minimal contact with their children after divorce, a situation that their new wives try to remedy. Vinick referred to these women as "carpenters" because they "repair" relationships between their husbands and their children.

In addition to problems determining their roles within stepfamilies, stepmothers have been demonized across cultures for centuries (Church 2004). In fact, no other family position has been held in such low regard. Stepmothers are stereotyped as "evil" and "wicked." Young children have an early introduction to this stereotype through many old and beloved fairy tales. Because of the stigma surrounding stepmothers, the chief goal of many of them is to avoid the "wicked" label. Unfortunately, there are no clear guidelines for doing so.

It is evident from the research that stepmothers have quite different experiences, depending on whether or not they share a residence on a daily basis or only see their stepchildren occasionally. There are also differences depending on the age of the stepchildren, and whether or not the stepmother shares a mutual child with her partner. Unfortunately, clinicians and most researchers do not distinguish between the various types of stepmothers. To understand the nature of stepmothering, far more attention needs to be paid to these variables in stepfamily research. Considering the difficulties that clinicians and researchers identify that stepmothers have in negotiating their roles within stepfamilies, it is unfortunate that we have so little empirical evidence to guide them.

SEE ALSO: Childhood; Divisions of Household Labor; Divorce; Family Diversity; Family Structure and Child Outcomes; Gender Ideology and Gender Role Ideology; Motherhood; Stepfamilies; Stepfathering

REFERENCES AND SUGGESTED READINGS

Ambert, A. M. (1986) Being a Stepparent: Live-in and Visiting Stepchildren. *Journal of Marriage and the Family* 48: 795–804.

Bernstein, A. (1989) *Yours, Mine, and Ours.* Scribner's, New York.

Church, E. (2004) *Understanding Stepmothers.* Harper Collins, Toronto.

Coleman, M., Ganong, L., & Fine, M. (2000) Reinvestigating Remarriage: Another Decade of Progress. *Journal of Marriage and the Family* 62: 1288–307.

Ganong, L. & Coleman, M. (2004) *Stepfamily Relationships: Development, Dynamics, and Interventions.* Kluwer/Plenum, New York.

Hayes, S. (1996) *The Cultural Contradictions of Motherhood.* Yale University Press, New Haven.

MacDonald, W. L. & DeMaris, A. (1996) Parenting Stepchildren and Biological Children: The Effects of Stepparent's Gender and New Biological Children. *Journal of Family Issues* 17: 5–25.

Morrison, K. & Thompson-Guppy, A. (1985) Cinderella's Stepmother Syndrome. *Canadian Journal of Psychiatry* 30: 521–9.

Nielsen, L. (1999) Stepmothers: Why So Much Stress? A Review of the Literature. *Journal of Divorce and Remarriage* 30: 115–48.

Stephens, L. S. (1996) Will Johnny See Daddy This Week? An Empirical Test of Three Theoretical Perspectives of Postdivorce Contact. *Journal of Family Issues* 17: 75–89.

Sturgess, W., Dunn, J., & Davies, L. (2001) Young Children's Perceptions of their Relationships with Family Members: Links with Family Setting, Friendships, and Adjustment. *International Journal of Behavioral Development* 25: 521–9.

Vinick, B. H. (1998) Is Blood Thicker Than Water? Remarried Mothers' Relationships with Grown Children from Previous Marriages. Paper presented at the Gerontological Society of America Annual Meeting, Philadelphia.

Visher, E. B. & Visher, J. S. (1979) *Stepfamilies: A Guide to Working with Stepparents and Stepchildren.* Brunner/Mazel, New York.

Weaver, S. E. & Coleman, M. (in press) A Mothering but not a Mother Role. *Journal of Social and Personal Relationships.*